Marketing Management

THIRTEENTH EDITION

PHILIP KOTLER
Northwestern University

KEVIN LANE KELLER
Dartmouth College

Prentice-Hall of India Private Limited
New Delhi-110001
2008

This Indian Reprint—Rs. 550.00
(Original U.S. Edition—Rs. 5648.00)

MARKETING MANAGEMENT, 13th Ed.
by Philip Kotler and Kevin Lane Keller

Credits and acknowledgments borrowed from other sources and reproduced, with permission, in this textbook appear on the appropriate page within text and on page C1.

ISBN-978-81-203-3570-7

Published by Asoke K. Ghosh, Prentice-Hall of India Private Limited, M-97, Connaught Circus, New Delhi-110001 and Printed by Tarun Offset Printers, New Delhi-110064.

This book is dedicated to my wife and best friend, Nancy, with love.

– PK

This book is dedicated to my wife, Punam, and my two daughters, Carolyn and Allison, with much love and thanks.

– KLK

ABOUT THE AUTHORS

Philip Kotler *is one of the world's leading authorities on marketing. He is the S. C. Johnson & Son Distinguished Professor of International Marketing at the Kellogg School of Management, Northwestern University. He received his master's degree at the University of Chicago and his Ph.D. at MIT, both in economics. He did postdoctoral work in mathematics at Harvard University and in behavioral science at the University of Chicago.*

Dr. Kotler is the coauthor of *Principles of Marketing* and *Marketing: An Introduction*. His *Strategic Marketing for Nonprofit Organizations*, now in its seventh edition, is the best seller in that specialized area. Dr. Kotler's other books include *Marketing Models; The New Competition; Marketing Professional Services; Strategic Marketing for Educational Institutions; Marketing for Health Care Organizations; Marketing Congregations; High Visibility; Social Marketing; Marketing Places; The Marketing of Nations; Marketing for Hospitality and Tourism; Standing Room Only—Strategies for Marketing the Performing Arts; Museum Strategy and Marketing; Marketing Moves; Kotler on Marketing; Lateral Marketing: Ten Deadly Marketing Sins*; and *Corporate Social Responsibility*.

In addition, he has published more than one hundred articles in leading journals, including the *Harvard Business Review, Sloan Management Review, Business Horizons, California Management Review*, the *Journal of Marketing*, the *Journal of Marketing Research, Management Science*, the *Journal of Business Strategy*, and *Futurist*. He is the only three-time winner of the coveted Alpha Kappa Psi award for the best annual article published in the *Journal of Marketing*.

Professor Kotler was the first recipient of the American Marketing Association's (AMA) Distinguished Marketing Educator Award (1985). The European Association of Marketing Consultants and Sales Trainers awarded him their Prize for Marketing Excellence. He was chosen as the Leader in Marketing Thought by the Academic Members of the AMA in a 1975 survey. He also received the 1978 Paul Converse Award of the AMA, honoring his original contribution to marketing. In 1995, the Sales and Marketing Executives International (SMEI) named him Marketer of the Year. In 2002, Professor Kotler received the Distinguished Educator Award from The Academy of Marketing Science. He has received honorary doctoral degrees from Stockholm University, the University of Zurich, Athens University of Economics and Business, DePaul University, the Cracow School of Business and Economics, Groupe H.E.C. in Paris, the Budapest School of Economic Science and Public Administration, and the University of Economics and Business Administration in Vienna.

Professor Kotler has been a consultant to many major U.S. and foreign companies, including IBM, General Electric, AT&T, Honeywell, Bank of America, Merck, SAS Airlines, Michelin, and others in the areas of marketing strategy and planning, marketing organization, and international marketing.

He has been Chairman of the College of Marketing of the Institute of Management Sciences, a Director of the American Marketing Association, a Trustee of the Marketing Science Institute, a Director of the MAC Group, a member of the Yankelovich Advisory Board, and a member of the Copernicus Advisory Board. He was a member of the Board of Governors of the School of the Art Institute of Chicago and a member of the Advisory Board of the Drucker Foundation. He has traveled extensively throughout Europe, Asia, and South America, advising and lecturing to many companies about global marketing opportunities.

ABOUT THE AUTHORS

***Kevin Lane Keller** is the E. B. Osborn Professor of Marketing at the Tuck School of Business at Dartmouth College. Professor Keller has degrees from Cornell, Carnegie-Mellon, and Duke universities. At Dartmouth, he teaches MBA courses on marketing management and strategic brand management and lectures in executive programs on those topics.*

Previously, Professor Keller was on the faculty of the Graduate School of Business at Stanford University, where he also served as the head of the marketing group. Additionally, he has been on the marketing faculty at the University of California at Berkeley and the University of North Carolina at Chapel Hill, been a visiting professor at Duke University and the Australian Graduate School of Management, and has two years of industry experience as Marketing Consultant for Bank of America.

Professor Keller's general area of expertise lies in marketing strategy and planning, and branding. His specific research interest is in how understanding theories and concepts related to consumer behavior can improve marketing strategies. His research has been published in three of the major marketing journals—the *Journal of Marketing*, the *Journal of Marketing Research*, and the *Journal of Consumer Research*. He also has served on the Editorial Review Boards of those journals. With over sixty published papers, his research has been widely cited and has received numerous awards. Two of his articles, "Consumer Evaluations of Brand Extensions" and "Conceptualizing, Measuring, and Managing Customer-Based Brand Equity" were named by INFORMS Society for Marketing Science in March 2007 to its list of Top 20 marketing science papers written in the past 25 years that have most affected the practice of marketing science.

Professor Keller is acknowledged as one of the international leaders in the study of brands, branding, and strategic brand management. Actively involved with industry, he has worked on a host of different types of marketing projects. He has served as a consultant and advisor to marketers for some of the world's most successful brands, including Accenture, American Express, Disney, Ford, Intel, Levi Strauss, Procter & Gamble, and SAB Miller. Additional brand consulting activities have been with other top companies such as Allstate, Beiersdorf (Nivea), BlueCross BlueShield, Campbell's, Eli Lilly, ExxonMobil, General Mills, Goodyear, Kodak, Mayo Clinic, Nordstrom, Shell Oil, Starbucks, Unilever, and Young & Rubicam. He has also served as an academic trustee for the Marketing Science Institute. A popular speaker, he has conducted marketing seminars to top executives in a variety of forums.

Professor Keller is currently conducting a variety of studies that address strategies to build, measure, and manage brand equity. His textbook on those subjects, *Strategic Brand Management*, has been adopted at top business schools and leading firms around the world and has been heralded as the "bible of branding."

An avid sports, music, and film enthusiast, in his so-called spare time, he has served as executive producer for one of Australia's great rock and roll treasures, The Church, as well as American power-pop legends Dwight Twilley and Tommy Keene. He is also on the Board of Directors for The Doug Flutie, Jr. Foundation for Autism. Professor Keller lives in Etna, NH with his wife, Punam (also a Tuck marketing professor), and his two daughters, Carolyn and Allison.

BRIEF CONTENTS

CONTENTS

CONTENTS

CONTENTS

CONTENTS

CONTENTS

CONTENTS

CONTENTS

CONTENTS

CONTENTS

CONTENTS

CONTENTS

CONTENTS

CONTENTS

CONTENTS

CONTENTS

CONTENTS

CONTENTS

CONTENTS

CONTENTS

PEARSON ONE

Each title in the Pearson One series is part of a collaborative global editorial development process that harnesses the talent and expertise of Pearson authors, editors, and production people from all over the world. And we combine content from many cultures, giving students greater insight into what they have in common with the world, and at the same time, we offer material that is locally relevant.

::: Our History

Pearson imprints have a rich heritage of academic, business, and professional books. For more than 100 years, we have provided educational tools to more than 100 million people across the globe. Our diverse network of brands encompasses a comprehensive range of solutions in testing, assessment, and enterprise software; the very best in online consumer and professional learning; and textbooks written by the most notable authors for higher education around the world. We help teachers teach and students learn across the globe.

::: The First in the Pearson One Series

Readers of the U.S. edition will benefit from these local perspectives and expertise through our international case studies, authored by our partners worldwide. These cases will be identified by a marginal note in each chapter linked to relevant content and available through links on our Companion Website.

::: What Is Marketing Management All About?

Marketing Management is the leading marketing text because its content and organization consistently reflect changes in marketing theory and practice. The very first edition of *Marketing Management*, published in 1967, introduced the concept that companies must be customer-and-market driven. But there was little mention of what have now become fundamental topics such as segmentation, targeting, and positioning. Concepts such as brand equity, customer value analysis, database marketing, e-commerce, value networks, hybrid channels, supply chain management, and integrated marketing communications were not even part of the marketing vocabulary then. *Marketing Management* continues to reflect the changes in the marketing discipline over the past forty years.

Firms now sell goods and services through a variety of direct and indirect channels. Mass advertising is not nearly as effective as it was, so marketers are exploring new forms of communication, such as experiential, entertainment, and viral marketing. Customers are telling companies what types of product or services they want and when, where, and how they want to buy them. They are increasingly reporting to other consumers what they think of specific companies and products—using e-mail, blogs, podcasts, and other digital media to do so. Company messages are becoming a smaller fraction of the total "conversation" about products and services.

In response, companies have shifted gears from managing product portfolios to managing *customer* portfolios, compiling databases on individual customers so they can understand them better and construct individualized offerings and messages. They are doing less product and service standardization and more niching and customization. They are replacing monologues with customer dialogues. They are improving their methods of measuring customer profitability and customer lifetime value. They are intent on measuring the return on their marketing investment and its impact on shareholder value. They are also concerned with the ethical and social implications of their marketing decisions.

As companies change, so does their marketing organization. Marketing is no longer a company department charged with a limited number of tasks—it is a company-wide undertaking. It drives the company's vision, mission, and strategic planning. Marketing includes decisions like who the company wants as its customers; which of their needs to satisfy; what products and services to offer; what prices to set; what communications to send and receive; what channels of distribution to use; and what partnerships to develop. Marketing succeeds only when all departments work together to achieve goals: when engineering designs the right products, finance furnishes the required funds, purchasing buys high-quality materials, production makes high-quality products on time, and accounting measures the profitability of different customers, products, and areas.

To address all these different shifts, good marketers are practicing holistic marketing. *Holistic marketing* is the development, design, and implementation of marketing programs, processes, and activities that recognize the breadth and interdependencies of today's marketing environment. Four key dimensions of holistic marketing are:

1. **Internal marketing**—ensuring everyone in the organization embraces appropriate marketing principles, especially senior management.
2. **Integrated marketing**—ensuring that multiple means of creating, delivering, and communicating value are employed and combined in the best way.
3. **Relationship marketing**—having rich, multifaceted relationships with customers, channel members, and other marketing partners.
4. **Performance marketing**—understanding returns to the business from marketing activities and programs, as well as addressing broader concerns and their legal, ethical, social, and environmental effects.

These four dimensions are woven throughout the book and at times spelled out explicitly. The text specifically addresses the following tasks that constitute modern marketing management in the 21st century:

PREFACE

1. Developing marketing strategies and plans
2. Capturing marketing insights and performance
3. Connecting with customers
4. Building strong brands
5. Shaping the market offerings
6. Delivering and communicating value
7. Creating successful long-term growth

::: What Makes *Marketing Management* the Marketing Leader?

Marketing is of interest to everyone, whether they are marketing goods, services, properties, persons, places, events, information, ideas, or organizations. As it has maintained its respected position among students, educators, and businesspeople, *Marketing Management* has kept up-to-date and contemporary. Students (and instructors) feel that the book is talking directly to them in terms of both content and delivery.

Marketing Management owes its marketplace success to its ability to maximize three dimensions that characterize the best marketing texts—depth, breadth, and relevance—as measured by the following criteria:

- **Depth.** Does the book have solid academic grounding? Does it contain important theoretical concepts, models, and frameworks? Does it provide conceptual guidance to solve practical problems?
- **Breadth.** Does the book cover all the right topics? Does it provide the proper amount of emphasis on those topics?
- **Relevance.** Does the book engage the reader? Is it interesting to read? Does it have lots of compelling examples?

The thirteenth edition builds on the fundamental strengths of past editions that collectively distinguish it from all other marketing management texts:

- **Managerial Orientation.** The book focuses on the major decisions that marketing managers and top management face in their efforts to harmonize the organization's objectives, capabilities, and resources with marketplace needs and opportunities.
- **Analytical Approach.** *Marketing Management* presents conceptual tools and frameworks for analyzing recurring problems in marketing management. Cases and examples illustrate effective marketing principles, strategies, and practices.
- **Multidisciplinary Perspective.** The book draws on the rich findings of various scientific disciplines—economics, behavioral science, management theory, and mathematics—for fundamental concepts and tools directly applicable to marketing challenges.
- **Universal Applications.** The book applies strategic thinking to the complete spectrum of marketing: products, services, persons, places, information, ideas and causes; consumer and business markets; profit and nonprofit organizations; domestic and foreign companies; small and large firms; manufacturing and intermediary businesses; and low- and high-tech industries.
- **Comprehensive and Balanced Coverage.** *Marketing Management* covers all the topics an informed marketing manager needs to understand to execute strategic, tactical, and administrative marketing.

Other features include new concepts, examples, guidelines, and developments as detailed below.

PREFACE

::: Revision Strategy for the *Thirteenth Edition*

As marketing techniques and organization have changed, so has this text. The thirteenth edition is designed not only to preserve the strengths of previous editions, but also to introduce new material and organization to further enhance learning. We retained the key theme of holistic marketing, and the recognition that "everything matters" with marketing and that a broad, integrated perspective is often necessary. This theme is not developed so deeply, however, that it would restrict or inhibit an instructor's flexibility and teaching approach. To provide flexibility in the classroom, we also retained the new modular structure and eight parts corresponding to the eight key marketing management tasks. The thirteenth edition was changed to include the following:

- All chapters have brief commentary and new introductory vignettes that set the stage for the chapter material to follow. By covering topical brands or companies, the vignettes serve as great discussion starters.
- Breakthrough Marketing boxes replace the Marketing Spotlight boxes from the twelfth edition. Each chapter has one box appearing in an appropriate spot to highlight innovative, insightful marketing accomplishments by leading organizations.
- Approximately four Marketing Insight and Marketing Memo boxes are included in each chapter; at least half, on average, are new. **Marketing Insight** boxes delve into important marketing topics, often highlighting current research findings. **Marketing Memo** boxes offer practical advice and direction in dealing with various decisions at all stages of the marketing management process.
- About ten in-text boxes are included in each chapter, with roughly two-thirds new. These in-text boxes provide vivid illustrations of chapter concepts using actual companies and situations. The boxes cover a variety of products, services, and markets, and many have accompanying illustrations in the form of ads or product shots.
- Chapters are updated throughout, especially in terms of academic references.
- At the end of each chapter, the *Marketing Applications* section has two practical exercises to challenge students: *Marketing Debate* suggests opposing points of view on an important marketing topic from the chapter and asks students to take a side. *Marketing Discussion* identifies provocative marketing issues and allows for a personal point of view.

::: Chapter-by-Chapter Changes

Once again, this edition has been both streamlined and expanded to bring essentials and classic examples into sharper focus, while covering new concepts and ideas in depth. Following is an overview of some of the new or expanded material in each chapter:

Chapter 1

- Role of Chief Marketing Officer (CMO)
- What makes a great marketer
- Internal marketing and effective marketing departments

Chapter 2

- Market sensing and becoming more market-driven
- Assigning resources to SBUs
- Corporate culture and innovative marketing

Chapter 3

- Database marketing
- Important new marketplace trends
- Generations and cohorts
- Green marketing

Chapter 4

- Ethnographic research
- Brain science
- Marketing dashboards
- Marketing-mix modeling

Chapter 5

- Measuring customer satisfaction
- Methods to calculate customer lifetime value
- The new customer empowerment

Chapter 6

- New consumer trends
- Consumer decision-making

Chapter 7

- Customer references
- Lead generation
- Customer value proposition

Chapter 8

- Niche marketing and the "long tail"
- Consumers trading up and down
- Brand funnel

Chapter 9

- Brand equity models
- Internal branding
- Brand valuation
- Customer equity

Chapter 10

- Creating new markets and categories
- Building a breakaway brand

Chapter 11

- Value innovation ("blue ocean thinking")
- Selecting customers
- Competing with value-based rivals

Chapter 12

- Product returns
- Product and product line simplification

Chapter 13

- Customer empowerment
- Coproduction
- Customer interface systems
- Service strategies for product companies

Chapter 14

- The changing pricing environment
- "Freemium" pricing strategies
- Price optimization
- Strategies to fight low-cost rivals

Chapter 15

- Channel stewardship
- E-marketing
- M-marketing

Chapter 16

- The new retail environment
- "Fast forward" retailers
- RFIDs
- Private-label competition

Chapter 17

- The changing marketing communication environment
- Interactive marketing
- Word-of-mouth marketing

Chapter 18

- New developments in place advertising
- Advergames and Second Life
- New developments in marketing events and experiences

Chapter 19

- Consumer-generated ads
- Types of interactive marketing
- Word of mouth, buzz and viral marketing, blogs, and podcasts

Chapter 20

- Innovation imperative
- "Connect and develop" innovation approaches

- Generating ideas from customers
- Designing brainstorming sessions

Chapter 21

- Emerging markets ("BRICS")
- Regionalization
- Gray markets and counterfeit products

Chapter 22

- New developments in social responsibility
- Cause marketing guidelines
- Marketing metrics
- Marketing creativity and discipline

ACKNOWLEDGMENTS

The thirteenth edition bears the imprint of many people.

From Phil Kotler: My colleagues and associates at the Kellogg School of Management at Northwestern University continue to have an important impact on my thinking: Nidhi Agrawal, Eric T. Anderson, James C. Anderson, Robert C. Blattberg, Miguel C. Brendl, Bobby J. Calder, Gregory S. Carpenter, Alex Chernev, Anne T. Coughlan, David Gal, Kent Grayson, Karsten Hansen, Dipak C. Jain, Lakshman Krishnamurti, Angela Lee, Vincent Nijs, Yi Qian, Mohanbir S. Sawhney, Louis W. Stern, Brian Sternthal, Alice M. Tybout, and Andris A. Zoltners. I also want to thank the S. C. Johnson Family for the generous support of my chair at the Kellogg School. Completing the Northwestern team is my former Dean, Donald P. Jacobs, and my current Dean, Dipak Jain, both of whom have provided generous support for my research and writing.

Several former faculty members of the marketing department had a great influence on my thinking when I first joined the Kellogg marketing faculty, specifically Richard M. Clewett, Ralph Westfall, Harper W. Boyd, and Sidney J. Levy. I also want to acknowledge Gary Armstrong for our work on *Principles of Marketing.*

I am indebted to the following coauthors of international editions of *Marketing Management* and *Principles of Marketing* who have taught me a great deal as we worked together to adapt marketing management thinking to the problems of different nations:

- Swee-Hoon Ang and Siew-Meng Leong: National University of Singapore
- Chin-Tiong Tan: Singapore Management University
- Friedhelm W. Bliemel: Universitat Kaiserslautern (Germany)
- Linden Brown; Stewart Adam: Deakin University; Suzan Burton: Macquarie Graduate School of Management; and Sara Denize: University of Western Sydney (Australia)
- Bernard Dubois: Groupe HEC School of Management (France); and Delphine Manceau: ESCP-EAP European School of Management
- John Saunders (Loughborough University) and Veronica Wong (Warwick University, United Kingdom)
- Jacob Hornick: Tel Aviv University (Israel)
- Walter Giorgio Scott: Universita Cattolica del Sacro Cuore (Italy)
- Peggy Cunningham: Queen's University (Canada)

I also want to acknowledge how much I have learned from working with coauthors on more specialized marketing subjects: Alan Andreasen, Christer Asplund, Paul N. Bloom, John Bowen, Roberta C. Clarke, Karen Fox, David Gertner, Michael Hamlin, Thomas Hayes, Donald Haider, Hooi Den Hua, Dipak Jain, Somkid Jatusripitak, Hermawan Kartajaya, Neil Kotler, Nancy Lee, Sandra Liu, Suvit Maesincee, James Maken, Waldemar Pfoertsch, Gustave Rath, Irving Rein, Eduardo Roberto, Joanne Scheff, Norman Shawchuck, Joel Shalowitz, Ben Shields, Francois Simon, Robert Stevens, Martin Stoller, Fernando Trias de Bes, Bruce Wrenn, and David Young.

My overriding debt continues to be to my lovely wife, Nancy, who provided me with the time, support, and inspiration needed to prepare this edition. It is truly our book.

From Kevin Lane Keller: I continually benefit from the wisdom of my colleagues at Tuck—Scott Neslin, Punam Keller, Kusum Ailawadi, Praveen Kopalle, Koen Pauwels, Petia Petrova, Jackie Luan, Fred Webster, Gert Assmus, and John Farley—as well as the leadership of Dean Paul Danos. I also gratefully acknowledge the invaluable research and teaching contributions from my faculty colleagues and collaborators through the years. I owe a considerable debt of gratitude to Duke University's Jim Bettman and Rick Staelin for helping to get my academic career started and serving as positive role models. I am also appreciative of all that I have learned from working with industry executives who have generously shared their insights and experiences. Finally, I give special thanks to Punam, my wife, and Carolyn and Allison, my daughters, who make it all happen and make it all worthwhile.

ACKNOWLEDGMENTS

We are indebted to the following colleagues at other universities who reviewed this new edition:

- Homero Aguirre, TAMIU
- Parimal Bhagat, Indiana University of Pennsylvania
- Michael Bruce, Anderson University
- Yun Chu, Frostburg State University
- Hugh Daubek, Purdue University
- Kathleen Dominick, Rider University
- Tad Duffy, Golden Gate University
- Mohan Dutta, Purdue University
- Barbara Dyer, University of North Carolina at Greensboro
- Jackie Eastman, Valdosta State University
- Steve Edison, University of Arkansas–Little Rock
- Barb Finer, Suffolk University
- Renee Foster, Delta State University
- Chic Fojtik, Pepperdine University
- Robert Galka, De Paul University
- Rashi Glazer, University of California, Berkeley
- Lewis Hershey, Fayetteville State University
- Thomas Hewett, Kaplan University
- Mary Higby, University of Detroit–Mercy
- Michelle Kunz, Morehead State University
- Even Lanseng, Norwegian School of Management
- Michael Lodato, California Lutheran University
- Henry Loehr, Pfeiffer University–Charlotte
- Susan Mann, Bluefield State College
- Charles Martin, Wichita State University
- John McKeever, University of Houston
- Robert Mika, Monmouth University
- Mark Mitchell, Coastal Carolina University
- Nnamdi Osakwe, Bryant & Stratton College
- Young-Hoon Park, Cornell University
- Koen Pauwels, Dartmouth College
- Keith Penney, Webster University
- Patricia Perry, University of Alabama
- Mike Powell, North Georgia College and State University
- William Rice, California State University–Fresno
- Bill Robinson, Purdue University
- Jan Napoleon Saykiewicz, Duquesne University
- Larry Schramm, Oakland University
- Jim Skertich, Upper Iowa University
- Allen Smith, Florida Atlantic University
- Joe Spencer, Anderson University
- Nancy Stephens, Arizona State University

ACKNOWLEDGMENTS

- Thomas Tellefsen, The College of Staten Island–CUNY
- Daniel Turner, University of Washington
- Edward Volchok, Stevens Institute of Management
- D.J. Wasmer, St. Mary-of-the-Woods College
- Zac Williams, Mississippi State University

We would also like to thank colleagues who have reviewed previous editions of *Marketing Management:*

Alan Au, University of Hong Kong
Hiram Barksdale, University of Georgia
Boris Becker, Oregon State University
Sandy Becker, Rutgers University
Sunil Bhatla, Case Western Reserve University
Frederic Brunel, Boston University
John Burnett, University of Denver
Lisa Cain, University of California at Berkeley and Mills College
Surjit Chhabra, DePaul University
Dennis Clayson, University of Northern Iowa
Bob Cline, University of Iowa
Brent Cunningham, Ph.D., Jacksonville State University
John Deighton, University of Chicago
Alton Erdem, University of Houston at Clear Lake
Elizabeth Evans, Concordia University
Ralph Gaedeke, California State University, Sacramento
Betsy Gelb, University of Houston at Clear Lake
Dennis Gensch, University of Wisconsin, Milwaukee
David Georgoff, Florida Atlantic University
Bill Gray, Keller Graduate School of Management
Barbara Gross, California State University at Northridge
Arun Jain, State University of New York, Buffalo
Eric Langer, Johns Hopkins University
Ron Lennon, Barry University
Bart Macchiette, Plymouth University
H. Lee Matthews, Ohio State University
Paul McDevitt, University of Illinois at Springfield
Mary Ann McGrath, Loyola University, Chicago
Kenneth P. Mead, Central Connecticut State University
Henry Metzner, University of Missouri, Rolla
Francis Mulhern, Northwestern University
Pat Murphy, University of Notre Dame
Jim Murrow, Drury College
Zhou Nan, University of Hong Kong
Nicholas Nugent, Boston College
Donald Outland, University of Texas, Austin
Albert Page, University of Illinois, Chicago
Lisa Klein Pearo, Cornell University
Hank Pruden, Golden Gate University

ACKNOWLEDGMENTS

Christopher Puto, Arizona State University
Abe Qstin, Lakeland University
Lopo Rego, University of Iowa
Richard Rexeisen, University of St. Thomas
Scott D. Roberts, Northern Arizona University
Robert Roe, University of Wyoming
Alex Sharland, Hofstra University
Dean Siewers, Rochester Institute of Technology
Anusorn Singhapakdi, Old Dominion University
Mark Spriggs, University of St. Thomas
Michael Swenso, Brigham Young University, Marriott School
Sean Valentine, University of Wyoming
Ann Veeck, West Michigan University
R. Venkatesh, University of Pittsburgh
Greg Wood, Canisius College
Kevin Zeng Zhou, University of Hong Kong

A warm welcome and many thanks to the following people who contributed to the global case studies developed for the thirteenth edition:

Mairead Brady, Trinity College
John R. Brooks, Jr., Houston Baptist University
Sylvain Charlebois, University of Regina
Geoffrey da Silva, Temasek Business School
Malcolm Goodman, Durham University
Torben Hansen, Copenhagen Business School
Abraham Koshy, Sanjeev Tripathi, and Abhishek, Indian Institute of Management Ahmedabad
Peter Ling, Edith Cowan University
Marianne Marando, Seneca College
Lu Taihong, Sun Yat-Sen University

The talented staff at Prentice Hall deserves praise for their role in shaping the thirteenth edition. We want to thank our Editor Melissa Sabella, for her contribution to this revision. We also want to thank our project manager, Melissa Pellerano, for making sure everything was moving along and falling into place in such a personable way, both with regard to the book and supplements. We benefited greatly from the superb editorial help of Elisa Adams, who lent her considerable talents as a development editor to this edition. We thank Nancy Brandwein, who again researched and updated the examples. We also want to acknowledge the fine production work of Judy Leale, the creative design work of Steve Frim, and the editorial assistance of Christine Ietto. We thank Denise Vaughn for her work on the media package. We also thank our Marketing Manager, Anne Fahlgren.

Philip Kotler
S. C. Johnson Distinguished Professor of International Marketing
Kellogg School of Management
Northwestern University
Evanston, Illinois

Kevin Lane Keller
E. B. Osborn Professor of Marketing
Tuck School of Business
Dartmouth College
Hanover, New Hampshire

Marketing Management

PART

1

UNDERSTANDING MARKETING MANAGEMENT

IN THIS CHAPTER, WE WILL ADDRESS THE FOLLOWING QUESTIONS:

1. Why is marketing important?
2. What is the scope of marketing?
3. What are some fundamental marketing concepts?
4. How has marketing management changed?
5. What are the tasks necessary for successful marketing management?

CHAPTER 1 ::: DEFINING MARKETING FOR THE 21ST CENTURY

one

Marketing is everywhere. Formally or informally, people and organizations engage in a vast number of activities that we could call marketing. Good marketing has become an increasingly vital ingredient for business success. And marketing profoundly affects our day-to-day lives. It is embedded in everything we do—from the clothes we wear, to the Web sites we click on, to the ads we see:

Two teenage girls walk into their local Starbucks, which happens to be in Shanghai. One goes to the crowded counter and waits to hand the barista cards for two free peppermint lattes. The other sits at a table and opens her Lenovo ThinkPad R60 notebook computer. Within a few seconds she connects to the Internet, courtesy of Starbucks' deal with China Mobile to provide its customers with wireless access to HotSpots on the China Mobile Network. Once on the Net, the girl uses Baidu.com—the Chinese search engine market leader—to search for information about the latest online game release from China's Shanda Interactive. In addition to links to various reviews, news sites, and fan pages, Baidu's search results feature a link to a chat room where hundreds of other gamers are discussing the game. The girl enters the chat room to ask whether people who have played the game recommend it. The response is overwhelmingly positive, so she clicks on a sponsored link from the results page, which >>>

Downtown Shanghai, a live demonstration of the many faces of marketing today.

generates a silver of paid-search revenue for Baidu and takes her to Shanda's official site, where she sets up an account.

Now her friend has returned with lattes in hand. She's eager to show off her parents' New Year's gift to her: a hot pink Motorola RAZR cell phone created by a team of young Chicago-based designers after months of market research and consumer tests. The two girls are admiring the slender phone when it receives a text ad announcing the availability of Shanda's latest game for mobile download. The girls turn to the laptop so they can gauge the online buzz for the mobile version of the game.

Good marketing is no accident, but a result of careful planning and execution. It is both an art and a science there's a constant tension between its formulated side and its creative side. It's easier to learn the formulated side, which will occupy most of out attention in this book, but we will also describe how real creativity and passion operate in many companies. In this chapter, we lay the foundation for our study by reviewing a number of important marketing concepts, tools, frameworks, and issues.

::: The Importance of Marketing

Financial success often depends on marketing ability. Finance, operations, accounting, and other business functions will not really matter if there isn't sufficient demand for products and services so the company can make a profit. There must be a top line for there to be a bottom line. Many companies have now created a Chief Marketing Officer, or CMO, position to put marketing on a more equal footing with other C-level executives, such as the Chief Executive Officer (CEO) and Chief Financial Officer (CFO). Press releases from organizations of all kinds—from consumer goods makers to health care insurers and from nonprofit organizations to industrial product manufacturers—trumpet their latest marketing achievements on their Web sites. In the business press, countless articles are devoted to marketing strategies and tactics.

In stating their business priorities, CEOs acknowledge the importance of marketing. One survey of the top 10 challenges CEOs face around the world in 2006 revealed that among the top 5 were both "sustained and steady top line growth" and "customer loyalty/retention," challenges whose achievement depends heavily on marketing.[1] CEOs also recognize the importance of marketing to building brands and a loyal customer base, intangible assets that make up a large percentage of the value of a firm.

Marketing is tricky, however, and it has been the Achilles' heel of many formerly prosperous companies. Sears, Levi's, General Motors, Kodak, Sony, and Xerox all have confronted newly empowered customers and new competitors and have had to rethink their business models.

Even market leaders such as Intel, Microsoft, and Wal-Mart recognize that they cannot afford to relax as their leadership is challenged. Jack Welch, GE's former CEO, repeatedly warned his company: "Change or die."

XEROX

Xerox has had to become more than just a copier company. Now the blue-chip icon with the name that became a verb sports the broadest array of imaging products in the world and dominates the market for high-end printing systems. And it's making a huge product-line transition as it moves away from the old-line "light lens" technology to digital systems. Xerox is preparing for a world that is no longer black and white, and in which most pages are printed in color (which, not incidentally, generates five times the revenue of black and white). In addition to revamping its machines, Xerox is beefing up sales by providing annuity-like products and services that are ordered again and again: document management, ink, and toners. Having been slow at one time to respond to the emergence of Canon and the small copier market, Xerox is doing everything it can to stay ahead of the game.[2]

Making the right decisions about change isn't always easy. Marketing managers must decide what features to design into a new product, what prices to offer customers, where to sell products, and how much to spend on advertising, sales, or the Internet. They must also decide on details such as the exact wording or color for new packaging. The companies at greatest risk are those that fail to carefully monitor their customers and competitors and to continuously improve their value offerings. They take a short-term, sales-driven view of their business and ultimately they fail to satisfy their stockholders, employees, suppliers, and channel partners. Skillful marketing is a never-ending pursuit.

::: The Scope of Marketing

To prepare to be a marketer, you need to understand what marketing is, how it works, what is marketed, and who does the marketing.

What Is Marketing?

Marketing is about identifying and meeting human and social needs. One of the shortest good definitions of marketing is "meeting needs profitably." When eBay recognized that people were unable to locate some of the items they desired most, it created an online auction clearinghouse. When IKEA noticed that people wanted good furniture at a substantially lower price, it created knockdown furniture. These two firms demonstrated marketing savvy and turned a private or social need into a profitable business opportunity.

The American Marketing Association offers the following formal definition: *Marketing is an organizational function and a set of processes for creating, communicating, and delivering value to customers and for managing customer relationships in ways that benefit the organization and its stakeholders.*[3] Coping with these exchange processes calls for a considerable amount of work and skill. *Marketing management* takes place when at least one party to a potential exchange thinks about the means of achieving desired responses from other parties. Thus we see **marketing management** as *the art and science of choosing target markets and getting, keeping, and growing customers through creating, delivering, and communicating superior customer value.*

We can distinguish between a social and a managerial definition of marketing. A social definition shows the role marketing plays in society; for example, one marketer has said that marketing's role is to "deliver a higher standard of living." Here is a social definition that serves our purpose: *Marketing is a societal process by which individuals and groups obtain what they need and want through creating, offering, and freely exchanging products and services of value with others.*

Managers sometimes think of marketing as "the art of selling products," but many people are surprised when they hear that selling is *not* the most important part of marketing! Selling is only the tip of the marketing iceberg. Peter Drucker, a leading management theorist, puts it this way:

> There will always, one can assume, be need for some selling. But the aim of marketing is to make selling superfluous. The aim of marketing is to know and understand the customer so well that the product or service fits him and sells itself. Ideally, marketing should result in a customer who is ready to buy. All that should be needed then is to make the product or service available.[4]

A successful new product is the result of careful marketing homework.

When Sony designed its Play Station 3 game system, when Apple launched its iPod Nano digital music player, and when Toyota introduced its Prius hybrid automobile, these manufacturers were swamped with orders because they had designed the "right" product, based on doing careful marketing homework.

What Is Marketed?

Marketing people market 10 types of entities: goods, services, events, experiences, persons, places, properties, organizations, information, and ideas. Let's take a quick look at these categories.

GOODS Physical goods constitute the bulk of most countries' production and marketing efforts. Each year, U.S. companies alone market billions of fresh, canned, bagged, and frozen food products and millions of cars, refrigerators, television sets, machines, and various other mainstays of a modern economy. Not only do companies market their goods, but thanks in part to the Internet, even individuals can effectively market goods.

RUBBER CHICKEN CARDS

A struggling actor who made ends meet by waiting tables, landing bit parts in TV series, teaching high school, and managing an office, Steve Rotblatt found a way to keep his acting dream alive by running a profitable small business out of his home. Rubber Chicken Cards (rubberchickencards.com) is a Santa Monica company that's generating online buzz with electronic greeting cards that combine voice-over acting—by Rotblatt and partner Richard Zobel—with irreverent humor. It didn't hurt that Classmates.com selected the company to develop a lighthearted card to help its 40 million members reconnect with old friends, or that the social networking site Me.com chose Rubber Chicken over dozens of competing vendors to create an electronic birthday card for its members. Founded in 2000, the company expected annual sales to reach $300,000 in 2006, up 60% from the prior year. Rotblatt and Zobel's business strategy: use our talents and spend as little as possible.[5]

SERVICES As economies advance, a growing proportion of their activities focuses on the production of services. The U.S. economy today consists of a 70–30 services-to-goods mix. Services include the work of airlines, hotels, car rental firms, barbers and beauticians, maintenance and repair people, and accountants, bankers, lawyers, engineers, doctors, software programmers, and management consultants. Many market offerings consist of a variable mix of goods and services. At a fast-food restaurant, for example, the customer consumes both a product and a service.

EVENTS Marketers promote time-based events, such as major trade shows, artistic performances, and company anniversaries. Global sporting events such as the Olympics and the World Cup are promoted aggressively to both companies and fans.

EXPERIENCES By orchestrating several services and goods, a firm can create, stage, and market experiences. Walt Disney World's Magic Kingdom represents this kind of experiential marketing, allowing customers to visit a fairy kingdom, a pirate ship, or a haunted house. There is also a market for customized experiences, such as spending a week at a baseball camp playing with retired baseball greats, conducting the Chicago Symphony Orchestra for five minutes, or climbing Mount Everest.[6]

PERSONS Celebrity marketing is a major business. Artists, musicians, CEOs, physicians, high-profile lawyers and financiers, and other professionals all get help from celebrity marketers.[7] Some people have done a masterful job of marketing themselves—think of David Beckham, Oprah Winfrey, and the Rolling Stones. Management consultant Tom Peters, himself a master at self-branding, has advised each person to become a "brand."

PLACES Cities, states, regions, and whole nations compete actively to attract tourists, factories, company headquarters, and new residents.[8] Place marketers include economic development specialists, real estate agents, commercial banks, local business associations, and advertising and public relations agencies. The Las Vegas Convention & Tourism Authority spent about $80 million on a provocative ad campaign, "What Happens Here, Stays Here." Returning to its roots as an "adult playground," Las Vegas hoped the campaign would lead to an increase from 37.4 million visitors in 2004 to 43 million visitors by 2009.[9]

PROPERTIES Properties are intangible rights of ownership of either real property (real estate) or financial property (stocks and bonds). Properties are bought and sold, and these exchanges require marketing. Real estate agents work for property owners or sellers, or they buy and sell residential or commercial real estate. Investment companies and banks market securities to both institutional and individual investors.

ORGANIZATIONS Organizations actively work to build a strong, favorable, and unique image in the minds of their target publics. In the United Kingdom, Tesco's "Every Little Helps" marketing program reflects the food marketer's attention to detail in everything it does, within as well as outside the store in the community and the environment. The campaign has vaulted Tesco to the top of the UK supermarket chain industry. Universities, museums, performing arts organizations, and nonprofits all use marketing to boost their public images and to compete for audiences and funds. Corporate identity campaigns are the result of intensive market research programs. This is certainly the case with Philips "Sense and Simplicity" campaign.

ROYAL PHILIPS

Philips researchers asked 1,650 consumers and 180 customers in dozens of in-depth and quantitative interviews and focus groups what was most important to them in using technology. Respondents from the UK, United States, France, Germany, the Netherlands, Hong Kong, China, and Brazil agreed on one thing: they wanted the benefits of technology without the hassles. With its "Sense and Simplicity" advertising campaign and focus, Philips believes, "our brand now reflects our belief that simplicity can be a goal of technology. It just makes sense." The campaign consists of print, online, and television advertising directed by five experts from the worlds of health care, lifestyle, and technology whose role is to provide "additional outside perspectives on the journey to simplicity."[10]

INFORMATION Information is essentially what books, schools, and universities produce, market, and distribute at a price to parents, students, and communities. Magazines such as *Road and Track*, *PC World*, and *Vogue* supply information about the car, computer, and fashion worlds, respectively. The production, packaging, and distribution of information are some of our society's major industries.[11] Even companies that sell physical products attempt to add value through the use of information. For example, the CEO of Siemens Medical Systems, Tom McCausland, says, "[our product] is not necessarily an X-ray or an MRI, but information. Our business is really health care information technology, and our end product is really an electronic patient record: information on lab tests, pathology, and drugs as well as voice dictation."[12]

IDEAS Every market offering includes a basic idea. Charles Revson of Revlon once observed: "In the factory, we make cosmetics; in the store we sell hope." Products and services are platforms for delivering some idea or benefit. Social marketers are busy promoting such ideas as "Friends Don't Let Friends Drive Drunk" and "A Mind Is a Terrible Thing to Waste."

Who Markets?

MARKETERS AND PROSPECTS A **marketer** is someone who seeks a response—attention, a purchase, a vote, a donation—from another party, called the **prospect**. If two parties are seeking to sell something to each other, we call them both marketers.

Marketing can help to promote powerful ideas.

Marketers are indeed skilled at stimulating demand for their company's products, but that's too limited a view of the tasks they perform. Just as production and logistics professionals are responsible for supply management, marketers are responsible for demand management. Marketing managers seek to influence the level, timing, and composition of demand to meet the organization's objectives. Eight demand states are possible:

1. ***Negative demand***—Consumers dislike the product and may even pay a price to avoid it.
2. ***Nonexistent demand***—Consumers may be unaware of or uninterested in the product.
3. ***Latent demand***—Consumers may share a strong need that cannot be satisfied by an existing product.
4. ***Declining demand***—Consumers begin to buy the product less frequently or not at all.
5. ***Irregular demand***—Consumer purchases vary on a seasonal, monthly, weekly, daily, or even hourly basis.
6. ***Full demand***—Consumers are adequately buying all products put into the marketplace.
7. ***Overfull demand***—More consumers would like to buy the product than can be satisfied.
8. ***Unwholesome demand***—Consumers may be attracted to products that have undesirable social consequences.

In each case, marketers must identify the underlying cause(s) of the demand state and then determine a plan of action to shift the demand to a more desired state.

MARKETS Traditionally, a "market" was a physical place where buyers and sellers gathered to buy and sell goods. Economists describe a *market* as a collection of buyers and sellers who transact over a particular product or product class (such as the housing market or the grain market). Modern economies abound in such markets.

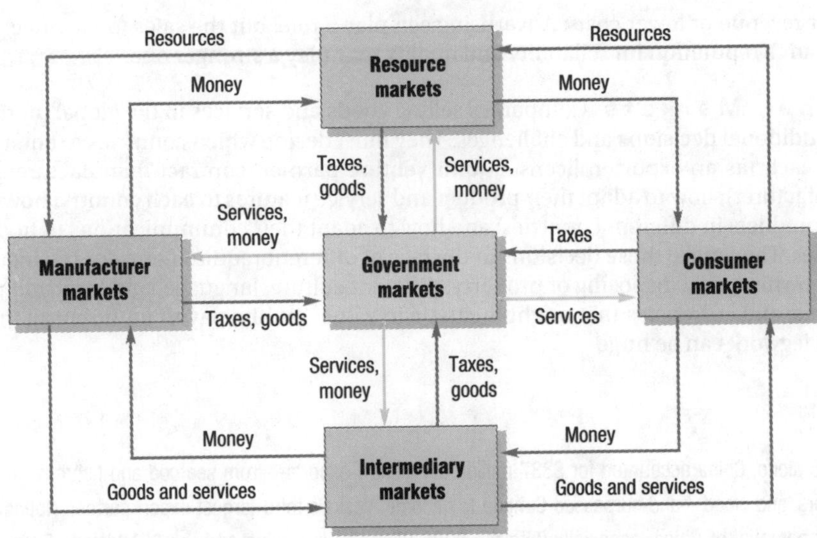

FIG. 1.1

Structure of Flows in a Modern Exchange Economy

Five basic markets and their connecting flows are shown in Figure 1.1. Manufacturers go to resource markets (raw material markets, labor markets, money markets), buy resources and turn them into goods and services, and then sell finished products to intermediaries, who sell them to consumers. Consumers sell their labor and receive money with which they pay for goods and services. The government collects tax revenues to buy goods from resource, manufacturer, and intermediary markets and uses these goods and services to provide public services. Each nation's economy, and the global economy, consists of complex interacting sets of markets linked through exchange processes.

Marketers often use the term **market** to cover various groupings of customers. They view sellers as constituting the industry and buyers as constituting the market. They talk about need markets (the diet-seeking market), product markets (the shoe market), demographic markets (the youth market), and geographic markets (the French market); or they extend the concept to cover other markets, such as voter markets, labor markets, and donor markets.

Figure 1.2 shows the relationship between the industry and the market. Sellers and buyers are connected by four flows. The sellers send goods and services and communications such as ads and direct mail to the market; in return they receive money and information such as customer attitudes and sales data. The inner loop shows an exchange of money for goods and services; the outer loop shows an exchange of information.

KEY CUSTOMER MARKETS Consider the following key customer markets: consumer, business, global, and nonprofit.

Consumer Markets Companies selling mass consumer goods and services such as soft drinks, cosmetics, air travel, and athletic shoes and equipment spend a great deal of time trying to establish a superior brand image. Much of a brand's strength depends on developing a superior product and packaging, ensuring its availability, and backing it with engaging communications and reliable service.

Business Markets Companies selling business goods and services often face well-trained and well-informed professional buyers who are skilled at evaluating competitive offerings. Business buyers buy goods in order to make or resell a product to others at a profit. Business marketers must demonstrate how their products will help these buyers achieve

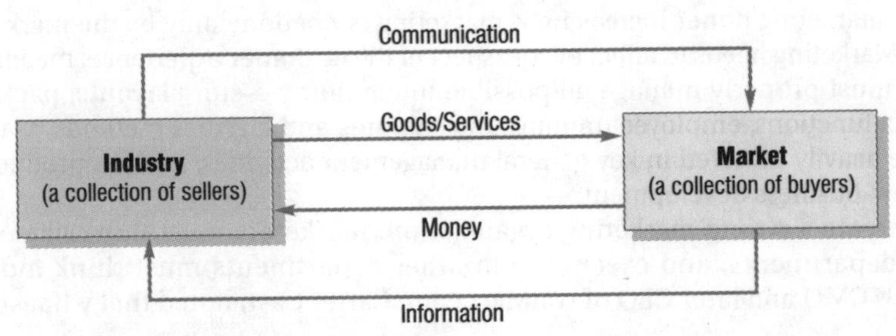

FIG. 1.2

A Simple Marketing System

higher revenue or lower costs. Advertising can play a role, but the sales force, price, and the company's reputation for reliability and quality may play a stronger one.

Global Markets Companies selling goods and services in the global marketplace face additional decisions and challenges. They must decide which countries to enter; how to enter each (as an exporter, licenser, joint venture partner, contract manufacturer, or solo manufacturer); how to adapt their product and service features to each country; how to price their products in different countries; and how to adapt their communications to fit different cultures. They make these decisions in the face of different requirements for buying, negotiating, owning, and disposing of property; different culture, language, and legal and political systems; and currencies that might fluctuate in value. Yet, the payoff for doing all this additional legwork can be huge.

ALASKA DEPARTMENT OF COMMERCE, WAL-MART

In 2005 alone, China accounted for $337 million of Alaska's exports—from seafood and fishmeal to minerals, fertilizers, and wood—and surpassed Canada to become Alaska's third-largest export partner. Noting the huge market potential of China, especially with the 2008 Olympics in Beijing and the 2010 World Expo slated for Shanghai, Wal-Mart purchased about $140,000 of Alaska seafood for its China stores. In order to compete with white fish and farmed salmon from Norway, five Wal-Mart stores hired Alaska officials to host cooking demonstrations of wild Alaska sockeye salmon and black cod during a 14-day span. Although they were labor intensive, the demonstrations gave an immediate taste test to China's young, sophisticated urban residents, who can pay the high prices these fish command.[13]

Nonprofit and Governmental Markets Companies selling their goods to nonprofit organizations such as churches, universities, charitable organizations, and government agencies need to price carefully, because these buyers have limited purchasing power. Lower selling prices affect the features and quality the seller can build into the offering. Much government purchasing calls for bids, and buyers often favor the lowest bid in the absence of extenuating factors.

MARKETPLACES, MARKETSPACES, AND METAMARKETS The *marketplace* is physical, such as a store you shop in; *marketspace* is digital, as when you shop on the Internet.[14]

Northwestern University's Mohan Sawhney has proposed the concept of a *metamarket* to describe a cluster of complementary products and services that are closely related in the minds of consumers, but spread across a diverse set of industries. The automobile metamarket consists of automobile manufacturers, new car and used car dealers, financing companies, insurance companies, mechanics, spare parts dealers, service shops, auto magazines, classified auto ads in newspapers, and auto sites on the Internet.

In purchasing a car, a buyer will get involved in many parts of this metamarket, and this creates an opportunity for *metamediaries* to assist buyers in moving seamlessly through these groups, although they are disconnected in physical space. One example is Edmund's (www.edmunds.com), a Web site where a car buyer can find the stated features and prices of different automobiles and easily click to other sites to search for the lowest-price dealer for financing, for car accessories, and for used cars at bargain prices. Metamediaries also serve other metamarkets, such as the home ownership market, the parenting and baby care market, and the wedding market.[15]

Marketing in Practice

How is marketing done? Increasingly, marketing is *not* done only by the marketing department. Marketing needs to affect every aspect of the customer experience, meaning that marketers must properly manage all possible touch points—store layouts, package designs, product functions, employee training, and shipping and logistics methods. Marketing must also be heavily involved in key general management activities, such as product innovation and new-business development.

To create a strong marketing organization, marketers must think like executives in other departments, and executives in other departments must think more like marketers.[16] CMO and later CEO of WalMart.com, Carter Cast, noted that what surprised him

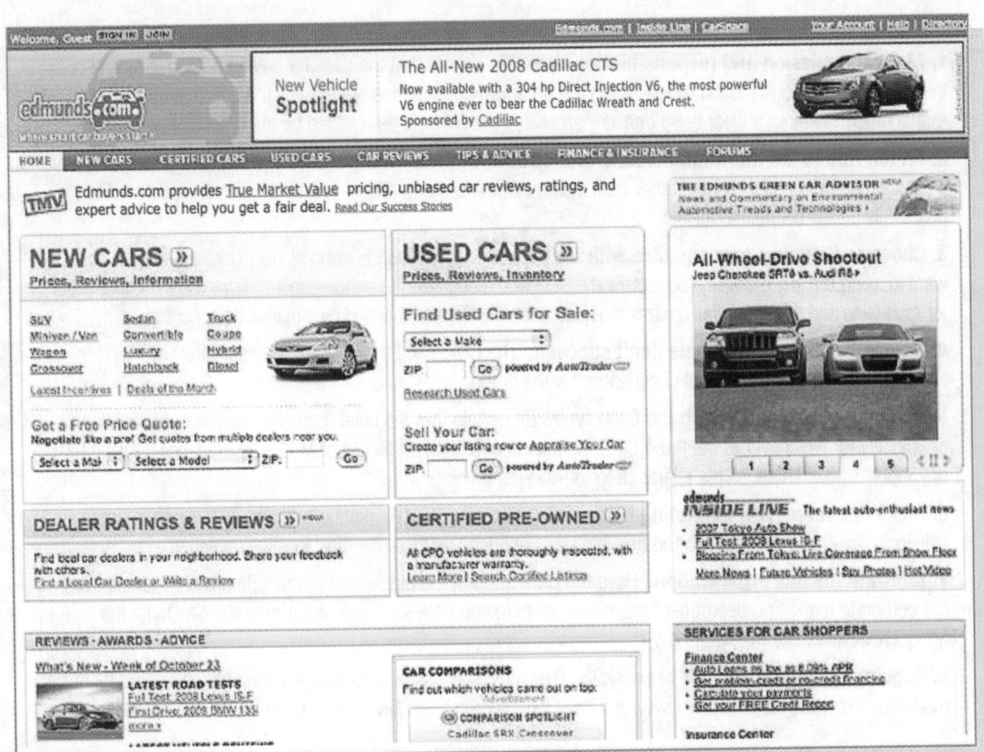

Edmund's is a metamediary Web site that helps prospective car buyers navigate the automobile metamarket online.

most when he became CMO was "that I would interact so much with functions outside of marketing. I didn't realize it is a holistic assignment. Then I realized I really had to understand things like product supply, cost break-evens, and accounting."[17]

Companies generally establish a marketing department to be responsible for creating and delivering customer value, but as the late David Packard of Hewlett-Packard observed, "Marketing is far too important to leave to the marketing department." Companies now know that every employee has an impact on the customer and must see the customer as the source of the company's prosperity. So they're beginning to emphasize interdepartmental teamwork to manage key processes. They're also placing more emphasis on the smooth management of core business processes, such as new-product realization, customer acquisition and retention, and order fulfillment.

In practice, marketing follows a logical process. The marketing *planning* process consists of analyzing marketing opportunities, selecting target markets, designing marketing strategies, developing marketing programs, and managing the marketing effort. In highly competitive marketplaces, however, marketing planning is more fluid and is continually refreshed. Companies must always be moving forward with marketing programs, innovating products and services, staying in touch with customer needs, and seeking new advantages rather than relying on past strengths.

The changing new marketing environment is putting considerable demands on marketing executives. Marketers must have diverse quantitative and qualitative skills, an entrepreneurial attitude, and a keen understanding of how marketing can create value within their organization.[18] They must work in harmony with the sales function.

There are five key functions for a CMO in leading marketing within the organization:

1. Strengthening the brands
2. Measuring marketing effectiveness
3. Driving new product development based on customer needs
4. Gathering meaningful customer insights
5. Utilizing new marketing technology

Harvard's John Quelch and Gail McGovern note that there is tremendous variability in the responsibilities and job descriptions for CMOs.[19] They offer eight ways to improve CMO success (see Figure 1.3).

FIG. 1.3

Improving CMO Success

Source: Gail McGovern and John A. Quelch, "The Fall and Rise of the CMO," *Strategy&Business*, Winter 2004, Reprinted by permission.

1. Make the mission and responsibilities clear. Be certain that the case for having a CMO is strong and the mission is well understood by leaders in the organization, particularly the CEO, the board, and line management. Without a clear need (real or perceived), the role will be rejected by the organization.

2. Fit the role to the marketing culture and structure. Avoid having a CMO in a marketing-led company that has many individual brands rather than a single corporate umbrella—unless the person appointed to the position is a well-connected insider.

3. Choose a CMO who is compatible with the CEO. Beware of the CEO who wants to hire a CMO but doesn't want to relinquish any marketing control. Find a CEO who recognizes his or her responsibility to be the cheerleader for marketing and the brand, but realizes the need to be guided and coached by a marketing specialist.

4. Remember that showpeople don't succeed. The CMO should work hard to ensure the CEO is successful at being the principal cheerleader for the brand.

5. Match the personality with the CMO type. Be certain that the chief marketer has the right skills and personality for whichever of the three CMO models he or she might fill (VP of Marketing Services, Classic CMO, or "Super" CMO). There is little tolerance for on-the-job training.

6. Make line managers marketing heroes. By stretching their marketing budgets, CMOs can improve a division's marketing productivity and help business unit leaders increase their top-line revenues.

7. Infiltrate the line organization. Have the CMO support the placement of marketing professionals from the corporate marketing department into divisional marketing roles. Provide input from the CMO into the annual reviews of line marketers.

8. Require right-brain and left-brain skills. The most successful CMO will have strong creative and technical marketing expertise, be politically savvy, and have the interpersonal skills to be a great leader and manager.

::: Core Marketing Concepts

To understand the marketing function, we need to understand the following core set of concepts.

Needs, Wants, and Demands

Needs are the basic human requirements. People need air, food, water, clothing, and shelter to survive. People also have strong needs for recreation, education, and entertainment. These needs become *wants* when they are directed to specific objects that might satisfy the need. A consumer in the United States needs food but may want a hamburger, french fries, and a soft drink. A person in Mauritius needs food but may want a mango, rice, lentils, and beans. Wants are shaped by our society.

Demands are wants for specific products backed by an ability to pay. Many people want a Mercedes; only a few are willing and able to buy one. Companies must measure not only how many people want their product, but also how many would actually be willing and able to buy it.

These distinctions shed light on the frequent criticism that "marketers create needs" or "marketers get people to buy things they don't want." Marketers do not create needs: Needs preexist marketers. Marketers, along with other societal factors, influence wants. Marketers might promote the idea that a Mercedes would satisfy a person's need for social status. They do not, however, create the need for social status.

Understanding customer needs and wants is not always simple. Some customers have needs of which they are not fully conscious, or they cannot articulate these needs, or they use words that require some interpretation. What does it mean when the customer asks for a "powerful" lawnmower, a "fast" lathe, an "attractive" bathing suit, or a "restful" hotel? The marketer must probe further. We can distinguish among five types of needs:

1. Stated needs (The customer wants an inexpensive car.)
2. Real needs (The customer wants a car whose operating cost, not its initial price, is low.)
3. Unstated needs (The customer expects good service from the dealer.)

4. Delight needs (The customer would like the dealer to include an onboard navigation system.)
5. Secret needs (The customer wants friends to see him as a savvy consumer.)

Responding only to the stated need may shortchange the customer. Many consumers do not know what they want in a product. Consumers did not know much about cellular phones when they were first introduced, and Nokia and Ericsson fought to shape consumer perceptions of them. Simply giving customers what they want isn't enough any more—to gain an edge companies must help customers learn what they want.

Target Markets, Positioning, and Segmentation

A marketer can rarely satisfy everyone in a market. Not everyone likes the same cereal, hotel room, restaurant, automobile, college, or movie. Therefore, marketers start by dividing the market into segments. They identify and profile distinct groups of buyers who might prefer or require varying product and service mixes by examining demographic, psychographic, and behavioral differences among buyers.

WAL-MART

Wal-Mart uses segmentation to reach customers in different geographic markets, with its new Store of the Community concept. Now over two dozen Wal-Mart stores have been designed to reflect the communities in which they are located. For instance, there's a Wal-Mart with a Western flair in Ft. Collins, Colorado, and a two-level art-deco-inspired unit to draw in wealthy African Americans in Baldwin Hills, California. In an effort to cater to the country's fourth-largest Amish community, the Middlefield, Ohio, Wal-Mart offers hitching posts outside for horse and buggies, block ice for refrigerators, and a huge assortment of denim fabric for making work pants.

After identifying market segments, the marketer then decides which present the greatest opportunity—which are its *target markets.* For each, the firm develops a *market offering* that it *positions* in the minds of the target buyers as delivering some central benefit(s). For example, Volvo develops its cars for buyers to whom safety is a major concern. Volvo, therefore, positions its car as the safest a customer can buy. Companies do best when they choose their target market(s) carefully and prepare tailored marketing programs.

The art-deco styling of this new Wal-Mart store is meant to appeal to the wealthy shoppers in its California neighborhood.

Offerings and Brands

Companies address needs by putting forth a **value proposition**, a set of benefits that they offer to customers to satisfy their needs. The intangible value proposition is made physical by an *offering,* which can be a combination of products, services, information, and experiences.

A *brand* is an offering from a known source. A brand name such as McDonald's carries many associations in people's minds that make up the brand image: hamburgers, fun, children, fast food, convenience, and golden arches. All companies strive to build a strong, favorable, and unique brand image.

Value and Satisfaction

The offering will be successful if it delivers value and satisfaction to the target buyer. The buyer chooses between different offerings based on which she perceives to deliver the most value. *Value* reflects the sum of the perceived tangible and intangible benefits and costs to customers. It's primarily a combination of quality, service, and price ("qsp"), called the "customer value triad." Value increases with quality and service and decreases with price, although other factors can also play an important role in our perceptions of value.

Value is a central marketing concept. We can think of marketing as the identification, creation, communication, delivery, and monitoring of customer value. *Satisfaction* reflects a person's judgments of a product's perceived performance (or outcome) in relationship to expectations. If the performance falls short of expectations, the customer is dissatisfied and disappointed. If it matches expectations, the customer is satisfied. If it exceeds them, the customer is delighted.

Marketing Channels

To reach a target market, the marketer uses three kinds of marketing channels. *Communication channels* deliver and receive messages from target buyers and include newspapers, magazines, radio, television, mail, telephone, billboards, posters, fliers, CDs, audiotapes, and the Internet. Beyond these, just as we convey messages by our facial expressions and clothing, firms communicate through the look of their retail stores, the appearance of their Web sites, and many other media. Marketers are increasingly adding dialogue channels such as e-mail, blogs, and toll-free numbers to familiar monologue channels such as ads.

The marketer uses *distribution channels* to display, sell, or deliver the physical product or service(s) to the buyer or user. They include distributors, wholesalers, retailers, and agents.

The marketer also uses *service channels* to carry out transactions with potential buyers. Service channels include warehouses, transportation companies, banks, and insurance companies that facilitate transactions. Marketers clearly face a design challenge in choosing the best mix of communication, distribution, and service channels for their offerings.

Supply Chain

The supply chain is a longer channel stretching from raw materials to components to final products that are carried to final buyers. The supply chain for women's purses starts with hides and moves through tanning, cutting, manufacturing, and the marketing channels to bring products to customers. Each company captures only a certain percentage of the total value generated by the supply chain's value delivery system. When a company acquires competitors or expands upstream or downstream, its aim is to capture a higher percentage of supply chain value.

Competition

Competition includes all the actual and potential rival offerings and substitutes a buyer might consider. Suppose an automobile company is planning to buy steel for its cars. There are several possible levels of competitors. The manufacturer can buy steel from U.S. Steel in the United States, it can buy from a foreign firm in Japan or Korea, it can buy from a minimill such as Nucor at a cost savings, or it can buy aluminum from Alcoa for certain parts to reduce the car's weight or engineered plastics from Saudi Basic Industries Corporation (SABIC), purchasers of GE Plastics, for bumpers instead of steel. Clearly, U.S. Steel would be thinking too narrowly about its competition if it thought only of other integrated steel companies. In fact, in the long run U.S. Steel is more likely to be hurt by substitute products than by other steel companies.

Marketing Environment

The marketing environment consists of the task environment and the broad environment. The *task environment* includes the actors engaged in producing, distributing, and promoting the offering. These are the company, suppliers, distributors, dealers, and the target customers. In the supplier group are material suppliers and service suppliers, such as marketing research agencies, advertising agencies, banking and insurance companies, transportation companies, and telecommunications companies. Distributors and dealers include agents, brokers, manufacturer representatives, and others who facilitate finding and selling to customers.

The *broad environment* consists of six components: demographic environment, economic environment, physical environment, technological environment, political-legal environment, and social-cultural environment. Marketers must pay close attention to the trends and developments in these environments and make timely adjustments to their marketing strategies.

::: The New Marketing Realities

We can say with some confidence that "the marketplace isn't what it used to be." Marketers must attend and respond to a number of significant developments.

Major Societal Forces

Today the marketplace is radically different as a result of major, and sometimes interlinking, societal forces that have created new behaviors, new opportunities, and new challenges:

- ***Network information technology.*** The digital revolution has created an Information Age. The Industrial Age was characterized by mass production and mass consumption, stores stuffed with inventory, ads everywhere, and rampant discounting. The Information Age promises to lead to more accurate levels of production, more targeted communications, and more relevant pricing.
- ***Globalization.*** Technological advances in transportation, shipping, and communication have made it easier for companies to market in other countries, and easier for consumers to buy products and services from marketers in other countries.
- ***Deregulation.*** Many countries have deregulated industries to create greater competition and growth opportunities. In the United States, laws restricting financial services, telecommunications, and electric utilities have all been loosened in the spirit of greater competition.
- ***Privatization.*** Many countries have converted public companies to private ownership and management to increase their efficiency, such as British Airways and British Telecom in the United Kingdom.
- ***Heightened competition.*** Brand manufacturers are facing intense competition from domestic and foreign brands, resulting in rising promotion costs and shrinking profit margins. They are being further buffeted by powerful retailers that command limited shelf space and are putting out their own store brands in competition with national brands. Many strong brands are extending into related product categories, creating megabrands with much presence and reputation.
- ***Industry convergence.*** Industry boundaries are blurring at an incredible rate as companies are recognizing that new opportunities lie at the intersection of two or more industries. The computing and consumer electronics industries are converging as the giants of the computer world such as Dell, Gateway, and Hewlett-Packard release a stream of entertainment devices—from MP3 players to plasma TVs and camcorders. The shift to digital technology is fueling this massive convergence.[20]
- ***Consumer resistance.*** A 2004 Yankelovich study found record levels of marketing resistance from consumers.[21] A majority of those surveyed reported negative opinions about marketing and advertising, stating that they avoid products that they feel overmarket. The increased popularity of digital video recorders such as TiVo make it easier for consumers to skip or "zap" TV commercials, in part reflecting their desire for marketing avoidance.

Retail transformation. Small retailers are succumbing to the growing power of giant retailers and "category killers." Store-based retailers face competition from catalog houses; direct-mail firms; newspaper, magazine, and TV direct-to-customer ads; home shopping TV; and e-commerce on the Internet. In response, entrepreneurial retailers are building entertainment into their stores with coffee bars, lectures, demonstrations, and performances, marketing an "experience" rather than a product assortment.

MAC COSMETICS INC.

A division of cosmetics giant Estée Lauder, MAC Cosmetics is considered a significant reason for Lauder's 13% net makeup sales increase. Yet, MAC's 1,000 stores worldwide don't simply sell Small Eye Shadow, Studio Fix, Lustreglass, and Pro Longwear Lipcoulour. Instead, they rely on highly paid "artists" to bond with each customer during a free makeup consultation and application lesson. Although this tack is hardly new in the world of retail makeup, what's unique is that MAC's artists are not out there to bump up their commissions and load customers down with more products. Rather, they're trained to collaborate with customers so they'll leave the store with $50 or more of MAC products *and* the feeling, "I can definitely do this at home." The goal, says Matthew Waitesmith, MAC's head of "artist training and development," is for each customer to feel she's had an authentically artistic experience "that hopefully means they'll return to the place that makes them feel like an artist."[22]

Disintermediation. The amazing success of early online dot-coms, such as AOL, Amazon.com, Yahoo!, eBay, E*TRADE, and dozens of others that created *disintermediation* in the delivery of products and services by intervening between the traditional flow of goods through distribution channels, struck terror into the hearts of many established manufacturers and retailers. In response, many traditional companies engaged in *reintermediation* and became "brick-and-click" retailers, adding online services to their existing offerings. Many brick-and-click competitors became stronger contenders than pure-click firms, because they had a larger pool of resources to work with and well-established brand names.

The societal forces that spawned this Information Age have resulted in many new consumer and company capabilities.

New Consumer Capabilities

Customers today perceive fewer real product differences and show less brand loyalty, and they are becoming more price and quality sensitive in their search for value. Consider what consumers have today that they didn't have yesterday:

A substantial increase in buying power. Buyers are only a click away from comparing competitor prices and product attributes on the Internet. They can even name their price for a hotel room, airline ticket, or mortgage. Business buyers can run a *reverse auction* in which sellers compete to capture their business. They can readily join with others to aggregate their purchases and achieve deeper volume discounts.

A greater variety of available goods and services. Amazon.com quickly became the world's largest bookstore but has since branched into retail sales of music and movies, clothing and accessories, consumer electronics, health and beauty aids, and home and garden products. Buyers can order goods online from anywhere in the world, bypassing limited local offerings and realizing great savings by ordering in countries with lower prices.

A great amount of information about practically anything. People can read almost any newspaper in any language from anywhere in the world. They can access online encyclopedias, dictionaries, medical information, movie ratings, consumer reports, and countless other information sources.

Greater ease in interacting and placing and receiving orders. Today's buyers can place orders from home, office, or mobile phone 24 hours a day, 7 days a week, and quickly receive goods at their home or office.

An ability to compare notes on products and services. Social networking sites bring together buyers with a common interest. At CarSpace.com auto enthusiasts talk about chrome rims, the latest BMW model, and where to find a great mechanic in their local area. Marketers are eying the success of the site, given that 35% of young, first-time car buyers consider the Internet their most important shopping tool.[23]

An amplified voice to influence peer and public opinion. The Internet fuels personal connections and user-generated content through social media such as MySpace and single-use social networks such as Flickr (photos), Del.cio.us (links), Digg (news stories),

Wikipedia (encyclopedia articles), and YouTube (video).[24] In late 2004, Kryptonite, a firm that makes high-priced bike locks, found itself in an awkward position when several blogs showed how the firm's U-shaped locks could be easily picked using only the plastic casing of a Bic pen.[25]

KFC, CONVERSE, WM. WRIGLEY JR.

Although Chinese citizens are still prohibited from criticizing the government online, they have thousands of online forums for airing grievances about poor customer service, misleading ad campaigns, shoddy products, safety standards, and more. Chinese consumers are vocal and active, and when enough of them voice a complaint, companies listen. When a Chinese TV spot for Yum! Brand Inc.'s KFC Corp. depicted a hard-working student who didn't pass his exams and two carefree children who enjoyed KFC fried chicken and did, KFC received so many complaints for suggesting hard work doesn't pay that it changed the ad to show all three children doing well. Smart companies are enlisting their opinionated Internet consumers to give input before a product is launched. Converse and Wm. Wrigley Jr. conducted a joint promotion encouraging Chinese consumers to come up with their own cool designs for Converse sneakers that featured Wrigley's Juicy Fruit logo. [26]

New Company Capabilities

New forces also have combined to generate a new set of capabilities for today's companies:

- Marketers can use the Internet as a powerful information and sales channel, augmenting their geographical reach to inform customers and promote their businesses and products worldwide. By establishing one or more Web sites, they can list their products and services, history, its business philosophy, job opportunities, and other information of interest to visitors.
- Researchers can collect fuller and richer information about markets, customers, prospects, and competitors. They can also conduct fresh marketing research using the Internet to arrange for focus groups, send out questionnaires, and gather primary data in several other ways.
- Managers can facilitate and speed internal communication among their employees by using the Internet as a private intranet. Employees can query one another, seek advice, and download or upload needed information from and to the company's main computer.
- Companies can also facilitate and speed external communication among customers by creating online and off-line "buzz" through brand advocates and user communities. In 2003, the Rock Bottom Brew pub chain reported a 76% jump in revenues after hiring BzzAgent and 1,000-plus of its "agents" to launch a 13-week word-of-mouth campaign.[27] BzzAgent has assembled a nationwide volunteer army of 260,000 consumers who join promotional programs for products and services they deem worth talking about.[28]
- Target marketing and two-way communication are easier thanks to the proliferation of special-interest magazines, TV channels, and Internet newsgroups. Extranets linking suppliers and distributors let firms send and receive information, place orders, and make payments more efficiently. The company can also interact with each customer individually to *personalize* messages, services, and the relationship. Discount brokerage Charles Schwab spent 25% of its marketing communication budget online in 2005 to support its "Talk to Chuck" campaign, up from 8% in 2003.[29]
- Marketers can send ads, coupons, samples, and information to customers who have requested them or have given the company permission to send them. They can now assemble information about individual customers' purchases, preferences, demographics, and profitability. British supermarket giant Tesco is outpacing its rival store, Sainsbury, by using its Clubcard data to personalize offers according to individual customer attributes.[30]
- Companies can reach consumers on the move with mobile marketing. Using GPS technology, for instance, consumers can download company logos so they can spot brands such as Dunkin' Donuts or Baskin Robbins when they're on the road.[31] Firms can also advertise on video iPods and reach consumers on their cell phones through mobile marketing.[32] General Motors Corp. launched its Pontiac G6 with a promotion asking consumers to

More and more companies can produce individually differentiated goods, even consumer products like these.

take photos of the sports sedan on their camera phones and send them to GM in return for a free classic punk rock ring tone and a chance to win $1 million in cash. About 18,500 photos were sent, mostly from the G6 target market of young males under the age of 25.[33]

- Firms can produce individually differentiated goods, whether they're ordered in person, on the phone, or online, thanks to advances in factory customization, computers, the Internet, and database marketing software. For a price, customers can buy M&M candies with their names on them, Wheaties boxes or Jones soda cans with their pictures on the front, and Heinz ketchup bottles with customized messages.[34] BMW's technology now allows buyers to design their own models from among 350 variations, with 500 options, 90 exterior colors, and 170 trims. The company claims that 80% of the cars bought by individuals in Europe and up to 30% bought in the United States are built to order.

- Managers can improve purchasing, recruiting, training, and internal and external communications. Aerospace and defense contractor Boeing has joined large, high-profile companies Walt Disney, General Motors, and McDonald's in embracing corporate blogging to communicate with the public, customers, and employees. External blogs allow dialogues with a marketing vice president and a glimpse into the flight testing of the new 777 model; internal blogs allow conversations on hot topics and anonymous feedback.[35]

- Corporate buyers can achieve substantial savings by using the Internet to compare sellers' prices and to purchase materials at auction or by posting their own terms. Companies can improve logistics and operations to reap substantial cost savings, at the same time improving accuracy and service quality.

- Firms can also recruit new employees online, and many are also preparing Internet training products for download to employees, dealers, and agents.

::: Company Orientation toward the Marketplace

Given these new marketing realities, what philosophy should guide a company's marketing efforts? Increasingly, marketers operate consistent with a holistic marketing concept. Let's review the evolution of earlier marketing ideas.

The Production Concept

The production concept is one of the oldest concepts in business. It holds that consumers will prefer products that are widely available and inexpensive. Managers of production-oriented businesses concentrate on achieving high production efficiency, low costs, and mass distribution. This orientation makes sense in developing countries such as China, where the largest PC manufacturer, Lenovo, and domestic appliances giant Haier take advantage of the country's huge and inexpensive labor pool to dominate the market. Marketers also use the production concept when a company wants to expand the market.[36]

The Product Concept

The product concept proposes that consumers favor products that offer the most quality, performance, or innovative features. Managers in these organizations focus on making superior products and improving them over time. However, these managers are sometimes caught up in a love affair with their products. They might commit the "better-mousetrap" fallacy, believing that a better mousetrap will lead people to beat a path to their door. A new or improved product will not necessarily be successful unless it's priced, distributed, advertised, and sold properly.

The Selling Concept

The selling concept holds that consumers and businesses, if left alone, won't buy enough of the organization's products. The organization must, therefore, undertake an aggressive selling and promotion effort. The selling concept is expressed in the thinking of Sergio Zyman, Coca-Cola's former vice president of marketing, who said: "The purpose of marketing is to sell more stuff to more people more often for more money in order to make more profit."[37]

The selling concept is practiced most aggressively with unsought goods, goods that buyers normally do not think of buying, such as insurance, encyclopedias, and cemetery plots. Most firms also practice the selling concept when they have overcapacity. Their aim is to sell what they make, rather than make what the market wants. However, marketing based on hard selling carries high risks. It assumes that customers who are coaxed into buying a product will like it, and that if they don't, they not only won't return or bad-mouth it or complain to consumer organizations, but they might even buy it again.

The Marketing Concept

To learn how Tata applied the marketing concept to deepen its understanding of customers in India, visit www.pearsoned.co.in/marketingmanagementindia.

The marketing concept emerged in the mid-1950s.[38] Instead of a product-centered, "make-and-sell" philosophy, business shifted to a customer-centered, "sense-and-respond" philosophy. The job is not to find the right customers for your products, but to find the right products for your customers. Dell Computer doesn't prepare a perfect computer for its target market. Rather, it provides product platforms on which each person customizes the features he desires in the computer.

The marketing concept holds that the key to achieving organizational goals is being more effective than competitors in creating, delivering, and communicating superior customer value to your chosen target markets.

Theodore Levitt of Harvard drew a perceptive contrast between the selling and marketing concepts:

> Selling focuses on the needs of the seller; marketing on the needs of the buyer. Selling is preoccupied with the seller's need to convert his product into cash; marketing with the idea of satisfying the needs of the customer by means of the product and the whole cluster of things associated with creating, delivering, and finally consuming it.[39]

Several scholars have found that companies that embrace the marketing concept achieve superior performance.[40] This was first demonstrated by companies practicing a *reactive market orientation*—understanding and meeting customers' expressed needs. Some critics say this means companies develop only very basic innovations. Narver and his colleagues argue that more advanced, high-level innovation is possible if the focus is on customers' latent needs. Narver calls this a *proactive marketing orientation.*[41] Companies such as 3M, Hewlett Packard, and Motorola have made a practice of researching latent needs through a "probe-and-learn" process. Companies that practice both a reactive and a proactive marketing orientation are implementing a *total market orientation* and are likely to be the most successful.

Nike is widely acknowledged as one of the most skilled marketers around.

The Holistic Marketing Concept

Without question, the trends and forces defining the 21st century are leading business firms to a new set of beliefs and practices. Today's best marketers recognize the need to have a more complete, cohesive approach that goes beyond traditional applications of the marketing concept. "Marketing Memo: Marketing Right and Wrong" suggests where companies go wrong—and how they can get it right—in their marketing.

The **holistic marketing** concept is based on the development, design, and implementation of marketing programs,

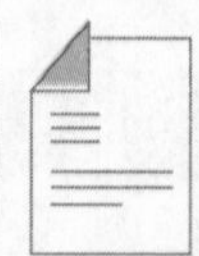

MARKETING **MEMO** | MARKETING RIGHT AND WRONG

The Ten Deadly Sins of Marketing	The Ten Commandments of Marketing
1. The company is not sufficiently market focused and customer driven.	**1.** The company segments the market, chooses the best segments, and develops a strong position in each chosen segment.
2. The company does not fully understand its target customers.	**2.** The company maps its customers' needs, perceptions, preferences, and behavior and motivates it stakeholders to obsess about serving and satisfying the customers.
3. The company needs to better define and monitor its competitors.	**3.** The company knows its major competitors and their strengths and weaknesses.
4. The company has not properly managed its relationships with its stakeholders.	**4.** The company builds partners out of its stakeholders and generously rewards them.
5. The company is not good at finding new opportunities.	**5.** The company develops systems for identifying opportunities, ranking them, and choosing the best ones.
6. The company's marketing plans and planning process are deficient.	**6.** The company manages a marketing planning system that leads to insightful long-term and short-term plans.
7. The company's product and service policies need tightening.	**7.** The company exercises strong control over its product and service mix.
8. The company's brand-building and communications skills are weak.	**8.** The company builds strong brands by using the most cost-effective communication and promotion tools.
9. The company is not well organized to carry on effective and efficient marketing.	**9.** The company builds marketing leadership and a team spirit among its various departments.
10. The company has not made maximum use of technology.	**10.** The company constantly adds technology that gives it a competitive advantage in the marketplace.

Adapted Source: Philip Kotler, *Ten Deadly Marketing Sins* (Hoboken, NJ: John Wiley & Sons, 2004).

processes, and activities that recognizes their breadth and interdependencies. Holistic marketing recognizes that "everything matters" in marketing—and that a broad, integrated perspective is often necessary.

Holistic marketing is thus an approach that attempts to recognize and reconcile the scope and complexities of marketing activities. Figure 1.4 provides a schematic overview of four broad components characterizing holistic marketing: relationship marketing, integrated marketing, internal marketing, and performance marketing. We'll examine these major themes throughout this book. Successful companies will be those that can keep their marketing changing with the changes in their marketplace—and marketspace. "Breakthrough Marketing: Nike" describes how that company has successfully changed—and thrived—through the years.

Relationship Marketing

Increasingly, a key goal of marketing is to develop deep, enduring relationships with people and organizations that could directly or indirectly affect the success of the firm's marketing activities. **Relationship marketing** aims to build mutually satisfying long-term relationships with key constituents in order to earn and retain their business.[42]

Four key constituents for relationship marketing are customers, employees, marketing partners (channels, suppliers, distributors, dealers, agencies), and members of the financial community (shareholders, investors, analysts). Marketers must respect the need to create prosperity among all these constituents and develop policies and strategies to balance the

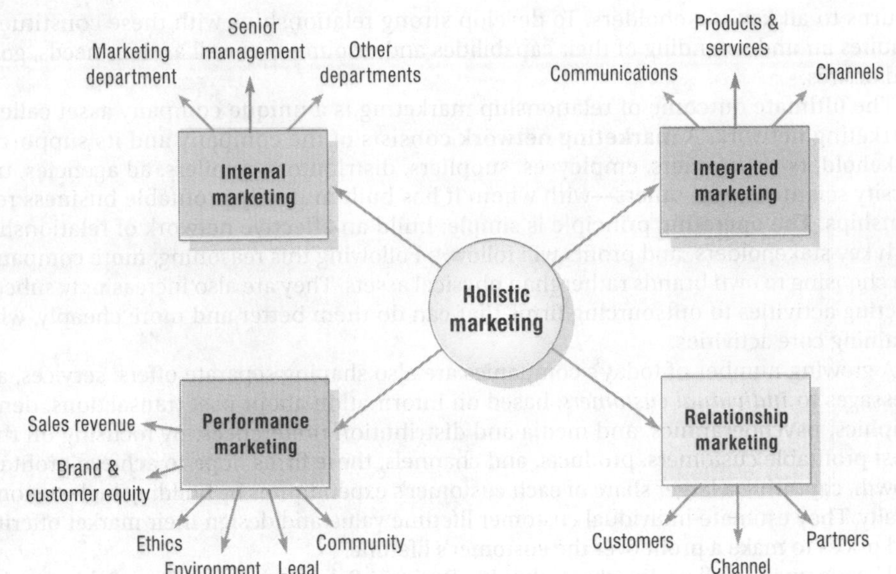

FIG. 1.4

Holistic Marketing Dimensions

BREAKTHROUGH MARKETING | NIKE

Nike hit the ground running in 1962. Originally known as Blue Ribbon Sports, the company focused on providing high-quality running shoes designed especially for athletes by athletes. Founder Philip Knight believed that high-tech shoes for runners could be manufactured at competitive prices if imported from abroad. The company's commitment to designing innovative footwear for serious athletes helped it build a cult following among U.S. consumers.

Nike believed in a "pyramid of influence" where product and brand choices were influenced by the preferences and behavior of a small percentage of top athletes. Therefore, from the start, Nike's marketing campaigns featured winning athletes as spokespeople. Nike's first spokesperson, runner Steve Prefontaine, had an irreverent attitude that matched the company's spirit.

In 1985, Nike signed up then-rookie guard Michael Jordan as a spokesperson. Jordan was still an up-and-comer, but he personified superior performance. Nike's bet paid off: The Air Jordan line of basketball shoes flew off the shelves, with revenues of over $100 million in the first year alone.

In 1988, Nike aired the first ads in its $20 million "Just Do It" ad campaign. The campaign, which ultimately featured 12 TV spots in all, subtly challenged a generation of athletic enthusiasts to chase their goals; it was a natural manifestation of Nike's attitude of self-empowerment through sports.

As Nike began expanding overseas to Europe, however, it found that its U.S.-style ads were seen there as too aggressive. Nike realized it had to "authenticate" its brand in Europe the way it had in the United States. That meant building credibility and relevance in European sports, especially soccer (known outside the United States as football). Nike became actively involved as a sponsor of youth leagues, local clubs, and national teams.

Authenticity also required that consumers see athletes using the product, especially athletes who win. The big break came in 1994, when the Brazilian team (the only national team for which Nike had any real sponsorships) won the World Cup. That victory in the world's most popular sport helped Nike succeed in other international markets such as China, where Nike came to command 10% of the shoe market. By 2003 overseas revenues surpassed U.S. revenues for the first time, and by 2006 international divisions generated nearly $7.3 billion in revenue, compared to $5.7 billion from the United States.

In addition to expanding overseas, Nike moved into new athletic footwear, apparel, and equipment product categories. These included the Nike Golf brand of footwear, apparel, and equipment, which were all endorsed by megastar Tiger Woods. In 2005, Nike introduced an urban-themed collection of retro footwear and apparel bearing the name of the original company, Blue Ribbon Sports. Blue Ribbon Sports designs—which included jeans, belts, sweaters, and woven shirts—were sold at high-end retailers such as Barney's and Fred Segal.

Today, Nike dominates the athletic footwear market. Swooshes abound on everything from wristwatches to golf clubs to swimming caps. As a result of its expansion across geographic markets and product categories, Nike is the top athletic apparel and footwear manufacturer in the world, with corporate fiscal 2007 revenues of nearly $16 billion.

Sources: Justin Ewers and Tim Smart, "A Designer Swooshes In," *U.S. News & World Report*, January 26, 2004, p. 12; "Corporate Media Executive of the Year," *Delaney Report*, January 12, 2004, p. 1; "10 Top Nontraditional Campaigns," *Advertising Age*, December 22, 2003, p. 24; Chris Zook and James Allen, "Growth Outside the Core," *Harvard Business Review* 8 (December 2003): 66.

returns to all key stakeholders. To develop strong relationships with these constituents requires an understanding of their capabilities and resources, as well as their needs, goals, and desires.

The ultimate outcome of relationship marketing is a unique company asset called a marketing network. A **marketing network** consists of the company and its supporting stakeholders—customers, employees, suppliers, distributors, retailers, ad agencies, university scientists, and others—with whom it has built mutually profitable business relationships. The operating principle is simple: build an effective network of relationships with key stakeholders, and profits will follow.[43] Following this reasoning, more companies are choosing to own brands rather than physical assets. They are also increasingly subcontracting activities to outsourcing firms that can do them better and more cheaply, while retaining core activities.

A growing number of today's companies are also shaping separate offers, services, and messages to *individual customers,* based on information about past transactions, demographics, psychographics, and media and distribution preferences. By focusing on their most profitable customers, products, and channels, these firms hope to achieve profitable growth, capturing a larger share of each customer's expenditures by building high customer loyalty. They estimate individual customer lifetime value and design their market offerings and prices to make a profit over the customer's lifetime.

These activities fall under what Columbia Business School professor Larry Selden and his wife and business consulting partner, Yoko Sugiura Selden, call "customer centricity." They offer the Royal Bank of Canada as an example:

ROYAL BANK OF CANADA

In thinking of its business in terms of customer segments rather than product segments, Royal Bank of Canada (RBC) has tagged each of its roughly 11 million clients and put them into meaningful segments. Now it can focus on measuring and managing the customer profitability of these segments. In the process, RBC discovered a sizeable subsegment of customers hidden within its broader categories of "wealth preservers" and "wealth accumulators." Dubbed "snowbirds," these individuals spent a number of months each winter in Florida, where they were experiencing difficulties establishing credit as well as missing their Canadian communities, particularly the familiarity of the French-Canadian accent and fluency in French. In order to meet their unique needs, RBC created a Canadian banking experience in Florida.[44]

Another goal of relationship marketing is to place much more emphasis on customer retention. Attracting a new customer may cost five times as much as doing a good enough job to retain an existing one. A bank aims to increase its share of the customer's wallet; the supermarket aims to capture a larger share of the customer's "stomach." Companies build customer share by offering a larger variety of goods to existing customers. They train their employees in cross-selling and up-selling.

Marketing must skillfully conduct not only customer relationship management (CRM), but partner relationship management (PRM) as well. Companies are deepening their partnering arrangements with key suppliers and distributors, thinking of these intermediaries not as customers but as partners in delivering value to final customers so everybody benefits. For example, tired of having its big rigs return empty as often as 15% of the time after making a delivery, General Mills entered a program with Fort James and a dozen other companies to combine one-way shipping routes into a cross-country loop served by a tag team of contracted trucks. As a result, General Mills reduced its empty-truck time to 6%, saving 7% on shipping costs in the process.[45]

Integrated Marketing

The marketer's task is to devise marketing activities and assemble fully integrated marketing programs to create, communicate, and deliver value for consumers. Marketing activities come in all forms.[46] McCarthy classified these activities as *marketing-mix* tools of four broad kinds, which he called *the four Ps* of marketing: product, price, place, and promotion.[47]

FIG. **1.5**

The Four P Components of the Marketing Mix

The particular marketing variables under each P are shown in Figure 1.5. Marketers make marketing-mix decisions for influencing their trade channels as well as their final consumers. Once they understand these groups, marketers make or customize an offering or solution, inform consumers—recognizing that many other sources of information also exist—set a price that offers real value, and choose places where the offering will be accessible.

The firm can change its price, sales force size, and advertising expenditures in the short run. It can develop new products and modify its distribution channels only in the long run. Thus the firm typically makes fewer period-to-period marketing-mix changes in the short run than the number of marketing-mix decision variables might suggest.

The four Ps represent the sellers' view of the marketing tools available for influencing buyers. From a buyer's point of view, each marketing tool is designed to deliver a customer benefit. A complementary breakdown of marketing activities has been proposed that centers on customers. Its four dimensions (SIVA) and the corresponding customer questions these are designed to answer are:[48]

1. Solution: How can I solve my problem?
2. Information: Where can I learn more about it?
3. Value: What is my total sacrifice to get this solution?
4. Access: Where can I find it?

Winning companies satisfy customer needs and surpass their expectations economically and conveniently and with effective communication.

Two key themes of integrated marketing are that (1) many different marketing activities communicate and deliver value and (2) when coordinated, marketing activities maximize their joint effects. In other words, marketers should design and implement any one marketing activity with all other activities in mind.

For example, using an integrated communication strategy means choosing communication options that reinforce and complement each other. A marketer might selectively employ television, radio, and print advertising, public relations and events, and PR and Web site communications, so that each contributes on its own as well as improving the effectiveness of the others. Each communication must also deliver a consistent brand image to customers at every brand contact. Applying an integrated channel strategy ensures that direct and indirect channels, such as online and retail sales, work together to maximize sales and brand equity.

Online marketing activities play an increasingly prominent role in building brands and selling products and services. Created for $300,000 and no additional promotional expense, online site Carnival Connections made it easy for cruise fans to compare notes on cruise destinations and onboard entertainment, from casinos to conga lines. In a few short months, 2,000 of the site's 13,000 registered users planned trips aboard Carnival's 22 ships, generating an estimated $1.6 million in revenue for the company.[49]

Carnival Connections' online marketing activities include an interactive site where cruise fans can compare notes. The site has generated about $1.6 million in bookings.

Internal Marketing

Holistic marketing incorporates *internal marketing*, ensuring that everyone in the organization embraces appropriate marketing principles, especially senior management. Internal marketing is the task of hiring, training, and motivating able employees who want to serve customers well. Smart marketers recognize that marketing activities within the company can be as important or even more important than marketing activities directed outside the company. It makes no sense to promise excellent service before the company's staff is ready to provide it.

Internal marketing must take place on two levels. At one level, the various marketing functions—sales force, advertising, customer service, product management, marketing research—must work together. Too often, the sales force thinks product managers set prices or sale quotas "too high"; or the advertising director and a brand manager cannot agree on an advertising campaign. All these marketing functions must be coordinated from the customer's point of view. The following example highlights the coordination problem:

> The marketing vice president of a major European airline wants to increase the airline's traffic share. His strategy is to build up customer satisfaction by providing better food, cleaner cabins, better-trained cabin crews, and lower fares, yet he has no authority in these matters. The catering department chooses food that keeps food costs down; the maintenance department uses cleaning services that keep cleaning costs down; the human resources department hires people without regard to whether they are naturally friendly; the finance department sets the fares. Because these departments generally take a cost or production point of view, the vice president of marketing is stymied in his efforts to create an integrated marketing mix.

At the second level, other departments must embrace marketing; they must also "think customer." Marketing is not a department so much as a company orientation.[50] See Table 1.1.

Internal marketing thus requires vertical alignment with senior management and horizontal alignment with other departments, so everyone understands, appreciates, and supports the marketing effort. As former Yahoo! CMO Cammie Dunaway states, "You

TABLE 1.1

Assessing Which Company Departments Are Customer Minded

H & D

- They spend time meeting customers and listening to their problems.
- They welcome the involvement of marketing, manufacturing, and other departments to each new project.
- They benchmark competitors' products and seek "best of class" solutions.
- They solicit customer reactions and suggestions as the project progresses.
- They continuously improve and refine the product on the basis of market feedback.

Purchasing

- They proactively search for the best suppliers.
- They build long-term relationships with fewer but more reliable, high-quality suppliers.
- They don't compromise quality for price savings.

Manufacturing

- They invite customers to visit and tour their plants.
- They visit customer plants.
- They willingly work overtime to meet promised delivery schedules.
- They continuously search for ways to produce goods faster and/or at lower cost.
- They continuously improve product quality, aiming for zero defects.
- They meet customer requirements for "customization" where possible.

Marketing

- They study customer needs and wants in well-defined market segments.
- They allocate marketing effort in relation to the long-run profit potential of the targeted segments.
- They develop winning offers for each target segment.
- They measure company image and customer satisfaction on a continuous basis.
- They continuously gather and evaluate ideas for new products, product improvements, and services.
- They urge all company departments and employees to be customer centered.

Sales

- They have specialized knowledge of the customer's industry.
- They strive to give the customer "the best solution."
- They make only promises that they can keep.
- They feed back customers' needs and ideas to those in charge of product development.
- They serve the same customers for a long period of time.

Logistics

- They set a high standard for service delivery time and meet this standard consistently.
- They operate a knowledgeable and friendly customer service department that can answer questions, handle complaints, and resolve problems in a satisfactory and timely manner.

Accounting

- They prepare periodic "profitability" reports by product, market segment, geographic areas (regions, sales territories), order sizes, channels, and individual customers.
- They prepare invoices tailored to customer needs and answer customer queries courteously and quickly.

Finance

- They understand and support marketing expenditures (e.g., image advertising) that produce long-term customer preference and loyalty.
- They tailor the financial package to the customer's financial requirements.
- They make quick decisions on customer creditworthiness.

Public Relations

- They send out favorable news about the company and "damage control" unfavorable news.
- They act as an internal customer and public advocate for better company policies and practices.

Source: Philip Kotler, *Kotler on Marketing* (New York: Free Press, 1999), pp. 21_22. Reprinted with permission of The Free Press, a Division of Simon & Schuster Adult Publishing Group.

| FIG. 1.6 |

Types of Marketing Organizations (percent of sample population in parentheses)

Source: Based on *Booz Allen Hamilton/Assn. of National Advertisers Marketing Profiles*, in conjunction with *Brandweek* from Constantine von Hoffman, "Armed with Intelligence," *Brandweek*, May 29, 2006, pp. 17–20.

Growth Champions (14.7%) emphasize growth-support functions, leading such general-management activities as product innovation and new-business development.

Marketing Masters (38.4%) oversee company-wide marketing efforts and the customer-focused side of new product and service launches, although are typically not involved with strategic decisions.

Senior Counselors (16.9%) specialize in marketing strategy, advising the CEO and individual businesses, and may drive major communication programs, although not typically new product development.

Best Practices Advisors (8.9%) work with individual business units to improve their marketing effectiveness and, but are less likely to be linked with above-average growth than both the Growth Champions and the Marketing Masters.

Brand Builders (12.2%) support brands by providing marketing services like communications strategy, creative output, and campaign execution, but exhibit little strategic leadership.

Service Providers (14.7%) coordinate marketing communications, but often work in firms with lower revenue growth and profitability.

want to be connecting at the very senior levels of the organization, and you also want to be connecting in with the engineers and scientists who are doing a lot of the work on the front lines." Dunaway also emphasizes the importance of integrated marketing, comparing her job to that of an orchestra conductor: "You have to figure out how to pull all those instruments together in a way that's delivering great marketing accountability and engaging marketing programs."[51]

A study conducted by Booz Allen Hamilton and the Association of National Advertisers, in conjunction with *Brandweek* magazine, asked 2,000 executives to describe the marketing structure within their organizations and to detail the tasks they consider integral to their missions. The researchers identified six types of marketing organizations (see Figure 1.6 for a breakdown and descriptions). In the most successful type, Growth Champions, marketing heavily influenced all aspects of the organization. Growth Champions were 20% more likely to deliver revenue growth and profitability than the other types of marketing organizations.

Performance Marketing

Holistic marketing incorporates *performance marketing* and understanding the returns to the business from marketing activities and programs, as well as addressing broader concerns and their legal, ethical, social, and environmental effects. Top management is going beyond sales revenue to examine the marketing scorecard and interpret what is happening to market share, customer loss rate, customer satisfaction, product quality, and other measures.

FINANCIAL ACCOUNTABILITY Marketers are thus being increasingly asked to justify their investments to senior management in financial and profitability terms, as well as in terms of building the brand and growing the customer base.[52] As a consequence, they're employing a broader variety of financial measures to assess the direct and indirect value their marketing efforts create. They're also recognizing that much of their firms' market value comes from intangible assets, particularly their brands, customer base, employees, distributor and supplier relations, and intellectual capital.

SOCIAL RESPONSIBILITY MARKETING The effects of marketing clearly extend beyond the company and the customer to society as a whole. Marketers must carefully consider their role in broader terms, and the ethical, environmental, legal, and social context of their activities.[53] Increasingly, consumers demand such behavior, as Starbucks Chairman Howard Schultz has observed:[54]

> We see a fundamental change in the way consumers buy their products and services. . . . Consumers now commonly engage in a cultural audit of providers. People want to know your value and ethics demonstrated by how you treat employees, the community in which you operate. The implication for marketers is to strike the balance between profitability and social consciousness and sensitivity. . . . It is not a program or a quarterly promotion, but rather a way of life. You have to integrate this level of social responsibility into your operation.

This realization calls for a new term that enlarges the marketing concept. We propose calling it the "societal marketing concept." The *societal marketing concept* holds that the organization's task is to determine the needs, wants, and interests of target markets and to deliver the desired satisfactions more effectively and efficiently than competitors in a way that preserves or enhances the consumer's and society's long-term well-being. Sustainability has become a major corporate concern in the face of challenging environmental forces. Firms such as Hewlett-Packard have introduced recyclable computers and printers and reduced greenhouse emissions; McDonald's strives for a "socially responsible supply system" encompassing everything from healthy fisheries to redesigned packaging.[55]

The societal marketing concept calls upon marketers to build social and ethical considerations into their marketing practices. They must balance and juggle the often conflicting criteria of company profits, consumer want satisfaction, and public interest. Table 1.2 displays some different types of corporate social initiatives, illustrated by McDonald's.[56]

As goods become more commoditized, and as consumers grow more socially conscious, some companies—including the Body Shop, Timberland, and Patagonia—are adding social responsibility as a way to differentiate themselves from competitors, build consumer preference, and achieve notable sales and profit gains. They believe customers will increasingly look for signs of good corporate citizenship.

TABLE 1.2 Corporate Social Initiatives

Type	Description	Example
Corporate social marketing	Supporting behavior change campaigns	McDonald's promotion of a statewide childhood immunization campaign in Oklahoma
Cause marketing	Promoting social issues through efforts such as sponsorships, licensing agreements, and advertising	McDonald's sponsorship of Forest (a gorilla) at Sydney's Zoo—a 10-year sponsorship commitment, aimed at preserving this endangered species
Cause-related marketing	Donating a percentage of revenues to a specific cause based on the revenue occurring during the announced period of support	McDonald's earmarking of $1 for Ronald McDonald Children's Charities from the sale of every Big Mac and pizza sold on McHappy Day
Corporate philanthropy	Making gifts of money, goods, or time to help nonprofit organizations, groups, or individuals	McDonald's contributions to Ronald McDonald House Charities
Corporate community involvement	Providing in-kind or volunteer services in the community	McDonald's catering meals for firefighters in the December 1997 bushfires in Australia
Socially responsible business practices	Adapting and conducting business practices that protect the environment and human and animal rights	McDonald's requirement that suppliers increase the amount of living space for laying hens on factory farms

Source: Philip Kotler and Nancy Lee, *Corporate Social Responsibility: Doing the Most Good for Your Company and Your Cause* (Hoboken, NJ: Wiley, 2004). Copyright © 2005 by Philip Kotler and Nancy Lee. Used by permission of John Wiley & Sons, Inc.

BEN & JERRY'S

When they founded Ben & Jerry's, Ben Cohen and Jerry Greenfield embraced the performance marketing concept by dividing the traditional financial bottom line into a "double" bottom line, which would include a measurement of the environmental impact of their products and processes. That "double bottom line" later expanded into a "triple bottom line," to represent in objective terms the social impacts, both negative and positive, of the firm's entire range of business activities. Cohen and Greenfield informed their senior managers that they were going to be held accountable to maintain two bottom lines: "To improve the quality of life in the communities in which we operate, and to make a reasonable profit." Ben & Jerry's also recognized that just as companies require outside auditors to measure financial performance, they also require outside auditors to measure their performance along the environmental and social dimensions. As one of those outside auditors later recalled: "Measurement is a key tool to convince boards of directors and core executives that the socially responsible company is a sound business strategy. As companies make more data from their efforts available, the story becomes more compelling. . . . To advocate transparency in business and for all of us to ascribe to that—that's the ultimate acid test."[57]

::: Marketing Management Tasks

With the holistic marketing philosophy as a backdrop, we can identify a specific set of tasks that make up successful marketing management and marketing leadership. We'll use the following situation to illustrate these tasks in the context of the plan of the book. (The "Marketing Memo: Marketers' Frequently Asked Questions" is a good checklist for the questions marketing managers ask, all of which we examine in this book.)

> Zeus Inc. (name disguised) operates in several industries, including chemicals, cameras, and film. The company is organized into SBUs. Corporate management is considering what to do with its Atlas camera division, which produces a range of 35 mm and digital cameras. Although Zeus has a sizable share and is producing revenue, the 35 mm market itself is rapidly declining and its market share is slipping. In the faster-growing digital camera segment, Zeus faces strong competition and has been slow to gain sales. Zeus's corporate management wants Atlas's marketing group to produce a strong turnaround plan for the division.

Developing Marketing Strategies and Plans

The first task facing Atlas is to identify its potential long-run opportunities, given its market experience and core competencies (see Chapter 2). Atlas can design its cameras with better features. It can make a line of video cameras, or it can use its core competency in optics to design a line of binoculars and telescopes. Whichever direction it chooses, it must develop concrete marketing plans that specify the marketing strategy and tactics going forward.

Capturing Marketing Insights

Atlas needs a reliable marketing information system to closely monitor its marketing environment. Its microenvironment consists of all the players who affect its ability to produce and sell cameras—suppliers, marketing intermediaries, customers, and competitors. Its macroenvironment includes demographic, economic, physical, technological, political-legal, and social-cultural forces that affect sales and profits (see Chapter 3).

Atlas also needs a dependable marketing research system. To transform marketing strategy into marketing programs, marketing managers must measure market potential, forecast demand, and make basic decisions about marketing expenditures, marketing activities, and marketing allocation.[58] To make these allocations, marketing managers may use sales-response functions that show how the amount of money spent in each application will affect sales and profits (see Chapter 4).

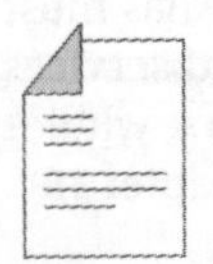

MARKETING MEMO | MARKETERS' FREQUENTLY ASKED QUESTIONS

1. How can we spot and choose the right market segment(s)?
2. How can we differentiate our offerings?
3. How should we respond to customers who buy on price?
4. How can we compete against lower-cost, lower-price competitors?
5. How far can we go in customizing our offering for each customer?
6. How can we grow our business?
7. How can we build stronger brands?
8. How can we reduce the cost of customer acquisition?
9. How can we keep our customers loyal for longer?
10. How can we tell which customers are more important?
11. How can we measure the payback from advertising, sales promotion, and public relations?
12. How can we improve sales force productivity?
13. How can we establish multiple channels and yet manage channel conflict?
14. How can we get the other company departments to be more customer oriented?

Connecting with Customers

Atlas must consider how to best create value for its chosen target markets and develop strong, profitable, long-term relationships with customers (see Chapter 5). To do so, it needs to understand consumer markets (see Chapter 6). Who buys cameras, and why do they buy? What are they looking for in the way of features and prices, and where do they shop? Atlas also sells cameras to business markets, including large corporations, professional firms, retailers, and government agencies (see Chapter 7), where purchasing agents or buying committees make the decisions. Atlas needs to gain a full understanding of how organizational buyers buy. It needs a sales force that is well trained in presenting product benefits.

Atlas will not want to market to all possible customers. It must divide the market into major market segments, evaluate each one, and target those it can best serve (see Chapter 8).

Building Strong Brands

Atlas must understand the strengths and weaknesses of the Zeus brand as customers see it (see Chapter 9). Is its 35 mm film heritage a handicap in the digital camera market? Suppose Atlas decides to focus on the consumer market and develop a positioning strategy (see Chapter 10). Should it position itself as the "Cadillac" brand, offering superior cameras at a premium price with excellent service and strong advertising? Should it build a simple, low-priced camera aimed at more price-conscious consumers? Or something in between?

Atlas must also pay close attention to competitors (see Chapter 11), anticipating its competitors' moves and knowing how to react quickly and decisively. It may want to initiate some surprise moves, in which case it needs to anticipate how its competitors will respond.

Shaping the Market Offerings

At the heart of the marketing program is the product—the firm's tangible offering to the market, which includes the product quality, design, features, and packaging (see Chapter 12). To gain a competitive advantage, Atlas may provide leasing, delivery, repair, and training as part of its product offering (see Chapter 13).

A critical marketing decision relates to price (see Chapter 14). Atlas must decide on wholesale and retail prices, discounts, allowances, and credit terms. Its price should match well with the offer's perceived value; otherwise, buyers will turn to competitors' products.

Delivering Value

Atlas must also determine how to properly deliver to the target market the value embodied in its products and services. Channel activities include those the company undertakes to make the product accessible and available to target customers (see Chapter 15). Atlas must identify, recruit, and link various marketing facilitators to supply its products and services efficiently to the target market. It must understand the various types of retailers, wholesalers, and physical-distribution firms and how they make their decisions (see Chapter 16).

Communicating Value

Atlas must also adequately communicate to the target market the value embodied by its products and services. It will need an integrated marketing communication program that maximizes the individual and collective contribution of all communication activities (see Chapter 17). Atlas needs to set up mass communication programs consisting of advertising, sales promotion, events, and public relations (see Chapter 18). It also needs to plan more personal communications, in the form of direct and interactive marketing, as well as hire, train, and motivate salespeople (see Chapter 19).

Creating Long-Term Growth

Based on its product positioning, Atlas must initiate new-product development, testing, and launching as part of its long-term view (see Chapter 20). The strategy should take into account changing global opportunities and challenges (see Chapter 21).

Finally, Atlas must build a marketing organization that's capable of implementing the marketing plan (see Chapter 22). Because surprises and disappointments can occur as marketing plans unfold, Atlas will need feedback and control to understand the efficiency and effectiveness of its marketing activities and how it can improve them.[59]

SUMMARY :::

1. From a managerial point of view, marketing is an organizational function and a set of processes for creating, communicating, and delivering value to customers and for managing customer relationships in ways that benefit the organization and its stakeholders. Marketing management is the art and science of choosing target markets and getting, keeping, and growing customers through creating, delivering, and communicating superior customer value.
2. Marketers are skilled at managing demand: they seek to influence the level, timing, and composition of demand. Marketers are involved in marketing many types of entities: goods, services, events, experiences, persons, places, properties, organizations, information, and ideas. They also operate in four different marketplaces: consumer, business, global, and nonprofit.
3. Marketing is not done only by the marketing department. Marketing needs to affect every aspect of the customer experience. To create a strong marketing organization, marketers must think like executives in other departments, and executives in other departments must think more like marketers.
4. Today's marketplace is fundamentally different as a result of major societal forces that have resulted in many new consumer and company capabilities. These forces have created new opportunities and challenges, and marketing management has changed significantly in recent years as companies seek new ways to achieve marketing excellence.
5. There are five competing concepts under which organizations can choose to conduct their business: the production concept, the product concept, the selling concept, the marketing concept, and the holistic marketing concept. The first three are of limited use today.
6. The holistic marketing concept is based on the development, design, and implementation of marketing programs, processes, and activities that recognize their breadth and interdependencies. Holistic marketing recognizes that "everything matters" with marketing and that a broad, integrated perspective is often necessary. Four components of holistic marketing are relationship marketing, integrated marketing, internal marketing, and socially responsible marketing.
7. The set of tasks necessary for successful marketing management includes developing marketing strategies and plans, capturing marketing insights, connecting with customers, building strong brands, shaping the market offerings, delivering and communicating value, and creating long-term growth.

APPLICATIONS :::

Marketing Debate Does Marketing Create or Satisfy Needs?

Marketing has often been defined in terms of satisfying customers' needs and wants. Critics, however, maintain that marketing goes beyond that and creates needs and wants that did not exist before. According to these critics, marketers encourage consumers to spend more money than they should on goods and services they really do not need.

Take a position: Marketing shapes consumer needs and wants *versus* Marketing merely reflects the needs and wants of consumers.

Marketing Discussion

Consider the broad shifts in marketing. Are there any themes that emerge in these shifts? Can they be related to the major societal forces? Which force has contributed to which shift?

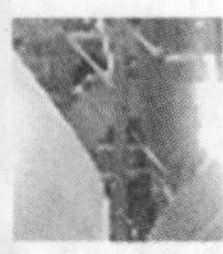

IN THIS CHAPTER, WE WILL ADDRESS THE FOLLOWING QUESTIONS:

1. How does marketing affect customer value?
2. How is strategic planning carried out at different levels of the organization?
3. What does a marketing plan include?

Key ingredients of the marketing management process are insightful, creative marketing strategies and plans that can guide marketing activities. Developing the right marketing strategy over time requires a blend of discipline and flexibility. Firms must stick to a strategy but also find new ways to constantly improve it. Increasingly, marketing must also develop strategies for a range of products and services within the organization. As a highly successful business-to-business marketer, Siemens, for instance, must continually design and implement marketing activities at many levels and for many units of the organization.

Siemens AG is one of the largest global electronics and engineering companies in the world, with 460,000 employees in 190 countries and worldwide sales of $96 billion in fiscal 2005. During 2005, Siemens grew organically through new-product innovation and was the world's fifth-largest corporate spender in research and development. Siemens also grew through strategic acquisition in the areas of medical imaging, clean-coal technology, pollution control, wind power, and water technologies. Senior management were faithful to their vow that problem businesses would be fixed, sold, or closed, divesting the money-losing cellular handset unit to Taiwan's BenQ Corp. and realigning the ailing telecommunications network equipment unit in a joint venture with global handset supplier giant Nokia.[1]

Siemens AG is a leading energy company focused on a growth strategy.

This chapter begins by examining some of the strategic marketing implications in creating customer value. We'll look at several perspectives on planning and describe how to draw up a formal marketing plan.

::: Marketing and Customer Value

Marketing is about satisfying consumers' needs and wants. The task of any business is to deliver customer value at a profit. In a hypercompetitive economy with increasingly rational buyers faced with abundant choices, a company can win only by fine-tuning the value delivery process and choosing, providing, and communicating superior value.

The Value Delivery Process

The traditional view of marketing is that the firm makes something and then sells it. In this view, marketing takes place in the second half of the process. Companies that subscribe to this view have the best chance of succeeding in economies marked by goods shortages where consumers are not fussy about quality, features, or style—for example, basic staple goods in developing markets.

This traditional view of the business process, however, will not work in economies where people face abundant choices. There, the "mass market" is actually splintering into numerous micromarkets, each with its own wants, perceptions, preferences, and buying criteria. The smart competitor must design and deliver offerings for well-defined target markets. This realization inspired a new view of business processes that places marketing at the *beginning* of planning. Instead of emphasizing making and selling, companies now see themselves as part of a value delivery process.

The value creation and delivery sequence can be divided into three phases. The first phase, *choosing the value,* represents the "homework" marketing must do before any product exists. The marketing staff must segment the market, select the appropriate market target, and develop the offering's value positioning. The formula "segmentation, targeting, positioning (STP)" is the essence of strategic marketing. Once the business unit has chosen the value, the second phase is *providing the value.* Marketing must determine specific product features, prices, and distribution. The task in the third phase is *communicating the value* by utilizing the sales force, sales promotion, advertising, and other communication tools to announce and promote the product. Each of these value phases has cost implications. It is also the case that the value delivery process begins before there is a product and continues while it is being developed and after it becomes available.

NIKE

Critics of Nike often complain that its shoes cost almost nothing to make, yet cost the consumer so much. True, the raw materials and manufacturing costs of a sneaker are relatively cheap, but marketing the product to the consumer is expensive. Materials, labor, shipping, equipment, import duties, and suppliers' costs generally total less than $25 a pair. Compensating the sales team, distributors, administration, and endorsers, as well as paying for advertising and R&D, adds $15 or so to Nike's total. Nike sells its product to retailers to make a profit of $7. The retailer therefore pays roughly $47 to put a pair of Nikes on the shelf. Factoring in the retailer's overhead (typically $30 covering human resources, lease, and equipment), along with a $10 profit, the shoe costs the consumer over $80.

London Business School's Nirmalya Kumar has put forth a "3 Vs" approach to marketing: (1) define the *value segment* or customers (and their needs); (2) define the *value proposition*; and (3) define the *value network* that will deliver the promised service.[2] Dartmouth's Frederick Webster views marketing in terms of: (1) *value-defining processes* such as market research and company self-analysis; (2) *value-developing processes* including new-product development, sourcing strategy, and vendor selection; and (3) *value-delivering processes* such as advertising and managing distribution.[3]

The Value Chain

Michael Porter of Harvard has proposed the **value chain** as a tool for identifying ways to create more customer value (see Figure 2.1).[4] According to this model, every firm is a synthesis of activities performed to design, produce, market, deliver, and support its product. The value chain identifies nine strategically relevant activities—five primary and four support activities—that create value and cost in a specific business.

The *primary activities* are inbound logistics or bringing materials into the business; operations or converting them into final products; outbound logistics or shipping out final products; marketing them, which includes sales; and servicing them. The *support activities*—procurement, technology development, human resource management, and firm infrastructure—are handled in specialized departments. The firm's infrastructure covers the costs of general management, planning, finance, accounting, legal, and government affairs.

The firm's task is to examine its costs and performance in each value-creating activity and to look for ways to improve it. Managers should estimate their competitors' costs and performances as *benchmarks* against which to compare their own costs and performance. And they should go further and study the "best of class" practices of the world's best companies.[5]

CISCO SYSTEMS INC.

Although Cisco Systems continues to grow, it is not growing at the breakneck speed of the 1990s, so its supply base needs have changed. The company has reduced its number of suppliers and aligned itself more closely with the remaining suppliers for each of its product-based teams—from Application Specific Integrated Circuits (ASIC) to microprocessors and broadband chips. Steve Darendinger, vice president of supply chain management for Cisco, says, "With ASIC we have gone from more than 20 suppliers to 3 suppliers," and "the three have a greater level of ASIC leverage . . . " Involving suppliers in new-product development lets Cisco tap into its partners' expertise in improving time to volume, cutting costs, and improving supplier quality.[6]

The firm's success depends not only on how well each department performs its work, but also on how well the company coordinates departmental activities to conduct *core business processes*.[7] These core business processes include:

- ***The market-sensing process.*** All the activities in gathering market intelligence, disseminating it within the organization, and acting on the information
- ***The new-offering realization process.*** All the activities in researching, developing, and launching new high-quality offerings quickly and within budget
- ***The customer acquisition process.*** All the activities in defining target markets and prospecting for new customers
- ***The customer relationship management process.*** All the activities in building deeper understanding, relationships, and offerings to individual customers
- ***The fulfillment management process.*** All the activities in receiving and approving orders, shipping the goods on time, and collecting payment

Strong companies are reengineering their work flows and building cross-functional teams to be responsible for each process.[8] At Xerox, a Customer Operations Group links

Rite Aid is hoping its use of cross-functional teams will improve its business processes enough to make it number one among retail drug chains.

sales, shipping, installation, service, and billing so these activities flow smoothly into one another. Winning companies are those that excel at managing core business processes through cross-functional teams. AT&T, Polaroid, and Motorola have reorganized their employees into cross-functional teams; cross-functional teams are also found in nonprofit and government organizations as well. Drugstore chain Rite Aid is using cross-functional teams to try to push its store from third to first place in the drugstore hierarchy. The company has created teams to focus on sales and margin growth, operational excellence, market optimization, continued supply chain improvements, and continued cost control.[9]

To be successful, a firm also needs to look for competitive advantages beyond its own operations, into the value chains of suppliers, distributors, and customers. Many companies today have partnered with specific suppliers and distributors to create a superior **value delivery network**, also called a **supply chain.**

Core Competencies

Traditionally, companies owned and controlled most of the resources that entered their businesses—labor power, materials, machines, information, and energy—but this situation is changing. Many companies today outsource less-critical resources if they can obtain better quality or lower cost. India has developed a reputation as a country that can provide ample outsourcing support.

The key, then, is to own and nurture the resources and competencies that make up the *essence* of the business. Nike, for example, does not manufacture its own shoes, because certain Asian manufacturers are more competent in this task; instead Nike nurtures its superiority in shoe design and merchandising, its two core competencies. A **core competency** has three characteristics: (1) It is a source of competitive advantage in that it makes a significant contribution to perceived customer benefits. (2) It has applications in a wide variety of markets. (3) It is difficult for competitors to imitate.[10]

Competitive advantage also accrues to companies that possess distinctive capabilities. Whereas "core competencies" refers to areas of special technical and production expertise, *distinctive capabilities* describes excellence in broader business processes. Consider Netflix, the pioneer online DVD rental service, based in Silicon Valley.[11]

NETFLIX

Back in 1997, while most people were still fumbling with programming their VCRs, Netflix founder Reed Hastings became convinced that DVDs were the home video medium of the future. He raised $120 million, attracted hundreds of thousands of customers for his online movie DVD rental business, and took the company public in 2002, gaining another $90 million. Netflix has distinctive capabilities that promise to keep the company on top even as competitors such as Blockbuster and Wal-Mart try to muscle in on its turf. These distinctive capabilities are no late fees, (mostly) overnight delivery, and a deep catalog of over 65,000 movie titles, linked to systematic proprietary search software that allows customers to easily search for obscure films and discover new ones. Netflix is now making all of Hollywood—not just movie rental businesses—react. With its online communities of people who provide reviews and feedback, Netflix can identify potential fans for films. For instance, the company is credited with single-handedly building audiences for such quirky independent films as *Capturing the Friedmans*, a documentary about sexual abuse in a Long Island family.

Netflix became a success in the DVD rental business by exploiting its distinctive capabilities—state-of-the-art software that supports its product recommendations, merchandising, and inventory control.

Reprinted by permission of Netflix, Inc. Copyright © 2007 Netflix, Inc. All rights reserved.

Wharton's George Day sees market-driven organizations as excelling in three distinctive capabilities: market sensing, customer linking, and channel bonding.[12] In terms of market sensing, he believes that tremendous opportunities and threats often begin as "weak signals" from the "periphery" of a business.[13] He offers a systematic process for developing peripheral vision, and practical tools and strategies for building "vigilant organizations" attuned to changes in the environment, by asking questions in three categories (see Table 2.1).

Competitive advantage ultimately derives from how well the company has fitted its core competencies and distinctive capabilities into tightly interlocking "activity systems." Competitors find it hard to imitate companies such as Southwest Airlines, Dell, and IKEA because they are unable to copy their activity systems.

TABLE 2.1

Becoming a Vigilant Organization

- *Learning from the past*
  - What have been our past blind spots?
  - What instructive analogies do other industries offer?
  - Who in the industry is skilled at picking up weak signals and acting on them?
- *Evaluating the present*
  - What important signals are we rationalizing away?
  - What are our mavericks, outliers, complainers, and defectors telling us?
  - What are our peripheral customers and competitors really thinking?
- *Envisioning the future*
  - What future surprises could really hurt or help us?
  - What emerging technologies could change the game?
  - Is there an unthinkable scenario that might disrupt our business?

Source: George S. Day and Paul J. H. Schoemaker, *Peripheral Vision: Detecting the Weak Signals That Will Make or Break Your Company* (Boston: Harvard Business School Press, 2006).

Business realignment may be necessary to maximize core competencies. It has three steps: (1) (re)defining the business concept or "big idea"; (2) (re)shaping the business scope; and (3) (re)positioning the company's brand identity. Consider what Kodak is doing to realign its business:

KODAK

With the advent of the digital era and consumers' new capacity to store, share, and print photos using their PCs, Kodak faces more competition than ever, both in-store and online. In 2004, after being bumped from the Dow Jones Industrial Average, where it had held a spot for more than 70 years, the company started the painful process of transformation. It started off by expanding its line of digital cameras, printers, and other equipment, and it also set out to increase market share in the lucrative medical imaging business. Making shifts is not without challenges, however. The company announced in the summer of 2006 that it would outsource the making of its digital cameras. Kodak eliminated almost 30,000 jobs between 2004 and 2007 and it spent money acquiring a string of companies for its graphics communications unit. Not only must Kodak convince consumers to buy its digital cameras and home printers, but it also must become known as the most convenient and affordable way to process digital images. So far, the company faces steep competition from Sony, Canon, and Hewlett-Packard.[14]

A Holistic Marketing Orientation and Customer Value

A holistic marketing orientation can also help capture customer value. One view of holistic marketing sees it as "integrating the value exploration, value creation, and value delivery activities with the purpose of building long-term, mutually satisfying relationships and coprosperity among key stakeholders."[15] According to this view, holistic marketers succeed by managing a superior value chain that delivers a high level of product quality, service, and speed. Holistic marketers achieve profitable growth by expanding customer share, building customer loyalty, and capturing customer lifetime value. Figure 2.1, a holistic marketing framework, shows how the interaction between relevant actors and value-based activities helps to create, maintain, and renew customer value.

The holistic marketing framework is designed to address three key management questions:

1. ***Value exploration***—How can a company identify new value opportunities?
2. ***Value creation***—How can a company efficiently create more promising new value offerings?
3. ***Value delivery***—How can a company use its capabilities and infrastructure to deliver the new value offerings more efficiently?

Let's look at how marketers can answer them.

FIG. 2.1

A Holistic Marketing Framework

Source: P. Kotler, D. C. Jain, and S. Maesincee, "Formulating a Market Renewal Strategy," in *Marketing Moves* (Part 1), Fig. 1-1 (Boston: Harvard Business School Press, 2002), p. 29. Copyright © 2002 by President and Fellows of Harvard College. All rights reserved.

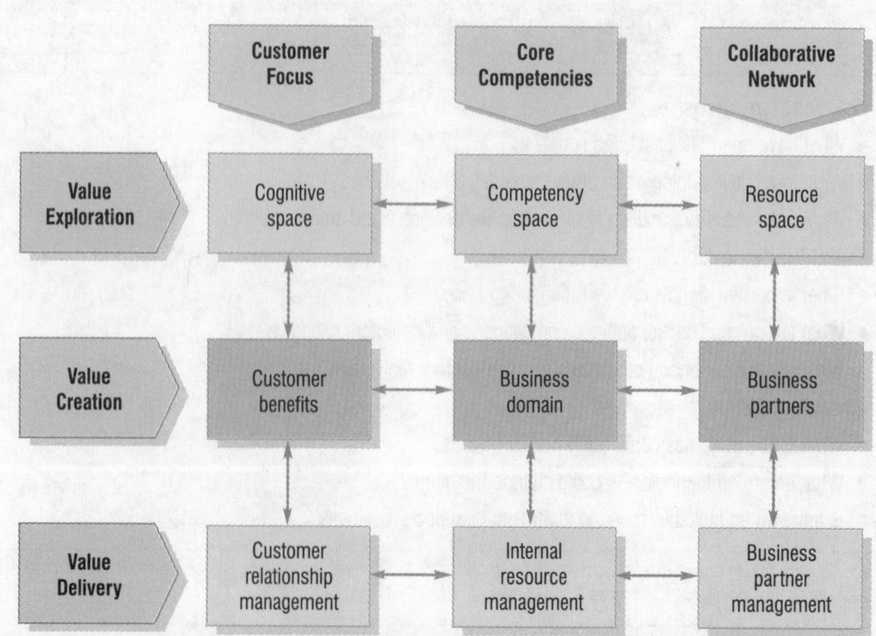

VALUE EXPLORATION Finding new value opportunities is a matter of understanding the relationships among three spaces: (1) the customer's cognitive space; (2) the company's competence space; and (3) the collaborator's resource space. The customer's *cognitive space* reflects existing and latent needs and includes dimensions such as the need for participation, stability, freedom, and change.[16] We can describe the company's *competency space* in terms of breadth—broad versus focused scope of business; and depth—physical versus knowledge-based capabilities. The collaborator's *resource space* includes horizontal partnerships, with partners chosen for their ability to exploit related market opportunities, and vertical partnerships, with partners who can serve the firm's value creation.

VALUE CREATION Value-creation skills for marketers include identifying new customer benefits from the customer's view; utilizing core competencies from its business domain; and selecting and managing business partners from its collaborative networks. To create new customer benefits, marketers must understand what the customer thinks about, wants, does, and worries about and observe whom customers admire and interact with, and who influences them.

VALUE DELIVERY Delivering value often means making substantial investments in infrastructure and capabilities. The company must become proficient at customer relationship management, internal resource management, and business partnership management. *Customer relationship management* allows the company to discover who its customers are, how they behave, and what they need or want. It also enables the company to respond appropriately, coherently, and quickly to different customer opportunities. To respond effectively, the company requires *internal resource management* to integrate major business processes, such as order processing, general ledger, payroll, and production, within a single family of software modules. Finally, *business partnership management* allows the company to handle complex relationships with its trading partners to source, process, and deliver products.

The Central Role of Strategic Planning

Successful marketing thus requires companies to have capabilities such as understanding customer value, creating customer value, delivering customer value, capturing customer value, and sustaining customer value. Only a select group of companies stand out as master marketers: Procter & Gamble, Southwest Airlines, Nike, Disney, Nordstrom, Barnes & Noble, Starbucks, Wal-Mart, Target, Enterprise Rent-A-Car, Progressive Insurance, McDonald's, Ritz-Carlton, and several Asian (Sony, Toyota, Samsung, Canon) and European (IKEA, Club Med, Bang & Olufsen, Electrolux, Nokia, Lego, Tesco, and Virgin) companies. "Breakthrough Marketing: Intel" describes how that company created customer value and built a brand in a category for which most people thought branding impossible.

These companies focus on the customer and are organized to respond effectively to changing customer needs. They all have well-staffed marketing departments, and all their other departments accept the concept that the customer is king.

To ensure that they select and execute the right activities, marketers must give priority to strategic planning in three key areas: managing a company's businesses as an investment portfolio, assessing each business's strength by considering the market's growth rate and the company's position and fit in that market, and establishing a strategy. For each business, the company must develop a game plan for achieving its long-run objectives.

Most large companies consist of four organizational levels: the corporate level, the division level, the business unit level, and the product level. Corporate headquarters is responsible for designing a corporate strategic plan to guide the whole enterprise; it makes decisions on the amount of resources to allocate to each division, as well as on which businesses to start or eliminate. Each division establishes a plan covering the allocation of funds to each business unit within the division. Each business unit develops a strategic plan to carry that business unit into a profitable future. Finally, each product level (product line, brand) within a business unit develops a marketing plan for achieving its objectives in its product market.

The **marketing plan** is the central instrument for directing and coordinating the marketing effort. The marketing plan operates at two levels: strategic and tactical. The **strategic marketing plan** lays out the target markets and the value proposition the firm will offer,

BREAKTHROUGH MARKETING | INTEL

Intel makes the microprocessors that are found in 80% of the world's personal computers. In the early days, Intel microprocessors were known simply by their engineering numbers, such as "80386" or "80486." Intel positioned its chips as the most advanced. The trouble was, as Intel soon learned, numbers can't be trademarked. Competitors came out with their own "486" chips, and Intel had no way to distinguish itself from the competition. Worse, Intel's products were hidden from consumers, buried deep inside PCs. With a hidden, untrademarked product, Intel had a hard time convincing consumers to pay more for its high-performance products.

Intel's response was a marketing campaign that created history. The company chose a trademarkable name—Pentium—and launched the "Intel Inside" marketing campaign to build awareness of the brand and get its name outside the PC and into the minds of consumers.

Intel used an innovative cooperative scheme to extend the reach of the campaign: It would help computer makers who used Intel processors to advertise their PCs if the makers also included the Intel logo in their ads. Intel also gave computer manufacturers a co-op reimbursement on Intel processors if they agreed to place an "Intel Inside" sticker on the outside of their PCs and laptops.

Intel continues its integrated ingredient campaigns to this day. For example, when launching its Centrino mobile microprocessor platform, Intel began with TV ads that aired in the United States and 11 other countries. These ads include the animated logo and now familiar five-note brand signature melody. Print, online, and outdoor advertising followed shortly thereafter. Intel created eight-page inserts for major newspapers that urged the wired world to not only "unwire," but also "Untangle. Unburden. Uncompromise. Unstress."

Intel even held a "One Unwired Day" event that took place in major cities such as New York, Chicago, San Francisco, and Seattle. In addition to allowing free trial Wi-Fi access, the company held festivals in each city that included live music, product demonstrations, and prize giveaways.

The "Unwired" campaign was another Intel success in marketing. The $300 million total media effort for the Centrino mobile platform, which also included cooperative advertising with manufacturers, helped generate $2 billion in revenue for Intel during the first nine months of the campaign.

Going forward, Intel launched a new brand identity in 2006, supported by a $2 billion global marketing campaign. The company introduced a new logo with a different font and updated visual look and also created a new slogan: "Leap Ahead." In addition to the new logo and slogan, Intel developed a new microprocessor platform called Viiv (rhymes with "five") aimed at home entertainment enthusiasts. These moves were designed to create the impression of Intel as a "warm and fuzzy consumer company," with products that went beyond the PC. Intel remained one of the most valuable brands in the world, its $32 billion brand valuation earning it fifth place in the 2006 Interbrand/*BusinessWeek* ranking of the Best Global Brands.

Sources: Don Clark, "Intel to Overhaul Marketing in Bid to Go beyond PCs," *Wall Street Journal*, December 30, 2005; Cliff Edwards, "Intel Everywhere?" *BusinessWeek*, March 8, 2004, pp. 56–62; Scott Van Camp, "ReadMe.1st," *Brandweek*, February 23, 2004, p. 17; and David Kirkpatrick, "At Intel, Speed Isn't Everything," *Fortune*, February 9, 2004, p. 34; "How to Become a Superbrand," *Marketing*, January 8, 2004, p. 15; Roger Slavens, "Pam Pollace, VP-Director, Corporate Marketing Group, Intel Corp," *B to B*, December 8, 2003, p. 19; Kenneth Hein, "Study: New Brand Names Not Making Their Mark," *Brandweek*, December 8, 2003, p. 12; Heather Clancy, "Intel Thinking Outside the Box," *Computer Reseller News*, November 24, 2003, p. 14; Cynthia L. Webb, "A Chip Off the Old Recovery?" Washingtonpost.com, October 15, 2003; "Intel Launches Second Phase of Centrino Ads," *Technology Advertising & Branding Report*, October 6, 2003.

based on an analysis of the best market opportunities. The **tactical marketing plan** specifies the marketing tactics, including product features, promotion, merchandising, pricing, sales channels, and service.

Today, teams develop the marketing plan with inputs and sign-offs from every important function. Management then implements these plans at the appropriate levels of the organization, monitors results, and takes necessary corrective action. The complete planning, implementation, and control cycle is shown in Figure 2.2. We next consider planning at each of these four levels of the organization.

FIG. 2.2

The Strategic Planning, Implementation, and Control Processes

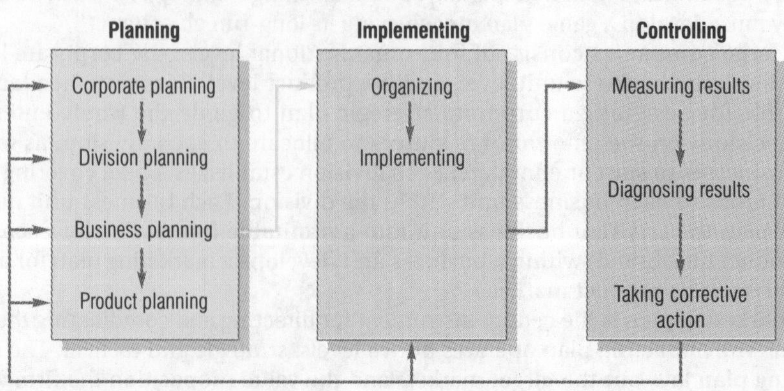

Ads like this were part of Intel's strategy for building a brand in a product area where no brand name had ever existed before—microprocessors.

::: Corporate and Division Strategic Planning

Some corporations give their business units a lot of freedom to set their own sales and profit goals and strategies. Others set goals for their business units but let them develop their own strategies. Still others set the goals and participate in developing individual business unit strategies.[17]

All corporate headquarters undertake four planning activities:

1. Defining the corporate mission
2. Establishing strategic business units
3. Assigning resources to each SBU
4. Assessing growth opportunities

We'll look at each process.

Defining the Corporate Mission

An organization exists to accomplish something: to make cars, lend money, provide a night's lodging, and so on. Over time the mission may change, to take advantage of new opportunities or respond to new market conditions. Amazon.com changed its mission from being the world's largest online bookstore to aspiring to become the world's largest online store; and eBay changed its mission from running online auctions for collectors to running online auctions of all kinds of goods.

To define its mission, a company should address Peter Drucker's classic questions:[18] What is our business? Who is the customer? What is of value to the customer? What will our business be? What should our business be? These simple-sounding questions are among the most difficult a company will ever have to answer. Successful companies continuously raise them and answer them thoughtfully and thoroughly.[19]

Organizations develop **mission statements** to share with managers, employees, and (in many cases) customers. A clear, thoughtful mission statement provides employees with a shared sense of purpose, direction, and opportunity.

Mission statements are at their best when they reflect a vision, an almost "impossible dream" that provides a direction for the company for the next 10 to 20 years. Sony's former president, Akio Morita, wanted everyone to have access to "personal portable sound," so his company created the Walkman and portable CD player. Fred Smith wanted to deliver mail anywhere in the United States before 10:30 AM the next day, so he created FedEx. Table 2.2 lists three sample mission statements.

Good mission statements have five major characteristics. First, they focus on a limited number of goals. The statement "We want to produce the highest-quality products, offer the most service, achieve the widest distribution, and sell at the lowest prices" claims too much. Second, mission statements stress the company's major policies and values. They narrow the range of individual discretion so that employees act consistently on important issues. Third, they define the major competitive spheres within which the company will operate.

- ***Industry.*** Some companies will operate in only one industry; some only in a set of related industries; some only in industrial goods, consumer goods, or services; and some in any industry. For example, DuPont prefers to operate in the industrial market, whereas Dow is willing to operate in the industrial and consumer markets.
- ***Products and applications.*** Firms define the range of products and applications they will supply. St. Jude Medical aims to "serve physicians worldwide with high-quality products for cardiovascular care."
- ***Competence.*** The firm identifies the range of technological and other core competencies it will master and leverage. Japan's NEC has built its core competencies in computing, communications, and components to support production of laptop computers, television receivers, and handheld telephones.
- ***Market segment.*** The type of market or customers a company will serve is the market segment. Aston Martin makes only high-performance sports cars. Gerber serves primarily the baby market.
- ***Vertical.*** The vertical sphere is the number of channel levels, from raw material to final product and distribution, in which a company will participate. At one extreme are companies with a large vertical scope; at one time Ford owned its own rubber plantations, sheep farms, glass manufacturing plants, and steel foundries. At the other extreme are "hollow corporations" or "pure marketing companies" consisting of a person with a phone, fax, computer, and desk who contracts out every service, including design, manufacture, marketing, and physical distribution.[20]
- ***Geographical.*** The range of regions, countries, or country groups in which a company will operate defines its geographical sphere. Some companies operate in a specific city or

TABLE 2.2

Sample Mission Statements

Rubbermaid Commercial Products Inc.

"Our Vision is to be the Global Market Share Leader in each of the markets we serve. We will earn this leadership position by providing to our distributor and end-user customers innovative, high-quality, cost-effective, and environmentally responsible products. We will add value to these products by providing legendary customer service through our Uncompromising Commitment to Customer Satisfaction."

Motorola

"The purpose of Motorola is to honorably serve the needs of the community by providing products and services of superior quality at a fair price to our customers; to do this so as to earn an adequate profit which is required for the total enterprise to grow; and by so doing provide the opportunity for our employees and shareholders to achieve their reasonable personal objectives."

eBay

"We help people trade practically anything on earth. We will continue to enhance the online trading experiences of all—collectors, dealers, small businesses, unique item seekers, bargain hunters, opportunity sellers, and browsers."

state. Others are multinationals such as Unilever and Caterpillar, which operate in almost every country in the world.

The fourth characteristic of mission statements is that they take a long-term view. They should be enduring; management should change the mission only when it ceases to be relevant. Finally, a good mission statement is as short, memorable, and meaningful as possible. Marketing consultant Guy Kawasaki even advocates developing short three- to four-word corporate mantras rather than mission statements, like "peace of mind" for Federal Express.[21] Compare the rather vague missions statements on the left with Google's mission statement and philosophy on the right:

To build total brand value by innovating to deliver customer value and customer leadership faster, better, and more completely than our competition.

We build brands and make the world a little happier by bringing our best to you.

Google Mission:

To organize the world's information and make it universally accessible and useful.

Google Philosophy:

Never settle for the best.

1. Focus on the user and all else will follow.
2. It's best to do one thing really, really well.
3. Fast is better than slow.
4. Democracy on the Web works.
5. You don't need to be at your desk to need an answer.
6. You can make money without doing evil.
7. There is always more information out there.
8. The need for information crosses all borders.
9. You can be serious without a suit.
10. Great just isn't good enough.[22]

Establishing Strategic Business Units

Companies often define their businesses in terms of products: They are in the "auto business" or the "clothing business." But Harvard's famed marketing professor Ted Levitt argued that *market definitions* of a business are superior to product definitions. In other words, companies must see their business as a customer-satisfying process, not a goods-producing process. Products are transient; basic needs and customer groups endure forever. Transportation is a need: the horse and carriage, the automobile, the railroad, the airline, and the truck are products that meet that need.

Viewing businesses in terms of customer needs can suggest additional growth opportunities. IBM redefined itself from a hardware and software manufacturer to a "builder of networks." Table 2.3 gives several examples of companies that have moved from a product to a market definition of their business. It highlights the difference between a target market definition and a strategic market definition.

TABLE 2.3 | Product-Oriented versus Market-Oriented Definitions of a Business

Company	Product Definition	Market Definition
Missouri-Pacific Railroad	We run a railroad.	We are a people-and-goods mover.
Xerox	We make copying equipment.	We help improve office productivity.
Standard Oil	We sell gasoline.	We supply energy.
Columbia Pictures	We make movies.	We market entertainment.
Encyclopaedia Britannica	We sell encyclopedias.	We distribute information.
Carrier	We make air conditioners and furnaces.	We provide climate control in the home.

A *target market definition* tends to focus on selling a product or service to a current market. Pepsi could define its target market as everyone who drinks a cola beverage, and competitors would therefore be other cola companies. A *strategic market definition,* however, focuses also on the potential market. If Pepsi considered everyone who might drink something to quench their thirst, their competition would also include noncola soft drinks, bottled water, fruit juices, tea, and coffee. To better compete, Pepsi might decide to sell additional beverages whose growth rate appears to be promising.

A business can define itself in terms of three dimensions: customer groups, customer needs, and technology.[23] Consider a small company that defines its business as designing incandescent lighting systems for television studios. Its customer group is television studios; the customer need is lighting; and the technology is incandescent lighting. The company might want to expand. It could make lighting for other customer groups, such as homes, factories, and offices; or it could supply other services needed by television studios, such as heating, ventilation, or air conditioning. It could design other lighting technologies for television studios, such as infrared or ultraviolet lighting.

Large companies normally manage quite different businesses, each requiring its own strategy. General Electric has classified its businesses into 49 **strategic business units, SBUs**. An SBU has three characteristics:

1. It is a single business, or a collection of related businesses, that can be planned separately from the rest of the company.
2. It has its own set of competitors.
3. It has a manager responsible for strategic planning and profit performance, who controls most of the factors affecting profit.

The purpose of identifying the company's strategic business units is to develop separate strategies and assign appropriate funding. Senior management knows that its portfolio of businesses usually includes a number of "yesterday's has-beens" as well as "tomorrow's breadwinners."[24]

Assigning Resources to Each SBU[25]

Once it has defined SBUs, management must decide how to allocate corporate resources to each. The 1970s saw several portfolio-planning models introduced to provide an analytical means for making investment decisions. The GE/McKinsey Matrix classifies each SBU according to the extent of its competitive advantage and the attractiveness of its industry. Management would want to grow, "harvest" or draw cash from, or hold on to the business. Another model, the BCG's Growth-Share Matrix, uses relative market share and annual rate of market growth as criteria to make investment decisions.

Portfolio-planning models like these have fallen out of favor as oversimplified and subjective. More recent methods firms use to make internal investment decisions are based on shareholder value analysis, and whether the market value of a company is greater with an SBU or without it (whether it is sold or spun off). These value calculations assess the potential of a business based on potential growth opportunities from global expansion, repositioning or retargeting, and strategic outsourcing.

Assessing Growth Opportunities

Assessing growth opportunities includes planning new businesses, downsizing, and terminating older businesses. If there is a gap between future desired sales and projected sales, corporate management will need to develop or acquire new businesses to fill it.

Figure 2.3 illustrates this strategic-planning gap for a major manufacturer of blank compact disks called Musicale (name disguised). The lowest curve projects the expected sales over the next five years from the current business portfolio. The highest curve describes desired sales over the same period. Evidently, the company wants to grow much faster than its current businesses will permit. How can it fill the strategic-planning gap?

The first option is to identify opportunities to achieve further growth within current businesses (intensive opportunities). The second is to identify opportunities to build or acquire businesses that are related to current businesses (integrative opportunities). The third option is to identify opportunities to add attractive businesses unrelated to current businesses (diversification opportunities).

INTENSIVE GROWTH Corporate management's first course of action should be a review of opportunities for improving existing businesses. One useful framework for detecting new intensive growth opportunities is called a "product–market expansion grid" (Figure 2.4).[26]

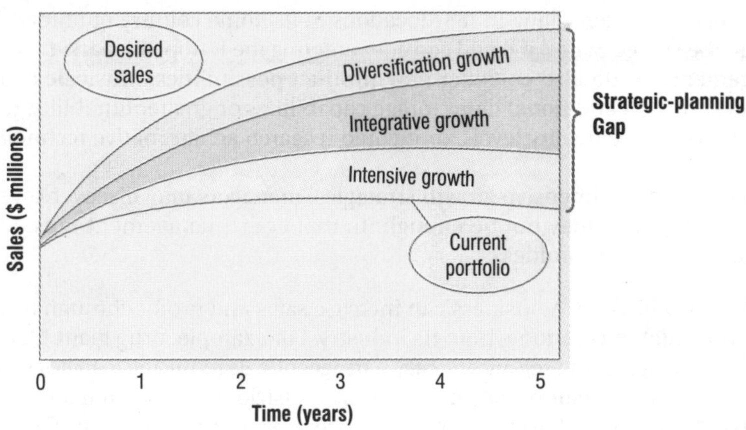

FIG. 2.3

The Strategic-Planning Gap

The company first considers whether it could gain more market share with its current products in their current markets, using a *market-penetration strategy.* Next it considers whether it can find or develop new markets for its current products, in a *market-development strategy.* Then it considers whether it can develop new products of potential interest to its current markets with a *product-development strategy.* Later the firm will also review opportunities to develop new products for new markets in a *diversification strategy.*

STARBUCKS

When Howard Schultz, Starbucks' CEO until 2000, came to the company in 1982, he recognized an unfilled niche for cafés serving gourmet coffee directly to customers. This became Starbucks' market-penetration strategy and helped the company attain a loyal customer base in Seattle. The market-development strategy marked the next phase in Starbucks' growth: It applied the same successful formula that had worked wonders in Seattle, first to other cities in the Pacific Northwest, then throughout North America, and finally, across the globe. Once the company had established itself as a presence in thousands of cities internationally, Starbucks sought to increase the number of purchases by existing customers with a product-development strategy that led to new in-store merchandise, including compilation CDs, a Starbucks Duetto Visa card that allows customers to receive points toward Starbucks purchases whenever they use it, and high-speed wireless Internet access at thousands of Starbucks "HotSpots" through a deal with T-Mobile. Finally, Starbucks pursued diversification into grocery store aisles with Frappuccino® bottled drinks, Starbucks brand ice cream, and the purchase of tea retailer Tazo® Tea.[27]

So how might Musicale use these three major intensive growth strategies to increase its sales? It could try to encourage its current customers to buy more by demonstrating the benefits of using compact disks for data storage in addition to music storage. Musicale could also try to attract competitors' customers if it noticed major weaknesses in competitors' products or marketing programs. Finally, Musicale could try to convince nonusers of compact disks to start using them.

How can Musicale use a market-development strategy? First, it might try to identify potential user groups in the current sales areas. If Musicale has been selling compact disks only to consumer markets, it might go after office and factory markets. Second, it might seek additional distribution channels in its present locations. If it has been selling its disks only through stereo equipment dealers, it might add mass-merchandising or online channels. Third, the

	Current Products	New Products
Current Markets	1. Market-penetration strategy	3. Product-development strategy
New Markets	2. Market-development strategy	(Diversification strategy)

FIG. 2.4

Three Intensive Growth Strategies: Ansoff's Product–Market Expansion Grid

Source: Adapted and reprinted by permission, *Harvard Business Review.* From "Strategies for Diversification," by Igor Ansoff, September–October 1957. Copyright © 1957 by the President and Fellows of Harvard College. All rights reserved.

company might consider selling in new locations in its home country or abroad. If Musicale sold only in the United States, it could consider entering the European market.

Management should also consider new-product possibilities. Musicale could develop new features, such as additional data storage capabilities or greater durability. It could offer the CD at two or more quality levels, or it could research an alternative technology such as flash drives.

By examining these intensive growth strategies, managers may discover several ways to grow. Still, that growth may not be enough. In that case, management must also look for integrative growth opportunities.

INTEGRATIVE GROWTH A business can increase sales and profits through backward, forward, or horizontal integration within its industry. For example, drug giant Merck has gone beyond just developing and selling ethical pharmaceuticals requiring a doctor's prescription. It purchased Medco, a mail-order pharmaceutical distributor, formed a joint venture with DuPont to establish more basic research, and began another joint venture with Johnson & Johnson to bring some of its ethical products into the over-the-counter market.

Media companies have long reaped the benefits of integrative growth. Here's how one business writer explains the potential that NBC could reap from its merger with Vivendi Universal Entertainment to become NBC Universal. Although it's a far-fetched example, it gets across the possibilities inherent in this growth strategy:[28]

> [When] the hit movie *Seabiscuit* (produced by Universal Pictures) comes to television, it would air on Bravo (owned by NBC) or USA Network (owned by Universal), followed by the inevitable bid to make the movie into a TV series (by Universal Television Group), with the pilot being picked up by NBC, which passes on the show, but it's then revived in the "Brilliant But Canceled" series on cable channel Trio (owned by Universal) where its cult status leads to a Spanish version shown on Telemundo (owned by NBC) and the creation of a popular amusement-park attraction at Universal Studios.

How might Musicale achieve integrative growth? The company might acquire one or more of its suppliers, such as plastic material producers, to gain more control or generate more profit through backward integration. It might acquire some wholesalers or retailers, especially if they are highly profitable, in forward integration. Finally, Musicale might acquire one or more competitors, provided that the government does not bar this horizontal integration. However, these new sources may still not deliver the desired sales volume. In that case, the company must consider diversification.

DIVERSIFICATION GROWTH Diversification growth makes sense when good opportunities exist outside the present businesses—the industry is highly attractive and the company has the right mix of business strengths to be successful. For example, from its origins as an animated film producer, Walt Disney Company has moved into licensing characters for merchandised goods, entering the broadcast industry with its own Disney Channel as well as ABC and ESPN acquisitions, and developing theme parks and vacation and resort properties.

CISCO SYSTEMS INC.

Known for years as a mass producer of routers and switches, Cisco is attempting to diversify beyond these nuts and bolts products into the business of changing how consumers communicate and view television. With its recent $6.9 billion acquisition of Scientific-Atlanta Inc., widely recognized for its expertise in video delivery, Cisco hopes to enter consumers' living rooms with items such as home-networking equipment and wirelessly networked DVD players and services such as video on demand. The diversification move is already paying off: Scientific-Atlanta produced 7% of Cisco's $8 billion in revenue in the fourth quarter of 2006.[29]

Several types of diversification are possible for Musicale. First, the company could choose a concentric strategy and seek new products that have technological or marketing synergies with existing product lines, though the new products themselves may appeal to a different group of customers. It might start a laser disk manufacturing operation, because it knows how to manufacture compact discs. Second, the company might use a horizontal strategy to search for new products that could appeal to current customers, even though the new products are technologically unrelated to its current product line. Musicale might produce compact disc cases, for example, though they require a different manufacturing process. Finally, the company might seek new businesses that have no relationship to its current technology, products, or markets, adopting a conglomerate strategy to consider such new businesses as making application software or personal organizers.

DOWNSIZING AND DIVESTING OLDER BUSINESSES Weak businesses require a disproportionate amount of managerial attention. Companies must carefully prune, harvest, or divest tired old businesses in order to release needed resources to other uses and reduce costs. To focus on its travel and credit card operations, American Express in 2005 spun off American Express Financial Advisors, which provided insurance, mutual funds, investment advice, and brokerage and asset management services (it was renamed Ameriprise Financial).

HEALTHSOUTH CORP.

In 2006, HealthSouth Corp., one of the nation's largest providers of rehabilitative health care, announced it was planning to get rid of its large network of outpatient services. The company, still reeling from a $2.7 billion fraud scandal in 2003, planned to increase its stockholder value by focusing on the areas that account for 58% of the company's net operating revenue and 86% of its operating earnings: post-acute-care inpatient services. "We intend to focus HealthSouth's resources on establishing a 'pure play,' post-acute company that builds on our core competencies," said Jay Grinney, CEO and president. "At the same time, we believe our outpatient, surgery, and diagnostic divisions will be well positioned to succeed under new owners who will place strategic priority on strengthening each individual business."[30]

Organization and Organizational Culture

Strategic planning happens within the context of the organization. A company's **organization** consists of its structures, policies, and corporate culture, all of which can become dysfunctional in a rapidly changing business environment. Whereas managers can change structures and policies (with difficulty), the company's culture is very hard to change. Yet adapting the culture is often the key to successfully implementing a new strategy.

What exactly is a **corporate culture**? Most businesspeople would be hard-pressed to describe this elusive concept, which some define as "the shared experiences, stories, beliefs, and norms that characterize an organization." Yet, walk into any company and the first thing that strikes you is the corporate culture—the way people dress, talk to one another, and greet customers.

A customer-centric culture can affect all aspects of an organization. As one expert says, "To me, being consumer-centric is more a principle—the driving value of a company—than a process. It's in a company's DNA, top to bottom. It means you recognize the diversity across the face of consumers, and that you are open to observations and opinions other than your own; this allows you to be an advocate for the consumer—whether you are a leading innovator or packing boxes in the warehouse. . . . The question is, Do you see consumers as the driving life force of your company for as long as it exists, or do you see them as simply a hungry group of people that needs to be satisfied so your business will grow in the short term?"[31]

Sometimes corporate culture develops organically and is transmitted directly from the CEO's personality and habits to the company employees. Mike Lazaridis, president and co-CEO of Blackberry producer Research in Motion, is a scientist in his own right, winning an Academy Award for technical achievement in film. He hosts a weekly, innovation-centered "Vision Series" at company headquarters to focus on new research and company goals. As he states, "I think we have a culture of innovation here, and [engineers] have absolute access to me. I live a life that tries to promote innovation."[32]

Marketing Innovation

Innovation in marketing is critical. The traditional view is that senior management hammers out the strategy and hands it down. Gary Hamel offers the contrasting view that imaginative ideas on strategy exist in many places within a company.[33] Senior management should identify

Research in Motion, the company that developed the Blackberry wireless device, fosters a culture of innovation that CEO Mike Lazaridis carefully cultivates and values highly.

and encourage fresh ideas from three groups that tend to be underrepresented in strategy making: employees with youthful perspectives; employees who are far removed from company headquarters; and employees who are new to the industry. Each group is capable of challenging company orthodoxy and stimulating new ideas. Jump Associates, an innovative strategy firm, offers five key strategies for managing change in an organization:[34]

1. ***Avoid the innovation title***—Pick a name for the innovation team that won't alienate coworkers.
2. ***Use the buddy system***—Find a like-minded collaborator within the organization.
3. ***Set the metrics in advance***—Establish different sets of funding, testing, and performance criteria for incremental, experimental, and potentially disruptive innovations.
4. ***Aim for quick hits first***—Start with easily implemented ideas that will work to demonstrate that things can get done, before quickly switching to bigger initiatives.
5. ***Get data to back up your gut***—Use testing to get feedback and improve an idea.

"Marketing Insight: Creating Innovative Marketing" describes how some leading companies approach innovation.

Firms develop strategy by identifying and selecting among different views of the future. The Royal Dutch/Shell Group has pioneered **scenario analysis**, which consists of developing plausible representations of a firm's possible future that make different assumptions about forces driving the market and that include different uncertainties. Managers need to think through each scenario with the question: "What will we do if it happens?" They need to adopt one scenario as the most probable and watch for signposts that might confirm or disconfirm it.[35]

::: Business Unit Strategic Planning

The business unit strategic-planning process consists of the steps shown in Figure 2.5. We examine each step in the sections that follow.

The Business Mission

Each business unit needs to define its specific mission within the broader company mission. Thus, a television-studio-lighting-equipment company might define its mission as, "To tar-

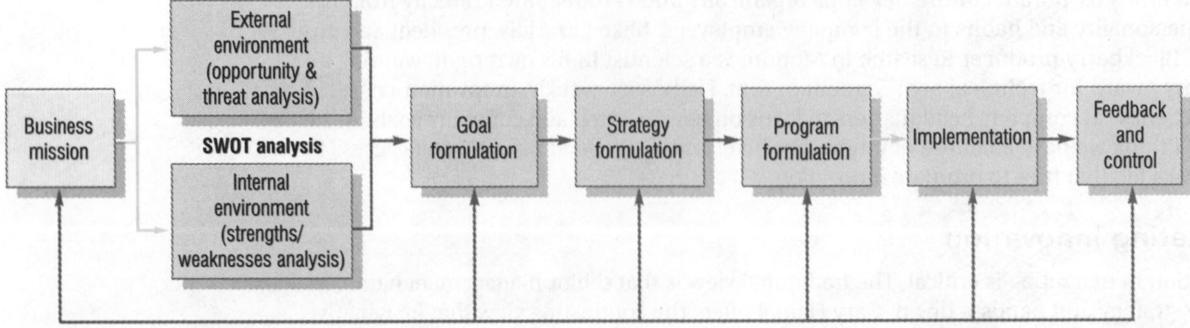

FIG. 2.5 The Business Unit Strategic-Planning Process

MARKETING INSIGHT | CREATING INNOVATIVE MARKETING

When IBM surveyed top CEOs and government leaders about their agenda priorities, their answers about innovation were revealing. Business-model innovation and coming up with unique ways of doing things scored high. IBM's own drive for business-model innovation led to much collaboration, both within IBM itself and externally with companies, governments, and educational institutions. CEO Samuel Palmisano noted how the breakthrough Cell processor, based on the company's Power architecture, would not have happened without collaboration with Sony and Nintendo, as well as competitors Toshiba and Microsoft.

Procter & Gamble similarly has made it a goal for 50% of the new company's products to come from outside P&G's labs—from inventors, scientists, and suppliers whose new-product ideas can be developed in-house.

Business guru Jim Collins' research emphasizes the importance of systematic, broad-based innovation: "Always looking for the one big breakthrough, the one big idea, is contrary to what we found: To build a truly great company, it's decision upon decision, action upon action, day upon day, month upon month. . . . It's cumulative momentum and no one decision defines a great company." He cites the success of Walt Disney with theme parks and Wal-Mart with retailing as examples of companies who were successful after having executed against a big idea brilliantly over such a long period of time.

Northwestern's Mohanbir Sawhney and his colleagues outline 12 dimensions of business innovation that make up the "innovation radar" (see Table 2.4) and suggest that business innovation is about increasing customer *value*, not just creating new *things*; business innovation comes in many flavors and can take place on any dimension of a business system; and business innovation is systematic and requires careful consideration of all aspects of a business.

Business writer C.K. Prahalad believes much innovation in industries from financial and telecom services to health care and automobiles can come from developments in emerging markets such as India. Forced to do more with less, Indian companies and foreign competitors are finding new ways to maximize minimal resources and offer quality products and services at low prices. Consider Bangalore's Narayana Hrudayalaya hospital, which charges a flat fee of $1,500 for heart bypass surgery that would cost 50 times that much in the United States. The low cost is a result of the hospital's low labor and operating expenses and an assembly-line view of care that has specialists focus just on their own area. The approach works—the hospital's mortality rates are half those of U.S. hospitals. Narayana also operates on hundreds of infants for free and profitably insures 2.5 million poor Indians against serious illness for 11 cents a month.

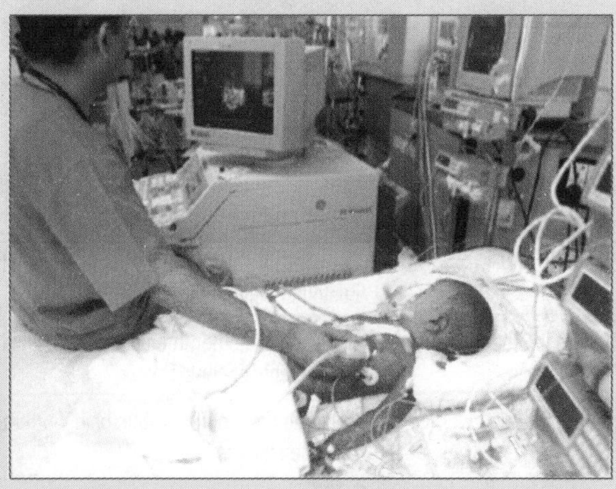

Low labor costs allow India's Narayana Hrudayalaya hospital to innovate through its pricing strategies.

Finally, to find breakthrough ideas, some companies find ways to immerse a range of employees in solving marketing problems. Samsung's Value Innovation Program (VIP) isolates product development teams of engineers, designers, and planners with a timetable and end date in the company's center just south of Seoul, Korea, while 50 specialists help guide their activities. To help make tough trade-offs, team members draw "value curves" that rank attributes such as a product's sound or picture quality on a scale from 1 to 5. To develop a new car, BMW similarly mobilizes specialists in engineering, design, production, marketing, purchasing, and finance at its Research and Innovation Center or Project House.

Sources: Steve Hamm, "Innovation: The View From the Top," *BusinessWeek*, April 3, 2006, pp. 52–53; Jena McGregor, "The World's Most Innovative Companies," *BusinessWeek*, April 24, 2006, pp. 63–74; Rich Karlgard, "Digital Rules," *Forbes*, March 13, 2006, p. 31; Jennifer Rooney and Jim Collins, "Being Great Is *Not* Just a Matter of Big Ideas," *Point*, June 2006, p. 20; Moon Ihiwan, "Camp Samsung," *BusinessWeek*, July 3, 2006, pp. 46–47; Mohanbir Sawhney, Robert C. Wolcott, and Inigo Arroniz, "The 12 Different Ways for Companies to Innovate," *MIT Sloan Management Review*, Spring 2006, pp. 75–85; Pete Engardio, "Business Prophet: How C.K. Prahalad Is Changing the Way CEO's Think," *BusinessWeek*, January 23, 2006, pp. 68–73.

get major television studios and become their vendor of choice for lighting technologies that represent the most advanced and reliable studio lighting arrangements." Notice that this mission does not attempt to win business from smaller television studios, win business by being lowest in price, or venture into nonlighting products.

SWOT Analysis

The overall evaluation of a company's strengths, weaknesses, opportunities, and threats is called SWOT analysis. It's a way of monitoring the external and internal marketing environment.

TABLE 2.4 | The 12 Dimensions of Business Innovation

Dimension	Definition	Examples
Offerings (WHAT)	Develop innovative new products or services.	■ Gillette Mach3Turbo razor ■ Apple iPod music player and iTunes music service
Platform	Use common components or building blocks to create derivative offerings.	■ General Motors OnStar telematics platform ■ Disney animated movies
Solutions	Create integrated and customized offerings that solve end-to-end customer problems.	■ UPS logistics services Supply Chain Solutions ■ DuPont Building Innovations for construction
Customers (WHO)	Discover unmet customer needs or identify underserved customer segments.	■ Enterprise Rent-A-Car focus on replacement car renters ■ Green Mountain Energy focus on "green power"
Customer Experience	Redesign customer interactions across all touch points and all moments of contact.	■ Washington Mutual Occasio retail banking concept ■ Cabela's "store as entertainment experience" concept
Value Capture	Redefine how company gets paid or create innovative new revenue streams.	■ Google paid search ■ Blockbuster revenue sharing with movie distributors
Processes (HOW)	Redesign core operating processes to improve efficiency and effectiveness.	■ Toyota Production System for operations ■ General Electric Design for Six Sigma (DFSS)
Organization	Change form, function, or activity scope of the firm.	■ Cisco partner-centric networked virtual organization ■ Procter & Gamble front-back hybrid organization for customer focus
Supply Chain	Think differently about sourcing and fulfillment.	■ Moen ProjectNet for collaborative design with suppliers ■ General Motors Celta use of integrated supply and online sales
Presence (WHERE)	Create new distribution channels or innovative points of presence, including the places where offerings can be bought or used by customers.	■ Starbucks music CD sales in coffee stores ■ Diebold RemoteTeller System for banking
Networking	Create network-centric intelligent and integrated offerings.	■ Otis Remote Elevator Monitoring service ■ Department of Defense Network-Centric Warfare
Brand	Leverage a brand into new domains.	■ Virgin Group "branded venture capital" ■ Yahoo! as a lifestyle brand

Source: Mohanbir Sawhney, Robert C. Wolcott, and Inigo Arroniz, "The 12 Different Ways for Companies to Innovate," *MIT Sloan Management Review*, Spring 2006, p. 78.

EXTERNAL ENVIRONMENT (OPPORTUNITY AND THREAD) ANALYSIS A business unit must monitor key *macroenvironment forces* and significant *microenvironment factors* that affect its ability to earn profits. The business unit should set up a marketing intelligence system to track trends and important developments and any related opportunities and threats.

Good marketing is the art of finding, developing, and profiting from these opportunities.[36] A **marketing opportunity** is an area of buyer need and interest that a company has a high probability of profitably satisfying. There are three main sources of market opportunities.[37] The first is to supply something that is in short supply. This requires little marketing talent, as the need is fairly obvious. The second is to supply an existing product or service in a new or superior way. There are several ways to uncover possible product or service improvements: the *problem detection method* asks consumers for their suggestions, the *ideal method* has them imagine an ideal version of the product or service, and the *consumption chain method* asks consumers to chart their steps in acquiring, using, and disposing of a product. This last method often leads to a totally new product or service.

Opportunities can take many forms, and marketers need to be good at spotting them. Consider the following:

- A company may benefit from converging industry trends and introduce hybrid products or services that are new to the market. For example: At least five major cell phone manufacturers released phones with digital photo capabilities.

- A company may make a buying process more convenient or efficient. Consumers can now use the Internet to find more books than ever and search for the lowest price with a few clicks.
- A company can meet the need for more information and advice. Guru.com facilitates finding professional experts in a wide range of fields.
- A company can customize a product or service that was formerly offered only in a standard form. Timberland allows customers to choose colors for different sections of their boots, add initials or numbers to their boots, and choose different stitching and embroidery.
- A company can introduce a new capability. Consumers can now create and edit digital "iMovies" with the new iMac and upload them to an Apple Web server or Web site such as YouTube to share with friends around the world.
- A company may be able to deliver a product or a service faster. FedEx discovered a way to deliver mail and packages much more quickly than the U.S. Post Office.
- A company may be able to offer a product at a much lower price. Pharmaceutical firms have created generic versions of brand-name drugs.

To evaluate opportunities, companies can use **market opportunity analysis (MOA)** to determine their attractiveness and probability of success by asking questions like:

1. Can we articulate the benefits convincingly to a defined target market(s)?
2. Can we locate the target market(s) and reach them with cost-effective media and trade channels?
3. Does our company possess or have access to the critical capabilities and resources we need to deliver the customer benefits?
4. Can we deliver the benefits better than any actual or potential competitors?
5. Will the financial rate of return meet or exceed our required threshold for investment?

In the opportunity matrix in Figure 2.6(a), the best marketing opportunities facing the TV-lighting-equipment company are listed in the upper-left cell (#1). The opportunities in the lower-right cell (#4) are too minor to consider. The opportunities in the upper-right cell (#2) and lower-left cell (#3) are worth monitoring in the event that any improve in attractiveness and success probability.

An **environmental threat** is a challenge posed by an unfavorable trend or development that would lead, in the absence of defensive marketing action, to lower sales or profit. Figure 2.6(b) illustrates the threat matrix facing the TV-lighting-equipment company. The

(a) Opportunity Matrix

Attractiveness \ Success Probability	High	Low
High	1	2
Low	3	4

1. Company develops more powerful lighting system
2. Company develops device to measure energy efficiency of any lighting system
3. Company develops device to measure illumination level
4. Company develops software program to teach lighting fundamentals to TV studio personnel

(b) Threat Matrix

Seriousness \ Probability of Occurrence	High	Low
High	1	2
Low	3	4

1. Competitor develops superior lighting system
2. Major prolonged economic depression
3. Higher costs
4. Legislation to reduce number of TV studio licenses

FIG. 2.6

Opportunity and Threat Matrices

threats in the upper-left cell are major, because they can seriously hurt the company and they have a high probability of occurrence. To deal with them, the company needs contingency plans. The threats in the lower-right cell are very minor and can be ignored. The firm will want to carefully monitor threats in the upper-right and lower-left cells in the event they grow more serious.

INTERNAL ENVIRONMENT (STRENGTHS AND WEAKNESSES) ANALYSIS It's one thing to find attractive opportunities, and another to be able to take advantage of them. Each business needs to evaluate its internal strengths and weaknesses.

LOAN BRIGHT

At the Web site of Loan Bright, an online mortgage company, potential homebuyers can get a personalized list of lenders and available terms. At first Loan Bright made its money by selling the homebuyer data to high-end mortgage lenders, including Wells Fargo, Bank of America, and Chase Manhattan Mortgages. These firms turned the data into leads for their sales teams. But worrisome internal issues arose. For one thing, Loan Bright had to please every one of its big clients, yet each was becoming tougher to satisfy, eating up time and resources. The company's top managers gathered to analyze the market and Loan Bright's strengths and weaknesses. They decided that instead of serving a few choice clients, they would shift down-market to serve many more individual loan officers, who responded to the company's Google ads and only wanted to buy a few leads. The switch required revamping the way Loan Bright salespeople brought in new business, including using a one-page contract instead of the old 12-page contract and creating a separate customer service department.[38]

Businesses can evaluate their own strengths and weaknesses by using a form like the one shown in "Marketing Memo: Checklist for Performing Strengths/Weaknesses Analysis."

Clearly, the business doesn't have to correct *all* its weaknesses, nor should it gloat about all its strengths. The big question is whether the firm should limit itself to those opportunities for which it possesses the required strengths, or consider those that might require it to find or develop new strengths. For example, managers at Texas Instruments (TI) were split between those who wanted TI to stick to industrial electronics, where it has clear strength, and those who wanted the company to continue introducing consumer products, where it lacks some required marketing strengths.

Sometimes a business does poorly not because its people lack the required strengths, but because they don't work together as a team. In one major electronics company, engineers look down on the salespeople as "engineers who couldn't make it," and salespeople look down on the service people as "salespeople who couldn't make it." It's critical to assess interdepartmental working relationships as part of the internal environmental audit.

Goal Formulation

Once the company has performed a SWOT analysis, it can proceed to develop specific goals for the planning period. This stage of the process is called **goal formulation**. Goals are objectives that are specific with respect to magnitude and time.

Most business units pursue a mix of objectives, including profitability, sales growth, market share improvement, risk containment, innovation, and reputation. The business unit sets these objectives and then manages by objectives (MBO). For an MBO system to work, the unit's objectives must meet four criteria:

1. ***They must be arranged hierarchically, from the most to the least important.*** For example, the business unit's key objective for the period may be to increase the rate of return on investment. Managers can increase profit by increasing revenue and reducing expenses. They can grow revenue, in turn, by increasing market share and prices.
2. ***Objectives should be quantitative whenever possible.*** The objective "to increase the return on investment (ROI)" is better stated as the goal "to increase ROI to 15% within two years."
3. ***Goals should be realistic.*** Goals should arise from an analysis of the business unit's opportunities and strengths, not from wishful thinking.

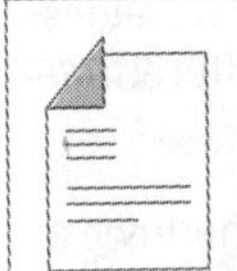

MARKETING MEMO | CHECKLIST FOR PERFORMING STRENGTHS/WEAKNESSES ANALYSIS

	Performance					Importance		
	Major Strength	Minor Strength	Neutral	Minor Weakness	Major Weakness	High	Med	Low
Marketing								
1. Company reputation	____	____	____	____	____	____	____	____
2. Market share	____	____	____	____	____	____	____	____
3. Customer satisfaction	____	____	____	____	____	____	____	____
4. Customer retention	____	____	____	____	____	____	____	____
5. Product quality	____	____	____	____	____	____	____	____
6. Service quality	____	____	____	____	____	____	____	____
7. Pricing effectiveness	____	____	____	____	____	____	____	____
8. Distribution effectiveness	____	____	____	____	____	____	____	____
9. Promotion effectiveness	____	____	____	____	____	____	____	____
10. Sales force effectiveness	____	____	____	____	____	____	____	____
11. Innovation effectiveness	____	____	____	____	____	____	____	____
12. Geographical coverage	____	____	____	____	____	____	____	____
Finance								
13. Cost or availability of capital	____	____	____	____	____	____	____	____
14. Cash flow	____	____	____	____	____	____	____	____
15. Financial stability	____	____	____	____	____	____	____	____
Manufacturing								
16. Facilities	____	____	____	____	____	____	____	____
17. Economies of scale	____	____	____	____	____	____	____	____
18. Capacity	____	____	____	____	____	____	____	____
19. Able, dedicated workforce	____	____	____	____	____	____	____	____
20. Ability to produce on time	____	____	____	____	____	____	____	____
21. Technical manufacturing skill	____	____	____	____	____	____	____	____
Organization								
22. Visionary, capable leadership	____	____	____	____	____	____	____	____
23. Dedicated employees	____	____	____	____	____	____	____	____
24. Entrepreneurial orientation	____	____	____	____	____	____	____	____
25. Flexible or responsive	____	____	____	____	____	____	____	____

4. ***Objectives must be consistent.*** It's not possible to maximize sales and profits simultaneously.

Other important trade-offs include short-term profit versus long-term growth, deep penetration of existing markets versus developing new markets, profit goals versus nonprofit goals, and high growth versus low risk. Each choice calls for a different marketing strategy.[39]

Many believe that adopting the goal of strong market share growth may mean foregoing strong short-term profits. For years, Compaq priced aggressively in order to build its share in the computer market. Compaq later decided to pursue profitability at the expense of growth. Yet management experts Charan and Tichy believe that most businesses can be growth businesses *and* grow profitably.[40] They cite success stories such as GE Medical, Allied Signal, Citibank, and GE Capital, all enjoying profitable growth. Some so-called trade-offs may not be trade-offs at all.

To understand the importance of staying focused in competitive marketing strategy and knowing exactly where to excel in terms of product and service differentiation, read about Singapore Airlines at www.pearsoned-asia.com/marketingmanagementasia.

Strategic Formulation

Goals indicate what a business unit wants to achieve; **strategy** is a game plan for getting there. Every business must design a strategy for achieving its goals, consisting of a *marketing strategy* and a compatible *technology strategy* and *sourcing strategy.*

PORTER'S GENERIC STRATEGIES Michael Porter has proposed three generic strategies that provide a good starting point for strategic thinking: overall cost leadership, differentiation, and focus.[41]

- ***Overall cost leadership.*** Firms pursuing this strategy work hard to achieve the lowest production and distribution costs so they can price lower than their competitors and win a large market share. They need less skill in marketing. The problem with this strategy is that other firms will usually compete with still-lower costs and hurt the firm that rested its whole future on cost.
- ***Differentiation.*** The business concentrates on uniquely achieving superior performance in an important customer benefit area valued by a large part of the market. Thus the firm seeking quality leadership, for example, must make products with the best components, put them together expertly, inspect them carefully, and effectively communicate their quality.
- ***Focus.*** The business focuses on one or more narrow market segments. The firm gets to know these segments intimately and pursues either cost leadership or differentiation within the target segment.

BELKIN CORPORATION

For most people, a surge protector is a necessary item you buy at a hardware store and hide behind your PC within a jumble of dust bunnies and cable cords. Yet, one company decided to focus not on the utilitarian aspect of the surge protector but on its aesthetic aspect. An example of both focus and differentiation, Belkin Corporation's surge protectors organize consumers' workspaces and protect their equipment. Its Concealed Surge Protector organizes cables and keeps them out of view with a unique closing cover. By differentiating itself from the average surge protector, which costs about $15.00, Belkin can charge $50.00.[42]

The online air travel industry provides a good example of these three strategies: Travelocity is pursuing a differentiation strategy by offering the most comprehensive range of services to the traveler. Lowestfare is pursuing a lowest-cost strategy; and Last Minute is pursuing a niche strategy in focusing on travelers who have the flexibility to travel on very short notice.

According to Porter, firms pursuing the same strategy directed to the same target market constitute a **strategic group**. The firm that carries out that strategy best will make the most profits. International Harvester went out of the farm equipment business because it did not stand out in its industry as lowest in cost, highest in perceived value, or best in serving some market segment.[43]

Porter draws a distinction between operational effectiveness and strategy. Competitors can quickly copy the operationally effective company using benchmarking and other tools, thus diminishing the advantage of operational effectiveness. Porter defines strategy as "the creation of a unique and valuable position involving a different set of activities." A company can claim that it has a strategy when it "performs different activities from rivals or performs similar activities in different ways."

STRATEGIC ALLIANCES Even giant companies—AT&T, IBM, Philips, and Nokia—often cannot achieve leadership, either nationally or globally, without forming alliances with domestic or multinational companies that complement or leverage their capabilities and resources.

Just doing business in another country may require the firm to license its product, form a joint venture with a local firm, or buy from local suppliers to meet "domestic content" requirements. As a result, many firms are rapidly developing global strategic networks, and victory is going to those who build the better global network. The Star Alliance, for example, brings together 18 airlines, including Lufthansa, United Airlines, Singapore Airlines, Air New Zealand, and South Africa Airways, into a huge global partnership that allows travelers to make nearly seamless connections to hundreds of destinations.

Many strategic alliances take the form of marketing alliances. These fall into four major categories.

1. ***Product or service alliances***—One company licenses another to produce its product, or two companies jointly market their complementary products or a new product. The credit card industry is a complicated combination of cards jointly marketed by banks

such as Bank of America, credit card companies such as Visa, and affinity companies such as Alaska Airlines.

2. ***Promotional alliances***—One company agrees to carry a promotion for another company's product or service. McDonald's, for example, teamed up with Disney for 10 years to offer products related to current Disney films as part of its meals for children.
3. ***Logistics alliances***—One company offers logistical services for another company's product. For example, Abbott Laboratories warehouses and delivers 3M's medical and surgical products to hospitals across the United States.
4. ***Pricing collaborations***—One or more companies join in a special pricing collaboration. Hotel and rental car companies often offer mutual price discounts.

Companies need to give creative thought to finding partners that might complement their strengths and offset their weaknesses. Well-managed alliances allow companies to obtain a greater sales impact at less cost. To keep their strategic alliances thriving, corporations have begun to develop organizational structures to support them, and many have come to view the ability to form and manage partnerships as core skills called **partner relationship management, PRM.**[44]

Both pharmaceutical and biotech companies are starting to make partnership a core competency. For example, Erbitux, a new drug to aid treatment of colorectal cancer, is the result of just such a partnership. The drug was originally discovered in biotech company ImClone Systems' clinical labs, and marketed via ImClone's partnership with pharmaceutical giant Bristol-Myers Squibb.[45]

Program Formulation and Implementation

Even a great marketing strategy can be sabotaged by poor implementation. If the unit has decided to attain technological leadership, it must plan programs to strengthen its R&D department, gather technological intelligence, develop leading-edge products, train the technical sales force, and develop ads to communicate its technological leadership.

Once they have formulated marketing programs, the marketing people must estimate their costs. Is participating in a particular trade show worth it? Will a specific sales contest pay for itself? Will hiring another salesperson contribute to the bottom line? Activity-based cost accounting (ABC) can help determine whether each marketing program is likely to produce sufficient results to justify its cost.[46]

Today's businesses are also increasingly recognizing that unless they nurture other stakeholders—customers, employees, suppliers, distributors—they may never earn sufficient profits for the stockholders. For example, a company might aim to delight its customers, perform well for its employees, and deliver a threshold level of satisfaction to its suppliers. In setting these levels, a company must be careful not to violate any stakeholder group's sense of fairness about the treatment they're receiving relative to the others.[47]

A dynamic relationship connects the stakeholder groups. A smart company creates a high level of employee satisfaction, which leads to higher effort, which leads to higher-quality products and services, which creates higher customer satisfaction, which leads to more repeat business, which leads to higher growth and profits, which leads to high stockholder satisfaction, which leads to more investment, and so on. This is the virtuous circle that spells profits and growth. "Marketing Insight: Marketing's Contribution to Shareholder Value" highlights the increasing importance of the proper bottom-line view to marketing expenditures.

According to McKinsey & Company, strategy is only one of seven elements—all of which start with the letter "s"—in successful business practice.[48] The first three—strategy, structure, and systems—are considered the "hardware" of success. The next four—style, skills, staff, and shared values—are the "software."

The first "soft" element, *style,* means that company employees share a common way of thinking and behaving. McDonald's employees smile at the customer, and IBM employees are very professional in their customer dealings. The second element, *skills,* means employees have the skills needed to carry out the company's strategy. *Staffing* means the company has hired able people, trained them well, and assigned them to the right jobs. The fourth element, *shared values,* means employees share the same guiding values. When these elements are present, companies are usually more successful at strategy implementation.[49]

Another study of management practices found that superior performance over time depended on flawless execution, a company culture based on aiming high, a structure that is flexible and responsive, and a strategy that is clear and focused.[50]

MARKETING INSIGHT | MARKETING'S CONTRIBUTION TO SHAREHOLDER VALUE

Companies normally focus on profit maximization rather than on shareholder value maximization. The late Peter Doyle, in his *Value-Based Marketing,* charges that profit maximization leads to short-term planning and underinvestment in marketing, promoting a focus on building sales, market share, and current profits. It also leads to cost cutting and shedding assets to produce quick improvements in earnings and erodes a company's long-term competitiveness by eliminating investment in new market opportunities.

Companies normally measure their profit performance using ROI (return on investment, calculated by dividing profits by investment). This method presents two problems:

1. Profits are arbitrarily measured and subject to manipulation. Cash flow is more important. As someone observed: "Profits are a matter of opinion; cash is a fact."
2. Investment ignores the real value of the firm. More of a company's value resides in its intangible marketing assets—brands, market knowledge, customer relationships, and partner relationships—than in its balance sheet. These assets are the drivers of long-term profits.

Doyle argues that marketing will not mature as a profession until it can demonstrate the impact of marketing on shareholder value, the market value of a company minus its debt. The market value is the share price times the number of shares outstanding. The share price reflects what investors estimate is the present value of the future lifetime earnings of a company. When management is choosing a marketing strategy, Doyle wants it to apply shareholder value analysis (SVA) to see which alternative course of action will maximize shareholder value.

If we accept Doyle's arguments, instead of seeing marketing as a specific function concerned only with increasing sales or market share, senior management will see it as an integral part of the whole management process. It will judge marketing by how much it contributes to shareholder value.

Source: Based on Peter Doyle, *Value-Based Marketing: Marketing Strategies for Corporate Growth and Shareholder Value* (Chichester, England: John Wiley & Sons, 2000).

Feedback and Control

A company's strategic fit with the environment will inevitably erode, because the market environment changes faster than the company's seven Ss. Thus, a company might remain efficient while it loses effectiveness. Peter Drucker pointed out that it is more important to "do the right thing"—to be effective—than "to do things right"—to be efficient. The most successful companies excel at both.

Once an organization fails to respond to a changed environment, it becomes increasingly hard to recapture its lost position. Consider what happened to Lotus Development Corporation. Its Lotus 1-2-3 software was once the world's leading software program, and now its market share in desktop software has slipped so low that analysts do not even bother to track it.

Organizations, especially large ones, are subject to inertia. It's difficult to change one part without adjusting everything else. Yet organizations can be changed through strong leadership, preferably in advance of a crisis. The key to organizational health is willingness to examine the changing environment and adopt new goals and behaviors.

::: Product Planning: The Nature and Contents of a Marketing Plan

Working within the plans set by the levels above them, product managers come up with a marketing plan for individual products, lines, brands, channels, or customer groups. Each product level, whether product line or brand, must develop a marketing plan for achieving its goals. A **marketing plan** is a written document that summarizes what the marketer has learned about the marketplace and indicates how the firm plans to reach its marketing objectives.[51] It contains tactical guidelines for the marketing programs and financial allocations over the planning period.[52] It's one of the most important outputs of the marketing process.

Marketing plans are becoming more customer and competitor oriented, better reasoned, and more realistic than in the past. They draw more inputs from all the functions and are team developed. Planning is becoming a continuous process to respond to rapidly changing market conditions.

MARKETING MEMO | MARKETING PLAN CRITERIA

Here are some questions to ask in evaluating a marketing plan.

1. *Is the plan simple?* Is it easy to understand and act on? Does it communicate its content clearly and practically?
2. *Is the plan specific?* Are its objectives concrete and measurable? Does it include specific actions and activities, each with specific dates of completion, specific persons responsible, and specific budgets?
3. *Is the plan realistic?* Are the sales goals, expense budgets, and milestone dates realistic? Has a frank and honest self-critique been conducted to raise possible concerns and objections?
4. *Is the plan complete?* Does it include all the necessary elements? Does it have the right breadth and depth?

Source: Adapted from Tim Berry and Doug Wilson, *On Target: The Book on Marketing Plans* (Eugene, OR: Palo Alto Software, 2000).

Most marketing plans cover one year in 5 to 50 pages. The most frequently cited shortcomings of current marketing plans, according to marketing executives, are lack of realism, insufficient competitive analysis, and a short-run focus. (See "Marketing Memo: Marketing Plan Criteria" for some guideline questions to ask in developing marketing plans.)

What, then, does a marketing plan look like? What does it contain?

- ***Executive summary and table of contents.*** The marketing plan should open with a brief summary for senior management of the main goals and recommendations. A table of contents outlines the rest of the plan and all the supporting rationale and operational detail.
- ***Situation analysis.*** This section presents relevant background data on sales, costs, the market, competitors, and the various forces in the macroenvironment. How do we define the market, how big is it, and how fast is it growing? What are the relevant trends? What is the product offering and what critical issues do we face? Firms will use all this information to carry out a SWOT (strengths, weaknesses, opportunities, threats) analysis.
- ***Marketing strategy.*** Here the product manager defines the mission, marketing and financial objectives, and groups and needs that the market offerings are intended to satisfy. The manager then establishes the product line's competitive positioning, which will inform the "game plan" to accomplish the plan's objectives. All this requires inputs from other areas, such as purchasing, manufacturing, sales, finance, and human resources.
- ***Financial projections.*** Financial projections include a sales forecast, an expense forecast, and a break-even analysis. On the revenue side, the projections show the forecasted sales volume by month and product category. On the expense side, they show the expected costs of marketing, broken down into finer categories. The break-even analysis shows how many units the firm must sell monthly to offset its monthly fixed costs and average per-unit variable costs.
- ***Implementation controls.*** The last section of the marketing plan outlines the controls for monitoring and adjusting implementation of the plan. Typically, it spells out the goals and budget for each month or quarter, so management can review each period's results and take corrective action as needed. Firms must also take a number of different internal and external measures to assess progress and suggest possible modifications. Some organizations include contingency plans outlining the steps management would take in response to specific environmental developments, such as price wars or strikes.

Sample Marketing Plan: Pegasus Sports International*

www.mplans.com/spv/3407/index.cfm?affiliate=mplans

1.0 Executive Summary

Pegasus Sports International is a start-up aftermarket inline skating accessory manufacturer. In addition to the aftermarket products, Pegasus is developing SkateTours, a service that takes clients out, in conjunction with a local skate shop, and provides them with an afternoon of skating using inline skates and some of Pegasus' other accessories such as SkateSails. The aftermarket skate accessory market has been largely ignored. Although there are several major manufacturers of the skates themselves, the accessory market has not been addressed. This provides Pegasus with an extraordinary opportunity for market growth. Skating is a booming sport. Currently, most of the skating is recreational. There are, however, a growing number of skating competitions, including team-oriented competitions such as skate hockey as well as individual competitions such as speed skate racing. Pegasus will work to grow these markets and develop the skate transportation market, a more utilitarian use of skating. Several of Pegasus' currently developed products have patents pending, and local market research indicates that there is great demand for these products. Pegasus will achieve fast, significant market penetration through a solid business model, long-range planning, and a strong management team that is able to execute this exciting opportunity. The three principals on the management team have over 30 years of combined personal and industry experience. This extensive experience provides Pegasus with the empirical information as well as the passion to provide the skating market with much-needed aftermarket products. Pegasus will sell its products initially through its Web site. This "Dell" direct-to-the-consumer approach will allow Pegasus to achieve higher margins and maintain a close relationship with the customers, which is essential for producing products that have a true market demand. By the end of the year, Pegasus will have also developed relationships with different skate shops and will begin to sell some of its products through retailers.

2.0 Situation Analysis

Pegasus is entering its first year of operation. Its products have been well received, and marketing will be key to the development of brand and product awareness as well as the growth of the customer base. Pegasus International offers several different aftermarket skating accessories, serving the growing inline skating industry.

2.1 Market Summary

Pegasus possesses good information about the market and knows a great deal about the common attributes of the most prized customer. This information will be leveraged to better understand who is served, what their specific needs are, and how Pegasus can better communicate with them.

Target Markets

Recreational

Fitness

Speed

Hockey

Extreme

2.1.1 Market Demographics

The profile for the typical Pegasus customer consists of the following geographic, demographic, and behavior factors:

Geographics

- Pegasus has no set geographic target area. By leveraging the expansive reach of the Internet and multiple delivery services, Pegasus can serve both domestic and international customers.
- The total targeted population is 31 million users.

*Adapted from a sample plan provided by and copyrighted by Palo Alto Software, Inc. Find more complete sample marketing plans at www.mplans.com.

TABLE 2.1 Target Market Forecast

Target Market Forecast							
Potential Customers	**Growth**	**2007**	**2008**	**2009**	**2010**	**2011**	**CAGR***
Recreational	10%	19,142,500	21,056,750	23,162,425	25,478,668	28,026,535	10.00%
Fitness	15%	6,820,000	7,843,000	9,019,450	10,372,368	11,928,223	15.00%
Speed	10%	387,500	426,250	468,875	515,763	567,339	10.00%
Hockey	6%	2,480,000	2,628,800	2,786,528	2,953,720	3,130,943	6.00%
Extreme	4%	2,170,000	2,256,800	2,347,072	2,440,955	2,538,593	4.00%
Total	10.48%	31,000,000	34,211,600	37,784,350	41,761,474	46,191,633	10.48%

*Compound Annual Growth Rate

Demographics

- There is an almost equal ratio between male and female users.
- Ages 13–46, with 48% clustering around ages 23–34. The recreational users tend to cover the widest age range, including young users through active adults. The fitness users tend to be ages 20–40. The speed users tend to be in their late twenties and early thirties. The hockey players are generally in their teens through their early twenties. The extreme segment is of similar age to the hockey players.
- Of the users who are over 20, 65% have an undergraduate degree or substantial undergraduate coursework.
- The adult users have a median personal income of $47,000.

Behavior Factors

- Users enjoy fitness activities not as a means for a healthy life, but as an intrinsically enjoyable activity in itself.
- Users spend money on gear, typically sports equipment.
- Users have active lifestyles that include some sort of recreation at least two to three times a week.

2.1.2 Market Needs

Pegasus is providing the skating community with a wide range of accessories for all variations of skating. The company seeks to fulfill the following benefits that are important to its customers:

- ***Quality craftsmanship.*** The customers work hard for their money and do not enjoy spending it on disposable products that work for only a year or two.
- ***Well-thought-out designs.*** The skating market has not been addressed by well-thought-out products that serve skaters' needs. Pegasus' industry experience and personal dedication to the sport will provide it with the needed information to produce insightfully designed products.
- ***Customer service.*** Exemplary service is required to build a sustainable business that has a loyal customer base.

2.1.3 Market Trends

Pegasus will distinguish itself by marketing products not previously available to skaters. The emphasis in the past has been to sell skates and very few replacement parts. The number of skaters is not restricted to any one single country, continent, or age group, so there is a world market. Pegasus has products for virtually every group of skaters. The fastest-growing segment of this sport is the fitness skater. Therefore, the marketing is being directed toward this group. BladeBoots will enable users to enter establishments without having to remove their skates. BladeBoots will be aimed at the recreational skater, the largest segment. SkateAids, on the other hand, are great for everyone.

The sport of skating will also grow through SkateSailing. This sport is primarily for the medium-to-advanced skater, and its growth potential is tremendous. The sails that Pegasus has manufactured have been sold in Europe, following a pattern similar to windsurfing. Windsailing originated in Santa Monica but did not take off until it had already grown big in Europe.

Another trend is group skating. More and more groups are getting together on skating excursions in cities all over the world. For example, San Francisco has night group skating that attracts hundreds of people. The market trends are showing continued growth in all directions of skating.

2.1.4 Market Growth

With the price of skates going down due to competition by so many skate companies, the market has had steady growth throughout the world, although sales had slowed down in some markets. The growth statistics for 2007 were estimated to be over 35 million units. More and more people are discovering—and in many cases rediscovering—the health benefits and fun of skating.

2.2 SWOT Analysis

The following SWOT analysis captures the key strengths and weaknesses within the company and describes the opportunities and threats facing Pegasus.

2.2.1 Strengths

- In-depth industry experience and insight
- Creative, yet practical product designers
- The use of a highly efficient, flexible business model utilizing direct customer sales and distribution

2.2.2 Weaknesses

- The reliance on outside capital necessary to grow the business
- A lack of retailers who can work face-to-face with the customer to generate brand and product awareness
- The difficulty of developing brand awareness as a start-up company

2.2.3 Opportunities

- Participation within a growing industry
- Decreased product costs through economy of scale
- The ability to leverage other industry participants' marketing efforts to help grow the general market

2.2.4 Threats

- Future/potential competition from an already established market participant
- A slump in the economy that could have a negative effect on people's spending of discretionary income on fitness/recreational products
- The release of a study that calls into question the safety of skating or the inability to prevent major skating-induced traumas

2.3 Competition

Pegasus Sports International is forming its own market. Although there are a few companies that do make sails and foils that a few skaters are using, Pegasus is the only brand that is truly designed for and by skaters. The few competitors' sails on the market are not designed for skating, but for windsurfing or for skateboards. In the case of foils, storage and carrying are not practical. There are different indirect competitors who are manufacturers of the actual skates. After many years in the market, these companies have yet to become direct competitors by manufacturing accessories for the skates that they make.

2.4 Product Offering

Pegasus Sports International now offers several products:

- The first product that has been developed is BladeBoots, a cover for the wheels and frame of inline skates, which allows skaters to enter places that normally would not allow them in with skates on. BladeBoots come with a small pouch and belt which converts to a well-designed skate carrier.
- The second product is SkateSails. These sails are specifically designed for use while skating. Feedback that Pegasus has received from skaters indicates skatesailing could become a very popular sport. Trademarking this product is currently in progress.
- The third product, SkateAid, will be in production by the end of the year. Other ideas for products are under development, but will not be disclosed until Pegasus can protect them through pending patent applications.

2.5 Keys to Success

The keys to success are designing and producing products that meet market demand. In addition, Pegasus must ensure total customer satisfaction. If these keys to success are achieved, it will become a profitable, sustainable company.

2.6 Critical Issues

As a start-up business, Pegasus is still in the early stages. The critical issues are for Pegasus to:

- Establish itself as the premier skating accessory company.
- Pursue controlled growth that dictates that payroll expenses will never exceed the revenue base. This will help protect against recessions.
- Constantly monitor customer satisfaction, ensuring that the growth strategy will never compromise service and satisfaction levels.

3.0 Marketing Strategy

The key to the marketing strategy is focusing on the speed, health and fitness, and recreational skaters. Pegasus can cover about 80% of the skating market because it produces products geared toward each segment. Pegasus is able to address all of the different segments within the market because, although each segment is distinct in terms of its users and equipment, its products are useful to all of the different segments.

3.1 Mission

Pegasus Sports International's mission is to provide the customer with the finest skating accessories available. "We exist to attract and maintain customers. With a strict adherence to this maxim, success will be ensured. Our services and products will exceed the expectations of the customers."

3.2 Marketing Objectives

- Maintain positive, strong growth each quarter (notwithstanding seasonal sales patterns).
- Achieve a steady increase in market penetration.
- Decrease customer acquisition costs by 1.5% per quarter.

3.3 Financial Objectives

- Increase the profit margin by 1% per quarter through efficiency and economy-of-scale gains.
- Maintain a significant research and development budget (as a percentage relative to sales) to spur future product developments.
- Achieve a double- to triple-digit growth rate for the first three years.

3.4 Target Markets

With a world skating market of over 31 million that is steadily growing (statistics released by the Sporting Goods Manufacturers Association), the niche has been created. Pegasus' aim is to expand this market by promoting SkateSailing, a new sport that is popular in both Santa Monica and Venice Beach in California. The Sporting Goods Manufacturers Association survey indicates that skating now has more participation than football, softball, skiing, and snowboarding combined. The breakdown of participation in skating is as follows: 1+% speed (growing), 8% hockey (declining), 7% extreme/aggressive (declining), 22% fitness (nearly 7 million—the fastest growing), and 61% recreational (first-timers). Pegasus' products are targeting the fitness and recreational groups, because they are the fastest growing. These groups are gearing themselves toward health and fitness, and combined, they can easily grow to 85% (or 26 million) of the market in the next five years.

3.5 Positioning

Pegasus will position itself as the premier aftermarket skating accessory company. This positioning will be achieved by leveraging Pegasus' competitive edge: industry experience and passion. Pegasus is a skating company formed by skaters for skaters. Its management is able to use its vast experience and personal passion for the sport to develop innovative, useful accessories for a broad range of skaters.

3.6 Strategies

The single objective is to position Pegasus as the premier skating accessory manufacturer, serving the domestic market as well as the international market. The marketing strategy will seek to first create customer awareness concerning the offered products and services and then develop the customer base. The message that Pegasus will seek to communicate is that it offers the best-designed, most useful skating accessories. This message will be communicated through a variety of methods. The first will be the Pegasus Web site, which will provide a rich source of product information and offer consumers the opportunity to purchase. A lot of time and money will be invested in the site to provide the customer with the perception of total professionalism and utility for Pegasus' products and services.

The second marketing method will be advertisements placed in numerous industry magazines. The skating industry is supported by several different glossy magazines designed to promote the industry as a whole. In addition, a number of smaller periodicals serve the smaller market segments within the skating industry. The last method of communication is the use of printed sales literature. The two previously mentioned marketing methods will create demand for the sales literature, which will be sent out to customers. The cost of the sales literature will be fairly minimal, because it will use the already-compiled information from the Web site.

3.7 Marketing Mix

Pegasus' marketing mix is comprised of the following approaches to pricing, distribution, advertising and promotion, and customer service.

- ***Pricing.*** This will be based on a per-product retail price.
- ***Distribution.*** Initially, Pegasus will use a direct-to-consumer distribution model. Over time, it will use retailers as well.
- ***Advertising and promotion.*** Several different methods will be used for the advertising effort.
- ***Customer service.*** Pegasus will strive to achieve benchmarked levels of customer care.

3.8 Marketing Research

Pegasus is blessed with the good fortune of being located in the center of the skating world: Venice, California. It will be able to leverage this opportune location by working with many of the different skaters that live in the area. Pegasus was able to test all of its products not only with its principals, who are accomplished skaters, but also with the many other dedicated and "newbie" users located in Venice. The extensive product testing by a wide variety of users provided Pegasus with valuable product feedback and has led to several design improvements.

4.0 Financials

This section will offer the financial overview of Pegasus related to marketing activities. Pegasus will address break-even analysis, sales forecasts, expense forecast, and indicate how these activities link to the marketing strategy.

4.1 Break-Even Analysis

The break-even analysis indicates that $7,760 will be required in monthly sales revenue to reach the break-even point.

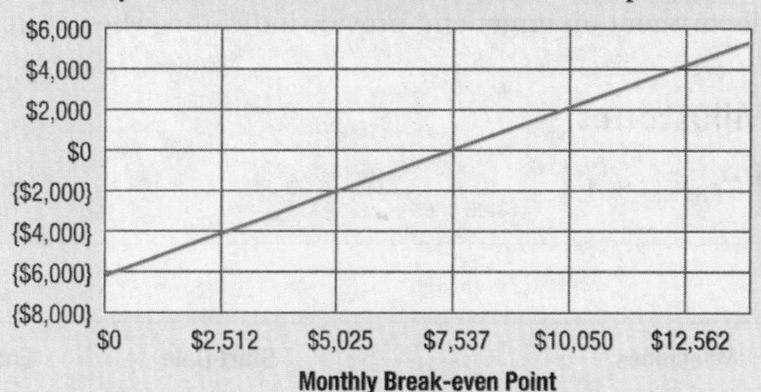

Reprinted by permission of Palo Alto Software.

TABLE 4.1 Break-Even Analysis

Break-even Analysis:	
Monthly Units Break-even	62
Monthly Sales Break-even	$ 7,760
Assumptions:	
Average Per-Unit Revenue	$125.62
Average Per-Unit Variable Cost	$ 22.61
Estimated Monthly Fixed Cost	$ 6,363

4.2 Sales Forecast

Pegasus feels that the sales forecast figures are conservative. It will steadily increase sales as the advertising budget allows. Although the target market forecast (Table 2.1) listed all of the potential customers divided into separate groups, the sales forecast groups customers into two categories: recreational and competitive. Reducing the number of categories allows the reader to quickly discern information, making the chart more functional.

Monthly Sales Forecast

TABLE 4.2 Sales Forecast

Sales Forecast			
Sales	**2007**	**2008**	**2009**
Recreational	$455,740	$598,877	$687,765
Competitive	$ 72,918	$ 95,820	$110,042
Total Sales	$528,658	$694,697	$797,807
Direct Cost of Sales	**2007**	**2008**	**2009**
Recreational	$ 82,033	$107,798	$123,798
Competitive	$ 13,125	$ 17,248	$ 19,808
Subtotal Cost of Sales	$ 95,158	$125,046	$143,606

4.3 Expense Forecast

The expense forecast will be used as a tool to keep the department on target and provide indicators when corrections/modifications are needed for the proper implementation of the marketing plan.

Milestones

TABLE 5.1 Milestones

	Plan				
Milestones	**Start Date**	**End Date**	**Budget**	**Manager**	**Department**
Marketing plan completion	1/1/07	2/1/07	$ 0	Stan	Marketing
Web site completion	1/1/07	3/15/07	$20,400	outside firm	Marketing
Advertising campaign #1	1/1/07	6/30/07	$ 3,500	Stan	Marketing
Advertising campaign #2	3/1/07	12/30/07	$ 4,550	Stan	Marketing
Development of the retail channel	1/1/07	11/30/07	$ 0	Stan	Marketing
Totals			$28,450		

Monthly Expense Budget

TABLE 4.3 Marketing Expense Budget

Marketing Expense Budget	2007	2008	2009
Web site	$ 25,000	$ 8,000	$ 10,000
Advertisements	$ 8,050	$ 15,000	$ 20,000
Printed Material	$ 1,725	$ 2,000	$ 3,000
Total Sales and Marketing Expenses	$ 34,775	$ 25,000	$ 33,000
Percent of Sales	6.58%	3.60%	4.14%
Contribution Margin	$398,725	$544,652	$621,202
Contribution Margin/Sales	75.42%	78.40%	77.86%

5.0 Controls

The purpose of Pegasus' marketing plan is to serve as a guide for the organization. The following areas will be monitored to gauge performance:

- Revenue: monthly and annual
- Expenses: monthly and annual
- Customer satisfaction
- New-product development

5.1 Implementation

The following milestones identify the key marketing programs. It is important to accomplish each one on time and on budget.

5.2 Marketing Organization

Stan Blade will be responsible for the marketing activities.

5.3 Contingency Planning

Difficulties and Risks

- Problems generating visibility, a function of being an Internet-based start-up organization
- An entry into the market by an already-established market competitor

Worst-Case Risks

- Determining that the business cannot support itself on an ongoing basis
- Having to liquidate equipment or intellectual capital to cover liabilities

SUMMARY :::

1. The value delivery process involves choosing (or identifying), providing (or delivering), and communicating superior value. The value chain is a tool for identifying key activities that create value and costs in a specific business.
2. Strong companies develop superior capabilities in managing core business processes such as new-product realization, inventory management, and customer acquisition and retention. Managing these core processes effectively means creating a marketing network in which the company works closely with all parties in the production and distribution chain, from suppliers of raw materials to retail distributors. Companies no longer compete—marketing networks do.
3. According to one view, holistic marketing maximizes value exploration by understanding the relationships between the customer's cognitive space, the company's competence space, and the collaborator's resource space; maximizes value creation by identifying new customer benefits from the customer's cognitive space, utilizing core competencies from its business domain, and selecting and managing business partners from its collaborative networks; and maximizes value delivery by becoming proficient at customer relationship management, internal resource management, and business partnership management.
4. Market-oriented strategic planning is the managerial process of developing and maintaining a viable fit between the organization's objectives, skills, and resources and its changing market opportunities. The aim of strategic planning is to shape the company's businesses and products so that they yield target profits and growth. Strategic planning takes place at four levels: corporate, division, business unit, and product.
5. The corporate strategy establishes the framework within which the divisions and business units prepare their strategic plans. Setting a corporate strategy entails four activities: defining the corporate mission, establishing strategic business units (SBUs), assigning resources to each SBU based on its market attractiveness and business strength, and planning new businesses and downsizing older businesses.
6. Strategic planning for individual businesses entails the following activities: defining the business mission, analyzing external opportunities and threats, analyzing internal strengths and weaknesses, formulating goals, formulating strategy, formulating supporting programs, implementing the programs, and gathering feedback and exercising control.
7. Each product level within a business unit must develop a marketing plan for achieving its goals. The marketing plan is one of the most important outputs of the marketing process.

APPLICATIONS :::

Marketing Debate What Good Is a Mission Statement?

Virtually all firms have mission statements to help guide and inspire employees as well as signal what is important to the firm to those outside the firm. Mission statements are often the product of much deliberation and discussion. At the same time, some critics claim that mission statements sometimes lack "teeth" and specificity. Moreover, critics also maintain that, in many cases, mission statements do not vary much from firm to firm and make the same empty promises.

Take a position: Mission statements are critical to a successful marketing organization *versus* Mission statements rarely provide useful marketing value.

Marketing Discussion

Consider Porter's value chain and the holistic marketing orientation model. What implications do they have for marketing planning? How would you structure a marketing plan to incorporate some of their concepts?

PART

2

CAPTURING MARKETING INSIGHTS

IN THIS CHAPTER, WE WILL ADDRESS THE FOLLOWING QUESTIONS:

1. What are the components of a modern marketing information system?
2. What are useful internal records?
3. What is involved in a marketing intelligence system?
4. What are the key methods for tracking and identifying opportunities in the macroenvironment?
5. What are some important macroenvironment developments?

CHAPTER 3 ::: GATHERING INFORMATION AND SCANNING THE ENVIRONMENT

three

Developing and implementing marketing plans requires a number of decisions. Making those decisions is both an art and a science. To provide insight into and inspiration for marketing decision making, companies must possess comprehensive, up-to-date information about macro trends, as well as about micro effects particular to their business. Holistic marketers recognize that the marketing environment is constantly presenting new opportunities and threats, and they understand the importance of continuously monitoring and adapting to that environment.

Under CEO Lee Scott, Wal-Mart has made a determined effort to become more environmentally friendly, stating it will invest $500 million in sustainability projects. In a company-wide speech in November 2005, Scott vowed to increase the efficiency of its vehicle fleet by 25% over the next 3 years and double it in 10 years; eliminate 30% of the energy used in stores; and reduce solid waste from U.S. stores by 25% in 3 years. Little decisions can make big differences for the retail giant. From eliminating excessive packaging on its private label line of toys, Kid Connection, >>>

Wal-Mart has made a number of changes in recent years in how it conducts its business.

the company estimated savings of $2.4 million a year in shipping costs, 3,800 trees, and one million barrels of oil. By wrapping four kinds of produce in a polymer derived from corn instead of oil, the company believes it could save as much as 800,000 gallons of gas. Major environmental groups have been pleased, but Wal-Mart still faces criticism from union leaders and liberal activists about its wage rates, employee health care, gender discrimination, and treatment of local competition. The company has responded by citing progress in each area.[1]

Wal-Mart isn't alone in making adjustments to the way it does business. Virtually every industry is facing up to changes in the natural environment. In this chapter, we consider how firms can develop processes to track trends. We also identify a number of important macroenvironment trends. Chapter 4 will review how marketers can conduct more customized research that addresses specific marketing problems or issues.

::: Components of a Modern Marketing Information System

Although every manager in an organization needs to observe the outside environment, the major responsibility for identifying significant marketplace changes falls to the company's marketers. They have two advantages: they have disciplined methods for collecting information, and they spend more time than anyone else interacting with customers and observing competition and other outside firms and groups.

Some firms have developed marketing information systems that provide management with rich detail about buyer wants, preferences, and behavior.

DUPONT

DuPont commissioned marketing studies to uncover personal pillow behavior for its Dacron Polyester unit, which supplies filling to pillow makers and sells its own Comforel brand. One challenge is that people don't give up their old pillows: 37% of one sample described their relationship with their pillow as being like that of "an old married couple," and an additional 13% said their pillow was like a "childhood friend." Respondents fell into distinct groups in terms of pillow behavior: stackers (23%), plumpers (20%), rollers or folders (16%), cuddlers (16%), and smashers, who pound their pillows into a more comfy shape (10%). Women were more likely to plump, men to fold. The prevalence of stackers led the company to sell more pillows packaged as pairs, as well as to market different levels of softness or firmness.[2]

Marketers also have extensive information about how consumption patterns vary across countries. On a per capita basis within Western Europe, for example, the Swiss consume the

TABLE 3.1

Information Needs Probes

1. What decisions do you regularly make?
2. What information do you need to make these decisions?
3. What information do you regularly get?
4. What special studies do you periodically request?
5. What information would you want that you are not getting now?
6. What information would you want daily? Weekly? Monthly? Yearly?
7. What magazines and trade reports would you like to see on a regular basis?
8. What topics would you like to be kept informed of?
9. What data analysis programs would you want?
10. What are the four most helpful improvements that could be made in the present marketing information system?

most chocolate, the Greeks eat the most cheese, the Irish drink the most tea, and the Austrians smoke the most cigarettes.

Nevertheless, many business firms are not sophisticated about gathering information. Many do not have a marketing research department. Others have a department that limits its work to routine forecasting, sales analysis, and occasional surveys. Some managers complain about not knowing how to get hold of critical information; getting too much information that they cannot use and too little that they really need; and getting important information too late. Companies with superior information enjoy a competitive advantage. They can choose their markets better, develop better offerings, and execute better marketing planning.

Every firm must organize and distribute a continuous flow of information to its marketing managers. A **marketing information system, MIS,** consists of people, equipment, and procedures to gather, sort, analyze, evaluate, and distribute needed, timely, and accurate information to marketing decision makers. A marketing information system relies on internal company records, marketing intelligence activities, and marketing research. We'll discuss the first two topics here, and the third one in the next chapter.

The company's marketing information system should be a cross between what managers think they need, what they really need, and what is economically feasible. An internal MIS committee can interview a cross section of marketing managers to discover their information needs. Table 3.1 displays some useful questions.

::: Internal Records and Marketing Intelligence

Marketing managers rely on internal reports of orders, sales, prices, costs, inventory levels, receivables, payables, and so on. By analyzing this information, they can spot important opportunities and problems.

The Order-to-Payment Cycle

The heart of the internal records system is the order-to-payment cycle. Sales representatives, dealers, and customers send orders to the firm. The sales department prepares invoices, transmits copies to various departments, and back-orders out-of-stock items. Shipped items generate shipping and billing documents that go to various departments.

Today's companies need to perform these steps quickly and accurately, because customers favor firms that can promise timely delivery. An increasing number of companies are using the Internet and extranets to improve the speed, accuracy, and efficiency of the order-to-payment cycle. Cisco Connection Online allows the computer-networking leader to connect with all its suppliers, manufacturers, customers, and resellers online. By reducing payment cycles for suppliers, eliminating paper-based purchasing, and reducing inventory levels, Cisco saved more than $24 million in material costs and $51 million in labor costs annually in the first years of the program's operations.[3]

Sales Information Systems

Marketing managers need timely and accurate reports on current sales. Wal-Mart operates a sales and inventory data warehouse that captures data on every item, for every customer, for every store, every day and refreshes it every hour. For example, the IT staff at headquarters tapped into the data warehouse the morning after Thanksgiving and noticed that East Coast sales of a computer-monitor holiday special were far below expectations. Marketing staff contacted stores and learned the computers and monitors weren't being displayed together, so potential buyers couldn't see what they were getting for the posted price. Calls went out to Wal-Mart stores across the country to rearrange the displays. By 9:30 that morning, the pace of sales could be seen picking up in the company's database.[4] Wal-Mart also transmits nightly orders to its many suppliers for new shipments of replacement stock, even entrusting some companies such as Procter & Gamble with the management of its inventory.[5]

And companies that make good use of "cookies," records of Web site usage stored on personal browsers, are smart users of targeted marketing. Although the perception is that most people delete cookies out of concern for their privacy, the numbers tell a different story. A recent survey showed that only 8% of people very frequently delete cookies, down from 18% in 2004, and 24% of respondents said they never delete cookies. Not only do customers *not* delete cookies, but they also expect customized marketing appeals and deals once they accept cookies.

UNICA CORPORATION

A marketing software provider in Lincoln, Massachusetts, Unica feels that its customers appreciate the informed messaging that the company is able to provide based on the cookies it receives. "They don't just come to the Unica site and register," says Andrew Halley, senior director of marketing at Unica. Instead, customers have a specific need and are searching for a strong vendor. Halley says the cookies allow Unica to better target its communications, like following up on a phone call or meeting at an appropriate event, such as a "Webinar," a Web-based seminar.[6]

Technological gadgets are revolutionizing sales information systems and allowing representatives to have up-to-the-second information. In visiting any of the 10,000 golf shops around the country, sales reps for TaylorMade used to spend up to two hours counting golf clubs in stock before filling new orders by hand. Since the company adopted handheld devices with bar-code readers and Internet connections, the reps simply point their handhelds at the bar codes and automatically tally inventory. By using the two hours they save to focus on boosting sales to retail customers, sales reps improved productivity by 20%.[7]

Companies must carefully interpret the sales data so as not to draw the wrong conclusions. Michael Dell gave this illustration: "If you have three yellow Mustangs sitting on a dealer's lot and a customer wants a red one, the salesman may be really good at figuring out how to sell the yellow Mustang. So the yellow Mustang gets sold, and a signal gets sent back to the factory that, hey, people want yellow Mustangs."

Databases, Data Warehousing, and Data Mining

Today companies organize their information into databases—customer databases, product databases, salesperson databases—and then combine data from the different databases. For example, the customer database will contain every customer's name, address, past transactions, and sometimes even demographics and psychographics (activities, interests, and opinions). Instead of sending a mass "carpet bombing" mailing of a new offer to every customer in its database, a company will rank its customers according to purchase recency, frequency, and monetary value (RFM) and send the offer to only the highest-scoring customers. Besides saving on mailing expenses, this manipulation of data can often achieve a double-digit response rate.

Companies warehouse these data and make them easily accessible to decision makers. Furthermore, by hiring analysts skilled in sophisticated statistical methods, they can "mine" the data and garner fresh insights into neglected customer segments, recent customer trends, and other useful information. Managers can cross-tabulate customer information with product and salesperson information to yield still-deeper insights. Using its own in-house technology, for example, Wells Fargo has developed the ability to track and analyze every bank transaction made by its 10 million retail customers—whether at ATMs, bank branches, or online. When transaction data are combined with personal information provided by customers, Wells Fargo can come up with targeted offerings to coincide with a customer's life-changing event. As a result, compared with the industry average of 2.2 products per customer, Wells Fargo sells 4.[8] Many other firms are also taking advantage of these new rich databases (see "Marketing Insight: The Big Dig").

If customers want red Mustangs but buy yellow because red isn't available, marketers might draw an incorrect message from the sales data about what color people really want.

The Marketing Intelligence System

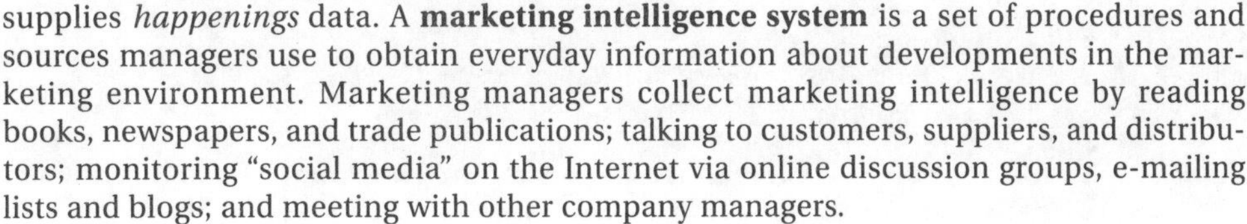

The internal records system supplies *results* data, but the marketing intelligence system supplies *happenings* data. A **marketing intelligence system** is a set of procedures and sources managers use to obtain everyday information about developments in the marketing environment. Marketing managers collect marketing intelligence by reading books, newspapers, and trade publications; talking to customers, suppliers, and distributors; monitoring "social media" on the Internet via online discussion groups, e-mailing lists and blogs; and meeting with other company managers.

A company can take several steps to improve the quality of its marketing intelligence.

- ***Train and motivate the sales force to spot and report new developments.*** The company must "sell" its sales force on their importance as intelligence gatherers. Grace Performance Chemicals, a division of W. R. Grace, supplies materials and chemicals to the construction and packaging industries. Grace sales reps were instructed to observe the innovative ways customers used its products in order to suggest possible new products. For example, some customers were using Grace waterproofing materials to soundproof their cars and patch boots and tents. Seven new-product ideas emerged, worth millions in sales.[9]

- ***Motivate distributors, retailers, and other intermediaries to pass along important intelligence.*** Many companies hire specialists to gather marketing intelligence.[10] Service providers and retailers often send mystery shoppers to their stores to assess cleanliness of facilities, product quality, and the way employees treat customers. Mystery shoppers for McDonald's discovered that only 46% of its restaurants nationwide met internal speed-of-service standards, forcing the company to rethink processes and training.[11] Health care facilities that use mystery shoppers say the reports have led to a number of changes in the patient experience, including improved estimates of wait times, better explanations of medical procedures, and even less-stressful programming on the television in the waiting room.[12]

- ***Network externally.*** The firm can purchase competitors' products; attend open houses and trade shows; read competitors' published reports; attend stockholders' meetings; talk to employees, dealers, distributors, suppliers, and freight agents; collect competitors' ads; and look up news stories about competitors. Software developer Cognos created an internal Web site called Street Fighter, where any of the firm's 3,000 workers can submit scoops about competitors and win prizes.[13]

MARKETING INSIGHT | THE BIG DIG

As companies gather more and more information, their ability to collect and analyze data to generate insights is more critical. Here is what several leading companies are doing.

Best Buy has assembled a 15-plus terabyte database with seven years of data on 75 million households. The company captures information about every transaction and interaction—from phone calls and mouse clicks to delivery and rebate-check addresses—and then deploys sophisticated match-and-merge algorithms to classify over three-quarters of its customers, or more than 100 million individuals. Best Buy places its core customers into profiled categories, such as "Buzz" (the young technology buff), "Jill" (the suburban soccer mom), "Barry" (the wealthy professional guy), and "Ray" (the family man). The firm also applies a customer lifetime value model that measures transaction-level profitability and factors in a host of customer behaviors that either increase or decrease the value of the relationship. Knowing so much about consumers allows Best Buy to employ precision marketing and customer-triggered incentive programs with more favorable response rates.

Some companies have applied their database knowledge to drive media purchases. To assess the effectiveness of various advertising media, a leading industry group, Interactive Advertising Bureau, conducted a series of tests over an 18-month period for 30 blue-chip companies. Analyzing customer behavior, the study concluded that Ford Motor Co. could have sold an additional $625 million worth of trucks if it had increased its online budget from 2.5% to 6%. After seeing the results, Ford announced in August 2005 that it would shift up to 30% of its $1 billion ad budget into media targeted to individual customers, half of it through online advertising.

Capturing online customer behavior can yield a wealth of insights. A new customer signing up with Microsoft to get a free Hotmail e-mail account is required to give the company his name, age, gender, and zip code. Microsoft can then combine those facts with information such as observed online behavior and characteristics of the area in which the customer lives, to help advertisers better understand whether, when, and how to contact that customer. Although Microsoft must be careful to preserve consumer privacy—the company claims it won't purchase an individual's income history—it can still provide advertising clients with behavioral targeting information. For example, it can help a Dinners To Go franchisee to zero in on working moms aged 30–40 in a given neighborhood with ads designed to reach them before 10 AM when they're most likely to be planning their evening meal.

Sources: "Jeff Zabin, "The Importance of Being Analytical," *Brandweek*, July 24, 2006, p. 21. Stephen Baker, "Math Will Rock Your World," *BusinessWeek*, January 23, 2006, pp. 54–62. Michelle Kessler and Byron Acohido, "Data Miners Dig a Little Deeper," *USA Today*, July 11, 2006.

Of course, before the Internet, sometimes you just had to go out in the field, literally, and watch the competition. This is what oil and gas entrepreneur T. Boone Pickens did. Describing how he learned about a rival's drilling activity, Pickens recalls, "We would have someone who would watch [the rival's] drilling floor from a half mile away with field glasses. Our competitor didn't like it but there wasn't anything they could do about it. Our spotters would watch the joints and drill pipe. They would count them; each [drill] joint was 30 feet long. By adding up all the joints, you would be able to tally the depth of the well." Pickens knew that the deeper the well, the more costly it would be for his rival to get the oil or gas up to the surface, and this information provided him with an immediate competitive advantage.[14]

Companies can still gain useful information in the field. On a fact-finding trip to Asia for a U.S. textile company, Fuld & Co., a Cambridge consulting firm that specializes in competitive intelligence, snapped a photo of a goat munching grass on a field. This wasn't just any goat, but proof that the rival company's much-heralded new Indonesian plant wasn't where it was rumored to be. Armed with that information, the textile company could change its defensive strategy.[15]

Competitive intelligence gathering must be legal and ethical, though. Procter & Gamble reportedly paid a multimillion-dollar settlement to Unilever when some external operatives hired as part of a P&G corporate intelligence program to learn about Unilever's hair care products were found to have engaged in such unethical behavior as "dumpster diving."[16]

- ***Set up a customer advisory panel.*** Members might include representative customers or the company's largest customers or its most outspoken or sophisticated customers. Many business schools have advisory panels made up of alumni and recruiters who provide valuable feedback on the curriculum.
- ***Take advantage of government data resources.*** The 2000 U.S. Census provides an in-depth look at the population swings, demographic groups, regional migrations, and chang-

ing family structure of 281,421,906 people. Census marketer Claritas cross-references census figures with consumer surveys and its own grassroots research for clients such as Procter & Gamble, Dow Jones, and Ford Motor Co. Partnering with "list houses" that provide customer phone and address information, Claritas can help firms select and purchase mailing lists with specific clusters.[17]

- ***Purchase information from outside suppliers.*** Well-known data suppliers include the A.C. Nielsen Company and Information Resources Inc. (see Table 3.2). These research firms gather consumer-panel data at a much lower cost than the company could manage on its own. Biz360 has specialized databases to provide reports from 7,000 sources on the extent and nature of print, broadcast, and online media coverage, including blogs and message boards, a company is receiving.[18]
- ***Use online customer feedback systems to collect competitive intelligence.*** Online customer review boards, discussion forums, chat rooms, and blogs can distribute one customer's evaluation of a product or a supplier to a large number of other potential buyers and, of course, to marketers seeking information about the competition. Chat rooms allow users to share experiences and impressions, but their unstructured nature makes it difficult for marketers to find relevant messages. Thus some companies have adopted structured systems, such as customer discussion boards or customer reviews. See "Marketing Memo: Clicking on the Competition" for a summary of the major categories of structured online feedback systems.[19]

Best Buy uses data to profile its customers into highly differentiated categories with archetype names such as "Buzz," "Barry," and "Jill."

GLAXOSMITHKLINE PLC

GlaxoSmithKline PLC, Kraft, and Hewlett-Packard are learning how to use the Internet to harness customer input. They aren't going it alone but teaming up with Communispace Corp., a start-up that hosts private online communities. For instance, Glaxo sponsors an online community devoted to weight loss and says it is learning far more than it could have gleaned from focus groups on topics that range from advice on packaging its first weight-loss pill to where to place in-store marketing. Most importantly, members give Glaxo insights into their own battles with weight loss and dieting.[20]

TABLE 3.2

Secondary Commercial Data Sources

- Nielsen Company: Data on products and brands sold through retail outlets (Retail Index Services), supermarket scanner data (Scantrack), data on television audiences (Media Research Services), magazine circulation data (Neodata Services Inc.), and others.
- MRCA Information Services: Data on weekly family purchases of consumer products (National Consumer Panel) and data on home food consumption (National Menu Census).
- Information Resources Inc.: Supermarket scanner data (InfoScan) and data on the impact of supermarket promotions (PromotioScan).
- SAMI/Burke: Reports on warehouse withdrawals to food stores in selected market areas (SAMI reports) and supermarket scanner data (SamScan).
- Simmons Market Research Bureau (MRB Group): Annual reports covering television markets, sporting goods, and proprietary drugs, with demographic data by sex, income, age, and brand preferences (selective markets and media reaching them).
- Other commercial research houses selling data to subscribers include the Audit Bureau of Circulation; Arbitron Audits and Surveys; Dun & Bradstreet's; National Family Opinion; Standard Rate & Data Service; and Starch.

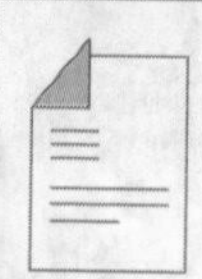

MARKETING MEMO — CLICKING ON THE COMPETITION

There are four main ways marketers can find relevant online information about competitors' product strengths and weaknesses, as well as summary comments and overall performance ratings of a product, service, or supplier.

- ***Independent customer goods and service review forums.*** Independent forums include Web sites such as Epinions.com, Rateital.com, Consumerreview.com, and Bizrate.com. Bizrate.com is a consumer feedback network that collects millions of consumer reviews of stores and products each year from two sources: its 1.3 million members, who have volunteered to provide ratings and feedback to assist other shoppers, and survey results on service quality from stores that have agreed to allow BizRate.com to collect feedback directly from their customers as they make purchases.
- ***Distributor or sales agent feedback sites.*** Feedback sites offer both positive and negative product or service reviews, but the stores or distributors have built the sites themselves. Amazon.com, for instance, offers an interactive feedback opportunity through which buyers, readers, editors, and others may review all products listed in the site, especially books. Elance.com is an online professional services provider that allows contractors to describe their experience and level of satisfaction with subcontractors.
- ***Combo sites offering customer reviews and expert opinions.*** Combination sites are concentrated in financial services and high-tech products that require professional knowledge. Zdnet.com, an online advisor on technology products, offers customer comments and evaluations based on ease of use, features, and stability, along with expert reviews. The advantage of this type of review site is that a product supplier can compare opinions from the experts with those from consumers.
- ***Customer complaint sites.*** Customer complaint forums are designed mainly for dissatisfied customers. For instance, Planetfeedback.com allows customers to voice unfavorable experiences with specific companies. Another site, Complaints.com, is devoted to customers who want to vent their frustrations with particular firms or their offerings.
- ***Public blogs.*** Tens of millions of blogs exist online and their numbers continue to grow. Firms such as BuzzMetrics, Umbria, and other consultancies analyze blogs and social networks to provide firms with insights into consumer sentiment: Drug firms want to know what questions are on patients' minds when they hear about problems with a medication; car companies are looking for better ways to spot defects and work out what to do about them.

Source: "The Blogs in the Corporate Machine," *The Economist*, February 11, 2006, pp. 55–56; also adapted from Robin T. Peterson and Zhilin Yang, "Web Product Reviews Help Strategy," *Marketing News*, April 7, 2004, p. 18.

Some companies circulate marketing intelligence. The staff scans the Internet and major publications, abstracts relevant news, and disseminates a news bulletin to marketing managers. The competitive intelligence function works best when intelligence operations collaborate closely with key users in the decision-making process. In contrast, organizations where intelligence is seen as a distinct, separate function that only produces reports and doesn't get involved are less effective.[21]

::: Analyzing the Macroenvironment

Successful companies recognize and respond profitably to unmet needs and trends.

Needs and Trends

Enterprising individuals and companies manage to create new solutions to unmet needs. FedEx was created to meet the need for next-day mail delivery. Dockers was created to meet the needs of baby boomers who could no longer really wear—or fit into!—their jeans and wanted a physically and psychologically comfortable pair of pants.

We distinguish among fads, trends, and megatrends. A **fad** is "unpredictable, short-lived, and without social, economic, and political significance." A company can cash in on a fad such as Beanie Babies, Furbies, and Tickle Me Elmo dolls, but getting it right is more a matter of luck and good timing than anything else.[22]

A **trend** is a direction or sequence of events that has some momentum and durability. Trends are more predictable and durable than fads. A trend reveals the shape of the future and provides many opportunities. For example, the percentage of people who value physical fitness and well-being has risen steadily over the years, especially in the under-30 group, young women, upscale consumers, and people living in the West.

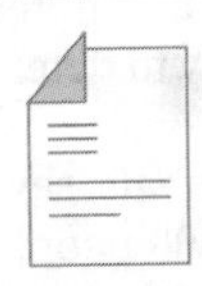

MARKETING MEMO — TRENDS SHAPING THE BUSINESS LANDSCAPE

Management consulting firm McKinsey believes that macroeconomic factors, environmental and social issues, and business and industry developments will profoundly shape the business landscape in the coming years. Here are some of the main trends they have highlighted.

Macroeconomic trends

1. ***Centers of economic activity will shift profoundly, not just globally, but also regionally.*** Today, Asia (excluding Japan) accounts for 13% of world GDP, and Western Europe accounts for more than 30%. Within the next 20 years the two will nearly converge. Some industries and functions—manufacturing and IT services, for example—will shift even more dramatically.
2. ***Public-sector activities will balloon, making productivity gains essential.*** The unprecedented aging of populations across the developed world will call for new levels of efficiency and creativity from the public sector. Many emerging-market governments will also have to decide what level of social services to provide to citizens who increasingly demand state-provided protections such as health care and retirement security. Private-sector approaches will likely become pervasive in the provision of social services.
3. ***The consumer landscape will change and expand significantly.*** Almost a billion new consumers will enter the global marketplace in the next decade as economic growth in emerging markets pushes them beyond the threshold level of $5,000 in annual household income—a point when people generally begin to spend on discretionary goods. Shifts within consumer segments in developed economies will also be profound. For example, by 2015 the Hispanic population in the United States will have spending power equivalent to that of 60% of all Chinese consumers.

Social and environmental trends

4. *Technological connectivity will transform the way people live and interact.* More transformational than technology itself is the shift in behavior that it enables. Communities and relationships are being formed in new ways (12% of U.S. newlyweds in 2005 met online). More than two billion people now use cell phones and nine trillion e-mails are sent a year. A billion Google searches occur every day, more than half in languages other than English.
5. *The battlefield for talent will shift.* The movement to knowledge-intensive industries highlights the importance and scarcity of well-trained talent. The 33 million university-educated young professionals in developing countries is more than double the number in developed ones. For many companies and governments, global labor and talent strategies will become as important as global sourcing and manufacturing strategies.
6. ***The role and behavior of big business will come under increasingly sharp scrutiny.*** The tenets of current global business ideology—for example, shareholder value, free trade, intellectual-property rights, and profit repatriation—are not understood, let alone accepted, in many parts of the world. Business leaders need to argue and demonstrate more forcefully the intellectual, social, and economic case for business in society and the massive contributions business makes to social welfare.
7. ***Demand for natural resources will grow, as will the strain on the environment.*** Natural resources are being used at unprecedented rates. Oil demand is projected to grow by 50% in the next two decades, and without large new discoveries or radical innovations, supply is unlikely to keep up. Water shortages will be the key constraint to growth in many countries. And one of our scarcest natural resources—the atmosphere—will require dramatic shifts in human behavior to escape further depletion.

Business and industry trends

8. ***New global industry structures are emerging.*** In many industries, a barbell-like structure is appearing, with a few giants on top, a narrow middle, and then a flourish of smaller, fast-moving players on the bottom. Similarly, corporate borders are becoming blurrier as interlinked "ecosystems" of suppliers, producers, and customers emerge.
9. ***Management will go from art to science.*** Long gone is the day of the "gut instinct" management style. Today's business leaders are adopting algorithmic decision-making techniques and using highly sophisticated software to run their organizations. Scientific management is becoming the ante that gives companies the right to play the game.
10. ***Ubiquitous access to information is changing the economics of knowledge.*** Open-source approaches to knowledge development are arising as communities, not individuals, become responsible for innovations. Knowledge production itself is growing: worldwide patent applications, for example, rose from 1990 to 2004 at a rate of 20% annually.

Source: Ian Davis and Elizabeth Stephenson, "Ten Trends to Watch in 2006," *McKinsey Quarterly* (January 2006). Used with permission from McKinsey & Company.

Megatrends have been described as "large social, economic, political, and technological changes [that] are slow to form, and once in place, they influence us for some time—between seven and ten years, or longer."[23] See "Marketing Memo: Trends Shaping the Business Landscape" for a look into some of the broad forces that are likely to come into play during the next decade or so.

A new market opportunity doesn't guarantee success, even if the product is technically feasible. For example, some companies sell portable "electronic books" or "e-books"; but there may not be a sufficient number of people interested in reading a book on a computer screen or willing to pay the required price. This is why market research is necessary to determine an opportunity's profit potential.

To help marketers spot cultural shifts that might bring new opportunities or threats, several firms offer social-cultural forecasts. The Yankelovich Monitor interviews 2,500 people nationally each year and has tracked 35 social trends since 1971, such as "anti-bigness," "mysticism," "living for today," "away from possessions," and "sensuousness."

Identifying the Major Forces

Companies and their suppliers, marketing intermediaries, customers, competitors, and publics all operate in a macroenvironment of forces and trends, increasingly global, that shape opportunities and pose threats. These forces represent "noncontrollables," which the company must monitor and to which it must respond.

The beginning of the new century brought a series of new challenges: the steep decline of the stock market, which affected savings, investment, and retirement funds; increasing unemployment; corporate scandals; and of course, the rise of terrorism. These dramatic events were accompanied by the continuation of existing trends that have already profoundly influenced the global landscape. In 2005, more transistors were produced (and at a lower cost) than grains of rice; the U.S. blog-reading audience is already 20% of the size of the newspaper-reading population; and insatiable world oil consumption is expected to rise 50% by 2030.[24]

Within the rapidly changing global picture, the firm must monitor six major forces: demographic, economic, social-cultural, natural, technological, and political-legal. We'll describe these forces separately, but marketers must pay attention to their interactions, because these will lead to new opportunities and threats. For example, explosive population growth (demographic) leads to more resource depletion and pollution (natural), which leads consumers to call for more laws (political-legal), which stimulate new technological solutions and products (technological), which, if they are affordable (economic), may actually change attitudes and behavior (social-cultural). "Breakthrough Marketing: Google" describes how that company has successfully capitalized on the new marketing environment.

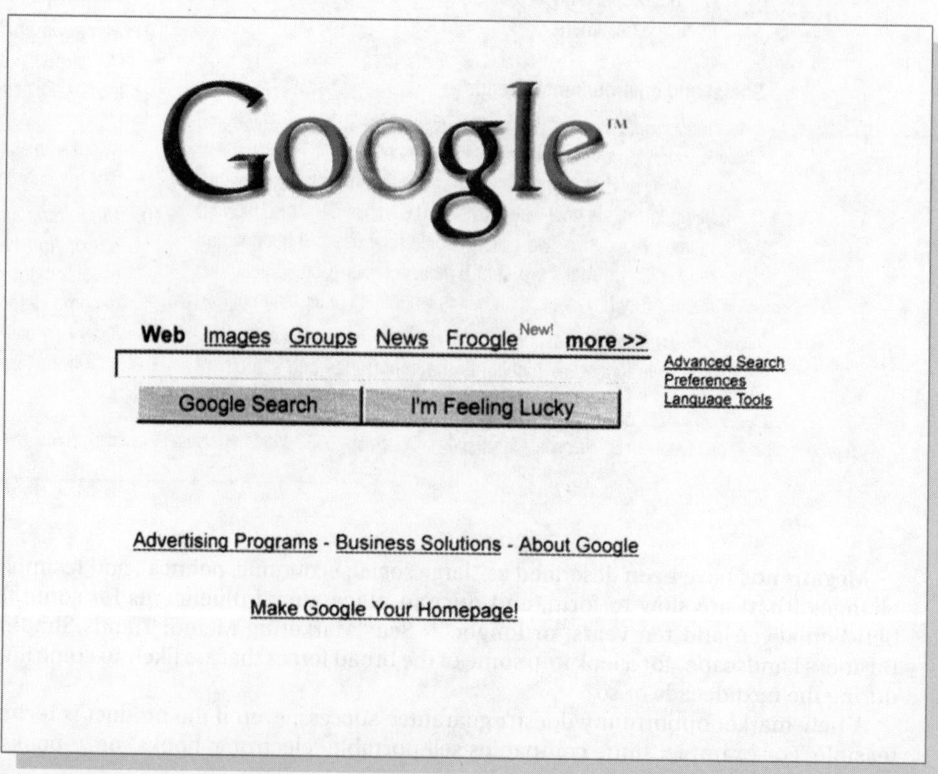

The simplicity of Google's home page has received high marks from consumers for usability.

BREAKTHROUGH **MARKETING** | GOOGLE

Founded in 1998 by two Stanford University PhD students, search engine Google's name is a play on the word *googol*—the number represented by a 1 followed by 100 zeroes—a reference to the massive quantity of data available online, which the company helps users make sense of. Google's stated corporate mission is "To organize the world's information and make it universally accessible and useful."

The company has become the market leader for search engines through its business focus and constant innovation. As Google grew into a primary destination for Web users searching for information online, it attracted a host of online advertisers. These advertisers drove Google's revenue by buying what are called "search ads," little text-based boxes shown alongside search results that advertisers pay for only when users click on them. Google's search ad program, called AdWords, sells space on its search pages to ads linked with specific keywords. Google auctions off the keyword ads, with the prime key words and prime page locations going to the highest bidder. The advertisers pay only if Internet users click on their ads.

In addition to offering prime online "real estate" for advertisers, Google adds value to advertisers by providing them with a variety of means to better target their ads to users and better understand the effectiveness of their marketing. Google Analytics, which Google provides free to advertisers, provides advertisers with a custom report, or dashboard, detailing how Internet users found the site, what ads they saw and/or clicked on, how they behaved while at the site, and how much traffic was generated. Google client Discount Tire was able to identify where visitors to the site encountered problems that led them to abandon a purchase midstream. After modifying its site and updating its keyword search campaign, Discount Tire measured a 14% increase in sales within a week.

With its ability to deploy data that enable up-to-the-minute improvements of a Web marketing program, Google supported a style of marketing where the advertising resources and budget could be constantly monitored and optimized. Google called this approach "marketing asset management," implying that advertising should be managed like assets in a portfolio, with management marshaling certain resources at one time or place online and others at a different time or place, depending on the market conditions. Rather than follow a marketing plan that had been developed months in advance, companies could use the real-time data collected on their campaigns to optimize the campaign's effectiveness by making it more responsive to the market.

Google has augmented its search capabilities with additional services and features for Internet users, including Google Maps, Google Local, Google Finance, Gmail (a Google e-mail service), and Google Video (which was bolstered by the $1.65 billion acquisition of video hosting site YouTube in 2006). These new efforts all offered opportunities for Google to grow by selling the additional targeted advertising space that was created.

Sources: www.google.com; Catherine P. Taylor, "Google Flex," *Adweek*, March 20, 2006, cover story; Richard Karpinski, "Keywords, Analytics Help Define User Lifetime Value," *Advertising Age*, April 24, 2006, p. S2; Danny Gorog, "Survival Guide," *Herald Sun*, March 29, 2006; Julie Schlosser, "Google," *Fortune*, October 31, 2005, pp. 168–69; Jefferson Graham, "Google's Profit Sails Past Expectations," *USA Today*, October 21, 2005.

::: The Demographic Environment

There's little excuse for being surprised by demographic developments. The Singer Company should have known for years that its sewing machine business would be hurt by smaller families and more working wives, yet it was slow in responding.

The main demographic force that marketers monitor is *population*, because people make up markets. Marketers are keenly interested in the size and growth rate of population in cities, regions, and nations; age distribution and ethnic mix; educational levels; household patterns; and regional characteristics and movements.

Worldwide Population Growth

The world population is showing explosive growth: it totaled 6.1 billion in 2000 and will exceed 7.9 billion by the year 2025.[25] Here is an interesting picture:

> If the world were a village of 1,000 people, it would consist of 520 females and 480 males, 330 children, 60 people over age 65, 10 college graduates, and 335 illiterate adults. The village would contain 52 North Americans, 55 Russians, 84 Latin Americans, 95 Eastern and Western Europeans, 124 Africans, and 584 Asians. Communication would be difficult because 165 people would speak Mandarin, 86 English, 83 Hindi/Urdu, 64 Spanish, 58 Russian, and 37 Arabic, and the rest would speak one of over 200 other languages. There would be 329 Christians, 178 Muslims, 132 Hindus, 62 Buddhists, 3 Jews, 167 nonreligious, 45 atheists, and 84 others.[26]

The population explosion has been a source of major concern. Moreover, population growth is highest in countries and communities that can least afford it. The less-developed regions of the world currently account for 76% of the world population and are growing at 2% per year, whereas the population in more developed countries is growing at only 0.6% per year. In developing countries, the death rate has been falling as a result of modern medicine, but the birthrate has remained fairly stable. Feeding, clothing, and educating children, although it can also raise the standard of living, is nearly impossible in these countries.

Explosive population growth has major implications for business. A growing population does not mean growing markets, unless these markets have sufficient purchasing power. Nonetheless, companies that carefully analyze their markets can find major opportunities.

Population Age Mix

National populations vary in their age mix. At one extreme is Mexico, a country with a very young population and rapid population growth. At the other extreme is Japan, a country with one of the world's oldest populations. Milk, diapers, school supplies, and toys will be more important products in Mexico than in Japan. In general, there is a global trend toward an aging population. By 2005, the population of people aged 60 or over surpassed the proportion of under-fives, and it is unlikely that there will ever again be more toddlers than seniors.[27]

Marketers generally divide the population into six age groups: preschool children, school-age children, teens, young adults age 20 to 40, middle-aged adults age 40 to 65, and older adults age 65 and up. Some marketers like to focus on cohorts. **Cohorts** are groups of individuals who are born during the same time period and travel through life together. The "defining moments" they experience as they become adults can stay with them for a lifetime and influence their values, preferences, and buying behaviors. "Marketing Insight: Friends for Life" summarizes one breakdown of cohorts in the U.S. market.

MARKETING INSIGHT | FRIENDS FOR LIFE

Schewe and Meredith have developed a generational cohort segmentation scheme based on the concept that the key defining moments that occur when a person comes of age (roughly ages 17–24) imprints core values that remain largely intact throughout life. They divide the U.S. adult population into seven distinct cohorts, each with its own unique value structure, demographic makeup, and markers.

Depression Cohort: Born from 1912 to 1921, ages 87 to 96 in 2008. This rapidly dwindling group's coming-of-age years were marked by economic strife and elevated unemployment rates. Financial security—what they most lacked when coming of age—rules their thinking. They are no longer in the workforce, but they have had a clear impact on many of today's management practices.

World War II Cohort: Born from 1922 to 1927, aged 81 to 86 in 2008. Sacrifice for the common good was widely accepted among members of the World War II cohort. This cohort was focused on defeating a common enemy during their coming-of-age years, and its members are team oriented and patriotic.

Postwar Cohort: Born from 1928 to 1945, ages 63 to 80 in 2008. These individuals experienced a time of remarkable economic growth and social tranquility, along with McCarthyism and the Korean conflict. They participated in the rise of the middle class, sought a sense of security and stability, and expected prosperous times to continue indefinitely.

Leading-Edge Baby Boomer Cohort: Born from 1946 to 1954, ages 54 to 62 in 2008. The loss of John F. Kennedy had the largest influence on this cohort's values. They became adults during the Vietnam War and watched as the first man walked on the moon. Leading-edge boomers championed causes (Greenpeace, civil rights, women's rights) yet were simultaneously hedonistic and self-indulgent (pot, free love, sensuality).

Trailing-Edge Baby Boomer Cohort: Born from 1955 to 1965, ages 43 to 53 in 2008. This group witnessed the fall of Vietnam, Watergate, and Nixon's resignation. The oil embargo, the raging inflation rate, and the more than 30% decline in the S&P Index led these individuals to be less optimistic about their financial future than the leading-edge boomers.

Generation X Cohort: Born from 1966 to 1976, ages 32 to 42 in 2008. Many members of this cohort were latch-key children or have parents who divorced. They have delayed marriage and children, and they don't take those commitments lightly. More than other groups, this cohort accepts cultural diversity and puts personal life ahead of work life. Members show a spirit of entrepreneurship unmatched by any other cohort.

N Generation Cohort: Born from 1977, ages 31 and under in 2008. The advent of the Internet is a defining event for them, and they will be the engine of growth over the next two decades. Although still a work in progress, their core value structure is different from that of Gen X. They are more idealistic and social-cause oriented, without the cynical, what's-in-it-for-me, free-agent mindset of many Xers.

Sources: Charles D. Schewe and Geoffrey Meredith, "Segmenting Global Markets by Generational Cohort: Determining Motivations by Age," *Journal of Consumer Behavior* 4 (October 2004): 51–63; Geoffrey E. Meredith and Charles D. Schewe, *Managing by Defining Moments: America's 7 Generational Cohorts, Their Workplace Values, and Why Managers Should Care* (Wiley, New York: Hungry Minds, 2002); Geoffrey E. Meredith, Charles D. Schewe, and Janice Karlovich, *Defining Markets Defining Moments* (Wiley, New York: Hungry Minds, 2001).

Ethnic and Other Markets

Countries also vary in ethnic and racial makeup. At one extreme is Japan, where almost everyone is Japanese; at the other is the United States, where people come from virtually all nations.

According to the 2000 census, the U.S. population of 276.2 million was 72% White. African Americans constituted 13%, and Hispanics 11%. The Hispanic population had been growing fast, with the largest subgroups of Mexican (5.4%), Puerto Rican (1.1%), and Cuban (0.4%) descent. By 2020, Hispanics are expected to make up 18.9% of the population. Asian Americans constituted 3.8% of the U.S. population, with the Chinese as the largest group, followed by the Filipinos, Japanese, Asian Indians, and Koreans, in that order. Hispanic and Asian American consumers were originally concentrated in the far western and southern parts of the country, but increasing dispersal is taking place. Moreover, nearly 25 million people living in the United States—more than 9% of the population—were born in another country.

A frequently noted megatrend, the increase in the percentage of Hispanics in the total population, represents a major shift in the nation's center of gravity. Hispanics made up half of all new workers in the past decade and will bump up to 25% of workers in two generations. Despite their lagging family incomes, their buying power is soaring. Disposable income in recent years has soared at double the pace of the rest of the population, to $760 billion. From the food U.S. consumers eat, to the clothing they wear, the music they listen to, and the cars they buy, Hispanics are having a huge impact.

Companies are scrambling to refine their products and their marketing to reach this fastest-growing and most influential consumer group:[28] Hispanic media giant Univision touts research that 70% of Spanish-language viewers are more likely to buy a product when advertised in Spanish. Targeting Hispanics also affects the actual message that is communicated. Fisher-Price, recognizing that many Hispanic mothers did not grow up with their brand, shifted their ad campaigns away from appeals to their heritage. Instead, ads targeting the Hispanic market have emphasized the joy of mother and child playing together with the toys.[29]

MTVTr3s

Replacing the all-Spanish-language MTV en Español, MTVTr3s (pronounced MTV*tres*) is concentrating on young Latinos between the ages of 12 and 34 and expects to reach 15 million households through cable, satellite, and broadcast channels. Changes in the program—which segues back and forth between Spanish and English, often in the same show—are based on market research showing that although U.S.-born Hispanics might speak only English, they preserve a pride and sense of uniqueness based on their Hispanic heritage. On MTVTr3s the VJs speckle their English with Spanish words and expressions and use playlists that put Daddy Yankee next to Justin Timberlake, for instance. Instead of *Pimp My Ride*, the popular car-customizing series, MTVTr3s viewers watch *Pimpeando*, where the talk is all about low riders and paint jobs with images of Aztecs and the Virgin of Guadalupe. For MTVTr3s and other companies trying to reach this market, it seems that attitude is more important than language and encompasses an individualistic approach to life, less rebellion against parents, and a less-rigid sense of privacy.[30]

Several food, clothing, and furniture companies have directed their products and promotions to one or more ethnic groups.[31] Yet marketers must be careful not to overgeneralize. Within each ethnic group are consumers who are quite different from each other. "There is really no such thing as an Asian market," says Greg Macabenta, whose ethnic advertising agency specializes in the Filipino market. Macabenta emphasizes that the five major Asian American groups have their own very specific market characteristics, speak different languages, consume different cuisines, practice different religions, and represent very distinct national cultures.[32]

This is no less true for the African American market, which marketers often treat as a monolithic group. Yet, subsections are divided less by culture than by economic aspirations and attainment. For instance, a 2005 Yankelovich MONITOR Multicultural Marketing study showed that marketers can separate the African American market into six socio-behavioral segments: Emulators, Seekers, Reachers, Attainers, Elites, and Conservers. The largest and perhaps most influential of these subsegments are the Reachers (24%) and the Attainers

(27%), each with very different needs. Reachers tend to be older, around 40, and are slowly working toward the American dream. Often single parents who are also caring for elderly relatives, they have median income of $28,000 and seek the greatest value for the money. Attainers have a more defined sense of self and solid plans for the future. Their median income is $55,000, and they want ideas and information to improve their quality of life.[33]

Diversity goes beyond ethnic and racial markets. More than 50 million U.S. consumers have disabilities, and they constitute a market for home delivery companies, such as Peapod, and for various medical services.

Educational Groups

The population in any society falls into five educational groups: illiterates, high school dropouts, high school diplomas, college degrees, and professional degrees. Over two-thirds of the world's 785 million illiterate adults are found in only eight countries (India, China, Bangladesh, Pakistan, Nigeria, Ethiopia, Indonesia, and Egypt); of all the illiterate adults in the world, two-thirds are women.[34] The United States has one of the world's highest percentages of college-educated citizens, around 36%. The large number of educated people in the United States spells a high demand for quality books, magazines, and travel, and a high supply of skills.

Household Patterns

The "traditional household" consists of a husband, wife, and children (and sometimes grandparents). Yet, by 2010, only one in five U.S. households will consist of married couples with children under the age of 18. Other projected household compositions are single live-alones (27%), single-parent families (8%), childless married couples and empty nesters (32%), living with nonrelatives only (5%), and other family structures (8%).[35]

More people are divorcing or separating, choosing not to marry, marrying later, or marrying without the intention to have children. Each group has a distinctive set of needs and buying habits. For example, people in the SSWD group (single, separated, widowed, divorced) need smaller apartments; inexpensive and smaller appliances, furniture, and furnishings; and smaller-size food packages. Products such as the George Foreman grill that target people who live alone and value convenience can be successful.[36]

Marketers must increasingly consider the special needs of nontraditional households, now growing more rapidly than traditional households. Academics and marketing experts estimate that the gay and lesbian population ranges between 4% and 8% of the total U.S. population, with an even higher percentage in urban areas.[37] Compared to the average U.S. consumer, respondents who classify themselves as gay are over 10 times more likely to be in professional jobs, almost 2 times as likely to own a vacation home, 8 times more likely to own a notebook computer, and 2 times as likely to own individual stocks.[38] Companies such as Absolut, American Express, IKEA, Procter & Gamble, and Subaru have recognized the potential of this market and the nontraditional household market as a whole.

Yet, in focusing the gay market or the recently targeted "metrosexual,"—straight urban men with gay shopping styles—marketers may miss out on other male markets just under their nose. For instance, millions of boomer dads shop a lot more than their fathers or grandfathers did. They married later and are much more involved in raising their kids. For instance, many of today's dads actually push strollers, and they don't want to be seen behind some fussy-looking contraption of yesteryear. So the maker of the high-concept Bugaboo stroller designed a stroller with a sleek design and tires resembling those of a dirt bike. Dyson, the high-end vacuum company, is reaching out to involved dads with ads geared to appeal to their inner geek, focusing on the machine's revolutionary technology. Before Dyson entered the U.S. market, men weren't even on the radar for vacuum cleaner sales. Now they make up 40% of Dyson's customers.[39]

Geographical Shifts in Population

This is a period of great migratory movements between and within countries. Although the United States experienced a rural rebound in the 1990s when nonmetropolitan counties attracted large numbers of urban refugees, the twenty-first century saw urban markets grow more rapidly again, due to a higher birth rate, a lower death rate, and rapid growth from foreign immigration.[40]

Marketers also look at where consumers are gathering. Almost one in two people over the age of five (120 million) moved at least one time between 1995 and 2000, according to a Census 2000 brief. State-by-state analysis clearly shows that the shift has been toward the Sunbelt states, away from the Midwest and Northeast.[41] From Virginia to Florida and western Sunbelt states such as Texas, Nevada, or Arizona, these "hot" states are luring more roamers.

The movement to the Sunbelt states has lessened the demand for warm clothing and home heating equipment and increased the demand for air conditioning. Those who live in large cities such as New York, Chicago, and San Francisco account for most of the sales of expensive furs, perfumes, luggage, and works of art. These cities also support the opera, ballet, and other forms of culture.

People living in the suburbs lead more casual lives, do more outdoor living, and have greater neighbor interaction, higher incomes, and younger families. Suburbanites buy vans, home workshop equipment, outdoor furniture, lawn and gardening tools, and outdoor cooking equipment. There are also regional differences: People in Seattle buy more toothbrushes per capita than people in any other U.S. city; people in Salt Lake City eat more candy bars; people from New Orleans use more ketchup; and people in Miami drink more prune juice. And nearly 40 million U.S. workers are working from their homes with the help of electronic conveniences such as computers, cell phones, fax machines, and personal organizers.

::: Other Major Macroenvironments

Other macroenvironment forces profoundly affect the fortunes of marketers. Here we review developments in the economic, social-cultural, natural, technological, and political-legal environments.

Economic Environment

The available purchasing power in an economy depends on current income, prices, savings, debt, and credit availability. Marketers must pay careful attention to trends affecting purchasing power, because they can have a strong impact on business, especially for companies whose products are geared to high-income and price-sensitive consumers.

INCOME DISTRIBUTION There are four types of industrial structures: *subsistence economies* like Papua New Guinea, with few opportunities for marketers; *raw-material-exporting economies* like Democratic Republic of Congo (copper) and Saudi Arabia (oil), with good markets for equipment, tools, supplies, and luxury goods for the rich; *industrializing economies* like India, Egypt, and the Philippines, where a new rich class and a growing middle class demand new types of goods; and *industrial economies* like countries in Western Europe, which are rich markets for all sorts of goods.

Marketers often distinguish countries using five different income-distribution patterns: (1) very low incomes; (2) mostly low incomes; (3) very low, very high incomes; (4) low, medium, high incomes; and (5) mostly medium incomes. Consider the market for Lamborghinis, an automobile costing more than $150,000. The market would be very small in countries with type (1) or (2) income patterns. One of the largest single markets for Lamborghinis turns out to be Portugal (income pattern 3)—one of the poorer countries in Western Europe, but one with enough wealthy families to afford expensive cars.

Over the past three decades in the United States, the rich have grown richer, the middle class has shrunk, and the poor have remained poor. From 1973 to 1999, earnings for U.S. households in the top 5% of the income distribution grew 65%, compared with growth of 11% for the middle one-fifth of households during the same period. This is leading to a two-tier U.S. market, with affluent people able to buy expensive goods and working-class people having to spend more carefully, shopping at discount stores and factory outlet malls, and selecting less-expensive store brands.

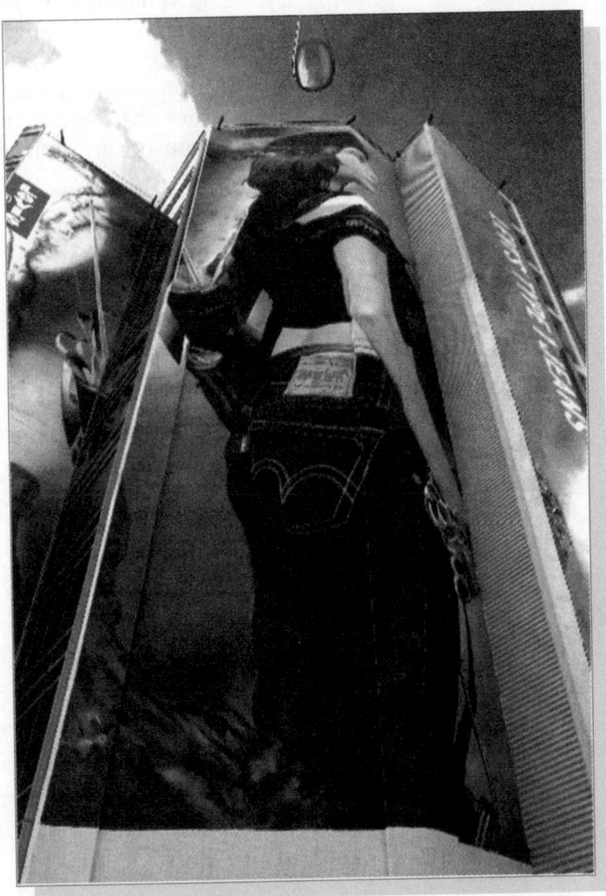

Levi's has responded to changes in income distribution in the United States by additionally segmenting its offerings with the upscale Capital E and the mass-market Signature lines.

Conventional retailers who offer medium-priced goods are the most vulnerable to these changes. Companies that respond to the trend by tailoring their products and pitches to these two very different Americas stand to gain.[42] Recognizing that it could be trapped in "no-man's land," given its channel strategy that emphasized retailers like Sears selling primarily to the middle class, Levi-Strauss introduced premium lines such as Levi's Capital E to upscale retailers Bloomingdales, Barney's New York, and others while also introducing the less-expensive Levis Strauss Signature line to mass-market retailers such as Wal-Mart.

SAVINGS, DEBT, AND CREDIT Consumer expenditures are affected by savings, debt, and credit availability. U.S. consumers have a high debt-to-income ratio, which slows down further expenditures on housing and large-ticket items. Credit is readily available in the United States but at fairly high interest rates, especially to lower-income borrowers. An economic issue of increasing importance to many unemployed U.S. consumers is the migration of manufacturers and service jobs off shore. From India, Infosys provides outsourcing services for Cisco, Nordstrom, Microsoft, and others. The 15,000 employees that the fast-growing $1.6 billion company hires every year receive training in Infosys' $120 million facility outside Bangalore. There they learn technical skills as well as "softer" skills concerning team building, interpersonal communication, and the importance of being an ambassador for the brands they serve.[43]

To learn about challenges in conducting market research in China, visit www.pearsoned-asia.com/marketingmanagementchina.

Social-Cultural Environment

Society shapes the beliefs, values, and norms that largely define consumer tastes and preferences. People absorb, almost unconsciously, a world view that defines their relationships to themselves, to others, to organizations, to society, to nature, and to the universe.

- ***Views of themselves.*** In the United States during the 1960s and 1970s, "pleasure seekers" sought fun, change, and escape. Others sought "self-realization." People bought dream cars and dream vacations and spent more time in health activities (jogging, tennis), in introspection, and in arts and crafts (see Table 3.3 for a summary of top consumer leisure-time activities and how they have changed over the past decade). Today, some people are adopting more conservative behaviors and ambitions.

TABLE 3.3

Top Leisure-Time Activities (Spontaneous, Unaided Responses) "What are your two or three most favorite leisure-time activities?" Base: All Adults

	1995	2004
	%	%
Reading	28	35
TV watching	25	21
Spending time with family/kids	12	20
Going to movies	8	10
Fishing	10	8
Computer activities	2	7
Gardening	9	6
Renting movies	5	6
Walking	8	6
Exercise (aerobics, weights)	2	6
Listening to music	5	6
Entertaining	7	5
Hunting	4	5
Playing team sports	9	5
Shopping	3	5

Adapted from ©2004, Harris Interactive Inc.

- ***Views of others.*** People are concerned about the homeless, crime and victims, and other social problems. At the same time, they seek out their "own kind" for serious and long-lasting relationships and avoid strangers. These trends portend a growing market for social-support products and services that promote direct relationships between human beings, such as health clubs, cruises, and religious activity. They also suggest a growing market for "social surrogates" such as television, home video games, and chat rooms on the Internet.
- ***Views of organizations.*** After a wave of company downsizings and corporate accounting scandals, there has been an overall decline in organizational loyalty.[44] Many people today see work not as a source of satisfaction, but as a required chore to earn money to enjoy their nonwork hours. Companies need to find new ways to win back consumer and employee confidence. They need to make sure they are good corporate citizens and that their consumer messages are honest.[45]
- ***Views of society.*** Some people defend society (preservers), some run it (makers), some take what they can from it (takers), some want to change it (changers), some are looking for something deeper (seekers), and still others want to leave it (escapers).[46] Consumption patterns often reflect social attitude. Makers tend to be high achievers who eat, dress, and live well. Changers usually live more frugally, drive smaller cars, and wear simpler clothes. Escapers and seekers are a major market for movies, music, surfing, and camping.
- ***Views of nature.*** People have awakened to nature's fragility and the finiteness of its resources. Business has responded to increased interest in being in harmony with and experiencing nature by producing wider varieties of camping, hiking, boating, and fishing gear such as boots, tents, backpacks, and accessories.
- ***Views of the universe.*** Most U.S. citizens are monotheistic, although religious conviction and practice have been waning through the years. Certain evangelical movements are reaching out to bring people back into organized religion. Some of the religious impulse has been redirected into an interest in Eastern religions, mysticism, the occult, and the human potential movement.

A growing appreciation of nature is among the elements of the social-cultural environment, to which marketers have responded with outdoor gear and wilderness trips.

Other cultural characteristics of interest to marketers are the persistence of core cultural values and the existence of subcultures. Let's look at both.

HIGH PERSISTENCE OF CORE CULTURAL VALUES Most people in the United States still believe in work, in getting married, in giving to charity, and in being honest. *Core beliefs* and values are passed on from parents to children and reinforced by major social institutions—schools, churches, businesses, and governments. *Secondary beliefs* and values are more open to change. Believing in the institution of marriage is a core belief; believing that people ought to get married early is a secondary belief.

Marketers have some chance of changing secondary values, but little chance of changing core values. For instance, the nonprofit organization Mothers Against Drunk Drivers (MADD) does not try to stop the sale of alcohol, but it does promote lower legal blood-alcohol levels for driving and more-limited operating hours for businesses permitted to sell alcohol. Although core values are fairly persistent, cultural swings do take place. In the 1960s, hippies, the Beatles, Elvis Presley, and other cultural phenomena had a major impact on young people's hairstyles, clothing, sexual norms, and life goals. Today's young people are influenced by new heroes and new activities: U2's Bono, the NBA's LeBron James, and skateboarder Tony Hawk.

EXISTENCE OF SUBCULTURES Each society contains **subcultures**, groups with shared values, beliefs, preferences, and behaviors emerging from their special life experiences or circumstances. There are sometimes unexpected rewards in targeting subcultures. Marketers have always loved teenagers because they are society's trendsetters in fashion, music, entertainment, ideas, and attitudes. Marketers also know that if they attract someone as a teen, there's a good chance they will keep the person as a customer later in life. Frito-Lay, which draws 15% of its sales from teens, said it saw a rise in chip snacking by grown-ups. "We think it's because we brought them in as teenagers," said Frito-Lay's marketing director.[47]

Natural Environment

The deterioration of the natural environment is a major global problem. There is great concern about "greenhouse gases" in the atmosphere due to the burning of fossil fuels; about the depletion of the ozone layer due to certain chemicals and global warming; and about growing shortages of water. In Western Europe, "green" parties have vigorously pressed for public action to reduce industrial pollution. In the United States, experts have documented ecological deterioration, and watchdog groups such as the Sierra Club and Friends of the Earth carry these concerns into political and social action.

New regulations hit certain industries very hard. Steel companies and public utilities have had to invest billions of dollars in pollution-control equipment and more environmentally friendly fuels. The soap industry increased its products' biodegradability. Great opportunities await companies and marketers who can create solutions that reconcile prosperity with environmental protection. Consider how the auto industry has adjusted to environmental concerns.[48]

TOYOTA PRIUS

Some auto experts scoffed when Toyota launched its Prius sedans with hybrid gas-and-electric engines in 2001 and predicted sales of 300,000 cars within five years. But by 2004, the Prius was such a huge hit that it had a six-month waiting list. Toyota's winning formula consists of a powerful electric motor and the ability to quickly switch power sources—resulting in 55 miles per gallon for city and highway driving—with the roominess and power of a family sedan and an eco-friendly design and look, for a little over $20,000. The lesson? Products that consumers see as good for the environment and that are functionally successful can offer enticing options. Toyota is now rolling out hybrids throughout its auto lineup, and U.S. automakers have followed suit.

Consumers often appear conflicted about product decisions that affect the natural environment. One research study showed that although 80% of U.S. consumers said environmental safety influenced their decision to buy a product, only a little over half asserted that they bought recycled or environmentally safe products.[49] Young people especially were more likely to feel that nothing they did personally made a difference in solving environmental problems. Increasing the number of green products they buy requires consumers to break their loyalty habits, overcome skepticism about the motives behind the introduction of the products and their quality level, and change their attitudes about the role such products play in environmental protection. (See "Marketing Insight: Green Marketing.")

Corporate environmentalism is the recognition of the importance of environmental issues facing the firm and the integration of those issues into the firm's strategic plans.[50] Marketers practicing corporate environmentalism need to be aware of the threats and opportunities associated with four major trends in the natural environment: the shortage of raw materials, especially water; the increased cost of energy; increased pollution levels; and the changing role of governments.

- The earth's raw materials consist of the infinite, the finite renewable, and the finite nonrenewable. *Finite nonrenewable resources*—oil, coal, platinum, zinc, silver—pose a particularly serious problem as the point of depletion approaches. Firms making products that require these increasingly scarce minerals face substantial cost increases. Firms engaged in research and development have an excellent opportunity to develop substitute materials.
- One finite nonrenewable resource, oil, has created serious problems for the world economy. As oil prices soar to record levels, companies are searching for practical means to harness solar, nuclear, wind, and other alternative forms of energy.
- Some industrial activity will inevitably damage the natural environment. A large market has been created for pollution-control solutions, such as scrubbers, recycling centers,

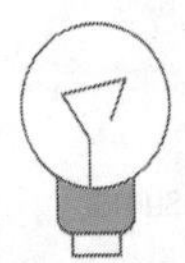

MARKETING INSIGHT | GREEN MARKETING

Gallup polls reveal that the percentage of U.S. consumers who report that they worry about the environment a great deal or a fair amount increased from 62% to 77% between 2004 and 2006. Membership in the Sierra Club increased by roughly a third between 2003 and 2006.

Environmental concerns are manifested in many behaviors. A Roper survey in 2002 reported that 58% of U.S. consumers try to save electricity at home, 46% recycle newspapers, 45% return bottles or cans, and 23% buy products made from, or packaged in, recycled materials. But people vary in their environmental sensitivity. The Roper survey breaks consumers into five groups based on their degree of environmental sensitivity (see Figure 3.1).

A new Bank of America tower in Manhattan designed by Cook & Fox takes sustainability to new heights. Every drop of rain that falls on its roof will be captured for use; scraps from the cafeteria will be fermented in the building to produce methane as a supplementary fuel for a generator designed to produce more than half the building's electricity; and the waste heat from the generator will both warm the offices and power a refrigeration plant to cool them. Little things can add up. When Anheuser-Busch developed an aluminum can that was 33% lighter than previous cans, the reduced use of aluminum combined with an overall recycling plan saved the company $200 million a year.

From a branding perspective, however, "green marketing" programs have not been entirely successful. Two main problems are that (1) consumers may believe the product is of inferior quality as a result of being green and (2) they may feel the product is not really that green to begin with. Successful green products convincingly overcome both these concerns to persuade consumers they are acting in their own and society's long-run interest at the same time, such as with organic foods that are seen as healthier, tastier, and safer, and energy-efficient appliances that cost less to run. Ottman and her colleagues refer to the tendency to overly focus on a product's greenness as "green marketing myopia." Figure 3.2 displays their recommendations for avoiding myopia by following three key principles: consumer value positioning, calibration of consumer knowledge, and the credibility of product claims.

Many top companies such as McDonald's, Nike, GE, and DuPont are embracing sustainability and green marketing. UPS and FedEx have introduced alternative-fuel and hybrid electric diesel vehicles to their fleets. Citicorp, Barclays, and other major banks have agreed to meet environmental- and social-impact standards when financing public work projects, such as dams and power plants, especially in developing markets. HP's "e-inclusion" programs are designed to increase access to technology and accelerate economic development in underserved communities all around the world.

Sources: Jerry Adler, "Going Green," *Newsweek*, July 17, 2006, pp. 43–52; Jacquelyn A. Ottman, Edwin R. Stafford, and Cathy L. Hartman, "Avoiding Green Marketing Myopia," *Environment* (June 2006): 22–36; Jill Meredith Ginsberg and Paul N. Bloom, "Choosing the Right Green Marketing Strategy," *MIT Sloan Management Review* (Fall 2004): 79–84; Marc Gunther, "Tree Huggers, Soy Lovers, and Profits," *Fortune*, June 23, 2003, pp. 98–104; Roper ASW, "Green Gauge Report 2002," (New York: Roper ASW, 2002); Jacquelyn Ottman, *Green Marketing: Opportunity for Innovation*, 2nd ed. (Chicago: NTC/Contemporary Publishing Company, 1998).

and landfill systems. Its existence leads to a search for alternative ways to produce and package goods.

- **Governments vary in their concern for and efforts to promote a clean environment. Many poor nations are doing little about pollution, largely because they lack the funds or the political will. It is in the richer nations' interest to help the poorer nations control their pollution, but even the richer nations today lack the necessary funds.**

- True Blue Greens (30%): True Blues are the environmental leaders and activists. They are characterized by a strong knowledge of environmental issues. They are more likely than the average consumer to engage in environmentally conscious behavior, such as recycling.
- Greenback Greens (10%): Greenbacks do not have the time or inclination to behave entirely green. However, they are more likely to purchase green.
- Sprouts (26%): Sprouts are environmental fence sitters. They feel some environmental issues are worth supporting, but not others. They will purchase an environmentally conscious product, but only if it meets their needs.
- Grousers (15%): Grousers believe that their individual behavior cannot improve environmental conditions. They are generally uninvolved and disinterested in environmental issues.
- Apathetics (18%): Apathetics are not concerned enough about the environment to do anything about it. They also believe that environmental indifference is mainstream.

| FIG. 3.1 |

Consumer Environmental Segments

Source: GfK Roper Green Gauge®, 2007, GfK Roper Consulting, New York, NY.

| FIG. 3.2 |

Three Keys to Avoiding Green Marketing Myopia

Source: Jacquelyn A. Ottman, Edwin R. Stafford, and Cathy L. Hartman, "Avoiding Green Marketing Myopia," *Environment* (June 2006): 22-36.

Consumer Value Positioning

- Design environmental products to perform as well as (or better than) alternatives.
- Promote and deliver the consumer-desired value of environmental products and target relevant consumer market segments (such as market health benefits among health-conscious consumers).
- Broaden mainstream appeal by bundling (or adding) consumer-desired value into environmental products (such as fixed pricing for subscribers of renewable energy).

Calibration of Consumer Knowledge

- Educate consumers with marketing messages that connect environmental product attributes with desired consumer value (for example, "pesticide-free produce is healthier"; "energy-efficiency saves money"; or "solar power is convenient").
- Frame environmental product attributes as "solutions" for consumer needs (for example, "rechargeable batteries offer longer performance").
- Create engaging and educational Internet sites about environmental products' desired consumer value (for example, Tide Coldwater's interactive Web site allows visitors to calculate their likely annual money savings based on their laundry habits, utility source [gas or electricity], and zip code location).

Credibility of Product Claims

- Employ environmental product and consumer benefit claims that are specific, meaningful, unpretentious, and qualified (that is, compared with comparable alternatives or likely usage scenarios).
- Procure product endorsements or eco-certifications from trustworthy third parties, and educate consumers about the meaning behind those endorsements and eco-certifications.
- Encourage consumer evangelism via consumers' social and Internet communication networks with compelling, interesting, and/or entertaining information about environmental products (for example, Tide's "Coldwater Challenge" Web site included a map of the United States so visitors could track and watch their personal influence spread when their friends requested a free sample).

Technological Environment

One of the most dramatic forces shaping people's lives is technology. Through the years, technology has released such wonders as penicillin, open-heart surgery, and the birth control pill, and such horrors as the hydrogen bomb, nerve gas, and the submachine gun. It has also released such mixed blessings as cell phones and video games.

Every new technology is a force for "creative destruction." Transistors hurt the vacuum-tube industry, xerography hurt the carbon-paper business, autos hurt the railroads, and television hurt the newspapers. Instead of moving into the new technologies, many old industries fought or ignored them, and their businesses declined. Yet it is the essence of market capitalism to be dynamic and tolerate the creative destructiveness of technology as the price of progress.

The number of major new technologies we discovered affects the economy's growth rate. Unfortunately, technological discoveries do not arise evenly through time—the railroad industry created a lot of investment, and then investment petered out until the auto industry emerged. In the time between major innovations, an economy can stagnate. In the meantime, minor innovations fill the gap: freeze-dried coffee, combination shampoo and conditioner, antiperspirants and deodorants, and the like. They require less risk, but they can also divert research effort away from major breakthroughs.

New technology also creates major long-run consequences that are not always foreseeable. The contraceptive pill, for example, helped lead to smaller families, more working wives, and larger discretionary incomes—resulting in higher expenditures on vacation travel, durable goods, and luxury items. Cell phones, video games, and Internet are not only reducing attention to traditional media, they are reducing face-to-face social interaction as people listen to music, watch a movie on their cellphone, and so on. Technologies also compete with each other. Consider the variety of means to view video material, as shown in Table 3.4.

TABLE 3.4

Video Venues

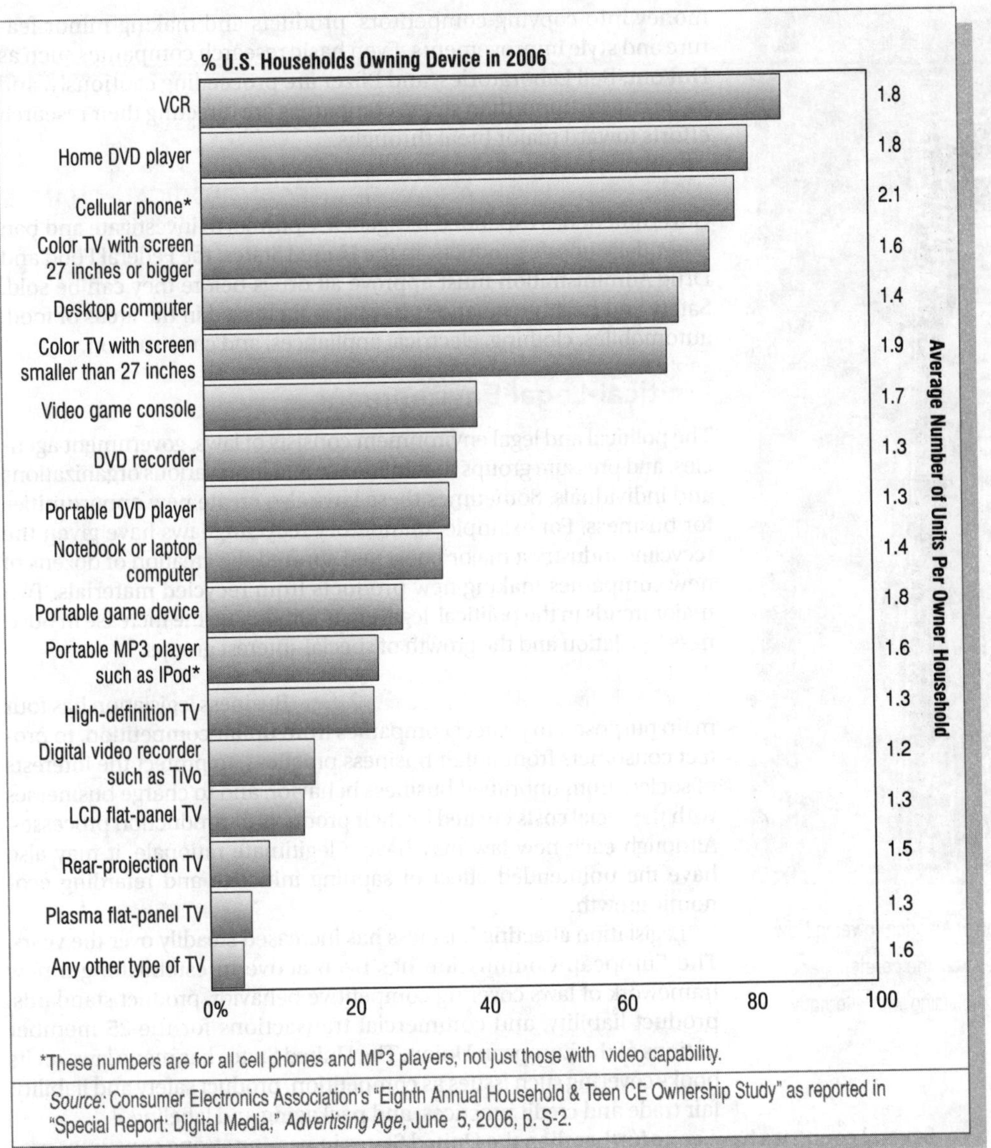

Device	% U.S. Households Owning Device in 2006	Average Number of Units Per Owner Household
VCR	[bar]	1.8
Home DVD player	[bar]	1.8
Cellular phone*	[bar]	2.1
Color TV with screen 27 inches or bigger	[bar]	1.6
Desktop computer	[bar]	1.4
Color TV with screen smaller than 27 inches	[bar]	1.9
Video game console	[bar]	1.7
DVD recorder	[bar]	1.3
Portable DVD player	[bar]	1.3
Notebook or laptop computer	[bar]	1.4
Portable game device	[bar]	1.8
Portable MP3 player such as IPod*	[bar]	1.6
High-definition TV	[bar]	1.3
Digital video recorder such as TiVo	[bar]	1.2
LCD flat-panel TV	[bar]	1.3
Rear-projection TV	[bar]	1.5
Plasma flat-panel TV	[bar]	1.3
Any other type of TV	[bar]	1.6

*These numbers are for all cell phones and MP3 players, not just those with video capability.

Source: Consumer Electronics Association's "Eighth Annual Household & Teen CE Ownership Study" as reported in "Special Report: Digital Media," *Advertising Age*, June 5, 2006, p. S-2.

Marketers should monitor the following four trends in technology: the accelerating pace of change, the unlimited opportunities for innovation, varying R&D budgets, and the increased regulation of technological change.

ACCELERATING PACE OF CHANGE Many of today's common products were not available 40 years ago. Electronic researchers are building smarter chips to make our cars, homes, and offices connected and more responsive to changing conditions. More ideas than ever are in the works, and the time between the appearance of new ideas and their successful implementation is all but disappearing. So is the time between introduction and peak production. Apple quickly ramped up in a little over five years to sell 23.5 million iPod's in 2006.

UNLIMITED OPPORTUNITIES FOR INNOVATION Some of the most exciting work today is taking place in biotechnology, computers, microelectronics, telecommunications, robotics, and designer materials. The Human Genome project promises to usher in the Biological Century as biotech workers create new medical cures, new foods, and new materials. Researchers are working on AIDS vaccines, totally safe contraceptives, and nonfattening foods. They are designing robots for firefighting, underwater exploration, and home nursing.

VARYING R&D BUDGETS A growing portion of U.S. R&D expenditures is going into the development side of R&D as opposed to the research side, raising concerns about whether the United States can maintain its lead in basic science. Many companies are content to put their

Taking sustainability to new heights, the Bank of America tower in New York City will recycle rain from the roof, waste from the cafeteria, and excess heat from the generator to provide the building with alternative sources of fuel and power.

money into copying competitors' products and making minor feature and style improvements. Even basic research companies such as DuPont, Bell Laboratories, and Pfizer are proceeding cautiously, and more consortiums than single companies are directing their research efforts toward major breakthroughs.

INCREASED REGULATION OF TECHNOLOGICAL CHANGE Government has expanded its agencies' powers to investigate and ban potentially unsafe products. In the United States, the Federal Food and Drug Administration must approve all drugs before they can be sold. Safety and health regulations have also increased in the areas of food, automobiles, clothing, electrical appliances, and construction.

Political-Legal Environment

The political and legal environment consists of laws, government agencies, and pressure groups that influence and limit various organizations and individuals. Sometimes these laws also create new opportunities for business. For example, mandatory recycling laws have given the recycling industry a major boost and spurred the creation of dozens of new companies making new products from recycled materials. Two major trends in the political-legal environment are the increase in business legislation and the growth of special-interest groups.

INCREASE IN BUSINESS LEGISLATION Business legislation has four main purposes: to protect companies from unfair competition, to protect consumers from unfair business practices, to protect the interests of society from unbridled business behavior, and to charge businesses with the social costs created by their products or production processes. Although each new law may have a legitimate rationale, it may also have the unintended effect of sapping initiative and retarding economic growth.

Legislation affecting business has increased steadily over the years. The European Commission has been active in establishing a new framework of laws covering competitive behavior, product standards, product liability, and commercial transactions for the 25 member nations of the European Union. The United States has many laws on its books covering such issues as competition, product safety and liability, fair trade and credit practices, and packaging and labeling.[51]

Several countries have gone further than the United States in passing strong consumer protection legislation. Norway bans several forms of sales promotion—trading stamps, contests, premiums—as inappropriate or "unfair" instruments for promoting products. Thailand requires food processors selling national brands to market low-price brands also, so that low-income consumers can find economy brands. In India, food companies need special approval to launch brands that duplicate what already exists on the market, such as another cola drink or brand of rice.

Companies generally establish legal review procedures and promulgate ethical standards to guide their marketing managers, and as more business takes place in cyberspace, marketers must establish new parameters for doing electronic business ethically.

GROWTH OF SPECIAL-INTEREST GROUPS Political action committees (PACs) lobby government officials and pressure business executives to pay more attention to consumers' rights, women's rights, senior citizens' rights, minority rights, and gay rights.

Many companies have established public affairs departments to deal with these groups and issues. An important force affecting business is the **consumerist movement**—an organized movement of citizens and government to strengthen the rights and powers of buyers in relationship to sellers. Consumerists have advocated and won the right to know the true interest cost of a loan, the true cost per standard unit of competing brands (unit pricing), the basic ingredients in a product, the nutritional quality of food, the freshness of products, and the true benefits of a product.

With consumers increasingly willing to swap personal information for customized products from firms—as long as they can be trusted—privacy issues will continue to be a public policy hot button.[52] Consumers worry that they will be robbed or cheated; that private information will be used against them; that someone will steal their identity; that they will be bombarded by solicitations; and that children will be targeted.[53] Wise companies establish consumer affairs departments to help formulate policies and resolve and respond to consumer complaints.

Clearly, new laws and growing numbers of pressure groups have put more restraints on marketers. Marketers must clear their plans with the company's legal, public relations, public affairs, and consumer affairs departments. Insurance companies directly or indirectly affect the design of smoke detectors; scientific groups affect the design of spray products. In essence, many private marketing transactions have moved into the public domain.

SUMMARY :::

1. To carry out their analysis, planning, implementation, and control responsibilities, marketing managers need a marketing information system (MIS). The role of the MIS is to assess the managers' information needs, develop the needed information, and distribute that information in a timely manner.
2. An MIS has three components: (a) an internal records system, which includes information on the order-to-payment cycle and sales information systems; (b) a marketing intelligence system, a set of procedures and sources used by managers to obtain everyday information about pertinent developments in the marketing environment; and (c) a marketing research system that allows for the systematic design, collection, analysis, and reporting of data and findings relevant to a specific marketing situation.
3. Marketers find many opportunities by identifying trends (directions or sequences of events that have some momentum and durability) and megatrends (major social, economic, political, and technological changes that have long-lasting influence).
4. Within the rapidly changing global picture, marketers must monitor six major environmental forces: demographic, economic, social-cultural, natural, technological, and political-legal.
5. In the demographic environment, marketers must be aware of worldwide population growth; changing mixes of age, ethnic composition, and educational levels; the rise of nontraditional families; and large geographic shifts in population.
6. In the economic arena, marketers need to focus on income distribution and levels of savings, debt, and credit availability.
7. In the social-cultural arena, marketers must understand people's views of themselves, others, organizations, society, nature, and the universe. They must market products that correspond to society's core and secondary values and address the needs of different subcultures within a society.
8. In the natural environment, marketers need to be aware of the public's increased concern about the health of the environment. Many marketers are now embracing sustainability and green marketing programs that provide better environmental solutions as a result.
9. In the technological arena, marketers should take account of the accelerating pace of technological change, opportunities for innovation, varying R&D budgets, and the increased governmental regulation brought about by technological change.
10. In the political-legal environment, marketers must work within the many laws regulating business practices and with various special-interest groups.

APPLICATIONS :::

Marketing Debate Is Consumer Behavior More a Function of a Person's Age or Generation?

One of the widely debated issues in developing marketing programs that target certain age groups is how much consumers change over time. Some marketers maintain that age differences are critical and that the needs and wants of a 25-year-old in 2002 are not that different from those of a 25-year-old in 1972. Others dispute that contention and argue that cohort and generation effects are critical, and that marketing programs must therefore suit the times.

Take a position: Age differences are fundamentally more important than cohort effects *versus* Cohort effects can dominate age differences.

Marketing Discussion

What brands and products do you feel successfully "speak to you" and effectively target your age group? Why? Which ones do not? What could they do better?

IN THIS CHAPTER, WE WILL ADDRESS THE FOLLOWING QUESTIONS:

1. What constitutes good marketing research?
2. What are good metrics for measuring marketing productivity?
3. How can marketers assess their return on investment of marketing expenditures?
4. How can companies more accurately measure and forecast demand?

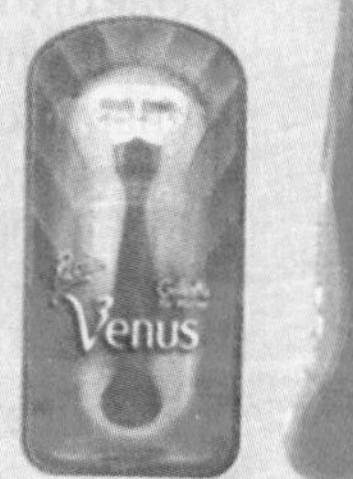

CHAPTER 2 ::: CONDUCTING MARKETING RESEARCH AND FORECASTING DEMAND

four

Good marketers want insights to help them interpret past performance as well as plan future activities. They nned timely, accurate, and actionable information about consumers, competition, and their brands. They also need to make the best possible tactical decisions in the short run and strategic decisions in the long run. Discovering a consumer insight and understanding its marketing implications can often lead to a successful product launch or spur the growth of a brand.

As part of a $300 million budget for the development of its first razor designed solely for women, Gillette conducted extensive consumer research and performed numerous market tests. The razor, called Venus, was a marked departure from previous women's razor designs, which had essentially been colored or repackaged versions of men's razors. After research revealed that women change their grip on a razor about 30 times during each shaving session, Gillette designed the Venus with a wide, sculpted rubberized handle offering superior grip and control, and oval-shaped blade in a storage case that could stick to shower walls. Research also indicated that women were reluctant to leave the shower in order to replace a dull blade, so the case held spare blade cartridges. The research paid off for Gillette, as the Venus brand accounted for more than $2 billion in >>>

Marketing research led to many of the successful features of Gillette's Venus, the first razor designed for women.

revenues in the four years following its 2001 retail launch and now holds more than 50% of the global women's shaving market. More recently, Gillette successfully leveraged customer insights in creating the six-bladed Fusion.[1]

In this chapter, we review the steps involved in the marketing research process. We also consider how marketers can develop effective metrics for measuring marketing productivity. Finally, we outline how marketers can develop good sales forecasts.

::: The Marketing Research System

Marketing managers often commission formal marketing studies of specific problems and opportunities. They may request a market survey, a product-preference test, a sales forecast by region, or an advertising evaluation. It's the job of the marketing researcher to produce insight into the customer's attitudes and buying behavior. **Marketing insights** provide diagnostic information about how and why we observe certain effects in the marketplace, and what that means to marketers.[2] We define **marketing research** as the systematic design, collection, analysis, and reporting of data and findings relevant to a specific marketing situation facing the company. Spending on marketing research topped $24 billion globally in 2006, according to ESOMAR, the World Association of Opinion and Market Research Professionals.[3]

Most large companies have their own marketing research departments, which often play crucial roles within the organization. Procter & Gamble's Consumer & Market Knowledge (CMK) market research function has dedicated CMK groups working for P&G businesses around the world to improve both their brand strategies and program execution, as well as a relatively smaller, centralized corporate CMK group that focuses on a variety of big-picture concerns that transcend any specific line of business. Yet, marketing research is not limited to large companies with big budgets and marketing research departments. Often at much smaller companies, everyone carries out marketing research—including the customers.

Companies normally budget marketing research at 1% to 2% of company sales. A large percentage of that is spent on the services of outside firms. Marketing research firms fall into three categories:

1. ***Syndicated-service research firms***—These firms gather consumer and trade information, which they sell for a fee. Examples: Nielsen Media Research, SAMI/Burke.
2. ***Custom marketing research firms***—These firms are hired to carry out specific projects. They design the study and report the findings.
3. ***Specialty-line marketing research firms***—These firms provide specialized research services. The best example is the field-service firm, which sells field interviewing services to other firms.

Small companies can hire the services of a marketing research firm or conduct research in creative and affordable ways, such as:

1. ***Engaging students or professors to design and carry out projects***—Companies such as American Express, GE, Hilton Hotels, IBM, Mars, and Whirlpool engage in "crowdcasting" and are sponsors of competitions such as the Innovation Challenge, where top MBA students compete in teams. The payoff to the students is experience and visibility; the payoff to the companies is fresh sets of eyes to solve problems at a fraction of the costs that consultants would charge.[4]

2. ***Using the Internet***—A company can collect considerable information at very little cost by examining competitors' Web sites, monitoring chat rooms, and accessing published data.
3. ***Checking out rivals***—Many small companies routinely visit their competitors. Tom Coohill, a chef who owns two Atlanta restaurants, gives managers a food allowance to dine out and bring back ideas.[5]

Most companies use a combination of marketing research resources to study their industries, competitors, audiences, and channel strategies.

::: The Marketing Research Process

Effective marketing research follows the six steps shown in Figure 4.1. We illustrate them with the following situation:[6]

> American Airlines (AA) was one of the first companies to install phone handsets on its planes. Now it's reviewing many new ideas, especially to cater to its first-class passengers on very long flights, mainly businesspeople whose high-priced tickets pay most of the freight. Among these ideas are: (1) an Internet connection with limited access to Web pages and e-mail messaging; (2) 24 channels of satellite cable TV; and (3) a 50-CD audio system that lets each passenger create a customized in-flight play list. The marketing research manager was assigned to investigate how first-class passengers would rate these services, specifically the Internet connection, and how much extra they would be willing to pay for it. One source estimates revenues of $70 billion from in-flight Internet access over 10 years, if enough first-class passengers paid $25. AA could thus recover its costs in a reasonable time. Making the connection available would cost the airline $90,000 per plane.[7]

Step 1: Define the Problem, the Decision Alternatives, and the Research Objectives

Marketing managers must be careful not to define the problem too broadly or too narrowly for the marketing researcher. A marketing manager who says, "Find out everything you can about first-class air travelers' needs," will collect a lot of unnecessary information. One who says, "Find out whether enough passengers aboard a B747 flying direct between Chicago and Tokyo would be willing to pay $25 for an Internet connection for American Airlines to break even in one year on the cost of offering this service," is taking too narrow a view of the problem.

The marketing researcher might even ask, "Why does the Internet connection have to be priced at $25 as opposed to $10, $50, or some other price? Why does American have to break even on the cost of the service, especially if it attracts new customers?" Another relevant question is: How important is it to be first in the market, and how long can the company sustain its lead?

The marketing manager and marketing researcher agreed to define the problem as follows: "Will offering an in-flight Internet service create enough incremental preference and profit for American Airlines to justify its cost against other possible investments in service enhancements American might make?" To help in designing the research, management should first spell out the decisions it might face and then work backward. Suppose management outlines these decisions: (1) Should American offer an Internet connection? (2) If so, should we offer the service to first-class only, or include business class, and possibly economy class? (3) What price(s) should we charge? (4) On what types of planes and lengths of trips should we offer the service?

Now management and marketing researchers are ready to set specific research objectives: (1) What types of first-class passengers would respond most to using an in-flight Internet service? (2) How many first-class passengers are likely to use the Internet service at different price levels? (3) How many extra first-class passengers might choose American because of this new service? (4) How much long-term goodwill will this service add to American Airlines' image? (5) How important is Internet service to first-class passengers relative to other services, such as a power plug or enhanced entertainment?

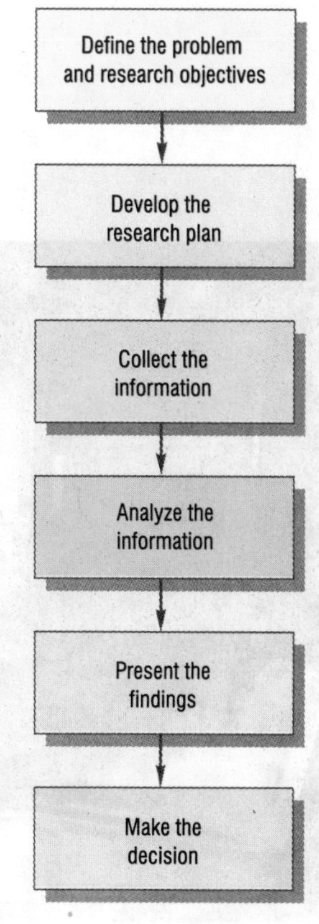

FIG. 4.1

The Marketing Research Process

Not all research projects can be this specific. Some research is *exploratory*—its goal is to shed light on the real nature of the problem and to suggest possible solutions or new ideas. Some research is *descriptive*—it seeks to quantify demand, such as how many first-class passengers would purchase in-flight Internet service at $25. Some research is *causal*—its purpose is to test a cause-and-effect relationship.

Step 2: Develop the Research Plan

The second stage of marketing research is where we develop the most efficient plan for gathering the needed information and what that will cost. Suppose the company made a prior estimate that launching in-flight Internet service would yield a long-term profit of $50,000. If the manager believes that doing the marketing research will lead to an improved pricing and promotional plan and a long-term profit of $90,000, he should be willing to spend up to $40,000 on this research. If the research will cost more than $40,000, it's not worth doing.[8]

To design a research plan, we need to make decisions about the data sources, research approaches, research instruments, sampling plan, and contact methods.

DATA SOURCES The researcher can gather secondary data, primary data, or both. *Secondary data* are data that were collected for another purpose and already exist somewhere. *Primary data* are data freshly gathered for a specific purpose or for a specific research project.

Researchers usually start their investigation by examining some of the rich variety of low-cost and readily available secondary data, to see whether they can partly or wholly solve the problem without collecting costly primary data. For instance, auto advertisers looking to get a better return on their online car ads might purchase a copy of J.D. Power and Associates' "Online Media Study—Wave 1," a survey that gives insights into who buys specific brands and where on the Web advertisers can find them. Among the helpful findings they would discover in the report are:

- The 6% of adults per year who buy a new car are six times more likely to frequent financial sites such as MSN Money and Yahoo! Finance than the average Web user.
- People who bought mid-sized pick-up trucks spent more time on sports Web sites.
- Women who purchase minivans and large SUVs also used Disney's online and game sites.[9]

When the needed data don't exist or are dated, inaccurate, incomplete, or unreliable, the researcher will need to collect primary data. Most marketing research projects do include some primary-data collection.

RESEARCH APPROACHES Marketers collect primary data in five main ways: through observation, focus groups, surveys, behavioral data, and experiments.

Observational Research Researchers can gather fresh data by observing the relevant actors and settings, unobtrusively observing as they shop or as they consume products.[10] Sometimes they equip consumers with pagers and instruct them to write down what they're doing whenever prompted, or they hold informal interview sessions at a café or bar. Photographs can also provide a wealth of detailed information.

A picture is worth 1,000 words to skilled marketing researchers, who can glean a number of insights from a photo of a Swedish kitchen like this.

Ethnographic Research is a particular observational research approach that uses concepts and tools from anthropology and other social science disciplines to provide deep understanding of how people live and work.[11] The goal is to immerse the researcher into consumers' lives to uncover unarticulated desires that might not surface in any other form of research.[12] Firms such as IBM, Intel, and Steelcase have embraced ethnographic research to design breakthrough products.

Bank of America's ethnographic research following baby-boomer women at home and while they shopped yielded two insights—they rounded up financial transactions because it was more convenient, and those with children found it difficult to save. Subsequent research led to the launch of "Keep the Change," a debit card program whereby purchases are rounded up to the nearest dollar amount and the added difference is automatically transferred from a checking account to a savings account. Since the launch, 2.5 million customers have signed up for the program, opening 700,000 new checking accounts and 1 million new savings accounts in the process.[13]

Many other companies have benefited from ethnographic research.[14]

- After observing the popularity of Chinese-character text messaging in Shanghai, Motorola developed the A732 cell phone, with which users could write messages directly on the keypad using a finger.
- After finding that many of their guests turned their bedrooms into work spaces, TownePlace Suites replaced a dining table with a flexible modular wall unit that could serve as either an office or a place to eat.
- After interviewing contractors and home renovators, OXO developed a set of professional-grade tools for consumers that included a hammer with a fiberglass core to cut vibration and a rubber bumper on top to avoid leaving marks when removing nails.
- After studying how people listen to music, read magazines, and watch TV, Sirius developed a portable satellite-radio player that is easily loaded with up to 50 hours of digital music for later playback.

The development of Sirius' portable satellite radios, such as the Stiletto 10, benefitted from ethnographic research.

Ethnographic research isn't limited just to consumer companies in developed markets. GE's ethnographic research into the plastic-fiber industry showed the firm that it wasn't in a commodity business driven by price as much as it was in an artisanal industry with customers who wanted collaborations at the earliest stages of development. GE completely reoriented the way it interacted with the companies in the plastic-fiber industry as a result. Ethnographic research can be particularly useful in developing markets, especially far-flung rural areas, where companies do not know consumers as well.[15]

The American Airlines researchers might meander around first-class lounges to hear how travelers talk about the different carriers and their features. They can fly on competitors' planes to observe in-flight service.

Focus Group Research A **focus group** is a gathering of 6 to 10 people carefully selected by researchers based on certain demographic, psychographic, or other considerations and brought together to discuss various topics of interest at length. Participants are normally paid a small sum for attending. A professional research moderator provides questions and probes based on the marketing managers' discussion guide or agenda.

Moderators try to discern consumers' real motivations and why they say and do certain things. They typically record the sessions, and marketing managers often remain behind two-way mirrors in the next room. Focus-group research is a useful exploratory step, but researchers must avoid generalizing from focus-group participants to the whole market, because the sample size is too small and the sample is not drawn randomly.

A focus group in session, with marketing people observing through a two-way mirror.

In fact, an increasing number of marketers are relying on other means of collecting information that they believe are less artificial. "Focus groups confirm what you already know," says Eva Steensig, a sociologist at DDB Denmark. DDB, part of the Omnicom Group, introduced a new service called SignBank, which uses the Internet and the advertising agency's global office network to collect thousands of snippets of information about cultural change, identify trends within the data, and advise clients about what it means to them. Consumers are not experts on their own consumption patterns, says Steensig, and this makes them easily led by focus group moderators. DDB and some other advertisers feel it is better to "read the signs" of consumption than ask consumers to self-consciously comment on their own patterns. For instance, DDB's sign spotters in several markets noticed that dinner-party guests were bringing their hosts flowers instead of chocolate, in a nod to current concerns over obesity and health. Anthon Berg, a Danish chocolate company and DDB client, plans to use that information to more closely associate its chocolate with different social occasions.[16]

"Marketing Insight: Conducting Informative Focus Groups" has some practical tips to improve the quality of focus groups. In the American Airlines research, the moderator might start with a broad question, such as, "How do you feel about first-class air travel?" Questions then move to how people view the different airlines, different existing services, different proposed services, and specifically, Internet service.

Survey Research Companies undertake surveys to learn about people's knowledge, beliefs, preferences, and satisfaction and to measure these magnitudes in the general population. A company such as American Airlines might prepare its own survey instrument to gather the information it needs, or it might add questions to an omnibus survey that carries the questions of several companies, at a much lower cost. It can also put the questions to an ongoing consumer panel run by itself or another company. It may do a mall intercept study by having researchers approach people in a shopping mall and ask them questions.

As we'll discuss in more detail later in this chapter, many marketers are taking their surveys online where they can easily develop, administer, and collect e-mail and Web-based questionnaires. "Companies are doing this on a much more frequent basis now, and they're using surveys as more of a performance-management tool; they tie the results to managers' compensation," says Charles Cornwell, a senior vice president at TNS Custom Research of North America. Cornwell reports that business at his division, which creates and conducts surveys, has increased 20% to 30% over the past two years. However they conduct their surveys—online, by phone, or in person—companies must feel the information they're getting from the mounds of data makes it all worthwhile. Here are two that do:

- ***Comcast Corp.*** This cable TV giant surveys between 10,000 and 15,000 customers each month by phone. Customer feedback has resulted in a more accommodating installation schedule that allows customers who sign up for cable TV or broadband Internet service to get a visit from a technician on Saturday afternoon or at 7 PM on weeknights. No more staying home all day waiting for "the cable guy."
- ***Wells Fargo.*** The San Francisco-based bank collects more than 50,000 customer surveys each month through its bank branches. It has used customers' comments to begin more stringent new wait-time standards designed to improve customer satisfaction.

Of course by putting out so many surveys each month, companies may run the risk of creating "survey burnout" and seeing response rates plummet. Keeping a survey short and simple and contacting customers no more than once a month are two keys to drawing people into the data collection effort. Offering incentives is another way companies get consumers to respond. Both Gap Inc. and Jack in the Box Inc. offer coupons for discount merchandise or the chance to win a cash prize.[17]

MARKETING INSIGHT | CONDUCTING INFORMATIVE FOCUS GROUPS

Focus groups allow marketers to observe how and why consumers accept or reject concepts, ideas, or any specific notion. The key to using focus groups successfully is to *listen and observe.* Marketers should eliminate their own biases as much as possible. Although many useful insights can emerge from thoughtfully run focus groups, questions can arise about their validity, especially in today's marketing environment.

Some researchers believe that consumers have been so bombarded with ads, they unconsciously (or perhaps cynically) parrot back what they've already heard instead of what they really think. There's always a concern that participants are just trying to maintain their self-image and public persona or have a need to identify with the other members of the group. Participants also may not be willing to admit in public—or may not even recognize—their behavior patterns and motivations. And the "loudmouth" or "know-it-all" problem often crops up when one highly opinionated person drowns out the rest of the group. It may be expensive to recruit qualified subjects who meet the sampling criteria ($3,000 to $5,000 per group), but getting the right participants is crucial.

Even when marketers use multiple focus groups, it may be difficult to generalize the results to a broader population. For example, within the United States, focus-group findings often vary from region to region. One firm specializing in focus-group research claimed that the best city to conduct groups was Minneapolis, because it could get a sample of fairly well-educated people who were honest and forthcoming with their opinions. Many marketers interpret focus groups in New York and other northeastern cities carefully, because the people in these areas tend to be highly critical and generally don't report that they like much.

Participants must feel as relaxed as possible and strongly motivated to be truthful. Physical surroundings can be crucial to achieving the right atmosphere. At one agency an executive noted, "We wondered why people always seemed grumpy and negative—people were resistant to any idea we showed them." Finally in one session a fight broke out between participants. The problem was the room itself: cramped, stifling, forbidding. "It was a cross between a hospital room and a police interrogation room." To fix the problem, the agency gave the room a makeover. Other firms are adapting the look of the room to fit the theme of the topic—such as designing the room to look like a playroom when speaking to children.

Many firms are substituting observational research for focus groups, but ethnographic observation can be expensive and tricky: Researchers must be highly skilled and participants on the level. Then there are mounds of data to analyze. The beauty of focus groups, as one marketing executive noted, is that "it's still the most cost-effective, quickest, dirtiest way to get information in rapid time on an idea." In analyzing the pros and cons, Wharton's Americus Reed might have said it best: "A focus group is like a chain saw. If you know what you're doing, it's very useful and effective. If you don't, you could lose a limb."

Sources: Naomi R. Henderson, "Beyond Top of Mind," *Marketing Research,* September 1, 2005; Rebecca Harris, "Do Focus Groups Have a Future?" *Marketing,* June 6, 2005, p. 17; Malcolm Gladwell, *Blink: The Power of Thinking Without Thinking* (New York: Little Brown, 2005); Linda Tischler, "Every Move You Make," *Fast Company* (April 2004): 73–75; Alison Stein Wellner, "The New Science of Focus Groups," *American Demographics* (March 2003): 29–33; Dennis Rook, "Out-of-Focus Groups," *Marketing Research* 15, no. 2 (Summer 2003): 11; Dennis W. Rook, "Loss of Vision: Focus Groups Fail to Connect Theory, Current Practice," *Marketing News,* September 15, 2003, p. 40; Sarah Jeffrey Kasner, "Fistfights and Feng Shui," *Boston Globe,* July 21, 2001.

Behavioral Data Customers leave traces of their purchasing behavior in store scanning data, catalog purchases, and customer databases. Marketers can learn much by analyzing these data. Actual purchases reflect consumers' preferences and often are more reliable than statements they offer to market researchers. For example, grocery shopping data show that high-income people don't necessarily buy the more expensive brands, contrary to what they might state in interviews; and many low-income people buy some expensive brands. Clearly, American Airlines can learn many useful things about its passengers by analyzing ticket purchase records and online behavior.

Experimental Research The most scientifically valid research is **experimental research**, designed to capture cause-and-effect relationships by eliminating competing explanations of the observed findings. If the experiment is well designed and executed, research and marketing managers can have confidence in the conclusions.

Experiments call for selecting matched groups of subjects, subjecting them to different treatments, controlling extraneous variables, and checking whether observed response differences are statistically significant. If we can eliminate or control extraneous factors, we can relate the observed effects to the variations in the treatments or stimuli. American Airlines might introduce in-flight Internet service on one of its regular flights from Chicago to Tokyo and charge $25 one week and $15 the next week. If the plane carried approximately the same number of first-class passengers each week and the particular weeks made no difference, the airline could relate any significant difference in the number of passengers using the service to the different prices charged.

RESEARCH INSTRUMENTS Marketing researchers have a choice of three main research instruments in collecting primary data: questionnaires, qualitative measures, and technological devices.

Questionnaires A **questionnaire** consists of a set of questions presented to respondents. Because of its flexibility, it is by far the most common instrument used to collect primary data. Researchers need to carefully develop, test, and debug questionnaires before administering them on a large scale. The form, wording, and sequence of the question can all influence the response. *Closed-end questions* specify all the possible answers and provide answers that are easier to interpret and tabulate. *Open-end questions* allow respondents to answer in their own words and often reveal more about how people think. They are especially useful in exploratory research, where the researcher is looking for insight into how people think rather than measuring how many people think a certain way. Table 4.1 provides examples of both types of questions; also see "Marketing Memo: Questionnaire Dos and Don'ts."

Qualitative Measures Some marketers prefer more qualitative methods for gauging consumer opinion, because consumer actions don't always match their answers to survey questions. *Qualitative research techniques* are relatively unstructured measurement approaches that permit a range of possible responses. Their variety is limited only by the creativity of the marketing researcher.

MOBILTEC

Mobiltec, a San Mateo, California-based company that offers content management software for wireless service providers, has an ingenious way of conducting global research on what teens want on their cell phones in terms of media, ringtones, games, music, and TV. The Mobiltec Lab consists of 11 teens aged 13–17 from around the world. Each month these teens find, access, use, and pay for different types of mobile content and then rate their experiences at every stage of the process. In their first assignment, for instance, Mobiltec asked Lab members to use their phones to download four mobile games: two specific ones (Jamdat Bowling, PacMan, or Tetris) and two games of their choice. The teens then rated their experience in downloading the game as well as things such as price. Because the teens expected the same ease, speed, graphics, sound, and marketing they get on the Internet, they were frustrated, for example, if a game took more than 10 seconds to load. They all felt the price, from $2 in India to $7 in Europe and the United States, was too high for length and quality.[18]

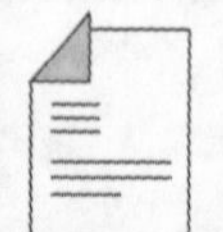

MARKETING MEMO | QUESTIONNAIRE DOS AND DON'TS

1. Ensure that questions are without bias. Don't lead the respondent into an answer.
2. Make the questions as simple as possible. Questions that include multiple ideas or two questions in one will confuse respondents.
3. Make the questions specific. Sometimes it's advisable to add memory cues. For example, be specific with time periods.
4. Avoid jargon or shorthand. Avoid trade jargon, acronyms, and initials not in everyday use.
5. Steer clear of sophisticated or uncommon words. Only use words in common speech.
6. Avoid ambiguous words. Words such as "usually" or "frequently" have no specific meaning.
7. Avoid questions with a negative in them. It is better to say, "Do you ever . . .?" than "Do you never . . .?"
8. Avoid hypothetical questions. It's difficult to answer questions about imaginary situations. Answers aren't necessarily reliable.
9. Do not use words that could be misheard. This is especially important when administering the interview over the telephone. "What is your opinion of sects?" could yield interesting but not necessarily relevant answers.
10. Desensitize questions by using response bands. To ask people their age or ask companies about employee turnover rates, offer a range of response bands instead of precise numbers.
11. Ensure that fixed responses do not overlap. Categories used in fixed-response questions should be distinct and not overlap.
12. Allow for "other" in fixed-response questions. Precoded answers should always allow for a response other than those listed.

Source: Adapted from Paul Hague and Peter Jackson, *Market Research: A Guide to Planning, Methodology, and Evaluation* (London: Kogan Page, 1999). See also, Hans Baumgartner and Jan-Benedict E. M. Steenkamp, "Response Styles in Marketing Research: A Cross-National Investigation," *Journal of Marketing Research* (May 2001): 143–56.

TABLE 4.1 Types of Questions

Name	Description	Example
A. Closed-End Questions		
Dichotomous	A question with two possible answers	In arranging this trip, did you personally phone American? Yes No
Multiple choice	A question with three or more answers	With whom are you traveling on this flight? ☐ No one ☐ Children only ☐ Spouse ☐ Business associates/friends/relatives ☐ Spouse and children ☐ An organized tour group
Likert scale	A statement with which the respondent shows the amount of agreement/disagreement	Small airlines generally give better service than large ones. Strongly disagree 1___ Disagree 2___ Neither agree nor disagree 3___ Agree 4___ Strongly agree 5___
Semantic differential	A scale connecting two bipolar words. The respondent selects the point that represents his or her opinion.	American Airlines Large ---------- Small Experienced ---------- Inexperienced Modern ---------- Old-fashioned
Importance scale	A scale that rates the importance of some attribute	Airline in-flight service to me is Extremely important 1___ Very important 2___ Somewhat important 3___ Not very important 4___ Not at all important 5___
Rating scale	A scale that rates some attribute from "poor" to "excellent"	American in-flight service is Excellent 1___ Very Good 2___ Good 3___ Fair 4___ Poor 5___
Intention-to-buy scale	A scale that describes the respondent's intention to buy	If an in-flight telephone were available on a long flight, I would Definitely buy 1___ Probably buy 2___ Not sure 3___ Probably not buy 4___ Definitely not buy 5___
B. Open-End Questions		
Completely unstructured	A question that respondents can answer in an almost unlimited number of ways	What is your opinion of American Airlines?
Word association	Words are presented, one at a time, and respondents mention the first word that comes to mind.	What is the first word that comes to your mind when you hear the following? Airline___ American___ Travel___
Sentence completion	An incomplete sentence is presented and respondents complete the sentence.	When I choose an airline, the most important consideration in my decision is ___.
Story completion	An incomplete story is presented, and respondents are asked to complete it.	"I flew American a few days ago. I noticed that the exterior and interior of the plane had very bright colors. This aroused in me the following thoughts and feelings. . . ." Now complete the story.
Picture	A picture of two characters is presented, with one making a statement. Respondents are asked to identify with the other and fill in the empty balloon.	WELL HERE'S THE FOOD.
Thematic Apperception Test (TAT)	A picture is presented and respondents are asked to make up a story about what they think is happening or may happen in the picture.	

Because of the freedom afforded both researchers in their probes and consumers in their responses, qualitative research can often be a useful first step in exploring consumers' brand and product perceptions, but it has its drawbacks. Marketers must temper the in-depth insights that emerge with the fact that the samples are often very small and may not necessarily generalize to broader populations. And different researchers examining the same qualitative results may draw very different conclusions. "Marketing Insight:

MARKETING INSIGHT | GETTING INTO CONSUMERS' HEADS WITH QUALITATIVE RESEARCH

Here are some popular qualitative research approaches to getting inside consumers' minds and finding out what they think or feel about brands and products:

1. ***Word associations.*** Ask subjects what words come to mind when they hear the brand's name. "What does the Timex name mean to you? Tell me what comes to mind when you think of Timex watches." The primary purpose of free-association tasks is to identify the range of possible brand associations in consumers' minds. But they may also provide some rough indication of the relative strength, favorability, and uniqueness of brand associations.
2. ***Projective techniques.*** Give people an incomplete stimulus and ask them to complete it, or give them an ambiguous stimulus and ask them to make sense of it. One such approach is "bubble exercises" in which empty bubbles, like those found in cartoons, appear in scenes of people buying or using certain products or services. Subjects fill in the bubble, indicating what they believe is happening or being said. Another technique is comparison tasks in which people compare brands to people, countries, animals, activities, fabrics, occupations, cars, magazines, vegetables, nationalities, or even other brands.
3. ***Visualization.*** Visualization requires people to create a collage from magazine photos or drawings to depict their perceptions. The ZMET technique asks participants in advance to select a minimum of 12 images from their own sources (magazines, catalogs, family photo albums) to represent their thoughts and feelings about the research topic. In a one-on-one interview the study administrator uses advanced interview techniques to explore the images with the participant and reveal hidden meanings. Finally, the participants use a computer program to create a collage with these images that communicates their subconscious thoughts and feelings about the topic. In one ZMET study about pantyhose, some of the respondents' pictures showed fence posts encased in plastic wrap or steel bands strangling trees, suggesting that pantyhose are tight and inconvenient. Another picture showed tall flowers in a vase, suggesting that the product made a woman feel thin, tall, and sexy.
4. ***Brand personification.*** Ask subjects what kind of person they think of when the brand is mentioned: "If the brand were to come alive as a person, what would it be like, what would it do, where would it live, what would it wear, who would it talk to if it went to a party (and what would it talk about)?" For example, the John Deere brand might make someone think of a rugged Midwestern male who is hardworking and trustworthy. The brand personality delivers a picture of the more human qualities of the brand.
5. ***Laddering.*** A series of increasingly more specific "why" questions can reveal consumer motivation and consumers' deeper, more abstract goals. Ask why someone wants to buy a Nokia cellular phone. "They look well built" (attribute). "Why is it important that the phone be well built?" "It suggests that the Nokia is reliable" (a functional benefit). "Why is reliability important?" "Because my colleagues or family can be sure to reach me" (an emotional benefit). "Why must you be available to them at all times?" "I can help them if they're in trouble" (brand essence). The brand makes this person feel like a Good Samaritan, ready to help others.

Drawings or other pictures that express consumers' feelings about products are part of ZMET studies. This drawing shows what one antismoking campaign research participant felt.

Sources: Catherine Marshall and Gretchen B. Rossman, *Designing Qualitative Research*, 4th ed. (Thousand Oaks, CA: Sage Publications, 2006); Bruce L. Berg, *Qualitative Research Methods for the Social Sciences*, 6th ed. (Boston: Allyn & Bacon, 2006); Norman K. Denzin and Yvonna S. Lincoln, eds., *The Sage Handbook of Qualitative Research*, 3rd ed. (Thousand Oaks, CA: Sage Publications, 2005); Linda Tischler, "Every Move You Make," *Fast Company* (April 2004): 73–75; Gerald Zaltman, *How Customers Think: Essential Insights into the Mind of the Market* (Boston: Harvard Business School Press, 2003).

Getting into Consumers' Heads with Qualitative Research" describes some popular approaches.

Technological Devices Technological devices are occasionally useful in marketing research. Galvanometers can measure the interest or emotions aroused by exposure to a specific ad or picture. The tachistoscope flashes an ad to a subject with an exposure interval that may range from less than one hundredth of a second to several seconds. After each exposure, the respondent describes everything he recalls. Eye cameras study respondents' eye movements to see where their eyes land first, how long they linger on a given item, and so on.

Technology has now advanced to such a degree that marketers can use devices such as skin sensors, brain wave scanners, and full body scanners to get consumer responses.[19] TACODA, an advertising technology company, is studying the eye movements and brain activity of Web surfers to see which ads grab their attention.[20] "Marketing Insight: Understanding Brain Science" provides a glimpse into some new marketing research frontiers studying the brain.

Technology has replaced the diaries that participants in media surveys used to keep. Audiometers attached to television sets in participating homes now record when the set is on and to which channel it is tuned. Electronic devices can record the number of radio programs a person is exposed to during the day, or, using Global Positioning System (GPS) technology, how many billboards a person may walk by or drive by during a day. Technology is also used to capture consumer reactions to programming content.

MARKETING INSIGHT | UNDERSTANDING BRAIN SCIENCE

As an alternative to traditional consumer research, some researchers have begun to develop sophisticated techniques from neuroscience that monitor brain activity to better gauge consumer responses to marketing stimuli.

For example, a group of researchers at UCLA used functional magnetic resonance imaging (fMRI) to measure how consumers' brains responded to 2006 Super Bowl advertisements. The research demonstrated how consumers' stated preferences often contradict their inner thoughts and emotions. The fMRI showed that the "I'm going to Disney World" ad featuring members of both teams rehearsing the famous line elicited the highest levels of positive brain activity, followed by a Sierra Mist commercial starring an airport security screener and a traveler. Yet in a consumer poll conducted independently, a Bud Light ad rated highest, despite not generating significant positive reaction in the fMRI tests.

Although it can be more effective in uncovering inner emotions than conventional techniques, neurological research is costly, running as much as $100,000 per project. One major finding to emerge from neurological consumer research is that many purchase decisions are characterized less by the logical weighing of variables than was previously assumed and more "as a largely unconscious habitual process, as distinct from the rational, conscious, information-processing model of economists and traditional marketing textbooks." Even basic decisions, such as the purchase of gasoline, are influenced by brain activity at the subrational level.

Neurological research can be used to measure the type of emotional response that consumers exhibit when presented with marketing stimuli. A group of researchers in England used an electroencephalograph (EEG) to monitor cognitive functions related to memory recall and attentiveness for 12 different regions of the brain as subjects were exposed to advertising. Brain wave activity in different regions indicated different emotional responses. For example, heightened activity in the left prefrontal cortex is characteristic of an "approach" response to an ad and indicates an attraction to the stimulus. In contrast, a spike in brain activity in the right prefrontal cortex is indicative of a strong revulsion to the stimulus. In yet another part of the brain, the degree of memory formation activity correlates with purchase intent. Other research has shown that people activate different regions of the brain in assessing the personality traits of people versus brands.

The term *neuromarketing* has been used to describe brain research on the effect of marketing stimuli. By adding neurological techniques to their research arsenal, marketers are trying to move toward a more complete picture of what goes on inside consumers' heads. Given the complexity of the human brain, however, many researchers caution that neurological research should not form the sole basis for marketing decisions. These research activities have not been universally applauded though. Critics think that such a development will only lead to more marketing manipulation by companies.

Sources: Carolyn Yoon, Angela H. Gutchess, Fred Feinberg, and Thad A. Polk, "A Functional Magnetic Resonance Imaging Study of Neural Dissociations between Brand and Person Judgments," *Journal of Consumer Research* 33 (June 2006): 31–40; Daryl Travis, "Tap Buyers' Emotions for Marketing Success," *Marketing News*, February 1, 2006, pp. 21–22; Deborah L. Vence, "Pick Someone's Brain," *Marketing News*, May 1, 2006, pp. 11–13; Louise Witt, "Inside Intent," *American Demographics* (March 2004): 34–39; Samuel M. McClure, Jian Li, Damon Tomlin, Kim S. Cypert, Latané M. Montague, and P. Read Montague, "Neural Correlates of Behavioral Preference for Culturally Familiar Drinks," *Neuron* 44, October 14, 2004, pp. 379–87; Melanie Wells, "In Search of the Buy Button," *Forbes*, September 1, 2003.

ASI ENTERTAINMENT

Television networks use marketing research to test their TV pilot ideas. ASI, the largest testing company, counts all the major broadcast and cable TV networks among its clients. In a small screening room outfitted with two-way mirrors and video cameras, 48 voluntary subjects take their seats and watch pilots on twin TV sets at the front of the room. At each seat the subjects use a handset to register their reaction, turning the dial from a neutral position to a minus, double minus, plus, or double plus. If they think a show is really poor, they can hit a red button to indicate they'd turn it off at home. Networks such as CBS and Fox pay as much as $20,000 per two-hour session to find their shows' weak points. Testing isn't perfect, however. Three shows that would have hit the cutting room floor if marketers had listened to test results are *All in the Family, Seinfeld,* and *Lost.*[21]

SAMPLING PLAN After deciding on the research approach and instruments, the marketing researcher must design a sampling plan. This calls for three decisions:

1. ***Sampling unit: Who should we survey?*** In the American Airlines survey, should the sampling unit consist only of first-class business travelers, first-class vacation travelers, or both? Should it include travelers under age 18? Both husbands and wives? Once they have determined the sampling unit, marketers must develop a sampling frame so that everyone in the target population has an equal or known chance of being sampled.
2. ***Sample size: How many people should we survey?*** Large samples give more reliable results, but it's not necessary to sample the entire target population to achieve reliable results. Samples of less than 1% of a population can often provide good reliability, with a credible sampling procedure.
3. ***Sampling procedure: How should we choose the respondents?*** Probability sampling allows confidence limits to be calculated for sampling error and makes the sample more representative. Thus, after choosing the sample the conclusion could be that "the interval five to seven trips per year has 95 chances in 100 of containing the true number of trips taken annually by first-class passengers flying between Chicago and Tokyo." Three types of probability sampling are described in Table 4.2 part A. When the cost or time to use probability sampling is too high, marketing researchers will take nonprobability samples. Table 4.2 part B describes three types.

CONTACT METHODS Now the marketing researcher must decide how to contact the subjects: by mail, by telephone, in person, or online.

Mail Questionnaire The *mail questionnaire* is the best way to reach people who would not give personal interviews or whose responses might be biased or distorted by the interviewers. Mail questionnaires require simple and clearly worded questions. Unfortunately, the response rate is usually low or slow.

TABLE 4.2

Probability and Nonprobability Samples

A. Probability Sample	
Simple random sample	Every member of the population has an equal chance of selection.
Stratified random sample	The population is divided into mutually exclusive groups (such as age groups), and random samples are drawn from each group.
Cluster (area) sample	The population is divided into mutually exclusive groups (such as city blocks), and the researcher draws a sample of the groups to interview.
B. Nonprobability Sample	
Convenience sample	The researcher selects the most accessible population members.
Judgment sample	The researcher selects population members who are good prospects for accurate information.
Quota sample	The researcher finds and interviews a prescribed number of people in each of several categories.

Telephone Interview *Telephone interviewing* is the best method for gathering information quickly; the interviewer is also able to clarify questions if respondents do not understand them. The response rate is typically higher than for mailed questionnaires, but interviews must be brief and not too personal. Telephone interviewing in the United States is getting more difficult because of consumers' growing antipathy toward telemarketers. In late 2003, Congress passed legislation allowing the Federal Trade Commission to restrict telemarketing calls through its "Do Not Call" registry, and consumers have since registered over 125 million phone numbers. Marketing research firms are exempt from the ruling, but many think it spells the beginning of the end for telephone surveys as a marketing research method in the United States. In other parts of the world, such restrictive legislation does not exist. One in nine Africans now owns a phone, so cell phones in Africa are used to convene focus groups in rural areas and to interact with text messages.[22]

Personal Interview *Personal interviewing* is the most versatile method. The interviewer can ask more questions and record additional observations about the respondent, such as dress and body language. At the same time, however, personal interviewing is the most expensive method, is subject to interviewer bias, and requires more administrative planning and supervision. Personal interviewing takes two forms. In *arranged interviews*, marketers contact respondents for an appointment and often offer a small payment or incentive. In *intercept interviews*, researchers stop people at a shopping mall or busy street corner and request an interview on the spot. Intercept interviews must be quick, and they run the risk of including nonprobability samples.

Online Interview There are so many ways to use the Internet to do research. A company can embed a questionnaire on its Web site in different ways and offer an incentive to answer it, or it can place a banner on a frequently visited site such as Yahoo!, inviting people to answer some questions and possibly win a prize. Marketers can also sponsor a chat room or bulletin board and introduce questions from time to time or host a real-time consumer panel or virtual focus group. The company can learn about individuals who visit its site by tracking how they *clickstream* through the Web site and move to other sites. It can post different prices, use different headlines, and offer different product features on different Web sites or at different times to learn the relative effectiveness of its offerings. Online product testing, in which companies float trial balloons for new products, is also growing and providing information much faster than traditional new-product marketing research techniques.

Online research was estimated to make up 33% of all survey-based research in 2006, and Internet-based questionnaires also accounted for nearly one-third of U.S. spending on market research surveys in the same year.[23] Yet, as popular as online research methods are, smart companies are choosing to use them to augment rather than replace more traditional methods. At Kraft Foods, online research is a supplement to traditional research, said Seth Diamond, director of consumer insights and strategy. "Online is not a solution in and of itself to all of our business challenges," he said, "but it does expand our toolkit." For example, insights from Kraft-sponsored online communities helped the company develop its popular line of 100-calorie snacks.[24]

"Marketing Memo: Pros and Cons of Online Research" outlines some of the advantages and disadvantages of online research thus far. Online researchers have also begun to use instant messaging (IM) in various ways—to conduct a chat with a respondent, to probe more deeply with a member of an online focus group, or to direct respondents to a Web site.[25] IM is also a useful way to get teenagers to open up on topics.

Step 3: Collect the Information

The data collection phase of marketing research is generally the most expensive and the most prone to error. Four major problems arise in surveys. Some respondents will not be at home and must be contacted again or replaced. Other respondents will refuse to cooperate. Still others will give biased or dishonest answers. Finally, some interviewers will be biased or dishonest.

Data collection methods are rapidly improving thanks to computers and telecommunications. Some telephone research firms interview from a central location, using professional interviewers to read a set of questions from a monitor and type the respondent's answers into a computer. This procedure eliminates editing and coding, reduces errors, saves time, and produces all the required statistics. Other research firms have set up interactive terminals in shopping centers, where respondents sit at a terminal, read questions from the monitor, and type in their answers. Here's what one firm did to develop its panel.

To learn how Nokia applied market research to develop a mobile handset especially suited for India, visit www.pearsoned.co.in/marketingmanagementindia.

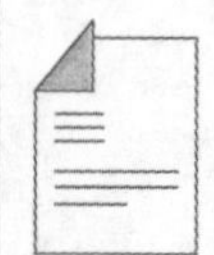

MARKETING MEMO | PROS AND CONS OF ONLINE RESEARCH

Advantages

- ***Online research is inexpensive.*** A typical e-mail survey can cost between 20% and 50% less than what a conventional survey costs, and return rates can be as high as 50%.
- ***Online research is fast.*** Online surveys are fast because the survey can automatically direct respondents to applicable questions and transmit results immediately. One estimate says that 75% to 80% of a survey's targeted response can be generated in 48 hours using online methods, compared to a telephone survey that can take 70 days to obtain 150 interviews.
- ***People tend to be honest online.*** Britain's online polling company YouGov.com surveyed 250 people via intercom in a booth and the other half online, asking questions such as "Should there be more aid to Africa?" Online answers were deemed much more honest. People may be more open about their opinions when they can respond privately and not to another person whom they feel might be judging them, especially on sensitive topics.
- ***Online research is versatile.*** Increased broadband penetration offers online research even more flexibility and capabilities. For instance, virtual reality software lets visitors inspect 3-D models of products such as cameras, cars, and medical equipment and manipulate product characteristics. Even at the basic tactile level, online surveys can make answering a questionnaire easier and more fun than paper-and-pencil versions.

Disadvantages

- ***Samples can be small and skewed.*** Some 33% of households are without Internet access in the United States; the percentage is even higher among lower-income groups, in rural areas, and in most parts of Asia, Latin America, and Central and Eastern Europe, where socioeconomic and education levels also differ. Although it's certain that more and more people will go online, online market researchers must find creative ways to reach population segments on the other side of the "digital divide." One option is to combine offline sources with online findings. Providing temporary Internet access at locations such as malls and recreation centers is another strategy. Some research firms use statistical models to fill in the gaps in market research left by offline consumer segments.
- ***Online market research is prone to technological problems and inconsistencies.*** Because online research is relatively new, many market researchers have not gotten survey designs right. Others overuse technology, concentrating on the bells and whistles and graphics while ignoring basic survey design guidelines. Problems also arise because browser software varies. The Web designer's final product may look very different on the research subject's screen.

Sources: www.consumeraffairs.com, "Survey: Internet Should Remain Open to All," January 25, 2006; www.nclnet.org/, "Highlights from the National Consumers League's Survey on Consumers and Communications Technologies: Current and Future Use," July 21, 2005; Catherine Arnold, "Not Done Net; New Opportunities Still Exist in Online Research," *Marketing News*, April 1, 2004, p. 17; Louella Miles, "Online, on Tap," *Marketing*, June 16, 2004, pp. 39–40; Suzy Bashford, "The Opinion Formers," *Revolution* (May 2004): 42–46; Nima M. Ray and Sharon W. Tabor, "Contributing Factors; Several Issues Affect e-Research Validity," *Marketing News*, September 15, 2003, p. 50; Bob Lamons, "Eureka! Future of B-to-B Research Is Online," *Marketing News*, September 24, 2001, pp. 9–10.

MARKETTOOLS INC.

MarketTools Inc. launched a Hispanic-targeted research panel in 2005, gathering more than 100,000 participants through a combination of off- and online recruitment. MarketTools also works with a direct marketing agency to reach off-line parties and make sure the panel represents the varying degrees of Hispanic acculturation in the United States. Those Hispanics who are almost fully unacculturated, such as seniors and lower-income Hispanics, are almost impossible to reach online, so their off-line responses are blended with the online ones.[26]

One of the biggest obstacles to collecting information internationally is the need to achieve consistency.[27] Nan Martin, global accounts director for Synovate Inc., a market research firm with offices in 46 countries, says: "In global research, we have to adapt culturally to how, where, and with whom we are doing the research. . . . A simple research study conducted globally becomes much more complicated as a result of the cultural nuances, and it's necessary for us to be sensitive to those nuances in data collection and interpretation." Latin American respondents may be more uncomfortable with the impersonal nature of the Internet and need interactive elements in a survey so they feel like they're talking to a real person. On the other hand, in Asia, respondents may feel more pressure to conform and may therefore not be as forthcoming in focus groups as online.

Step 4: Analyze the Information

The next-to-last step in the process is to extract findings by tabulating the data and developing frequency distributions. The researchers now compute averages and measures of dispersion for the major variables and apply some advanced statistical techniques and decision models in the hope of discovering additional findings. They may test different hypotheses and theories, applying sensitivity analysis to test assumptions and the strength of the conclusions.

Step 5: Present the Findings

As the last step, the researcher presents findings relevant to the major marketing decisions facing management. Researchers increasingly are being asked to play a more proactive, consulting role in translating data and information into insights and recommendations.[28] They're also considering ways to present research findings in as understandable and compelling a fashion as possible.

For example, some researchers try to bring data to life for the marketers in their organization.[29] Delta Airlines created a video of its primary business customers, personified in a character called "Ted," and showed it to flight attendants and airport personnel. Chrysler designed rooms for two fictional characters—28-year-old single male Roberto Moore and 30-year-old pharmaceutical rep Jenny Sieverson—and decorated them to reflect the personality, lifestyles, and brand choices of these key targets for the Dodge Caliber and Jeep Compass. Specialty tool and equipment maker Campbell Hausfeld relied on its many suppliers, including Home Depot and Lowe's, to keep it in touch with consumers. After developing eight consumer profiles, including a female do-it-yourselfer and an elderly consumer, the firm was able to successfully launch new products such as drills that weighed less or that included a level for picture hanging.

The main survey findings for the American Airlines case show that:

1. The chief reasons for using in-flight Internet service are to pass the time surfing and to send and receive messages from colleagues and family. Passengers would charge the cost and their companies would pay.
2. At \$25, about 5 of 10 first-class passengers would use Internet service during a flight; about 6 would use it at \$15. Thus, a fee of \$15 would produce less revenue (\$90 = 6 × \$15) than \$25 (\$125 = 5 × \$25). Assuming the same flight takes place 365 days a year, AA could collect \$45,625 (= \$125 × 365) annually. Given an investment of \$90,000, it would take two years to break even.
3. Offering in-flight Internet service would strengthen the public's image of American Airlines as an innovative and progressive airline. American would gain some new passengers and customer goodwill.

Step 6: Make the Decision

The managers who commissioned the research need to weigh the evidence. If their confidence in the findings is low, they may decide against introducing the in-flight Internet service. If they are predisposed to launching the service, the findings support their inclination. They may even decide to study the issues further and do more research. The decision is theirs, but rigorously done research provides them with insight into the problem (see Table 4.3).[30]

A growing number of organizations are using a marketing decision support system to help their marketing managers make better decisions. MIT's John Little defines a **marketing decision support system (MDSS)** as a coordinated collection of data, systems, tools, and techniques, with supporting software and hardware, by which an organization gathers and interprets relevant information from business and environment and turns it into a basis for marketing action.[31]

A classic MDSS example is the CALLPLAN model that helps salespeople determine the number of calls to make per period to each prospect and current client. The model takes into account travel time as well as selling time. When launched, it was tested at United Airlines with an experimental group that increased its sales by 8 percentage points over a matched control group.[32] Once a year, *Marketing News* lists hundreds of current marketing and sales software programs that assist in designing marketing research studies, segmenting markets, setting prices and advertising budgets, analyzing media, and planning sales force activity.

Overcoming Barriers to the Use of Marketing Research

In spite of the rapid growth of marketing research, many companies still fail to use it sufficiently or correctly, for several reasons:[33]

- ***A narrow conception of the research.*** Many managers see marketing research as a fact-finding operation. They expect the researcher to design a questionnaire, choose a sample, conduct interviews, and report results, often without their providing a careful definition of

TABLE 4.3

The Seven Characteristics of Good Marketing Research

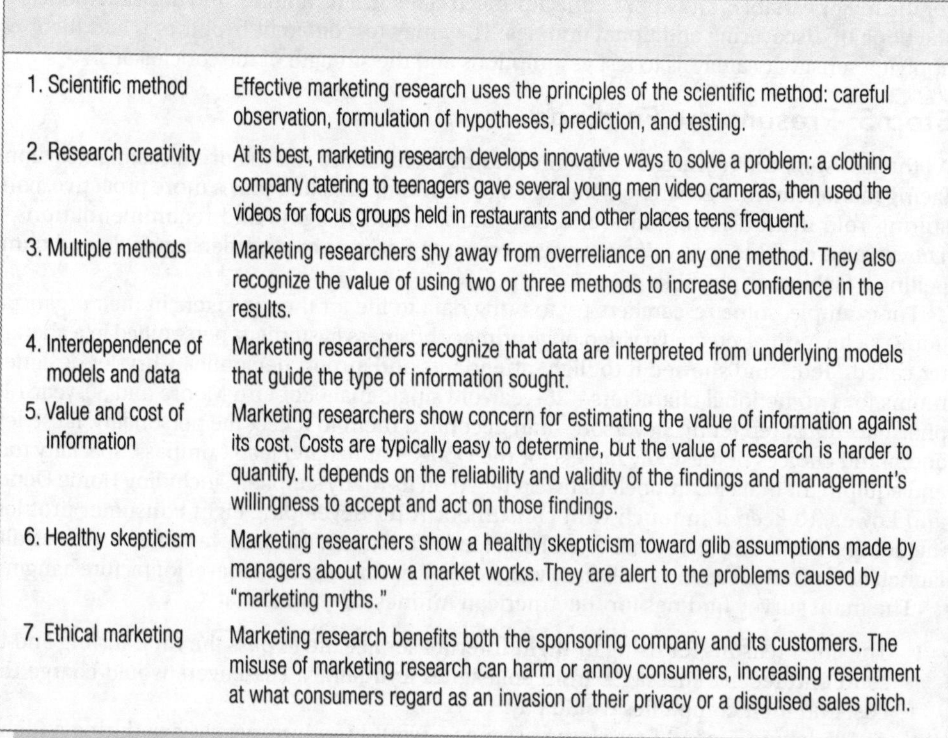

1. Scientific method	Effective marketing research uses the principles of the scientific method: careful observation, formulation of hypotheses, prediction, and testing.
2. Research creativity	At its best, marketing research develops innovative ways to solve a problem: a clothing company catering to teenagers gave several young men video cameras, then used the videos for focus groups held in restaurants and other places teens frequent.
3. Multiple methods	Marketing researchers shy away from overreliance on any one method. They also recognize the value of using two or three methods to increase confidence in the results.
4. Interdependence of models and data	Marketing researchers recognize that data are interpreted from underlying models that guide the type of information sought.
5. Value and cost of information	Marketing researchers show concern for estimating the value of information against its cost. Costs are typically easy to determine, but the value of research is harder to quantify. It depends on the reliability and validity of the findings and management's willingness to accept and act on those findings.
6. Healthy skepticism	Marketing researchers show a healthy skepticism toward glib assumptions made by managers about how a market works. They are alert to the problems caused by "marketing myths."
7. Ethical marketing	Marketing research benefits both the sponsoring company and its customers. The misuse of marketing research can harm or annoy consumers, increasing resentment at what consumers regard as an invasion of their privacy or a disguised sales pitch.

the problem. When fact-finding fails to be useful, management's idea of the limited usefulness of marketing research is reinforced.

- ***Uneven caliber of researchers.*** Some managers view marketing research as little more than a clerical activity and treat it as such. They hire less-competent marketing researchers, whose weak training and low creativity lead to unimpressive results. The disappointing results reinforce management's prejudice against marketing research, and low salaries perpetuate the basic problem.
- ***Poor framing of the problem.*** The famous failure of New Coke was largely due to a failure to set up the research problem correctly, from a marketing perspective. The real issue was how consumers felt about Coca-Cola as a brand, not how they felt about its taste in isolation.
- ***Late and occasionally erroneous findings.*** Managers want results that are accurate and conclusive. They may want the results tomorrow. Yet good marketing research takes time and money. Managers are disappointed when marketing research costs too much or takes too much time.
- ***Personality and presentational differences.*** Differences between the styles of line managers and marketing researchers often get in the way of productive relationships. To a manager who wants concreteness, simplicity, and certainty, a marketing researcher's report may seem abstract, complicated, and tentative. Yet in the more progressive companies, marketing researchers are being included as members of the product management team, and their influence on marketing strategy is growing.

Failure to use marketing research properly has led to numerous gaffes, including this historic one:

STAR WARS

In the 1970s, a successful research executive left General Foods to try a daring gambit: bringing market research to Hollywood, to give film studios access to the same research that had spurred General Foods' success. A major film studio handed him a science fiction film proposal and asked him to research and predict its success or failure. His views would inform the studio's decision about whether to back the film. The executive concluded the film would fail. For one, he argued, Watergate had made the United States less trusting of institutions and, as a result, its citizens in the 1970s prized realism and authenticity over science fiction. This particular film also had the word "war" in its title; he reasoned that viewers, suffering from post-Vietnam hangover, would stay away in droves. The film was *Star Wars*. What this researcher delivered was information, not insight. He failed to study the script itself, to see that it was a fundamentally human story—of love, conflict, loss, and redemption—that happened to play out against the backdrop of space.[34]

One company that has benefited from research-driven insights is IDEO. "Breakthrough Marketing: IDEO" shows how that company has used clever marketing research to come up with innovative product and service designs.

BREAKTHROUGH MARKETING — IDEO

IDEO is the largest industrial-design firm in the United States. The company has created some of the most recognizable design icons of the technology age, including the first laptop computer, the first mouse (for Apple), the Palm V PDA, and the Treo mobile phone. Beyond its high-tech wizardry, the company has designed household items such as the Swiffer Sweeper and the Crest Neat Squeeze toothpaste tube, both for Procter & Gamble. IDEO's diverse roster of clients also includes AT&T, Ford Motor Company, PepsiCo, Nike, Marriott, Caterpillar, Lilly, Lufthansa, Prada, and the Mayo Clinic.

IDEO's success is predicated on its design philosophy of creating products that consumers actively want to use because they offer a superior experience. In order to achieve these consumer-friendly designs, IDEO tries to uncover deep insights through a variety of research methods to better understand how consumers purchase, interact with, use, and even dispose of products. This customer-focused approach has run counter to the prevailing wisdom of many high-tech firms who focus more on their own capabilities when designing products. "Tech companies design from the inside out, whereas we design from the outside in so that we can put customers first," said David Blakely, head of IDEO's technology group.

For example, IDEO often uses observational research techniques to conduct "deep dives" into consumer behavior. The company's "human factors" team shadows consumers, taking pictures or videos of them during product purchase or use occasions, and afterward conducts in-depth interviews with them to further evaluate their experiences. For example, for apparel-maker Warnaco the company's designers shadowed eight women as they shopped for lingerie. The "shop-alongs" revealed that most of their experience buying Warnaco's lingerie was negative. They had difficulty locating the lingerie section in the department store and finding the right size in the overcrowded display, plus the fitting rooms were too small. IDEO developed a new merchandising environment that included larger fitting rooms, "concierges" to give shoppers information, and improved displays, which Warnaco worked with department stores to implement.

IDEO also employs a number of other observational methods. One such method is a "behavioral mapping," which creates a photographic log of people within a certain area (e.g., an airline departure lounge, a hospital waiting room, or a food court at a shopping mall) over a period of days to gauge how the experience can be improved. Another method is "camera journals" that participants keep in which they record their visual impressions of a given product or category. A third such method is "storytelling," where consumers are asked to share personal narratives about their experiences with a product or service.

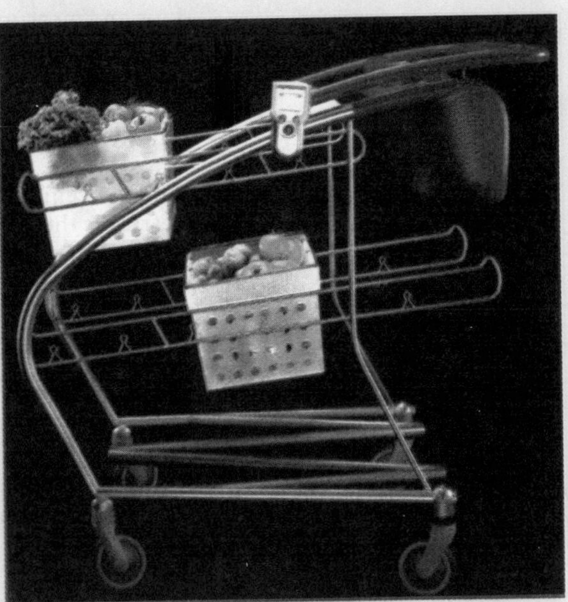

IDEO has designed a number of highly innovative products for consumers. This unique-looking shopping cart was designed to demonstrate its process for innovation for an episode of ABC's late-night news show Nightline.

IDEO also encourages its clients, even senior executives, to participate in the research so they too get a sense for the actual consumer experience with their product or service. For example, AT&T executives were sent on a scavenger hunt designed to test the company's location software for its mMode mobile phones. The executives soon realized that the software was not user-friendly; one exec resorted to calling his wife so she could use Google to help him find an item on the list. IDEO helped AT&T redesign the interface to be more intuitive to the average user.

IDEO's novel consumer-led approach to design has led to countless success stories for its clients, and for the firm itself. In 2005, it generated $70 million in revenues from more than 500 projects. The company also committed to a donation of $35 million to create a new design school at Stanford University that would share the consumer-focused design approach to a new generation of designers.

Sources: Lisa Chamberlain, "Going off the Beaten Path for New Design Ideas," *New York Times*, March 12, 2006; Cindy Taylor, "School of Bright Ideas," *Time*, March 14, 2005, Inside Business/Innovation p. A8; Scott Morrison, "Sharp Focus Gives Design Group the Edge," *Financial Times*, February 18, 2005, Business Life p. 8; Bruce Nussbaum, "The Power of Design," *BusinessWeek*, May 17, 2004, p. 86.

::: Measuring Marketing Productivity

An important task of marketing research is to assess the efficiency and effectiveness of marketing activities.[35] Marketers increasingly are being held accountable for their investments and must be able to justify marketing expenditures to senior management.[36] One survey of top U.S. marketers revealed that around half were not satisfied with their ability to measure the return on their marketing investments.[37] Another revealed that 63% of senior management were dissatisfied with their marketing performance measurement system and wanted marketing to supply prior and posterior estimates of the impact of marketing programs.[38]

Marketing research can help address this increased need for accountability. Two complementary approaches to measuring marketing productivity are: (1) *marketing metrics* to assess marketing effects and (2) *marketing-mix modeling* to estimate causal relationships and measure how marketing activity affects outcomes. *Marketing dashboards* are a structured way to disseminate the insights gleaned from these two approaches within the organization.

Marketing Metrics

Marketers employ a wide variety of measures to assess marketing effects.[39] **Marketing metrics** is the set of measures that helps them quantify, compare, and interpret their marketing performance. Marketing metrics can be used by brand managers to justify and design marketing programs and by senior management to decide on financial allocations.[40]

London Business School's Tim Ambler suggests that if firms think they are already measuring marketing performance adequately, they should ask themselves five questions:[41]

1. Do you routinely research consumer behavior (retention, acquisition, usage) and why consumers behave that way (awareness, satisfaction, perceived quality)?
2. Do you routinely report the results of this research to the board in a format integrated with financial marketing metrics?
3. In those reports, do you compare the results with the levels previously forecasted in the business plans?
4. Do you also compare them with the levels achieved by your key competitor using the same indicators?
5. Do you adjust short-term performance according to the change in your marketing-based asset(s)?

Ambler believes firms must give priority to measuring and reporting marketing performance through marketing metrics. He believes evaluation can be split into two parts: (1) short-term results and (2) changes in brand equity. Short-term results often reflect profit-and-loss concerns as shown by sales turnover, shareholder value, or some combination of the two. Brand-equity measures could include customer awareness, attitudes, and behaviors; market share; relative price premium; number of complaints; distribution and availability; total number of customers; perceived quality, and loyalty and retention.[42] DoubleClick Inc., which places roughly two trillion ads a month for clients, offers 50 different types of metrics to monitor campaigns.[43]

Companies can also monitor an extensive set of metrics internal to the company, such as innovation. For example, 3M tracks the proportion of sales resulting from its recent innovations. Ambler also recommends developing employee measures and metrics, arguing that "end users are the ultimate customers, but your own staff are your first; you need to measure the health of the internal market." Table 4.4 summarizes a list of popular internal and external marketing metrics from Ambler's survey in the United Kingdom.[44]

Marketing-Mix Modeling

Marketing accountability also means that marketers must more precisely estimate the effects of different marketing investments. *Marketing-mix models* analyze data from a variety of sources, such as retailer scanner data, company shipment data, pricing, media, and

TABLE 4.4

Sample Marketing Metrics

I. External	II. Internal
Awareness	Awareness of goals
Market share (volume or value)	Commitment to goals
Relative price (market share value/volume)	Active innovation support
Number of complaints (level of dissatisfaction)	Resource adequacy
Consumer satisfaction	Staffing/skill levels
Distribution/availability	Desire to learn
Total number of customers	Willingness to change
Perceived quality/esteem	Freedom to fail
Loyalty/retention	Autonomy
Relative perceived quality	Relative employee satisfaction

Source: Tim Ambler, "What Does Marketing Success Look Like?" *Marketing Manaement* (Spring 2001): 13--18.

promotion spending data, to understand more precisely the effects of specific marketing activities.[45] To deepen understanding, marketers can conduct multivariate analyses, such as regression analysis, to sort through how each marketing element influences marketing outcomes such as brand sales or market share.[46]

Especially popular with packaged-goods marketers such as Procter & Gamble, Clorox, and Colgate, the findings from marketing-mix modeling help allocate or reallocate expenditures. Analyses explore which part of ad budgets are wasted, what optimal spending levels are, and what minimum investment levels should be.[47]

Although marketing-mix modeling helps to isolate effects, it is less effective at assessing how different marketing elements work in combination. Wharton's Dave Reibstein also notes three other shortcomings:[48]

- Marketing-mix modeling focuses on incremental growth instead of baseline sales or long-term effects.
- Despite their importance, the integration of metrics such as customer satisfaction, awareness, and brand equity into marketing-mix modeling is limited.
- Marketing-mix modeling generally fails to incorporate metrics related to competitors, the trade, or the sales force (the average business spends far more on the sales force and trade promotion than on advertising or consumer promotion).

Marketing Dashboards

Firms are also employing organizational processes and systems to make sure they maximize the value of all these different metrics. Management can assemble a summary set of relevant internal and external measures in a *marketing dashboard* for synthesis and interpretation. Marketing dashboards are like the instrument panel in a car or plane, visually displaying real-time indicators to ensure proper functioning. They are only as good as the information on which they're based, but sophisticated visualization tools are helping bring data alive to improve understanding and analysis.[49]

Some companies are also appointing marketing controllers to review budget items and expenses. Increasingly, these controllers are using business intelligence software to create digital versions of marketing dashboards that aggregate data from disparate internal and external sources.

As input to the marketing dashboard, companies should include two key market-based scorecards that reflect performance and provide possible early warning signals.

- A **customer-performance scorecard** records how well the company is doing year after year on such customer-based measures as those shown in Table 4.5. Management should set norms for each measure and take action when results get out of bounds.

TABLE 4.5

Sample Customer-Performance Scorecard Measures

- Percentage of new customers to average number of customers
- Percentage of lost customers to average number of customers
- Percentage of win-back customers to average number of customers
- Percentage of customers falling into very dissatisfied, dissatisfied, neutral, satisfied, and very satisfied categories
- Percentage of customers who say they would repurchase the product
- Percentage of customers who say they would recommend the product to others
- Percentage of target market customers who have brand awareness or recall
- Percentage of customers who say that the company's product is the most preferred in its category
- Percentage of customers who correctly identify the brand's intended positioning and differentiation
- Average perception of company's product quality relative to chief competitor
- Average perception of company's service quality relative to chief competitor

- A **stakeholder-performance scorecard** tracks the satisfaction of various constituencies who have a critical interest in and impact on the company's performance: employees, suppliers, banks, distributors, retailers, and stockholders. Again, management should take action when one or more groups register increased or above-norm levels of dissatisfaction.[50]

Some executives worry that they'll miss the big picture if they focus too much on a set of numbers on a dashboard. Some critics are concerned about privacy and the pressure the technique places on employees. But most experts feel the rewards offset the risks.[51] "Marketing Insight: Marketing Dashboards to Improve Effectiveness and Efficiency" provides practical advice about the development of these marketing tools.

MARKETING INSIGHT | MARKETING DASHBOARDS TO IMPROVE EFFECTIVENESS AND EFFICIENCY

Marketing consultant Pat LaPointe sees marketing dashboards as providing all the up-to-the-minute information necessary to run the business operations for a company—such as sales versus forecast, distribution channel effectiveness, brand equity evolution, and human capital development. According to LaPointe, an effective dashboard will focus thinking, improve internal communications, and reveal where marketing investments are paying off and where they aren't.

LaPointe observes four common measurement "pathways" marketers are pursuing today (see Figure 4.2).

- The *customer metrics pathway* looks at how prospects become customers, from awareness to preference to trial to repeat purchase. Many companies track progression through a "hierarchy of effects" model to follow the evolution of broad market potential to specific revenue opportunities.
- The *unit metrics pathway* reflects what marketers know about sales of product/service units—how much is sold by product line and/or by geography; the marketing cost per unit sold as an efficiency yardstick; and where and how margin is optimized in terms of characteristics of the product line or distribution channel.
- The *cash-flow metrics pathway* focuses on how well marketing expenditures are achieving short-term returns. Program and campaign ROI models measure the immediate impact or net present value of profits expected from a given investment.
- The *brand metrics pathway* tracks the development of the longer-term impact of marketing through brand equity measures that assess both the perceptual health of the brand from customer and prospective customer perspectives as well as the overall financial health of the brand.

LaPointe feels a marketing dashboard can present insights from all the pathways in a graphically related view that helps management see subtle links between them. A well-constructed dashboard can have a series of "tabs" that allow the user to toggle easily between different "families" of metrics organized by customer, product, experience, brand, channels, efficiency, organizational development, or macroenvironmental factors. Each tab presents the three or four most insightful metrics, with data filtered by business unit, geography, or customer segment based upon the users' needs. (See Figure 4.3 for example.)

Ideally, the number of metrics presented in the marketing dashboard would be reduced to a handful of key drivers over time. Important, the process of developing and refining the marketing dashboard will undoubtedly raise and resolve many key questions about the business.

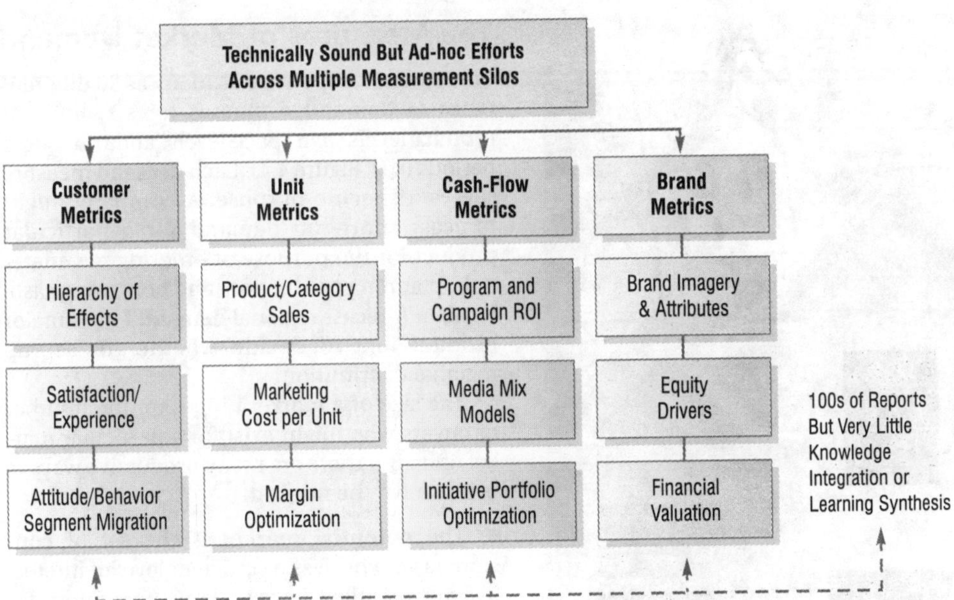

FIG. 4.2

Marketing Measurement Pathway

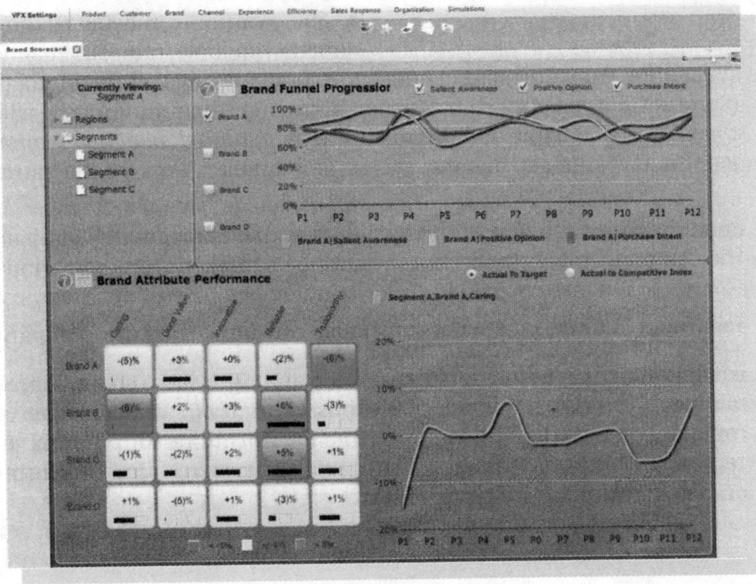

FIG. 4.3

Example of a Marketing Dashboard

Adapted from Patrick LaPointe, *Marketing by the Dashboard Light —How to Get More Insight, Foresight, and Accountability from Your Marketing Investments*, © 2005, Patrick LaPointe.

::: Forecasting and Demand Measurement

One major reason for undertaking marketing research is to identify market opportunities. Once the research is complete, the company must measure and forecast the size, growth, and profit potential of each market opportunity. Sales forecasts are used by finance to raise the needed cash for investment and operations; by the manufacturing department to establish capacity and output levels; by purchasing to acquire the right amount of supplies; and by human resources to hire the needed number of workers. Marketing is responsible for preparing the sales forecasts. If its forecast is far off the mark, the company will face excess or inadequate inventory.

Sales forecasts are based on estimates of demand. Managers need to define what they mean by market demand. Dupont's Performance Materials group doesn't see DuPont Tyvek as having a 70% share of the $100 million market for air barrier membranes. Rather, they evaluate the brand much more broadly in terms of the entire $7 billion U.S. home construction market.[52]

Forecasting demand of products, including building materials such as Tyvek, is part of the job of marketing.

The Measures of Market Demand

Companies can prepare as many as 90 different types of demand estimates for six different product levels, five space levels, and three time periods (see Figure 4.4). Each demand measure serves a specific purpose. A company might forecast short-run demand for a particular product for the purpose of ordering raw materials, planning production, and borrowing cash. It might forecast regional demand for its major product line to decide whether to set up regional distribution.

The size of a market hinges on the number of buyers who might exist for a particular market offer. But there are many productive ways to break down the market:

- The **potential market** is the set of consumers who profess a sufficient level of interest in a market offer. However, consumer interest is not enough to define a market for marketers unless they also have sufficient income and access to the product.
- The **available market** is the set of consumers who have interest, income, *and* access to a particular offer. For some market offers, the company or government may restrict sales to certain groups. For example, a particular state might ban motorcycle sales to anyone under 21 years of age. Eligible adults constitute the *qualified available market*—the set of consumers who have interest, income, access, and qualifications for the particular market offer.
- The **target market** is the part of the qualified available market the company decides to pursue. The company might decide to concentrate its marketing and distribution effort on the East Coast.
- The **penetrated market** is the set of consumers who are buying the company's product.

These definitions are a useful tool for market planning. If the company isn't satisfied with its current sales, it can take a number of actions. It can try to attract a larger percentage of buyers from its target market. It can lower the qualifications for potential buyers. It can expand its available market by opening distribution elsewhere or lowering its price, or it can reposition itself in the minds of its customers.

FIG. 4.4

Ninety Types of Demand Measurement (6 × 5 × 3)

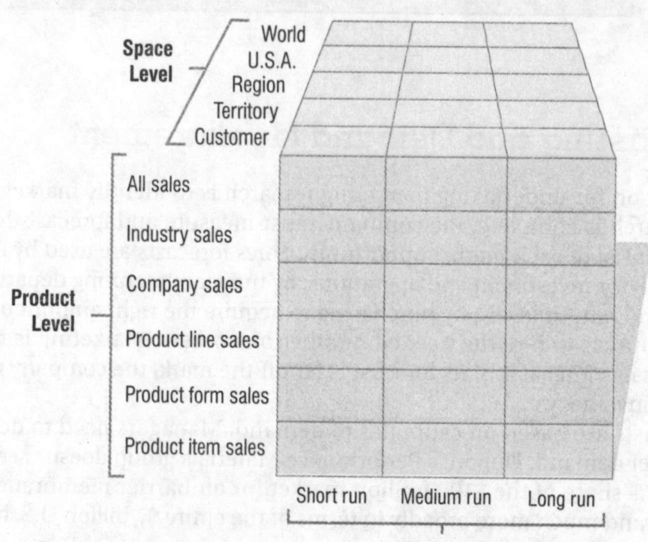

A Vocabulary for Demand Measurement

The major concepts in demand measurement are market demand and company demand. Within each, we distinguish among a demand function, a sales forecast, and a potential.

MARKET DEMAND The marketer's first step in evaluating marketing opportunities is to estimate total market demand. **Market demand** for a product is the total volume that would be bought by a defined customer group in a defined geographical area in a defined time period in a defined marketing environment under a defined marketing program.

Market demand is not a fixed number, but rather a function of the stated conditions. For this reason, we can call it the *market demand function*. The dependence of total market demand on underlying conditions is illustrated in Figure 4.5(a). The horizontal axis shows different possible levels of industry marketing expenditure in a given time period. The vertical axis shows the resulting demand level. The curve represents the estimated market demand associated with varying levels of industry marketing expenditure.

Some base sales—called the *market minimum* and labeled Q_1 in the figure—would take place without any demand-stimulating expenditures. Higher levels of industry marketing expenditures would yield higher levels of demand, first at an increasing rate, then at a decreasing rate. Take fruit juices. Given all the indirect competition they face from other types of beverages, increased marketing expenditures would be expected to help fruit juice products stand out and increase demand and sales. Marketing expenditures beyond a certain level would not stimulate much further demand, thus suggesting an upper limit to market demand, called the *market potential* and labeled Q_2 in the figure.

The distance between the market minimum and the market potential shows the overall *marketing sensitivity of demand*. We can think of two extreme types of market, the expansible and the nonexpansible. An *expansible market*, such as the market for racquetball playing, is very much affected in size by the level of industry marketing expenditures. In terms of Figure 4.5(a), the distance between Q_1 and Q_2 is relatively large. A *nonexpansible market*—for example, the market for weekly trash or garbage removal—is not much affected by the level of marketing expenditures; the distance between Q_1 and Q_2 is relatively small. Organizations selling in a nonexpansible market must accept the market's size—the level of *primary demand* for the product class—and direct their efforts toward winning a larger **market share** for their product, that is, a higher level of selective demand for their product.

It pays to compare the current and potential levels of market demand. The result is called the **market-penetration index.** A low market-penetration index indicates substantial growth potential for all the firms. A high market-penetration index suggests it will be expensive to attract the few remaining prospects. Generally, price competition increases and margins fall when the market-penetration index is already high.

A company should also compare its current and potential market shares. The result is called the company's **share-penetration index**. A low share-penetration index indicates the company can greatly expand its share. The factors holding it back could be many: low brand awareness, low availability, benefit deficiencies, and high price. A firm should calculate the share-penetration increases that would occur if it removed each factor, to see which investments produce the greatest improvement.[53]

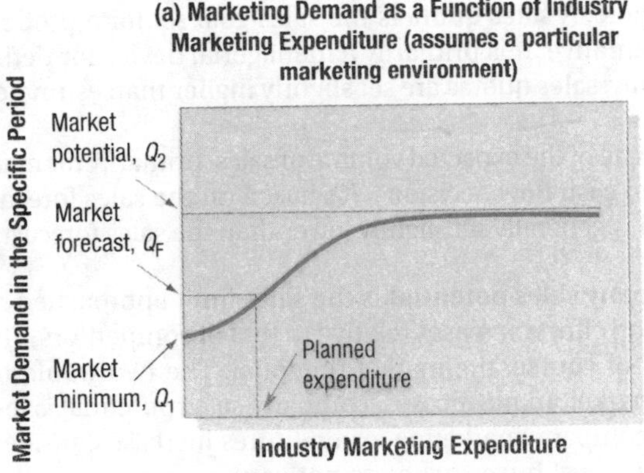

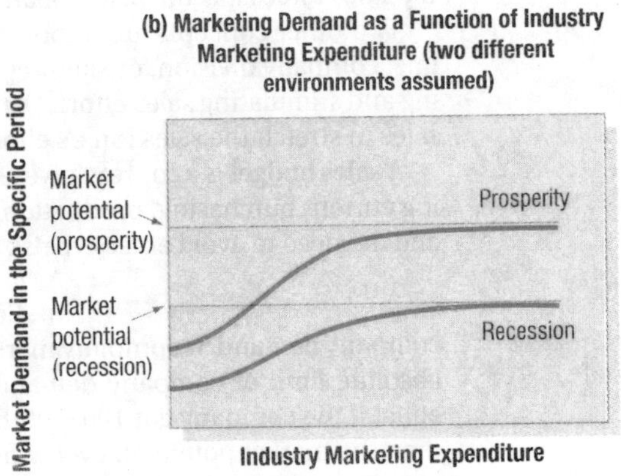

FIG. **4.5** Market Demand Functions

Remember that the market demand function is not a picture of market demand over time. Rather, the curve shows alternative current forecasts of market demand associated with possible levels of industry marketing effort.

MARKET FORECAST Only one level of industry marketing expenditure will actually occur. The market demand corresponding to this level is called the **market forecast**.

MARKET POTENTIAL The market forecast shows expected market demand, not maximum market demand. For the latter, we need to visualize the level of market demand resulting from a "very high" level of industry marketing expenditure, where further increases in marketing effort would have little effect in stimulating further demand. **Market potential** is the limit approached by market demand as industry marketing expenditures approach infinity for a given marketing environment.

The phrase "for a given market environment" is crucial. Consider the market potential for automobiles. It's higher during prosperity than during a recession. The dependence of market potential on the environment is illustrated in Figure 4.5(b). Market analysts distinguish between the position of the market demand function and movement along it. Companies cannot do anything about the position of the market demand function, which is determined by the marketing environment. However, they influence their particular location on the function when they decide how much to spend on marketing.

Companies interested in market potential have a special interest in the **product-penetration percentage**, which is the percentage of ownership or use of a product or service in a population. Companies assume that the lower the product-penetration percentage, the higher the market potential, although this assumes that everyone will eventually be in the market for every product.

COMPANY DEMAND **Company demand** is the company's estimated share of market demand at alternative levels of company marketing effort in a given time period. It depends on how the company's products, services, prices, and communications are perceived relative to the competitors'. If other things are equal, the company's market share will depend on the relative scale and effectiveness of its market expenditures. Marketing model builders have developed sales response functions to measure how a company's sales are affected by its marketing expenditure level, marketing mix, and marketing effectiveness.[54]

COMPANY SALES FORECAST Once marketers have estimated company demand, their next task is to choose a level of marketing effort. The **company sales forecast** is the expected level of company sales based on a chosen marketing plan and an assumed marketing environment.

We represent the company sales forecast graphically with sales on the vertical axis and marketing effort on the horizontal axis, as in Figure 4.5. We often hear that the company should develop its marketing plan on the basis of its sales forecast. This forecast-to-plan sequence is valid if "forecast" means an estimate of national economic activity, or if company demand is nonexpansible. The sequence is not valid, however, where market demand is expansible or where "forecast" means an estimate of company sales. The company sales forecast does not establish a basis for deciding what to spend on marketing. On the contrary, the sales forecast is the result of an assumed marketing expenditure plan.

Two other concepts are important here. A **sales quota** is the sales goal set for a product line, company division, or sales representative. It is primarily a managerial device for defining and stimulating sales effort. Generally, sales quotas are set slightly higher than estimated sales to stretch the sales force's effort.

A **sales budget** is a conservative estimate of the expected volume of sales, primarily for making current purchasing, production, and cash flow decisions. It's based on the sales forecast and the need to avoid excessive risk and is generally set slightly lower than the sales forecast.

COMPANY SALES POTENTIAL **Company sales potential** is the sales limit approached by company demand as company marketing effort increases relative to that of competitors. The absolute limit of company demand is, of course, the market potential. The two would be equal if the company got 100% of the market. In most cases, company sales potential is less than the market potential, even when company marketing expenditures increase considerably. Each competitor has a hard core of loyal buyers who are not very responsive to other companies' efforts to woo them.

Estimating Current Demand

We are now ready to examine practical methods for estimating current market demand. Marketing executives want to estimate total market potential, area market potential, and total industry sales and market shares.

TOTAL MARKET POTENTIAL **Total market potential** is the maximum amount of sales that might be available to all the firms in an industry during a given period, under a given level of industry marketing effort and environmental conditions. A common way to estimate total market potential is to multiply the potential number of buyers by the average quantity each purchases, times the price.

If 100 million people buy books each year, and the average book buyer buys three books a year, and the average price of a book is $20, then the total market potential for books is $6 billion (100 million × 3 × $20). The most difficult component to estimate is the number of buyers for the specific product or market. We can always start with the total population in the nation, say, 261 million people. Next we eliminate groups that obviously would not buy the product. Assume that illiterate people and children under 12 don't buy books and constitute 20% of the population. This means 80% of the population, or 209 million people, are in the potentials pool. We might do further research and find that people of low income and low education don't read books, and they constitute over 30% of the potentials pool. Eliminating them, we arrive at a prospect pool of approximately 146.3 million book buyers. We use this number of prospective buyers to calculate total market potential.

A variation on this method is the *chain-ratio method,* which multiplies a base number by several adjusting percentages. Suppose a brewery is interested in estimating the market potential for a new light beer especially designed to accompany food. It can make an estimate with the following calculation:

Demand for the new light beer	=	Population	×	Average percentage of personal discretionary income per capita spent on food	×	Average percentage of amount spent on food that is spent on beverages	×	Average percentage of amount spent on beverages that is spent on alcoholic beverages	×	Average percentage of amount spent on alcoholic beverages that is spent on beer	×	Expected percentage of amount spent on beer that will be spent on light beer.

AREA MARKET POTENTIAL Because companies must allocate their marketing budget optimally among their best territories, they need to estimate the market potential of different cities, states, and nations. Two major methods of assessing area market potential are the market-buildup method, used primarily by business marketers, and the multiple-factor index method, used primarily by consumer marketers.

Market-Buildup Method The **market-buildup method** calls for identifying all the potential buyers in each market and estimating their potential purchases. This method produces accurate results if we have a list of all potential buyers and a good estimate of what each will buy. Unfortunately, this information is not always easy to gather.

Consider a machine-tool company that wants to estimate the area market potential for its wood lathe in the Boston area. Its first step is to identify all potential buyers of wood lathes in the area, primarily manufacturing establishments that shape or ream wood as part of their operations. The company could compile a list from a directory of all manufacturing establishments in the Boston area. Then it could estimate the number of lathes each industry might purchase, based on the number of lathes per thousand employees or per $1 million of sales in that industry.

An efficient method of estimating area market potentials makes use of the *North American Industry Classification System (NAICS),* developed by the U.S. Bureau of the Census in conjunction with the Canadian and Mexican governments.[55] The NAICS classifies all manufacturing into 20 major industry sectors and further breaks each sector into a six-digit, hierarchical structure as follows.

51	Industry sector (information)
513	Industry subsector (broadcasting and telecommunications)
5133	Industry group (telecommunications)
51332	Industry (wireless telecommunications carriers, except satellite)
513321	National industry (U.S. paging)

For each six-digit NAICS number, a company can purchase CD-ROMs of business directories that provide complete company profiles of millions of establishments, subclassified by location, number of employees, annual sales, and net worth.

To use the NAICS, the lathe manufacturer must first determine the six-digit NAICS codes that represent products whose manufacturers are likely to require lathe machines. To get a full picture of all six-digit NAICS industries that might use lathes, the company can (1) determine past customers' NAICS codes; (2) go through the NAICS manual and check off all the six-digit industries that might have an interest in lathes; (3) mail questionnaires to a wide range of companies inquiring about their interest in wood lathes.

The company's next task is to determine an appropriate base for estimating the number of lathes that each industry will use. Suppose customer industry sales are the most appropriate base. Once the company estimates the rate of lathe ownership relative to the customer industry's sales, it can compute the market potential.

Multiple-Factor Index Method Like business marketers, consumer companies also need to estimate area market potentials, but the customers of consumer companies are too numerous to list. The method most commonly used in consumer markets is a straightforward index method. A drug manufacturer, for example, might assume that the market potential for drugs is directly related to population size. If the state of Virginia has 2.28% of the U.S. population, the company might assume that Virginia would be a market for 2.28% of total drugs sold.

A single factor, however, is rarely a complete indicator of sales opportunity. Regional drug sales are also influenced by per capita income and the number of physicians per 10,000 people. Thus it makes sense to develop a multiple-factor index, with each factor assigned a specific weight. The numbers are the weights attached to each variable. For example, suppose Virginia has 2.00% of the U.S. disposable personal income, 1.96% of U.S. retail sales, and 2.28% of U.S. population, and the respective weights are 0.5, 0.3, and 0.2. The buying-power index for Virginia is then 2.04 [0.5(2.00) + 0.3(1.96) + 0.2(2.28)]. Thus 2.04% of the nation's drug sales (not 2.28%) might be expected to take place in Virginia.

The weights in the buying-power index are somewhat arbitrary, and companies can assign others if appropriate. A manufacturer might also want to adjust the market potential for additional factors, such as competitors' presence in that market, local promotional costs, seasonal factors, and local market idiosyncrasies.

Many companies compute other area indexes as a guide to allocating marketing resources. Suppose the drug company is reviewing the six cities listed in Table 4.6. The first two columns show its percentage of U.S. brand and category sales in these six cities. Column 3 shows the **brand development index (BDI)**, which is the index of brand sales to category sales. Seattle, for example, has a BDI of 114 because the brand is relatively more developed than the category in Seattle. Portland has a BDI of 65, which means that the brand in Portland is relatively underdeveloped. Normally, the lower the BDI, the higher the market opportunity, in that there is room to grow the brand. However, other marketers would argue the opposite—that marketing funds should go into the brand's *strongest* markets, where it might be important to reinforce loyalty or more easily capture additional brand share.[56]

TABLE 4.6

Calculating the Brand Development Index (BDI)

Territory	(a) Percent of U.S. Brand Sales	(b) Percent of U.S. Category Sales	BDI (a ÷ b) × 100
Seattle	3.09	2.71	114
Portland	6.74	10.41	65
Boston	3.49	3.85	91
Toledo	.97	.81	120
Chicago	1.13	.81	140
Baltimore	3.12	3.00	104

After the company decides on the city-by-city allocation of its budget, it can refine each city allocation down to census tracts or zip+4 code centers. *Census tracts* are small, locally defined statistical areas in metropolitan areas and some other counties. They generally have stable boundaries and a population of about 4,000. Zip+4 code centers (which were designed by the U.S. Post Office) are a little larger than neighborhoods. Data on population size, median family income, and other characteristics are available for these geographical units, and marketers have found them extremely useful for identifying high-potential retail areas within large cities or for buying mailing lists to use in direct-mail campaigns (see Chapter 8).

INDUSTRY SALES AND MARKET SHARES Besides estimating total potential and area potential, a company needs to know the actual industry sales taking place in its market. This means identifying competitors and estimating their sales.

The industry trade association will often collect and publish total industry sales, although it usually does not list individual company sales separately. With this information, however, each company can evaluate its own performance against the whole industry. If a company's sales are increasing by 5% a year, and industry sales are increasing by 10%, the company is losing its relative standing in the industry.

Another way to estimate sales is to buy reports from a marketing research firm that audits total sales and brand sales. Nielsen Media Research audits retail sales in various product categories in supermarkets and drugstores and sells this information to interested companies. These audits let a company compare its performance to the total industry or to any particular competitor to see whether it is gaining or losing share either overall or on a brand-by-brand basis.

Because distributors typically will not supply information about how much of competitors' products they are selling, business-goods marketers operate with less knowledge of their market share results.

Estimating Future Demand

The few products or services that lend themselves to easy forecasting generally enjoy an absolute level or a fairly constant trend and competition that is either nonexistent (public utilities) or stable (pure oligopolies). In most markets, in contrast, good forecasting is a key factor in success.

Companies commonly prepare a macroeconomic forecast first, followed by an industry forecast, followed by a company sales forecast. The macroeconomic forecast calls for projecting inflation, unemployment, interest rates, consumer spending, business investment, government expenditures, net exports, and other variables. The end result is a forecast of gross national product, which the firm uses, along with other environmental indicators, to forecast industry sales. The company derives its sales forecast by assuming that it will win a certain market share.

How do firms develop their forecasts? They may create their own or buy forecasts from outside sources such as marketing research firms, which interview customers, distributors, and other knowledgeable parties. Specialized forecasting firms produce long-range forecasts of particular macroenvironmental components, such as population, natural resources, and technology. Some examples are Global Insight (a merger of Data Resources and Wharton Econometric Forecasting Associates), Forrester Research, and the Gartner Group. Futurist research firms produce speculative scenarios; three examples are the Institute for the Future, Hudson Institute, and the Futures Group.

All forecasts are built on one of three information bases: what people say, what people do, or what people have done. Using what people say requires surveying the opinions of buyers or those close to them, such as salespeople or outside experts, with surveys of buyer's intentions, composites of sales force opinions, and expert opinion. Building a forecast on what people do means putting the product into a test market to measure buyer response. To use the final basis—what people have done—firms analyze records of past buying behavior or use time-series analysis or statistical demand analysis.

SURVEY OF BUYERS' INTENTIONS **Forecasting** is the art of anticipating what buyers are likely to do under a given set of conditions. For major consumer durables such as appliances, several research organizations conduct periodic surveys of consumer buying intentions and ask questions like this: *Do you intend to buy an automobile within the next six months?* and put the answers on a **purchase probability scale**:

0.00	0.20	0.40	0.60	0.80	1.00
No chance	Slight possibility	Fair possibility	Good possibility	High possibility	Certain

Surveys also inquire into consumers' present and future personal finances and their expectations about the economy. They combine various bits of information into a consumer confidence measure (Conference Board) or a consumer sentiment measure (Survey Research Center of the University of Michigan).

For business buying, research firms can carry out buyer-intention surveys regarding plant, equipment, and materials. Their estimates tend to fall within a 10% error band around the actual outcomes. Buyer-intention surveys are particularly useful in estimating demand for industrial products, consumer durables, product purchases where advanced planning is required, and new products. The value of a buyer-intention survey increases to the extent that buyers are few, the cost of reaching them is low, and they have clear intentions that they willingly disclose and implement.

COMPOSITE OF SALES FORCE OPINIONS When buyer interviewing is impractical, the company may ask its sales representatives to estimate their future sales.

Few companies use sales force estimates without making some adjustments. Sales representatives might be pessimistic or optimistic, they might not know how their company's marketing plans will influence future sales in their territory, and they might deliberately underestimate demand so the company will set a low sales quota. To encourage better estimating, the company could offer incentives or assistance, such as information about marketing plans or past forecasts compared to actual sales.

Sales force forecasts bring a number of benefits. Sales reps might have better insight into developing trends than any other group, and forecasting might give them greater confidence in their sales quotas and more incentive to achieve them. Also, a "grassroots" forecasting procedure provides detailed estimates broken down by product, territory, customer, and sales rep.

EXPERT OPINION Companies can also obtain forecasts from experts, including dealers, distributors, suppliers, marketing consultants, and trade associations. Dealer estimates are subject to the same strengths and weaknesses as sales force estimates. Many companies buy economic and industry forecasts from well-known economic-forecasting firms that have more data available and more forecasting expertise.

Occasionally, companies will invite a group of experts to prepare a forecast. The experts exchange views and produce an estimate as a group (*group-discussion method*) or individually, in which case another analyst might combine them into a single estimate (*pooling of individual estimates*). Further rounds of estimating and refining follow (this is the Delphi method).[57]

PAST-SALES ANALYSIS Firms can develop sales forecasts on the basis of past sales. *Time-series analysis* breaks past time series into four components (trend, cycle, seasonal, and erratic) and projects them into the future. *Exponential smoothing* projects the next period's sales by combining an average of past sales and the most recent sales, giving more weight to the latter. *Statistical demand analysis* measures the impact of a set of causal factors (such as income, marketing expenditures, and price) on the sales level. Finally, *econometric analysis* builds sets of equations that describe a system and statistically derives the different parameters that make up the equations statistically.

MARKET-TEST METHOD When buyers don't plan their purchases carefully, or experts are unavailable or unreliable, a direct-market test can help forecast new-product sales or established product sales in a new distribution channel or territory. (We discuss market testing in detail in Chapter 20.)

SUMMARY :::

1. Companies can conduct their own marketing research or hire other companies to do it for them. Good marketing research is characterized by the scientific method, creativity, multiple research methods, accurate model building, cost-benefit analysis, healthy skepticism, and an ethical focus.
2. The marketing research process consists of defining the problem, decision alternatives, and research objectives, developing the research plan, collecting the information, analyzing the information, presenting the findings to management, and making the decision.
3. In conducting research, firms must decide whether to collect their own data or use data that already exist. They must also decide which research approach (observational, focus group, survey, behavioral data, or experimental) and which research instruments (questionnaire, qualitative measures, or technological devices) to use. In addition, they must decide on a sampling plan and contact methods (by mail, by phone, in person, or online).
4. Two complementary approaches to measuring marketing productivity are: (1) marketing metrics to assess marketing effects and (2) marketing-mix modeling to estimate causal relationships and measure how marketing activity affects outcomes. Marketing dashboards are a structured way to disseminate the insights gleaned from these two approaches within the organization.
5. There are two types of demand: market demand and company demand. To estimate current demand, companies attempt to determine total market potential, area market potential, industry sales, and market share. To estimate future demand, companies survey buyers' intentions, solicit their sales force's input, gather expert opinions, analyze past sales, or engage in market testing. Mathematical models, advanced statistical techniques, and computerized data collection procedures are essential to all types of demand and sales forecasting.

APPLICATIONS :::

Marketing Debate What Is the Best Type of Marketing Research?

Many market researchers have their favorite research approaches or techniques, although different researchers often have different preferences. Some researchers maintain that the only way to really learn about consumers or brands is through in-depth, qualitative research. Others contend that the only legitimate and defensible form of marketing research involves quantitative measures.

Take a position: The best marketing research is quantitative in nature *versus* The best marketing research is qualitative in nature.

Marketing Discussion

When was the last time you participated in a survey? How helpful do you think was the information you provided? How could the research have been done differently to make it more effective?

PART 3

CONNECTING WITH CUSTOMERS

IN THIS CHAPTER, WE WILL ADDRESS THE FOLLOWING QUESTIONS:

1. What are customer value, satisfaction, and loyalty, and how can companies deliver them?
2. What is the lifetime value of customers and how can marketers maximize it?
3. How can companies cultivate strong customer relationships?
4. How can companies both attract and retain customers?
5. What is database marketing?

CHAPTER 5 ::: CREATING CUSTOMER VALUE, SATISFACTION, AND LOYALTY

five

Today, companies face their toughest competition ever. Moving from a product-and-sales philosophy to a holistic marketing philosophy, however, gives them a better chance of outperforming competition. And the cornerstone of a well-conceived marketing orientation is strong customer relationships. Marketers must connect with customers—informing, engaging, and maybe even energizing them in the process. John Chambers, CEO of Cisco Systems, put it well when he said to "Make your customer the center of your culture." Customer-centered companies are adept at building customer relationships, not just products; they are skilled in market engineering, not just product engineering.

The Ritz-Carlton hotel chain, owned by Marriott International, is known throughout the world for its singular focus on providing guests with luxurious amenities and exceptional service. This customer-centered approach is expressed by the company's motto:"We are ladies and gentlemen serving ladies and gentlemen."Guests at any of the 62 Ritz-Carlton hotels in 21 countries notice the brand's famed personal touch immediately upon checking in, when they are greeted by name. To ensure guests' total experience at the hotel is of the utmost quality, Ritz-Carlton creates a daily "Service Quality Index" (SQI) at each of its locations, so employees can continually monitor key guest service processes and swiftly address potential problem areas. At the brand's corporate headquarters in Maryland, >>>

Ritz-Carlton's focus on its guests helped it win the prestigious Baldrige award twice and placed it among the Top 20 in the Brand Keys Customer Loyalty Index.

SQIs for each hotel are displayed in a central command room, allowing instant analysis of how well a single location is performing. Other customer service initiatives include the CLASS (Customer Loyalty Anticipation Satisfaction System) database, which contains preferences and requirements of repeat Ritz-Carlton guests, and a room maintainence system known as CARE (Clean and Repair Everything), which ensures all guestrooms are free of defects every 90 days. These initiatives helped Ritz-Carlton win its second Malcolm Baldrige National Quality Award in 1999, becoming the only service company to win twice. Its dedication to its customers also enables Ritz-Carlton to forge lasting relationships with them, as evidenced by the hotel's Top 20 ranking on the Brand Keys 2006 Customer Loyalty Index.[1]

As Ritz-Carlton's experience shows, successful marketers are the ones that fully satisfy their customers profitably. In this chapter, we spell out in detail the ways companies can go about winning customers and beating competitors. The answer lies largely in doing a better job of meeting or exceeding customer expectations.

::: Building Customer Value, Satisfaction, and Loyalty

Creating loyal customers is at the heart of every business.[2] As marketing experts Don Peppers and Martha Rogers say:[3]

> The only value your company will ever create is the value that comes from customers—the ones you have now and the ones you will have in the future. Businesses succeed by getting, keeping, and growing customers. Customers are the only reason you build factories, hire employees, schedule meetings, lay fiber-optic lines, or engage in any business activity. Without customers, you don't have a business.

Managers who believe the customer is the company's only true "profit center" consider the traditional organization chart in Figure 5.1—a pyramid with the president at the top, management in the middle, and frontline people and customers at the bottom—obsolete.[4]

Successful marketing companies invert the chart (Figure 5.1b). At the top are customers; next in importance are frontline people who meet, serve, and satisfy customers; under them are the middle managers, whose job is to support the frontline people so they can serve customers well; and at the base is top management, whose job is to hire and support good middle managers. We have added customers along the sides of Figure 5.1(b) to indicate that managers at every level must be personally involved in knowing, meeting, and serving customers.

Some companies have been founded with the customer-on-top business model, and customer advocacy has been their strategy—and competitive advantage—all along. With the rise of digital technologies such as the Internet, today's increasingly informed consumers expect companies to do more than connect with them, more than satisfy them, and even more than delight them. They expect companies to *listen* to them.[5] When CompUSA permitted customer reviews on its site—which can then show up in online searches—it found that 20,000 more customers than before visited the site in a month, with a 50% greater propensity to buy.[6] When Ebates, an online shopping portal that offers members cash back for shopping on the Web, switched to online survey software to better monitor customer responses, the site redesign and other changes that resulted from customer feedback brought increases in virtually all aspects of business performance, including sales.[7]

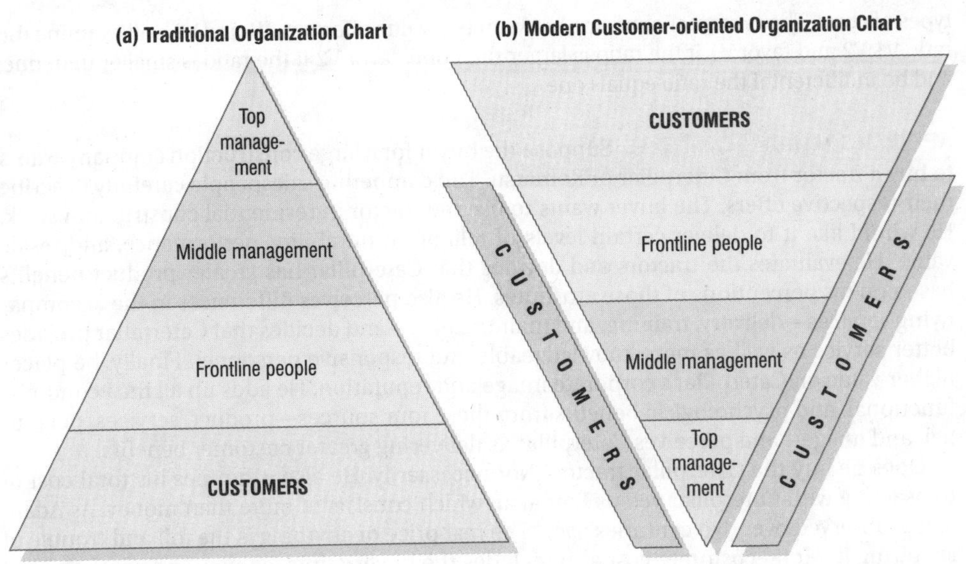

FIG. 5.1

Traditional Organization versus Modern Customer-Oriented Company Organization

Customer Perceived Value

Consumers are more educated and informed than ever, and they have the tools to verify companies' claims and seek out superior alternatives.[8]

HEWLETT-PACKARD CO., DELL INC.

Hewlett-Packard is beginning to outpace Dell in terms of customer perceived value. Dell rode to success by offering low-priced computers, logistical efficiency, and after-sales service. Dell's maniacal focus on low costs has been a key ingredient to that business model success. When the company shifted its customer-service call centers to India and the Philippines to cut costs, understaffed call centers led to frequent 30-minute waits for customers. Almost half the calls required at least one transfer. To discourage customer calls, Dell even removed its toll-free service number from its Web site. With customer satisfaction slipping and competitors matching its product quality and prices and offering improved service, Dell's market share and stock price both declined sharply. Dell ended up hiring more North American call center employees. "The team was managing cost instead of managing service and quality," Michael Dell confesses. In contrast, Hewlett-Packard is aggressively pursuing a solutions approach based on strengthening its channel partner relationships. Don Ritchie, CEO of Sequel Data Systems, an exclusive HP partner, says he sees no threat from Dell as he continues to deliver enterprise solutions in concert with HP and says, "One of the easiest sales Sequel has is to go into an account that has been serviced by Dell."[9]

How then do customers ultimately make choices? They tend to be value maximizers, within the bounds of search costs and limited knowledge, mobility, and income. Customers estimate which offer will deliver the most perceived value and act on it (Figure 5.2). Whether the offer lives up to expectation affects customer satisfaction and the probability that the customer will purchase the product again.

Customer-perceived value (CPV) is the difference between the prospective customer's evaluation of all the benefits and all the costs of an offering and the perceived alternatives. **Total customer benefit** is the perceived monetary value of the bundle of economic, functional, and psychological benefits customers expect from a given market offering because of the products, services, personnel, and image involved. **Total customer cost** is the perceived bundle of costs customers expect to incur in evaluating, obtaining, using, and disposing of the given market offering, including monetary, time, energy, and psychological costs.

Customer-perceived value is thus based on the difference between what the customer gets and what he or she gives for different possible choices. The customer gets benefits and assumes costs. The marketer can increase the value of the customer offering by some combination of raising economic, functional, or emotional benefits and/or reducing one or more of the various

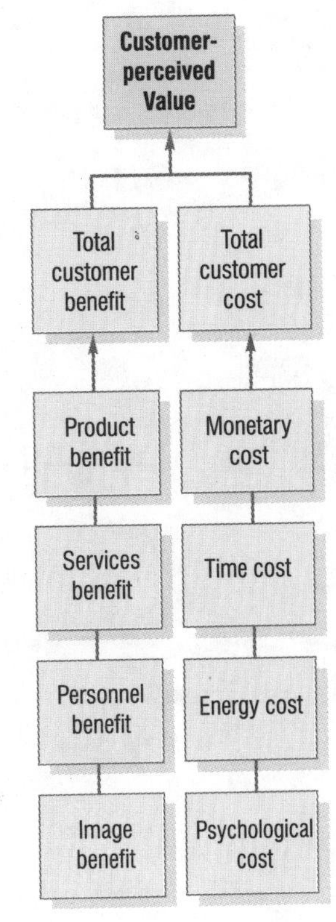

FIG. 5.2

Determinants of Customer-Perceived Value

types of costs. The customer choosing between two value offerings, V1 and V2, will examine the ratio V1:V2 and favor V1 if the ratio is larger than one, favor V2 if the ratio is smaller than one, and be indifferent if the ratio equals one.

APPLYING VALUE CONCEPTS Suppose the buyer for a large construction company wants to buy a tractor from Caterpillar or Komatsu. The competing salespeople carefully describe their respective offers. The buyer wants to use the tractor in residential construction work. He would like it to deliver certain levels of reliability, durability, performance, and resale value. He evaluates the tractors and decides that Caterpillar has greater product benefits based on his perceptions of those attributes. He also perceives differences in the accompanying services—delivery, training, and maintenance—and decides that Caterpillar provides better service as well as more knowledgeable and responsive personnel. Finally, he places higher value on Caterpillar's corporate image and reputation. He adds up all the economic, functional, and psychological benefits from these four sources—product, services, personnel, and image—and perceives Caterpillar as delivering greater customer benefits.

Does he buy the Caterpillar tractor? Not necessarily. He also examines his total cost of transacting with Caterpillar versus Komatsu, which consists of more than money. As Adam Smith observed over two centuries ago, "The real price of anything is the toil and trouble of acquiring it." Total customer cost also includes the buyer's time, energy, and psychological costs expended in product acquisition, usage, maintenance, ownership, and disposal. The buyer evaluates these elements together with the monetary cost to form a total customer cost. Then he considers whether Caterpillar's total customer cost is too high in relationship to the total customer benefits Caterpillar delivers. If it is, the buyer might choose Komatsu. The buyer will choose whichever source he thinks delivers the highest perceived value.

Now let's use this decision-making theory to help Caterpillar succeed in selling to this buyer. Caterpillar can improve its offer in three ways. First, it can increase total customer benefit by improving economic, functional, and psychological benefits of its product, services, personnel, and/or image. Second, it can reduce the buyer's nonmonetary costs by reducing the time, energy, and psychological costs. Third, it can reduce its product's monetary cost to the buyer.

Suppose Caterpillar concludes that the buyer sees its offer as worth $20,000. Further, suppose Caterpillar's cost of producing the tractor is $14,000. This means Caterpillar's offer potentially generates $6,000 over the company's cost, so Caterpillar needs to charge a price between $14,000 and $20,000. If it charges less than $14,000, it won't cover its costs; if it charges more than $20,000, it will price itself out of the market.

The price Caterpillar charges will determine how much value will be delivered to the buyer and how much will flow to Caterpillar. For example, if Caterpillar charges $19,000, it is creating $1,000 of customer perceived value and keeping $5,000 for itself. The lower Caterpillar sets its price, the higher the customer perceived value and, therefore, the higher the customer's incentive to purchase. To win the sale, Caterpillar must offer more customer perceived value than Komatsu does.[10]

Very often, managers conduct a **customer value analysis** to reveal the company's strengths and weaknesses relative to those of various competitors. The steps in this analysis are:

1. ***Identify the major attributes and benefits that customers value***—Customers are asked what attributes, benefits, and performance levels they look for in choosing a product and vendors.
2. ***Assess the quantitative importance of the different attributes and benefits***—Customers are asked to rate the importance of the different attributes and benefits. If their ratings diverge too much, the marketer should cluster them into different segments.
3. ***Assess the company's and competitors' performances on the different customer values against their rated importance***—Customers describe where they see the company's and competitors' performances on each attribute and benefit.
4. ***Examine how customers in a specific segment rate the company's performance against a specific major competitor on an individual attribute or benefit basis***—If the company's offer exceeds the competitor's offer on all important attributes and benefits, the company can charge a higher price (thereby earning higher profits), or it can charge the same price and gain more market share.
5. ***Monitor customer values over time***—The company must periodically redo its studies of customer values and competitors' standings as the economy, technology, and features change.

CHOICES AND IMPLICATIONS Some marketers might argue that the process we have described is too rational. Suppose the customer chooses the Komatsu tractor. How can we explain this choice? Here are three possibilities.

1. ***The buyer might be under orders to buy at the lowest price***—The Caterpillar salesperson's task is to convince the buyer's manager that buying on price alone will result in lower long-term profits and customer value.
2. ***The buyer will retire before the company realizes that the Komatsu tractor is more expensive to operate***—The buyer will look good in the short run; he is maximizing personal benefit. The Caterpillar salesperson's task is to convince other people in the customer company that Caterpillar delivers greater customer value.
3. ***The buyer enjoys a long-term friendship with the Komatsu salesperson***—In this case, Caterpillar's salesperson needs to show the buyer that the Komatsu tractor will draw complaints from the tractor operators when they discover its high fuel cost and need for frequent repairs.

The point of these examples is clear: Buyers operate under various constraints and occasionally make choices that give more weight to their personal benefit than to the company's benefit.

Customer-perceived value is a useful framework that applies to many situations and yields rich insights. Here are its implications:

First, the seller must assess the total customer benefit and total customer cost associated with each competitor's offer in order to know how his or her offer rates in the buyer's mind.

Second, the seller who is at a customer-perceived-value disadvantage has two alternatives: to increase total customer benefit or to decrease total customer cost. The former calls for strengthening or augmenting the economical, functional, and psychological benefits of the offering's product, services, personnel, and image. The latter calls for reducing the buyer's costs by reducing the price or cost of ownership and maintenance, simplifying the ordering and delivery process, or absorbing some buyer risk by offering a warranty.[11]

DELIVERING HIGH CUSTOMER VALUE Consumers have varying degrees of loyalty to specific brands, stores, and companies. Oliver defines **loyalty** as "A deeply held commitment to rebuy or repatronize a preferred product or service in the future despite situational influences and marketing efforts having the potential to cause switching behavior."[12] Table 5.1 displays brands with the greatest degree of customer loyalty according to one 2006 survey.[13]

The **value proposition** consists of the whole cluster of benefits the company promises to deliver; it is more than the core positioning of the offering. For example, Volvo's core positioning has been "safety," but the buyer is promised more than just a safe car; other benefits include a long-lasting car, good service, and a long warranty period. The value proposition is a statement about the experience customers will gain from the company's market offering and from their relationship with the supplier. The brand must represent a promise about the total experience customers can expect. Whether the promise is kept depends on the company's ability to manage its value delivery system.[14] The **value delivery system** includes all the experiences the customer will have on the way to obtaining and using the offering. At the heart of a good value delivery system is a set of core business processes that help to deliver distinctive consumer value.[15]

Safety is a leading, but not the only, benefit promised in Volvo's value proposition.

TABLE 5.1

Top 20 Brands in Customer Loyalty

1. Avis	11. Verizon long distance
2. Google	12. KeySpan Energy
3. L.L. Bean catalog	13. Miller Genuine Draft
4. Samsung mobile phones	14. Amazon
5. Yahoo!	15. Target
6. Canon office copiers	16. Motorola mobile phones
7. Land's End catalog	17. BlackBerry
8. Coors	18. Diet Pepsi
9. Hyatt hotels	19. Netscape
10. Marriott hotels	20. Ritz-Carlton Hotels

Source: 2006 Brand Keys Customer Loyalty Leaders List, as summarized in Kenneth Hein, "Brand Loyalty Shows There's No Place Like Home," *Brandweek*, October 23, 2006, p. 11.

Here's a company that is a master at delivering customer value.[16]

SUPERQUINN

Superquinn is Ireland's largest supermarket chain and its founder, Feargal Quinn, is Ireland's master marketer. A greeter is posted at the store entrance to welcome and help customers and even offer coffee, and to provide carryout service to customers' cars and umbrellas in case of rain. Department managers post themselves in the aisles to interact with customers and answer questions. There is a high-quality salad bar, fresh bread baked every four hours, and indications of when produce arrived, including the farmers' pictures. Superquinn also operates a child care center. It offers a loyalty program that gives points for the amount purchased and for discovering anything wrong with the store, such as dented cans or bad tomatoes. A dozen other firms (a bank, gas station, and others) that give points for purchases at their establishments recognize the loyalty card. Because everything is done to exceed normal customer expectations, Superquinn stores enjoy an almost cultlike following. In August 2006, Superquinn was sold to a consortium, Select Retail Holdings for $590 million.

Total Customer Satisfaction

Whether the buyer is satisfied after purchase depends on the offer's performance in relationship to the buyer's expectations, and whether the buyer interprets any deviations between the two.[17] In general, **satisfaction** is a person's feelings of pleasure or disappointment that result from comparing a product's perceived performance (or outcome) to their expectations.[18] If the performance falls short of expectations, the customer is dissatisfied. If the performance matches the expectations, the customer is satisfied. If the performance exceeds expectations, the customer is highly satisfied or delighted.[19] Customer assessments of product performance depend on many factors, especially the type of loyalty relationship the customer has with the brand.[20] Consumers often form more favorable perceptions of a product with a brand they already feel positive about.

Although the customer-centered firm seeks to create high customer satisfaction, that is not its ultimate goal. If the company increases customer satisfaction by lowering its price or increasing its services, the result may be lower profits. The company might be able to increase its profitability by means other than increased satisfaction (for example, by improving manufacturing processes or investing more in R&D). Also, the company has many stakeholders, including employees, dealers, suppliers, and stockholders. Spending more to increase customer satisfaction might divert funds from increasing the satisfaction of other "partners." Ultimately, the company must operate on the philosophy that it is trying to deliver a high level of customer satisfaction subject to delivering acceptable levels of satisfaction to the other stakeholders, given its total resources.[21]

Joie de Vivre's boutique hotels offer personal touches that exceed customer expectations.

How do buyers form their expectations? Expectations result from past buying experience; friends' and associates' advice; and marketers' and competitors' information and promises. If marketers raise expectations too high, the buyer is likely to be disappointed. However, if the company sets expectations too low, it won't attract enough buyers (although it will satisfy those who do buy).[22] Some of today's most successful companies are raising expectations and delivering performances to match. Korean automaker Kia found success in the United States by launching low-cost, high-quality cars with enough reliability so that it could offer 10-year warranties.

A customer's decision to be loyal or to defect is the sum of many small encounters with the company. Many companies now strive to create a "branded customer experience." Here's how San Francisco's Joie de Vivre chain does this.[23]

JOIE DE VIVRE

Joie de Vivre Hospitality Inc. operates a chain of boutique hotels, restaurants, and resorts in the San Francisco area. Each property's unique décor, quirky amenities, and thematic style are often loosely based on popular magazines. For example, the Hotel del Sol—a converted motel bearing a yellow exterior and surrounded by palm trees wrapped with festive lights—is described as "kind of *Martha Stewart Living* meets *Islands* magazine."[24] Two Silicon Valley hotels offer guests high-speed Internet connections in their rooms and by the pool.[25] The boutique concept enables the hotels to offer personal touches, such as vitamins in place of chocolates on pillows. Joie de Vivre now owns the largest number of independent hotel properties in the Bay Area.

Monitoring Satisfaction

Many companies are systematically measuring how well they treat their customers, identifying the factors shaping satisfaction, and making changes in their operations and marketing as a result.[26] For example, Wachovia Securities employs mystery shoppers to assess how well employees are satisfying customers, linking part of employees' compensation to their ratings. The emphasis on customer service seems to be working—a research study by Brand Keys during the first quarter of 2006 found that Wachovia did a better job of meeting the expectations of its loyal customers than any other bank.[27]

A company would be wise to measure customer satisfaction regularly, because one key to customer retention is customer satisfaction.[28] A highly satisfied customer generally stays loyal longer, buys more as the company introduces new products and upgrades existing products, talks favorably to others about the company and its products, pays less attention to competing brands and is less sensitive to price, offers product or service ideas to the company, and costs less to serve than new customers because transactions can become routine.[29] Greater customer satisfaction has also been linked to higher returns and lower risk in the stock market.[30]

The link between customer satisfaction and customer loyalty, however, is not proportional. Suppose customer satisfaction is rated on a scale from one to five. At a very low level of customer satisfaction (level one), customers are likely to abandon the company and even bad-mouth it. At levels two to four, customers are fairly satisfied but still find it easy to switch when a better offer comes along. At level five, the customer is very likely to repurchase and even spread good word of mouth about the company. High satisfaction or delight creates an emotional bond with the brand or company, not just a rational preference. Xerox's senior management found out that its "completely satisfied" customers were six times more likely to repurchase Xerox products over the following 18 months than its "very satisfied" customers.[31]

When customers rate their satisfaction with an element of the company's performance—say, delivery—the company needs to recognize that customers vary in how they define good performance. Good delivery could mean early delivery, on-time delivery, order completeness, and so on. The company must also realize that two customers can report being "highly satisfied" for different reasons. One may be easily satisfied most of the time and the other might be hard to please but was pleased on this occasion.[32]

MEASUREMENT TECHNIQUES A number of methods exist to measure customer satisfaction. *Periodic surveys* can track customer satisfaction directly and also ask additional questions to measure repurchase intention and the respondent's likelihood or willingness to recommend the company and brand to others. Paramount attributes the success of its five theme parks to the thousands of Web-based guest surveys it sends to customers who have agreed to be contacted. During a recent year, the company conducted more than 55 of these surveys and netted 100,000 individual responses that described guest satisfaction on topics including rides, dining, shopping, games, and shows.[33] "Marketing Insight: Net Promoter and Customer Satisfaction" describes why some companies believe just one well-designed question is all that is necessary to assess customer satisfaction.[34]

Besides conducting periodic surveys, companies can monitor their *customer loss rate* and contact customers who have stopped buying or who have switched to another supplier to find out why. Finally, companies can hire *mystery shoppers* to pose as potential buyers and report on strong and weak points experienced in buying the company's and competitors' products. Managers themselves can enter company and competitor sales situations where they are unknown and experience firsthand the treatment they receive, or they can phone their own company with questions and complaints to see how employees handle the calls.

In addition to tracking customer value expectations and satisfaction for their own firms, companies need to monitor their competitors' performance in these areas. One company was pleased to find that 80% of its customers said they were satisfied. Then the CEO found out that its leading competitor had a 90% customer satisfaction score. He was further dismayed when he learned that this competitor was aiming for a 95% satisfaction score.

INFLUENCE OF CUSTOMER SATISFACTION For customer-centered companies, customer satisfaction is both a goal and a marketing tool. Companies need to be especially concerned today with their customer satisfaction level because the Internet provides a tool for consumers to quickly spread bad word of mouth—as well as good word of mouth—to the rest of the world. Some customers even set up their own Web sites to air their grievances and dissatisfaction, targeting high-profile brands such as United Airlines, Wal-Mart, and Mercedes-Benz.[36] Describing events and actions as being wronged by the company, these Web sites often attempt to galvanize consumer discontent and protest.

Companies that do achieve high customer satisfaction ratings make sure their target market knows it. Once they achieved number-one status on J.D. Power's customer satisfaction ratings, Countrywide home mortgage lenders, Continental airlines, and Kyocera copiers all advertised that fact.

The University of Michigan's Claes Fornell has developed the American Customer Satisfaction Index (ACSI) to measure the perceived satisfaction consumers feel with different firms, industries, economic sectors, and national economies.[37] Examples of firms that led their respective industries with high ACSI scores in 2005 are Heinz (91), Toyota (87), Apple (83), and Google (82).

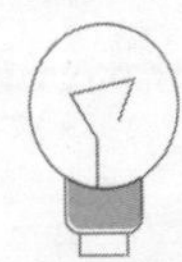

MARKETING INSIGHT | NET PROMOTER AND CUSTOMER SATISFACTION

Measuring customer satisfaction is a top priority for many companies, but a difference of opinion exists as to how they should go about doing that. Bain's Frederick Reichheld suggests that perhaps only one customer question really matters: "How likely is it that you would recommend this product or service to a friend or colleague?" According to Reichheld, a customer's willingness to recommend to a friend results from how well the customer is treated by frontline employees, which in turn is determined by all the functional areas that contribute to a customer's experience.[35]

Reichheld was inspired in part by the experiences of Enterprise Rent-A-Car. When the company cut its customer satisfaction survey from 18 to 2 questions in 1998—one about the quality of their rental experience and the other about the likelihood they would rent from the company again—it found that customers who gave the highest ratings to their rental experience were three times as likely to rent again than those who gave the company the second highest rating. The firm also found that the diagnostic information its managers collected from dissatisfied customers helped the company fine-tune its operations.

In a typical Net Promoter survey that follows Reicheld's thinking, customers are asked to rate their likelihood to recommend on a 0–10-point scale. Marketers then subtract *detractors* (those who gave a 0 to 6) from *promoters* (those who gave a 9 or 10) to arrive at the Net Promoter Score (NPS). Customers who rate the brand with a 7 or 8 are deemed *passively satisfied* and are not included in the final score. A typical set of NPS scores falls in the 10% to 30% range, but world-class companies can score over 50%. Some firms with top NPS scores include USAA (82%), Harley-Davidson (81%), Costco (79%), Amazon (73%), and eBay (71%).

Reichheld is gaining a number of believers. GE, American Express, and Microsoft, among others, have all adopted the NPS metric. GE has tied 20% of its manager's bonuses to its NPS scores. When the European unit of GE Healthcare scored low, follow-up research revealed that response times to customers were a major problem. After it overhauled its call center and put more specialists in the field, GE Healthcare's Net Promoter scores jumped 10 to 15 points. BearingPoint found that clients who gave it high Net Promoter scores showed the highest revenue growth.

Reichheld says he developed NPS in response to what he saw as overly complicated—and thus ineffective—customer surveys. So it's not surprising that client firms praise its simplicity and its strong relationship to financial performance. Companies such as GE stress the importance of the explanations customers provide to explain or justify their ratings. When Intuit applied Net Promoter to its TurboTax software, feedback revealed dissatisfaction with TurboTax's rebate procedure. After dropping the proof-of-purchase requirement as a result, Intuit saw sales jump 6%.

Enterprise Rent-a-Car was able to learn a great deal about customer loyalty by cutting the number of customer satisfaction questions down to just two.

Sources: Fred Reichheld, *Ultimate Question: For Driving Good Profits and True Growth* (Cambridge, MA: Harvard Business School Press, 2006); Matthew Creamer, "Do You Know Your Score?" Advertising Age, July 3, 2006, pp. 1–24; Jena McGregor, "Would You Recommend Us?" *BusinessWeek*, January 30, 2006, pp. 94–95; Kathryn Kranhold, "Client-Satisfaction Tool Takes Root," *Wall Street Journal*, July 10, 2006; Todd Wasserman, "Net Promoter Approaches ROI Question with Question," *Brandweek*, April 17, 2006, p. 13; Fred Reichheld, "The One Number You Need to Grow," *Harvard Business Review*, December 2003.

J.D. Power's customer satisfaction ratings make powerful advertising copy for customer-centered firms.

PULTE HOMES INC.

One of the nation's largest and most diversified new homebuilders, Pulte Homes has won more awards in J.D. Power's annual survey of customers than any other new homebuilder. The 55-year-old company doesn't rely on J.D. Power to get a bead on its customers' satisfaction level, however. Pulte Homes constantly measures how well it's doing with customers by tracking them over a long period of time. The builder first surveys buyers to get a feel of what the experience was like just after they bought their home. Then, several years later, Pulte goes back to those same buyers to make sure they're still happy. When Pulte was dissatisfied with the marks it was getting from customers for overall satisfaction in 2001, it created a customer relations department of 1,200 people and a program to ensure that it paid closer attention to customers' desires throughout the entire sales and building process. Erik Pekarski, national vice president of customer relations at Pulte, says that the jump in repeat and referral business following this initiative is "proof that the stronger relationship increases our bottom line." Pekarski also stresses that Pulte's focus is on preventing customer problems and complaints and that's why the firm uses the term "customer relations" instead of "customer service."[38]

CUSTOMER COMPLAINTS Some companies think they're getting a sense of customer satisfaction by tallying complaints, but studies of customer dissatisfaction show that customers are dissatisfied with their purchases about 25% of the time but that only about 5% complain.

The other 95% either feel complaining is not worth the effort, or they do not know how or to whom to complain, and they just stop buying.[39]

Of the customers who register a complaint, between 54% and 70% will do business with the organization again if their complaint is resolved. The figure goes up to a staggering 95% if the customer feels the complaint was resolved *quickly*. Customers who have complained to an organization and had their complaints satisfactorily resolved tell an average of 5 people about the good treatment they received.[40] The average dissatisfied customer, however, gripes to 11 people. If each of them tells still other people, the number of people exposed to bad word of mouth may grow exponentially.

The fact is, no matter how perfectly designed and implemented a marketing program is, mistakes will happen. The best thing a company can do is to make it easy for the customer to complain. Suggestion forms, toll-free numbers, Web sites, and e-mail addresses allow for quick, two-way communication. The 3M Company claims that over two-thirds of its product improvement ideas come from listening to customer complaints.

Given the potential downside of having an unhappy customer, it's critical that marketers deal with the negative experience properly.[41] Beyond that, the following procedures can help to recover customer goodwill:[42]

1. Set up a 7-day, 24-hour toll-free "hotline" (by phone, fax, or e-mail) to receive and act on customer complaints.
2. Contact the complaining customer as quickly as possible. The slower the company is to respond, the more dissatisfaction may grow and lead to negative word of mouth.
3. Accept responsibility for the customer's disappointment; don't blame the customer.
4. Use customer-service people who are empathic.
5. Resolve the complaint swiftly and to the customer's satisfaction. Some complaining customers are not looking for compensation so much as a sign that the company cares.

Product and Service Quality

Satisfaction will also depend on product and service quality. What exactly is quality? Various experts have defined it as "fitness for use," "conformance to requirements," "freedom from variation," and so on. We will use the American Society for Quality Control's definition: **Quality** is the totality of features and characteristics of a product or service that bear on its ability to satisfy stated or implied needs.[43] This is clearly a customer-centered definition. We can say that the seller has delivered quality whenever its product or service meets or exceeds the customers' expectations. A company that satisfies most of its customers' needs most of the time is called a quality company, but we need to distinguish between *conformance* quality and *performance* quality (or grade). A Lexus provides higher performance quality than a Hyundai: The Lexus rides smoother, goes faster, and lasts longer. Yet we can say that both a Lexus and a Hyundai deliver the same conformance quality if all the units deliver their respective promised quality.

According to GE's former chairman, John F. Welch Jr., "Quality is our best assurance of customer allegiance, our strongest defense against foreign competition, and the only path to sustained growth and earnings."[44] The drive to produce goods that are superior in world markets has led some countries—and groups of countries—to recognize or award prizes to companies that exemplify the best quality practices, such as the Deming Prize in Japan, the Malcolm Baldrige National Quality Award in the United States, and the European Quality Award.

IMPACT OF QUALITY Product and service quality, customer satisfaction, and company profitability are intimately connected. Higher levels of quality result in higher levels of customer satisfaction, which support higher prices and (often) lower costs. Studies have shown a high correlation between relative product quality and company profitability.[45] Companies that have lowered costs to cut corners have paid the price when the quality of the customer experience suffers:[46]

- When Home Depot decided to expand into the contractor supply business, while also cutting costs and streamlining operations in 1,816 U.S. stores, it replaced many full-time workers with part-time employees who soon made up about 40% of store staff. The chain's ACS index of customer satisfaction dropped to the bottom among major U.S. retailers, 11 points behind customer-friendly competitor Lowe's, and Home Depot's share price slid 24% during the biggest home improvement boom in history.

- Although Northwest Airlines stopped offering free magazines, pillows, movies, and even minibags of pretzels on domestic flights, the carrier also raised prices and reduced its flight schedule. As one frequent flier noted, "Northwest acts low cost without *being* low cost." Not surprisingly, Northwest came in last of all top U.S. airlines in both the ACS index and J.D. Power & Associates customer satisfaction poll.

Quality is clearly the key to value creation and customer satisfaction.

TOTAL QUALITY Total quality is everyone's job, just as marketing is everyone's job. Marketers play several roles in helping their companies define and deliver high-quality goods and services to target customers. First, they bear the major responsibility for correctly identifying the customers' needs and requirements. Second, they must communicate customer expectations properly to product designers. Third, they must make sure that customers' orders are filled correctly and on time. Fourth, they must check that customers have received proper instructions, training, and technical assistance in the use of the product. Fifth, they must stay in touch with customers after the sale to ensure that they are satisfied and remain satisfied. Sixth, they must gather customer ideas for product and service improvements and convey them to the appropriate departments. When marketers do all this, they are making substantial contributions to total quality management and customer satisfaction, as well as to customer and company profitability.

::: Maximizing Customer Lifetime Value

Ultimately, marketing is the art of attracting and keeping profitable customers. Yet every company loses money on some of its customers. The well-known 20–80 rule says that the top 20% of the customers often generates 80% or more of the company's profits. In some cases the profit distribution may be more extreme—the most profitable 20% of customers (on a per capita basis) may contribute as much as 150% to 300% of profitability. The least profitable 10% to 20% of customers, on the other hand, can actually reduce profits between 50% to 200% per account, with the middle 60% to 70% breaking even.[47] Figure 5.3 displays one customer profit distribution. The implication is that a company could improve its profits by "firing" its worst customers.

It's not always the company's largest customers who yield the most profit. The largest customers can demand considerable service and receive the deepest discounts. The smallest customers pay full price and receive minimal service, but the costs of transacting with them can reduce their profitability. The midsize customers who receive good service and pay nearly full price are often the most profitable.

Customer Profitability

What makes a customer profitable? A **profitable customer** is a person, household, or company that over time yields a revenue stream that exceeds by an acceptable amount the

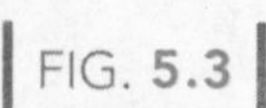

FIG. 5.3

The 150-20 Rule: "The 20% most profitable customers generate as much as 150% of the profits of a company; the 20% least profitable lose 100% of the profits."

Source: Larry Selden and Yoko S. Selden, "Profitable Customer: The Key to Great Brands," *Point* (July–August 2006): 9.

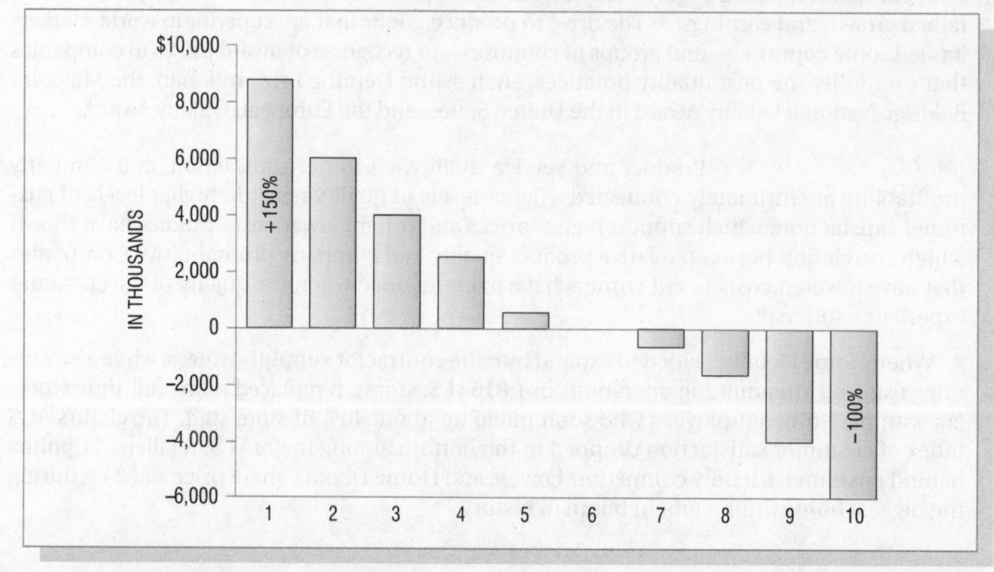

company's cost stream for attracting, selling, and servicing that customer. Note that the emphasis is on the *lifetime* stream of revenue and cost, not on the profit from a particular transaction.[48] Marketers can assess customer profitability individually, by market segment, or by channel.

Although many companies measure customer satisfaction, most companies fail to measure individual customer profitability.[49] Banks claim this is a difficult task, because each customer uses different banking services and the transactions are logged in different departments. However, the number of unprofitable customers in their customer base has appalled banks that have succeeded in linking customer transactions. Some banks report losing money on over 45% of their retail customers.

CUSTOMER PROFITABILITY ANALYSIS A useful type of profitability analysis is shown in Figure 5.4.[50]

Customers are arrayed along the columns and products along the rows. Each cell contains a symbol representing the profitability of selling that product to that customer. Customer 1 is very profitable; he buys two profit-making products (P1 and P2). Customer 2 yields a picture of mixed profitability; he buys one profitable product (P1) and one unprofitable product (P3). Customer 3 is a losing customer because he buys one profitable product (P1) and two unprofitable products (P3 and P4).

What can the company do about customers 2 and 3? (1) It can raise the price of its less profitable products or eliminate them, or (2) it can try to sell customers 2 and 3 its profit-making products. Unprofitable customers who defect should not concern the company. In fact, the company should encourage these customers to switch to competitors.

Customer profitability analysis (CPA) is best conducted with the tools of an accounting technique called activity-based costing (ABC). The company estimates all revenue coming from the customer, less all costs. The costs should include not only the cost of making and distributing the products and services, but also of taking phone calls from the customer, traveling to visit the customer, paying for entertainment and gifts—all the company's resources that go into serving that customer.

When a company does this for each customer, it can classify customers into different profit tiers: *platinum customers* (most profitable), *gold customers* (profitable), *iron customers* (low profitability but desirable for volume), and *lead customers* (unprofitable and undesirable). The company can then move iron customers into the gold tier and gold customers into the platinum tier, while dropping the lead customers or making them profitable by raising their prices or lowering the cost of serving them. More generally, marketers must segment customers into those worth pursuing and those potentially less-lucrative customers that should receive less attention, if any at all.

CUSTOMER PORTFOLIOS Marketers are recognizing the need to manage customer portfolios, made up of different groups of customers[51] defined in terms of their loyalty, profitability, and other factors. One perspective is that a firm's portfolio consists of a combination of "acquaintances," "friends," and "partners" that are constantly changing.[52] The three types of customers will differ in their product needs, their buying, selling, and servicing activities, and their acquisition costs and competitive advantages.

Products	Customers: C_1	C_2	C_3	
P_1	+	+	+	Highly profitable product
P_2	+			Profitable product
P_3		–	–	Unprofitable product
P_4			–	Highly unprofitable product
	High-profit customer	Mixed-bag customer	Losing customer	

FIG. 5.4

Customer-Product Profitability Analysis

Another perspective compares the individuals who make up the firm's customer portfolio to the stocks that make up an investment portfolio.[53] In marketing, as in investments, it's important to calculate the beta, or risk-reward value, for each portfolio item and then diversify accordingly. From this perspective, firms should assemble portfolios of negatively correlated individuals so that the financial contributions of one offset the deficits of another to maximize the portfolio's risk-adjusted lifetime value.

Measuring Customer Lifetime Value

The case for maximizing long-term customer profitability is captured in the concept of customer lifetime value.[54] **Customer lifetime value (CLV)** describes the net present value of the stream of future profits expected over the customer's lifetime purchases. The company must subtract from its expected revenues the expected costs of attracting, selling, and servicing the account of that customer, applying the appropriate discount rate (say, between 10% and 20%, depending on cost of capital and risk attitudes). Lifetime value calculations for a product or service can add up to tens of thousands of dollars or even into six figures.[55]

Many methods exist to measure customer lifetime value.[56] "Marketing Memo: Calculating Customer Lifetime Value" illustrates one.

CLV calculations provide a formal quantitative framework for planning customer investment and help marketers adopt a long-term perspective. One challenge in applying CLV concepts, however, is to arrive at reliable cost and revenue estimates. Marketers who use CLV concepts must also take into account the short-term, brand-building marketing activities that help increase customer loyalty.

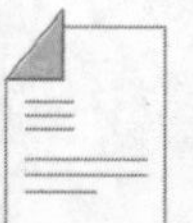

MARKETING MEMO — CALCULATING CUSTOMER LIFETIME VALUE

Researchers and practitioners have used many different approaches for modeling and estimating customer lifetime value (CLV). Columbia's Don Lehmann and Harvard's Sunil Gupta recommend the following formula to estimate the CLV for a not-yet-acquired customer:

$$CLV = \sum_{t=0}^{T} \frac{(p_t - c_t)r_t}{(1+i)^t} - AC$$

where, p_t = price paid by a consumer at time t,

c_t = direct cost of servicing the customer at time t,

i = discount rate or cost of capital for the firm,

r_t = probability of customer repeat buying or being "alive" at time t,

AC = acquisition cost,

T = time horizon for estimating CLV.

A key decision is what time horizon to use for estimating CLV. Typically, three to five years is reasonable. With this information and estimates of other variables, we can calculate CLV using spreadsheet analysis.

Gupta and Lehmann illustrate their approach by calculating the CLV of 100 customers over a 10-year period (see Table 5.2). In this example, the firm acquires 100 customers with an acquisition cost per customer of $40. Therefore, in year 0, it spends $4,000. Some of these customers defect each year. The present value of the profits from this cohort of customers over 10 years is $13,286.52. The net CLV (after deducting acquisition costs) is $9,286.52 or $92.87 per customer.

Using an infinite time horizon avoids using an arbitrary time horizon for calculating CLV. In the case of an infinite time horizon, researchers have shown that if margins (price minus cost) and retention rates stay constant over time, then the future CLV of an existing customer simplifies to the following:

$$CLV = \sum_{t=1}^{\infty} \frac{mr^t}{(1+i)^t} = m\frac{r}{(1+i-r)}$$

In other words, CLV simply becomes margin (m) times a *margin multiple* $[r/(1+i-r)]$.

Table 5.3 shows the margin multiple for various combinations of r and i. This table shows a simple way to estimate CLV of a customer. For example, when retention rate is 80% and discount rate is 12%, the margin multiple is about two-and-a-half. Therefore, the future CLV of an existing customer in this scenario is simply his or her annual margin multiplied by 2.5.

Sources: Sunil Gupta and Donald R. Lehmann, "Models of Customer Value," in *Handbook of Marketing Decision Models*, ed. Berend Wierenga (Berlin, Germany: Springer Science and Business Media, 2007); Sunil Gupta and Donald R. Lehmann, "Customers as Assets," *Journal of Interactive Marketing* 17, no. 1 (Winter 2006): 9–24; Sunil Gupta and Donald R. Lehmann, *Managing Customers as Investments* (Upper Saddle River, NJ: Wharton School Publishing, 2005); Peter Fader, Bruce Hardie, and Ka Lee, "RFM and CLV: Using Iso-Value Curves for Customer Base Analysis," *Journal of Marketing Research* 42, no. 4, (November 2005): 415–30; Sunil Gupta, Donald R. Lehmann, and Jennifer Ames Stuart, "Valuing Customers," *Journal of Marketing Research* 41, no. 1 (February 2004): 7–18; Werner J. Reinartz and V. Kumar, "On the Profitability of Long-Life Customers in a Noncontractual Setting: An Empirical Investigation and Implications for Marketing," *Journal of Marketing* 64 (October 2000): 17–35.

TABLE 5.2 A Hypothetical Example to Illustrate CLV Calculations

	Year 0	Year 1	Year 2	Year 3	Year 4	Year 5	Year 6	Year 7	Year 8	Year 9	Year 10
Number of Customers	100	90	80	72	60	48	34	23	12	6	2
Revenue per Customer		100	110	120	125	130	135	140	142	143	145
Variable Cost per Customer		70	72	75	76	78	79	80	81	82	83
Margin per Customer		30	38	45	49	52	56	60	61	61	62
Acquisition Cost per Customer	40										
Total Cost or Profit	−4000	2700	3040	3240	2940	2496	1904	1380	732	366	124
Present Value	−4000	2454.55	2512.40	2434.26	2008.06	1549.82	1074.76	708.16	341.48	155.22	47.81

TABLE 5.3 Margin Multiple $\frac{r}{1+i-r}$

Retention Rate	Discount Rate 10%	12%	14%	16%
60%	1.20	1.5	1.11	1.07
70%	1.75	1.67	1.59	1.52
80%	2.67	2.50	2.35	2.22
90%	4.50	4.09	3.75	3.46

::: Cultivating Customer Relationships

Maximizing customer value means cultivating long-term customer relationships. Companies are now moving away from wasteful mass marketing to precision marketing designed to build strong customer relationships.[57] Today's economy is supported by information businesses. Information has the advantages of being easy to differentiate, customize, personalize, and dispatch over networks at incredible speed.

But information cuts both ways. For instance, customers now have a quick and easy means of doing comparison shopping through sites such as BizRate.com, Shopping.com, and Pricegrabber.com. The Internet also facilitates communication between customers. Web sites such as Epinions.com and Amazon.com enable customers to share information about their experiences with various products and services.

Customer empowerment has become a way of life for many companies that have had to adjust to a shift in the power with their customer relationships. "Marketing Insight: Company Response to Customer Empowerment" describes some of the changes companies have made in their marketing practices as a result.

Customer Relationship Management

Customer relationship management (CRM) is the process of carefully managing detailed information about individual customers and all customer "touch points" to maximize customer loyalty.[58] A *customer touch point* is any occasion on which a customer encounters the brand and product—from actual experience to personal or mass communications to casual observation. For a hotel, the touch points include reservations, check-in and checkout, frequent-stay programs, room service, business services, exercise facilities, laundry service, restaurants, and bars. For instance, the Four Seasons relies on personal touches, such as a staff that always addresses guests by name, high-powered employees who understand the

MARKETING INSIGHT | COMPANY RESPONSE TO CUSTOMER EMPOWERMENT

Often seen as the flag bearer for marketing best practices, P&G's chairman A. G. Lafley created shockwaves for marketers with his Association of National Advertiser's speech in October 2006. "The power is with the consumer," proclaimed Lafley, and "marketers and retailers are scrambling to keep up with her. Consumers are beginning in a very real sense to own our brands and participate in their creation. We need to learn to let go." In support of his contention, Lafley pointed out how a teenager had created an animated spot for Pringles snacks that was posted on YouTube; how Pantene, the hair care products company, had created a campaign that encouraged women to cut their hair and donate the clippings to make wigs for cancer patients; and how sales of Cover Girl Outlast lipstick increased 25% after the firm put mirrored ads in women's restrooms asking, "Is your lipstick still on?" and ran targeted five-second TV ads with the same theme.

Other marketers have begun to advocate a "bottom-up" grassroots approach to marketing, rather than the more traditional "top-down" approach where the marketers feel they are calling the shots. Burger King has launched edgy campaigns on consumer-friendly new media such as YouTube, MySpace, video games, and iPods. Allowing the customer to take charge just makes sense for a brand whose slogan is "Have It Your Way" and whose main rival, McDonald's, already owns the more staid family market.

To provide a little more control, Yahoo! engages in "participation marketing" by tapping consumers who already like a particular brand, rather than just casting a wide net. For example, to create a new music video, Yahoo! Music asked fans of the singer Shakira to contribute video clips of themselves performing her song "Hips Don't Lie," which then provided the visual content. Reflecting the company philosophy, Yahoo! CMO Cammie Dunaway noted, "Content is no longer something you push out; content is an invitation to engage with your brand."

Even the 2007 Super Bowl, the most expensive media event on the planet, had two homemade consumer commercials. To capitalize on the buzz of user-generated content, both Frito-Lay and Chevrolet created ad contests, with the winners receiving prizes and getting their ads aired during the game telecast. Perhaps the most compelling example of the new brand world comes from master marketer Nike. As part of its *Joga Bonito* (Portuguese for "play beautiful") World Cup Sponsorship, Nike spent $100 million on a multilayered campaign. The centerpiece, however, was Joga.com, a social networking Web site available in 140 countries. One million members blogged, downloaded videos, created fan communities for their favorite players or teams, and expressed their passions on bulletin-board-type debates. Nike CEO Mark Parker sums up the new marketing equation well, "A strong relationship is created when someone joins a Nike community or invites Nike into their community."

Sources: Stuart Elliott, "Letting Consumers Control Marketing: Priceless," *New York Times*, October 9, 2006; Louise Story, "Super Bowl Glory for Amateurs with Video Cameras," *New York Times*, September 27, 2006; Todd Wasserman and Jim Edwards, "Marketers' New World Order," *Brandweek*, October 9, 2006, pp. 4–6; Heather Green and Robert D. Hof, "Your Attention Please," *BusinessWeek*, July 24, 2006, pp. 48–53; Brian Sternberg, "The Marketing Maze," *Wall Street Journal*, July 10, 2006.

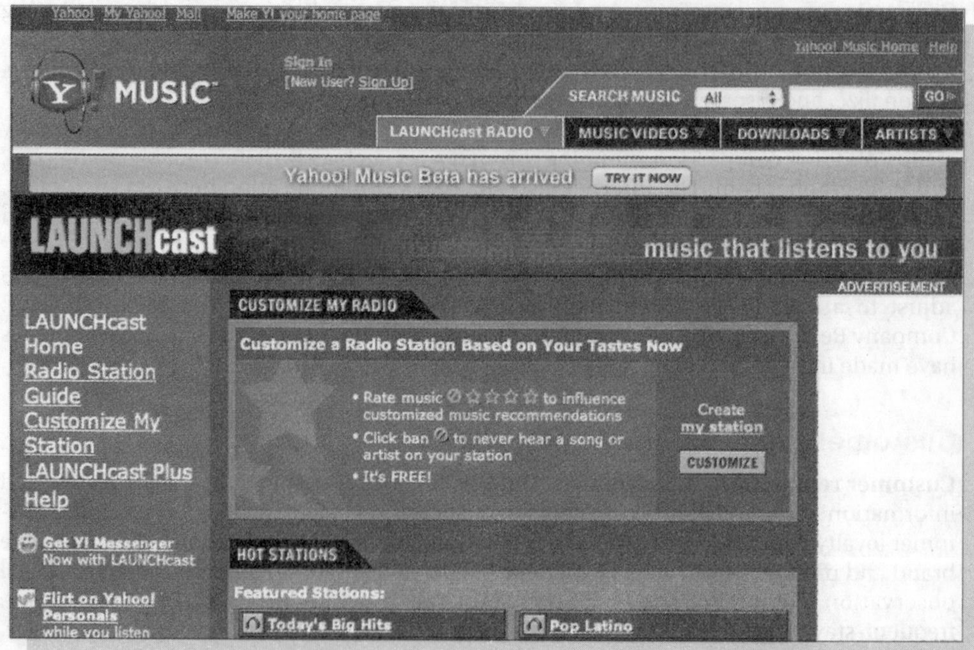

Web sites such as Yahoo! music that empower visitors, allow them to post comments or pictures, or encourage the formation of active communities can benefit companies and customers alike.

needs of sophisticated business travelers, and at least one best-in-region facility, such as a premier restaurant or spa.[59]

Sometimes touch points are where you least expect, such as in customer billing. Microsoft's Global CRM product manager, Karen Smith, related what happened when a telecommunications company converted to unified billing—one bill for all lines—to cut company costs. One of the customers requested a slightly modified version of unified billing to suit his expense submission purposes, but the service rep replied, "No, Sir, we can't do that. We use unified billing." The frustrated customer then switched his two business lines to another telecommunications company but lost his volume discount with the original provider, which still had his personal accounts. Even more frustrated, the customer then moved all his business to the new telecommunications company. Says Smith, "We may think that something will be great to do for our customers, but before we take action we need to really step into their shoes. Companies often focus on CRM functionality and integration, but they forget about some of the most basic touch points."[60]

Customer relationship management enables companies to provide excellent real-time customer service through the effective use of individual account information. Based on what they know about each valued customer, companies can customize market offerings, services, programs, messages, and media. CRM is important because a major driver of company profitability is the aggregate value of the company's customer base.[61] A pioneer in the application of CRM techniques is Harrah's Entertainment.

HARRAH'S

In 1997, Harrah's Entertainment Inc., in Las Vegas, launched a pioneering loyalty program that pulled all customer data into a centralized warehouse and provided sophisticated analysis to better understand the value of the investments the casino makes in its customers. Harrah's has fine-tuned its Total Rewards system to achieve near-real-time analysis: As customers interact with slot machines, check into casinos, or buy meals, they receive reward offers based on the predictive analyses. The company has now identified hundreds of customer segments among its more than 26 million slot players. By targeting offers to highly specific customer segments, the company has been able to almost double its share of customers' gaming budgets, from 26% in 1997 to 50% in 2005. Harrah's has over 6 million active members in its Total Rewards loyalty program who have used their card.[62]

ONE-TO-ONE MARKETING Some of the groundwork for customer relationship management was laid by Don Peppers and Martha Rogers.[63] Peppers and Rogers outline a four-step framework for one-to-one marketing that can be adapted to CRM marketing as follows:

To read how Tesco built, maintains, and mines a rich customer database in the United Kingdom, visit www.pearsoned.co.uk/marketingmanagementeurope.

1. ***Identify your prospects and customers***—Don't go after everyone. Build, maintain, and mine a rich customer database with information derived from all the channels and customer touch points.
2. ***Differentiate customers in terms of (1) their needs and (2) their value to your company***—Spend proportionately more effort on the most valuable customers (MVCs). Apply activity-based costing and calculate customer lifetime value. Estimate net present value of all future profits coming from purchases, margin levels, and referrals, less customer-specific servicing costs.
3. ***Interact with individual customers to improve your knowledge about their individual needs and to build stronger relationships***—Formulate customized offerings that you can communicate in a personalized way.
4. ***Customize products, services, and messages to each customer***—Facilitate customer–company interaction through the company contact center and Web site.

The practice of one-to-one marketing, however, is not for every company: The required investment in information collection, hardware, and software may exceed the payout. It works best for companies that normally collect a great deal of individual customer information, carry a lot of products that can be cross-sold, carry products that need periodic replacement or upgrading, and sell products of high value.

INCREASING VALUE OF THE CUSTOMER BASE A key driver of shareholder value is the aggregate value of the customer base. Winning companies improve the value of their customer base by excelling at strategies such as the following:

- ***Reducing the rate of customer defection.*** Selecting and training employees to be knowledgeable and friendly increases the likelihood that the inevitable shopping questions from customers will be answered satisfactorily. Whole Foods, the world's largest retailer of natural and organic foods, woos customers with a commitment to marketing the best foods and a team concept for employees.
- ***Increasing the longevity of the customer relationship.*** The more involved a customer is with the company, the more likely he is to stick around. Some companies treat their customers as partners—especially in business-to-business markets—soliciting their help in the design of new products or improving their customer service. Instant Web Companies (IWCO), a Chanhassen, Minnesota, direct-mail printer, launched a monthly Customer Spotlight program where guest companies provide an overview of their business and direct-mail programs and comment on IWCO practices, products, and services. IWCO's staff not only gains exposure to customers but also develops a broader perspective on customers' business and marketing objectives and how to add value and identify options that help meet its customers' goals.[64]
- ***Enhancing the growth potential of each customer through "share-of-wallet," cross-selling, and up-selling.***[65] Increase sales from existing customers with new offerings and opportunities. Harley-Davidson sells more than motorcycles and accessories (such as gloves, leather jackets, helmets, and sunglasses). Its dealerships sell more than 3,000 items of clothing—some shops even have fitting rooms. Licensed goods sold by others range from predictable items (shot glasses, cue balls, and Zippo cigarette lighters) to the more surprising (cologne, dolls, and cell phones).
- ***Making low-profit customers more profitable or terminating them.*** To avoid the direct need for termination, marketers can encourage unprofitable customers to buy more or in larger quantities, forgo certain features or services, or pay higher amounts or fees. Banks, phone companies, and travel agencies are all now charging for once-free services to ensure minimum customer revenue levels.
- ***Focusing disproportionate effort on high-value customers.*** The most valuable customers can be treated in a special way. Thoughtful gestures such as birthday greetings, small gifts, or invitations to special sports or arts events can send a strong positive signal to the customer.

Attracting and Retaining Customers

Companies seeking to expand their profits and sales must spend considerable time and resources searching for new customers. To generate leads, they develop ads and place them in media that will reach new prospects; send direct mail and make phone calls to possible new prospects; send their salespeople to participate in trade shows where they might find new leads; purchases names from list brokers; and so on.

CITIZENS BANK.

In Boston's fiercely competitive banking market, Citizens Bank distinguishes itself by substituting the dog biscuit for the ubiquitous lollipop, which banks have long used to attract and retain customers with young children. Citizens gives out dog biscuits to canine-loving customers with their pooches in tow, distributing 14,000 in 2005. Because dog lovers keep coming back and bringing their dog-loving friends, Citizens' South End Boston branch went a step further and installed the Dog Spot, a dedicated area in the lobby where dogs can hang out while their owners take care of their banking needs. This 10-foot-wide space has turf, a doghouse, water bowls, plants, and biscuits. Since the Dog Spot opened, the bank has seen a spike in new customers, and its branch manager noted that sometimes dogs force owners in even if there's no banking to be done.[66]

TABLE 5.4

Customer Acquisition Costs by Marketing Activity

Activity	Cost per New Customer	Cost per Solicitation
Personal selling	$550	$110.00
Direct mail	$130	$ 1.70
Telemarketing	$105	$ 3.75
Web site, e-mail	$ 35	$ 0.07

1. Costs are based upon typical industry averages. Response rates are implied.
2. Actual costs vary from business to business depending on the complexity of the sales process.

For discussion, see: Justin Zohn, "Customer Acquisition Cost—A Key Marketing Metric," *National Petroleum News* (April 2003).

Table 5.4 displays one analysis of some typical acquisition costs. Different types of acquisition methods can yield different types of customers with varying CLVs. One study showed that customers acquired through the offer of a 35% discount had about one-half the long-term value of customers acquired without any discount.[67]

REDUCING DEFECTION It is not enough, however, to attract new customers; the company must keep them and increase their business.[68] Too many companies suffer from high **customer churn** or defection. Adding customers here is like adding water to a leaking bucket. Cellular carriers and cable TV operators, for example, are plagued with "spinners," customers who switch carriers at least three times a year looking for the best deal. Many lose 25% of their subscribers each year, at an estimated cost of $2 billion to $4 billion.

To reduce the defection rate, the company must:

1. Define and measure its retention rate. For a magazine, subscription renewal rate is a good measure of retention. For a college, it could be the first- to second-year retention rate, or the class graduation rate.
2. Distinguish the causes of customer attrition and identify those that can be managed better. Not much can be done about customers who leave the region or go out of business, but much can be done about those who leave because of poor service, shoddy products, or high prices.[69]
3. Compare the lost profit equal to the customer's lifetime value from a lost customer to the costs to reduce the defection rate. As long as the cost to discourage defection is lower than the lost profit, the company should spend the money to try to retain the customer.

RETENTION DYNAMICS Figure 5.5 shows the main steps in the process of attracting and retaining customers. The starting point is everyone who might conceivably buy the product or service. These *potentials* are people or organizations who might conceivably have an interest in buying the company's product or service, but may not have the means or intention to buy. The next task is to identify which potentials are really good *prospects*—people with the motivation, ability, and opportunity to make a purchase—by interviewing them, checking on their financial standing, and so on. Marketing efforts can then concentrate on converting the prospects into *first-time customers,* and then into *repeat customers,* and then into *clients*—people to whom the company gives very special and knowledgeable treatment. The next challenge is to turn clients into *members* by starting a membership program that offers benefits to customers who join, and then turning members into *advocates,* customers who enthusiastically recommend the company and its products and services to others. The ultimate challenge is to turn advocates into *partners.*

Unfortunately, much marketing theory and practice centers on the art of attracting new customers, rather than on retaining and cultivating existing ones. The emphasis traditionally has been on making sales rather than on building relationships; on preselling and selling rather than on caring for the customer afterward. More companies now recognize the importance of satisfying and retaining customers.

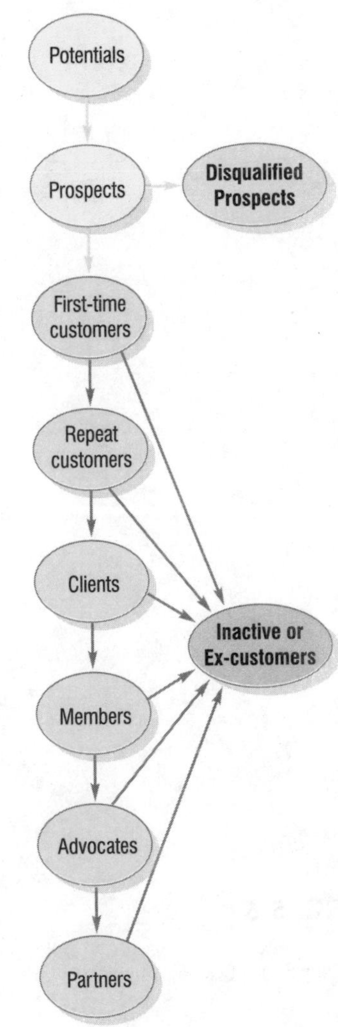

FIG. 5.5

The Customer-Development Process

Source: See Jill Griffin, *Customer Loyalty: How to Earn It, How to Keep It* (New York: Lexington Books, 1995), p. 36. Also see Murray Raphel and Neil Raphel, *Up the Loyalty Ladder: Turning Sometime Customers into Full-Time Advocates Your Business* (New York: HarperBusiness, 1995

Satisfied customers constitute the company's *customer relationship capital.* If the company were to be sold, the acquiring company would pay not only for the plant and equipment and the brand name, but also for the delivered *customer base,* the number and value of the customers who would do business with the new firm. Here are some interesting facts that bear on customer retention:[70]

- Acquiring new customers can cost five times more than satisfying and retaining current customers. It requires a great deal of effort to induce satisfied customers to switch away from their current suppliers.
- The average company loses 10% of its customers each year.
- A 5% reduction in the customer defection rate can increase profits by 25% to 85%, depending on the industry.
- The customer profit rate tends to increase over the life of the retained customer due to increased purchases, referrals, and price premiums and reduced operating costs to service.

Building Loyalty

Creating a strong, tight connection to customers is the dream of any marketer and often the key to long-term marketing success. Companies that want to form strong customer bonds need to attend to a number of different considerations (see Figure 5.6). One set of researchers see retention-building activities as adding financial benefits, social benefits, or structural ties.[71] The following sections explain four important types of marketing activities that companies are using to improve loyalty and retention.

INTERACTING WITH CUSTOMERS Listening to customers is crucial to customer relationship management. Some companies have created an ongoing mechanism that keeps senior managers permanently plugged in to frontline customer feedback.

- MBNA, the credit card giant, asks every executive to listen in on telephone conversations in the customer-service area or customer recovery units.
- Deere & Company, which makes John Deere tractors and has a superb record of customer loyalty—nearly 98% annual retention in some product areas—has used retired employees to interview defectors and customers.[72]
- Chicken of the Sea has 80,000 members in its Mermaid Club, a core-customer group treated to coupons and special offers. In return, club members provide valuable feedback on what the company is doing and is thinking of doing. When the company considered introducing canned whitefish, members emphatically rejected the product concept and the company chose not to introduce it.[73]

But listening is only part of the story. It is also important to be a customer advocate and, as much as possible, take the customers' side on issues, understanding their point of view.[74] USAA Insurance's legendary quality of service has led to the highest customer satisfaction in

FIG. 5.6 | Forming Strong Customer Bonds

- Create superior products, services, and experiences for the target market.
- Get cross-departmental participation in planning and managing the customer satisfaction and retention process.
- Integrate the "Voice of the Customer" to capture their stated and unstated needs or requirements in all business decisions.
- Organize and make accessible a database of information on individual customer needs, preferences, contacts, purchase frequency, and satisfaction.
- Make it easy for customers to reach appropriate company personnel and express their needs, perceptions, and complaints.
- Assess the potential of frequency programs and club marketing programs.
- Run award programs recognizing outstanding employees.

the industry. USAA subscribers will often tell stories about how the company looks out for them, even counseling them not to take out more insurance than they need. With such levels of trust, USAA enjoys high levels of customer loyalty and significant cross-selling opportunities.[75] "Marketing Memo: Creating Customer Evangelists" describes six keys to creating customers who feel so strongly about companies and brands that they go way beyond just purchasing and consuming their products and services.

DEVELOPING LOYALTY PROGRAMS Two customers loyalty programs that companies can offer are frequency programs and club marketing programs. **Frequency programs (FPs)** are designed to provide rewards to customers who buy frequently and in substantial amounts.[76] They can help build long-term loyalty with high CLV customers, creating cross-selling opportunities in the process. Originally pioneered by the airlines, hotels, and credit card companies, FPs now exist in many other types of businesses. For example, today most supermarket chains offer price club cards, which provide member customers with discounts on particular items.[77]

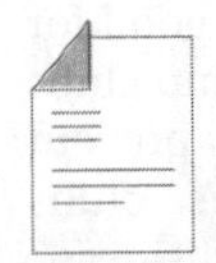

MARKETING MEMO — CREATING CUSTOMER EVANGELISTS

Authors Ben McConnell and Jackie Huba assert that *customer evangelists* not only buy a company's products or services but believe in them so much that they are compelled to spread the word and voluntarily recruit their friends and colleagues on the company's behalf. McConnell and Huba studied brands such as Macintosh, Krispy Kreme, the Dallas Mavericks, Linux, Pallotta TeamWorks, SolutionPeople, and others created and sustained by customer evangelists. On their own "Church of the Customer" blog site (www.churchofthecustomer.com), they offer six tips for marketing evangelism:

- ***Customer Plus-Delta.*** Understand what evangelists love by continuously gathering their input. Build-a-Bear Workshop uses a "Cub Advisory Board" as a feedback and decision-input body. The board is made up of twenty 8-to-12-year-olds who review new-product ideas and give a "paws up or down." Many products in the stores are customer ideas.
- ***Napsterize Your Knowledge.*** Release your own knowledge, data or intellectual property into a fast-moving distribution network. Sharing knowledge freely makes it more accessible, reducing your biggest threat: obscurity. It's liable to fall into the hands of people who will tell others about it. People talking about your knowledge increases its perceived and actual value.
- ***Build the Buzz.*** Keep customer evangelists talking by providing them tools, programs, and features to demonstrate their passion. Sneaker company Converse asked amateur filmmakers to submit 30-second short films that demonstrated their inspiration from the iconic brand. The best of the 1,800 submissions were showcased in the Converse Gallery Web site (conversegallery.com). Converse used the best of the best films as TV commercials. One key outcome of the gallery: Sales of shoes via the Web site doubled in the month after the gallery's launch.
- ***Create Community.*** Provide like-minded customers the chance to meet. Paetec provides telecommunications services to hotels, universities, and other companies. It has grown into a $500 million company in six years, and its growth is due entirely to evangelism. Paetec's primary marketing strategy: Host informal dinners around the country for customers. Current customers and key prospects are invited to dine on Paetec's tab and meet one another. No boring PowerPoint presentations here, just customers talking about their telecommunications challenges and their unfiltered experiences of being a Paetec customer. Prospects are sold on the company by other customers.
- ***Make Bite-Size Chunks.*** Bite-size chunks of products and services reduce risk, improve sales cycles, and offer upfront value. Even if a customer doesn't purchase, he or she may spread favorable word of mouth. This is largely the marketing strategy of beverage maker Izze. The company's slightly carbonated juice drinks appear at high-profile charity events. In what surely must be confounding to some brand marketers, Izze insists that event organizers do not display Izze logos or banners anywhere at the event. The outcome is serendipity: Attendees feel as if they have "discovered" a new drink without a marketer hawking it to them. The discovery process inspires them to tell others. The result: Starbucks, Whole Foods, and Target have all sought out Izze to stock the beverages in their stores, without requiring the typical slotting fees.
- ***Create a Cause.*** Companies that strive for a higher purpose—such as supporting "freedom," as Harley-Davidson and Southwest do—often find that customers, vendors, suppliers, and employees naturally root for their success. Customer evangelists crave emotional connection and validation; a well-defined cause generates emotional commitment. When your brand, product, or service aspires to change the world, altruism and capitalism converge.

Sources: Ben McConnell and Jackie Huba, "Learning to Leverage the Lunatic Fringe," *Point* (July–August 2006): 14–15; Michael Krauss, "Work to Convert Customers into Evangelists," *Marketing News*, December 15, 2006, p. 6; Ben McConnell and Jackie Huba, *Creating Customer Evangelists: How Loyal Customers Become a Loyal Sales Force* (New York: Kaplan Business, 2003).

HERSHEY CO.

In the Spring of 2006, Hershey's started an unusual loyalty program in conjunction with online auction giant eBay. Consumers who collect WrapperCash points—codes printed on one billion single-serve Hershey products—could bank those points at the Hershey's Web site and then use them to outbid other players for big-ticket items in an online auction powered by eBay. That means customers may have had to eat a lot of candy to post a winning bid, but they could also win a sports car for a pretty low number of wrappers. The program successfully integrated consumers' off-line and online experiences with the brand. For instance, the big-ticket items, such as the chance to be a master chocolatier for a day, spurred consumers to visit Hersheys.com to register and bank their codes.[78]

Typically, the first company to introduce an FP in an industry gains the most benefit, especially if competitors are slow to respond. After competitors respond, FPs can become a financial burden to all the offering companies, but some companies are more efficient and creative in managing FPs.

Many companies have created club membership programs. **Club membership programs** can be open to everyone who purchases a product or service, or it can be limited to an affinity group or to those willing to pay a small fee. Although open clubs are good for building a database or snagging customers from competitors, limited membership clubs are more powerful long-term loyalty builders. Fees and membership conditions prevent those with only a fleeting interest in a company's products from joining. These clubs attract and keep those customers who are responsible for the largest portion of business.

Some highly successful clubs include the following:

Local user groups have proliferated among Apple owners, thanks to links on the Apple Web site that help visitors locate them. The groups help executives such as Steve Jobs keep in close touch with the company's customers and their needs.

APPLE

Apple encourages owners of its computers to form local Apple-user groups. By 2001, there were over 600, ranging in size from fewer than 25 members to over 1,000 members. The user groups provide Apple owners with opportunities to learn more about their computers, share ideas, and get product discounts. They sponsor special activities and events and perform community service. A visit to Apple's Web site will help a customer find a nearby user group.[79]

HARLEY-DAVIDSON

The world-famous motorcycle company sponsors the Harley Owners Group (H.O.G.), which now numbers one million members in over 1,200 chapters. The first-time buyer of a Harley-Davidson motorcycle gets a free one-year H.O.G. membership. H.O.G. benefits include a magazine called *Hog Tales*, a touring handbook, emergency road service, a specially designed insurance program, theft reward service, discount hotel rates, and a Fly & Ride program enabling members to rent Harleys while on vacation. The company also maintains an extensive Web site devoted to H.O.G., which includes information on club chapters, events, and a special members-only section.[80]

PERSONALIZING MARKETING Company personnel can create strong bonds with customers by individualizing and personalizing relationships. In essence, thoughtful companies turn their customers into clients. One distinction that has been drawn:

> Customers may be nameless to the institution; clients cannot be nameless. Customers are served as part of the mass or as part of larger segments; clients are served on an individual basis. Customers are served by anyone who happens to be available; clients are served by the professional assigned to them.[81]

TABLE 5.5 | Breaking Down Customer Relationship Management: What Customer Relationship Management Really Comprises

CRM Imperative				
Acquiring the right customer	Crafting the right value proposition	Instituting the best processes	Motivating employees	Learning to retain customers
You Get It When . . .				
■ You've identified your most valuable customers. ■ You've calculated your share of their wallet for your goods and services.	■ You've studied what products or services your customers need today and will need tomorrow. ■ You've surveyed what products or services your competitors offer today and will offer tomorrow. ■ You've spotted what products or services you should be offering.	■ You've researched the best way to deliver your products or services to customers, including the alliances you need to strike, the technologies you need to invest in, and the service capabilities you need to develop or acquire.	■ You know what tools your employees need to foster customer relationships. ■ You've identified the HR systems you need to institute in order to boost employee loyalty.	■ You've learned why customers defect and how to win them back. ■ You've analyzed what your competitors are doing to win your high-value customers. ■ Your senior management monitors customer defection metrics.
CRM Technology Can Help . . .				
■ Analyze customer revenue and cost data to identify current and future high-value customers. ■ Target your direct-marketing efforts better.	■ Capture relevant product and service behavior data. ■ Create new distribution channels. ■ Develop new pricing models. ■ Build communities.	■ Process transactions faster. ■ Provide better information to the front line. ■ Manage logistics and the supply chain more efficiently. ■ Catalyze collaborative commerce.	■ Align incentives and metrics. ■ Deploy knowledge management systems.	■ Track customer defection and retention levels. ■ Track customer service satisfaction levels.

Source: Darrel K. Rigby, Frederick F. Reichheld, and Phil Schefter, "Avoid the Four Perils of CRM," *Harvard Business Review* (February 2002): 106.

An increasingly essential ingredient for the best relationship marketing today is the right technology. Table 5.5 highlights five imperatives of CRM and shows where technology fits in. GE Plastics could not target its e-mail effectively to different customers if it were not for advances in database software. Dell Computer could not customize computer ordering for its global corporate customers without advances in Web technology. Companies are using e-mail, Web sites, call centers, databases, and database software to foster continuous contact between company and customer. Here is how one company used technology to build customer value:

AMERITRADE

The discount brokerage service Ameritrade provides detailed information to its customers, which helps to create strong bonds. It offers customized e-mail alerts to the device of the customer's choice, detailing stock movements and analysts' recommendations. The company's Web site permits online trading and provides access to a variety of research tools. Ameritrade developed an investing tutorial called Darwin, which it offered free on CD-ROM to its customers. Customers responded to this new focus on their needs: Ameritrade grew from fewer than 100,000 accounts in 1997 to over 3 million in 2004. A research study in 2005 showed Ameritrade customers were among the most active online traders in the industry.[82]

E-commerce companies looking to attract and retain customers are discovering that personalization goes beyond creating customized information.[83] For example, the Lands' End Live Web site offers visitors the opportunity to talk with a customer service representative. Nordstrom takes a similar approach with its Web site to ensure that online buyers are as satisfied with the company's customer service as the in-store visitors. Even the BBC, British archetype of an old media company, is reaping the benefits of customizing its offerings, a practice that is taking it well beyond its commercial rivals in UK broadcasting:

BRITISH BROADCASTING CORP.

MyBBC player, now in trials, lets British users download current radio and TV programs up to seven days after broadcast. Not only can viewers download content, they can also build on it and share it. One project, for instance, lets Britons download footage from BBC news and science shows, remix them, and eventually share them online. Even more radical is http://backstage.bbc.co.uk, which provides data, resources, and support for Internet developers and designers—inside and outside the BBC—to share in order to build prototypes of new concepts using BBC material. One consumer-created prototype called Sport Map allows people to find the nearest soccer team on the map and get its latest news—a service bound to be popular in a country full of avid soccer fans.[84]

At the same time, online companies need to make sure their attempts to create relationships with customers don't backfire, as when customers are bombarded by computer-generated recommendations that consistently miss the mark. Buy a lot of baby gifts on Amazon.com, and your personalized recommendations suddenly don't look so personal! E-tailers need to recognize the limitations of online personalization at the same time that they try harder to find technology and processes that really work.[85]

Companies are also recognizing the importance of the personal component to CRM and what happens once customers make actual contact. As Stanford's business guru Jeffrey Pfeffer puts it, "the best companies build cultures in which frontline people are empowered to do what's needed to take care of the customer." He cites examples of firms such as SAS, the Scandinavian airline, which engineered a turnaround based in part on the insight that a customer's impressions of a company are formed through myriad small interactions—checking in, boarding the plane, eating a meal.[86]

CREATING INSTITUTIONAL TIES The company may supply customers with special equipment or computer links that help customers manage orders, payroll, and inventory. Customers are less inclined to switch to another supplier when this would involve high capital costs, high search costs, or the loss of loyal-customer discounts. A good example is McKesson Corporation, a leading pharmaceutical wholesaler, which invested millions of dollars in EDI capabilities to help independent pharmacies manage inventory, order-entry processes, and shelf space. Another example is Milliken & Company, which provides proprietary software programs, marketing research, sales training, and sales leads to loyal customers.

Win-Backs

Regardless of the nature of the category or how hard companies may try, some customers inevitably become inactive or drop out. The challenge is to reactivate dissatisfied customers through win-back strategies.[87] It's often easier to reattract ex-customers (because the company knows their names and histories) than to find new ones. The key is to analyze the causes of customer defection through exit interviews and lost-customer surveys and win back only those who have strong profit potential.[88]

::: Customer Databases and Database Marketing

Marketers must know their customers.[89] And in order to know the customer, the company must collect information and store it in a database from which to conduct database marketing. A **customer database** is an organized collection of comprehensive information about individual customers or prospects that is current, accessible, and actionable for such marketing purposes as lead generation, lead qualification, sale of a product or service, or maintenance of customer relationships. **Database marketing** is the process of building, maintaining, and using customer databases and other databases (products, suppliers, resellers) to contact, transact, and build customer relationships.

Customer Databases

Many companies confuse a customer mailing list with a customer database. A **customer mailing list** is simply a set of names, addresses, and telephone numbers. A customer database contains much more information, accumulated through customer transactions, registration information, telephone queries, cookies, and every customer contact.

Ideally, a customer database also contains the consumer's past purchases, demographics (age, income, family members, birthdays), psychographics (activities, interests, and opinions), mediagraphics (preferred media), and other useful information. The catalog company Fingerhut possesses some 1,400 pieces of information about each of the 30 million households in its massive customer database.

Ideally, a **business database** would contain business customers' past purchases; past volumes, prices, and profits; buyer team member names (and ages, birthdays, hobbies, and favorite foods); status of current contracts; an estimate of the supplier's share of the customer's business; competitive suppliers; assessment of competitive strengths and weaknesses in selling and servicing the account; and relevant buying practices, patterns, and policies.

For example, a Latin American unit of the Swiss pharmaceutical firm Novartis keeps data on 100,000 of Argentina's farmers, knows their crop protection chemical purchases, groups them by value, and treats each group differently. "Breakthrough Marketing: Tesco" describes how the U.K. supermarket giant has found ways to use its database to attract and engage customers.

Data Warehouses and Datamining

Savvy companies are capturing information every time a customer comes into contact with any of their departments. Touch points include a customer purchase, a customer-requested service call, an online query, or a mail-in rebate card. Banks and credit card companies, telephone companies, catalog marketers, and many other companies have a great deal of information about their customers, including not only addresses and phone numbers, but also transactions and enhanced data on age, family size, income, and other demographic information.

These data are collected by the company's contact center and organized into a **data warehouse** where marketers can capture, query, and analyze it to draw inferences about an individual customer's needs and responses. Telemarketers can respond to customer inquiries based on a total picture of the customer relationship.

Through **datamining**, marketing statisticians can extract useful information about individuals, trends, and segments from the mass of data. Datamining uses sophisticated statistical and mathematical techniques such as cluster analysis, automatic interaction detection, predictive modeling, and neural networking.[90]

Some observers believe that a proprietary database can provide a company with a significant competitive advantage. MCI Communications Corporation, the long-distance carrier, sifts through 1 trillion bytes of customer phoning data to create new discount calling plans for different types of customers. Lands' End can tell which of its 2 million customers should receive special mailings of specific clothing items that would fit their wardrobe needs. (See Figure 5.7 for additional examples.)

In general, companies can use their databases in five ways:

1. ***To identify prospects***—Many companies generate sales leads by advertising their product or service. The ads generally contain a response feature, such as a business reply card or toll-free phone number, and the company builds its database from customer responses. It sorts through the database to identify the best prospects, then contacts them by mail, phone, or personal call to try to convert them into customers.
2. ***To decide which customers should receive a particular offer***—Companies are interested in selling, up-selling, and cross-selling their products and services. Companies

BREAKTHROUGH MARKETING | TESCO

If you asked a customer of U.K. supermarket chain Tesco what the shopping experience there was like in the early 1980s, "customer friendly" would probably not be the answer. Though it began upgrading its stores and product selection in 1983, Tesco continued to suffer from a reputation as a "pile it high and sell it cheap" mass-market retailer, lagging behind the more upscale market leader Sainsbury's. To gain share against Sainsbury's, Tesco needed to reverse the public perception of its stores. It decided to improve the shopping experience and highlight improvements with an image campaign to "lift us out of the mold in our particular sector," as its 1989 agency brief put it.

British retailer Tesco's strong customer focus has spurred its growth in the U.K. and allowed it to successfully enter other countries such as China.

Between 1990 and 1992, Tesco launched 114 separate initiatives to improve the quality of its stores, including adding baby-changing rooms, stocking specialty items such as French free-range chickens, and introducing a value-priced line of products. It developed a campaign titled "Every Little Helps" to communicate these improvements with 20 ads, each focusing on a different aspect of its approach—"doing right by the customer." As a result, between 1990 and 1995, Tesco attracted 1.3 million new customers, who pushed revenues and market share steadily upward until Tesco surpassed Sainsbury's as the market leader in 1995.

Tesco then introduced an initiative that would make it a world-class example of how to build lasting relationships with customers: the Tesco Clubcard frequent-shopper program. Essentially a loyalty card that offered discounts and special offers tailored to individual shoppers, the Clubcard was also a powerful data-gathering tool enabling Tesco to understand the shopping patterns and preferences of its customers better than any competitor could. Using Clubcard data, Tesco created a unique "DNA profile" for each customer based on shopping habits. To build this profile, it classified each product purchased by a customer on a set of up to 40 dimensions, including price, size, brand, ecofriendliness, convenience, and healthiness. Based on their DNA profile, Tesco shoppers received one of 4 million different variations of the quarterly Clubcard statement, which contained targeted special offers and other promotions. The company also installed kiosks in its stores where Clubcard shoppers could get customized coupons.

The Clubcard data also helped Tesco run its business more efficiently. Tracking Clubcard purchases helped uncover price elasticities and set promotional schedules saving over $500 million. Tesco used customer data to determine the range of products and the nature of merchandising for each store, and even the location of new stores. Within 15 months of introduction, more than 8 million Clubcards had been issued, of which 5 million were used regularly. The customer focus enhanced by the Clubcard helped propel Tesco to even greater success than in the early 1990s. The company's market share in the United Kingdom rose to 15% by 1999, and that year other British companies voted Tesco Britain's most admired company for the second year in a row.

In the following years, Tesco continued to apply its winning formula of using customer data to dominate the British retail landscape, moving beyond supermarkets to "big-box" retailing of general merchandise, or nonfood products. Not only was Tesco providing additional convenience to consumers who preferred shopping under one roof, it was also improving its profitability. The average margin of nonfood products was 9%, as opposed to 5% for food. By 2003, nearly 20% of Tesco's revenues came from nonfood items, and the company was selling more CDs than Virgin Megastores, and its apparel line, Cherokee, was the fastest-growing brand in the United Kingdom.

Tesco also undertook extensive customer research with telephone and written surveys and customer panels to extend its lead in the grocery market. By 2005, the company had a 35% share of supermarket spending in the united Kingdom, almost twice that of its nearest competitor, and a 14% share of total retail sales. Tesco used the same customer-centered strategy to expand overseas. In 2005, it had 648 stores outside the United Kingdom and was the supermarket leader in Poland, Hungary, Thailand, Ireland, and Slovakia. In 2006, it was Britain's largest company and the sixth-largest retailer in the world.

Sources: Richard Fletcher, "Leahy Shrugs Off Talk of a 'Brain Drain'," *Sunday Times* (London), January 29, 2006; Elizabeth Rigby, "Prosperous Tesco Takes Retailing to a New Level," *Financial Times*, September 21, 2005, p. 23; Laura Cohn, "A Grocery War That's Not about Food," *BusinessWeek*, October 20, 2003, p. 30; "The Prime Minister Launches the 10th Tesco Computers for Schools Scheme," *M2 Presswire*, January 26, 2001; Ashleye Sharpe and Joanna Bamford, "Tesco Stores Ltd." (paper presented at Advertising Effectiveness Awards, 2000); Hamish Pringle and Marjorie Thompson, *Brand Spirit* (New York: John Wiley, 1999).

FIG. 5.7

Examples of Database Marketing

Qwest Twice a year Qwest sifts through its customer list looking for customers that have the potential to be more profitable. The company's database contains as many as 200 observations about each customer's calling patterns. By looking at demographic profiles, plus the mix of local versus long-distance calls or whether a consumer has voice mail, Qwest can estimate potential spending. Next, the company determines how much of the customer's likely telecom budget is already coming its way. Armed with that knowledge, Qwest sets a cutoff point for how much to spend on marketing to this customer.

Royal Caribbean Royal Caribbean uses its database to offer spur-of-the-moment cruise packages to fill all the berths on its ships. It focuses on retired people and single people because they are more able to make quick commitments. Fewer empty berths mean maximized profits for the cruise line.

Fingerhut The skillful use of database marketing and relationship building has made catalog house Fingerhut one of the nation's largest direct-mail marketers. Not only is its database full of demographic details such as age, marital status, and number of children, but it also tracks customers' hobbies, interests, and birthdays. Fingerhut tailors mail offers based on what each customer is likely to buy. Fingerhut stays in continuous touch with customers through regular and special promotions, such as annual sweepstakes, free gifts, and deferred billing. Now the company has applied its database marketing to its Web sites.

Mars Mars is a market leader not only in candy, but also in pet food. In Germany, Mars has compiled the names of virtually every cat-owning family by contacting veterinarians and by advertising a free booklet titled "How to Take Care of Your Cat." Those who request the booklet fill out a questionnaire, so Mars knows the cat's name, age, and birthday. Mars now sends a birthday card to each cat each year, along with a new-cat-food sample or money-saving coupons for Mars brands.

American Express It is no wonder that, at its secret location in Phoenix, security guards watch over American Express's 500 billion bytes of data on how its customers have used the company's 35 million green, gold, and platinum charge cards. Amex uses the database to include precisely targeted offers in its monthly mailing of millions of customer bills.

set up criteria describing the ideal target customer for a particular offer. Then they search their customer databases for those who most closely resemble the ideal type. By noting response rates, a company can improve its targeting precision over time. Following a sale, it can set up an automatic sequence of activities: One week later, send a thank-you note; five weeks later, send a new offer; ten weeks later (if customer has not responded), phone the customer and offer a special discount.

3. ***To deepen customer loyalty***—Companies can build interest and enthusiasm by remembering customer preferences and by sending appropriate gifts, discount coupons, and interesting reading material.
4. ***To reactivate customer purchases***—Companies can install automatic mailing programs (automatic marketing) that send out birthday or anniversary cards, Christmas shopping reminders, or off-season promotions. The database can help the company make attractive or timely offers.
5. ***To avoid serious customer mistakes***—A major bank confessed to a number of mistakes it had made by not using its customer database well. In one case, the bank charged a customer a penalty for late payment on his mortgage, failing to note he headed a company that was a major depositor in this bank. He quit the bank. In a second case, two different staff members of the bank phoned the same mortgage customer offering a home equity loan at different prices. Neither knew that the other had made the call. In a third case, the bank gave a premium customer only standard service in another country.

The Downside of Database Marketing and CRM

Having covered the good news about database marketing, we also need to cover the bad news. Four problems can prevent a firm from effectively using CRM. The first is that building and maintaining a customer database requires a large investment in computer hardware, database software, analytical programs, communication links, and skilled personnel. It's difficult to collect the right data, especially to capture all the occasions of company interaction with individual customers. Building a customer database would not be worthwhile in the following cases: (1) when the product is a once-in-a-lifetime purchase (a grand piano); (2) when customers show little loyalty to a brand (there is lots of customer churn); (3) when the unit sale is very small (a candy bar); and (4) when the cost of gathering information is too high.

The second problem is the difficulty of getting everyone in the company to be customer oriented and to use the available information. Employees find it far easier to carry on traditional transaction marketing than to practice customer relationship marketing. Effective database marketing requires managing and training employees as well as dealers and suppliers.

The third problem is that not all customers want a relationship with the company, and they may resent knowing that the company has collected that much personal information about them. Marketers must be concerned about customer attitudes toward privacy and security. American Express, long regarded as a leader on privacy issues, does not sell information about specific customer transactions. However, the company found itself the target of consumer outrage when it announced a partnership with KnowledgeBase Marketing Inc. that would have made data about 175 million U.S. customers available to any merchant that accepted American Express cards. American Express killed the partnership. AOL, also targeted by privacy advocates, junked a plan to sell subscribers' telephone numbers. Online companies would be smart to explain their privacy policies and to give consumers the right not to have their information stored in a database. European countries do not look favorably upon database marketing and are more protective of consumers' private information. The European Union passed a law handicapping the growth of database marketing in its 15 member countries.

A fourth problem is that the assumptions behind CRM may not always hold true.[91] For example, it may not cost less to serve more loyal customers. High-volume customers often know their value to a company and can leverage it to extract premium service and/or price discounts. Loyal customers may expect and demand more from the firm and resent any attempt to charge full or higher prices. They may also be jealous of attention lavished on other customers. When eBay began to chase big corporate customers such as IBM, Disney, and Sears, some small mom-and-pop businesses that helped to build the brand felt abandoned.[92] Loyal customers may not necessarily be the best ambassadors for the brand. One study found that customers who scored high on behavioral loyalty and bought a lot of a company' products were less active word-of-mouth marketers than customers who scored high on attitudinal loyalty and expressed greater commitment to the firm.

Thus, the benefits of database marketing do not come without heavy costs, not only in collecting the original customer data, but also in maintaining them and mining them. When it works, a data warehouse yields more than it costs, but the data must be in good condition, and the discovered relationships must be valid.

Database marketing is most frequently used by business marketers and service providers (hotels, banks, airlines; and insurance, credit card, and telephone companies) that normally and easily collect a lot of customer data. Other types of companies in the best position to invest in CRM are those that do a lot of cross-selling and up-selling (such as GE and Amazon.com) or whose customers have highly differentiated needs and are of highly differentiated value to the company. Packaged-goods retailers and consumer packaged-goods companies use database marketing less frequently, though some (such as Kraft, Quaker Oats, Ralston Purina, and Nabisco) have built databases for certain brands. Businesses with low CLV, high churn, and no direct contact between the seller and ultimate buyer may not benefit as much from CRM. Some businesses cited as CRM successes include Enterprise Rent-A-Car, Pioneer Hi-Bred Seeds, Fidelity Investments, Lexus, Intuit, and Capital One.[93]

Deloitte Consulting found that 70% of firms found little or no improvement through CRM implementation. The reasons are many: The CRM system was poorly designed, it became too expensive, users didn't make much use of it or report much benefit, and collaborators ignored the system. One set of business commentators suggested the following as the four main perils of CRM:[94]

1. Implementing CRM before creating a customer strategy
2. Rolling out CRM before changing the organization to match
3. Assuming more CRM technology is better
4. Stalking, not wooing, customers

Wharton's George Day concludes that one of the reasons many CRM failures occur is that companies concentrate on customer contact processes without making corresponding changes in internal structures and systems.[95] His recommendation? Change the configuration before installing CRM: "Our survey results confirm that a superior customer-relating capability has everything to do with how a business builds and manages its organization and not much to do with the CRM tools and technologies it employs." All this points to the need for each company to determine how much (and where) to invest in building and using database marketing to conduct its customer relationships.

SUMMARY :::

1. Customers are value maximizers. They form an expectation of value and act on it. Buyers will buy from the firm that they perceive to offer the highest customer-delivered value, defined as the difference between total customer benefits and total customer cost.
2. A buyer's satisfaction is a function of the product's perceived performance and the buyer's expectations. Recognizing that high satisfaction leads to high customer loyalty, many companies today are aiming for TCS—total customer satisfaction. For such companies, customer satisfaction is both a goal and a marketing tool.
3. Losing profitable customers can dramatically affect a firm's profits. The cost of attracting a new customer is estimated to be five times the cost of keeping a current customer happy. The key to retaining customers is relationship marketing.
4. Quality is the totality of features and characteristics of a product or service that bear on its ability to satisfy stated or implied needs. Marketers play a key role in achieving high levels of total quality so that firms remain solvent and profitable.
5. Marketing managers must calculate customer lifetime values of their customer base to understand their profit implications. They must also determine ways to increase the value of the customer base.
6. Companies are also becoming skilled in customer relationship management (CRM), which focuses on developing programs to attract and retain the right customers and meeting the individual needs of those valued customers.
7. Customer relationship management often requires building a customer database and doing datamining to detect trends, segments, and individual needs.

APPLICATIONS :::

Marketing Debate Online versus Off-line Privacy

As more and more firms practice relationship marketing and develop customer databases, privacy issues are emerging as an important topic. Consumers and public interest groups are scrutinizing—and sometimes criticizing—the privacy policies of firms and raising concerns about potential theft of online credit card information or other potentially sensitive or confidential financial information. Others maintain that the online privacy fears are unfounded and that security issues are every bit as much a concern in the off-line world. They argue that the opportunity to steal information exists virtually everywhere and that it's up to the consumer to protect their interests.

Take a position: (1) Privacy is a bigger issue in the online world than the off-line world *versus* Privacy is no different online than off-line.

Marketing Discussion

Consider the lifetime value of customers (CLV). Choose a business and show how you would go about developing a quantitative formulation that captures the concept. How would that business change if it totally embraced the customer equity concept and maximized CLV?

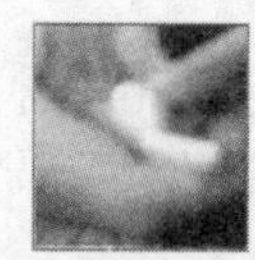

IN THIS CHAPTER, WE WILL ADDRESS THE FOLLOWING QUESTIONS:

1. How do consumer characteristics influence buying behavior?
2. What major psychological processes influence consumer responses to the marketing program?
3. How do consumers make purchasing decisions?
4. How do marketers analyze consumer decision making?

CHAPTER 6 ::: ANALYZING CONSUMER MARKETS

The aim of marketing is to meet and satisfy target customers' needs and wants better than competitors. Marketers are always looking for emerging customer trends that suggest new marketing opportunities. For example, the emergence of the mobile phone, especially with teens and young adults, has marketers rethinking their practices

With over 2.6 billion mobile subscribers in the world at the end of 2006—more than 200 million of whom were in the United States—cell phones represent a major opportunity for advertisers to reach consumers on the "third screen" (after the TV and the computer). Wireless carriers have a wealth of information about their customers that marketers find valuable, such as demographic data, geographic location, and content purchasing habits. Major wireless carriers in the United States had long been reluctant to allow advertising to customers via their networks, but with a shift in consumer attitudes towards mobile marketing came the introduction in 2006 of text ads, search-based ads, and even banner ads to Web-enabled phones. A 2006 study by Harris Interactive found that 80% of respondents were open to receiving marketing messages on their mobile phones, provided the ads were targeted. Young people are an extremely attractive target. In the United Kingdom alone, 99% of 15- to 19-year-olds have cell phones, spending $202.9 million on downloadable content and $570 million >>>

Cell phones are among the newest marketing frontiers for wireless advertising messages.

on test messages in 2005. Major advertisers have begun embracing mobile marketing. For example, Procter & Gamble developed a mobile efforts for its Crest Whitening Plus Scope Extreme Toothpaste, in which consumers were prompted by a series of guerrilla ads on bar napkins and club bathroom signs to text the letters "IQ" to a specific number in order to take a quiz that tested their "Irresistability IQ." From this small start, mobile advertising is expected to grow significantly, providing revenues of $11 billion by 2011 according to Informa Telecoms & Media.[1]

Successful marketing requires that companies fully connect with their customers. Adopting a holistic marketing orientation means understanding customers—gaining a 360-degree view of both their daily lives and the changes that occur during their lifetimes so that the right products are marketed to the right customers in the right way. This chapter explores individual consumer buying dynamics; the next chapter explores the buying dynamics of business buyers.

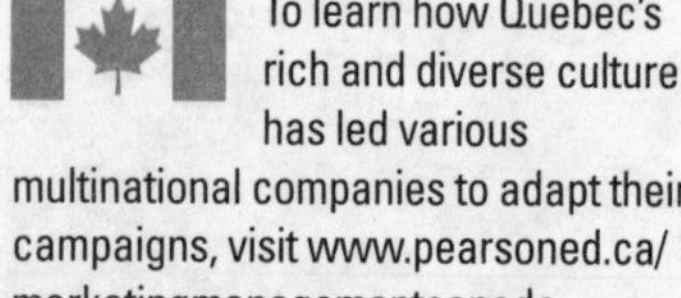
To learn how Quebec's rich and diverse culture has led various multinational companies to adapt their campaigns, visit www.pearsoned.ca/marketingmanagementcanada.

::: What Influences Consumer Behavior?

Consumer behavior is the study of how individuals, groups, and organizations select, buy, use, and dispose of goods, services, ideas, or experiences to satisfy their needs and wants.[2] Marketers must fully understand both the theory and reality of consumer behavior. Table 6.1 profiles U.S. consumers in 2005, and "Marketing Insight: The Future of American Hyperconsumption" looks ahead to how broad demographic trends might bring changes in the level of consumer demand.

A consumer's buying behavior is influenced by cultural, social, and personal factors. Cultural factors exert the broadest and deepest influence.

Cultural Factors

Culture, subculture, and social class are particularly important influences on consumer buying behavior. **Culture** is the fundamental determinant of a person's wants and behavior. Through family and other key institutions, a child growing up in the United States is exposed to the following values: achievement and success, activity, efficiency and practicality, progress, material comfort, individualism, freedom, external comfort, humanitarianism, and youthfulness.[3] A child growing up in another country might have a different view of self, relationship to others, and rituals. Marketers must closely attend to cultural values in every country to understand how to best market their existing products and find opportunities for new products.

Each culture consists of smaller **subcultures** that provide more specific identification and socialization for their members. Subcultures include nationalities, religions, racial groups, and geographic regions. When subcultures grow large and affluent enough, companies often design specialized marketing programs to serve them.

TABLE 6.1

American Consumer Almanac

Expenditures

Average U.S. outlays for goods and services in 2005:

- Housing: 32.1%
- Transportation: 18%
- Food at home: 7.7%
- Food away from home: 5.6%
- Alcohol: 1.1%
- Tobacco: 0.7%
- Health care: 5.9%
- Entertainment: 5.1%
- Reading: 0.3%
- Apparel: 4.2%
- Education: 2.1%
- Life insurance, pensions, Social Security contributions: 11.1%
- Cash contributions: 3.2%
- Personal care: 1.3%
- Miscellaneous: 1.6%

Ownership

- Average number of vehicles per household: 1.9
- Percentage of households that own homes: 68%
- Percentage of households that own their homes "free and clear": 26%

Time (per day)

- Sleeping & personal care: 9.34 hours
- Leisure & sports: 5.18 hours
- Work: 3.65 hours: 7.9 hours (during workweek)
- Household activities: 1.80 hours
- Eating & drinking: 1.24 hours
- Shopping: 0.81 hours
- Caring for household members: 0.56 hours
- Education: 0.50 hours
- Volunteering, civic groups, & religion: 0.32 hours
- Caring for non-household members: 0.27 hours
- Phone calls, mail, e-mail: 0.18 hours
- Miscellaneous: 0.15 hours

Media

The average consumer was estimated to spend 9 hours and 35 minutes a day using media in 2006 (including media multitasking).

- TV: 256 minutes
- Radio: 160 minutes
- Internet: 31 minutes
- Newspapers: 29 minutes
- Recorded music: 29 minutes
- Magazines: 20 minutes
- Books: 17 minutes
- Prerecorded DVD & VCR: 14 minutes
- Video games: 14 minutes
- Wireless content: 3 minutes
- Movie theater: 2 minutes

Source: "The American Consumer 2006," *Advertising Age*, January 2, 2006.

DAVID'S BRIDAL

As Latinos make up a greater proportion of the population in the United States and their purchasing power grows, the Quinceañera is attracting marketers' attention. A social and religious celebration of a girl's transition to womanhood on her 15th birthday, the Quinceañera resembles a groomless wedding and features a processional entrance and a waltz. Not surprisingly, then, big retail chains such as David's Bridal, with 250 stores, now market to the Quinceañera customer. For instance, David's Bridal started a Spanish-language version of its Web site, and its 2007 line featured more dresses in pink and blue to cater to the Quinceañera celebrant. The company's senior vice president says, "We hope we're going to be there for her for events later in life. It's a relationship business."[4]

MARKETING INSIGHT | THE FUTURE OF AMERICAN HYPERCONSUMPTION

As a group, U.S. consumers outspend every other nation's consumers. In 2005, total U.S. household consumption in the average week exceeded Finland's gross domestic product for an entire year. Yet ongoing shifts in the makeup of the U.S. consumer base bring questions as to whether this hyperconsumption will continue to grow. Here are three trends that may lessen demand and three that may increase it.

Lessening Demand

1. ***Higher Growth in Low-Income Households***—Low-income households are projected to grow through 2010 for two main reasons. One, the growth rate of single mothers is projected to increase, while the growth rate of married mothers with children living at home will decrease. Single mothers have a median annual income of less than $27,000, approximately one-third of the median annual income for married couples with children. Second, the Hispanic population is projected to grow 14% through 2010, while the non-Hispanic White population will grow 1% in the same time. The average Hispanic annual household income is $45,900, compared with $65,300 for White non-Hispanics.
2. ***Widening Wealth Disparity***—Between 2000 and 2004, the number of U.S. citizens living in poverty rose 17% to 37 million. By contrast, the number of very affluent people—with individual incomes above $90,000—rose 16% in real terms to 11.9 million. It is expected that this gap between rich and poor will continue to widen. Furthermore, as the United States shifts from a manufacturing- to a knowledge-based economy, wages for unskilled labor may fall, leading to an increase in the number of its citizens living in poverty.
3. ***Male College Enrollment Dropping***—Among those aged 18–24, U.S. men slightly outnumber women, yet in this group there are 23% more women enrolled in college than men. In 2004, fully employed college graduates earned twice as much as fully employed high-school graduates, on average. As fewer men go to college, their total spending power will drop. Compounding the problem is the fact that women with bachelor's degrees currently earn 32% less on average than men with the same qualifications.

Increasing Demand

1. ***Female Economic Power Growing***—Women are rapidly narrowing the wage gap. Women between 25 and 64 who worked full time saw their inflation-adjusted income rise an average of 4% between 2000 and 2005, compared with a 3% decline for men. As a greater percentage of women earn advanced degrees than their male counterparts, women will also attain a greater proportion of high-paying jobs for which these qualifications are essential. Though they represented only 47% of the workforce in 2005, women held nearly 52% of all professional or managerial positions and 64% of sales and other white-collar jobs.
2. ***Rise of the Mass Affluent***—The superrich are growing, and spending. The number of households with total spending of more than $100,000 a year is growing at an annual rate of 7%, compared to total household growth of 1%. As the knowledge-based economy continues to grow, the mass affluent segment—which contains many white-collar workers and entrepreneurs—will continue to reap the benefits.
3. ***Baby Boomer Population Aging***—Baby Boomers, the approximately 76 million U.S. consumers born between 1946 and 1964, represent 26% of the U.S. population and control roughly one-third of the country's wealth. The average annual income for households headed by people between the ages of 50 and 59 was $75,000 in 2005. Rather than retire as they get older, many of them will continue to work and, consequently, continue to spend.

Source: Adapted from Peter Francese, "U.S. Consumer—Like No Other on the Planet," *Advertising Age*, January 2, 2006, p. 3.

Multicultural marketing grew out of careful marketing research, which revealed that different ethnic and demographic niches did not always respond favorably to mass-market advertising.

Companies have capitalized on well-thought-out multicultural marketing strategies in recent years (see "Marketing Insight: Marketing to Cultural Market Segments"). As countries become more culturally diverse, however, many marketing campaigns targeting a specific cultural target can spill over and positively influence other cultural groups.[5]

Virtually all human societies exhibit *social stratification,* most often in the form of **social classes**, relatively homogeneous and enduring divisions in a society, hierarchically ordered and with members who share similar values, interests, and behavior. One classic depiction of social classes in the United States defined seven ascending levels, as follows: (1) lower lowers, (2) upper lowers, (3) working class, (4) middle class, (5) upper middles, (6) lower uppers, and (7) upper uppers.[6]

Social classes have several characteristics. First, those within each class tend to be more alike in dress, speech patterns, and recreational preferences than persons from

MARKETING INSIGHT | MARKETING TO CULTURAL MARKET SEGMENTS

Hispanic Americans

Hispanic Americans have become the largest minority in the country with annual purchasing power expected to reach $1 trillion in 2010. The Hispanic American segment can be difficult for marketers. Roughly two dozen nationalities can be classified as "Hispanic American," including Cuban, Mexican, Puerto Rican, Dominican, and other Central and South American groups with a mix of cultures, physical types, racial backgrounds, and aspirations.

Nickelodeon has been hugely successful in creating a "Pan-Latina" character, the bilingual *Dora the Explorer.* Dora's creators enlisted the help of a team of consultants with Latin American backgrounds. As a result, kids might see Dora up in the Andes or with a cocky, a frog that's an important part of Puerto Rican folklore. The research paid off; the show, which airs on both Nick Jr. and sister network Noggin, is the most watched preschool show on commercial television, not only by Hispanic Americans but also by all preschoolers. Dora also soon became a licensing powerhouse, generating over $30 million in 2005 from sales of more than 250 licensed items.

Despite their differences, Hispanic Americans often share strong family values, a need for respect, brand loyalty, and a keen interest in product quality. Marketers are reaching out to Hispanic Americans with targeted promotions, ads, or Web sites, but need to be careful to capture the nuances of cultural and market trends. Although Hispanic Americans share a common language, significant differences exist across regional and national dialects. For example, the word used in Argentina for insect is the same word that people from the Caribbean use to describe the male reproductive organ, which could have serious consequences for the maker of an insect repellent.

U.S.-born Hispanic Americans also have different needs and tastes than their foreign-born counterparts and, though bilingual, often prefer to communicate in English. To cater to this U.S.-born audience, which in 2006 comprised 60% of all Hispanic Americans, Toyota ran an ad for its hybrid cars during the 2006 Super Bowl that featured a Hispanic father and son in a bilingual conversation that compared the cars' use of gas and electricity to their family's use of Spanish and English.

Some marketers are partnering closely with Hispanic-based media: Miller Brewing's three-year, $100 million deal with Spanish-language media giant Univision includes TV, radio, and online ads; numerous sponsorships; and significant brand integration.

African Americans

The purchasing power of the country's 36 million African Americans exploded during the prosperous 1990s and reached $800 billion in 2006, or 8.4% of total U.S. buying power. Based on survey findings, African Americans are the most fashion conscious of all racial and ethnic groups and are strongly motivated by quality and selection. They're also more likely to be influenced by their children when selecting a product for purchase, and less likely to buy brands that are not familiar to them. African Americans watch television and listen to the radio more than other groups, and they buy more DVDs than any except Hispanics.

Many companies have been successful at tailoring products to meet the needs of African Americans. In 1987, Hallmark Cards launched its African American-targeted Mahogany line with only 16 greeting cards; today it offers 800 cards and a line of stationary. Sara Lee Corporation's L'eggs discontinued its separate line of pantyhose for black women; now shades and styles popular among black women make up half the company's general-focus sub-brands. Similarly, in 2004 L'Oreal launched its TrueMatch line of cosmetic foundation, designed to match any skin tone. L'Oreal's move reflected its understanding of the diversity of pigmentation not just across ethnic groups, but also within them.

Asian Americans

According to the U.S. Census Bureau, "Asian" refers to people having origins in any of the original peoples of the Far East, Southeast Asia, or the Indian subcontinent. Six countries represent 79% of the Asian U.S. population: China (21%), the Philippines (18%), India (11%), Vietnam (10%), Korea (10%), and Japan (9%). As a group, Asian Americans represented $427 billion in purchasing power in 2006, or 4.5% of the total. Yet the Asian American market received only a small fraction—less than 2%—of the total multicultural marketing expenditure in the United States in 2004, with Hispanic Americans and African Americans garnering 68% and 30%, respectively. For this reason, many experts on Asian American marketing called it the "invisible market."

Asian Americans tend to be more brand conscious than other minority groups, yet are the least loyal to particular brands. They also tend to care more about what others think (for instance, whether their neighbors will approve of them). The most computer-literate group, Asian Americans are more likely to use the Internet on a daily basis. The diverse national identities that make up the Asian American ethnicity limit the effectiveness of pan-Asian marketing appeals. Bank of America prospered by targeting Asians in San Francisco with separate TV campaigns aimed at Chinese, Korean, and Vietnamese consumers.

Sources: Lisa Sanders, "How to Target Blacks? First You Gotta Spend," *Advertising Age,* July 3, 2006, p. 19; "The 'Invisible' Market," *Brandweek,* January 30, 2006; Samar Farah, "Latino Marketing Goes Mainstream," *Boston Globe,* July 9, 2006; Dianne Solis, "Latino Buying Power Still Surging," *Dallas Morning News,* September 1, 2006; Joseph Tarnowski, "Assimilate or Perish," *Progressive Grocer,* February 1, 2006; Pepper Miller and Herb Kemp, *What's Black about It? Insights to Increase Your Share of a Changing African American Market* (Ithaca, NY: Paramount Market Publishing, 2005); Paula Lyon Andrus, "Mass Appeal: 'Dora' Translates Well," *Marketing News,* October 13, 2003, p. 8; Mindy Charski, "Old Navy to Tailor Message to Hispanics," *Adweek,* August 4, 2003, p. 9.

two different social classes. Second, persons are perceived as occupying inferior or superior positions according to social class. Third, a *cluster* of variables—for example, occupation, income, wealth, education, and value orientation—indicates social class, rather than any single variable. Fourth, individuals can move up or down the social-class ladder during their lifetimes. How easily and how far depends on how rigid the social stratification is.

Social classes show distinct product and brand preferences in many areas, including clothing, home furnishings, leisure activities, and automobiles. They also differ in media preferences, with upper-class consumers often preferring magazines and books and lower-class consumers often preferring television. Even within a category such as TV, upper-class consumers tend to prefer news and drama, and lower-class consumers tend to prefer soap operas and sports programs. There are also language differences—advertising copy and dialogue must ring true to the targeted social class.

Social Factors

In addition to cultural factors, social factors such as reference groups, family, and social roles and statuses affect our buying behavior.

REFERENCE GROUPS A person's **reference groups** are all the groups that have a direct (face-to-face) or indirect influence on their attitudes or behavior. Groups having a direct influence are called **membership groups**. Some of these are **primary groups** with whom the person interacts fairly continuously and informally, such as family, friends, neighbors, and coworkers. People also belong to **secondary groups**, such as religious, professional, and trade-union groups, which tend to be more formal and require less continuous interaction.

Reference groups influence members in at least three ways. They expose an individual to new behaviors and lifestyles, they influence attitudes and self-concept, and they create pressures for conformity that may affect product and brand choices. People are also influenced by groups to which they do *not* belong. **Aspirational groups** are those a person hopes to join; **dissociative groups** are those whose values or behavior an individual rejects.

Where reference group influence is strong, marketers must determine how to reach and influence the group's opinion leaders. An **opinion leader** is the person who offers informal advice or information about a specific product or product category, such as which of several brands is best or how a particular product may be used.[7] Opinion leaders are often highly confident, socially active, and involved with the category. Marketers try to reach opinion leaders by identifying their demographic and psychographic characteristics, identifying the media they read, and directing messages at them.

CHRYSLER

To reach opinion leaders involved with their African American communities, Chrysler is taking its cars to church. As part of its "Inspired Drives" tour, in which the company sets up tracks around the country for customers to test its latest models, Chrysler is locating test drives at influential megachurches. New Birth Missionary Baptist Church in Lithonia, Georgia, is one. Situated on 250 acres, it has 25,000 members and a charismatic senior pastor, Bishop Eddie L. Long. Bishop Long hosts a weekly program on the Trinity Broadcasting Network and is an occasional advisor to government policy makers. By locating test drives at megachurches—and partnering with them at fundraising events, such as a Patti Labelle concert to raise funds for cancer research—Chrysler has found a powerful way to reach customers.[8]

In the United States, the hottest trends in teenage music, language, and fashion often start in the inner cities. Clothing companies such as Hot Topic, which hope to appeal to the fickle and fashion-conscious youth market, have made a concerted effort to monitor urban opinion leaders' style and behavior.

HOT TOPIC

With over 600 stores in malls in 49 states and Puerto Rico, Hot Topic has been hugely successful at using antiestablishment style in its fashions. The chain also sells books, comics, jewelry, CDs, records, posters, and other paraphernalia. Hot Topic's slogan, "Everything about the music," reflects its operating premise: Whether a teen is into rock, pop-punk, emo, acid rap, rave, or rockabilly—or even more obscure musical tastes—Hot Topic has the right T-shirt. In order to keep up with music trends, all Hot Topic staffers, from the CEO to the lowliest store employee, regularly attend concerts by up-and-coming and established bands to scout who's wearing what. It's a perk for store clerks, who get reimbursed for concert tickets if they turn in a fashion write-up later. Hot Topic's Web site solicits suggestions from customers, and the CEO reads more than 1,000 customer comment cards and e-mails a month.[9]

FAMILY The family is the most important consumer buying organization in society, and family members constitute the most influential primary reference group.[10] There are two families in the buyer's life. The **family of orientation** consists of parents and siblings. From parents a person acquires an orientation toward religion, politics, and economics and a sense of personal ambition, self-worth, and love.[11] Even if the buyer no longer interacts very much with their parents, their influence on behavior can be significant. Almost 40% of families have auto insurance with the same company as the husband's parents.

A more direct influence on everyday buying behavior is the **family of procreation**—namely, one's spouse and children. In the United States, husband–wife involvement in purchases has traditionally varied widely by product category. The wife has usually acted as the family's main purchasing agent, especially for food, sundries, and staple clothing items. Now traditional purchasing roles are changing, and marketers would be wise to see both men and women as possible targets.

For expensive products and services such as cars, vacations, or housing, the vast majority of husbands and wives engage in joint decision making.[12] And marketers are realizing that women actually buy more technology than men do, but consumer electronics stores have been slow to catch on to this fact. Some savvy electronics stores are starting to heed women's complaints of being ignored, patronized, or offended by salespeople. RadioShack Corp., a 7,000-store chain, began actively recruiting female store managers so that now a woman manages about one of every seven stores.[13]

Nevertheless, men and women may respond differently to marketing messages.[14] One study showed that women valued connections and relationships with family and friends and placed a high priority on people. Men, on the other hand, related more to competition and placed a high priority on action. Marketers are taking more direct aim at women with new products such as Quaker's Nutrition for Women cereals and Crest Rejuvenating Effects toothpaste. Sherwin-Williams recently designed a Dutch Boy easy-to-use "Twist and Pour" paint can targeted specifically at women.

Another shift in buying patterns is an increase in the amount of dollars spent and the direct and indirect influence wielded by children and teens. Direct influence describes children's hints, requests, and demands—"I want to go to McDonald's." Indirect influence means that parents know the brands, product choices, and preferences of their children without hints or outright requests ("I think Tommy would want to go to McDonald's"). One researcher estimates that children under 14 influenced as much as 47% of American household spending in 2005, amounting to more than $700 billion, with roughly an equal split between direct and indirect influence.[15]

To make women customers feel more at ease, some electronics retailers like RadioShack are making it a point to recruit female store managers and employees.

Research has shown that teenagers are playing a more active role than before in helping parents choose a car, audio/video equipment, or a vacation spot.[16] In fact, a J.D. Power study revealed that 62% of parents say their child "actively participated in the car-buying decision." That's why automakers are upping their marketing programs for children as young as five.

GENERAL MOTORS

In August 2006, GM's Hummer division teamed up with McDonald's to put tiny toy Hummers in McDonald's Happy Meals—the first time a carmaker directly offered toy versions of its vehicles in the meals. At the same time, GM rolled out its Hummerkids.com Web site with games and printable coloring pages of H3 models. Hummer's licensed goods geared to kids are also increasing in volume—from a Hummer kids' bike to a children's tent.[17]

Recognizing the power of kids, marketers are pouring money into programs targeting them. Advertising directed at children is estimated at over $15 billion annually—about 2.5 times more than in 1992.[18]

Television can be powerful in reaching children, and marketers are using television to target children at younger ages than ever before. By the time children are around 2 years old, they can often recognize characters, logos, and specific brands. They can distinguish between advertising and programming by about ages 6 or 7. A year or so later, they can understand the concept of persuasive intent on the part of advertisers. By 9 or 10, they can understand the discrepancies between message and product.[19] Marketers are tapping into that audience with product tie-ins, placed at a child's eye level, on just about everything—from Scooby Doo vitamins to Elmo juice and cookies.[20]

Millions of kids under the age of 17 are also online. Marketers have jumped online with them, offering freebies in exchange for personal information. Many have come under fire for this practice and for not clearly differentiating ads from games or entertainment. Establishing ethical and legal boundaries in marketing to children online and off-line continues to be a hot topic as consumer advocates decry the commercialism they believe such marketing engenders, as discussed in Chapter 8.

ROLES AND STATUS A person participates in many groups—family, clubs, organizations. Groups often are an important source of information and help to define norms for behavior. We can define a person's position in each group to which he belongs in terms of role and status. A **role** consists of the activities a person is expected to perform. Each role carries a **status**. A senior vice president of marketing has more status than a sales manager, and a sales manager has more status than an office clerk. People choose products that reflect and communicate their role and actual or desired status in society. Marketers must be aware of the status-symbol potential of products and brands.

Personal Factors

A buyer's decisions are also influenced by personal characteristics. These include the buyer's age and stage in the life cycle; occupation and economic circumstances; personality and self-concept; and lifestyle and values. Because many of these characteristics have a very direct impact on consumer behavior, it is important for marketers to follow them closely. See how well you do with "Marketing Memo: The Average U.S. Consumer Quiz."

AGE AND STAGE IN THE LIFE CYCLE Our taste in food, clothes, furniture, and recreation is often related to our age. Consumption is also shaped by the *family life cycle* and the number, age, and gender of people in the household at any point in time. U.S. households are increasingly fragmented—the traditional family of four with a husband, wife, and two kids makes up a much smaller percentage of total households than it once did. In addition, *psychological* life-cycle stages may matter. Adults experience certain "passages" or "transformations" as they go through life.[21] Yet, the behavior people exhibit as they go through these passages, such as becoming a parent, is not necessarily fixed but changes with the times.

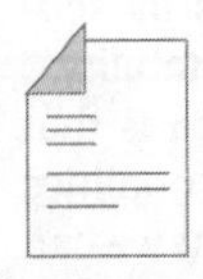

MARKETING MEMO

Listed below is a series of statements used in attitude surveys of U.S. consumers. For each statement, estimate what percent of *married* U.S. men and women agreed with it in 2005 and write your answer, a number between 0% and 100%, in the columns to the right. Then check your results against the correct answers in the footnote.*

Statements	Percent of consumers agreeing % Men	% Women
1. A store's brand is usually a better buy than a nationally advertised brand.	______	______
2. I went fishing at least once in the past 12 months.	______	______
3. I am a homebody.	______	______
4. Information from advertising helps me make better buying decisions.	______	______
5. I like to pay cash for everything I buy.	______	______
6. A woman's place is in the home.	______	______
7. I am interested in spices and seasonings.	______	______
8. The father should be the boss in the house.	______	______
9. You have to use disinfectants to get things really clean.	______	______
10. I believe beings from other planets have visited Earth.	______	______

Note: Only *married* U.S. men and women participated and were selected as representative of a broad cross section of U.S. consumers based on a quota sample, balanced on age, income, geographical area, and population density.

***Answers:** 1. M=55%, W=57%; 2. M=39%, W=24%; 3. M=63%, W=68%; 4. M=53%, W=56%; 5. M=57%, W=57%; 6. M=26%, W=20%; 7. M=68%, W=75%; 8. M=49%, W=28%; 9. M=64%, W=65%; 10. M=41%, W=39%. These numbers are based on the 2005 DDB Life Style Study™ courtesy of Marty Horn. For an interesting application and analysis of the quiz, see Stephen J. Hoch, "Who Do We Know: Predicting the Interests and Opinions of the American Consumer," *Journal of Consumer Research* 15 (December 1998): 315–24.

Marketers should also consider *critical life events or transitions*—marriage, childbirth, illness, relocation, divorce, career change, widowhood—as giving rise to new needs. These should alert service providers—banks, lawyers, and marriage, employment, and bereavement counselors—to ways they can help.[22]

OCCUPATION AND ECONOMIC CIRCUMSTANCES Occupation also influences consumption patterns. A blue-collar worker will buy work clothes, work shoes, and lunchboxes. A company president will buy dress suits, air travel, and country club memberships. Marketers try to identify the occupational groups that have above-average interest in their products and services and even tailor products for certain occupational groups: Computer software companies, for example, design different products for brand managers, engineers, lawyers, and physicians.

Product choice is greatly affected by economic circumstances: spendable income (level, stability, and time pattern), savings and assets (including the percentage that is liquid), debts, borrowing power, and attitudes toward spending and saving. Luxury-goods makers such as Gucci, Prada, and Burberry can be vulnerable to an economic downturn. If economic indicators point to a recession, marketers can take steps to redesign, reposition, and reprice their products or introduce or increase the emphasis on discount brands so they can continue to offer value to target customers.

PERSONALITY AND SELF-CONCEPT Each person has personality characteristics that influence his or her buying behavior. By **personality**, we mean a set of distinguishing human psychological traits that lead to relatively consistent and enduring responses to environmental stimuli (including buying behavior). We often describe it in terms of such traits as self-confidence, dominance, autonomy, deference, sociability, defensiveness, and adaptability.[23] Personality can be a useful variable in analyzing consumer brand choices. The idea is that brands also have personalities, and consumers are likely to choose brands whose personalities match their own. We define **brand personality** as the specific mix of human traits that we can attribute to a particular brand.

Stanford's Jennifer Aaker researched brand personalities and identified the following traits:[24]

1. Sincerity (down-to-earth, honest, wholesome, and cheerful)
2. Excitement (daring, spirited, imaginative, and up-to-date)
3. Competence (reliable, intelligent, and successful)
4. Sophistication (upper-class and charming)
5. Ruggedness (outdoorsy and tough)

She analyzed some well-known brands and found that a number of them tended to be strong on one particular trait: Levi's with "ruggedness"; MTV with "excitement"; CNN with "competence"; and Campbell's with "sincerity." The implication is that these brands will attract persons who are high on the same personality traits. A brand personality may have several attributes: Levi's suggests a personality that is also youthful, rebellious, authentic, and American.

A cross-cultural study exploring the generalizability of Aaker's scale outside the United States found that three of the five factors applied in Japan and Spain, but a "peacefulness" dimension replaced "ruggedness" both in Japan and Spain, and a "passion" dimension emerged in Spain instead of "competency."[25] Research on brand personality in Korea revealed two culture-specific factors—passive likeableness and ascendancy—reflecting the importance of Confucian values in Korea's social and economic systems.[26]

Consumers often choose and use brands that have a brand personality consistent with their own *actual self-concept* (how we view ourselves), although the match may instead be based on the consumer's *ideal self-concept* (how we would like to view ourselves) or even on *others' self-concept* (how we think others see us).[27] These effects may also be more pronounced for publicly consumed products than for privately consumed goods.[28] On the other hand, consumers who are high "self-monitors"—that is, sensitive to how others see them—are more likely to choose brands whose personalities fit the consumption situation.[29] Finally, often consumers have multiple aspects of self (serious professional, caring family member,

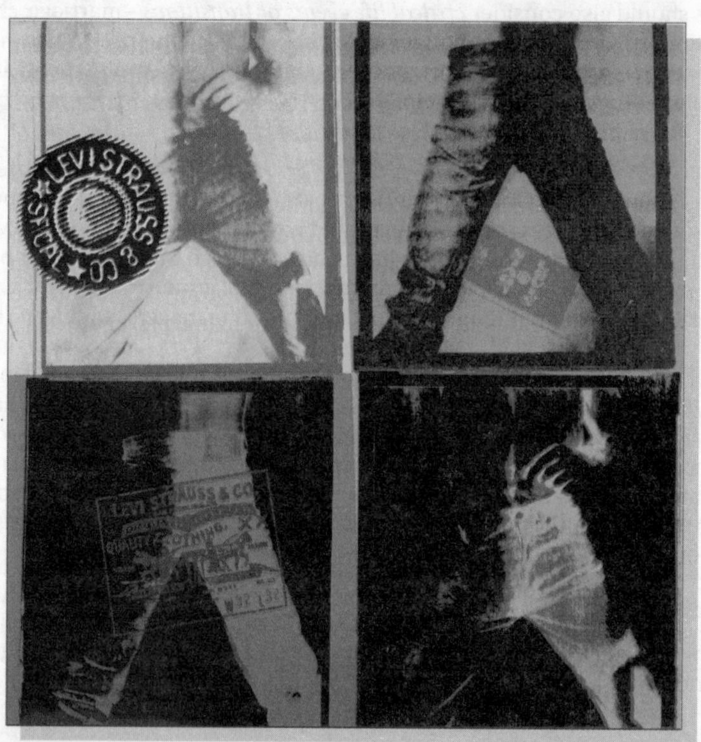

Levi's iconic brand image and personality has endured for years. Here is Andy Warhol's take on the brand.

active fun-lover) that may be evoked differently in different situations or around different types of people.

LIFESTYLE AND VALUES People from the same subculture, social class, and occupation may lead quite different lifestyles.

INDIA'S "GEN NEXT"

Within the 54% of India's population that is under 30, approximately 16 million, or 3%, are high-earning targets of youth lifestyle brands connoting high status and an affluent lifestyle. Members of India's so-called Gen Next spend most of their money on personal clothing and accessories, food, entertainment, and consumer durables as well as on exotic holidays in India and abroad. Luxury cars and shiny motorbikes are the most sought-after status symbols among these newly prosperous young people, most of whom work in India's burgeoning IT sector. Harley-Davidson has set its sights on the Indian market, and LeviStrauss India (Pvt.) Ltd., a subsidiary of the U.S.-based clothing giant, regards India as one of the fastest-growing markets for Levi's in the world.[30]

A **lifestyle** is a person's pattern of living in the world as expressed in activities, interests, and opinions. It portrays the "whole person" interacting with his environment. Marketers search for relationships between their products and lifestyle groups. For example, a computer manufacturer might find that most computer buyers are achievement oriented and then aim the brand more clearly at the achiever lifestyle. Here's an example of one of the latest lifestyle trends businesses are targeting:

LOHAS

Consumers who worry about the environment, want products to be produced in a sustainable way, and spend money to advance their personal health, development, and potential have been named "LOHAS," an acronym standing for *lifestyles of health and sustainability*. The market for LOHAS products encompasses organic foods, energy-efficient appliances and solar panels, as well as alternative medicine, yoga tapes, and ecotourism. Taken together, these accounted for a $230 billion market in 2000. One estimate placed 30% of the adults in the United States, or 50 million people, in the LOHAS or "Cultural Creatives" category. Table 6.2 breaks the LOHAS market into five segments with estimated size, and product and service interests.[31]

TABLE 6.2

LOHAS Market Segments

Sustainable Economy	***Ecological Lifestyles***
Green building and industrial goods	Ecological home and office products
Renewable energy	Organic / recycled fiber products
Resource-efficient products	Environmentally friendly appliances
Socially responsible investing	Ecotourism and travel
Alternative transportation	*US Market—$81.19 billion*
Environmental management	***Alternative Health Care***
US Market—$76.47 billion	Health and wellness solutions
Healthy Lifestyles	Acupuncture, homeopathy, naturopathy, etc.
Natural, organics; nutritional products	Holistic disease prevention
Food and beverage	Complementary medicine
Dietary supplements	*US Market—$30.7 billion*
Personal care	***Personal Development***
US Market—$30 billion	Mind, body, and spirit products such as CDs, books, tapes, seminars
	Yoga, fitness, weight loss
	Spiritual products and services
	US Market—$10.63 billion

Source: Reprinted by permission of LOHAS.

Lifestyles are shaped partly by whether consumers are *money constrained* or *time constrained.* Companies aiming to serve money-constrained consumers will create lower-cost products and services. By appealing to thrifty consumers, Wal-Mart has become the largest company in the world. Its "everyday low prices" have wrung tens of billions of dollars out of the retail supply chain, passing the larger part of savings along to shoppers in the form of rock-bottom bargain prices.[32] "Breakthrough Marketing: IKEA" outlines IKEA's global success formula of appealing to price-conscious shoppers in the furniture market.

Consumers who experience time famine are prone to **multitasking**, doing two or more things at the same time. They will also pay others to perform tasks because time is more important than money. Companies aiming to serve them will create convenient products and services for this group.

In some categories, notably food processing, companies targeting time-constrained consumers need to be aware that these very same people want to believe they're *not* operating within time constraints. Marketers call those who seek both convenience and some involvement in the cooking process the "convenience involvement segment."[33]

Tonight, I will turn this hamburger into a great meal.
Tonight, my skillet will sizzle.
Tonight, you're getting a big hug.
Tonight, you're having a home-cooked meal.
Hamburger Helper
Cheeseburger Macaroni
One pound. One pan. One happy family.™

The "convenience involvement segment" of the food market is receptive to time-savers such as Hamburger Helper that still allow them to feel good about investing some time or effort in meal preparation.

HAMBURGER HELPER

Launched in 1971 in response to tough economic times, the inexpensive pasta-and-powdered mix Hamburger Helper was designed to quickly and inexpensively stretch a pound of meat into a family meal. With an estimated 44% of evening meals prepared in under 30 minutes and strong competition from fast-food drive-through windows, restaurant deliveries, and precooked grocery store dishes, Hamburger Helper's days of prosperity might seem numbered. Market researchers found, however, that some consumers don't want the fastest microwaveable solution possible—they also want to feel good about how they prepare a meal. In fact, on average, they prefer to use at least one pot or pan and 15 minutes of time. To remain attractive to this segment, marketers of Hamburger Helper are always introducing new flavors to tap into the latest consumer taste trends.[34]

Consumer decisions are also influenced by **core values**, the belief systems that underlie attitudes and behaviors. Core values go much deeper than behavior or attitude and determine, at a basic level, people's choices and desires over the long term. Marketers who target consumers on the basis of their values believe that with appeals to people's inner selves, it is possible to influence their outer selves—their purchase behavior.

::: Key Psychological Processes

The starting point for understanding consumer behavior is the stimulus-response model shown in Figure 6.1. Marketing and environmental stimuli enter the consumer's consciousness, and a set of psychological processes combine with certain consumer characteristics to result in decision processes and purchase decisions. The marketer's task is to understand what happens in the consumer's consciousness between the arrival of the outside marketing stimuli and the ultimate purchase decisions. Four key psychological

BREAKTHROUGH MARKETING | IKEA

Swedish furniture retailer IKEA excels at appealing to price-conscious shoppers around the world with stylish items carefully selected for each country's market.

IKEA was founded in 1943 by a 17-year-old Swede named Ingvar Kamprad. The company, which initially sold pens, Christmas cards, and seeds from a shed on Kamprad's family farm, eventually grew into a retail titan in home furnishings and a global cultural phenomenon, what *BusinessWeek* called a "one-stop sanctuary for coolness" and "the quintessential cult brand."

IKEA inspires remarkable levels of devotion from its customers, who visit in numbers that average 1.1 million per day. When a new location debuted in London in 2005, 6,000 people arrived before the doors opened. A contest in Atlanta crowned five winners "Ambassador of Kul" (Swedish for "fun") who, in order to collect their prizes, had to live in the IKEA store for three full days before it opened, which they gladly did.

IKEA achieved this level of success by offering a unique value proposition to consumers: leading-edge Scandinavian design at bargain prices. The company's fashionable bargains include Klippan sofas for $249, Billy bookcases for $120, and Lack side tables for $13. In Scandinavian markets, IKEA has even sold 2,500 prefabricated homes for around $45,000, depending on local housing prices. The company is able to offer such low prices in part because most items come boxed and require complete assembly at home, meaning they are easier to transport, take up less shelf space, and seldom require delivery, which reduces costs.

IKEA's mission of providing value is predicated on founder Kamprad's statement that "People have very thin wallets. We should take care of their interests." IKEA adheres to this philosophy by reducing prices across its products by 2% to 3% annually. Its focus on value also benefits the bottom line: IKEA enjoys 10% margins, higher than competitors such as Target (7.7%) and Pier 1 Imports (5%).

Many of its products are sold uniformly throughout the world, but IKEA also caters to local tastes. In China, for example, it stocked 250,000 plastic placemats with Year of the Rooster themes, which quickly sold out after the holiday. When employees realized U.S. shoppers were buying vases as drinking glasses because they considered IKEA's regular glasses too small, the company developed larger glasses for the U.S. market.

IKEA managers visited Europeans and U.S. consumers in their homes and learned that Europeans generally hang their clothes, whereas U.S. shoppers prefer to store them folded. Wardrobes for the U.S. market were designed with deeper drawers. Visits to Hispanic households in California led IKEA to add seating and dining space in its California stores, brighten the color palettes, and hang more picture frames on the walls.

IKEA evolved into a retail empire with 264 stores and revenues of $22.2 billion in 2006 and still had excellent growth opportunities. IKEA planned to double the number of U.S. outlets by 2010, and in 2006, it rolled out 6 new stores worldwide.

Sources: Kerry Capell, "IKEA: How the Swedish Retailer Became a Global Cult Brand," *BusinessWeek*, November 14, 2005, p. 96; "Need a Home to Go with That Sofa?" *BusinessWeek*, November 14, 2005, p. 106; www.ikea.com.

processes—motivation, perception, learning, and memory—fundamentally influence consumer responses.[35]

Motivation: Freud, Maslow, Herzberg

We all have many needs at any given time. Some needs are *biogenic*; they arise from physiological states of tension such as hunger, thirst, or discomfort. Other needs are *psychogenic*; they arise from psychological states of tension such as the need for recognition, esteem, or

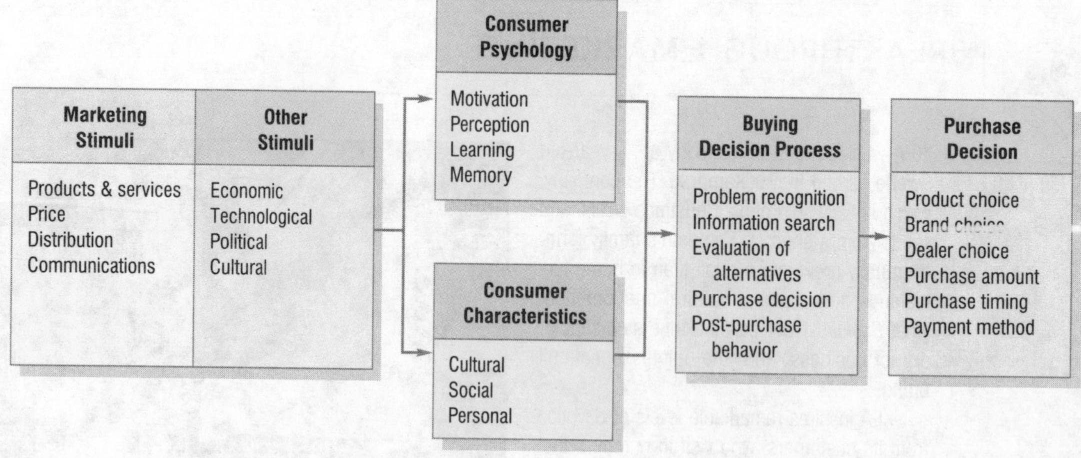

FIG. **6.1** Model of Consumer Behavior

belonging. A need becomes a **motive** when it is aroused to a sufficient level of intensity to drive us to act. Motivation has both direction—we select one goal over another—and intensity—the vigor with which we pursue the goal.

Three of the best-known theories of human motivation—those of Sigmund Freud, Abraham Maslow, and Frederick Herzberg—carry quite different implications for consumer analysis and marketing strategy.

FREUD'S THEORY Sigmund Freud assumed that the psychological forces shaping people's behavior are largely unconscious, and that a person cannot fully understand his or her own motivations. When a person examines specific brands, she will react not only to their stated capabilities, but also to other, less conscious cues such as shape, size, weight, material, color, and brand name. A technique called *laddering* lets us trace a person's motivations from the stated instrumental ones to the more terminal ones. Then the marketer can decide at what level to develop the message and appeal.[36]

Motivation researchers often collect "in-depth interviews" with a few dozen consumers to uncover deeper motives triggered by a product. They use various *projective techniques* such as word association, sentence completion, picture interpretation, and role playing, many pioneered by Ernest Dichter, a Viennese psychologist who settled in the United States.[37]

Today motivational researchers continue the tradition of Freudian interpretation. Jan Callebaut identifies different motives a product can satisfy. For example, whisky can meet the need for social relaxation, status, or fun. Different whisky brands need to be motivationally positioned in one of these three appeals.[38] Another motivation researcher, Clotaire Rapaille, works on breaking the "code" behind a lot of product behavior.[39]

CHRYSLER

When Chrysler decided to offer a new sedan, it had already done a great deal of traditional market research that suggested U.S. consumers wanted excellent gas mileage, safety, and prices. However, it was only through qualitative research that Chrysler discovered what cultural anthropologist Clotaire Rapaille calls "the code"—the unconscious meaning people give to a particular market offering. First interviewers took on the role of "a visitor from another planet," asking participants to help them understand the product in question. Then, participants told stories about the product, and finally, after a relaxation exercise they wrote about their first experiences with the product. In this way, Chrysler learned that "cookie-cutter" sedans were "off-code," and it used information from the sessions to create the PT Cruiser. With its highly distinctive retro design, this sedan was one of the most successful U.S. car launches in recent history.[40]

MASLOW'S THEORY Abraham Maslow sought to explain why people are driven by particular needs at particular times.[41] His answer is that human needs are arranged in a hierarchy

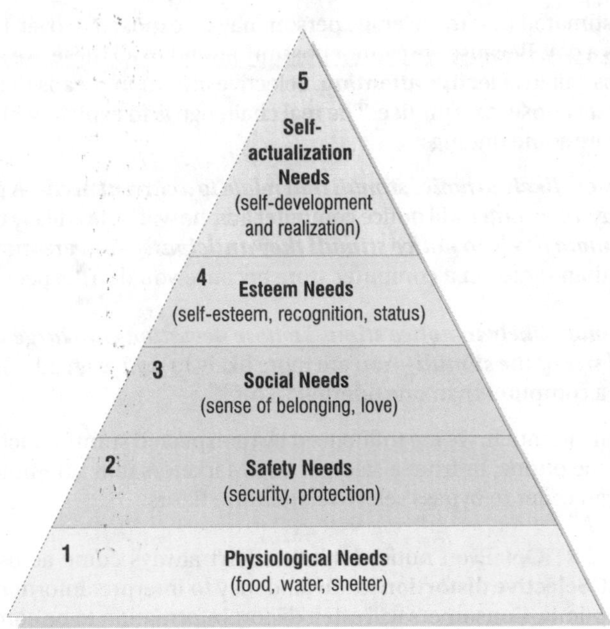

FIG. 6.2

Maslow's Hierarchy of Needs

Source: A.H. Maslow, *Motivation and Personality*, 2nd ed. (Upper Saddle River, NJ: Prentice Hall, 1970). Reprinted by permission of Prentice Hall Inc.

from most to least pressing—physiological needs, safety needs, social needs, esteem needs, and self-actualization needs (see Figure 6.2). People will try to satisfy their most important needs first. When a person succeeds in satisfying an important need, he will then try to satisfy the next-most-important need. For example, a starving man (need 1) will not take an interest in the latest happenings in the art world (need 5), nor in how he is viewed by others (need 3 or 4), nor even in whether he is breathing clean air (need 2); but when he has enough food and water, the next-most-important need will become salient.

HERZBERG'S THEORY Frederick Herzberg developed a two-factor theory that distinguishes *dissatisfiers* (factors that cause dissatisfaction) from *satisfiers* (factors that cause satisfaction).[42] The absence of dissatisfiers is not enough to motivate a purchase; satisfiers must be present. For example, a computer that does not come with a warranty would be a dissatisfier. Yet the presence of a product warranty would not act as a satisfier or motivator of a purchase, because it is not a source of intrinsic satisfaction. Ease of use would be a satisfier.

Herzberg's theory has two implications. First, sellers should do their best to avoid dissatisfiers (for example, a poor training manual or a poor service policy). Although these things will not sell a product, they might easily unsell it. Second, the seller should identify the major satisfiers or motivators of purchase in the market and then supply them.

Perception

A motivated person is ready to act. *How* she acts is influenced by her view of the situation. In marketing, perceptions are more important than the reality, because it's perceptions that affect consumers' actual behavior. **Perception** is the process by which we select, organize, and interpret information inputs to create a meaningful picture of the world.[43] The key point is that it depends not only on the physical stimuli, but also on the stimuli's relationship to the surrounding field and on conditions within each of us. One person might perceive a fast-talking salesperson as aggressive and insincere; another, as intelligent and helpful. Each will respond differently to the salesperson.

In marketing, perceptions are more important than the reality, as it is perceptions that will affect consumers' actual behavior. People can emerge with different perceptions of the same object because of three perceptual processes: selective attention, selective distortion, and selective retention.

SELECTIVE ATTENTION Attention is the allocation of processing capacity to some stimulus. Voluntary attention is something purposeful; involuntary attention is grabbed by someone or something. It's estimated that the average person may be exposed to over 1,500 ads or brand communications a day. Because we cannot possibly attend to all these, we screen most stimuli out—a process called **selective attention**. Selective attention means that marketers must work hard to attract consumers' notice. The real challenge is to explain which stimuli people will notice. Here are some findings:

1. ***People are more likely to notice stimuli that relate to a current need***—A person who is motivated to buy a computer will notice computer ads; he will be less likely to notice DVD ads.
2. ***People are more likely to notice stimuli they anticipate***—You are more likely to notice computers than radios in a computer store because you don't expect the store to carry radios.
3. ***People are more likely to notice stimuli whose deviations are large in relationship to the normal size of the stimuli***—You are more likely to notice an ad offering $100 off the list price of a computer than one offering $5 off.

Though we screen out much, we are influenced by unexpected stimuli, such as sudden offers in the mail, over the phone, or from a salesperson. Marketers may attempt to promote their offers intrusively in order to bypass selective attention filters.

SELECTIVE DISTORTION Even noticed stimuli don't always come across in the way the senders intended. **Selective distortion** is the tendency to interpret information in a way that fits our preconceptions. Consumers will often distort information to be consistent with prior brand and product beliefs and expectations.[44]

For a stark demonstration of the power of consumer brand beliefs, consider that in "blind" taste tests, one group of consumers samples a product without knowing which brand it is, while another group knows. Invariably, the groups have different opinions, despite consuming *exactly the same product.*

When consumers report different opinions of branded and unbranded versions of identical products, it must be the case that their brand and product beliefs, created by whatever means (past experiences, marketing activity for the brand, or the like), have somehow changed their product perceptions. We can find examples with virtually every type of product.[45] When Coors changed its label from "Banquet Beer" to "Original Draft," consumers claimed the taste had changed even though the formulation had not.

Selective distortion can work to the advantage of marketers with strong brands when consumers distort neutral or ambiguous brand information to make it more positive. In other words, beer may seem to taste better, a car may seem to drive more smoothly, the wait in a bank line may seem shorter, depending on the particular brands involved.

SELECTIVE RETENTION Most of us don't remember much of the information to which we're exposed, but we do retain information that supports our attitudes and beliefs. Because of **selective retention**, we're likely to remember good points about a product we like and forget good points about competing products. Selective retention again works to the advantage of strong brands. It also explains why marketers need to use repetition—to make sure their message is not overlooked.

SUBLIMINAL PERCEPTION The selective perception mechanisms require consumers' active engagement and thought. A topic that has fascinated armchair marketers for ages is **subliminal perception**. They argue that marketers embed covert, subliminal messages in ads or packaging. Consumers are not consciously aware of them, yet they affect behavior. Although it's clear that mental processes include many subtle subconscious effects,[46] no evidence supports the notion that marketers can systematically control consumers at that level, especially in terms of changing moderately important or strongly held beliefs.[47]

Learning

When we act, we learn. **Learning** induces changes in our behavior arising from experience. Most human behavior is learned, although much learning is incidental. Learning theorists believe that learning is produced through the interplay of drives, stimuli, cues, responses, and reinforcement. Two popular approaches to learning are classical conditioning and operant (instrumental) conditioning.

A **drive** is a strong internal stimulus impelling action. **Cues** are minor stimuli that determine when, where, and how a person responds. Suppose you buy an HP computer. If your experience is rewarding, your response to computers and HP will be positively reinforced. Later on, when you want to buy a printer, you may assume that because HP makes good computers, HP also makes good printers. In other words, you *generalize* your response to similar stimuli. A countertendency to generalization is discrimination. **Discrimination** means we have learned to recognize differences in sets of similar stimuli and can adjust our responses accordingly.

Learning theory teaches marketers that they can build demand for a product by associating it with strong drives, using motivating cues, and providing positive reinforcement. A new company can enter the market by appealing to the same drives that competitors use and by providing similar cues, because buyers are more likely to transfer loyalty to similar brands (generalization); or the company might design its brand to appeal to a different set of drives and offer strong cue inducements to switch (discrimination).

Some researchers prefer more active, cognitive approaches when learning depends upon the inferences or interpretations consumers make about outcomes (was an unfavorable consumer experience due to a bad product or did the consumer fail to follow instructions properly?). The **hedonic bias** says people have a general tendency to attribute success to themselves and failure to external causes. Consumers are thus more likely to blame a product than themselves, putting pressure on marketers to carefully explicate product functions in well-designed packaging and labels, instructive ads and Web sites, and so on.

Memory

All the information and experiences we encounter as we go through life can end up in our long-term memory. Cognitive psychologists distinguish between **short-term memory (STM)**—a temporary and limited repository of information—and **long-term memory (LTM)**—a more permanent, essentially unlimited repository.

Most widely accepted views of long-term memory structure assume we form some kind of associative model.[48] For example, the **associative network memory model** views LTM as a set of nodes and links. *Nodes* are stored information connected by *links* that vary in strength. Any type of information can be stored in the memory network, including verbal, visual, abstract, and contextual. A spreading activation process from node to node determines how much we retrieve and what information we can actually recall in any given situation. When a node becomes activated because we're encoding external information (when we read or hear a word or phrase) or retrieving internal information from LTM (when we think about some concept), other nodes are also activated if they're strongly enough associated with that node.

In this model, we can think of consumer brand knowledge as a node in memory with a variety of linked associations. The strength and organization of these associations will be important determinants of the information we can recall about the brand. **Brand associations** consist of all brand-related thoughts, feelings, perceptions, images, experiences, beliefs, attitudes, and so on that become linked to the brand node.

BAHLSEN

Germany's largest cookie company takes an unusual tack to embed cues in consumers' minds so the next time they're in the cookie aisle, they'll reach for Bahlsen cookies. Bahlsen is concentrating on a mostly neglected aspect of the cookie-eating experience: sound. Steffen Heise, Bahlsen's director of R&D, says, "Imagine, you would see a cookie on a plate and it looks to you very crunchy, it appears crunchy and when you eat it, you would find something very soft and unpleasant." Bahlsen has hired a team of testers who use special microphones in their ears to record the crunching. Then Bahlsen adjusts the dough recipes to get just the right crunch. For cookies aimed at young people, Bahlsen aims for a loud, crisp, exciting sound. Elderly people, they have found, are not interested in noisy or stressful situations and prefer a softer crunch. While all this may sound a little far-fetched, sound design in other industries has been part of the brand experience for a long time. Engineers fiddle with everything from the buzz of an electric razor to the way a car door sounds when it slams—all to create a pleasing subconscious association for the consumer.[49]

| FIG. 6.3 |

Hypothetical State Farm Mental Map

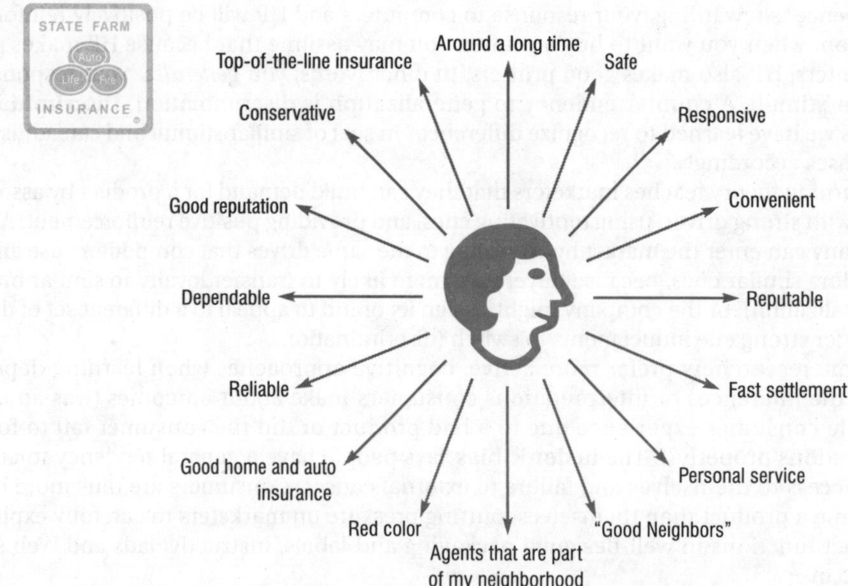

We can think of marketing as a way of making sure consumers have the right types of product and service experiences to create the right brand knowledge structures and maintain them in memory. Companies such as Procter & Gamble like to create mental maps of consumers that depict their knowledge of a particular brand in terms of the key associations that are likely to be triggered in a marketing setting, and their relative strength, favorability, and uniqueness to consumers. Figure 6.3 displays a very simple mental map highlighting brand beliefs for a hypothetical consumer for State Farm insurance.

MEMORY PROCESSES Memory is a very constructive process, because we don't remember information and events completely and accurately. Often we remember bits and pieces and fill in the rest based upon whatever else we know.

Memory encoding describes how and where information gets into memory. The strength of the resulting association depends on how much we process the information at encoding (how much we think about it, for instance) and in what way.[50]

In general, the more attention we pay to the meaning of information during encoding, the stronger the resulting associations in memory will be.[51] When a consumer actively thinks about and "elaborates" on the significance of product or service information, stronger associations are created in memory. It's also easier for consumers to create an association to new information when extensive, relevant knowledge structures already exist in memory. One reason personal experiences create such strong brand associations is that information about the product is likely to be related to existing knowledge.

The ease with which we can integrate new information into established knowledge structures also clearly depends on its simplicity, vividness, and concreteness. Repeated exposures to information, too, provide greater opportunity for processing and thus the potential for stronger associations. Recent advertising research in a field setting, however, suggests that high levels of repetition for an uninvolving, unpersuasive ad are unlikely to have as much sales impact as lower levels of repetition for an involving, persuasive ad.[52]

MEMORY RETRIEVAL **Memory retrieval** is the way information gets out of memory. According to the associative network memory model, a strong brand association is both more accessible and more easily recalled by "spreading activation." Our successful recall of brand information doesn't depend only on the initial strength of that information in memory. Three factors are particularly important.

First, the presence of *other* product information in memory can produce interference effects and cause us to either overlook or confuse new data. One marketing challenge in a category crowded with many competitors—for example, airlines, financial services, and insurance companies—is that consumers may mix up brands.

Second, the time between exposure to information and encoding matters—the longer the time delay, the weaker the association. The time elapsed since the last exposure opportunity, however, has been shown generally to produce only gradual decay. Cognitive psychologists believe memory is extremely durable, so that once information becomes stored in memory, its strength of association decays very slowly.[53]

Third, information may be *available* in memory but not be *accessible* (able to be recalled) without the proper retrieval cues or reminders. The particular associations for a brand that come to mind depend on the context in which we consider it. The more cues linked to a piece of information, however, the greater the likelihood that we can recall it. The effectiveness of retrieval cues is one reason marketing *inside* a supermarket or any retail store is so critical—the actual product packaging, the use of in-store minibillboard displays, and so on. The information they contain and the reminders they provide of advertising or other information already conveyed outside the store will be prime determinants of consumer decision making.

Memory can often be reconstructive, however, and consumers may remember an experience with a brand differently after the fact due to intervening factors or other events.[54]

::: The Buying Decision Process: The Five-Stage Model

These basic psychological processes play an important role in understanding how consumers actually make their buying decisions.[55] Table 6.3 provides a list of some key consumer behavior questions in terms of "who, what, when, where, how, and why."

Smart companies try to fully understand the customers' buying-decision process—all their experiences in learning, choosing, using, and even disposing of a product.[56] Bissel developed its Steam n' Clean vacuum cleaner based on the product trial experiences of a local PTA group near corporate headquarters in Grand Rapids, Michigan. The result was a name change, color-coded attachments, and an infomercial highlighting its special features.[57]

Marketing scholars have developed a "stage model" of the buying-decision process (see Figure 6.4). The consumer passes through five stages: problem recognition, information search, evaluation of alternatives, purchase decision, and postpurchase behavior. Clearly, the buying process starts long before the actual purchase and has consequences long afterward.[58]

TABLE 6.3

Understanding Consumer Behavior

Who buys our product or service?
Who makes the decision to buy the product?
Who influences the decision to buy the product?
How is the purchase decision made? Who assumes what role?
What does the customer buy? What needs must be satisfied?
Why do customers buy a particular brand?
Where do they go or look to buy the product or service?
When do they buy? Any seasonality factors?
How is our product perceived by customers?
What are customers' attitudes toward our product?
What social factors might influence the purchase decision?
Do customers' lifestyles influence their decisions?
How do personal or demographic factors influence the purchase decision?

Source: Based on list from George Belch and Michael Belch, *Advertising and Communication Management*, 6th ed. (Homewood, IL: Irwin, 2003).

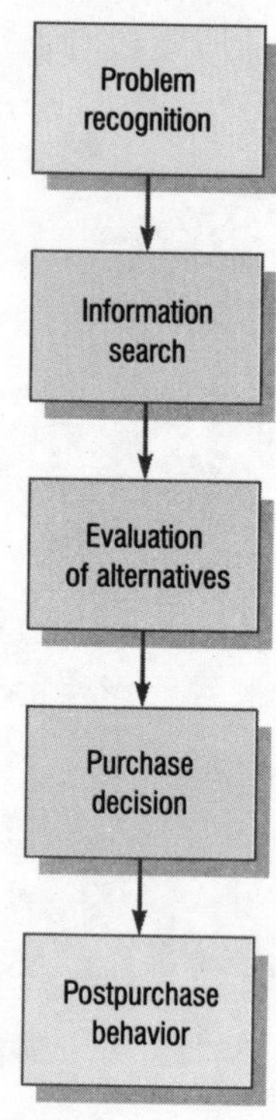

| FIG. 6.4 |

Five-Stage Model of the Consumer Buying Process

Consumers don't always pass through all five stages in buying a product. They may skip or reverse some. When you buy your regular brand of toothpaste, you go directly from the need for toothpaste to the purchase decision, skipping information search and evaluation. The model in Figure 6.4 provides a good frame of reference, however, because it captures the full range of considerations that arise when a consumer faces a highly involving new purchase.[59]

Problem Recognition

The buying process starts when the buyer recognizes a problem or need triggered by internal or external stimuli. With an internal stimulus, one of the person's normal needs—hunger, thirst, sex—rises to a threshold level and becomes a drive; or a need can be aroused by an external stimulus. A person may admire a neighbor's new car or see a television ad for a Hawaiian vacation, which triggers thoughts about the possibility of making a purchase.

Marketers need to identify the circumstances that trigger a particular need by gathering information from a number of consumers. They can then develop marketing strategies that trigger consumer interest. Particularly for discretionary purchases such as luxury goods, vacation packages, and entertainment options, marketers may need to increase consumer motivation so a potential purchase gets serious consideration.

Information Search

Surprisingly, consumers often search for limited amounts of information. Surveys have shown that for durables, half of all consumers look at only one store, and only 30% look at more than one brand of appliances. We can distinguish between two levels of involvement with search. The milder search state is called *heightened attention.* At this level a person simply becomes more receptive to information about a product. At the next level, the person may enter an *active information search:* looking for reading material, phoning friends, going online, and visiting stores to learn about the product.

INFORMATION SOURCES Major information sources to which consumers will turn fall into four groups:

- ***Personal.*** Family, friends, neighbors, acquaintances
- ***Commercial.*** Advertising, Web sites, salespersons, dealers, packaging, displays
- ***Public.*** Mass media, consumer-rating organizations
- ***Experiential.*** Handling, examining, using the product

The relative amount and influence of these sources vary with the product category and the buyer's characteristics. Generally speaking, the consumer receives the most information about a product from commercial—that is, marketer-dominated—sources. However, the most effective information often comes from personal sources or public sources that are independent authorities.

Each information source performs a different function in influencing the buying decision. Commercial sources normally perform an information function, whereas personal sources perform a legitimizing or evaluation function. For example, physicians often learn of new drugs from commercial sources but turn to other doctors for evaluations.

SEARCH DYNAMICS Through gathering information, the consumer learns about competing brands and their features. The first box in Figure 6.5 shows the *total set* of brands available to the consumer. The individual consumer will come to know only a subset of these brands, the *awareness set.* Some brands, the *consideration set,* will meet initial buying criteria. As the consumer gathers more information, only a few, the *choice set,* will remain strong contenders. The consumer makes a final choice from this set.[60]

Marketers need to identify the hierarchy of attributes that guide consumer decision making in order to understand different competitive forces and how these various sets get formed. This process of identifying the hierarchy is called **market partitioning**. Years ago, most car buyers first decided on the manufacturer and then on one of its car divisions (*brand-dominant hierarchy*). A buyer might favor General Motors cars and, within this set,

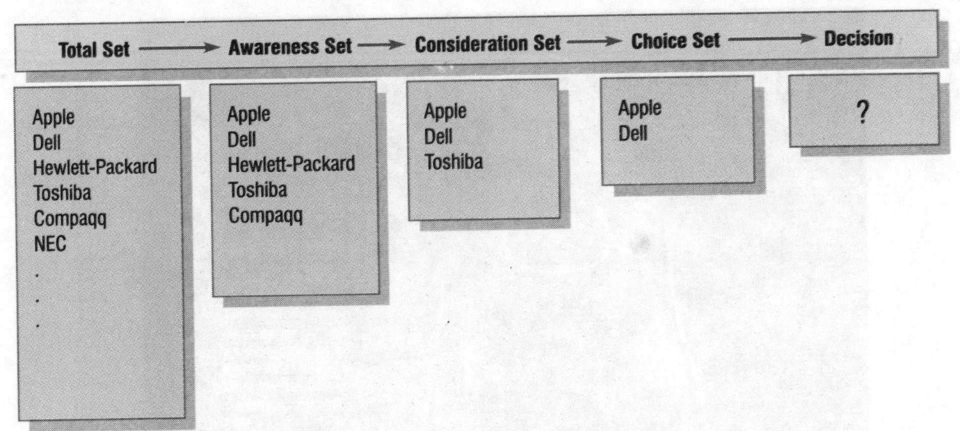

FIG. 6.5

Successive Sets Involved in Consumer Decision Making

Pontiac. Today, many buyers decide first on the nation from which they want to buy a car (*nation-dominant hierarchy*). Buyers may first decide they want to buy a Japanese car, then Toyota, and then the Corolla model of Toyota.

The hierarchy of attributes also can reveal customer segments. Buyers who first decide on price are price dominant; those who first decide on the type of car (sports, passenger, station wagon) are type dominant; those who first decide on the car brand are brand dominant. Type/price/brand-dominant consumers make up a segment; quality/service/type buyers make up another. Each segment may have distinct demographics, psychographics, and mediagraphics and different awareness, consideration, and choice sets.[61]

Figure 6.5 makes it clear that a company must strategize to get its brand into the prospect's awareness, consideration, and choice sets. If a food store owner arranges yogurt first by brand (such as Dannon and Yoplait) and then by flavor within each brand, consumers will tend to select their flavors from the same brand. However, if all the strawberry yogurts are together, then all the vanilla and so forth, consumers will probably choose which flavors they want first, and then choose the brand name they want for that particular flavor. Australian supermarkets arrange meats by the way they might be cooked, and stores use more descriptive labels, such as "a 10-minute herbed beef roast." The result is that Australians buy a greater variety of meats than U.S. shoppers, who choose from meats laid out by animal type—beef, chicken, pork, and so on.[62]

The company must also identify the other brands in the consumer's choice set so that it can plan the appropriate competitive appeals. In addition, the company should identify the consumer's information sources and evaluate their relative importance. Asking consumers how they first heard about the brand, what information came later, and the relative importance of the different sources will help the company prepare effective communications for the target market.

Evaluation of Alternatives

How does the consumer process competitive brand information and make a final value judgment? No single process is used by all consumers, or by one consumer in all buying situations. There are several processes, and the most current models see the consumer forming judgments largely on a conscious and rational basis.

Some basic concepts will help us understand consumer evaluation processes: First, the consumer is trying to satisfy a need. Second, the consumer is looking for certain benefits from the product solution. Third, the consumer sees each product as a bundle of attributes with varying abilities for delivering the benefits sought to satisfy this need. The attributes of interest to buyers vary by product—for example:

1. ***Hotels***—Location, cleanliness, atmosphere, price
2. ***Mouthwash***—Color, effectiveness, germ-killing capacity, taste/flavor, price
3. ***Tires***—Safety, tread life, ride quality, price

Consumers will pay the most attention to attributes that deliver the sought-after benefits. We can often segment the market for a product according to attributes important to different consumer groups.

The Got Milk campaign successfully reminds consumers of existing attitudes instead of trying to change them.

BELIEFS AND ATTITUDES Through experience and learning, people acquire beliefs and attitudes. These in turn influence buying behavior. A **belief** is a descriptive thought that a person holds about something. Just as important are **attitudes**, a person's enduring favorable or unfavorable evaluations, emotional feelings, and action tendencies toward some object or idea.[63] People have attitudes toward almost everything: religion, politics, clothes, music, food.

Attitudes put us into a frame of mind: liking or disliking an object, moving toward or away from it. They lead us to behave in a fairly consistent way toward similar objects. Because attitudes economize on energy and thought, they can be very difficult to change. A company is well advised to fit its product into existing attitudes rather than to try to change attitudes. Here's an example of an organization that used ad campaigns to remind consumers of their attitudes, with handsome results:

CALIFORNIA MILK PROCESSOR BOARD

After a 20-year decline in milk consumption among Californians, in 1993 milk processors from across the state formed the California Milk Processor Board (CMPB) with one goal in mind: to get people to drink more milk. The ad agency commissioned by the CMPB developed a novel approach to pitching milk's benefits. Research had shown that most consumers already believed milk was good for them. So the campaign would remind consumers of the inconvenience and annoyance of running out of milk, which became known as "milk deprivation." The "Got Milk?" tagline reminded consumers to make sure they had milk in their refrigerators. A year after the launch, sales volume increased 1.07%. In 1995, the "Got Milk?" campaign was licensed to the

National Dairy Board. In 1998, the National Fluid Milk Processor Education Program, which had been using the "milk mustache" campaign since 1994 to boost sales, bought the rights to the "Got Milk?" tagline. The "Got Milk?" campaign continues to pay strong dividends by halting the decline in sales of milk in California more than 13 years after its launch.[64]

EXPECTANCY-VALUE MODEL The consumer arrives at attitudes toward various brands through an attribute evaluation procedure.[65] She develops a set of beliefs about where each brand stands on each attribute. The **expectancy-value model** of attitude formation posits that consumers evaluate products and services by combining their brand beliefs—the positives and negatives—according to importance.

Suppose Linda has narrowed her choice set to four laptop computers (A, B, C, D). Assume she's interested in four attributes: memory capacity, graphics capability, size and weight, and price. Table 6.4 shows her beliefs about how each brand rates on the four attributes. If one computer dominated the others on all the criteria, we could predict that Linda would choose it. But, as is often the case, her choice set consists of brands that vary in their appeal. If Linda wants the best memory capacity, she should buy C; if she wants the best graphics capability, she should buy A; and so on.

If we knew the weights Linda attaches to the four attributes, we could more reliably predict her computer choice. Suppose she assigned 40% of the importance to the computer's memory capacity, 30% to graphics capability, 20% to size and weight, and 10% to price. To find Linda's perceived value for each computer, according to the expectancy-value model, we multiply her weights by her beliefs about each computer's attributes. This computation leads to the following perceived values:

$$\text{Computer A} = 0.4(8) + 0.3(9) + 0.2(6) + 0.1(9) = 8.0$$

$$\text{Computer B} = 0.4(7) + 0.3(7) + 0.2(7) + 0.1(7) = 7.0$$

$$\text{Computer C} = 0.4(10) + 0.3(4) + 0.2(3) + 0.1(2) = 6.0$$

$$\text{Computer D} = 0.4(5) + 0.3(3) + 0.2(8) + 0.1(5) = 5.0$$

An expectancy-model formulation predicts that Linda will favor computer A, which (at 8.0) has the highest perceived value.[66]

Suppose most computer buyers form their preferences the same way. Knowing this, the marketer of computer B, for example, could apply the following strategies to stimulate greater interest in brand B:

- ***Redesign the computer.*** This technique is called *real repositioning.*
- ***Alter beliefs about the brand.*** Attempting to alter beliefs about the brand is called *psychological repositioning.*
- ***Alter beliefs about competitors' brands.*** This strategy, called *competitive depositioning,* makes sense when buyers mistakenly believe a competitor's brand has more quality than it actually has.

TABLE 6.4

A Consumer's Brand Beliefs about Laptop Computers

Laptop Computer	Attribute			
	Memory Capacity	Graphics Capability	Size and Weight	Price
A	8	9	6	9
B	7	7	7	7
C	10	4	3	2
D	5	3	8	5

Note: Each attribute is rated from 0 to 10, where 10 represents the highest level on that attribute. Price, however, is indexed in a reverse manner, with a 10 representing the lowest price, because a consumer prefers a low price to a high price.

- ***Alter the importance weights.*** The marketer could try to persuade buyers to attach more importance to the attributes in which the brand excels.
- ***Call attention to neglected attributes.*** The marketer could draw buyers' attention to neglected attributes, such as styling or processing speed.
- ***Shift the buyer's ideals.*** The marketer could try to persuade buyers to change their ideal levels for one or more attributes.[67]

Purchase Decision

In the evaluation stage, the consumer forms preferences among the brands in the choice set. The consumer may also form an intention to buy the most preferred brand. In executing a purchase intention, the consumer may make up to five subdecisions: brand (brand A), dealer (dealer 2), quantity (one computer), timing (weekend), and payment method (credit card).

NONCOMPENSATORY MODELS OF CONSUMER CHOICE The expectancy-value model is a compensatory model, in that perceived good things for a product can help to overcome perceived bad things. But consumers often take "mental shortcuts" using simplifying choice heuristics. **Heuristics** are rules of thumb or mental shortcuts in the decision process.

With **noncompensatory models** of consumer choice, positive and negative attribute considerations don't necessarily net out. Evaluating attributes in isolation makes decision making easier for a consumer, but it also increases the likelihood that she would have made a different choice if she had deliberated in greater detail. We highlight three such choice heuristics here.

1. With the **conjunctive heuristic**, the consumer sets a minimum acceptable cutoff level for each attribute and chooses the first alternative that meets the minimum standard for all attributes. For example, if Linda decided all attributes had to rate at least a 5, she would choose computer B.
2. With the **lexicographic heuristic**, the consumer chooses the best brand on the basis of its perceived most important attribute. With this decision rule, Linda would choose computer C.
3. With the **elimination-by-aspects heuristic**, the consumer compares brands on an attribute selected probabilistically—where the probability of choosing an attribute is positively related to its importance—and eliminates brands that do not meet minimum acceptable cutoffs.

Our brand or product knowledge, the number and similarity of brand choices and time pressure involved, and the social context (such as the need for justification to a peer or boss) all may affect whether and how we use choice heuristics.[68]

Consumers don't necessarily use only one type of choice rule. Sometimes, they adopt a phased decision strategy that combines two or more. For example, they might use a noncompensatory decision rule such as the conjunctive heuristic to reduce the number of brand choices to a more manageable number, and then evaluate the remaining brands. One reason for the runaway success of the Intel Inside campaign in the 1990s was that it made the brand the first cutoff for many consumers—they would only buy a personal computer that had an Intel microprocessor. Personal computer makers such as IBM, Dell, and Gateway had no choice but to support Intel's marketing efforts.

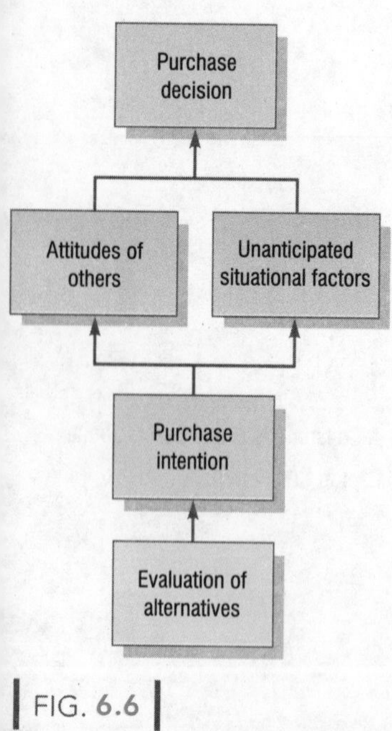

FIG. 6.6

Steps between Evaluation of Alternatives and a Purchase Decision

INTERVENING FACTORS Even if consumers form brand evaluations, two general factors can intervene between the purchase intention and the purchase decision (Figure 6.6).[69] The first is the *attitudes of others.* The extent to which another person's attitude reduces our preference for an alternative depends on two things: (1) the intensity of the other person's negative attitude toward our preferred alternative and (2) our motivation to comply with the other person's wishes.[70] The more intense the other person's negativism and the closer the other person is to us, the more we will adjust our purchase intention. The converse is also true.

Related to the attitudes of others is the role played by infomediaries who publish their evaluations. Examples include *Consumer Reports,* which provides unbiased expert reviews of all types of products and services; J.D. Power, which provides consumer-based ratings of cars, financial services, and travel products and services; professional movie, book, and music reviewers; customer reviews of books and music on Amazon.com; and the increasing number of chat rooms, bulletin boards, blogs, and so on where people discuss products, services, and companies. Consumers are undoubtedly influenced by these evaluations, as evidenced by the success of a small-budget movie such as *Napoleon Dynamite,* which cost only $400,000 to make but grossed over $44 million at the box office in 2004 thanks to a slew of favorable reviews by moviegoers on many Web sites.

The second factor is *unanticipated situational factors* that may erupt to change the purchase intention. Linda might lose her job, some other purchase might become more urgent, or a store salesperson may turn her off. Preferences and even purchase intentions are not completely reliable predictors of purchase behavior.

A consumer's decision to modify, postpone, or avoid a purchase decision is heavily influenced by *perceived risk.*[71] Consumers may perceive many types of risk in buying and consuming a product:

1. ***Functional risk***—The product does not perform up to expectations.
2. ***Physical risk***—The product poses a threat to the physical well-being or health of the user or others.
3. ***Financial risk***—The product is not worth the price paid.
4. ***Social risk:*** The product results in embarrassment from others.
5. ***Psychological risk***—The product affects the mental well-being of the user.
6. ***Time risk***—The failure of the product results in an opportunity cost of finding another satisfactory product.

The amount of perceived risk varies with the amount of money at stake, the amount of attribute uncertainty, and the amount of consumer self-confidence. Consumers develop routines for reducing the uncertainty and negative consequences of risk, such as decision avoidance, information gathering from friends, and preferences for national brand names and warranties. Marketers must understand the factors that provoke a feeling of risk in consumers and provide information and support to reduce perceived risk.

Postpurchase Behavior

After the purchase, the consumer might experience dissonance that stems from noticing certain disquieting features or hearing favorable things about other brands and will be alert to information that supports his or her decision. Marketing communications should supply beliefs and evaluations that reinforce the consumer's choice and help him feel good about the brand.

The marketer's job therefore doesn't end with the purchase. Marketers must monitor postpurchase satisfaction, postpurchase actions, and postpurchase product uses.

POSTPURCHASE SATISFACTION Satisfaction is a function of the closeness between expectations and the product's perceived performance.[72] If performance falls short of expectations, the consumer is *disappointed;* if it meets expectations, the consumer is *satisfied;* if it exceeds expectations, the consumer is *delighted.* These feelings make a difference in whether the customer buys the product again and talks favorably or unfavorably about it to others.

The larger the gap between expectations and performance, the greater the dissatisfaction. Here the consumer's coping style comes into play. Some consumers magnify the gap when the product isn't perfect and are highly dissatisfied; others minimize it and are less dissatisfied.[73]

POSTPURCHASE ACTIONS If the consumer is satisfied, she is more likely to purchase the product again. The satisfied customer will also tend to say good things about the brand to others. On the other hand, dissatisfied consumers may abandon or return the product. They may seek information that confirms its high value. They may take public action by complaining to the company, going to a lawyer, or complaining to other groups (such as business, private, or government agencies). Private actions include deciding to stop buying the product (*exit option*) or warning friends (*voice option*).[74]

Chapter 5 described CRM programs designed to build long-term brand loyalty. Postpurchase communications to buyers have been shown to result in fewer product returns and order cancellations. Computer companies, for example, can send a letter to new owners congratulating them on having selected a fine computer. They can place ads showing satisfied brand owners. They can solicit customer suggestions for improvements and list the location of available services. They can write intelligible instruction booklets. They can send

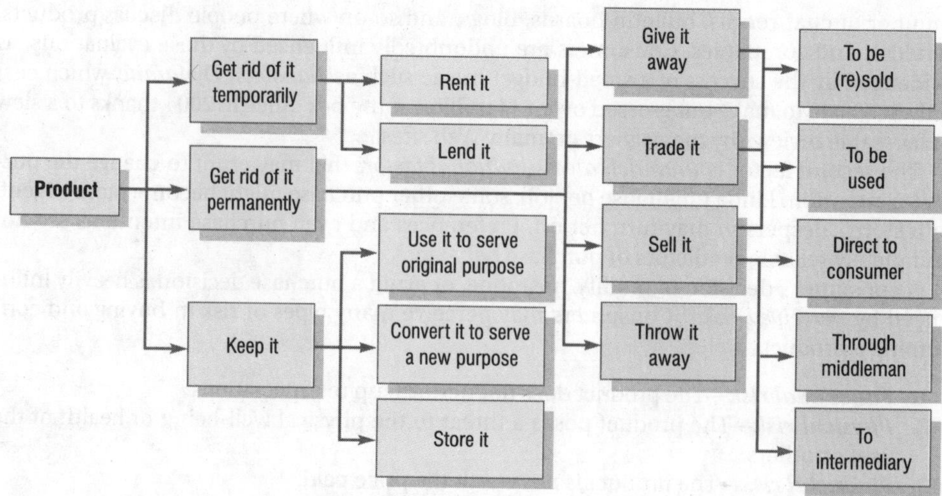

FIG. 6.7

How Customers Use or Dispose of Products

Source: Jacob Jacoby, Carol K. Berning, and Thomas F. Dietvorst, "What about Disposition?" *Journal of Marketing* (July 1977): 23. Reprinted with permission of the American Marketing Association.

owners a magazine containing articles describing new computer applications. In addition, they can provide good channels for speedy redress of customer grievances.

POSTPURCHASE USE AND DISPOSAL Marketers should also monitor how buyers use and dispose of the product (Figure 6.7). A key driver of sales frequency is product consumption rate—the more quickly buyers consume a product, the sooner they may be back in the market to repurchase it.

One opportunity to increase frequency of product use occurs when consumers' perceptions of their usage differ from reality. Consumers may fail to replace products with relatively short life spans soon enough because they overestimate its product life.[75] One strategy to speed up replacement is to tie the act of replacing the product to a certain holiday, event, or time of year.

For example, Oral B has run toothbrush promotions tied in with the springtime switch to daylight savings time. Another strategy is to provide consumers with better information about either: (1) when they first used the product or need to replace it or (2) its current level of performance. Batteries have built-in gauges that show how much power they have left; toothbrushes have color indicators to indicate when the bristles are worn; and so on. Perhaps the simplest way to increase usage is to learn when actual usage is less than recommended and persuade customers of the merits of more regular usage, overcoming potential hurdles.

If consumers throw the product away, the marketer needs to know how they dispose of it, especially if—like batteries, beverage containers, electronic equipment, and disposable diapers—it can damage the environment.

::: Other Theories of Consumer Decision Making

The consumer decision process may not always develop in a carefully planned fashion. Here are some other theories and approaches to explaining it.

Level of Consumer Involvement

The expectancy-value model assumes a high level of involvement on the part of the consumer. We can define **consumer involvement** in terms of the level of engagement and active processing the consumer undertakes in responding to a marketing stimulus.

ELABORATION LIKELIHOOD MODEL Richard Petty and John Cacioppo's *elaboration likelihood model,* an influential model of attitude formation and change, describes how consumers make evaluations in both low- and high-involvement circumstances.[76] There are two means of persuasion in their model: the *central route,* where attitude formation or change stimulates much thought and is based on a diligent, rational consideration of the most important product information; and the *peripheral route,* where attitude formation or change provokes much less thought and results from the association of a brand with either positive or negative peripheral cues. *Peripheral cues* for consumers include a celebrity endorsement, a credible source, or any object that generates positive feelings.

Consumers follow the central route only if they possess sufficient motivation, ability, and opportunity. In other words, consumers must want to evaluate a brand in detail, have the necessary brand and product or service knowledge in memory, and have sufficient time and the proper setting. If any of those factors is lacking, consumers tend to follow the peripheral route and consider less central, more extrinsic factors in their decisions.

LOW-INVOLVEMENT MARKETING STRATEGIES Many products are bought under conditions of low involvement and the absence of significant brand differences. Consider salt. Consumers have little involvement in this product category. If they keep reaching for the same brand, it's out of habit, not strong brand loyalty. Evidence suggests consumers have low involvement with most low-cost, frequently purchased products.

Marketers use four techniques to try to convert a low-involvement product into one of higher involvement. First, they can link the product to some involving issue, as when Crest linked its toothpaste to avoiding cavities. Second, they can link the product to some involving personal situation—for example, fruit juice makers began to include vitamins such as calcium to fortify their drinks. Third, they might design advertising to trigger strong emotions related to personal values or ego defense, as when cereal makers began to advertise to adults the heart-healthy nature of cereals and the importance of living a long time to enjoy family life. Fourth, they might add an important feature—for example, when GE light bulbs introduced "Soft White" versions. These strategies at best raise consumer involvement from a low to a moderate level; they do not necessarily propel the consumer into highly involved buying behavior.

If, regardless of what the marketer can do, consumers will have low involvement with a purchase decision, they are likely to follow the peripheral route. Marketers must pay special attention to giving consumers one or more positive cues to justify their brand choice. For instance, frequent ad repetition, visible sponsorships, and vigorous PR are all ways to enhance brand familiarity. Other peripheral cues that can tip the balance in favor of the brand include a beloved celebrity endorser, attractive packaging, and an appealing promotion.[77]

VARIETY-SEEKING BUYING BEHAVIOR Some buying situations are characterized by low involvement but significant brand differences. Here consumers often do a lot of brand switching. Think about cookies. The consumer has some beliefs about cookies, chooses a brand without much evaluation, and evaluates the product during consumption. Next time, the consumer may reach for another brand out of a wish for a different taste. Brand switching occurs for the sake of variety, rather than dissatisfaction.

The market leader and the minor brands in this product category have different marketing strategies. The market leader will try to encourage habitual buying behavior by dominating the shelf space with a variety of related but different product versions, avoiding out-of-stock conditions, and sponsoring frequent reminder advertising. Challenger firms will encourage variety seeking by offering lower prices, deals, coupons, free samples, and advertising that tries to break the consumer's purchase and consumption cycle and presents reasons for trying something new.

Decision Heuristics and Biases

We've seen that consumers don't always process information or make decisions in a deliberate, rational manner. "Marketing Insight: How Consumers Really Make Decisions" highlights some recent advances from the thriving academic study of how consumers make decisions.

Behavioral decision theorists have identified many different heuristics and biases in everyday consumer decision making. They come into play when consumers forecast the likelihood of future outcomes or events.[78]

1. The **availability heuristic**—Consumers base their predictions on the quickness and ease with which a particular example of an outcome comes to mind. If an example comes to mind too easily, consumers might overestimate the likelihood of its happening. For example, a recent product failure may lead a consumer to inflate the likelihood of a future product failure and make him more inclined to purchase a product warranty.

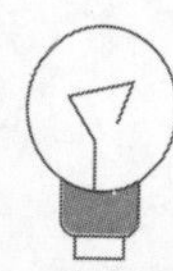

MARKETING INSIGHT | HOW CONSUMERS REALLY MAKE DECISIONS

One of the most active academic research areas in marketing is behavioral decision theory (BDT). Researchers have uncovered many fascinating influences and outcomes in consumer decision making, often challenging predictions from economic theory and assumptions about rationality.[79]

- Consumers are more likely to choose an alternative (a home bread bakery) after a relatively inferior option (a slightly better but significantly more expensive bakery) is added to the choice set.
- Consumers are more likely to choose an alternative that appears to be a compromise in the particular choice set under consideration.
- The choices that consumers make influence their assessment of their own tastes.
- Shifting attention to one of two considered alternatives tends to enhance the perceived attractiveness and choice probability of that alternative.
- The manner in which consumers compare products that vary in terms of price and perceived quality (features, brand name) and the way those products are displayed in the store (by brand or by model type) affect their willingness to pay more for additional features or a better-known brand.
- Consumers who think about the possibility that their purchase decisions will turn out to be wrong are more likely to choose better-known brands.
- Consumers for whom possible feelings of regret are made more relevant are more likely to choose a product that is currently on sale rather than wait for a better sale or buy a higher-priced item.
- Consumers' choices are influenced by subtle (and theoretically inconsequential) changes in the way alternatives are described.
- Consumers who make purchases for later consumption appear to make systematic errors in predicting their future preferences.
- Consumer's predictions of their future tastes are not accurate—they do not really know how they will feel after consuming the same flavor of yogurt or ice cream several times.
- Consumers often overestimate the duration of their overall emotional reactions to future events (moves, financial windfalls, outcomes of sporting events).
- Consumers often overestimate their future consumption, especially if there is limited availability (which may explain why Black Jack and other gums have higher sales when availability is limited to several months per year than when they are offered year round).
- In anticipating future consumption opportunities, consumers often assume they will want or need more variety than they actually do.
- Consumers are less likely to choose alternatives with product features or promotional premiums that have little or no value, even when these features and premiums are optional (like the opportunity to purchase a Collector's Plate) and do not reduce the actual value of the product in any way.
- Consumers are less likely to choose products selected by other consumers for reasons that they find irrelevant, even though these other reasons would not suggest anything positive or negative about the products' values.
- Consumers' interpretations and evaluations of past experiences are greatly influenced by the ending and trend of events. A positive event at the end of a service experience can color later reflections and evaluations of the experience as a whole.

What all these and other studies reinforce is that consumer behavior is very constructive and that the context of decisions really matter. Understanding how these effects show up in the marketplace can be crucial for marketers.

Sources: For an overview of some issues involved, see James R. Bettman, Mary Frances Luce, and John W. Payne, "Constructive Consumer Choice Processes," *Journal of Consumer Research* 25 (December 1998): 187–217; and Itamar Simonson, "Getting Closer to Your Customers by Understanding How They Make Choices," *California Management Review* 35 (Summer 1993): 68–84. For examples of classic studies in this area, see some of the following: Dan Ariely and Ziv Carmon, "Gestalt Characteristics of Experiences: The Defining Features of Summarized Events," *Journal of Behavioral Decision Making* 13, no. 2 (April 2000): 191–201; Ravi Dhar and Klaus Wertenbroch, "Consumer Choice between Hedonic and Utilitarian Goods," *Journal of Marketing Research* 37 (February 2000): 60–71; Itamar Simonson and Amos Tversky, "Choice in Context: Tradeoff Contrast and Extremeness Aversion," *Journal of Marketing Research* 29 (August 1992): 281–95; Itamar Simonson, "The Effects of Purchase Quantity and Timing on Variety-Seeking Behavior," *Journal of Marketing Research* 27 (May 1990): 150–62.

2. The **representativeness heuristic**—Consumers base their predictions on how representative or similar the outcome is to other examples. One reason that package appearances may be so similar for different brands in the same product category is that they want to be seen as representative of the category as a whole.
3. The **anchoring and adjustment heuristic**—Consumers arrive at an initial judgment and then adjust it based on additional information. For services marketers, it is critical to make a strong first impression to establish a favorable anchor, so that subsequent experiences are interpreted in a more favorable light.

Note that marketing managers also may use heuristics and be subject to biases in their decision making. "Marketing Memo: Decision Traps" reveals 10 common mistakes managers make in their decisions.

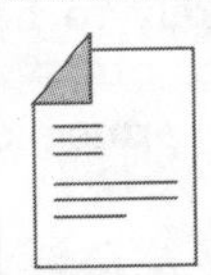

MARKETING MEMO | DECISION TRAPS

In *Decision Traps*, Jay Russo and Paul Schoemaker reveal the 10 most common mistakes managers make in their decisions.

1. ***Plunging In***—Beginning to gather information and reach conclusions without taking a few minutes to think about the crux of the issue you're facing or how you believe decisions like this one should be made.
2. ***Allowing Frame Blindness***—Setting out to solve the wrong problem because you've created a mental framework for your decision with little thought, causing you to overlook the best options or to lose sight of important objectives.
3. ***Lacking Frame Control***—Failing to consciously define the problem in more ways than one, or being unduly influenced by the frames of others.
4. ***Being Overconfident in Your Judgment***—Failing to collect key factual information because you are too sure of your assumptions and opinions.
5. ***Using Shortsighted Shortcuts***—Relying inappropriately on "rules of thumb" such as implicitly trusting the most readily available information or anchoring too much on convenient facts.
6. ***Shooting from the Hip***—Believing you can keep straight all the information you've discovered, "winging it" rather than following a systematic procedure when making the final choice.
7. ***Allowing Group Failure***—Assuming that with many smart people involved, good choices will follow automatically, and therefore failing to manage the group decision-making process.
8. ***Fooling Yourself about Feedback***—Failing to interpret the evidence from past outcomes for what it really says, because you are protecting your ego or hindsight effects trick you.
9. ***Not Keeping Track***—Assuming that experience will make its lessons available automatically, and therefore failing to keep systematic records to track the results of your decisions and analyze them in ways that reveal their key lessons.
10. ***Failing to Audit Your Decision Process***—Failing to create an organized approach to understanding your own decision making, so you remain constantly exposed to all the other nine decision traps.

Sources: J. Edward Russo and Paul J. H. Schoemaker, *Decision Traps: Ten Barriers to Brilliant Decision Making and How to Overcome Them* (New York: Doubleday, 1990); see also, J. Edward Russo and Paul J. H. Schoemaker, *Winning Decisions: Getting It Right the First Time* (New York: Doubleday, 2001).

Mental Accounting

Researchers have found that consumers use mental accounting when they handle their money.[80] **Mental accounting** refers to the way consumers code, categorize, and evaluate financial outcomes of choices. Formally, it is "the tendency to categorize *funds* or items of value even though there is no logical *basis* for the categorization, e.g., individuals often segregate their savings into separate accounts to meet different goals even though funds from any of the accounts can be applied to any of the goals."[81]

For example, assume you spend $50 to buy a ticket to see a concert.[82] As you arrive at the show, you realize you've lost your ticket. You may be unsure about purchasing another ticket for $50. Assume, on the other hand, that you realize you lost $50 on the way to buy the ticket. You might be much more likely to go ahead and buy the ticket anyway. Although you lost the same amount in each case—$50—in the first case, you may have mentally allocated $50 for going to a concert. Buying another ticket would exceed your mental concert budget. In the second case, the money you lost did not belong to any account, so you had not yet exceeded your mental concert budget.

According to Chicago's Richard Thaler, mental accounting is based on a set of key core principles:

1. Consumers tend to *segregate gains*. When a seller has a product with more than one positive dimension, it's desirable to have the consumer evaluate each dimension separately. Listing multiple benefits of a large industrial product, for example, can make the sum of the parts seem greater than the whole.
2. Consumers tend to *integrate losses*. Marketers have a distinct advantage in selling something if its cost can be added to another large purchase. House buyers are more inclined to view additional expenditures favorably given the high price of buying a house.
3. Consumers tend to *integrate smaller losses with larger gains*. The "cancellation" principle might explain why withholding taxes from monthly paychecks is less aversive than

large, lump-sum tax payments—the smaller withholdings are more likely to be absorbed by the larger pay amount.

4. Consumers tend to *segregate small gains from large losses.* The "silver lining" principle might explain the popularity of rebates on big-ticket purchases such as cars.

The principles of mental accounting are derived in part from prospect theory. **Prospect theory** maintains that consumers frame their decision alternatives in terms of gains and losses according to a value function. Consumers are generally loss averse. They tend to overweight very low probabilities and underweight very high probabilities.

Profiling the Customer Buying-Decision Process

How can marketers learn about the stages in the buying process for their product? They can think about how they themselves would act, in the *introspective method.* They can interview a small number of recent purchasers, asking them to recall the events leading to their purchase, in the *retrospective method.* They can use the *prospective method* to locate consumers who plan to buy the product and ask them to think out loud about going through the buying process, or they can ask consumers to describe the ideal way to buy the product, in the *prescriptive method.* Each method yields a picture of the steps in the process.

Trying to understand the customer's behavior in connection with a product has been called mapping the customer's *consumption system,*[83] *customer activity cycle,*[84] or *customer scenario.*[85] Marketers can do this for such activity clusters as doing laundry, preparing for a wedding, or buying a car. Buying a car, for example, includes a whole cluster of activities—choosing the car, financing the purchase, buying insurance, buying accessories, and so on.

SUMMARY :::

1. Consumer behavior is influenced by three factors: cultural (culture, subculture, and social class); social (reference groups, family, and social roles and statuses); and personal (age, stage in the life cycle, occupation, economic circumstances, lifestyle, personality, and self-concept). Research into all these factors can provide marketers with clues to reach and serve consumers more effectively.
2. Four main psychological processes affect consumer behavior: motivation, perception, learning, and memory.
3. To understand how consumers actually make buying decisions, marketers must identify who makes and has input into the buying decision; people can be initiators, influencers, deciders, buyers, or users. Different marketing campaigns might be targeted to each type of person.
4. The typical buying process consists of the following sequence of events: problem recognition, information search, evaluation of alternatives, purchase decision, and postpurchase behavior. The marketers' job is to understand the behavior at each stage. The attitudes of others, unanticipated situational factors, and perceived risk may all affect the decision to buy, as will consumers' levels of postpurchase product satisfaction, use and disposal, and actions on the part of the company.
5. Consumers are constructive decision makers and subject to many contextual influences. Consumers often exhibit low involvement in their decisions, using many heuristics as a result.

APPLICATIONS :::

Marketing Debate Is Target Marketing Ever Bad?

As marketers increasingly develop marketing programs tailored to certain target market segments, some critics have denounced these efforts as exploitive. For example, the preponderance of billboards advertising cigarettes, alcohol, and other vices in low-income urban areas is seen as taking advantage of a vulnerable market segment. Critics can be especially harsh in evaluating marketing programs that target African Americans and other minority groups, claiming they often employ stereotypes and inappropriate depictions. Others counter that targeting and positioning is critical to marketing and that these marketing programs are an attempt to be relevant to a certain consumer group.

Take a position: Targeting minorities is exploitive *versus* Targeting minorities is a sound business practice.

Marketing Discussion What Are Your Mental Accounts?

What mental accounts do you have in your mind about purchasing products or services? Do you have any rules you employ in spending money? Are they different from what other people do? Do you follow Thaler's four principles in reacting to gains and losses?

cisco.

Welcome to You, Inc.

One thing is constant in business. It's change. New competitors appear daily. And customers are always demanding more. How do you keep up? Welcome to You, Inc., a smart, new way of doing business with highly secure Cisco networks designed for small to medium-sized businesses. Today, people like you are Web conferencing Shanghai in a mouse click. And tracking inventory in Ottawa from a cab in New York. It's world of constant change and unprecedented opportunity. Find out what businesses like yours are doing at cisco.com.

welcome to
the human network. cisco.

IN THIS CHAPTER, WE WILL ADDRESS THE FOLLOWING QUESTIONS:

1. What is the business market, and how does it differ from the consumer market?
2. What buying situations do organizational buyers face?
3. Who participates in the business-to-business buying process?
4. How do business buyers make their decisions?
5. How can companies build strong relationships with business customers?
6. How do institutional buyers and government agencies do their buying?

CHAPTER 7 ::: ANALYZING BUSINESS MARKETS

seven

Business organizations do not only sell; they also buy vast quantities of raw materials, manufactured components, plant and equipment, supplies, and business services. There are over 6 million businesses with paid employees in the United States alone. To create and capture value, sellers need to understand these organizations' needs, resources, policies, and buying procedures.

Cisco, the network communications equipment manufacturer that leads the market in the switches and routers that direct traffic on the Internet, sought growth by directing considerable research and marketing resources at an underserved market: small- and medium-sized business (SMB) customers, which the company defined as businesses with fewer than 250 employees.[1] To better understand buyer behavior, Cisco conducted customer research that segmented the overall SMB market into four tiers by networking expenditure and purchase patterns. Tier-1 and tier-2 companies, who view networking as the core of their business, make up 30% of the SMB space, but account for 75% of total networking expenditures. Tier-3 and tier-4 companies make up 70% of the market, but are hesitant to invest heavily in networking technology. Based on this understanding of the market, Cisco was able to target these segments with products and services designed specifically for them. It developed a program called the "Smart Business >>>

Network equipment manufacturer Cisco discovered that about a third of the firms in the small- to medium-sized segment of its market account for about 75% of total networking expenditures, pointing the way to a lucrative growth opportunity.

Roadmap" that matched common business issues faced by SMB customer types with long-term technology solutions. One of these solutions was Linksys One, a hosted communications service offering telephone, video, data, and Internet networking on one high-speed connection that debuted in 2005. Overall, Cisco raised its R&D budget for the SMB market to $2 billion and directed 40% of its total marketing expenditure toward this market. The program generated 22% growth in Cisco's business with SMBs.

Some of the world's most valuable brands belong to business marketers: ABB, Caterpiller, DuPont, FedEx, GE, Hewlett-Packard, IBM, Intel, and Siemens to name a few. Many principles of basic marketing also apply to business marketers. They need to embrace holistic marketing principles, such as building strong relationships with their customers, just like any marketer. But they also face some unique considerations in selling to other businesses. In this chapter, we will highlight some of the crucial similarities and differences for marketing in business markets.[2]

::: What Is Organizational Buying?

Webster and Wind define **organizational buying** as the decision-making process by which formal organizations establish the need for purchased products and services and identify, evaluate, and choose among alternative brands and suppliers.[3]

The Business Market versus the Consumer Market

The **business market** consists of all the organizations that acquire goods and services used in the production of other products or services that are sold, rented, or supplied to others. The major industries making up the business market are agriculture, forestry, and fisheries; mining; manufacturing; construction; transportation; communication; public utilities; banking, finance, and insurance; distribution; and services.

More dollars and items change hands in sales to business buyers than to consumers. Consider the process of producing and selling a simple pair of shoes. Hide dealers must sell hides to tanners, who sell leather to shoe manufacturers, who sell shoes to wholesalers, who sell shoes to retailers, who finally sell them to consumers. Each party in the supply chain also buys many other goods and services to support their operations.

Business marketers face many of the same challenges as consumer marketers. In particular, understanding their customers and what they value is of paramount importance to both.[4] Table 7.1 summarizes the business-to-business challenges identified in the 2005–2007 ISBM Trends Study.

Business marketers, however, have several characteristics that contrast sharply with those of consumer markets:

- ***Fewer, larger buyers.*** The business marketer normally deals with far fewer, much larger buyers than the consumer marketer does, particularly in such industries as aircraft engines and defense weapons. The fate of Goodyear Tire Company and other automotive part suppliers depends on getting contracts from just a handful of major automakers. It's also true, however, that as a slowing economy has put a stranglehold on large corporations' purchasing

TABLE 7.1

The Top Business Marketing Challenges for 2005–2007

1. Expand understanding of customer needs, market segments, and the drivers of customer value.
2. Competing globally as China and India reshape markets.
3. Master analytical tools and improving quantitative skills.
4. Reinstate innovation as an engine of growth.
5. Create new organizational models and linkages.
6. Improve return on marketing investment (ROMI) decision making.
7. Demonstrate and document delivered customer value, and price accordingly.

Source: *Marketplace*, Winter 2006, Institute for the Study of Business Markets

departments, the small and midsize business market is offering new opportunities for suppliers.[5] See "Marketing Insight: Big Sales to Small Business," for more on this important B2B market.

- ***Close supplier–customer relationship.*** Because of the smaller customer base and the importance and power of the larger customers, suppliers are frequently expected to customize their offerings to individual business customer needs.

TEXAS INSTRUMENTS INC.

Texas Instruments is a maker of analog- and digital-signal-processing (DSP) chips that has learned it's worthwhile to pay attention to some of the smallest business customers. After reinventing itself as a more innovative company, TI is exploring sales leads for customers it used to ignore, such as tiny LifeSize Communications, which as a two-person startup was too small for TI's attention ten years ago. Recently, TI brought several engineers and salespeople to LifeSize and spent half a day talking to its four employees and asking them what they wanted. The result is LifeSize Room, an $8,000 to $12,000 system that delivers high definition video and CD quality sound over the Internet. LifeSize has sold over 1,000 of the systems, with 75 TI components each, to customers such as a casting agency that allows actors on one coast to audition for roles on the opposite coast via teleconference.[6]

PPG INDUSTRIES

At Pittsburgh-based PPG industries, a specific program has buyers and suppliers of maintenance, repair, and operating (MRO) goods and services working together more closely than ever. It's called $AVE for Supplier Added Value Effort. Through this program, PPG challenges its suppliers to deliver on annual value-added/cost-savings proposals equaling at least 5% of their total annual sales to PPG. One preferred supplier (one that PPG designates for providing a particular commodity) submitted a suggestion to $AVE that reduced costs by $160,000 for a lighting project by negotiating discounted prices for new fixtures and fluorescent bulbs.[7]

Goodyear Tire Company exemplifies many suppliers that depend on a market of fewer, but larger, business buyers.

Business buyers often select suppliers who also buy from them. A paper manufacturer might buy from a chemical company that buys a considerable amount of its paper.

- ***Professional purchasing.*** Business goods are often purchased by trained purchasing agents, who must follow their organizations'

MARKETING INSIGHT | BIG SALES TO SMALL BUSINESS

Small businesses—defined as those with fewer than 500 employees—hire half of all private sector workers and have generated 60% to 80% of net new jobs annually over the past decade. According to the Small Business Administration's Office of Advocacy, 670,000 small businesses opened in the United States in 2005. Those new ventures all need capital equipment, technology, supplies, and services. Look beyond the United States to new ventures around the world and you have a huge and growing B2B market. Here's how some companies are reaching it:

- With its new suite of run-your-business software, **Microsoft** is counting on sales to 45 million small to midsize businesses worldwide to add $10 billion to annual revenue by 2010. Yet even Microsoft can't afford to send reps to all its customers. Instead, the company is unleashing an army of 24,000 independent computer consulting companies and adding 300 sales managers to support resellers and customers.
- **IBM** counts small to midsize customers as 20% of its business and has launched Express, a line of hardware, software services, and financing, for this market. IBM sells through regional reps as well as independent software vendors and resellers, and it supports its small–midsize push with millions of dollars in advertising annually, including in publications such as *American Banker* and *Inc.* The company also directly targets gay business owners with ads in *The Advocate* and *Out* and partners with nonprofits to reach racial and ethnic minority segments.
- **American Express** has been steadily adding new features to its credit card for small business, which some small companies use to cover hundreds of thousands of dollars a month in cash needs. It has also created a small business network called OPEN (www.openamericanexpress.com) to bring together various services, Web tools, and discount programs with other giants such as ExxonMobil, Dell, FedEx, and Staples. With OPEN, American Express not only allows customers to save money on common expenses, it also encourages them to do much of their record-keeping on its Web site.

Midsize businesses present a huge opportunity, and huge challenges. The market is large and fragmented by industry, size, and number of years in operation. Small business owners are notably averse to long-range planning and have an "I'll buy it when I need it" decision-making style. Here are some guidelines for selling to small businesses:

- ***Don't lump small and midsize businesses together.*** There's a big gap between $1 million in revenue and $50 million, or between a start-up with 10 employees and a more mature business with 100. IBM customizes its small and midsize business portal (www-ibm.com/businesscenter/us) with call-me or text-chat buttons connected to products for different market segments.
- ***Don't waste their time.*** That means no cold calls, entertaining sales shows, or sales pitches over long lavish lunches.
- ***Do keep it simple.*** Simplicity means one point of contact with a supplier for all service problems, or one bill for all services and products. AT&T corporation, which serves 3.9 million businesses with fewer than 100 employees, bundles data management, networking, and other abilities into convenient single packages for this market.
- ***Do use the Internet.*** Hewlett-Packard found that time-strapped small-business decision makers prefer to buy, or at least research, products and services online. So it designed a site targeted to small and midsize businesses and pulls visitors through extensive advertising, direct mail, e-mail campaigns, catalogs, and events.
- ***Don't forget about direct contact.*** Even if a small business owner's first point of contact is via the Internet, you still need to offer phone or face time. In major metropolitan areas, Sprint connects with small businesses through its Sprint Experience Centers, where Sprint reps or dealer reps can invite prospects to interact with the technologies.
- ***Do provide support after the sale.*** Small businesses want partners, not pitchmen. When The DeWitt Company, a 100-employee landscaping products business, purchased a large piece of machinery from Moeller, a German company, the company's president paid DeWitt's CEO a personal visit and stayed until the machine was up and running properly.
- ***Do your homework.*** The realities of small or midsize business management are different from those of a large corporation. Microsoft created a small, fictional executive research firm, Southridge, and baseball-style trading cards of its key decision makers in order to help Microsoft employees tie sales strategies to small business realities.

Sources: Based on Barnaby J. Feder, "When Goliath Comes Knocking on David's Door," *New York Times,* May 6, 2003; Jay Greene, "Small Biz: Microsoft's Next Big Thing?" *BusinessWeek,* April 21, 2003, pp. 72–73; Jennifer Gilbert, "Small but Mighty," *Sales & Marketing Management* (January 2004): 30–35; Verne Kopytoff, "Businesses Click on eBay," *San Francisco Chronicle,* July 28, 2003; Matt Krantz, "Firms Jump on the eBay Wagon," *USA Today,* May 3, 2004.

purchasing policies, constraints, and requirements. Many of the buying instruments—for example, requests for quotations, proposals, and purchase contracts—are not typically found in consumer buying. Professional buyers spend their careers learning how to buy better. Many belong to the National Association of Purchasing Managers (NAPM), which seeks to improve professional buyers' effectiveness and status. This means that business marketers must provide greater technical data about their product and its advantages over competitors' products.

- ***Multiple buying influences.*** More people typically influence business buying decisions. Buying committees consisting of technical experts and even senior management are common in the purchase of major goods. Business marketers need to send well-trained sales representatives and sales teams to deal with the well-trained buyers.

- ***Multiple sales calls.*** A study by McGraw-Hill found that it takes four to four and a half calls to close an average industrial sale. In the case of capital equipment sales for large projects, it may take many attempts to fund a project, and the sales cycle—between quoting a job and delivering the product—is often measured in years.[8]
- ***Derived demand.*** The demand for business goods is ultimately derived from the demand for consumer goods. For this reason, the business marketer must closely monitor the buying patterns of ultimate consumers. For instance, the Big Three automakers in Detroit have been driving the boom in demand for steel-bar products. Much of that demand in turn is derived from the sustained growth in sales of minivans and other light trucks, which consume far more steel than cars. Business buyers must also pay close attention to current and expected economic factors, such as the level of production, investment, consumer spending, and the interest rate. In a recession, they reduce their investment in plant, equipment, and inventories. Business marketers can do little to stimulate total demand in this environment. They can only fight harder to increase or maintain their share of the demand.
- ***Inelastic demand.*** The total demand for many business goods and services is inelastic—that is, not much affected by price changes. Shoe manufacturers are not going to buy much more leather if the price of leather falls, nor will they buy much less leather if the price rises, unless they can find satisfactory substitutes. Demand is especially inelastic in the short run because producers cannot make quick changes in production methods. Demand is also inelastic for business goods that represent a small percentage of the item's total cost, such as shoelaces.
- ***Fluctuating demand.*** The demand for business goods and services tends to be more volatile than the demand for consumer goods and services. A given percentage increase in consumer demand can lead to a much larger percentage increase in the demand for plant and equipment necessary to produce the additional output. Economists refer to this as the *acceleration effect.* Sometimes a rise of only 10% in consumer demand can cause as much as a 200% rise in business demand for products in the next period; a 10% fall in consumer demand may cause a complete collapse in business demand.
- ***Geographically concentrated buyers.*** More than half of U.S. business buyers are concentrated in seven states: New York, California, Pennsylvania, Illinois, Ohio, New Jersey, and Michigan. The geographical concentration of producers helps to reduce selling costs. At the same time, business marketers need to monitor regional shifts of certain industries.
- ***Direct purchasing.*** Business buyers often buy directly from manufacturers rather than through intermediaries, especially items that are technically complex or expensive such as mainframes or aircraft.

Buying Situations

The business buyer faces many decisions in making a purchase. The number depends on the buying situation: complexity of the problem being solved, newness of the buying requirement, number of people involved, and time required. Three types of buying situations are the straight rebuy, modified rebuy, and new task.[9]

STRAIGHT REBUY In a straight rebuy, the purchasing department reorders supplies such as office supplies and bulk chemicals on a routine basis and chooses from suppliers on an approved list. The suppliers make an effort to maintain product and service quality and often propose automatic reordering systems to save time. "Out-suppliers" attempt to offer something new or to exploit dissatisfaction with a current supplier. Their goal is to get a small order and then enlarge their purchase share over time.

MODIFIED REBUY The buyer wants to modify product specifications, prices, delivery requirements, or other terms. The modified rebuy usually involves additional participants on both sides. The in-suppliers become nervous and want to protect the account. The out-suppliers see an opportunity to propose a better offer to gain some business.

NEW TASK A purchaser buys a product or service for the first time (an office building, a new security system). The greater the cost or risk, the larger the number of participants and the greater their information gathering—and therefore the longer the time to a decision.[10]

Orica Ltd.'s success grew from its realization that it could provide more than just explosives to its mining customers. Now it researches the efficiency of different kinds of explosions and manages the entire blast for its clients.

The business buyer makes the fewest decisions in the straight rebuy situation and the most in the new-task situation. Over time, new-buy situations become straight rebuys and routine purchase behavior.

New-task buying is the marketer's greatest opportunity and challenge. The process passes through several stages: awareness, interest, evaluation, trial, and adoption.[11] Mass media can be most important during the initial awareness stage; salespeople often have their greatest impact at the interest stage; and technical sources can be most important during the evaluation stage.

In the new-task situation, the buyer must determine product specifications, price limits, delivery terms and times, service terms, payment terms, order quantities, acceptable suppliers, and the selected supplier. Different participants influence each decision, and the order in which these decisions are made varies.

Because of the complicated selling involved, many companies use a *missionary sales force* consisting of their most effective salespeople. The brand promise and the manufacturer's brand name recognition will be important in establishing trust and the customer's willingness to consider change.[12] The marketer also tries to reach as many key participants as possible and provide helpful information and assistance.

Once a customer is acquired, in-suppliers are continually seeking ways to add value to their market offer to facilitate rebuys. Data storage leader EMC successfully acquired a series of computer software leaders to reposition the company to manage—and not just store—information, often by giving customers customized information.[13]

ORICA LTD.

Orica Ltd., formerly ICI Australia, competes in the cutthroat commercial explosives business. Its customers are quarries that use explosives to blast solid rock face into aggregate of a specified size. Orica is constantly trying to minimize the cost of explosives. The firm realized it could create significant value by improving the efficiency of the blast. To do this, it established over 20 parameters that influenced the success of the blast and began collecting data from customers on the input parameters as well as the outcomes of individual blasts. By collating the data, Orica engineers came to understand the conditions that produced different outcomes. It then could offer customers a contract for "broken rock" that would almost guarantee the desired outcome. The success of Orica's approach—of managing the entire blast for the quarry rather than simply selling explosives—entrenched the company as the world's leading supplier of commercial explosives.[14]

Customers considering dropping six or seven figures on one transaction for big-ticket goods and services want all the information they can get. One way to entice new buyers is to create a customer reference program in which satisfied existing customers act in concert with the company's sales and marketing department by agreeing to serve as references. Technology companies such as HP, Lucent, and Unisys have all employed such programs. "Marketing Memo: Maximizing Customer References" provides some tips for developing activities and programs with impact.

Systems Buying and Selling

Many business buyers prefer to buy a total solution to a problem from one seller. Called *systems buying,* this practice originated with government purchases of major weapons and communications systems. The government would solicit bids from *prime contractors,* who

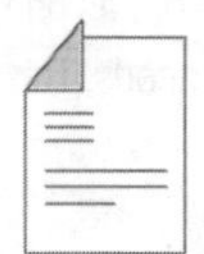

MARKETING MEMO | MAXIMIZING CUSTOMER REFERENCES

Many firms depend on the opinions and experiences of others in evaluating a new business proposal from a new company. Here is some industry wisdom as to what works and doesn't work when developing customer information and reference programs to respond to these demands.

Five Common Mistakes in Developing Customer Reference Stories

1. ***Failing to state the customer's need and its implications with specificity***—Clearly state why customers had a need and how the company's products would resolve it. Such detailed information can better allow salespeople to assess whether a prospect has similar needs and could obtain similar pay-offs.
2. ***Failing to quantify your customer's results***—Although outside companies may seem reluctant to share too much hard data, it may just reflect the fact that they don't have the information readily accessible. Assist them in getting it.
3. ***Failing to describe business benefits of any kind (quantified or not)***—Don't focus on your expertise in various technologies and industries without telling how it specifically helped customers to enter or grow markets. Make an obvious cause-and-effect link between the solution provided and the claims for your product.
4. ***Failing to differentiate your offerings from competition***—Make it clear why it was the case that not just any company's products or services could have led to the same solution.
5. ***Failing to provide a concise, accessible summary of the story***—Make sure you package the customer reference story in a way that a prospect can easily and quickly understand. Here are seven ways to do so.

Seven Keys to Successfully Developing Customer Reference Stories

1. State the customer's needs in compelling terms.
2. Emphasize the barriers in satisfying customer needs.
3. Describe your company's solution in terms of value.
4. List quantified results, especially those that affect ROI.
5. Differentiate your offering from those of competitors.
6. Provide a brief comprehensive summary.
7. Include numerous customer quotes.

Source: Based on a white paper, Bill Lee, "Success Stories: The Top 5 Mistakes," www.lee-communications.com/.

assembled the package or system. The contractor who was awarded the contract would be responsible for bidding out and assembling the system's subcomponents from *second-tier contractors*. The prime contractor would thus provide a turnkey solution, so-called because the buyer simply had to turn one key to get the job done.

Sellers have increasingly recognized that buyers like to purchase in this way, and many have adopted systems selling as a marketing tool. One variant of systems selling is *systems contracting*, where a single supplier provides the buyer with his entire requirement of MRO (maintenance, repair, operating) supplies. During the contract period, the supplier manages the customer's inventory. For example, Shell Oil manages the oil inventory of many of its business customers and knows when it requires replenishment. The customer benefits from reduced procurement and management costs and from price protection over the term of the contract. The seller benefits from lower operating costs because of a steady demand and reduced paperwork.

Systems selling is a key industrial marketing strategy in bidding to build large-scale industrial projects, such as dams, steel factories, irrigation systems, sanitation systems, pipelines, utilities, and even new towns. Project engineering firms must compete on price, quality, reliability, and other attributes to win contracts. With systems selling, customers present potential suppliers with a list of project specifications and requirements. Suppliers, however, are not just at the mercy of these customer demands. Ideally, they're involved with customers early in the process to influence the actual development of the specifications. Or they can go beyond the specifications to offer additional value in various ways, as the following example shows.

JAPAN AND INDONESIA

The Indonesian government requested bids to build a cement factory near Jakarta. A U.S. firm made a proposal that included choosing the site, designing the cement factory, hiring the construction crews, assembling the materials and equipment, and turning over the finished factory to the Indonesian government. A Japanese firm, in outlining its proposal, included all these services, plus hiring and training the workers to run the factory, exporting the cement through its trading companies, and using the cement to build roads and new office buildings in Jakarta. Although the Japanese proposal involved more money, it won the contract. Clearly, the Japanese viewed the problem not just as one of building a cement factory (the narrow view of systems selling) but as one of contributing to Indonesia's economic development. They took the broadest view of the customer's needs. This is true systems selling.

::: Participants in the Business Buying Process

Who buys the trillions of dollars' worth of goods and services needed by business organizations? Purchasing agents are influential in straight-rebuy and modified-rebuy situations, whereas other department personnel are more influential in new-buy situations. Engineering personnel usually have a major influence in selecting product components, and purchasing agents dominate in selecting suppliers.[15,16]

The Buying Center

Webster and Wind call the decision-making unit of a buying organization *the buying center.* It consists of "all those individuals and groups who participate in the purchasing decision-making process, who share some common goals and the risks arising from the decisions."[17] The buying center includes all members of the organization who play any of seven roles in the purchase decision process.

1. ***Initiators***—Users or others in the organization who request that something be purchased.
2. ***Users***—Those who will use the product or service. In many cases, the users initiate the buying proposal and help define the product requirements.
3. ***Influencers***—People who influence the buying decision, often by helping define specifications and providing information for evaluating alternatives. Technical personnel are particularly important influencers.
4. ***Deciders***—People who decide on product requirements or on suppliers.
5. ***Approvers***—People who authorize the proposed actions of deciders or buyers.
6. ***Buyers***—People who have formal authority to select the supplier and arrange the purchase terms. Buyers may help shape product specifications, but they play their major role in selecting vendors and negotiating. In more complex purchases, buyers might include high-level managers.
7. ***Gatekeepers***—People who have the power to prevent sellers or information from reaching members of the buying center. For example, purchasing agents, receptionists, and telephone operators may prevent salespersons from contacting users or deciders.

Several people can occupy a given role such as user or influencer, and one person may occupy multiple roles.[18] A purchasing manager, for example, often occupies the roles of buyer, influencer, and gatekeeper simultaneously: She can determine which sales reps can call on other people in the organization; what budget and other constraints to place on the purchase; and which firm will actually get the business, even though others (deciders) might select two or more potential vendors that can meet the company's requirements.

The typical buying center has a minimum of five or six members and often has dozens. Some may be outside the organization, such as government officials, consultants, technical advisors, and other members of the marketing channel. One study found that 3.5 more people on average were involved in making a purchase decision in 2005 than in 2001.[19]

Buying Center Influences

Buying centers usually include several participants with differing interests, authority, status, and persuasiveness and sometimes very different decision criteria. For example, engineering personnel may want to maximize the performance of the product; production personnel may want ease of use and reliability of supply; financial personnel focus on the economics of the purchase; purchasing may be concerned with operating and replacement costs; union officials may emphasize safety issues.

Business buyers also have personal motivations, perceptions, and preferences that are influenced by their age, income, education, job position, personality, attitudes toward risk, and culture. Buyers definitely exhibit different buying styles. There are "keep-it-simple" buyers, "own-expert" buyers, "want-the-best" buyers, and "want-everything-done" buyers. Some younger, highly educated buyers are computer experts who conduct rigorous analyses of competitive proposals before choosing a supplier. Other buyers are "toughies" from the old school who pit the competing sellers against one another, and in some companies, the purchasing powers-that-be are legendary.

GENERAL MOTORS

Every year Bo I. Andersson, General Motors VP of global purchasing, is charged with knocking a whopping $2 billion from GM's purchasing bill. A former Swedish army officer, Andersson is a hands-on individual who buys $85 billion worth of wheels, axles, seats, bolts, and other parts in a purchasing bill topped only by the U.S. military. Yet, he isn't focused so much on squeezing suppliers as he is on squeezing inefficiencies out of the system, such as getting GM's vehicles to share more parts. (GM currently makes 26 versions of seat frames, whereas Toyota makes 2.) Still, Andersson does not suffer inefficiency from suppliers. If they don't meet his standards, he will drop them even if it means forcing them into bankruptcy. In 2006, for instance, he decided to jettison 3,200 suppliers. Perhaps that's why GM ranks last in an annual supplier satisfaction survey![20]

Webster cautions that ultimately, individuals, not organizations, make purchasing decisions.[21] Individuals are motivated by their own needs and perceptions in attempting to maximize the rewards (pay, advancement, recognition, and feelings of achievement) offered by the organization. Personal needs motivate the behavior of individuals, but organizational needs legitimate the buying-decision process and its outcomes. People are not buying "products." They are buying solutions to two problems: the organization's economic and strategic problem and their own personal need for individual achievement and reward. In this sense, industrial buying decisions are both "rational" and "emotional," as they serve both the organization's and the individual's needs.[22]

For example, research conducted by one industrial component manufacturer found that although top executives at small- and medium-size companies stated they were comfortable in general with buying from other companies, they appeared to harbor subconscious insecurities about buying the manufacturer's product. Constant changes in technology had left them concerned about the internal effects within the company. Recognizing this unease, the manufacturer retooled its selling approach to emphasize more emotional appeals and how its product line actually enabled the customer's employees to improve their performance, relieving management of the complications and stress with component use.[23]

Recognizing these extrinsic, interpersonal influences, more industrial firms have put greater emphasis on strengthening their corporate brand. At one time, Emerson Electric, global provider of power tools, compressors, electrical equipment, and engineering solutions, was a conglomerate of 60 autonomous—and sometimes anonymous—companies. A new CMO aligned the previously independent brands under a new global brand architecture and identity, allowing Emerson to achieve a broader presence so that it could sell locally while leveraging its global brand name. Record sales and stock price highs soon followed.[24]

SAS INSTITUTE INC.

With sales of more than $1.1 billion and a huge "fan club" of IT customers, SAS, the business intelligence software firm, seemed to be in an enviable position in 1999. Yet, its image was what one industry observer called "a geek brand." In order to extend the company's reach beyond IT managers with PhDs in math or statistical analysis, the company needed to connect with C-level executives in the largest companies—the kind of people who either didn't have a clue what SAS's software was and what to do with it, or who didn't think business intelligence was a strategic issue. Working with its first outside ad agency ever, SAS emerged with a new logo, a new slogan, "The Power to Know," and a series of TV spots and print ads in business publications such as *Business Week, Forbes,* and *The Wall Street Journal.* One TV spot that exemplifies SAS's rebranding effort ran like this:

> *The problem is not harvesting the new crop of e-business information. It's making sense of it. With e-intelligence from SAS, you can harness the information. And put the knowledge you need within reach. SAS. The power to know.*

Subsequent research showed that SAS had made the transition to a mainstream business decision-making support brand, both user friendly and necessary.[25]

Recognizable brands are important to business buyers, as Emerson Electric found when it created a new global brand identity for its 60 autonomous companies.

Buying Center Targeting

To target their efforts properly, business marketers need to figure out: Who are the major decision participants? What decisions do they influence? What is their level of influence? What evaluation criteria do they use? Consider the following example:

> A company sells nonwoven disposable surgical gowns to hospitals. The hospital personnel who participate in this buying decision include the vice president of purchasing, the operating-room administrator, and the surgeons. The vice president of purchasing analyzes whether the hospital should buy disposable gowns or reusable gowns. If the findings favor disposable gowns, then the operating-room administrator compares various competitors' products and prices and makes a choice. This administrator considers absorbency, antiseptic quality, design, and cost and normally buys the brand that meets the functional requirements at the lowest cost. Surgeons influence the decision retroactively by reporting their satisfaction with the particular brand.

The business marketer is not likely to know exactly what kind of group dynamics take place during the decision process, although whatever information he can obtain about personalities and interpersonal factors is useful.

Small sellers concentrate on reaching the *key buying influencers.* Larger sellers go for *multilevel in-depth selling* to reach as many participants as possible. Their salespeople virtually "live" with high-volume customers. Companies must rely more heavily on their communications programs to reach hidden buying influences and keep current customers informed.[26]

SYMANTEC CORPORATION

Internet security provider Symantec Corporation has moved from being primarily a provider of consumer software (under the Norton name) to a provider of enterprise security solutions for financial services, health care, and utilities industries, as well as key accounts for the U.S. Department of Defense. To reach these new markets,

Symantec had to restructure its sales force to develop high-level relationships. So Symantec launched the Executive Sponsorship Program in 2003. The 13 Symantec executives enrolled in the program are paired with vice presidents or C-level executives within 19 key customer organizations in industries ranging from banking to telecommunications and manufacturing. The goal of the program is to foster better understanding of Symantec's customers and their business concerns. So far the program has enabled Symantec to be seen as a valued partner and has given its executives insights into how they can develop products that fit customers' needs.[27]

Business marketers must periodically review their assumptions about buying center participants. For years, Kodak sold X-ray film to hospital lab technicians, but research indicated that professional administrators were increasingly making purchasing decisions. As a result, Kodak revised its marketing strategy and developed new advertising to reach out to these decision makers.

::: The Purchasing/Procurement Process

In principle, business buyers seek to obtain the highest benefit package (economic, technical, service, and social) in relation to a market offering's costs. To make comparisons, they will try to translate all costs and benefits into monetary terms. A business buyer's incentive to purchase will be a function of the difference between perceived benefits and perceived costs.[28] The marketer's task is to construct a profitable offering that delivers superior customer value to the target buyers.

Supplier diversity is a benefit that may not have a price tag but that business buyers overlook at their risk. As the CEOs of many of the country's largest companies see it, a diverse supplier base is a business imperative. Minority suppliers are the fastest-growing segment of today's business landscape.

PFIZER

One of the biggest names in pharmaceuticals, Pfizer views its supplier-diversity program as an essential tool in connecting with customers. Gwendolyn Turner, manager of supplier diversity, says the company spent about $700M with 2,400 minority and women suppliers. "Our business touches all kinds of customers, so it only makes sense that our supplier base represents a broad range of people as well." Pfizer has even developed a mentoring program that identifies the women and minority suppliers who need help growing, whether it's designing a better Web site or building a better business plan. Pfizer managers meet with the owners, often on-site, to figure out what they need.[29]

Purchasing Department Perceptions

In the past, purchasing departments occupied a low position in the management hierarchy, in spite of often managing more than half the company's costs. Recent competitive pressures have led many companies to upgrade their purchasing departments and elevate administrators to vice presidential rank. These new, more strategically oriented purchasing departments have a mission to seek the best value from fewer and better suppliers. Some multinationals have even elevated them to "strategic supply deparments" with responsibility for global sourcing and partnering. At Caterpillar, for example, purchasing, inventory control, production scheduling, and traffic have been combined into one department. Lockheed Martin and McDonald's are two companies that have improved their business buying practices.

LOCKHEED MARTIN

Defense contractor Lockheed Martin, which spends $13.2 billion annually, created a Strategic Sourcing Solutions Group to centralize the company's purchasing functions across divisions and consolidate redundancies. The group has 52 employees with cross-functional experience, and its mission is "to be an integrated, leading-edge team that provides industry-recognized supply chain intelligence and innovative sourcing strategies, while fully optimizing customer value." As an example of the group's strategic focus, Lockheed Martin found it was spending roughly 25% to 40% more than it should on machining. A machining council was assigned to look into driving down the number of suppliers and consolidating among the preferred ones. It reduced the supply base by driving more business to preferred suppliers, negotiating more often, and introducing reverse auctions where appropriate.[30]

MCDONALD'S

As director of global technology supplier management for McDonald's, Joseph Youssef's mandate is to segment and measure suppliers and then manage them based on the measurements. And, mind you, Youssef oversees only one aspect of McDonald's huge supplier base, its IT services and equipment. As McDonald's began to see positive results from applying its supplier relationship management methods to one of its IT suppliers, it extended the strategy to its other IT contracts such as its network systems, Verizon and MCI, and its restaurant point-of-sale systems. McDonalds will now go on to apply supplier management strategies to its indirect materials suppliers.[31]

The upgrading of purchasing means that business marketers must upgrade their sales personnel to match the higher caliber of the business buyers.

Purchasing Organization and Administration

Most purchasing professionals describe their jobs as more strategic, technical, team oriented, and involving more responsibility than ever before. "Purchasing is doing more cross-functional work than it did in the past," says David Duprey, a buyer for Anaren Microwave Inc. Sixty-one percent of buyers surveyed said the buying group was more involved in new-product design and development than it was five years ago; and more than half the buyers participate in cross-functional teams, with suppliers well represented.[32]

Some companies have started to centralize purchasing. Headquarters identifies materials purchased by several divisions and buys them centrally, gaining more purchasing clout. For the business marketer, this development means dealing with fewer and higher-level buyers and using a national account sales group to deal with large corporate buyers. At the same time, companies are decentralizing some purchasing operations by empowering employees to purchase small-ticket items, such as special binders, coffeemakers, or Christmas trees, through corporate purchasing cards issued by credit card organizations.

::: Stages in the Buying Process

We're ready to describe the general stages in the business buying-decision process. Robinson and his associates identified eight stages and called them *buyphases*.[33] The model in Table 7.2 is the *buygrid* framework.

In modified-rebuy or straight-rebuy situations, some stages are compressed or bypassed. For example, the buyer normally has a favorite supplier or a ranked list of suppliers and can skip the search and proposal solicitation stages. Here are some important considerations in each of the eight stages.

TABLE 7.2

Buygrid Framework: Major Stages (Buyphases) of the Industrial Buying Process in Relation to Major Buying Situations (Buyclasses)

		Buyclasses		
		New Task	**Modified Rebuy**	**Straight Rebuy**
BUYPHASES	1. Problem recognition	Yes	Maybe	No
	2. General need description	Yes	Maybe	No
	3. Product specification	Yes	Yes	Yes
	4. Supplier search	Yes	Maybe	No
	5. Proposal solicitation	Yes	Maybe	No
	6. Supplier selection	Yes	Maybe	No
	7. Order-routine specification	Yes	Maybe	No
	8. Performance review	Yes	Yes	Yes

Problem Recognition

The buying process begins when someone in the company recognizes a problem or need that can be met by acquiring a good or service. The recognition can be triggered by internal or external stimuli. Internal stimuli might be that the company decides to develop a new product and needs new equipment and materials, or a machine breaks down and requires new parts. Or purchased material turns out to be unsatisfactory and the company searches for another supplier, or lower prices or better quality. Externally, the buyer may get new ideas at a trade show, see an ad, or receive a call from a sales representative who offers a better product or a lower price. Business marketers can stimulate problem recognition by direct mail, telemarketing, and calling on prospects.

General Need Description and Product Specification

Next, the buyer determines the needed item's general characteristics and required quantity. For standard items, this is simple. For complex items, the buyer will work with others—engineers, users—to define characteristics such as reliability, durability, or price. Business marketers can help by describing how their products meet or even exceed the buyer's needs.

The buying organization now develops the item's technical specifications. Often, the company will assign a product-value-analysis engineering team to the project. *Product value analysis (PVA)* is an approach to cost reduction that studies components to determine whether they can be redesigned or standardized or made by cheaper methods of production. The PVA team will identify overdesigned components, for instance, that last longer than the product itself. Tightly written specifications will allow the buyer to refuse components that are too expensive or that fail to meet specified standards. Suppliers can use product value analysis as a tool for positioning themselves to win an account.

Supplier Search

The buyer next tries to identify the most appropriate suppliers through trade directories, contacts with other companies, trade advertisements, trade shows, and the Internet.[34] The move to Internet purchasing has far-reaching implications for suppliers and will change the shape of purchasing for years to come.[35] Companies that purchase over the Internet are utilizing electronic marketplaces in several forms:

- ***Catalog sites.*** Companies can order thousands of items through electronic catalogs distributed by e-procurement software, such as Grainger's.
- ***Vertical markets.*** Companies buying industrial products such as plastics, steel, or chemicals or services such as logistics or media can go to specialized Web sites (called e-hubs). For example, Plastics.com allows plastics buyers to search for the best prices among thousands of plastics sellers.
- ***"Pure Play" auction sites.*** Online marketplaces such as eBay and Freemarkets.com could not have been realized without the Internet. Freemarkets.com provides online auctions for buyers and sellers of industrial parts, raw materials, commodities, and services in over 50 product categories and has facilitated over $40 billion worth of commerce since 1995.
- ***Spot (or exchange) markets.*** On spot electronic markets, prices change by the minute. ChemConnect.com is an exchange for buyers and sellers of bulk chemicals such as benzene, and it's a B2B success in an arena littered with failed online exchanges. First to market, it is now the biggest online exchange for chemical trading, with 1 million barrels traded daily. Customers such as Vanguard Petroleum Corp. in Houston conduct about 15% of their spot purchases and sales of natural gas liquids on ChemConnect's commodities trading site.
- ***Private exchanges.*** Hewlett-Packard, IBM, and Wal-Mart operate private exchanges to link with specially invited groups of suppliers and partners over the Web.
- ***Barter markets.*** In barter markets, participants offer to trade goods or services.
- ***Buying alliances.*** Several companies buying the same goods join together to form purchasing consortia such as Transora and Covisint to gain deeper discounts on volume purchases.

Online business buying offers several advantages: It shaves transaction costs for both buyers and suppliers, reduces time between order and delivery, consolidates purchasing systems, and forges more direct relationships between partners and buyers. On the downside, it may help to erode supplier–buyer loyalty and create potential security problems.

E-PROCUREMENT Web sites are organized around two types of e-hubs: *vertical hubs* centered on industries (plastics, steel, chemicals, paper) and *functional hubs* (logistics, media buying, advertising, energy management). In addition to using these Web sites, companies can use e-procurement in other ways:

- ***Set up direct extranet links to major suppliers.*** For example, a company can set up a direct e-procurement account at Dell or Office Depot, and its employees can make their purchases this way.
- ***Form buying alliances.*** A number of major retailers and manufacturers such as Ace Hardware, Coca-Cola, Colgate Palmolive, Johnson & Johnson, Kraft, Kroger, Lowe's, Nestle, Office Depot, PepsiCo, Procter & Gamble, Sara Lee, Staples, Wal-Mart, and Wegmans Food Markets are part of a data-sharing alliance called 1SYNC. Several auto companies (GM, Ford, DaimlerChrysler) formed Covisint for the same reason. Covisint is the leading provider of services that can integrate crucial business information and processes between partners, customers, and suppliers. The company has now also targeted health care to provide similar services.
- ***Set up company buying sites.*** General Electric formed the Trading Process Network (TPN), where it posts *requests for proposals (RFPs)*, negotiates terms, and places orders.

Moving into e-procurement means more than acquiring software; it requires changing purchasing strategy and structure. However, the benefits are many: Aggregating purchasing across multiple departments yields larger, centrally negotiated volume discounts, a smaller purchasing staff, and less buying of substandard goods from outside the approved list of suppliers.

LEAD GENERATION The supplier's task is to ensure it is considered when customers are—or could be—in the market and searching for a supplier. Identifying good leads and converting them to sales requires the whole marketing and sales organizations to work in a coordinated, multichannel approach in the role of trusted advisor to prospective customers. Marketing must work together with sales to define what makes a "sales ready" prospect and cooperate to send the right messages via sales calls, tradeshows, online activities, PR, events, direct mail, and referrals.[36]

To proactively generate leads, suppliers need to know about their customers. They can obtain background information from vendors such as Dun & Bradstreet and infoUSA or information-sharing Web sites such as Jigsaw and LinkedIn.[37]

Suppliers that lack the required production capacity or suffer from a poor reputation will be rejected. Those who qualify may be visited by the buyer's agents, who will examine the suppliers' manufacturing facilities and meet their personnel. After evaluating each company, the buyer will end up with a short list of qualified suppliers. Many professional buyers have forced suppliers to change their marketing to increase their likelihood of making the cut.

Proposal Solicitation

The buyer next invites qualified suppliers to submit proposals. If the item is complex or expensive, the buyer will require a detailed written proposal from each qualified supplier. After evaluating the proposals, the buyer will invite a few suppliers to make formal presentations.

Business marketers must be skilled in researching, writing, and presenting proposals. Written proposals should be marketing documents that describe value and benefits in customer terms. Oral presentations must inspire confidence and position the company's capabilities and resources so they stand out from the competition. Proposals and selling are often team efforts. Pittsburgh-based Cutler-Hammer developed "pods" of salespeople focused on a particular geographic region, industry, or market concentration. Salespeople can leverage the knowledge and expertise of coworkers instead of working in isolation.[38]

Supplier Selection

Before selecting a supplier, the buying center will specify desired supplier attributes and indicate their relative importance. To rate and identify the most attractive suppliers, buying centers often use a supplier-evaluation model such as the one shown in Table 7.3.

TABLE 7.3

An Example of Vendor Analysis

Attributes	Importance Weights	Rating Scale Poor (1)	Fair (2)	Good (3)	Excellent (4)
Price	.30				X
Supplier reputation	.20			X	
Product reliability	.30				X
Service reliability	.10		X		
Supplier flexibility	.10			X	
Total Score: .30(4) + .20(3) + .30(4) + .10(2) + .10(3) = 3.5					

To develop compelling value propositions, business marketers need to better understand how business buyers arrive at their valuations.[39] Researchers studying how business marketers assess customer value found eight different *customer value assessment (CVA)* methods. Companies tended to use the simpler methods, although the more sophisticated ones promise to produce a more accurate picture of customer-perceived value. (See "Marketing Memo: Developing Compelling Customer Value Propositions.")

The choice and importance of different attributes varies with the type of buying situation. Delivery reliability, price, and supplier reputation are important for routine-order products. For procedural-problem products, such as a copying machine, the three most important attributes are technical service, supplier flexibility, and product reliability. For political-problem products that stir rivalries in the organization (such as the choice of a computer system), the most important attributes are price, supplier reputation, product reliability, service reliability, and supplier flexibility.

OVERCOMING PRICE PRESSURES The buying center may attempt to negotiate with preferred suppliers for better prices and terms before making the final selection. Despite moves toward strategic sourcing, partnering, and participation in cross-functional teams, buyers still spend a large chunk of their time haggling with suppliers on price. The number of price-oriented buyers can vary by country depending on customer preferences for different service configurations and characteristics of the customer's organization.[40]

Marketers can counter requests for a lower price in a number of ways. They may be able to show evidence that the "total cost of ownership," that is, the "life-cycle cost" of using their product, is lower than for competitors' products. They can cite the value of the services the buyer now receives, especially if they are superior to those offered by competitors. Research shows that service support and personal interactions, as well as a supplier's know-how and ability to improve customers' time to market, can be useful differentiators in achieving key-supplier status.[41]

Improving productivity helps alleviate price pressures. Burlington Northern ties 30% of employee bonuses to improvements in the number of railcars shipped per mile.[42] Some firms are using technology to devise novel customer solutions. With Web technology and tools, VistaPrint printers can offer professional printing to small businesses that previously could not afford it.[43]

Some companies handle price-oriented buyers by setting a lower price but establishing restrictive conditions: (1) limited quantities, (2) no refunds, (3) no adjustments, and (4) no services.[44]

- ***Cardinal Health*** set up a bonus-dollars scheme and gave points according to how much the customer purchased. The points could be turned in for extra goods or free consulting.
- ***GE*** is installing diagnostic sensors in its airline engines and railroad engines. It is now compensated for hours of flight or railroad travel.
- ***IBM*** is now more of a service company aided by products than a product company aided by services. It can sell computer power on demand (like video on demand) as an alternative to selling computers.

Solution selling can also alleviate price pressure and comes in different forms. Here are three examples.[45]

MARKETING MEMO | DEVELOPING COMPELLING CUSTOMER VALUE PROPOSITIONS

To command price premiums in competitive B2B markets, firms must create compelling customer value propositions. The first step is to research the customer. Here are a number of productive research methods:

1. ***Internal engineering assessment***—Have company engineers use laboratory tests to estimate the product's performance characteristics. Weakness: Ignores the fact that in different applications, the product will have different economic value.
2. ***Field value-in-use assessment***—Interview customers about how costs of using a new product compare to those of using an incumbent. The task is to assess how much each cost element is worth to the buyer.
3. ***Focus-group value assessment***—Ask customers in a focus group what value they would put on potential market offerings.
4. ***Direct survey questions***—Ask customers to place a direct dollar value on one or more changes in the market offering.
5. ***Conjoint analysis***—Ask customers to rank their preferences for alternative market offerings or concepts. Use statistical analysis to estimate the implicit value placed on each attribute.
6. ***Benchmarks***—Show customers a "benchmark" offering and then a new-market offering. Ask how much more they would pay for the new offering or how much less they would pay if certain features were removed from the benchmark offering.
7. ***Compositional approach***—Ask customers to attach a monetary value to each of three alternative levels of a given attribute. Repeat for other attributes, then add the values together for any offer configuration.
8. ***Importance ratings***—Ask customers to rate the importance of different attributes and their suppliers' performance on each.

Having done this research, you can specify the customer value proposition, following a number of important principles. First, clearly substantiate value claims by concretely specifying the differences between your offerings and those of competitors on the dimensions that matter most to the customer. For example, Rockwell Automation determined the cost savings customers would realize from purchasing its pump solution instead of a competitor's by using industry-standard metrics of functionality and performance: kilowatt-hours spent, number of operating hours per year, and dollars per kilowatt-hour. Also, make the financial implications obvious.

Rockwell Automation's marketers quantified its customers' potential cost savings by applying industry-standard measures of performance to its products.

Second, document the value delivered by creating written accounts of costs savings or added value that existing customers have actually captured by using your offerings. Chemical producer Akzo Nobel conducted a two-week pilot on a production reactor at a prospective customer's facility to document points-of-parity and points-of-difference of its high-purity metal organics product.

Finally, make sure the customer value proposition is well implemented within the company, and train and reward employees for developing a compelling one. Quaker Chemical conducts training programs for its managers that include a competition to develop the best proposals.

Source: James C. Anderson, James A. Narus, and Wouter van Rossum, "Customer Value Propositions in Business Markets," *Harvard Business Review* (March 2006): 2–10; James C. Anderson and James A. Narus, "Business Marketing: Understanding What Customers Value," *Harvard Business Review* (November 1998): 53–65; James C. Anderson and James A. Narus, "Capturing the Value of Supplementary Services," *Harvard Business Review* (January 1995): 75–83; James C. Anderson, Dipak C. Jain, and Pradeep K. Chintagunta, "A Customer Value Assessment in Business Markets: A State-of-Practice Study," *Journal of Business-to-Business Marketing* 1, no. 1 (January 1993): 3–29.

- ***Solutions to Enhance Customer Revenues.*** Hendrix Voeders used its sales consultants to help farmers deliver an incremental animal weight gain of 5% to 10% over competitors.
- ***Solutions to Decrease Customer Risks.*** ICI Explosives formulated a safer way to ship explosives for quarries.
- ***Solutions to Reduce Customer Costs.*** W.W. Grainger employees work at large customer facilities to reduce materials-management costs.

More and more firms are seeking solutions that increase benefits and reduce costs enough to overcome any low price concerns. Consider the following example.

Lincoln Electric is a successful industrial products company that works with its customers to build strong relationships by lowering their costs.

LINCOLN ELECTRIC

Lincoln Electric has a decades-long tradition of working with its customers to reduce costs through its Guaranteed Cost Reduction Program. When a customer insists that a Lincoln distributor lower prices to match competitors, the company and the particular distributor may guarantee that, during the coming year, they will find cost reductions in the customer's plant that meet or exceed the price difference between Lincoln's products and the competition's. For example, The Holland Binkley Company, a major manufacturer of components for tractor trailers including landing gear, suspension undercarriages, and custom parts, had been purchasing Lincoln Electric welding wire for years. When Binkley began to shop around for a better price on wire, Lincoln Electric developed a package of reducing costs and working together that called for a $10,000 savings but eventually led to a six-figure savings, a growth in business, and a strong, long-term partnership between customer and supplier.[46]

Risk and gain sharing can offset requested price reductions from customers. For example, say Medline, a hospital supplier, signs an agreement with Highland Park Hospital promising $350,000 in savings over the first 18 months in exchange for a tenfold increase in the hospitals' share of supplies. If Medline achieves less than this promised savings, it will make up the difference. If Medline achieves substantially more than promised, it participates in the extra savings. To make such arrangements work, the supplier must be willing to help the customer to build a historical database, reach an agreement for measuring benefits and costs, and devise a dispute resolution mechanism.

NUMBER OF SUPPLIERS As part of the buyer selection process, buying centers must decide how many suppliers to use. Companies are increasingly reducing the number of suppliers. Ford, Motorola, and Honeywell have cut the number of suppliers by 20% to 80%. These companies want their chosen suppliers to be responsible for a larger component system, they want them to achieve continuous quality and performance improvement, and at the same time they want them to lower prices each year by a given percentage. These companies expect their suppliers to work closely with them during product development, and they value their suggestions. There is even a trend toward single sourcing.

Companies that use multiple sources often cite the threat of a labor strike as the biggest deterrent to single sourcing. Another reason companies may be reluctant to use a single source is that they fear they'll become too comfortable in the relationship and lose their competitive edge.

Order-Routine Specification

After selecting suppliers, the buyer negotiates the final order, listing the technical specifications, the quantity needed, the expected time of delivery, return policies, warranties, and so on. Many industrial buyers lease heavy equipment such as machinery and trucks. The lessee gains a number of advantages: conserving capital, getting the latest products, receiving better service, and gaining some tax advantages. The lessor often ends up with a larger net income and the chance to sell to customers that could not afford outright purchase.

In the case of maintenance, repair, and operating items, buyers are moving toward blanket contracts rather than periodic purchase orders. A blanket contract establishes a long-term relationship in which the supplier promises to resupply the buyer as needed, at agreed-upon prices, over a specified period of time. Because the seller holds the stock, blanket contracts are sometimes called *stockless purchase plans.* The buyer's computer automatically sends an order to the seller when stock is needed. This system locks suppliers in tighter with the buyer and makes it difficult for out-suppliers to break in unless the buyer becomes dissatisfied with the in-supplier's prices, quality, or service.

Companies that fear a shortage of key materials are willing to buy and hold large inventories. They will sign long-term contracts with suppliers to ensure a steady flow of materials. DuPont, Ford, and several other major companies regard long-term supply planning as a major responsibility of their purchasing managers. For example, General Motors wants to buy from fewer suppliers, who must be willing to locate close to its plants and produce high-quality components. Business marketers are also setting up extranets with important customers to facilitate and lower the cost of transactions. The customers enter orders directly on the computer that are automatically transmitted to the supplier. Some companies go further and shift the ordering responsibility to their suppliers in systems called *vendor-managed inventory.* These suppliers are privy to the customer's inventory levels and take responsibility for replenishing it automatically through *continuous replenishment programs.*

Performance Review

The buyer periodically reviews the performance of the chosen supplier(s) using one of three methods. The buyer may contact the end users and ask for their evaluations; the buyer may rate the supplier on several criteria using a weighted-score method; or the buyer might aggregate the cost of poor performance to come up with adjusted costs of purchase, including price. The performance review may lead the buyer to continue, modify, or end a supplier relationship.

Many companies have set up incentive systems to reward purchasing managers for good buying performance, in much the same way that sales personnel receive bonuses for good selling performance. These systems lead purchasing managers to increase pressure on sellers for the best terms.

::: Managing Business-to-Business Customer Relationships

To improve effectiveness and efficiency, business suppliers and customers are exploring different ways to manage their relationships.[47] Closer relationships are driven in part by supply chain management, early supplier involvement, and purchasing alliances.[48] Cultivating the right relationships with business is paramount for any holistic marketing program. A master at business-to-business marketing is GE, as chronicled in "Breakthrough Marketing: General Electric."

The Benefits of Vertical Coordination

Much research has advocated greater vertical coordination between buying partners and sellers, so they can transcend merely transacting and instead engage in activities that create more value for both parties.[49] Building trust is one prerequisite to healthy long-term relationships. "Marketing Insight: Establishing Corporate Trust and Credibility" identifies some key dimensions to such trust. Knowledge that is specific and relevant to a relationship partner is also an important factor in the strength of interfirm ties between partners.[50]

Consider the mutual benefits from the following arrangement.

MOTOMAN INC. AND STILLWATER TECHNOLOGIES

Motoman Inc., a leading supplier of industry robotic systems, and Stillwater Technologies, a contract tooling and machinery company and a key supplier to Motoman, are tightly integrated. Not only do they occupy office and manufacturing space in the same facility, but their telephone and computer systems are linked, and they share

BREAKTHROUGH MARKETING | GENERAL ELECTRIC

GE is made up of six recently reorganized major divisions that operate in areas as diverse as home appliances, jet engines, security systems, wind turbines, and financial services. The company is so large (2005 revenues of $150 billion) that if each of its six business units were ranked separately, all would appear in the *Fortune* 500. If GE were a country, it would be one of the 50 largest, ahead of Finland, Israel, and Ireland.

Founded by Thomas Edison as the Edison Electric Light Company in 1878, GE was an early pioneer in light bulbs and electrical appliances. It also served the electrical needs of various industries, such as transportation, utilities, manufacturing, and broadcasting. It became the acknowledged pioneer in business-to-business marketing in the 1950s and 1960s when its tagline was "Live Better Electrically." As the company diversified its product lines, it created new campaigns, including "Progress for People" and "We Bring Good Things to Life."

In 2003, GE faced a new challenge: how to promote its diversified brand globally with a unified message. Its major new campaign, called "Imagination at Work," highlighted its renewed focus on innovation and new technology. The award-winning campaign promoted units such as GE Aircraft Engines, GE Medical Systems, and GE Plastics, focusing on the breadth of GE's product offerings. GE spends some $150 million on corporate advertising—a large expenditure, but one that creates efficiencies by focusing on the core GE brand. The goal was to unify these divisions under the GE brand while giving them a voice. "When you're a company like ours, with 11 different businesses, brand is really important in pulling the identity of the company together," said former Chief Marketing Officer Beth Comstock. "Integration was important in communicating the brand across the organization and to all of our constituents."

The new integrated campaign got results. "Research indicates GE is now being associated with attributes such as being high tech, leading edge, innovative, contemporary, and creative," said Judy Hu, GE's general manager for global advertising and branding. Just as encouraging, survey respondents still associate GE with some of its traditional attributes, such as being trustworthy and reliable.

In 2005, the company extended the campaign with its next initiative, "Ecomagination," which highlighted the company's efforts to develop environmentally friendly "green" technologies. It leveraged the "Imagination" tagline again with a 2006 campaign called "Health Care Re-Imagined" that featured innovative GE health care products for detecting, preventing, and curing diseases.

While the campaign unites all GE business units, GE's success rests on its ability to understand the business market and the business buying process, putting itself in the shoes of its business customers. Consider its approach to pricing its aircraft engines. GE is aware that purchasing an aircraft engine is a multi-million-dollar expenditure ($21 million for each large engine). And it doesn't end with the purchase of the engine—customers (airlines) face substantial maintenance costs to meet FAA guidelines and ensure reliability of the engines. So in 1999, GE pioneered a new pricing option. The concept, called "Power by the Hour," gives customers an opportunity to pay a fixed fee each time they run the engine. In return, GE performs all the maintenance and guarantees the engine's reliability. When demand for air travel is uncertain, GE gives its customers a lower cost of ownership.

This kind of B2B marketing savvy helped GE cement its top position in the *Financial Times* "World's Most Respected Companies" survey for six consecutive years. Its understanding of the business markets, its way of doing business, and its brand marketing have kept GE's brand equity growing. Indeed, its brand equity was valued at $49 billion in the 2006 Interbrand/*BusinessWeek* ranking of the top 100 Global Brands, placing it fourth among all brands. "The GE brand is what connects us all and makes us so much better than the parts," Chief Marketing Officer Comstock said.

Sources: Geoffrey Colvin, "What Makes GE Great?" *Fortune*, March 6, 2006, pp. 90–104; Thomas A. Stewart, "Growth as a Process," *Harvard Business Review* (June 2006): 60–70; Kathryn Kranhold, "The Immelt Era, Five Years Old, Transforms GE," *Wall Street Journal*, September 11, 2006; Daniel Fisher, "GE Turns Green," *Forbes*, August 15, 2005, pp. 80– 85; John A. Byrne, "Jeff Immelt," *Fast Company* (July 2005): 60–65.

a common lobby, conference room, and employee cafeteria. Philip V. Morrison, chairman and CEO of Motoman, says it is like "a joint venture without the paperwork." Short delivery distances are just one benefit of the unusual partnership. Also key is the fact that employees of both companies have ready access to one another and can share ideas on improving quality and reducing costs. This close relationship has opened the door to new opportunities. Both companies had been doing work for Honda Motor Company, and Honda suggested that they work together on systems projects. The integration makes the two bigger than they are individually.[51]

One historical study of four very different business-to-business relationships found that several factors, by affecting partner interdependence and/or environmental uncertainty, influenced the development of a relationship between business partners.[52] The relationship between advertising agencies and clients illustrates these findings:

1. ***In the relationship formation stage, one partner experienced substantial market growth***—Manufacturers capitalizing on mass-production techniques developed national brands, which increased the importance and amount of mass-media advertising.

MARKETING INSIGHT | ESTABLISHING CORPORATE TRUST AND CREDIBILITY

Corporate credibility is the extent to which customers believe a firm can design and deliver products and services that satisfy their needs and wants. It reflects the supplier's reputation in the marketplace and is the foundation for a strong relationship.

Corporate credibility depends in turn on three factors:

- ***Corporate expertise*** the extent to which a company is seen as able to make and sell products or conduct services.
- ***Corporate trustworthiness*** the extent to which a company is seen as motivated to be honest, dependable, and sensitive to customer needs.
- ***Corporate likability*** the extent to which a company is seen as likable, attractive, prestigious, dynamic, and so on.

In other words, a credible firm is good at what it does; it keeps its customers' best interests in mind and is enjoyable to work with.

Trust is the willingness of a firm to rely on a business partner. It depends on a number of interpersonal and interorganizational factors, such as the firm's perceived competence, integrity, honesty, and benevolence. Personal interactions with employees of the firm, opinions about the company as a whole, and perceptions of trust will evolve with experience. Figure 7.1 provides a summary of some core dimensions of trust.

Building trust can be especially tricky in online settings, and firms often impose more stringent requirements on their online business partners than on others. Business buyers worry that they won't get products of the right quality delivered to the right place at the right time. Sellers worry about getting paid on time—or at all—and how much credit they should extend. Some firms, such as transportation and supply chain management company Ryder System, use automated credit-checking applications and online trust services to determine the creditworthiness of trading partners.

Sources: Bob Violino, "Building B2B Trust," *Computerworld*, June 17, 2002, p. 32; Richard E. Plank, David A. Reid, and Ellen Bolman Pullins, "Perceived Trust in Business-to-Business Sales: A New Measure," *Journal of Personal Selling and Sales Management* 19, no. 3 (Summer 1999): 61–72; Kevin Lane Keller and David A. Aaker, "Corporate-Level Marketing: The Impact of Credibility on a Company's Brand Extensions," *Corporate Reputation Review* 1 (August 1998): 356–78; Robert M. Morgan and Shelby D. Hunt, "The Commitment–Trust Theory of Relationship Marketing," *Journal of Marketing* 58, no. 3 (July 1994): 20–38; Christine Moorman, Rohit Deshpande, and Gerald Zaltman, "Factors Affecting Trust in Market Research Relationships," *Journal of Marketing* 57 (January 1993): 81–101.

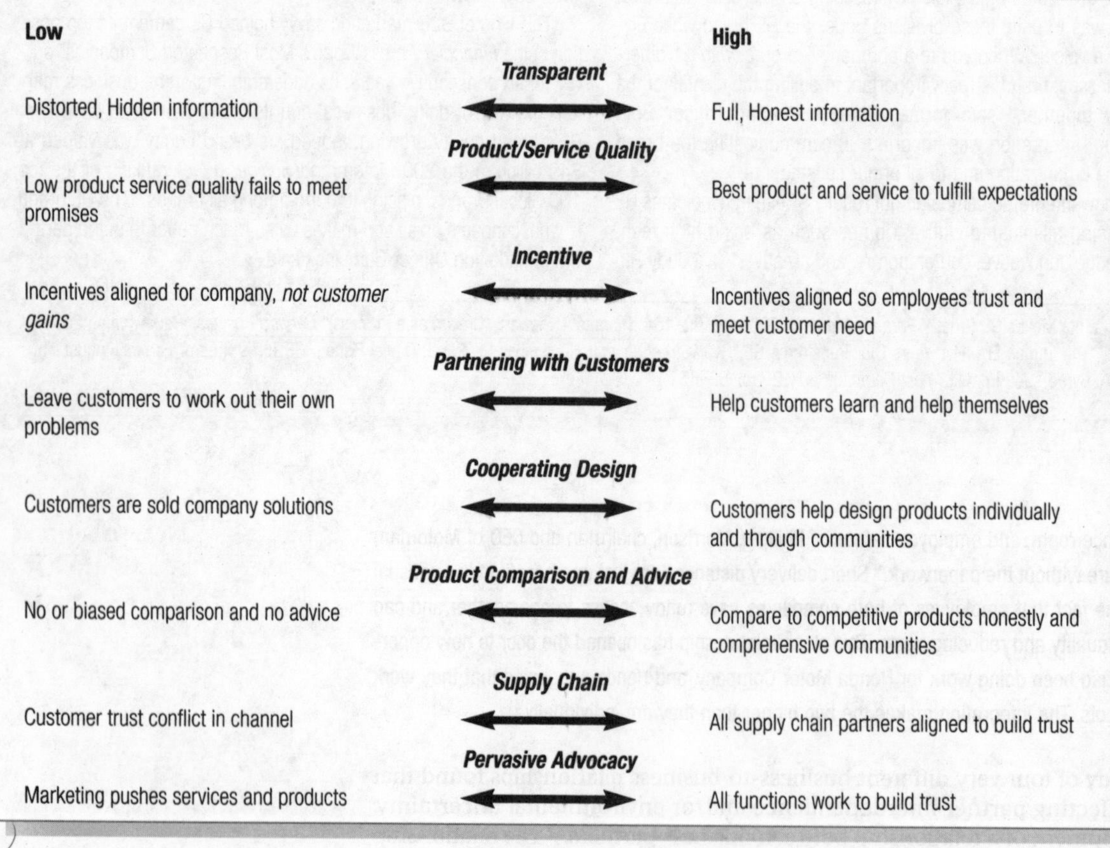

FIG. 7.1 | Trust Dimensions

Source: Glen Urban, "Where Are You Positioned on the Trust Dimensions?" *Don't Just Relate-Advocate: A Blueprint for Profit in the Era of Customer Power,* Wharton School Publishers, 2005, p. 99.

2. ***Information asymmetry between partners was such that a partnership would generate more profits than if the partner attempted to invade the other firm's area***—Advertising agencies had specialized knowledge that their clients would have had difficulty obtaining.
3. ***At least one partner had high barriers to entry that would prevent the other partner from entering the business***—Advertising agencies could not easily become national manufacturers, and for years, manufacturers were not eligible to receive media commissions.
4. ***Dependence asymmetry existed such that one partner was more able to control or influence the other's conduct***—Advertising agencies had control over media access.
5. ***One partner benefited from economies of scale related to the relationship***—Ad agencies gained by providing the same market information to multiple clients.

Research has found that buyer–supplier relationships differ according to four factors: availability of alternatives; importance of supply; complexity of supply; and supply market dynamism. Based on these four factors, they classified buyer–supplier relationships into eight different categories:[53]

1. ***Basic buying and selling***—These are simple, routine exchanges with moderate levels of cooperation and information exchange.
2. ***Bare bones***—These relationships require more adaptation by the seller and less cooperation and information exchange.
3. ***Contractual transaction***—These exchanges are defined by formal contract and generally have low levels of trust, cooperation, and interaction.
4. ***Customer supply***—In this traditional custom supply situation, competition rather than cooperation is the dominant form of governance.
5. ***Cooperative systems***—The partners in cooperative systems are united in operational ways, but neither demonstrates structural commitment through legal means or adaptation.
6. ***Collaborative***—In collaborative exchanges, much trust and commitment lead to true partnership.
7. ***Mutually adaptive***—Buyers and sellers make many relationship-specific adaptations, but without necessarily achieving strong trust or cooperation.
8. ***Customer is king***—In this close, cooperative relationship, the seller adapts to meet the customer's needs without expecting much adaptation or change in exchange.

Over time, however, the roles and nature of a relationship may shift and be activated depending on different circumstances.[54] Some needs can be satisfied with fairly basic supplier performance. Buyers then neither want nor require a close relationship with a supplier. Likewise, some suppliers may not find it worth their while to invest in customers with limited growth potential.

One study found that the closest relationships between customers and suppliers arose when the supply was important to the customer and there were procurement obstacles, such as complex purchase requirements and few alternative suppliers.[55] Another study suggested that greater vertical coordination between buyer and seller through information exchange and planning is usually necessary only when high environmental uncertainty exists and specific investments (described below) are modest.[56]

Business Relationships: Risks and Opportunism

To understand how Dome Coffee worked its business relationships to grow its operations from Australia to an international presence, visit www.pearsoned.com.au/marketingmanagementaustralia.

Researchers have noted that establishing a customer–supplier relationship creates tension between safeguarding and adaptation. Vertical coordination can facilitate stronger customer–seller ties but at the same time may increase the risk to the customer's and supplier's specific investments. *Specific investments* are those expenditures tailored to a particular company and value chain partner (investments in company-specific training, equipment, and operating procedures or systems).[57] They help firms grow profits and achieve their positioning.[58] For example, Xerox has worked closely with its suppliers to develop customized processes and components that reduced its copier-manufacturing costs by 30% to 40%. In return, suppliers received sales and volume guarantees, an enhanced understanding of their customer needs, and a strong position with Xerox for future sales.[59]

Specific investments, however, also entail considerable risk to both customer and supplier. Transaction theory from economics maintains that because these investments are partially sunk, they lock the firms that make them into a particular relationship. Sensitive cost and process information may need to be exchanged. A buyer may be vulnerable to holdup because of switching costs; a supplier may be more vulnerable to holdup in future contracts because of dedicated assets and/or expropriation of technology/knowledge. In terms of the latter risk, consider the following example.[60]

> An automobile component manufacturer wins a contract to supply an under-hood component to an original equipment manufacturer (OEM). A one-year, sole-source contract safeguards the supplier's OEM-specific investments in a dedicated production line. However, the supplier may also be obliged to work (noncontractually) as a partner with the OEM's internal engineering staff, using linked computing facilities to exchange detailed engineering information and coordinate frequent design and manufacturing changes over the term of the contract. These interactions could reduce costs and/or increase quality by improving the firm's responsiveness to marketplace changes. But they could also magnify the threat to the supplier's intellectual property.

When buyers cannot easily monitor supplier performance, the supplier might shirk or cheat and not deliver the expected value. *Opportunism* is "some form of cheating or undersupply relative to an implicit or explicit contract."[61] It may entail blatant self-interest and deliberate misrepresentation that violates contractual agreements. In creating the 1996 version of the Ford Taurus, Ford Corporation chose to outsource the whole process to one supplier, Lear Corporation. Lear committed to a contract that, for various reasons, it knew it was unable to fulfill. According to Ford, Lear missed deadlines, failed to meet weight and price objectives, and furnished parts that did not work.[62] A more passive form of opportunism might be a refusal or unwillingness to adapt to changing circumstances.

Opportunism is a concern because firms must devote resources to control and monitoring that they could otherwise allocate to more productive purposes. Contracts may become inadequate to govern supplier transactions when supplier opportunism becomes difficult to detect, when firms make specific investments in assets that they cannot use elsewhere, and when contingencies are harder to anticipate. Customers and suppliers are more likely to form a joint venture (instead of signing a simple contract) when the supplier's degree of asset specificity is high, monitoring the supplier's behavior is difficult, and the supplier has a poor reputation.[63] When a supplier has a good reputation, it is more likely to avoid opportunism to protect this valuable intangible asset.

The presence of a significant future time horizon and/or strong solidarity norms typically causes customers and suppliers to strive for joint benefits. As a result, there is a shift in specific investments from expropriation (increased opportunism on the receiver's part) to bonding (reduced opportunism).[64]

::: Institutional and Government Markets

Our discussion has concentrated largely on the buying behavior of profit-seeking companies. Much of what we have said also applies to the buying practices of institutional and government organizations. However, we want to highlight certain special features of these markets.

The **institutional market** consists of schools, hospitals, nursing homes, prisons, and other institutions that must provide goods and services to people in their care. Many of these organizations are characterized by low budgets and captive clienteles. For example, hospitals must decide what quality of food to buy for patients. The buying objective here is not profit, because the food is provided as part of the total service package; nor is cost minimization the sole objective, because poor food will cause patients to complain and hurt the hospital's reputation. The hospital purchasing agent must search for institutional-food vendors whose quality meets or exceeds a certain minimum standard and whose prices are low. In fact, many food vendors set up a separate division to sell to institutional buyers because of these buyers' special needs and characteristics. Heinz produces, packages, and prices its ketchup differently to meet the requirements of hospitals, colleges, and prisons. Aramark Corp., which provides food services for stadiums, arenas, campuses, businesses, and schools, also has a competitive advantage for providing food for the nation's prisons, a direct result of refining its purchasing practices and supply chain management:

ARAMARK CORP.

Where Aramark once merely selected products from lists provided by potential suppliers, it now collaborates with suppliers to develop products that it customizes to meet the needs of individual segments. In the corrections segment, quality has historically been sacrificed to meet food costs that operators outside the market would find impossible to work with. "When you go after business in the corrections field, you are making bids that are measured in hundredths of a cent," says John Zillmer, president of Aramark's Food & Support Services, "So any edge we can gain on the purchasing side is extremely valuable." Aramark sourced a series of protein products with unique partners at price points it never could have imagined before. These partners were unique because they understood the chemistry of proteins and knew how to lower the price while still creating a product very acceptable to Aramark's customers, allowing Aramark to drive down costs. Then Aramark replicated this process with 163 different items formulated exclusively for corrections. Rather than reducing food costs by increments of a penny or so a meal, the previous norm for this market, Aramark took five to nine cents off—while maintaining or even improving quality.[65]

Aramark Corp., a food supplier to the corrections market, worked with its own suppliers in turn to offer its customers dramatic savings.

In most countries, government organizations are a major buyer of goods and services. They typically require suppliers to submit bids and often award the contract to the lowest bidder. In some cases, the government unit will make allowance for superior quality or a reputation for completing contracts on time. Governments will also buy on a negotiated contract basis, primarily in the case of complex projects involving major R&D costs and risks, and in cases where there is little competition.

A major complaint of multinationals operating in Europe was that each country showed favoritism toward its nationals despite superior offers from foreign firms. Although such practices are fairly entrenched, the European Union is attempting to remove this bias.

Because their spending decisions are subject to public review, government organizations require considerable paperwork from suppliers, who often complain about bureaucracy, regulations, decision-making delays, and frequent shifts in procurement personnel. But the fact remains that the U.S. government buys goods and services valued at $200 billion, making it the largest and therefore most potentially attractive customer in the world.

It is not just the dollar figure that is large, but the number of individual acquisitions. According to the General Sources Administration Procurement Data Center, over 20 million individual contract actions are processed every year. Although most items purchased cost between $2,500 and $25,000, the government also makes purchases in the billions, many in technology. But government decision makers often think technology vendors have not done their homework. In addition, vendors do not pay enough attention to cost justification, which is a major activity for government procurement professionals. Companies hoping to be government contractors need to help government agencies see the bottom-line impact of products.

Just as companies provide government agencies with guidelines about how best to purchase and use their products, governments provide would-be suppliers with detailed guidelines describing how to sell to the government. Failure to follow the guidelines or to fill out forms and contracts correctly can create a legal nightmare.[66]

ADI TECHNOLOGY

The federal government has always been ADI Technology Corporation's most important client, accounting for about 90% of its nearly $6 million in annual revenues. Yet managers at this professional services company often shake their heads at all the work that goes into winning the coveted government contracts. A comprehensive bid proposal will run from 500 to 700 pages because of federal paperwork requirements. The company's president estimates that the firm has spent as much as $20,000, mostly in worker hours, to prepare a single bid proposal.

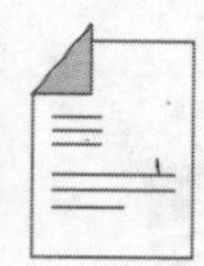

MARKETING MEMO | SELLING TECH TO THE GOVERNMENT

A large chunk of this U.S. government business, isn't contracted out at all. Through the General Services Administration (GSA) and other government organizations, companies can sell directly to agencies without formal bidding. Here are three tips for tapping into that market.

1. ***Get in the Government IT Catalog***—The GSA runs an online catalog of goods and services for government agencies. About 28% of federal spending flows through the catalog's Schedule 70, which includes more than 2,000 tech vendors. Getting a business listed can be important. Apply electronically and remember to spell out pricing structure carefully.
2. ***Work Your Way In***—Small businesses—especially those owned by women and minorities—are often needed by large businesses to satisfy small business set-asides. To maximize that probability:
   - ***Make sure contractors can find you.*** Get listed on the Small Business Administration's Subcontracting Network (wed.sba.gov/subnet) or use the U.S. Chamber of Commerce Web site.
   - ***Stay on top of key contracts.*** Several Web sites provide updates for the latest deals that might provide opportunities (www.fedbizopps.gov; www.dodbusopps.com; prod.nais.nasa.gov/pub/fedproc/home.hml).
   - ***Work the angles.***Meet with prospective bidders and explain your qualifications.
3. ***Network Actively***—Attend one of the large trade shows, such as FOSE, GSA Expo, or E-Gov.

Source: Owen Thomas, "How to Sell Tech to the Feds," *Business 2.0* (March 2003): 111–12.

Fortunately for businesses of all sizes, the federal government has been trying to simplify the contracting procedure and make bidding more attractive. Some reforms place more emphasis on buying commercial off-the-shelf items instead of items built to the government's specs; online communication with vendors to eliminate the massive paperwork; and a "debriefing" from the appropriate government agency for vendors who lose a bid, enabling them to increase their chances of winning the next time around.[67] More purchasing is being done online via Web-based forms, digital signatures, and electronic procurement cards (P-cards).[68]

Several federal agencies that act as purchasing agents for the rest of the government have launched Web-based catalogs that allow authorized defense and civilian agencies to buy everything from medical and office supplies to clothing online. "Marketing Memo: Selling Tech to the Government" provides some tips for attacking that multibillion-dollar market. The General Services Administration, for example, not only sells stocked merchandise through its Web site but also creates direct links between buyers and contract suppliers.

In spite of these reforms, for a number of reasons many companies that sell to the government have not used a marketing orientation. Some, though, have pursued government business by establishing separate government marketing departments. Companies such as Gateway, Rockwell, Kodak, and Goodyear anticipate government needs and projects, participate in the product specification phase, gather competitive intelligence, prepare bids carefully, and produce strong communications to describe and enhance their companies' reputations.

SUMMARY :::

1. Organizational buying is the decision-making process by which formal organizations establish the need for purchased products and services, then identify, evaluate, and choose among alternative brands and suppliers. The business market consists of all the organizations that acquire goods and services used in the production of other products or services that are sold, rented, or supplied to others.
2. Compared to consumer markets, business markets generally have fewer and larger buyers, a closer customer–supplier relationship, and more geographically concentrated buyers. Demand in the business market is derived from demand in the consumer market and fluctuates with the business cycle. Nonetheless, the total demand for many business goods and services is quite price inelastic. Business marketers need to be aware of the role of professional purchasers and their influencers, the need for multiple sales calls, and the importance of direct purchasing, reciprocity, and leasing.
3. The buying center is the decision-making unit of a buying organization. It consists of initiators, users, influencers, deciders, approvers, buyers, and gatekeepers. To influence these parties, marketers must be aware of environmental, organizational, interpersonal, and individual factors.
4. The buying process consists of eight stages called buyphases: (1) problem recognition, (2) general need description, (3) product specification, (4) supplier search, (5) proposal solicitation, (6) supplier selection, (7) order-routine specification, and (8) performance review.
5. Business marketers must form strong bonds and relationships with their customers and provide them added value. Some customers, however, may prefer more of a transactional relationship.
6. The institutional market consists of schools, hospitals, nursing homes, prisons, and other institutions that provide goods and services to people in their care. Buyers for government organizations tend to require a great deal of paperwork from their vendors and to favor open bidding and domestic companies. Suppliers must be prepared to adapt their offers to the special needs and procedures found in institutional and government markets.

APPLICATIONS :::

Marketing Debate How Different Is Business-to-Business Marketing?

Many business-to-business marketing executives lament the challenges of business-to-business marketing, maintaining that many traditional marketing concepts and principles do not apply. For a number of reasons, they assert that selling products and services to a company is fundamentally different from selling to individuals. Others disagree, claiming that marketing theory is still valid and only involves some adaptation in the marketing tactics.

Take a position: Business-to-business marketing requires a special, unique set of marketing concepts and principles *versus* Business-to-business marketing is really not that different and the basic marketing concepts and principles apply.

Marketing Discussion

Consider some of the consumer behavior topics from Chapter 6. How might you apply them to business-to-business settings? For example, how might noncompensatory models of choice work? Mental accounting?

IN THIS CHAPTER, WE WILL ADDRESS THE FOLLOWING QUESTIONS:

1. What are the different levels of market segmentation?
2. How can a company divide a market into segments?
3. How should a company choose the most attractive target markets?
4. What are the requirements for effective segmentation?

CHAPTER 8 ::: IDENTIFYING MARKET SEGMENTS AND TARGETS

eight

Companies cannot connect with all customers in large, broad, or diverse markets. But they can divide such markets into groups of consumers or segments with distinct needs and wants. A company then needs to identify which market segments it can serve effectively. This decision requires a keen understanding of consumer behavior and careful strategic thinking. To develop the best marketing plans, managers need to understand what makes each segment unique and different.

One lucrative market segment is the Baby Boomers, the approximately 76 million U.S. consumers born between 1946 and 1964. Though baby boomers represent a wealthy target, possessing $1.2 trillion in annual spending power and controlling three-quarters of the country's wealth, marketers often overlook them. For example, in network television circles, viewers over 50 are referred to as "undesirables," because advertisers are primarily interested in 18- to 49-year-olds. Yet with many baby boomers into their 60s and even the last wave turning 40, demand for products to turn back the hands of time has exploded. According to one survey, half of all boomers were depressed that they were no longer young, and nearly one in five were actively resisting the aging process. As they search for the fountain of youth, sales of hair replacement and hair coloring aids. health >>>

Ameriprise, a spin-off from American Express, provides financial planning and advice. It has set its sights on baby boomers as a prime target, given the impending retirement of many members of this group.

club memberships, home gym equipment, skin-tightening creams, nutritional supplements, and organic foods have all soared. Furthermore, contrary to the conventional marketing wisdom that the brand preferences of consumers over 50 are fixed, one study found that 52% of boomers are willing to change brands, in line with the total population. The boomer market will only grow in importance in the coming years: by 2020 the proportion of U.S. adults over 65 will be 20% compared with just 12% in 2005.[1]

To compete more effectively, many companies are now embracing target marketing. Instead of scattering their marketing efforts, they're focusing on those consumers they have the greatest chance of satisfying.

Effective target marketing requires that marketers:

1. Identify and profile distinct groups of buyers who differ in their needs and preferences (market seqmentation).
2. Select one or more market seqments to enter (market targeting).
3. For each target segment, establish and communicate the distinctive benefit(s) of the company's market offering (market positioning).

This chapter will focus on the first two steps. Chapter 10 discusses the third step, brand and market positioning.

::: Levels of Market Segmentation

The starting point for discussing segmentation is **mass marketing**. In mass marketing, the seller engages in the mass production, mass distribution, and mass promotion of one product for all buyers. Henry Ford epitomized this strategy when he offered the Model-T Ford in one color, black. Coca-Cola also practiced mass marketing when it sold only one kind of Coke in a 6.5-ounce bottle.

The argument for mass marketing is that it creates the largest potential market, which leads to the lowest costs, which in turn can lead to lower prices or higher margins. However, many critics point to the increasing splintering of the market, and the proliferation of advertising media and distribution channels, which are making it difficult and increasingly expensive to reach a mass audience. Some claim that mass marketing is dying. Most companies are turning to *micromarketing* at one of four levels: segments, niches, local areas, and individuals.

Segment Marketing

A *market segment* consists of a group of customers who share a similar set of needs and wants. Rather than creating the segments, the marketer's task is to identify them and decide which one(s) to target. Segment marketing offers key benefits over mass marketing. The company can often better design, price, disclose, and deliver the product or service and also can fine-tune the marketing program and activities to better reflect competitors' marketing.

However, even a segment is partly a fiction, in that not everyone wants exactly the same thing. Business-to-business marketing experts Anderson and Narus have urged marketers to present flexible market offerings to all members of a segment.[2] A **flexible market offering** consists of two parts: a *naked solution* containing the product and service elements that all segment members value, and *discretionary options* that some segment members value. Each option might carry an additional charge. For example, Siemens Electrical Apparatus Division sells metal-clad boxes to small manufacturers at prices that include free delivery and a warranty, but it also offers installation, tests, and communication peripherals as extra-cost options. Delta Airlines offers all economy passengers a seat and soft drinks and charges extra for alcoholic beverages, snacks, and meals.

We can characterize market segments in different ways. One way is to identify *preference segments.* **Homogeneous preferences** exist when all consumers have roughly the same preferences; the market shows no natural segments. At the other extreme, consumers in **diffused preferences** vary greatly in their preferences. If several brands are in the market, they are likely to position themselves throughout the space and show real differences to match differences in consumer preference. Finally, **clustered preferences** result when natural market segments emerge from groups of consumers with shared preferences.

Niche Marketing

A niche is a more narrowly defined customer group seeking a distinctive mix of benefits. Marketers usually identify niches by dividing a segment into subsegments. For example, whereas Hertz, Avis, Alamo, and others specialize in airport rental cars for business and leisure travelers, Enterprise has attacked the low-budget, insurance-replacement market by primarily renting to customers whose cars have been wrecked or stolen. By creating unique associations to low cost and convenience in an overlooked niche market, Enterprise has been highly profitable.

What does an attractive niche look like? The customers have a distinct set of needs; they will pay a premium to the firm that best satisfies them; the niche is fairly small but has size, profit, and growth potential and is unlikely to attract many other competitors; and the nicher gains certain economies through specialization.

Larger companies, such as IBM, have lost pieces of their market to nichers: These confrontations have been labeled "guerrillas against gorillas."[3] This is happening in the online social networking market, where MySpace and Facebook are becoming mature service providers.

MYSPACE, FACEBOOK

A drop in traffic numbers has made headlines for the nation's biggest social networking sites, MySpace and Facebook. The sites, with 130 million and 12 million users respectively, rely on advertising revenue to survive and risk losing out by trying to be all things to all people. A host of upstart social networking nichers hope to capitalize on the tendency of individuals to want to congregate with others who share their own particular passions, however arcane. For instance, there is now 1Up.com, a content-heavy social site where online gaming fanatics can trade tips, stories, opinions, and gossip. Gather.com is a social network for the so-called NPR crowd: people in the prime of their career who, unlike students, have disposable income to burn. Then there's Dogster, an ultra-niche site that has 3,500 active communities for dog owners and is already attracting scads of advertisers.[4]

Hallmark targets several market segments including young women, African Americans, Hispanics, and Jews. It also promotes targeted products lines including Warm Wishes (inexpensive greetings cards) and Shoebox Greetings (humorous cards).

Some large companies have even turned to niche marketing. Hallmark personal expression products can be found in more than 43,000 retail outlets nationwide, and they account for one of every two greeting cards purchased in the United States. Hallmark's success in part has been due to its vigorously segmenting its greeting card business. In addition to popular subbranded card lines such as the humorous

Shoebox Greetings, Hallmark has introduced lines targeting specific market segments. Fresh Ink targets 18- to 39-year-old women. Hallmark Warm Wishes offers hundreds of 99-cent cards. Hallmark's three ethnic lines—Mahogany, Sinceramente Hallmark, and Tree of Life—target African American, Hispanic, and Jewish consumers respectively.

Niche marketers aim to understand their customers' needs so well that the customers willingly pay a premium. Tom's of Maine was acquired by Colgate-Palmolive for $100 million in part because its all-natural personal care products and charitable donation programs appeal to consumers who have been turned off by big businesses. The brand commands a 30% premium as a result.[5]

As marketing efficiency increases, niches that were seemingly too small may become more profitable.[6] The low cost of setting up shop on the Internet has led to many small business start-ups aimed at niches. The recipe for Internet niching success: Choose a hard-to-find product that customers don't need to see and touch. "Marketing Insight: Chasing the Long Tail" outlines how provocative are the implications of Internet niching.

INTERNET NICHING

The experience of Dan Myrick, director of *The Blair Witch Project,* illustrates what can happen when you move away from targeting the mass market. In 1999, just two years out of film school, Myrick spent eight days in the woods of Maryland shooting *The Blair Witch Project.* The crudely made film netted nearly $250 million on a $35,000 production budget, largely from audiences drawn to the movie through Myrick's Web site. Myrick has also used the Web to distribute *The Strand,* a series of "Webisodes" set in Venice Beach, California. He says, "The great thing about the Internet is it opens up this realm of micromarkets and I don't need an 8 or 9 or 10 Nielson share to be a success. NBC will cancel a show if it didn't get $3 million."[7]

Local Marketing

Target marketing is leading to marketing programs tailored to the needs and wants of local customer groups in trading areas, neighborhoods, even individual stores. Retail firms such as Starbucks, Costco, Trader Joe's, and REI have all found great success emphasizing local marketing initiatives, but other types of firms are also jumping into action.[8] Citibank provides different mixes of banking services in its branches, depending on neighborhood demographics. Curves, an exercise chain aimed at middle-aged women, places paper bags in local businesses such as ice cream shops, pizza parlors, and other places where guilt can strike. In 2004, Baskin-Robbins dropped all TV advertising for its ice cream specialty stores for the first time in 17 years to focus on "three-mile marketing," with more emphasis on local events and promotions, remodeled stores with vibrant new colors, and improved customer service from greater employee training.

To emphasize its new drive toward "three-mile marketing" with a heavily local concentration, Baskin-Robbins stopped advertising on TV for the first time in 17 years.

Local marketing reflects a growing trend called *grassroots marketing.* Marketing activities concentrate on getting as close and personally relevant to individual customers as possible. Much of Nike's initial success comes from engaging target consumers through grassroots marketing such as sponsorship of local school teams, expert-conducted clinics, and provision of shoes, clothing, and equipment. "Breakthrough Marketing: HSBC" profiles another success story.

Those who favor localized marketing see national advertising as wasteful because it is too "arm's length" and fails to address local needs. Those against local marketing argue that it drives up manufacturing and marketing costs by reducing economies of scale and magnifying logistical problems. A brand's overall image might be diluted if the product and message are different in different localities.

Individual Marketing

The ultimate level of segmentation leads to "segments of one," "customized marketing," or "one-to-one marketing."[9] Today customers are taking more individual initiative in determining what and how to buy. They log onto the Internet; look up information and evaluations of

MARKETING INSIGHT | CHASING THE LONG TAIL

The advent of online commerce, made possible by technology and epitomized by Amazon.com, iTunes, and Netflix, has led to a shift in consumer buying patterns, according to Chris Anderson, editor-in-chief of *Wired* magazine and author of *The Long Tail*.

In most markets, the distribution of product sales conforms to a curve weighted heavily to one side—the "head"—where the bulk of sales are generated by a few products. The curve falls rapidly toward zero and hovers just above it far along the X-axis—the "long tail"—where the vast majority of products generate very little sales. The mass market traditionally focused on generating "hit" products that occupy the head, disdaining the low-revenue market niches comprising the tail.

Anderson asserts that as a result of consumers' embrace of the Internet as a shopping medium, the long tail harbors significantly more value than before. In fact, Anderson argues, the Internet has directly contributed to the shifting of demand "down the tail, from hits to niches" in a number of product categories, including music, books, clothing, and movies.

On his blog, Anderson boils down his argument as follows: "The Long Tail equation is simple: (1) The lower the cost of distribution, the more you can economically offer without having to predict demand. (2) The more you can offer, the greater the chance that you will be able to tap latent demand for minority tastes that was unreachable through traditional retail. (3) Aggregate enough minority taste, and you'll often find a big new market."

Anderson identifies two aspects of Internet shopping that contribute to this shift. First, greater choice is permitted by increased inventory and variety. Given a choice between 10 hit products, consumers are forced to select one of the 10. If, however, the choice set is expanded to 1,000, then the top 10 hits will be chosen less frequently. Second, the "search costs" of finding relevant new products are lowered due to the wealth of information sources available online, the filtering of product recommendations based on user preferences that vendors can provide, and the word-of-mouth network of Internet users.

Anderson sees the long tail effect as particularly pronounced in media, a category that's historically hit-driven but that benefits enormously from these two aspects of online shopping. He points to the success of niche media properties such as the book *Touching the Void*, the band My Chemical Romance, and the documentary film *Capturing the Friedmans*, which all benefited from the choice and information-organization aspects of Internet shopping to achieve greater success than was expected.

The long tail thesis was also supported by researchers Erik Brynjolfsson and Yu "Jeffrey" Hu at MIT and Michael D. Smith at Carnegie Mellon, who conducted two studies to measure the tail in online versus off-line book selling and clothing retail. The book-selling study concluded that the increased product variety offered by online bookstores increased consumer welfare by $731 million to $1.03 billion in 2000. In the case of online clothing retail, the study found that consumers who used both online and catalog channels of a midsize retailer purchased a more even distribution of products than through the catalog.

New consumer buying patterns, aided by the Internet, are highlighting the revenue potential of "the long tail" of the market, where many seemingly niche products can find broader success. My Chemical Romance is an example of a hit band that emerged from this "long tail."

The same companies that compete in the business of creating hits are beginning to develop ways to evolve niche successes in the long tail. For example, in 2006 the Universal Music Group released 3,000 out-of-print European recordings in download-only digital format on the Internet. The release generated 250,000 individual downloads of the songs, and after this encouraging start Universal planned to eventually release more than 100,000 out-of-print recordings. In a press release, Universal even stated, "Overall, these results lend weight to author Chris Anderson's The Long Tail theory."

Yet companies like Universal may soon face additional competition from unconventional sources. Anderson predicts that as a result of the proliferation of free user-generated content, the variety popularized by YouTube, the end of the long tail where this content resides will be a "nonmonetary economy."

Others have countered that, especially in entertainment, the "head" where the hits are concentrated is valuable to consumers, not only to the content creators. An article in *The Economist* argued that "most hits are popular because they are of high quality," and a critique in the *New Yorker* notes that the majority of products and services making up the long tail originate from a small concentration of "long-tail aggregators"—sites such as Amazon.com, eBay, iTunes, and Netflix. This observation challenges the premise that old business paradigms have changed as much as Anderson suggests.

Sources: Chris Anderson, *The Long Tail* (New York: Hyperion, 2006); "Reading the Tail," interview with Chris Anderson, *Wired*, July 8, 2006, p. 30; "Wag the Dog: What the Long Tail Will Do," *The Economist*, July 8, 2006, p. 77; Erik Brynjolfsson, Yu "Jeffrey" Hu, and Michael D. Smith, "From Niches to Riches: Anatomy of a Long Tail," *MIT Sloan Management Review* (Summer 2006): 67; John Cassidy, "Going Long," *New Yorker*, July 10, 2006; www.longtail.com.

BREAKTHROUGH MARKETING | HSBC

HSBC wants to be known as the "world's local bank." This tagline reflects HSBC's positioning as a globe-spanning financial institution with unique focus on serving local markets. Originally the Hong Kong and Shanghai Banking Corporation Limited, HSBC was established in 1865 to finance the growing trade between China and the United Kingdom. It's now the second-largest bank in the world. Despite serving over 100 million customers through 9,500 branches in 79 countries, the bank works hard to maintain a local presence and local knowledge in each area. Its fundamental operating strategy is to remain close to its customers. As HSBC chairman Sir John Bond said, "Our position as the world's local bank enables us to approach each country uniquely, blending local knowledge with a worldwide operating platform."

Ads for the "World's Local Bank" campaign depicted the way two different cultures interpret the same objects or events. One TV spot showed a U.S. businessman hitting a hole-in-one during a round in Japan with his Japanese counterparts. He is surprised to find that rather than paying for a round of drinks in the clubhouse, as in the United States, by Japanese custom he must buy expensive gifts for his playing partners. The ad shows a subsequent round, with the Japanese players sporting expensive-looking new clothes and watches. The commercial closes with the U.S. player aiming his tee shot into the trees, only to have it ricochet directly into the hole. Ads for the campaign differed by region, where, according to the ad agency, "Each country has developed its own variations on the initial idea."

HSBC demonstrated its local knowledge with marketing efforts dedicated to specific locations. For example, in 2005 it set out to prove to jaded New Yorkers that the London-based financial behemoth was a bank with local knowledge. The company held a "New York City's Most Knowledgeable Cabbie" contest, in which the winning cabbie got paid to drive an HSBC-branded BankCab full-time for a year. HSBC customers could win, too. Any customer showing an HSBC bankcard, checkbook, or bank statement was able to get a free ride in the BankCab. HSBC also ran an integrated campaign highlighting the diversity of New Yorkers, which appeared on subways, taxis, bus shelters, kiosks, coffee cups, and a Times Square billboard, as well as print, radio, and TV.

More than 8,000 miles away, HSBC undertook a two-part "Support Hong Kong" campaign to revitalize the local economy hit hard by the 2003 SARS outbreak. First, HSBC delayed interest payments for personal-loan customers who worked in industries most affected by SARS (cinemas, hotels, restaurants, and travel agencies). Second, the bank offered discounts and rebates for HSBC credit card users when they shopped and dined out. More than 1,500 local merchants participated in the promotion.

HSBC also targets consumer niches with unique products and services. For example, it found a little-known product area growing at 125% a year: pet insurance. The bank now distributes nationwide pet insurance to its depositors through its HSBC Insurance agency. In Malaysia, HSBC offered a "smart card" and no-frills credit cards to the underserved student segment and targeted high-value customers with special "Premium Centers" bank branches.

The bank pulls its worldwide businesses together under a single global brand with the "world's local bank" slogan. The aim is to link its international size with close relationships in each of the countries in which it operates. HSBC spends $600 million annually on global marketing, which it consolidated in 2004 under the WPP group of agencies. Going forward, it will be seeking to leverage its position as "The World's Local Bank" to improve on its $11.6 billion brand value, which placed it 28th on the 2006 Interbrand/*BusinessWeek* global brand rankings.

Sources: Carrick Mollenkamp, "HSBC Stumbles in Bid to Become Global Deal Maker," *Wall Street Journal*, October 5, 2006; Kate Nicholson, "HSBC Aims to Appear Global Yet Approachable," *Campaign*, December 2, 2005, p. 15; Deborah Orr, "New Ledger," *Forbes*, March 1, 2004, pp. 72–73; "HSBC's Global Marketing Head Explains Review Decision," *Adweek*, January 19, 2004; "Now Your Customers Can Afford to Take Fido to the Vet," *Bank Marketing* (December 2003): 47; Kenneth Hein, "HSBC Bank Rides the Coattails of Chatty Cabbies," *Brandweek*, December 1, 2003, p. 30; Sir John Bond and Stephen Green, "HSBC Strategic Overview," presentation to investors, November 27, 2003; "Lafferty Retail Banking Awards 2003," *Retail Banker International*, November 27, 2003, pp. 4–5; "Ideas that Work," *Bank Marketing* (November 2003): 10; "HSBC Enters the Global Branding Big League," *Bank Marketing International* (August 2003): 1–2; Normandy Madden, "HSBC Rolls out Post-SARS Effort," *Advertising Age*, June 16, 2003, p. 12; www.hsbc.com.

product or service offers; conduct dialogue with suppliers, users, and product critics; and in many cases, design the product they want.

Wind and Rangaswamy see a movement toward "customerizing" the firm.[10] **Customerization** combines operationally driven mass customization with customized marketing in a way that empowers consumers to design the product and service offering of their choice. The firm no longer requires prior information about the customer, nor does the firm need to own manufacturing. The firm provides a platform and tools and "rents" out to customers the means to design their own products. A company is customerized when it is able to respond to individual customers by customizing its products, services, and messages on a one-to-one basis.[11]

Customization is certainly not for every company.[12] It may be very difficult to implement for complex products such as automobiles. Customization can also raise the cost of goods by more than the customer is willing to pay. Some customers don't know what they want until they see actual products. They also cannot cancel the order after the company has started to work on the product. The product may be hard to repair and have little sales value. In spite of this, customization has worked well for some products.

JACKRABBIT, SBR MULTISPORTS, SIGNATURE

"Custom bikes are on the rise, and we're nowhere near the saturation point," said Megan Tompkins, editor of *Bicycle Retailer and Industry News.* As if to prove her point, three custom bike shops have opened in New York City in the past two years: JackRabbit, SBR MultiSports, and Signature. The main market for custom-made bikes is made up of wealthy, aging baby boomers with worn-out knees who have embraced cycling as a low-impact, aerobic alternative to basketball, tennis, or running. When they come to these tony shops seeking a custom-made bike, they face a detailed interview process similar to an adoption proceeding. Yet, with custom bikes selling for $9,000 or $10,000, consumers need to be sure the bikes fit their needs and desires. At JackRabbit, $9,000 can buy you a brushed silver bike called a Guru and made of titanium, known for its high performance, ultralight strength, and lifetime durability. However, it's not geeks who are shopping at the custom stores, but those who seek custom bikes as status accessories and who revel in the personalized service. In the typical bike shop, "customer service" is an oxymoron. As one industry executive said, "It's one of the few retail industries where a condition for employment seems to be utter contempt for the customer." Contrast that with Signature, where customers are offered a glass of Courvoisier while discussing their cycling habits.[13]

::: Bases for Segmenting Consumer Markets

To learn how BMW studies changing consumer lifestyles to match product development to segmentation, visit www.pearsoned.co.uk/marketingmanagementeurope.

We use two broad groups of variables to segment consumer markets. Some researchers try to define segments by looking at descriptive characteristics: geographic, demographic, and psychographic. Then they examine whether these customer segments exhibit different needs or product responses. For example, they might examine the differing attitudes of "professionals," "blue collars," and other groups toward, say, "safety" as a car benefit.

Other researchers try to define segments by looking at behavioral considerations, such as consumer responses to benefits, use occasions, or brands. The researcher then sees whether different characteristics are associated with each consumer-response segment. For example, do people who want "quality" rather than "low price" in an automobile purchase differ in their geographic, demographic, and psychographic makeup?

Regardless of which type of segmentation scheme we use, the key is adjusting the marketing program to recognize customer differences. The major segmentation variables—geographic, demographic, psychographic, and behavioral segmentation—are summarized in Table 8.1.

Geographic Segmentation

Geographic segmentation calls for dividing the market into different geographical units such as nations, states, regions, counties, cities, or neighborhoods. The company can operate in one or a few areas, or operate in all, but pay attention to local variations. For example, Hilton Hotels customizes rooms and lobbies according to location. Northeastern hotels are sleeker and more cosmopolitan. Southwestern hotels are more rustic. Major retailers such as Wal-Mart; Sears, Roebuck & Co.; and Kmart all allow local managers to stock products that suit the local community.[14]

Local Bed Bath & Beyond managers choose most of their own merchandise, allowing stores separated by only a few miles to address the different taste preferences of city and suburbia with unique product mixes for each.

BED BATH & BEYOND

Home furnishing retailer Bed Bath & Beyond's ability to cater to local tastes has fueled its phenomenal growth. The firm's managers pick 70% of their own merchandise, and this fierce local focus has helped the chain evolve from bed linens to the "beyond"

part—products from picture frames and pot holders to imported olive oil and designer door mats. In Manhattan stores, for instance, managers are beginning to stock wall paint. You won't find paint in suburban stores, where customers can go to Home Depot or Lowe's. One manager says that several customers have been surprised to find out the store is part of a national chain and not a mom-and-pop operation. That's the ultimate compliment.[15]

More and more, regional marketing means marketing right down to a specific zip code.[16] Many companies use mapping software to show the geographic locations of their customers. The software may show a retailer that most of his customers are within only a 10-mile radius of his store, and further concentrated within certain zip+4 areas. By mapping the densest areas, the retailer can rely on *customer cloning,* assuming the best prospects live where most of his customers come from.

TABLE 8.1

Major Segmentation Variables for Consumer Markets

Geographic region	Pacific Mountain, West North Central, West South Central, East North Central, East South Central, South Atlantic, Middle Atlantic, New England
City or metro size	Under 5,000; 5,000–20,000; 20,000–50,000; 50,000–100,000; 100,000–250,000; 250,000–500,000; 500,000–1,000,000; 1,000,000–4,000,000; 4,000,000 or over
Density	Urban, suburban, rural
Climate	Northern, southern
Demographic age	Under 6, 6–11, 12–19, 20–34, 35–49, 50–64, 64+
Family size	1–2, 3–4, 5+
Family life cycle	Young, single; young, married, no children; young, married, youngest child under 6; young; married, youngest child 6 or over; older, married, with children; older, married, no children under 18; older, single; other
Gender	Male, female
Income	Under \$10,000; \$10,000–\$15,000; \$15,000–\$20,000; \$20,000–\$30,000; \$30,000–\$50,000; \$50,000–\$100,000; \$100,000 and over
Occupation	Professional and technical; managers, officials, and proprietors; clerical sales; craftspeople; forepersons; operatives; farmers; retired; students; homemakers; unemployed
Education	Grade School or less; some high school; high school graduate; some college; college graduate
Religion	Catholic, Protestant, Jewish, Muslim, Hindu, other
Race	White, Black, Asian, Hispanic
Generation	Baby boomers, Generation Xers
Nationality	North American, South American, British, French, German, Italian, Japanese
Social class	Lower lowers, upper lowers, working class, middle class, upper middles, lower uppers, upper uppers
Psychographic lifestyle	Culture-oriented, sports-oriented, outdoor-oriented
Personality	Compulsive, gregarious, authoritarian, ambitious
Behavioral occasions	Regular occasion, special occasion
Benefits	Quality, service, economy, speed
User status	Nonuser, ex-user, potential user, first-time user, regular user
Usage rate	Light user, medium user, heavy user
Loyalty status	None, medium, strong, absolute
Readiness stage	Unaware, aware, informed interested, desirous, intending to buy
Attitude toward product	Enthusiastic, positive, indifferent, negative, hostile

Some approaches combine geographic data with demographic data to yield even richer descriptions of consumers and neighborhoods. Claritas Inc. has developed a geoclustering approach called PRIZM (Potential Rating Index by Zip Markets) NE that classifies over half a million U.S. residential neighborhoods into 14 distinct groups and 66 distinct lifestyle segments called PRIZM Clusters.[17] The groupings take into consideration 39 factors in five broad categories: (1) education and affluence, (2) family life cycle, (3) urbanization, (4) race and ethnicity, and (5) mobility. The neighborhoods are broken down by zip code, zip+4, or census tract and block group. The clusters have descriptive titles such as *Blue Blood Estates, Winner's Circle, Hometown Retired, Latino America, Shotguns and Pickups,* and *Back Country Folks.* The inhabitants in a cluster tend to lead similar lives, drive similar cars, have similar jobs, and read similar magazines. Here are four new PRIZM clusters:[18]

- ***Young Digerati.*** Young Digerati are the nation's tech-savvy singles and couples living in fashionable neighborhoods on the urban fringe. Affluent, highly educated, and ethnically mixed, Young Digerati communities are typically filled with trendy apartments and condos, fitness clubs and clothing boutiques, casual restaurants, and all types of bars—from juice to coffee to microbrew.
- ***Beltway Boomers.*** One segment of the huge Baby Boomer cohort—college-educated, upper-middle-class, and home owning—is Beltway Boomers. Like many of their peers who married late, these Boomers are still raising children in comfortable suburban subdivisions, and they're pursuing kid-centered lifestyles.
- ***The Cosmopolitans.*** These immigrants and descendants of mulitcultural backgrounds in multiracial, multilingual neighborhoods typify the American Dream. Single parents and married couples with and without children are affluent from working hard at multiple trades and public service jobs. They have big families, unusual for their social group, Urban Uptown.
- ***Old Milltowns.*** Once-thriving mining and manufacturing towns have aged—as have the residents in Old Milltowns communities. Today, the majority of residents are retired singles and couples, living on downscale incomes in pre-1960 homes and apartments. For leisure, they enjoy gardening, sewing, socializing at veterans clubs, or eating out at casual restaurants.

Marketers can use PRIZM to answer questions such as: Which geographic areas (neighborhoods or zip codes) contain our most valuable customers? How deeply have we already penetrated these segments? Which distribution channels and promotional media work best in reaching our target clusters in each area? Geoclustering captures the increasing diversity of the U.S. population.

Ace Hardware has used PRIZM segmentation to help guide decisions in a number of areas: direct mail, advertising, partnerships, site selection, new concepts, and local store marketing. Based on a successful pilot with *Veggie Tales* concerts, Clear Channel Communications is using geoclustering information to target e-mails to prospects for national tours in all entertainment venues.[19]

Marketing to microsegments has become accessible even to small organizations as database costs decline, PCs proliferate, software becomes easier to use, data integration increases, and the Internet grows.[20]

Demographic Segmentation

In demographic segmentation, we divide the market into groups on the basis of variables such as age, family size, family life cycle, gender, income, occupation, education, religion, race, generation, nationality, and social class. One reason demographic variables are so popular with marketers is that they're often associated with consumer needs and wants. Another is that they're easy to measure. Even when we describe the target market in nondemographic terms (say, by personality type), we may need the link back to demographic characteristics in order to estimate the size of the market and the media we should use to reach it efficiently.

Here's how certain demographic variables have been used to segment markets.

AGE AND LIFE-CYCLE STAGE Consumer wants and abilities change with age. Toothpaste brands such as Crest and Colgate offer three main lines of products to target kids, adults, and older consumers. Age segmentation can be even more refined. Pampers divides its market into prenatal, new baby (0–5 months), baby (6–12 months), toddler (13–23 months), and preschooler (24 months+).

To market the new Fit model, Honda used what it had learned from the launch of the Element—that baby boomers hanging on to their youthful image were just as interested in the stylish new cars as the original target audience, 21-year-old drivers.

Nevertheless, age and life cycle can be tricky variables.[21] In some cases, the target market for products may be the psychologically young. For example, Honda tried to target 21-year-olds with its boxy Element, which company officials described as a "dorm room on wheels." So many baby boomers were attracted to the car's ads depicting sexy college kids partying near the car at a beach, however, that the average age of buyers turned out to be 42! With baby boomers seeking to stay young, Honda decided that the lines between age groups were getting blurred. When it was ready to launch a new subcompact called the Fit, Honda deliberately targeted Gen Y buyers as well as their empty-nest parents.[22]

LIFE STAGE People in the same part of the life cycle may differ in their life stage. **Life stage** defines a person's major concern, such as going through a divorce, going into a second marriage, taking care of an older parent, deciding to cohabit with another person, deciding to buy a new home, and so on. These life stages present opportunities for marketers who can help people cope with their major concerns.

The wedding industry attracts marketers of a whole host of products and services. Recognizing that 80% of Broadway musicals fail to make money, producers of the $11 million show "The Wedding Singer" negotiated advertising partnerships with wedding Web sites such as The Knot and magazines such as Modern Bride, product placements with NBC's "Today" show, and promotional packages with large New York city bridal retailer, Kleinfeld.[23] But marketing opportunities don't end when couples say "I do."

NEWLYWEDS

Newlyweds in the United States spend a total of about $70 billion on their households in the first year after marriage—and they buy more in the first six months than an established household does in five years! Marketers know that marriage often means two sets of shopping habits and brand preferences must be blended into one. Companies such as Procter & Gamble, Clorox, and Colgate-Palmolive include their products in "Newlywed Kits" distributed when couples apply for their marriage license. JC Penney has identified "Starting Outs" as one of its two major customer groups. Marketers pay a premium for name lists to assist their direct marketing because, as one marketer noted, newlywed names "are like gold."[24]

GENDER Men and women have different attitudes and behave differently, based partly on genetic makeup and partly on socialization.[25] For example, women tend to be more communal minded and men tend to be more self-expressive and goal directed; women tend to take in more of the data in their immediate environment; men tend to focus on the part of the environment that helps them achieve a goal. A research study examining how men and women shop found that men often need to be invited to touch a product, whereas women are likely to pick it up without prompting. Men often like to read product information; women may relate to a product on a more personal level.

According to some studies, women in the United States and the United Kingdom control or influence over 80% of consumer goods and services, make 75% of the decisions about buying new homes, and purchase 60% of new cars outright. Gender differentiation has long been applied in clothing, hairstyling, cosmetics, and magazines. Avon has built a $6 billion-plus business selling beauty products to women. Some products have been positioned as more masculine or feminine. Gillette's Venus is the most successful female shaving line ever, with over 50% of the market, and has appropriate product design, packaging, and advertising cues to reinforce a female image.[26]

A marketing bonanza to the bridal industry and marketers targeting newlyweds, the hit Broadway show "The Wedding Singer" entered advertising partnerships with wedding Web sites and bridal magazines.

But it's not enough to tout a product as masculine or feminine. Hypersegmentation is now occurring within both male and female personal care segments. To expand beyond the metrosexual market, Unilever's Axe brand includes "Snake Eel Shower Scrub with Desert Minerals + Cactus Oil," whose ingredients sound more rugged than "exfoliating liquid soap with plant oils."[27] And Unilever earned kudos by targeting women who don't look like, or aspire to look like, fashion models, with its award-winning "Dove Campaign for Real Beauty".

DOVE

Dove's Campaign for Real Beauty features women of all shapes, sizes, and colors posing proudly in their underwear. The company claims that the ad series, developed by Ogilvy & Mather, was not just a vehicle to sell more soap but "aims to change the status quo and offer in its place a broader, healthier, more democratic view of beauty." The springboard was a global study sponsored by Dove that researched women's attitudes toward themselves and beauty. Only 2% of women in the study considered themselves beautiful, so not only women, but everyone, took notice when the pictures of beaming full-figured or average-looking women began appearing. Even the National Organization for Women (NOW), not known for approving of depictions of women in advertising, has called the campaign "a step forward for the advertising industry."[28]

Media have emerged to make gender targeting easier. Marketers can reach women more easily on Lifetime, Oxygen, and WE television networks and through scores of women's magazines; men are more likely to be found at ESPN, Comedy Central, Fuel, and Spike TV channels and through magazines such as *Maxim* and *Men's Health*.[29]

Some traditionally more male-oriented markets, such as the automobile industry, are beginning to recognize gender segmentation and are changing the way they design and sell cars.[30] Women shop differently for cars than men; they are more interested in environmental impact, care more about interior than exterior styling, and view safety in terms of features that help survive an accident rather than handling to avoid an accident.[31]

Armed with research suggesting that 80% of home improvement projects are now initiated by women, Lowe's designed its stores with wider aisles—to make it easier for shopping carts to get around—and to include more big-ticket appliances and high-margin home furnishings. Half its clientele is now female, forcing its more traditional competitor, Home Depot, to

So-called New Luxury products, including premium hotels, personal care products, and Kendall- Jackson wines, are riding a number of demographic and cultural trends that allow consumers to "trade up" their purchase decisions.

introduce "Ladies' Night at the Depot" to appeal to women.[32] Another hot retail trend is athletic stores and boutiques such as Lucy, Paiva, and NikeWomen that target women.[33]

INCOME Income segmentation is a long-standing practice in such categories as automobiles, clothing, cosmetics, financial services, and travel. However, income does not always predict the best customers for a given product. Blue-collar workers were among the first purchasers of color television sets; it was cheaper for them to buy these sets than to go to movies and restaurants.

Many marketers are deliberately going after lower-income groups, in some cases discovering fewer competitive pressures or greater consumer loyalty.[34] Casual Male created a big-and-tall brand aimed at the lower-income market. Procter & Gamble launched two discount-priced brand extensions—Bounty Basic and Charmin Basic. Prepaid debit cards and wireless service accounts are the fastest-growing segments in those respective markets.

Yet, at the same time, other marketers are finding success with premium-priced products. When Whirlpool launched a pricey Duet washer line, sales doubled forecasts in a weak economy, due primarily to middle-class shoppers who traded up.

Increasingly, companies are finding that their markets are "hourglass shaped" as middle-market U.S. consumers migrate toward both discount *and* premium products.[35] Companies that miss out on this new market risk being "trapped in the middle" and seeing their market share steadily decline. General Motors was caught in the middle, between highly engineered German imports in the luxury market and high-value Japanese and Korean models in the economy class, and has seen its market share continually slide.[36] "Marketing Insight: Trading Up (and Down): The New Consumer" describes the factors creating this trend and what it means to marketers.

MARKETING INSIGHT | TRADING UP (AND DOWN): THE NEW CONSUMER

A new pattern in consumer behavior has emerged in recent years, according to Michael Silverstein and Neil Fiske, the authors of *Trading Up*. In unprecedented numbers, middle-market consumers are periodically trading up to what Silverstein and Fiske call "New Luxury" products and services "that possess higher levels of quality, taste, and aspiration than other goods in the category but are not so expensive as to be out of reach." For example, these consumer might trade up to an imported French wine, use a premium skin cream, or stay in a luxury hotel for a few nights on vacation, depending on the emotional benefits gained in the trade. In 2003, 96% of U.S. consumers said they were willing to pay a premium for at least one type of product. Silverstein and Fiske calculate that this percentage translates to almost 122 million U.S. consumers who are willing and able to trade up.

The authors identify a number of broad demographic and cultural explanations for the trend. In general, people have more money to spend than in years past. Average U.S. household income has risen in the past 30 years, with growth highest for the top 20% of households, those earning over $82,000 per year. More women are entering the workforce and are commanding higher salaries than before. They feel entitled to spend the money they earn; women accounted for 75% of discretionary spending. And, as baby boomers find themselves with empty nests, as adults continue to marry later and divorce more often, the typical U.S. consumer has fewer mouths to feed. In 2003, only 24% of households had a married couple with children living at home. Finally, U.S. consumers today are better educated and more comfortable analyzing and satisfying their emotional needs, which New Luxury goods often target. As a result, the authors assert, the typical U.S. consumer has been transformed into "a sophisticated and discerning consumer with high aspirations and substantial buying power and clout."

Thanks to the trading-up trend, New Luxury goods sell at higher volumes than traditional luxury goods, although priced higher than conventional mid-market items. The authors identify three main types of New Luxury products:

- *Accessible superpremium products*, such as Victoria's Secret underwear and Kettle gourmet potato chips, carry a significant premium over middle-market brands, yet consumers can readily trade up to them because they are relatively low-ticket items in affordable categories.
- *Old Luxury brand extensions* extend historically high-priced brands down-market while retaining their cachet, such as the Mercedes-Benz C-class and the American Express Blue card.
- *Masstige goods*, such as Kiehl's skin care and Kendall-Jackson wines, are priced between average middle-market brands and superpremium Old Luxury brands. They are "always based on emotions, and consumers have a much stronger emotional engagement with them than with other goods."

The authors note that in order to trade up on the brands that offered these emotional benefits, consumers often "trade down" by shopping at discounters such as Wal-Mart and Costco for staple items or goods that confer no emotional benefit but still deliver quality and functionality. In a subsequent book titled *Treasure Hunt*, Michael Silverstein notes that 82% of U.S. consumers trade down in five or more categories (what he calls "treasure hunting"), whereas 62% focus on trading up in the two categories that provide the most emotional benefits. This makes the new consumer "part martyr and part hedonist," willingly sacrificing on a number of purchases in order to experience enhanced benefits from a handful of others.

Silverstein reasons that with the trading-up segment of the market expected to rise from $605 billion in 2005 to $1 trillion in 2010, and trading-down segment predicted to grow from $1.1 trillion to $1.5 trillion in the same period, the firms that succeed will offer one of two kinds of value: New Luxury or Treasure Hunting. The remaining firms, which occupy the middle market, will continue to see their market share shrink as they get "trapped in the middle." Traditional grocers and department stores are already suffering, having experienced market share declines of 30% and 50%, respectively. Silverstein argues that most middle-market companies do not offer the economic, functional, and emotional value that modern consumers are searching for. Brands that offer opportunities to trade up, such as Coach, Victoria's Secret, Grey Goose, and Bath & Body Works, or to trade down, such as Best Value Inn, Kohls, Dollar General, and IKEA, are optimally positioned to deliver the value that modern consumers seek.

Sources: Michael J. Silverstein, *Treasure Hunt: Inside the Mind of the New Consumer* (New York: Portfolio, 2006); Jeff Cioletti, "Movin' on Up," *BeverageWorld* (June 2006): 20; Michael J. Silverstein and Neil Fiske, *Trading Up: The New American Luxury* (New York: Portfolio, 2003).

GENERATION Each generation is profoundly influenced by the times in which it grows up—the music, movies, politics, and defining events of that period. Demographers call these generational groups *cohorts.* Members share the same major cultural, political, and economic experiences and have similar outlooks and values. Marketers often advertise to a cohort by using the icons and images prominent in its experiences. "Marketing Insight: Marketing to Gen Y" provides insight into that key age cohort. "Marketing Memo: Cheat Sheet for 20-Somethings" looks at a key part of Gen Y.

Although we can make distinctions between them, different generational cohorts also influence each other. For instance, because so many members of Generation Y—"Echo Boomers"—are living with their boomer parents, parents are being influenced by what demographers are calling a "boom-boom effect." The same products that appeal to 21-year-olds are appealing to

MARKETING INSIGHT | MARKETING TO GENERATION Y

They're dubbed "Echo Boomers" or "Generation Y." They grew up amid economic abundance, followed by years of economic recession. Their world was defined by a long period of national calm disrupted by events such as Columbine and 9/11. They've been "wired" almost from birth—playing computer games, navigating the World Wide Web, downloading music, connecting with friends via instant messaging and mobile phones. They have a sense of entitlement and abundance from growing up during the economic boom and being pampered by their boomer parents. They are selective, confident, and impatient. They want what they want when they want it—and they often get it by using plastic. The average 21-year-old carries almost $3,000 in credit card debt.

The influences that shaped Gen Y are incredibly important to marketers because this cohort will shape consumer and business markets for years to come. Born between 1977 and 1994, Generation Y is three times the size of Generation X with roughly 78 million members. Their annual spending power is estimated at $187 billion. If you factor in career growth and household and family formation, and multiply by another 53 years of life expectancy, you're in the $10 trillion range in consumer spending over the life span of today's 21-year-olds.

It's not surprising, then, that market researchers and advertisers are racing to get a bead on Gen Y's buying behavior. Because its members are often turned off by overt branding practices and a "hard sell," marketers have tried many different approaches to reach and persuade them.

1. ***Online buzz***—Rock band Foo Fighters created a digital street team that sends targeted e-mail blasts to members who "get the latest news, exclusive audio/video sneak previews, tons of chances to win great Foo Fighters prizes, and become part of the Foo Fighters Family."
2. ***Student ambassadors***—Red Bull enlists college students as Red Bull Student Brand Managers to distribute samples, research drinking trends, design on-campus marketing initiatives, and write stories for student newspapers.
3. ***Unconventional sports***—Dodge automobiles sponsors the World Dodgeball Association, which is taking the sport "to a new level by emphasizing teamwork, strategy, and skill."
4. ***Cool events***—The U.S. Open of Surfing attracted sponsors such as Honda, Philips Electronics, and, of course, O'Neill Clothing, originators of the first wet suit. Spring break in Florida has been the launch site of such products as Old Spice Cool Contact Refreshment Towels and Calvin Klein's CK swimwear line.
5. ***Computer games***—Product placement is not restricted to movies or TV: Mountain Dew, Oakley, and Harley-Davidson all made deals to put logos on Tony Hawk's Pro Skater 3 from Activision.
6. ***Videos***—Burton snowboards ensures that its boards and riders are clearly visible in any videos that are shot.
7. ***Street teams***—As part of an antismoking crusade, The American Legacy hires teens as the "Truth Squad" to hand out T-shirts, bandanas, and dog tags at teen-targeted events.

Sources: Anonymous, "Gen Y and the Future of Mall Retailing," *American Demographics* (December 2002–January 2003): J1–J4; Michael J. Weiss, "To Be about to Be," *American Demographics* (September 2003): 28–36; John Leo, "The Good-News Generation," *U.S. News & World Report,* November 3, 2003, p .60; Kelly Pate, "Not 'X,' but 'Y' Marks the Spot: Young Generation a Marketing Target," *Denver Post,* August 17, 2003; Bruce Horovitz, "Gen Y: A Tough Crowd to Sell," *USA Today,* April 22, 2002; Bruce Horovitz, "Marketers Revel with Spring Breakers," *USA Today,* March 12, 2002; Martha Irvine, "Labels Don't Fit Us, Gen Y Insists," *Denver Post,* April 19, 2001; J. M. Lawrence, "Trends: X-ed Out: Gen Y Takes Over," *Boston Herald,* February 2, 1999.

youth-obsessed baby boomers. The multiseason success of MTV's reality show *The Osbournes,* starring heavy-metal rocker Ozzy Osbourne and his family, was fueled as much by boomer parents as by their MTV-loving kids. This is what writer and corporate consultant Christopher Noxon has called the "rejuvenile" mindset. Here are two examples of the rejuvenilization phenomenon:

- Adult gadgets, such as cell phones, automobiles, and even housewares have been transformed from purely utilitarian to toylike. Vacuums come in candy-apple red and baby blue, and Target sells a Michael Graves version of a toaster shaped like a fluffy cartoon cloud. Cars such as lemon yellow Mini Coopers look like they're designed for the toddler set.
- Half the adults who visit Disney World every day do so without kids, and Noxon found that Disney enthusiasts return to the Magic Kingdom to recapture the safety and serenity of childhood.[37]

SOCIAL CLASS Social class has a strong influence on preferences in cars, clothing, home furnishings, leisure activities, reading habits, and retailers, and many companies design products and services for specific social classes. The tastes of social classes change with the years, however. The 1990s were about greed and ostentation for the upper classes. Affluent tastes now run more conservatively, although luxury-goods makers such as Coach, Tiffany, Burberry, TAG Heuer, and Louis Vuitton still successfully sell to those seeking the good life.[38]

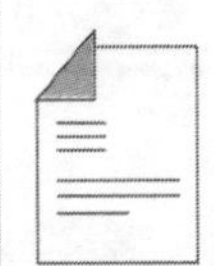

MARKETING MEMO | **CHEAT SHEET FOR 20-SOMETHINGS**

In 2003, 4.1 million U.S. consumers turned 21. Here are some facts you need to know about them:

41%—Share of 21-year-olds who currently live with mom and/or dad

60%—Share of college students who plan to move back home after graduation

1-in-4—Odds that a 21-year-old was raised by a single parent

70%—Share of 21-year-olds who have a full- or part-time job

47%—Share of 21-year-olds who own a mobile phone

23 million—Number of ad impressions received thus far by the average 21-year-old

$2,241,141—Amount the average 21-year-old will spend between now and the end of his or her life

$3,000—Credit card debt of the average 21-year-old

5.8—Years until the average 21-year-old man marries for the first time

4.1—Years until the average 21-year-old woman marries for the first time

10—Years until the average 21-year-old buys his or her first vacation home

43%—Share of 21-year-olds who have a tattoo or a body piercing

62%—Share of 21-year-olds who are non-Hispanic Whites

Source: Cheat Sheet for 21 Year-olds from John Fetto, "Twenty-One, and Counting . . .," *American Demographics,* September 2003, p. 48. Reprinted with permission of Primedia BMMG.

Psychographic Segmentation

Psychographics is the science of using psychology and demographics to better understand consumers. In *psychographic segmentation,* buyers are divided into different groups on the basis of psychological/personality traits, lifestyle, or values. People within the same demographic group can exhibit very different psychographic profiles.

One of the most popular commercially available classification systems based on psychographic measurements is SRI Consulting Business Intelligence's (SRIC-BI) VALS™ framework. VALS, signifying values and lifestyles, classifies U.S. adults into eight primary groups based on responses to a questionnaire featuring 4 demographic and 35 attitudinal questions. The VALS system is continually updated with new data from more than 80,000 surveys per year (see Figure 8.1).[39] You can find out which VALS type you are by going to SRIC-BI's Web site (www.sric-bi.com).

The main dimensions of the VALS segmentation framework are consumer motivation (the horizontal dimension) and consumer resources (the vertical dimension). Consumers are inspired by one of three primary motivations: ideals, achievement, and self-expression. Those primarily motivated by ideals are guided by knowledge and principles. Those motivated by achievement look for products and services that demonstrate success to their peers. Consumers whose motivation is self-expression desire social or physical activity, variety, and risk. Personality traits such as energy, self-confidence, intellectualism, novelty seeking, innovativeness, impulsiveness, leadership, and vanity—in conjunction with key demographics—determine an individual's resources. Different levels of resources enhance or constrain a person's expression of his primary motivation.

The four groups with higher resources are:

1. ***Innovators***—Successful, sophisticated, active, "take-charge" people with high self-esteem. Purchases often reflect cultivated tastes for relatively upscale, niche-oriented products and services.
2. ***Thinkers***—Mature, satisfied, and reflective people who are motivated by ideals and who value order, knowledge, and responsibility. They seek durability, functionality, and value in products.
3. ***Achievers***—Successful, goal-oriented people who focus on career and family. They favor premium products that demonstrate success to their peers.
4. ***Experiencer***—Young, enthusiastic, impulsive people who seek variety and excitement. They spend a comparatively high proportion of income on fashion, entertainment, and socializing.

FIG. 8.1

The VALS Segmentation System: An Eight-Part Typology

Source: VALS™ ©, SRI Consulting Business Intelligence. Used with permissioion.

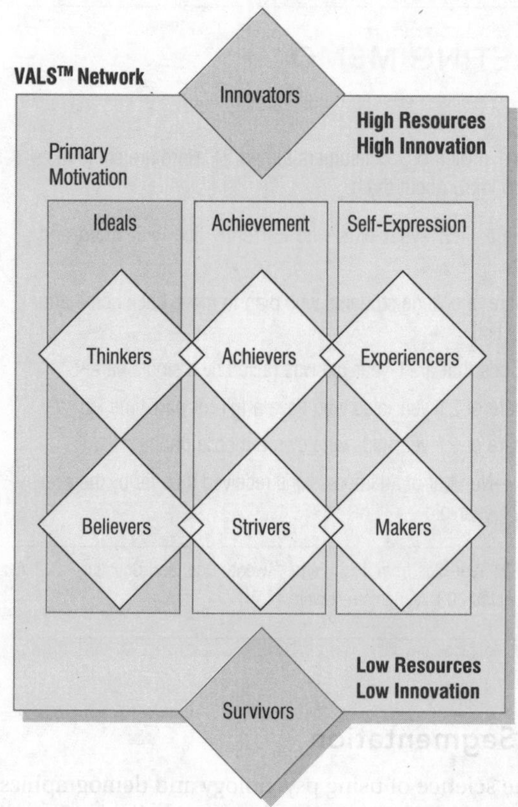

The four groups with lower resources are:

1. ***Believers***—Conservative, conventional, and traditional people with concrete beliefs. They prefer familiar, U.S. products and are loyal to established brands.
2. ***Strivers***—Trendy and fun-loving people who are resource constrained. They favor stylish products that emulate the purchases of those with greater material wealth.
3. ***Makers***—Practical, down-to-earth, self-sufficient people who like to work with their hands. They seek U.S.-made products with a practical or functional purpose.
4. ***Survivors***—Elderly, passive people who are concerned about change. They are loyal to their favorite brands.

Sharper Image is an example of a retailer who used VALS segments to guide their target market and site selections.

Marketers can apply their understanding of VALS segments to marketing planning. For example, Transport Canada, the agency that operates major Canadian airports, found that Actualizers, who desire to express independence and taste, made up a disproportionate percentage of air travelers. Given that segment's profile, stores such as Sharper Image and Nature Company were expected to do well in the firm's airports.

Psychographic segmentation schemes are often customized by culture. The Japanese version of VALS, Japan VALS™, divides society into 10 consumer segments on the basis of two key concepts: life orientation (traditional ways, occupations, innovation, and self-expression) and attitudes to social change (sustaining, pragmatic, adapting, and innovating).

Behavioral Segmentation

In behavioral segmentation, marketers divide buyers into groups on the basis of their knowledge of, attitude toward, use of, or response to a product.

DECISION ROLES It's easy to identify the buyer for many products. In the United States, men normally choose their shaving equipment and women choose their pantyhose; but even here marketers must be careful in making their targeting decisions, because buying roles change. When ICI, the giant British chemical company, discovered that women made 60% of decisions on the brand of household paint, it decided to advertise its DuLux brand to women.

People play five roles in a buying decision: *Initiator, Influencer, Decider, Buyer,* and *User.* For example, assume a wife initiates a purchase by requesting a new treadmill for her birthday. The husband may then seek information from many sources, including his best friend who has a treadmill and is a key influencer in what models to consider. After presenting the alternative choices to his wife, he then purchases her preferred model which, as it turns out, ends up being used by the entire family. Different people are playing different roles, but all are crucial in the decision process and ultimate consumer satisfaction.

BEHAVIORAL VARIABLES Many marketers believe behavioral variables—occasions, benefits, user status, usage rate, buyer-readiness stage, loyalty status, and attitude—are the best starting points for constructing market segments.

Occasions Occasions can be defined in terms of the time of day, week, month, year, or in terms of other well-defined temporal aspects of a consumer's life. We can distinguish buyers according to the occasions when they develop a need, purchase a product, or use a product. For example, air travel is triggered by occasions related to business, vacation, or family. Occasion segmentation can help expand product usage. During the 1960s and 1970s, Ocean Spray Cranberries Inc. was essentially a single-purpose, single-usage product: Consumption of cranberries was almost entirely confined to cranberry sauce served as a side dish with Thanksgiving and Christmas dinners. After a pesticide scare one Thanksgiving drastically cut sales and almost put growers out of business, the Ocean Spray cooperative embarked on a program to diversify and create a year-round market by producing cranberry-based juice drinks and other products.[40]

Marketers also can extend activities associated with certain holidays to other times of the year. Although Christmas, Mother's Day, and Valentine's Day are the major gift-giving holidays, these and other events account for just over half of givers' budgets. That leaves the rest available throughout the year for occasions such as birthdays, weddings, anniversaries, housewarming, and new babies.[41]

Benefits Not everyone who buys a product wants the same benefits from it. Constellation Wines U. S. identified six different benefit segments in the premium wine market ($5.50 a bottle and up).[42]

- ***Enthusiast*** (12% of the market). Skewing female, their average income is about $76,000 a year. About 3% are "luxury enthusiasts" who skew more male with a higher income.
- ***Image Seekers*** (20%). The only segment that skews male, with an average age of 35. They use wine basically as a badge to say who they are, and they're willing to pay more to make sure they're getting the right bottle.
- ***Savvy Shoppers*** (15%). They love to shop and believe they don't have to spend a lot to get a good bottle of wine. Happy to use the bargain bin.
- ***Traditionalist*** (16%). With very traditional values, they like to buy brands they've heard of and from wineries that have been around a long time. Their average age is 50 and they are 68% female.
- ***Satisfied Sippers*** (14%). Not knowing much about wine, they tend to buy the same brands. About half of what they drink is white zinfandel.
- ***Overwhelmed*** (23%). A potentially attractive target market, they find purchasing wine confusing.

User Status Every product has its nonusers, ex-users, potential users, first-time users, and regular users. Blood banks cannot rely only on regular donors to supply blood; they must also recruit new first-time donors and contact ex-donors, each with a different marketing strategy. The key to attracting potential users, or even possibly nonusers, is understanding the reasons they are not using. Do they have deeply held attitudes, beliefs, or behaviors or just lack knowledge of the product or brand benefits and usage?

Included in the potential-user group are consumers who will become users in connection with some life stage or life event. Mothers-to-be are potential users who will turn into heavy users. Producers of infant products and services learn their names and shower them with products and ads to capture a share of their future purchases. Market share leaders tend to focus on attracting potential users because they have the most to gain. Smaller firms focus on trying to attract current users away from the market leader.

Usage Rate Markets can be segmented into light, medium, and heavy product users. Heavy users are often a small percentage of the market but account for a high percentage of total consumption. For example, heavy beer drinkers account for 87% of the beer consumed—almost seven times as much as light drinkers. Marketers would rather attract one heavy user than several light users. A potential problem, however, is that heavy users are often either extremely loyal to one brand or never loyal to any brand and always looking for the lowest price. They also may have less room to expand their purchase and consumption.

Buyer-Readiness Stage Some people are unaware of the product, some are aware, some are informed, some are interested, some desire the product, and some intend to buy. To help characterize how many people are at different stages and how well they have converted people from one stage to another, some marketers employ a marketing funnel. Figure 8.2 displays a funnel for two hypothetical brands, A and B. Brand B performs poorly compared to Brand A at converting one-time triers to more recent triers (only 46% convert for Brand A as compared to 61% for Brand B).

The relative numbers of consumers at different stages make a big difference in designing the marketing program. Suppose a health agency wants to encourage women to have an annual Pap test to detect cervical cancer. At the beginning, most women may be unaware of the Pap test. The marketing effort should go into awareness-building advertising using a simple message. Later, the advertising should dramatize the benefits of the Pap test and the risks of not taking it. A special offer of a free health examination might motivate women to actually sign up for the test.

Loyalty Status Marketers usually envision four groups based on brand loyalty status:

1. ***Hard-core loyals***—Consumers who buy only one brand all the time
2. ***Split loyals***—Consumers who are loyal to two or three brands
3. ***Shifting loyals***—Consumers who shift loyalty from one brand to another
4. ***Switchers***—Consumers who show no loyalty to any brand[43]

A company can learn a great deal by analyzing the degrees of brand loyalty: Hard-core loyals can help identify the products' strengths; split loyals can show the firm which brands are most competitive with its own; and by looking at customers who are shifting away from its brand, the company can learn about its marketing weaknesses and

FIG. 8.2

Brand Funnel

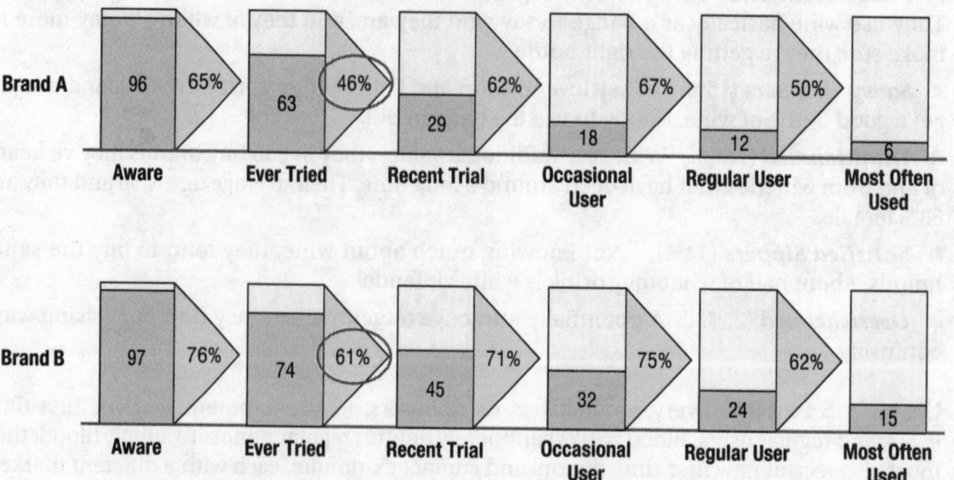

attempt to correct them. One caution: What appear to be brand-loyal purchase patterns may reflect habit, indifference, a low price, a high switching cost, or the unavailability of other brands.

Attitude Five attitudes about products are: enthusiastic, positive, indifferent, negative, and hostile. Door-to-door workers in a political campaign use voter attitude to determine how much time to spend with that voter. They thank enthusiastic voters and remind them to vote; they reinforce those who are positively disposed; they try to win the votes of indifferent voters; they spend no time trying to change the attitudes of negative and hostile voters.

Combining different behavioral bases can help to provide a more comprehensive and cohesive view of a market and its segments. Figure 8.3 depicts one possible way to break down a target market by various behavioral segmentation bases.

THE CONVERSION MODEL The Conversion Model measures the strength of consumers' psychological commitment to brands and their openness to change.[44] To determine how easily a consumer can be converted to another choice, the model assesses commitment based on factors such as consumer attitudes toward, and satisfaction with, current brand choices in a category and the importance of the decision to select a brand in the category.[45]

The model segments *users* of a brand into four groups based on strength of commitment, from low to high, as follows:

1. ***Convertible*** (most likely to defect)
2. ***Shallow*** (uncommitted to the brand and could switch—some are actively considering alternatives)

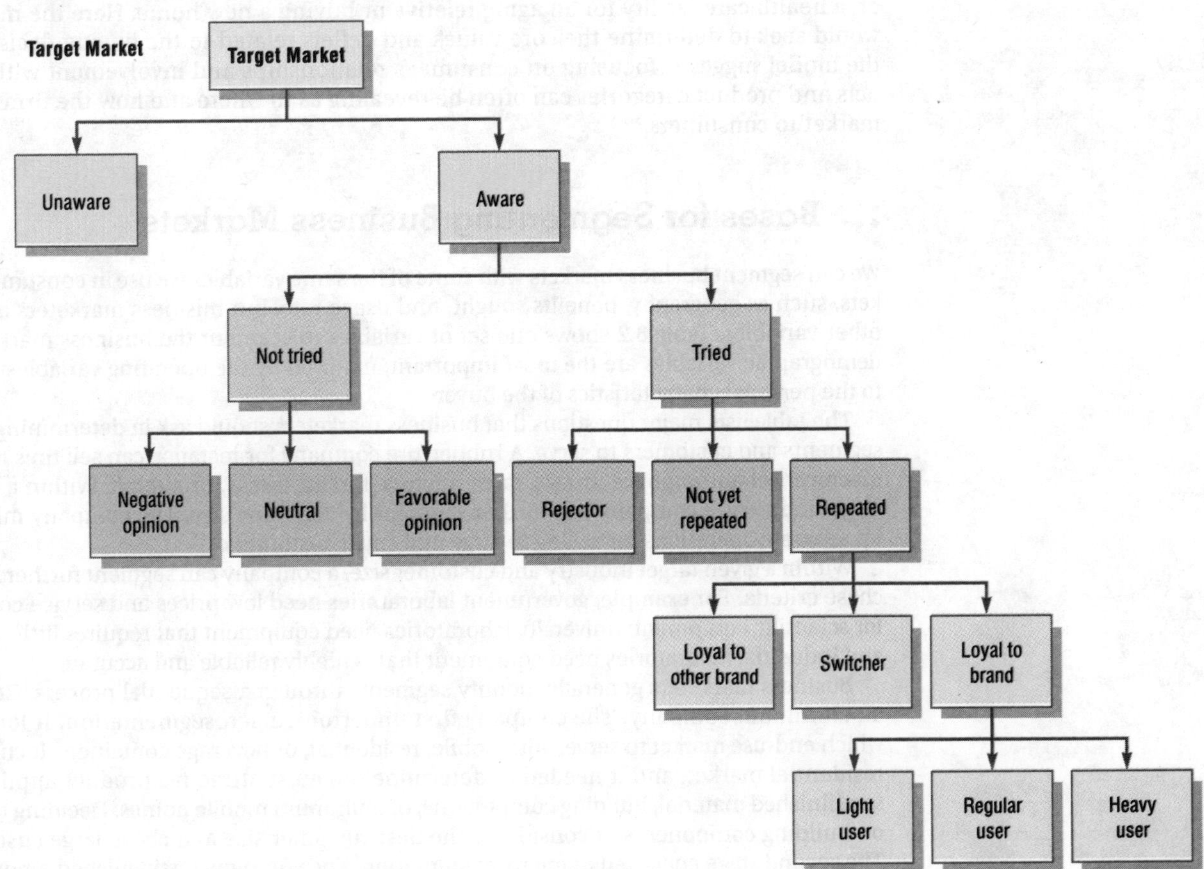

FIG. 8.3 | Behavioral Segmentation Breakdown

3. ***Average*** (also committed to the brand they are using, but not as strongly—they are unlikely to switch brands in the short term)
4. ***Entrenched*** (strongly committed to the brand they are currently using—they are highly unlikely to switch brands in the foreseeable future)

The model also classifies *nonusers* of a brand into four other groups based on their "balance of disposition" and openness to trying the brand, from low to high, as follows:

1. ***Strongly unavailable*** (unlikely to switch to the brand—their preference lies strongly with their current brands)
2. ***Weakly unavailable*** (not available to the brand because their preference lies with their current brand, although not strongly)
3. ***Ambivalent*** (as attracted to the brand as they are to their current brands)
4. ***Available*** (most likely to be acquired in the short run)

In an application of the Conversion Model, Lloyds TSB bank discovered that the profitability of its "least committed" clients had fallen by 14% in a 12-month period, whereas for the "most committed" it had increased by 9%. Those who were "committed" were 20% more likely to increase the number of products they held during the 12-month period. As a result, the bank took action to attract and retain high-value committed customers, which resulted in increased profitability.

Finally, a related method of behavioral segmentation has recently been proposed that looks more at the expectations a consumer brings to a particular kind of transaction and locates those expectations on a "Gravity of Decision Spectrum." On the shallow end of the spectrum, consumers seek products and services they think will save them time, effort, and money, such as toiletries and snacks. Segmentation for these items would tend to measure consumers' price sensitivity, habits, and impulsiveness. At the other end of the spectrum, the deep end, are those decisions in which consumers' emotional investment is greatest and their core values most engaged, such as deciding on a health care facility for an aging relative or buying a new home. Here the marketer would seek to determine the core values and beliefs related to the buying decision. As the model suggests, focusing on consumer's relationships and involvement with products and product categories can often be revealing as to where and how the firm should market to consumers.[46]

::: Bases for Segmenting Business Markets

We can segment business markets with some of the same variables we use in consumer markets, such as geography, benefits sought, and usage rate, but business marketers also use other variables. Table 8.2 shows one set of variables to segment the business market. The demographic variables are the most important, followed by the operating variables—down to the personal characteristics of the buyer.

The table lists major questions that business marketers should ask in determining which segments and customers to serve. A rubber-tire company for instance can sell tires to manufacturers of automobiles, trucks, farm tractors, forklift trucks, or aircraft. Within a chosen target industry, a company can further segment by company size. The company might set up separate operations for selling to large and small customers.

Within a given target industry and customer size, a company can segment further by purchase criteria. For example, government laboratories need low prices and service contracts for scientific equipment; university laboratories need equipment that requires little service; and industrial laboratories need equipment that is highly reliable and accurate.

Business marketers generally identify segments through a sequential process. Consider an aluminum company: The company first undertook macrosegmentation. It looked at which end-use market to serve: automobile, residential, or beverage containers. It chose the residential market, and it needed to determine the most attractive product application: semifinished material, building components, or aluminum mobile homes. Deciding to focus on building components, it considered the best customer size and chose large customers. The second stage consisted of microsegmentation. The company distinguished among customers buying on price, service, or quality. Because the aluminum company had a high-service profile, it decided to concentrate on the service-motivated segment of the market.

TABLE 8.2

Major Segmentation Variables for Business Markets

Demographic

1. *Industry:* Which industries should we serve?
2. *Company size:* What size companies should we serve?
3. *Location:* What geographical areas should we serve?

Operating Variables

4. *Technology:* What customer technologies should we focus on?
5. *User or nonuser status:* Should we serve heavy users, medium users, light users, or nonusers?
6. *Customer capabilities:* Should we serve customers needing many of few services?

Purchasing Approaches

7. *Purchasing-function organization:* Should we serve companies with highly centralized or decentralized purchasing organization?
8. *Power structure:* Should we serve companies that are engineering dominated, financially dominated, and so on?
9. *Nature of existing relationship:* Should we serve companies with which we have strong relationship or simply go after the most desirable companies?
10. *General purchasing policies:* Should we serve companies that prefer leasing? Service contract? Systems purchases? Sealed bidding?
11. *Purchasing criteria:* Should we serve companies that are seeking quality? Service? Price?

Situational Factors

12. *Urgency:* Should we serve companies that need quick and sudden delivery or service?
13. *Specific application:* Should we focus on certain application of our product rather than all applications?
14. *Size or order:* Should we focus on large or small orders?

Personal Characteristics

15. *Buyer-seller similarity:* Should we serve companies whose people and values are similar to ours?
16. *Attitude toward risk:* Should we serve risk-taking or risk-avoiding customers?
17. *Loyalty:* Should we serve companies that show high loyalty to their suppliers?

Source: Adapted from Thomas V. Bonoma and Benson P. Shapiro, *Segmenting the Industrial Market* (Lexington MA: Lexington Books, 1983).

::: Market Targeting

There are many statistical techniques for developing market segments.[47] Once the firm has identified its market-segment opportunities, it must decide how many and which ones to target. Marketers are increasingly combining several variables in an effort to identify smaller, better-defined target groups. Thus, a bank may not only identify a group of wealthy retired adults, but within that group distinguish several segments depending on current income, assets, savings, and risk preferences. This has led some market researchers to advocate a *needs-based market segmentation approach.* Roger Best proposed the seven-step approach shown in Table 8.3.

Effective Segmentation Criteria

Not all segmentation schemes are useful. For example, table salt buyers could be divided into blond and brunette customers, but hair color is undoubtedly irrelevant to the purchase of salt. Furthermore, if all salt buyers buy the same amount of salt each month, believe all salt is the same, and would pay only one price for salt, this market would be minimally segmentable from a marketing point of view.

TABLE 8.3

Steps in the Segmentation Process

	Description
1. Needs-Based Segmentation	Group customers into segments based on similar needs and benefits sought by customer in solving a particular consumption problem.
2. Segment Identification	For each needs-based segment, determine which demographics, lifestyles, and usage behaviors make the segment distinct and identifiable (actionable).
3. Segment Attractiveness	Using predetermined segment attractiveness criteria (such as market growth, competitive intensity, and market access), determine the overall attractiveness of each segment.
4. Segment Profitability	Determine segment profitability.
5. Segment Positioning	For each segment, create a "value proposition" and product-price positioning strategy based on that segment's unique customer needs and characteristics.
6. Segment "Acid Test"	Create "segment storyboard" to test the attractiveness of each segment's positioning strategy.
7. Marketing-Mix Strategy	Expand segment positioning strategy to include all aspects of the marketing mix: product, price, promotion, and place.

Source: Adapted from Roger J. Best, *Market-Based Management* 4th ed. (Upper Saddle River NJ: Prentice Hall, 2005).

To be useful, market segments must rate favorably on five key criteria:

- ***Measurable.*** The size, purchasing power, and characteristics of the segments can be measured.
- ***Substantial.*** The segments are large and profitable enough to serve. A segment should be the largest possible homogeneous group worth going after with a tailored marketing program. It would not pay, for example, for an automobile manufacturer to develop cars for people who are less than four feet tall.
- ***Accessible.*** The segments can be effectively reached and served.
- ***Differentiable.*** The segments are conceptually distinguishable and respond differently to different marketing-mix elements and programs. If married and unmarried women respond similarly to a sale on perfume, they do not constitute separate segments.
- ***Actionable.*** Effective programs can be formulated for attracting and serving the segments.

Evaluating and Selecting the Market Segments

In evaluating different market segments, the firm must look at two factors: the segment's overall attractiveness and the company's objectives and resources. How well does a potential segment score on the five criteria? Does a potential segment have characteristics that make it generally attractive, such as size, growth, profitability, scale economies, and low risk? Does investing in the segment make sense given the firm's objectives, competencies, and resources? Some attractive segments may not mesh with the company's long-run objectives, or the company may lack one or more necessary competencies to offer superior value.

After evaluating different segments, the company can consider five patterns of target market selection, shown in Figure 8.4. We describe each of them next.

SINGLE-SEGMENT CONCENTRATION Volkswagen concentrates on the small-car market—its foray into the large-car market with the Phaeton was a failure in the United States—and Porsche on the sports car market. Through concentrated marketing, the firm gains a strong knowledge of the segment's needs and achieves a strong market presence. Furthermore, the firm enjoys operating economies through specializing its production, distribution, and promotion. If it captures segment leadership, the firm can earn a high return on its investment.

However, there are risks. A particular market segment can turn sour or a competitor may invade the segment: When digital camera technology took off, Polaroid's earnings fell sharply. For these reasons, many companies prefer to operate in more than one segment. If selecting more than one segment to serve, a company should pay close attention to segment interrelationships on the cost, performance, and technology side. A company carrying fixed costs (sales force, store outlets) can add products to absorb and share some costs. The sales force will sell additional products, and a fast-food outlet will offer additional menu items. Economies of scope can be just as important as economies of scale.

Companies can try to operate in supersegments rather than in isolated segments. A **supersegment** is a set of segments sharing some exploitable similarity. For example, many symphony orchestras target people who have broad cultural interests, rather than only those who regularly attend concerts.

SELECTIVE SPECIALIZATION A firm selects a number of segments, each objectively attractive and appropriate. There may be little or no synergy among the segments, but each promises to be a moneymaker. This multisegment strategy has the advantage of diversifying the firm's risk. When Procter & Gamble launched Crest Whitestrips, initial target segments included newly engaged women and brides-to-be as well as gay males.

PRODUCT SPECIALIZATION The firm makes a certain product that it sells to several different market segments. A microscope manufacturer, for instance, sells to university, government, and commercial laboratories. The firm makes different microscopes for the different customer groups and builds a strong reputation in the specific product area. The downside risk is that the product may be supplanted by an entirely new technology.

MARKET SPECIALIZATION The firm concentrates on serving many needs of a particular customer group. For instance, a firm can sell an assortment of products only to university laboratories. The firm gains a strong reputation in serving this customer group and becomes a channel for additional products the customer group can use. The downside risk is that the customer group may suffer budget cuts or shrink in size.

FULL MARKET COVERAGE The firm attempts to serve all customer groups with all the products they might need. Only very large firms such as Microsoft (software market), General Motors (vehicle market), and Coca-Cola (nonalcoholic beverage market) can undertake a full market coverage strategy. Large firms can cover a whole market in two broad ways: through undifferentiated marketing or differentiated marketing.

In *undifferentiated marketing*, the firm ignores segment differences and goes after the whole market with one offer. It designs a product and a marketing program that will endow the product with a superior image and appeal to the broadest number of buyers, and it relies on mass distribution and advertising. Undifferentiated marketing is "the marketing counterpart to standardization and mass production in manufacturing."[48] The narrow product line keeps down the costs of research and development, production, inventory, transportation, marketing research, advertising, and product management. The undifferentiated advertising program also reduces advertising costs. The company can turn its lower costs into lower prices to win the price-sensitive segment of the market.

In *differentiated marketing*, the firm operates in several market segments and designs different products for each. Cosmetics firm Estée Lauder markets brands that appeal to women (and men) of different tastes: The flagship brand, the original Estée Lauder, appeals to older consumers; Clinique caters to middle-aged women; M.A.C. to youthful hipsters; Aveda to aromatherapy enthusiasts; and Origins to ecoconscious consumers who want cosmetics made from natural ingredients.[49]

Single-segment Concentration

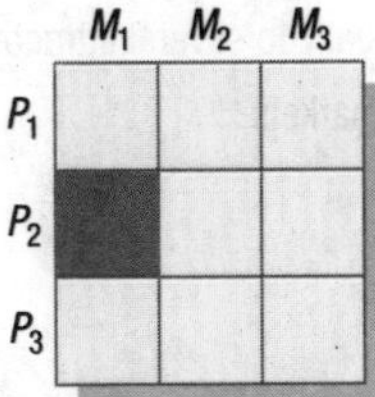

Selective Specialization

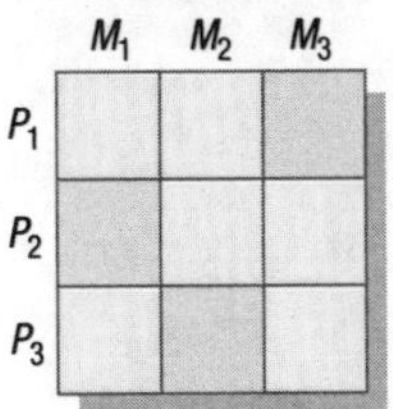

Product Specialization

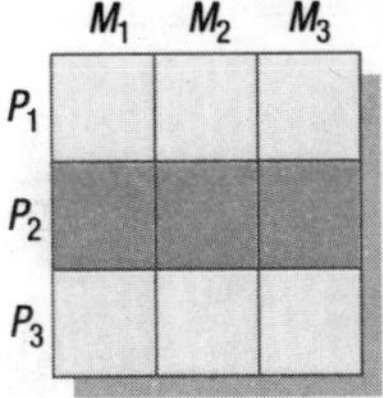

Market Specialization

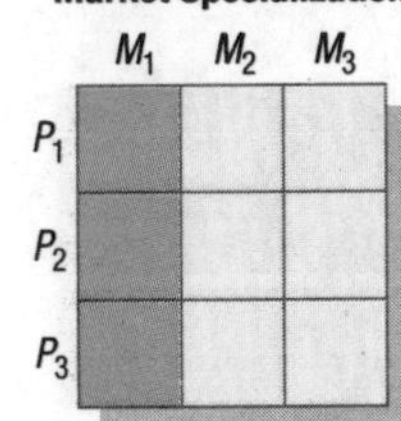

Full Market Coverage

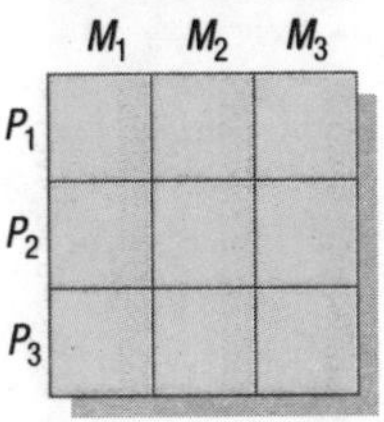

P = Product M = Market

FIG. 8.4

Five Patterns of Target Market Selection

Source: Adopted from Derek F. Abell, *Defining the Business: The Starting Point of Strategic Planning* (Upper Saddle River, NJ: Prentice Hall, 1980), chapter 8, pp. 192-96.

STARWOOD HOTELS & RESORTS

In its rebranding attempt to go "beyond beds," Starwood Hotels & Resorts has differentiated its hotels along emotional, experiential lines. In order to quickly provide distinctive definitions for each Starwood brand, the company took an innovative co-branding approach, creating alliances for each brand that helped telegraph that brand's particular identity. At upscale Westin Hotels the key definition became "renewal." Not only are guests welcomed with herbal drinks, candles, and soft music, but each room features Westin's own "Heavenly Beds," sold exclusively in the retail market through Nordstrom's, thus enhancing the brand's upscale image.

Multisegment strategies work well for products like Crest Whitestrips that appeal equally to several attractive but separate markets.

Somewhat less upscale, Sheraton's core value centers on "connections," an image aided by the hotel's alliance with Yahoo!, which cofounded the Yahoo! Link@Sheraton lobby kiosks and cyber cafés. Four Points by Sheraton is a more value-oriented Sheraton chain that uses "comfort" as its watchword and links with the American Pie Council, Nestlé Waters, and Seattle's Best Coffee to reinforce that positioning (free coffee and bottled water are offered in each room). The Four Points ads feature apple pies and talk about providing guests with "the comforts of home."[50]

Differentiated marketing typically creates more total sales than undifferentiated marketing. However, it also increases the costs of doing business. Because differentiated marketing leads to both higher sales and higher costs, nothing general can be said about the profitability of this strategy. Companies should be cautious about oversegmenting their markets. If this happens, they may want to turn to *countersegmentation* to broaden the customer base. For example, Johnson & Johnson broadened its target market for its baby shampoo to include adults. Smith Kline Beecham launched its Aquafresh toothpaste to attract three benefit segments simultaneously: those seeking fresh breath, whiter teeth, and cavity protection.

Additional Considerations

Two other considerations in evaluating and selecting segments are segment-by-segment invasion plans and ethical choice of market targets.

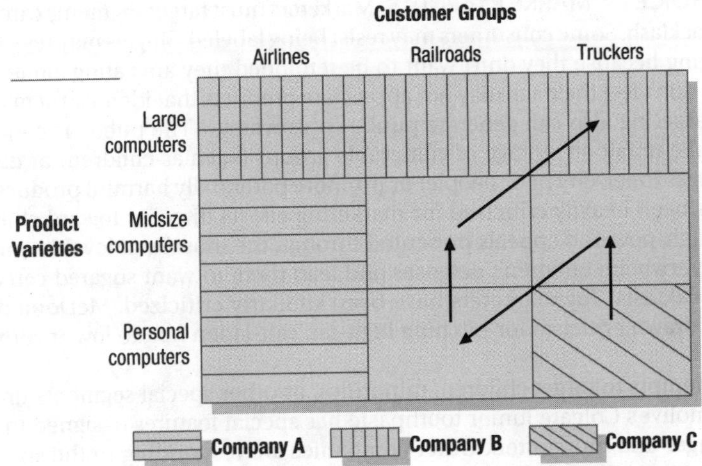

FIG. 8.5

Segment-by-Segment Invasion Plan

SEGMENT-BY-SEGMENT INVASION PLANS A company would be wise to enter one segment at a time. Competitors must not know to what segment(s) the firm will move into next. Segment-by-segment invasion plans are illustrated in Figure 8.5. Three firms, A, B, and C, have specialized in adapting computer systems to the needs of airlines, railroads, and trucking companies. Company A meets all the computer needs of airlines. Company B sells large computer systems to all three transportation sectors. Company C sells personal computers to trucking companies.

Where should company C move next? Arrows added to the chart show the planned sequence of segment invasions. Company C will next offer midsize computers to trucking companies. Then, to allay company B's concern about losing some large computer business with trucking companies, C's next move will be to sell personal computers to railroads. Later, C will offer midsize computers to railroads. Finally, it may launch a full-scale attack on company B's large computer position in trucking companies. Of course, C's hidden planned moves are provisional in that much depends on competitors' segment moves and responses.

Unfortunately, too many companies fail to develop a long-term invasion plan. PepsiCo is an exception. It first attacked Coca-Cola in the grocery market, then in the vending-machine market, then in the fast-food market, and so on. Japanese firms also plot their invasion sequence. They first gain a foothold in a market, then enter new segments with new products. Toyota began by introducing small cars (Tercel, Corolla), then expanded into midsize cars (Camry, Avalon), and finally into luxury cars (Lexus).

A company's invasion plans can be thwarted when it confronts blocked markets. The invader must then figure out a way to break in, which usually calls for a megamarketing approach. **Megamarketing** is the strategic coordination of economic, psychological, political, and public relations skills, to gain the cooperation of a number of parties in order to enter or operate in a given market. Pepsi used megamarketing to enter the Indian market.

PEPSICO

After Coca-Cola left India, Pepsi worked with an Indian business group to gain government approval for its entry, over the objections of domestic soft drink companies and antimultinational legislators. Pepsi offered to help India export some agricultural products in a volume that would more than cover the cost of importing soft-drink concentrate. Pepsi also promised to help rural areas in their economic development. It further offered to transfer food-processing, packaging, and water-treatment technology to India. Pepsi's bundle of benefits won the support of various Indian interest groups.

ETHICAL CHOICE OF MARKET TARGETS Marketers must target segments carefully to avoid consumer backlash. Some consumers may resist being labeled. Singles may reject single-serve food packaging because they don't want to be reminded they are eating alone. Elderly consumers who don't feel their age may not appreciate products that identify them as "old."

Market targeting also can generate public controversy.[51] The public is concerned when marketers take unfair advantage of vulnerable groups (such as children) or disadvantaged groups (such as inner-city poor people) or promote potentially harmful products. The cereal industry has been heavily criticized for marketing efforts directed toward children. Critics worry that high-powered appeals presented through the mouths of lovable animated characters will overwhelm children's defenses and lead them to want sugared cereals or poorly balanced breakfasts. Toy marketers have been similarly criticized. McDonald's and other chains have drawn criticism for pitching high-fat, salt-laden fare to low-income, inner-city residents.

Not all attempts to target children, minorities, or other special segments draw criticism. Colgate-Palmolive's Colgate Junior toothpaste has special features designed to get children to brush longer and more often. Other companies are responding to the special needs of minority segments. Black-owned ICE theaters noticed that although moviegoing by Blacks has surged, there were few inner-city theaters. Starting in Chicago, ICE partnered with the Black communities in which it operates theaters, using local radio stations to promote films and featuring favorite food items at concession stands.[52] Thus the issue is not who is targeted, but rather, how and for what. Socially responsible marketing calls for targeting that serves not only the company's interests, but also the interests of those targeted.

This is the case being made by many companies marketing to the nation's preschoolers. With nearly four million youngsters attending some kind of organized child care, the potential market—including kids and parents—is too great to pass up. So in addition to stocking the usual standards such as art easels, gerbil cages, and blocks, the nation's preschools are likely to have Care Bear worksheets, Pizza Hut reading programs, and Nickelodeon magazines.

Teachers and parents are divided in their feelings about the ethics of this increasing preschool marketing push. Some side with groups such as Stop Commercial Exploitation of Children, who feel that preschoolers are incredibly susceptible to advertising and that schools' endorsements of products make children believe the product is good for them—no matter what it is. Yet, many preschools and day care centers operating on tight budgets welcome the free resources.[53]

SUMMARY :::

1. Target marketing includes three activities: market segmentation, market targeting, and market positioning.
2. We can target markets at four levels: segments, niches, local areas, and individuals. Market segments are large, identifiable groups within a market. A niche is a more narrowly defined group. Globalization and the Internet have made niche marketing more feasible to many. Marketers appeal to local markets through grassroots marketing for trading areas, neighborhoods, and even individual stores.
3. More companies now practice individual and mass customization. The future is likely to see more self-marketing, a form of marketing in which individual consumers take the initiative in designing products and brands.
4. There are two bases for segmenting consumer markets: consumer characteristics and consumer responses. The major segmentation variables for consumer markets are geographic, demographic, psychographic, and behavioral. Marketers use them singly or in combination.
5. Business marketers use all these variables along with operating variables, purchasing approaches, and situational factors.
6. To be useful, market segments must be measurable, substantial, accessible, differentiable, and actionable.
7. A firm must evaluate the various segments and decide how many and which ones to target: a single segment, several segments, a specific product, a specific market, or the full market. If it serves the full market, it must choose between differentiated and undifferentiated marketing. Firms must also monitor segment relationships and seek economies of scope and the potential for marketing to supersegments.
8. Marketers must develop segment-by-segment invasion plans and choose target markets in a socially responsible manner at all times.

APPLICATIONS :::

Marketing Debate Is Mass Marketing Dead?

With marketers increasingly adopting more and more refined market segmentation schemes—fueled by the Internet and other customization efforts—some critics claim that mass marketing is dead. Others counter that there will always be room for large brands that employ marketing programs targeting the mass market.

Take a position: Mass marketing is dead *versus* Mass marketing is still a viable way to build a profitable brand.

Marketing Discussion

Descriptive versus Behavioral Market Segmentation Schemes

Think of various product categories. How would you classify yourself in terms of the various segmentation schemes? How would marketing be more or less effective for you depending on the segment involved? How would you contrast demographic versus behavioral segment schemes? Which ones do you think would be most effective for marketers trying to sell to you?

PART

4

BUILDING STRONG BRANDS

IN THIS CHAPTER, WE WILL ADDRESS THE FOLLOWING QUESTIONS:

1. What is a brand and how does branding work?
2. What is brand equity?
3. How is brand equity built, measured, and managed?
4. What are the important decisions in developing a branding strategy?

CHAPTER 9 ::: CREATING BRAND EQUITY

nine

At the heart of a successful brand is a great product or service, backed by careful planning, a great deal of long-term commitment, and creatively designed and executed marketing. A strong brand commands intense consumer loyalty.

ESPN (the Entertainment and Sports Programming Network) was launched in 1978 in Bristol, Connecticut, with a single satellite, broadcasting regional sports and obscure international sporting contests such as the "World's Strongest Man." Through its singular focus on providing sports programming and news, it grew into the biggest name in sports. Its slogan, "Worldwide Leader in Sports," embodies its position as the sports authority, but one with a youthful, slightly irreverent personality. In the early 1990s, the company crafted a well-thought-out plan: wherever sports fans watched, read, and discussed sports, ESPN was going to be there. The network pursued this strategy by expanding its brand into a number of new categories relevant to sports fans. By 2006, the ESPN brand had been extended to encompass a total of 10 cable channels, a Web site, a magazine, a restaurant chain, more than 600 local radio affiliates, original movies and television series, book publishing, a sports merchandise catalog and online store, music and video games, and a mobile service.

>>>

While its core ESPN cable channel now reaches 99% of cable customers in the United States, the ESPN brand has grown rapidly and includes 10 cable channels, a Web site, a magazine, a restaurant chain, more than 600 local radio affiliates, as well as other media and publishing ventures.

The core ESPN cable channel was still thriving too: in 2006 it was distributed on 99% of cable systems in the United States and the $2.96-per-subscriber monthly license fee it charged cable system operators was the highest for any cable channel. ESPN continues to expand its brand footprint. Its failed seven-month foray into the fiercely competitive cell phone market in 2006 left the company undaunted, and next it launched a credit card. Now owned by The Walt Disney Company, ESPN earns $5 billion a year in revenue, but perhaps the greatest tribute to the power of its brand came from the mouth of one male focus group respondent: "If ESPN was a woman, I'd marry her."[1]

Marketers of successful 21st-century brands must excel at the strategic brand management process. Strategic brand management combines the design and implementation of marketing activities and programs to build, measure, and manage brands to maximize their value. The strategic brand management process has four main steps:

- Identifying and establishing brand positioning
- Planning and implementing brand marketing
- Measuring and interpreting brand performance
- Growing and sustaining brand value

Chapter 10 deals with brand positioning. The remaining topics are discussed in this chapter.[2] Chapter 11 reviews important concepts dealing with competition.

::: What is Brand Equity?

Perhaps the most distinctive skill of professional marketers is their ability to create, maintain, enhance, and protect brands. Starbucks, Sony, and Nike brands command a price premium and elicit deep customer loyalty. Newer brands such as Google, Red Bull, and JetBlue capture the imagination of consumers and the financial community alike.

The American Marketing Association defines a **brand** as "a name, term, sign, symbol, or design, or a combination of them, intended to identify the goods or services of one seller or group of sellers and to differentiate them from those of competitors." A brand is thus a product or service whose dimensions differentiate it in some way from other products or services designed to satisfy the same need. These differences may be functional, rational, or tangible—related to product performance of the brand. They may also be more symbolic, emotional, or intangible—related to what the brand represents.

Branding has been around for centuries as a means to distinguish the goods of one producer from those of another.[3] The earliest signs of branding in Europe were the medieval guilds' requirement that craftspeople put trademarks on their products to protect themselves and their customers against inferior quality. In the fine arts, branding began with artists signing their works. Brands today play a number of important roles that improve consumers' lives and enhance the financial value of firms.

The Role of Brands

Brands identify the source or maker of a product and allow consumers—either individuals or organizations—to assign responsibility for its performance to a particular manufacturer or distributor. Consumers may evaluate the identical product differently depending on how it is branded. They learn about brands through past experiences with the product and its marketing program, finding out which brands satisfy their needs and which do not. As consumers' lives become more complicated, rushed, and time starved, the ability of a brand to simplify decision making and reduce risk is invaluable.[4]

Brands also perform valuable functions for firms.[5] First, they simplify product handling or tracing. Brands help to organize inventory and accounting records. A brand also offers the firm legal protection for unique features or aspects of the product.[6] The brand name can be protected through registered trademarks; manufacturing processes can be protected through patents; and packaging can be protected through copyrights and proprietary designs. These intellectual property rights ensure that the firm can safely invest in the brand and reap the benefits of a valuable asset.

Brands signal a certain level of quality so that satisfied buyers can easily choose the product again.[7] Brand loyalty provides predictability and security of demand for the firm, and it creates barriers to entry that make it difficult for other firms to enter the market. Loyalty also can translate into customer willingness to pay a higher price—often 20% to 25% more than competing brands.[8] Although competitors may duplicate manufacturing processes and product designs, they cannot easily match lasting impressions left in the minds of individuals and organizations by years of product experience and marketing activity. In this sense, branding can be a powerful means to secure a competitive advantage.[9]

Sometimes marketers don't see the real importance of brand loyalty until they change a crucial element of the brand, as Federated Department Stores realized when it bought the fabled Chicago retailer Marshall Field's.

MARSHALL FIELD'S & MACY'S

To consolidate its retail properties, Federated Department Stores had rechristened a number of regional department stores with the Macy's brand. Whereas in some markets, this wouldn't have caused much of a stir, in Chicago it caused an uproar among customers loyal to the Marshall Field's store, which opened in 1852. The store has long been synonymous with Chicago itself, attracting some 9 million visitors a year, and is considered one of Chicago's most popular tourist spots. Its rebranding as Macy's, a name widely associated with New York, was greeted with largely negative reactions including an online petition to retain the Marshall Field's name, which garnered nearly 60,000 signatures. Federated, which owns Macy's, quickly realized it had to preserve some elements of the original brand. Federated eventually retained the Marshal Field's name on the flagship State Street store's brass name plate and on some merchandise, including the beloved Frango chocolate mints, sold at Marshall Field's. Although the slogan "As Chicago as It Gets" was replaced by Macy's "Way to Shop," Macy's promised it would continue local traditions in Chicago during and after the transition, such as the Great Tree at Christmas and Glamorama, its signature fashion show.[10]

Customer Sensitivity to changes in a beloved brand surprised Federated Stores when it rebranded the famous Marshall Field's store in Chicago with the Macy's name.

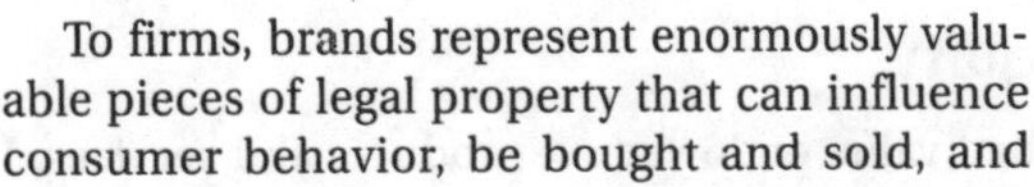

To firms, brands represent enormously valuable pieces of legal property that can influence consumer behavior, be bought and sold, and provide the security of sustained future revenues to their owner. Companies have paid large earning multiples for brands in mergers or acquisitions, often justifying the price premium on the basis of the extra profits to be extracted and sustained from the brands, as well as the tremendous difficulty and expense of creating similar brands from scratch. Wall Street believes strong brands result in better earnings and profit performance for firms, which, in turn, create greater value for shareholders.[11] One of the master marketers at creating brands is Procter & Gamble, as described in "Breakthrough Marketing: Procter & Gamble."

The Scope of Branding

How do you "brand" a product? Although firms provide the impetus to brand creation through marketing programs and other activities, ultimately a brand resides in the minds of consumers. It is a perceptual entity rooted in reality but reflecting the perceptions and idiosyncrasies of consumers.

Branding is endowing products and services with the power of a brand. It's all about creating differences between products. Marketers need to teach consumers "who" the product is—by giving it a name and other brand elements to identify it—as well as what the product does and why consumers should care. Branding creates mental structures that help consumers organize their knowledge about products and services in a way that clarifies their decision making and, in the process, provides value to the firm.

For branding strategies to be successful and brand value to be created, consumers must be convinced there are meaningful differences among brands in the product or service category. Brand differences are often related to attributes or benefits of the product itself. Gillette, Merck, 3M, and others have been leaders in their product categories for decades, due, in part, to continual innovation. Other brands create competitive advantages through nonproduct-related means. Gucci, Chanel, Louis Vuitton, and others have become leaders in their product categories by understanding consumer motivations and desires and creating relevant and appealing images around their products.

Marketers can apply branding virtually anywhere a consumer has a choice. It's possible to brand a physical good (Pantene shampoo, Ford Mustang automobiles, or Lipitor cholestoral medication), a service (Singapore Airlines, Bank of America, or BlueCross BlueShield medical insurance), a store (Nordstrom department store, Foot Locker specialty store, or Safeway supermarket), a person (Tony Hawk, Jay-Z, or Andre Agassi), a place (the city of Sydney, state of Texas, or country of Spain), an organization (UNICEF, American Automobile Association, or U2), or an idea (abortion rights, free trade, or freedom of speech).[12]

Colonial Williamsburg was the nation's first successful geographic brand and now licenses its name to home décor with a modern twist.

COLONIAL WILLIAMSBURG

Colonial Williamsburg, created on a Revolutionary War site in Virginia was the nation's first successful geographic brand, established by John D. Rockefeller 70 years ago. The first license to use the "Williamsburg" brand was awarded to Wedgewood for a line of fine china based on a pottery shard excavated at the site. Licensees continued in this vein, producing high-end bone china, brass, and rugs, until five years ago, when Williamsburg adopted an aggressive, focused program to expand the brand beyond "Colonial" to contemporary home décor with a "revolutionary," cheeky twist. Now it includes historically accurate paint (Sherwin Williams), comforter covers (Pine Cone Hill), and a little verse dish (Mottahedeh) that says "A little rebellion now and then is a good thing,"—a sentiment that sounds hip and modern but was actually penned by Thomas Jefferson.

"Marketing Insight: Brand Cooking with Jamie Oliver" looks at how the popular English chef has become a brand in his own right.

Defining Brand Equity

Brand equity is the added value endowed on products and services. It may be reflected in the way consumers think, feel, and act with respect

BREAKTHROUGH MARKETING | PROCTER & GAMBLE

Procter & Gamble (P&G) is one of the most skillful marketers of consumer packaged goods. The company's scope and accomplishments are staggering. It employs 138,000 people in more than 180 countries; is a global leader in the majority of the 22 different product categories in which it competes; has 23 billion-dollar global brands; spends more than $5 million a day on R&D; and has total worldwide sales of more than $76 billion a year. Its sustained market leadership rests on a number of different capabilities and philosophies:

Procter & Gamble successfully markets nearly 300 brands in 160 countries by focusing on quality, innovation, and unmatched brand-management and extension strategies.

- ***Customer knowledge:*** P&G studies its customers—both end consumers and trade partners—through continuous marketing research and intelligence gathering. It spends more than $100 million annually on more than 10,000 formal consumer research projects every year and generates more than 3 million consumer contacts via its e-mail and phone center. It also puts more emphasis on getting its marketers and researchers out into the field, where they can interact with consumers and retailers in their natural environment.
- ***Long-term outlook:*** P&G takes the time to analyze each opportunity carefully and prepare the best product, then commits itself to making this product a success. It struggled with Pringles potato chips for almost a decade before achieving market success.
- ***Product innovation:*** P&G is an active product innovator, devoting $1.8 billion (3.5% of sales) to research and development, an impressively high amount for a packaged-goods company. It employs more science PhDs than Harvard, Berkeley, and MIT combined and applies for roughly 3,000 patents each year. Part of its innovation process is developing brands that offer new consumer benefits. Recent examples include Febreze, an odor-eliminating fabric spray; Swiffer, a new cleaning system that more effectively removes dust, dirt, and hair from floors and other hard surfaces; and Mr. Clean Magic Eraser, a innovative cleaning sponge that contains a specialty chemical compound developed by BASF.
- ***Quality strategy:*** P&G designs products of above-average quality and continuously improves them. When P&G says "new and improved," it means it. Recent examples include Pantene Ice Shine shampoo, conditioner, and styling gel, and Pampers BabyDry with Caterpillar Flex, a diaper designed to prevent leaks when babies' stomachs shrink at night.
- ***Brand extension strategy:*** P&G produces its brands in several sizes and forms. This strategy gains more shelf space and prevents competitors from moving in to satisfy unmet market needs. P&G also uses its strong brand names to launch new products with instant recognition and much less advertising outlay. The Mr. Clean brand has been extended from household cleaner to bathroom cleaner, and even to a carwash system. Old Spice was successfully extended from men's fragrances to deodorant.
- ***Multibrand strategy:*** P&G markets several brands in the same product category, such as Luvs and Pampers diapers and Oral-B and Crest toothbrushes. Each brand meets a different consumer want and competes against specific competitors' brands. At the same time, P&G has begun carefully not to sell too many brands and has reduced its vast array of products, sizes, flavors, and varieties in recent years to assemble a stronger brand portfolio.
- ***Communication pioneer:*** With its acquisition of Gillette, P&G became the nation's largest advertiser, spending over $5 billion a year on advertising. A pioneer in using the power of television to create strong consumer awareness and preference, P&G is now taking a leading role in building its brands on the Web. It's also infusing stronger emotional appeals into its communications to create deeper consumer connections.
- ***Aggressive sales force:*** P&G's sales force has been named one of the top 25 sales forces by *Sales & Marketing Management* magazine. A key to its success is the close ties its sales force forms with retailers, notably Wal-Mart. The 150-person team that serves the retail giant works closely with Wal-Mart to improve both the products that go to the stores and the process by which they get there.
- ***Manufacturing efficiency and cost cutting:*** P&G's reputation as a great marketing company is matched by its excellence as a manufacturing company. P&G spends large sums developing and improving production operations to keep its costs among the lowest in the industry, allowing it to reduce the premium prices at which some of its goods sell.
- ***Brand-management system:*** P&G originated the brand-management system, in which one executive is responsible for each brand. The system has been copied by many competitors but not often with P&G's success. Recently, P&G modified its general management structure so that each brand category is now run by a category manager with volume and profit responsibility. Although this new organization does not replace the brand-management system, it helps to sharpen strategic focus on key consumer needs and competition in the category.

It's easy to see that P&G's success is based not on doing one thing well, but on successfully orchestrating the myriad factors that contribute to market leadership.

Sources: Robert Berner, "Detergent Can Be So Much More," *BusinessWeek*, May 1, 2006, pp. 66–68; "A Post-Modern Proctoid," *The Economist*, April 15, 2006, p. 68; *P&G Fact Sheet* (December 2006); John Galvin, "The World on a String," *Point* (February 2005): 13–24; Jack Neff, "P&G Kisses Up to the Boss: Consumers," *Advertising Age*, May 2, 2005, p. 18; www.pg.com.

MARKETING INSIGHT | BRAND COOKING WITH JAMIE OLIVER

Jamie Oliver got his start as a chef at London's River Café. In 1997, when he was prominently featured in a TV documentary about the restaurant, his engaging personality led five different TV production companies to contact him the next day. His resulting television show on cooking, "The Naked Chef," became a worldwide hit, and a celebrity chef was born. Oliver has since leveraged his cooking fame and reputation to launch a number of successful new products:

- Seven books published internationally in 26 languages with over 14 million sold worldwide
- Eleven different television series with over 123 episodes shown in over 60 countries
- Eleven DVDs distributed in 25 countries
- Two U.K.-based newspaper columns syndicated in 5 countries
- Jamie Oliver Professional Series of pots and pans, bakeware, and kitchen accessories, licensed by Tefal (American spelling is T-Fal) and sold in department stores in 15 countries
- Porcelain tableware and serveware licensed by Royal Worcester
- New products such as the Flavour Shaker, traditional Italian pasta sauces, antipasti, olive oils, and vinegars
- A Web site, jamieoliver.com, that logs 250,000 unique visitors per month

An endorser for U.K. supermarket giant Sainsbury since 2000, Jamie Oliver is also credited with helping the chain's "Recipe for Success" campaign deliver a staggering £1.12 billion of incremental revenue. The company believes the campaign has been 65% more effective than any of its other campaigns.

Besides these commercial ventures, Oliver has a philanthropic side. For instance, he created the Fifteen Foundation whose mission is to "inspire young people." An important activity was the introduction of the Fifteen restaurant in London in 2002 that trains 15 disadvantaged young people to work in the hospitality industry. Additional restaurants in Amsterdam, Melbourne, and Cornwall have followed. Oliver next turned his sights on a high-profile campaign "to ban the junk in schools and get kids eating fresh, tasty, nutritious food instead." Dialogue, publicity, and new school food standards have resulted.

Jamie Oliver has skillfully managed his career as a brand.

Jamie Oliver clearly has a strong brand and benefits from all its advantages. And like any strong brand, his has a well-defined brand image and appealing brand promise. Figure 9.1 displays a BrandPrint assembled to help his marketing brand trust to better understand and explain their brand. Oliver's success in brand building is reflected in the profitable financial performance of the company he created to manage his businesses, Sweet as Candy Limited.

Source: Tessa Graham, Sweet as Candy Limited.

to the brand, as well as in the prices, market share, and profitability the brand commands for the firm.

Marketers and researchers use various perspectives to study brand equity.[13] Customer-based approaches view it from the perspective of the consumer—either an individual or an organization.[14] The premise of customer-based brand equity models is that the power of a brand lies in what customers have seen, read, heard, learned, thought, and felt about the brand over time.[15]

Customer-based brand equity is the differential effect that brand knowledge has on consumer response to the marketing of that brand.[16] A brand has *positive* customer-based brand equity when consumers react more favorably to a product and the way it is marketed when the brand is *identified,* than when it is not identified. A brand has negative customer-based brand equity if consumers react less favorably to marketing activity for the brand under the same circumstances. There are three key ingredients of customer-based brand equity.

First, brand equity arises from differences in consumer response. If no differences occur, then the brand name product is essentially a commodity or generic version of the product.[17] Competition will probably be based on price.

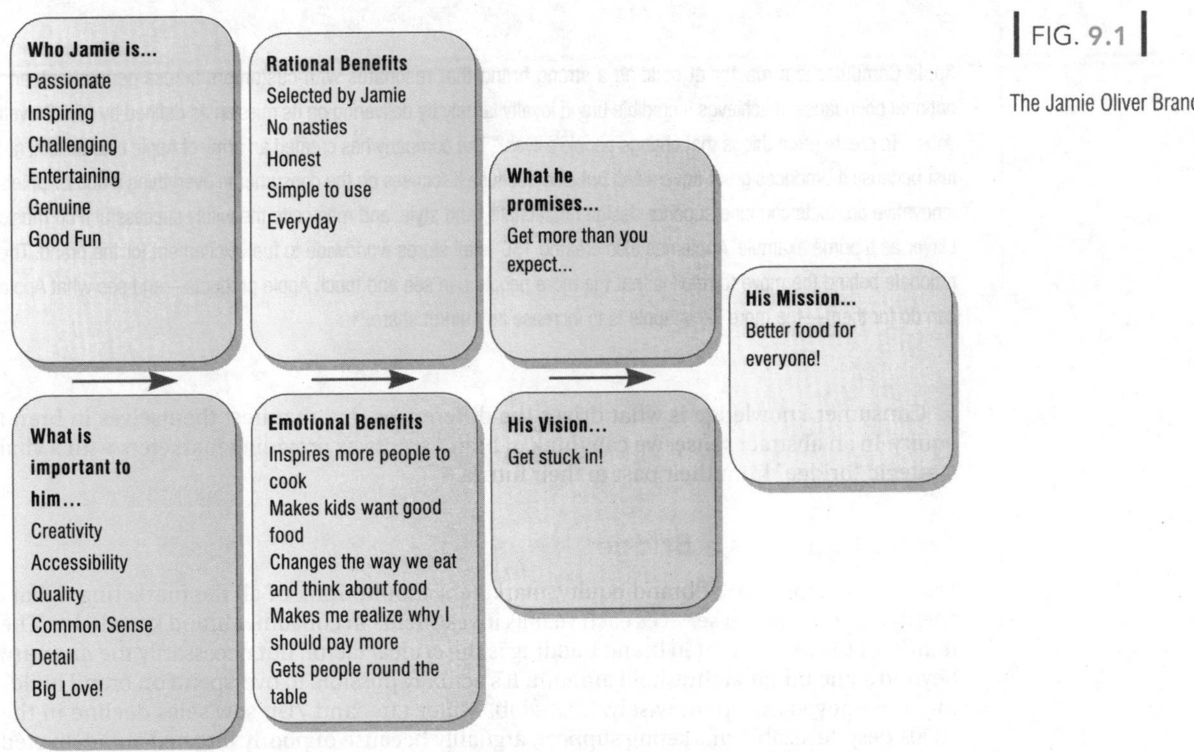

FIG. 9.1

The Jamie Oliver Brand Print

Second, differences in response are a result of consumer's knowledge about the brand. **Brand knowledge** consists of all the thoughts, feelings, images, experiences, beliefs, and so on that become associated with the brand. In particular, brands must create strong, favorable, and unique brand associations with customers, as have Volvo *(safety)*, Hallmark *(caring)*, and Harley-Davidson *(adventure)*.

Third, the differential response by consumers that makes up brand equity is reflected in perceptions, preferences, and behavior related to all aspects of the marketing of a brand. Stronger brands lead to greater revenue.[18] Table 9.1 summarizes some of these key benefits of brand equity.

The challenge for marketers in building a strong brand is therefore ensuring that customers have the right type of experiences with products, services, and their marketing programs to create the desired brand knowledge.

TABLE 9.1

Marketing Advantages of Strong Brands

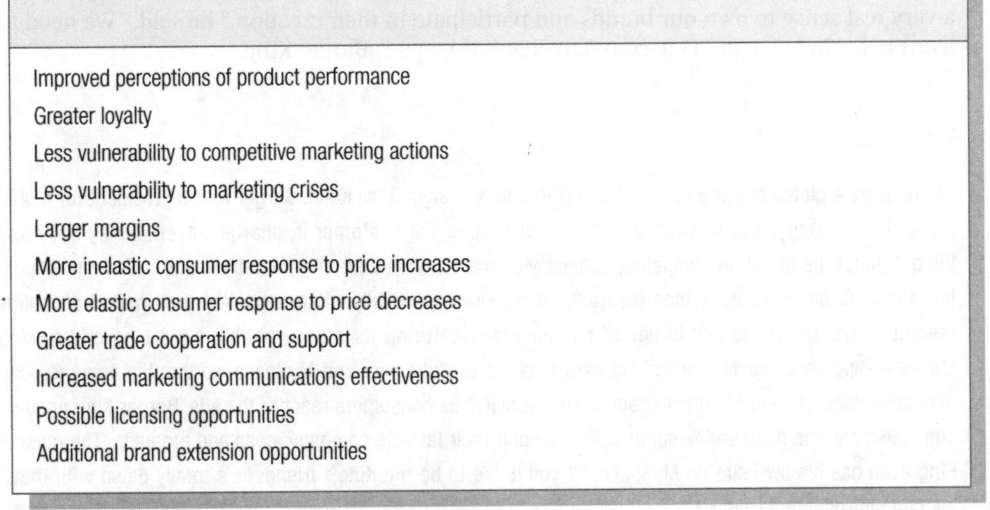

Improved perceptions of product performance
Greater loyalty
Less vulnerability to competitive marketing actions
Less vulnerability to marketing crises
Larger margins
More inelastic consumer response to price increases
More elastic consumer response to price decreases
Greater trade cooperation and support
Increased marketing communications effectiveness
Possible licensing opportunities
Additional brand extension opportunities

APPLE COMPUTER

Apple Computer is a master at building a strong brand that resonates with customers across generations and national boundaries. It achieves incredible brand loyalty largely by delivering on its mission as defined by CEO Steven Jobs: "To create great things that change people's lives." The company has created an army of Apple evangelists, not just because it produces great advertising but also because it focuses on the consumer in everything it does. Apple's innovative products combine superior design functionality and style, and many cite the wildly successful iPod music player as a prime example. Apple has also created 150 retail stores worldwide to fuel excitement for the brand. The rationale behind the move to retail is that the more people can see and touch Apple products—and see what Apple can do for them—the more likely Apple is to increase its market share.[19]

Consumer knowledge is what drives the differences that manifest themselves in brand equity. In an abstract sense, we can think of brand equity as providing marketers with a vital strategic "bridge" from their past to their future.[20]

Brand Equity as a Bridge

From the perspective of brand equity, marketers should think of all the marketing dollars spent on products and services each year as investments in consumer brand knowledge. The *quality* of the investment in brand building is the critical factor, not necessarily the *quantity*, beyond some minimal threshold amount. It's actually possible to overspend on brand building, if money is not spent wisely. Michelob, Miller Lite, and 7Up saw sales decline in the 1990s despite sizable marketing support, arguably because of poorly targeted and delivered marketing campaigns.

At the same time, the brand knowledge created by marketing investments dictates appropriate future directions for the brand. Consumers will decide, based on what they think and feel about the brand, where (and how) they believe the brand should go and grant permission (or not) to any marketing action or program. New products such as Crystal Pepsi, Levi's Tailored Classic suits, Fruit of the Loom laundry detergent, and Cracker Jack cereal failed because consumers found them inappropriate extensions for the brand.

A **brand promise** is the marketer's vision of what the brand must be and do for consumers. At the end of the day, the true value and future prospects of a brand rest with consumers, their knowledge about the brand, and their likely response to marketing activity as a result of this knowledge. Understanding consumer brand knowledge—all the different things that become linked to the brand in the minds of consumers—is thus of paramount importance because it is the foundation of brand equity.

Oxford University's Douglas Holt believes for companies to build iconic, leadership brands, they must assemble cultural knowledge, strategize according to cultural branding principles, and hire and train cultural experts.[21] Even Procter & Gamble, a company that has long orchestrated how shoppers perceive its products, has started on what its chief executive, A. G. Lafley, calls "a learning journey" with the consumer. "Consumers are beginning in a very real sense to own our brands and participate in their creation," he said. "We need to learn to begin to let go." One company that has let go is Burger King.

BURGER KING

"If you have a global brand promise, 'Have It Your Way'," says Russ Klein, Burger King's president for global marketing, strategy, and innovation; "it's about putting the customer in charge," even if they say "bad things" about the brand. In competing against McDonald's, with its family-friendly image, "it's more important for us to be provocative than pleasant," adds Klein, especially when appealing to a market of mainly teenage boys. Burger King's brash ad campaigns—featuring its creepy bobble-head king and talking chicken—appear on social networking sites such as YouTube.com and MySpace, so that the company can take advantage of what Klein calls "social connectivity" as consumers react to the ads. Burger King encourages customers to build online communities around their favorite company icons and products. The mascot King even has his own site on MySpace. "If you'd like to be the King's friend, he's totally down with that," his page introduction says.[22]

Brand Equity Models

Although marketers agree about basic branding principles, a number of models of brand equity offer some different perspectives. Here we highlight four of the more-established ones.

BRAND ASSET VALUATOR Advertising agency Young and Rubicam (Y&R) developed a model of brand equity called brand asset valuator (BAV). Based on research with almost 500,000 consumers in 44 countries, BAV provides comparative measures of the brand equity of thousands of brands across hundreds of different categories. There are five key components—or pillars—of brand equity, according to BAV:

- ***Differentiation*** measures the degree to which a brand is seen as different from others.
- ***Energy*** measures the brand's sense of momentum.
- ***Relevance*** measures the breadth of a brand's appeal.
- ***Esteem*** measures how well the brand is regarded and respected.
- ***Knowledge*** measures how familiar and intimate consumers are with the brand.

Differentiation, Energy, and Relevance combine to determine *Energized Brand Strength.* These three pillars point to the brand's future value. Esteem and Knowledge together create *Brand Stature,* which is more of a "report card" on past performance.

The relationships among these dimensions—a brand's "pillar pattern"—reveal much about a brand's current and future status. Energized Brand Strength and Brand Stature combined form the *Power Grid,* depicting the stages in the cycle of brand development—each with characteristic pillar patterns—in successive quadrants (see Figure 9.2). Strong new brands show higher levels of Differentiation and Energy than Relevance, whereas both Esteem and Knowledge are lower still. Leadership brands show high levels on all pillars. Finally, declining brands show high Knowledge—evidence of past performance—a lower level of Esteem, and even lower Relevance, Energy, and Differentiation.

BRANDZ Marketing research consultants Millward Brown and WPP have developed the BRANDZ model of brand strength, at the heart of which is the BrandDynamics pyramid. According to this model, brand building follows a sequential series of steps, each contingent upon successfully accomplishing the preceding one (see Figure 9.3).

"Bonded" consumers, those at the top of the pyramid, build stronger relationships with the brand and spend more on it than those at lower levels. More consumers, however, will be found at the lower levels. The challenge for marketers is to develop activities and programs that help consumers move up the pyramid.

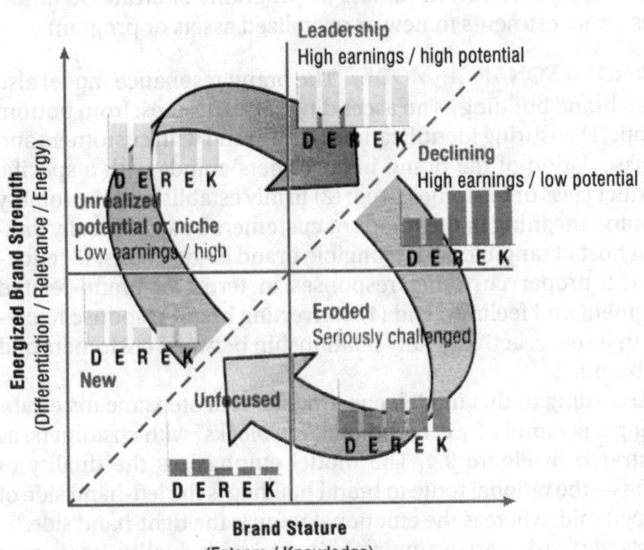

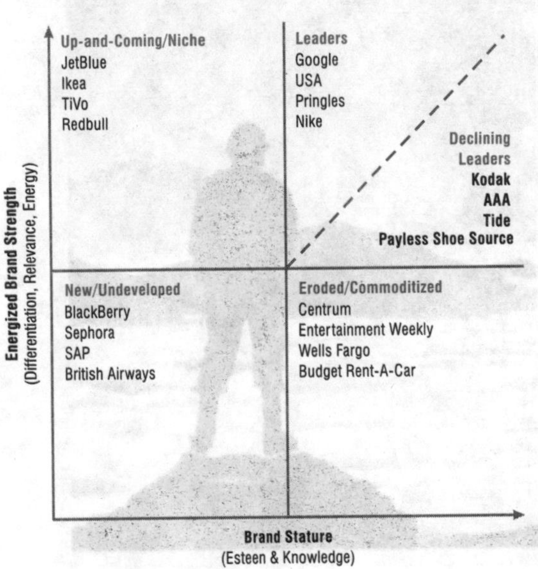

FIG. 9.2 BAV Power Grid

FIG. 9.3

BrandDynamics™ Pyramid

Source: BrandDynamics™ Pyramid. Reprinted by permission of MillwardBrown.

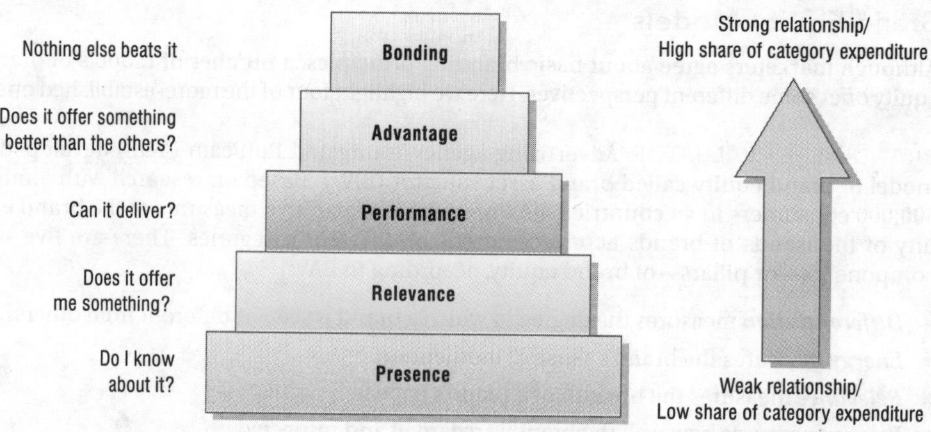

AAKER MODEL Former UC-Berkeley marketing professor David Aaker views brand equity as the brand awareness, brand loyalty, and brand associations that combine to add to or subtract from the value provided by a product or service.[23] According to Aaker, brand management starts with developing a *brand identity*—the unique set of brand associations that represent what the brand stands for and promises to customers, an aspirational brand image.[24] Brand identity is typically 8 to 12 elements that represent concepts such as product scope, product attributes, quality/value, uses, users, country of origin, organizational attributes, brand personality, and symbols. The most important of these, which will drive brand-building programs, are the *core identity elements.* The others, *extended identity elements,* add texture and guidance. In addition, a *brand essence* can communicate the brand identity in a compact and inspiring way.

For example, according to Aaker, Ajax, a large industrial service company, has a brand essence of "Commitment to Excellence—Anytime, Anywhere, Whatever It Takes"; a core identity of "Spirit of Excellence," "Team Solutions," and "Technology That Fits"; and an extended identity of "Worldly But Informal," "Confident and Competent," "Open Communicator," "Global Network of Local Experts," and a "Supporter of World Health." The "Team Solutions" core identity was aspirational for a firm that consisted of several autonomous divisions, but necessary to support its strategy going forward.

Aaker maintains that the identity should be differentiating on some dimensions, suggest parity on others, resonate with customers, drive brand-building programs, reflect the culture and strategy of the business, and be credible. Credibility can be based on proof points, current assets or programs or strategic initiatives, or investments in new or revitalized assets or programs.

MasterCard appeals to "the head and the heart" in its long-running Priceless ad.

BRAND RESONANCE MODEL The brand resonance model also views brand building as an ascending series of steps, from bottom to top: (1) ensuring identification of the brand with customers and an association of the brand in customers' minds with a specific product class or customer need; (2) firmly establishing the totality of brand meaning in the minds of customers by strategically linking a host of tangible and intangible brand associations; (3) eliciting the proper customer responses in terms of brand-related judgment and feelings; and (4) converting brand response to create an intense, active loyalty relationship between customers and the brand.

According to this model, enacting the four steps means establishing a pyramid of six "brand building blocks" with customers, as illustrated in Figure 9.4. The model emphasizes the duality of brands—the rational route to brand building is the left-hand side of the pyramid, whereas the emotional route is the right-hand side.[25]

MasterCard is an example of a brand with duality, because it emphasizes both the rational advantages of the credit card—its acceptance at establishments worldwide, as well as the emotional advantages—expressed in the award-winning "Priceless" adver-

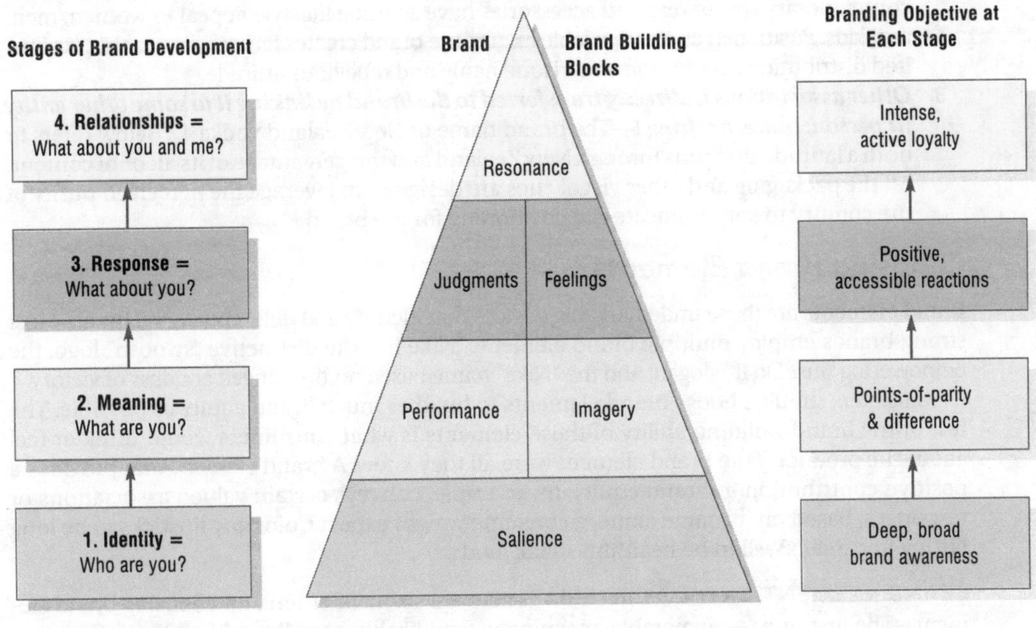

FIG. 9.4 Brand Resonance Pyramid

tising campaign, which shows people buying items to reach a certain goal. The goal itself—a feeling, an accomplishment, or other intangible—is "priceless" ("There are some things money can't buy; for everything else, there's MasterCard.").

The creation of significant brand equity requires reaching the top or pinnacle of the brand pyramid, which occurs only if the right building blocks are put into place.

- ***Brand salience*** is how often and how easily customers think of the brand under various purchase or consumption situations.
- ***Brand performance*** is how well the product or service meets customers' functional needs.
- ***Brand imagery*** describes the extrinsic properties of the product or service, including the ways in which the brand attempts to meet customers' psychological or social needs.
- ***Brand judgments*** focus on customers' own personal opinions and evaluations.
- ***Brand feelings*** are customers' emotional responses and reactions with respect to the brand.
- ***Brand resonance*** refers to the nature of the relationship customers have with the brand and the extent to which they feel they're "in sync" with it.

Resonance is the intensity or depth of the psychological bond customers have with the brand, as well as the level of activity engendered by this loyalty.[26] Brands with high resonance include Harley-Davidson, Apple, and eBay. Fox News has found that the higher levels of resonance and engagement its programs engender often leads to greater recall of the ads it runs.[27]

::: Building Brand Equity

Marketers build brand equity by creating the right brand knowledge structures with the right consumers. This process depends on *all* brand-related contacts—whether marketer initiated or not. From a marketing management perspective, however, there are three main sets of *brand equity drivers:*

1. ***The initial choices for the brand elements or identities making up the brand (brand names, URLs, logos, symbols, characters, spokespeople, slogans, jingles, packages, and signage)***—By creating a line of nontoxic household cleaning products with bright colors and sleek designs totally unique to the category, Method racked up $32 million in sales in 2005. Because of a limited advertising budget, the company believes its attractive packaging and innovative products must work harder to express the brand positioning.[28]
2. ***The product and service and all accompanying marketing activities and supporting marketing programs***—Liz Claiborne's fastest-growing label is Juicy Couture, whose edgy,

contemporary sportswear and accessories have a strong lifestyle appeal to women, men, and kids. Positioned as an affordable luxury, the brand creates its exclusive cachet via limited distribution and a somewhat risque name and rebellious attitude.[29]

3. ***Other associations indirectly transferred to the brand by linking it to some other entity (a person, place, or thing)***—The brand name of New Zealand vodka 42 Below refers to both a latitude that runs through New Zealand and the percentage of its alcohol content. All the packaging and other visual cues are designed to leverage the perceived purity of the country to communicate the positioning for the brand.[30]

Choosing Brand Elements

Brand elements are those trademarkable devices that identify and differentiate the brand. Most strong brands employ multiple brand elements. Nike has the distinctive "swoosh" logo, the empowering "Just Do It" slogan, and the "Nike" name based on the winged goddess of victory.

Marketers should choose brand elements to build as much brand equity as possible. The test of the brand-building ability of these elements is what consumers would think or feel about the product *if* the brand element were all they knew. A brand element that provides a positive contribution to brand equity, for example, conveys certain valued associations or responses. Based on its name alone, a consumer might expect ColorStay lipsticks to be long lasting and SnackWell to be healthful snack foods.

BRAND ELEMENT CHOICE CRITERIA There are six main criteria for choosing brand elements. The first three—memorable, meaningful, and likable—are "brand building." The latter three—transferable, adaptable, and protectable—are "defensive" and deal with how to leverage and preserve the equity in a brand element in the face of opportunities and constraints.

1. ***Memorable***—How easily is the brand element recalled and recognized? Is this true at both purchase and consumption? Short names such as Tide, Crest, and Puffs are memorable brand elements.
2. ***Meaningful***—Is the brand element credible and suggestive of the corresponding category? Does it suggest something about a product ingredient or the type of person who might use the brand? Consider the inherent meaning in names such as DieHard auto batteries, Mop & Glo floor wax, and Lean Cuisine low-calorie frozen entrees.
3. ***Likable***—How aesthetically appealing is the brand element? Is it likable visually, verbally, and in other ways? Concrete brand names such as Sunkist, Spic and Span, and Thunderbird evoke much imagery.
4. ***Transferable***—Can the brand element be used to introduce new products in the same or different categories? Does it add to brand equity across geographic boundaries and market segments? Although initially an online book seller, Amazon.com was smart enough not to call itself "Books 'R' Us." The Amazon is famous as the world's biggest river, and the name suggests the wide variety of goods that could be shipped, an important descriptor of the diverse range of products the company now sells.
5. ***Adaptable***—How adaptable and updatable is the brand element? The face of Betty Crocker has received more than eight makeovers over her 75 years and she doesn't look a day over 35!
6. ***Protectible***—How legally protectible is the brand element? How competitively protectible? Names that become synonymous with product categories—such as Kleenex, Kitty Litter, Jell-O, Scotch Tape, Xerox, and Fiberglass—should retain their trademark rights and not become generic.

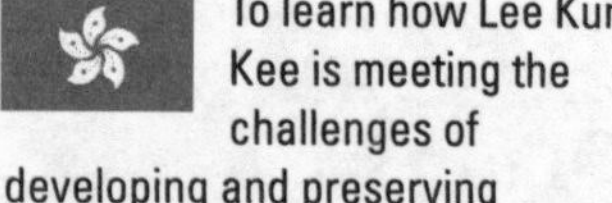
To learn how Lee Kum Kee is meeting the challenges of developing and preserving traditional Asian brands in Hong Kong, visit www.pearsoned-asia.com/marketingmanagementasia.

DEVELOPING BRAND ELEMENTS Brand elements can play a number of brand-building roles.[31] If consumers don't examine much information in making their product decisions, brand elements should be easy to recognize and recall and inherently descriptive and persuasive. The likability and appeal of brand elements may also play a critical role in awareness and associations leading to brand equity.[32] The Keebler elves reinforce home-style baking quality and a sense of magic and fun for their line of cookies.

Of course, brand names aren't the only important brand element. Often, the less concrete brand benefits are, the more important it is that brand elements capture intangible characteristics. Many insurance firms have used symbols of strength (the Rock of Gibraltar for Prudential and the stag for Hartford), security (the "good hands" of Allstate, Traveller's umbrella, and the hard hat of Fireman's Fund), or some combination of the two (the castle for Fortis).

Like brand names, slogans are an extremely efficient means to build brand equity. They can function as useful "hooks" or "handles" to help consumers grasp what the brand is and what makes it special, summarizing and translating the intent of a marketing program. Think of the inherent brand meaning in slogans such as "Like a Good Neighbor, State Farm Is There," "Nothing Runs Like a Deere," and "We Try Harder" for Avis rental cars.

AVIS GROUP HOLDINGS INC.

A classic example of a slogan that builds brand equity is Avis's 41-year-old "We Try Harder." In 1963, when the campaign was developed, Avis was losing money and widely considered the number-two car rental company next to market leader Hertz. When account executives from DDB ad agency met with Avis managers, they asked: "What can you do that we can say you do better than your competitors?" An Avis manager replied, "We try harder because we have to." Someone at DDB wrote this down and it became the heart of the campaign. Avis was hesitant to air the campaign because of its blunt, break-the-rules honesty, but also because the company had to deliver on that promise. Yet, by creating buy-in on "We Try Harder" from all Avis employees, especially its frontline employees at the rental desks, the company was able to create a company culture and brand image from an advertising slogan that lives to this day.[33]

But choosing a name with inherent meaning creates less flexibility, making it harder to add a different meaning or update the positioning.[34]

Designing Holistic Marketing Activities

Brands are not built by advertising alone. Customers come to know a brand through a range of contacts and touch points: personal observation and use, word of mouth, interactions with company personnel, online or telephone experiences, and payment transactions. A **brand contact** is any information-bearing experience, whether positive or negative, a customer or prospect has with the brand, the product category, or the market that relates to the marketer's product or service.[35] The company must put as much effort into managing these experiences as into producing its ads.[36]

The strategy and tactics behind marketing programs have changed dramatically in recent years.[37] Marketers are creating brand contacts and building brand equity through many avenues, such as clubs and consumer communities, trade shows, event marketing, sponsorship, factory visits, public relations and press releases, and social cause marketing. Marketers of Mountain Dew created the multicity Dew Action Sports Tour where athletes compete in skateboarding, BMX, and freestyle motocross events to reach the coveted but fickle 12–24-year-old target market.[38]

Regardless of the particular tools or approaches they choose, holistic marketers emphasize three important new themes in designing brand-building marketing programs: personalization, integration, and internalization.

PERSONALIZATION The rapid expansion of the Internet has created opportunities to personalize marketing.[39] Marketers are increasingly abandoning the mass-market practices that built brand powerhouses in the 1950s, 1960s, and 1970s for new approaches that are in fact a throwback to marketing practices from a century ago, when merchants literally knew their customers by name. *Personalizing marketing* is about making sure the brand and its marketing are as relevant as possible to as many customers as possible—a challenge, given that no two customers are identical.

JONES SODA

Peter van Stolk founded Jones Soda on the premise that Gen Y consumers would be more accepting of a new soft-drink brand if they felt they discovered it themselves. Jones Soda initially was sold only in shops that sell surfboards, snowboards, and skateboards. The Jones Soda Web site encourages fans to send in personal photos for possible use on Jones Soda labels. Although only a small number can be picked from the tens of thousands of entries, the approach helps to create relevance and an emotional connection. Customers can also purchase bottles with customized labels. Famous for unusual flavors such as Turkey and Gravy, Pineapple Upside Down, Berry White (a pun on singer Barry White), Purple Carrot, and Lemon Drop Dead, the company also adds pithy words of wisdom from customers under the bottle cap to create additional relevance and distinctiveness. The approach has worked—revenue for 2006 exceeded $39 million and has been growing at 15–30% annually.[40]

Initially sold only in sporting-goods stores that cater to surfing and snowboarding, Jones Soda has forged a unique connection with customers by offering personalized bottles and by encouraging customers to send personal photos as candidates for product labels.

To adapt to the increased consumer desire for personalization, marketers have embraced concepts such as experiential marketing, one-to-one marketing, and permission marketing. From a branding point of view, these different concepts are about getting consumers more actively involved with a brand.

Permission marketing, the practice of marketing to consumers only after gaining their express permission, is based on the premise that marketers can no longer use "interruption marketing" via mass-media campaigns. According to Seth Godin, a pioneer in the technique, marketers can develop stronger consumer relationships by respecting consumers' wishes and sending messages only when they express a willingness to become more involved with the brand.[41] Godin believes permission marketing works because it is "anticipated, personal, and relevant."

Permission marketing, like other personalization concepts, does presume consumers know what they want. But in many cases, consumers have undefined, ambiguous, or conflicting preferences. "Participatory marketing" may be a more appropriate concept than permission marketing, because marketers and consumers need to work together to find out how the firm can best satisfy consumers.

INTEGRATION The traditional "marketing-mix" concept and the notion of the "four Ps" do not adequately describe modern marketing programs. **Integration marketing** is about mixing and matching marketing activities to maximize their individual and collective effects.[42] To achieve it, marketers need a variety of different marketing activities that reinforce the brand promise. The Olive Garden has become the second-largest casual dining restaurant chain in the United States, with $2.6 billion in sales and record profits in 2005 from their 582 North American restaurants, in part through establishing a fully integrated marketing program.

THE OLIVE GARDEN

The Olive Garden brand promise is "the idealized Italian family meal" characterized by "fresh, simple, delicious Italian food," "complemented by a great glass of wine," served by "people who treat you like family," "in a comfortable homelike setting." To live up to that brand promise, The Olive Garden sends select managers and servers on cultural immersion trips to Italy; launched the Culinary Institute of Tuscany in Italy to inspire new dishes; conducts wine training workshops for employees and in-restaurant wine sampling for customers; and remodeled restaurants to give them a Tuscan farmhouse look. Communications include in-store, employee, and mass-media messages that all reinforce the brand promise and ad slogan, "When You're Here, You're Family."[43]

We can evaluate all integrated marketing activities in terms of the effectiveness and efficiency with which they affect brand awareness and create, maintain, or strengthen brand image.

Let's distinguish between brand identity and image. *Identity* is the way a company aims to identify or position itself or its product. *Image* is the way the public actually perceives them. For the right image to be established in the minds of consumers, the marketer must convey brand identity through every available communication vehicle and brand contact.

Identity should be diffused in ads, annual reports, brochures, catalogs, packaging, company stationery, and business cards. If "IBM means service," this message must be expressed in symbols, colors and slogans, atmosphere, events, and employee behavior. Although it's fast becoming an economic powerhouse, China is late in the game when it comes to developing these aspects of branding—both image and identity—but some Chinese companies are learning fast.

HAIER

If one company can subvert China's old reputation for producing low-cost but shoddy products, it's the white-goods manufacturer Haier (pronounced *higher*). Adopting the strategy of successful Japanese and Korean companies, Haier concentrated on building a big market at home and then going on the offensive overseas. Since entering the U.S. market in 1999, it has become the top-selling brand of compact refrigerators, the kind in college dorm rooms. Yet, the company had to rely on innovation to get past a reputation for producing me-too products. The product that really got Haier noticed was a free-standing home wine cooler—a more convenient way of storing wine for the growing number of wine aficionados. Another way Haier is going for a more premium-priced image is by producing a line of eco-friendly, technology-rich appliances, priced at $600–$1,500, compared with the $200–$300 range of its white goods. Its Genesis top-loading washing machine and a dishwasher with a particle sensor to detect when plates are clean and an automatic shutoff to save energy are among its newest offerings.[44]

Different marketing activities have different strengths and can accomplish different objectives. Marketers should therefore engage in a mixture of activities, each of which plays a specific role in building or maintaining brand equity. Although Michelin may invest in R&D and engage in advertising, promotions, and other communications to reinforce its "safety" brand association, it may also choose to sponsor events to make sure it is seen as contemporary and up-to-date. Marketing programs should be put together so that the whole is greater than the sum of the parts. In other words, the effects of any one option should be enhanced or complemented by the presence of another.

INTERNALIZATION Marketers must now "walk the walk" to deliver the brand promise. They must adopt an *internal* perspective to be sure employees and marketing partners appreciate and understand basic branding notions and how they can help—or hurt—brand equity.[45] **Internal branding** is activities and processes that help to inform and inspire employees.[46] It is critical for service companies and retailers that all employees have an up-to-date, deep understanding of the brand and its promise. Holistic marketers must go even further and train and encourage distributors and dealers to serve their customers well. Poorly trained dealers can ruin the best efforts to build a strong brand image.

Brand bonding occurs when customers experience the company as delivering on its brand promise. All the customers' contacts with company employees and company communications must be positive.[47] *The brand promise will not be delivered unless everyone in the company lives the brand.* Disney is so successful at internal branding and having employees support its brand that it holds seminars on the "Disney Style" for employees from other companies.

ELI LILLY

In 2000, Eli Lilly launched a new brand-building initiative with the slogan, "Answers That Matter." The aim was to establish Eli Lilly as a pharmaceutical firm that could give doctors, patients, hospitals, HMOs, and governments trustworthy answers to questions of concern to them. To make sure everyone at Eli Lilly could deliver the right answers, the company developed a comprehensive Brand-to-Action training program. These sessions educated and engaged employees in the role of the corporate brand, Lilly's intended positioning, and how employees' behavior affected the customer experience and key touch points. Lilly also set up a brand governance structure, began to measure their corporate brand image, and developed a communications plan for the corporate branding effort.[48]

When employees care about and believe in the brand, they're motivated to work harder and feel greater loyalty to the firm. Some important principles for internal branding are:[49]

1. ***Choose the right moment***—Turning points are ideal opportunities to capture employees' attention and imagination. BP found that after it ran an internal branding campaign to accompany its external repositioning, "Beyond Petroleum," most employees were positive about the new brand and thought the company was going in the right direction.
2. ***Link internal and external marketing***—Internal and external messages must match. IBM's e-business campaign not only helped to change public perceptions of the company in the marketplace, it also sent a signal to employees that IBM was determined to be a leader in the use of Internet technology.
3. ***Bring the brand alive for employees***—A professional branding campaign should be based on marketing research and supervised by the marketing department. Internal communications should be informative and energizing. To improve employee morale, Miller Brewing has tapped into its brewing heritage to generate some pride and passion.

Leveraging Secondary Associations

The third and final way to build brand equity is, in effect, to "borrow" it. That is, create brand equity by linking the brand to other information in memory that conveys meaning to consumers (see Figure 9.5).

These "secondary" brand associations can link the brand to sources, such as the company itself (through branding strategies), to countries or other geographical regions (through identification of product origin), and to channels of distribution (through channel strategy); as well as to other brands (through ingredient or co-branding), characters (through licensing), spokespeople (through endorsements), sporting or cultural events (through sponsorship), or some other third-party sources (through awards or reviews).

FIG. 9.5

Secondary Sources of Brand Knowledge

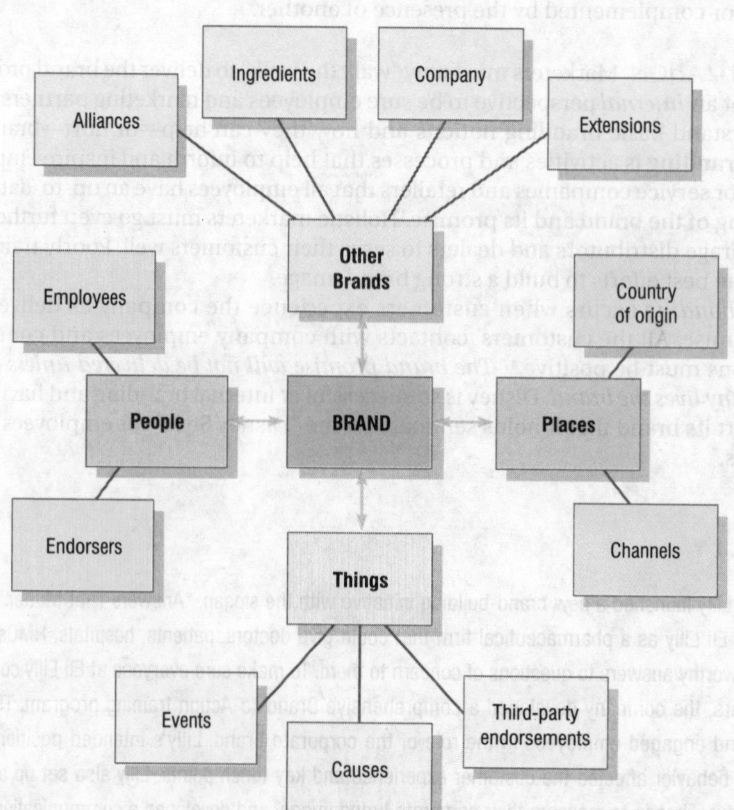

For example, assume Burton—makers of snowboards as well as ski boots, bindings, clothing, and outerwear—decided to introduce a new surfboard called "The Dominator." Burton has gained over a third of the snowboard market by closely aligning itself with top professional riders and creating a strong amateur snowboarder community around the country. In creating the marketing program to support the new Dominator surfboard, Burton could attempt to leverage secondary brand knowledge in a number of different ways:

- It could leverage associations to the corporate brand by "subbranding" the product, calling it "Dominator by Burton." Consumers' evaluations of the new product would be influenced by how they felt about Burton and how they felt that such knowledge predicted the quality of a Burton surfboard.
- Burton could rely on its rural New England origins, but such a geographical location would seem to have little relevance to surfing.
- Burton could also sell through popular surf shops in the hope that its credibility would "rub off" on the Dominator brand.
- Burton could co-brand by identifying a strong ingredient brand for its foam or fiberglass materials (as Wilson did by incorporating Goodyear tire rubber on the soles of its ProStaff Classic tennis shoes).
- Burton could find one or more top professional surfers to endorse the surfboard, or it could sponsor a surfing competition or even the entire Association of Surfing Professionals (ASP) World Tour.
- Burton could secure and publicize favorable ratings from third-party sources such as *Surfer* or *Surfing* magazine.

Thus, independent of the associations created by the surfboard itself, its brand name, or any other aspects of the marketing program, Burton could build equity by linking the brand to these other entities.

::: Measuring Brand Equity

Given that the power of a brand resides in the minds of consumers and the way it changes their response to marketing, there are two basic approaches to measuring brand equity. An *indirect* approach assesses potential sources of brand equity by identifying and tracking consumer brand knowledge structures.[50] A *direct* approach assesses the actual impact of brand knowledge on consumer response to different aspects of the marketing. "Marketing Insight: The Brand Value Chain" shows how to link the two approaches.[51]

The two general approaches are complementary, and marketers can employ both. In other words, for brand equity to perform a useful strategic function and guide marketing decisions, marketers need to fully understand (1) the sources of brand equity and how they affect outcomes of interest, as well as (2) how these sources and outcomes change, if at all, over time. Brand audits are important for the former; brand tracking for the latter.

A **brand audit** is a consumer-focused series of procedures to assess the health of the brand, uncover its sources of brand equity, and suggest ways to improve and leverage its equity. Marketers should conduct a brand audit whenever they're considering important shifts in strategic direction. Conducting brand audits on a regular basis, such as annually, allows marketers to keep their fingers on the pulse of their brands so they can manage them more proactively and responsively. Audits are particularly useful background for managers as they set up their marketing plans.

Brand-tracking studies collect quantitative data from consumers on a routine basis over time to provide marketers with consistent, baseline information about how their brands and marketing programs are performing on key dimensions. Tracking studies are a means of understanding where, how much, and in what ways brand value is being created, to facilitate day-to-day decision making.

MARKETING INSIGHT | THE BRAND VALUE CHAIN

The **brand value chain** is a structured approach to assessing the sources and outcomes of brand equity and the manner in which marketing activities create brand value (see Figure 9.6). It is based on several premises.

First, the brand value creation process is assumed to begin when the firm invests in a marketing program targeting actual or potential customers. Any marketing program investment that can be attributed to brand value development, intentional or not, falls into this category—product research, development, and design; trade or intermediary support; and marketing communications.

Next, customers' mindsets are assumed to change as a result of the marketing program. The question is how. This change, in turn, is assumed to affect the way the brand performs in the marketplace through the collective impact of individual customers deciding how much to purchase and when, how much they'll they pay, and so on. Finally, the investment community considers market performance and other factors such as replacement cost and purchase price in acquisitions to arrive at an assessment of shareholder value in general and the value of a brand in particular.

The model also assumes that a number of linking factors intervene between these stages and determine the extent to which value created at one stage transfers to the next stage. Three sets of multipliers moderate the transfer between the marketing program and the subsequent three value stages—the program multiplier, the customer multiplier, and the market multiplier.

The *program multiplier* determines the marketing program's ability to affect the customer mind-set and is a function of the quality of the program investment. The *customer multiplier* determines the extent to which value created in the minds of customers affects market performance. This result depends on contextual factors external to the customer.

Three such factors are:

- competitive superiority—how effective the quantity and quality of the marketing investment of other competing brands are
- channel and other intermediary support—how much brand reinforcement and selling effort various marketing partners are putting forth
- customer size and profile—how many and what types of customers, profitable or not, are attracted to the brand

The *market multiplier* determines the extent to which the value shown by the market performance of a brand is manifested in shareholder value. It depends, in part, on the actions of financial analysts and investors.

Sources: Kevin Lane Keller and Don Lehmann, "How Do Brands Create Value," *Marketing Management* (May–June 2003): 27–31. See also, Marc J. Epstein and Robert A. Westbrook, "Linking Actions to Profits in Strategic Decision Making," *MIT Sloan Management Review* (Spring 2001): 39–49; and Rajendra K. Srivastava, Tasadduq A. Shervani, and Liam Fahey, "Market-Based Assets and Shareholder Value," *Journal of Marketing* 62, no. 1 (January 1998): 2–18.

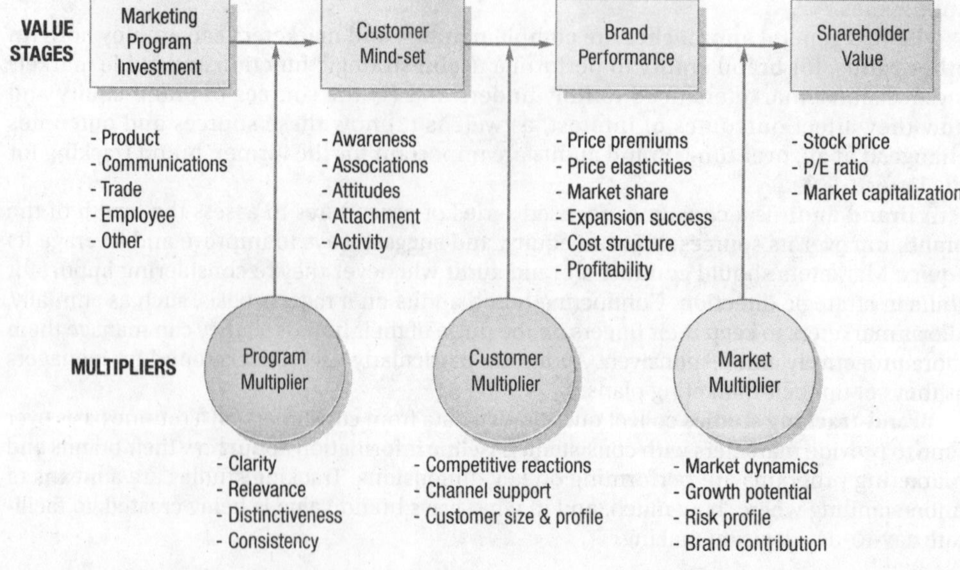

FIG. 9.6 Brand Value Chain

Source: Kevin Lane Keller, Strategic Brand Management, 3rd ed. (Upper Saddle River, NJ: Prentice Hall, 2008). Reproduced by permission of Pearson Education, Inc. Upper Saddle River, New Jersey.

TABLE 9.2

The World's 10 Most Valuable Brands in 2006

Rank	Brand	2006 Brand Value (Billions)
1	Coca-Cola	$67.00
2	Microsoft	$56.93
3	IBM	$56.20
4	GE	$48.91
5	Intel	$38.32
6	Nokia	$30.13
7	Toyota	$27.94
8	Disney	$27.85
9	McDonald's	$27.50
10	Mercedes-Benz	$22.13

Brand Valuation

Marketers should distinguish brand equity from **brand valuation**, which is the job of estimating the total financial value of the brand. Table 9.2 displays the world's most valuable brands in 2006 according to one ranking.[52] In these well-known companies, brand value is typically over half the total company market capitalization. John Stuart, cofounder of Quaker Oats, said: "If this business were split up, I would give you the land and bricks and mortar, and I would take the brands and trademarks, and I would fare better than you." U.S. companies do not list brand equity on their balance sheets because of the arbitrariness of the estimate. However, brand equity is given a value by some companies in the United Kingdom, Hong Kong, and Australia. "Marketing Insight: What Is a Brand Worth?" reviews one popular valuation approach.

::: Managing Brand Equity

Effective brand management requires a long-term view of marketing actions. Because consumer responses to marketing activity depend on what they know and remember about a brand, short-term marketing actions, by changing brand knowledge, necessarily increase or decrease the long-term success of future marketing actions.

Brand Reinforcement

As a company's major enduring asset, a brand needs to be carefully managed so that its value does not depreciate.[53] Many brand leaders of 70 years ago remain brand leaders today—Wrigley's, Coca-Cola, Heinz, and Campbell Soup—but only by constantly striving to improve their products, services, and marketing.

Brand equity is reinforced by marketing actions that consistently convey the meaning of the brand in terms of: (1) What products the brand represents, what core benefits it supplies, and what needs it satisfies, as well as (2) how the brand makes products superior, and which strong, favorable, and unique brand associations should exist in the minds of consumers.[54] Nivea, one of Europe's strongest brands, has expanded its scope from a skin cream brand to a skin care and personal care brand through carefully designed and implemented brand extensions reinforcing the Nivea brand promise of "mild," "gentle," and "caring" in a broader arena.

Reinforcing brand equity requires innovation and relevance throughout the marketing program. The brand must always be moving forward—but moving forward in the right direction, with new and compelling offerings and ways to market them. Brands that fail to move foreward—such as Kmart, Levi Strauss, Montgomery Ward, Oldsmobile, and Polaroid—find that their market leadership dwindles or even disappears.

MARKETING INSIGHT | WHAT IS A BRAND WORTH?

Top brand management firm Interbrand has developed a model to formally estimate the dollar value of a brand. Interbrand defines Brand Value as the net present value of the earnings a brand is expected to generate in the future and believes both marketing and financial analyses are equally important in determining the value of a brand. Its process follows the following five steps (see Figure 9.7 for a schematic overview):

1. **Market Segmentation**—The first step in the brand valuation process is to divide the market(s) in which the brand is sold into mutually exclusive segments of customers that help to determine the variances in the brand's economic value.
2. **Financial Analysis**—Interbrand assesses purchase price, volume, and frequency to help calculate accurate forecasts of future brand sales and revenues. Specifically, Interbrand performs a detailed review of the brand's equities, industry and customer trends, and historic financial performance across each segment. Once it has established Branded Revenues, it deducts all associated operating costs to derive earnings before interest and tax (EBIT). It also deducts the appropriate taxes and a charge for the capital employed to operate the underlying business, leaving Intangible Earnings, that is, the earnings attributed to the intangible assets of the business.
3. **Role of Branding**—Interbrand next attributes a proportion of intangible earnings to the brand in each market segment, by first identifying the various drivers of demand, then determining the degree to which the brand directly influences each. The Role of Branding assessment is based on market research, client workshops, and interviews and represents the percentage of intangible earnings the brand generates. Multiplying the Role of Branding by Intangible Earnings yields brand earnings.
4. **Brand Strength**—Interbrand then assesses the brand's strength profile to determine the likelihood that the brand will realize forecast earnings. This step relies on competitive benchmarking and a structured evaluation of the brand's market, stability, leadership position, growth trend, support, geographic footprint, and ability to be legally protected. For each segment, Interbrand applies industry and brand equity metrics to determine a risk premium for the brand. The company's analysts derive the overall Brand Discount Rate by adding a brand-risk premium to the risk-free rate, represented by the yield on government bonds. The Brand Discount Rate, applied to the brand earnings forecast, yields the net present value of the Brand Earnings. The stronger the brand, the lower the discount rate, and vice versa.
5. **Brand Value Calculation**—Brand Value is the net present value (NPV) of the forecast Brand Earnings, discounted by the Brand Discount Rate. The NPV calculation comprises both the forecast period and the period beyond, reflecting the ability of brands to continue generating future earnings.

Increasingly, Interbrand uses brand value assessments as a dynamic, strategic tool to identify and maximize return on brand investment across a whole host of areas.

Source: Interbrand, the Interbrand Brand Glossary, and Jeff Swystun.

An important part of reinforcing brands is providing marketing support that's consistent in amount and kind. Consistency doesn't mean uniformity with no changes: Many tactical changes may be necessary to maintain the strategic thrust and direction of the brand. Unless there is some change in the marketing environment, however, there is little need to deviate from a successful positioning. When change *is* necessary, marketers should vigorously preserve and defend sources of brand equity.

VOLVO

In an attempt to woo a different audience, Volvo drifted away from its heritage of safety in the late 1990s to push driving fun, speed, and performance. Purchased by Ford in 1999, the company dropped its ReVOLVOlution-themed ad campaign for the brand and went back to its roots in an attempt to revive sagging sales. Volvo's positioning was updated, however, to convey "active safety" to transcend the brand's boxy, sturdy "passive safety" image. With product introductions that maximized safety but that still encompassed style, performance, and luxury, Volvo's sales set records in 2003.[55]

In managing brand equity, marketers must recognize the trade-offs between activities that fortify the brand and reinforce its meaning, such as a well-received new product improvement or a creatively designed ad campaign, and those that leverage or borrow from existing brand equity to reap some financial benefit, such as a short-term promotional discount that just emphasizes the lower price.[56] At some point, failure to reinforce the brand will diminish brand awareness and weaken brand image.

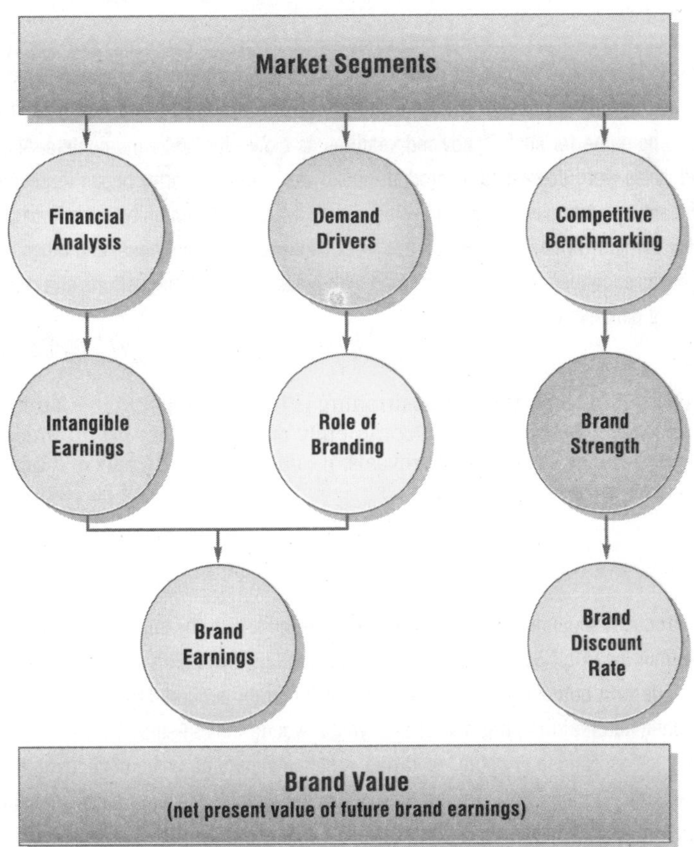

FIG. 9.7

Interbrand Brand Valuation Method

Brand Revitalization

Changes in consumer tastes and preferences, the emergence of new competitors or new technology, or any new development in the marketing environment can affect the fortunes of a brand. In virtually every product category, once-prominent and admired brands—such as Smith Corona, Zenith, and TWA—have fallen on hard times or even disappeared.[57] Nevertheless, a number of brands have managed to make impressive comebacks in recent years, as marketers have breathed new life into their customer franchises. Volkswagen, Dr. Scholl's, and Hyperion Solutions software have all seen their brand fortunes successfully turned around to varying degrees in recent years.

Often, the first thing to do in revitalizing a brand is to understand what the sources of brand equity were to begin with. Are positive associations losing their strength or uniqueness? Have negative associations become linked to the brand? Then decide whether to retain the same positioning or create a new one, and if so, which new one. Sometimes the actual marketing program is the source of the problem, because it fails to deliver on the brand promise. Then a "back to basics" strategy may make sense, as it did for Harley-Davidson.

Harley recovered from a brush with bankruptcy and revitalized its brand with a renewed commitment to quality and to grassroots marketing efforts that appeal to its image-conscious customers.

HARLEY-DAVIDSON

Founded in 1903 in Milwaukee, Wisconsin, Harley-Davidson has twice narrowly escaped bankruptcy but is today one of the most recognized motor vehicle brands in the world. In dire financial straits in the 1980s, Harley desperately licensed its name for such ill-advised ventures as cigarettes and wine coolers. Although consumers loved the brand, sales were depressed by product-quality problems, so Harley began its return to greatness by improving manufacturing processes. It also developed a strong brand community in the form of an owners' club, called the Harley Owners Group (HOG), which sponsors bike rallies, charity rides, and other motorcycle events. Harley-Davidson has continued to promote its brand with grassroots marketing efforts and now finds itself in the enviable position of demand exceeding supply.[58]

In other cases, however, the old positioning is just no longer viable and a "reinvention" strategy is necessary. Mountain Dew completely overhauled its brand image to become a soft-drink powerhouse. As its history reveals, it is often easier to revive a brand that is alive but has been more or less forgotten.

MOUNTAIN DEW

Pepsi initially introduced Mountain Dew in 1969 and marketed it with the countrified tagline "Yahoo Mountain Dew! It'll Tickle Your Innards." By the 1990s, the brand was languishing on store shelves despite an attempt to evolve the image with outdoor action scenes. To turn the brand around, Mountain Dew updated the packaging and launched ads featuring a group of anonymous young males—the "Dew Dudes"—participating in extreme sports such as bungee jumping, skydiving, and snowboarding while consuming Mountain Dew. The brand slogan became "Do the Dew." The brand's successful pursuit of young soda drinkers led to Mountain Dew's passing Diet Pepsi and challenging Diet Coke to become the number-four selling soft drink in terms of market share by 2005.

There is obviously a continuum of revitalization strategies, with pure "back to basics" at one end, pure "reinvention" at the other, and many combinations in between. Brand revitalizations of almost any kind start with the product. General Motors' turnaround of its fading Cadillac brand was fueled by new designs that redefined the Cadillac look and styling, such as the CTS sedan, XLR roadster, and ESV sport utility vehicle.[59]

::: Devising a Branding Strategy

A firm's **branding strategy** reflects the number and nature of both common and distinctive brand elements it applies to the products it sells. Deciding how to brand new products is especially critical. When a firm introduces a new product, it has three main choices:

1. It can develop new brand elements for the new product.
2. It can apply some of its existing brand elements.
3. It can use a combination of new and existing brand elements.

When a firm uses an established brand to introduce a new product, the product is called a **brand extension**. When marketers combine a new brand with an existing brand, the brand extension can also be called a **subbrand**, such as Hershey Kisses candy, Adobe Acrobat software, Toyota Camry automobiles, and American Express Blue cards. The existing brand that gives birth to a brand extension or subbrand is the **parent brand**. If the parent brand is already associated with multiple products through brand extensions, it can also be called a **family brand**.

Brand extensions fall into two general categories:[60] In a **line extension**, the parent brand covers a new product within a product category it currently serves, such as with new flavors, forms, colors, ingredients, and package sizes. Dannon has introduced several types of Dannon yogurt line extensions through the years—Fruit on the Bottom, All Natural Flavors, and Fruit Blends. In a **category extension**, the parent brand is used to enter a different product category from the one it currently serves, such as Swiss Army watches. Honda has used its company name to cover such different products as automobiles, motorcycles, snowblowers, lawnmowers, marine engines, and snowmobiles. This allows Honda to advertise that it can fit "six Hondas in a two-car garage."

A **brand line** consists of all products—original as well as line and category extensions—sold under a particular brand. A **brand mix** (or brand assortment) is the set of all brand lines that a particular seller makes available to buyers. Many companies are now introducing **branded variants**, which are specific brand lines supplied to specific retailers or distribution channels. They result from the pressure retailers put on manufacturers to provide distinctive offerings. A camera company may supply its low-end cameras to mass merchandisers while limiting its higher-priced items to specialty camera shops. Valentino may design and supply different lines of suits and jackets to different department stores.[61]

A **licensed product** is one whose brand name has been licensed to other manufacturers that actually make the product. Corporations have seized on licensing to push their company name and image across a wide range of products—from bedding to shoes—making licensing a $35 billion business.[62] Jeep's licensing program, which now has 600 products and 150 licensees, includes everything from strollers (built for a father's longer arms) to apparel (with teflon in the denim)—as long they fit the brand's positioning of "Life without Limits." Licensing revenue rose by 20% from 2004 to 2006.[63]

Branding Decisions

The first branding strategy decision is whether to develop a brand name for a product. Today, branding is such a strong force that hardly anything goes unbranded. Assuming a firm decides to brand its products or services, it must then choose which brand names to use. Four general strategies are often used:

- ***Individual names.*** General Mills uses individual names, such as Bisquick, Gold Medal flour, Nature Valley granola bars, Old El Paso Mexican foods, Pop Secret popcorn, Wheaties cereal, and Yoplait yogurt. A major advantage of an individual-names strategy is that the company does not tie its reputation to the product. If the product fails or appears to have low quality, the company's name or image is not hurt. Companies often use different brand names for different quality lines within the same product class. Delta branded its low-fare air carrier Song in part to protect the equity of its Delta Airlines brand, a prophetic move given the eventual demise of the new carrier.[64] UTC Technologies also relies on individual names.

UTC TECHNOLOGIES

UTC's brand portfolio includes Otis Elevators, Carrier air conditioners, Sikorsky helicopters, and Pratt & Whitney jet engines. Most of its brands are the names of the individuals who invented the product or created the company decades ago—they have more power and are more recognizable in the business buying marketplace. The parent brand, UTC, is advertised only to small but influential audiences—the financial community and opinion leaders in New York and Washington, D.C. After all, the parent trademark dates to 1972, and employees are loyal to the individual companies owned by UTC. "My philosophy has always been to use the power of the trademarks of the subsidiaries to improve the recognition and brand acceptance, awareness, and respect for the parent company itself," said UTC CEO George David.[65]

- ***Blanket family names.*** Many firms, such as Heinz and General Electric, use their corporate brand across their range of products.[66] Development costs are lower with blanket names because there's no need to run "name" research or spend heavily on advertising to create recognition. Campbell's introduces new soups under its brand name with extreme simplicity and achieves instant recognition. Sales of the new product are likely to be strong if the manufacturer's name is good. Corporate-image associations of innovativeness, expertise, and trustworthiness have been shown to directly influence consumer evaluations.[67] Finally, a corporate branding strategy can lead to greater intangible value for the firm.[68]
- ***Separate family names for all products.*** Sears uses separate family names such as Kenmore for appliances, Craftsman for tools, and Homart for major home installations. If a

company produces quite different products like these, one blanket name is often not desirable. Swift and Company developed separate family names for its hams (Premium) and fertilizers (Vigoro).

- ***Corporate name combined with individual product names.*** Kellogg combines corporate and individual names in Kellogg's Rice Krispies, Kellogg's Raisin Bran, and Kellogg's Corn Flakes, as do Honda, Sony, and Hewlett-Packard for their products. The company name legitimizes, and the individual name individualizes, the new product.

Individual names and blanket family names are sometimes referred to as a "house of brands" and a "branded house," respectively, and they represent two ends of a brand relationship continuum. Separate family names comes in between the two, and corporate-plus-individual names combine them. Not every company follows one strategy. For instance, when FedEx acquired copier chain Kinko's, the branding decision was trickier. Named Kinko's for founder Paul Orfalea's headfull of kinky red hair, the copying service had enough brand equity that FedEx didn't want to throw the name out. After numerous focus groups, FedEx decided to co-brand the chain. Hence, the name "FedEx Kinko's."

So, although firms rarely adopt a pure example of any of the four strategies, deciding which general strategy to emphasize depends on several factors, as evidenced by Table 9.3.

Two key components of virtually any branding strategy are brand extensions and brand portfolios.

Brand Extensions

Many firms have decided to leverage their most valuable asset by introducing a host of new products under their strongest brand names. Most new products are in fact line extensions—typically 80% to 90% in any one year. Moreover, many of the most successful new products, as rated by various sources, are extensions. Among the most successful new products in 2005 were Nabisco 100 Calorie Packs, Tide with a touch of Downy laundry detergent, the Microsoft Xbox video game system, Apple's iPod digital music player, and the Nokia 6800 cell phone. Nevertheless, many new products are introduced each year as new brands, such as the mood stabilizer drug Zyprexa, TiVo digital video recorders, and the Mini Cooper automobile.

ADVANTAGES OF BRAND EXTENSIONS Two main advantages of brand extensions are that they can facilitate new-product acceptance and provide positive feedback to the parent brand and company.

Improved Odds of New-Product Success Consumers can make inferences and form expectations about the composition and performance of a new product based on what they already know about the parent brand and the extent to which they feel this information is relevant to the new product.[69] For example, when Sony introduced a new personal computer tailored for multimedia applications, the Vaio, consumers may have felt

TABLE 9.3

Selecting a Brand Relationship Spectrum Position

Toward a Branded House	Toward a House of Brands
Does the parent brand contribute to the offering by adding:	**Is there a compelling need for a separate brand because it will:**
—Associations enhancing the value proposition?	—Create and own an association?
—Credibility through organizational associations?	—Represent a new, different offering?
—Visibility?	—Retain/capture customer/brand bond?
—Communication efficiencies?	—Deal with channel conflict?
Will the master brand be strengthened by associating with the new offering?	**Will the business support a new brand name?**

Source: Figure 4.6, page 120 adapted with the permission of The Free Press, a Division of Simon & Schuster Adult Publishing Group, from BRAND LEADERSHIP by David A. Aaker and Erich Joachimsthaler.

comfortable with its anticipated performance because of their experience with and knowledge of other Sony products.

By setting up positive expectations, extensions reduce risk.[70] It also may be easier to convince retailers to stock and promote a brand extension because of increased customer demand. From a marketing communications perspective, an introductory campaign for an extension doesn't need to create awareness of both the brand *and* the new product, but instead it can concentrate on the new product itself.[71]

Extensions can thus reduce costs of the introductory launch campaign, important given that establishing a new brand name in the U.S. marketplace for a mass-consumer-packaged good can cost $100 million! Extensions also can avoid the difficulty—and expense—of coming up with a new name and allow for packaging and labeling efficiencies. Similar or identical packages and labels can result in lower production costs for extensions and, if coordinated properly, more prominence in the retail store via a "billboard" effect. For example, Stouffers offers a variety of frozen entrees with identical orange packaging that increases their visibility when they're stocked together in the freezer. With a portfolio of brand variants within a product category, consumers who need a change—because of boredom, satiation, or whatever—can switch to a different product type without having to leave the brand family. Business-to-business companies are even finding that brand extensions are a powerful way to enter consumer markets, as these two name brand rubber companies discovered.

GROUPE MICHELIN, GOODYEAR

Both Groupe Michelin and Goodyear, known primarily for their rubber tires, have launched a number of brand extensions in recent years. Although Michelin's extensions have mainly been in the auto accessories area—from inflation- and pressure-monitoring goods to automotive floor mats—its sports and leisure category now has the potential to overtake the auto accessories line. So far its brand extensions fall into three categories: (1) automotive and cycle-related products, (2) footwear, apparel, accessories, and equipment for work, sports, and leisure, and (3) personal accessories—gifts and collectibles promoting Michelin culture and heritage featuring Bibendum, the trademark "Michelin Man." Like Michelin, Goodyear has a category of products closely aligned to the automotive industry—such as jack stands and auto repair tools, but it, too, has branched out into consumer areas. The company is selling its own line of cleaning wipes for windows and upholstery, mechanic's gloves, and garden hose nozzles, among other products, at Home Depot stores.[72]

Positive Feedback Effects Besides facilitating acceptance of new products, brand extensions can also provide feedback benefits.[73] They can help to clarify the meaning of a brand and its core brand values or improve consumer loyalty and perceptions of the credibility of the company behind the extension.[74] Thus, through brand extensions, Crayola means "colorful crafts for kids," Aunt Jemima means "breakfast foods," and Weight Watchers means "weight loss and maintenance."

Line extensions can renew interest and liking for the brand and benefit the parent brand by expanding market coverage. The goal of Kimberly-Clark's Kleenex unit is to have facial tissue in every room of the home. This philosophy has led to a wide variety of Kleenex facial tissues and packaging, including scented, ultra-soft, and lotion-impregnated tissues; boxes with drawings of dinosaurs and dogs for children's rooms; colorful, stylish designs to match room décor; and a "man-sized" box with tissues 50% larger than regular Kleenex.

One benefit of a successful extension is that it may also serve as the basis for subsequent extensions.[75] During the 1970s and 1980s, Billabong established its brand credibility with the young surfing community as a designer and producer of quality surf apparel. This success permitted it to extend into other youth-oriented areas, such as snowboarding and skateboarding.

DISADVANTAGES OF BRAND EXTENSIONS On the downside, line extensions may cause the brand name to be less strongly identified with any one product.[76] Ries and Trout call this the "line-extension trap."[77] By linking its brand to mainstream food products such as mashed potatoes, powdered milk, soups, and beverages, Cadbury ran the risk of losing its more specific meaning as a chocolates and candy brand.[78] **Brand dilution** occurs when consumers no longer associate a brand with a specific product or highly similar products and start thinking less of the brand.

If a firm launches extensions consumers deem inappropriate, they may question the integrity of the brand or become confused and perhaps even frustrated: Which version of the product is the "right one" for them? Retailers reject many new products and brands because they don't have the shelf or display space for them. And the firm itself may become overwhelmed. When Lego decided to become a lifestyle brand and launch its own lines of clothes, watches, and video games, as well as design programs to attract more girls into the brand franchise, it neglected its core market of five- to nine-year-old boys. When plunging profits led to layoffs of almost half its employees in 2004, the firm streamlined its brand portfolio to emphasize its core businesses.[79]

The worst possible scenario is for an extension not only to fail, but also to harm the parent brand image in the process. Fortunately, such events are rare. "Marketing failures," where insufficient consumers were attracted to a brand, are typically much less damaging than "product failures," where the brand fundamentally fails to live up to its promise. Even then, product failures dilute brand equity only when the extension is seen as very similar to the parent brand. The Audi 5000 car suffered from a tidal wave of negative publicity and word of mouth in the mid-1980s when it was alleged to have a "sudden acceleration" problem. The adverse publicity also spilled over to the 4000 model. But the Quattro was relatively insulated from negative repercussions, because it was distanced from the 5000 by its more distinct branding and advertising strategy.[80]

Even if sales of a brand extension are high and meet targets, the revenue may be coming from consumers switching to the extension from existing parent-brand offerings—in effect *cannibalizing* the parent brand. Intrabrand shifts in sales may not necessarily be undesirable if they're a form of *preemptive cannibalization.* In other words, consumers might have switched to a competing brand instead of the line extension if the extension hadn't been introduced. Tide laundry detergent maintains the same market share it had 50 years ago because of the sales contributions of its various line extensions—scented and unscented powder, tablet, liquid, and other forms.

One easily overlooked disadvantage of brand extensions is that the firm forgoes the chance to create a new brand with its own unique image and equity. Consider the advantages to Disney of having introduced more-adult-oriented Touchstone films; to Levi's of creating casual Dockers pants; and to Black and Decker of introducing high-end Dewalt power tools.

SUCCESS CHARACTERISTICS Marketers must judge each potential brand extension by how effectively it leverages existing brand equity from the parent brand, as well as how effectively, in turn, it contributes to the parent brand's equity.[81] Crest White Strips leveraged the strong reputation of Crest and dental care to provide reassurance in the teeth-whitening arena, while also reinforcing its dental authority image. The most important consideration with extensions is that there should be a "fit" in the mind of the consumer, based on common physical attributes, usage situations, or user types.

Figure 9.8 lists a number of academic research findings on brand extensions.[82] One major mistake in evaluating extension opportunities is failing to take *all* consumers' brand knowledge structures into account and focusing instead on one or perhaps a few brand associations as a potential basis of fit.

BIC

The French company Société Bic, by emphasizing inexpensive, disposable products, was able to create markets for nonrefillable ball-point pens in the late 1950s; disposable cigarette lighters in the early 1970s; and disposable razors in the early 1980s. It unsuccessfully tried the same strategy in marketing Bic perfumes in the United States and Europe in 1989. The perfumes—two for women ("Nuit" and "Jour") and two for men ("Bic for Men" and "Bic Sport for Men")—were packaged in quarter-ounce glass spray bottles that looked like fat cigarette lighters and sold for $5 each. The products were displayed on racks at checkout counters throughout Bic's extensive distribution channels. At the time, a Bic spokeswoman described the new products as extensions of the Bic heritage—"high quality at affordable prices, convenient to purchase, and convenient to use." The brand extension was launched with a $20 million advertising and promotion campaign containing images of stylish people enjoying themselves with the perfume and using the tagline "Paris in Your Pocket." Nevertheless, Bic was unable to overcome its lack of cachet and negative image associations, and the extension was a failure.[83]

FIG. 9.8

Research Insights on Brand Extensions

Academics have studied brand extensions closely. Here is a summary of some of their key research findings.

- Successful brand extensions occur when the parent brand is seen as having favorable associations and there is a perception of fit between the parent brand and the extension product.
- There are many bases of fit: product-related attributes and benefits, as well as nonproduct-related attributes and benefits related to common usage situations or user types.
- Depending on consumer knowledge of the categories, perceptions of fit may be based on technical or manufacturing commonalties or more surface considerations such as necessary or situational complementarity.
- High-quality brands stretch farther than average-quality brands, although both types of brands have boundaries.
- A brand that is seen as prototypical of a product category can be difficult to extend outside the category.
- Concrete attribute associations tend to be more difficult to extend than abstract benefit associations.
- Consumers may transfer associations that are positive in the original product class but become negative in the extension context.
- Consumers may infer negative associations about an extension, perhaps even based on other inferred positive associations.
- It can be difficult to extend into a product class that is seen as easy to make.
- A successful extension can not only contribute to the parent brand image but also enable a brand to be extended even farther.
- An unsuccessful extension hurts the parent brand only when there is a strong basis of fit between the two.
- An unsuccessful extension does not prevent a firm from "backtracking" and introducing a more-similar extension.
- Vertical extensions can be difficult and often require subbranding strategies.
- The most effective advertising strategy for an extension emphasizes information about the extension (rather than reminders about the parent brand).

Source: Kevin Lane Keller, *Strategic Brand Management*, 3rd ed. (Upple Saddle River, NJ: Prentice Hall, 2008). Reproduced by permission of Pearson Education, Inc., Upper Saddle River, NJ.

Brand Portfolios

All brands have boundaries—a brand can only be stretched so far, and all the segments the firm would like to target may not view the same brand equally favorably. Marketers often need multiple brands in order to pursue these multiple segments. Some other reasons for introducing multiple brands in a category include:[84]

1. Increasing shelf presence and retailer dependence in the store
2. Attracting consumers seeking variety who may otherwise have switched to another brand
3. Increasing internal competition within the firm
4. Yielding economies of scale in advertising, sales, merchandising, and physical distribution

The **brand portfolio** is the set of all brands and brand lines a particular firm offers for sale in a particular category or market segment.

ARMANI

Armani has set out to create a product line differentiated by style, luxury, customization, and price to compete in three distinct price tiers. In the most expensive Tier I, it sells Giorgio Armani and Giorgio Armani Privé, which are custom-made runway couture products that sell for thousands of dollars. In the more moderately priced Tier II, it offers Emporio Armani, young and modern with more affordable prices, as well as the informal Armani jeans that focus on technology and ecology. In the lower-priced Tier III, the firm sells the more youthful and street-savvy translation of Armani style, AIX Armani Exchange, at retail locations in cities and suburban malls.

Armani's line of luxury clothing is differentiated to appeal to three distinct price tiers, each with different styles and levels of luxury and customization.

The hallmark of an optimal brand portfolio is the ability of each brand in it to maximize equity in combination with all the other brands in it. Marketers generally need to trade off market coverage with costs and profitability. If they can increase profits by dropping brands, a portfolio is too big; if they can increase profits by *adding* brands, it's not big enough. The basic principle in designing a brand portfolio is to *maximize market coverage*, so that no potential customers are being ignored, but to *minimize brand overlap*, so brands are not competing for customer approval. Each brand should be clearly differentiated and appealing to a sizable enough marketing segment to justify its marketing and production costs.[85]

Marketers carefully monitor brand portfolios over time to identify weak brands and kill unprofitable ones.[86] Brand lines with poorly differentiated brands are likely to be characterized by much cannibalization and require pruning.[87] Kellogg's Eggo frozen waffles come in over two dozen flavors. Investors can choose among thousands of mutual funds. Students can choose among hundreds of business schools. For the seller, this spells hypercompetition. For the buyer, it may mean too much choice.

Brands can also play a number of specific roles as part of a portfolio.

FLANKERS Flanker or "fighter" brands are positioned with respect to competitors' brands so that more important (and more profitable) *flagship brands* can retain their desired positioning. Procter & Gamble markets Luvs diapers in a way that flanks the more premium Pampers. Marketers walk a fine line in designing fighter brands, which must not be so attractive that they take sales away from their higher-priced comparison brands. At the same time, if fighter brands are seen as connected to other brands in the portfolio in any way—say, by virtue of a common branding strategy—then they also can't be designed so cheaply that they reflect poorly on these other brands.

CASH COWS Some brands may be kept around despite dwindling sales because they still manage to hold on to enough customers and maintain their profitability with virtually no marketing support. Companies can effectively "milk" these "cash cow" brands by capitalizing on their reservoir of existing brand equity. For example, despite the fact that technological advances have moved much of its market to the newer Mach III and Fusion brands of razors, Gillette still sells the older Trac II, Atra, and Sensor brands. Because withdrawing them may not necessarily move customers to another Gillette brand, it may be more profitable for Gillette to keep them in its brand portfolio for razor blades.

LOW-END ENTRY LEVEL The role of a relatively low-priced brand in the portfolio often may be to attract customers to the brand franchise. Retailers like to feature these "traffic builders" because they are able to "trade up" customers to a higher-priced brand. For example, BMW introduced certain models into its 3-series automobiles in part as a means of bringing new customers into the brand franchise, with the hope of later "moving them up" to higher-priced models when they decided to trade in their cars.

HIGH-END PRESTIGE The role of a relatively high-priced brand often is to add prestige and credibility to the entire portfolio. For example, one analyst argued that the real value to Chevrolet of its high-performance Corvette sports car was "its ability to lure curious customers into showrooms and at the same time help improve the image of other Chevrolet cars. It does not mean a hell of a lot for GM profitability, but there is no question that it is a traffic builder."[88] Corvette's technological image and prestige cast a halo over the entire Chevrolet line.

::: Customer Equity

Brand equity should be a top priority for any organization. "Marketing Memo: Twenty-First-Century Branding" offers some contemporary perspectives on enduring brand leadership.

Finally, we can relate brand equity to one other important marketing concept, **customer equity**. The aim of customer relationship management (CRM) is to produce high customer equity.[89] Although we can calculate it in different ways, one definition of customer equity is "the sum of lifetime values of all customers."[90]As Chapter 5 reviewed, customer lifetime value is affected by revenue and cost considerations related to customer acquisition, retention, and cross-selling.[91]

- *Acquisition* is affected by the number of prospects, the acquisition probability of a prospect, and acquisition spending per prospect.
- *Retention* is influenced by the retention rate and retention spending level.
- *Add-on spending* is a function of the efficiency of add-on selling, the number of add-on selling offers given to existing customers, and the response rate to new offers.

The brand equity and customer equity perspectives certainly share many common themes.[92] Both emphasize the importance of customer loyalty and the notion that value is created by having as many customers as possible pay as high a price as possible.

As they've been put into practice, however, the two perspectives emphasize different things. The customer equity perspective focuses on bottom-line financial value. Its clear benefit is its quantifiable measures of financial performance. But it offers limited guidance for go-to-market strategies. It largely ignores some of the important advantages of creating a strong brand, such as the ability to attract higher-quality employees; elicit stronger support from channel and supply chain partners; and create growth opportunities through line and category extensions and licensing. The customer equity approach can overlook the "option value" of brands and their potential to affect future revenues and costs. It does not always fully account for competitive moves and countermoves, or for social network effects, word-of-mouth, and customer-to-customer recommendations.

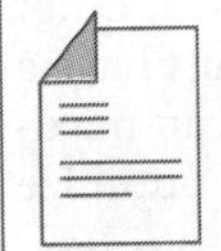

MARKETING MEMO | TWENTY-FIRST-CENTURY BRANDING

One of the most successful marketers of the past fifteen years, Scott Bedbury played a key role in the rise of both Nike and Starbucks. In his insightful book, *A New Brand World*, he offers the following branding principles:

1. ***Relying on brand awareness has become marketing fool's gold***—Smart brands are more concerned with brand relevance and brand resonance.
2. ***You have to know it before you can grow it***—Most brands don't know who they are, where they've been, and where they're going.
3. ***Always remember the Spandex rule of brand expansion***—Just because you can, doesn't mean you should.
4. ***Great brands establish enduring customer relationships***—They have more to do with emotions and trust than with footwear cushioning or the way a coffee bean is roasted.
5. ***Everything matters***—Even your restroom.
6. ***All brands need good parents***—Unfortunately, most brands come from troubled homes.
7. ***Big is no excuse for being bad***—Truly great brands use their superhuman powers for good and place people and principles before profits.
8. ***Relevance, simplicity, and humanity***—Rather than technology, these will distinguish brands in the future.

Source: Scott Bedbury, *A New Brand World* (New York: Viking Press, 2002). Copyright © 2001 by Scott Bedbury. Used by permission of Viking Penguin, a division of Penguin Group (USA) Inc.

Brand equity, on the other hand, tends to emphasize strategic issues in managing brands and creating and leveraging brand awareness and image with customers. It provides much practical guidance for specific marketing activities. With a focus on brands, however, managers don't always develop detailed customer analyses in terms of the brand equity they achieve or the resulting long-term profitability they create.[93] Brand equity approaches could benefit from sharper segmentation schemes afforded by customer-level analyses and more consideration of how to develop personalized, customized marketing programs for individual customers—whether individuals or organizations such as retailers. There are generally fewer financial considerations put into play with brand equity than with customer equity.

Nevertheless, both brand equity and customer equity matter. There are no brands without customers and no customers without brands. Brands serve as the "bait" that retailers and other channel intermediaries use to attract customers from whom they extract value. Customers serve as the tangible profit engine for brands to monetize their brand value.

SUMMARY :::

1. A brand is a name, term, sign, symbol, design, or some combination of these elements, intended to identify the goods and services of one seller or group of sellers and to differentiate them from those of competitors. The different components of a brand—brand names, logos, symbols, package designs, and so on—are brand elements.
2. Brands offer a number of benefits to customers and firms. Brands are valuable intangible assets that need to be managed carefully. The key to branding is that consumers perceive differences among brands in a product category.
3. Brand equity should be defined in terms of marketing effects uniquely attributable to a brand. That is, brand equity relates to the fact that different outcomes result in the marketing of a product or service because of its brand, as compared to the results if that same product or service was not identified by that brand.
4. Building brand equity depends on three main factors: (1) The initial choices for the brand elements or identities making up the brand; (2) the way the brand is integrated into the supporting marketing program; and (3) the associations indirectly transferred to the brand by linking the brand to some other entity (e.g., the company, country of origin, channel of distribution, or another brand).
5. Brand equity needs to be measured in order to be managed well. Brand audits measure "where the brand has been," and tracking studies measure "where the brand is now" and whether marketing programs are having the intended effects.
6. A branding strategy for a firm identifies which brand elements a firm chooses to apply across the various products it sells. In a brand extension, a firm uses an established brand name to introduce a new product. Potential extensions must be judged by how effectively they leverage existing brand equity to a new product, as well as how effectively the extension, in turn, contributes to the equity of the existing parent brand.
7. Brands can play a number of different roles within the brand portfolio. Brands may expand coverage, provide protection, extend an image, or fulfill a variety of other roles for the firm. Each brand name product must have a well-defined positioning. In that way, brands can maximize coverage and minimize overlap and thus optimize the portfolio.
8. Customer equity is a complimentary concept to brand equity that reflects the sum of lifetime values of all customers for a brand.

APPLICATIONS :::

Marketing Debate Are Brand Extensions Good or Bad?

Some critics vigorously denounce the practice of brand extensions, as they feel that too often companies lose focus and consumers become confused. Other experts maintain that brand extensions are a critical growth strategy and source of revenue for the firm.

Take a position: Brand extensions can endanger brands *versus* Brand extensions are an important brand-growth strategy.

Marketing Discussion

How can you relate the different models of brand equity presented in this chapter? How are they similar? How are they different? Can you construct a brand-equity model that incorporates the best aspects of each model?

IN THIS CHAPTER, WE WILL ADDRESS THE FOLLOWING QUESTIONS:

1. How can a firm choose and communicate an effective positioning in the market?
2. How are brands differentiated?
3. What marketing strategies are appropriate at each stage of the product life cycle?
4. What are the implications of market evolution for marketing strategies?

CHAPTER 10 ::: CRAFTING THE BRAND POSITIONING

ten

No company can win if its products and services resemble every other product and offering. As part of the strategic brand management process, each offering must represent a compelling, distinctive big idea in the mind of the target market.

Victoria's Secret, purchased by Limited Brands in 1982, has become one of the most identifiable brands in retailing through skillful marketing of women's clothing, lingerie, and beauty products. Most U.S. women a generation ago did their underwear shopping in department stores and owned few items that could be considered "lingerie." After witnessing women buying expensive lingerie as fashion items from small boutiques in Europe, Limited Brands founder Leslie Wexner felt a similar store model could work on a mass scale in the United States, though it was unlike anything the average shopper would have encountered amid the bland racks at department stores. Wexner, however, had reason to believe that U.S. women would relish the opportunity to have a European-style lingerie shopping experience. "Women need underwear, but women want lingerie," he observed. Wexner's assumption proved correct: A little more than a decade after he bought the business, Victoria's Secret's average customer bought 8 to 10 bras per year, compared with the national average of two. To enhance its upscale reputation and glamorous appeal, the brand is >>>

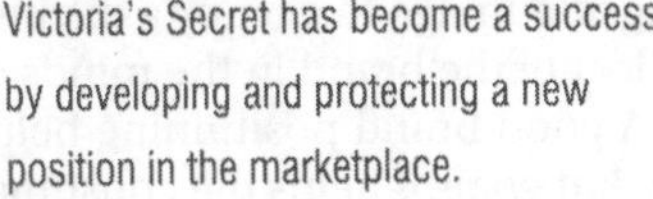
Victoria's Secret has become a success by developing and protecting a new position in the marketplace.

endorsed by high-profile supermodels in ads and fashion shows. Since 1985, Victoria's Secret has delivered 25% annual sales growth, selling through its stores, catalogs, and company Web site, posting $3.2 billion in revenues in 2006.[1]

As the success of Victoria's Secret demonstrates, a company can reap the benefits of carving out a unique position in the marketplace. But circumstances often dictate that companies reformulate their marketing strategies and offerings several times. Economic conditions change, competitors launch new assaults, and products pass through new stages of buyer interest and requirements. Marketers must develop strategies for each stage in the product's life cycle. This chapter explores specific ways a company can effectively position and differentiate its offerings to achieve a competitive advantage throughout the entire life cycle of a product or an offering.

::: Developing and Communicating a Positioning Strategy

To understand how the local enterprise Nice Group has used a positioning strategy to succeed in China, visit www.pearsoned-asia.com/marketingmanagementchina.

All marketing strategy is built on STP—segmentation, targeting, and positioning. A company discovers different needs and groups in the marketplace, targets those it can satisfy in a superior way, and then positions its offering so the target market recognizes the company's distinctive offering and image. If a company does a poor job of positioning, the market will be confused. This is what happened when National Car Company and Alamo Rent-a-Car were combined by their former parent, ANC Rental Corp., following its Chapter 11 bankruptcy court filing in 2001.

NATIONAL CAR RENTAL AND ALAMO RENT-A-CAR

Premium brand National Car Rental traditionally catered to business travelers, whereas Alamo Rent-a-Car has been getting 90% of its business from leisure travelers. After the two merged, the dual Alamo/National logos were plastered on everything from airport shuttle buses to workers' polo shirts. Customers of both Alamo and National had problems distinguishing between the brands, even though National's cars typically rent for 10% to 20% more than Alamo's. After all, the customers would stand in the same line at the same airport counter, receive service from the same rental agents, ride the same shuttle buses, and drive cars from the same fleet. National was most hurt by the lack of differentiation at these key touch points, and its market share fell 5% to 10%. Interestingly, after consolidation of the brands, shuttle bus frequency improved 38% and business travelers were given even more options to bypass the rental counter entirely. Still, in surveys, National renters *perceived* the buses to be slower, the lines longer, and customer service poorer. The clear implication was that in order for the two brands to maintain their integrity and their positioning with their respective market segments, they needed to be separated.[2]

Positioning is the act of designing the company's offering and image to occupy a distinctive place in the minds of the target market.[3] The goal is to locate the brand in the minds of consumers to maximize the potential benefit to the firm. A good brand positioning helps guide marketing strategy by clarifying the brand's essence, what goals it helps the consumer achieve, and how it does so in a unique way. Everyone in the organization should understand the brand positioning and use it as context for making decisions.

TABLE 10.1 | Examples of Value Propositions

Company and Product	Target Customers	Benefits	Price	Value Proposition
Perdue (chicken)	Quality-conscious consumers of chicken	Tenderness	10% premium	More tender golden chicken at a moderate premium price
Volvo (station wagon)	Safety-conscious "upscale" families	Durability and safety	20% premium	The safest, most durable wagon in which your family can ride
Domino's (pizza)	Convenience-minded pizza lovers	Delivery speed and good quality	15% premium	A good hot pizza, delivered promptly to your door, at a moderate price

The result of positioning is the successful creation of a *customer-focused value proposition,* a cogent reason why the target market should buy the product. Table 10.1 shows how three companies—Perdue, Volvo, and Domino's—have defined their value proposition given their target customers, benefits, and prices.

Positioning requires that similarities and differences between brands be defined and communicated. Specifically, deciding on a positioning requires determining a frame of reference by identifying the target market and the competition and identifying the ideal points-of-parity and points-of-difference brand associations. "Breakthrough Marketing: UPS" chronicles how UPS has successfully positioned itself against a formidable opponent, FedEx.

Competitive Frame of Reference

A starting point in defining a competitive frame of reference for a brand positioning is to determine **category membership**—the products or sets of products with which a brand competes and which function as close substitutes. As we discuss in Chapter 11, competitive analysis will consider a whole host of factors—including the resources, capabilities, and likely intentions of various other firms—in choosing those markets where consumers can be profitably served.

Deciding to target a certain type of consumer, in particular, can define the nature of competition, because certain firms have decided to target that segment in the past (or plan to do so in the future), or because consumers in that segment may already look to certain products or brands in their purchase decisions. To determine the proper competitive frame of reference, marketers need to understand consumer behavior and the consideration sets consumers use in making brand choices. In the United Kingdom, for example, the Automobile Association positioned itself as the fourth "emergency service"—along with police, fire, and ambulance—to convey greater credibility and urgency. And look at how DiGiorno's positioned itself:

DIGIORNO'S PIZZA

DiGiorno's is a frozen pizza whose crust rises when the pizza is heated. Instead of putting it in the frozen pizza category, the marketers positioned it in the delivered pizza category. One of their ads shows party guests asking which pizza delivery service the host used. Then he says: "It's not delivery, it's DiGiorno!" This helped highlight DiGiorno's fresh quality and superior taste. Through this clever positioning, DiGiorno's sales went from essentially nothing in 1995 to $514 million in 2005, making it the frozen pizza leader by far.[4]

Points-of-Difference and Points-of-Parity

Once marketers have fixed the competitive frame of reference for positioning by defining the customer target market and the nature of the competition, they can define the appropriate points-of-difference and points-of-parity associations.[5]

POINTS-OF-DIFFERENCE **Points-of-difference (PODs)** are attributes or benefits consumers strongly associate with a brand, positively evaluate, and believe they could not find to the same extent with a competitive brand. Associations that make up points-of-difference may be based on virtually any type of attribute or benefit. Examples are Apple (*design*), Nike (*performance*), and Lexus (*quality*). Creating strong, favorable, and unique associations is a real challenge, but essential in terms of competitive brand positioning.

BREAKTHROUGH MARKETING | UPS

The United Parcel Service was founded by James E. Casey in 1907 to fill a gap in the shipping market: local parcel deliveries. Parcels, which might be sent by stores and restaurants to customers' homes, were too large to be efficiently and cost-effectively sent via the post office. UPS spent the following decades establishing a national presence before becoming the first package delivery company to ship to every address in the lower 48 states in 1975.

As the first and largest national package delivery company, UPS enjoyed a dominant position in the shipping industry. Yet its authority was challenged in the 1980s, when upstart Federal Express (as it was then called) began offering customers a unique "triple play": overnight service, shipment tracking, and volume discounts. UPS launched its next-day service in 1982 and pushed aggressively in this market for the remainder of the decade. In 1987, it expanded its air fleet by adding 110 planes at a cost of $1.8 billion, thereby forming the 10th-largest airline in the United States. By 1990, next-day service accounted for 21% of UPS total business.

Although it attempted to keep pace with FedEx in overnight shipping, UPS sought to differentiate itself by building the largest international shipping network. Between 1988 and 1990, UPS entered 145 countries in Europe and Asia, primarily by buying small local couriers. These acquisitions pushed its share of the foreign shipping market up to 6% from 2% in 1988. These moves abroad enabled UPS to position itself as the "provider of the broadest range of package distribution services and solutions in the world." Whereas FedEx offered essentially one service—express air delivery—UPS offered a wider range of shipping options in the air and on the ground, and it shipped to more locations. As a result of its broader scope, by 2000, UPS held a much higher share of on-time package delivery (55%) than FedEx (25%).

UPS extended its range of services and solutions in the Internet-enabled world, adding a host of capabilities for e-commerce customers and launching a logistics business that offered manufacturing, warehousing, and supply-chain services. By 2001, UPS was the clear leader in e-commerce shipments, handling 55% of all online purchases, compared to 10% for FedEx. At the same time, UPS's logistics business was growing 40% annually, whereas FedEx was strugging to reverse a decline in its own logistics operations. One of UPS's major wins in this business was designing an online system for Ford that tracked shipments of cars to dealers, which saved Ford an estimated $1 billion in 2001 by reducing the average number of vehicles in inventory. UPS supported its new suite of shipping and logistics services with the 2002 launch of an approximately $50 million ad campaign titled "What Can Brown Do for You?"

UPS was the first to serve the local package delivery market but has had to protect its dominant position at home and abroad against strong competition from younger rival FedEx.

UPS expanded its service offering again in 2003, when it rebranded more than 3,000 Mail Boxes Etc. nationwide franchises it had acquired in 2001 as The UPS Store. UPS Stores provided one-stop convenience for customers' shipping needs and offered standardized shipping rates that were 20% less than the previous average Mail Boxes Etc. rates. In test markets, average UPS shipments from joint-branded stores rose 70% annually. FedEx mirrored UPS's move later that year by acquiring Kinko's and establishing FedEx Kinko's joint-branded stores.

In 2006, UPS addressed an area where it was perceived to lag behind FedEx: speed. The resulting campaign, which used the tagline "Covering more ground faster than ever," highlighted UPS's "fast lane" initiative to speed up shipments between 11 major business centers in the United States. And its "expanded early AM" effort to increase the destinations it serves before 7 AM ads depicted UPS trucks shuttling between distant destinations in the United States as if the drive took only seconds. Another series of ads showcased the same speed in Europe. At the time of the campaign, UPS's business was in good condition. Total revenues for 2005 had risen 16% to $42.6 billion, and profits had risen 13% to $12.8 billion in the same period. Furthermore, it remained the dominant player in the domestic package delivery market, with a 65% share in 2006.

Sources: UPS Annual Report, 2005 and 2002; "Up with Brown," *Brandweek*, January 27, 2003; Charles Haddad, "Ground Wars," *BusinessWeek*, May 21, 2001, p. 64; Brian O'Reilly, "They've Got Mail!" *Fortune*, February 7, 2000, p. 100; Stephen Smith, "Brand Surfin' Safari," *Brandweek*, June 24, 1996, p. 17; Todd Vogel, "Can UPS Deliver the Goods in a New World?" *BusinessWeek*, June 4, 1990, p. 80.

POINTS-OF-PARITY **Points-of-parity (POPs)**, on the other hand, are associations that are not necessarily unique to the brand but may in fact be shared with other brands.[6] These types of associations come in two basic forms: category and competitive.

Category points-of-parity are associations consumers view as essential to a legitimate and credible offering within a certain product or service category. In other words, they represent necessary—but not sufficient—conditions for brand choice. Consumers might not consider a travel agency truly a travel agency unless it is able to make air and hotel reservations, provide advice about leisure packages, and offer various ticket payment and delivery options. Category points-of-parity may change over time due to technological advances, legal developments, or consumer trends, but they are the "greens fees" to play the marketing game.

Competitive points-of-parity are associations designed to negate *competitors'* points-of-difference. If, in the eyes of consumers, a brand can "break even" in those areas where the competitors are trying to find an advantage *and* achieve advantages in other areas, the brand should be in a strong—and perhaps unbeatable—competitive position. Consider the introduction of Miller Lite beer.[7]

MILLER LITE

The initial advertising strategy for Miller Lite beer had two goals—ensuring parity with key competitors in the category by stating that it "tastes great," while at the same time creating a point-of-difference: It contained one-third fewer calories and was thus "less filling" than regular, full-strength beers. As is often the case, the point-of-parity and point-of-difference were somewhat conflicting, as consumers tend to equate taste with calories. To overcome potential resistance, Miller employed credible spokespeople, primarily popular former professional athletes, who would presumably not drink a beer unless it tasted good. These ex-jocks humorously debated which of the two product benefits—"tastes great" or "less filling"—was more descriptive of the beer. The ads ended with the clever tagline "Everything You've Always Wanted in a Beer . . . and Less."

POINTS-OF-PARITY VERSUS POINTS-OF-DIFFERENCE For an offering to achieve a point-of-parity (POP) on a particular attribute or benefit, a sufficient number of consumers must believe the brand is "good enough" on that dimension. There is a zone or range of tolerance or acceptance with points-of-parity. The brand does not literally need to be seen as equal to competitors, but consumers must feel that the brand does well enough on that particular attribute or benefit. If they do, they may be willing to base their evaluations and decisions on other factors potentially more favorable to the brand. A light beer presumably would never taste as good as a full-strength beer, but it would need to taste close enough to be able to effectively compete.

With points-of-difference, however, the brand must demonstrate clear superiority. Consumers must be convinced that Louis Vuitton has the most stylish handbags, Energizer is the longest-lasting battery, and Merrill Lynch offers the best financial advice and planning.

Often, the key to positioning is not so much achieving a point-of-difference (POD) as achieving points-of-parity!

VISA VERSUS AMERICAN EXPRESS

Visa's POD in the credit card category is that it is the most widely available card, which underscores the category's main benefit of convenience. American Express, on the other hand, has built the equity of its brand by highlighting the prestige associated with the use of its card. Having established their PODs, Visa and American Express now compete by attempting to blunt each others' advantage to create POPs. Visa offers gold and platinum cards to enhance the prestige of its brand and advertises, "It's Everywhere You Want to Be" in settings that reinforce exclusivity and acceptability. American Express has substantially increased the number of merchants that accept its cards and created other value enhancements.

Establishing Category Membership

Target customers are aware that Maybelline is a leading brand of cosmetics, Cheerios is a leading brand of cereal, Accenture is a leading consulting firm, and so on. Often, however, marketers must inform consumers of a brand's category membership. Perhaps the most obvious situation is the introduction of new products, especially when category identification itself is not apparent.

Category membership can be a special problem for high-tech products. When GO Corporation created the first pen-based tablet computer in the early 1990s, analysts and the media responded enthusiastically to the concept, but consumer interest never materialized. GO was eventually purchased by AT&T for use in a pen computer venture that folded in

American Express built its credit card brand with appeals based on prestige and now defends itself against Visa and other competitors by increasing the number of merchants that accept the card.

1994. With the current development of tablet PCs, however, the pen-computing idea has achieved new life.[8]

There are also situations where consumers know a brand's category membership, but may not be convinced that the brand is a valid member of the category. For example, consumers may be aware that Hewlett-Packard produces digital cameras, but they may not be certain whether Hewlett-Packard cameras are in the same class as Sony, Olympus, Kodak, and Nikon. In this instance, HP might find it useful to reinforce category membership.

Brands are sometimes affiliated with categories in which they do *not* hold membership. This approach is one way to highlight a brand's point-of-difference, providing that consumers know the brand's actual membership.

UMPQUA BANK

Most consumers would never describe a bank transaction as soul satisfying, but Oregon-based Umpqua Bank isn't your average bank. Umpqua has become affiliated with the café/retail categories in order to establish points-of-difference between itself and other banks. About a decade ago, when Umpqua trailed U.S. Bank and Wells Fargo in market share, its new CEO decided to go into totally new territory: Think bank crossed with your local Starbucks. No longer called "banks" or "branches," Umpqua's "stores" were designed to stimulate cozy connections between customers and feature a computer café with wi-fi access and branded merchandise, including Umpqua's own blend of coffee (a must in the coffee-obsessed Northwest). Like Starbucks, Umpqua has also made music a part of its product mix. Working with Portland's Rumblefish, it created something called "Discover Local Music." Listening stations with headphones allow bank customers to browse and sample songs and even purchase customized CDs. After-hours activities such as movies, knitting, and yoga classes are encouraged just as much as financial events. However, creating the cool, inviting environment is just half the equation. Umpqua also fosters what it calls "extreme service." Every new employee receives guest service education through the Ritz-Carlton Hotel training group, well known for its award-winning service. Not only has Umpqua managed to go from $140 million in assets in 1994 to $7 billion in 2006, but the company was also heralded in *BusinessWeek*'s "Best Ideas of 2005," in an article that said, " . . . customers aren't just paying for a cup of coffee at Starbucks or, say, simply doing transactions at Umpqua Bank. They're paying admission to a club—one that delivers something to satisfy the soul."[9]

With this approach, however, it's important not to be trapped between categories. Consumers should understand what the brand stands for, and not just what it's not. The Konica e-mini M digital camera and MP3 player was marketed as the "four-in-one entertainment solution," but it suffered from functional deficiencies in each of its product applications and languished in the marketplace.[10]

The typical approach to positioning is to inform consumers of a brand's membership before stating its point-of-difference. Presumably, consumers need to know what a product is and what function it serves before deciding whether it dominates the brands against which it competes. For new products, initial advertising often concentrates on creating brand awareness, and subsequent advertising attempts to craft the brand image.

Umpqua Bank competes in the Pacific Northwest by turning the idea of brand categories upside down. Its "stores" offer music, coffee, wi-fi access, and of course—banking services.

STRADDLE POSITIONING Occasionally, a company will try to straddle two frames of reference.

BMW

When BMW first made a strong competitive push into the U.S. market in the early 1980s, it positioned the brand as the only automobile that offered both luxury *and* performance. At that time, consumers saw American luxury cars as lacking performance, and American performance cars as lacking luxury. By relying on the design of its cars, its German heritage, and other aspects of a well-conceived marketing program, BMW was able to simultaneously achieve: (1) a point-of-difference on luxury and a point-of-parity on performance with respect to performance cars and (2) a point-of-difference on performance and a point-of-parity on luxury with respect to luxury cars. The clever slogan "The Ultimate Driving Machine" effectively captured the newly created umbrella category—luxury performance cars.

Although a straddle positioning often is attractive as a means of reconciling potentially conflicting consumer goals and creating a "best-of-both-worlds" solution, it also carries an extra burden. If the points-of-parity and points-of-difference with respect to both categories are not credible, the brand may not be viewed as a legitimate player in either category and may end up in "no-man's-land." Many early PDAs that unsuccessfully tried to straddle categories ranging from pagers to laptop computers provide a vivid illustration of this risk.

COMMUNICATING CATEGORY MEMBERSHIP There are three main ways to convey a brand's category membership:

1. ***Announcing category benefits***—To reassure consumers that a brand will deliver on the fundamental reason for using a category, marketers frequently use benefits to announce category membership. Thus, industrial tools might claim to have durability and antacids might announce their efficacy. A brownie mix might attain membership in the baked desserts category by claiming the benefit of great taste and support this claim by including high-quality ingredients (performance) or by showing users delighting in its consumption (imagery).
2. ***Comparing to exemplars***—Well-known, noteworthy brands in a category can also help a brand specify its category membership. When Tommy Hilfiger was an unknown, advertising announced his membership as a great American designer by associating him with Geoffrey Beene, Stanley Blacker, Calvin Klein, and Perry Ellis, who were recognized members of that category.
3. ***Relying on the product descriptor***—The product descriptor that follows the brand name is often a concise means of conveying category origin. Ford Motor Co. invested more than $1 billion on a radical new 2004 model called the X-Trainer, which combined the attributes of an SUV, a minivan, and a station wagon. To communicate its unique position—and to avoid association with its Explorer and Country Squire models—the vehicle, later called Freestyle, was designated a "sports wagon."[11]

BMW has achieved market success in the U.S. with a straddle positioning strategy that emphasizes both luxury and performance.

Choosing POPs and PODs

Points-of-parity are driven by the needs of category membership (to create category POPs) and the necessity of negating competitors' PODs (to create competitive POPs). In addition to distinctiveness, two other important considerations in choosing points-of-difference are that consumers find the POD desirable and that the firm has the capabilities to deliver on it. As Table 10.2 shows, three criteria can judge both desirability and deliverability.

Marketers must decide at which level(s) to anchor the brand's points-of-differences. At the lowest level are the *brand attributes*; at the next level are the *brand benefits*; and at the top are the *brand values*. Thus marketers of Dove soap can talk about its attribute of one-quarter cleansing cream; or its benefit of softer skin; or its value of being more attractive. Attributes are typically the least desirable level to position. First, the buyer is more interested in benefits. Second, competitors can easily copy attributes. Third, current attributes may become less desirable over time.

Research has shown, however, that brands can sometimes be successfully differentiated on seemingly irrelevant attributes, *if* consumers infer the proper benefit.[12] Procter & Gamble differentiates its Folger's instant coffee by its "flaked coffee crystals," created through a "unique patented process." In reality, the shape of the coffee particles is irrelevant because the crystals immediately dissolve in the hot water. Saying that a brand of coffee is "mountain grown" is irrelevant because most coffee is mountain grown. "Marketing Memo: Writing a Positioning Statement" outlines how marketers can express positioning formally.

Creating POPs and PODs

One common difficulty in creating a strong, competitive brand positioning is that many of the attributes or benefits that make up the points-of-parity and points-of-difference are negatively correlated. For example, it might be difficult to position a brand as "inexpensive" and at the same time assert that it is "of the highest quality." Con-Agra must convince consumers that Healthy Choice frozen foods are good for you and taste good. Table 10.3 displays some other examples of negatively correlated attributes and benefits. Moreover, individual attributes and benefits often have positive *and* negative aspects. For example, consider a long-lived brand such as La-Z-Boy recliners. The brand's heritage could suggest experience, wisdom, and expertise. On the other hand, it could also imply being old-fashioned and not up-to-date.[13]

TABLE 10.2 Judging Desirability and Deliverability for Points-of-Difference

Desirability Criteria	Deliverability Criteria
Relevance Target consumers must find the POD personally relevant and important. ■ The Westin Stamford hotel in Singapore advertised that it was the world's tallest hotel, but a hotel's height is not important to many tourists. ***Distinctiveness*** Target consumers must find the POD distinctive and superior. ■ Splenda sugar substitute overtook Equal and Sweet'N Low to become the leader in its category in 2003 by differentiating itself on its authenticity as a product derived from sugar, without any of the associated drawbacks.[14] ***Believability*** Target consumers must find the POD believable and credible. A brand must offer a compelling reason for choosing it over the other options. ■ Mountain Dew may argue that it is more energizing than other soft drinks and support this claim by noting that it has a higher level of caffeine. ■ Chanel No. 5 perfume may claim to be the quintessential elegant French perfume and support this claim by noting the long association between Chanel and haute couture.	***Feasibility*** The product design and marketing offering must support the desired association. Does communicating the desired association require real changes to the product itself, or just perceptual shifts in the way the consumer thinks of the product or brand? The latter is typically easier. ■ General Motors has had to work to overcome public perceptions that Cadillac is not a youthful, contemporary brand. ***Communicability*** Consumers must be given a compelling reason and understandable rationale as to why the brand can deliver the desired benefit. What factual, verifiable evidence or "proof points" can ensure consumers will actually believe in the brand and its desired associations? ■ Substantiators often come in the form of patented, branded ingredients, such as Nivea Wrinkle Control Crème with Q10 co-enzyme or Herbal Essences hair conditioner with Hawafena. ***Sustainability*** The firm must be sufficiently committed and willing to devote enough resources to create an enduring positioning. Is the positioning preemptive, defensible, and difficult to attack? Can the favorability of a brand association be reinforced and strengthened over time? ■ It is generally easier for market leaders such as ADM, Visa, and SAP, whose positioning is based in part on demonstrable product or service performance, to sustain their positioning than for market leaders such as Fendi, Prada, and Hermes, whose positioning is based on fashion and is thus subject to the whims of a more fickle market.

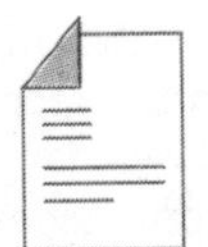

MARKETING MEMO | WRITING A POSITIONING STATEMENT

To communicate a company or brand positioning, marketing plans often include a *positioning statement.* The statement should follow the form: To *(target group and need)*, our *(brand)* is *(the concept)* that *(what the point-of-difference is or does)*. For example: "To *busy professionals who need to stay organized, Palm Pilot* is *an electronic organizer* that *allows you to back up files on your PC more easily and reliably than competitive products.*" Sometimes the positioning statement is more detailed:

> *Mountain Dew:* To young, active soft-drink consumers who have little time for sleep, Mountain Dew is the soft drink that gives you more energy than any other brand because it has the highest level of caffeine. With Mountain Dew, you can stay alert and keep going even when you haven't been able to get a good night's sleep.

Note that the positioning first states the product's membership in a category (Mountain Dew is a soft drink) and then shows its point-of-difference from other members of the group (it has more caffeine). The product's membership in the category suggests the points-of-parity that it might have with other products in the category, but the case for the product rests on its points-of-difference. Sometimes the marketer will put the product in a surprisingly different category before indicating the points of difference.

Sources: Bobby J. Calder and Steven J. Reagan, "Brand Design," in *Kellogg on Marketing*, ed. Dawn Iacobucci (New York: John Wiley & Sons, 2001), p. 61; Alice M. Tybout and Brian Sternthal, "Brand Positioning," in *Kellogg on Marketing*, ed. Dawn Iacobucci (New York: John Wiley & Sons, 2001), p. 54.

TABLE 10.3

Examples of Negatively Correlated Attributes and Benefits

Low price vs. High quality	Powerful vs. Safe
Taste vs. Low calories	Strong vs. Refined
Nutritious vs. Good tasting	Ubiquitous vs. Exclusive
Efficacious vs. Mild	Varied vs. Simple

BURBERRY LTD.

In recent years the trademark Burberry plaid has become one of the world's most recognizable symbols. From its staid place on Burberry raincoats, the plaid began showing up on dog collars, taffeta dresses, bikinis, on gear worn by British soccer hooligans, and unfortunately, on an increasing number of counterfeit goods. This integral part of Burberry's heritage, called "the check" by those in the fashion industry, had suddenly become a liability due to overexposure. Consequently, Burberry's sales are sluggish and its CEO, Angela Ahrendt, is attempting to jump-start sales growth in numerous ways. For one, she has studied Burberry's 150-year history to create new brand symbols, such as an equestrian-knight logo that was trademarked by the company in 1901. Handbags will allude to the brand's tradition as a trench coat maker by featuring leather belt buckles or the quilt pattern that lined Burberry's outerwear. The other tactic Ms. Ahrendt is pushing is to invest aggressively in selling Burberry accessories—handbags, shoes, scarves, and belts—rather than apparel, which now accounts for 75% of the company's sales. Not only do these accessories have higher profit margins, but they are also less exposed than clothing to changes in fashion.[15]

A straddle brand positioning can help convince customers that the product can accomplish two or more seemingly conflicting benefits, such as Gore-Tex's promise to deliver both breathability and water protection.

Unfortunately, consumers typically want to maximize *both* the negatively correlated attributes or benefits. Much of the art and science of marketing is dealing with trade-offs, and positioning is no different. The best approach clearly is to develop a product or service that performs well on both dimensions. BMW was able to establish its "luxury and performance" straddle positioning due in large part to product design, and the fact that the car was in fact seen as both luxurious and high performance. Gore-Tex® was able to overcome the seemingly conflicting product image of "breathable" and "waterproof" through technological advances.

Some marketers have adopted other approaches to address attribute or benefit trade-offs: launching two different marketing campaigns, each one devoted to a different brand attribute or benefit; linking themselves to any kind of entity (person, place, or thing) that possesses the right kind of equity as a means to establish an attribute or benefit as a POP or POD; and even attempting to convince consumers that the negative relationship between attributes and benefits, if they consider it differently, is in fact positive.

::: Differentiation Strategies

To avoid the commodity trap, marketers must start with the belief that you can differentiate anything. (See "Marketing Memo: How to Derive Fresh Consumer Insights to Differentiate Products and Services.") **Competitive advantage** is a company's ability to perform in one or more ways that competitors cannot or will not match. Michael Porter urged

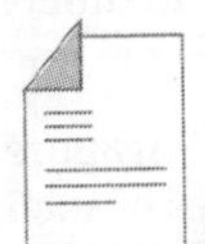

MARKETING MEMO | HOW TO DERIVE FRESH CONSUMER INSIGHTS TO DIFFERENTIATE PRODUCTS AND SERVICES

In "Discovering New Points of Differentiation," Ian C. MacMillan and Rita Gunther McGrath argue that if companies examine customers' entire experience with a product or service—the consumption chain—they can uncover opportunities to position their offerings in ways that neither they nor their competitors thought possible. MacMillan and McGrath list a set of questions marketers can use to help them identify new, consumer-based points of differentiation.

- How do people become aware of their need for your product and service?
- How do consumers find your offering?
- How do consumers make their final selection?
- How do consumers order and purchase your product or service?
- What happens when your product or service is delivered?
- How is your product installed?
- How is your product or service paid for?
- How is your product stored?
- How is your product moved around?
- What is the consumer really using your product for?
- What do consumers need help with when they use your product?
- What about returns or exchanges?
- How is your product repaired or serviced?
- What happens when your product is disposed of or no longer used?

Source: Ian C. MacMillan and Rita Gunther McGrath, "Discovering New Points of Differentiation," *Harvard Business Review* (July–August 1997): 133–45.

companies to build a sustainable competitive advantage.[16] But few competitive advantages are sustainable. At best, they may be leverageable. A *leverageable advantage* is one that a company can use as a springboard to new advantages, much as Microsoft has leveraged its operating system to Microsoft Office and then to networking applications. In general, a company that hopes to endure must be in the business of continuously inventing new advantages.

Customers must see any competitive advantage as a *customer advantage.* For example, if a company delivers faster than its competitors, it won't be a customer advantage if customers don't value speed. Select Comfort has made a splash in the mattress industry with its Sleep Number beds, which allows consumers to adjust the support and fit of the mattress for optimal comfort with a simple numbering index.[17] Companies must also focus on building customer advantages.[18] Then they will deliver high customer value and satisfaction, which leads to high repeat purchases and ultimately to high company profitability.

Marketers can differentiate brands on the basis of many variables. Southwest Airlines is a good example.

SOUTHWEST AIRLINES

The Dallas-based carrier Southwest Airlines carved its niche in short-haul flights with low prices, reliable service, and a healthy sense of humor. Southwest keeps costs low by offering only basic in-flight service (no meals, no movies) and rapid turnaround at the gates to keep the planes in the air. But Southwest knew it couldn't differentiate on price alone, because competitors could try to muscle into the market with their own cheaper fares. So it has also distinguished itself as a "fun" airline, noted for humorous in-flight commentary from pilots and cabin crew members. Another popular feature of Southwest flights is the first-come, first-served open seating: Passengers are given numbered cards based on when they arrive at the gate. Southwest is now the nation's largest airline in terms of passengers flown and holds the distinction of being the only low-fare airline to achieve long-term financial success.[19]

The obvious means of differentiation, and often most compelling ones to consumers, relate to aspects of the product and service (reviewed in Chapters 12 and 13). Swatch offers colorful, fashionable watches. Subway differentiates itself in terms of healthy sandwiches as an alternative to fast food. In competitive markets, however, firms may need to go beyond these. Consider these other dimensions, among the many that a company can use to differentiate its market offerings:

- ***Personnel differentiation.*** Companies can have better-trained employees. Singapore Airlines is well regarded in large part because of its flight attendants. The sales forces of such companies as General Electric, Cisco, Frito-Lay, Northwestern Mutual Life, and Pfizer enjoy an excellent reputation.[20]
- ***Channel differentiation.*** Companies can more effectively and efficiently design their distribution channels' coverage, expertise, and performance. Back in 1946, pet food was cheap, not too nutritious, and sold exclusively in supermarkets and the occasional feed store. Dayton, Ohio–based Iams found success selling premium pet food through regional veterinarians, breeders, and pet stores.
- ***Image differentiation.*** Companies can craft powerful, compelling images. The primary explanation for Marlboro's extraordinary worldwide market share (around 30%) is that Marlboro's "macho cowboy" image has struck a responsive chord with much of the cigarette-smoking public. Wine and liquor companies also work hard to develop distinctive images for their brands. Even a seller's physical space can be a powerful image generator. Hyatt Regency hotels developed a distinctive image through its atrium lobbies.

::: Product Life-Cycle Marketing Strategies

A company's positioning and differentiation strategy must change as the product, market, and competitors change over the *product life cycle* (PLC). To say that a product has a life cycle is to assert four things:

1. Products have a limited life.
2. Product sales pass through distinct stages, each posing different challenges, opportunities, and problems to the seller.
3. Profits rise and fall at different stages of the product life cycle.
4. Products require different marketing, financial, manufacturing, purchasing, and human resource strategies in each life-cycle stage.

Product Life Cycles

Most product life-cycle curves are portrayed as bell-shaped (see Figure 10.1). This curve is typically divided into four stages: introduction, growth, maturity, and decline.[21]

1. ***Introduction***—A period of slow sales growth as the product is introduced in the market. Profits are nonexistent because of the heavy expenses of product introduction.
2. ***Growth***—A period of rapid market acceptance and substantial profit improvement.
3. ***Maturity***—A slowdown in sales growth because the product has achieved acceptance by most potential buyers. Profits stabilize or decline because of increased competition.
4. ***Decline***—Sales show a downward drift and profits erode.

FIG. 10.1

Sales and Profit Life Cycles

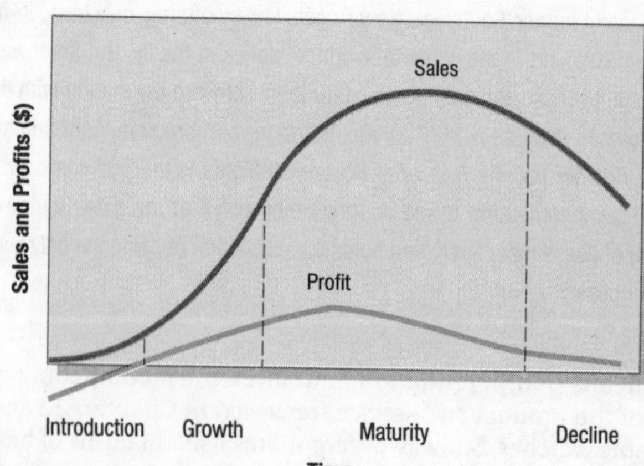

FIG. 10.2 | Common Product Life-Cycle Patterns

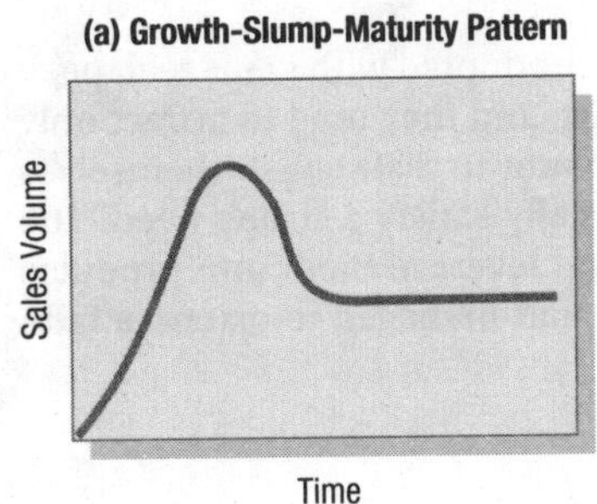

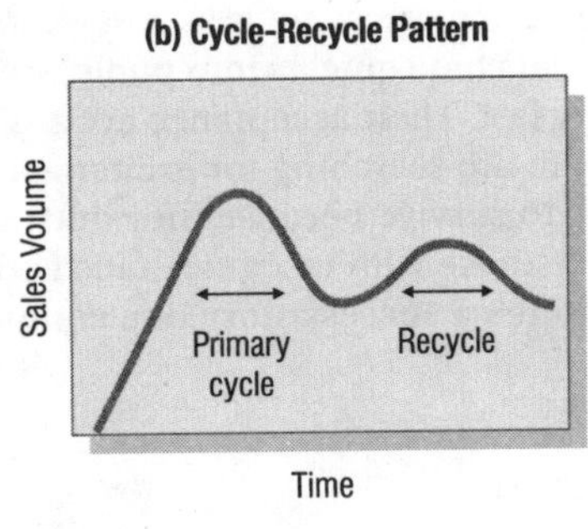

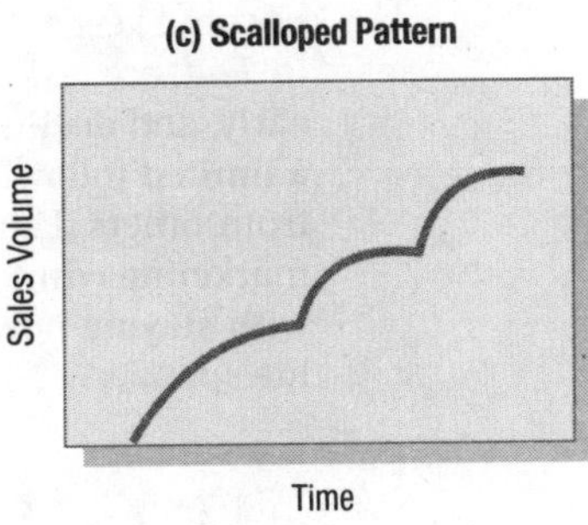

We can use the PLC concept to analyze a product category (liquor), a product form (white liquor), a product (vodka), or a brand (Smirnoff). Not all products exhibit a bell-shaped PLC.[22] Three common alternate patterns are shown in Figure 10.2.

Figure 10.2(a) shows a *growth-slump-maturity pattern*, often characteristic of small kitchen appliances such as handheld mixers and bread makers. Sales grow rapidly when the product is first introduced and then fall to a "petrified" level that is sustained by late adopters buying the product for the first time and early adopters replacing it.

The *cycle-recycle pattern* in Figure 10.2(b) often describes the sales of new drugs. The pharmaceutical company aggressively promotes its new drug, and this produces the first cycle. Later, sales start declining and the company gives the drug another promotion push, which produces a second cycle (usually of smaller magnitude and duration).[23]

Another common pattern is the *scalloped PLC* in Figure 10.2(c). Here sales pass through a succession of life cycles based on the discovery of new-product characteristics, uses, or users. The sales of nylon, for example, show a scalloped pattern because of the many new uses—parachutes, hosiery, shirts, carpeting, boat sails, automobile tires—that continue to be discovered over time.[24]

Style, Fashion, and Fad Life Cycles

We need to distinguish three special categories of product life cycles—styles, fashions, and fads (Figure 10.3). A *style* is a basic and distinctive mode of expression appearing in a field of human endeavor. Styles appear in homes (colonial, ranch, Cape Cod); clothing (formal, casual, funky); and art (realistic, surrealistic, abstract). A style can last for generations and go in and out of vogue. A *fashion* is a currently accepted or popular style in a given field. Fashions pass through four stages: distinctiveness, emulation, mass fashion, and decline.[25]

The length of a fashion cycle is hard to predict. One point of view is that fashions end because they represent a purchase compromise, and consumers start looking for the missing attributes.[26] For example, as automobiles become smaller, they become less comfortable, and then a growing number of buyers start wanting larger cars. Another explanation is that too many consumers adopt the fashion, thus turning others away. Still another is that

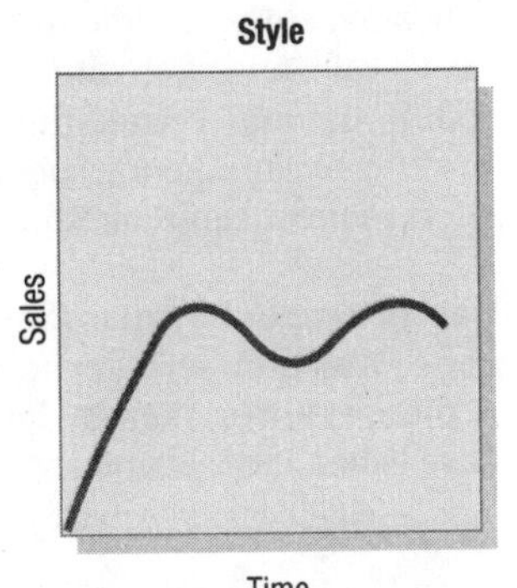

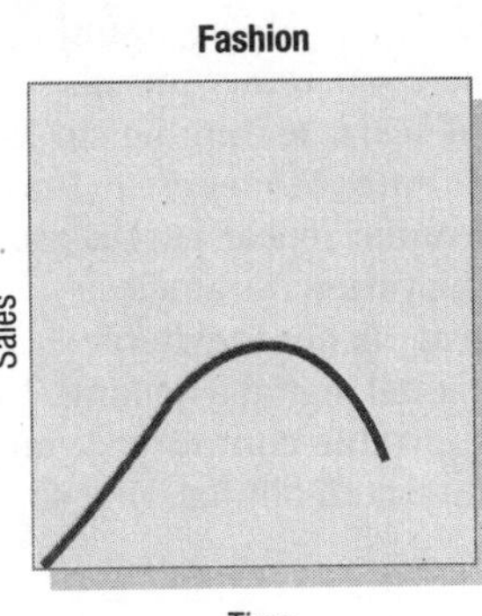

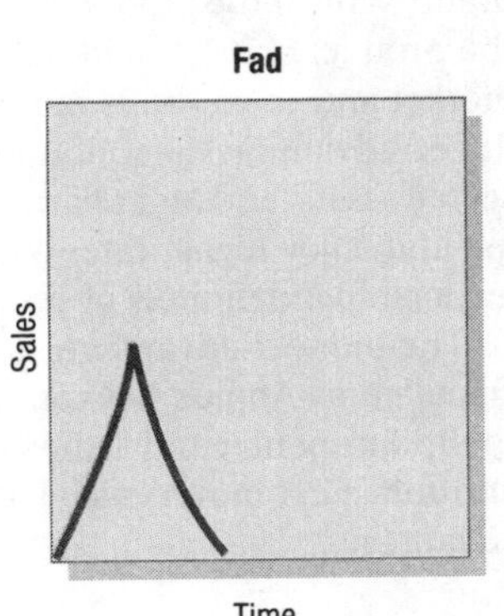

FIG. 10.3 | Style, Fashion, and Fad Life Cycles

the length of a particular fashion cycle depends on the extent to which the fashion meets a genuine need, is consistent with other trends in the society, satisfies societal norms and values, and keeps within technological limits as it develops.[27]

Fads are fashions that come quickly into public view, are adopted with great zeal, peak early, and decline very fast. Their acceptance cycle is short, and they tend to attract only a limited following who are searching for excitement or want to distinguish themselves from others. Fads fail to survive because they don't normally satisfy a strong need. The marketing winners are those who recognize fads early and leverage them into products with staying power. Here's a success story of a company that managed to extend a fad's life span:

TRIVIAL PURSUIT

Since its debut at the International Toy Fair in 1982, Trivial Pursuit has sold 80 million copies in 18 languages in 32 countries, and it remains one of the best-selling adult games. Parker Brothers has kept the product's popularity going by making a new game with updated questions every year. It also keeps creating offshoots—travel packs, a children's version, Trivial Pursuit Genus IV, and themed versions tapping into niches tied to various sports, movies, and decades. The game is available in a variety of platforms: an interactive CD-ROM from Virgin Entertainment Interactive; online with its own Web site (www.trivialpursuit.com), and a mobile edition that can be accessed via cell phones. If you're having trouble making dinner conversation on a date—no problem: NTN Entertainment Network has put Trivial Pursuit in about 3,000 restaurants.[28]

Marketing Strategies: Introduction Stage and the Pioneer Advantage

Because it takes time to roll out a new product, work out the technical problems, fill dealer pipelines, and gain consumer acceptance, sales growth tends to be slow in the introduction stage.[29] Profits are negative or low, and promotional expenditures are at their highest ratio to sales because of the need to (1) inform potential consumers, (2) induce product trial, and (3) secure distribution in retail outlets.[30] Firms focus on those buyers who are the most ready to buy, usually in higher-income groups. Prices tend to be high because costs are high.

Companies that plan to introduce a new product must decide when to enter the market. To be first can be rewarding, but risky and expensive. To come in later makes sense if the firm can bring superior technology, quality, or brand strength.

Speeding up innovation time is essential in an age of shortening product life cycles. Being early has been shown to pay. One prior study found that products that came out six months late—but on budget—earned an average of 33% less profit in their first five years; products that came out on time but 50% over budget cut their profits by only 4%.[31]

Most studies indicate that the market pioneer gains the greatest advantage.[32] Companies such as Campbell, Coca-Cola, Hallmark, and Amazon.com developed sustained market dominance. Carpenter and Nakamoto found that 19 of 25 companies that were market leaders in 1923 were still the market leaders in 1983, 60 years later.[33] Robinson and Min found that in a sample of industrial-goods businesses, 66% of pioneers survived at least 10 years, versus 48% of the early followers.[34]

What are the sources of the pioneer's advantage?[35] Early users will recall the pioneer's brand name if the product satisfies them. The pioneer's brand also establishes the attributes the product class should possess. The pioneer's brand normally aims at the middle of the market and so captures more users. Customer inertia also plays a role; and there are producer advantages: economies of scale, technological leadership, patents, ownership of scarce assets, and other barriers to entry. Pioneers can have more effective marketing spending and enjoy higher rates of consumer repeat purchases. An alert pioneer can maintain its leadership indefinitely by pursuing various strategies.[36]

The pioneer advantage, however, is not inevitable.[37] Look at the fate of Bowmar (hand calculators), Apple's Newton (personal digital assistant), Netscape (Web browser), Reynolds (ballpoint pens), and Osborne (portable computers), market pioneers overtaken by later entrants. First movers also have to watch out for what some have called the "second mover advantage."

Wikipedia, the Web's first and most popular reader-created encyclopedia, may soon face competition from second-in-the-market Citizendium, a similar site created by Wikipedia's founder.

WIKIPEDIA.ORG, CITIZENDIUM.ORG

Launched in January 2001, the collaborative Internet encyclopedia Wikipedia has ridden its pioneer advantage to become as familiar as eBay and Google. Its 5 million pages of content are created entirely by volunteers and are available, free, to users in 250 languages. It might seem that no other Internet encyclopedia could hope to eclipse Wikipedia's reach and brand equity at this point. Yet, who better than Wikipedia's cofounder, Larry Sanger, to try? Sanger believes his new site, Citizendium, enjoys certain "second mover" advantages that can help it overtake his old site. First, second movers avoid heavy investment in R&D by replicating the first mover's approach. Citizendium will open up as an exact copy of Wikipedia, saving five years of development time. Next, second movers enjoy the advantage of positioning. Because Sanger knows exactly how Wikipedia is perceived, he can use that data to aim Citizendium at what he calls "different social niches." Finally, second movers learn from the pioneer's mistakes. Citizendium is introducing site sponsorship and an editorial team of experts who can prove their expertise in their respective subjects. Wikipedia, watch your back![38]

Steven Schnaars studied 28 industries where the imitators surpassed the innovators.[39] He found several weaknesses among the failing pioneers, including new products that were too crude, were improperly positioned, or appeared before there was strong demand; product-development costs that exhausted the innovator's resources; a lack of resources to compete against entering larger firms; and managerial incompetence or unhealthy complacency. Successful imitators thrived by offering lower prices, improving the product more continuously, or using brute market power to overtake the pioneer. None of the companies that now dominate in the manufacture of personal computers—including Dell, Gateway, and Compaq—were first movers.[40]

Golder and Tellis raise further doubts about the pioneer advantage.[41] They distinguish between an *inventor*, first to develop patents in a new-product category, a *product pioneer*, first to develop a working model, and a *market pioneer*, first to sell in the new-product category. They also include nonsurviving pioneers in their sample. They conclude that although pioneers may still have an advantage, a larger number of market pioneers fail than has been reported, and a larger number of early market leaders (though not pioneers) succeed. Examples of later entrants overtaking market pioneers are IBM over Sperry in mainframe computers, Matsushita over Sony in VCRs, and GE over EMI in CAT scan equipment.

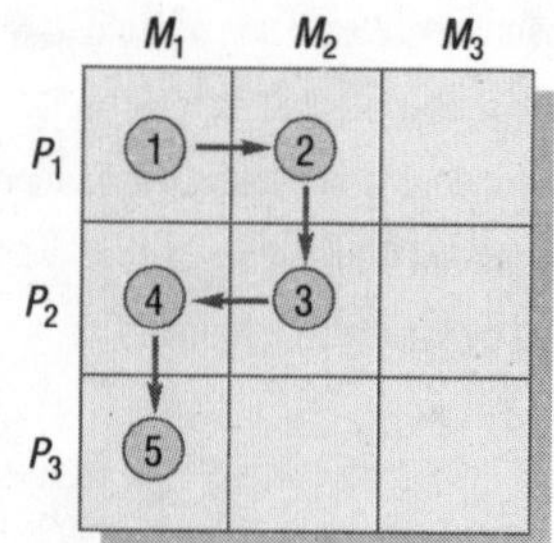

FIG. 10.4

Long-Range Product Market Expansion Strategy (P_i = product i; M_j = market j)

In a more recent study, Tellis and Golder identify the following five factors as underpinning long-term market leadership: vision of a mass market, persistence, relentless innovation, financial commitment, and asset leverage.[42] Other research has highlighted the importance of the novelty of the product innovation.[43] When a pioneer starts a market with a really new product, as was the case with Segway Human Transporter, survival can be very challenging. In contrast, when the market is started by an incremental innovation, as was the case with MP3 players with video capabilities, pioneers' survival rates are much higher.

The pioneer should visualize the various product markets it could initially enter, knowing it cannot enter all of them at once. Suppose market-segmentation analysis reveals the product market segments shown in Figure 10.4. The pioneer should analyze the profit potential of each product market singly and in combination and decide on a market expansion path. Thus the pioneer in Figure 10.4 plans first to enter product market P_1M_1, then move the product into a second market (P_1M_2), then surprise the competition by developing a second product for the second market (P_2M_2), then take the second product back into the first market (P_2M_1), and then launch a third product for the first market (P_3M_1). If this game plan works, the pioneer firm will own a good part of the first two segments and serve them with two or three products.

Marketing Strategies: Growth Stage

The growth stage is marked by a rapid climb in sales. Early adopters like the product, and additional consumers start buying it. New competitors enter, attracted by the opportunities. They introduce new product features and expand distribution.

Prices remain where they are or fall slightly, depending on how fast demand increases. Companies maintain their promotional expenditures at the same or at a slightly increased level to meet competition and to continue to educate the market. Sales rise much faster than promotional expenditures, causing a welcome decline in the promotion–sales ratio. Profits increase during this stage as promotion costs are spread over a larger volume and unit manufacturing costs fall faster than price declines, owing to the producer learning effect. Firms must watch for a change from an accelerating to a decelerating rate of growth in order to prepare new strategies. AthenaHealth Inc. is at this stage of the product life cycle.

ATHENAHEALTH INC.

Rated one of the fastest-growing U.S. private companies for two years running, AthenaHealth experienced a whopping 347% revenue increase from 2002 to 2005. Run by Jonathan Bush, President George W. Bush's first cousin, AthenaHealth has grown by tackling physicians' most heinous tasks: insurance bill submission and recordkeeping. Its unique pitch to physicians is that its fee is based solely on the amount of reimbursements it recovers. This gives AthenaHealth an incentive to work fast, something doctors appreciate when the average time between submission and reimbursement stretches past two months. Even with its stellar growth, AthenaHealth has ample room to grow even more. Only about 1% of the nation's doctors are signed up as clients so far and the company hasn't yet turned a profit. As a high-growth company, it's putting its eggs in these two baskets: wooing venture capital and wooing more clients. To do the latter, AthenaHealth is adding staffers to its headcount of 500 full-time employees, and it has signed a sales partnership with hospital IT company Eclipsys to reach the over 50% of U.S. doctors who work in very small private practices—so small they don't have the staff to keep up with their billing. Competitors include McKesson, which now owns one of the largest outsourced-billing providers for medical offices. To keep ahead of the game, CEO Bush spends half his time on the road talking up the company.[44]

During the growth stage, the firm uses several strategies to sustain rapid market growth:

- It improves product quality and adds new product features and improved styling.
- It adds new models and flanker products (i.e., products of different sizes, flavors, and so forth that protect the main product).
- It enters new market segments.

- It increases its distribution coverage and enters new distribution channels.
- It shifts from product-awareness advertising to product-preference advertising.
- It lowers prices to attract the next layer of price-sensitive buyers.

These market-expansion strategies strengthen the firm's competitive position. Consider how Yahoo! has fueled growth.

YAHOO!

Founded in 1994 by Web-surfing Stanford University grad students, Yahoo! has become the number-one place to be on the Web, averaging 129 million unique visitors a month, representing almost 80% of the online population. The company grew into more than just a search engine; it became a portal, offering a full-blown package of information and services, from e-mail to online shopping malls. Yahoo!'s revenues, which exceeded $6 billion in 2005, come from a number of sources—banner ads, paid search, subscriptions for services such as personals, and a broadband partnership with SBC Communications. Yahoo!'s $1.6 billion acquisition of Overture Services in 2003, a key paid-search competitor of Google, helped strengthen its claim as a one-stop shop for advertisers. Subsequent years have seen many additional acquisitions to expand the company's online capabilities and services, including online social event calendar Upcoming.org, online video editing site Jumpcut, and online social contest site bix.com. Yahoo! also continued to grow globally with strong emphasis on Europe and Asia, helped in part by the acquisition of Kelkoo, a European comparison-shopping site, for $579 million and 46% of Alibaba, a Chinese e-commerce company, for $1 billion in cash in 2005.[45]

A firm in the growth stage faces a trade-off between high market share and high current profit. By spending money on product improvement, promotion, and distribution, it can capture a dominant position. It forgoes maximum current profit in the hope of making even greater profits in the next stage.

Marketing Strategies: Maturity Stage

At some point, the rate of sales growth will slow, and the product will enter a stage of relative maturity. This stage normally lasts longer than the previous stages and poses big challenges to marketing management. Most products are in the maturity stage of the life cycle.

The maturity stage divides into three phases: growth, stable, and decaying maturity. In the first phase, the sales growth rate starts to decline. There are no new distribution channels to fill. New competitive forces emerge (see "Marketing Insight: Competitive Category Dynamics"). In the second phase, sales flatten on a per capita basis because of market saturation. Most potential consumers have tried the product, and future sales are governed by population growth and replacement demand. In the third phase, decaying maturity, the absolute level of sales starts to decline, and customers begin switching to other products.

The third phase of maturity poses the most challenges. The sales slowdown creates overcapacity in the industry, which leads to intensified competition. Competitors scramble to find niches. They engage in frequent markdowns. They increase advertising and trade and consumer promotion. They increase R&D budgets to develop product improvements and line extensions. They make deals to supply private brands. A shakeout begins, and weaker competitors withdraw. The industry eventually consists of well-entrenched competitors whose basic drive is to gain or maintain market share.

Dominating the industry are a few giant firms—perhaps a quality leader, a service leader, and a cost leader—that serve the whole market and make their profits mainly through high volume and lower costs. Surrounding these dominant firms is a multitude of market nichers, including market specialists, product specialists, and customizing firms. The issue facing a firm in a mature market is whether to struggle to become one of the "big three" and achieve profits through high volume and low cost, or to pursue a niching strategy and achieve profits through low volume and a high margin. Sometimes, however, the market will become polarized between low- and high-end segments, and the firms in the middle see their market share steadily erode. Here's how Swedish appliance manufacturer, Electrolux, has coped with this situation.

MARKETING INSIGHT | COMPETITIVE CATEGORY DYNAMICS

One of marketing's most astute observers, former U.C. Berkeley professor David Aaker notes that because new categories can represent strategically important threats or opportunities, marketers must be very attentive to the forces that drive their emergence. He cites seven such dynamics that result in new categories.

1. ***A new product or service dimension expands the boundaries of an existing category***—In the yogurt business, the "eat-on-the-go" trend led Yoplait to develop Go-Gurt, delivered in a colorful nine-inch tube designed to enhance portability and to appeal to kids. Go-Gurt helped Yoplait forge ahead of Danone's Dannon, a brand it had trailed for decades. A new subcategory had been created in which Dannon was not relevant.
2. ***A new product or set of products carves out a fresh niche in an existing category***—The energy-bar market created by PowerBar ultimately fragmented into a variety of subcategories, including those directed at specific segments (such as Luna bars for women) and some possessing specific attributes (such as the protein-associated Balance and the calorie-control bar Pria). Each represented a subcategory for which the original PowerBar was not relevant.
3. ***A new competitor devises a way to bundle existing categories into a supercategory***—In the late 1990s, Siebel created Internet-based customer relationship management software by pulling together a host of applications, including customer loyalty programs, customer acquisition, call centers, customer service, customer contact, and sales force automation. In doing so, Siebel rendered irrelevant, for some customers, the more specialized application programs of competitors.
4. ***A new competitor repositions existing products or services to create an original category***—In the United Kingdom, Ford positioned its Galaxy minivan in relation to first-class air travel—comfortable enough to be suitable for busy executives. By highlighting attributes far different from those that would appeal to a buyer looking for a family vehicle, the automaker created a new minivan subcategory.
5. ***Customer needs propel a new product category or subcategory***—Dual trends—wellness and the use of herbs and natural supplements—have supported a huge new beverage category, healthy refreshment beverages. It now contains a host of subcategories, including enhanced teas, fruit drinks, soy-based drinks, and specialty waters. The pioneer and category leader is SoBe, which started in 1996 with SoBe Black Tea 3G with ginseng, ginkgo, and guarana and now has an extensive line of teas, juices, and energy drinks.
6. ***A new technology leads the development of a product category or subcategory***—Asahi reshaped the Japanese beer market by introducing an innovative brewing process that reduced "body" and bitterness while increasing alcohol content. Its new product, Asahi Super Dry, had a very different taste from that of other Japanese lagers and generated a new category, dry beer. As a result, Kirin, for decades the leading brand with a dominant 60% share of market, suddenly was not relevant for the many customers attracted to the new category. Asahi's market share—8% when Super Dry was launched in 1986—rose continually until it took share leadership in 1998.
7. ***A company exploits changing technologies to invent a new category***—TiVo Inc. created a new category for home television viewing by combining the personal video player, a computer hard drive, and an electronic program guide, changing the way people watch television. Any new entrant must define itself with respect to TiVo.

Sources: Reprinted from David A. Aaker, "The Relevance of Brand Relevance," *Strategy+Business* 35 (Summer 2004): 1–10. See also David A. Aaker, *Brand Portfolio Strategy: Creating Relevance, Differentiation, Energy, Leverage, and Clarity* (New York: Free Press, 2004).

ELECTROLUX AB

In 2002, Electrolux began facing a rapidly polarizing appliance market. At one end, low-cost Asian companies such as Haier, LG, and Samsung were applying downward price pressure. At the other end, premium competitors such as Bosch, Sub-Zero, and Viking were continuing to grow at the expense of the middle-of-the-road brands. Electrolux's new CEO Hans Stråberg, who took over the reins just as the middle was dropping out of the market, decided to escape the middle by rethinking Electrolux's customers' wants and needs. For instance, rather than accept the stratification between low and high, Stråberg segmented the market according to the lifestyle and purchasing patterns of about 20 different types of consumers—"20 product positions" as he calls them. Electrolux now successfully markets its steam ovens to health-oriented consumers, for example, and its compact dishwashers, originally developed for smaller kitchens, to a broader consumer segment interested in washing dishes more often. To companies finding themselves stuck in the middle of a mature market, Stråberg offers these words of advice: "Start with consumers and understand what their latent needs are and what problems they experience . . . then put the puzzle together yourself to discover what people really want to have. Henry Ford is supposed to have said, 'If I had asked people what they really wanted, I would have made faster horses' or something like that. You need to figure out what people really want, although they can't express it."[46]

Some companies abandon weaker products to concentrate on more-profitable and new products. Yet they may be ignoring the high potential many mature markets and old products still have. Industries widely thought to be mature—autos, motorcycles, television, watches, cameras—were proved otherwise by the Japanese, who found ways to offer new value to customers. Seemingly moribund brands such as RCA, Jell-O, and Ovaltine have achieved sales revivals through the exercise of marketing imagination.

Three potentially useful ways to change the course for a brand are market, product, and marketing program modifications.

MARKET MODIFICATION A company might try to expand the market for its mature brand by working with the two factors that make up sales volume: Volume = number of brand users × usage rate per user, as in Table 10.4.

PRODUCT MODIFICATION Managers also try to stimulate sales by modifying the product's characteristics through quality improvement, feature improvement, or style improvement.

Quality improvement aims at increasing the product's functional performance. A manufacturer can often overtake its competition by launching a "new and improved" product. Grocery manufacturers call this a "plus launch" and promote a new additive or advertise something as "stronger," "bigger," or "better." This strategy is effective to the extent that the quality is improved, buyers accept the claim, and a sufficient number will pay for it. In the case of the canned coffee industry, manufacturers are using "freshness" to better position their brands in the face of fierce competition from premium rivals, such as store brands that let customers grind their own beans in the store. Kraft's Maxwell House touts coffee sold in its new Fresh Seal packaging and P&G's Folger's ads show how its AromaSeal canisters—plastic, peel-top, resealable, and easy-grip packages—keep its ground beans fresher.[47]

Feature improvement aims at adding new features such as size, weight, materials, additives, and accessories that expand the product's performance, versatility, safety, or convenience. This strategy has several advantages. New features build the company's image as an innovator and win the loyalty of market segments that value these features. They provide an opportunity for free publicity and they generate sales force and distributor enthusiasm. The chief disadvantage is that feature improvements are easily imitated; unless the marketer realizes a permanent gain from being first, the feature improvement might not pay off in the long run.[50]

Style improvement aims at increasing the product's esthetic appeal. The periodic introduction of new car models is largely about style competition, as is the introduction of new packaging for consumer products. A style strategy might give the product a unique market

TABLE 10.4

Alternative Ways to Increase Sales Volume

Expand the Number of Brand Users	Increase the Usage Rates Among Users
■ *Convert nonusers.* The key to the growth of air freight service is the constant search for new users to whom air carriers can demonstrate the benefits of using air freight rather than ground transportation.	■ *Have consumers use the product on more occasions.* Serve Campbell's soup for a snack. Use Heinz vinegar to clean windows. Take Kodak pictures of your pets.
■ *Enter new market segments.* When Goodyear decided to sell its tires via Wal-Mart, Sears, and Discount Tire, it boosted market share from 14% to 16% in the first year.[48]	■ *Have consumers use more of the product on each occasion.* Drink a larger glass of orange juice.
■ *Attract competitors' customers.* Marketers of Puffs facial tissues are always wooing Kleenex customers.	■ *Have consumers use the product in new ways.* Use Tums antacid as a calcium supplement.[49]

identity. Yet style competition has problems. First, it's difficult to predict whether people—and which people—will like a new style. Second, a style change usually requires discontinuing the old style, and the company risks losing customers.

Regardless of the type of improvement, marketers must beware of a possible backlash. Customers are not always willing to accept an "improved" product, as the now-classic tale of New Coke illustrates.

COCA-COLA

Battered by competition from the sweeter Pepsi-Cola, Coca-Cola decided in 1985 to replace its old formula with a sweeter variation, dubbed New Coke. Coca-Cola spent $4 million on market research. Blind taste tests showed that Coke drinkers preferred the new, sweeter formula, but the launch of New Coke provoked a national uproar. Market researchers had measured the taste but had failed to measure the emotional attachment consumers had to Coca-Cola. There were angry letters, formal protests, and even lawsuit threats to force the retention of "The Real Thing." Ten weeks later, the company withdrew New Coke and reintroduced its century-old formula as "Classic Coke," giving the old formula even stronger status in the marketplace.

MARKETING PROGRAM MODIFICATION Product managers might also try to stimulate sales by modifying other marketing program elements. They should ask the following questions:

- ***Prices.*** Would a price cut attract new buyers? If so, should we lower the list price or lower prices through price specials, volume or early-purchase discounts, freight cost absorption, or easier credit terms? Or would it be better to *raise* the price, to signal higher quality?
- ***Distribution.*** Can the company obtain more product support and display in existing outlets? Can it penetrate more outlets? Can the company introduce the product into new distribution channels?
- ***Advertising.*** Should we increase advertising expenditures? Change the message or ad copy? The media mix? What about the timing, frequency, or size of ads?
- ***Sales promotion.*** Should the company step up sales promotion—trade deals, cents-off coupons, rebates, warranties, gifts, and contests?
- ***Personal selling.*** Should we increase the number or quality of salespeople? Should we change the basis for sales force specialization? Revise sales territories or sales force incentives? Can we improve sales-call planning?
- ***Services.*** Can the company speed up delivery? Can we extend more technical assistance to customers? More credit?

Marketing Strategies: Decline Stage

Sales decline for a number of reasons, including technological advances, shifts in consumer tastes, and increased domestic and foreign competition. All can lead to overcapacity, increased price cutting, and profit erosion. The decline might be slow, as in the case of sewing machines, or rapid, as in the case of 5.25 floppy disks. Sales may plunge to zero, or they may petrify at a low level.

As sales and profits decline, some firms withdraw from the market. Those remaining may reduce the number of products they offer. They may withdraw from smaller market segments and weaker trade channels, and they may cut their promotion budgets and reduce prices further. Unfortunately, most companies have not developed a policy for handling aging products.

Unless strong reasons for retention exist, carrying a weak product is very costly to the firm—and not just by the amount of uncovered overhead and profit: There are many hidden costs. Weak products often consume a disproportionate amount of management's time; require frequent price and inventory adjustments; incur expensive setup for short production runs; draw both advertising and sales force attention that might be better used to make healthy products more profitable; and cast a shadow on the company's image. The biggest cost might well lie in the future. Failing to eliminate weak products delays the aggressive search for replacement products. The weak products create a lopsided product mix, long on yesterday's breadwinners and short on tomorrow's.

In handling aging products, a company faces a number of tasks and decisions. The first task is to establish a system for identifying weak products. Many companies appoint a product-review committee with representatives from marketing, R&D, manufacturing, and finance who, based on all available information, makes a recommendation for each product—leave it alone, modify its marketing strategy, or drop it.[51]

Some firms abandon declining markets earlier than others. Much depends on the height of exit barriers in the industry.[52] The lower the exit barriers, the easier it is for firms to leave the industry, and the more tempting it is for the remaining firms to stay and attract the withdrawing firms' customers. For example, Procter & Gamble stayed in the declining liquid-soap business and improved its profits as others withdrew.

The appropriate strategy also depends on the industry's relative attractiveness and the company's competitive strength in that industry. A company that is in an unattractive industry but possesses competitive strength should consider shrinking selectively. A company that is in an attractive industry but has competitive strength should consider strengthening its investment. Companies that successfully restage or rejuvenate a mature product often do so by adding value to the original offering.

If the company were choosing between harvesting and divesting, its strategies would be quite different. *Harvesting* calls for gradually reducing a product or business's costs while trying to maintain sales. The first step is to cut R&D costs and plant and equipment investment. The company might also reduce product quality, sales force size, marginal services, and advertising expenditures. It would try to cut these costs without letting customers, competitors, and employees know what is happening. Harvesting is difficult to execute. Yet many mature products warrant this strategy. It can substantially increase the company's current cash flow.[53]

When a company decides to drop a product, it faces further decisions. If the product has strong distribution and residual goodwill, the company can probably sell it to another firm. If the company can't find any buyers, it must decide whether to liquidate the brand quickly or slowly. It must also decide on how much inventory and service to maintain for past customers.

Evidence on the Product Life-Cycle Concept

Based on the above discussion, Table 10.5 summarizes the characteristics, marketing objectives, and marketing strategies of the four stages of the PLC. The PLC concept helps marketers interpret product and market dynamics, conduct planning and control, and do forecasting. One recent research study of 30 product categories unearthed a number of interesting findings concerning the PLC:[54]

- New consumer durables show a distinct takeoff, after which sales increase by roughly 45% a year, but also show a distinct slowdown, when sales decline by roughly 15% a year.
- Slowdown occurs at 34% penetration on average, well before the majority of households own a new product.
- The growth stage lasts a little over eight years and does not seem to shorten over time.
- Informational cascades exist, meaning that people are more likely to adopt over time if others already have, instead of by making careful product evaluations. One implication, however, is that product categories with large sales increases at takeoff tend to have larger sales decline at slowdown.

Critique of the Product Life-Cycle Concept

PLC theory has its share of critics. They claim that life-cycle patterns are too variable in shape and duration to be generalized, and that marketers can seldom tell what stage their product is in. A product may appear to be mature when actually it has reached a plateau prior to another upsurge. Critics also charge that, rather than an inevitable course that sales must follow, the PLC pattern is the self-fulfilling result of marketing strategies and that

TABLE 10.5 Summary of Product Life-Cycle Characteristics, Objectives, and Strategies

	Introduction	Growth	Maturity	Decline
Characteristics				
Sales	Low sales	Rapidly rising sales	Peak sales	Declining sales
Costs	High cost per customer	Average cost per customer	Low cost per customer	Low cost per customer
Profits	Negative	Rising profits	High profits	Declining profits
Customers	Innovators	Early adopters	Middle majority	Laggards
Competitors	Few	Growing number	Stable number beginning to decline	Declining number
Marketing Objectives				
	Create product awareness and trial	Maximize market share	Maximize profit while defending market share	Reduce expenditure and milk the brand
Strategies				
Product	Offer a basic product	Offer product extensions, service, warranty	Diversify brands and items models	Phase out weak products
Price	Charge cost-plus	Price to penetrate market	Price to match or best competitors'	Cut price
Distribution	Build selective distribution	Build intensive distribution	Build more intensive distribution	Go selective: phase out unprofitable outlets
Advertising	Build product awareness among early adopters and dealers	Build awareness and interest in the mass market	Stress brand differences and benefits	Reduce to level needed to retain hard-core loyals
Sales Promotion	Use heavy sales promotion to entice trial	Reduce to take advantage of heavy consumer demand	Increase to encourage brand switching	Reduce to minimal level

Sources: Chester R. Wasson, *Dynamic Competitive Strategy and Product Life Cycles* (Austin, TX: Austin Press, 1978); John A. Weber, "Planning Corporate Growth with Inverted Product Life Cycles," *Long Range Planning* (October 1976): 12–29; Peter Doyle, "The Realities of the Product Life Cycle," *Quarterly Review of Marketing* (Summer 1976).

skillful marketing can in fact lead to continued growth.[55] "Marketing Memo: How to Build a Breakaway Brand" provides 10 rules for long-term marketing success.

Market Evolution

Because the PLC focuses on what's happening to a particular product or brand rather than on what's happening to the overall market, it yields a product-oriented picture rather than a market-oriented picture. Firms also need to visualize a *market's* evolutionary path as it is affected by new needs, competitors, technology, channels, and other developments.[56] In the course of a product's or brand's existence, its positioning must change to keep pace with market developments. Like products, markets evolve through four stages: emergence, growth, maturity, and decline.

EMERGENCE Before a market materializes, it exists as a latent market. For example, for centuries people have wanted faster means of calculation. The market satisfied this need with abacuses, slide rules, and large adding machines. Suppose an entrepreneur recognizes this need and imagines a technological solution in the form of a small, handheld electronic calculator. He now must determine the product attributes, including physical size and number of mathematical functions. Because he is market oriented, he interviews potential buyers and finds that target customers vary greatly in their preferences. Some want a four-function calculator (adding, subtracting, multiplying, and dividing) and others want more functions (calculating percentages, square roots, and logs). Some want a small hand calculator and others want a large one. This type of market, in which buyer preferences scatter evenly, is called a *diffused-preference market.*

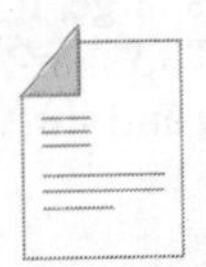

MARKETING MEMO | HOW TO BUILD A BREAKAWAY BRAND

Arnold Worldwide marketing experts Francis Kelly and Barry Silverstein define a *breakaway brand* as one that stands out, not just in its own product category but from all other brands, and that achieves significant results in the marketplace. Here is a summary of their 10 tips for building a breakaway brand:

1. Make a Commitment

Your entire organization, from the top down, needs to make a commitment to build and support a breakaway brand. Get your company behind developing new products that have breakaway attributes.

2. Get a "Chief" Behind It

Few breakaway branding initiatives have a chance of success without the enthusiastic support of your CEO, COO, or CMO. A senior executive at your company must play the role of brand visionary, brand champion, and brand architect.

3. Find Your Brand Truth

Ultimately, the DNA of your breakaway brand is its brand truth. It is what defines and differentiates every breakaway brand. It is the single most important weapon a brand will ever have in the battle for increased awareness, profitability, market share, and even share price.

4. Target a Winning Mind-set

The winning mind-set is the potent, aspirational, shared "view of life" among all core audience segments. It becomes the filter through which all of your advertising and promotional activities should flow.

5. Create a Category of One

To be a breakaway brand, your brand needs not only to stand apart from others in its own category but also to transcend categories and open a defining gap between itself and its competitors. Then it becomes a category of one.

6. Demand a Great Campaign

Great campaigns are a team sport—they require a partnership between you and your agency to create a campaign that breaks away. Never compromise on a campaign, because without a great campaign, your breakaway brand can fizzle.

7. Tirelessly Integrate

Integration is the name of the game. Depending on the audience you're trying to reach, your campaign might integrate both network and cable TV, print and online advertising, direct mail, e-mail, radio, and nontraditional media—from street marketing to publicity stunts to contests.

8. Take Risks

Today, 80% of brands are merely treading water in a sea of gray. Only 20% are making waves. You can't afford to have your product sink in the sea—and that may mean taking a calculated risk or two—or three—to ensure your brand rises above the others.

9. Accelerate New-Product Development

Nothing is more important than differentiating a product in the marketplace—but the only way to rise above me-too branding is to innovate and do something different and unique with the product. It may mean throwing away an old product brand and reinventing it. Or it may mean starting from scratch.

10. Invest as If Your Brand Depends on It

Building a breakaway brand is serious business, so it takes a serious business investment. Invest in the product, of course—but also in the packaging and a smart integrated marketing campaign. Invest wisely . . . as if your brand depends on it.

Source: Adapted from Francis J. Kelly III and Barry Silverstein, *The Breakaway Brand* (New York: McGraw-Hill, 2005).

The entrepreneur's problem is to design an optimal product for this market. There are three options:

1. Design the new product to meet the preferences of one of the corners of the market—*a single-niche strategy.*
2. Launch two or more products simultaneously to capture two or more parts of the market—*a multiple-niche strategy.*
3. Design the new product for the middle of the market—*a mass-market strategy.*

A small firm doesn't have the resources for capturing and holding the mass market, so a single-niche market strategy makes the most sense. A large firm might go after the mass market by designing a product that's medium in size and in its number of functions. Assume our pioneer firm is large and designs its product for the mass market. Once it has launched the product, the *emergence* stage begins.[57]

GROWTH If the new product sells well, new firms will enter the market, ushering in a *market-growth stage.* Where will a second firm enter the market, assuming the first firm established itself in the center? If the second firm is small, it's likely to avoid head-on competition with the

(a) Market-fragmentation Stage

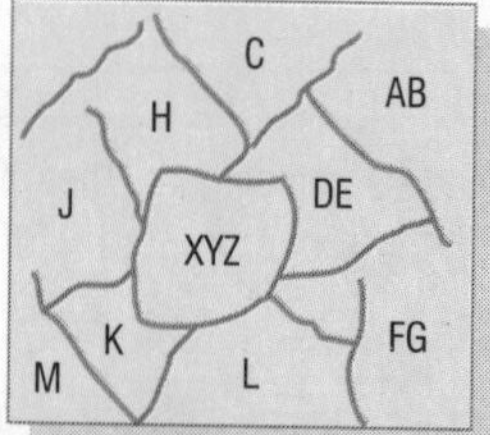

(b) Market-consolidation Stage

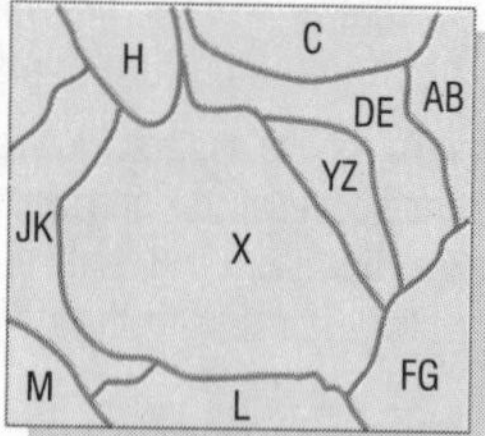

FIG. 10.5

Market-Fragmentation and Market-Consolidation Strategies

pioneer and to launch its brand in one of the market corners. If the second firm is large, it might launch its brand in the center against the pioneer. The two firms can easily end up sharing the mass market. Or a large second firm can implement a multiple-niche strategy and surround and box in the pioneer.

MATURITY Eventually, the competitors cover and serve all the major segments and the market enters the *maturity stage.* In fact, the competitors go further and invade each others' segments, reducing everyone's profits in the process. As market growth slows down, the market splits into finer segments and high *market fragmentation* occurs. This situation is illustrated in Figure 10.5(a) where the letters represent different companies supplying various segments. Note that two segments are unserved because they're too small to yield a profit.

Market fragmentation is often followed by a *market consolidation,* caused by the emergence of a new attribute that has strong appeal. This situation is illustrated in Figure 10.5(b) and the expansive size of the X territory.

However, even a consolidated market condition will not last. Other companies will copy a successful brand, and the market will eventually splinter again. Mature markets swing between fragmentation brought about by competition and consolidation brought about by innovation. Consider the evolution of the paper towel market.

PAPER TOWELS

Originally, homemakers used cotton and linen dishcloths and towels in their kitchens. A paper company, looking for new markets, developed paper towels. This development crystallized a latent market, and other manufacturers entered. The number of brands grew and created market fragmentation. Industry overcapacity led manufacturers to search for new features. One manufacturer, hearing consumers complain that paper towels were not absorbent, introduced "absorbent" towels and increased its market share. This market consolidation didn't last long because competitors came out with their own versions of absorbent paper towels. The market fragmented again. Then another manufacturer introduced a "superstrength" towel. It was soon copied. Another manufacturer introduced a "lint-free" paper towel, which was subsequently copied. Thus, paper towels evolved from a single product to one with various absorbencies, strengths, and applications. Market evolution was driven by the forces of innovation and competition.

DECLINE Eventually, demand for the current products will begin to decrease, and the market will enter the *decline stage.* Either society's total need level declines, or a new technology replaces the old. For example, shifts in tradition and a trend toward cremation have caused casket makers and funeral homes to reconsider how to conduct their business.[58]

SUMMARY :::

1. Deciding on positioning requires the determination of a frame of reference—by identifying the target market and the nature of the competition—and the ideal points-of-parity and points-of-difference brand associations. To determine the proper competitive frame of reference, one must understand consumer behavior and the considerations consumers use in making brand choices.
2. Points-of-difference are those associations unique to the brand that are also strongly held and favorably evaluated by consumers. Points-of-parity are those associations not necessarily unique to the brand but perhaps shared with other brands. Category point-of-parity associations are associations consumers view as being necessary to a legitimate and credible product offering within a certain category. Competitive point-of-parity associations are those associations designed to negate competitors' points-of-difference.
3. The key to competitive advantage is relevant brand differentiation—consumers must find something unique and meaningful about a market offering. These differences may be based directly on the product or service itself or on other considerations related to factors such as personnel, channels, or image.
4. Because economic conditions change and competitive activity varies, companies normally find it necessary to reformulate their marketing strategy several times during a product's life cycle. Technologies, product forms, and brands also exhibit life cycles with distinct stages. The general sequence of stages in any life cycle is introduction,

growth, maturity, and decline. The majority of products today are in the maturity stage.

5. Each stage of the product life cycle calls for different marketing strategies. The introduction stage is marked by slow growth and minimal profits. If successful, the product enters a growth stage marked by rapid sales growth and increasing profits. There follows a maturity stage in which sales growth slows and profits stabilize. Finally, the product enters a decline stage. The company's task is to identify the truly weak products; develop a strategy for each one; and phase out weak products in a way that minimizes the hardship to company profits, employees, and customers.
6. Like products, markets evolve through four stages: emergence, growth, maturity, and decline.

APPLICATIONS :::

Marketing Debate Do Brands Have Finite Lives?

Often, after a brand begins to slip in the marketplace or disappears altogether, commentators observe, "all brands have their day." Their rationale is that all brands, in some sense, have a finite life and cannot be expected to be leaders forever. Other experts contend, however, that brands can live forever, and their long-term success depends on the skill and insight of the marketers involved.

Take a position: Brands cannot be expected to last forever *versus* There is no reason for a brand to ever become obsolete.

Marketing Discussion

Identify other negatively correlated attributes and benefits not included in Table 10.3. What strategies do firms use to try to position themselves on the basis of pairs of attributes and benefits?

IN THIS CHAPTER, WE WILL ADDRESS THE FOLLOWING QUESTIONS:

1. How do marketers identify primary competitors?
2. How should we analyze competitors' strategies, objectives, strengths, and weaknesses?
3. How can market leaders expand the total market and defend market share?
4. How should market challengers attack market leaders?
5. How can market followers or nichers compete effectively?

PROGRESSIVE

#1 INSURANCE WEB SITE · 2007 KEYNOTE

1-800-PROGRESSIVE

HOME | CAR & VEHICLE INSURANCE | HOME & PROPERTY INSURANCE | INSURANCE BASICS | ARTICLES & BLOGS | VEHICLE RESOURCES

» Claims & Concierge

Immediate Response Vehicles
Reporting A Claim
Concierge Service
Claims Offices
Catastrophe Claims
Windshield & Glass
Repair Estimates
Roadside Assistance

You Could **Save Over $400** on Your Car Insurance!
Rates & coverage options in about 6 minutes*

Quote & Compare

Buy online and print your insurance card!

Select:
Auto
ZIP Code:

QUOTE & COMPARE

RETRIEVE A SAVED QUOTE

Or, shop with a local agent:

FIND AGENT / GET AGENT QUOTE

Home > Claims & Concierge > **Immediate Response Vehicles**

Immediate Response® Vehicles

ADJUST FONT: A A A

Print | Send Page | Link to | Bookmark

Since 1994, Progressive has used Immediate Response Vehicles (IRVs) — those white SUVs with the Progressive logo on the side — to give your car insurance claim a head start. IRVs transport our claims professionals wherever you need them: to repair shops, tow yards, your house — even the scene of an accident — to help resolve your claim quickly and accurately.

SHARE

BLOG

ALSO ON PROGRESSIVE.COM

UPDATED!
Auto Tech
Why Can't I Get the Kind of Mileage on the Window Stick

NEW!
Understanding Insurance
What's Covered If Someone Breaks Into Your Car?

NEW!
Driving Destinations
Amazing Art Parks in Public Places

CHAPTER 11 ::: DEALING WITH COMPETITION

eleven

Building strong brands requires a keen understanding of competitors, and competition grows more intense every year. New competition is coming from all directions—from global competitors eager to grow sales in new markets; from online competitors seeking cost-efficient ways to expand distribution; from private-label and store brands designed to provide low-price alternatives; and from brand extensions from strong megabrands leveraging their strengths to move into new categories. One good way to start to deal with competition is through creatively designed and well-executed marketing programs.

When it was still a relatively minor player in the insurance industry, Progressive Insurance specialized in a small niche of the auto insurance business that most other insurers ignored: "nonstandard" insurance, typically purchased by motorists whose driving records are marred by accidents and moving violations. By collecting and analyzing loss data in automobile insurance better than anyone else, Progressive acquired a solid understanding of what it costs to serve various types of customers and how to make a profit serving potentially lucrative but high-risk customers no one else wanted to cover. But Progressive gained its truly sustainable competitive advantage in the mid-1990s when it became one of the first auto insurance companies to sell direct to consumers via the Internet. The company's early >>>

Progressive Insurance became a profitable business by targeting an underserved market segment for auto insurance and figuring out how to do what the competition wasn't—giving customers price comparisons for auto coverage and settling claims at the accident site.

adoption of technology enabled it to offer a unique service: In addition to providing free online quotes for its own policies, Progressive also provided quotes from up to three competitors, information that until then had been available only through insurance agents. In addition to saving its customers time, Progressive was able to save them money by showing that, in many cases, its policies were more competitively priced. Once Progressive won new customers' business, it mobilized an army of 12,000 claims adjusters who speed right to an accident scene__and often cut a check right on the spot. It has further enhanced its competitiveness by adding innovative service features such as an "accident concierge," who handles all aspects of the claims and repair process for customers, and online policy management that enables customers to make payments and change coverage any time. From 1996 to 1005, Progressive grew an average of 17% per year, from $3.4 billion to $14 billion, and by 2006, it was the 3rd-biggest auto insurer in the United States, up from 48th in 1980, with 12 million customers.[1]

To effectively devise and implement the best possible brand-positioning strategies, companies must pay keen attention to their competitors. Markets have become too competitive to focus on the consumer alone. This chapter examines the role competition plays and how marketers can best manage their brands depending on their market position.[2]

::: Competitive Forces

Michael Porter has identified five forces that determine the intrinsic long-run attractiveness of a market or market segment: industry competitors, potential entrants, substitutes, buyers, and suppliers. His model is shown in Figure 11.1. The threats these forces pose are as follows:

1. ***Threat of intense segment rivalry***—A segment is unattractive if it already contains numerous, strong, or aggressive competitors. It's even more unattractive if it's stable or declining, if plant capacity must be added in large increments, if fixed costs or exit barriers are high, or if competitors have high stakes in staying in the segment. These conditions will lead to frequent price wars, advertising battles, and new-product introductions and will make it expensive to compete. The cellular phone market has seen fierce competition due to segment rivalry.
2. ***Threat of new entrants***—The most attractive segment is one in which entry barriers are high and exit barriers are low.[3] Few new firms can enter the industry, and poorly performing firms can easily exit. When both entry and exit barriers are high, profit potential is high, but firms face more risk because poorer-performing firms stay in and fight it out. When both entry and exit barriers are low, firms easily enter and leave the industry, and the returns are stable and low. The worst case is when entry barriers are low and exit barriers are high: Here firms enter during good times but find it hard to leave during bad times. The result is chronic overcapacity and depressed earnings for all. The airline industry has low entry barriers but high exit barriers, leaving all carriers struggling during economic downturns.

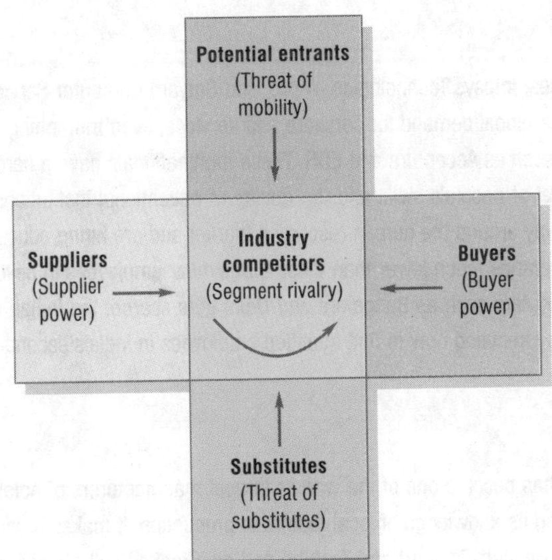

FIG. 11.1

Five Forces Determining Segment Structural Attractiveness

Source: Adapted with the permission of The Free Press, a Division of Simon & Schuster Adult Publishing Group, from *Competitive Advantage: Creating and Sustaining Superior Performance* by Michael E. Porter. Copyright © 1985, 1998 by Michael E. Porter. All rights reserved.

3. ***Threat of substitute products***—A segment is unattractive when there are actual or potential substitutes for the product. Substitutes place a limit on prices and on profits. If technology advances or competition increases in these substitute industries, prices and profits are likely to fall. Greyhound and Amtrak have seen profitability threatened by the rise of air travel.
4. ***Threat of buyers' growing bargaining power***—A segment is unattractive if buyers possess strong or growing bargaining power. The rise of retail giants such as Wal-Mart has led some analysts to conclude that the potential profitability of packaged-goods companies will become curtailed. Buyers' bargaining power grows when they become more concentrated or organized, when the product represents a significant fraction of the buyers' costs, when the product is undifferentiated, when buyers' switching costs are low, when buyers are price sensitive because of low profits, or when they can integrate upstream. To protect themselves, sellers might select buyers who have the least power to negotiate or switch suppliers. A better defense consists of developing superior offers that strong buyers cannot refuse.
5. ***Threat of suppliers' growing bargaining power***—A segment is unattractive if the company's suppliers are able to raise prices or reduce quantity supplied. Oil companies such as ExxonMobil, Shell, BP, and Chevron-Texaco are at the mercy of the limited amount of oil reserves and the actions of oil-supplying cartels such as OPEC. Suppliers tend to be powerful when they are concentrated or organized, when there are few substitutes, when the supplied product is an important input, when the costs of switching suppliers are high, and when the suppliers can integrate downstream. The best defenses are to build win–win relationships with suppliers or use multiple supply sources.

::: Identifying Competitors

It would seem a simple task for a company to identify its competitors. PepsiCo knows that Coca-Cola's Dasani is the major bottled-water competitor for its Aquafina brand; Citigroup knows that Bank of America is a major banking competitor; and PetSmart.com knows that a major online competitor for pet food and supplies is Petco.com. However, the range of a company's actual and potential competitors can be much broader than the obvious. And a company is more likely to be hurt by emerging competitors or new technologies than by current competitors.

In recent years, for instance, a number of new "emerging giants" have arisen from developing countries, and these nimble competitors are not only competing with multinationals on their home turf but also becoming global forces in their own right. They have gained competitive advantage by exploiting their knowledge about local factors of production—capital and talent—and supply chains in order to build world-class businesses.

INDIAN SOFTWARE & SERVICES COMPANIES

Tata Consultancy Services, Infosys Technologies, Wipro, and Satyam Computer Services, all of India, have succeeded in catering to the global demand for software and services, even triumphing against multinational software service providers such as Accenture and EDS. These multinationals have a hard time sorting out talent in a market where the level of people's skills and the quality of educational institutions vary dramatically. Indian companies know their way around the human resources market and are hiring educated, skilled engineers and technical graduates at salaries much lower than those that similar employees in developed markets earn. Even as the talent in urban centers such as Bangalore and Delhi gets scarce, the Indian companies will keep their competitive advantage by knowing how to find qualified employees in India's second-tier cities.[4]

INVENTEC

Taiwan-based Inventec has become one of the world's largest manufacturers of notebook computers, PCs, and servers, also by exploiting its knowledge of local factors of production. It makes products in China and supplies them to giants such as Hewlett-Packard and Toshiba and also makes cell phones and MP3 players for other multinational customers. Inventec's customers get the low cost of manufacturing products in China without investing in factories there, and they can also use China's talented software and hardware professionals. It won't be long, however, before Inventec begins competing directly with its own customers; it has already started selling computers in Taiwan and China under its own retail brand name.[5]

We can examine competition from both an industry and a market point of view.[6] An **industry** is a group of firms that offer a product or class of products that are close substitutes for one another. Marketers classify industries according to number of sellers; degree of product differentiation; presence or absence of entry, mobility, and exit barriers; cost structure; degree of vertical integration; and degree of globalization.

Using the market approach, we define *competitors* as companies that satisfy the same customer need. For example, a customer who buys a word-processing package really wants "writing ability"—a need that can also be satisfied by pencils, pens, or typewriters. Marketers must overcome "marketing myopia" and stop defining competition in traditional category and industry terms.[7] Coca-Cola, focused on its soft-drink business, missed seeing the market for coffee bars and fresh-fruit-juice bars that eventually impinged on its soft-drink business.

The market concept of competition reveals a broader set of actual and potential competitors than competition defined in just product category terms. Rayport and Jaworski suggest profiling a company's direct and indirect competitors by mapping the buyer's steps in obtaining and using the product. This type of analysis highlights both the opportunities and the challenges a company faces.[8] "Marketing Insight: High Growth Through Value Innovation" describes how firms can tap into new markets that minimizes competition from others.

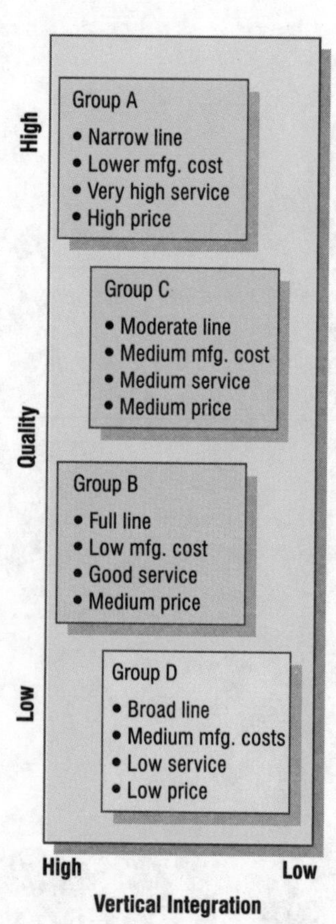

FIG. 11.2

Strategic Groups in the Major-Appliance Industry

::: Analyzing Competitors

Once a company identifies its primary competitors, it must ascertain their strategies, objectives, strengths, and weaknesses.[9]

Strategies

A group of firms following the same strategy in a given target market is a **strategic group.**[10] Suppose a company wants to enter the major-appliance industry. What is its strategic group?

The company develops the chart shown in Figure 11.2 and discovers four strategic groups based on product quality and level of vertical integration. Group A has one competitor (Maytag); group B has three (General Electric, Whirlpool, and Sears); group C has four; and group D has two. Important insights emerge from this exercise. First, the height of the entry barriers differs for each group. Second, if the company successfully enters a group, the members of that group become its key competitors.

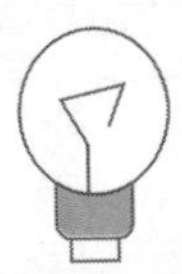

MARKETING INSIGHT | HIGH GROWTH THROUGH VALUE INNOVATION

INSEAD professors W. Chan Kim and Renée Mauborgne believe that too many firms engage in "red-ocean thinking"—seeking bloody, head-to-head battles with competitors based largely on incremental improvements in cost, quality, or both. They advocate engaging instead in "blue-ocean thinking" by creating products and services for which there are no direct competitors. Their belief is that instead of searching within the conventional boundaries of industry competition, managers should look beyond those boundaries to find unoccupied market positions that represent real value innovation.

The Belgian Kinepolis movie megaplex exemplifies "blue-ocean thinking"__a competitive strategy that focuses on finding unoccupied market positions. Here is an exterior shot of the megaplex in Antwerp, Belgium.

The authors cite as one example Bert Claeys, a Belgian movie theater operator, and its introduction of the 25-screen, 7,600-seat Kinepolis megaplex. Despite an industry slump, Kineoplis has thrived on a unique combination of features, such as ample, safe, and free parking; large screens and state-of-the-art sound and projection equipment; and roomy, comfortable, oversized seats with unobstructed views. Through smart planning and economies of scale, Bert Claeys creates Kinepolis's unique cinema experience at a lower cost.

This is classic blue-ocean thinking—designing creative business ventures to positively affect both a company's cost structure and its value proposition to consumers. Cost savings result from eliminating and reducing the factors affecting traditional industry competition; value to consumers comes from introducing factors the industry has never before offered. Over time, costs drop even more as superior value leads to higher sales volume, and that generates economies of scale.

Other examples of marketers that exhibit unconventional, blue-ocean thinking include:

- Southwest Airlines created an airline that offers reliable, fun, and convenient service at a low cost.
- Callaway Golf designed "Big Bertha," a golf club with a large head and expanded sweet spot that helped golfers frustrated by the difficulty of hitting a golf ball squarely.
- NetJets figured out how to offer private jet service to a larger group of customers through fractional ownership.
- Cirque du Soleil reinvented circus as a higher form of entertainment by eliminating high-cost elements such as animals and enhancing the theatrical experience instead.

Kim and Mauborgne propose four crucial questions for marketers to ask themselves in guiding blue-ocean thinking and creating value innovation:

1. Which of the factors that our industry takes for granted should we eliminate?
2. Which factors should we reduce well *below* the industry's standard?
3. Which factors should we raise well *above* the industry's standard?
4. Which factors should we create that the industry has never offered?

They maintain that the most successful blue-ocean thinkers took advantage of all three platforms on which value innovation can take place: *physical product*; *service* including maintenance, customer service, warranties and training for distributors and retailers; and *delivery*, meaning channels and logistics. Figure 11.3 summarizes key principles driving the successful formulation and execution of blue-ocean strategy.

Sources: W. Chan Kim and Renée Mauborgne, *Blue-Ocean Strategy: How to Create Uncontested Market Space and Make the Competition Irrelevant* (Cambridge, MA: Harvard Business School Press, 2005); W. Chan Kim and Renée Mauborgne, "Creating New Market Space," *Harvard Business Review* (January–February 1999); W. Chan Kim and Renée Mauborgne, "Value Innovation: The Strategic Logic of High Growth," *Harvard Business Review* (January–February 1997).

Objectives

Once a company has identified its main competitors and their strategies, it must ask: What is each competitor seeking in the marketplace? What drives each competitor's behavior? Many factors shape a competitor's objectives, including size, history, current management, and financial situation. If the competitor is a division of a larger company, it's important to know whether the parent company is running it for growth, profits, or milking it.

FIG. **11.3**

Key Principles of Blue-Ocean Strategy

Source: W. Chan Kim and Renée Mauborgne, *Blue-Ocean Strategy: How to Create Uncontested Market Space and Make the Competition Irrelevant* (Cambridge, MA: Harvard Business School Press, 2005). Copyright © 2005, by the Harvard Business School Publishing Corporation; all rights reserved.

FORMULATION PRINCIPLES

a. Reconstruct market boundaries
- Look across alternative industries
- Look across strategic groups within industries
- Look across chain of buyers
- Look across complementary product and service offerings
- Look across functional or emotional appeal to buyers
- Look across time

b. Focus on the big picture not the numbers

c. Reach beyond existing demand

d. Get the strategic sequence right
- Is there buyer utility?
- Is the price acceptable?
- Can we attain target cost?
- What are the adoption challenges?

EXECUTION PRINCIPLES

a. Overcome key organizational hurdles
- Cognitive hurdle
- Resource hurdle
- Motivational hurdle
- Political hurdle

b. Build execution into strategy

It's useful to assume that competitors strive to maximize profits. However, companies differ in the relative emphasis they put on short-term and long-term profits. Many U.S. firms have been criticized for operating on a short-run model, largely because current performance is judged by stockholders who might lose confidence, sell their stock, and cause the company's cost of capital to rise. Japanese firms operate largely on a market-share-maximization model. They receive much of their funds from banks at a lower interest rate and in the past have readily accepted lower profits. So another reliable assumption is that each competitor pursues some mix of objectives: current profitability, market share growth, cash flow, technological leadership, and service leadership.[11]

Finally, a company must monitor competitors' expansion plans. Figure 11.4 shows a product-market battlefield map for the personal computer industry. Dell, which started out as a strong force in the sale of personal computers to individual users, is now a major force in the commercial and industrial market. Other incumbents may try to set up mobility barriers to Dell's further expansion.

FIG. **11.4**

A Competitor's Expansion Plans

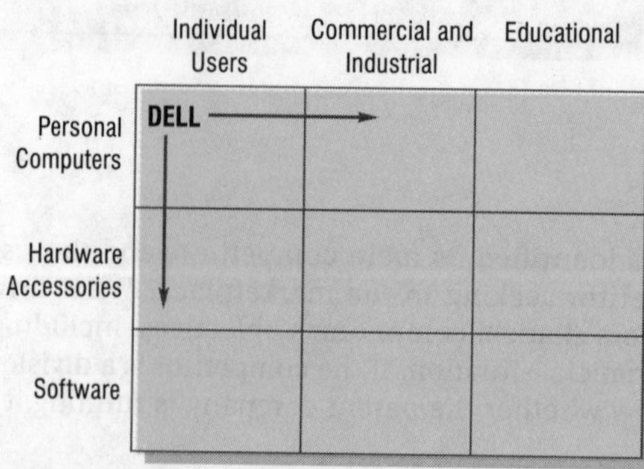

TABLE 11.1

Customers' Ratings of Competitors on Key Success Factors

	Customer Awareness	Product Quality	Product Availability	Technical Assistance	Selling Staff
Competitor A	E	E	P	P	G
Competitor B	G	G	E	G	E
Competitor C	F	P	G	F	F

Note: E = excellent, G = good, F = fair, P = poor.

Strengths and Weaknesses

A company needs to gather information about each competitor's strengths and weaknesses. Table 11.1 shows the results of a company survey that asked customers to rate its three competitors, A, B, and C, on five attributes. Competitor A turns out to be well known and respected for producing high-quality products sold by a good sales force but is poor at providing product availability and technical assistance. Competitor B is good across the board and excellent in product availability and sales force. Competitor C rates poor to fair on most attributes. This result suggests that the company could attack Competitor A on product availability and technical assistance and Competitor C on almost anything, but should not attack B, which has no glaring weaknesses.

In general, a company should monitor three variables when analyzing competitors:

1. ***Share of market***—The competitor's share of the target market
2. ***Share of mind***—The percentage of customers who named the competitor in responding to the statement, "Name the first company that comes to mind in this industry."
3. ***Share of heart***—The percentage of customers who named the competitor in responding to the statement, "Name the company from which you would prefer to buy the product."

There's an interesting relationship among these three measures. Table 11.2 shows them as recorded for the three competitors listed in Table 11.1. Competitor A enjoys the highest market share but is slipping. Its mind share and heart share are also slipping, probably because it's not providing good product availability and technical assistance. Competitor B is steadily gaining market share, probably due to strategies that are increasing its mind share and heart share. Competitor C seems to be stuck at a low level of market share, mind share, and heart share, probably because of its poor product and marketing attributes. We could generalize as follows: *Companies that make steady gains in mind share and heart share will inevitably make gains in market share and profitability.* Firms such as CarMax, Timberland, Jordan's Furniture, Wegmans, and Toyota are all reaping the financial benefits of providing emotional, experiential, social, and financial value to satisfy customers and all their constituents.[12]

To improve market share, many companies benchmark their most successful competitors, as well as other world-class performers.[13] The technique and its benefits are described in "Marketing Memo: Benchmarking to Improve Competitive Performance."

Selecting Competitors

After the company has conducted customer value analysis and examined its competitors carefully, it can focus its attack on one of the following classes of competitors: strong versus weak, close versus distant, and "good" versus "bad."

TABLE 11.2

Market Share, Mind Share, and Heart Share

	Market Share			Mind Share			Heart Share		
	2000	2001	2002	2000	2001	2002	2000	2001	2002
Competitor A	50%	47%	44%	60%	58%	54%	45%	42%	39%
Competitor B	30	34	37	30	31	35	44	47	53
Competitor C	20	19	19	10	11	11	11	11	8

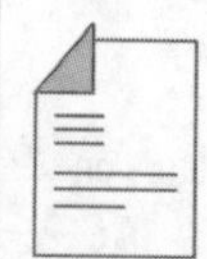

MARKETING MEMO | BENCHMARKING TO IMPROVE COMPETITIVE PERFORMANCE

Benchmarking is the art of learning from companies that perform certain tasks better than other companies. There can be as much as a tenfold difference between the quality, speed, and cost performance of a world-class company and that of an average company. The aim of benchmarking is to copy or improve on "best practices," either within an industry or across industries. Benchmarking has seven steps:

1. Determine which functions or processes to benchmark.
2. Identify the key performance variables to measure.
3. Identify the best-in-class companies.
4. Measure the performance of best-in-class companies.
5. Measure the company's performance.
6. Specify programs and actions to close the gap.
7. Implement and monitor results.

How can companies identify best-practice companies? A good starting point is consulting customers, suppliers, distributors, financial analysts, trade associations, and magazines to see whom they rate as doing the best job. Even the best companies can benchmark to improve their performance. To aid its corporate goal to be more innovative, GE has benchmarked against P&G as well as developing its own new best practices.

Sources: www.benchmarking.org; Patricia O'Connell, "Bringing Innovation to the Home of Six Sigma," *BusinessWeek*, August 1, 2005; John E. Prescott, Stephen H. Miller, and The Society of Competitive Intelligence Professionals, *Proven Strategies in Competitive Intelligence: Lessons from the Trenches* (New York: John Wiley & Sons, 2001); Robert Hiebeler, Thomas B. Kelly, and Charles Ketteman, *Best Practices: Building Your Business with Customer-Focused Solutions* (New York: Arthur Andersen/Simon & Schuster, 1998); Michael Hope, "Contrast and Compare," *Marketing*, August 28, 1997, pp. 11–13.

- ***Strong versus Weak.*** Most companies aim their shots at weak competitors, because this requires fewer resources per share point gained. Yet, the firm should also compete with strong competitors to keep up with the best. Even strong competitors have some weaknesses.
- ***Close versus Distant.*** Most companies compete with the competitors that resemble them the most. Chevrolet competes with Ford, not with Ferrari. Yet companies should also identify distant competitors. Coca-Cola recognizes that its number-one competitor is tap water, not Pepsi. U.S. Steel worries more about plastic and aluminum than about Bethlehem Steel; museums now worry about theme parks and malls.
- ***"Good" versus "Bad."*** Every industry contains "good" and "bad" competitors.[14] Good competitors play by the industry's rules; they set prices in reasonable relationship to costs; and they favor a healthy industry. Bad competitors try to buy share rather than earn it; they take large risks; they invest in overcapacity; and they upset industrial equilibrium. A company may find it necessary to attack its bad competitors to reduce or end their dysfunctional practices.

Selecting Customers

As part of the competitive analysis, firms must evaluate its customer base and think about which customers it's willing to lose and which it wants to retain. One way to divide up the customer base is in terms of whether a customer is valuable and vulnerable, creating a grid of four segments as a result; see Table 11.3. Each segment suggests different competitive activities.[15]

TABLE 11.3 | Customer Selection Grid

	Vulnerable	Not Vulnerable
Valuable	These customers are profitable but not completely happy with the company. Find out and address their sources of vulnerability to **retain them**.	These customers are loyal and profitable. Don't take them for granted but **maintain margins** and reap the benefits of their satisfaction.
Not Valuable	These customers are likely to defect. Let them go or even **encourage their departure**.	These unprofitable customers are happy. Try to **make them valuable or vulnerable**.

Source: John H. Roberts, "Defensive Marketing: How a Strong Incumbent Can Protect Its Position," *Harvard Business Review* (November 2005): 156. Copyright © 205 by the Harvard Business School Publishing Corporation; all rights reserved.

Australian telephone company, Telstra, conducted this type of segment analysis and developed a series of "Flex-Plan" products designed to retain the Valuable/Vulnerables but without losing the margin it realized on the Valuable/Not Vulnerables. The Flex Plans had a subscription fee but offered significant net savings. Because Valuable/Vulnerables were highly involved with the category, they were able to see how they could benefit from such plans, but Valuable/Not Vulnerable regarded the plans as unnecessary. As a result, the plans achieved the desired goals.

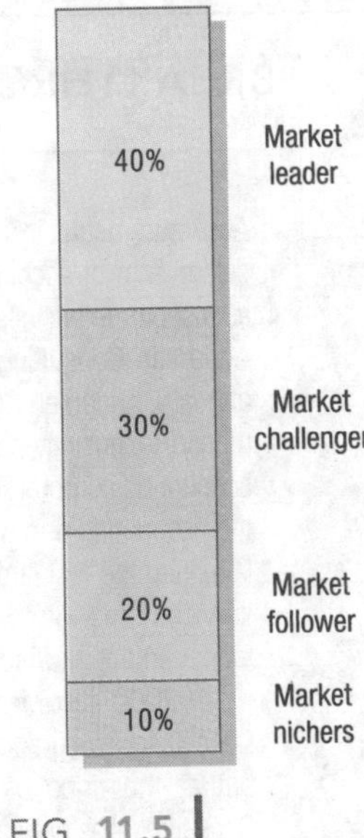

FIG. 11.5

Hypothetical Market Structure

::: Competitive Strategies for Market Leaders

We can gain further insight by classifying firms by the roles they play in the target market: leader, challenger, follower, or nicher. Suppose a market is occupied by the firms shown in Figure 11.5. Forty percent of the market is in the hands of a *market leader;* another 30% is in the hands of a *market challenger;* another 20% is in the hands of a *market follower,* a firm that is willing to maintain its market share and not rock the boat. The remaining 10% is in the hands of *market nichers,* firms that serve small market segments not being served by larger firms.

Many industries contain one firm that is the acknowledged market leader. This firm has the largest market share in the relevant product market and usually leads the other firms in price changes, new-product introductions, distribution coverage, and promotional intensity. Some historical market leaders are Microsoft (computer software), Countrywide (independent home mortgages), Gatorade (sports drinks), Best Buy (retail electronics), McDonald's (fast food), BlueCross BlueShield (health insurance), and Visa (credit cards). "Breakthrough Marketing: Accenture" summarizes how that firm has attained and maintained market leadership.

Although marketers assume well-known brands are distinctive in consumers' minds, unless a dominant firm enjoys a legal monopoly, it must maintain constant vigilance. A product innovation may come along and hurt the leader; a competitor might unexpectedly find a fresh new marketing angle or commit to a major marketing investment; or the leader might find its cost structure spiraling upward. One well-known brand and market leader that lost its way is Gap.

GAP

Nowadays when people think about Gap, they don't think of hip, contemporary clothes. They think quite literally, of a "gap"—what's missing from the company's 1,295 stores. Young people will be quick to tell you that the missing ingredient is a unique style. In an era when small niche fashion brands—Coach, Juicy Couture, Tahari, Laundry—have risen to success in U.S. retailing, Gap has continued to push timeless, simple, and some would say bland, casual clothing. The main problem is that Gap doesn't have a target customer but tries to appeal to

The Gap brand has become diluted in an effort to appeal to too-broad a market base, and the company plans several strategies to refocus it.

BREAKTHROUGH MARKETING | ACCENTURE

Accenture began in 1942 as Adminstrative Accounting Group, the consulting arm of accounting firm Arthur Andersen. In 1989, it launched as a separate business unit focused on IT consulting bearing the name Andersen Consulting. At that time, though it was earning $1 billion annually, Andersen Consulting had low brand awareness among information technology consultancies and was commonly mistaken for its accounting corporate parent. To build its brand and separate itself from the accounting firm with which it shared a name, Andersen Consulting launched the first large-scale advertising campaign in the professional services area. By the end of the decade, it was the world's largest management and technology consulting organization.

In 2000, following arbitration against its former parent, Andersen Consulting was granted its full independence from Arthur Andersen—but at the price of relinquishing the Andersen name. Andersen Consulting was given three months to find a name that was trademarkable in 47 countries, effective and inoffensive in over 200 languages, and acceptable to employees and clients—*and* that corresponded with an available URL. The effort that followed was one of the largest—and most successful—rebranding campaigns in corporate history.

As luck would have it, the company's new name came from a consultant at the company's Oslo office, who submitted "Accenture" as part of an internal name-generation initiative dubbed "Brandstorming." The consultant coined the Accenture name because it rhymed with "adventure" and connoted an "accent on the future." The name also retained the "Ac" of the original Andersen Consulting name (echoing the Ac.com Web site), which would help the firm retain some of its former brand equity. On midnight, December 31, 2000, Andersen Consulting officially adopted the Accenture name and launched a global marketing campaign targeting senior executives at Accenture's clients and prospects, all Accenture partners and employees, the media, leading industry analysts, potential recruits, and academia.

The results of the advertising, marketing, and communications campaigns were quick and impressive. Overall, the number of firms considering purchasing Accenture's services increased by 350%. Accenture's brand equity increased 11%. Awareness of Accenture's breadth and depth of services achieved 96% of its previous level. Globally, awareness of Accenture as a provider of management and technology consulting services was 76% of the former Andersen Consulting levels. These results enabled Accenture to successfully complete a $1.7 billion IPO in July 2001.

In 2002, Accenture unveiled a new positioning to reflect its new role as a partner to aid execution of strategy, summarized succinctly by the tagline "Innovation Delivered." This tagline was supported by the statement, "From innovation to execution, Accenture helps accelerate your vision." Accenture surveyed senior executives from different industries and countries and confirmed that they saw inability to execute and deliver on ideas as the number-one barrier to success.

Accenture saw its differentiator as the ability both to provide innovative ideas—ideas grounded in business processes as well as IT—and to execute them. Competitors such as McKinsey were seen as highly specialized at developing strategy, whereas other competitors such as IBM were seen as highly skilled with technological implementation. Accenture wanted to be seen as excelling at both. Ian Watmore, Accenture's U.K. chief, explained the need to have both strategy and execution: "Unless you can provide both transformational consulting and outsourcing capability, you're not going to win. Clients expect both."

In 2002, the business climate changed. After the dot-com crash and the economic downturn, innovation was no longer enough. Executives wanted bottom-line results. Accenture built upon the "Innovation Delivered" theme when it announced its new "High Performance Delivered" tagline in late 2003, featuring golfer Tiger Woods as the spokesperson. As part of its new commitment to helping clients achieve their business objectives, Accenture introduced a policy whereby many of its contracts contained incentives that it realized only if specific business targets were met. For instance, a contract with British travel agent Thomas Cook was structured such that Accenture's bonus depended on five metrics, including a cost-cutting one. In 2004, 30% of the company's contracts contained such incentives. The company's focus on improving the performance and results of its clients proved beneficial to the bottom line: 2006 revenues grew 13% to $17.1 billion and profits rose 36% to $940 million.

Sources: www.accenture.com; "Lessons Learned from Top Firms' Marketing Blunders," *Management Consultant International* (December 2003): 1; Sean Callahan, "Tiger Tees Off in New Accenture Campaign," *B to B*, October 13, 2003, p. 3; "Inside Accenture's Biggest UK Client," *Management Consultant International* (October 2003): 1–3; "Accenture's Results Highlight Weakness of Consulting Market," *Management Consultant International* (October 2003): 8–10; "Accenture Re-Branding Wins UK Plaudits," *Management Consultant International* (October 2002): 5.

everyone, from newborn babies to teenagers to senior citizens. "If you stand for everything in fashion today, you stand for nothing," says Paul R. Charron, the former chief executive of Liz Claiborne, who revitalized that ailing clothing company by buying Juicy Couture and Lucky Brand. By not being vigilant about responding to (or better, yet, envisioning) the changing retailing scene, Gap has seen sales fall dramatically. Sales at stores open at least a year have fallen or remained stagnant for 28 of the past 30 months. Still, the former leading brand is planning a number of strategies to get it out of the doldrums. Among them are selling other-branded merchandise inside its stores (as it used to sell Levi's and now sells Converse), shrinking the number of stores to cut back on overexposure, and focusing on a narrower group of consumers with clothing tailored to meet their needs.[16] ■

In many industries, a discount competitor has entered and undercut the leader's prices. "Marketing Insight: When Your Competitor Delivers More for Less" describes how leaders can respond to an aggressive competitive price discounter.

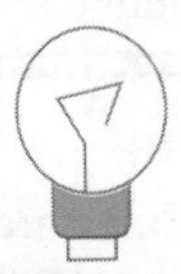

MARKETING INSIGHT | WHEN YOUR COMPETITOR DELIVERS MORE FOR LESS

Companies offering the powerful combination of low prices and high quality are capturing the hearts and wallets of consumers all over the world. In the United States, more than half the population now shops weekly at mass merchants such as Wal-Mart and Target, up from 25% in 1996. In the United Kingdom, premium retailers such as Boots and Sainsbury are scrambling to meet intensifying price—and quality—competition from ASDA and Tesco.

These and similar value players, such as Aldi, Dell, E*TRADE Financial, JetBlue Airways, Ryanair, and Southwest Airlines, are transforming the way consumers of nearly every age and income purchase groceries, apparel, airline tickets, financial services, and computers. As value-driven companies in a growing number of industries change the way they compete, traditional players are right to feel threatened. The formula these upstart firms often rely on includes focusing on one or a few consumer segments; providing better delivery of the basic product or one additional benefit; and matching low prices with highly efficient operations to keep costs down.

To compete with value-based rivals, mainstream companies must reconsider the perennial routes to business success: keeping costs in line, finding sources of differentiation, and managing prices effectively. To succeed in value-based markets, companies need to infuse these timeless strategies with greater intensity and focus, and then execute them flawlessly. Differentiation, for example, becomes less about the abstract goal of rising above competitive clutter and more about identifying opportunities left open by the value players' business models. Effective pricing means waging a transaction-by-transaction perception battle to win over those consumers who are predisposed to believe that value-oriented competitors are always cheaper.

Competitive outcomes will be determined, as always, on the ground—in product aisles, merchandising displays, reconfigured processes, and pricing stickers. When it comes to value-based competition, traditional players can't afford to drop a stitch. Value-driven competitors have changed consumer expectations about the trade-off between quality and price. This shift is gathering momentum, placing a new premium on—and adding new twists to—the old imperatives of differentiation and execution.

Differentiation

To counter value-based players, marketers will need to focus on areas where their business models give other companies room to maneuver. Successful differentiation calls for marshalling multiple tactics to provide superior delivery of a highly desired consumer benefit. Instead of trying to compete with Wal-Mart and other value retailers on price, for example, Walgreens emphasizes convenience across all elements of its business. It has expanded rapidly to make its stores ubiquitous, meanwhile ensuring that most are on corner locations with easy parking. In addition, Walgreens has overhauled its in-store layouts to speed consumers in and out, placing key categories such as convenience foods and one-hour photo services near the front. To protect pharmacy sales, the company has implemented a simple telephone and online preordering system, made it easy to transfer prescriptions between locations around the country, and installed drive-through windows at most freestanding stores. These steps helped it significantly increase its revenue from 1998 to 2006—to over $52 billion from $15 billion.

Execution

Value-based markets also place a premium on execution, particularly in prices and costs. Kmart's disastrous experience in trying to compete head-on with Wal-Mart highlights the difficulty of challenging value leaders on their own terms. Matching or even beating a value player's prices—as Kmart briefly did—won't necessarily win the battle of consumer perceptions against companies with reputations for the lowest prices. To effectively compete against value-based players, firms may need to downplay or even abandon some target market segments. To compete with Ryanair and easyJet, British Airways has put more emphasis on its long haul routes, where value-based players are not evident, and less on the highly competitive short-haul routes where low-cost carriers thrive.

Major airlines have also tried another competitive response, introducing their own low-cost airlines. But Continental's Lite, KLM's Buzz, SAS's Snowflake, and United's Shuttle have all been unsuccessful. One school of thought is that companies should set up low-cost operations only if: (1) the firm's existing businesses will be made more competitive as a result and (2) the new business will derive some advantages it would not have gained by being independent. The success of low-cost operations set up by HSBC, ING, Merrill Lynch, and Royal Bank of Scotland—First Direct, ING Direct, ML Direct, and Direct Line Insurance, respectively—is due in part to synergies between the old and new lines of business. Thus, success dictates the low-cost operation must be designed and launched to be a moneymaker in its own right, not just as a defensive play.

Sources: Adapted from two insightful articles: Nirmalya Kumar, "Strategies to Fight Low-Cost Rivals," *Harvard Business Review* (December 2006): 104–12; and Robert J. Frank, Jeffrey P. George, and Laxman Narasimhan, "When Your Competitor Delivers More for Less," *McKinsey Quarterly* (Winter 2004): 48–59.

Staying the number-one firm calls for action on three fronts. First, the firm must find ways to expand total market demand. Second, the firm must protect its current market share through good defensive and offensive actions. Third, the firm can try to increase its market share, even if market size remains constant. Let's look at each strategy.

To learn how clothing retailer Lululemon uses grass roots marketing techniques to position itself in Canada, visit www.pearsoned.ca/marketingmanagementcanada.

Expanding the Total Market

When the total market expands, the dominant firm usually gains the most. If U.S. consumers increase their consumption of ketchup, Heinz stands to gain the most because it sells almost two-thirds of the country's ketchup. If it can convince more people to use ketchup, or to use ketchup with more meals, or to use more ketchup on each occasion, Heinz will benefit considerably. In general, the market leader should look for new customers or more usage from existing customers.

NEW CUSTOMERS Every product class has the potential to attract buyers who are unaware of the product or who are resisting it because of price or lack of certain features. As Chapter 2 suggested, a company can search for new users among three groups: those who might use it but do not *(market-penetration strategy)*, those who have never used it *(new-market segment strategy)*, or those who live elsewhere *(geographical-expansion strategy)*.

Starbucks Coffee is one of the best-known brands in the world. Starbucks is able to sell a cup of coffee for $3 while the store next door can only get $1. (And if you want the popular café latte, it's $4.) Starbucks has more than 7,200 locations throughout North America, the Pacific Rim, Europe, and the Middle East, and its annual revenue for 2002 topped $3.3 billion. Its corporate Web site (www.starbucks.com) gives a peek into its multipronged approach to growth.[17]

> Starbucks purchases and roasts high-quality whole bean coffees and sells them along with fresh, rich-brewed, Italian-style espresso beverages, a variety of pastries and confections, and coffee-related accessories and equipment—primarily through its company-operated retail stores. In addition, Starbucks sells whole-bean coffees through a specialty sales group and supermarkets. Additionally, Starbucks produces and sells bottled Frappuccino® coffee drinks and a line of premium ice creams through its joint venture partnerships and offers a line of innovative premium teas produced by its wholly owned subsidiary, Tazo Tea Company. The company's objective is to establish Starbucks as the most recognized and respected brand in the world. To achieve this goal, the company plans to continue to rapidly expand its retail operations, grow its specialty sales and other operations, and selectively pursue opportunities to leverage the Starbucks brand through the introduction of new products and the development of new distribution channels.

MORE USAGE Marketers can try to increase the amount, level, or frequency of consumption. The *amount* of consumption can sometimes be increased through packaging or product redesign. Larger package sizes have been shown to increase the amount of product that consumers use at one time.[18] The usage of impulse consumption products such as soft drinks and snacks increases when the product is made more available.

Increasing *frequency* of consumption, on the other hand, requires either (1) identifying additional opportunities to use the brand in the same basic way or (2) identifying completely new and different ways to use the brand. Consumers may see the product as useful only in certain places and at certain times, especially if it has strong associations to particular usage situations or user types.

Among Starbucks' expansion efforts have been a new line of premium tea produced by Tazo Tea Company, a Starbucks subsidiary.

To generate additional opportunities to use the brand in the same basic way, a marketing program can communicate the appropriateness and advantages of using the brand more frequently in new or existing situations or remind consumers to actually use the brand as close as possible to those situations. Clorox has run ads stressing the many benefits of its bleach, such as how it eliminates kitchen odors. Another opportunity arises when consumers' perceptions of their usage differs from the reality. Consumers may fail to replace a short-lived product when they should, because they overestimate how long it stays fresh.[19]

One strategy to speed up product replacement is to tie the act of replacing the product to a holiday, event, or time of year. Another might be to provide consumers with better information about either (1) when they first used the product or need to replace it or (2) the current level of product performance. Gillette razor cartridges feature colored stripes that slowly fade with repeated use, signaling the user to move on to the next cartridge.

The second approach to increasing frequency of consumption is to identify completely new and different applications. For example, food product companies have long advertised recipes that use their branded products in entirely different ways. After discovering that consumers used Arm & Hammer baking soda brand as a refrigerator deodorant, the company launched a heavy promotion campaign focusing on this single use. After succeeding in getting half the homes in the United States to place an open box of baking soda in the refrigerator, the company expanded the brand into a variety of new product categories, such as toothpaste, antiperspirant, and laundry detergent.

Product development can also spur new uses. Chewing gum manufacturers such as Cadbury Schweppes, maker of Trident, are producing "nutraceutical" products to strengthen or whiten teeth. Aquafresh has successfully launched dental chewing gums with health and cosmetic benefits.[20]

Defending Market Share

While trying to expand total market size, the dominant firm must continuously and actively defend its current business: Boeing against Airbus; Staples against Office Depot; and Google against Yahoo! and Microsoft.[21] The success of online social network sites MySpace and Facebook has brought challenges from upstarts such as LinkedIn personal business network, Dogster for dog owners, and Eons and Vox for sharing photos and videos, and blog posts for baby boomers and older consumers.[22]

What can the market leader do to defend its terrain? The most constructive response is *continuous innovation.* The leader should lead the industry in developing new products and customer services, distribution effectiveness, and cost cutting. It keeps increasing its competitive strength and value to customers by providing comprehensive solutions.

MARTELLI LAVORAZIONI TESSILI

Consumers who wonder why it costs $200 or more to buy a pair of designer jeans might feel better about the high price tag if they strolled through a Martelli Lavorazioni Tessili factory in Vedelago, Italy. The market leader in the technology of "distressing" denim, Martelli counts Gucci, Armani, Dolce and Gabbana, and Yves St. Laurent among its clients on the high end and Levi-Strauss, Lee, Wrangler, and Gap on the low end. Martelli is uncontested in Europe; its only competitors are in the United States and Japan. The company stays on top by relentlessly innovating—investing at least $5 million a year to continually upgrade technology—and by finding cheap but skilled labor to carry out its bizarre but effective techniques. In its main factory with 900 workers, huge washing machines tumble jeans with pumice gravel. Workers wearing face masks put jeans legs over inflated balloons, which then are moved between sets of plastic brushes that scrub the denim. Some workers do painstaking hand work on individual jeans, applying discoloring chemicals with brushes, applying embroidered designs, or using handheld guns to blast jets of quartz sand. After experimenting with workers from Africa and Romania, Martelli has found that legal Chinese immigrants are the most skilled, patient, and cost effective.[23]

The market leader for "distressing jeans," Itlay's Martelli Lavorazioni Tessili counts Italian designers Stefano Gabbana and Domenico Dolce, shown here at Milan Fashion Week, as one of their customers.

In satisfying customer needs, we can draw a distinction between responsive marketing, anticipative marketing, and creative marketing. A *responsive* marketer finds a stated need and fills it. An *anticipative* marketer looks ahead into what needs customers may have in the near future. A *creative* marketer discovers and produces solutions customers did not ask for but to which they enthusiastically respond. Creative marketers are *market-driving firms,* not just market driven. Interactive ad agency, R/GA is one such market-driving firm.

R/GA

The advertising business has been turned upside down by increasing consumer control, the ascendance of digital media, and the fragmentation of one mass market into countless niche markets. Yet, rather than responding to trends in advertising, R/GA agency, headed by CEO Bob Greenberg, has become a trendsetter by creating a totally different type of ad agency, one in which technology is considered equal to creativity. By blending pioneering technological applications with "big picture" creative strategies, R/GA expanded revenue over 35% to an estimated $150 million in 2006 and was voted *Adweek*'s Interactive Agency of the Year. Clients include L'Oreal Interactive, Nike, Nokia, and Verizon. A typical out-of-the-box application is the "music mixer" R/GA created for Verizon. The feature combines video footage of famous beatbox artists and a sound mixer, inviting visitors to mix their own beats to forward to friends, post in a gallery, or embed in their blog. In addition to providing consumers with a rewarding, fun experience, the application drives home a big idea: It shows off the power of Verizon's broadband connectivity and links Verizon with "innovation" in the mind of its users.[24]

Market-driving firms become market leaders through superior value delivery of unmet—and maybe even unknown—consumer needs. Think of Sony. In the late 1970s, Akio Morita, the Sony founder, was working on a pet project that would revolutionize the way people listened to music: a portable cassette player he called the Walkman. Engineers at the company insisted there was little demand for such a product, but Morita refused to part with his vision. By the 20th anniversary of the Walkman, Sony had sold over 250 million in nearly 100 different models.[25]

Even when it does not launch offensives, the market leader must not leave any major flanks exposed. It must consider carefully which terrains are important to defend, even at a loss, and which can be surrendered. The aim of defensive strategy is to reduce the probability of attack, divert attacks to less-threatening areas, and lessen their intensity. The defender's speed of response can make an important difference in the profit consequences. A dominant firm can use the six defense strategies summarized in Figure 11.6.[26]

POSITION DEFENSE Position defense means occupying the most desirable market space in consumers' minds, making the brand almost impregnable, as Procter & Gamble has done with Tide detergent for cleaning, Crest toothpaste for cavity prevention, and Pampers diapers for dryness.

FLANK DEFENSE Although position defense is important, the market leader should also erect outposts to protect a weak front or possibly serve as an invasion base for counterattack. When Heublein's brand Smirnoff, which had 23% of the U.S. vodka market, was at-

FIG. 11.6

Six Types of Defense Strategies

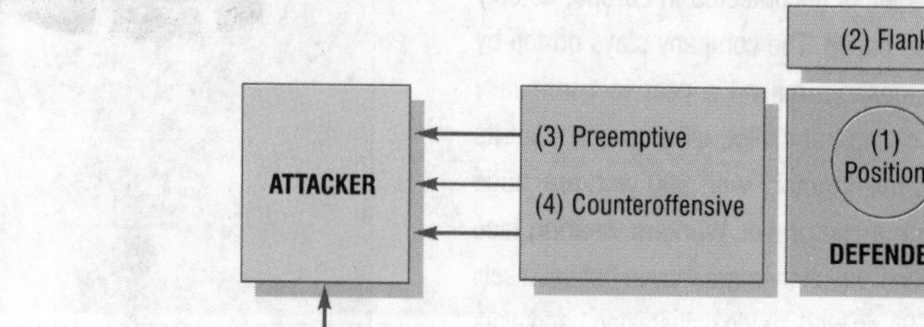

tacked by low-priced competitor Wolfschmidt, Heublein actually *raised* its price and put the increased revenue into advertising. At the same time, Heublein introduced another brand, Relska, to compete with Wolfschmidt and still another, Popov, to sell for less than Wolfschmidt. This strategy effectively bracketed Wolfschmidt and protected Smirnoff's flanks.

PREEMPTIVE DEFENSE A more aggressive maneuver is to attack *before* the enemy starts its offense. A company can launch a preemptive defense in several ways. It can wage guerrilla action across the market—hitting one competitor here, another there—and keep everyone off balance; or it can try to achieve a grand market envelopment. Bank of America's 17,000 ATMs and 5,700 retail branches nationwide provide steep competition to local and regional banks. In this way the firm can send out market signals to dissuade competitors from attacking.[27]

Marketers can introduce a stream of new products, making sure to precede them with *preannouncements*—deliberate communications regarding future actions.[28] Preannouncements can signal to competitors that they will need to fight to gain market share.[29] If Microsoft announces plans for a new-product development, smaller firms may choose to concentrate their development efforts in other directions to avoid head-to-head competition. Some high-tech firms have even been accused of engaging in selling "vaporware"—preannouncing products that miss delivery dates or are never introduced.[30]

COUNTEROFFENSIVE DEFENSE When attacked, most market leaders will respond with a counterattack. In a *counteroffensive,* the leader can meet the attacker frontally or hit its flank or launch a pincer movement. An effective counterattack is to invade the attacker's main territory so that it will pull back to defend it. After FedEx watched UPS successfully invade its airborne delivery system, FedEx invested heavily in ground delivery service through a series of acquisitions to challenge UPS on its home turf.[31]

Another common form of counteroffensive is the exercise of economic or political clout. The leader may try to crush a competitor by subsidizing lower prices for the vulnerable product with revenue from its more profitable products, or the leader may prematurely announce that a product upgrade will be available, to prevent customers from buying the competitor's product. Or the leader may lobby legislators to take political action to inhibit the competition.

MOBILE DEFENSE In mobile defense, the leader stretches its domain over new territories that can serve as future centers for defense and offense through market broadening and market diversification. *Market broadening* shifts focus from the current product to the underlying generic need. The company gets involved in R&D across the whole range of technology associated with that need. Thus "petroleum" companies such as BP sought to recast themselves as "energy" companies. Implicitly, this change demanded that they dip their research fingers into the oil, coal, nuclear, hydroelectric, and chemical industries.

Market diversification shifts into unrelated industries. When U.S. tobacco companies such as Reynolds and Philip Morris acknowledged the growing curbs on cigarette smoking, they were not content with position defense or even with looking for cigarette substitutes. Instead they moved quickly into new industries, such as beer, liquor, soft drinks, and frozen foods.

CONTRACTION DEFENSE Large companies sometimes must recognize that they can no longer defend all their territory. The best course of action then appears to be *planned contraction* (also called *strategic withdrawal*): giving up weaker territories and reassigning resources to stronger territories. In 2006, Sara Lee spun off products that accounted for almost 40% of the company's revenues, including its strong Hanes hosiery brand, so it could concentrate on its well-known food brands.[32]

Expanding Market Share

In many markets, one share point is worth tens of millions of dollars. No wonder competition has turned fierce in so many markets. Gaining increased share in the served market, however, does not automatically produce higher profits—especially for labor-intensive service companies that may not experience many economies of scale. Much depends on the company's strategy.[33]

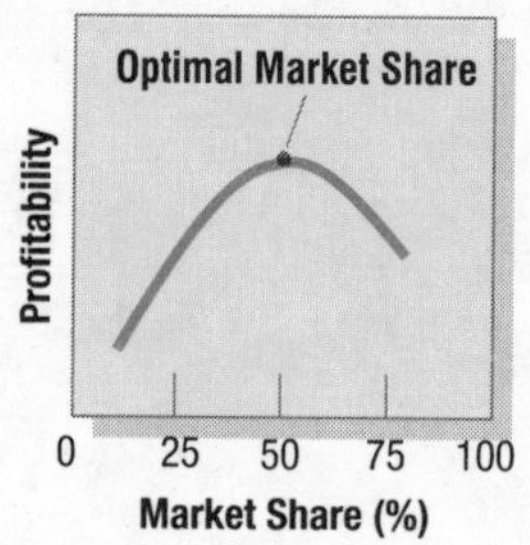

FIG. 11.7

The Concept of Optimal Market Share

Because the cost of buying higher market share may far exceed its revenue value, a company should consider four factors before pursuing increased share:

- ***The possibility of provoking antitrust action.*** Jealous competitors are likely to cry "monopoly" if a dominant firm makes further inroads. This rise in risk would diminish the attractiveness of pushing market share gains too far. Microsoft and Intel are examples of companies that have faced great scrutiny for their market leadership and practices.
- ***Economic cost.*** Figure 11.7 shows that profitability might *fall* with further market share gains after some level. In the illustration, the firm's *optimal market share* is 50%. The cost of gaining further market share might exceed the value. The "holdout" customers may dislike the company, be loyal to competitive suppliers, have unique needs, or prefer dealing with smaller suppliers. And the costs of legal work, public relations, and lobbying rise with market share. Pushing for higher share is less justified when there are few scale or experience economies, unattractive market segments exist, buyers want multiple sources of supply, and exit barriers are high. Some market leaders have even increased profitability by selectively *decreasing* market share in weaker areas.[34]
- ***Pursuing the wrong marketing activities.*** Companies successfully gaining share typically outperform competitors in three areas: new-product activity, relative product quality, and marketing expenditures.[35] On the other hand, companies that attempt to increase market share by cutting prices more deeply than competitors typically don't achieve significant gains, because enough rivals meet the price cuts and others offer other values so buyers don't switch. Competitive rivalry and price cutting have been shown to be most intense in industries with high fixed costs, high inventory costs, and stagnant primary demand, such as steel, auto, paper, and chemicals.[36]
- ***The effect of increased market share on actual and perceived quality.***[37] Too many customers can put a strain on the firm's resources, hurting product value and service delivery. America Online experienced growing pains when its customer base expanded, resulting in system outages and access problems. Consumers may also infer that "bigger is not better" and assume that growth will lead to a deterioration of quality. If "exclusivity" is a key brand benefit, existing customers may resent additional new customers.

::: Other Competitive Strategies

Firms that occupy second, third, and lower ranks in an industry are often called runner-up or trailing firms. Some, such as PepsiCo, Ford, Avis, and Texas Instruments, are quite large in their own right. These firms can adopt one of two postures. They can attack the leader and other competitors in an aggressive bid for further market share as *market challengers,* or they can play ball and not "rock the boat" as *market followers.*

Market-Challenger Strategies

Many market challengers have gained ground or even overtaken the leader. Toyota today produces more cars than General Motors, Lowe's is putting pressure on Home Depot, and AMD has been chipping away at Intel's market share.[38] Challengers set high aspirations, leveraging their resources while the market leader often runs the business as usual. Now let's examine the competitive attack strategies available to market challengers.[39]

DEFINING THE STRATEGIC OBJECTIVE AND OPPONENT(S) A market challenger must first define its strategic objective. Most aim to increase market share. The challenger must decide whom to attack:

- ***It can attack the market leader.*** This is a high-risk but potentially high-payoff strategy and makes good sense if the leader is not serving the market well. It often has the added benefit of distancing the firm from other challengers. When Miller Lite attacked Bud Lite on product quality during 2004–2005, Coors Lite was left out of the consumer conversation. An alternative strategy is to out-innovate the leader across the whole segment. Xerox wrested the copy market from 3M by developing a better copying process. Later, Canon grabbed a large chunk of Xerox's market by introducing desk copiers.

■ ***It can attack firms of its own size that are not doing the job and are underfinanced.*** These firms have aging products, are charging excessive prices, or are not satisfying customers in other ways.

■ ***It can attack small local and regional firms.*** Several major banks grew to their present size by gobbling up smaller regional banks, or "guppies."

CHOOSING A GENERAL ATTACK STRATEGY Given clear opponents and objectives, what attack options are available? We can distinguish among five attack strategies: frontal, flank, encirclement, bypass, and guerilla attacks.

Frontal Attack In a pure *frontal attack*, the attacker matches its opponent's product, advertising, price, and distribution. The principle of force says that the side with the greater resources will win. A modified frontal attack, such as cutting price, can work if the market leader doesn't retaliate, and if the competitor convinces the market that its product is equal to the leader's. Helene Curtis is a master at convincing the market that its brands—such as Suave and Finesse—are equal in quality but a better value than higher-priced brands.

Flank Attack An enemy's weak spots are natural targets. A *flank attack* can be directed along two strategic dimensions—geographic and segmental. In a geographic attack, the challenger spots areas where the opponent is underperforming. Although the Internet has siphoned newspaper readers and advertisers away in many markets, Independent News & Media, a 102-year-old Irish media company, sells a majority of its 175 newspaper and magazine titles in cities where the economy is strong but the Internet is still relatively weak—countries such as Ireland, South Africa, Australia, New Zealand, and India.[40] The other flanking strategy is to serve uncovered market needs. Ariat's cowboy boots have challenged long-time market leaders Justin Boots and Tony Lama by making boots that were every bit as ranch ready, but ergonomically designed to feel as comfortable as a running shoe—a totally new benefit in the category.[41]

A flanking strategy is another name for identifying shifts in market segments that are causing gaps to develop, then rushing in to fill the gaps and develop them into strong segments. Flanking is in the best tradition of modern marketing, which holds that the purpose of marketing is to discover needs and satisfy them. It's particularly attractive to a challenger with fewer resources than its opponent and much more likely to be successful than frontal attacks.

SEARCH ENGINES

Given Google's 45% share of the Internet search business, it might seem foolhardy for anybody to challenge it. A frontal attack on Google would mean building a better mousetrap—in this case a better search algorithm. Yet, a handful of smaller search companies are mounting flank attacks on Google, and they're confident they'll be able to swipe some of the search giant's market share. The flank these small companies are attacking is the one missing element in Google's searches: human intelligence and its ability to reason and contextualize. Jim Wales, cofounder of Wikipedia, the collaborative Internet encyclopedia, plans to create an open-source search engine called Wikia that uses human deduction as well as a machine-driven algorithm. Wales figures that humans are better at weeding out spam search results. ChaCha employs a similar strategy and has thrived in Korea, where Google has made few inroads. ChaCha, founded by MIT research scientist Scott A. Jones, uses 25,000 part- and full-time employees who can offer guided searches in real time. Anyone who has ever "googled" a topic and come up with thousands of Web pages, only of a handful of which are truly helpful, can see how guided search might be an attractive offering. ChaCha's human-guided searches can offer a smaller set of focused and relevant results. The expense of using human guides might be daunting, but ChaCha has managed to bring in 10,000 guides a month at $5 to $10 an hour; it offers them a financial incentive for bringing in others. For its part, Wikia plans to use thousands of volunteers, building on the model of its successful all-volunteer-run Wikipedia.[42]

Encirclement Attack The *encirclement* maneuver is an attempt to capture a wide slice of the enemy's territory through a blitz. It means launching a grand offensive on several fronts. Encirclement makes sense when the challenger commands superior resources and believes a swift encirclement will break the opponent's will. In making a stand against archrival Microsoft, Sun Microsystems licensed its Java software to hundreds of companies and millions of software developers for all sorts of consumer devices. As consumer electronics products began to go digital, Java started appearing in a wide range of gadgets.

Bypass Attack The most indirect assault strategy is *bypassing* the enemy altogether and attacking easier markets to broaden the firm's resource base. This strategy offers three lines of approach: diversifying into unrelated products, diversifying into new geographical markets, and leapfrogging into new technologies to supplant existing products. In the past decade, Pepsi has used a bypass strategy against Coke by: (1) aggressively rolling out Aquafina bottled water nationally in 1997 before Coke launched its Dasani brand; (2) purchasing orange juice giant Tropicana for $3.3 billion in 1998, which owned almost twice the market share of Coca-Cola's Minute Maid; and (3) purchasing The Quaker Oats Company, owner of market leader Gatorade sports drink, for $14 billion in 2000.[43]

Technological leapfrogging is a bypass strategy practiced in high-tech industries. The challenger patiently researches and develops the next technology and launches an attack, shifting the battleground to its own territory where it has an advantage. Nintendo's successful attack in the video-game market was precisely about wresting market share by introducing a superior technology and redefining the "competitive space." Then Sega/Genesis did the same with more advanced technology, and now Sony's PlayStation has grabbed the technological lead to gain almost half the video-game market.[44] Challenger Google used technological leapfrogging to overtake Yahoo! and become the market leader in search.

Guerrilla Warfare Guerrilla warfare consists of waging small, intermittent attacks to harass and demoralize the opponent and eventually secure permanent footholds. The guerrilla challenger uses both conventional and unconventional means of attack. These include selective price cuts, intense promotional blitzes, and occasional legal action. Princeton Review successfully challenged Kaplan Educational Centers, the largest test-preparation business in the United States, through e-mail horror stories about Kaplan and brash ads—"Stanley's a wimp," or "Friends don't let friends take Kaplan"—while always touting the Princeton Review's smaller, livelier classes.

A guerrilla campaign can be expensive, although less so than a frontal, encirclement, or flank attack. Guerrilla warfare is more a preparation for war than a war itself. Ultimately, it must be backed by a stronger attack if the challenger hopes to beat the opponent. Guerrilla marketing must, however, not cross lines of legality or morality. On January 31, 2007, several guerrilla-marketing magnetic light displays in and around the city of Boston Massachusetts, were mistaken for possible explosive devices. Subway stations, bridges, and a portion of Interstate 93 were closed as police examined, removed, and in some cases, destroyed the devices. The suspicious objects were revealed to be ads depicting characters from the Cartoon Network's animated television series *Aqua Teen Hunger Force*, resulting in a fine for network owner's Turner Broadcasting System and a wave of negative publicity.[45]

CHOOSING A SPECIFIC ATTACK STRATEGY The challenger must go beyond the five broad strategies and develop more specific strategies. Any aspect of the marketing program can serve as the basis for attack, such as lower-priced or discounted products, new or improved products and services, a wider variety of offerings, and innovative distribution strategies. A challenger's success depends on combining several strategies to improve its position over time. "Marketing Memo: Making Smaller Better" provides some additional tips for challenger brands.

Market-Follower Strategies

Some years ago, Theodore Levitt wrote an article entitled "Innovative Imitation," in which he argued that a strategy of *product imitation* might be as profitable as a strategy of *product innovation*.[46] The innovator bears the expense of developing the new product, getting it into distribution, and informing and educating the market. The reward for all this work and risk is normally market leadership. However, another firm can come along and copy or improve on the new product. Although it probably will not overtake the leader, the follower can achieve high profits because it did not bear any of the innovation expense.

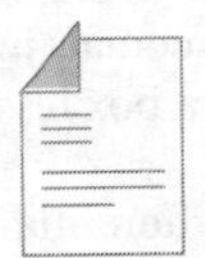

MARKETING MEMO | MAKING SMALLER BETTER

Adam Morgan offers eight suggestions on how small brands can better compete:

1. ***Break with your immediate past***—Don't be afraid to ask "dumb" questions to challenge convention and view your brand differently.
2. ***Build a "lighthouse identity"***—Establish values and communicate who and why you are. Apple excels at this task.
3. ***Assume thought leadership of the category***—Break convention in terms of what you say about yourself, where you say it, and what you do beyond talk.
4. ***Create symbols of reevaluation***—A rocket uses half its fuel in the first mile to break loose from Earth's gravitational pull—you may need to polarize people to get them to rethink your brand.
5. ***Sacrifice***—Focus your target, message, reach and frequency, distribution, and line extensions, and recognize that less can be more.
6. ***Overcommit***—Although you may do fewer things, do "big" things when you do them.
7. ***Use publicity and advertising to enter popular culture***—Unconventional communications can get people talking.
8. ***Be idea centered, not consumer centered***—Sustain challenger momentum by not losing sight of what the brand is about and can be, and redefine marketing support as the center of the company to reflect this vision.

Sources: Adam Morgan, *Eating the Big Fish: How Challenger Brands Can Compete against Brand Leaders* (New York: John Wiley & Sons, 1999). See also, Adam Morgan, *The Pirate Inside: Building a Challenger Brand Culture within Yourself and Your Organization* (West Sussex, England: John Wiley & Sons, 2004). Reprinted by permission of John Wiley & Sons, Inc.

S&S CYCLE

S&S Cycle is the biggest supplier of complete engines and major motor parts to more than 15 companies that build several thousand Harley-like cruiser bikes each year. These cloners charge as much as $30,000 for their customized creations. S&S has built its name by improving on Harley-Davidson's handiwork. Its customers are often would-be Harley buyers frustrated by long waiting lines at the dealers. Other customers simply want the incredibly powerful S&S engines. S&S stays abreast of its evolving market by ordering a new Harley bike every year and taking apart the engine to see what it can improve upon.[47]

Many companies prefer to follow rather than challenge the market leader. Patterns of "conscious parallelism" are common in capital-intensive, homogeneous-product industries, such as steel, fertilizers, and chemicals. The opportunities for product differentiation and image differentiation are low; service quality is often comparable; and price sensitivity runs high. The mood in these industries is against short-run grabs for market share because that strategy only provokes retaliation. Most firms decide against stealing one another's customers. Instead, they present similar offers to buyers, usually by copying the leader. Market shares show high stability.

That's not to say that market followers lack strategies. A market follower must know how to hold current customers and win a fair share of new ones. Each follower tries to bring distinctive advantages to its target market—location, services, financing. Because the follower is often a major target of attack by challengers, it must keep its manufacturing costs low and its product quality and services high. It must also enter new markets as they open up. The follower must define a growth path, but one that doesn't invite competitive retaliation. We distinguish four broad strategies:

S&S Cycle has become a successful market follower by appealing to would-be Harley owners.

1. ***Counterfeiter***—The counterfeiter duplicates the leader's product and packages and sells it on the black market or through disreputable dealers. Music firms, Apple, and Rolex have been plagued by the counterfeiter problem, especially in Asia.

2. ***Cloner***—The cloner emulates the leader's products, name, and packaging, with slight variations. For example, Ralcorp Holding Inc. sells imitations of name-brand cereals in look-alike boxes. Its Tasteeos, Fruit Rings, and Corn Flakes sell for nearly $1 a box less than the leading name brands.
3. ***Imitator***—The imitator copies some things from the leader but maintains differentiation in terms of packaging, advertising, pricing, or location. The leader doesn't mind the imitator as long as the imitator doesn't attack the leader aggressively. Fernandez Pujals grew up in Fort Lauderdale, Florida, and took Domino's home delivery idea to Spain, where he borrowed $80,000 to open his first store in Madrid. His TelePizza chain now operates almost 1,000 stores in Europe and Latin America.
4. ***Adapter***—The adapter takes the leader's products and adapts or improves them. The adapter may choose to sell to different markets, but often it grows into the future challenger, as many Japanese firms have done after improving products developed elsewhere.

What does a follower earn? Normally, less than the leader. For example, a study of food-processing companies showed the largest firm averaging a 16% return on investment; the number-two firm, 6%; the number-three firm, –1%, and the number-four firm, –6%. In this case, only the top two firms have profits. No wonder Jack Welch, former CEO of GE, told his business units that each must reach the number-one or -two position in its market or else! Followership is often not a rewarding path.

Market-Nicher Strategies

An alternative to being a follower in a large market is to be a leader in a small market, or niche, as we introduced in Chapter 8. Smaller firms normally avoid competing with larger firms by targeting small markets of little or no interest to the larger firms. But even large, profitable firms may choose to use niching strategies for some of their business units or companies.

ITW

Illinois Tool Works (ITW) manufactures thousands of products, including nails, screws, plastic six-pack holders for soda cans, bicycle helmets, backpacks, plastic buckles for pet collars, resealable food packages, and more. Since the late 1980s, the company has made between 30 and 40 acquisitions each year that added new products to the product line. ITW has more than 700 highly autonomous and decentralized business units in 48 countries employing 50,000 people. When one division commercializes a new product, the company spins the product and personnel off into a new entity.[48]

Firms with low shares of the total market can become highly profitable through smart niching. Such companies tend to offer high value, charge a premium price, achieve lower manufacturing costs, and shape a strong corporate culture and vision. Family-run Tire Rack sells two million specialty tires a year through the Internet, telephone, and mail from its South Bend, Indiana, location.[49] Houston-based VAALCO Energy decided that its odds of striking it rich were better in foreign territory than at home where they faced hundreds of wildcatters. Drilling in an oil field off the coast of Gabon in West Central Africa, it has met with a lot less competition. The company's revenues have risen so much it was deemed *BusinessWeek*'s number-one hot growth company in 2006.[50]

In a study of hundreds of business units, the Strategic Planning Institute found that the return on investment averaged 27% in smaller markets, but only 11% in larger markets.[51] Why is niching so profitable? The main reason is that the market nicher ends up knowing the target customers so well, it meets their needs better than other firms selling to this niche casually. As a result, the nicher can charge a substantial price over costs. The nicher achieves *high margin,* whereas the mass marketer achieves *high volume.*

Nichers have three tasks: creating niches, expanding niches, and protecting niches. Niching carries a major risk in that the market niche might dry up or be attacked. The company is then stuck with highly specialized resources that may not have high-value alternative uses.

ZIPPO

With smoking on a steady decline, Bradford, Pennsylvania–based Zippo Manufacturing is finding the market for its iconic metal cigarette lighter drying up. Zippo marketers now find themselves needing to diversify and to broaden their focus to "selling flame." With a goal of reducing reliance on tobacco-related products to 50% of revenue by 2010, the company introduced a long, slender multipurpose lighter for candles, grills, and fireplaces in 2001; it has explored licensing arrangements with suppliers of flame-related outdoor products; and it has acquired Case Cutlery, a knifemaker, and D.D.M. Italia, known throughout Europe for fine Italian leather goods.[52]

Because niches can weaken, the firm must continually create new ones. "Marketing Memo: Niche Specialist Roles" outlines some options. The firm should "stick to its niching" but not necessarily to its niche. That is why *multiple niching* is preferable to *single niching*. By developing strength in two or more niches, the company increases its chances for survival.

Firms entering a market should initially aim at a niche rather than the whole market. The cell phone industry has experienced phenomenal growth but is now facing fierce competition as the number of new potential users dwindles. An Irish upstart company, Digicel Group, has successfully tapped into one of the few remaining high-growth segments: poor people without cell phones.

DIGICEL GROUP

In 2001, Digicel CEO Denis O'Brien heard that the government of Jamaica was opening its local phone market, long monopolized by British telecom giant Cable & Wireless. O'Brien spent nearly $50 million for a license, using money from the sale of his first telecom venture, Esat Telecom Group PLC. O'Brien took the plunge because he knew that Jamaicans had to wait over two years for a landline, and only 4% of the population had cell phones. Within 100 days, Digicel had signed on 100,000 subscribers, luring them with inexpensive rates and phones and with improved service. Five years later, 70% of Jamaica's cell phone users—now 82% of the country's 2.7 million citizens—are Digicel customers. O'Brien has also homed in on the rest of the Caribbean and boasts three million subscribers in 22 countries throughout the Caribbean, Latin America, and even the South Pacific. In an ambitious move, O'Brien now plans to target the United States, specifically U.S. consumers who are young, poor, or immigrants—the kind of customers that giants such as TMobile and Verizon don't court.[53]

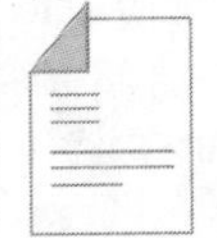

MARKETING MEMO | NICHE SPECIALIST ROLES

The key idea in successful nichemanship is specialization. Here are some possible niche roles:

- ***End-user specialist:*** The firm specializes in serving one type of end-use customer. For example, a *value-added reseller (VAR)* customizes the computer hardware and software for specific customer segments and earns a price premium in the process.
- ***Vertical-level specialist:*** The firm specializes at some vertical level of the production-distribution value chain. A copper firm may concentrate on producing raw copper, copper components, or finished copper products.
- ***Customer-size specialist:*** The firm concentrates on selling to either small, medium-sized, or large customers. Many nichers specialize in serving small customers neglected by the majors.
- ***Specific-customer specialist:*** The firm limits its selling to one or a few customers. Many firms sell their entire output to a single company, such as Sears or General Motors.
- ***Geographic specialist:*** The firm sells only in a certain locality, region, or area of the world.
- ***Product or product-line specialist:*** The firm carries or produces only one product line or product. A manufacturer may produce only lenses for microscopes. A retailer may carry only ties.
- ***Product-feature specialist:*** The firm specializes in producing a certain type of product or product feature. Zipcar's car-sharing services targets people who live and work in seven major U.S. cities, frequently use public transportation, but still need a car a few times a month.
- ***Job-shop specialist:*** The firm customizes its products for individual customers.
- ***Quality-price specialist:*** The firm operates at the low- or high-quality ends of the market. Hewlett-Packard specializes in the high-quality, high-price end of the handheld calculator market.
- ***Service specialist:*** The firm offers one or more services not available from other firms. A bank might take loan requests over the phone and hand-deliver the money to the customer.
- ***Channel specialist:*** The firm specializes in serving only one channel of distribution. For example, a soft-drink company decides to make a very large-sized serving available only at gas stations.

::: Balancing Customer and Competitor Orientations

We've stressed the importance of a company's positioning itself competitively as a market leader, challenger, follower, or nicher. Yet a company must not spend *all* its time focusing on competitors.

Competitor-Centered Companies

A *competitor-centered company* sets its course as follows:

Observed Situation

- Competitor W is going all out to crush us in Miami.
- Competitor X is improving its distribution coverage in Houston and hurting our sales.
- Competitor Y has cut its price in Denver, and we lost three share points.
- Competitor Z has introduced a new service feature in New Orleans, and we are losing sales.

Reactions

- We will withdraw from the Miami market because we cannot afford to fight this battle.
- We will increase our advertising expenditure in Houston.
- We will meet competitor Y's price cut in Denver.
- We will increase our sales promotion budget in New Orleans.

This kind of planning has some pluses and minuses. On the positive side, the company develops a fighter orientation. It trains its marketers to be on constant alert, to watch for weaknesses in its competitors' and its own position. On the negative side, the company is too reactive. Rather than formulating and executing a consistent, *customer-oriented* strategy, it determines its moves based on its competitors' moves. It does not move toward its own goals. It does not know where it will end up, because so much depends on what its competitors do.

Customer-Centered Companies

A *customer-centered company* focuses more on customer developments in formulating its strategies.

Observed Situation

- The total market is growing at 4% annually.
- The quality-sensitive segment is growing at 8% annually.
- The deal-prone customer segment is also growing fast, but these customers do not stay with any supplier very long.
- A growing number of customers have expressed an interest in a 24-hour hot line, which no one in the industry offers.

Reactions

- We will focus more effort on reaching and satisfying the quality segment of the market. We will buy better components, improve quality control, and shift our advertising theme to quality.
- We will avoid cutting prices and making deals because we do not want the kind of customer that buys this way.
- We will install a 24-hour hot line if it looks promising.

Clearly, the customer-centered company is in a better position to identify new opportunities and set a course that promises to deliver long-run profits. By monitoring customer needs, it can decide which customer groups and emerging needs are the most important to serve, given its resources and objectives. Jeff Bezos, founder of Amazon.com, strongly favors a customer-centered orientation: "Amazon.com's mantra has been that we were going to obsess over our customers and not our competitors. We watch our competitors, learn from them, see the things that they [were doing for customers] and copy those things as much as we can. But we were never going to obsess over them."[54]

SUMMARY :::

1. To prepare an effective marketing strategy, a company must study competitors as well as actual and potential customers. Marketers need to identify competitors' strategies, objectives, strengths, and weaknesses.
2. A company's closest competitors are those seeking to satisfy the same customers and needs and making similar offers. A company should also pay attention to latent competitors, who may offer new or other ways to satisfy the same needs. A company should identify competitors by using both industry- and market-based analyses.
3. A market leader has the largest market share in the relevant product market. To remain dominant, the leader looks for ways to expand total market demand, attempts to protect its current market share, and perhaps tries to increase its market share.
4. A market challenger attacks the market leader and other competitors in an aggressive bid for more market share. Challengers can choose from five types of general attack; challengers must also choose specific attack strategies.
5. A market follower is a runner-up firm willing to maintain its market share and not rock the boat. A follower can play the role of counterfeiter, cloner, imitator, or adapter.
6. A market nicher serves small market segments not being served by larger firms. The key to nichemanship is specialization. Nichers develop offerings to fully meet a certain group of customers' needs, commanding a premium price in the process.
7. As important as a competitive orientation is in today's global markets, companies should not overdo the emphasis on competitors. They should maintain a good balance of consumer and competitor monitoring.

APPLICATIONS :::

Marketing Debate How Do You Attack a Category Leader?

Attacking a leader is always difficult. Some strategists recommend attacking a leader "head-on" by targeting its strengths. Other strategists disagree and recommend flanking and attempting to avoid the leader's strengths.

Take a position: The best way to challenge a leader is to attack its strengths *versus* The best way to attack a leader is to avoid a head-on assault and to adopt a flanking strategy.

Marketing Discussion

Pick an industry. Classify firms according to the four different roles they might play: leader, challenger, follower, and nicher. How would you characterize the nature of competition? Do the firms follow the principles described in this chapter?

PART 5

SHAPING THE MARKET OFFERINGS

IN THIS CHAPTER, WE WILL ADDRESS THE FOLLOWING QUESTIONS:

1. What are the characteristics of products, and how do marketers classify products?
2. How can companies differentiate products?
3. How can a company build and manage its product mix and product lines?
4. How can companies combine products to create strong co-brands or ingredient brands?
5. How can companies use packaging, labeling, warranties, and guarantees as marketing tools?

CHAPTER 12 :::

SETTING PRODUCT STRATEGY

twelve

At the heart of a great brand is a great product. Product is a key element in the market offering. Market leaders generally offer products and services of superior quality that provide unsurpassed customer value.

Caterpillar has become a leading firm by maximizing total customer value in the construction-equipment industry, despite challenges from a number of able competitors, such as John Deere, J. I. Case, Komatsu, Volvo, and Hitachi. First, Caterpillar produces high-performance equipment known for its reliability and durability—key purchase considerations in the choice of heavy industrial equipment. The firm also makes it easy for customers to find the right product by providing a full line of construction equipment and offering a wide range of financial terms. Caterpillar maintains the largest number of independent construction-equipment dealers in the industry. These dealers all carry a complete line of Caterpillar products and are typically better trained and perform more reliably than competitors' dealers. Caterpillar has also built a worldwide parts and service system second to none in the industry. Customers recognize all the value that Caterpillar creates in its offerings, allowing the firm to command a premium price in the marketplace.[1]

High-performance equipment backed by Superior sales and service functions are at the heart of Caterpillar's successful product strategy.

Marketing planning begins with formulating an offering to meet target customers' needs or wants. The customer will judge the offering by three basic elements: product features and quality, services mix and quality, and price (see Figure 12.1). In this chapter, we examine product; in Chapter 13, services; and in Chapter 14, price. All three elements must be meshed into a competitively attractive offering.

FIG. 12.1

Components of the Market Offering

::: Product Characteristics and Classifications

Many people think a product is a tangible offering, but it can be more than that. Broadly, a **product** is anything that can be offered to a market to satisfy a want or need, including physical goods, services, experiences, events, persons, places, properties, organizations, information, and ideas.

Product Levels: The Customer-Value Hierarchy

In planning its market offering, the marketer needs to address five product levels (see Figure 12.2).[2] Each level adds more customer value, and the five constitute a **customer-value hierarchy**.

- The fundamental level is the **core benefit**: the service or benefit the customer is really buying. A hotel guest is buying "rest and sleep." The purchaser of a drill is buying "holes." Marketers must see themselves as benefit providers.
- At the second level, the marketer must turn the core benefit into a **basic product**. Thus a hotel room includes a bed, bathroom, towels, desk, dresser, and closet.
- At the third level, the marketer prepares an **expected product**, a set of attributes and conditions buyers normally expect when they purchase this product. Hotel guests expect a clean bed, fresh towels, working lamps, and a relative degree of quiet.
- At the fourth level, the marketer prepares an **augmented product** that exceeds customer expectations. In developed countries, brand positioning and competition take place at this level. In developing and emerging markets such as India and Brazil, however, competition takes place mostly at the expected product level.
- At the fifth level stands the **potential product**, which encompasses all the possible augmentations and transformations the product or offering might undergo in the future. Here is where companies search for new ways to satisfy customers and distinguish their offering.

FIG. 12.2

Five Product Levels

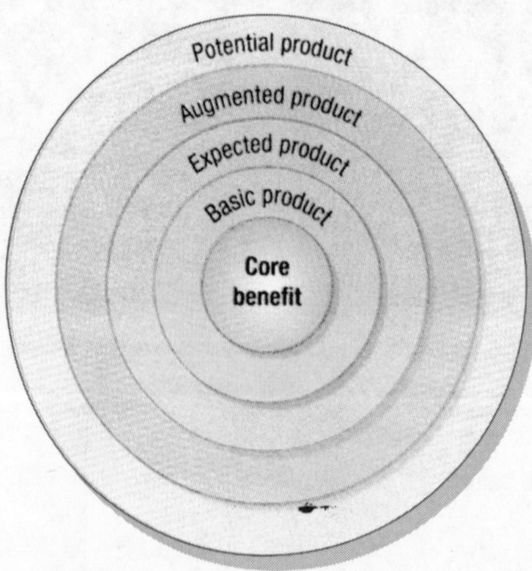

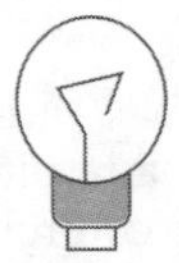

MARKETING INSIGHT | METAMARKETS AND METAMEDIARIES

There are some products whose purchase necessitates other purchases. The new-automobile market is a good example of a "metamarket." The consumer chooses an automobile but also must buy insurance from an insurance company and often must get a loan from a bank. A smart auto company or auto dealer would make all three purchases easy for the buyer by partnering with an insurance company and a bank. Such an auto dealer is performing as a "metamediary."

The wedding market is also a metamarket. The bride and groom need a bridal gown and tuxedo respectively, a chapel, a hotel for the wedding, a caterer, and possibly a wedding consultant. Here the wedding dress seller or the wedding consultant might perform as a wedding metamediary.

Metamarkets are the result of marketers observing the total consumption system and "packaging" a system that simplifies carrying out these related product/service activities. Professor Mohan Sawhney defines a metamarket as "a set of products and services that consumers need to perform a ***cognitively related*** set of activities. Other metamarkets that are organized around major assets or major life events include:

- Buying a home
- Giving birth to a child
- Getting a divorce
- Planning a vacation

Source: Adapted from Mohan Sawhney, "Rethinking Marketing and Mediation in the Networked Economy," Winning Strategies for E-Commerce Lecture at the Kellogg School of Management, April 7–10, 1999.

Differentiation arises and competition increasingly occurs on the basis of product augmentation, which also leads the marketer to look at the user's total **consumption system**: the way the user performs the tasks of getting and using products and related services.[3] Each augmentation adds cost, however, and augmented benefits soon become expected benefits and necessary points-of-parity. Today's hotel guests expect cable or satellite television with a remote control and high-speed Internet access or two phone lines. This means competitors must search for still other features and benefits.

As some companies raise the price of their augmented product, others offer a "stripped-down" version at a much lower price. Thus, alongside the growth of fine hotels such as Four Seasons and Ritz-Carlton, we see the emergence of lower-cost hotels and motels such as Motel 6 and Comfort Inn, which cater to clients who simply want the basic product.

JAMESTOWN CONTAINER COMPANY

What could be harder to differentiate than corrugated cardboard? Yet, Jamestown Container Company, the lead supplier of corrugated products for companies such as 3M, has formed strategic partnerships with area manufacturers to provide every part of the shipping system. It not only provides boxes but also offers tape, shrink-wrap, and everything else needed to display or to ship a customer's final product. "It's a combination for survival," says the company's chief operating officer. "More customers want to call one place for everything. We have to keep reinventing ourselves and form these kinds of relationships to remain competitive."[4]

Product Classifications

Marketers have traditionally classified products on the basis of durability, tangibility, and use (consumer or industrial). Each product type has an appropriate marketing-mix strategy.[5]

DURABILITY AND TANGIBILITY Marketers classify products into three groups according to durability and tangibility:

1. **Nondurable goods** are tangible goods normally consumed in one or a few uses, such as beer and soap. Because these goods are purchased frequently, the appropriate strategy is to make them available in many locations, charge only a small markup, and advertise heavily to induce trial and build preference.
2. **Durable goods** are tangible goods that normally survive many uses: refrigerators, machine tools, and clothing. Durable products normally require more personal selling

Marketers rely on well-trained salespeople to help customers compare quality and features of shopping goods such as appliances.

and service, command a higher margin, and require more seller guarantees.

3. **Services** are intangible, inseparable, variable, and perishable products. As a result, they normally require more quality control, supplier credibility, and adaptability. Examples include haircuts, legal advice, and appliance repairs.

CONSUMER-GOODS CLASSIFICATION We classify the vast array of goods consumers buy on the basis of shopping habits. We distinguish among convenience, shopping, specialty, and unsought goods.

The consumer usually purchases **convenience goods** frequently, immediately, and with a minimum of effort. Examples include soft drinks, soaps, and newspapers. Convenience goods can be further divided. *Staples* are goods consumers purchase on a regular basis. A buyer might routinely purchase Heinz ketchup, Crest toothpaste, and Ritz crackers. *Impulse goods* are purchased without any planning or search effort. Candy bars and magazines can be impulse goods. *Emergency goods* are purchased when a need is urgent—umbrellas during a rainstorm, boots and shovels during the first winter snow. Manufacturers of impulse and emergency goods will place them in those outlets where consumers are likely to experience an urge or compelling need to make a purchase.

Shopping goods are goods that the consumer characteristically compares on such bases as suitability, quality, price, and style. Examples include furniture, clothing, used cars, and major appliances. We further divide this category. *Homogeneous shopping goods* are similar in quality but different enough in price to justify shopping comparisons. *Heterogeneous shopping goods* differ in product features and services that may be more important than price. The seller of heterogeneous shopping goods carries a wide assortment to satisfy individual tastes and must have well-trained salespeople to inform and advise customers.

Specialty goods have unique characteristics or brand identification for which a sufficient number of buyers are willing to make a special purchasing effort. Examples include cars, stereo components, photographic equipment, and men's suits. A Mercedes is a specialty good because interested buyers will travel far to buy one. Specialty goods don't require comparisons; buyers invest time only to reach dealers carrying the wanted products. Dealers don't need convenient locations, although they must let prospective buyers know their locations.

Unsought goods are those the consumer does not know about or does not normally think of buying, such as smoke detectors. The classic examples of known but unsought goods are life insurance, cemetery plots, gravestones, and encyclopedias. Unsought goods require advertising and personal-selling support.

INDUSTRIAL-GOODS CLASSIFICATION Industrial goods can be classified in terms of their relative cost and how they enter the production process: materials and parts, capital items, and supplies and business services. **Materials and parts** are goods that enter the manufacturer's product completely. They fall into two classes: raw materials, and manufactured materials and parts. *Raw materials* fall into two major groups: *farm products* (wheat, cotton, livestock, fruits, and vegetables) and *natural products* (fish, lumber, crude petroleum, iron ore). Farm products are supplied by many producers, who turn them over to marketing intermediaries, who provide assembly, grading, storage, transportation, and selling services. Their perishable and seasonal nature gives rise to special marketing practices, whereas their commodity character results in relatively little advertising and promotional activity, with some exceptions. At times, commodity groups will launch campaigns to promote their product—potatoes, cheese, and beef. Some producers brand their products—Dole salads, Mott's apples, and Chiquita bananas.

Natural products are limited in supply. They usually have great bulk and low unit value and must be moved from producer to user. Fewer and larger producers often market them directly to industrial users. Because users depend on these materials, long-term supply contracts are common. The homogeneity of natural materials limits the amount of demand-creation activity. Price and delivery reliability are the major factors influencing the selection of suppliers.

Manufactured materials and parts fall into two categories: component materials (iron, yarn, cement, wires) and component parts (small motors, tires, castings). *Component materials* are usually fabricated further—pig iron is made into steel, and yarn is woven into cloth. The standardized nature of component materials usually means that price and supplier reliability are key purchase factors. *Component parts* enter the finished product with no further change in form, as when small motors are put into vacuum cleaners, and tires are put on automobiles. Most manufactured materials and parts are sold directly to industrial users. Price and service are major marketing considerations, and branding and advertising tend to be less important.

Capital items are long-lasting goods that facilitate developing or managing the finished product. They include two groups: installations and equipment. *Installations* consist of buildings (factories, offices) and heavy equipment (generators, drill presses, mainframe computers, elevators). Installations are major purchases. They are usually bought directly from the producer, whose sales force includes technical personnel, and a long negotiation period precedes the typical sale. Producers must be willing to design to specification and to supply postsale services. Advertising is much less important than personal selling.

Equipment includes portable factory equipment and tools (hand tools, lift trucks) and office equipment (personal computers, desks). These types of equipment don't become part of a finished product. They have a shorter life than installations but a longer life than operating supplies. Although some equipment manufacturers sell direct, more often they use intermediaries, because the market is geographically dispersed, the buyers are numerous, and the orders are small. Quality, features, price, and service are major considerations. The sales force tends to be more important than advertising, although advertising can be used effectively.

Supplies and business services are short-term goods and services that facilitate developing or managing the finished product. Supplies are of two kinds: *maintenance and repair items* (paint, nails, brooms) and *operating supplies* (lubricants, coal, writing paper, pencils). Together, they go under the name of MRO goods. Supplies are the equivalent of convenience goods; they are usually purchased with minimum effort on a straight-rebuy basis. They are normally marketed through intermediaries because of their low unit value and the great number and geographic dispersion of customers. Price and service are important considerations, because suppliers are standardized and brand preference is not high.

Business services include *maintenance and repair services* (window cleaning, copier repair) and *business advisory services* (legal, management consulting, advertising). Maintenance and repair services are usually supplied under contract by small producers or are available from the manufacturers of the original equipment. Business advisory services are usually purchased on the basis of the supplier's reputation and staff.

::: Differentiation

To be branded, products must be differentiated. Physical products vary in their potential for differentiation. At one extreme, we find products that allow little variation: chicken, aspirin, and steel. Yet even here, some differentiation is possible: Perdue chickens, Bayer aspirin, and India's Tata Steel have carved out distinct identities in their categories. Procter & Gamble makes Tide, Cheer, and Gain laundry detergents, each with a separate brand identity. At the other extreme are products capable of high differentiation, such as automobiles, commercial buildings, and furniture. Here the seller faces an abundance of differentiation possibilities, including form, features, customization, performance quality, conformance quality, durability, reliability, repairability, and style.[6] Design has become an increasingly important means of differentiation and we will discuss it separately.

Product Differentiation

FORM Many products can be differentiated in **form**—the size, shape, or physical structure of a product. Consider the many possible forms taken by products such as aspirin. Although aspirin is essentially a commodity, it can be differentiated by dosage size, shape, color, coating, or action time.

FEATURES Most products can be offered with varying **features** that supplement their basic function. A company can identify and select appropriate new features by surveying recent buyers and then calculating *customer value* versus *company cost* for each potential feature. The company should also consider how many people want each feature, how long it would take to introduce it, and whether competitors could easily copy it. To avoid "feature fatigue," the company also must be careful to prioritize those features that are included and find unobtrusive ways to provide information about how consumers can use and benefit from the feature.[7] Companies must also think in terms of feature bundles or packages. Auto companies often manufacture cars at several "trim levels." This lowers manufacturing and inventory costs. Each company must decide whether to offer feature customization at a higher cost or a few standard packages at a lower cost.

CUSTOMIZATION Marketers can differentiate products by making them customized to an individual. As companies have grown proficient at gathering information about individual customers and business partners (suppliers, distributors, retailers), and as their factories are being designed more flexibly, they have increased their ability to individualize market offerings, messages, and media. **Mass customization** is the ability of a company to meet each customer's requirements—to prepare on a mass basis individually designed products, services, programs, and communications.[8]

Although Levi's and Lands' End were among the first clothing manufacturers to introduce custom jeans, other players have introduced mass customization into other markets. The Architechtural Skylight Company uses an object-oriented design approach that allows it to design and manufacture custom skylights.[9] About 60% of the 40,000 Minis that BMW sells in the United States each year are customized. Two investment bankers even mounted shark fins atop the roofs of their Minis![10] Lego has embraced mass customization from the start.

LEGO

In a sense, Lego of Billund, Denmark, has always been mass customized. Every child who has ever had a set of the most basic Legos has built his or her own unique and amazing creations, brick by plastic brick. However, in 2005, Lego set up The Lego Factory, which, as it says on the company Web site, "lets you design, share, and build your very own custom Lego products." Using Lego's freely downloadable Digital Designer Software, customers can create any structure. The creations can exist—and be shared with other enthusiasts—solely online or, if customers want to build it, the software tabulates the pieces required and sends an order to Lego's Enfield, Connecticut, warehouse. The employees there put all the pieces into a box and send it off. Not only do Lego Factory customers have the pride of building their own creations, but they can also earn royalties if Lego decides the design is good enough to put in its own catalog. Some of the most creative models: a rendering of the Danish parliament building and of M.C. Escher's "Another World." And in 2006, The Lego Factory initiated a design competition in which eight contestants competed to be profiled on the Lego Factory Web site along with their creations.[11]

PERFORMANCE QUALITY Most products are established at one of four performance levels: low, average, high, or superior. **Performance quality** is the level at which the product's primary characteristics operate. Quality is becoming an increasingly important dimension for differentiation as companies adopt a value model and provide higher quality for less money. Firms, however, should not necessarily design the highest performance level possible. The manufacturer must design a performance level appropriate to the target market and competitors' performance levels. A company must also manage performance quality through time. Continuously improving the product can produce high returns and market share; failing to do so can have negative consequences.

MERCEDES-BENZ

From 2003 to 2006, Mercedes-Benz endured one of its most painful stretches in its 127-year history, as its stellar quality reputation took a beating in J.D. Power and other surveys, and BMW surpassed it in global sales. As a consequence, DaimlerChrysler Chief Executive Dieter Zetsche and his new management team initiated a major restructuring, organizing the company around functional elements of the car—motors, chassis, and electronic systems—instead of by model lines. To improve quality, the company also made a number of changes in product development. Engineers begin testing electronic systems a year earlier than in the past. Lab workers put each new model's electronic system through a battery of 10,000 tests that ran 24 hours a day for three weeks. Trying to uncover even the most unlikely event, Mercedes ferreted out more than 1,000 errors in the new S-Class. Mercedes now also uses three times as many prototypes of new designs, allowing engineers to drive a new model three million miles before it goes into production. As a result of these and other changes, the number of flaws in a car has dropped 72% from its peak in 2002 and warranty costs have decreased by 25% as well.[12]

Performance quality is such a critical part of Mercedes-Benz's product strategy that the company recently undertook a series of sweeping changes in its quality-control processes to reduce errors and flaws when its quality ratings fell.

CONFORMANCE QUALITY Buyers expect products to have a high **conformance quality**, which is the degree to which all the produced units are identical and meet the promised specifications. Suppose a Porsche 911 is designed to accelerate to 60 miles per hour within 10 seconds. If every Porsche 911 coming off the assembly line does this, the model is said to have high conformance quality. The problem with low conformance quality is that the product will disappoint some buyers.

DURABILITY **Durability**, a measure of the product's expected operating life under natural or stressful conditions, is a valued attribute for certain products. Buyers will generally pay more for vehicles and kitchen appliances that have a reputation for being long lasting. However, this rule is subject to some qualifications. The extra price must not be excessive. Furthermore, the product must not be subject to rapid technological obsolescence, as are personal computers and video cameras.

RELIABILITY Buyers normally will pay a premium for more reliable products. **Reliability** is a measure of the probability that a product will not malfunction or fail within a specified time period. Maytag, which manufactures major home appliances, has an outstanding reputation for creating reliable appliances. "Breakthrough Marketing: Toyota" describes how that company has excelled at making and selling high-quality, dependable automobiles.

REPAIRABILITY **Repairability** is a measure of the ease of fixing a product when it malfunctions or fails. Ideal repairability would exist if users could fix the product themselves with little cost in money or time. Some products include a diagnostic feature that allows service people to correct a problem over the telephone or advise the user how to correct it. Many computer hardware and software companies offer technical support over the phone, by fax or e-mail, or by real-time "chat" online.

STYLE **Style** describes the product's look and feel to the buyer. Car buyers pay a premium for Jaguars because of their extraordinary looks. Aesthetics play a key role in such brands as Absolut vodka, Apple computers, Montblanc pens, Godiva chocolate, and Harley-Davidson motorcycles.[13] Style has the advantage of creating distinctiveness that is difficult to copy. On the negative side, strong style does not always mean high performance. A car may look sensational but spend a lot of time in the repair shop.

BREAKTHROUGH MARKETING | TOYOTA

Toyota may have gotten its start in automaking by being a fast follower, but it is now the innovator. In 1936, Toyota admitted following Chrysler's landmark Airflow and patterning its engine after a 1933 Chevrolet engine. But by 2000, when it introduced the first hybrid electric-gasoline car, the Prius, Toyota was the leader. In 2002, when the second-generation Prius hit showrooms, dealers received 10,000 orders before the car was even available; GM followed with an announcement that it would enter the hybrid market with models of its own.

Toyota offers a full line of cars for the U.S. market, from family sedans to sport utility vehicles to trucks to minivans. Toyota also has products for different price points, from lower-cost Scions to mid-priced Camrys to the luxury Lexus. Designing these different products means listening to different customers, building the cars they want, and then crafting the marketing to reinforce each make's image. For example, Toyota spent four years carefully listening to teens before launching the Scion for first-time car buyers. It learned, for instance, that Scion's target age group of 16- to 21-year-olds wanted personalization. To meet that preference, Toyota builds the car "mono-spec" at the factory with just one well-equipped trim level but lets customers at dealerships choose from over 40 customization elements, from stereo components to wheels and even floor mats. Toyota markets the Scion at music events and will have showrooms where "young people feel comfortable hanging out and not a place where they just go stare at a car," said Scion vice president Jim Letz.

In contrast, Toyota's marketing strategy for the Lexus line focuses on perfection. The tagline for the global strategy is "Passionate Pursuit of Perfection." Dealerships offer white-glove treatment. Toyota markets Lexus globally and understands that each country defines perfection differently. In the United States, for example, perfection and luxury mean comfort, size, and dependability. In Europe, luxury means attention to detail and brand heritage. Therefore, although the core of Lexus marketing is similar (a consistent Lexus visual vocabulary, logo, font, and overall communication), the advertising varies by country.

A big reason behind Toyota's success is its manufacturing. Toyota's combination of manufacturing speed and flexibility is world class. It is the master of lean manufacturing and continuous improvement. Its plants can make as many as eight different models at the same time, which brings Toyota huge increases in productivity and market responsiveness. And it relentlessly innovates. A typical Toyota assembly line makes thousands of operational changes in the course of a single year. Toyota employees see their purpose as threefold: making cars, making cars better, and teaching everyone how to make cars better. The company encourages problem solving, always looking to improve the process by which it improves all other processes.

Toyota is integrating its assembly plants around the world into a single giant network. The plants will customize cars for local markets and be able to shift production quickly to satisfy any surges in demand from markets worldwide. With a manufacturing network, Toyota can build a wide variety of models much more inexpensively.

Toyota's product strategy is built on innovation and agility and has recently vaulted the firm into the number-one spot in the industry for the first time.

That means Toyota will be able to fill market niches as they emerge without building whole new assembly operations. "If there's a market or market segment where they aren't present, they go there," said Tatsuo Yoshida, auto analyst at Deutsche Securities Ltd. And with consumers being increasingly fickle about what they want in a car, such market agility gives Toyota a huge competitive edge.

In 2006, Toyota earned over $11 billion—more than all other major automakers *combined*. It now produces 50% more automobiles than it did in 2001, and 60% of the cars Toyota sells in North America are made here. In the first quarter of 2007, it edged past General Motors to become the world's largest carmaker, and its market cap of $110 billion is more than that of GM, Ford, and DaimlerChrysler combined.

Sources: Martin Zimmerman, "Toyota's First Quarter Global Sales Beat GM's Preliminary Numbers," *Los Angeles Times*, April 24, 2007; Charles Fishman, "No Satisfaction at Toyota," *Fast Company* (December 2006–January 2007): 82–90; Stuart F. Brown, "Toyota's Global Body Shop," *Fortune*, February 9, 2004, p. 120; James B. Treece, "Ford Down; Toyota Aims for No. 1," *Automotive News*, February 2, 2004, p.1; Brian Bemner and Chester Dawson, "Can Anything Stop Toyota?" *BusinessWeek*, November 17, 2003, pp. 114–22; and www.toyota.com.

Design

As competition intensifies, design offers a potent way to differentiate and position a company's products and services.[14] In increasingly fast-paced markets, price and technology are not enough. Design is the factor that will often give a company its competitive edge. **Design** is the totality of features that affect how a product looks, feels, and functions in terms of customer requirements.

Design is particularly important in making and marketing retail services, apparel, packaged goods, and durable equipment. The designer must figure out how much to invest in form, feature development, performance, conformance, durability, reliability, repairability, and style. To the company, a well-designed product is one that is easy to manufacture and distribute. To the customer, a well-designed product is one that is pleasant to look at and easy to open, install, use, repair, and dispose of. The designer must take all these factors into account.

The arguments for good design are particularly compelling for smaller consumer-products companies and start-ups that don't have big advertising dollars. A case in point is Method Products.

METHOD PRODUCTS

Named the seventh-fastest-growing company in the United States by *Inc.* magazine in 2006, Method Products is the brainchild of former high school buddies Eric Ryan and Adam Lowry. During the height of the dot-com frenzy, these two young San Francisco entrepreneurs shocked their friends by deciding to start up a cleaning and household products company. Now Ryan and Lowry are laughing, as the dot-coms went bust and their business has boomed. The company started with their realization that although household products is a huge category, taking up an entire supermarket aisle or more, it is an incredibly boring one. Ryan and Lowry designed a sleek, uncluttered dish soap container that also had a functional advantage—the bottle, shaped like a chess piece, was built to let soap flow out the bottom, so users would never have to turn it upside down. This signature product, with its pleasant fragrance, was designed by award-winning industrial designer Karim Rashid. "The cleaning product industry is very backwards, and many of the products have a 1950s language," Rashid said, "They are cluttered with graphics, too much information, and complicated ugly forms." Method's big break came with placement of its product in Target, known for partnering with well-known designers to produce stand-out products at affordable prices. Seven years later, Method has revenues of over $45 million and a phenomenal growth rate—contrast a growth rate of 68% for its liquid hand soap with 13% growth for industry leader Softsoap—all due to Method's refreshingly simple design. The challenge for Method now, however, is to differentiate beyond design to avoid copycats eroding the company's cachet. The company is riding the interest in green products and emphasizing its nontoxic, nonpolluting ingredients.[15]

Certain countries and companies are winning on design: Italian design in apparel and furniture; Scandinavian design for functionality, aesthetics, and environmental consciousness. Finland's Nokia was the first to introduce user-changeable covers for cell phones, the first to have elliptical-shaped, soft, and friendly forms, and the first with big screens, all contributing to its remarkable ascent. Braun, a German division of Gillette, has elevated design to a high art in its electric shavers, coffeemakers, hair dryers, and food processors. The company's design department enjoys equal status with engineering and manufacturing. The Danish firm Bang & Olufsen has received many kudos for the design of its stereos, TV equipment, and telephones.

Manufacturers, service providers, and retailers seek new designs to create differentiation and establish a more complete connection with consumers. Holistic marketers recognize the emotional power of design and the importance to consumers of how things look and feel. After seeing some of its brands lose share to competitors with stronger designs and aesthetics, Procter & Gamble appointed a chief design officer in 2001 and now hands out an A. G. Lafley Design award each fall. Lafley, P&G's CEO, is credited with pushing for more products to include design at the front end—not as an afterthought. These products, such as Crest Whitestrips, Olay Daily Facials, and the whole line of Swiffer Quick Clean products, have generated more trials, more repurchases, and more sales.[16]

In an increasingly visually oriented culture, translating brand meaning and positioning through design is critical. "In a crowded marketplace," writes Virginia Postrel in *The Substance of Style,* "aesthetics is often the only way to make a product stand out." Design can shift consumer perceptions to make brand experiences more rewarding. Consider the lengths Boeing went to in making its 777 airplane seem roomier and more comfortable. Raised center bins, side luggage bins, divider panels, gently arched ceilings, and raised seats make the aircraft interior seem bigger. As one design engineer noted, "If we do our jobs, people don't realize what we have done. They just say they feel more comfortable."

A bad design can also ruin a product's prospects. Sony's e-Villa Internet appliance was intended to allow consumers to have Internet access from their kitchens. But at nearly 32 pounds and 16 inches, the mammoth product was so awkward and heavy that the owner's manual recommended customers bend their legs, not their back, to pick it up. The product was withdrawn after three months.

Services Differentiation

When the physical product cannot easily be differentiated, the key to competitive success may lie in adding valued services and improving their quality. Rolls-Royce PLC has ensured its aircraft engines are in high demand by continuously monitoring the health of its 3,000 engines for 45 airlines through live satellite feeds. Under its TotalCare program, airlines pay Rolls a fee for every hour an engine is in flight, and Rolls assumes the risks and costs of downtime and repairs in return.[17]

The main service differentiators are ordering ease, delivery, installation, customer training, customer consulting, and maintenance and repair.

ORDERING EASE **Ordering ease** refers to how easy it is for the customer to place an order with the company. Baxter Healthcare has eased the ordering process by supplying hospitals with computer terminals through which they send orders directly to Baxter. Many financial service institutions offer secure online sites to help customers get information and do transactions more efficiently.

DELIVERY **Delivery** refers to how well the product or service is brought to the customer. It includes speed, accuracy, and care throughout the process. Today's customers have grown to expect delivery speed: pizza delivered in one-half hour, film developed in one hour, eyeglasses made in one hour, cars lubricated in 15 minutes. Levi Strauss, Benetton, and The Limited have adopted computerized *quick response systems* (QRS) that link the information systems of their suppliers, manufacturing plants, distribution centers, and retailing outlets. Cemex, a giant cement company based in Mexico, has transformed the cement business by promising to deliver concrete faster than pizza. Cemex equips every truck with a *global positioning system* (GPS) so that its real-time location is known and full information is available to drivers and dispatchers. Cemex is able to promise that if your load is more than 10 minutes late, you get a 20% discount.[18]

INSTALLATION **Installation** refers to the work done to make a product operational in its planned location. Buyers of heavy equipment expect good installation service. Differentiating at this point in the consumption chain is particularly important for companies with complex products. Ease of installation becomes a true selling point, especially when the target market is technology novices.

CUSTOMER TRAINING **Customer training** refers to training the customer's employees to use the vendor's equipment properly and efficiently. General Electric not only sells and installs expensive X-ray equipment in hospitals; it also gives extensive training to users of this equipment. McDonald's requires its new franchisees to attend Hamburger University in Oak Brook, Illinois, for two weeks, to learn how to manage the franchise properly.

CUSTOMER CONSULTING **Customer consulting** refers to data, information systems, and advice services that the seller offers to buyers.

HERMAN MILLER INC.

Herman Miller, a large office furniture company, has partnered with a California firm to show corporate clients how to get the full benefits from its furnishings. The firm, Future Industrial Technologies, specializes in workplace ergonomics training. Working through Herman Miller's dealership network, customers can arrange two-hour training sessions for small groups of employees. The sessions are run by some of the 1,200 physical therapists, occupational therapists, registered nurses, and chiropractors who work under contract to Future Industrial

Technologies. Although customer ergonomics training results in only modest revenue gains for Herman Miller, the company feels that teaching healthy work habits creates higher levels of satisfaction for customers and sets Herman Miller products apart.[19]

Herman Miller Inc.'s product strategy consists of more than designing and producing innovative office furniture. The company also helps train office workers in ergonomics, or the science of equipment design, to improve efficiency, comfort, and safety.

MAINTENANCE AND REPAIR **Maintenance and repair** describes the service program for helping customers keep purchased products in good working order. Hewlett-Packard offers online technical support, or "e-support," for its customers. In the event of a service problem, customers can use various online tools to find a solution. Those aware of the specific problem can search an online database for fixes; those unaware can use diagnostic software that finds the problem and searches the online database for an automatic fix. Customers can also seek online help from a technician.[20]

BEST BUY

As consolidation and competitive pricing among electronics retailers continues, companies are increasingly looking for new ways to stand out in the crowd. That's why Best Buy contracted with the Geek Squad, a small residential computer services company in its home market of Minnesota's Twin Cities, to revamp the chain's in-store computer repair services. Best Buy used to send PCs to regional repair facilities, a process that was time consuming and ultimately contributed to a high degree of consumer dissatisfaction. Now about half of all repairs are made in Best Buy stores. But the real differentiator is the Geek Squad's ability to make house calls (at a higher fee). Geek Squad house calls are called a "Beetle Roll" because of the squad's signature fleet of hip VW Beetles. Geek Squad employees even dress differently for house calls—they wear a distinctive "geek" look as opposed to the traditional Best Buy blue they wear at the in-store service centers.[21]

RETURNS Although product returns are undoubtedly a nuisance to customers, manufacturers, retailers, and distributors alike, they are also an unavoidable reality of doing business, especially with online purchases. Although the average return rate for online sales is roughly 5%, return and exchange policies are estimated to serve as a deterrent for one-third to one-half of online buyers. The cost of processing a return can be two to three times that of an outbound shipment, totaling an average of $30–$35 for items bought on the Internet.

COSTCO WHOLESALE CORP.

Costco's ultragenerous return policy was perhaps the cushiest in the retail electronics business. Until recently, a customer could buy an expensive plasma TV, use it indefinitely, and take it back any time. Then he or she could use the refund to buy a newer model—often at a cheaper price. However, what was the customer's gain was Costco's loss. The membership warehouse chain ended up losing "tens of millions of dollars" annually with this policy. In early 2007, Costco cut its return policy for electronics to (a still generous) 90 days in California with a subsequent rollout nationwide. Some customers, who had come to rely on the trust and generosity embodied in Costco's return policy, vowed to shop for electronics elsewhere. Yet, most realized the good times had to come to a halt. To Costco's credit, it is now offering more technical support for installing and operating the electronics it sells; the company had discovered that most returns were due not to problems with the items so much as customers' inability to set up today's very complicated electronic devices. And with the exception of electronics and computers—which now must be returned within 6 months—all other Costco items can still be returned for any reason at any time.[22]

We can think of product returns in two ways:[23]

- *Controllable returns* result from problems, difficulties, or errors of the seller or customer and can mostly be eliminated with proper strategies and programs by the company or its supply chain partners. Improved handling or storage, better packaging, and improved transportation and forward logistics can eliminate problems before they happen.
- *Uncontrollable returns* can't be eliminated by the company in the short-run through any of these means.

One basic returns strategy that companies can adopt is to attempt to eliminate the root causes of controllable returns while at the same time developing processes for handling uncontrollable product returns. The goal of a product return strategy is to have fewer products returned and a higher percentage of returns that can go back into the distribution pipeline to be sold again. San Diego–based Road Runner Sports sells running shoes, clothing, and equipment through multiple channels. The firm trains its salespeople to be as knowledgeable as possible when it comes to recommending the right products. As a result, its return rate on running shoes is 12%, noticeably below the industry average of 15%–20%. Road Runner also uses SmartLabels, which are prepaid, preaddressed, bar-coded return labels, to make returns quick and easy for those customers who do need to make a return.

::: Product and Brand Relationships

Each product can be related to other products to ensure that a firm is offering and marketing the optimal set of products.

The Product Hierarchy

The product hierarchy stretches from basic needs to particular items that satisfy those needs. We can identify six levels of the product hierarchy, using life insurance as an example:

1. ***Need family***—The core need that underlies the existence of a product family. Example: security.
2. ***Product family***—All the product classes that can satisfy a core need with reasonable effectiveness. Example: savings and income.
3. ***Product class***—A group of products within the product family recognized as having a certain functional coherence. Also known as a product category. Example: financial instruments.
4. ***Product line***—A group of products within a product class that are closely related because they perform a similar function, are sold to the same customer groups, are marketed through the same outlets or channels, or fall within given price ranges. A product line may consist of different brands, or a single family brand, or individual brand that has been line extended. Example: life insurance.
5. ***Product type***—A group of items within a product line that share one of several possible forms of the product. Example: term life insurance.
6. ***Item*** (also called ***stockkeeping unit*** or ***product variant***)—A distinct unit within a brand or product line distinguishable by size, price, appearance, or some other attribute. Example: Prudential renewable term life insurance.

To read about French carmaker Renault and its strategy for pursuing international growth, visit www.pearsoned.co.uk/marketingmanagementeurope.

Product Systems and Mixes

A **product system** is a group of diverse but related items that function in a compatible manner. For example, the PalmOne handheld and smartphone product lines come with attachable products including headsets, cameras, keyboards, presentation projectors, e-books, MP3 players, and voice recorders. A **product mix** (also called a **product assortment**) is the set of all products and items a particular seller offers for sale.

A product mix consists of various product lines. Seagate now makes 29 kinds of drives that are essential to servers, PCs, and consumer electronic products such as video games, DVRs, and cameras. In General Electric's Consumer Appliance Division, there are product-line managers for refrigerators, stoves, and washing machines. NEC's (Japan) product mix consists of communication products and computer products. Michelin has three product lines: tires, maps, and restaurant-rating services. At Northwestern University, there are separate academic deans for the medical school, law school, business school, engineering school, music school, speech school, journalism school, and liberal arts school.

TABLE 12.1 | Product-Mix Width and Product-Line Length for Procter & Gamble Products (including Dates of Introduction)

	Product-Mix Width				
	Detergents	**Toothpaste**	**Bar Soap**	**Disposable Diapers**	**Paper Products**
PRODUCT LINE LENGTH	Ivory Snow (1930) Dreft (1933) Tide (1946) Cheer (1950) Dash (1954) Bold (1965) Gain (1966) Era (1972)	Gleem (1952) Crest (1955)	Ivory (1879) Camay (1926) Zest (1952) Safeguard (1963) Oil of Olay (1993)	Pampers (1961) Luvs (1976)	Charmin (1928) Puffs (1960) Bounty (1965)

A company's product mix has a certain width, length, depth, and consistency. These concepts are illustrated in Table 12.1 for selected Procter & Gamble consumer products.

- The *width* of a product mix refers to how many different product lines the company carries. Table 12.1 shows a product-mix width of five lines. (In fact, P&G produces many additional lines.)
- The *length* of a product mix refers to the total number of items in the mix. In Table 12.1, it is 20. We can also talk about the average length of a line. We obtain this by dividing the total length (here 20) by the number of lines (here 5), for an average product-line length of 4.
- The *depth* of a product mix refers to how many variants are offered of each product in the line. If Tide comes in two scents (Mountain Spring and Regular), two formulations (liquid and powder), and two additives (with or without bleach), Tide has a depth of eight because there are eight distinct variants. We can calculate the average depth of P&G's product mix by averaging the number of variants within the brand groups.
- The *consistency* of the product mix refers to how closely related the various product lines are in end use, production requirements, distribution channels, or some other way. P&G's product lines are consistent insofar as they are consumer goods that go through the same distribution channels. The lines are less consistent insofar as they perform different functions for the buyers.

These four product-mix dimensions permit the company to expand its business in four ways. It can add new product lines, thus widening its product mix. It can lengthen each product line. It can add more product variants to each product and deepen its product mix. Finally, a company can pursue more product-line consistency. To make these product and brand decisions, it is useful to conduct product-line analysis.

Product-Line Analysis

In offering a product line, companies normally develop a basic platform and modules that can be added to meet different customer requirements. Car manufacturers build their cars around a basic platform. Homebuilders show a model home to which buyers can add additional features. This modular approach enables the company to offer variety and to lower production costs.

Product-line managers need to know the sales and profits of each item in their line in order to determine which items to build, maintain, harvest, or divest.[24] They also need to understand each product line's market profile.

SALES AND PROFITS Figure 12.3 shows a sales and profit report for a five-item product line. The first item accounts for 50% of total sales and 30% of total profits. The first two items account for 80% of total sales and 60% of total profits. If these two items were suddenly hurt by

FIG. 12.3

Product-Item Contributions to a Product Line's Total Sales and Profits

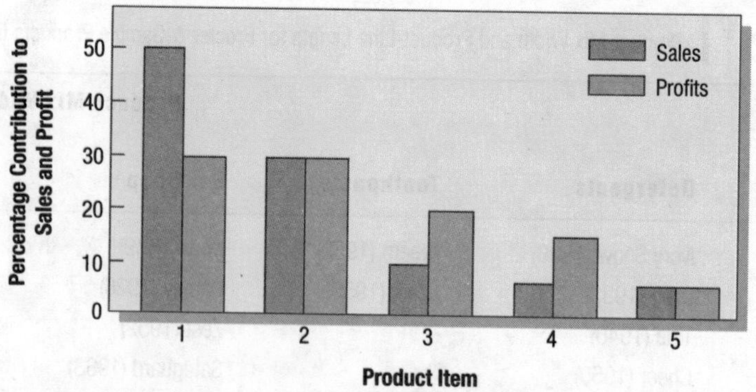

a competitor, the line's sales and profitability could collapse. These items must be carefully monitored and protected. At the other end, the last item delivers only 5% of the product line's sales and profits. The product-line manager may consider dropping this item unless it has strong growth potential.

Every company's product portfolio contains products with different margins. Supermarkets make almost no margin on bread and milk; reasonable margins on canned and frozen foods; and even better margins on flowers, ethnic food lines, and freshly baked goods. A local telephone company makes different margins on its core telephone service, call waiting, caller ID, and voice mail.

A company can classify its products into four types that yield different gross margins, depending on sales volume and promotion. To illustrate with laptop computers:

- ***Core products.*** Basic laptop computers that produce high sales volume and are heavily promoted but with low margins because they are viewed as undifferentiated commodities.
- ***Staples.*** Items with lower sales volume and no promotion, such as faster CPUs or bigger memories. These yield a somewhat higher margin.
- ***Specialties.*** Items with lower sales volume but that might be highly promoted, such as digital moviemaking equipment; or might generate income for services, such as personal delivery, installation, or on-site training.
- ***Convenience items.*** Peripheral items that sell in high volume but receive less promotion, such as carrying cases and accessories, upscale video or sound cards, and software. Consumers tend to buy them where they buy the original equipment because it is more convenient than making further shopping trips. These items can carry higher margins.

The main point is that companies should recognize that these items differ in their potential for being priced higher or advertised more as ways to increase their sales, their margins, or both.[25]

MARKET PROFILE The product-line manager must review how the line is positioned against competitors' lines. Consider paper company X with a paperboard product line.[26] Two paperboard attributes are weight and finish quality. Paper is usually offered at standard levels of 90, 120, 150, and 180 weight. Finish quality is offered at low, medium, and high levels. Figure 12.4 shows the location of the various product-line items of company X and four competitors, A, B, C, and D. Competitor A sells two product items in the extra-high weight class ranging from medium to low finish quality. Competitor B sells four items that vary in weight and finish quality. Competitor C sells three items in which the greater the weight, the greater the finish quality. Competitor D sells three items, all lightweight but varying in finish quality. Company X offers three items that vary in weight and finish quality.

The **product map** shows which competitors' items are competing against company X's items. For example, company X's low-weight, medium-quality paper competes against competitor D's and B's papers, but its high-weight, medium-quality paper has no direct competitor. The map also reveals possible locations for new items. No manufacturer offers a high-weight, low-quality paper. If company X estimates a strong unmet demand and can produce and price this paper at low cost, it could consider adding this item to its line.

Another benefit of product mapping is that it identifies market segments. Figure 12.4 shows the types of paper, by weight and quality, preferred by the general printing industry,

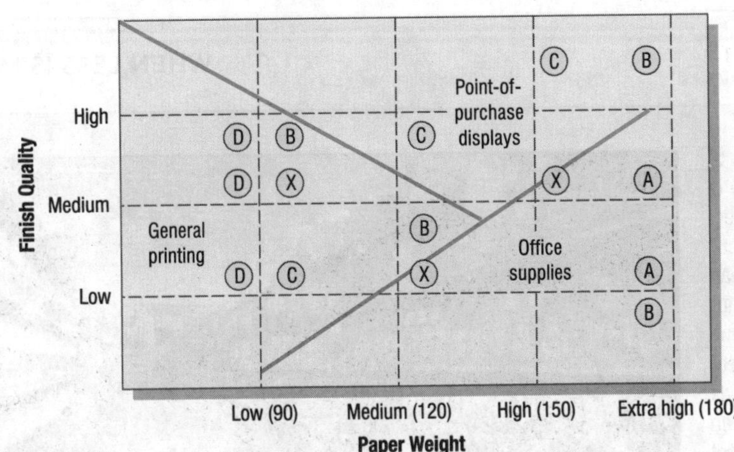

FIG. 12.4

Product Map for a Paper-Product Line

Source: Benson P. Shapiro, *Industrial Product Policy: Managing the Existing Product Line* (Cambridge, MA: Marketing Science Institute Report No.77–110). Copyright © 2003. Reprinted by permission of Marketing Science Institute and Benson P. Shapiro.

the point-of-purchase display industry, and the office supply industry. The map shows that company X is well positioned to serve the needs of the general printing industry but is less effective in serving the other two industries.

Product-line analysis provides information for two key decision areas—product-line length and product-mix pricing.

Product-Line Length

Company objectives influence product-line length. One objective is to create a product line to induce upselling: Thus General Motors would like to move customers up from the Chevrolet to the Buick to the Cadillac. A different objective is to create a product line that facilitates cross-selling: Hewlett-Packard sells printers as well as computers. Still another objective is to create a product line that protects against economic ups and downs; Electrolux offers white goods such as refrigerators, dishwashers, and vacuum cleaners under different brand names in the discount, middle-market, and premium segments, in part in case the economy moves up or down.[27] Companies seeking high market share and market growth will generally carry longer product lines. Companies that emphasize high profitability will carry shorter lines consisting of carefully chosen items.

Product lines tend to lengthen over time. Excess manufacturing capacity puts pressure on the product-line manager to develop new items. The sales force and distributors also pressure the company for a more complete product line to satisfy customers. But as items are added, costs rise: design and engineering costs, inventory-carrying costs, manufacturing-changeover costs, order-processing costs, transportation costs, and new-item promotional costs. Eventually, someone calls a halt: Top management may stop development because of insufficient funds or manufacturing capacity. The controller may call for a study of money-losing items. A pattern of product-line growth followed by massive pruning may repeat itself many times. Increasingly, consumers are growing weary of dense product lines, over-extended brands, and feature-laden products (see "Marketing Insight: When Less Is More").

A company lengthens its product line in two ways: line stretching and line filling.

LINE STRETCHING Every company's product line covers a certain part of the total possible range. For example, Mercedes automobiles are located in the upper price range of the automobile market. **Line stretching** occurs when a company lengthens its product line beyond its current range. The company can stretch its line down-market, up-market, or both ways.

Down-Market Stretch A company positioned in the middle market may want to introduce a lower-priced line for any of three reasons:

1. The company may notice strong growth opportunities as mass retailers such as Wal-Mart, Best Buy, and others attract a growing number of shoppers who want value-priced goods.
2. The company may wish to tie up lower-end competitors who might otherwise try to move up-market. If the company has been attacked by a low-end competitor, it often decides to counterattack by entering the low end of the market.
3. The company may find that the middle market is stagnating or declining.

MARKETING INSIGHT | WHEN LESS IS MORE

Although many consumers find the notion of having more choices appealing, the reality is that consumers can sometimes be overwhelmed by the choices involved. With thousands of new products introduced each year, consumers find it harder and harder to successfully navigate through store aisles. One study found that the average shopper spent 40 seconds or more in the supermarket soda aisle, compared to 25 seconds six or seven years ago. Another research study showed that although consumers expressed greater interest in shopping with a larger assortment of 24 different flavored jams than a smaller assortment of 6, they were 10 times more likely to actually make a selection with the smaller assortment.

Marketers are learning through sometimes painful experience that product lines can get too long, or products can become just too complicated.

Although consumers with well-defined preferences may benefit from more differentiated products that offer specific benefits to better suit their needs, too much product choice may be a source of frustration, confusion, and regret for other consumers. Product proliferation has another downside. Exposing the customer to constant product changes and introductions may nudge them into reconsidering their choices, resulting in their switching to a competitor's product as a result.

And not all the new choices may be winners anyway, as Nestlé found out with its KitKat bars, among the best-selling candy bars in the United Kingdom since they were invented there in the 1930s. To increase sales in 2004, the company rolled out a vast array of new flavors. The summer saw the launch of strawberries and cream, passion fruit and mango, and red berry versions; with winter came Christmas pudding, tiramisu (with real wine and marscapone), and low-carb versions. The new flavors were a disaster—the tastes were too sweet and unusual for many—and even worse, some consumers couldn't find the classic KitKat bars among all the new varieties. An ill-timed switch from the classic slogan, "Have a Break, Have a KitKat," didn't help, and sales dropped 18% as a result. The new flavors were then discontinued.

Smart marketers are also realizing that it's not just the product lines that are making consumer heads spin—many products themselves are just too complicated for the average consumer. Royal Philips Electronics learned its lesson when the company asked 100 top managers to take various Philips electronic products home one weekend and see whether they could make them work. The number of executives who returned frustrated and angry spoke volumes about the challenges the ordinary consumer faced. A Yankee Group research study in 2004 reinforces this fact: Almost a third of all home-networking products sold that year were returned because the consumer couldn't get them to work; almost half of potential digital camera buyers were delaying their purchase because they thought the products were too complicated; and about a quarter of consumers thought they already owned an HDTV (they didn't). Philips launched an initiative in September 2004 with a goal to make technology simpler, backed by a $100 million ad campaign "Sense and Simplicity."

Sources: Deborah Ball, "Flavor Experiment for KitKat Leaves Nestlé with a Bad Taste," *Wall Street Journal*, July 6, 2006; Barry Schwartz, *The Paradox of Choice: Why More Is Less* (New York: Harper Collins Ecco, 2004); Frisco Endt, "It Is Rocket Science," *Newsweek*, October 18, 2004, p. E8; Alexander Chernev, "When More Is Less and Less Is More: The Role of Ideal Point Availability and Assortment in Choice," *Journal of Consumer Research* 30 (September 2003): 170–83; Sheena S. Iyengar and Mark R. Lepper, "When Choice Is Demotivating: Can One Desire Too Much of a Good Thing?" *Journal of Personality and Social Psychology* 79, no. 6 (December 2000): 995–1006; Ravi Dhar, "Consumer Preference for a No-Choice Option," *Journal of Consumer Research* 27 (September 1997): 233–48.

A company faces a number of naming choices in deciding to move a brand down-market:

1. Use the parent brand name on all its offerings. Sony has used its name on products in a variety of price tiers.
2. Introduce lower-priced offerings using a subbrand name, such as P&G's Charmin Basics, Gillette Good News, and Ramada Limited.
3. Introduce the lower-priced offerings under a different name, such as The Gap's Old Navy brand. This strategy is expensive to implement, and consumers may not accept a new brand that lacks the equity of the parent brand name.

Moving down-market carries risks. Kodak introduced Kodak Funtime film to counter lower-priced brands, but it did not price it low enough to match the lower-priced film. It also found some of its regular customers buying Funtime, so it was cannibalizing its core brand. Kodak withdrew the product and may have also lost some of its quality image in the process. On the other hand, Mercedes successfully introduced its C-Class cars at $30,000 without injuring its ability to sell other Mercedes cars for $100,000. John Deere introduced a lower-priced line of lawn tractors called Sabre from John Deere while still selling its more expensive tractors under the John Deere name. In these cases, consumers may have been better able to compartmentalize the different brand offerings and understand and rationalize functional differences between offerings in higher and lower price tiers.

Up-Market Stretch Companies may wish to enter the high end of the market to achieve more growth, to realize higher margins, or simply to position themselves as full-line manufacturers. Many markets have spawned surprising upscale segments: Starbucks in coffee, Häagen-Dazs in ice cream, and Evian in bottled water. The leading Japanese auto companies have each introduced an upscale automobile: Toyota's Lexus; Nissan's Infiniti; and Honda's Acura. Note that they invented entirely new names rather than using or including their own names, because consumers may not have given the brand "permission" to stretch upward at the time when those different lines were first introduced.

Other companies have included their own name in moving up-market. Gallo introduced Gallo of Sonoma (priced at $10 to $30 a bottle) to compete in the premium wine segment, using the founder's grandchildren as spokespeople in an intensive push-and-pull campaign. With a hip, young, and fun image, the line was a critical and commercial success and was rebranded as Gallo Family Vineyards in 2006. General Electric introduced the GE Profile brand for its large appliance offerings in the upscale market.[28] Some brands have used modifiers to signal a noticeable, although presumably not dramatic, quality improvement, such as Ultra Dry Pampers, Extra Strength Tylenol, or PowerPro Dustbuster Plus.

Two-Way Stretch Companies serving the middle market might decide to stretch their line in both directions. Robert Mondavi Winery sells its $35 bottles of wines as the first premium "New World wine," but it also sells its $85 bottles of Mondavi Reserve at high-end wineries, restaurants, and vineyards and through direct order, as well as its $11 bottles of Woodbridge created during the grape oversupply of the mid-1990s. Consider how Purina Dog Food has stretched up and down to create a product line differentiated by benefits to dogs, breadth of varieties, ingredients, and price:

- Pro Plan ($22.49/20 lb bag)—helps dogs live long and healthy lives with high-quality ingredients (real meat, fish, and poultry)
- Purina ONE ($17.99/20 lb bag)—meets dog's changing and unique nutritional needs and provides superpremium nutrition for good health
- Purina Dog Chow ($11.49/22 lb bag)—provides dogs complete nutrition to build, replenish, and repair at each life stage
- Alpo by Purina ($8.99/17.6 lb bag)—offers beef, liver, and cheese flavor combinations and three meaty varieties

HOLIDAY INN

Holiday Inn Worldwide also has performed a two-way stretch of its hotel product line. The hotel chain broke its domestic hotels into five separate chains to tap into five different benefit segments—the upscale Crowne Plaza, the traditional Holiday Inn, the budget Holiday Inn Express, and the business-oriented Holiday Inn Select and Holiday Inn Suites & Rooms. Different branded chains received different marketing programs and emphasis. Holiday Inn Express has been advertised with the humorous "Stay Smart" advertising campaign showing the brilliant feats that ordinary people could attempt after staying at the chain. By basing the development of these brands on distinct consumer targets with unique needs, Holiday Inn is able to ensure against overlap between brands.

The relative position of a brand and its competitor context will also affect consumer acceptance. Research has shown that a high-end model of a low-end brand is favored over a low-end model of a high-end brand, even when information about competing categories is made available.[29]

LINE FILLING A firm can also lengthen its product line by adding more items within the present range. There are several motives for *line filling:* reaching for incremental profits, trying to satisfy dealers who complain about lost sales because of missing items in the line, trying to utilize excess capacity, trying to be the leading full-line company, and trying to plug holes to keep out competitors.

BMW AG

In four years BMW has morphed from a one-brand, 5-model carmaker into a three-brand, 10-model powerhouse. Not only has the carmaker expanded its product range downward with Mini Coopers and its compact 1-series models, but it has also built it upward with Rolls-Royce and filled the gaps in between with its X3 and X5 sports activity vehicles, the Z3 and Z4 roadsters, and a 6-series coupe. The company has used line filling successfully to boost its appeal to the rich, the super-rich, and the wannabe-rich, all without departing from its pure premium positioning.[30]

Line filling is overdone if it results in self-cannibalization and customer confusion. The company needs to differentiate each item in the consumer's mind with a *just-noticeable difference.* According to Weber's law, customers are more attuned to relative than to absolute difference.[31] They will perceive the difference between boards 2 and 3 feet long and boards 20 and 30 feet long, but not between boards 29 and 30 feet long. The company should also check that the proposed item meets a market need and is not being added simply to satisfy an internal need. The infamous Edsel automobile, on which Ford lost $350 million in the late 1950s, met Ford's internal positioning needs for a car between its Ford and Lincoln lines, but not the market's needs.

LINE MODERNIZATION, FEATURING, AND PRUNING Product lines need to be modernized. The issue is whether to overhaul the line piecemeal or all at once. A piecemeal approach allows the company to see how customers and dealers take to the new style. It is also less draining on the company's cash flow, but it allows competitors to see changes and to start redesigning their own lines.

In rapidly changing product markets, modernization is continuous. Companies plan improvements to encourage customer migration to higher-valued, higher-priced items. Microprocessor companies such as Intel and AMD, and software companies such as Microsoft and Oracle, continually introduce more-advanced versions of their products. A major issue is timing improvements so they do not appear too early (damaging sales of the current line) or too late (after the competition has established a strong reputation for more-advanced equipment).

The product-line manager typically selects one or a few items in the line to feature. Sears will announce a special low-priced washing machine to attract customers. At other times, managers will feature a high-end item to lend prestige to the product line. Sometimes a company finds one end of its line selling well and the other end selling poorly. The company may try to boost demand for the slower sellers, especially if they are produced in a factory that is idled by lack of demand; but it could be counterargued that the company should promote items that sell well rather than try to prop up weak items. Nike's Air Force 1 basketball shoe, introduced in the 1980s, is a billion-dollar brand that is still a consumer and retailer favorite and moneymaker for the company due to collectable designs and tight supplies.[32]

Product-line managers must periodically review the line for deadwood that is depressing profits.[33] The weak items can be identified through sales and cost analysis. One study found that for a big Dutch retailer, a major assortment reduction led to a short-term drop in category sales, caused mainly by fewer category purchases by former buyers, but it also attracted new category buyers at the same time. These new buyers partially offset the sales losses among former buyers of the delisted items.[34]

In 1999, Unilever announced its "Path to Growth" program designed to get the most value from its brand portfolio by eliminating three-quarters of its 1,600 distinct brands by 2003.[35] More than 90% of its profits came from just 400 brands, prompting Unilever cochairman Niall FitzGerald to liken the brand reduction to weeding a garden, so "the light and air get in to the blooms which are likely to grow the best." The company retained global brands such as Lipton, as well as regional brands and "local jewels" such as Persil, the leading detergent in the United Kingdom.

Multibrand companies all over the world are attempting to optimize their brand portfolios. In many cases, this has led to a greater focus on core brand growth and to concentrating energy and resources on the biggest and most established brands. Hasbro has designated a set of core toy brands, including GI Joe, Transformers, and My Little Pony, to emphasize in its marketing. Procter & Gamble's "back to basics strategy" concentrated on its brands with over $1 billion in revenue, such as Tide, Crest, Pampers, and Pringles. Every product in a product line must play a role, as must any brand in the brand portfolio.

Pruning slow-selling brands from product lines often benefits the brands that are left, such as Unilever's global bestsellers including Lipton worldwide or Persil in the United Kingdom.

VW

VW has four different brands to manage in its European portfolio. Initially, Audi and Seat had a sporty image and VW and Skoda had a family-car image. Audi and VW were in a higher price-quality tier than their respective counterparts. Skoda and Seat with their basic spartan interiors and utilitarian engine performance were clearly differentiated. With the goal of reducing costs, streamlining part/systems designs, and eliminating redundancies, Volkswagen upgraded the Seat and Skoda brands. Once viewed as subpar products by European consumers, Skoda and Seat have captured market share with splashy interiors, a full array of safety systems, and reliable powertrains borrowed from Volkswagen. The danger, of course, is that by borrowing from its upper-echelon Audi and Volkswagen products, Volkswagen may have diluted their cachet. Frugal European automotive consumers may convince themselves that a Seat or Skoda is almost identical to its VW sister, at several thousand Euros less.[36]

Product-Mix Pricing

Chapter 14 describes pricing concepts in detail, but let's quickly consider some basic product-mix pricing issues here. Marketers must modify their price-setting logic when the product is part of a product mix. In **product-mix pricing,** the firm searches for a set of prices that maximizes profits on the total mix. Pricing is difficult because the various products have demand and cost interrelationships and are subject to different degrees of competition. We can distinguish six situations calling for product-mix pricing: product-line pricing, optional-feature pricing, captive-product pricing, two-part pricing, by-product pricing, and product-bundling pricing.

PRODUCT-LINE PRICING Companies normally develop product lines rather than single products and introduce price steps. In many lines of trade, sellers use well-established price points for the products in their line. A men's clothing store might carry men's suits at three price levels: $200, $400, and $600. Customers will associate low-, average-, and high-quality suits with the three price points. The seller's task is to establish perceived quality differences that justify the price differences.

OPTIONAL-FEATURE PRICING Many companies offer optional products, features, and services along with their main product. The automobile buyer can order power window controls, remote adjustable mirrors, a sunroof, and theft protection. Pricing is a sticky problem, because companies must decide which items to include in the standard price and which to offer as options. For many years, U.S. auto companies advertised economy models to pull people into showrooms, but the cars were stripped of so many features that most buyers left the showroom spending thousands more.

Restaurants face a similar pricing problem. Many price their liquor high and their food low. The food revenue covers costs, and the liquor produces the profit. This explains why servers often press hard to get customers to order drinks. Other restaurants price their liquor low and food high to draw in a drinking crowd.

CAPTIVE-PRODUCT PRICING Some products require the use of ancillary products, or **captive products.** Manufacturers of razors, digital phones, and cameras often price them low and set high markups on razor blades and film. AT&T may give a cellular phone free if the person commits to buying two years of phone service.

HEWLETT-PACKARD

In 1996, Hewlett-Packard (HP) began drastically cutting prices on its printers, by as much as 60% in some cases. HP could afford to make such dramatic cuts because customers typically spend twice as much on replacement ink cartridges, toner, and specialty paper as on the actual printer over the life of the product. As the price of printers dropped, printer sales rose, as did the number of aftermarket sales. HP now owns about 40% of the worldwide printer business. Its inkjet supplies carry 35% profit margins and generated $2.2 billion in operating profits in 2002—over 70% of the company's total.[37]

There is a danger in pricing the captive product too high in the aftermarket, however. If parts and service are too expensive, counterfeiting and substitutions can erode sales. Consumers now can buy cartridge refills for their printers from discount suppliers and save 20% to 30% over what it would cost them to buy directly from the manufacturers.

TWO-PART PRICING Service firms engage in **two-part pricing**, consisting of a fixed fee plus a variable usage fee. Telephone users pay a minimum monthly fee plus charges for calls beyond a certain area. Amusement parks charge an admission fee plus fees for rides over a certain minimum. The service firm faces a problem similar to captive-product pricing—namely, how much to charge for the basic service and how much for the variable usage. The fixed fee should be low enough to induce purchase of the service; the profit can then come from the usage fees.

BY-PRODUCT PRICING The production of certain goods—meats, petroleum products, and other chemicals—often results in by-products. If the by-products have value to a customer group, they should be priced on their value. Any income earned on the by-products will make it easier for the company to charge a lower price on its main product if competition forces it to do so. Formed in 1855, Australia's CSR was originally named Colonial Sugar Refinery and its early reputation was forged as a sugar company. The company began to sell by-products of its sugar cane: waste sugar cane fiber was used to manufacture wallboard. Today, through product development and acquisition, the renamed CSR had become one of the top 10 companies in Australia selling building and construction materials.

PRODUCT-BUNDLING PRICING Sellers often bundle products and features. **Pure bundling** occurs when a firm offers its products only as a bundle. Michael Ovitz's former company, Artists Management Group, would sign up a "hot" actor if the film company would also accept other talents that Ovitz represented (directors, writers, scripts). This is a form of *tied-in sales.* In **mixed bundling**, the seller offers goods both individually and in bundles. When offering a mixed bundle, the seller normally charges less for the bundle than if the items were purchased separately. An auto manufacturer might offer an option package at less than the cost of buying all the options separately. A theater will price a season subscription at less than the cost of buying all the performances separately. Customers may not have planned to buy all the components, so the savings on the price bundle must be substantial enough to induce them to buy it.[38]

Some customers will want less than the whole bundle. Suppose a medical-equipment supplier's offer includes free delivery and training. A particular customer might ask to forgo the free delivery and training in exchange for a lower price. The customer is asking the seller to "unbundle" or "rebundle" its offer. If a supplier saves $100 by not supplying delivery and reduces the customer's price by $80, the supplier has kept the customer happy while increasing its profit by $20.

Studies have shown that as promotional activity increases on individual items in the bundle, buyers perceive less savings on the bundle and are less apt to pay for it. This research suggests the following guidelines for correctly implementing a bundling strategy:[39]

- Don't promote individual products in a package as frequently and cheaply as the bundle. The bundle price should be much lower than the sum of individual products or the consumer will not perceive its attractiveness.
- Limit promotions to a single item in the mix if you still want to promote individual products. Another option: alternate promotions, one after another, in order to avoid running conflicting promotions.
- If you decide to offer large rebates on individual products, make them the absolute exception and do it with discretion. Otherwise, the consumer uses the price of individual products as an external reference for the bundle, which then loses value.

Co-Branding and Ingredient Branding

CO-BRANDING Marketers often combine their products with products from other companies in various ways. In **co-branding**—also called dual branding or brand bundling—two or more well-known brands are combined into a joint product or marketed together in some fashion.[40] One form of co-branding is *same-company co-branding,* as when General Mills advertises Trix and Yoplait yogurt. Still another form is *joint-venture co-branding,* such as General Electric and Hitachi lightbulbs in Japan, and the Citibank AAdvantage credit card. There is *multiple-sponsor co-branding,* such as Taligent, a one-time technological alliance of Apple, IBM, and Motorola.[41] Finally, there is *retail co-branding* where two retail establishments use the same location as a way to optimize both space and profits, such as jointly owned Pizza Hut, KFC, and Taco Bell fast-food restaurants.

The main advantage of co-branding is that a product may be convincingly positioned by virtue of the multiple brands. Co-branding can generate greater sales from the existing target market as well as opening additional opportunities for new consumers and channels. It can also reduce the cost of product introduction, because it combines two well-known images and speeds adoption. And co-branding may be a valuable means to learn about consumers and how other companies approach them. Companies within the automotive industry have reaped all these benefits of co-branding.

The potential disadvantages of co-branding are the risks and lack of control in becoming aligned with another brand in the minds of consumers. Consumer expectations about the level of involvement and commitment with co-brands are likely to be high, so unsatisfactory performance could have negative repercussions for both brands. If the other brand has entered into a number of co-branding arrangements, overexposure may dilute the transfer of any association. It may also result in a lack of focus on existing brands.

For co-branding to succeed, the two brands must separately have brand equity—adequate brand awareness and a sufficiently positive brand image. The most important requirement is a logical fit between the two brands, such that the combined brand or marketing activity maximizes the advantages of each while minimizing their disadvantages. Research studies show that consumers are more apt to perceive co-brands favorably if the two brands are complementary rather than similar.[42]

Besides remembering these strategic considerations, managers must enter into co-branding ventures carefully. There must be the right kind of fit in values, capabilities, and goals, in addition to an appropriate balance of brand equity. There must be detailed plans to legalize contracts, make financial arrangements, and coordinate marketing programs. As one executive at Nabisco put it, "Giving away your brand is a lot like giving away your child—you want to make sure everything is perfect." The financial arrangement between brands may vary, although one common approach is for the brand more deeply involved in the production process to pay a licensing fee and royalty.

Brand alliances require a number of decisions.[43] What capabilities do you not have? What resource constraints are you faced with (people, time, money, etc.)? What are your growth goals or revenue needs? In assessing a joint branding opportunity, ask whether it's a profitable business venture. How does it help maintain or strengthen brand equity? Is there any risk of dilution of brand equity? Does the opportunity offer any extrinsic advantages such as learning opportunities?

INGREDIENT BRANDING **Ingredient branding** is a special case of co-branding. It creates brand equity for materials, components, or parts that are necessarily contained within other branded products. Some successful ingredient brands include Dolby noise reduction,

Gore-Tex water-resistant fibers, and Scotchgard fabrics. Some popular ingredient-branded products are Lunchables lunch combinations with Taco Bell tacos and Lay's potato chips made with KC Masterpiece barbecue sauce. Ingredient branding is taking off in an area known as "nutraceuticals," food products that have health-increasing properties. For example, there's Dannon's Activia yogurt that advertises its trademarked probiotic Bacilus Regularis, promoting healthy digestion, or Heinz Ketchup's bottles touting the inclusion of Lycopene, a "powerful antioxidant that gives tomatoes their red color."

CARGILL

Cargill, a Minneapolis-based major agribusiness manufacturer, is having success with branding its CoroWise nutraceutical. CoroWise is made of cholesterol reducing "plant sterols"—soybean byproducts that cooking-oil producers once discarded. It has made its appearance on cartons of Minute Maid's "heartwise" orange juice and has recently become a featured additive in bread. Mexican-owned Bimbo now sells Oroweat Whole Grain Wheat & Oat with CoroWise in 21 states west of the Mississippi. On the package Bimbo cites research findings that eating three slices a day will lower a typical person's LDL (bad) cholesterol by 12% in three weeks. Cargill must now fight off rival Archer Daniel Midlands, which has created its own naturally derived plant sterols, marketed as CardioAid, for the baking industry. With the proliferation of health-related claims, however, will come increased pressure to make sure the promises on the packaging are true.[44]

An interesting take on ingredient branding is "self-branding" in which companies advertise and even trademark their own branded ingredients. For instance, Westin Hotels advertises its "Heavenly Bed" and "Heavenly Shower." The Heavenly Bed has been so successful that Westin now sells the bed, pillows, sheets, and blankets via an online catalog, along with other "Heavenly" gifts and bath items. If it can be done well, it makes much more sense for companies to use self-brand ingredients because they have more control and can develop the ingredient to suit their purposes.[45]

An extreme example of self-branding is Westin Hotels' successful marketing of its popular "Heavenly Bed" and related bedding, gift, and bath items.

Ingredient brands try to create enough awareness and preference for their product so consumers will not buy a "host" product that doesn't contain the ingredient. DuPont has achieved success in marketing its products as ingredient brands.

DUPONT

Over the years, DuPont has introduced a number of innovative products, such as Corian® solid-surface material, for use in markets ranging from apparel to aerospace. Many of DuPont's products, such as Lycra® and Stainmaster® fabrics, Teflon® coating, and Kevlar® fiber, became household names as ingredient brands in consumer products manufactured by other companies. Several recent ingredient brands include Supro® isolated soy proteins used in food products and RiboPrinter® genetic fingerprinting technology.[46]

Many manufacturers make components or materials that enter into final branded products but lose their individual identity. One of the few component branders that have succeeded in building a separate identity is Intel. Intel's consumer-directed brand campaign convinced many personal computer buyers to buy only computer brands with "Intel Inside." As a result, major PC manufacturers—IBM, Dell, Compaq—purchase their chips from Intel at a premium price rather than buy equivalent chips from an unknown supplier. Most component manufacturers, however, would find it difficult to create a successful ingredient brand. "Marketing Memo: Making Ingredient Branding Work" outlines the characteristics of successful ingredient branding.

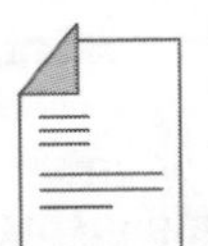

MARKETING MEMO | MAKING INGREDIENT BRANDING WORK

What are the requirements for success in ingredient branding?

1. Consumers must perceive that the ingredient matters to the performance and success of the end product. Ideally, this intrinsic value is easily seen or experienced.
2. Consumers must be convinced that not all ingredient brands are the same and that the ingredient is superior.
3. A distinctive symbol or logo must clearly signal to consumers that the host product contains the ingredient. Ideally, the symbol or logo would function like a "seal" and would be simple and versatile and credibly communicate quality and confidence.
4. A coordinated "pull" and "push" program must help consumers understand the importance and advantages of the branded ingredient. Channel members must offer full support. Often this will require consumer advertising and promotions and—sometimes in collaboration with manufacturers—retail merchandising and promotion programs.

Sources: Kevin Lane Keller, *Strategic Brand Management,* 3rd ed. (Upper Saddle River, NJ: Prentice Hall, 2008); Philip Kotler and Waldemar Pfoertsch, *B2B Brand Management* (New York: Springer, 2006); Paul F. Nunes, Stephen F. Dull, and Patrick D. Lynch, "When Two Brands Are Better Than One," *Outlook* (January 2003): 14–23.

::: Packaging, Labeling, Warranties, and Guarantees

Most physical products must be packaged and labeled. Some packages—such as the Coke bottle and the L'eggs container—are world famous. Many marketers have called packaging a fifth P, along with price, product, place, and promotion. Most marketers, however, treat packaging and labeling as an element of product strategy. Warranties and guarantees can also be an important part of the product strategy, which often appear on the package.

Packaging

We define **packaging** as all the activities of designing and producing the container for a product. Packages might include up to three levels of material. Cool Water cologne comes in a bottle (*primary package*) in a cardboard box (*secondary package*) in a corrugated box (*shipping package*) containing six dozen boxes.

Well-designed packages can build brand equity and drive sales. The package is the buyer's first encounter with the product and is capable of turning the buyer on or off. Packaging also affects consumers' later product experiences. Various factors have contributed to the growing use of packaging as a marketing tool:

- ***Self-service.*** An increasing number of products are sold on a self-service basis. In an average supermarket, which stocks 15,000 items, the typical shopper passes by some 300 items per minute. Given that 50% to 70% of all purchases are made in the store, the effective package must perform many of the sales tasks: attract attention, describe the product's features, create consumer confidence, and make a favorable overall impression.
- ***Consumer affluence.*** Rising consumer affluence means consumers are willing to pay a little more for the convenience, appearance, dependability, and prestige of better packages.
- ***Company and brand image.*** Packages contribute to instant recognition of the company or brand. In the store, packages for a brand can create a visible billboard effect, such as Garnier Fructis and their bright green packaging in the hair care aisle.
- ***Innovation opportunity.*** Innovative packaging can bring large benefits to consumers and profits to producers. Companies are incorporating unique materials and features such as resealable spouts and openings. Heinz's unique, colorful EZ Squirt ketchup and upside-down bottle have helped to revitalize the brand's sales.[47]

From the perspective of both the firm and consumers, packaging must achieve a number of objectives:[48]

1. Identify the brand.
2. Convey descriptive and persuasive information.
3. Facilitate product transportation and protection.

Kimberly Clark has dressed up its Kleenex products in any number of vivid new package designs including boxes with seasonal themes.

4. Assist at-home storage.
5. Aid product consumption.

To achieve the marketing objectives for the brand and satisfy the desires of consumers, marketers must choose the aesthetic and functional components of packaging correctly. Aesthetic considerations relate to a package's size and shape, material, color, text, and graphics. Blue is cool and serene, red is active and lively, yellow is medicinal and weak, pastel colors are feminine, and dark colors are masculine. Functionally, structural design is crucial. For example, innovations with food products over the years have resulted in packages that are resealable, tamperproof, and more convenient to use (easy to hold, easy to open, or squeezable). The packaging elements must harmonize with each other and with pricing, advertising, and other parts of the marketing program.

Packaging changes can have immediate impact on sales. A good example is the book publishing industry, where customers often quite literally choose a book by its cover: The number-one classics publisher, Penguin Books Ltd., repackaged most of its titles and spent $500,000 to promote them under the banner, "Classic Books, Fresh Looks." Sales increased 400% for Dorothy Parker's *Complete Stories,* 50% for a new translation of *Don Quixote,* and 43% for *Pride and Prejudice.*[49] Packaging changes can come in all forms. Kleenex tissues' seasonally themed oval-shaped boxes, Domino sugar's easy-to-store plastic canister, and Crest toothpaste's beauty-product-inspired Vivid White packaging all led to sales increases.[50]

After the company designs its packaging, it must test it. *Engineering tests* ensure that the package stands up under normal conditions; *visual tests,* that the script is legible and the colors harmonious; *dealer tests,* that dealers find the packages attractive and easy to handle; and *consumer tests,* that buyers will respond favorably. Eye tracking by hidden cameras can assess how much consumers notice and examine packages. For Comtrex cold medicine, tracking research was able to confirm that only 50% of consumers considered the old package on the shelf, versus 62% for a newly redesigned package.[51]

Although developing effective packaging may cost several hundred thousand dollars and take several months to complete, companies must pay attention to growing environmental and safety concerns to reduce packaging. Fortunately, many companies have gone "green" and are finding new ways to develop their packaging.

Labeling

The label may be a simple tag attached to the product or an elaborately designed graphic that is part of the package. It might carry only the brand name, or a great deal of information. Even if the seller prefers a simple label, the law may require more.

Labels perform several functions. First, the label *identifies* the product or brand—for instance, the name Sunkist stamped on oranges. The label might also *grade* the product; canned peaches are grade-labeled A, B, and C. The label might *describe* the product: who made it, where it was made, when it was made, what it contains, how it is to be used, and how to use it safely. Finally, the label might *promote* the product through attractive graphics. New technology allows for 360-degree shrink-wrapped labels to surround containers with bright graphics and accommodate more on-pack product information, replacing paper labels glued onto cans and bottles.[52]

Labels eventually become outmoded and need freshening up. The label on Ivory soap has been redone at least 18 times since the 1890s, with gradual changes in the size and design of the letters. Companies with labels that have become icons need to tread very carefully when initiating a redesign:

CAMPBELL SOUP COMPANY

The Campbell Soup Company has estimated that the average shopper sees its familiar red-and-white can 76 times a year, creating the equivalent of millions of dollars worth of advertising. Its label is such an icon that pop artist Andy Warhol immortalized it in one of his silk screens in the 1960s. The original Campbell's Soup label—with its scripted name and signature red and white—was designed in 1898, and the company did not redesign it until more than a century later, in 1999. With the goal of making the label more contemporary and making it easier for customers to find individual soups, Campbell made the famous script logo smaller and featured a photo of a steaming bowl of the soup flavor inside. In addition to the new graphic, the company put nutritional information on the packaging, with serving suggestions, quick dinner ideas, and colored bands that identify the six subgroups of condensed soup, that is, creams, broths, and so on.[53]

There is a long history of legal concerns surrounding labels, as well as packaging. In 1914, the Federal Trade Commission Act held that false, misleading, or deceptive labels or packages constitute unfair competition. The Fair Packaging and Labeling Act, passed by Congress in 1967, set mandatory labeling requirements, encouraged voluntary industry packaging standards, and allowed federal agencies to set packaging regulations in specific industries.

The Food and Drug Administration (FDA) has required processed-food producers to include nutritional labeling that clearly states the amounts of protein, fat, carbohydrates, and calories contained in products, as well as their vitamin and mineral content as a percentage of the recommended daily allowance.[54] The FDA has also taken action against the potentially misleading use of such descriptions as "light," "high fiber," and "low fat."

Warranties and Guarantees

All sellers are legally responsible for fulfilling a buyer's normal or reasonable expectations. **Warranties** are formal statements of expected product performance by the manufacturer. Products under warranty can be returned to the manufacturer or designated repair center for repair, replacement, or refund. Whether expressed or implied, warranties are legally enforceable.

MITSUBISHI MOTORS NORTH AMERICA

To counter consumer perceptions that Mitsubishi lags behind competitors when it comes to quality, the company began offering a 10-year, 100,000-mile powertrain warranty. This warranty, which came into effect in 2004, replaced its 7-year, 60,000-mile warranty. Mitsubishi hopes the new, longer-term warranty will signal to consumers that the company has confidence in the quality and reliability of its vehicles.[55]

Sometimes a warranty can be an incredibly smart marketing strategy.

SHOES FOR CREWS

Shoes for Crews makes work shoes that are absolutely guaranteed not to slip. No one had ever given much thought to the rather stalwart shoes before the company issued a warranty that most people would consider insane: a $5,000 warranty for a $50–$75 product. Yet, this was the smartest move the company ever made. A decade after CEO Matthew Smith instituted the warranty, 9 of the 10 largest restaurant chains in the country either buy the Shoes for Crews brand for their workers or urge them to do so. It works like this: If a restaurant or shop employee does happen to slip on the job while wearing a Shoes for Crews product, it can easily set an employer back $5,000 in worker's comp claims—$5,000 the employer gets back from Shoes for Crews. This kind of warranty is dubbed "risk reversal marketing." The idea behind it is to think about what your customers' biggest fear is when it comes to doing business with you, and then take on some of the risk yourself. Fortunately for Matthew Smith, Shoes for Crews shoes mainly live up to their guarantee. However, when Smith has honored the warranty—ranging from payouts of a few hundred dollars for an ambulance ride to the whole $5K for major surgery, the surprise and gratitude in his customers' voices makes the payout well worth it for him.[56]

Extended warranties can be extremely lucrative for manufacturers and retailers. Analysts estimated that warranty sales accounted for more than a third of Best Buy's and all of Circuit City's operating profits in 2005, prompting retail competitor Wal-Mart to offer lower-cost warranties on electronics to better compete.[57]

Many sellers offer either general guarantees or specific guarantees.[58] A company such as Procter & Gamble promises general or complete satisfaction without being more specific—"If you are not satisfied for any reason, return for replacement, exchange, or refund." Other companies offer specific and in some cases extraordinary guarantees:

- A. T. Cross guarantees its Cross pens and pencils for life. The customer mails the pen to A. T. Cross (mailing envelopes are provided at stores selling Cross writing instruments), and the pen is repaired or replaced at no charge.
- Oakley Millwork, a Chicago supplier of construction-industry products, offers customers "no sweat solutions" with a "no back-order guarantee," promising that if any of the 44,000 items in its catalog is unavailable for immediate delivery, the customer gets the item free.
- "Bugs" Burger Bugs Killers (BBBK), a pest extermination company serving the hospitality industry, offers the following guarantee: (1) no payment until all pests are eradicated; (2) if the effort fails, the customer receives a full refund to pay the next exterminator; (3) if guests on the client's premises spot a pest, BBBK will pay for the guest's room and send an apology letter; and (4) if the client's facility is closed down, BBBK will pay all fines, lost profits, and $5,000.

Guarantees reduce the buyer's perceived risk. They suggest that the product is of high quality and that the company and its service performance are dependable. They can be especially helpful when the company or product is not that well known or when the product's quality is superior to competitors.

SUMMARY :::

1. Product is the first and most important element of the marketing mix. Product strategy calls for making coordinated decisions on product mixes, product lines, brands, and packaging and labeling.
2. In planning its market offering, the marketer needs to think through the five levels of the product: the core benefit, the basic product, the expected product, the augmented product, and the potential product, which encompasses all the augmentations and transformations the product might ultimately undergo.
3. Products can be classified in several ways. In terms of durability and reliability, products can be nondurable goods, durable goods, or services. In the consumer-goods category, products are convenience goods (staples, impulse goods, emergency goods), shopping goods (homogeneous and heterogeneous), specialty goods, or unsought goods. In the industrial-goods category, products fall into one of three categories: materials and parts (raw materials and manufactured materials and parts), capital items (installations and equipment), or supplies and business services (operating supplies, maintenance and repair items, maintenance and repair services, and business advisory services).
4. Brands can be differentiated on the basis of a number of different product or service dimensions: product form, features, performance, conformance, durability, reliability, repairability, style, and design, as well as such service dimensions as ordering ease, delivery, installation, customer training, customer consulting, and maintenance and repair.
5. Most companies sell more than one product. A product mix can be classified according to width, length, depth, and consistency. These four dimensions are the tools for developing the company's marketing strategy and deciding which product lines to grow, maintain, harvest, and divest. To analyze a product line and decide how many resources should be invested in that line, product-line managers need to look at sales and profits and market profile.
6. A company can change the product component of its marketing mix by lengthening its product via line stretching (down-market, up-market, or both) or line filling, by modernizing its products, by featuring certain products, and by pruning its products to eliminate the least profitable.
7. Brands are often sold or marketed jointly with other brands. Ingredient brands and co-brands can add value, assuming they have equity and are perceived as fitting appropriately.
8. Physical products must be packaged and labeled. Well-designed packages can create convenience value for customers and promotional value for producers. In effect, they can act as "five-second commercials" for the product. Warranties and guarantees can offer further assurance to consumers.

APPLICATIONS :::

Marketing Debate With Products, Is It Form or Function?

The "form versus function" debate applies in many arenas, including marketing. Some marketers believe that product performance is the end all and be all. Other marketers maintain that the looks, feel, and other design elements of products are what really make the difference.

Take a position: Product functionality is the key to brand success *versus* Product design is the key to brand success.

Marketing Discussion

Consider the different means of differentiating products and services. Which ones have the most impact on your choices? Why? Can you think of certain brands that excel on a number of these different means of differentiation?

IN THIS CHAPTER, WE WILL ADDRESS THE FOLLOWING QUESTIONS:

1. How do we define and classify services, and how do they differ from goods?
2. How do we market services?
3. How can we improve service quality?
4. How do services marketers create strong brands?
5. How can goods marketers improve customer-support services?

CHAPTER 13 ::: DESIGNING AND MANAGING SERVICES

thirteen

As product companies find it harder and harder to differentiate their physical products, they turn to service differentiation. Many in fact find significant profitability in delivering superior service,[1] whether that means on-time delivery, better and faster answering of inquiries, or quicker resolution of complaints. Service providers know these advantages well. The Mayo Clinic has set new standards in the health care industry by considering all aspects of the patient experience.

The Mayo Clinic is the first and largest integrated not-for-profit medical group practice in the world. It has built one of the most powerful services brands on its firmly held brand beliefs and its relentless focus on the patient experience. Two interrelated core values that trace back to the clinic's founders, William and Charles Mayo, over a century ago are at the heart of all the organization does: placing the patient's interests above all others, and practicing teamwork. Every aspect of the patient experience is considered. From public exam rooms to laboratories, Mayo facilities have been designed so that, in the words of the architect of one of the buildings, "patients feel a little better before they see their doctors." The 20-story Gonda Building in Rochester, Minnesota, has spectacular wide-open spaces, and the lobby of the Mayo Clinic hospital in Scottsdale, Arizona, has an indoor waterfall and a wall of windows overlooking mountains. In pediatric exam >>>

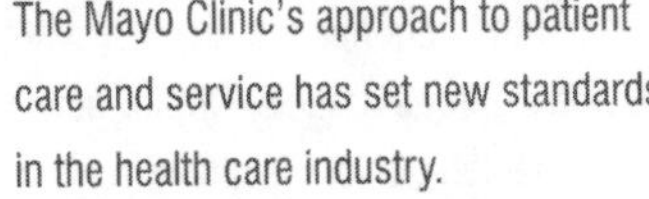

The Mayo Clinic's approach to patient care and service has set new standards in the health care industry.

rooms, resuscitation equipment is hidden behind a large cheery picture. Hospital rooms feature microwave ovens and chairs that really do convert to beds because, as one staff member explained, "People don't come to the hospital alone."[2]

Because it is critical to understand the special nature of services and what that means to marketers, in this chapter we systematically analyze services and how to market them most effectively.

::: The Nature of Services

The Bureau of Labor Statistics reports that the service-producing sector will continue to be the dominant employment generator in the economy, adding about 20 million jobs by 2014. Employment in the service-producing sector is expected to increase by 17% over the 2004–2014 period, whereas manufacturing employment is expected to decrease by 5%. In fact, manufacturing's share of total jobs is expected to decline from around 10% in 2004 to 8% in 2010.[3] These numbers and others have led to a growing interest in the special problems of marketing services.[4]

Service Industries Are Everywhere

The *government sector,* with its courts, employment services, hospitals, loan agencies, military services, police and fire departments, postal service, regulatory agencies, and schools, is in the service business. The *private nonprofit sector,* with its museums, charities, churches, colleges, foundations, and hospitals, is in the service business. A good part of the *business sector,* with its airlines, banks, hotels, insurance companies, law firms, management consulting firms, medical practices, motion picture companies, plumbing repair companies, and real estate firms, is in the service business. Many workers in the *manufacturing sector,* such as computer operators, accountants, and legal staff, are really service providers. In fact, they make up a "service factory" providing services to the "goods factory." And those in the *retail sector,* such as cashiers, clerks, salespeople, and customer-service representatives, are also providing a service.

We define a service as follows: A **service** is any act or performance one party can offer to another that is essentially intangible and does not result in the ownership of anything. Its production may or may not be tied to a physical product. Increasingly, however, manufacturers, distributors, and retailers are providing value-added services, or simply excellent customer service, to differentiate themselves.

LUXURY AUTOMOBILES

To operate effectively in the lucrative but highly competitive luxury automobile market, Lexus, Cadillac, and Porsche all are committed to making sure their customers have another car at their disposal if theirs happens to be in the shop. When Lexus had to recall the RX330 in 2006, it gave its inconvenienced customers a free iPod Nano. When customers balked about the price and value of early scheduled maintenance, Lexus implemented a new system that cut the average appointment time in half. For Cadillac, General Motors has put an early warning system for mechanical problems into its OnStar telematics system, standard in all models. OnStar service helps customers with related tasks including emergency services dispatch, stolen vehicle location, roadside assistance, remote diagnostics, and route support. Although the first year of OnStar is free to GM car owners, it now claims renewal rates as high as 80% at annual subscription fees ranging from $200 to more than $600.[5]

Many services though, include no physical products, and many pure service firms are now using the Internet to reach customers. State Farm insurance received a Webby award, which honors Internet sites for excellence, for its "Now What?" information Web site.[6] Some service firms are even purely online. Monster.com has a Webby award-winning Web site to support its online career advice and employment recruiting efforts. Done right, improvements in customer service can have a big payoff. Figure 13.1 summarizes some high-impact customer-service projects.

Categories of Service Mix

The service component can be a minor or a major part of the total offering. We distinguish five categories of offerings:

1. ***Pure tangible good***—The offering consists primarily of a tangible good such as soap, toothpaste, or salt. No services accompany the product.
2. ***Tangible good with accompanying services***—The offering consists of a tangible good accompanied by one or more services. Typically, the more technologically advanced the product, the greater the need for a broad range of high-quality supporting services. Services are often crucial for cars, computers, and cell phones.
3. ***Hybrid***—The offering consists of equal parts goods and services. For example, people patronize restaurants for both the food and its preparation.
4. ***Major service with accompanying minor goods and services***—The offering consists of a major service along with additional services or supporting goods. For example, though the trip includes a few tangibles such as snacks and drinks, what airline passengers buy

FIG. 13.1 | High-Impact Online Customer-Service Projects

	Project	Payoff
Zipcar	Zap busy signals by linking the car-sharing service's phone reservation system to its Web site and client databases. Customers are automatically recognized when they call and their requests are routed efficiently.	Cut in half the number of calls that needed operator assistance and improved service, contributing $3.5 million to 2005's estimated $15 million in sales.
Continental Airlines	Analyze data on the fly to improve customer care. One online system alerts the company when planes arrive late and assesses passengers' needs—delaying departures of other flights or sending carts to make connections easier.	After ranking last in the industry for customer satisfaction in the 1990s, Continental climbed into the top tier—ahead of American, United, and US Air.
Museum of Modern Art	As part of its $425 million rebuilding project, the museum's management pumped up the use of technology to cater better to visitors.	New services include podcast audio tours, on-demand printing of tickets, and a 35-foot flat-panel display featuring art and informational updates on shows and lectures.
Cremation Society of New Hampshire	Buck conventional wisdom by providing information for people researching cremations and letting them order the service online.	Cremations ordered online are expected to account for about 20% of the company's projected $1.8 million in revenues in 2005, up from 11% in 2004.
Enel Telegestore	Install meters for the customers of one of Italy's major electricity utilities and remotely monitor them.	Reaped nearly $600 million annually in savings and benefits by recommending shifts in usage from peak to nonpeak hours and slashing field service costs.
BT Group	Entirely revamp its self-service Web portal used by customers to manage telecom accounts. Link it to the system used by the company's customer-support staff to improve consistency.	Customer-support transactions done via the Web tripled from 2003 to 2006, and half of all new orders for broadband service are made online. Saved tens of millions annually in costs, and boosted customer satisfaction 40%.
Whirlpool	Sign up for Rearden Commerce, an online hub that provides employees at 10 companies with a one-stop shop for services from 130,000 suppliers, including booking travel, shipping packages, and restaurant reservations.	During the first phase of the rollout of the shipping service over a two month period, employees saved 10% and cut the time spent arranging for shipping by 52%.

Source: Catherine Yang, *BusinessWeek*, November 21, 2005, pp. 84–85.

is transportation. This service requires a capital-intensive good—an airplane—for its realization, but the primary item is a service.

5. ***Pure service***—The offering consists primarily of a service. Examples include babysitting, psychotherapy, and massage.

The range of service offerings makes it difficult to generalize without a few further distinctions.

- Services vary as to whether they are *equipment based* (automated car washes, vending machines) or *people based* (window washing, accounting services). People-based services vary by whether unskilled, skilled, or professional workers provide them.
- Service companies can choose among different *processes* to deliver their service. Restaurants have developed cafeteria-style, fast-food, buffet, and candlelight service formats.
- Some services need the *client's presence.* Brain surgery requires the client's presence, a car repair does not. If the client must be present, the service provider must be considerate of his or her needs. Thus beauty salon operators will invest in décor, play background music, and engage in light conversation with the client.
- Services may meet a *personal need* (personal services) or a *business need* (business services). Service providers typically develop different marketing programs for personal and business markets.
- Service providers differ in their *objectives* (profit or nonprofit) and *ownership* (private or public). These two characteristics, when crossed, produce four quite different types of organizations. The marketing programs of a private investor hospital will differ from those of a private charity hospital or a Veterans' Administration hospital.[7]

Customers cannot judge the technical quality of some services even after they have received them. Figure 13.2 shows various products and services according to difficulty of evaluation.[8] At the left are goods high in *search qualities*—that is, characteristics the buyer can evaluate before purchase. In the middle are goods and services high in *experience qualities*—characteristics the buyer can evaluate after purchase. At the right are goods and services high in *credence qualities*—characteristics the buyer normally finds hard to evaluate even after consumption.[9]

Because services are generally high in experience and credence qualities, there is more risk in purchase. This factor has several consequences. First, service consumers generally rely on word of mouth rather than advertising. Second, they rely heavily on price, personnel, and physical cues to judge quality. Third, they are highly loyal to service providers who satisfy them. Fourth, because switching costs are high, consumer inertia can make it challenging to entice a customer away from a competitor.

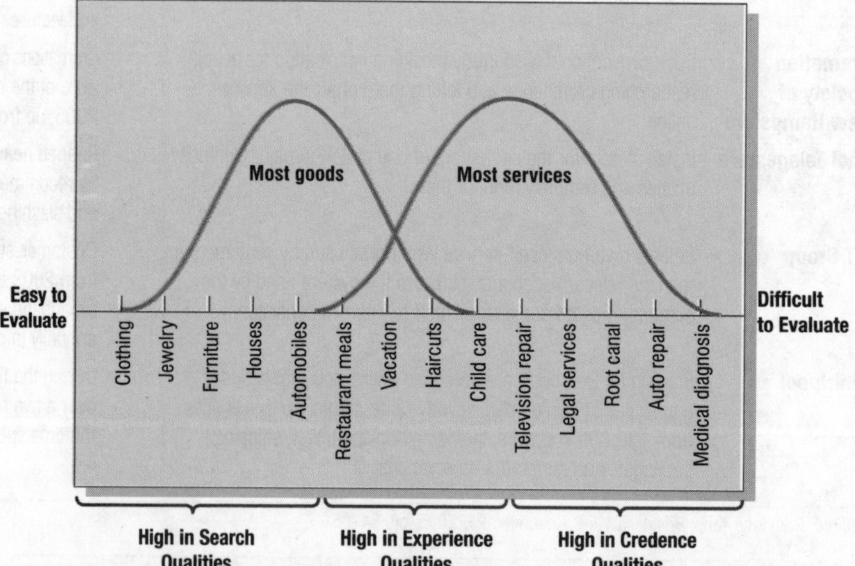

FIG. 13.2

Continuum of Evaluation for Different Types of Products

Source: Valarie A. Zeithaml, "How Consumer Evaluation Processes Differ between Goods and Services," in *Marketing of Services,* ed. James H. Donnelly and William R. George (Chicago: American Marketing Association, 1981). Reprinted with permission of the American Marketing Association.

Distinctive Characteristics of Services

Services have four distinctive characteristics that greatly affect the design of marketing programs: *intangibility, inseparability, variability,* and *perishability*.[10]

INTANGIBILITY Unlike physical products, services cannot be seen, tasted, felt, heard, or smelled before they are bought. A person getting cosmetic surgery cannot see the results before the purchase, and the patient in the psychiatrist's office cannot know the exact outcome of treatment. To reduce uncertainty, buyers will look for evidence of quality by drawing inferences from the place, people, equipment, communication material, symbols, and price. Therefore, the service provider's task is to "manage the evidence," to "tangibilize the intangible."[11]

Service companies can try to demonstrate their service quality through *physical evidence* and *presentation*.[12] A hotel will develop a look and a style of dealing with customers that realizes its intended customer-value proposition, whether it's cleanliness, speed, or some other benefit. Suppose a bank wants to position itself as the "fast" bank. It could make this positioning strategy tangible through any number of marketing tools:

1. ***Place***—The exterior and interior should have clean lines. The layout of the desks and the traffic flow should be planned carefully. Waiting lines should not get overly long.
2. ***People***—Personnel should be busy, but there should be a sufficient number of employees to manage the workload.
3. ***Equipment***—Computers, copying machines, and desks should be and look like "state of the art."
4. ***Communication material***—Printed materials—text and photos—should suggest efficiency and speed.
5. ***Symbols***—The name and symbol could suggest fast service.
6. ***Price***—The bank could advertise that it will deposit $5 in the account of any customer who waits in line for more than five minutes.

Service marketers must be able to transform intangible services into concrete benefits and a well-defined experience.[13] The Disney Company is a master at "tangibilizing the intangible" and creating magical fantasies in its theme parks; so are companies such as Jamba Juice and Barnes & Noble in their respective retail stores.[14] Washington Mutual has been highly successful in part through its careful branch designs and in-store policies.

WASHINGTON MUTUAL

Walk into most banks, and you'll notice that human contact is kept to a minimum. The scenario at a branch of Washington Mutual, known affectionately as "WaMu" (wa-moo) by its employees and loyal customers, is a sharp contrast. There are no teller windows. No ropes. If you need to open a checking account (with free checking), you step right up to the concierge station and a friendly person directs you to the right "nook." If your children are with you and get restless, you can send them to the WaMu Kids® corner to play. The bank's format, known as its Occasio™ style, which is Latin for "favorable opportunity," is carefully designed to promote a pleasing experience and facilitate cross-selling of products. To ensure that all frontline employees at the branches—tellers, financial advisors, and loan officers—are effective brand ambassadors, the company holds brand rallies around the country, with up to 3,000 employees at a time. Designed to reinforce the importance of executing the company's brand values of fairness, caring, and "being human" in all customer encounters, the 60–90-minute road show features speeches, trivia games, and vignettes led by professional actors and senior managers, many times including the "Chief Brand Ambassador" himself, CEO Kerry Killinger. To sustain the buzz that gets created, the

Washington Mutual has mastered the use of intangibles to make its brand seem friendlier to banking customers, and more "human."

company embeds these brand lessons in everything from recruitment processes and introduction programs to rewards and training programs. This fanatical focus on satisfying customers and living the brand has paid off. The formerly unknown Seattle thrift bank became a $346 billion major player in under a decade.[15]

INSEPARABILITY Whereas physical goods are manufactured, put into inventory, distributed through multiple resellers, and consumed later, services are typically produced and consumed simultaneously. A barber can't give a haircut without being present. If a person renders the service, then the provider is part of the service. Because the client is also often present as the service is produced, provider–client interaction is a special feature of services marketing.

In the case of entertainment and professional services, buyers are very interested in the specific provider. It's not the same concert if Mariah Carey is indisposed and replaced by Shania Twain, or if a corporate legal defense will be supplied by an intern because antitrust expert David Boies is unavailable. When clients have strong provider preferences, the provider can raise its price to ration its limited time.

Several strategies exist for getting around the limitations of inseparability. The service provider can learn to work with larger groups. Psychotherapists have moved from one-on-one therapy to small-group therapy to groups of over 300 people in a large hotel ballroom. The service provider can learn to work faster—the psychotherapist can spend 30 more-efficient minutes with each patient instead of 50 less-structured minutes and can see more patients. The service organization can train more service providers and build up client confidence, as H&R Block has tried to do with its national network of trained tax consultants. Creative artists have also developed techniques to overcome the limits of inseparability.

Entertainment, like that provided by the high-concept Blue Man Group, exhibits the quality of inseparability. As they expanded from 3 to 60 performers, the Blue Men created an intensive training program to ensure that the experience they provide their audiences would be consistent from cast to cast around the world.

BLUE MAN GROUP

Blue Man Group got its start in 1988 when the three original members—Matt Goldman, Phil Stanton, and Chris Wink—began performing on the streets of New York City. The company eventually moved into a theater, and the three performed every show for three straight years without the help of understudies. Wearing black clothing, bald caps and blue grease paint, the trio developed multimedia shows that captivated audiences. When the group opened a second show in Boston, the founders decided to add more Blue Men to help carry the weight. Today 60 different performers, including one woman, run the shows in cities around the world and enable the Blue Man Group to take on various projects, such as recording albums and DVDs, launching a Creativity Center for children of all ages, and designing instruments. Three full-time casting directors screen up to 3,000 people a year in search of the dozen or so who will qualify for the troupe's two-month training program.[16]

VARIABILITY Because the quality of services depends on who provides them, when and where, and to whom, services are highly variable. Some doctors have an excellent bedside manner; others are less empathic.

Service buyers are aware of this variability and often talk to others before selecting a service provider. To reassure customers, some firms offer *service guarantees* that may reduce consumer perceptions of risk.[17] Here are three steps service firms can take to increase quality control.

1. ***Invest in good hiring and training procedures***—Recruiting the right employees and providing them with excellent training is crucial, regardless of whether employees are highly skilled professionals or low-skilled workers. Better-trained personnel exhibit six characteristics: *Competence:* They possess the required skill and knowledge; *courtesy:* They are friendly, respectful, and considerate; *credibility:* They are trustworthy; *reliability:* They perform the service consistently and accurately; *responsiveness:* They respond quickly to customers' requests and problems; and *communication:* They make an effort to understand the customer and communicate clearly.[18] Given the diverse nature of its customer base in California, banking and mortgage giant Wells Fargo actively seeks and

trains a diverse work force. The average Wells Fargo customer uses 5.2 different bank products, roughly twice the industry average, thanks in part to the teamwork of its highly motivated staff.[19]

2. ***Standardize the service-performance process throughout the organization***—A *service blueprint* can simultaneously map out the service process, the points of customer contact, and the evidence of service from the customer's point of view.[20] Figure 13.3 shows a service blueprint for a guest spending a night at a hotel.[21] The guest's experience includes a series of steps he or she must enact before even getting to sleep. Behind the scenes, the hotel must skillfully help the guest move from one step to the next. Service blueprints can be helpful in developing new service, supporting a "zero defects" culture, and devising service recovery strategies.
3. ***Monitor customer satisfaction***—Employ suggestion and complaint systems, customer surveys, and comparison shopping. General Electric sends out 700,000 response cards a year asking households to rate its service people's performance. Citibank checks continuously on measures of ART (accuracy, responsiveness, and timeliness). Recognizing how customer needs may vary in different geographical areas can allow firms to develop region-specific programs to improve total customer satisfaction.[22] Firms can also develop customer information databases and systems to permit more personalized, customized service, especially online.[23]

PERISHABILITY Services cannot be stored, so their perishability can be a problem when demand fluctuates. For example, public transportation companies must own much more equipment because of rush-hour demand than if demand were even throughout the day. Some doctors charge patients for missed appointments because the service value (the doctor's availability) exists only at the time of the appointment.

Demand or yield management is critical—the right services must be available to the right customers at the right places at the right times and right prices to maximize profitability.

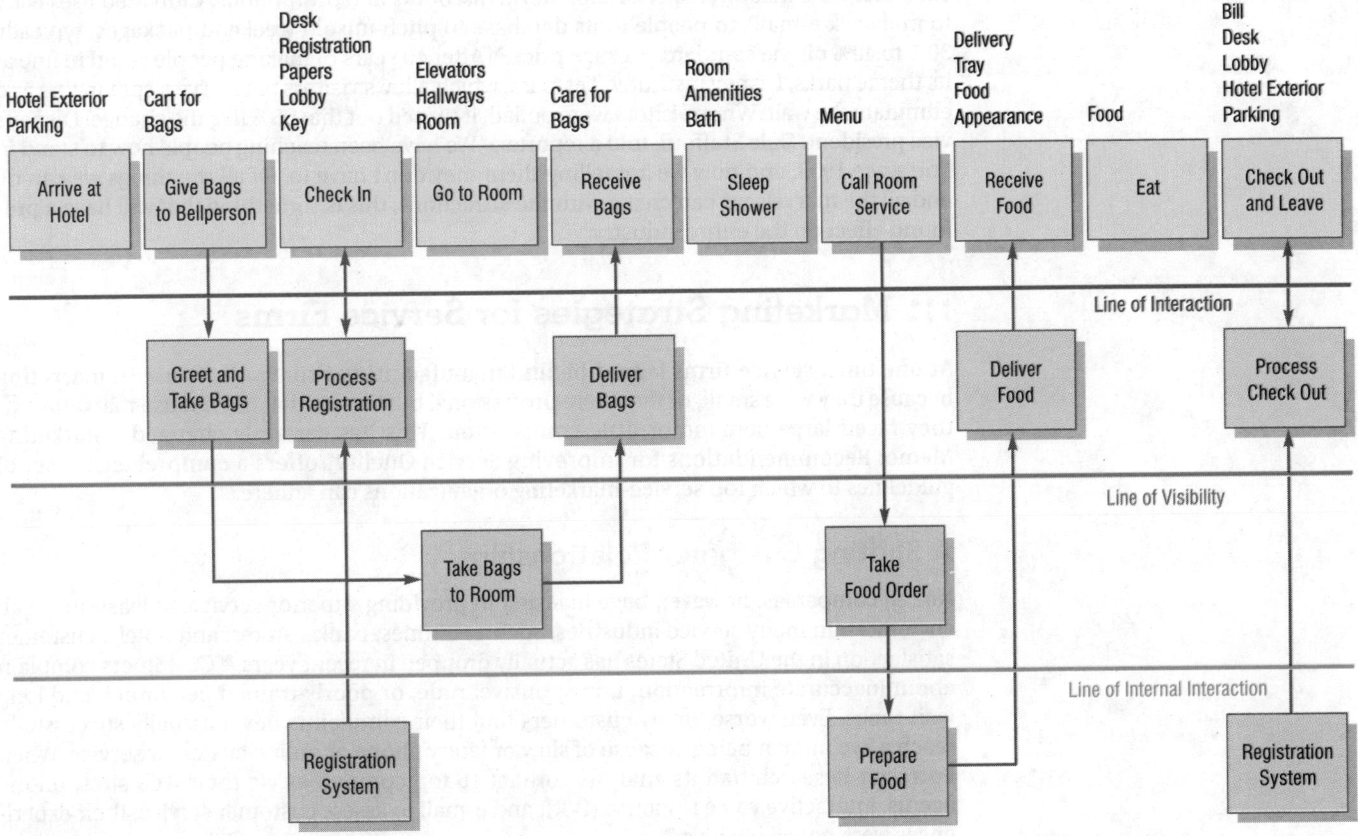

FIG. 13.3 | Blueprint for Overnight Hotel Stay

Source: Valarie Zeithaml, Mary Jo Bitner, and Dwayne D. Gremler, *Services Marketing: Integrating Customer Focus across the Firm*, 4th ed. (New York: McGraw-Hill, 2006).

Several strategies can produce a better match between demand and supply in a service business.[24] On the demand side:

- ***Differential pricing*** will shift some demand from peak to off-peak periods. Examples include low early-evening movie prices and weekend discounts for car rentals.[25]
- ***Nonpeak demand*** can be cultivated. McDonald's pushes breakfast service, and hotels promote minivacation weekends.
- ***Complementary services*** can provide alternatives to waiting customers, such as cocktail lounges in restaurants and automated teller machines in banks.
- ***Reservation systems*** are a way to manage the demand level. Airlines, hotels, and physicians employ them extensively.

On the supply side:

- ***Part-time employees*** can serve peak demand. Colleges add part-time teachers when enrollment goes up, stores hire extra clerks during holiday periods, and restaurants call in part-time servers when needed.
- ***Peak-time efficiency*** routines can allow employees to perform only essential tasks during peak periods. Paramedics assist physicians during busy periods.
- ***Increased consumer participation*** can be encouraged. Consumers fill out their own medical records or bag their own groceries.
- ***Shared services*** can improve offerings. Several hospitals can share medical-equipment purchases.
- ***Facilities for future expansion*** can be a good investment. An amusement park buys surrounding land for later development.

Many airlines, hotels, and resorts send e-mail alerts to self-selected segments of their customer base that offer special short-term discounts and promotions. Club Med uses early to midweek e-mails to people in its database to pitch unsold weekend packages, typically 30% to 40% off the standard package price.[26] After 40 years of making people stand in line at its theme parks, Disney instituted Fastpass, which allows visitors to reserve a spot in line and eliminate the wait. When visitors were polled, it turned out that 95% like the change. Disney's vice president, Dale Stafford, told a reporter, "We have been teaching people how to stand in line since 1955, and now we are telling them they don't have to. Of all the things we can do and all the marvels we can create with the attractions, this is something that will have a profound effect on the entire industry."[27]

::: Marketing Strategies for Service Firms

At one time, service firms lagged behind manufacturing firms in their use of marketing because they were small, or they were professional businesses that did not use marketing, or they faced large demand or little competition. This has certainly changed. "Marketing Memo: Recommendations for Improving Service Quality" offers a comprehensive set of guidelines to which top service-marketing organizations can adhere.

A Shifting Customer Relationship

Not all companies, however, have invested in providing superior service, at least not to all customers. In many service industries, such as airlines, banks, stores, and hotels, customer satisfaction in the United States has actually dropped in recent years.[28] Customers complain about inaccurate information; unresponsive, rude, or poorly trained personnel; and long wait times. Even worse, many customers find their complaints never actually successfully reach a live human being because of slow or faulty phone or online customer service. When Forrester Research had its analysts contact 16 top companies via their Web sites, phone agents, interactive voice response (IVR), and e-mail to assess customer service, their experiences were not all positive:[29]

- When analysts called Wal-Mart to track an order and collect additional information, the automated voice system politely told them that their complete satisfaction was a priority, then said "goodbye" and hung up.

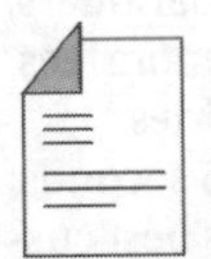

MARKETING MEMO | RECOMMENDATIONS FOR IMPROVING SERVICE QUALITY

Pioneers in conducting academic service research, Berry, Parasuraman, and Zeithaml offer 10 lessons that they maintain are essential for improving service quality across service industries.

1. ***Listening***—Understand what customers really want through continuous learning about the expectations and perceptions of customers and noncustomers (for instance, by means of a service-quality information system).
2. ***Reliability***—Reliability is the single most important dimension of service quality and must be a service priority.
3. ***Basic service***—Service companies must deliver the basics and do what they are supposed to do—keep promises, use common sense, listen to customers, keep customers informed, and be determined to deliver value to customers.
4. ***Service design***—Develop a holistic view of the service while managing its many details.
5. ***Recovery***—To satisfy customers who encounter a service problem, service companies should encourage customers to complain (and make it easy for them to do so), respond quickly and personally, and develop a problem-resolution system.
6. ***Surprising customers***—Although reliability is the most important dimension in *meeting* customers' service expectations, process dimensions such as assurance, responsiveness, and empathy are most important in *exceeding* customer expectations, for example, by surprising them with uncommon swiftness, grace, courtesy, competence, commitment, and understanding.
7. ***Fair play***—Service companies must make special efforts to *be* fair, and to *demonstrate* fairness, to customers and employees.
8. ***Teamwork***—Teamwork is what enables large organizations to deliver service with care and attentiveness by improving employee motivation and capabilities.
9. ***Employee research***—Marketers should conduct research with employees to reveal why service problems occur and what companies must do to solve problems.
10. ***Servant leadership***—Quality service comes from inspired leadership throughout the organization; from excellent service-system design; from the effective use of information and technology; and from a slow-to-change, invisible, all-powerful, internal force called corporate culture.

Sources: Leonard L. Berry, A. Parasuraman, and Valarie A. Zeithaml, "Ten Lessons for Improving Service Quality," *MSI Reports Working Paper Series, No.03-001* (Cambridge, MA: Marketing Science Institute, 2003), pp. 61–82. See also, Leonard L. Berry's books, *On Great Service: A Framework for Action* (New York: Free Press, 2006) and *Discovering the Soul of Service* (New York: Free Press, 1999), as well as his articles, Leonard L. Berry, Venkatesh Shankar, Janet Parish, Susan Cadwallader, and Thomas Dotzel, "Creating New Markets through Service Innovation," *Sloan Management Review* (Winter 2006): 56–63; Leonard L. Berry, Stephan H. Haeckel, and Lewis P. Carbone, "How to Lead the Customer Experience," *Marketing Management* (January–February 2003): 18–23; and Leonard L. Berry, Kathleen Seiders, and Dhruv Grewal, "Understanding Service Convenience," *Journal of Marketing* (July 2002): 1–17.

- When the researchers called RadioShack for digital camera recommendations, a sales agent told the caller to call back and request technical support, but the second call was transferred back to the same sales department again.
- Cingular's Web site provided forms for sending e-mail inquiries with a registered account, but the password for the account was sent via text message to a phone that had not been received yet.

It doesn't have to be that way. The makers of Butterball Turkey staff 55 operators to handle the 100,000 calls it receives annually on its 800 number—10,000 on Thanksgiving Day alone—about how to prepare, cook, and serve turkeys. Trained at Butterball University, the operators have all cooked turkeys dozens of different ways and can handle the myriad queries that come their way, from the danger of stashing turkeys in snow banks because of full freezers to the hazards of thawing turkeys in bathtubs.[30]

Hewlett-Packard tries to respond to every e-mail query within an hour, and usually answers within 10 minutes. The firm monitors its e-mail centers minute by minute to ensure it meets its service-quality standards. Because of its successful e-mail service centers, HP received 25% fewer calls to its call center between 2005 and 2006. E-mail volume rose, improving profits because an e-mail response costs HP 60% less than a phone call.

E-mail response must be implemented properly to be effective.[31] One expert believes companies should (1) send an automated reply to tell customers when a more complete answer will arrive (ideally within 24 hours); (2) ensure the subject line always contains the company name; (3) make the message easy to scan for relevant information; and (4) give customers an easy way to respond with follow-up questions.[32]

PROFIT TIERS Firms have decided to raise fees and lower service to those customers who barely pay their way and to coddle big spenders to retain their patronage as long as possible.

Good customer service can be done well, as the Butterball Turkey company proves every Thanksgiving with its 800 number customer hotline.

Customers in high-profit tiers get special discounts, promotional offers, and lots of special service; customers in lower-profit tiers may get more fees, stripped-down service, and voice messages to process their inquiries.

Charles Schwab's best customers get their calls answered in 15 seconds; other customers can wait longer. Sears sends a repairperson to its best customers within two hours; other customers wait four hours.[33] Companies that provide differentiated levels of service, however, must be careful about claiming superior service—the customers who receive poor treatment will bad-mouth the company and injure its reputation. Delivering services that maximize both customer satisfaction and company profitability can be challenging. "Breakthrough Marketing: Southwest Airlines" describes how that spunky airline took on the big boys and succeeded.

CUSTOMER EMPOWERMENT Customers are becoming more sophisticated about buying product-support services and are pressing for "services unbundling." They may want separate prices for each service element and the right to select the elements they want. Customers also increasingly dislike having to deal with a multitude of service providers handling different types of equipment. Some third-party service organizations now service a greater range of equipment.

Most important, the Internet has empowered customers by letting them vent their rage about bad service—or reward good service—and have their comments beamed around the world with a mouse click.[34] Ninety percent of angry customers reported that they shared their story with a friend. Now, they can share their stories with strangers via the Internet, or "word of mouth on steroids" as some say. With a few clicks on the Planetfeedback.com Web site, shoppers can send an e-mail complaint, compliment, suggestion, or question directly to a company with the option to post comments publicly at the site as well.

Most companies respond quickly, some within an hour. More important than simply responding to a disgruntled customer, however, is preventing dissatisfaction from occurring in the future. That may mean simply taking the time to nurture customer relationships and give customers attention from a real person. Columbia Records spent $10 million to improve its call center, and customers who phone the company can now "opt out" to reach an operator at any point in their call.

JETBLUE

CEO David Neeleman set the bar high for responding to enraged customers after the company's drastic Valentine's Day failure of 2007. During storms in New York City, JetBlue left hundreds of passengers stranded aboard grounded aircraft—some for longer than 9 hours—and cancelled more than 1,000 flights. JetBlue had built its reputation on being a more responsive, humane company in an era of minimal services and maximal delays for airline passengers. Hence, CEO Neeleman knew he had to act fast to stem another kind of storm: a whirlwind of customer defections. Within 24 hours, Neeleman had placed full-page ads in newspapers nationwide in which he personally responded to JetBlue's debacle. "We are sorry and embarrassed," the ads declared, "But most of all we are deeply sorry." Along with the heartfelt apology, JetBlue gave concrete reparations to passengers. Neeleman announced a new "customer bill of rights" that promises passengers travel credits for excessive waits. For instance, passengers who are unable to disembark from an arriving flight for 3 hours or more will receive vouchers worth the full value of their round-trip ticket. Waiting for as little as 30 minutes will bring smaller amounts. JetBlue will also hand out vouchers for the full amount of passengers' round trips if a flight is cancelled within 12 hours of a scheduled departure. The apology, backed by concrete benefits for the angry and inconvenienced passengers, netted kudos for the company from both the business press and JetBlue's own true blue customers. Neeleman eventually stepped down as CEO though, as new management was brought in to address some of the growth challenges the airlines faced.[35]

COPRODUCTION The reality is that customers do not merely purchase and use services, they play an active role in the delivery of that service every step of the way.[36] Their words and actions affect the quality of their service experiences and those of others, and the productivity of frontline employees. One study estimated that one-third of all service problems are

BREAKTHROUGH MARKETING | SOUTHWEST AIRLINES

Southwest Airlines entered the airline industry in 1971 with little money, but lots of personality. Marketing itself as the LUV airline, the company featured a bright red heart as its first logo. In the 1970s, flight attendants in red-orange hot pants served Love Bites (peanuts) and Love Potions (drinks). With little money for advertising in the early days, Southwest relied on its outrageous antics to generate word-of-mouth advertising.

Later ads showcased Southwest's low fares, frequent flights, on-time arrivals, and top safety record. Throughout all the advertising, the spirit of fun pervaded. For example, one TV spot showed a small bag of peanuts with the words, "This is what our meals look like at Southwest Airlines. . . . It's also what our fares look like." Southwest used ads with humor to poke fun at itself and to convey its personality.

Southwest can offer low fares because it streamlines operations. For example, it flies only Boeing 737s, which saves time and money because training is simplified for pilots, flight attendants, and mechanics; and management can substitute aircraft, reschedule flight crews, or transfer mechanics quickly. Southwest also bucks the traditional hub-and-spoke system and offers only point-to-point service; it chooses to fly to smaller airports that have lower gate fees and less congestion, which speeds aircraft turnaround. Southwest's 15- to 20-minute turnaround time from flight landing to departure is half the industry average, giving it better asset utilization (it flies more flights and more passengers per plane per day).

Southwest grows by entering new markets that are overpriced and underserved by current airlines. The company believes it can bring fares down by one-third to one-half whenever it enters a new market, and it grows the market in every city it serves by making flying affordable to people who previously could not afford to fly. Southwest currently serves 64 cities in 32 states.

Even though Southwest is a low-cost airline, it has pioneered many additional services and programs such as same-day freight service, senior discounts, Fun Fares, and Fun Packs. Despite Southwest's reputation for low fares and no-frills service, the company wins the hearts of customers. It consistently ranks at the top of lists of customer service for airlines, yet the average price of a flight is $105. Southwest has been ranked by *Fortune* magazine as the United States' most admired airline since 1997, as its fifth-most admired corporation in 2007, and as one of the top five best places to work. Southwest's financial results also shine: The company has been profitable for 34 straight years. It has been the only airline to report profits every quarter since September 11, 2001, and one of the few that has had no layoffs amid a travel slump created by the slow economy and the threat of terrorism.

Although the hot pants are long gone, the LUVing spirit remains at the heart of Southwest. The company's stock symbol on the NYSE is LUV and red hearts can be found everywhere across the company. These symbols embody the Southwest spirit of employees "caring about themselves, each other, and Southwest's customers." "Our fares can be matched; our airplanes and routes can be copied. But we pride ourselves on our customer service," said Sherry Phelps, director of corporate employment. That's why Southwest looks for and hires people who generate enthusiasm. In fact, having a sense of humor is a selection criteria it uses for hiring. As one employee explained, "We can train you to do any job, but we can't give you the right spirit." And the feeling is reciprocated. When Southwest needed to close reservation centers in three cities in 2004, it didn't fire a single employee but rather paid for relocation and commuting expenses.

Sources: Barney Gimbel, "Southwest's New Flight Plan," *Fortune*, May 16, 2005, pp. 93–98; Melanie Trottman, "Destination: Philadelphia," *Wall Street Journal*, May 4, 2004; Andy Serwer, "Southwest Airlines: The Hottest Thing in the Sky," *Fortune*, March 8, 2004; Colleen Barrett, "Fasten Your Seat Belts," *Adweek*, January 26, 2004, p. 17; "Southwest May Not Be No.1, but It Sure Looks Like the Leader," *Airline Financial News*, November 24, 2003; Eva Kaplan-Leiserson, "Strategic Service," *Training and Development* (November 2003): 14–16; www.southwest.com.

caused by the customer.[37] With an increasing shift to self-service technologies, this percentage can be expected to rise.

Preventing service failures from ever happening to begin with is crucial, as service recovery is always challenging. One of the biggest problems is attribution—customers will often feel that the firm is at fault or, even if not, that it is still responsible for righting any wrongs. Unfortunately, although many firms have well-designed and executed procedures to deal with their own failures, they find that managing customer failures is much more difficult.

Figure 13.4 displays the four broad categories of root causes for customer failures, although there often are multiple causes at work. Solutions come in all forms, as illustrated by some of the following examples:[38]

1. ***Redesign processes and redefine customer roles to simplify service encounters***—One of the keys to Netflix' success is that it charges a flat fee and allows customers to return DVDs by mail at their leisure, giving customers greater control and flexibility.
2. ***Incorporate the right technology to aid employees and customers***—Circuit City keeps a virtual copy of purchase information in case customers are unable to produce a receipt needed for a return.
3. ***Create high-performance customers by enhancing their role clarity, motivation, and ability***—Saturn coaches novice buyers about proper vehicle maintenance. USAA reminds policyholders who are in the military to suspend their car insurance when

FIG. 13.4

Root Causes of Customer Failure

Source: Stephen Tax, Mark Colgate, and David Bowen, *MIT Solan Management Review* (Spring 2006): 30–38.

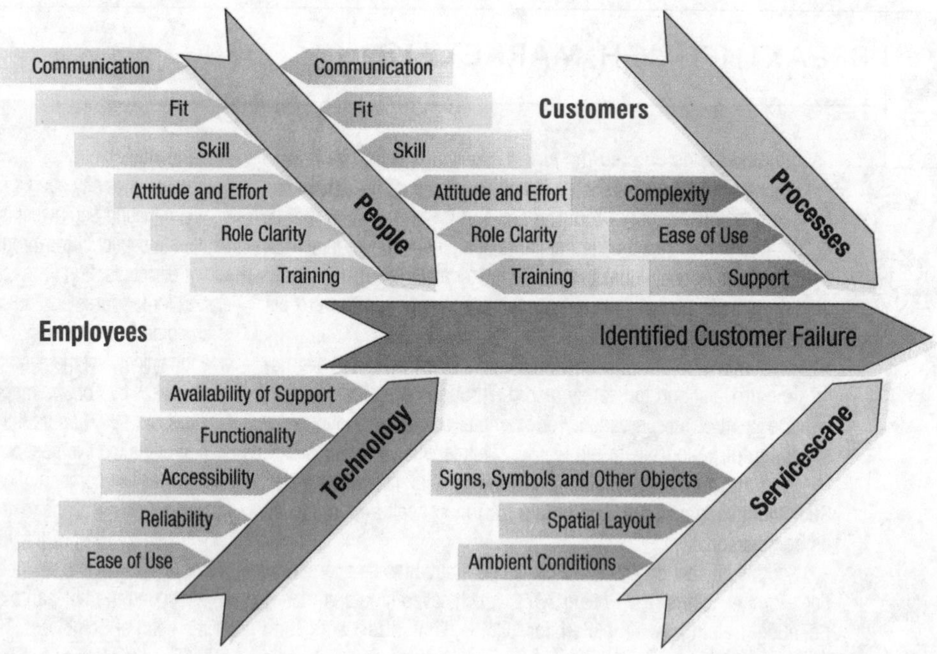

they are stationed overseas. Gordian Health Solutions, which offers integrated health management services to employers, provides instant incentives to employees, such as a 20% reduction in their contribution to health insurance premiums, to get them to participate in various health programs.

4. ***Encourage "customer citizenship" where customers help customers***—At golf courses, players can not only follow the rules by playing and behaving appropriately, they can encourage others to do so.

Holistic Marketing for Services

The service outcome, and whether people will remain loyal to a service provider, is influenced by a host of variables. One study identified more than 800 critical behaviors that cause customers to switch services.[39] These behaviors fall into eight categories (see Table 13.1).

Holistic marketing for services requires external, internal, and interactive marketing (see Figure 13.5).[40] *External marketing* describes the normal work of preparing, pricing, distributing, and promoting the service to customers. *Internal marketing* describes training and motivating employees to serve customers well. The most important contribution the marketing department can make is arguably to be "exceptionally clever in getting everyone else in the organization to practice marketing."[41]

Singapore Airlines adopts a holistic approach to its services, dividing its resources between training staff (employees), reviewing its processes (company), and creating new products and services (customers).

SINGAPORE AIRLINES (SIA)

Singapore Airlines is consistently recognized as the world's "best" airline—it wins so many awards, it has to update its Web site monthly to keep up to date—in large part due to its stellar efforts at holistic marketing. SIA continually strives to create a "wow effect" and surpass expectations of its customers. Famous for pampering passengers, it was the first to launch indi-

TABLE 13.1

Factors Leading to Customer Switching Behavior

Pricing	Response to Service Failure
■ High price	■ Negative response
■ Price increases	■ No response
■ Unfair pricing	■ Reluctant response
■ Deceptive pricing	**Competition**
Inconvenience	■ Found better service
■ Location/hours	**Ethical Problems**
■ Wait for appointment	■ Cheat
■ Wait for service	■ Hard sell
Core Service Failure	■ Unsafe
■ Service mistakes	■ Conflict of interest
■ Billing errors	**Involuntary Switching**
■ Service catastrophe	■ Customer moved
Service Encounter Failures	■ Provider closed
■ Uncaring	
■ Impolite	
■ Unresponsive	
■ Unknowledgeable	

Source: Susan M. Keaveney, "Customer Switching Behavior in Service Industries: An Exploratory Study," *Journal of Marketing* (April 1995): 71)_82. Copyright © 1995 American Marketing Association. Used with permission.

vidual video screens at airplane seats. To improve its food, SIA built the first-of-its-kind $1 million simulator to mimic the air pressure and humidity found inside a plane. Because taste buds change in the air, SIA found that, among other things, it needed to cut back on spices. SIA places a high emphasis on training through its "Transforming Customer Service (TCS)" program, which includes staff in five key operational areas: cabin crew, engineering, ground services, flight operations, and sales support. The TCS culture is embedded in all management training, company-wide. TCS also uses a 40-30-30 rule in its holistic approach to people, processes, and products: 40% of resources go to training and invigorating staff, 30% is spent on reviewing process and procedures, and the last 30% on creating new product and service ideas. In 2007, with its innovatively designed Boeing 777-300 ERS and Airbus A380 planes, SIA set new standards of comforts in all classes of service, from eight private minirooms in first class to wider seats, AC power supplies, and USB ports in coach.[42] ■

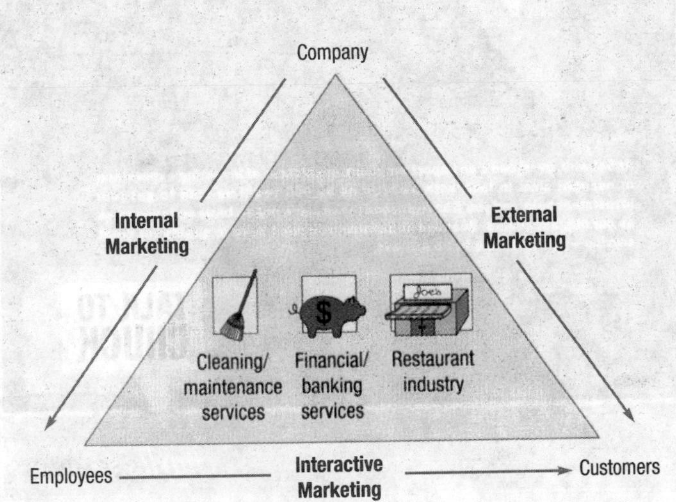

FIG. 13.5

Three Types of Marketing in Service Industries

Interactive marketing describes the employees' skill in serving the client. Clients judge service not only by its *technical quality* (Was the surgery successful?), but also by its *functional quality* (Did the surgeon show concern and inspire confidence?).[43] Teamwork is often key, and delegating authority to frontline employees can allow for greater flexibility and adaptability in service delivery through better problem solving, closer employee cooperation, and more efficient knowledge transfer.[44]

Technology also has great power to make service workers more productive. Many physicians and nurses now carry wireless laptop-like devices in their coat pockets from exam room to exam room. These devices contain all relevant patient information and charts, e-mail correspondence, suggested treatments for certain diagnoses, and billing information. They also allow the physicians to write prescriptions, and they store and automatically process all information entered during the patient visit.

PEDIATRIC ASSOCIATES

When Pediatric Associates in Cincinnati, Ohio, installed an electronic medical and practice management system, it eliminated nearly all the paperwork, freeing up doctors to see up to 25 patients a day and allowing a reduction in staff from attrition and flex-time so others could work at home. The $300,000 investment was recouped in 18 months, and the number of claims denied for coding errors dropped 87%. The average charge per patient visit increased by $20.[45]

Companies must avoid pushing productivity so hard, however, that they reduce perceived quality. Some methods lead to too much standardization. Service providers must deliver "high touch" as well as "high tech."

With its many "high-touch" services such as after-hours trading, the Schwab learning center, live events, online chats with customer-service representatives, and market updates by e-mail, the Charles Schwab brokerage house has become one of the nation's largest.

CHARLES SCHWAB

Charles Schwab, one of the nation's largest discount brokerage houses, uses the telephone, Internet, and wireless devices to create an innovative combination of high-tech and high-touch services. One of the first major brokerage houses to provide online trading, Schwab today services almost eight million individual and institutional accounts. It has avoided competing on price with low-priced competitors such as Ameritrade.com and instead has assembled the most comprehensive financial and company information resources to be found online. It offers account information and proprietary research from retail brokers; real-time quotes; an after-hours trading program; the Schwab learning center; live events; online chats with customer-service representatives; a global investing service; and market updates delivered by e-mail. Besides the discount brokerage, the firm offers mutual funds, annuities, bond trading, and now mortgages through its Charles Schwab Bank. Despite a lull in 2004, Schwab has fired back to lead its competitors by focusing on three areas: superior service (online, via phone, and in local branch offices), innovative products, and low prices.[46]

The Internet lets firms improve their service offerings and strengthen their relationships with customers by allowing for true interactivity, customer-specific and situational personalization, and real-time adjustments of the firm's offerings.[47] But as companies collect, store, and use more information about customers, concerns have arisen about security and privacy.[48] Companies must incorporate the proper safeguards and reassure customers about their efforts.

::: Managing Service Quality

The service quality of a firm is tested at each service encounter. If service personnel are bored, cannot answer simple questions, or are visiting with each other while customers are waiting, customers will think twice about doing business again with that seller.

Haier is the preferred brand in China for household appliances—a result of providing its customers with quality service. To learn about Haier's successful service strategies that propelled this company to its current position, visit www.pearsoned-asia.com/marketingmanagementchina.

Customer Expectations

Customers form service expectations from many sources, such as past experiences, word of mouth, and advertising. In general, customers compare the *perceived service* with the *expected service*.[49] If the perceived service falls below the expected service, customers are disappointed. Successful companies add benefits to their offering that not only *satisfy* customers but surprise and *delight* them. Delighting customers is a matter of exceeding expectations.[50]

RITZ-CARLTON HOTELS

Ritz-Carlton Hotels' legendary service starts with 100 hours of training annually for every employee. The goal? To treat every guest like royalty by being warm, friendly, gracious, courteous, and genuinely devoted to making sure every stay is a memorable one. Every manager and frontline employee carries a laminated card with 12 service values guidelines to help create the brand mystique that lures the luxury traveler, such as "I build strong relationships and create Ritz-Carlton guests for life" (#1) and "I am proud of my professional appearance, language, and behavior (#10). Every day at every Ritz-Carlton, employees around the world gather from every department for a 15-minute meeting known as "the line-up." They first review guest experiences, resolve issues, and discuss ways to improve service, before spending the bulk of the time on reinforcing one of the 12 service values. Every meeting each day also shares one "wow story" by a staff person who provided exemplary service by going above and beyond the call of duty. It's perhaps no surprise that Ritz-Carlton, with 35 properties in the United States and 25 outside, was the first two-time winner of the Malcolm Baldrige National Quality Award.[51]

The service-quality model in Figure 13.6 highlights the main requirements for delivering high service quality.[52] It identifies five gaps that cause unsuccessful delivery:

1. ***Gap between consumer expectation and management perception***—Management does not always correctly perceive what customers want. Hospital administrators may think patients want better food, but patients may be more concerned with nurse responsiveness.
2. ***Gap between management perception and service-quality specification***—Management might correctly perceive customers' wants but not set a performance

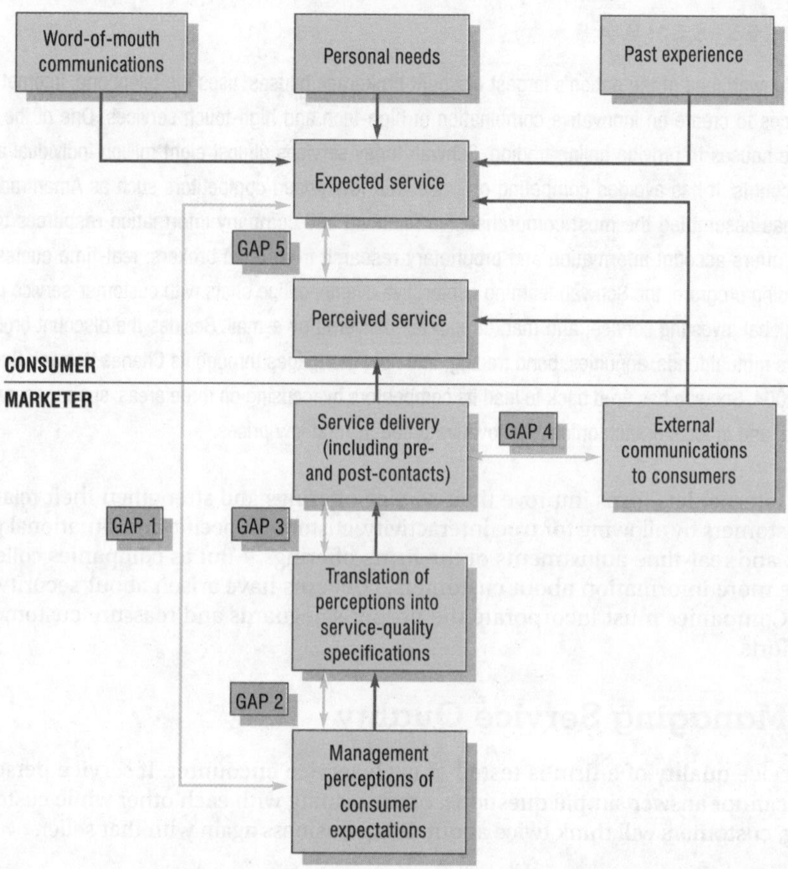

| FIG. 13.6 |

Service-Quality Model

Sources: A. Parasuraman Valarie A. Zeithaml, and Leonard L. Berry, "A Conceptual Model of Service Quality and Its Implications for Future Research," *Journal of Marketing* (Fall 1985): 44. Reprinted with permission of the American Marketing Association. The model is more fully discussed or elaborated in Valarie Zeithaml, Mary Jo Bitner, and Dwayne D. Gremler, *Services Marketing: Integrating Customer Focus across the Firm*, 4th ed. (New York: McGraw-Hill, 2006).

standard. Hospital administrators may tell the nurses to give "fast" service without specifying it in minutes.

3. ***Gap between service-quality specifications and service delivery***—Personnel might be poorly trained, or incapable of or unwilling to meet the standard; or they may be held to conflicting standards, such as taking time to listen to customers and serving them fast.
4. ***Gap between service delivery and external communications***—Consumer expectations are affected by statements made by company representatives and ads. If a hospital brochure shows a beautiful room, but the patient arrives and finds the room to be cheap and tacky looking, external communications have distorted the customer's expectations.
5. ***Gap between perceived service and expected service***—This gap occurs when the consumer misperceives the service quality. The physician may keep visiting the patient to show care, but the patient may interpret this as an indication that something really is wrong.

Based on this service-quality model, researchers identified the following five determinants of service quality, in order of importance.[53]

1. ***Reliability***—The ability to perform the promised service dependably and accurately.
2. ***Responsiveness***—The willingness to help customers and to provide prompt service.
3. ***Assurance***—The knowledge and courtesy of employees and their ability to convey trust and confidence.
4. ***Empathy***—The provision of caring, individualized attention to customers.
5. ***Tangibles***—The appearance of physical facilities, equipment, personnel, and communication materials.

Based on these five factors, the researchers developed the 21-item SERVQUAL scale (see Table 13.2).[54] They also note there is a *zone of tolerance* or a range where a service dimension would be deemed satisfactory, anchored by the minimum level consumers are willing to accept and the level they believe can and should be delivered. "Marketing Insight: The Role of Expectations in Service-Quality Perceptions" describes important recent research on services marketing. "Marketing Memo: Assessing E-Service Quality" reviews two models of online service quality.

TABLE 13.2 SERVQUAL Attributes

Reliability

- Providing service as promised
- Dependability in handling customers' service problems
- Performing services right the first time
- Providing services at the promised time
- Maintaining error-free records
- Employees who have the knowledge to answer customer questions

Responsiveness

- Keeping customer informed as to when services will be performed
- Prompt service to customers
- Willingness to help customers
- Readiness to respond to customers' requests

Assurance

- Employees who instill confidence in customers
- Making customers feel safe in their transactions
- Employees who are consistently courteous

Empathy

- Giving customers individual attention
- Employees who deal with customers in a caring fashion
- Having the customer's best interests at heart
- Employees who understand the needs of their customers
- Convenient business hours

Tangibles

- Modern equipment
- Visually appealing facilities
- Employees who have a neat, professional appearance
- Visually appealing materials associated with the service

Source: A. Parasuraman, Valarie A. Zeithaml, and Leonard L. Berry, "A Conceptual Model of Service Quality and Its Implications for Future Research," *Journal of Marketing* (Fall 1985): 41–50. Reprinted by permission of American Marketing Association.

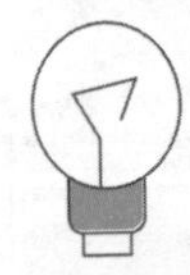

MARKETING INSIGHT | THE ROLE OF EXPECTATIONS IN SERVICE-QUALITY PERCEPTIONS

The service-quality model in Figure 13.6 highlights some of the gaps that cause unsuccessful service delivery. Subsequent research has extended the model to incorporate additional considerations. One *dynamic process model* of service quality was based on the premise that customer perceptions and expectations of service quality change over time, but at any one point they are a function of prior expectations about what *will* and what *should* happen during the service encounter, as well as the *actual* service delivered during the last contact. Tests of the model reveal that the two different types of expectations have opposite effects on perceptions of service quality.

1. ***Increasing*** customer expectations of what the firm *will* deliver can lead to improved perceptions of overall service quality.
2. ***Decreasing*** customer expectations of what the firm *should* deliver can lead to improved perceptions of overall service quality.

Much work has validated the role of expectations in consumers' interpretations and evaluations of the service encounter and the relationship they adopt with a firm over time. Consumers are often forward-looking with respect to their decision to keep or switch from a service relationship. Any marketing activity that affects current or expected future usage can help to solidify a service relationship.

With continuously provided services, such as public utilities, health care, financial services, computing services, insurance, and other professional, membership, or subscription services, customers have been observed to mentally calculate their *payment equity*—the perceived fairness of the level of economic benefits derived from service usage in relationship to the level of economic costs. Payment costs typically consist of some combination of an initial payment such as a membership fee or retainer; a fixed, periodic fee such as a monthly service charge; and a variable fee such as usage-based charges. Payment benefits depend on current payment and usage levels. The perceived fairness of the exchange determines service satisfaction and future usage. In other words, customers ask themselves, "Am I using this service enough, given what I pay for it?"

There can be a dark side to long-term service relationships. For example, with an ad agency, the client may feel that over time, the agency loses objectivity and becomes stale in its thinking or begins to take advantage of the relationship.

Sources: Roland T. Rust and Tuck Siong Chung, "Marketing Models of Service and Relationships," *Marketing Science* 25 (November–December 2006): 560–80; Katherine N. Lemon, Tiffany Barnett White, and Russell S. Winer, "Dynamic Customer Relationship Management: Incorporating Future Considerations into the Service Retention Decision," *Journal of Marketing* 6 (January 2002): 1–14; Ruth N. Bolton and Katherine N. Lemon, "A Dynamic Model of Customers' Usage of Services: Usage as an Antecedent and Consequence of Satisfaction," *Journal of Marketing* 36 (May 1999): 171–86; Kent Grayson and Tim Ambler, "The Dark Side of Long-Term Relationships in Marketing Services," *Journal of Marketing Research* 36 (February 1999): 132–41; William Boulding, Ajay Kalra, Richard Staelin, and Valarie A. Zeithaml, "A Dynamic Model of Service Quality: From Expectations to Behavioral Intentions," *Journal of Marketing Research* 30 (February 1993): 7–27.

MARKETING MEMO | ASSESSING E-SERVICE QUALITY

Academic researchers Zeithaml, Parasuraman, and Malhotra define online service quality as the extent to which a Web site facilitates efficient and effective shopping, purchasing, and delivery. They identified 11 dimensions of perceived e-service quality: access, ease of navigation, efficiency, flexibility, reliability, personalization, security/privacy, responsiveness, assurance/trust, site aesthetics, and price knowledge. Some of these service-quality dimensions were the same online as off-line, but some specific underlying attributes were different. Different dimensions emerged with e-service quality too. Empathy didn't seem to be as important online, unless there were service problems. Core dimensions of regular service quality were efficiency, fulfillment, reliability, and privacy; core dimensions of service recovery were responsiveness, compensation, and real-time access to help.

Another set of academic researchers, Wolfinbarger and Gilly, developed a reduced scale of online service quality with four key dimensions: reliability/fulfillment, Web site design, security/privacy, and customer service. The researchers interpret their study findings to suggest that the most basic building blocks of a "compelling online experience" are reliability and functionality to provide time savings, easy transactions, good selection, in-depth information, and the "right level" of personalization. Their 14-item scale is displayed here:

Reliability/Fulfillment

The product that came was represented accurately by the Web site.

You get what you ordered from this Web site.

The product is delivered by the time promised by the company.

Web Site Design

This Web site provides in-depth information.

The site doesn't waste my time.

It is quick and easy to complete a transaction at this Web site.

The level of personalization at this site is about right, not too much or too little.

This Web site has good selection.

Security/Privacy

I feel that my privacy is protected at this site.

I feel safe in my transactions with this Web site.

This Web site has adequate security transactions.

Customer Service

The company is willing and ready to respond to customer needs.

When you have a problem, the Web site shows a sincere interest in solving it.

Inquiries are answered promptly.

Sources: Mary Wolfinbarger and Mary C. Gilly, "E-TailQ: Dimensionalizing, Measuring, and Predicting E-Tail Quality," *Journal of Retailing* 79 (Fall 2003): 183–98; Valarie A. Zeithaml, A. Parsu Parasuraman, and Arvind Malhotra, "A Conceptual Framework for Understanding E-Service Quality: Implications for Future Research and Managerial Practice," *Marketing Science Institute Working Paper,* Report No. 00-115, 2000.

Best Practices of Service-Quality Management

Various studies have shown that well-managed service companies share the following common practices: a strategic concept, a history of top-management commitment to quality, high standards, self-service technologies, systems for monitoring service performance and customer complaints, and an emphasis on employee satisfaction. Rackspace, a San Antonio–based Web-hosting company that provides space on servers to make their clients' Web sites accessible on the Internet, embodies many of these practices.

RACKSPACE

In 1999, the Rackspace tech support team was lax about delivering great service and, indeed, was often hostile to customers. Its turnaround began with a new company mantra—to provide what the firm called "Fanatical Support." This concept was backed by a few simple rules: Criticizing a customer is a firing offense; Be reliable; No news is not good news—in other words, you must communicate frequently with customers; and Remove all obstacles that make it hard for customers to do business with you. Rackspace's setup allows every customer to call the same person every time and get a problem solved quickly. Technical support is available via phone 24 hours a day, 7 days a week, 365 days a year or via a dedicated technical service area of the Web site. Every month Rackspace gives the "straightjacket award" to the employee who best lives up to the company's "fanatical customer support" motto. Public recognition of employee achievement includes customer compliments posted on the walls and a "FANATIC" sign hanging prominently above the desk of straightjacket award winners. In recognition of its accomplishments, the company was named Best Customer-Service Organization by the American Business Awards in its 2005 ceremony.[55]

STRATEGIC CONCEPT Top service companies are "customer obsessed." They have a clear sense of their target customers and their needs. They have developed a distinctive strategy for satisfying these needs. At the Four Seasons luxury hotel chain, employees must pass four interviews before being hired. Each hotel also employs a "guest historian" to track guest preferences. With more branch offices in the United States than Starbucks has, Edward Jones brokerage stays close to customers by assigning a single financial advisor and one administrator to each office. Although costly, its intimate size fosters personal relationships.[56]

TOP-MANAGEMENT COMMITMENT Companies such as Marriott, Disney, and USAA have a thorough commitment to service quality. Their managements look not only at financial performance on a monthly basis, but also at service performance. Ray Kroc of McDonald's insisted on continually measuring each McDonald's outlet on its conformance to QSCV: quality, service, cleanliness, and value. Some companies insert a reminder along with employees' paychecks: BROUGHT TO YOU BY THE CUSTOMER. Sam Walton of Wal-Mart required the following employee pledge: "I solemnly swear and declare that every customer that comes within 10 feet of me, I will smile, look them in the eye, and greet them, so help me Sam."

HIGH STANDARDS The best service providers set high service-quality standards. Citibank aims to answer phone calls within 10 seconds and customer letters within 2 days. The standards must be set *appropriately* high. A 98% accuracy standard may sound good, but it would result in 64,000 lost FedEx packages a day; 6 misspelled words on each page of a book; 400,000 misfilled prescriptions daily; and unsafe drinking water 8 days a year. We can distinguish between companies offering "merely good" service and those offering "breakthrough" service, aimed at being 100% defect-free.[57]

A service company can differentiate itself by designing a better and faster delivery system. There are three levels of differentiation.[58] The first is *reliability:* Some suppliers are more reliable in their on-time delivery, order completeness, and order-cycle time. The second is *resilience:* Some suppliers are better at handling emergencies, product recalls, and answering inquiries. The third is *innovativeness:* Some suppliers create better information systems, introduce bar coding and mixed pallets, and in other ways help the customer. "Marketing Insight: Developing Customer Interface Systems" discusses how service marketers must reengineer their customer interface systems for optimal efficiency and effectiveness.

SELF-SERVICE TECHNOLOGIES (SSTs) Consumers value convenience in services.[59] Many person-to-person service interactions are being replaced by self-service technologies.[60] To the traditional vending machines we can add Automated Teller Machines (ATMs), self-pumping at gas stations, self-checkout at hotels, and a variety of activities on the Internet, such as ticket purchasing, investment trading, and customization of products.

Not all SSTs improve service quality, but they can make service transactions more accurate, convenient, and faster. Obviously they can also reduce costs. IBM saved $2 billion by shifting 99 million service telephone calls online.[61] Every company needs to think about improving its service using SSTs.

Some companies have found that the biggest obstacle is not the technology itself, but convincing customers to use it, especially for the first time. Customers must have a clear sense of their roles in the SST process, must see a clear benefit to SST, and must feel they have the ability to actually use it.[62] Delta has been successful in getting customers to use its self-service kiosks by employing a number of tactics such as advertising the advantages of self-service, providing customer reps to faciliate the process, and ensuring as many machines are available as possible.[63]

HOTEL FRONT DESKS

After a long journey—from taxi to plane to taxi to hotel—the hotel's front desk can sometimes seem like a barrier to the longed-for respite of the hotel room. In order to reduce lines and get guests to their rooms more quickly, many hotels are trying to streamline the process through self-service check-in kiosks in the hotel lobby. Hilton Hotels already has kiosks in 170 of its Embassy Suites properties and plans to add them in all domestic Hilton brand hotels by 2008. Travelers can slide in their credit cards and receive their purple key cards. The kiosk is no replacement for the front desk, but it allows front desk staff to truly serve a concierge function, devoting more time to guests who need attention. Hilton Hotels, then, is using a combination of high tech and high touch to give it a leg up in the fiercely competitive hotel industry. In contrast, Kimpton Hotels, a San Francisco-based chain of boutique hotels, is putting all its efforts into beefing up front desk services, going for high touch rather than high tech. The chain is teaching employees how to better read and respond to guest behavior—to differentiate between the hurried guest and the one who seeks more information, such as parents who want to know all the kid-friendly events and activities in the area. "Guests are looking for an expedient friendly process," said Niki Leondakis, chief operating officer of Kimpton Hotels, "but are also using the desk as a complete resource center for all services."[64]

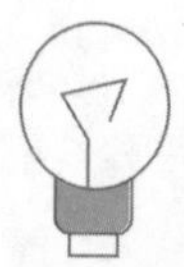

MARKETING INSIGHT | DEVELOPING CUSTOMER INTERFACE SYSTEMS

Marketing academics and consultants Jeffrey Rayport and Bernie Jaworski define a *customer-service interface* as any place at which a company seeks to manage a relationship with a customer, whether through people, technology, or some combination of the two. They believe that to deliver high levels of customer-perceived value, any interface should excel on four dimensions:

- ***Physical presence and appearance:*** Be on the scene in sufficient numbers and presentable in appearance. At the Four Seasons Hotel, the frontline staff is differentiated on appearance as uniformed, clean-cut, businesslike, courteous, individual, and authentic.
- ***Cognition:*** Be able to recognize patterns, draw intelligent conclusions, and communicate articulately. At Nordstrom, salespeople are skilled at recognizing and rewarding the store's best customers with appropriate service and attention.
- ***Emotion or attitude:*** Be respectful and attentive, displaying brand-consistent personality attributes, and be emotionally calibrated with the customer. Southwest Airline's flight crew's sense of humor and positive dispositions enhance passengers' travel experience.
- ***Connectedness:*** Remain well connected to other resources important to the customer's experience. Four Seasons, Nordstrom, and Southwest Airlines all coordinate communications and activities to provide a holistic, positive experience.

Rayport and Jaworski believe companies are facing a crisis in customer interaction and relationship management. Although many companies serve customers through a broad array of interfaces, from retail sales clerks to Web sites to voice-response telephone systems, these more often constitute an interface *collection,* not an actual interface *system,* as the whole set does not add up to the sum of its parts in its ability to provide superior service and build strong customer relationships. Rising complexity and costs, and customer dissatisfaction can result. Networked technologies, however, such as Web sites, kiosks, interactive voice-response units, vending machines, and touch screens let managers successfully introduce machines into front office roles that have long been held by humans. Here are a few examples they note:

- Borders deployed Title Sleuth self-service kiosks to take the burden of title searches off its employees. The three hundred machines handle up to 1.2 million customer searches per week, and customers using these machines spend 50% more per store visit and generate 20% more special-order sales.
- REI uses interactive kiosks in its stores to hold information about its 78,000 SKUs—information that would be impossible for even the most intelligent store clerks to store in their heads. Kiosk sales are growing at 30% a year, building revenues to the equivalent of an additional 25,000-square-foot brick-and-mortar store.
- Rite Aid is using prescription-dispensing robots and interactive voice-response units to fulfill an anticipated labor shortage—prescriptions filled in the United States are expected to grow by 30% over the next two years while the number of pharmacists is projected to expand by only 6%. Automation of rote tasks lets Rite Aid pharmacists use their time to personally attend to customer's needs, providing much-needed brand differentiation in a commoditized category of the retail sector.

According to Rayport and Jaworski, successfully integrating technology into the work force requires a comprehensive reengineering of the front office to identify what people do best, what machines do best, and how to deploy them separately and together. Managers can take the following steps in conducting a service interface reengineering project:

1. ***Understand the experience customers want***—Do customers seek information, advice, social exchange, affirmation, anonymity, discretion, efficiency, or something else? What interactions and relationships will shape those experiences? What are the implications of these experiences for the firm's own goals and objectives?
2. ***Understand the potential of technology***—What is the effectiveness and efficiency of possible technology? What new roles can technology assume?
3. ***Match the interface type to the task***—Should the interface be people dominant, machine dominant, or a hybrid of the two? What are the associated costs and customer outcomes?
4. ***Put work in its right place***—Should services be provided proximally (in stores or on-site) or remotely (through network connections to customers or operations off-site)?
5. ***Optimize performance across the system***—Whereas most customers use multiple channels, is the interface system able to capitalize on the economic potential of each?

Sources: Jeffrey F. Rayport and Bernard J. Jaworski, *Best Face Forward* (Boston: Harvard Business School Press, 2005); Jeffrey F. Rayport, Bernard J. Jaworski, and Ellie J. Kyung, "Best Face Forward," *Journal of Interactive Marketing* 19 (Autumn 2005): 67–80; Jeffrey F. Rayport and Bernard J. Jaworski, "Best Face Forward," *Harvard Business Review* 82 (December 2004): 47–58.

MONITORING SYSTEMS Top firms audit service performance, both their own and competitors', on a regular basis. They collect *voice of the customer (VOC) measurements* to probe customer satisfiers and dissatisfiers. They use comparison shopping, ghost shopping, customer surveys, suggestion and complaint forms, service-audit teams, and letters to the president.

Mystery shopping—the use of undercover shoppers who are paid to report back to the company—is now big business: $300 million in the United States and $500 million worldwide. Fast-food chains, big-box stores, gas stations, and even large government agencies are using mystery shoppers to pinpoint and fix customer-service problems.

We can judge services on *customer importance* and *company performance. Importance-performance analysis* rates the various elements of the service bundle and identifies what actions are required. Table 13.3 shows how customers rated 14 service elements or attributes of an automobile dealer's service department on importance and performance. For example, "Job done right the first time" (attribute 1) received a mean importance rating of 3.83 and a mean performance rating of 2.63, indicating that customers felt it was highly important but not performed well. The ratings of the 14 elements are displayed in Figure 13.7 and divided into four sections.

- Quadrant A shows important service elements that are not being performed at the desired levels; they include elements 1, 2, and 9. The dealer should concentrate on improving the service department's performance on these elements.
- Quadrant B shows important service elements that are being performed well; the company needs to maintain the high performance.
- Quadrant C shows minor service elements that are being delivered in a mediocre way but do not need any attention.
- Quadrant D shows that a minor service element, "Send out maintenance notices," is being performed in an excellent manner.

Perhaps the company should spend less on sending out maintenance notices and use the savings to improve performance on important elements. Management can enhance the analysis by checking on the competitors' performance levels on each element.[65]

SATISFYING CUSTOMER COMPLAINTS Every complaint is a gift if handled well. Companies that encourage disappointed customers to complain—and also empower employees to remedy the situation on the spot—have been shown to achieve higher revenues and greater

TABLE 13.3

Customer Importance and Performance Ratings for an Auto Dealership

Number Attribute	Attribute Description	Mean Importance Rating[a]	Mean Performance Rating[b]
1	Job done right the first time	3.83	2.63
2	Fast action on complaints	3.63	2.73
3	Prompt warranty work	3.60	3.15
4	Able to do any job needed	3.56	3.00
5	Service available when needed	3.41	3.05
6	Courteous and friendly service	3.41	3.29
7	Car ready when promised	3.38	3.03
8	Perform only necessary work	3.37	3.11
9	Low prices on service	3.29	2.00
10	Clean up after service work	3.27	3.02
11	Convenient to home	2.52	2.25
12	Convenient to work	2.43	2.49
13	Courtesy buses and cars	2.37	2.35
14	Send out maintenance notices	2.05	3.33

[a] Ratings obtained from a four-point scale of "extremely important" (4), "important" (3), "slightly important" (2), and "not important" (1).

[b] Ratings obtained from a four-point scale of "excellent" (4), "good" (3), "fair" (2), and "poor" (1). A "no basis for judgment" category was also provided.

FIG. 13.7

Importance-Performance Analysis

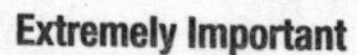

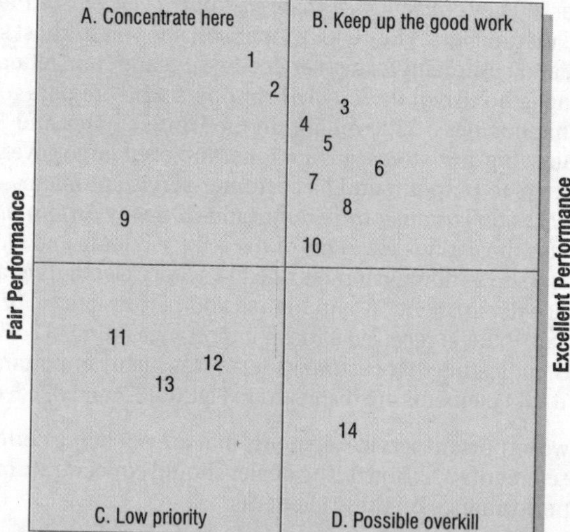

profits than companies that do not have a systematic approach for addressing service failures.[66] Pizza Hut prints its toll-free number on all pizza boxes. When a customer complains, Pizza Hut sends voice mail to the store manager, who must call the customer within 48 hours and resolve the complaint. Hyatt Hotels also gets high marks on many of these criteria.

Getting frontline employees to adopt *extra-role behaviors* and to advocate the interests and image of the firm to consumers, as well as take initiative and engage in conscientious behavior in dealing with customers, can be a critical asset in handling complaints.[67] Research has shown that customers evaluate complaint incidents in terms of the outcomes they receive, the procedures used to arrive at those outcomes, and the nature of the interpersonal treatment during the process.[68] Companies also are increasing the quality of their *call centers* and their *customer-service representatives* (CSRs).

Handling phone calls more efficiently can improve service, reduce complaints, and extend customer longevity. Yet more often than not the problem isn't poor quality but that customers are asked to use an automated voice-response system instead of interacting with a customer-service representative. Although some automated voices are actually popular with customers—the unfailingly polite and chipper voice of Amtrak's "Julie" consistently wins kudos from callers—most just incite frustration and even rage. One savvy entrepreneur took that rage and capitalized on it.

GETHUMAN.COM

Boston-based entrepreneur Paul English got so fed up with automated voice-response systems that he started a Web log listing all the ways callers could bypass them. The blog was so popular, he turned it into the gethuman.com Web site, which now lists over 500 companies and provides keys consumers can use to get around their telephone "trees" to reach a human. If you want to reach a person at Bank of America, for instance, the site directs you to press zero twice after each prompt. The gethuman.com Web site gets over 10,000 hits a day, proving that this issue has touched a nerve with today's consumers. But English is not only devoted to helping consumers, he also has amassed feedback on how companies can improve their automated response systems, which he has condensed into the "gethuman standard." Some of its suggestions are:

- Callers should always be able to press zero, or say "operator," to get to a human.
- The system should always give estimated wait times and updates every 60 seconds.
- Callers should not be forced to listen to long, verbose prompts.
- When a human is not available, callers should always be offered the option to be called back when one is.

For more suggestions and the gethuman core principles, you can go to www.gethuman.com.[69]

SATISFYING EMPLOYEES AS WELL AS CUSTOMERS Excellent service companies know that positive employee attitudes will promote stronger customer loyalty. Instilling a strong customer orientation in employees can also increase their job satisfaction and commitment, especially if they're in service settings that allow for a high degree of customer-contact time. Employees thrive in customer-contact positions when they have an internal drive to (1) pamper customers, (2) accurately read customer needs, (3) develop a personal relationship with customers, and (4) deliver quality service to solve customers' problems.[70]

Consistent with this reasoning, Sears found a high correlation between customer satisfaction, employee satisfaction, and store profitability. In companies such as Hallmark, John Deere, and Four Seasons Hotels, employees exhibit real company pride. Consider the crucial role of employees with Paychex Inc., a leading provider of payroll and human resource services.

PAYCHEX

Headquartered in Rochester, New York, Paychex has more than 100 offices and serves approximately 43,000 clients nationwide. In 2007, Paychex was ranked number 70 on *Fortune*'s very competitive annual "100 Best Companies to Work For" list. Paychex has made the list for four of the past six years for being a place where, in the words of its CEO Jonathan J. Judge, ". . . employees can't wait to get to work—a place where employees are genuinely valued and where their opinions matter." Benefits include two extra holidays a year, $4,000 in adoption aid, new flex schedules in which employees have the option of working four 10-hour days, tablet PCs replacing bulky laptops for all salespeople, and a generous tuition reimbursement policy. The University of Paychex, the company's training and development center, provided more than 1.2 million hours of training for Paychex employees during fiscal 2006, with an average of 121 hours of training per Paychex employee. The emphasis on training is the reason there's so much promotion from within. "The people who packed our payroll are now regional managers," says Keysha McDougal-Brown, a client service manager in one of Paychex's offices.[71]

Given the importance of positive employee attitudes to customer satisfaction, service companies must attract the best employees they can find. They need to market a career rather than just a job. They must design a sound training program and provide support and rewards for good performance. They can use the intranet, internal newsletters, daily reminders, and employee roundtables to reinforce customer-centered attitudes. Finally, they must audit employee job satisfaction regularly.

::: Managing Service Brands

Some of the world's strongest brands are services—consider financial service leaders such as Citicorp, American Express, JP Morgan, HSBC, and Goldman Sachs. Like any brand, service brands must be skillful at differentiating themselves and developing appropriate brand strategies.

Differentiating Services

Service marketers frequently complain about the difficulty of differentiating their services. The deregulation of several major service industries—communications, transportation, energy, banking—has resulted in intense price competition. To the extent that customers view a service as fairly homogeneous, they care less about the provider than about the price.

Marketers, however, can differentiate their service offerings in many ways, through people and processes that add value. The offering can include innovative features. What the customer expects is called the *primary service package.* Vanguard, the second-largest no-load mutual fund company, has a unique client ownership structure that lowers costs and permits better fund returns. Strongly differentiated from many competitors, the brand grew through word of mouth, PR, and viral marketing.[72]

The provider can add *secondary service features* to the package. In the hotel industry, various chains have introduced such secondary service features as merchandise for sale, free breakfast buffets, and loyalty award programs. Marriott is setting up hotel rooms for high-tech travelers who need accommodations that will support computers, fax machines, and e-mail.

Many companies are using the Web to offer secondary service features that were never possible before. Conversely, other service providers, including large drugstore chains, are adding a human element to combat competition from online businesses. As in-store pharmacies see competition from low-cost online mail-order drugstores, they are playing up the presence of on-site health care professionals. For instance, Brooks Pharmacy is establishing "RX Care Centers" in many of its remodeled stores. There are private consulting rooms where pharmacists can speak at length with patients about complicated prescription benefit plans, potentially dangerous drug interactions, and embarrassing subjects like urinary incontinence.[73]

Sometimes the company achieves differentiation through the sheer range of its service offerings and the success of its cross-selling efforts. The major challenge is that most service offerings and innovations are easily copied. Still, the company that regularly introduces innovations will gain a succession of temporary advantages over competitors.

SCHNEIDER NATIONAL

Schneider National is the world's largest long-haul truckload freight carrier, with $3 billion in revenues and more than 40,000 bright orange tractors and trailers on the roads. Although the core benefit is to move freight from one location to another, Don Schneider is in the *customer solutions* business. His company is expert at providing a cost-minimizing trailer for each load. Schneider offers service guarantees backed by monetary incentives for meeting tight schedules and runs driver-training programs to improve driver performance. Dispatchers are assigned to large customers. Schneider was the first to introduce a computerized tracking system in each truck, and the firm received the single top national prize in 2006 from The Institute for Operations Research and the Management Sciences for their use of modeling techniques. To actively recruit the best drivers, Schneider advertises on television shows such as *Trick My Truck*, satellite radio, newspapers, and online; employs Webinars and PR; and partners with AARP, local organizations, and veteran groups. Even painting the trucks orange was part of the branding strategy.[74]

Creativity and innovation is as vital in services as in any industry. There are always ways to improve the customer experience. When a group of hospitality and travel industry experts convened late in 2006 to share their insights into what the ideal 2025 hotel might look like, their visions suggested a totally transformed service experience. One idea, turning hotels into retail showrooms where guests can try out and buy displayed items, was later adopted by chains such as Hyatt and Kimpton. Some of the other ideas have yet to be implemented and may take more time, but they help point out how achieving service excellence is a never-ending process:[75]

1. Kinetic corridors could light up with a blanket of stars and illuminated signs to provide guests with an easy, relaxing entry to their rooms.
2. A multipurpose bed could be flipped over to create more work surfaces or rise all the way up to be a ceiling panel.
3. A multitask chair could be equipped with reading lights, fold-up tablet tray tables, integrated speakers near the ears, and a muscle massager.

Schneider National has differentiated its nationwide trucking business in a number of ways, including computerized tracking for each truck, monetary rewards for drivers who meet tight schedules, and unmistakably orange trucks.

Developing Brand Strategies for Services

Developing brand strategies for a service brand requires special attention to choosing brand elements, establishing image dimensions, and devising the branding strategy.

CHOOSING BRAND ELEMENTS Because services are intangible, and because customers often make decisions and arrangements about them away from the actual service location itself (at home or at work), brand recall becomes critically important. So an easy-to-remember brand name is critical.

Other brand elements—logos, symbols, characters, and slogans—can also "pick up the slack" and complement the brand name to build brand awareness and brand image. These brand elements often attempt to make the service and some of its key benefits more tangible, concrete, and real—for example, the "friendly skies" of United, the "good hands" of Allstate, and the "bullish" nature of Merrill Lynch.

Because a physical product does not exist, the physical facilities of the service provider—its primary and secondary signage, environmental design and reception area, apparel, collateral material, and so on—are especially important. All aspects of the service delivery process can be branded, which is why Allied Van Lines is concerned about the appearance of its drivers and laborers; why UPS has developed such strong equity with its brown trucks, and why DoubleTree hotels offers warm, fresh-baked cookies as a means of symbolizing care and friendliness.

ESTABLISHING IMAGE DIMENSIONS Given the human nature of services, it's no surprise that brand personality is an important image dimension for services. Starwood trains its hotel employees and call center operators to convey different experiences for the firm's different hotel chains: Sheraton is positioned as warm, comforting, and casual; Westin is positioned in terms of renewal and is a little more formal; Four Points by Sheraton is designed to be all about honest, uncomplicated comfort.[76]

Service firms can also design marketing communication and information programs so that consumers learn more about the brand than the information they get from service encounters alone. Comcast's "It's Comcastic!" ad campaign, created by their ad agency Goodby, Silverstein & Partners, was a multifaceted campaign designed to confidently, but humorously brand the cable provider as the premiere content provider for all entertainment needs. Backed by a vibrant Web site, the ads reinforced service benefits by cleverly using doctored archival footage from popular past TV shows. The ads were deemed the best campaign of 2005 by *Adweek* magazine.

DEVISING BRANDING STRATEGY Finally, services also must consider developing a brand hierarchy and brand portfolio that permits positioning and targeting of different market segments. Marketers can brand classes of service vertically on the basis of price and quality. Vertical extensions often require subbranding strategies that combine the corporate name with an individual brand name or modifier. In the hotel and airlines industries, brand lines and portfolios have been created by brand extension and introductions. Hilton Hotels has a portfolio of brands that includes Hilton Garden Inns to target budget-conscious business travelers and compete with the popular Courtyard by Marriott chain, as well as DoubleTree, Embassy Suites, Homewood Suites, and Hampton Inn. Cirque du Soleil has adopted a very disciplined branding strategy.[77]

CIRQUE DU SOLEIL

In its 25-year history, Cirque du Soleil (French for "circus of the sun") has continually broken loose from circus convention. It takes traditional ingredients such as trapeze artists, clowns, muscle men, and contortionists and places them in a nontraditional setting with lavish costumes, New Age music, and spectacular stage designs. And it eliminates other commonly observed elements—there are no animals. Each production is loosely tied together with a theme such as "a tribute to the nomadic soul" (*Varekai*) or "a phantasmagoria of urban life" (*Saltimbanco*). The group has grown from its Quebec street-performance roots to become a half-billion dollar enterprise with 3,000 employees on four continents entertaining audiences of millions annually. Part of the success is a company culture that encourages artistic creativity and innovation and carefully safeguards the brand (see Figure 13.8). Each new production is created in-house—roughly one a year—and is unique: There are no duplicate touring companies. In addition to using a varied mix of media and local promotion, an extensive interactive e-mail program to its million-plus-member Cirque Club creates an online community of fans—20% to 30% of all ticket sales for touring shows come from club members. The Cirque du Soleil brand has expanded to encompass a record label, a retail operation, and resident productions in Las Vegas (five in all), Orlando, and Tokyo. ■

Cirque du Soleil's branding strategy includes spectacular themed performances by circus players with elaborate costumes and New Age music—and no animals. Each touring production is unique; there are no duplicate casts, protecting the brand from overexposure and easy imitation.

FIG. 13.8

Flying High without a Net: Cirque du Soleil's Formula for Creative Success

1. **Cast teams for creative conflict.**
   Cirque officials generally make sure there's a mix of nationalities and viewpoints when they draft a creative team. Then they lock creators in a room with the instructions, "Don't come out till you have something great."
2. **Always shoot for the triple somersault.**
   Cirque's founder, Guy Laliberte, is famous for asking his people to stretch beyond the great to the jaw-dropping. "It's a commitment to a degree of sophistication and performance that distinguishes Cirque du Soleil productions from their less demanding peers," says coach Boris Verkhovsky.
3. **Recruit the near-great.**
   Elite athletes who just missed the national team generally have the same work ethic, the same tricks, and nearly the same skills as medal winners. The difference: They still have something to prove, and they're rarely prima donnas.
4. **Push the envelope—at the interview.**
   Cirque scouts routinely ask candidates to do something unexpected at their audition: Climb a rope . . . then sing a song when you get to the top ("Happy Birthday" is forbidden). It's a good way to find talent that's multidimensional and comfortable improvising, not to mention a great character test.
5. **Don't be greedy.**
   Cirque limits its show production to one a year. "If we want to have fun creating shows and pushing the boundaries, one show a year is good enough for us. We don't want to jeopardize quality," Lamarre says. Besides, "if there's not a creative challenge, we're not going to do a deal, regardless of the financial impact."
6. **Protect creative teams from business pressures.**
   Lamarre isolates his creative teams from the Cirque du Soleil "machine." "I want them to eat and breathe their show," he says, "and keeping them away from day-to-day operations is the best thing."

Source: Linda Tischler, "Join the Circus," *Fast Company* (July 2005): 53_58. Reprinted by permission of Fast Company via Copyright Clearance Center.

::: ManagingProduct-SupportServices

No less important than service industries are product-based industries that must provide a service bundle. Manufacturers of equipment—small appliances, office machines, tractors, mainframes, airplanes—all must provide *product-support services.* Product-support service is becoming a major battleground for competitive advantage.

Chapter 12 described how products could be augmented with key service differentiators—ordering ease, delivery, installation, customer training, customer consulting, maintenance, and repair. Some equipment companies, such as Caterpillar Tractor and John Deere, make over 50% of their profits from these services. In the global marketplace, companies that make a good product but provide poor local service support are seriously disadvantaged.

Identifying and Satisfying Customer Needs

Customers have three specific worries:[78]

- They worry about reliability and *failure frequency.* A farmer may tolerate a combine that will break down once a year, but not two or three times a year.
- They worry about *downtime.* The longer the downtime, the higher the cost. The customer counts on the seller's *service dependability*—the seller's ability to fix the machine quickly, or at least provide a loaner.[79]
- They worry about *out-of-pocket costs.* How much does the customer have to spend on regular maintenance and repair costs?

A buyer takes all these factors into consideration and tries to estimate the **life-cycle cost,** which is the product's purchase cost plus the discounted cost of maintenance and repair less the discounted salvage value. A one-computer office will need higher product reliability and faster repair service than an office where other computers are available if one breaks down. An airline needs 100% reliability in the air. Where reliability is important, manufacturers or service providers can offer guarantees to promote sales.

To provide the best support, a manufacturer must identify the services customers value most and their relative importance. In the case of expensive equipment, manufacturers offer *facilitating services* such as installation, staff training, maintenance and repair services, and financing. They may also add *value-augmenting services* that extend beyond the functioning and performance of the product itself. Johnson Controls introduced services that extended beyond its climate control equipment and components business to manage integrated facilities by offering products and services that optimize energy use and improve comfort and security.

A manufacturer can offer, and charge for, product-support services in different ways. One specialty organic-chemical company provides a standard offering plus a basic level of services. If the customer wants additional services, it can pay extra or increase its annual purchases to a higher level, in which case additional services are included. Many companies offer *service contracts* (also called *extended warranties*), in which sellers agree to provide free maintenance and repair services for a specified period of time at a specified contract price.

Product companies must understand their strategic intent and competitive advantage in developing services. Are service units supposed to support or protect existing product businesses or to grow as an independent platform? Are the sources of competitive advantage based on economies of scale or economies of skill?[80] See Figure 13.9 for examples of strategies of different service companies.

Postsale Service Strategy

The quality of customer-service departments varies greatly. At one extreme are departments that simply transfer customer calls to the appropriate person or department for action, with little follow-up. At the other extreme are departments eager to receive customer requests, suggestions, and even complaints and handle them expeditiously. Table 13.4 displays one ranking of companies providing the best customer service.

CUSTOMER-SERVICE EVOLUTION Manufacturers usually start out by running their own parts-and-service departments. They want to stay close to the equipment and know its problems. They also find it expensive and time consuming to train others, and discover that they can

FIG. 13.9 Service Strategies for Product Companies

Source of Competitive Advantage	Strategic Intent: Protect or Enhance Product	Strategic Intent: Expand Independent Service
Economies of scale	■ Apple's iPod music download and transaction management service (iTunes) ■ Otis Elevator's remote monitoring and diagnostics services ■ General Motors' OnStar auto remote diagnostics service ■ Symantec's virus protection and data security services	■ Cardinal Healthcare's hospital inventory-management services ■ Cincinnati Bell's billing services (now part of Convergys) ■ IBM's data-center-outsourcing services ■ Johnson Controls' integrated facilities-management services
Economies of skill	■ Cisco's network integration and maintenance services ■ EMC's storage-management and maintenance services ■ SAP Systems' integration services ■ UTC's utilities field support services	■ Cincinnati Bell's call-center-management services (now part of Convergys) ■ General Electric's aircraft-engine-maintenance services ■ GE Healthcare's hospital equipment—support and diagnostics services for hospital equipment ■ IBM's systems integration services

Source: Byron G. Auguste, Eric P. Harmon, and Vivek Pandit, "The Right Service Strategies for Product Companies," *The McKinsey Quarterly, Number 1,* (2006): 41–51. Reprinted by permission of McKinsey Quarterly.

TABLE 13.4

Top 25 Companies Providing Superior Customer Service

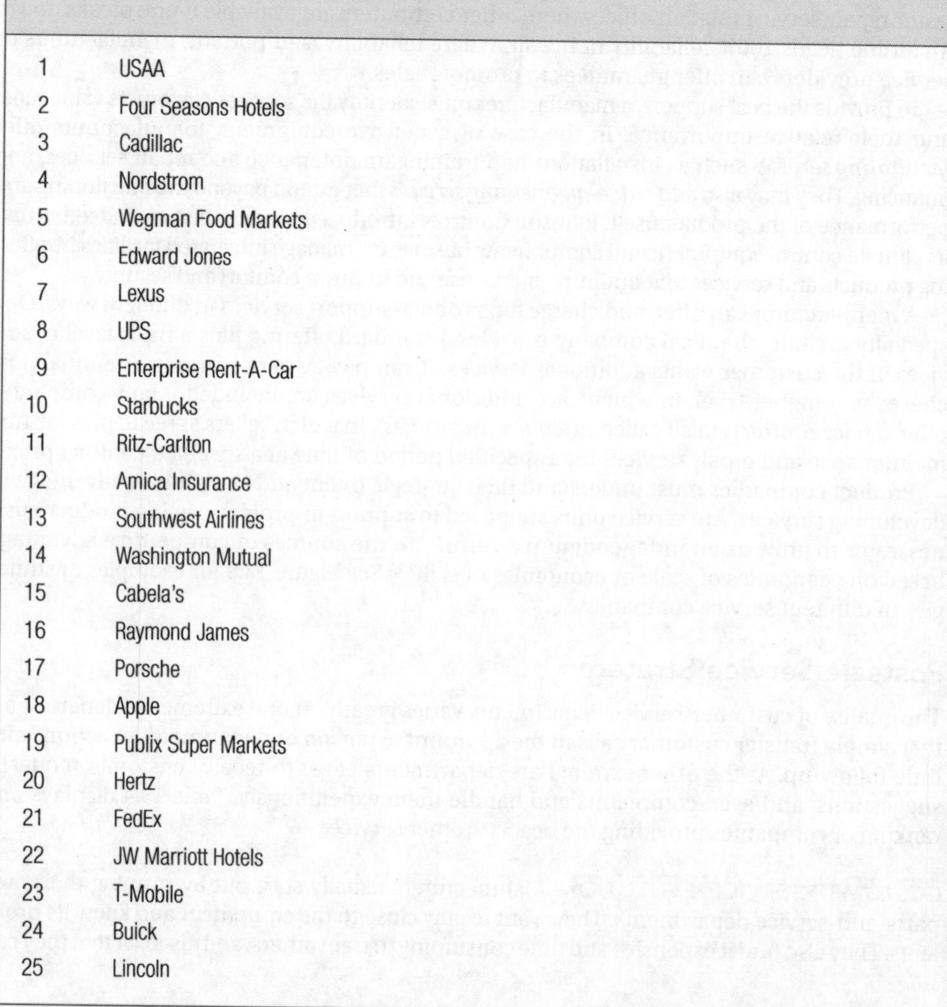

1	USAA
2	Four Seasons Hotels
3	Cadillac
4	Nordstrom
5	Wegman Food Markets
6	Edward Jones
7	Lexus
8	UPS
9	Enterprise Rent-A-Car
10	Starbucks
11	Ritz-Carlton
12	Amica Insurance
13	Southwest Airlines
14	Washington Mutual
15	Cabela's
16	Raymond James
17	Porsche
18	Apple
19	Publix Super Markets
20	Hertz
21	FedEx
22	JW Marriott Hotels
23	T-Mobile
24	Buick
25	Lincoln

Source: Jena McGregor, "Customer Service Champs," *BusinessWeek,* March 5, 2007, pp. 52–64. Based on J.D. Power's database and customer surveys of perceptions about a company's "processes" (e.g., its return policies or reservation procedures) and "people" (e.g., friendliness or expertise).

make good money running the parts-and-service business, especially if they are the only supplier of the needed parts and can charge a premium price. In fact, many equipment manufacturers price their equipment low and compensate by charging high prices for parts and service.

Over time, manufacturers switch more maintenance and repair service to authorized distributors and dealers. These intermediaries are closer to customers, operate in more locations, and can offer quicker service. Still later, independent service firms emerge and offer a lower price or faster service. A significant percentage of auto-service work is now done outside franchised automobile dealerships by independent garages and chains such as Midas Muffler, Sears, and JC Penney. Independent service organizations handle mainframes, telecommunications equipment, and a variety of other equipment lines.

THE CUSTOMER-SERVICE IMPERATIVE Customer-service choices are increasing rapidly, however, and equipment manufacturers increasingly must figure out how to make money on their equipment, independent of service contracts. Some new-car warranties now cover 100,000 miles before servicing. The increase in disposable or never-fail equipment makes customers less inclined to pay 2% to 10% of the purchase price every year for a service. A company with several hundred personal computers, printers, and related equipment might find it cheaper to have its own service personnel on-site.

SUMMARY :::

1. A service is any act or performance that one party can offer to another that is essentially intangible and does not result in the ownership of anything. It may or may not be tied to a physical product.
2. Services are intangible, inseparable, variable, and perishable. Each characteristic poses challenges and requires certain strategies. Marketers must find ways to give tangibility to intangibles; to increase the productivity of service providers; to increase and standardize the quality of the service provided; and to match the supply of services with market demand.
3. In the past, service industries lagged behind manufacturing firms in adopting and using marketing concepts and tools, but this situation has now changed. Service marketing must be done holistically: It calls not only for external marketing but also for internal marketing to motivate employees, and interactive marketing to emphasize the importance of both "high tech" and "high touch."
4. Customers' expectations play a critical role in their service experiences and evaluations. Companies must manage service quality by understanding the effects of each service encounter.
5. Top service companies excel at the following practices: a strategic concept, a history of top-management commitment to quality, high standards, self-service technologies, systems for monitoring service performance and customer complaints, and an emphasis on employee satisfaction.
6. To brand a service organization effectively, the company must differentiate its brand through primary and secondary service features and develop appropriate brand strategies. Effective branding programs for services often employ multiple brand elements. They also develop brand hierarchies and portfolios and establish image dimensions to reinforce or complement service offerings.
7. Even product-based companies must provide postpurchase service. To provide the best support, a manufacturer must identify the services customers value most and their relative importance. The service mix includes both presale services (facilitating and value-augmenting services) and postsale services (customer-service departments, repair and maintenance services).

APPLICATIONS :::

Marketing Debate Is Service Marketing Different from Product Marketing?

Some service marketers vehemently maintain that service marketing is fundamentally different from product marketing and that different skills are involved. Some traditional product marketers disagree, saying "good marketing is good marketing."

Take a position: Product and service marketing are fundamentally different *versus* Product and service marketing are highly related.

Marketing Discussion

Colleges, universities, and other educational institutions can be classified as service organizations. How can you apply the marketing principles developed in this chapter to your school? Do you have any advice as to how it could become a better service marketer?

IN THIS CHAPTER, WE WILL ADDRESS THE FOLLOWING QUESTIONS:

1. How do consumers process and evaluate prices?
2. How should a company set prices initially for products or services?
3. How should a company adapt prices to meet varying circumstances and opportunities?
4. When should a company initiate a price change?
5. How should a company respond to a competitor's price change?

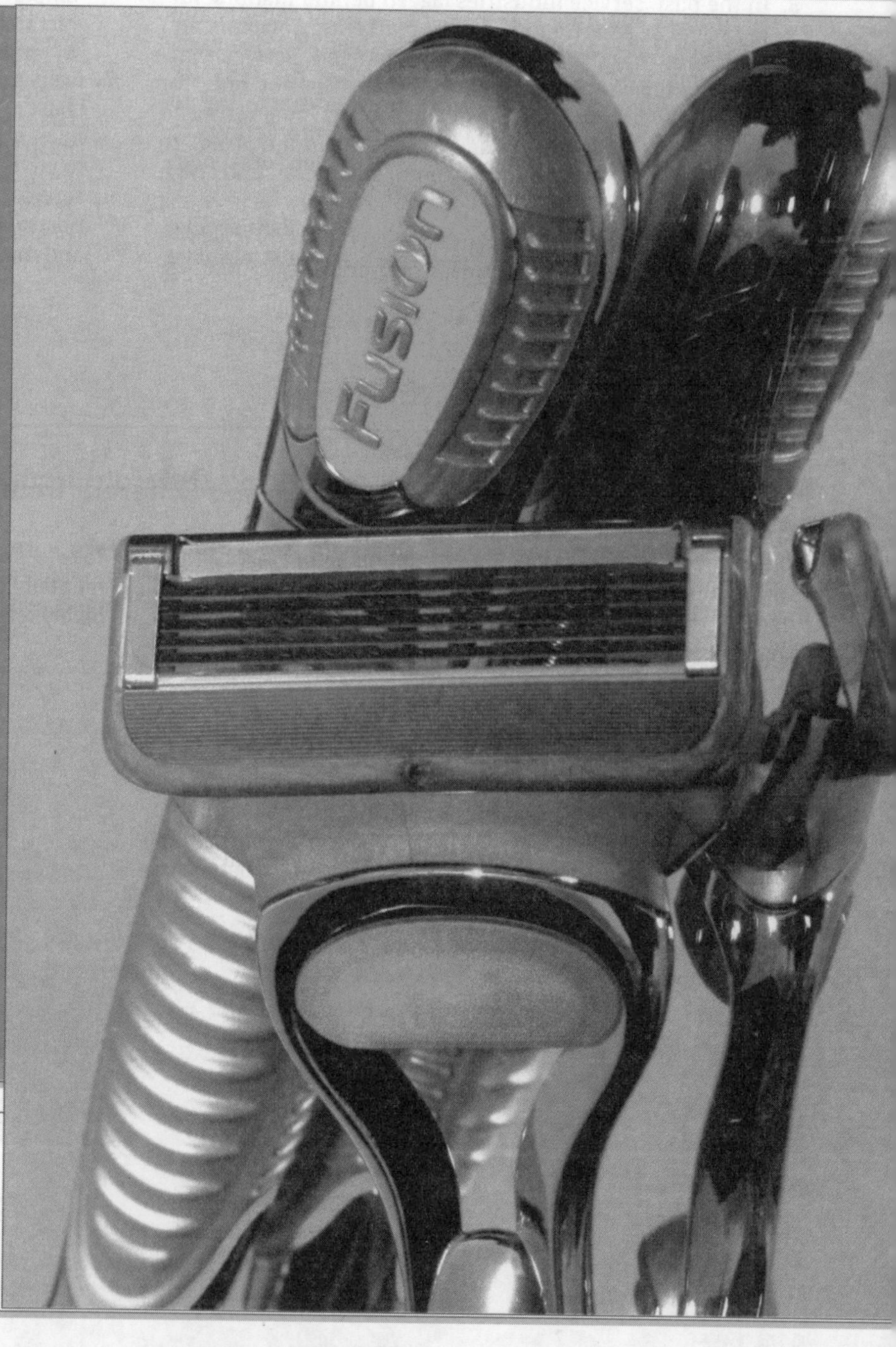

CHAPTER 14 ::: DEVELOPING PRICING STRATEGIES AND PROGRAMS

fourteen

Price is the one element of the marketing mix that produces revenue; the other elements produce costs. Prices are perhaps the easiest element of the marketing program to adjust; product features, channels, and even communications take more time. Price also communicates to the market the company's intended value positioning of its product or brand. A well-designed and marketed product can command a price premium and reap big profits. Consider Gillette.

Gillette has a tradition of product innovation, beginning with the invention of the safety razor by King C. Gillette in 1901. Subsequent product breakthroughs include the first twin-blade shaving system, Trac II, in 1971; the first razor with a pivoting head, Atra, in 1977; the first razor with spring-mounted twin blades, Sensor, in 1989; and the first triple-blade system, Mach3, in 1998. January 2006 saw the launch of the "best shave on the planet" with the six-bladed Fusion—five blades in the front for regular shaving and one in the back for trimming—in both power and nonpower versions. Gillette conducts exhaustive consumer research in designing its new products and markets aggressively to spread the word. Gillette spent over $1.2 billion on research and development after the Mach3 was introduced. About 9,000 men tested potential new products and preferred the new Fusion razor by a two-to-one margin over the older Mach3 >>>

Gillette's Fusion Power razor commands a premium price and about 70% of the global market.

varieties. To back the introduction, Procter & Gamble, which acquired Gillette in 2005 for $57 billion (a record five times sales), spent $200 million in the United States and over $1 billion worldwide. The payoff? Gillette enjoys enormous market leadership in the razors and blades categories, owning roughly 70% of the global market. Gillette also commands sizable price premiums. Refills for the Fusion Power cost $14 for a four-pack, compared to $5.29 for a 5-pack of Sensor Excel. All this adds up to significant, sustained profitability for corporate owner P&G.[1]

The Gillette example reveals the power of pricing. Pricing decisions are clearly complex and difficult though, and many marketers neglect their pricing strategies.[2] Holistic marketers must take into account many factors in making pricing decisions—the company, the customers, the competition, and the marketing environment. Pricing decisions must be consistent with the firm's marketing strategy and its target markets and brand positionings.

In this chapter, we provide concepts and tools to facilitate the setting of initial prices and adjusting prices over time and markets.

::: Understanding Pricing

Price is not just a number on a tag. Price comes in many forms and performs many functions. Rent, tuition, fares, fees, rates, tolls, retainers, wages, and commissions all may in some way be the price you pay for some good or service. It's also made up of many components. If you buy a new car, the sticker price may be adjusted by rebates and dealer incentives. Some firms allow for payment through multiple forms, such as $129 plus 25,000 frequent flier miles from an airline loyalty program.[3]

Throughout most of history, prices were set by negotiation between buyers and sellers. Bargaining is still a sport in some areas. Setting one price for all buyers is a relatively modern idea that arose with the development of large-scale retailing at the end of the nineteenth century. F. W. Woolworth, Tiffany and Co., John Wanamaker, and others advertised a "strictly one-price policy," because they carried so many items and supervised so many employees.

Traditionally, price has operated as the major determinant of buyer choice. Consumers and purchasing agents have more access to price information and price discounters. Consumers put pressure on retailers to lower their prices. Retailers put pressure on manufacturers to lower their prices. The result is a marketplace characterized by heavy discounting and sales promotion.

A Changing Pricing Environment

Pricing practices have changed significantly in recent years. Many firms are bucking the low-price trend and have been successful in trading consumers up to more expensive products and services by combining unique product formulations with engaging marketing campaigns. Even products in fiercely competitive supermarket categories have been able to enjoy price hikes for the right new offerings. Procter & Gamble launched Crest Pro-Health toothpaste at a 50% premium over other premium toothpastes, as well as Olay Definity mass-market skin care line with a $25-plus price point that rivaled the lower end of department store brands. Rival Unilever has struck gold with Axe deodorants, which have pushed prices in the category to over $4. Even Coca-Cola has been able to find higher price points, introducing the Coke Blāk line extension at about $2 per 8-ounce bottle, or roughly twice what it could receive for 2 liters of regular Coke.[4]

Today the Internet is also partially reversing the fixed pricing trend. As one industry observer noted, "We are moving toward a very sophisticated economy. It's kind of an arms race between merchant technology and consumer technology."[5] Here is a short list of how the Internet allows sellers to discriminate between buyers and buyers to discriminate between sellers.[6]

Buyers can:

- ***Get instant price comparisons from thousands of vendors.*** Customer can compare the prices offered by over two dozen online bookstores by just clicking mySimon.com. PriceScan.com lures thousands of visitors a day, most of them corporate buyers. Intelligent shopping agents ("bots") take price comparison a step further and seek out products, prices, and reviews from hundreds if not thousands of merchants.
- ***Name their price and have it met.*** On Priceline.com, the customer states the price he wants to pay for an airline ticket, hotel, or rental car, and Priceline checks whether any seller is willing to meet that price. Volume-aggregating sites combine the orders of many customers and press the supplier for a deeper discount.
- ***Get products free.*** Open Source, the free software movement that started with Linux, will erode margins for just about any company creating software. The biggest challenge confronting Microsoft, Oracle, IBM, and virtually every other major software producer is: How do you compete with programs that can be had for free? "Marketing Insight: Giving It All Away" describes how different firms have been successful with essentially free offerings.

Sellers can:

- ***Monitor customer behavior and tailor offers to individuals.*** GE Lighting, which gets 55,000 pricing requests a year, has Web programs that evaluate 300 factors that go into a pricing quote, such as past sales data and discounts, so it can reduce processing time from up to 30 days to 6 hours.
- ***Give certain customers access to special prices.*** CDNOW, an online vendor of music albums, e-mails certain buyers a special Web site address with lower prices. Business marketers are already using extranets to get a precise handle on inventory, costs, and demand at any given moment in order to adjust prices instantly.

Among the marketers attempting to swim against the trend toward low prices is Coca-Cola with its Coke Blāk.

Both buyers and sellers can:

- ***Negotiate prices in online auctions and exchanges.*** Want to sell hundreds of excess and slightly worn widgets? Post a sale on eBay. Want to purchase vintage baseball cards at a bargain price? Go to www.baseballplanet.com.

How Companies Price

Companies do their pricing in a variety of ways. In small companies, prices are often set by the boss. In large companies, pricing is handled by division and product-line managers. Even here, top management sets general pricing objectives and policies and often approves the prices proposed by lower levels of management. In industries where pricing is a key factor (aerospace, railroads, oil companies), companies will often establish a pricing department to set or assist others in determining appropriate prices. This department reports to the marketing department, finance department, or top management. Others who exert an influence on pricing include sales managers, production managers, finance managers, and accountants.

Executives complain that pricing is a big headache—and one that is getting worse by the day. Many companies do not handle pricing well and throw up their hands with "strategies" such as this: "We determine our costs and take our industry's traditional margins." Other common mistakes are not revising price often enough to capitalize on market changes; setting price independently of the rest of the marketing mix rather than as an intrinsic element of market-positioning strategy; and not varying price enough for different product items,

MARKETING INSIGHT | GIVING IT ALL AWAY

Giving away products for free via sampling has been a successful marketing tactic for years. Estée Lauder gave free samples of cosmetics to celebrities, and organizers at awards shows to this day like to lavish award winners with extensive free items or gifts known as "swag." Other manufacturers, such as Gillette and HP, have built their business model around selling the host product essentially at cost and making money on the sale of necessary supplies, such as razor blades and printer ink.

With the advent of the Internet, software companies began to adopt similar practices. Adobe gave away PDF Reader for free in 1994, as did Macromedia with its Shockwave player in 1995. In the process, the software became the industry standard, but the firms really made their money selling the product's authoring software. More recently, a number of Internet start-ups such as Blogger Weblog publishing tool, Flickr online photo management and sharing application, MySpace online community, and Skype Internet phone calls have all achieved some success with a "freemium" strategy—free online services with a premium component. Venture capitalists and entrepreneurs believe that successful online freemium strategies of this kind depend on a number of factors (see Figure 14.1).

Off-line, other firms are also adopting freemium-type strategies. In Europe, profits for discount air carrier Ryanair have been sky high thanks to its revolutionary business model. The secret? Founder Michael O'Leary thinks like a retailer, charging for almost everything but the seat itself:

1. A quarter of Ryanair's seats are free. O'Leary wants to double that within five years, with the ultimate goal of all seats for free. Passengers pay only taxes and fees of about \$10–\$24, with an average one-way fare of roughly \$52.
2. Passengers pay extra for basically everything else on the flight: checked luggage (\$9.50 per bag); snacks (\$5.50 for a hot dog, \$4.50 for chicken soup; and \$3.50 for water); and bus or train transportation into town from the far-flung airports that Ryanair uses (\$24).
3. Flight attendants sell a variety of merchandise, including digital cameras (\$137.50) and iPocket MP3 players (\$165). On-board gambling and cell phone service are projected new revenue sources.
4. Seats don't recline, window shades and seat-back pockets have been removed, and there is no entertainment. Seat-back trays now carry ads, and the exteriors of the planes are giant billboards for Vodafone Group, Jaguar, Hertz, and others.
5. More than 98% of tickets are sold online. The Web site also offers travel insurance, hotels, ski packages, and car rentals.
6. Only Boeing 737–800 jets are flown to reduce maintenance, and flight crews buy their own uniforms.

Ryanair wants to earn revenue on everything but the seats on its airplanes. In addition to charging passengers for baggage and snacks and eliminating frills like entertainment and reclining seats, the carrier sells ad space on the interior and exterior of its planes. This Ryanair Boeing 737 is painted in a special sponsored Vodaphone color scheme.

The formula works for Ryanair's customers, and the airline flies 42 million passengers annually to 127 cities. All the extras add up to 15% of revenue. Ryanair enjoys net margins of 18%, which are more than double the 7% margins Southwest has achieved. Some industry pundits even refer to Ryanair as "Wal-Mart with Wings!" European discount carrier EasyJet has adopted many of the same practices. Some U.S. airlines have now taken notice. Fellow discount carrier Spirit Airlines has begun to charge for checking bags and all drinks; and even nondiscount carriers such as American, Northwest, and Delta have begun to charge extra for aisle seats, headsets, and snacks.

market segments, distribution channels, and purchase occasions. GE CEO Jeffrey Immelt offers a lament to which many executives can relate.[7]

> We're getting the sales force better trained and equipped with better tools and metrics. A good example is what we're doing to create discipline around pricing. Not long ago, a guy here named Dave McCalpin did an analysis of our pricing in appliances and found out that about \$5 billion of it is discretionary. Given all the decisions that sales reps can make on their own, that's how much is in play. It was the most astounding number I'd ever heard—and that's just in appliances. Extrapolating across our businesses, there may be \$50 billion that few people are tracking or accountable for. We would never allow something like that on the cost side. When it

1. Have a product or service that truly stands out. Its performance, ease of use, and reliability should be superior to those of current offerings.

2. Know your up-selling plan from the beginning. Before you even go into beta, make sure you have at least one paid, add-on premium service up your sleeve. Better yet, have more than one.

3. Once you've decided that a product will be given away for free, don't change your mind. "The fundamental 'what's for free' and 'what's for pay' divide needs to be set early," says Adeo Ressi, CEO of Game Trust, a start-up that hosts 45 free games and sells enhancements online. If you make changes, Ressi says, you risk alienating customers accustomed to getting your product for free.

4. Access to your product should be just one click away. The fewer time-consuming plug-ins, downloads, and registration forms required, the better. Otherwise people may get bored or frustrated and abort.

5. Make sure the major bugs have been exterminated. Your product can be in beta, Rimer says, but not "so much in beta that it doesn't work well."

6. Harness the collective intelligence of your users. Måårten Mickos, CEO of MySQL, says customer suggestions can help speed up product improvements or inspire ideas for premium services.

7. Keep improving the product to give users more reasons to stick with it. "The reality is that offering a product for free can be far riskier than if you actually charged for your product," says Howard Anderson, a lecturer at the MIT Entrepreneurship Center. "Only one in 10 companies will succeed at pulling this off."

8. Identify a range of revenue sources. The Epocrates service, which offers medical professionals both free and premium access to reference material via PDAs, doesn't charge just for the premium information. It also charges fees to pharmaceutical firms for surveys it conducts of Epocrates customers. Similarly, MySQL makes money from customer service as well as from fees charged to firms that redistribute the software.

9. Timing is everything. Make sure that revenue from your premium service soon covers the cost of your free service. Otherwise, cut your losses and move on to the next start-up.

Sources: Peter J. Howe, "The Next Pinch: Fees to Check Bags," *Boston Globe,* March 8, 2007; Katherine Heires, "Why It Pays to Give Away the Store," *Business 2.0* (October 2006): 36–37; Kerry Capel, "'Wal-Mart with Wings,'" *BusinessWeek,* November 27, 2006, pp. 44–45; Matthew Maier, "A Radical Fix for Airlines: Make Flying Free," *Business 2.0* (April 2006): 32–34; Gary Stoller, "Would You Like Some Golf Balls with That Ticket," *USA Today,* October 30, 1996.

FIG. 14.1

Guidelines for a Successful Freemium Strategy

comes to the prices we pay, we study them, we map them, we work them. But with the prices we charge, we're too sloppy.

GE is responding by making pricing one of its top three initiatives and instituting a wholesale set of changes:[8]

- A matrix organization dedicated to pricing has been created.
- The CMO, reporting to the CEO, leads the pricing initiative.
- Dedicated pricing managers focus on product pricing, and in each business unit there is generally a VP or director of pricing reporting to the head of marketing.
- Pricing has been added to the GE executive education curriculum and is a mandatory initiative for the Commercial Excellence Council of Top 100 GE executives.
- A Global Pricing Council, made up of pricing leaders from each GE business unit, is looking for best pricing practices across GE and seeding them throughout the organization.
- Within large business units, specialized Industry Pricing Councils cater to unique industry needs.

For any organization, effectively designing and implementing pricing strategies requires a thorough understanding of consumer pricing psychology and a systematic approach to setting, adapting, and changing prices.

Consumer Psychology and Pricing

Many economists assume that consumers are "price takers" and accept prices at "face value" or as given. Marketers recognize that consumers often actively process price information, interpreting prices in terms of their knowledge from prior purchasing experience, formal communications (advertising, sales calls, and brochures), informal communications (friends, colleagues, or family members), point-of-purchase or online resources, or other factors.[9]

Purchase decisions are based on how consumers perceive prices and what they consider the current actual price to be—*not* the marketer's stated price. Customers may have a lower price threshold below which prices signal inferior or unacceptable quality, as well as an upper price threshold above which prices are prohibitive and seen as not worth the money. The following example helps illustrate the large part consumer psychology plays in determining three different prices for essentially the same item: a black T-shirt.

ARMANI, GAP, H&M

The black T-shirt for women looks pretty ordinary. In fact, it's not that different from the black T-shirt sold by Gap and by Swedish discount clothing chain, H&M. Yet the black Armani T-shirt costs $275.00, whereas the Gap item costs $14.90 and the H&M one $7.90. Customers who purchase the Armani T-shirt are paying for a T-shirt made of 70% nylon, 25% polyester, and 5% Elastine, whereas the Gap and H&M shirts are made mainly of cotton. True, the Armani T is a bit more stylishly cut than the other two and sports a "Made in Italy" label, but how does it command a $275 price tag? A luxury brand, Armani is primarily known for its suits, handbags, and evening gowns that it sells for thousands of dollars. In that context, it can hardly sell its T-shirts for $15 or even $100. And because there aren't many takers for $275 T-shirts, Armani doesn't make many, thus further enhancing the appeal for status seekers who like the idea of having a "limited edition" T-shirt. "Value is not only quality, function, utility, channel of distribution," says Arnold Aronson, managing director of retail strategies for Kurt Salmon Associates and former CEO of Saks Fifth Avenue; it's also a customer's perception of a brand's luxury connotations.[10]

Understanding how consumers arrive at their perceptions of prices is an important marketing priority. Here we consider three key topics—reference prices, price–quality inferences, and price endings.

REFERENCE PRICES Research has shown that although consumers may have fairly good knowledge of the range of prices involved, surprisingly few can accurately recall specific prices of products.[11] When examining products, however, consumers often employ **reference prices**, comparing an observed price to an internal reference price they remember or to an external frame of reference such as a posted "regular retail price."[12]

All types of reference prices are possible (see Table 14.1), and sellers often attempt to manipulate them. For example, a seller can situate its product among expensive competitors to imply that it belongs in the same class. Department stores will display women's apparel in separate departments differentiated by price; dresses found in the more expensive department are assumed to be of better quality.[13] Marketers also encourage reference-price thinking by stating a high manufacturer's suggested price, or by indicating that the product was priced much higher originally, or by pointing to a competitor's high price.[14]

TABLE 14.1

Possible Consumer Reference Prices

- "Fair Price" (what the product should cost)
- Typical Price
- Last Price Paid
- Upper-Bound Price (reservation price or what most consumers would pay)
- Lower-Bound Price (lower threshold price or the least consumers would pay)
- Competitor Prices
- Expected Future Price
- Usual Discounted Price

Source: Adapted from Russell S. Winer, "Behavioral Perspectives on Pricing: Buyers' Subjective Perceptions of Price Revisited," in *Issues in Pricing: Theory and Research,* ed. Timothy Devinney (Lexington, MA: Lexington Books, 1988), pp. 35–57.

CONSUMER ELECTRONICS

On JVC's Web site, the manufacturer's suggested retail price often bears no relationship to what a retailer would charge for the same item. For instance, in the Spring of 2007, for the GR-D370 model of a mini digital video camcorder, JVC suggests a retail price of $330.00, but Amazon.com was selling it through its RitzCamera merchant associate for $247.00 and eBay was selling a "like new" version at a "buy it for now" price of $149.00. Compared with other consumer items, from clothing to cars to furniture to toothbrushes, the gap between the prices routinely quoted by manufacturer and retailer in consumer electronics is large. "The simplest thing to say is that we have trained the consumer electronics buyer to think he is getting 20% or 30% or 40% off," said Robert Atkins, a vice president at Mercer Management Consulting. A product manager for Olympus America, primarily known for its cameras, defends the practice by saying that the high manufacturer's suggested retail price is a psychological tool, a reference price that makes people see they are getting something of value for less than top price.[15]

High reference prices in the consumer electronics industry have trained consumers to gravitate toward "sale" prices.

When consumers evoke one or more of these frames of reference, their perceived price can vary from the stated price.[16] Research on reference prices has found that "unpleasant surprises"—when perceived price is lower than the stated price—can have a greater impact on purchase likelihood than pleasant surprises.[17] Consumer expectations can also play a key role in price response. In the case of Internet auction sites, such as eBay, when consumers know similar goods will be available in future auctions, they will bid less in the current auction.[18]

Clever marketers try to frame the price to signal the best value possible. For example, a relatively more expensive item can look less expensive if the price is broken down into smaller units. A $500 annual membership may look more expensive than "under $50 a month" even if the totals are the same.[19]

PRICE–QUALITY INFERENCES Many consumers use price as an indicator of quality. Image pricing is especially effective with ego-sensitive products such as perfumes, expensive cars, and Armani T-shirts. A $100 bottle of perfume might contain $10 worth of scent, but gift givers pay $100 to communicate their high regard for the receiver.

Price and quality perceptions of cars interact.[20] Higher-priced cars are perceived to possess high quality. Higher-quality cars are likewise perceived to be higher priced than they actually are. Table 14.2 shows how consumer perceptions about cars can differ from reality. When alternative information about true quality is available, price becomes a less significant indicator of quality. When this information is not available, price acts as a signal of quality.

Some brands adopt exclusivity and scarcity as a means to signify uniqueness and justify premium pricing. Luxury-goods makers of watches, jewelry, perfume, and other products often emphasize exclusivity in their communication messages and channel strategies. For luxury-goods customers who desire uniqueness, demand may actually increase with higher prices, as they may believe that fewer other customers will be able to afford to purchase the product.[21]

TIFFANY & COMPANY

For its entire history, Tiffany's name has connoted diamonds and luxury. Yet, in the late 1990s during the stock market boom, there emerged the notion of "affordable luxuries." Tiffany seized the moment by creating a line of cheaper silver jewlery, and its "Return to Tiffany" silver bracelet became a must-have item for teens of a certain set. Sales skyrocketed after the introduction of the "Return to Tiffany" collection, rising 67% from 1997 to 2002,

For years the link between price and quality was what made Tiffany special. The luxury jeweler has recently tried to broaden its appeal to ever-younger consumers but must safeguard its high-end image.

with earnings more than doubling over the same time. But the rise in sales of cheaper silver jewlery brought on both an image and a pricing crisis for the company: What if all those teens who bought Tiffany charm bracelets grew up to think of Tiffany's only as a place where they got the jewlery of their girlhood? Starting in 2002, the company began hiking prices again. (The Return to Tiffany bracelet has gone from $110 to $175—a price increase of 30% from 2001.) At the same time, the company launched higher-end collections, renovated stores to feature expensive items that would appeal to more-mature buyers, and expanded agressively into new cities and shopping malls. When the slowdown came in 2005—with earnings and the stock price plunging—sales of items over $20,000 and $50,000 began growing and now lead the company in terms of growth. Still, the firm must be ever careful about diluting its high-end appeal. As one customer says of Tiffany's jewelry, "You used to aspire to be able to buy something at Tiffany, but now it's not that special anymore."[22] ■

PRICE ENDINGS Many sellers believe prices should end in an odd number. Customers see an item priced at $299 in the $200 rather than the $300 range. Research has shown that consumers tend to process prices in a "left-to-right" manner rather than by rounding.[23] Price encoding in this fashion is important if there is a mental price break at the higher, rounded price.

Another explanation for the popularity of "9" endings is that they convey the notion of a discount or bargain, suggesting that if a company wants a high-price image, it should avoid

TABLE 14.2

Consumer Perceptions versus Reality for Cars

Wall Street firm Morgan Stanley used J.D. Power and Associates' 2003 Vehicle Dependability Study, which tracks reliability over three years, and CNW Market Research's Perceived Quality Survey to find out which car brands were potentially over- and undervalued.

Brand	Percentage
Overvalued: Brands whose perceived quality exceeds actual quality by percentage	
Land Rover	75.3%
Kia	66.6%
Volkswagen	58.3%
Volvo	36.0%
Mercedes	34.2%
Undervalued: Brands whose actual quality exceeds perceived quality by percentage	
Mercury	42.3%
Infiniti	34.1%
Buick	29.7%
Lincoln	25.3%
Chrysler	20.8%

Source: David Kiley, "U.S. Automakers Get a Bum Rap." *USA Today,* January 15, 2004, p. B5. Copyright © 2004 USA TODAY. Reprinted with permission.

the odd-ending tactic.[24] One study even showed that demand was actually increased one-third when the price of a dress *rose* from $34 to $39 but was unchanged when the price increased from $34 to $44.[25]

Prices that end with 0 and 5 are also common in the marketplace; they are thought to be easier for consumers to process and retrieve from memory.[26] "Sale" signs next to prices have been shown to spur demand, but only if not overused: Total category sales are highest when some, but not all, items in a category have sale signs; past a certain point, sale signs may cause total category sales to fall.[27]

Pricing cues such as sale signs and prices that end in 9 become less effective the more they are employed. They are more influential when consumers' price knowledge is poor, when they purchase the item infrequently or are new to the category, and when product designs vary over time, prices vary seasonally, or quality or sizes vary across stores.[28] Limited availability (for example, "three days only") also can spur sales among consumers actively shopping for a product.[29]

::: Setting the Price

A firm must set a price for the first time when it develops a new product, when it introduces its regular product into a new distribution channel or geographical area, and when it enters bids on new contract work. The firm must decide where to position its product on quality and price.

Most markets have three to five price points or tiers. Marriott Hotels is good at developing different brands for different price points: Marriott Vacation Club—Vacation Villas (highest price), Marriott Marquis (high price), Marriott (high-medium price), Renaissance (medium-high price), Courtyard (medium price), Towne Place Suites (medium-low price), and Fairfield Inn (low price). Consumers often rank brands according to these price tiers in a category.[30]

The firm must consider many factors in setting its pricing policy.[31] Let's look in some detail at a six-step procedure: (1) selecting the pricing objective; (2) determining demand; (3) estimating costs; (4) analyzing competitors' costs, prices, and offers; (5) selecting a pricing method; and (6) selecting the final price.

Step 1: Selecting the Pricing Objective

The company first decides where it wants to position its market offering. The clearer a firm's objectives, the easier it is to set price. Five major objectives are: survival, maximum current profit, maximum market share, maximum market skimming, and product-quality leadership.

SURVIVAL Companies pursue *survival* as their major objective if they are plagued with overcapacity, intense competition, or changing consumer wants. As long as prices cover variable costs and some fixed costs, the company stays in business. Survival is a short-run objective; in the long run, the firm must learn how to add value or face extinction.

MAXIMUM CURRENT PROFIT Many companies try to set a price that will *maximize current profits.* They estimate the demand and costs associated with alternative prices and choose the price that produces maximum current profit, cash flow, or rate of return on investment. This strategy assumes that the firm has knowledge of its demand and cost functions; in reality, these are difficult to estimate. In emphasizing current performance, the company may sacrifice long-run performance by ignoring the effects of other marketing-mix variables, competitors' reactions, and legal restraints on price.

MAXIMUM MARKET SHARE Some companies want to *maximize their market share.* They believe that a higher sales volume will lead to lower unit costs and higher long-run profit. They set the lowest price, assuming the market is price sensitive. Texas Instruments (TI) practiced this **market-penetration pricing** for years. TI would build a large plant, set its price as low as possible, win a large market share, experience falling costs, and cut its price further as costs fell.

The following conditions favor adopting a market-penetration pricing strategy: (1) The market is highly price sensitive and a low price stimulates market growth; (2) production and distribution costs fall with accumulated production experience; and (3) a low price discourages actual and potential competition.

IKEA

IKEA is using market-penetration pricing to get a lock on China's surging market for home furnishings. When the Swedish home furnishings giant opened its first store in Beijing in 2002, shoppers would come in mainly to take advantage of the air-conditioning and the decorating ideas on display. Outside the store, shops were selling copies of IKEA's furniture designs at a fraction of IKEA's prices. The only way for IKEA to lure China's price-sensitive and frugal customers was to drastically slash its prices. By stocking its Chinese stores with Chinese-made products, IKEA has been able to slash prices as low as 70% below its own prices outside China. The move has worked. Customers are taking their low-priced goods to the check-out counters in droves, and IKEA is building its largest store in the world—aside from the flagship store in Stockholm—in Beijing. Western brands in China usually price products such as makeup and running shoes 20% to 30% higher than in their other markets, both to make up for China's high import taxes and to give their products added cachet. But with 43% market share in China's homewares segment alone, IKEA is proving that it pays to buck a pricing trend.[32]

MAXIMUM MARKET SKIMMING Companies unveiling a new technology favor setting high prices to *maximize market skimming.* Sony is a frequent practitioner of **market-skimming pricing**, in which prices start high and slowly drop over time. When Sony introduced the world's first high-definition television (HDTV) to the Japanese market in 1990, it was priced at $43,000. So that Sony could "skim" the maximum amount of revenue from the various segments of the market, the price dropped steadily through the years—a 28-inch Sony HDTV cost just over $6,000 in 1993 and a 40-inch Sony HDTV about $1,200 in 2007.

This strategy can be fatal, however, if a worthy competitor decides to price low. When Philips, the Dutch electronics manufacturer, priced its videodisc players to make a profit on each player, Japanese competitors priced low and succeeded in building their market share rapidly, which in turn pushed down their costs substantially.

Market skimming makes sense under the following conditions: (1) A sufficient number of buyers have a high current demand; (2) the unit costs of producing a small volume are not so high that they cancel the advantage of charging what the traffic will bear; (3) the high initial price does not attract more competitors to the market; (4) the high price communicates the image of a superior product.

PRODUCT-QUALITY LEADERSHIP A company might aim to be the *product-quality leader* in the market. Many brands strive to be "affordable luxuries"—products or services characterized by high levels of perceived quality, taste, and status with a price just high enough not to be out of consumers' reach. Brands such as Starbucks coffee, Aveda shampoo, Victoria's Secret lingerie, BMW cars, and Viking ranges have been able to position themselves as quality leaders in their categories, combining quality, luxury, and premium prices with an intensely loyal customer base.[33] Grey Goose and Absolut carved out a superpremium niche in the essentially odorless, colorless, and tasteless vodka category through clever on-premise and off-premise marketing that made the brands seem hip and exclusive.[34]

OTHER OBJECTIVES Nonprofit and public organizations may have other pricing objectives. A university aims for *partial cost recovery,* knowing that it must rely on private gifts and public grants to cover its remaining costs. A nonprofit hospital may aim for full cost recovery in its pricing. A nonprofit theater company may price its productions to fill the maximum number of theater seats. A social service agency may set a service price geared to client income.

Whatever the specific objective, businesses that use price as a strategic tool will profit more than those that simply let costs or the market determine their pricing. For art museums, which earn only an average of 5% of their revenues from admission charges, pricing can send a message that affects their public image and the amount of donations and sponsorships they receive.

THE METROPOLITAN MUSEUM OF ART

Should art museums be free? This question arose after New York's venerable Metropolitan Museum of Art hiked its recommended admissions fee to $20 from $15 in 2006, following the Museum of Modern Art's steep hike from $12 recommended to $20 mandatory admission when it reopened in 2004. The cost of operating the Met has risen sharply—from much higher insurance premiums after 9/11 to the cost of providing health insurance

Vodka has no taste or odor to differentiate brands, but Absolut has used sophisticated advertising to position itself as a superpremium brand.

for its employees and heating and cooling its vast spaces. However, only a narrow and perhaps elite segment of the community can pay up to $20 to enter, even though the price level is merely recommended. Attendance by nonwhite visitors at the Baltimore Museum tripled when it instituted limited free hours. Other museums that have eliminated admission, such as the Contemporary Art Museum of Houston, see not only the diversity of visitors but also the level of public donations increase, sometimes enough to make up for the loss of admissions income. Defenders of the Metropolitan Museum say that visitors can still pay as little as a penny, and in fact the use of the "recommended" sign is the Met's way of introducing variable pricing. Those who can afford to pay $20 do so, and they subsidize the others. "It's an imperfect system," said Judith Chevalier, a Yale economist who studies pricing, "but I'm not exactly sure what a better one is."[35]

Step 2: Determining Demand

Each price will lead to a different level of demand and will therefore have a different impact on a company's marketing objectives. The relationship between price and demand is captured in a demand curve (see Figure 14.2). In the normal case, the two are inversely related: The higher the price, the lower the demand. In the case of prestige goods, the demand curve sometimes slopes upward. One perfume company raised its price and sold more perfume rather than less! Some consumers take the higher price to signify a better product. However, if the price is too high, the level of demand may fall.

PRICE SENSITIVITY The demand curve shows the market's probable purchase quantity at alternative prices. It sums the reactions of many individuals who have different price sensitivities. The first step in estimating demand is to understand what affects price sensitivity. Generally speaking, customers are less price sensitive to low-cost items or items they buy infrequently. They are also less price sensitive when (1) there are few or no

FIG. 14.2

Inelastic and Elastic Demand

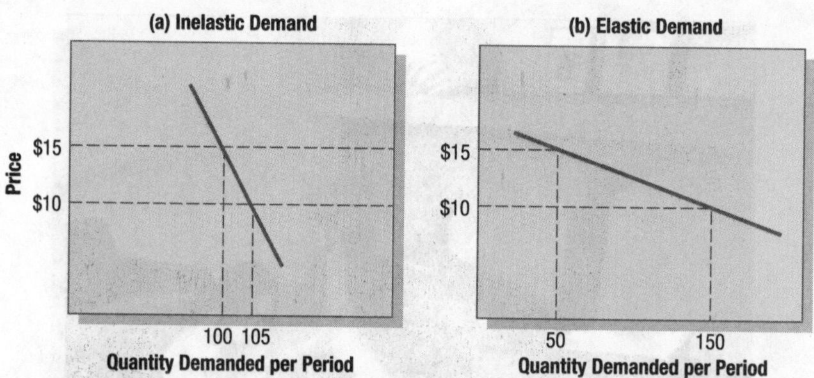

substitutes or competitors; (2) they do not readily notice the higher price; (3) they are slow to change their buying habits; (4) they think the higher prices are justified; and (5) price is only a small part of the total cost of obtaining, operating, and servicing the product over its lifetime.

A seller can charge a higher price than competitors and still get the business if it can convince the customer that it offers the lowest *total cost of ownership* (TCO). Marketers often do not realize the value they actually provide but think only in terms of product features. They treat the service elements in a product offering as sales incentives rather than as value-enhancing augmentations for which they can charge. In fact, pricing expert Tom Nagle believes the most common mistake manufacturers have made in recent years has been to offer all sorts of services to differentiate their products without charging for them in any way.[36]

Of course, companies prefer customers who are less price sensitive. Table 14.3 lists some characteristics associated with decreased price sensitivity. On the other hand, the Internet has the potential to *increase* price sensitivity. Research has found that in some established, fairly big-ticket categories such as auto retailing and term insurance, consumers pay lower prices as a result of the Internet. Car buyers use the Internet to gather information and to use the negotiating clout of an online buying service.[37] But customers must visit multiple sites to realize these savings, and they don't always do so. Targeting only price-sensitive consumers may in fact be "leaving money on the table."

ESTIMATING DEMAND CURVES Most companies make some attempt to measure their demand curves using several different methods.

- ***Surveys*** can explore how many units consumers would buy at different proposed prices, although there is always the chance they might understate their purchase intentions at higher prices to discourage the company from setting higher prices.

TABLE 14.3

Factors Leading to Less Price Sensitivity

- The product is more distinctive.
- Buyers are less aware of substitutes.
- Buyers cannot easily compare the quality of substitutes.
- The expenditure is a smaller part of the buyer's total income.
- The expenditure is small compared to the total cost of the end product.
- Part of the cost is borne by another party.
- The product is used in conjunction with assets previously bought.
- The product is assumed to have more quality, prestige, or exclusiveness.
- Buyers cannot store the product.

Source: Adapted from Thomas T. Nagle and Reed K. Holden, *The Strategy and Tactics of Pricing*, 3rd ed. (Upper Saddle River, NJ: Prentice Hall, 2001), chapter 4.

- ***Price experiments*** can vary the prices of different products in a store or charge different prices for the same product in similar territories to see how the change affects sales. Another approach is to use the Internet. An e-business could test the impact of a 5% price increase by quoting a higher price to every 40th visitor to compare the purchase response. However, it must do this carefully and not alienate customers.[38]
- ***Statistical analysis*** of past prices, quantities sold, and other factors can reveal their relationships. The data can be longitudinal (over time) or cross-sectional (from different locations at the same time). Building the appropriate model and fitting the data with the proper statistical techniques calls for considerable skill.

Advances in database management have improved marketers' abilities to optimize pricing. New York-based Duane Reade pharmacy chain uncovered a new strategy by analyzing its data—set the price markup on diapers as a function of a child's age. Making the newborn's sizes more expensive and big-kids pull-ups cheaper boosted the chain's baby care revenue by 27%. Table 14.4 displays some other examples of successful price-optimization analyses.[39]

In measuring the price–demand relationship, the market researcher must control for various factors that will influence demand.[40] The competitor's response will make a difference. Also, if the company changes other marketing-mix factors besides price, the effect of the price change itself will be hard to isolate.

PRICE ELASTICITY OF DEMAND Marketers need to know how responsive, or elastic, demand would be to a change in price. Consider the two demand curves in Figure 14.2. In demand curve (a), a price increase from $10 to $15 leads to a relatively small decline in demand from 105 to 100. In demand curve (b), the same price increase leads to a substantial drop in demand from 150 to 50. If demand hardly changes with a small change in price, we say the demand is *inelastic.* If demand changes considerably, demand is *elastic.*

The higher the elasticity, the greater the volume growth resulting from a 1% price reduction. If demand is elastic, sellers will consider lowering the price. A lower price will produce more total revenue. This makes sense as long as the costs of producing and selling more units do not increase disproportionately.[41]

Price elasticity depends on the magnitude and direction of the contemplated price change. It may be negligible with a small price change and substantial with a large price change. It may differ for a price cut versus a price increase, and there may be a *price indifference band* within which price changes have little or no effect.

Finally, long-run price elasticity may differ from short-run elasticity. Buyers may continue to buy from a current supplier after a price increase, but they may eventually switch suppliers. Here demand is more elastic in the long run than in the short run, or the reverse may happen: Buyers may drop a supplier after being notified of a price increase but return later. The distinction between short-run and long-run elasticity means that sellers will not know the total effect of a price change until time passes.

TABLE 14.4 Price Optimization to Boost Sales and Profits

Type of Retailer	Before	After
Drugstore	The drugstore was selling tooth-whitening chewing gum with all the other gum.	By putting the whitening gum with the whitening toothpaste and strips, the drugstore sold more whitening gum because it was in close proximity to other products that were often in the same basket.
Electronics retailer	The retailer sold four tiers of 27-inch televisions, with Toshiba as the priciest, then Philips, Sharp, and Sansui.	The retailer increased the price of Sansui and slightly lowered the price of Sharp, and demand rose for Sharp, the more expensive (and more profitable) TV set.
Hardware chain	The chain's best-selling item was a $1 paintbrush, but a new Wal-Mart store offered the same paintbrush for $1, potentially stealing sales.	The chain discontinued the $1 brush but the store lost no ground in brush sales, and profits went up because sales of paint determined brush sales, not price.

Source: Victoria Murphy Barret, "What the Traffic Will Bear," *Forbes,* July 3, 2006, pp. 69_70. Reprinted by Permission of Forbes Magazine © 2007 Forbes LLC.

One comprehensive study reviewing a 40-year period of academic research projects that investigated price elasticity yielded a number of interesting findings:[42]

- The average price elasticity across all products, markets, and time periods studied was –2.62.
- Price elasticity magnitudes were higher for durable goods than for other goods, and higher for products in the introduction/growth stages of the product life cycle than in the mature/decline stages.
- Inflation led to substantially higher price elasticities, especially in the short run.
- Promotional price elasticities were higher than actual price elasticities in the short run (although the reverse was true in the long run).
- Price elasticities were higher at the individual item or SKU level than at the overall brand level.

Step 3: Estimating Costs

Demand sets a ceiling on the price the company can charge for its product. Costs set the floor. The company wants to charge a price that covers its cost of producing, distributing, and selling the product, including a fair return for its effort and risk. Yet, when companies price products to cover their full costs, profitability isn't always the net result.

TYPES OF COSTS AND LEVELS OF PRODUCTION A company's costs take two forms, fixed and variable. **Fixed costs** (also known as **overhead**) are costs that do not vary with production level or sales revenue. A company must pay bills each month for rent, heat, interest, salaries, and so on regardless of output.

Variable costs vary directly with the level of production. For example, each hand calculator produced by Texas Instruments incurs the cost of plastic, microprocessor chips, and packaging. These costs tend to be constant per unit produced, but they're called *variable* because their total varies with the number of units produced.

Total costs consist of the sum of the fixed and variable costs for any given level of production. **Average cost** is the cost per unit at that level of production; it equals total costs divided by production. Management wants to charge a price that will at least cover the total production costs at a given level of production.

To price intelligently, management needs to know how its costs vary with different levels of production. Take the case in which a company such as TI has built a fixed-size plant to produce 1,000 hand calculators a day. The cost per unit is high if few units are produced per day. As production approaches 1,000 units per day, the average cost falls because the fixed costs are spread over more units. Short-run average cost *increases* after 1,000 units, however, because the plant becomes inefficient: Workers must line up for machines, getting in each other's way, and machines break down more often (see Figure 14.3a).

If TI believes it can sell 2,000 units per day, it should consider building a larger plant. The plant will use more efficient machinery and work arrangements, and the unit cost of producing 2,000 units per day will be lower than the unit cost of producing 1,000 units per day. This is shown in the long-run average cost curve (LRAC) in Figure 14.3b. In fact, a 3,000-capacity plant would be even more efficient according to Figure 14.3b, but a 4,000-daily production plant would be less so because of increasing diseconomies of scale: There are too many workers to manage, and paperwork slows things down. Figure 14.3b indicates that a 3,000-daily production plant is the optimal size if demand is strong enough to support this level of production.

There are more costs than those associated with manufacturing. To estimate the real profitability of selling to different types of retailers or customers, the manufacturer needs to use **activity-based cost (ABC) accounting** instead of standard cost accounting. ABC accounting tries to identify the real costs associated with serving each customer. It allocates indirect costs like clerical costs, office expenses, supplies, and so on, to the activities that use them, rather than in some proportion to direct costs. Both variable and overhead costs are tagged back to each customer.

Companies that fail to measure their costs correctly are also not measuring their profit correctly and are likely to misallocate their marketing effort. The key to effectively employing ABC is to define and judge "activities" properly. One proposed time-based solution calculates the cost of one minute of overhead and then decides how much of this cost each activity uses.[43]

ACCUMULATED PRODUCTION Suppose TI runs a plant that produces 3,000 hand calculators per day. As TI gains experience producing hand calculators, its methods improve. Work-

(a) Cost Behavior in a Fixed-Size Plant

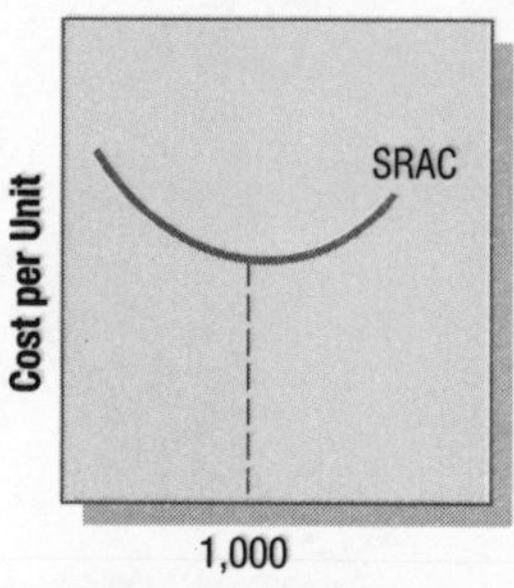

(b) Cost Behavior over Different-Size Plants

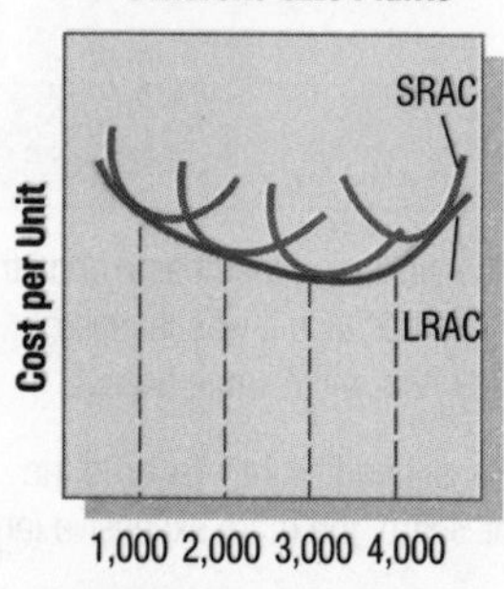

FIG. 14.3

Cost per Unit at Different Levels of Production per Period

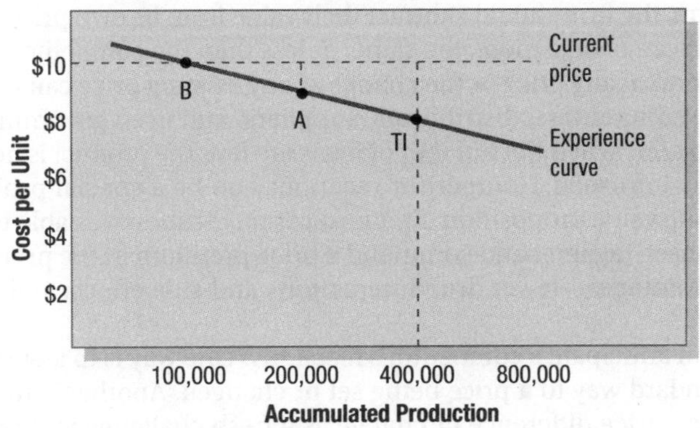

FIG. 14.4

Cost per Unit as a Function of Accumulated Production: The Experience Curve

ers learn shortcuts, materials flow more smoothly, and procurement costs fall. The result, as Figure 14.4 shows, is that average cost falls with accumulated production experience. Thus the average cost of producing the first 100,000 hand calculators is $10 per calculator. When the company has produced the first 200,000 calculators, the average cost has fallen to $9. After its accumulated production experience doubles again to 400,000, the average cost is $8. This decline in the average cost with accumulated production experience is called the **experience curve** or **learning curve**.

Now suppose three firms compete in this industry, TI, A, and B. TI is the lowest-cost producer at $8, having produced 400,000 units in the past. If all three firms sell the calculator for $10, TI makes $2 profit per unit, A makes $1 per unit, and B breaks even. The smart move for TI would be to lower its price to $9. This will drive B out of the market, and even A may consider leaving. TI will pick up the business that would have gone to B (and possibly A). Furthermore, price-sensitive customers will enter the market at the lower price. As production increases beyond 400,000 units, TI's costs will drop still further and faster and will more than restore its profits, even at a price of $9. TI has used this aggressive pricing strategy repeatedly to gain market share and drive others out of the industry.

Experience-curve pricing nevertheless carries major risks. Aggressive pricing might give the product a cheap image. The strategy also assumes that competitors are weak followers. It leads the company into building more plants to meet demand, but a competitor may choose to innovate with a lower-cost technology. The market leader is now stuck with the old technology.

Most experience-curve pricing has focused on manufacturing costs, but all costs can be improved on, including marketing costs. If three firms are each investing a large sum of money in marketing, the firm that has used it the longest might achieve the lowest costs. This firm can charge a little less for its product and still earn the same return, all other costs being equal.[44]

TARGET COSTING Costs change with production scale and experience. They can also change as a result of a concentrated effort by designers, engineers, and purchasing agents to reduce them through **target costing**.[45] Market research establishes a new product's desired functions and the price at which the product will sell, given its appeal and competitors' prices. Deducting the desired profit margin from this price leaves the target cost the marketer must achieve.

The firm must examine each cost element—design, engineering, manufacturing, sales—and consider different ways to bring down costs so the final cost projections are in the target cost range. If this is not possible, it may be necessary to stop developing the product because it cannot sell for the target price and make the target profit. To hit price and margin targets, marketers of 9Lives® brand of cat food employed target costing to bring their price down to "four cans for a dollar" through a reshaped package and redesigned manufacturing processes. Even with lower prices, profits for the brand doubled.

Step 4: Analyzing Competitors' Costs, Prices, and Offers

Within the range of possible prices determined by market demand and company costs, the firm must take competitors' costs, prices, and possible price reactions into account. The firm should first consider the nearest competitor's price. If the firm's offer contains features not offered by the nearest competitor, it should evaluate their worth to the customer and add that value to the competitor's price. If the competitor's offer contains some features not

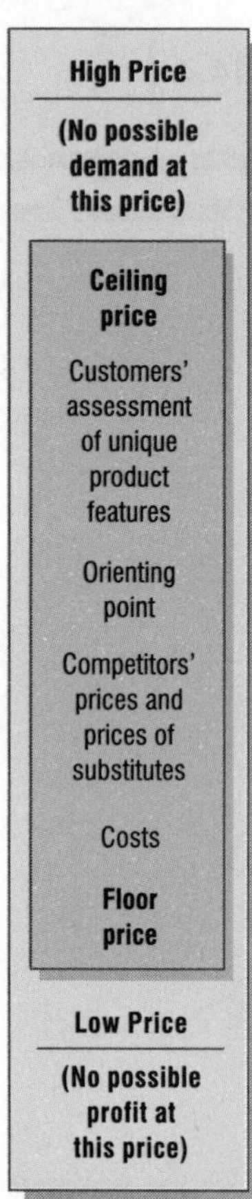

FIG. 14.5

The Three Cs Model for Price Setting

offered by the firm, the firm should subtract their value from its own price. Now the firm can decide whether it can charge more, the same, or less than the competitor.

The introduction of any price or the change of any existing price can provoke a response from customers, competitors, distributors, suppliers, and even government. Competitors are most likely to react when the number of firms are few, the product is homogeneous, and buyers are highly informed. Competitor reactions can be a special problem when these firms have a strong value proposition. Zantac ulcer medication was able to take share away from market pioneer Tagamet and command a price premium in the process because of its performance advantages—fewer drug interactions and side effects and more convenient dosing.[46]

How can a firm anticipate a competitor's reactions? One way is to assume the competitor reacts in the standard way to a price being set or changed. Another is to assume the competitor treats each price difference or change as a fresh challenge and reacts according to self-interest at the time. Now the company will need to research the competitor's current financial situation, recent sales, customer loyalty, and corporate objectives. If the competitor has a market share objective, it is likely to match price differences or changes.[47] If it has a profit-maximization objective, it may react by increasing the advertising budget or improving product quality.

The problem is complicated because the competitor can put different interpretations on lowered prices or a price cut: that the company is trying to steal the market, that the company is doing poorly and trying to boost its sales, or that the company wants the whole industry to reduce prices to stimulate total demand.

Step 5: Selecting a Pricing Method

Given the customers' demand schedule, the cost function, and competitors' prices, the company is now ready to select a price. Figure 14.5 summarizes the three major considerations in price setting: Costs set a floor to the price. Competitors' prices and the price of substitutes provide an orienting point. Customers' assessment of unique features establishes the price ceiling.

Companies select a pricing method that includes one or more of these three considerations. We will examine six price-setting methods: markup pricing, target-return pricing, perceived-value pricing, value pricing, going-rate pricing, and auction-type pricing.

MARKUP PRICING The most elementary pricing method is to add a standard **markup** to the product's cost. Construction companies submit job bids by estimating the total project cost and adding a standard markup for profit. Lawyers and accountants typically price by adding a standard markup on their time and costs.

Suppose a toaster manufacturer has the following costs and sales expectations:

Variable cost per unit	$10
Fixed costs	$300,000
Expected unit sales	50,000

The manufacturer's unit cost is given by:

$$\text{Unit cost} = \text{variable cost} + \frac{\text{fixed cost}}{\text{unit sales}} = \$10 + \frac{\$300{,}000}{50{,}000} = \$16$$

Now assume the manufacturer wants to earn a 20% markup on sales. The manufacturer's markup price is given by:

$$\text{Markup price} = \frac{\text{unit cost}}{(1 - \text{desired return on sales})} = \frac{\$16}{1 - 0.2} = \$20$$

The manufacturer would charge dealers $20 per toaster and make a profit of $4 per unit. The dealers in turn will mark up the toaster. If dealers want to earn 50% on their selling price, they will mark up the toaster 100% to $40. Markups are generally higher on seasonal items (to cover the risk of not selling), specialty items, slower-moving items, items with high storage and handling costs, and demand-inelastic items, such as prescription drugs.

Does the use of standard markups make logical sense? Generally, no. Any pricing method that ignores current demand, perceived value, and competition is not likely to lead to the optimal price. Markup pricing works only if the marked-up price actually brings in the expected level of sales. Consider what happened at Parker Hannifan.[48]

PARKER HANNIFAN

When Donald Washkewicz took over as CEO of Parker Hannifan, maker of 800,000 industrial parts for the aerospace, transportation, and manufacturing industries, pricing was done one way: Calculate how much it costs to make and deliver a product and then add a flat percentage (usually 35%). Even though this method was historically well received, Washkewicz set out to get the company to think more like a retailer and charge what customers were willing to pay. Encountering initial resistance from some of the company's 115 different divisions, Washkewicz assembled a list of the 50 most commonly given reasons why the new pricing scheme would fail and announced he would listen only to arguments that were not on the list. With the new pricing scheme, Parker Hannifan's products were put into one of four categories depending on how much competition existed. About one-third fell into niches where Parker offered unique value and there was little competition, and higher prices were appropriate. Each division now has a pricing guru or specialist who assists in strategic pricing. The division making industrial fittings reviewed 2,000 different items and concluded that 28% of the parts were priced too low, raising prices anywhere from 3% to 60%.

Still, markup pricing remains popular. First, sellers can determine costs much more easily than they can estimate demand. By tying the price to cost, sellers simplify the pricing task. Second, where all firms in the industry use this pricing method, prices tend to be similar and price competition is minimized. Third, many people feel that cost-plus pricing is fairer to both buyers and sellers. Sellers do not take advantage of buyers when the latter's demand becomes acute, and sellers earn a fair return on investment.

TARGET-RETURN PRICING In **target-return pricing**, the firm determines the price that would yield its target rate of return on investment (ROI). General Motors has priced its automobiles to achieve a 15% to 20% ROI. Public utilities, which need to make a fair return on investment, can also use this method.

Suppose the toaster manufacturer has invested \$1 million in the business and wants to set a price to earn a 20% ROI, specifically \$200,000. The target-return price is given by the following formula:

$$\text{Target-return price} = \text{unit cost} + \frac{\text{desired return} \times \text{invested capital}}{\text{unit sales}}$$

$$= \$16 + \frac{.20 \times \$1{,}000{,}000}{50{,}000} = \$20$$

The manufacturer will realize this 20% ROI provided its costs and estimated sales turn out to be accurate. But what if sales don't reach 50,000 units? The manufacturer can prepare a break-even chart to learn what would happen at other sales levels (see Figure 14.6). Fixed costs are \$300,000 regardless of sales volume. Variable costs, not shown in the figure, rise with volume. Total costs equal the sum of fixed costs and variable costs. The total revenue curve starts at zero and rises with each unit sold.

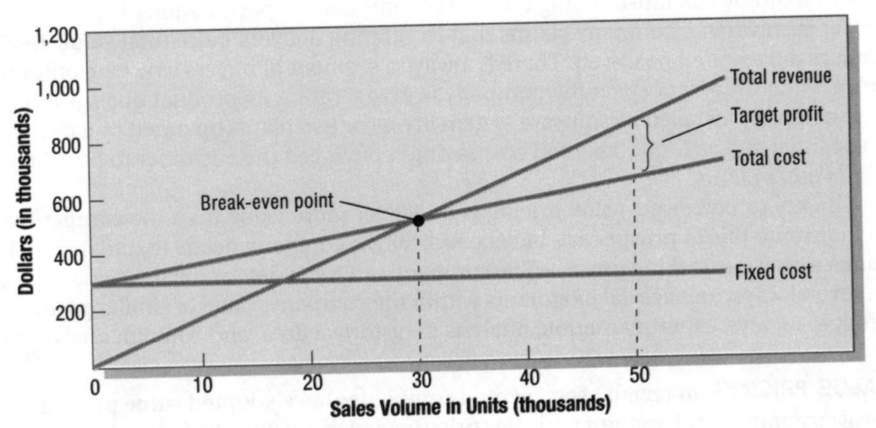

FIG. 14.6

Break-Even Chart for Determining Target-Return Price and Break-Even Volume

The total revenue and total cost curves cross at 30,000 units. This is the break-even volume. We can verify it by the following formula:

$$\text{Break-even volume} = \frac{\text{fixed cost}}{(\text{price} - \text{variable cost})} = \frac{\$300{,}000}{\$20 - \$10} = 30{,}000$$

The manufacturer, of course, is hoping the market will buy 50,000 units at $20, in which case it earns $200,000 on its $1 million investment, but much depends on price elasticity and competitors' prices. Unfortunately, target-return pricing tends to ignore these considerations. The manufacturer needs to consider different prices and estimate their probable impacts on sales volume and profits. The manufacturer should also search for ways to lower its fixed or variable costs, because lower costs will decrease its required break-even volume.

PERCEIVED-VALUE PRICING An increasing number of companies now base their price on the customer's **perceived value**. Perceived value is made up of several elements, such as the buyer's image of the product performance, the channel deliverables, the warranty quality, customer support, and softer attributes such as the supplier's reputation, trustworthiness, and esteem. Companies must deliver the value promised by their value proposition, and the customer must perceive this value. Firms use the other marketing-mix elements, such as advertising and sales force, to communicate and enhance perceived value in buyers' minds.[49]

Caterpillar uses perceived value to set prices on its construction equipment. It might price its tractor at $100,000, although a similar competitor's tractor might be priced at $90,000. When a prospective customer asks a Caterpillar dealer why he should pay $10,000 more for the Caterpillar tractor, the dealer answers:

$ 90,000	is the tractor's price if it is only equivalent to the competitor's tractor
$ 7,000	is the price premium for Caterpillar's superior durability
$ 6,000	is the price premium for Caterpillar's superior reliability
$ 5,000	is the price premium for Caterpillar's superior service
$ 2,000	is the price premium for Caterpillar's longer warranty on parts
$110,000	is the normal price to cover Caterpillar's superior value
–$10,000	discount
$100,000	final price

The Caterpillar dealer is able to indicate why Caterpillar's tractor delivers more value than the competitor's. Although the customer is asked to pay a $10,000 premium, he is actually getting $20,000 extra value! He chooses the Caterpillar tractor because he is convinced that its lifetime operating costs will be lower.

Ensuring that customers appreciate the total value of a product or service offering is crucial. For example, Paccar Inc., maker of Kenworth and Peterbilt trucks, is able to command a 10% premium by its relentless focus on all aspects of the customer experience to maximize total value. Contract Freighters trucking company, a loyal Paccar customer for 20 years, justified ordering another 700 new trucks in 2006, despite their higher price, because of their higher perceived quality—greater reliability, higher trade-in value, even the superior plush interiors that might attract better drivers. Paccar bucks the commoditization trend by custom-building its trucks to individual specifications.

Yet even when a company claims that its offering delivers more total value, not all customers will respond positively. There is always a segment of buyers who care only about the price. Other buyers suspect the company is exaggerating its product quality and services. One company installed its software system in one or two plants operated by a customer. The substantial and well-documented cost savings convinced the customer to buy the software for its other plants.

The key to perceived-value pricing is to deliver more value than the competitor and to demonstrate this to prospective buyers. Basically, a company needs to understand the customer's decision-making process. The company can try to determine the value of its offering in several ways: managerial judgments within the company, value of similar products, focus groups, surveys, experimentation, analysis of historical data, and conjoint analysis.[50]

VALUE PRICING In recent years, several companies have adopted **value pricing**: They win loyal customers by charging a fairly low price for a high-quality offering. Value pricing is thus not a matter of simply setting lower prices; it is a matter of reengineering the company's operations to become a low-cost producer without sacrificing quality, to attract a large number of value-conscious customers.

Among the best practitioners of value pricing are IKEA, Target, and Southwest Airlines. In the early 1990s, Procter & Gamble created quite a stir when it reduced prices on supermarket staples such as Pampers and Luvs diapers, liquid Tide detergent, and Folger's coffee to value price them. In the past, a brand-loyal family had to pay what amounted to a $725 premium over private-label or low-priced items for a year's worth of P&G products. To offer value prices, P&G underwent a major overhaul. It redesigned the way it developed, manufactured, distributed, priced, marketed, and sold products to deliver better value at every point in the supply chain.[51]

An important type of value pricing is **everyday low pricing (EDLP)**, which takes place at the retail level. A retailer that holds to an EDLP pricing policy charges a constant low price with little or no price promotions and special sales. These constant prices eliminate week-to-week price uncertainty and the "high-low" pricing of promotion-oriented competitors. In **high-low pricing**, the retailer charges higher prices on an everyday basis but then runs frequent promotions in which prices are temporarily lowered below the EDLP level.[52] The two different pricing strategies have been shown to affect consumer price judgments—deep discounts (EDLP) can lead customers to perceive lower prices over time than frequent, shallow discounts (high-low), even if the actual averages are the same.[53]

In recent years, high-low pricing has given way to EDLP at such widely different venues as General Motors' Saturn car dealerships and upscale department stores such as Nordstrom; but the king of EDLP is surely Wal-Mart, which practically defined the term. Except for a few sale items every month, Wal-Mart promises everyday low prices on major brands. "It's not a short-term strategy," says one Wal-Mart executive. "You have to be willing to make a commitment to it, and you have to be able to operate with lower ratios of expense than everybody else."

Some retailers have even based their entire marketing strategy around what could be called *extreme* everyday low pricing. Partly fueled by an economic downturn, once-unfashionable "dollar stores" are gaining popularity:

DOLLAR STORES

Dollar stores are shedding their stigma, stocking name brands, and attracting younger and more-affluent shoppers. These ultradiscounters are not dollar stores in a strict sense of the word—they sell many items over a dollar, although most are under $10. They have developed a successful formula for drawing shoppers from Target and even Wal-Mart: Build small, easy-to-navigate stores with parking handy; keep overhead low by limiting inventory; and spend sparingly on store décor and get free word-of-mouth publicity. The two biggest chains, Dollar General and Family Dollar, are breaking ground on new stores at a pace of more than one each day and now operate almost 15,000 stores nationwide. Dollar General stocks health and beauty aids, packaged food and refrigerated products, home cleaning supplies, housewares, stationery, seasonal goods, basic clothing, and domestics. In March 2007, Kohlberg Kravis Roberts, the private equity firm, announced plans to acquire Dollar General and take the company back to privately owned status.[54]

The most important reason retailers adopt EDLP is that constant sales and promotions are costly and have eroded consumer confidence in the credibility of everyday shelf prices. Consumers also have less time and patience for such time-honored traditions as watching for supermarket specials and clipping coupons. Yet, there is no denying that promotions create excitement and draw shoppers. For this reason, EDLP is not a guarantee of success. As supermarkets face heightened competition from their counterparts and from alternative channels, many find that the key to drawing shoppers is using a combination of high-low and everyday low pricing strategies, with increased advertising and promotions.

GOING-RATE PRICING In **going-rate pricing**, the firm bases its price largely on competitors' prices, charging the same, more, or less than major competitor(s). In oligopolistic industries that sell a commodity such as steel, paper, or fertilizer, all firms normally charge the same price. The smaller firms "follow the leader," changing their prices when the market leader's prices change rather than when their own demand or costs change. Some firms may charge a slight premium or slight discount, but they preserve the amount of difference. Thus

BREAKTHROUGH MARKETING | EBAY

Pierre Omidayar, a French-Iranian immigrant, created eBay as a way to help his girlfriend sell and trade her Pez candy dispenser collection. Soon the site grew into a broader auction site where consumers could auction collectibles such as baseball cards and Barbie dolls. The momentum continued, and soon small businesses discovered that eBay was an efficient way to reach consumers and other businesses. Large companies saw it as an opportunity to sell bulk lots of unsold inventory.

By helping buyers get the best price for their items and letting customers decide the price they want to pay, eBay created a pricing revolution. Customers gain control as they choose the price, and the efficiency and wide reach of the site lets sellers make good margins.

EBay generated $6 billion in consolidated new revenues in 36 merchandise categories in 2006. The site has 222 million registered users and receives 43 million unique visitors a month. More than 1 million of its members make their living from the site. Yet, eBay itself doesn't buy any inventory or own the products on its site. It earns its money by collecting a fee for the auction listing, plus a commission that ranges from 1% to 5% when the sale is completed. Merchants report profit margins of 40%. With eBay's expansion into a whole range of other categories—from boats and cars and travel and tickets to health and beauty and home and garden—collectibles now make up only 13% of eBay sales.

Consumer trust is a key element of eBay's success. The company tracks and publishes the reputations of both buyers and sellers on the basis of feedback from each transaction. EBay's millions of passionate users have a voice in all major decisions the company makes through its Voice of the Customer program. Every few months, eBay brings in as many as a dozen sellers and buyers and asks them questions about how they work and what else eBay needs to do. At least twice a week the company holds hour-long teleconferences to poll users on almost every new feature or policy. The result is that users (eBay's customers) feel like owners, and they have taken the initiative to expand the company into ever-new territory.

Although eBay began as an auction site, it has evolved to also offer a fixed-price "buy it now" option to those who don't want to wait for an auction and are willing to pay the price set by the seller. For years, buyers and sellers used eBay as an informal guide to market value. A consumer or businessperson—or even a company with a new-product design—who wanted to know the "going price" for anything from a copier to a new DVD player checked on eBay.

Current CEO Meg Whitman believes eBay's acquisitions of PayPal online payment service in 2002 and Skype Internet voice and video communication service in 2005 have synergistically expanded the company's auction capabilities and revenue sources: EBay buyers and sellers can talk over Skype (generating ad revenue for eBay); Skype callers can use Paypal to pay for any calls that require payment; and Skype will facilitate the further global expansion of PayPal's positioning itself to be a global giant; part international swap meet, part clearinghouse for the world's manufacturers and retailers.

Acquisitions of shopping.com, an online comparison shopping service, rent.com online, an apartment-listing service in 2005, and StubHub online ticket resale service in 2007 provided additional diversification, but eBay has also encountered increased competition from Google and new challenges as it expands globally into tough markets such as China. EBay will need to continue to transform the modern electronic marketplace to achieve lasting success.

Sources: Adam Lashinsky, "Building EBay 2.0," *Fortune*, October 16, 2006, pp. 161–64; Matthew Creamer, "A Million Marketers," *Advertising Age*, June 26, 2006, pp. 1, 71; Clive Thompson, "EBay Heads East," *Fast Company* (July–August 2006): 87–89; Betsy Streisand, "Make New Sales, but Keep the Old," *U.S. News & World Report*, February 16, 2004, p. 40; Glen L. Urban, "The Emerging Era of Customer Advocacy," *MIT Sloan Management Review* (Winter 2004): 77–82; Robert D. Hof, "The EBay Economy," *BusinessWeek*, August 25, 2003, pp. 125–28.

minor gasoline retailers usually charge a few cents less per gallon than the major oil companies, without letting the difference increase or decrease.

Going-rate pricing is quite popular. Where costs are difficult to measure or competitive response is uncertain, firms feel the going price is a good solution because it is thought to reflect the industry's collective wisdom.

AUCTION-TYPE PRICING Auction-type pricing is growing more popular, especially with the growth of the Internet. "Breakthrough Marketing: EBay" describes the ascent of that wildly successful Internet company. There are over 2,000 electronic marketplaces selling everything from pigs to used vehicles to cargo to chemicals. One major purpose of auctions is to dispose of excess inventories or used goods. Companies need to be aware of the three major types of auctions and their separate pricing procedures.

- ***English auctions (ascending bids)*** one seller and many buyers. On sites such as Yahoo! and eBay, the seller puts up an item and bidders raise the offer price until the top price is reached. The highest bidder gets the item. English auctions are used today for selling antiques, cattle, real estate, and used equipment and vehicles. After seeing eBay and other ticket brokers, scalpers, and middlemen reap millions by charging what the market would bear, Ticketmaster Corp. has overhauled the way it sells tickets, including running auctions for 30%

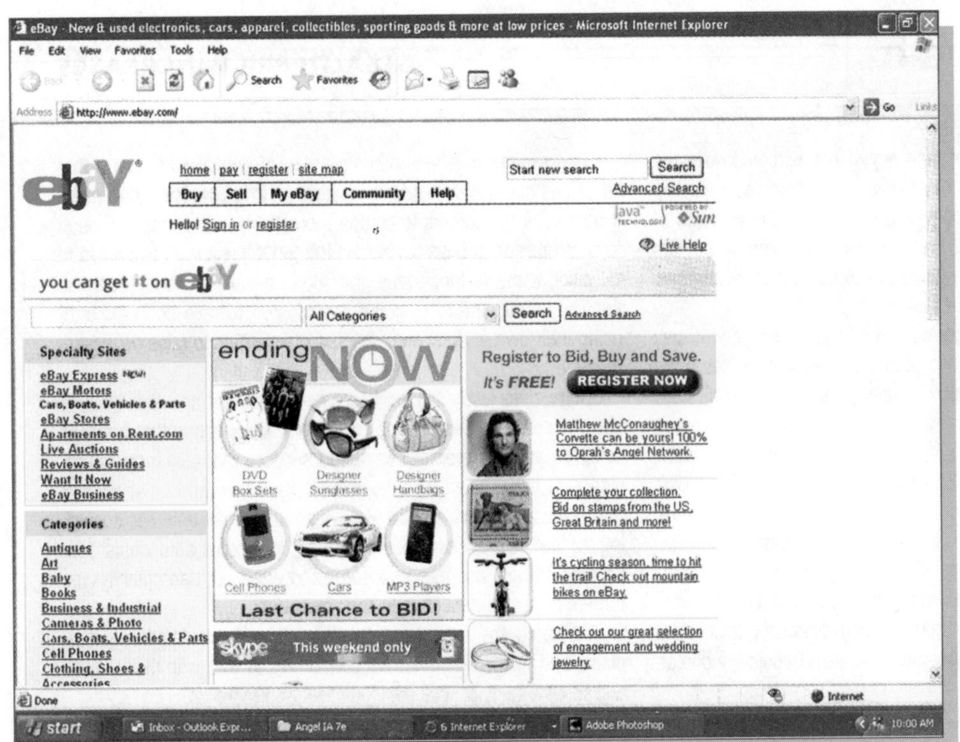

EBay has become the premier auction site on the Web by letting customers choose their price.

of major music tours for popular artists such as Barbara Streisand and Madonna and allowing some customers to resell their seats at its Web site.[55]

■ ***Dutch auctions (descending bids)*** one seller and many buyers, or one buyer and many sellers. In the first kind, an auctioneer announces a high price for a product and then slowly decreases the price until a bidder accepts the price. In the other, the buyer announces something he or she wants to buy, and potential sellers compete to get the sale by offering the lowest price. Each seller sees what the last bid is and decides whether to go lower. FreeMarkets.com—later acquired by Ariba—helped Royal Mail Group plc, the United Kingdom's public mail service company, save approximately 2.5 million pounds in 2003, in part via an auction where 25 airlines bid for its international freight business.[56]

■ ***Sealed-bid auctions*** would-be suppliers can submit only one bid and cannot know the other bids. The U.S. government often uses this method to procure supplies. A supplier will not bid below its cost but cannot bid too high for fear of losing the job. The net effect of these two pulls can be described in terms of the bid's *expected profit.* Using expected profit for setting price makes sense for the seller that makes many bids. The seller who bids only occasionally or who needs a particular contract badly will not find it advantageous to use expected profit. This criterion does not distinguish between a $1,000 profit with a 0.10 probability and a $125 profit with a 0.80 probability. Yet the firm that wants to keep production going would prefer the second contract to the first.

As more and more firms use online auctions for industrial buying, they need to recognize the possible effects it can have on their suppliers. If the increased savings a firm obtains in an online auction translates into decreased margins for an incumbent supplier, the supplier may feel the firm is opportunistically squeezing out price concessions.[57] Online auctions with a large number of bidders, greater economic stakes, and less visibility in pricing have been shown to result in greater overall satisfaction, more positive future expectations, and fewer perceptions of opportunism.

Step 6: Selecting the Final Price

Pricing methods narrow the range from which the company must select its final price. In selecting that price, the company must consider additional factors, including the impact of other marketing activities, company pricing policies, gain-and-risk-sharing pricing, and the impact of price on other parties.

MARKETING INSIGHT | STEALTH PRICE INCREASES

With consumers stubbornly resisting higher prices, companies are trying to figure out how to increase revenue without really raising prices. Increasingly, the solution has been through the addition of fees for what had once been free features. Although some consumers abhor "nickel-and-dime" pricing strategies, small additional charges can add up to a substantial source of revenue.

The numbers can be staggering. Fees for consumers who pay bills online, bounce checks, or use automated teller machines bring banks billions of dollars annually. Penalty fees for late credit card payments more than doubled over a 10-year span—from an average of $13 in 1995 to as much as $34 in 2005—and credit card companies collected $17.1 billion dollars in total late and over-the-limit penalty fees in 2006. The telecommunications industry in general has been aggressive at adding fees for setup, change-of-service, service termination, directory assistance, regulatory assessment, number portability, and cable hookup and equipment, costing consumers billions of dollars. By charging its long-distance customers a 99-cent monthly "regulatory assessment fee," AT&T could bring in as much as $475 million.

This explosion of fees has a number of implications. Given that list prices stay fixed, they may understate inflation. They also make it harder for consumers to compare competitive offerings. Although various citizens' groups have been formed to pressure companies to roll back some of these fees, they don't always get a sympathetic ear from state and local governments, which have been guilty of using their own array of fees, fines, and penalties to raise necessary revenue.

Companies justify the extra fees as the only fair and viable way to cover expenses without losing customers. Many argue that it makes sense to charge a premium for added services that cost more to provide, rather than charging all customers the same amount whether or not they use the extra service. Breaking out charges and fees according to the related services is a way to keep basic costs low. Companies also use fees as a means to weed out unprofitable customers or get them to change their behavior.

Ultimately, the viability of extra fees will be decided in the marketplace, and by the willingness of consumers to vote with their wallets and pay the fees, or vote with their feet and move on.

Sources: Adapted from Kathy Chu, "Credit Card Fees Can Suck You In," *USA Today*, December 15, 2006; Michael Arndt, "Fees! Fees! Fees!" *BusinessWeek*, September 29, 2003, pp. 99–104; "The Price Is Wrong," *The Economist*, May 25, 2002, pp. 59–60.

To read about Australia's Internet provider BigPond and its focus on advertising to drive sales, visit www.pearsoned.com.au/marketingmanagementaustralia.

IMPACT OF OTHER MARKETING ACTIVITIES The final price must take into account the brand's quality and advertising relative to the competition. In a classic study, Farris and Reibstein examined the relationships among relative price, relative quality, and relative advertising for 227 consumer businesses and found the following:

- Brands with average relative quality but high relative advertising budgets were able to charge premium prices. Consumers were willing to pay higher prices for known products than for unknown products.
- Brands with high relative quality and high relative advertising obtained the highest prices. Conversely, brands with low quality and low advertising charged the lowest prices.
- The positive relationship between high prices and high advertising held most strongly in the later stages of the product life cycle for market leaders.[58]

These findings suggest that price is not as important as quality and other benefits in the market offering. One study asked consumers to rate the importance of price and other attributes in using online retailing. Only 19% cared about price; far more cared about customer support (65%), on-time delivery (58%), and product shipping and handling (49%).[59]

COMPANY PRICING POLICIES The price must be consistent with company pricing policies. At the same time, companies are not averse to establishing pricing penalties under certain circumstances.[60]

Airlines charge $150 to those who change their reservations on discount tickets. Banks charge fees for too many withdrawals in a month or for early withdrawal of a certificate of deposit. Dentists, hotels, car rental companies, and other service providers charge penalties for no-shows who miss appointments or reservations. Although these policies are often justifiable, marketers must use them judiciously so as not to unnecessarily alienate customers. (See "Marketing Insight: Stealth Price Increases.")

Many companies set up a pricing department to develop policies and establish or approve decisions. The aim is to ensure that salespeople quote prices that are reasonable to customers and profitable to the company.

GAIN-AND-RISK-SHARING PRICING Buyers may resist accepting a seller's proposal because of a high perceived level of risk. The seller has the option of offering to absorb part or all the risk if it does not deliver the full promised value. Baxter Healthcare, a leading medical products firm, was able to secure a contract for an information management system from Columbia/HCA, a leading health care provider, by guaranteeing the firm several million dollars in savings over an eight-year period. An increasing number of companies, especially business marketers who promise great savings with their equipment, may have to stand ready to guarantee the promised savings, but also possibly participate in the upside if the gains are much greater than expected.

IMPACT OF PRICE ON OTHER PARTIES Management must also consider the reactions of other parties to the contemplated price.[61] How will distributors and dealers feel about it? If they don't make enough profit, they may not choose to bring the product to market. Will the sales force be willing to sell at that price? How will competitors react? Will suppliers raise their prices when they see the company's price? Will the government intervene and prevent this price from being charged?

Marketers need to know the laws regulating pricing. U.S. legislation states that sellers must set prices without talking to competitors: Price-fixing is illegal. Many federal and state statutes protect consumers against deceptive pricing practices. For example, it is illegal for a company to set artificially high "regular" prices, then announce a "sale" at prices close to previous everyday prices.

::: Adapting the Price

Companies usually do not set a single price, but rather develop a pricing structure that reflects variations in geographical demand and costs, market-segment requirements, purchase timing, order levels, delivery frequency, guarantees, service contracts, and other factors. As a result of discounts, allowances, and promotional support, a company rarely realizes the same profit from each unit of a product that it sells. Here we will examine several price-adaptation strategies: geographical pricing, price discounts and allowances, promotional pricing, and differentiated pricing.

Geographical Pricing (Cash, Countertrade, Barter)

In geographical pricing, the company decides how to price its products to different customers in different locations and countries.

PROCTER & GAMBLE

China is P&G's sixth-largest market, yet two-thirds of China's population earns less than $25 per month. So in 2003, P&G developed a tiered pricing initiative to help compete against cheaper local brands while still protecting the value of its global brands. P&G introduced a 320-gram bag of Tide Clean White for 23 cents, compared with 33 cents for 350 grams of Tide Triple Action. The Clean White version doesn't offer such benefits as stain removal and fragrance, but it costs less to make and, according to P&G, outperforms every other brand at that price level.[62]

Should the company charge higher prices to distant customers to cover the higher shipping costs, or a lower price to win additional business? How should it account for exchange rates and the strength of different currencies?

Another question is how to get paid. This issue is critical when buyers lack sufficient hard currency to pay for their purchases. Many buyers want to offer other items in payment, a practice known as **countertrade**. U.S. companies are often forced to engage in countertrade if they want the business. Countertrade may account for 15% to 25% of world trade and takes several forms:[63]

- ***Barter.*** The buyer and seller directly exchange goods, with no money and no third party involved.
- ***Compensation deal.*** The seller receives some percentage of the payment in cash and the rest in products. A British aircraft manufacturer sold planes to Brazil for 70% cash and the rest in coffee.

Procter & Gamble sets different prices for different customers in different locations, often by making slight changes in the product. Clean White, for instance, is the lower-priced version of its detergent for the Chinese market and lacks stain removal ingredients and fragrance.

- ***Buyback arrangement.*** The seller sells a plant, equipment, or technology to another country and agrees to accept as partial payment products manufactured with the supplied equipment. A U.S. chemical company built a plant for an Indian company and accepted partial payment in cash and the remainder in chemicals manufactured at the plant.
- ***Offset.*** The seller receives full payment in cash but agrees to spend a substantial amount of the money in that country within a stated time period. For example, PepsiCo sells its cola syrup to Russia for rubles and agrees to buy Russian vodka at a certain rate for sale in the United States.

Price Discounts and Allowances

Most companies will adjust their list price and give discounts and allowances for early payment, volume purchases, and off-season buying (see Table 14.5).[64] Companies must do this carefully or find their profits much lower than planned.[65]

Discount pricing has become the modus operandi of a surprising number of companies offering both products and services. Some product categories tend to self-destruct by always being on sale. Salespeople, in particular, are quick to give discounts in order to close a sale. But word can get around fast that the company's list price is "soft," and discounting becomes the norm. The discounts undermine the value perceptions of the offerings.

Some companies with overcapacity are tempted to give discounts or even begin to supply a retailer with a store-brand version of their product at a deep discount. Because the store brand is priced lower, however, it may start making inroads on the manufacturer's brand. Manufacturers should stop to consider the implications of supplying products to retailers at a discount, because they may end up losing long-run profits in an effort to meet short-run volume goals.

Kevin Clancy, chairman of Copernicus, a major marketing research and consulting firm, found that only 15% to 35% of buyers in most categories are price sensitive. People with higher incomes and higher product involvement willingly pay more for features, customer service, quality, added convenience, and the brand name. So it can be a mistake for a strong, distinctive brand to plunge into price discounting to respond to low-price attacks.[66] One such distinctive brand is financial information giant Bloomberg LP, which refuses to discount its product.

TABLE 14.5

Price Discounts and Allowances

Discount:	A price reduction to buyers who pay bills promptly. A typical example is "2/10, net 30," which means that payment is due within 30 days and that the buyer can deduct 2% by paying the bill within 10 days.
Quantity Discount:	A price reduction to those who buy large volumes. A typical example is "$10 per unit for fewer than 100 units; $9 per unit for 100 or more units." Quantity discounts must be offered equally to all customers and must not exceed the cost savings to the seller. They can be offered on each order placed or on the number of units ordered over a given period.
Functional Discount:	Discount (also called *trade discount*) offered by a manufacturer to trade-channel members if they will perform certain functions, such as selling, storing, and recordkeeping. Manufacturers must offer the same functional discounts within each channel.
Seasonal Discount:	A price reduction to those who buy merchandise or services out of season. Hotels, motels, and airlines offer seasonal discounts in slow selling periods.
Allowance:	An extra payment designed to gain reseller participation in special programs. *Trade-in allowances* are granted for turning in an old item when buying a new one. *Promotional allowances* reward dealers for participating in advertising and sales support programs.

BLOOMBERG LP

Bloomberg LP markets a subscription service that sells reams of financial data, analytic software to leverage the data's usefulness, trading tools, and even news. Users get all this data via a specialized terminal and a color-coded keyboard that pops the desired information onto the screen. The price is $1,800 a month, or just a little over $1,500 each for multiple setups in the same company, whether 2 or 2,000. Banking on the perceived worth of its product and strong user loyalty, Bloomberg knows it doesn't need to discount. Nor does it need to unbundle its data. Reuters, a competing service, actually has more terminals installed than Bloomberg, but it doesn't come close to getting as much revenue from each. Bloomberg's revenue, on the other hand, keeps going up. Revenues for 2006 were $4.7 billion, with operating profits of $1.5 billion and operating margins a healthy 30%. When Bloomberg needs to raise its rates, it has an equally simple, one-size-fits-all policy; it raises price 5% every two years (customers enter a two-year contract when they subscribe).[67]

At the same time, discounting can be a useful tool if a company can gain concessions in return, such as when the customer agrees to sign a longer contract, is willing to order electronically, thus saving the company money, or agrees to buy in truckload quantities.

Sales management needs to monitor the proportion of customers who are receiving discounts, the average discount, and the particular salespeople who are overrelying on discounting. Higher levels of management should conduct a **net price analysis** to arrive at the "real price" of the offering. The real price is affected not only by discounts, but by many other expenses that reduce the realized price (see promotional pricing section): Suppose the company's list price is $3,000. The average discount is $300. The company's promotional spending averages $450 (15% of the list price). Co-op advertising money of $150 is given to retailers to back the product. The company's net price is $2,100, not $3,000.

Promotional Pricing

Companies can use several pricing techniques to stimulate early purchase:

- ***Loss-leader pricing.*** Supermarkets and department stores often drop the price on well-known brands to stimulate additional store traffic. This pays if the revenue on the additional sales compensates for the lower margins on the loss-leader items. Manufacturers of loss-leader brands typically object because this practice can dilute the brand image and bring complaints from retailers who charge the list price. Manufacturers have tried to restrain intermediaries from loss-leader pricing through lobbying for retail-price-maintenance laws, but these laws have been revoked.

- ***Special-event pricing.*** Sellers will establish special prices in certain seasons to draw in more customers. Every August, there are back-to-school sales.
- ***Cash rebates.*** Auto companies and other consumer-goods companies offer cash rebates to encourage purchase of the manufacturers' products within a specified time period. Rebates can help clear inventories without cutting the stated list price.
- ***Low-interest financing.*** Instead of cutting its price, the company can offer customers low-interest financing. Automakers have used no-interest financing to try to attract more customers.
- ***Longer payment terms.*** Sellers, especially mortgage banks and auto companies, stretch loans over longer periods and thus lower the monthly payments. Consumers often worry less about the cost (the interest rate) of a loan and more about whether they can afford the monthly payment.
- ***Warranties and service contracts.*** Companies can promote sales by adding a free or low-cost warranty or service contract.
- ***Psychological discounting.*** This strategy sets an artificially high price and then offers the product at substantial savings; for example, "Was $359, now $299." The Federal Trade Commission and Better Business Bureaus fight illegal discount tactics. Discounts from normal prices are a legitimate form of promotional pricing.

Promotional-pricing strategies are often a zero-sum game. If they work, competitors copy them and they lose their effectiveness. If they don't work, they waste money that could have been put into other marketing tools, such as building up product quality and service or strengthening product image through advertising.

Differentiated Pricing

Companies often adjust their basic price to accommodate differences in customers, products, locations, and so on. Lands' End creates men's shirts in many different styles, weights, and levels of quality. A men's white button-down shirt may cost as little as $18.50 or as much as $48.00.[68]

Price discrimination occurs when a company sells a product or service at two or more prices that do not reflect a proportional difference in costs. In first-degree price discrimination, the seller charges a separate price to each customer depending on the intensity of his or her demand.

BALTIMORE ORIOLES

In the 2006 season, the Baltimore Orioles lost 9 of 27 games against the New York Yankees and the Boston Red Sox. Yet whereas Orioles fans may have been down in the dumps about a record like this, the Orioles' owners were pleased whenever the Yankees and Red Sox came to Camden Yards. The two teams are popular draws, often attracting droves of fans wearing their caps and jerseys. During a three-game stretch against the Yankees, for instance, the Orioles drew about 48,000 spectators a game, compared to the season average of 26,582. Thus, Orioles management is following the lead of many other major league baseball teams, including the Washington Nationals and Chicago White Sox, and instituting variable pricing. Beginning with its 2007 season, the organization is charging extra for single-game tickets to all games against the Yankees as well as for weekend dates with the Red Sox and Opening Day against the Detroit Tigers. Other teams vary their prices according to the time of the season or day of the week, not the popularity of the rival team. For instance, the Philadelphia Phillies, for the second year running, are increasing ticket prices between Memorial Day and Labor Day.[69]

Variable pricing has come to sports. The Orioles have joined many other major league teams in charging higher prices for weekends and opening day.

In second-degree price discrimination, the seller charges less to buyers who buy a larger volume. In third-degree price discrimination, the seller charges different amounts to different classes of buyers, as in the following cases:

- ***Customer-segment pricing.*** Different customer groups pay different prices for the same product or service. For example, museums often charge a lower admission fee to students and senior citizens.
- ***Product-form pricing.*** Different versions of the product are priced differently, but not proportionately to their costs. Evian prices a 48-ounce bottle of its mineral water at $2.00. It takes the same water and packages 1.7 ounces in a moisturizer spray for $6.00. Through product-form pricing, Evian manages to charge $3.50 an ounce in one form and about $.04 an ounce in another.
- ***Image pricing.*** Some companies price the same product at two different levels based on image differences. A perfume manufacturer can put the perfume in one bottle, give it a name and image, and price it at $10 an ounce. It can put the same perfume in another bottle with a different name and image and price it at $30 an ounce.
- ***Channel pricing.*** Coca-Cola carries a different price depending on whether the consumer purchases it in a fine restaurant, a fast-food restaurant, or a vending machine.
- ***Location pricing.*** The same product is priced differently at different locations even though the cost of offering it at each location is the same. A theater varies its seat prices according to audience preferences for different locations.
- ***Time pricing.*** Prices are varied by season, day, or hour. Public utilities vary energy rates to commercial users by time of day and weekend versus weekday. Restaurants charge less to "early bird" customers, and some hotels charge less on weekends.

The airline and hospitality industries use yield management systems and **yield pricing**, by which they offer discounted but limited early purchases, higher-priced late purchases, and the lowest rates on unsold inventory just before it expires.[70] Airlines charge different fares to passengers on the same flight, depending on the seating class; the time of day (morning or night coach); the day of the week (workday or weekend); the season; the person's employer, past business, or status (youth, military, senior citizen); and so on.

That's why on a flight from New York City to Miami you might have paid $200 and be sitting across from someone who has paid $1,290. Continental Airlines launches 2,000 flights a day and each flight has between 10 and 20 prices. Continental starts booking flights 330 days in advance, and every flying day is different from every other flying day. At any given moment the market has more than 7 million prices. And in a system that tracks the difference in prices and the price of competitors' offerings, airlines collectively change 75,000 different prices a day! It's a system designed to punish procrastinators by charging them the highest possible prices.

The phenomenon of offering different pricing schedules to different consumers and dynamically adjusting prices is exploding.[71] Many companies are using software packages that provide real-time controlled tests of actual consumer response to different pricing schedules. Constant price variation, however, can be tricky where consumer relationships are concerned. Research shows it tends to work best in situations where there's no bond between the buyer and the seller. One way to make it work is to offer customers a unique bundle of products and services to meet their needs precisely, making it harder for them to make price comparisons.

The tactic most companies favor, however, is to use variable prices as a reward for good behavior rather than as a penalty. For instance, shipping company APL Inc. rewards customers who can better predict how much cargo space they'll need with cheaper rates for booking early. Customers are also getting savvier about how to avoid buyer's remorse from overpaying. They are changing their buying behavior to accommodate the new realities of dynamic pricing—where prices vary frequently by channels, products, customers, and time.

Most consumers are probably not even aware of the degree to which they are the targets of discriminatory pricing. For instance, catalog retailers such as Victoria's Secret routinely send out catalogs that sell identical goods at different prices. Consumers who live in a more free-spending zip code may see only the higher prices. Office product superstore Staples also sends out office supply catalogs with different prices.

We've seen that some forms of price discrimination (in which sellers offer different price terms to different people within the same trade group) are illegal. However, price discrimination is legal if the seller can prove that its costs are different when selling different volumes or different qualities of the same product to different retailers. Predatory pricing—selling below cost with the intention of destroying competition—is unlawful.[72] Even if legal, some differentiated pricing may meet with a hostile reaction. Coca-Cola considered using wireless technology to raise its vending machine soda prices on hot days and lower them on cold days. Customers so disliked the idea that Coke abandoned it.

For price discrimination to work, certain conditions must exist. First, the market must be segmentable and the segments must show different intensities of demand. Second, members in the lower-price segment must not be able to resell the product to the higher-price segment. Third, competitors must not be able to undersell the firm in the higher-price segment. Fourth, the cost of segmenting and policing the market must not exceed the extra revenue derived from price discrimination. Fifth, the practice must not breed customer resentment and ill will. Sixth, of course, the particular form of price discrimination must not be illegal.[73]

::: Initiating and Responding to Price Changes

Companies often need to cut or raise prices.

Initiating Price Cuts

Several circumstances might lead a firm to cut prices. One is *excess plant capacity*: The firm needs additional business and cannot generate it through increased sales effort, product improvement, or other measures. Companies sometimes initiate price cuts in a *drive to dominate the market through lower costs.* Either the company starts with lower costs than its competitors, or it initiates price cuts in the hope of gaining market share and lower costs.

Cutting prices to keep customers or beat competitors often encourages customers to demand price concessions, however, and trains salespeople to offer them.[74] A price-cutting strategy can lead to other possible traps:

- ***Low-quality trap.*** Consumers assume quality is low.
- ***Fragile-market-share trap.*** A low price buys market share but not market loyalty. The same customers will shift to any lower-priced firm that comes along.

	Before	After	
Price	$ 10	$10.10	(a 1% price increase)
Units sold	100	100	
Revenue	$1,000	$1,010	
Costs	–970	–970	
Profit	$ 30	$ 40	(a 33⅓% profit increase)

TABLE 14.6

Profits Before and After a Price Increase

- ***Shallow-pockets trap.*** Higher-priced competitors match the lower prices but have longer staying power because of deeper cash reserves.
- ***Price-war trap.*** Competitors respond by lowering their prices even more, triggering a price war.

Customers often question the motivation behind price changes.[75] They may assume the item is about to be replaced by a new model; the item is faulty and is not selling well; the firm is in financial trouble; the price will come down even further; or the quality has been reduced. The firm must monitor these attributions carefully.

Initiating Price Increases

A successful price increase can raise profits considerably. For example, if the company's profit margin is 3% of sales, a 1% price increase will increase profits by 33% if sales volume is unaffected. This situation is illustrated in Table 14.6. The assumption is that a company charged $10 and sold 100 units and had costs of $970, leaving a profit of $30, or 3% on sales. By raising its price by 10 cents (a 1% price increase), it boosted its profits by 33%, assuming the same sales volume.

A major circumstance provoking price increases is *cost inflation.* Rising costs unmatched by productivity gains squeeze profit margins and lead companies to regular rounds of price increases. Companies often raise their prices by more than the cost increase, in anticipation of further inflation or government price controls, in a practice called *anticipatory pricing.*

Another factor leading to price increases is *overdemand.* When a company cannot supply all its customers, it can raise its prices, ration supplies to customers, or both. The price can be increased in the following ways, each of which has a different impact on buyers.

- ***Delayed quotation pricing.*** The company does not set a final price until the product is finished or delivered. This pricing is prevalent in industries with long production lead times, such as industrial construction and heavy equipment.
- ***Escalator clauses.*** The company requires the customer to pay today's price and all or part of any inflation increase that takes place before delivery. An escalator clause bases price increases on some specified price index. Escalator clauses are found in contracts for major industrial projects, such as aircraft construction and bridge building.
- ***Unbundling.*** The company maintains its price but removes or prices separately one or more elements that were part of the former offer, such as free delivery or installation. Car companies sometimes add antilock brakes and passenger-side airbags as supplementary extras to their vehicles.
- ***Reduction of discounts.*** The company instructs its sales force not to offer its normal cash and quantity discounts.

Although there is always a chance that a price increase can carry some positive meanings to customers—for example, that the item is "hot" and represents an unusually good value—consumers generally dislike higher prices. In passing price increases on to customers, the company must avoid looking like a price gouger.[76] Consumer concern and dissatisfaction with high gasoline and prescription drug prices, Coca-Cola's proposed smart vending machines that would raise prices as temperatures rose, and Amazon.com's dynamic pricing experiment whereby prices varied by purchase occasion became front-page news. The more similar the products or offerings from a company, the more likely consumers are to interpret any pricing differences as unfair. Product customization and differentiation and communications that clarify differences are thus critical.[77]

Generally, consumers prefer small price increases on a regular basis to sudden, sharp increases. Their memories are long, and they can turn against companies they perceive as price gougers. Price hikes without corresponding investments in the value of the brand increase vulnerability to lower-priced competition. Consumers may be willing to "trade down" because they no longer can justify to themselves that the higher-priced brand is worth it.

Several techniques help consumers avoid sticker shock and a hostile reaction when prices rise: One is that a sense of fairness must surround any price increase, and customers must be given advance notice so they can do forward buying or shop around. Sharp price increases need to be explained in understandable terms. Making low-visibility price moves first is also a good technique: Eliminating discounts, increasing minimum order sizes, and curtailing production of low-margin products are some examples; and contracts or bids for long-term projects should contain escalator clauses based on such factors as increases in recognized national price indexes.[78]

Given strong consumer resistance to price hikes, marketers go to great lengths to find alternative approaches that will allow them to avoid increasing prices when they otherwise would have done so. Here are a few popular ones.

- Shrinking the amount of product instead of raising the price. (Hershey Foods maintained its candy bar price but trimmed its size. Nestlé maintained its size but raised the price.)
- Substituting less-expensive materials or ingredients. (Many candy bar companies substituted synthetic chocolate for real chocolate to fight price increases in cocoa.)
- Reducing or removing product features. (Sears engineered down a number of its appliances so they could be priced competitively with those sold in discount stores.)
- Removing or reducing product services, such as installation or free delivery.
- Using less-expensive packaging material or larger package sizes.
- Reducing the number of sizes and models offered.
- Creating new economy brands. (Jewel food stores introduced 170 generic items selling at 10% to 30% less than national brands.)

Responding to Competitors' Price Changes

How should a firm respond to a price cut initiated by a competitor? In general, the best response varies with the situation. The company must consider the product's stage in the life cycle, its importance in the company's portfolio, the competitor's intentions and resources, the market's price and quality sensitivity, the behavior of costs with volume, and the company's alternative opportunities.

In markets characterized by high product homogeneity, the firm can search for ways to enhance its augmented product. If it cannot find any, it may need to meet the price reduction. If the competitor raises its price in a homogeneous product market, other firms might not match it if the increase will not benefit the industry as a whole. Then the leader will need to roll back the increase.

GENERAL MILLS

General Mills ran into some trouble by not responding to competitors' price changes. While both private-label cereals and name-brand competitors, such as Kellogg, decreased package sizes and either lowered cereal prices or kept them static, General Mills banked on its brand-name reputation for quality and innovation and kept its prices at premium level. But many customers were reluctant to pay above $4.00 for a box of Cheerios or Lucky Charms. As a result, Kellogg took the lead in the cereal category in terms of dollar share, with 33.8% compared to General Mills' 29.7%. Finally, in 2007, General Mills announced its "right size, right price" strategy, adjusting package sizes downward (as its rivals already had) and lowering its prices.[79]

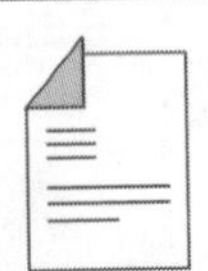

MARKETING MEMO | HOW TO FIGHT LOW-COST RIVALS

London Business School's Nirmalya Kumar spent five years studying 50 incumbents and 25 low-cost businesses to better understand the threats posed by disruptive, low-cost competitors. He notes that successful price warriors, such as Germany's Aldi supermarkets, India's Aravind Eye Hospitals, and Israel's Teva Pharmaceuticals, are changing the nature of competition all over the world by employing several key tactics, such as focusing on just one or a few consumer segments, delivering the basic product or providing one benefit better than rivals do, and backing low prices with superefficient operations.

Kumar believes ignoring low-cost rivals is a mistake, because they eventually force companies to vacate entire market segments. He doesn't see price wars as the answer either: Slashing prices usually lowers profits for incumbents without driving the low-cost entrants out of business. In the race to the bottom, he says, the challengers always come out ahead of the incumbents. Instead, he offers three possible responses that will vary in their success depending on different factors, as outlined in Figure 14.7.

The first approach to competing against cut-price players is to differentiate the product or service through various means:

- Design cool products (Apple; Bang & Olufsen)
- Continually innovate (Gillette; 3M)
- Offer unique product mix (Sharper Image; Whole Foods)
- Brand a community (Harley-Davidson; Red Bull)
- Sell experiences (Four Seasons; Starbucks)

Kumar cautions that three conditions will determine the success of a differentiation response:

1. ***Companies must not use differentiation tactics in isolation.*** Bang & Olufsen has competed effectively against low-cost electronics manufacturers in part because of its strong design capabilities, but also because the company continually introduces new products, cultivates an upscale brand image, and supports modern-looking retail outlets.
2. ***Companies must be able to persuade consumers to pay for added benefits.*** Charging a small premium for greater services or benefits, as Target and Walgreens have done, can be a powerful defense.
3. ***Companies must first bring costs and benefits in line.*** HP's resurgence in the PC industry can be attributed in part to its success in cutting Dell's cost advantage from 20% to 10%.

Kumar cautions that unless sizable numbers of consumers demand additional benefits, companies may need to yield some markets to price warriors. For example, British Airways has relinquished some short-haul routes to low-cost rivals easyJet and Ryanair. Kumar also believes strategies that help an incumbent firm coexist with low-cost rivals can work initially, but over the long haul, consumers migrate to low-cost options as they become more familiar with them.

Another approach that many companies have tried in responding to low-cost competitors is to introduce a low-cost venture themselves. Citing the failure of no-frills second carriers such as Continental Lite, Delta's Song, KLM's Buzz, SAS's Snowflake, US Airways' MetroJet, and United's Shuttle, however, Kumar asserts that companies should set up low-cost operations only if (1) the traditional operation will become more competitive as a result and (2) the new business will derive some advantages that it would not have gained as an independent entity.

A dual strategy succeeds only if companies can generate synergies between the existing businesses and the new ventures, as financial service providers HSBC and ING did. The low-cost venture most likely includes a unique brand name or identity, adequate resources, and a willingness to endure some cannibalization between the two businesses.

If there are no synergies between traditional and low-cost businesses, companies should consider two other options: They can switch from selling products to selling solutions, or even convert themselves into low-cost players. In the former approach, Kumar believes that by offering products and services as an integrated package, companies can expand the segment of the market that is willing to pay more for additional benefits. Selling solutions requires managing customers' processes and increasing their revenues or lowering their costs and risks.

And if all else fails, the best solution may be reinvention as a low-cost player. After all, as noted above, Ryanair was an unprofitable, high-cost traditional airline before it completely—and quite successfully—transformed itself into a low-cost carrier.

In nonhomogeneous product markets, a firm has more latitude. It needs to consider the following issues: (1) Why did the competitor change the price? To steal the market, to utilize excess capacity, to meet changing cost conditions, or to lead an industry-wide price change? (2) Does the competitor plan to make the price change temporary or permanent? (3) What will happen to the company's market share and profits if it does not respond? Are other companies going to respond? (4) What are the competitors' and other firms' responses likely to be to each possible reaction?

Market leaders often face aggressive price cutting by smaller firms trying to build market share. Using price, Fuji has attacked Kodak, Schick has attacked Gillette, and AMD has attacked Intel. Brand leaders also face lower-priced private-label store brands. The brand leader can respond in several ways. "Marketing Memo: How to Fight Low-Cost Rivals" highlights some possible responses.

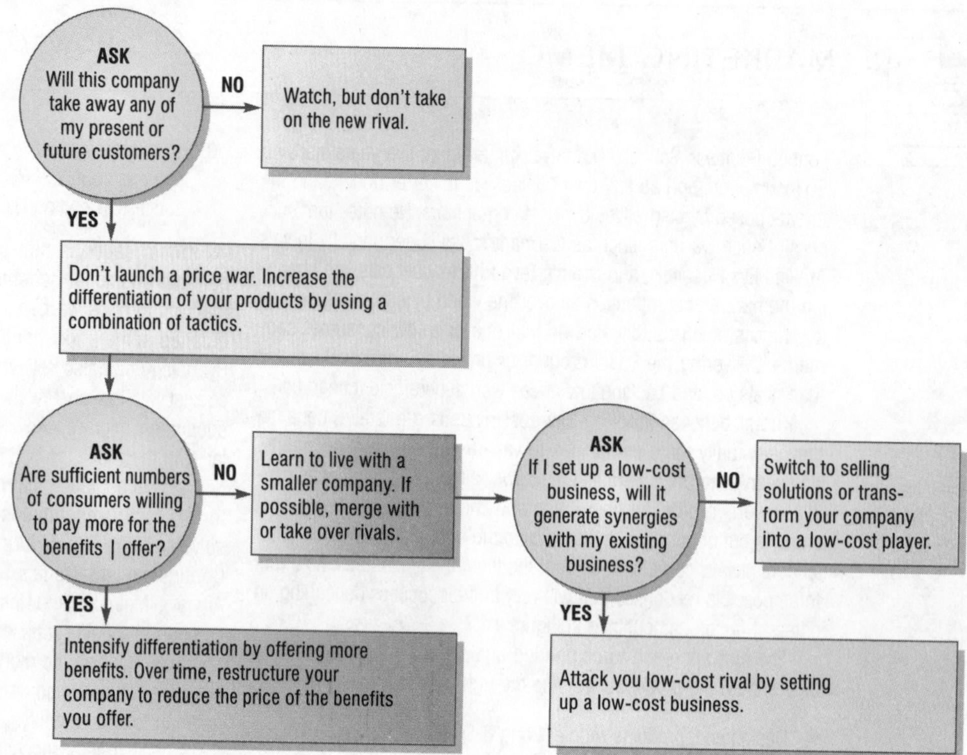

FIG. 14.7

A Framework for Responding to Low-Cost Rivals

Source: Nirmalya Kumar, "Strategies to Fight Low-Cost Rivals," *Harvard Business Review* (December 2006): 104–12.

An extended analysis of alternatives may not always be feasible when the attack occurs. The company may have to react decisively within hours or days, especially in those industries where price changes occur with some frequency and where it is important to react quickly, such as the meatpacking, lumber, or oil industries. It would make better sense to anticipate possible competitors' price changes and prepare contingent responses.

SUMMARY :::

1. Despite the increased role of nonprice factors in modern marketing, price remains a critical element of the marketing mix. Price is the only element that produces revenue; the others produce costs.
2. In setting pricing policy, a company follows a six-step procedure. It selects its pricing objective. It estimates the demand curve, the probable quantities it will sell at each possible price. It estimates how its costs vary at different levels of output, at different levels of accumulated production experience, and for differentiated marketing offers. It examines competitors' costs, prices, and offers. It selects a pricing method. It selects the final price.
3. Companies do not usually set a single price, but rather a pricing structure that reflects variations in geographical demand and costs, market-segment requirements, purchase timing, order levels, and other factors. Several price-adaptation strategies are available: (1) geographical pricing; (2) price discounts and allowances; (3) promotional pricing; and (4) discriminatory pricing.
4. After developing pricing strategies, firms often face situations in which they need to change prices. A price decrease might be brought about by excess plant capacity, declining market share, a desire to dominate the market through lower costs, or economic recession. A price increase might be brought about by cost inflation or overdemand. Companies must carefully manage customer perceptions in raising prices.
5. Companies must anticipate competitor price changes and prepare contingent responses. A number of responses are possible in terms of maintaining or changing price or quality.
6. The firm facing a competitor's price change must try to understand the competitor's intent and the likely duration of the change. Strategy often depends on whether a firm is producing homogeneous or nonhomogeneous products. A market leader attacked by lower-priced competitors can seek to better differentiate itself, introduce its own low-cost competitor, or transform itself more completely.

APPLICATIONS :::

Marketing Debate Is the Right Price a Fair Price?

Prices are often set to satisfy demand or to reflect the premium that consumers are willing to pay for a product or service. Some critics shudder, however, at the thought of $2 bottles of water, $150 running shoes, and $500 concert tickets.

Take a position: Prices should reflect the value that consumers are willing to pay *versus* Prices should primarily just reflect the cost involved in making a product or service.

Marketing Discussion

Think of the various pricing methods described in this chapter—markup pricing, target-return pricing, perceived-value pricing, value pricing, going-rate pricing, and auction-type pricing. As a consumer, which method do you personally prefer to deal with? Why? If the average price were to stay the same, which would you prefer: (1) for firms to set one price and not deviate or (2) to employ slightly higher prices most of the year, but slightly lower discounted prices or specials for certain occasions?

PART

6

DELIVERING VALUE

IN THIS CHAPTER, WE WILL ADDRESS THE FOLLOWING QUESTIONS:

1. What is a marketing channel system and value network?
2. What work do marketing channels perform?
3. How should channels be designed?
4. What decisions do companies face in managing their channels?
5. How should companies integrate channels and manage channel conflict?
6. What are the key issues with e-commerce?

CHAPTER 15 ::: DESIGNING AND MANAGING INTEGRATED MARKETING CHANNELS

fifteen

Successful value creation needs successful value delivery. Holistic marketers are increasingly taking a value network view of their businesses. Instead of limiting their focus to their immediate suppliers, distributors, and customers, they are examining the whole supply chain that links raw materials, components, and manufactured goods and shows how they move toward the final consumers. Companies are looking at their suppliers' suppliers upstream and at their distributors' customers downstream. They are looking at customer segments and considering a wide range of different possible means to sell, distribute, and service their offerings.

Royal Philips Electronics of the Netherlands is one of the world's biggest electronics companies and Europe's largest, with sales of over $36 billion in 2006. Philips' electronics products are channeled towards the consumer primarily through local and international retailers. The company offers a brand range of products from high to low price/value quartiles, relying on a diverse distribution model that includes mass merchants, retail chains, independents, and small specialty stores. In order to work in the most effective way with these retail channels, Philips has created an organization designed around its retail customers, with dedicated global key account managers serving leading retailers such as Best Buy, Carrefour, Costco, Dixons, Tesco, and Country Ambassadors. Like many modern firms, Philips also sells via the Web through its own online store as well as through a number of other online retailers.[1]

>>>

Royal Philips Electronics has mastered a wide array of marketing channels including an online store and a worldwide network of retailers of every size and price range, some of whom have been assigned their own Philips key account managers.

Companies today must build and manage a continuously evolving and increasingly complex channel system and value network. In this chapter, we consider strategic and tactical issues with integrating marketing channels and developing value networks. We will examine marketing channel issues from the perspective of retailers, wholesalers, and physical distribution agencies in Chapter 16.

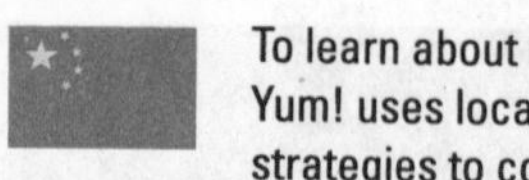

To learn about how Yum! uses localization strategies to compete in China, visit www.pearsoned-asia.com/marketingmanagement china.

::: Marketing Channels and Value Networks

Most producers do not sell their goods directly to the final users; between them stands a set of intermediaries performing a variety of functions. These intermediaries constitute a marketing channel (also called a trade channel or distribution channel). Formally, **marketing channels** are sets of interdependent organizations involved in the process of making a product or service available for use or consumption. They are the set of pathways a product or service follows after production, culminating in purchase and use by the final end user.[2]

Some intermediaries—such as wholesalers and retailers—buy, take title to, and resell the merchandise; they are called *merchants.* Others—brokers, manufacturers' representatives, sales agents—search for customers and may negotiate on the producer's behalf but do not take title to the goods; they are called *agents.* Still others—transportation companies, independent warehouses, banks, advertising agencies—assist in the distribution process but neither take title to goods nor negotiate purchases or sales; they are called *facilitators.*

The Importance of Channels

A **marketing channel system** is the particular set of marketing channels a firm employs, and decisions about it are among the most critical ones management faces. In the United States, channel members collectively have earned margins that account for 30% to 50% of the ultimate selling price. In contrast, advertising typically has accounted for less than 5% to 7% of the final price.[3] Marketing channels also represent a substantial opportunity cost. One of the chief roles of marketing channels is to convert potential buyers into profitable customers. Marketing channels must not just *serve* markets, they must also *make* markets.[4]

The channels chosen affect all other marketing decisions. The company's pricing depends on whether it uses mass merchandisers or high-quality boutiques. The firm's sales force and advertising decisions depend on how much training and motivation dealers need. In addition, channel decisions include relatively long-term commitments with other firms as well as a set of policies and procedures. When an automaker signs up independent dealers to sell its automobiles, the automaker cannot buy them out the next day and replace them with company-owned outlets. But at the same time, channel choices themselves depend on the company's marketing strategy with respect to segmentation, targeting, and positioning. Holistic marketers ensure that marketing decisions in all these different areas are made to collectively maximize value.

In managing its intermediaries, the firm must decide how much effort to devote to push versus pull marketing. A **push strategy** uses the manufacturer's sales force, trade promotion money, or other means to induce intermediaries to carry, promote, and sell the product to end users. Push strategy is appropriate where there is low brand loyalty in a category, brand choice is made in the store, the product is an impulse item, and product benefits are well understood. In a **pull strategy** the manufacturer uses advertising, promotion, and other forms of communication to persuade consumers to demand the product from intermediaries, thus inducing the intermediaries to order it. Pull strategy is appropriate when there is high brand loyalty and high involvement in the category, when consumers are able to perceive differences between brands, and when they choose the brand before they go to the store. For years, drug companies aimed ads solely at doctors and hospitals, but in 1997 the

FDA issued guidelines for TV ads that opened the way for pharmaceuticals to reach consumers directly. This is particularly evident in the burgeoning business of prescription sleep aids.

SEPRACOR INC.

The increased use of prescription sleep aids is due not so much to an increase in the number of insomniacs, as to the billions of dollars the drug companies are spending on print and TV advertising. Consider Sepracor's ads for Lunesta, featuring a pale green Luna moth flitting around the head of a peaceful sleeper. Sepracor spent $2.98 million in consumer advertising in 2006, and its stock and sales have jumped due to its successful campaign. The drug industry as a whole spent more than $4 billion on consumer ads in 2005, more than a fivefold increase in 10 years. Its aggressive pull marketing strategy has, however, prompted intense debate and scrutiny from Congress. After all, while aggressive advertising of Merck's Vioxx generated huge profits, it exposed thousands of U.S. adults to heart attack risks. Critics of the new drug ads say the drugs they tout treat symptoms rather than spurring consumers to discover the reason they can't sleep (which can range from simple stress to serious illness). Proponents of such ads say that in an era of managed care and shortened doctor visits, ads educate patients and spark important conversations with doctors. Although the pharmaceutical industry is unlikely to pull back, Bristol-Myers Squibb Co. has won some kudos for voluntarily banning ads during the first year new drugs are on the market.[5]

Top marketing companies such as Coca-Cola, Intel, and Nike skillfully employ both push and pull strategies. Marketing activities directed towards the channel as part of a push strategy are more effective when accompanied by a well-designed and well-executed pull strategy that activates consumer demand. On the other hand, without at least some consumer interest, it can be very difficult to gain much channel acceptance and support.

Channel Development

A new firm typically starts as a local operation selling in a fairly circumscribed market, using existing intermediaries. The number of such intermediaries is apt to be limited: a few manufacturers' sales agents, a few wholesalers, several established retailers, a few trucking companies, and a few warehouses. Deciding on the best channels might not be a problem; the problem is often to convince the available intermediaries to handle the firm's line.

If the firm is successful, it might branch into new markets and use different channels in different markets. In smaller markets, the firm might sell directly to retailers; in larger markets, it might sell through distributors. In rural areas, it might work with general-goods merchants; in urban areas, with limited-line merchants. In one part of the country, it might grant exclusive franchises; in another, it might sell through all outlets willing to handle the merchandise. In one country, it might use international sales agents; in another, it might partner with a local firm.

International markets pose distinct challenges. Customers' shopping habits can vary by countries, and many retailers such as Germany's Aldi, the United Kingdom's Tesco, and Spain's Zara have redefined themselves to a certain degree when entering a new market to better tailor their image to local needs and wants. Retailers that have largely stuck to the same selling formula regardless of geography, such as Eddie Bauer, Marks & Spencer, and Wal-Mart, have sometimes encountered trouble in entering new markets.[6]

No-frills, limited-assortment Aldi, the giant German discount supermarket chain, adapted its marketing strategy for its entrance into the U.S. market to stock different national manufacturer brands.

In short, the channel system evolves as a function of local opportunities and conditions, emerging threats and opportunities, company resources and capabilities, and other factors. Consider some of the challenges Dell has encountered in recent years.

DELL

Dell revolutionized the personal computer category by selling products directly to customers via the telephone and later the Internet, rather than through retailers or resellers. Customers could custom design the exact PC they wanted, and rigorous cost cutting allowed for low everyday prices. Sound like a winning formula? It was for almost two decades. But 2006 saw the company encounter a number of problems that led to a steep stock price decline. First, reinvigorated competitors such as HP narrowed the gap in productivity and price. Always focused more on the business market, Dell struggled to sell effectively to the consumer market. A shift in consumer preferences to buy in retail stores as opposed to buying direct didn't help, but self-inflicted damage from an ultra-efficient supply chain model that squeezed costs—and quality—out of customer service was perhaps the most painful. Managers evaluated call center employees primarily on how long they stayed on each call—a recipe for disaster as scores of customers felt their problems were ignored or not properly handled. A lack of R&D spending that hindered new-product development and led to a lack of differentiation didn't help either. Clearly, Dell was entering a new chapter in its history that would require a fundamental rethinking of its channel strategy and its marketing approach as a whole.[7]

Hybrid Channels

Today's successful companies are also multiplying the number of "go-to-market" or **hybrid channels** in any one market area. In contrast to Dell, HP has used its sales force to sell to large accounts, outbound telemarketing to sell to medium-sized accounts, direct mail with an inbound number to sell to small accounts, retailers to sell to still smaller accounts, and the Internet to sell specialty items. Staples markets through its traditional retail channel, a direct-response Internet site, virtual malls, and thousands of links on affiliated sites.

Companies that manage hybrid channels must make sure these channels work well together and match each target customer's preferred ways of doing business. Customers expect *channel integration*, characterized by features such as:

- the ability to order a product online and pick it up at a convenient retail location
- the ability to return an online-ordered product to a nearby store of the retailer
- the right to receive discounts and promotional offers based on total online and off-line purchases

Circuit City estimated in-store pick-ups accounted for more than half its online sales in 2006.[8] Here's a specific example of a company that has carefully managed its multiple channels.

REI

What's more frustrating: buying hiking boots that cripple your feet, or trying on the perfect pair only to find the store is out of stock in the size or style you want? At Recreational Equipment Inc. (REI), the largest consumer cooperative in the United States with 2.5 million active members, outdoor enthusiasts can easily avoid both problems. In 90 REI stores across the country, customers are lighting up gas stoves, pitching tents, and snuggling deep into sleeping bags. REI stores are designed to give an experience, not just sell goods. If an item is out of stock, all customers need do is tap into the store's Internet kiosk to order it from REI's Web site. Less Internet-savvy customers can even get clerks to place the order for them at the checkout counters. REI has been lauded by industry analysts for the seamless integration of its retail store, Web site, Internet kiosks, mail-order catalogs, value-priced outlets, and toll-free order number. And REI not only generates store-to-Internet traffic, it also sends Internet shoppers into its stores. If a customer browses REI's site and stops to read an REI "Learn and Share" article on backpacking, the site might highlight an in-store promotion on hiking boots. Like many retailers, REI has found that dual-channel shoppers spend significantly more than single-channel shoppers, and that tri-channel shoppers spend even more.[9]

Understanding Customer Needs

Consumers may choose the channels they prefer based on a number of factors: the price, product assortment, and convenience of a channel option, as well as their own particular shopping goals (economic, social, or experiential).[10] As with products, segmentation exists, and marketers employing different types of channels must be aware that different consumers have different needs during the purchase process.

Researchers Nunes and Cespedes argue that, in many markets, buyers fall into one of four categories.[11]

1. ***Habitual shoppers*** purchase from the same places in the same manner over time.
2. ***High-value deal seekers*** know their needs and "channel surf" a great deal before buying at the lowest possible price.
3. ***Variety-loving shoppers*** gather information in many channels, take advantage of high-touch services, and then buy in their favorite channel, regardless of price.
4. ***High-involvement shoppers*** gather information in all channels, make their purchase in a low-cost channel, but take advantage of customer support from a high-touch channel.

One study of 40 grocery and clothing retailers in France, Germany, and the United Kingdom found that retailers in those countries served three types of shoppers: (1) ***Service/quality customers*** who cared most about the variety and performance of products in stores as well as the service provided; (2) ***Price/value customers*** who were most concerned about spending their money wisely; and (3) ***Affinity customers*** who primarily sought stores that suited people like themselves or the members of groups they aspired to join. As Figure 15.1 shows, customer profiles for these types of retailers differed across the three markets: In France, shoppers placed more importance on service and quality, in the United Kingdom, affinity, and in Germany, price and value.[12]

Even the same consumer, though, may choose to use different channels for different functions in making a purchase. For instance, someone may choose to browse through a catalog before visiting a store or take a test-drive at a dealer before ordering a car online. Consumers may also seek different types of channels depending on the particular types of goods involved. Some consumers are willing to "trade up" to retailers offering higher-end goods such as TAG Heuer watches or Callaway golf clubs; these same consumers are also

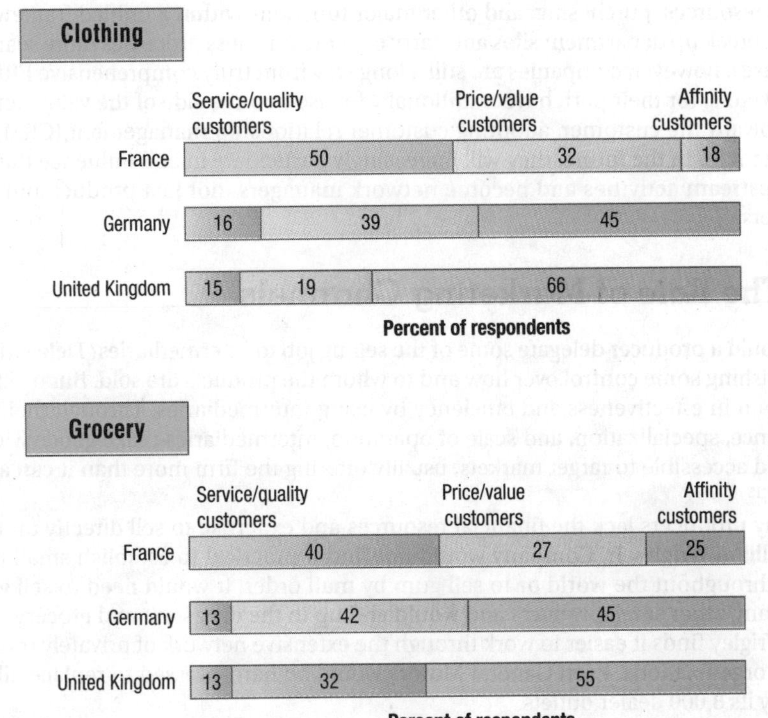

FIG. 15.1

What Do European Consumers Value?

Source: Peter N. Child, Suzanne Heywood, and Michael Kliger, "Do Retail Brands Travel?" *The McKinsley Quarterly* (January 2002): 11–13. Reprinted by permission.

willing to "trade down" to discount retailers to buy private-label paper towels, detergent, or vitamins.[13]

Value Networks

A supply chain view of a firm sees markets as destination points and amounts to a linear view of the flow. The company should first think of the target market, however, and then design the supply chain backward from that point. This view has been called **demand chain planning**. Northwestern's Don Schultz says: "A demand chain management approach doesn't just push things through the system. It emphasizes what solutions consumers are looking for, not what products we are trying to sell them." Schultz has suggested that the traditional marketing "four Ps" be replaced by a new acronym, SIVA, which stands for solutions, information, value, and access.[14]

An even broader view sees a company at the center of a **value network**—a system of partnerships and alliances that a firm creates to source, augment, and deliver its offerings. A value network includes a firm's suppliers and its suppliers' suppliers, and its immediate customers and their end customers. The value network includes valued relations with others such as university researchers and government approval agencies.

A company needs to orchestrate these parties in order to deliver superior value to the target market. Palm, the leading manufacturer of handheld devices, consists of a whole community of suppliers and assemblers of semiconductor components, plastic cases, LCD displays, and accessories; of off-line and online resellers; of 275,000 developers in the Palm Developer Network who have created over 21,000 software programs and 100 hardware add-ons for the Palm operating systems for handheld computers and smartphones.

Demand chain planning yields several insights. First, the company can estimate whether more money is made upstream or downstream, in case it might want to integrate backward or forward. Second, the company is more aware of disturbances anywhere in the supply chain that might cause costs, prices, or supplies to change suddenly. Third, companies can go online with their business partners to carry on faster and more accurate communications, transactions, and payments to reduce costs, speed up information, and increase accuracy. For example, Ford not only manages numerous supply chains but also sponsors or transacts on many B2B Web sites and exchanges as needs arise.

Managing this value network has required companies to make increasing investments in information technology (IT) and software. Firms have introduced supply chain management (SCM) software and invited such software firms as SAP and Oracle to design comprehensive *enterprise resource planning* (ERP) systems to manage cash flow, manufacturing, human resources, purchasing, and other major functions within a unified framework. They hope to break up department silos and carry out core business processes more seamlessly. In most cases, however, companies are still a long way from truly comprehensive ERP systems.

Marketers, for their part, have traditionally focused on the side of the value network that looks toward the customer, adopting customer relationship management (CRM) software and practices. In the future, they will increasingly participate in and influence their companies' upstream activities and become network managers, not just product and customer managers.

::: The Role of Marketing Channels

Why would a producer delegate some of the selling job to intermediaries? Delegation means relinquishing some control over how and to whom the products are sold. But producers can often gain in effectiveness and efficiency by using intermediaries. Through their contacts, experience, specialization, and scale of operation, intermediaries make goods widely available and accessible to target markets, usually offering the firm more than it can achieve on its own.[15]

Many producers lack the financial resources and expertise to sell directly on their own. The William Wrigley Jr. Company would not find it practical to establish small retail gum shops throughout the world or to sell gum by mail order. It would need to sell gum along with many other small products and would end up in the drugstore and grocery store business. Wrigley finds it easier to work through the extensive network of privately owned distribution organizations. Even General Motors would be hard-pressed to replace all the tasks done by its 8,000 dealer outlets.

TABLE 15.1

Channel Member Functions

- Gather information about potential and current customers, competitors, and other actors and forces in the marketing environment.
- Develop and disseminate persuasive communications to stimulate purchasing.
- Reach agreements on price and other terms so that transfer of ownership or possession can be effected.
- Place orders with manufacturers.
- Acquire the funds to finance inventories at different levels in the marketing channel.
- Assume risks connected with carrying out channel work.
- Provide for the successive storage and movement of physical products.
- Provide for buyers' payment of their bills through banks and other financial institutions.
- Oversee actual transfer of ownership from one organization or person to another.

Channel Functions and Flows

A marketing channel performs the work of moving goods from producers to consumers. It overcomes the time, place, and possession gaps that separate goods and services from those who need or want them. Members of the marketing channel perform a number of key functions (see Table 15.1).

Some functions (physical, title, promotion) constitute a *forward flow* of activity from the company to the customer; other functions (ordering and payment) constitute a *backward flow* from customers to the company. Still others (information, negotiation, finance, and risk taking) occur in both directions. Five flows are illustrated in Figure 15.2 for the marketing of forklift trucks. If these flows were superimposed in one diagram, the tremendous complexity of even simple marketing channels would be apparent.

A manufacturer selling a physical product and services might require three channels: a *sales channel*, a *delivery channel*, and a *service channel*. To sell its Bowflex fitness equipment, the Nautilus Group historically has emphasized direct marketing via television infomercials and ads, inbound/outbound call centers, response mailings, and the Internet

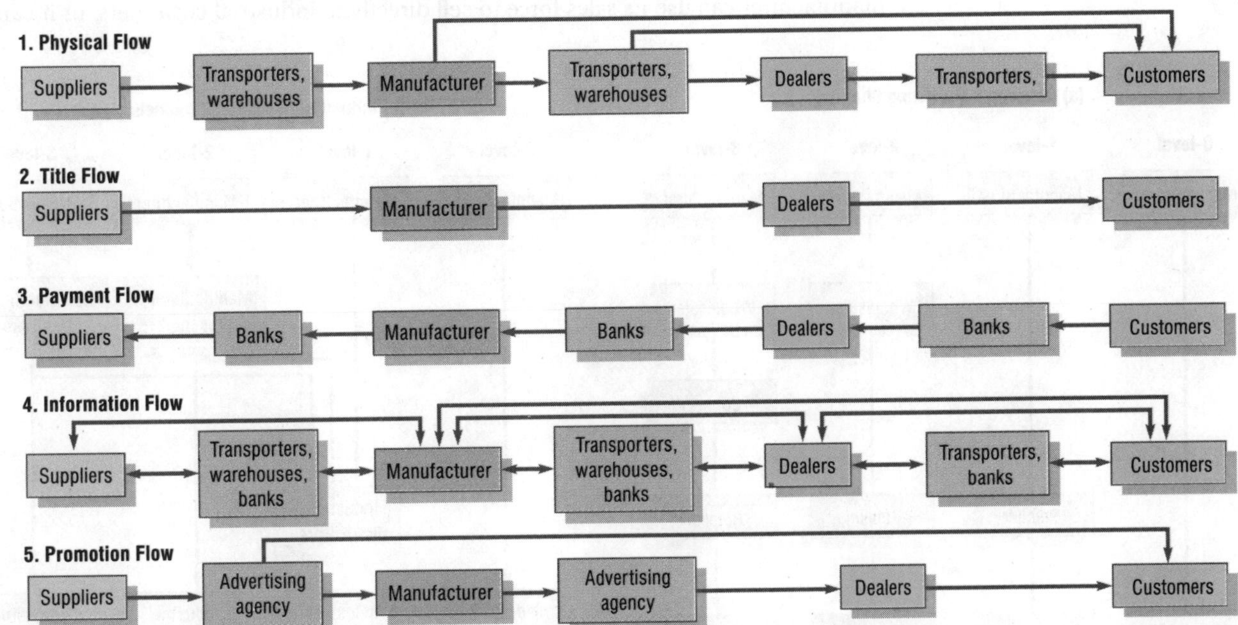

FIG. 15.2 Five Marketing Flows in the Marketing Channel for Forklift Trucks

as sales channels; UPS ground service as the delivery channel; and local repair people as the service channel. Reflecting shifting consumer buying habits, Nautilus now also sells Bowflex through commercial, retail, and specialty retail channels.

The question is not *whether* various channel functions need to be performed—they must be—but rather, *who* is to perform them. All channel functions have three things in common: They use up scarce resources; they can often be performed better through specialization; and they can be shifted among channel members. When the manufacturer shifts some functions to intermediaries, the producer's costs and prices are lower, but the intermediary must add a charge to cover its work. If the intermediaries are more efficient than the manufacturer, prices to consumers should be lower. If consumers perform some functions themselves, they should enjoy even lower prices. Changes in channel institutions thus largely reflect the discovery of more efficient ways to combine or separate the economic functions that provide assortments of goods to target customers.

Channel Levels

The producer and the final customer are part of every channel. We will use the number of intermediary levels to designate the length of a channel. Figure 15.3a illustrates several consumer-goods marketing channels of different lengths.

A **zero-level channel** (also called a **direct marketing channel**) consists of a manufacturer selling directly to the final customer. The major examples are door-to-door sales, home parties, mail order, telemarketing, TV selling, Internet selling, and manufacturer-owned stores. Avon sales representatives sell cosmetics door-to-door; Tupperware representatives sell kitchen goods through home parties; Franklin Mint sells collectibles through mail order; Verizon uses the telephone to prospect for new customers or to sell enhanced services to existing customers; Time-Life sells music and video collections through TV commercials or longer "infomercials"; Red Envelope sells gifts online; and Apple sells computers and other consumer electronics through its own stores.

A *one-level channel* contains one selling intermediary, such as a retailer. A *two-level channel* contains two intermediaries. In consumer markets, these are typically a wholesaler and a retailer. A *three-level channel* contains three intermediaries. In the meatpacking industry, wholesalers sell to jobbers, who sell to small retailers. In Japan, food distribution may include as many as six levels. From the producer's point of view, obtaining information about end users and exercising control becomes more difficult as the number of channel levels increases.

Figure 15.3b shows channels commonly used in B2B marketing. An industrial-goods manufacturer can use its sales force to sell directly to industrial customers; or it can sell to

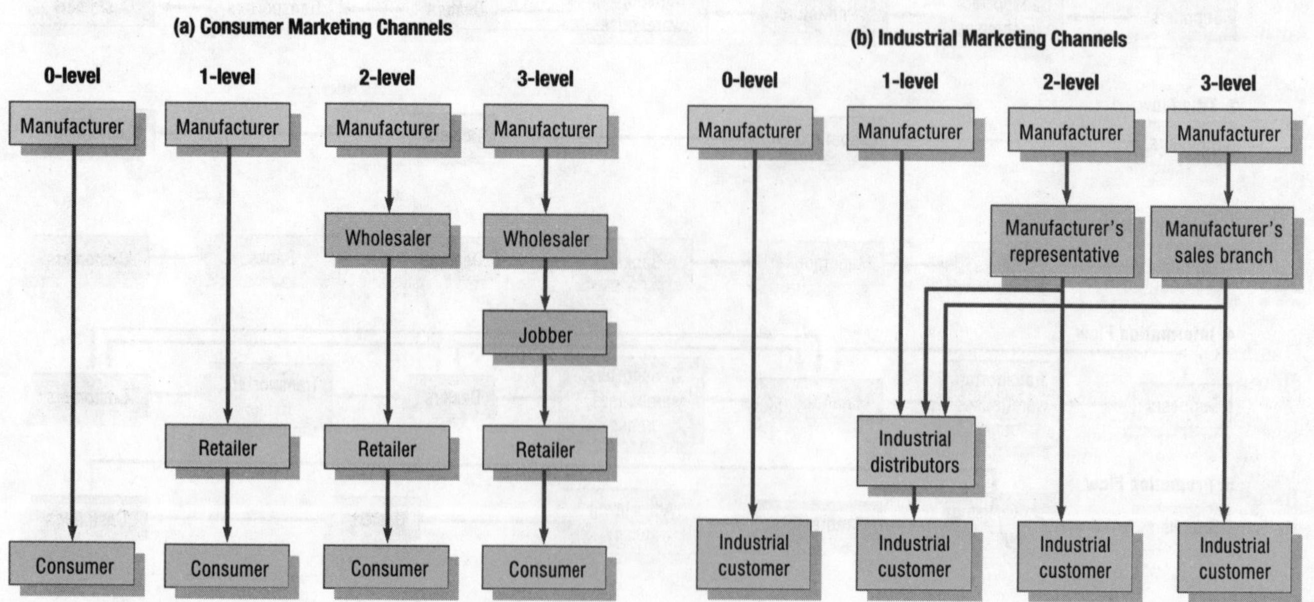

FIG. 15.3 | Consumer and Industrial Marketing Channels

industrial distributors, who sell to the industrial customers; or it can sell through manufacturer's representatives or its own sales branches directly to industrial customers, or indirectly to industrial customers through industrial distributors. Zero-, one-, and two-level marketing channels are quite common.

Channels normally describe a forward movement of products from source to user, but there are also *reverse-flow channels.* These are important in the following cases: (1) to reuse products or containers (such as refillable chemical-carrying drums); (2) to refurbish products (such as circuit boards or computers) for resale; (3) to recycle products (such as paper); and (4) to dispose of products and packaging (waste products). Several intermediaries play a role in reverse-flow channels, including manufacturers' redemption centers, community groups, traditional intermediaries such as soft-drink intermediaries, trash-collection specialists, recycling centers, trash-recycling brokers, and central processing warehousing.[16]

Service Sector Channels

Marketing channels are not limited to the distribution of physical goods. Producers of services and ideas also face the problem of making their output available and accessible to target populations. Schools develop "educational-dissemination systems" and hospitals develop "health-delivery systems." These institutions must figure out agencies and locations for reaching a population spread out over an area.

WHARTON

Founded in 1881 as the world's first collegiate school of business, Wharton reaches a wide variety of business students and executives. It offers undergraduate, MBA, executive MBA, and doctoral degree programs, as well as nondegree executive education programs and certificate programs for working professionals. Additionally, Wharton has a publishing arm for books, audio books, e-documents, CD-ROMs, and videos. It also offers a monthly electronic newsletter, Wharton@Work, and an online business journal, Knowledge@Wharton.

Marketing channels also keep changing in "person" marketing. Besides live and programmed entertainment, entertainers, musicians, and other artists can reach prospective and existing fans online in many ways—via their own Web sites, social community sites such as MySpace, and third-party Web sites. Even legendary former Beatle Paul McCartney decided to end his 45-year relationship with music conglomerate E.M.I. to launch his new album, *Memory Almost Full,* in June 2007 as the debut release from Hear Music, a record label cofounded by Starbucks, to be sold at the company's coffee shops, as well as record stores and on iTunes.[17] Politicians also must choose a mix of channels—mass media, rallies, coffee hours, spot TV ads, direct mail, billboards, faxes, e-mail, blogs, podcasts, Web sites—for delivering their messages to voters.[18]

As Internet and other technologies advance, service industries such as banking, insurance, travel, and stock buying and selling are operating through new channels. Kodak offers its customers four different ways to print their digital photos—minilabs in retail outlets, home printers, online services with the Kodak-owned Ofoto Web site, and self-service kiosks. Kodak, the world leader with 80,000 kiosks including 2,000 at Wal-Mart, makes money both by selling kiosks and by supplying the units with the chemical and paper used to make the prints.[19]

::: Channel-Design Decisions

Designing a marketing channel system requires analyzing customer needs, establishing channel objectives, and identifying and evaluating major channel alternatives.

Analyzing Customers' Desired Service Output Levels

In designing the marketing channel, the marketer must understand the service output levels its target customers want. Channels produce five service outputs:

1. ***Lot size***—The number of units the channel permits a typical customer to purchase on one occasion. In buying cars for its fleet, Hertz prefers a channel from which it can buy a large lot size; a household wants a channel that permits buying a lot size of one.

2. ***Waiting and delivery time***—The average time customers of that channel wait for receipt of the goods. Customers increasingly prefer faster and faster delivery channels.
3. ***Spatial convenience***—The degree to which the marketing channel makes it easy for customers to purchase the product. Chevrolet, for example, offers greater spatial convenience than Cadillac, because there are more Chevrolet dealers. Chevrolet's greater market decentralization helps customers save on transportation and search costs in buying and repairing an automobile.
4. ***Product variety***—The assortment breadth provided by the marketing channel. Normally, customers prefer a greater assortment because more choices increase the chance of finding what they need.
5. ***Service backup***—The add-on services (credit, delivery, installation, repairs) provided by the channel. The greater the service backup, the greater the work provided by the channel.[20]

The marketing channel designer knows that providing greater service outputs also means increasing channel costs and raising prices for customers. Different customers have different service needs. The success of discount stores indicates that many consumers are willing to accept smaller service outputs if they can save money.

Establishing Objectives and Constraints

Marketers should state their channel objectives in terms of targeted service output levels. Under competitive conditions, channel institutions should arrange their functional tasks to minimize total channel costs and still provide desired levels of service outputs.[21] Usually, planners can identify several market segments that want different service levels. Effective planning requires determining which market segments to serve and choosing the best channels for each.

Channel objectives vary with product characteristics. Perishable products require more direct marketing. Bulky products, such as building materials, require channels that minimize the shipping distance and the amount of handling. Nonstandard products, such as custom-built machinery and specialized business forms, are sold directly by company sales representatives. Products requiring installation or maintenance services, such as heating and cooling systems, are usually sold and maintained by the company or by franchised dealers. High-unit-value products such as generators and turbines are often sold through a company sales force rather than intermediaries.

A number of other factors affect channel objectives. In entering new markets, for instance, firms often closely observe what other firms from their home market are doing in those markets. France's Auchan considered the presence of its French rivals Leclerc and Casino in Poland, a key driver for it to also enter that market.[22]

Marketers must adapt their channel objectives to the larger environment. When economic conditions are depressed, producers want to move their goods to market using shorter channels and without services that add to the final price of the goods. Legal regulations and restrictions also affect channel design. U.S. law looks unfavorably on channel arrangements that substantially lessen competition or create a monopoly.

Identifying and Evaluating Major Channel Alternatives

Companies can choose from a wide variety of channels for reaching customers—from sales forces to agents, distributors, dealers, direct mail, telemarketing, and the Internet. Each channel has unique strengths as well as weaknesses. Sales forces can handle complex products and transactions, but they are expensive. The Internet is much less expensive, but it may not be as effective with complex products. Distributors can create sales, but the company loses direct contact with customers. Manufacturers' reps are able to contact customers at a low cost per customer because several clients share the cost, but the selling effort per customer is less intense than if company sales reps did the selling.

The problem is further complicated by the fact that most companies now use a mix of channels. The idea is that each channel reaches a different segment of buyers and delivers the right products at the least cost. When this doesn't happen, there is usually channel conflict and excessive cost.

TABLE 15.2

Channel Alternatives for a Cellular Car Phone Maker

- The company could sell its car phones to automobile manufacturers to be installed as original equipment.
- The company could sell its car phones to auto dealers.
- The company could sell its car phones to retail automotive-equipment dealers through a direct sales force or through distributors.
- The company could sell its car phones to car phone specialist dealers through a direct sales force or dealers.
- The company could sell its car phones through mail-order catalogs.
- The company could sell its car phones through mass merchandisers such as Best Buy or Circuit City.

A channel alternative is described by three elements: the types of available business intermediaries, the number of intermediaries needed, and the terms and responsibilities of each channel member.

TYPES OF INTERMEDIARIES A firm needs to identify the types of intermediaries available to carry on its channel work. Table 15.2 lists channel alternatives identified by a consumer electronics company that produces cellular car phones.

Companies should search for innovative marketing channels. Medion sold 600,000 PCs in Europe, mostly via major one- or two-week "burst promotions" at Aldi's supermarkets.[23] Columbia House has successfully merchandised music albums through the mail and Internet. Other sellers such as Harry and David and Calyx & Corolla have creatively sold fruit and flowers, respectively, through direct delivery. (See "Marketing Insight: How CarMax Is Transforming the Auto Business.")

Sometimes a company chooses a new or unconventional channel because of the difficulty, cost, or ineffectiveness of working with the dominant channel. The advantage is that the company will encounter less competition during the initial move into this channel. Years ago, after trying to sell its inexpensive Timex watches through regular jewelry stores, the U.S. Time Company placed them instead in fast-growing mass-merchandise outlets. Frustrated with a printed catalog it saw as out-of-date and unprofessional, commercial lighting company Display Supply & Lighting developed an interactive online catalog that drove down costs, sped up the sales process, and increased revenue.[24]

High-quality gift baskets of hand-packed fruit, cake, and cookies have made Harry and David a consistently successful direct delivery firm.

NUMBER OF INTERMEDIARIES Companies must decide on the number of intermediaries to use at each channel level. Three strategies are available: exclusive distribution, selective distribution, and intensive distribution.

Exclusive distribution means severely limiting the number of intermediaries. It's appropriate when the producer wants to maintain control over the service level and outputs offered by the resellers, and it often includes *exclusive dealing* arrangements. By granting exclusive distribution, the producer hopes to obtain more dedicated and knowledgeable selling. Exclusive distribution requires a closer partnership between seller and reseller and is used in the distribution of new automobiles, some major appliances, and some women's apparel brands. Exclusive deals between suppliers and retailers are becoming a mainstay for specialists looking for an edge in a business world that is increasingly driven by price.[25] When the legendary Italian designer label Gucci found its image severely tarnished by overexposure from licensing and discount stores, it

MARKETING INSIGHT | HOW CARMAX IS TRANSFORMING THE AUTO BUSINESS

For years, buying a used car was considered a dangerous and risky business; used-car salespeople were stock figures in comedy routines. Then CarMax emerged to change the face of the industry and its standards.

Circuit City, a major retailer of electronic products, started CarMax, the Auto Superstore, in 1993 in Richmond, Virginia, where its headquarters are located. CarMax is now the nation's leading specialty retailer of used cars; it operates 80 used-car superstores in 19 states. CarMax also operates a number of new-car franchises that are integrated with or in its used-car superstores and annually sells a total of over 300,000 cars.

What's so special about CarMax? The company locates its used-car superstores, each carrying around 500 cars, on large lots on the outskirts of a city near a major highway. Customers enter an attractive display room, where a sales associate finds out what kind of car they want and then escorts them to a computer kiosk. Using a touch screen, the associate retrieves a full listing of the cars in stock that meet the customer's criteria. A color display of each car can be shown along with the vehicle's features and its fixed selling price. The company has over 15,000 cars in all, nearly every make and model.

There is no price negotiation. The salesperson, paid a commission on the number of cars sold rather than their value, has no incentive to push higher-priced cars. The customer is informed that CarMax mechanics have carried out a 110-point inspection and made any necessary repairs beforehand. Furthermore, a car buyer receives a 5-day money-back guarantee and a 30-day comprehensive warranty. If the buyer wants financing, the CarMax associate can arrange it in 20 minutes. The entire process typically takes less than one hour.

But tight margins mean that CarMax must run a tight ship, buying and selling cars at the right price. Here are some key facts and figures that underlie its business model:

- 25%—percentage of sellers who say yes to CarMax's offer
- 6—number of days it takes to recondition a car
- $1,000—average money spent reconditioning a car
- 30—number of days before a car sells
- 80%—percentage of buyers who finance at CarMax
- $1,807—average gross profit on a sale

CarMax uses a sophisticated inventory system to keep track of which models sell and when demand shifts. Each car is fitted with a RFID tag to track how long it sits and when a test drive occurs. Eight hundred CarMax buyers draw on the company's voluminous databases to appraise trade-in vehicles at exactly the right price to make sure that any transaction that occurs is profitable to the company. Although the major U.S. auto makers have experienced a decline in sales and profitability in recent years, CarMax has thrived, with revenue approaching $8 billion.

CarMax has streamlined the used-car purchase and revolutionized the business with its unique database of over 15,000 cars.

Sources: Jonathan Fahey, "Used Cars, New," *Forbes*, March 27, 2006, pp. 98–100; Michael Myser, "The Wal-Mart of Used Cars," *Business 2.0* (September 2006): 58–59; Laura Heller, "Circuit City Restructures, Spins Off CarMax Unit," *DSN Retailing Today*, March 11, 2002, pp. 3–4; Arlena Sawyers, "CarMax Is out of the Red, in the Pink," *Automotive News*, April 16, 2001, p. 28.

decided to end contracts with third-party suppliers, control its distribution, and open its own stores to bring back some of the luster.[26]

Selective distribution relies on more than a few but less than all of the intermediaries willing to carry a particular product. It makes sense for established companies and for new companies seeking distributors. The company does not need to worry about too many outlets; it can gain adequate market coverage with more control and less cost than intensive distribution. Stihl is a good example of selective distribution.

STIHL

Stihl manufactures handheld outdoor power equipment. All its products are branded under one name and it does not make private labels for other companies. Stihl is best known for chain saws, but it has expanded into string trimmers, blowers, hedge trimmers, and cut-off machines. It sells exclusively to seven independent U.S. distributors and five Stihl-owned marketing and distribution centers, which sell Stihl products to a nationwide network of more than 8,000 servicing retail dealers. The company also is a worldwide exporter of U.S.–manufactured Stihl products to 130 countries. Stihl is one of the few outdoor-power-equipment companies that does not sell its products through mass merchants, catalogs, or the Internet.[27]

In **intensive distribution** the manufacturer places the goods or services in as many outlets as possible. This strategy is generally used for items such as snack foods, soft drinks, newspapers, candies and gum, products the consumer seeks to buy frequently or in a variety of locations. Convenience stores such as 7-Eleven, Circle K, and gas-station-linked stores such as ExxonMobil's On the Run have survived by selling items that provide just that—location and time convenience.

Manufacturers are constantly tempted to move from exclusive or selective distribution to more intensive distribution to increase coverage and sales. This strategy may help in the short term, but it can hurt long-term performance. Intensive distribution increases product and service availability but may also encourage retailers to compete aggressively. Price wars can then erode profitability, potentially dampening retailer interest in supporting the product and harming brand equity. Some firms avoid intensive distribution and do not want to be sold everywhere. After Sears department stores acquired discount chain Kmart in 2005, Nike pulled all its products from Sears to make sure that Kmart could not carry the brand.[28]

TERMS AND RESPONSIBILITIES OF CHANNEL MEMBERS Each channel member must be treated respectfully and given the opportunity to be profitable.[29] The main elements in the "trade-relations mix" are price policies, conditions of sale, territorial rights, and specific services to be performed by each party.

- ***Price policy*** calls for the producer to establish a price list and schedule of discounts and allowances that intermediaries see as equitable and sufficient.
- ***Conditions of sale*** refers to payment terms and producer guarantees. Most producers grant cash discounts to distributors for early payment. Producers might also provide distributors a guarantee against defective merchandise or price declines. A guarantee against price declines gives distributors an incentive to buy larger quantities.
- ***Distributors' territorial rights*** define the distributors' territories and the terms under which the producer will enfranchise other distributors. Distributors normally expect to receive full credit for all sales in their territory, whether or not they did the selling.
- ***Mutual services and responsibilities*** must be carefully spelled out, especially in franchised and exclusive-agency channels. McDonald's provides franchisees with a building, promotional support, a recordkeeping system, training, and general administrative and technical assistance. In turn, franchisees are expected to satisfy company standards for the physical facilities, cooperate with new promotional programs, furnish requested information, and buy supplies from specified vendors.

Evaluating the Major Alternatives

Each channel alternative needs to be evaluated against economic, control, and adaptive criteria.

ECONOMIC CRITERIA Each channel alternative will produce a different level of sales and costs. Figure 15.4 shows how six different sales channels stack up in terms of the value added per sale and the cost per transaction. For example, in the sale of industrial products costing between $2,000 and $5,000, the cost per transaction has been estimated at $500 (field sales), $200 (distributors), $50 (telesales), and $10 (Internet). In the sale of retail banking services, a

| FIG. 15.4 |

The Value-Adds versus Costs of Different Channels

Source: Oxford Associates, adapted from Dr. Rowland T. Moriarty, Cubex Corp.

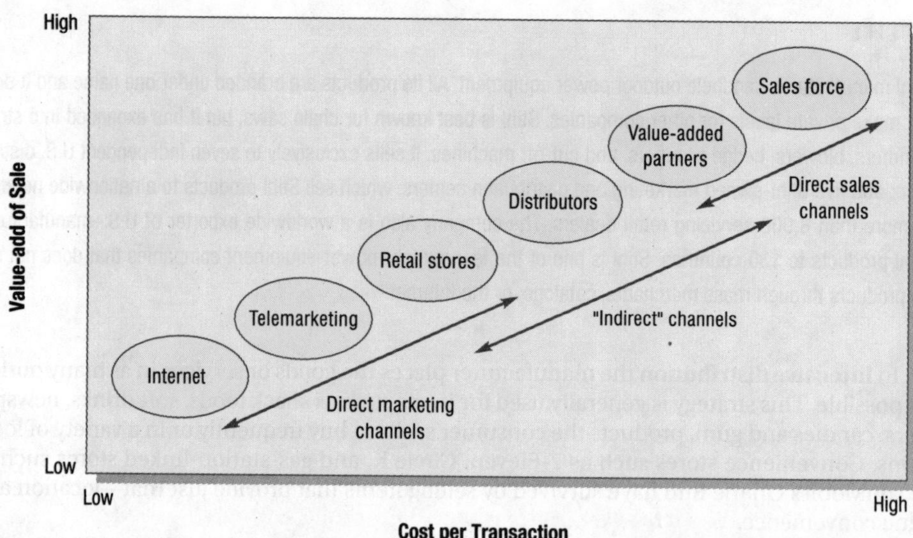

Booz Allen Hamilton study shows the average transaction at a full-service branch costs the bank $4.07, a phone transaction costs 54 cents, and an ATM transaction 27 cents, but a typical Web-based transaction costs only 1 cent.[30]

Firms will try to align customers and channels to maximize demand at the lowest overall cost. Clearly, sellers try to replace high-cost channels with low-cost channels as long as the value added per sale is sufficient. Asset manager Vanguard's service representatives set out to train customers to use its Web sites over the telephone. As a result, Vanguard was able to cut staff in half, an important accomplishment given that a phone call to a rep cost the company $9 versus pennies for a Web log-in.[31]

As an example of an economic analysis of channel choices, consider the following situation:

> A North Carolina furniture manufacturer wants to sell its line to retailers on the West Coast. The manufacturer is trying to decide between two alternatives: One calls for hiring 10 new sales representatives who would operate out of a sales office in San Francisco. They would receive a base salary plus commissions. The other alternative would be to use a San Francisco manufacturers' sales agency that has extensive contacts with retailers. The agency has 30 sales representatives who would receive a commission based on their sales.

The first step in the analysis is to estimate how many sales are likely to be generated by a company sales force or a sales agency. On one hand, a company sales force will concentrate on the company's products; will be better trained to sell those products; will be more aggressive because each rep's future depends on the company's success; and will be more successful because many customers prefer to deal directly with the company. On the other hand, the sales agency has 30 representatives, not just 10; it may be just as aggressive as a direct sales force, depending on the commission level; it may be better received by customers as more independent; and it may have extensive contacts and marketplace knowledge. The marketer needs to evaluate all these factors in formulating a demand function for the two different channels.

The next step is to estimate the costs of selling different volumes through each channel. The cost schedules are shown in Figure 15.5. The fixed costs of engaging a sales agency are lower than those of establishing a new company sales office, but costs rise faster through an agency because sales agents get a larger commission than company salespeople.

The final step is comparing sales and costs. As Figure 15.5 shows, there is one sales level (S_B) at which selling costs are the same for the two channels. The sales agency is thus the better channel for any sales volume below S_B, and the company sales branch is better at any volume above S_B. Given this information, it is not surprising that sales agents tend to be used by smaller firms, or by large firms in smaller territories where the volume is low.

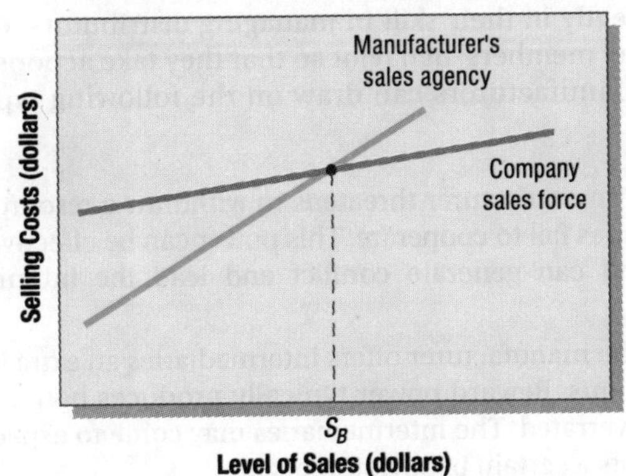

FIG. 15.5

Break-Even Cost Chart for the Choice between a Company Sales Force and a Manufacturer's Sales Agency

CONTROL AND ADAPTIVE CRITERIA Using a sales agency poses a control problem. A sales agency is an independent firm seeking to maximize its profits. Agents may concentrate on the customers who buy the most, not necessarily on those who buy the manufacturer's goods. Furthermore, agents might not master the technical details of the company's product or handle its promotion materials effectively.

To develop a channel, members must make some degree of commitment to each other for a specified period of time. Yet these commitments invariably lead to a decrease in the producer's ability to respond to a changing marketplace. In rapidly changing, volatile, or uncertain product markets, the producer needs channel structures and policies that provide high adaptability.

::: Channel-Management Decisions

After a company has chosen a channel system, it must select, train, motivate, and evaluate individual intermediaries for each channel. It must also modify channel design and arrangements over time.

Selecting Channel Members

To customers, the channels are the company. Consider the negative impression customers would get of McDonald's, Shell Oil, or Mercedes-Benz if one or more of their outlets or dealers consistently appeared dirty, inefficient, or unpleasant.

To facilitate channel member selection, producers should determine what characteristics distinguish the better intermediaries. They should evaluate the number of years in business, other lines carried, growth and profit record, financial strength, cooperativeness, and service reputation. If the intermediaries are sales agents, producers should evaluate the number and character of other lines carried and the size and quality of the sales force. If the intermediaries are department stores that want exclusive distribution, the producer should evaluate locations, future growth potential, and type of clientele.

Training and Motivating Channel Members

A company needs to view its intermediaries in the same way it views its end users. It needs to determine intermediaries' needs and construct a channel positioning such that its channel offering is tailored to provide superior value to these intermediaries.

Being able to stimulate channel members to top performance starts with understanding their needs and wants. The company should plan and implement careful training programs, market research programs, and other capability-building programs to improve intermediaries' performance. Microsoft requires third-party service engineers to complete a set of courses and take certification exams. Those who pass are formally recognized as Microsoft Certified Professionals, and they can use this designation to promote their own business. Others use customer surveys rather than exams. The company must constantly communicate its view that the intermediaries are partners in a joint effort to satisfy end users of the product.

Producers vary greatly in their skill in managing distributors. **Channel power** is the ability to alter channel members' behavior so that they take actions they would not have taken otherwise.[32] Manufacturers can draw on the following types of power to elicit cooperation:

- ***Coercive power.*** A manufacturer threatens to withdraw a resource or terminate a relationship if intermediaries fail to cooperate. This power can be effective, but its exercise produces resentment and can generate conflict and lead the intermediaries to organize countervailing power.
- ***Reward power.*** The manufacturer offers intermediaries an extra benefit for performing specific acts or functions. Reward power typically produces better results than coercive power, but it can be overrated. The intermediaries may come to expect a reward every time the manufacturer wants a certain behavior to occur.
- ***Legitimate power.*** The manufacturer requests a behavior that is warranted under the contract. As long as the intermediaries view the manufacturer as a legitimate leader, legitimate power works.
- ***Expert power.*** The manufacturer has special knowledge the intermediaries value. Once the intermediaries acquire this expertise, however, expert power weakens. The manufacturer must continue to develop new expertise so that the intermediaries will want to continue cooperating.
- ***Referent power.*** The manufacturer is so highly respected that intermediaries are proud to be associated with it. Companies such as IBM, Caterpillar, and Hewlett-Packard have high referent power.[33]

Coercive and reward power are objectively observable; legitimate, expert, and referent power are more subjective and depend on the ability and willingness of parties to recognize them.

Most producers see gaining intermediaries' cooperation as a huge challenge.[34] They often use positive motivators, such as higher margins, special deals, premiums, cooperative advertising allowances, display allowances, and sales contests. At times they will apply negative sanctions, such as threatening to reduce margins, slow down delivery, or terminate the relationship. The weakness of this approach is that the producer is using crude, stimulus-response thinking.

More sophisticated companies try to forge a long-term partnership with distributors. The manufacturer clearly communicates what it wants from its distributors in the way of market coverage, inventory levels, marketing development, account solicitation, technical advice and services, and marketing information. The manufacturer seeks distributor agreement with these policies and may introduce a compensation plan for adhering to the policies.

To streamline the supply chain and cut costs, many manufacturers and retailers have adopted *efficient consumer response (ECR) practices* to organize their relationships in three areas: (1) *demand side management* or collaborative practices to stimulate consumer demand by promoting joint marketing and sales activities, (2) *supply side management* or collaborative practices to optimize supply (with a focus on joint logistics and supply chain activities), and (3) *enablers and integrators,* or collaborative information technology and process improvement tools to support joint activities that reduce operational problems, allow greater standardization, and so on. Research has shown that although ECR has a positive impact on manufacturers' economic performance and capability development, it may also generate greater perceptions of inequity on the manufacturer's part in that they feel they are inequitably sharing the burdens of ECR adoption and not getting as much as they deserve.[35]

Evaluating Channel Members

Producers must periodically evaluate intermediaries' performance against such standards as sales-quota attainment, average inventory levels, customer delivery time, treatment of damaged and lost goods, and cooperation in promotional and training programs. A producer will occasionally discover that it is paying particular intermediaries too much for what they are actually doing. One manufacturer compensating a distributor for holding inventories found that the inventories were actually held in a public warehouse at its own expense. Producers should set up functional discounts in which they pay specified amounts for the trade channel's performance of each agreed-upon service. Underperformers need to be counseled, retrained, motivated, or terminated.

Modifying Channel Design and Arrangements

A producer must periodically review and modify its channel design and arrangements. It will want to modify them when the distribution channel is not working as planned, consumer buying patterns change, the market expands, new competition arises, innovative distribution channels emerge, and the product moves into later stages in the product life cycle.

No marketing channel will remain effective over the whole product life cycle. Early buyers might be willing to pay for high-value-added channels, but later buyers will switch to lower-cost channels. Small office copiers were first sold by manufacturers' direct sales forces, later through office equipment dealers, still later through mass merchandisers, and now by mail-order firms and Internet marketers.

In competitive markets with low entry barriers, the optimal channel structure will inevitably change over time. The change could mean adding or dropping individual channel members, adding or dropping particular market channels, or developing a totally new way to sell goods. Consider Apple.

APPLE STORES

When Apple stores were launched in 2001, many critics questioned their prospects and BusinessWeek published an article titled, "Sorry Steve, Here's Why Apple Stores Won't Work." Fast-forward five years, and Apple was celebrating the launch of its spectacular new Manhattan showcase store. With over 175 locations and annual sales per square foot of $4,032—compared to Tiffany's $2,666, Best Buy's $930, and Saks' $362—Apple stores were an unqualified success. Opened because of the company's frustration with its poor retail presentation by others, the stores sell Apple products exclusively and target tech-savvy customers with in-store product presentations and workshops; a full line of Apple products, software, and accessories; and a "Genius Bar" staffed by Apple specialists who provide technical support often free of charge. Although the move upset existing retailers, Apple has worked hard to smooth relationships, in part justifying the decision to add its own stores as a natural evolution of its already existing online sales channel.[36]

Adding or dropping individual channel members requires an incremental analysis. What would the firm's profits look like with and without this intermediary? A producer may drop any intermediary whose sales drop below a certain level. Increasingly more detailed customer shopping information stored in databases and sophisticated means to analyze that data can provide guidance into those decisions.[37]

Perhaps the most difficult decision of all is whether to revise the overall channel strategy.[38] Distribution channels clearly become outmoded, and a gap arises between the existing distribution system and the ideal system that would satisfy target customers' needs and desires. Examples abound: Avon's door-to-door system for selling cosmetics was modified as more women entered the workforce. In retail banking, despite a belief that technological advances such as automated teller machines, online banking, and telephone call centers would reduce customers' reliance on their neighborhood branches, banks have found that

To preserve its channel relationships, Apple has justified the opening of hundreds of its own retail stores as a natural extension of its online sales channel. The stores have proven extremely profitable.

many people still want "high touch" over "high tech," or at least the choice. Banks are responding by opening more branches and developing more cross-selling and up-selling practices to take advantage of the face-to-face contact that results.

::: Channel Integration and Systems

Distribution channels don't stand still. New wholesaling and retailing institutions emerge, and new channel systems evolve. We'll look at the recent growth of vertical, horizontal, and multichannel marketing systems; the next section examines how these systems cooperate, conflict, and compete.

Vertical Marketing Systems

One of the most significant recent channel developments is the rise of vertical marketing systems. A **conventional marketing channel** comprises an independent producer, wholesaler(s), and retailer(s). Each is a separate business seeking to maximize its own profits, even if this goal reduces profit for the system as a whole. No channel member has complete or substantial control over other members.

A **vertical marketing system (VMS)**, by contrast, comprises the producer, wholesaler(s), and retailer(s) acting as a unified system. One channel member, the *channel captain*, owns the others or franchises them or has so much power that they all cooperate. "Marketing Insight: The Importance of Channel Stewards" provides some perspective on how *channel stewards*, a closely related concept, should work.

Vertical marketing systems (VMSs) arose as a result of strong channel members' attempts to control channel behavior and eliminate the conflict that results when independent members pursue their own objectives. VMSs achieve economies through size, bargaining power, and elimination of duplicated services. Business buyers of complex products and systems have been shown to value the extensive exchange of information they can obtain from a VMS.[39] VMSs have become the dominant mode of distribution in the U.S. consumer marketplace, serving between 70% and 80% of the total market. There are three types of VMS: corporate, administered, and contractual.

CORPORATE VMS A *corporate VMS* combines successive stages of production and distribution under single ownership. For example, Sears obtains over 50% of the goods it sells from companies that it partly or wholly owns. Sherwin-Williams makes paint but also owns and operates 3,000 retail outlets.

As part of its vertical marketing system, Sherwin-Williams both manufactures paint and sells it directly in its own retail outlets.

ADMINISTERED VMS An *administered VMS* coordinates successive stages of production and distribution through the size and power of one of the members. Manufacturers of a dominant brand are able to secure strong trade cooperation and support from resellers. Thus Kodak, Gillette, and Campbell Soup are able to command high levels of cooperation from their resellers in connection with displays, shelf space, promotions, and price policies.

The most advanced supply-distributor arrangement for administered VMSs relies on **distribution programming**, which builds a planned, professionally managed, vertical marketing system that meets the needs of both manufacturer and distributors. The manufacturer establishes a department within the company called *distributor relations planning*. Its job is to identify distributor needs and build up merchandising programs to help each distributor operate as efficiently as possible. This

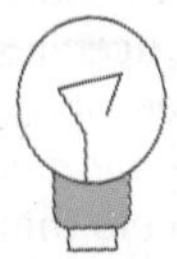

MARKETING INSIGHT | THE IMPORTANCE OF CHANNEL STEWARDS

Harvard's V. Kasturi Rangan believes that companies should adopt a new approach to going to market—channel stewardship. He defines **channel stewardship** as the ability of a given participant in a distribution channel—a steward—to create a go-to-market strategy that simultaneously addresses customers' best interests and drives profits for all channel partners. A channel steward might be the maker of the product or service (such as Procter & Gamble or American Airlines); the maker of a key component (such as microchip maker Intel); the supplier or assembler (such as Dell or Arrow Electronics); or the distributor (such as W. W. Grainger) or retailer (such as Wal-Mart). Within a company, Rangan notes the stewardship function might reside with the CEO, a top manager, or a team of senior managers.

The concept of channel stewardship is meant to appeal to any organization in the distribution channel that wants to bring a disciplined approach to channel strategy. An effective channel steward considers the channel from the customer's point of view. With that view in mind, the steward then advocates for change among all participants, transforming disparate entities into partners having a common purpose.

Channel stewardship has two important outcomes. One is to expand value for the steward's customers and increase the size of the market or existing customers' purchases through the channel in the process. A second outcome is to create a more tightly woven, and yet adaptable, channel where valuable members are suitably rewarded and the less valuable members are weeded out.

Rangan outlines three key disciplines of channel management:

1. ***Mapping*** is undertaken at an industry level to gain a sense of what the key determinants of channel strategy are and how they are evolving. It gives an idea of current best practices and gaps, and it projects what the future requirements might be.
2. ***Building and editing*** is an assessment of the producer's own channels with a view to identifying any deficits in meeting customers' needs and/or competitive best practices.
3. ***Aligning and influencing*** closes the gaps and works out a compensation package in tune with effort and performance for channel members that add or could add value.

Rangan maintains that the beauty of the channel stewardship discipline is that it works at the level of customer needs and not at the level of channel institutions. As a result, channel managers can evolve and change their fulfillment of customer needs without having to change channel structure all at once. An evolutionary approach to channel change, it requires constant monitoring, learning, and adaptation, but all in the best interests of customers, channel partners, and the channel steward. Rangan also notes that a channel steward need not be a huge company or market leader, citing a number of smaller players, such as Haworth and Atlas Copco, as well as distributors and retailers such as Wal-Mart, Best Buy (consumer electronics), and HEB (supermarkets).

Source: V. Kasturi Rangan, *Transforming Your Go-to-Market Strategy: The Three Disciplines of Channel Management* (Boston: Harvard Business School Press, 2006).

department and the distributors jointly plan merchandising goals, inventory levels, space and visual merchandising plans, sales-training requirements, and advertising and promotion plans. The aim is to convert the distributors from thinking that they make their money primarily on the buying side (through tough negotiation with the manufacturer) to seeing that they make their money on the selling side (by being part of a sophisticated, vertical marketing system).

CONTRACTUAL VMS A *contractual VMS* consists of independent firms at different levels of production and distribution, integrating their programs on a contractual basis to obtain more economies or sales impact than they could achieve alone. Johnston and Lawrence call them "value-adding partnerships" (VAPs).[40] Contractual VMSs now constitute one of the most significant developments in the economy. They are of three types:

1. ***Wholesaler-sponsored voluntary chains***—Wholesalers organize voluntary chains of independent retailers to help them standardize their selling practices and achieve buying economies in order to compete with large chain organizations.
2. ***Retailer cooperatives***—Retailers take the initiative and organize a new business entity to carry on wholesaling and possibly some production. Members concentrate their purchases through the retailer co-op and plan their advertising jointly. Profits pass back to members in proportion to their purchases. Nonmember retailers can also buy through the co-op but do not share in the profits.
3. ***Franchise organizations***—A channel member called a *franchisor* might link several successive stages in the production-distribution process. Franchising has been the fastest-growing retailing development in recent years.

Although the basic idea is an old one, some forms of franchising are quite new. The traditional system is the *manufacturer-sponsored retailer franchise.* Ford, for example, licenses dealers to sell its cars. The dealers are independent businesspeople who agree to meet specified conditions of sales and services. Another is the *manufacturer-sponsored wholesaler franchise.* Coca-Cola, for example, licenses bottlers (wholesalers) in various markets that buy its syrup concentrate and then carbonate, bottle, and sell it to retailers in local markets. A newer system is the *service-firm-sponsored retailer franchise.* A service firm organizes a whole system for bringing its service efficiently to consumers. We find examples in the auto-rental business (Hertz and Avis), fast-food-service business (McDonald's and Burger King), and motel business (Howard Johnson and Ramada Inn). Some franchising is done via a dual distribution system in which firms use both vertical integration (where the franchisor actually owns and runs the units) and market governance (in which the franchisor licenses the units to other franchisees).[41]

THE NEW COMPETITION IN RETAILING Many independent retailers that have not joined VMSs have developed specialty stores that serve special market segments. The result is a polarization in retailing between large vertical marketing organizations and independent specialty stores, which creates a problem for manufacturers. They are strongly tied to independent intermediaries but must eventually realign themselves with the high-growth vertical marketing systems on less attractive terms. Furthermore, vertical marketing systems constantly threaten to bypass large manufacturers and set up their own manufacturing. *The new competition in retailing is no longer between independent business units but between whole systems of centrally programmed networks (corporate, administered, and contractual) competing against one another to achieve the best cost economies and customer response.*

Horizontal Marketing Systems

Another channel development is the **horizontal marketing system**, in which two or more unrelated companies put together resources or programs to exploit an emerging marketing opportunity. Each company lacks the capital, know-how, production, or marketing resources to venture alone, or it is afraid of the risk. The companies might work with each other on a temporary or permanent basis or create a joint venture company.

IN-STORE BANKING

Many supermarket chains have arrangements with local banks to offer in-store banking. Citizens Bank has over 500 in-store branches in supermarkets, which makes up roughly 30% of its total branch network. To reflect the different clientele, Citizens' staff members in the supermarket locations are more sales oriented, younger, and more likely to have some retail sales background than staff in the traditional brick-and-mortar branches.[42]

Horizontal marketing systems include Citizens Bank's arrangement with supermarkets that house about 30% of its branches.

Integrating Multichannel Marketing Systems

Most companies today have adopted multichannel marketing. Disney sells its DVDs through five main channels: movie rental stores such as Blockbuster; Disney Stores (now owned and run by The Children's Place); retail stores such as Best Buy; online retailers such as Amazon.com and Disney's own online Disney Stores; and the Disney catalog and other catalog sellers. These varied channels afford Disney maximum market coverage and enable the company to offer its videos at a number of price points.[43]

Multichannel marketing occurs when a single firm uses two or more marketing channels to reach one or more customer segments. An **integrated marketing channel system** is one in which the strategies and tactics of selling through one channel reflect the strategies and tactics of selling through other channels.

By adding more channels, companies can gain three important benefits. The first is increased market coverage. Not only are more customers able to shop for the company's products in more places, but customers who buy in more than one channel are often more profitable than single-channel customers.[44] The second is lower channel cost—selling by phone is cheaper than selling via personal visits to small customers. The third is more customized selling—such as adding a technical sales force to sell more-complex equipment. The gains from adding new channels come at a price, however. New channels typically introduce conflict and problems with control. Two or more channels may end up competing for the same customers. The new channels may be more independent and make cooperation more difficult. "Marketing Memo: Multichannel Shopping Checklist" offers some concrete advice on channel integration of online and off-line channels.

Clearly, companies need to think through their channel architecture. They must determine which channels should perform which functions. Figure 15.6 shows a simple grid to help make channel architecture decisions. The grid consists of major marketing channels (as rows) and the major channel tasks that must be completed (as columns).[45]

The grid illustrates why using only one channel is not efficient. Consider using only a direct sales force. A salesperson would have to find leads, qualify them, presell, close the sale, provide service, and manage account growth. It's more efficient for the company to perform the earlier tasks, leaving the salesperson to invest his or her costly time primarily in closing the sale. The company's marketing department would run a preselling campaign informing prospects about the company's products through advertising, direct mail, and telemarketing; generate leads through telemarketing, direct mail, advertising, and trade shows; and qualify leads into hot, warm, and cool. The salesperson comes to the prospect when the prospect is ready to talk business. This multichannel architecture optimizes coverage, customization, and control while minimizing cost and conflict.

Channels should be designed to work together effectively. Outdoor accessories retailer Smith & Hawken has seen its Web site sales blossom to 20% of total sales while catalog sales have declined to 15% in recent years. But the company would never abandon paper

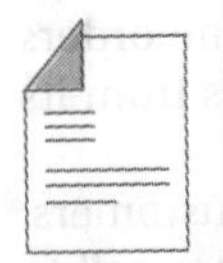

MARKETING MEMO | MULTICHANNEL SHOPPING CHECKLIST

During the 2003 "back-to-school" season, the e-tailing group, an e-commerce consulting firm in Chicago, sent mystery shoppers to visit retail locations of 16 e-tailers to test their claims of an integrated shopping experience in the online/retail returns process. Overall, the study found that 44% of in-store returns of merchandise purchased online required a store manager to override the retail system in order to accept the return. In response to this and several other inadequacies revealed by the study, the e-tailing group created a "Best of Breed Multichannel Shopping Checklist" to help marketers better integrate online and off-line channels:

- Train all store associates on processes for online merchandise returns.
- List your company's 800 number on the Web homepage, and be sure your customer-service hours of operation are easily accessible.
- Provide an information center that is easy to navigate and includes contact information, FAQs, guarantees, return policies, and tips for first-time customers.
- Implement a store locator feature that includes store locations, hours, and events.
- Make store pickup for purchases an option and include real-time inventory levels, where applicable.
- Post the store's weekly circular online for a more complete multichannel experience.
- Offer gift certificates that can be redeemed online and off-line.
- Send e-mail notifications of the order, shipping, and return credit; include a reminder of the returns process in notifications as well as a link to your store locator.
- Supply all pertinent/compatible information for store return of merchandise on the packing slip or invoice.

Source: Excerpted from Hallie Mummert, "Multichannel Marketers Earn a 'C+' on Returns," *Target Marketing* (October 2003): 158.

Demand-generation Tasks

Marketing Channels and Methods — VENDOR	Better communication information	Disseminate communication	Reach price agreements	Pace orders	Acquire funds for inventories	Assume risks	Facilitate product storage & movement	Facilitate payment	Oversee ownership terms
Internet									
National account management									
Direct sales									
Telemarketing									
Direct mail									
Retail stores									
Distributors									
Dealers and value-added resellers									
Advertising									

CUSTOMER

FIG. 15.6 The Hybrid Grid

Source: Adapted from Rowland T. Moriarty and Ursula Moran, "Marketing Hybrid Marketing Systems," *Harvard Business Review* (November–December 1990): 150.

catalogs, because it believes they are the most effective way to make an emotional appeal and the best method to convince customers to go online. Catalogs have actually grown in an Internet world as more firms use them as branding devices. Victoria's Secret ships 400 million catalogs a year, or 1.33 for every U.S. citizen, and catalog and online orders account for nearly 28% of its overall revenue, growing at double the rate of sales from its stores.[46]

Companies should use different channels for selling to different-size business customers. A company can use its direct sales force to sell to large customers, telemarketing to sell to midsize customers, and distributors to sell to small customers; but these gains can be compromised by an increased level of conflict over who has account ownership. For example, territory-based sales representatives may want credit for all sales in their territories, regardless of the marketing channel used.

Multichannel marketers also need to decide how much of their product to offer in each of the channels. Patagonia views the Web as the ideal channel for showing off its entire line of goods, given that its 14 stores and 5 outlets are limited by space to offering a selection only, and even its catalog offers less than 70% of its total merchandise.[47] Other marketers prefer to limit their online offerings on the theory that customers look to Web sites and catalogs for a "best of" array of merchandise and don't want to have to click through dozens of pages.

::: Conflict, Cooperation, and Competition

No matter how well channels are designed and managed, there will be some conflict, if for no other reason than that the interests of independent business entities do not always coincide. **Channel conflict** is generated when one channel member's actions prevent another channel from achieving its goal. Software giant Oracle Corp., plagued by channel conflict between its sales force and its vendor partners, decided to roll out new "All Partner

Territories" where all deals except for specific strategic accounts would go through select Oracle partners.[48]

Channel coordination occurs when channel members are brought together to advance the goals of the channel, as opposed to their own potentially incompatible goals.[49] Here we examine three questions: What types of conflict arise in channels? What causes channel conflict? What can marketers do to resolve conflict situations?

Types of Conflict and Competition

Suppose a manufacturer sets up a vertical channel consisting of wholesalers and retailers. The manufacturer hopes for channel cooperation that will produce greater profits for each channel member. Yet vertical, horizontal, and multichannel conflict can occur.

Vertical channel conflict means conflict between different levels within the same channel. General Motors came into conflict with its dealers in trying to enforce policies on service, pricing, and advertising.

Greater retailer consolidation—the 10 largest U.S. retailers accounted for 80% of the average manufacturer's business in 2005 versus roughly 30% a decade earlier—has led to increased price pressure and influence from retailers.[50] Wal-Mart, for example, is the principal buyer for many manufacturers, including Disney, Procter & Gamble, and Revlon, and is able to command concessions from its suppliers through reduced prices or quantity discounts.[51]

Horizontal channel conflict is conflict between members at the same level within the channel. Some Pizza Inn franchisees complained about other Pizza Inn franchisees cheating on ingredients, providing poor service, and hurting the overall Pizza Inn image.

Multichannel conflict exists when the manufacturer has established two or more channels that sell to the same market. It's likely to be especially intense when the members of one channel get a lower price (based on larger-volume purchases) or work with a lower margin. When Goodyear began selling its popular tire brands through Sears, Wal-Mart, and Discount Tire, it angered its independent dealers. It eventually placated them by offering exclusive tire models that would not be sold in other retail outlets. Other strategies to reduce multichannel conflict are creating and enforcing rules of engagement beforehand (rather than mediating disputes after the fact) and compensating both parties that participate in a sale regardless of which one books the order.[52]

Causes of Channel Conflict

Some causes of channel conflict are easy to resolve, others are not. Conflict may arise from:

- ***Goal incompatibility.*** For example, the manufacturer may want to achieve rapid market penetration through a low-price policy. Dealers, in contrast, may prefer to work with high margins and pursue short-run profitability.
- ***Unclear roles and rights.*** HP may sell personal computers to large accounts through its own sales force, but its licensed dealers may also be trying to sell to large accounts. Territory boundaries and credit for sales often produce conflict.
- ***Differences in perception.*** The manufacturer may be optimistic about the short-term economic outlook and want dealers to carry higher inventory. Dealers may be pessimistic. In the beverage category, it is not uncommon for disputes to arise between manufacturers and their distributors about the optimal advertising strategy.
- ***Intermediaries' dependence on the manufacturer.*** The fortunes of exclusive dealers, such as auto dealers, are profoundly affected by the manufacturer's product and pricing decisions. This situation creates a high potential for conflict.

Managing Channel Conflict

As companies add channels to grow sales, they run the risk of creating channel conflict. Some channel conflict can be constructive and lead to better adaptation to a changing environment, but too much conflict is dysfunctional.[53] The challenge is not to eliminate conflict but to manage it better. Here's an example of how one B2B company added a potentially conflicting e-commerce channel and still managed to build trust—and not stir up conflict—with its distributors:[54]

AB DICK

Printing equipment manufacturer AB Dick was on the verge of bypassing an important distributor channel for a direct e-commerce channel. Instead, the company developed a tiered dealer model and formed strategic supply chain partnerships with influential distributors. AB Dick would deal directly via the Web with all customers in a respective dealer's territory for sales of supplies. The dealer would act as the distribution point, bill and collect from the customer, maintain the relationship in terms of high-end equipment sales, earn incremental margins from the online sales of supplies (even though the transaction would be direct from AB Dick to the end user), and remain the local contact for equipment sales. According to AB Dick's vice president of technology, the dealers were happy because they picked up margin on business they never had, but they also picked up collections, freight, transportation, and labor. AB Dick benefited from reduced costs per online transaction and incremental sales. It had to balance the efficiencies and convenience of direct online ordering for its end users with the need to maintain its dealers as local points of distribution and customer contact.

There are several mechanisms for effective conflict management (see Table 15.3).[55] One is the adoption of superordinate goals. Channel members come to an agreement on the fundamental goal they are jointly seeking, whether it is survival, market share, high quality, or customer satisfaction. They usually do this when the channel faces an outside threat, such as a more efficient competing channel, an adverse piece of legislation, or a shift in consumer desires.

A useful step is to exchange persons between two or more channel levels. General Motors executives might agree to work for a short time in some dealerships, and some dealership owners might work in GM's dealer policy department. The hope is that the participants will grow to appreciate each other's point of view.

Similarly, marketers can accomplish much by encouraging joint membership in and between trade associations. For example, there is good cooperation between the Grocery Manufacturers of America and the Food Marketing Institute, which represents most of the food chains; this cooperation led to the development of the universal product code (UPC). The associations can consider issues between food manufacturers and retailers and resolve them in an orderly way.

Co-optation is an effort by one organization to win the support of the leaders of another organization by including them in advisory councils, boards of directors, and the like. As long as the initiating organization treats the leaders seriously and listens to their opinions, co-optation can reduce conflict, but the initiating organization may need to compromise its policies and plans to win their support.

When conflict is chronic or acute, however, the parties may need to resort to diplomacy, mediation, or arbitration. *Diplomacy* takes place when each side sends a person or group to meet with its counterpart to resolve the conflict. *Mediation* means resorting to a neutral third party skilled in conciliating the two parties' interests. *Arbitration* occurs when the two parties agree to present their arguments to one or more arbitrators and accept the arbitration decision.

Finally, when none of these methods proves effective, a company or a channel partner may choose to file a lawsuit. Coca-Cola came into conflict with several of its key bottlers when the company decided to distribute Powerade thirst quencher directly to Wal-Mart's regional warehouses. After 60 bottlers complained that the practice would undermine their core direct-store-distribution (DSD) duties and filed a lawsuit, a compromise settlement

TABLE 15.3

Strategies to Manage Channel Conflict

Adoption of superordinate goals
Exchange of employees
Joint membership in trade associations
Co-optation
Diplomacy, mediation, or arbitration
Legal recourse

was reached that allowed for the mutual exploration of new service and distribution systems to supplement the DSD system.[56]

Dilution and Cannibalization

Marketers must also be careful not to dilute their brands through inappropriate channels. This is especially a concern with luxury brands whose images are often built on the basis of exclusivity and personalized service. The images of brands such as Calvin Klein and Tommy Hilfiger took a hit when they sold too many of their products in discount channels. Coach has worked hard to avoid diluting its image.

Coach avoids brand dilution while enjoying multichannel distribution by keeping its full-price store shoppers separate from its discount shoppers, even locating its factory outlets a minimum of 60 miles from its retail stores.

COACH

Handbag maker Coach's sustained double-digit growth through 2004–5 was the result of some timely product introductions, but also a well-designed expansion in channels. As it turned out, the fastest-growing segment of Coach's business was factory outlets selling discontinued or older styles at 25% discounts. The company manages its channels carefully, however, and seeks to keep discount shoppers separate from more upscale and profitable clientele. Coach maintains full price in its 199 regular stores and doesn't discount. Merchandise that doesn't sell is not reduced in price but instead is sent to factory outlets located at least 60 miles away. As evidence of the firm's success in distinguishing the two channels, the average full-price shopper (a 35-year-old, college-educated, and single or newly married working woman) is very different from the average factory outlet shopper (a 45-year-old, college-educated married woman who buys 80% of her Coach purchases from outlets).[57]

To help tap into affluent shoppers who work long hours and have little time to shop, high-end fashion brands such as Dior, Louis Vuitton, and Fendi have unveiled e-commerce sites. These luxury makers also see their Web sites as a way for customers to research items before walking into a store and a means to help combat fakes sold over the Internet. Given the lengths these brands go to pamper their customers in their stores—doormen, glasses of champagne, extravagant surroundings—they have had to work hard to provide a high-quality experience online.[58]

Legal and Ethical Issues in Channel Relations

For the most part, companies are legally free to develop whatever channel arrangements suit them. In fact, the law seeks to prevent companies from using exclusionary tactics that might keep competitors from using a channel. Here we briefly consider the legality of certain practices, including exclusive dealing, exclusive territories, tying agreements, and dealers' rights.

Many producers like to develop exclusive channels for their products. A strategy in which the seller allows only certain outlets to carry its products is called exclusive distribution. When the seller requires that these dealers not handle competitors' products, this is called exclusive dealing. Both parties benefit from exclusive arrangements: The seller obtains more loyal and dependable outlets, and the dealers obtain a steady source of supply of special products and stronger seller support. Exclusive arrangements are legal as long as they do not substantially lessen competition or tend to create a monopoly, and as long as both parties enter into the agreement voluntarily.

Exclusive dealing often includes exclusive territorial agreements. The producer may agree not to sell to other dealers in a given area, or the buyer may agree to sell only in its own territory. The first practice increases dealer enthusiasm and commitment. It is also perfectly legal—a seller has no legal obligation to sell through more outlets than it wishes. The second practice, whereby the producer tries to keep a dealer from selling outside its territory, has become a major legal issue. One bitter lawsuit was brought by GT Bicycles of Santa Ana,

California, against the giant Price-Costco chain, which sold 2,600 of its high-priced mountain bikes at a huge discount, upsetting GT's other U.S. dealers. GT alleges that it first sold the bikes to a dealer in Russia and that they were meant for sale only in Russia. The firm maintains that when discounters work with middlemen to get exclusive goods, it constitutes fraud.[59]

Producers of a strong brand sometimes sell it to dealers only if they will take some or all of the rest of the line. This practice is called full-line forcing. Such **tying agreements** are not necessarily illegal, but they do violate U.S. law if they tend to lessen competition substantially.

Producers are free to select their dealers, but their right to terminate dealers is somewhat restricted. In general, sellers can drop dealers "for cause," but they cannot drop dealers if, for example, the dealers refuse to cooperate in a doubtful legal arrangement, such as exclusive dealing or tying agreements.

::: E-Commerce Marketing Practices

E-business describes the use of electronic means and platforms to conduct a company's business.[60] **E-commerce** means that the company or site offers to transact or facilitate the selling of products and services online. E-commerce has given rise in turn to e-purchasing and e-marketing. **E-purchasing** means companies decide to purchase goods, services, and information from various online suppliers. Smart e-purchasing has already saved companies millions of dollars. **E-marketing** describes company efforts to inform buyers, communicate, promote, and sell its products and services over the Internet.

Online retail sales have exploded, growing at 30% a year. It's easy to see why. Online retailers can predictably provide convenient, informative, and personalized experiences for vastly different types of consumers and businesses. By not having to bear the cost of maintaining retail floor space, staff, and inventory, online retailers can sell low-volume products to niche markets. Online retailers compete among themselves in terms of three key aspects of a transaction: (1) customer interaction with the Web site, (2) delivery of the product, and (3) ability to address problems when they occur.[61]

We can distinguish between **pure-click** companies, those that have launched a Web site without any previous existence as a firm, and **brick-and-click** companies, existing companies that have added an online site for information or e-commerce.

Pure-Click Companies

There are several kinds of pure-click companies: search engines, Internet service providers (ISPs), commerce sites, transaction sites, content sites, and enabler sites. Commerce sites sell all types of products and services, notably books, music, toys, insurance, stocks, clothes, financial services, and so on. Commerce sites use various strategies to compete: AutoNation, a leading metamediary of car buying and related services; Hotels.com, the information leader in hotel reservations; Buy.com, the low-price leader; and Winespectator, a single-category specialist. "Breakthrough Marketing: Amazon.com" describes that quintessential online retailer.

Companies must set up and operate their e-commerce Web sites carefully. Customer service is critical. Often, online shoppers select an item for purchase but fail to complete the transaction—the conversion rate of Internet shoppers among the top 100 Internet retailers is only about 5%, much lower than the norm from similar top firms using traditional channels.[62] Worse, only 1.8% of visits to online retailers lead to sales, compared with 5% of visits to department stores.

Consumer surveys suggest that the most significant inhibitors of online shopping are the absence of pleasurable experiences, social interaction, and personal consultation with a company representative.[63] Firms are responding. For example, Ritz Camera and others use live online chat to give potential customers immediate advice about products for sale on their Web sites.[64] Another benefit of providing live sales assistance is the ability to sell additional items. When a representative is involved in the sale, the average amount per order is typically higher. Online footwear retailer Zappos offers fast turnaround and free returns for a wide selection of shoes and finds that two-thirds of purchases during any one day are from repeat customers.[65] B2B marketers also need to put a human face on their e-commerce pres-

BREAKTHROUGH MARKETING | AMAZON.COM

Founded by Jeff Bezos, Amazon.com started as the "world's largest bookstore in July 1995. A virtual bookstore that physically owned no books, Amazon.com promised to revolutionize retailing. Although some may debate whether that was accomplished, Bezos clearly blazed an e-commerce trail of innovations that many have studied and followed.

Amazon.com set out to create personalized storefronts for each customer by providing more useful information and more choices than could be found in your typical neighborhood bookstore. Readers can review books and evaluate them on a one- to five-star rating system, and browsers can rate which reviews are helpful and which are not. Amazon.com's personal recommendation service aggregates data on buying patterns to infer who might like which book. The site offers peeks into books' contents, index, and beginning pages with a "search inside the book" feature that lets customers search the entire text of 120,000 books—about as many titles as are in a Barnes & Noble bookstore. Amazon.com's one-click shopping lets buyers make purchases with one click.

Amazon.com also established itself as an electronic marketplace by enabling merchants of all kinds to sell items on Amazon.com. It powers and operates retail Web sites for Target, the NBA, Timex, and Marks & Spencer. Amazon.com derives about 40% of its sales from its million-plus affiliates called "Associates," independent sellers or businesses that receive commissions for referring to the Amazon.com site customers who then make a purchase.

To overcome the lag between purchase and delivery of product, Amazon.com has offered fast, inexpensive shipping. For a $79 annual fee, Amazon.com Prime offers unlimited free express shipping for most items. Amazon.com has also diversified its product lines into DVDs, music CDs, computer software, video games, electronics, apparel, furniture, food, toys, and more. It has established separate Web sites in Canada, the United Kingdom, Germany, Austria, France, China, and Japan and moved into the black in 2003. Revenue exceeded $10 billion in 2006.

One key to Amazon.com's success in all these different ventures was a willingness to invest in the latest Internet technology to make shopping online faster, easier, and more personally rewarding. The Amazon.com Web project, launched in 2002, opened up its databases to more than 65,000 programmers and businesses that, in turn, have built moneymaking Web sites, new online shopping interfaces, and innovative services for Amazon.com's 800,000 or so active sellers. One application was a service, ScoutPal, that turned cell phones into mobile bar-code scanners.

Amazon.com's next move? The firm is spending heavily on development to allow consumers to download video, music, and books. As Jeff Bezos wrote in his letter to shareholders in 1997, which he reprinted in Amazon.com's 2005 annual report, "It's all about the long term."

Sources: "Click to Download," *Economist*, August 19, 2006, pp. 57–58; Robert D. Hof, "Jeff Bezos' Risky Bet," *BusinessWeek*, November 13, 2006; Erick Schonfield, "The Great Giveaway," *Business 2.0* (April 2005): 80–86; Elizabeth West, "Who's Next?" *Potentials* (February 2004): 7–8; Robert D. Hof, "The Wizard of Web Retailing," *BusinessWeek*, December 20, 2004, p. 18; Chris Taylor, "Smart Library," *Time*, November 17, 2003, p. 68.

ence, and some are doing so by taking advantage of Web 2.0 technologies such as virtual environments, blogs, online videos, and click-to-chat.

CISCO SYSTEMS

Cisco is experimenting with a variety of Web 2.0 applications such as posting videos of its "human network" campaign on YouTube, holding analyst briefings in the virtual world of Second Life, and especially using click-to-chat. "The single biggest home run we've achieved in the last month is click-to-chat," said Michael Metz, Cisco's senior director of Web marketing and strategy. When users, who tend to be small-business customers, click on a button in the technical portion of Cisco's Web site, they are connected to a call center representative who helps them solve their problem. Then Cisco added a more sales-oriented click-to-chat feature. If a user comes back to a product page several times to look at a particular item, a chat box comes up saying, "Can we help you with product X?" So-called proactive chat enabled Cisco to improve its lead conversion rate by 50% in just the first three months.[66]

To increase the entertainment and information value and the customer satisfaction from Web-based shopping experiences, some firms are employing *avatars*, graphical representations of virtual, animated characters that can act as company representatives. Avatars can provide a more interpersonal shopping experience by serving as identification figures, as personal shopping assistants, as Web site guides, or as conversation partners. Research has shown that avatars can enhance the effectiveness of a Web-based sales channel, especially if they are seen as expert or attractive.[67]

SUE'S CREW PRINTING

Andre McReynolds runs a silkscreen T-shirt business out of his home in Chicago's South Side that boasts corporate customers all across the country. But however messy his basement operation gets, purchasing agents shopping at his Web site would never know it, in part due to McReynolds' use of an attractive avatar as the public face of his 16-year-old company. As soon as you go to SuesCrewPrinting.com, you're greeted by an animated character with green eyes and a pink blouse who says, "Welcome and thank you for visiting SuesCrewPrinting.com." Her voice is a little mechanical and sometimes a bit out of synch, but McReynolds says orders have spiked since he installed the avatar, and he's proud that his site has become "stickier," with people spending more time on it and clicking through more pages. McReynolds got the idea for installing an avatar from another Web site. "They were like tour guides and they would tell you to go to this page to get this information, go to that page to get that information, and then they would send you back to the homepage to make the complete sales pitch, and I said, hmmmm, that's a very good idea." Unlike human customer-service reps, avatars work 24/7 and never get tired. Still, they're robots, only as smart as their programming. They're unlikely to replace customer service or sales reps yet, but they do provide a polished, friendly face for small e-businesses that operate out of basements or garages.[68]

Ensuring security and privacy online remains important. Customers must find the Web site trustworthy, even if it represents an already highly credible off-line firm such as Kodak. Investments in Web site design and processes can help reassure customers sensitive to online risk.[69] Online retailers are also trying new technologies, such as blogs, social networks, and mobile marketing, to attract new shoppers.

Although the popular press has given the most attention to business-to-consumer (B2C) Web sites, even more activity is being conducted on business-to-business (B2B) sites. These are changing the supplier–customer relationship in profound ways. Firms are using B2B auction sites, spot exchanges, online product catalogs, barter sites, and other online resources to obtain better prices. LendingTree brokers millions of loans on behalf of over 200 lenders. Retail loans are an ideal commodity to trade online: they're highly standardized, the lending industry is fragmented, and large volumes of transactions allow small profit margins to add up.[70]

The purpose of B2B sites is to make markets more efficient. In the past, buyers exerted a lot of effort to gather information on worldwide suppliers. With the Internet, buyers have easy access to a great deal of information. They can get information from: (1) supplier Web sites; (2) *infomediaries,* third parties that add value by aggregating information about alternatives; (3) *market makers,* third parties that create markets linking buyers and sellers; and (4) *customer communities,* Web sites where buyers can swap stories about suppliers' products and services.[71] Ironically, the largest of the B2B market makers is homegrown in China, a country where businesses have faced decades of Communist antipathy to private enterprise.

ALIBABA

The brainchild of 42-year-old Jack Ma, Alibaba has become the world's largest online B2B marketplace, Asia's most popular online auction site, and now, with its acquisition of Yahoo! China, the 12th most popular Web site in the world. At its heart are two B2B Web sites, alibaba.com and china.alibaba. The former is a marketplace for companies around the globe to buy and sell in English, and the latter is a domestic Chinese marketplace. Whereas Alibaba's rivals, such as Commerce One, were founded with the goal of slashing procurement costs, the Chinese powerhouse has a more nationalist agenda: to build markets for China's vast number of small and medium-sized businesses. Alibaba enables them to both trade with each other and link to global supply chains. Of his focus on SMEs, Jack Ma says, "We are interested in catching shrimp, not the whales. When you catch the shrimp, then you will also catch the whales." European importers are particularly drawn to the "shrimp" in Alibaba's B2B net, in large part because Alibaba has set up a system by which businesses can easily establish trust. When membership in Alibaba's B2B exchange was free, members complained, "I don't trust this guy!" says Jack Ma; so he set up TrustPass, in which users pay Alibaba a fee to hire a third party that verifies them. Users must have five people vouch for them and provide a list of all their certificates/business licenses. Finally, anyone on Alibaba who has done business with a user is encouraged to comment on the firm, in the same way buyers comment on sellers in Amazon.com's or eBay's marketplace. This feature was not very common in the online B2B world, but Alibaba has made it a standard. Businesses are even starting to print "TrustPass" on their business cards, a true sign of Alibaba's B2B credibility.[72]

The net impact of these mechanisms is to make prices more transparent.[73] In the case of undifferentiated products, price pressure will increase. For highly differentiated products, buyers will gain a better picture of the items' true value. Suppliers of superior products will be able to offset price transparency with value transparency; suppliers of undifferentiated products will need to drive down their costs in order to compete.

Brick-and-Click Companies

Many brick-and-mortar companies debated whether to add an online e-commerce channel for fear that selling their products or services online might produce channel conflict with their off-line retailers, agents, or their own stores.[74] Most eventually added the Internet as a distribution channel after seeing how much business their online competitors were generating.

Yet adding an e-commerce channel creates the threat of a backlash from retailers, brokers, agents, and other intermediaries. The question is how to sell both through intermediaries and online. There are at least three strategies for trying to gain acceptance from intermediaries. One, offer different brands or products on the Internet. Two, offer off-line partners higher commissions to cushion the negative impact on sales. Three, take orders on the Web site but have retailers deliver and collect payment. Harley-Davidson treaded carefully before going online.

HARLEY-DAVIDSON

Given that Harley sells more than $500 million worth of parts and accessories to its loyal followers, an online venture was an obvious next step to generate even more revenue. Harley needed to be careful, however, to avoid the wrath of 650 dealers who benefited from the high margins on those sales. Harley's solution was to send customers seeking to buy accessories online to the company's Web site. Before they can buy anything, they are prompted to select a participating Harley-Davidson dealer. When the customer places the order, it is transmitted to the selected dealer for fulfillment, ensuring that the dealer still remains the focal point of the customer experience. Dealers, in turn, had to agree to a number of standards, such as checking for orders twice a day and shipping orders promptly. The Web site now gets more than one million visitors a month.[75]

It's difficult to launch a new brand successfully, so most companies brand their online ventures under their existing brand names. In June 1999, Bank One launched a spin-off venture called WingspanBank to get into the online banking business, but it developed it as a separate entity. WingspanBank customers could not use Bank One branches to do their banking in person. No wonder it garnered only 144,000 accounts and had to be closed down as a separate venture.

M-Commerce

Consumers and businesspeople no longer need to be near a computer to send and receive information. All they need is a cell phone or personal digital assistant (PDA). While they're on the move, they can connect to the Internet to check stock prices, the weather, and sports scores; send and receive e-mail messages; and place online orders. A whole field called *telematics* places wireless Internet-connected computers in the dashboards of cars and trucks, and makes more home appliances (such as computers) wireless so they can be used anywhere in or near the home. Many see a big future in what is now called *m-commerce* (m for mobile).[76]

SHOPTEXT INC.

ShopText Inc., a small New York City company, is making a big splash with technology that opens a whole new channel for marketers. Started in 2005 within an ad agency, ShopText worked with the PayPal unit of eBay to build text-message shopping tools. When the firm receives text messages to donate money or buy products and services, it charges the credit card it has on file for the buyer (who registers on ShopText as you would register on PayPal, for instance) and ships the product from one of its warehouses around the country. Among the first marketers to leap on the text-to-buy bandwagon:

- *Details, CosmoGIRL!, Glamour,* and *Brides* have included print ads in recent issues.
- National CineMedia produced a promotion for DVDs of *An Inconvenient Truth*, the documentary by Al Gore.

- Country music singer Tim McGraw is selling CDs through text-to-buy and also soliciting charitable donations for brain cancer research.
- The Knitting Factory in New York City is selling concert tickets through text messages.[77]

Consider the fast growth of Internet-connected phones. In Japan, millions of teenagers carry DoCoMo phones available from NTT (Nippon Telephone and Telegraph). They can also use their phones to order goods. Each month, the subscriber receives a bill from NTT listing the monthly subscriber fee, the usage fee, and the cost of all the transactions. The person can then pay the bill at the nearest 7-11 store.

The potential market opportunities for location-based services are enormous. Imagine some not-too-distant possibilities:

- Getting a Coke by pointing and clicking the phone at a vending machine. The bottle drops down and an appropriate amount is deducted from your bank account.
- Using the phone to search for a nearby restaurant that meets the criteria you entered
- Watching stock prices on the phone while sitting in the restaurant and deciding to place a purchase order
- Clicking the phone to pay the bill for your meal
- Coming home and clicking a combination of keys on the phone to open your door

Some see positive benefits, such as locating people making emergency 911 calls or checking on the whereabouts of children late at night. Others worry about privacy issues. What if an employer learns that an employee is being treated for AIDS at a local clinic, or a wife finds her husband is out clubbing? Like so many new technologies, location-based services have potential for good or harm and ultimately will warrant public scrutiny and regulation.

SUMMARY :::

1. Most producers do not sell their goods directly to final users. Between producers and final users stands one or more marketing channels, a host of marketing intermediaries performing a variety of functions.
2. Marketing channel decisions are among the most critical decisions facing management. The company's chosen channel(s) profoundly affect all other marketing decisions.
3. Companies use intermediaries when they lack the financial resources to carry out direct marketing, when direct marketing is not feasible, and when they can earn more by doing so. The most important functions performed by intermediaries are information, promotion, negotiation, ordering, financing, risk taking, physical possession, payment, and title.
4. Manufacturers have many alternatives for reaching a market. They can sell direct or use one-, two-, or three-level channels. Deciding which type(s) of channel to use calls for analyzing customer needs, establishing channel objectives, and identifying and evaluating the major alternatives, including the types and numbers of intermediaries involved in the channel.
5. Effective channel management calls for selecting intermediaries and training and motivating them. The goal is to build a long-term partnership that will be profitable for all channel members.
6. Marketing channels are characterized by continuous and sometimes dramatic change. Three of the most important trends are the growth of vertical marketing systems, horizontal marketing systems, and multichannel marketing systems.
7. All marketing channels have the potential for conflict and competition resulting from such sources as goal incompatibility, poorly defined roles and rights, perceptual differences, and interdependent relationships. Companies can manage conflict by striving for superordinate goals, exchanging people among two or more channel levels, coopting the support of leaders in different parts of the channel, encouraging joint membership in and between trade associations, employing diplomacy, mediation, or arbitration, or pursuing legal recourse.
8. Channel arrangements are up to the company, but there are certain legal and ethical issues to be considered with regard to practices such as exclusive dealing or territories, tying agreements, and dealers' rights.
9. E-commerce has grown in importance as companies have adopted "brick-and-click" channel systems. Channel integration must recognize the distinctive strengths of online and off-line selling and maximize their joint contributions. An emerging new area is m-commerce and marketing through cell phones and PDAs.

APPLICATIONS :::

Marketing Debate Does It Matter Where You Are Sold?

Some marketers feel that the image of the particular channel in which they sell their products does not matter—all that matters is that the right customers shop there and the product is displayed in the right way. Others maintain that channel images—such as a retail store—can be critical and must be consistent with the image of the product.

Take a position: Channel images do not really affect the brand images of the products they sell that much *versus* Channel images must be consistent with the brand image.

Marketing Discussion

Think of your favorite retailers. How have they integrated their channel system? How would you like their channels to be integrated? Do you use multiple channels from them? Why?

IN THIS CHAPTER, WE WILL ADDRESS THE FOLLOWING QUESTIONS:

1. What major types of marketing intermediaries occupy this sector?
2. What marketing decisions do these marketing intermediaries make?
3. What are the major trends with marketing intermediaries?

CHAPTER 16 ::: MANAGING RETAILING, WHOLESALING, AND LOGISTICS

sixteen

In the previous chapter, we examined marketing intermediaries from the viewpoint of manufacturers who wanted to build and manage marketing channels. In this chapter, we view these intermediaries—retailers, wholesalers, and logistical organizations—as requiring and forging their own marketing strategies. Intermediaries also strive for marketing excellence and can reap the benefits like any other company.

Spain's Zara has become Europe's leading apparel retailer in recent years by adopting a different retail model. The firm's strategy is to give customers a lot of variety at affordable prices. It can make 20,000 different items in a year, about triple what The Gap would do. Zara distributes all its merchandise, regardless of origin, from Spain and is willing to experience occasional shortages to preserve an image of exclusivity. Unlike some other retailers, Zara doesn't spend lavish amounts of money on advertising or on deals with designers, and instead invests more in its store locations. Zara places its stores—over 90% of which it owns—in heavily trafficked, high-end retail zones. These practices help it to sell more at full price—85% of its merchandise—than the industry average of 60%. By controlling all aspects of the supply chain, Zara can take an idea and make it a reality on the store floor in about five weeks, compared to the months needed by a typical clothing manufacturer.[1]

>>>

Zara's nimble retailing model enables it to bring new fashions from drawing board to selling floor in a matter of weeks and to sell most of its merchandise at full price.

But while "fast-forward" retailers such as Zara, Sweden's H&M, Spain's Mango, and Britain's Topshop have thrived in recent years, others such as former U.S. stars The GAP, Home Depot, and Kmart have struggled. Many of the more successful intermediaries use strategic planning, advanced information systems, and sophisticated marketing tools. They measure performance more on a return-on-investment basis than on a profit-margin basis. They segment their markets, improve their market targeting and positioning, and aggressively pursue market expansion and diversification strategies. In this chapter, we consider marketing excellence in retailing, wholesaling, and logistics.

::: Retailing

Retailing includes all the activities in selling goods or services directly to final consumers for personal, nonbusiness use. A **retailer** or **retail store** is any business enterprise whose sales volume comes primarily from retailing.

Any organization selling to final consumers—whether it is a manufacturer, wholesaler, or retailer—is doing retailing. It doesn't matter *how* the goods or services are sold (in person, by mail, telephone, vending machine, or on the Internet) or *where* (in a store, on the street, or in the consumer's home).

Types of Retailers

Consumers today can shop for goods and services at store retailers, nonstore retailers, and retail organizations. Perhaps the best-known type of retailer is the department store. Japanese department stores such as Takashimaya and Mitsukoshi attract millions of shoppers each year and feature art galleries, restaurants, cooking classes, fitness clubs, and children's playgrounds.

Department stores are the best-known type of retailer. Japan's Takashimaya attracts millions each year with special offerings such as art galleries, playgrounds, and restaurants.

Retail-store types pass through stages of growth and decline that we can think of as the *retail life cycle.*[2] Department stores took 80 years to reach maturity, whereas warehouse retail outlets reached maturity in 10 years. The most important retail-store types are described in Table 16.1.

LEVELS OF SERVICE The *wheel-of-retailing* hypothesis explains one reason that new store types emerge.[3] Conventional retail stores typically increase their services and raise their prices to cover the costs. These higher costs provide an opportunity for new store forms to offer lower prices and less service. New store types meet widely different consumer preferences for service levels and specific services.

Retailers position themselves as offering one of four levels of service:

1. ***Self-service***—Self-service is the cornerstone of all discount operations. Many customers are willing to carry out their own locate-compare-select process to save money.
2. ***Self-selection***—Customers find their own goods, although they can ask for assistance.

| TABLE 16.1 |

Major Retailer Types

Specialty store: Narrow product line. Athlete's Foot, The Limited, The Body Shop.
Department store: Several product lines. Sears, JCPenney, Nordstrom, Bloomingdale's.
Supermarket: Large, low-cost, low-margin, high-volume, self-service store designed to meet total needs for food and household products. Kroger, Safeway, Food Emporium.
Convenience store: Small store in residential area, often open 24/7, limited line of high-turnover convenience products plus takeout. 7-Eleven, Circle K.
Discount store: Standard or specialty merchandise; low-price, low-margin, high-volume stores. Wal-Mart, Kmart, Circuit City.
Off-price retailer: Leftover goods, overruns, irregular merchandise sold at less than retail. Factory outlets; independent off-price retailers Filene's Basement, TJ Maxx; warehouse clubs Sam's Club, Costco, BJ's Wholesale.
Superstore: Huge selling space, routinely purchased food and household items, plus services (laundry, shoe repair, dry cleaning, check cashing). Category killer (deep assortment in one category) such as Petsmart, Staples, Home Depot; combination store such as Jewel-Osco; hypermarket (huge stores that combine supermarket, discount, and warehouse retailing) such as Carrefour in France and Meijer's in the Netherlands.
Catalog showroom: Broad selection of high-markup, fast-moving, brand-name goods sold by catalog at discount. Customers pick up merchandise at the store. Inside Edge Ski and Bike.

3. ***Limited service***—These retailers carry more shopping goods and services such as credit and merchandise-return privileges. Customers need more information and assistance.
4. ***Full service***—Salespeople are ready to assist in every phase of the locate-compare-select process. Customers who like to be waited on prefer this type of store. The high staffing cost, along with the higher proportion of specialty goods and slower-moving items and the many services, result in high-cost retailing.

By combining these different service levels with different assortment breadths, we can distinguish the four broad positioning strategies available to retailers, as shown in Figure 16.1.

1. ***Bloomingdale's***—Stores that feature a broad product assortment and high value added pay close attention to store design, product quality, service, and image. Their profit margin is high, and if they have high enough volume, they will be very profitable.
2. ***Tiffany***—Stores that feature a narrow product assortment and high value added cultivate an exclusive image and operate on high margin and low volume.
3. ***Sunglass Hut***—Stores that feature a narrow line and low value added keep costs and prices low by centralizing buying, merchandising, advertising, and distribution.

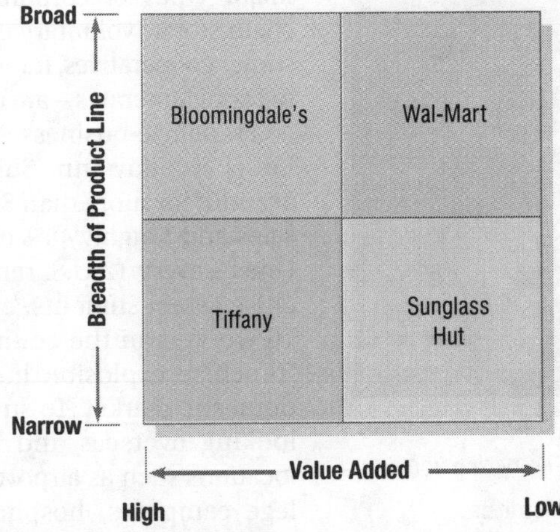

| FIG. 16.1 |

Retail Positioning Map

Source: William T. Gregor and Eileen M. Friars, *Money Merchandising: Retail Revolution in Consumer Financial Service* (Cambridge, MA: The MAC Group, 1982).

4. ***Wal-Mart***—Stores that feature a broad line and low value added focus on keeping prices low and have the image of a place for good buys. High volume makes up for low margin.

Although the overwhelming bulk of goods and services—97%—is sold through stores, *nonstore retailing* has been growing much faster than store retailing. Nonstore retailing falls into four major categories: direct selling, direct marketing (which includes telemarketing and Internet selling), automatic vending, and buying services:

1. ***Direct selling***, also called *multilevel selling* and *network marketing*, is a multibillion-dollar industry, with hundreds of companies selling door-to-door or at home sales parties. Well-known in one-to-one selling are Avon, Electrolux, and Southwestern Company of Nashville (Bibles). Tupperware and Mary Kay Cosmetics are sold one-to-many: A salesperson goes to the home of a host who has invited friends; the salesperson demonstrates the products and takes orders. Pioneered by Amway, the multilevel (network) marketing sales system works by recruiting independent businesspeople who act as distributors. The distributor's compensation includes a percentage of sales made by those he or she recruits, as well as earnings on direct sales to customers. These direct-selling firms, now finding fewer consumers at home, are developing multidistribution strategies.
2. ***Direct marketing*** has roots in direct-mail and catalog marketing (Lands' End, L.L.Bean); it includes *telemarketing* (1-800-FLOWERS), *television direct-response marketing* (Home Shopping Network, QVC), and *electronic shopping* (Amazon.com, Autobytel.com). As people become more accustomed to shopping on the Internet, they are ordering a greater variety of goods and services from a wider range of Web sites. In the United States, online sales were estimated to be 25% higher in 2005 versus 2004. Travel was the biggest category ($64 billion), followed by computer equipment and software ($14 billion), automobiles ($13 billion), clothing ($11 billion), and home furnishings ($8 billion).[4]
3. ***Automatic vending*** offers a variety of merchandise, including impulse goods such as cigarettes, soft drinks, coffee, candy, newspapers, magazines, and other products such as hosiery, cosmetics, hot food, condoms, and paperbacks. Vending machines are found in factories, offices, large retail stores, gasoline stations, hotels, restaurants, and many other places. They offer 24-hour selling, self-service, and merchandise that is always fresh. Japan has the most vending machines per person—Coca-Cola has over 1 million machines there and annual vending sales of $50 billion—twice that in the United States.
4. ***Buying service*** is a storeless retailer serving a specific clientele—usually employees of large organizations—who are entitled to buy from a list of retailers that have agreed to give discounts in return for membership.

Vending machines are enormously popular retail outlets in Japan, dispensing everything from jeans to expensive food. Coca-Cola alone operates more than a million drink machines there.

CORPORATE RETAILING Although many retail stores are independently owned, an increasing number are part of a **corporate retailing** organization. These organizations achieve economies of scale, greater purchasing power, wider brand recognition, and better-trained employees than independent stores can usually gain alone. The major types of corporate retailing—corporate chain stores, voluntary chains, retailer and consumer cooperatives, franchises, and merchandising conglomerates—are described in Table 16.2.

Franchise businesses such as Subway, Jiffy-Lube, Holiday Inn, Supercuts, and 7-Eleven account for more than $1 trillion of annual U.S. sales and roughly 40% of all retail transactions. One of every 12 U.S. retail businesses are franchise establishments, employing one in every 16 workers in the country.[5] In recent years a franchise explosion has helped saturate the domestic market. To sustain growth, firms are looking overseas and in nontraditional site locations such as airports, sports stadiums, college campuses, hospitals, gambling casinos,

TABLE 16.2

Major Types of Corporate Retail Organizations

Corporate chain store: Two or more outlets owned and controlled, employing central buying and merchandising, and selling similar lines of merchandise. GAP, Pottery Barn, Hold Everything.

Voluntary chain: A wholesaler-sponsored group of independent retailers engaged in bulk buying and common merchandising. Independent Grocers Alliance (IGA).

Retailer cooperative: Independent retailers using a central buying organization and joint promotion efforts. Associated Grocers, ACE Hardware.

Consumer cooperative: A retail firm owned by its customers. Members contribute money to open their own store, vote on its policies, elect a group to manage it, and receive dividends.

Franchise organization: Contractual association between a franchisor and franchisees, popular in a number of product and service areas. McDonald's, Subway, Pizza Hut, Jiffy Lube, 7-Eleven.

Merchandising conglomerate: A corporation that combines several diversified retailing lines and forms under central ownership, with some integration of distribution and management. Allied Domeq PLC with Dunkin' Donuts and Baskin-Robbins, plus a number of British retailers and a wine and spirits group.

theme parks, convention halls, and even riverboats. And franchises that offer a unique product or service can always find customers. The aging population in developed, English-speaking countries is driving the success of one unusual franchise.

COMFORT KEEPERS

Comfort Keepers began in 1997 when a registered nurse in Springfield, Ohio, Kris Clum, was frustrated that she was allowed to meet only her clients' medical needs. Many of her in-home clients also needed someone to pick up a loaf of bread or drive them to the doctor, to bathe them, or simply to sit and chat. With her husband she founded the Comfort Keepers franchise, which now has 550 franchised offices in the United States, Canada, The United Kingdom, Ireland, Australia, and even Singapore. Comfort Keepers provides a wide range of personal in-home care services to thousands of elderly or home-bound individuals, and visits range from a few hours a week to round-the-clock care. The number of employees at each franchise is driven by the local needs. For instance, Martin Duncan, a Comfort Keepers franchisee in Hazleton, Pennsylvania, has 54 employees and in 2006 had an enviable growth rate of 49%. According to Franchising.com, 6,000 persons in the United States turn 65 every day, and one in five will be older than 65 by the year 2030. That's the kind of statistic that signals opportunity for Comfort Keepers.[6]

In a franchising system, individual *franchisees* are a tightly knit group of enterprises whose systematic operations are planned, directed, and controlled by the operation's innovator, called a *franchisor.* Franchises are distinguished by three characteristics:

1. The franchisor owns a trade or service mark and licenses it to franchisees in return for royalty payments.
2. The franchisee pays for the right to be part of the system. Start-up costs include rental and lease equipment and fixtures, and usually a regular license fee. McDonald's franchisees may invest as much as $1.6 million in total start-up costs and fees. The franchisee then pays McDonald's a certain percentage of sales plus a monthly rent.
3. The franchisor provides its franchisees with a system for doing business. McDonald's requires franchisees to attend "Hamburger University" in Oak Brook, Illinois, for two weeks to learn how to manage the business. Franchisees must follow certain procedures in buying materials.

Franchising benefits both franchisor and franchisee. Franchisors gain the motivation and hard work of employees who are entrepreneurs rather than "hired hands," the franchisees' familiarity with local communities and conditions, and the enormous purchasing power of being a franchisor. Franchisees benefit from buying into a business with a well-known and accepted brand name. They find it easier to borrow money for their business from financial institutions, and they receive support in areas ranging from marketing and advertising to site selection and staffing. Franchisees do walk a line between being independent and loyal to the franchisor. Their independence can allow them more flexibility.

The New Retail Environment

To find out how malls in Malaysia are addressing the challenges of intense competition, visit www.pearsoned-asia.com/marketingmanagementasia.

In the past, retailers secured customer loyalty by offering convenient locations, special or unique assortments of goods, greater or better services than competitors, and store credit cards. All this has changed. Retail-store assortments have grown more alike as national-brand manufacturers place their branded goods in more and more places. Service differentiation also has eroded. Many department stores have trimmed services, and many discounters have increased theirs. Customers have become smarter shoppers. They don't want to pay more for identical brands, especially when service differences have diminished; nor do they need credit from a particular store, because bank credit cards are almost universally accepted.

Retailers must react or risk going out of business. In the face of increased competition from discount houses and specialty stores, department stores are waging a comeback war. In addition to locations in the centers of cities, many have branches in suburban shopping centers, where parking is plentiful and family incomes are higher. Bloomingdale's opened a store in downtown SoHo to attract young, well-heeled New Yorkers who would rarely venture up to the flagship midtown store.[7] To better compete, other department stores update merchandise more frequently, remodel their stores, introduce their own brands, and sell through mail-order catalogs, online Web sites, and the phone.[8]

Similarly, supermarkets have opened larger stores, carry a larger number and variety of items, and are upgrading facilities. They've also increased their promotional budgets and moved heavily into private labels. Others have sought to create stronger differentiation.

WHOLE FOODS MARKET

In 194 stores in North America and the United Kingdom, Whole Foods creates celebrations of food. The markets are bright and well staffed, and food displays are bountiful and seductive. Whole Foods is the largest organic and natural foods grocer in the country, offering more than 1,500 items in four lines of private-label products (such as the premium Whole Foods and a line of organic products for children, Whole Kids). Whole Foods offers lots of information about its food. If you want to know, for instance, whether the chicken in the display case lived a happy, free-roaming life, you can get a 16-page booklet and an invitation to visit the farm in Pennsylvania where it was raised. If you can't find the information you need, you have only to ask a well-trained and knowledgeable employee. Whole Foods' approach is working, especially for consumers who view organic and artisanal food as an affordable luxury. From 2004–2006, the company enjoyed double-digit growth in overall and comparable-store, year-to-year sales.[9]

Many characteristics of Whole Foods' outlets exemplify the new retail environment, such as helpful employees and unique products.

Here are some of the other retail developments that are changing the way consumers buy and manufacturers and retailers sell.

- ***New Retail Forms and Combinations.*** Some supermarkets include bank branches. Bookstores feature coffee shops. Gas stations include food stores. Loblaw's Supermarkets have added fitness clubs to their stores. Shopping malls and bus and train stations have peddlers' carts in their aisles. Retailers are also experimenting with limited-time-only stores called "pop-ups" that let retailers promote brands, reach seasonal shoppers for a few weeks in busy areas and create buzz. JCPenney unveiled designer Chris Madden's home, bath, and kitchen line in a 2,500-square-foot Rockefeller Center space for one month only. The pop-up offered four PCs for Web buying, so that customers were exposed to a wider selection of JCPenney merchandise.[10]

  Some stores such as Galeries Lafayette in Paris and Selfridges in London not only sell other companies' brands but get the vendors of those brands to take responsibility for stock, staff, and even the selling space. The vendors then hand over a percentage of the sales to the store's owner. This translates into lower gross margins for the department store, but also lower operating costs. The showcase store needs to keep droves of customers coming in, and that means it needs to be an entertainment destination in its own right. Galeries Lafayette's flagship Paris store offered free lessons from professional striptease artists to promote the opening of its huge new lingerie department.[11]

- ***Growth of Intertype Competition.*** Department stores can't worry just about other department stores—discount chains such as Wal-Mart and Tesco are expanding into product areas such as clothing, health, beauty, and electrical appliances.[12] Different types of stores—discount stores, catalog showrooms, department stores—all compete for the same consumers by carrying the same type of merchandise. The biggest winners: retailers that have helped shoppers to be economically cautious, simplified their increasingly busy and complicated lives, and provided an emotional connection, including supercenters, dollar stores, warehouse clubs, and the Internet.[13]

- ***Competition between Store-Based and Non-Store-Based Retailing.*** Consumers now receive sales offers through direct-mail letters and catalogs, and over television, computers, and telephones. These non-store-based retailers are taking business away from store-based retailers. Although some store-based retailers such as Home Depot initially saw online retailing as a definite threat, they are now finding it advantageous to work with online retailers. Most major retailers such as Wal-Mart and Kmart have developed their own Web sites, and some online retailers own or manage physical outlets, either retail stores or warehouses.

- ***Growth of Giant Retailers.*** Through their superior information systems, logistical systems, and buying power, giant retailers such as Wal-Mart are able to deliver good service and immense volumes of product at appealing prices to masses of consumers. They are crowding out smaller manufacturers that cannot deliver enough quantity and often dictate to the most powerful manufacturers what to make, how to price and promote, when and how to ship, and even how to improve production and management. Manufacturers need these accounts; otherwise they would lose 10% to 30% of the market. Some giant retailers are *category killers* that concentrate on one product category, such as pet food (Petco), home improvement (Home Depot), or office supplies (Staples). Others are *supercenters* that combine grocery items with a huge selection of nonfood merchandise (Wal-Mart).

- ***Decline of Middle-Market Retailers.*** Today we can characterize the retail market as hourglass or dog-bone shaped: Growth seems to be centered at the top (with luxury offerings from retailers such as Nordstrom and Neiman Marcus) and at the bottom (with discount pricing from retailers such as Target and Wal-Mart). Opportunities are scarcer in the middle where retailers such as Sears, CompuUSA, and others have struggled or gone out of business like Montgomery Ward. Supermarkets, department stores, and drugstores are most at risk or on the brink—fewer consumers have shopped these channels weekly in recent years as newer, more relevant places have come to serve their needs.[14] As discount retailers improve their quality and image, consumers have been willing to trade down. Target offers Todd Oldham designs and Kmart sells an extensive line of Joe Boxer underwear and sleepwear.[15]

  Kohl's has found some success going after middle-market consumers by bringing in trendy names such as Vera Wang, Elle magazine, skateboard icon Tony Hawk, and the Food Network to design exclusive lines. In addition to more up-market merchandise, Kohl's also adapted the stores themselves to make the shopping experience more convenient and pleasant.[16] Marks and Spencer in the United Kingdom features in-house brands and has built a strong retail brand image. Although these stores tend to have high operating costs, they command high margins if their in-house brands are both fashionable and popular.[17]

- ***Growing Investment in Technology.*** Retailers are using computers to produce better forecasts, control inventory costs, order electronically from suppliers, send e-mail between stores, and even sell to customers within stores. Some retailers are borrowing technological tactics from other industries, and with great success.

WENDY'S INTERNATIONAL INC.

Drive-thru business accounts for a sizable percentage of fast-food sales, but the system is dogged by two major profit killers: (1) employee theft (when late-night drive-thru employees give food to their friends and pocket the cash) and (2) slowness. No one wants to sit in a hot car waiting for cold french fries to arrive. Now, Wendy's, McDonald's, and a host of fast-food companies are adopting call center technology to fill orders even faster.

When you pull into one of the drive-thru lanes at the Wendy's in Burbank, California, the voice that takes your order will be coming from Nashua, New Hampshire, 3,000 miles away. It's connected to the computer of a call center employee using Internet calling technology, who needs a mere 40 milliseconds to transfer your order to a screen in the drive-thru kitchen. Call centers not only free employees to put orders together faster; they also make orders more accurate and more profitable. Call center employees are trained to urge customers to order extras, such as a larger order of fries or a drink with each order. It's a win-win strategy, especially for Wendy's, which differentiates itself on its drive-thru speed and has been the industry's speediest server for seven straight years. With call center technology, Wendy's expects to complete orders in under 90 seconds.[18]

Retailers are also adopting checkout scanning systems,[19] electronic funds transfer, electronic data interchange,[20] in-store television, store traffic radar systems,[21] and improved merchandise-handling systems. Some employ goggle-like devices that record what test customers see by projecting an infrared beam onto the wearer's retina. One finding was that many shoppers ignored products at eye level—the optimum location was between their waist and chest level.[22]

Retailers are also introducing features to help customers as they shop. Some supermarkets are installing personal shopping "assistants" on shopping carts that help customers locate items in the store, find out about sales and special offers, and even place a deli order.[23]

■ ***Global Profile of Major Retailers.*** Retailers with unique formats and strong brand positioning are increasingly appearing in other countries.[24] U.S. retailers such as The Limited and The GAP have become globally prominent. Wal-Mart operates over 2,700 stores abroad where it does 20% of its business. Dutch retailer Ahold, and Belgian retailer Delhaize earn almost 80% of their sales in nondomestic markets. Among foreign-based global retailers in the United States are Britain's Marks and Spencer, Italy's Benetton, France's Carrefour hypermarkets, Sweden's IKEA home furnishings stores, and Japan's Uniqlo casual apparel retailer and Yaohan supermarkets.[25]

Marketing Decisions

With this new retail environment as a backdrop, we will examine retailers' marketing decisions in the areas of target market, product assortment and procurement, prices, services and store atmosphere, store activities and experiences, communications, and location.

TARGET MARKET Until it defines and profiles the target market, the retailer cannot make consistent decisions about product assortment, store decor, advertising messages and media, price, and service levels. Ann Taylor has an external client panel of 3,000 customers who provide feedback on its merchandise and even its marketing campaign. The firm also solicits employees' input.[26]

Mistakes in choosing or switching target markets can be costly. When historically mass-market jeweler Zales decided to chase upscale customers, it replaced one-third of its merchandise, dropping inexpensive, low-quality diamond jewelry for high-margin, fashionable 14-karat gold and silver pieces and also shifting its ad campaign in the process. The move was a disaster. Zales lost many of its traditional customers without winning over the new customers it had hoped to attract.[27]

To better hit their targets, retailers are slicing the market into finer and finer segments and introducing new lines of stores to provide a more relevant set of offerings to exploit niche markets: Gymboree launched Janie and Jack, selling apparel and gifts for babies and toddlers; Hot Topic introduced Torrid, selling fashions for plus-sized teen girls.

PRODUCT ASSORTMENT The retailer's product assortment must match the target market's shopping expectations. The retailer must decide on product-assortment *breadth* and *depth*. A restaurant can offer a narrow and shallow assortment (small lunch counters), a narrow and deep assortment (delicatessen), a broad and shallow assortment (cafeteria), or a broad and deep assortment (large restaurant). Table 16.3 provides an illustration of how Borders developed category assortment within a section of its stores.

Product assortment can be especially challenging in fast-moving industries such as technology or fashion. Urban Outfitters ran into trouble when it strayed from its "hip, but not too hip" formula, moving to embrace new styles too quickly. Sales fell over 25% during 2006.[28] On the other hand, active and casual apparel retailer Aeropostale has found success by carefully matching its product assortment to its young teen target market's needs.

TABLE 16.3 | Retail Category Management

Step	What It Means	How Borders Applied It
1. Define the category.	Decide where you draw the line between product categories. For example, do your customers view alcohol and soft drinks as one beverage category, or should you manage them separately?	Named the cookbook section Food and Cooking because consumers expected to see books on nutrition there as well.
2. Figure out its role.	Determine how the category fits into the whole store. For example, "destination" categories lure folks in, so they get maximum marketing push, whereas "fill-ins" carry a minimal assortment.	Decided to make Food and Cooking a destination category.
3. Assess performance.	Analyze sales data from AC Nielsen, Information Resources Inc., and others. Identify opportunities.	Learned that cookbooks sell faster than expected during holidays. Responded by creating gift promotions.
4. Set goals.	Agree on the category's objectives, including sales, profit, and average-transaction targets, as well as customer satisfaction levels.	Aimed to grow cookbook sales faster than the store average and to grab market share from competition.
5. Choose the audience.	Sharpen your focus within the category for maximum effect.	Decided to go after repeat buyers. "Since 30% of shoppers buy 70% of the cookbooks sold, we are aiming at the enthusiast," says Borders' chief marketing officer Mike Spinozzi.
6. Figure out tactics.	Decide the best product selection, promotion merchandising, and pricing to achieve the category's goals.	Gave more prominent display to books by celebrity chefs such as Mario Batali. Created a more approachable product selection by reducing the number of titles on certain subjects.
7. Implement the plan.	Set the timetable and execute the tactics.	Introduced changes to its cooking sections as of November 2002.

Source: Andrew Raskin, "Who's Minding the Store?" *Business 2.0* (February 2003): 73.

AEROPOSTALE INC.

Rather than compete head-on with trend-setting Abercrombie & Fitch or American Eagle Outfitters Inc., Aeropostale has chosen to embrace a key reality of its target market: 11-to-18-year-old young men and women, and especially those on the young end, who often want to look like other teens. So while Abercrombie and American Eagle might choose to reduce the number of cargo pants on the sales floor, Aeropostale will keep an ample supply on hand and at an affordable price. Staying on top of the right trends isn't easy, but Aeropostale is among the most diligent of teen retailers when it comes to consumer research. In addition to high school focus groups and in-store product tests, Aeropostale launched an Internet-based program that seeks online shoppers' input in creating new styles. The company targets 10,000 of its best customers for each of these tests and averages 3,500 participants in each of 20 tests a year. Aeropostale has gone from being a lackluster performer with only 100 stores to a powerhouse with 736 mall stores in 47 states and earnings that jumped 16.5% in fiscal year 2006.[29]

When it comes to product assortment, fashion retailers have a particularly hard time staying on top of the right trends. Aeropostale has succeeded by using product tests, focus groups, and online research among its teenage customers.

The real challenge begins after defining the store's product assortment, and that is to develop a product-differentiation strategy. Here are some possibilities:

- ***Feature exclusive national brands that are not available at competing retailers.*** Saks might get exclusive rights to carry the dresses of a well-known international designer.
- ***Feature mostly private-label merchandise.*** Benetton and GAP design most of the clothes carried in their stores. Many supermarket and drug chains carry private-label merchandise.
- ***Feature blockbuster distinctive merchandise events.*** Bloomingdale's will run month-long shows featuring the goods of another country, such as India or China, throughout the store.
- ***Feature surprise or ever-changing merchandise.*** Off-price apparel retailer TJ Maxx offers surprise assortments of distress merchandise (goods the owner must sell immediately because it needs cash), overstocks, and closeouts, totaling 10,000 new items each week.
- ***Feature the latest or newest merchandise first.*** Hot Topic sells hip clothing and hard-to-find pop culture merchandise to teens, catching trends in order to launch new products in six to eight weeks, literally months before traditional competitors using off-shore suppliers.[30]
- ***Offer merchandise-customizing services.*** Harrod's of London will make custom-tailored suits, shirts, and ties for customers, in addition to ready-made menswear.
- ***Offer a highly targeted assortment.*** Lane Bryant carries goods for the larger woman. Brookstone offers unusual tools and gadgets for the person who wants to shop in a "toy store for grown-ups."[31]

Merchandise may vary by geographical market. Electronics superstore Best Buy reviewed each of its 25,000 SKUs to adjust its merchandise according to income level and buying habits of shoppers. They will also put different store formats and staffs in different areas—a location with computer sophisticates gets a different store treatment than one with less technically sophisticated computer users.[32] Bed Bath & Beyond allows store managers to pick 70% of their own merchandise to ensure that stores cater to local interests.[33]

As Chapter 15 explained, retailers that use multiple selling channels must integrate them effectively. Century-old department store chain JCPenney has ensured that its Internet, store, and catalog businesses are fully intertwined. It sells a vast variety of goods online; has made Internet access available at its 35,000 checkout registers; and allows online shoppers to pick up and return orders at stores and check which clothes are in stock in their local stores. These strategies—as well as the introduction of a.n.a., a stylish line of women's clothing—have helped give JCPenney a younger, more upscale image.[34]

PROCUREMENT After deciding on the product-assortment strategy, the retailer must establish merchandise sources, policies, and practices. In the corporate headquarters of a supermarket chain, specialist buyers (sometimes called *merchandise managers*) are responsible for developing brand assortments and listening to salespersons' presentations. In some chains, buyers have the authority to accept or reject new items. In other chains, they are limited to screening "obvious rejects" and "obvious accepts"; they bring other items to the buying committee for approval. Even when an item is accepted by a chain-store buying committee, individual stores in the chain may not carry it. About one-third of the items must be stocked, and about two-thirds are stocked at the discretion of each store manager.

Manufacturers face a major challenge trying to get new items onto store shelves. They offer the nation's supermarkets between 150 and 250 new items each week, of which store buyers reject over 70%. Manufacturers need to know the acceptance criteria used by buyers, buying committees, and store managers. A. C. Nielsen Company interviewed store managers and found they are most influenced by (in order of importance) strong evidence of consumer acceptance, a well-designed advertising and sales promotion plan, and generous financial incentives to the trade.

Retailers are rapidly improving their skills in demand forecasting, merchandise selection, stock control, space allocation, and display. They use computers to track inventory, compute economic order quantities, order goods, and analyze dollars spent on vendors and products. Supermarket chains use scanner data to manage their merchandise mix on a store-by-store basis, and soon all stores will probably rely on "smart tags" to track goods, in real time, as they move from factories to supermarkets to shopping baskets. For more on the possible uses—and abuses—of this technology, see "Marketing Insight: Making Labels Smarter."

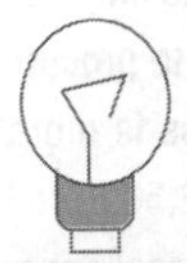

MARKETING INSIGHT | MAKING LABELS SMARTER

Radio frequency identification (RFID) systems are made up of "smart" tags—microchips attached to tiny radio antennas—and electronic readers. The smart tags can be embedded on products or stuck on labels, and when the tag is near a reader, it transmits a unique identifying number to its computer database. The use of RFIDs has been exploding, with an estimated 1.3 billion tags sold in 2006. Radio-tagging products allow retailers to alert manufacturers before shelves go bare, and consumer-goods manufacturers can further perfect their supply chain so they don't produce or distribute too few or too many goods.

Gillette maintains that retailers and consumer-goods firms lose around $30 billion a year from being out of stock on crucial items. The firm is using smart tags to let store owners know they need to reorder, as well as to provide alerts if a large decrease on a shelf may be the result of shoplifting. Gillette also is using smart tags to improve logistics and shipping from factories. RFID technology enabled Gillette to get the new Fusion razor on store shelves 11 days faster than its normal turnaround time. Gillette forecasts a 25% return on its RFID investment over the next 10 years, through increased sales and productivity savings.

Gillette isn't alone. Coca-Cola is embedding RFID readers in 200,000 of its one million vending machines in Japan to allow consumers to buy a Coke using wallet phones with RFID chips. Dutch bookseller Selexyz is tagging every title it stocks after a pilot study showed a 25% increase in sales. RFID-tagged books make for easier inventory control, consumer search, and checkout at the register.

The ability to link product IDs with databases containing the life histories and whereabouts of products makes RFID useful for preventing counterfeiting and even ensuring food and drug safety. A food company could program a system to alert plant managers when cases of meat sit too long unrefrigerated. The FDA is already pushing for the widespread tagging of medicines to keep counterfeit pharmaceuticals from entering the market. Some retailers are using RFID to prevent shoplifting.

Although a potential boon to marketers, smart tags raise issues of consumer privacy. Take tagged medications. Electronic readers in office buildings might detect the type of medication carried by employees—an invasion of privacy. Or what about RFID-enabled customer loyalty cards that encode all sorts of personal and financial data? Already more than 40 public-interest groups have called for strict public-notification rules, the right to demand deactivation of the tag when people leave stores, and overall limits on the technology's use until privacy concerns have been better addressed. To bolster privacy protection, at least seven states including New Hampshire, California, Utah, and Missouri have been debating RFID bills with various restrictions and measures.

Sources: Diane Anderson, "RFID Technology Getting Static in New Hampshire," *Brandweek*, January 23, 2006, p. 13; Mary Catherine O'Conner, "Gillette Fuses RFID with Product Launch," *RFID Journal*, March 27, 2006; "The End of Privacy?" *Consumer Reports* (June 2006): 33–40; Erick Schonfeld, "Tagged for Growth," *Business 2.0* (December 2006): 58–61.

When retailers do study the economics of buying and selling individual products, they typically find that a third of their square footage is tied up in products that don't make an economic profit for them (above the cost of capital). Another third is typically allocated to product categories that break even. The final third of the space creates more than 100% of the economic profit. Yet, most retailers are unaware of which third of their products generate the profit.[35]

Stores are using **direct product profitability (DPP)** to measure a product's handling costs (receiving, moving to storage, paperwork, selecting, checking, loading, and space cost) from the time it reaches the warehouse until a customer buys it in the retail store. Users learn to their surprise that the gross margin on a product often bears little relation to the direct product profit. Some high-volume products may have such high handling costs that they are less profitable and deserve less shelf space than low-volume products.

To better differentiate themselves and generate consumer interest, some luxury retailers are making their stores and merchandise more varied. Chanel has expanded its "ultralux" goods, including $26,000 aligator bags, while ensuring an ample supply of "must-haves" that are consistently strong sellers.[36] Burberry's sells antique cufflinks and made-to-measure Scottish kilts only in London and customized trench coats only in New York.[37]

Trader Joe's has differentiated itself on its innovative procurement strategy.

TRADER JOE'S INC.

Los Angeles–based Trader Joe's began 45 years ago as a convenience store and has carved out a special niche as a "gourmet food outlet discount warehouse hybrid," selling a constantly rotating assortment of upscale specialty food and wine at lower-than-average prices. Trader Joe's also sells roughly 80% of what it

Trader Joe's has an unbeatable international procurement network, enabling it to introduce new products all the time and ensure that no unpopular items remain in the store for long.

stocks under private labels (compared to only 16% at most supermarkets). When it comes to procurement, Trader Joe's has adopted a "less is more" philosophy. Every store carries about 2,500 products, compared to 25,000 at a conventional supermarket, and it carries only what it can buy and sell at a good price, even if that means changing stock weekly. Its 18 expert buyers go directly to hundreds of suppliers, not to intermediaries, and 20% to 25% of its suppliers are overseas. With thousands of vendor relationships all around the world, Trader Joe's has a success formula that's difficult to copy. In addition, a product finds a space on the shelf only if it's approved by a tasting panel; there's one on each coast to satisfy regional tastes. Even if a product makes it onto the shelf, there is no guarantee it will be popular. The company introduces as many as 20 products a week to replace unpopular items.[38] ■

PRICES Prices are a key positioning factor and must be decided in relation to the target market, the product-and-service assortment mix, and the competition.[39] All retailers would like high *turns x earns* (high volumes and high gross margins), but the two don't usually go together. Most retailers fall into the *high-markup, lower-volume* group (fine specialty stores) or the *low-markup, higher-volume* group (mass merchandisers and discount stores). Within each of these groups are further gradations. Bijan's on Rodeo Drive in Beverly Hills prices suits starting at $1,000 and shoes at $400. At the other end, Target has skillfully combined a hip image with discount prices to offer customers a strong value proposition. "Breakthrough Marketing: Target" describes how Target was able to hit the retail sweet spot.

Retailers must also pay attention to pricing tactics. Most retailers will put low prices on some items to serve as traffic builders or loss leaders or to signal their pricing policies.[40] They will run storewide sales. They will plan markdowns on slower-moving merchandise. Shoe retailers, for example, expect to sell 50% of their shoes at the normal markup, 25% at a 40% markup, and the remaining 25% at cost.

As Chapter 14 notes, some retailers such as Wal-Mart have abandoned "sales pricing" in favor of everyday low pricing (EDLP). EDLP can lead to lower advertising costs, greater pricing stability, a stronger image of fairness and reliability, and higher retail profits. Research has shown that supermarket chains practicing everyday low pricing can be more profitable than those practicing hi-lo sale pricing, but only in certain circumstances.[41]

SERVICES The services mix is a key tool for differentiating one store from another. Retailers must decide on the *services mix* to offer customers:

- Prepurchase services include accepting telephone and mail orders, advertising, window and interior display, fitting rooms, shopping hours, fashion shows, and trade-ins.
- Postpurchase services include shipping and delivery, gift wrapping, adjustments and returns, alterations and tailoring, installations, and engraving.
- Ancillary services include general information, check cashing, parking, restaurants, repairs, interior decorating, credit, rest rooms, and baby-attendant service.

Retailers also need to consider differentiation based on unerringly reliable customer service, whether it is face-to-face, across phone lines, or even via a technological innovation. Frontline employees can be a means of differentiating and positioning a retailer's brand. Barnes & Noble hires clean-cut people with a passion for customer service and a general love of books. Borders employees are likely to be tattooed or have multiple body piercings. The company prides itself on the diversity of its employees and hires people who radiate excitement about particular books and music, rather than simply finding a book for a customer.[42]

BREAKTHROUGH MARKETING | TARGET

Target's roots go back to 1902, when George Dayton founded Goodfellows department store in downtown Minneapolis. The Dayton Company (now the Target Corporation) entered the discount merchandising category in 1962 by opening the first Target store in Roseville, Minnesota. By 1979, Target had 80 stores and revenues exceeding $1 billion.

In the mid-1980s, Kmart was the dominant mass retailer, and Wal-Mart was growing rapidly. Sensing a gap in the market for "cheap chic" retail, Target strove to set itself apart from the other "big box" retailers. As CEO Bob Ulrich explained, "Both [Kmart and Wal-Mart] had merchandise we didn't think was particularly inspiring. And we didn't think it would benefit our guests to offer them the same."

To position itself against its bigger rivals, Target began to enhance the design quality of its product selection, focusing on merchandise that was contemporary and unique. The company's team of merchandisers traveled the world looking for the next hot items and trends to bring to the shelves. Target also differentiated its merchandising layout, using low shelves, halogen and track lighting, and wider aisles and avoiding "visual clutter" in stores.

Target also sought to build an up-market cachet for its brand, without losing its relevance for price-conscious consumers. In 1998, the company became the first discounter whose advertisements were accepted by *Vogue* and *Elle*. That same year, Target introduced a line of designer products from world-renowned designer Michael Graves, further establishing its image as an "upscale discounter." Target's stable of design partners expanded over time to include 12 star designers, including Isaac Mizrahi, Mossimo Giannulli, and Liz Lange.

Target's marketing activity also contributed to its success. In 1999, the company unveiled a campaign to build equity in its bull's-eye logo. The campaign featured "Bull's-Eye World," full of "funky, retro pop culture" settings where the bull's-eye dominated the landscape, but no product shots appeared. The campaign helped Target win *Advertising Age*'s Marketer of the Year for 2000.

Target also developed experiential marketing efforts that generate buzz both locally and globally. It built a 220-foot floating shop, called the *U.S.S. Target*, at a pier on Manhattan's West Side during the 2002 holiday season. In 2003, Target established a temporary boutique showcasing Isaac Mizrahi designs in New York City's Rockefeller Center. It created a "vertical fashion show" in New York in 2005, where models with climbing gear sauntered down a vertical "runway" attached to the side of Rockefeller Center. These campaigns enticed local customers to shop on the spot while generating press coverage for Target around the world.

Target has kept innovating with its merchandising model. In 2006, it introduced U.S. consumers to the concept of "fast fashion," already popular in Europe, to help keep the product selection fresh, which in turn led to more frequent shopper visits.

With its unique merchandising approach and world-class branding and marketing, Target achieved enduring financial success. Between 1995 and 2005, the company's stock rose 721%, compared with 254% for Wal-Mart. During that same period, Target's revenues climbed from $21 billion to $52 billion. Revenues climbed further still in 2006 to $59 billion, and the company was poised for further growth.

Sources: www.Target.com; Ann Zimmerman, "Staying on Target," *Wall Street Journal*, May 7, 2007; Mya Frazier, "The Latest European Import: Fast Fashion," *Advertising Age*, January 9, 2006, p. 6; Julie Schlosser, "How Target Does It," *Fortune*, October 18, 2004, p. 100; Michelle Conlin, "Mass with Class," *Forbes*, January 11, 1999, p. 50; Shelly Branch, "How Target Got Hot," *Fortune*, May 24, 1999, p. 169.

Whatever retailers do to enhance customer service, they must keep women in mind. Approximately 85% of everything sold in the United States is bought or influenced by a woman, and women are fed up with the decline in customer service. They are finding every possible way to get around the system, from ordering online, to resisting fake sales or just doing without.[43] And when they do shop, they want well-organized layouts, helpful staff, and speedy checkouts.[44]

STORE ATMOSPHERE *Atmosphere* is another element in the store arsenal. Every store has a look, and a physical layout that makes it hard or easy to move around. (see "Marketing Memo: Helping Stores to Sell"). Kohl's employs a floor plan modeled after a racetrack. Designed to convey customers smoothly past all the merchandise in the store, the eight-foot-wide main aisle moves them in a circle around the store. The design also includes a middle aisle that hurried shoppers can use as a shortcut. The racetrack loop yields higher spending levels than many competitors.[45] Here's how Safeway increased profits by thoroughly reinventing the look of its stores:[46]

Walls. Replaced plain old white walls with earthy tones to convey freshness and wholesomeness

- **Lighting.** Replaced bright glaring lights with warm accent lights that direct attention to products and departments
- **Signage.** Added big pictures of healthy food, as well as display stations throughout the store to suggest meal ideas for time-starved shoppers
- **Produce department.** Enlarged organic section, moving it from a case against the wall to wooden crates at the center of the floor, suggesting a farmer's market

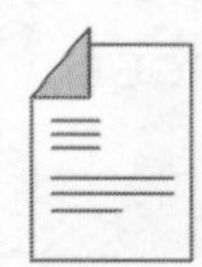

MARKETING MEMO | HELPING STORES TO SELL

In the pursuit of higher sales volume, retailers are studying their store environments for ways to improve the shopper experience. Paco Underhill is managing director of the retail consultant Envirosell Inc., whose clients include McDonald's, Starbucks, Estée Lauder, Blockbuster, Citibank, The Gap, Burger King, CVS, and Wells Fargo. He offers the following advice for fine-tuning retail space in order to keep shoppers spending:

- ***Attract shoppers and keep them in the store.*** The amount of time shoppers spend in a store is perhaps the single most important factor in determining how much they will buy. To increase shopping time, give shoppers a sense of community; recognize them in some way, manner, or form; give them ways to deal with their accessories, such as husbands and children; and keep an environment that is both familiar and fresh each time they come in.
- ***Honor the "transition zone."*** On entering a store, people need to slow down and sort out the stimuli, which means they will likely be moving too fast to respond positively to signs, merchandise, or sales clerks in the zone they cross before making that transition. Make sure there are clear sight lines. Create a focal point for information within the store.
- ***Don't make them hunt.*** Put the most popular products up front to reward busy shoppers and encourage leisurely shoppers to look more. At Staples, ink cartridges are one of the first products shoppers encounter after entering.
- ***Make merchandise available to the reach and touch.*** It is hard to overemphasize the importance of customers' hands. A store can offer the finest, cheapest, sexiest goods, but if the shopper cannot reach or pick them up, much of their appeal can be lost.
- ***Note that men do not ask questions.*** Men always move faster than women do through a store's aisles. In many settings, it is hard to get them to look at anything they had not intended to buy. Men also do not like asking where things are. If a man cannot find the section he is looking for, he will wheel about once or twice, then leave the store without ever asking for help.
- ***Remember women need space.*** A shopper, especially a woman, is far less likely to buy an item if her derriere is brushed, even lightly, by another customer when she is looking at a display. Keeping aisles wide and clear is crucial.
- ***Make checkout easy.*** Be sure to have the right high-margin goods near cash registers to satisfy impulse shoppers. And people love to buy candy when they check out—so satisfy their sweet tooth.

Some of Paco Underhill's additional words of wisdom for modern retailers include: (1) Develop expertise in the mature market; (2) sell both to and through your customer; (3) localize your presence; (4) extend your brand—use your history better; (5) build on the Internet-to-phone-to-store connection; (6) find your customers where they are; (7) refine the details of each point of sale; and (8) go undercover as your reality check.

Source: Paco Underhill, *Call of the Mall: The Geography of Shopping* (New York: Simon & Schuster, 2004); Paco Underhill, *Why We Buy: The Science of Shopping* (New York: Simon & Schuster, 1999). See also, Kenneth Hein, "Shopping Guru Sees Death of Detergent Aisle," *Brandweek*, March 27, 2006, p. 11; "Monday Keynote: Why They Buy," *Loupe Online* 15 (Fall 2006); Bob Parks, "5 Rules of Great Design," *Business 2.0* (March 2003): 47–49; Keith Hammonds, "How We Sell," *Fast Company* (November 1999): 294; www.envirosell.com.

- ***Floors.*** Installed hardwood floors in perishables department to provide a natural feel
- ***Bakery.*** Knocked down walls to show off bread baking in wood-fired oven; added island in center of department that offers custom bread slicing

Retailers must consider all the senses in shaping the customer's experience. Supermarkets have found that varying the tempo of music affects average time spent in the store and average expenditures. Retailers are adding fragrances to stimulate certain moods. SonyStyle stores are seasoned with a specially designed subtle vanilla and mandarin orange fragrance. Every surface in a SonyStyle store is also designed to be touchable, from etched glass with beveled edges on countertops to silk paper to maple paneling. Bloomingdale's uses different essences in different departments: baby powder in the baby store; suntan lotion in the bathing suit area; lilacs in lingerie; and cinnamon and pine scent during the holiday season.[47]

STORE ACTIVITIES AND EXPERIENCES The growth of e-commerce has forced traditional brick-and-mortar retailers to respond. In addition to their natural advantages, such as products that shoppers can actually see, touch, and test, real-life customer service, and no delivery lag time for small or medium-sized purchases, they also provide a shopping experience as a strong differentiator.[48]

Brick-and-mortar retailers are adopting practices as simple as calling each shopper a "guest" and as grandiose as building an indoor amusement park. The store atmosphere should match the basic motivations of the shopper—if target consumers are more likely to be in a task-oriented and functional mindset, then a simpler, more restrained in-store environment may be better.[49]

Consistent with this reasoning, some retailers of experiential products are creating in-store entertainment to attract customers who want fun and excitement:

- REI, seller of outdoor gear and clothing products, allows consumers to test climbing equipment on 25-foot or even 65-foot walls in the store and to try Gore-Tex raincoats under a simulated rain shower.[50]
- Victoria's Secret, retailer of lingerie, other women's clothing, and beauty products, works on the concept of "retail theater": Customers feel they are in a romance novel, with lush music and faint floral scents in the background.
- Bass Pro Shops, a retailer of outdoor sports equipment, features giant aquariums, waterfalls, trout ponds, archery and rifle ranges, putting greens, and classes in everything from ice fishing to conservation—all free.
- The Discovery Zone, a chain of children's play spaces, offers indoor spaces where kids can go wild without breaking anything and stressed-out parents can exchange stories.

REI has responded strongly to the threat of online competition by making its retail outlets exciting destinations full of popular attractions such as play spaces and climbing walls.

COMMUNICATIONS Retailers use a wide range of communication tools to generate traffic and purchases. They place ads, run special sales, issue money-saving coupons, and run frequent-shopper-reward programs, in-store food sampling, and coupons on shelves or at checkout points. They will also work with manufacturers to design point-of-sale materials that reflect the retailer's image as well as that of the manufacturer's brand.[51] Fine stores will place tasteful, full-page ads in magazines such as *Vogue, Vanity Fair,* or *Esquire* and carefully train salespeople to greet customers, interpret their needs, and handle complaints. Off-price retailers will arrange their merchandise to promote bargains and savings, while conserving on service and sales assistance.

LOCATION DECISION The three keys to retail success are "location, location, and location." Department store chains, oil companies, and fast-food franchisers exercise great care in selecting regions of the country in which to open outlets, then particular cities, and then particular sites. A supermarket chain might decide to operate in the Midwest; in the cities of Chicago, Milwaukee, and Indianapolis; and in 14 locations, mostly suburban, within the Chicago area.

Retailers can place their stores in the following locations:

- ***Central business districts.*** The oldest and most heavily trafficked city areas, often known as "downtown"
- ***Regional shopping centers.*** Large suburban malls containing 40 to 200 stores, typically featuring one or two nationally known anchor stores, such as JCPenney or Lord & Taylor or a combination of big-box stores such as Petco, Circuit City, Bed Bath & Beyond, and a great number of smaller stores, many under franchise operation[52]
- ***Community shopping centers.*** Smaller malls with one anchor store and between 20 and 40 smaller stores
- ***Shopping strips.*** A cluster of stores, usually housed in one long building, serving a neighborhood's needs for groceries, hardware, laundry, shoe repair, and dry cleaning
- ***A location within a larger store.*** Certain well-known retailers—McDonald's, Starbucks, Nathan's, Dunkin' Donuts—locate new, smaller units as concession space within larger stores or operations, such as airports, schools, or department stores.

In view of the relationship between high traffic and high rents, retailers must decide on the most advantageous locations for their outlets, using traffic counts, surveys of consumer shopping habits, and analysis of competitive locations.[53] Several models for site location have also been formulated.[54]

Retailers can assess a particular store's sales effectiveness by looking at four indicators: (1) number of people passing by on an average day; (2) percentage who enter the store; (3) percentage who buy; and (4) average amount per sale.

::: Private Labels

A **private-label brand** (also called a reseller, store, house, or distributor brand) is a brand that retailers and wholesalers develop. Benetton, The Body Shop, and Marks and Spencer carry mostly own-brand merchandise. In Britain, the largest food chains, Sainsbury and Tesco, sell 50% and 45% store-label goods, respectively.

For many manufacturers, retailers can be both collaborators and competitors. According to the Private Label Manufacturers' Association, store brands now account for one of every five items sold in U.S. supermarkets, drug chains, and mass merchandisers; 41% of U.S. shoppers now describe themselves as frequent store-brand buyers, up from 36% just five years ago; and store brands were a $65 billion business at retail in 2006.[55] AC Nielsen reports that 72% of shoppers said "national brands are not worth the extra cost," whereas 68% believed private labels are "an extremely good value."[56]

Private labels are rapidly gaining ascendance in a way that has many manufacturers of name brands running scared. Consider the following:[57]

- Wal-Mart's Ol'Roy dog food has surpassed Nestlé's venerable Purina brand as the top-selling dog chow.
- One in every two ceiling fans sold in the United States is from Home Depot and most of those are its own Hampton Bay brand.
- *Consumer Reports* rated Winn-Dixie supermarket's chocolate ice cream ahead of brand name Breyer's.
- Grocery giant Kroger cranks out 4,300 of its own-label food and drink items from the 41 factories it owns and operates.

Some experts believe though that 50% is the natural limit for volume of private labels to carry because (1) consumers prefer certain national brands, and (2) many product categories are not feasible or attractive on a private-label basis.[58]

Role of Private Labels

Why do intermediaries bother to sponsor their own brands? First, they can be more profitable. Intermediaries search for manufacturers with excess capacity that will produce the private label at a low cost. Other costs, such as research and development, advertising, sales promotion, and physical distribution are also much lower, so private labels can be sold at a lower price yet generate a higher profit margin. Second, retailers develop exclusive store brands to differentiate themselves from competitors. Many consumers prefer store brands in certain categories.

A store brand can become a global one if the product is a good as Loblaw's President's Choice line from Canada.

LOBLAW

Since 1984, when its President's Choice line of foods made its debut, the term "private label" has brought Loblaw instantly to mind. Toronto-based Loblaw's Decadent Chocolate Chip Cookie quickly became a Canadian leader and showed how innovative store brands could compete effectively with national brands by matching or even exceeding their quality. A finely tuned brand strategy for its premium President's Choice line and no-frills, yellow-labeled No Name line has helped differentiate its stores and build Loblaw into a powerhouse in Canada and the United States. The President's Choice line of products has become so successful that Loblaw is licensing it to noncompetitive retailers in other countries, thus turning a local store brand into—believe it or not—a global brand.[59]

Some retailers have returned to a "no branding" strategy for certain staple consumer goods and pharmaceuticals. Carrefours, the originator of the French hypermarket, introduced a line of "no brands" or generics in its stores in the early 1970s. Today, a Japanese retailer has taken Carrefours' strategy a step further by successfully defining its stores with the no-brand concept.

MUJIRUSHI RYOHIN

Mujirushi Ryohin's full name translates into "no-brand quality products." The Japanese retailer, known simply as "Muji," has become a huge success, with 387 outlets in 15 countries, including 34 in Europe. Until recently, it has been known in the United States only through products carried in the New York Museum of Modern Art store—an $8.00 aluminum business card holder and $42 collapsible speakers. But the no-brand retailer—which carries 7,000 products ranging from $4.00 socks to $115,000 prefab homes—is opening a 5,000-square-foot store in mid-town Manhattan. Its biggest challenge will be deciding what to charge for its wares. In Japan, low prices are a huge part of Muji's appeal. Another challenge will be to stay true to its no-brand ethos. Muji's intended audience is young 20–30-year-olds who are tired of in-your-face logos and designer goods. But its sleek, functional postindustrial products will probably seem anything but generic to U.S. consumers. Muji's products resonate with the minimalism of Japan's gardens and haiku poetry, and this is how the company will differentiate itself among the competition and—whether it wants to or not—become an identifiable brand.[60]

Generics are unbranded, plainly packaged, less expensive versions of common products such as spaghetti, paper towels, and canned peaches. They offer standard or lower quality at a price that may be as much as 20% to 40% lower than nationally advertised brands and 10% to 20% lower than the retailer's private-label brands. The lower price of generics is made possible by lower-quality ingredients, lower-cost labeling and packaging, and minimal advertising. Generic drugs have become big business. Pharma giant Novartis is one of the world's top five makers of branded drugs, with such successes as Diovan for high blood pressure and Gleevac for cancer, but it is also the world's second-largest maker of generic drugs following its acquisition of Sandoz, Hexal, Eon Labs, and others.[61]

The Private-Label Threat

In the confrontation between manufacturers' and private labels, retailers have many advantages and increasing market power.[62] Because shelf space is scarce, many supermarkets now charge a *slotting fee* for accepting a new brand, to cover the cost of listing and stocking it. Retailers also charge for special display space and in-store advertising space. They typically give more prominent display to their own brands and make sure they are well stocked. Retailers are now building better quality into their store brands and are emphasizing attractive packaging. Some are even advertising aggressively: Safeway ran a $100 million integrated communication program in 2005 that featured TV and print ads, touting the store brand's quality.[63]

The growing power of store brands is not the only factor weakening national brands. Many consumers are more price sensitive. Competing manufacturers and national retailers copy and duplicate the qualities of the best brands. The continuous barrage of coupons and price specials has trained a generation of shoppers to buy on price. The fact that companies have reduced advertising to 30% of their total promotion budget has in some cases weakened their brand equity. A steady stream of brand extensions and line extensions has blurred brand identity at times and led to a confusing amount of product proliferation.

To maintain their power, leading brand marketers are investing significantly in R&D to bring out new brands, line extensions, features, and quality improvements to stay a step ahead of the store brands. They are also investing in strong "pull" advertising programs to maintain high consumer brand recognition and preference and overcome the in-store marketing advantage that private labels can enjoy. Top brand marketers also are seeking ways to partner with major mass distributors in a joint search for logistical economies and competitive strategies that produce savings. Cutting all unnecessary costs allows national brands to command a price premium, although it can't exceed the value perceptions of consumers.[64] "Marketing Memo: How to Compete Against Store Brands" reflects on the severity of the private-label challenge and what leading brand marketers must do in response.[65]

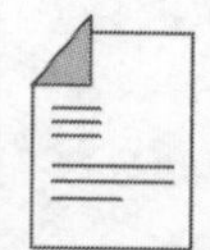

MARKETING MEMO | HOW TO COMPETE AGAINST STORE BRANDS

University of North Carolina's Jan-Benedict E. M. Steenkamp and London Business School's Nirmalya Kumar have identified what they feel are the most successful strategies for launching, leveraging, and competing against store brands. Based on extensive research, Kumar and Steenkamp begin their analysis with a number of observations of the sometimes surprising realities of private labels in the marketplace.

- ***Private labels are ubiquitous.*** Currently, store brands are present in over 95% of consumer packaged-goods categories and have made huge inroads in a variety of other industries, from apparel to books, from financial services to pharmaceuticals.
- ***Consumers accept private labels.*** Two-thirds of consumers around the world believe that "supermarket-owned brands are a good alternative to other brands."
- ***Private-label buyers come from all socioeconomic strata.*** It is considered "smart" shopping to purchase private-label products of comparable quality for a much lower price, rather than being "ripped off" by high-priced manufacturer brands.
- ***Private labels are not a recessionary phenomenon.*** Part of private-label growth in a recession is permanent, caused by consumer learning. As consumers learn about the improved quality of private labels in recessions, a significant proportion of them remain loyal to private labels, even after the necessity to save money is over.
- ***Consumer loyalty shifts from manufacturers to retailers.*** Consumers are becoming first and foremost loyal to a specific retailer.
- ***Profits flow from manufacturers to retailers.*** Between 1996 and 2003, retailers gained five share points of the combined manufacturer and retailer profit pool and more than 50% of the system profit growth.

Kumar and Steenkamp believe manufacturer brands must accept these new private-label realities and respond aggressively. They offer four key sets of strategic recommendations for manufacturers to compete against or collaborate with private labels.

- Fight selectively where manufacturers can win against private labels and add value for consumers, retailers, and shareholders. This is typically where the brand is one or two in the category or occupying a premium niche position.
- Partner effectively by seeking win-win relationships with retailers through strategies that complement the retailer's private labels.
- Innovate brilliantly with new products to help beat private labels. Continuously launching incremental new products keeps the manufacturer brands looking fresh, but this must be punctuated by periodically launching radical new products.
- Create winning value propositions by imbuing brands with symbolic imagery as well as functional quality that beats private labels. Too many manufacturer brands have let private labels equal and sometimes better them on functional quality. In addition, to have a winning value proposition, the pricing needs to be monitored closely to ensure that perceived benefits are equal to the price premium.

Source: Jan-Benedict E. M. Steenkamp and Nirmalya Kumar, *Private Label Strategy: How to Meet the Store-Brand Challenge* (Boston: Harvard Business School Press, 2007).

::: Wholesaling

Wholesaling includes all the activities in selling goods or services to those who buy for resale or business use. It excludes manufacturers and farmers because they are engaged primarily in production, and it excludes retailers. The major types of wholesalers are described in Table 16.4.

Wholesalers (also called *distributors*) differ from retailers in a number of ways. First, wholesalers pay less attention to promotion, atmosphere, and location because they are dealing with business customers rather than final consumers. Second, wholesale transactions are usually larger than retail transactions, and wholesalers usually cover a larger trade area than retailers. Third, the government deals with wholesalers and retailers differently in terms of legal regulations and taxes.

Why do manufacturers not sell directly to retailers or final consumers? Why are wholesalers used at all? In general, wholesalers are more efficient in performing one or more of the following functions:

- ***Selling and promoting.*** Wholesalers' sales forces help manufacturers reach many small business customers at a relatively low cost. They have more contacts, and buyers often trust them more than they trust a distant manufacturer.
- ***Buying and assortment building.*** Wholesalers are able to select items and build the assortments their customers need, saving them considerable work.
- ***Bulk breaking.*** Wholesalers achieve savings for their customers by buying large carload lots and breaking the bulk into smaller units.

TABLE 16.4

Major Wholesaler Types

Merchant wholesalers: Independently owned businesses that take title to the merchandise they handle. They are full-service and limited-service jobbers, distributors, mill supply houses.

Full-service wholesalers: Carry stock, maintain a sales force, offer credit, make deliveries, provide management assistance. Wholesale merchants sell primarily to retailers: Some carry several merchandise lines, some carry one or two lines, others carry only part of a line. Industrial distributors sell to manufacturers and also provide services such as credit and delivery.

Limited-service wholesalers: *Cash and carry wholesalers* sell a limited line of fast-moving goods to small retailers for cash. *Truck wholesalers* sell and deliver a limited line of semiperishable goods to supermarkets, grocery stores, hospitals, restaurants, hotels. *Drop shippers* serve bulk industries such as coal, lumber, heavy equipment. They assume title and risk from the time an order is accepted to its delivery. *Rack jobbers* serve grocery retailers in nonfood items. Delivery people set up displays, price goods, keep inventory records; they retain title to goods and bill retailers only for goods sold to end of year. *Producers' cooperatives* assemble farm produce to sell in local markets. *Mail-order wholesalers* send catalogs to retail, industrial, and institutional customers; orders are filled and sent by mail, rail, plane, or truck.

Brokers and agents: Facilitate buying and selling, on commission of 2% to 6% of the selling price; limited functions; generally specialize by product line or customer type. *Brokers* bring buyers and sellers together and assist in negotiation; paid by the party hiring them. Food brokers, real estate brokers, insurance brokers. *Agents* represent buyers or sellers on a more permanent basis. Most manufacturers' agents are small businesses with a few skilled salespeople: Selling agents have contractual authority to sell a manufacturer's entire output; purchasing agents make purchases for buyers and often receive, inspect, warehouse, and ship merchandise; commission merchants take physical possession of products and negotiate sales.

Manufacturers' and retailers' branches and offices: Wholesaling operations conducted by sellers or buyers themselves rather than through independent wholesalers. Separate branches and offices are dedicated to sales or purchasing. Many retailers set up purchasing offices in major market centers.

Specialized wholesalers: Agricultural assemblers (buy the agricultural output of many farms), petroleum bulk plants and terminals (consolidate the output of many wells), and auction companies (auction cars, equipment, etc., to dealers and other businesses).

- ***Warehousing.*** Wholesalers hold inventories, thereby reducing inventory costs and risks to suppliers and customers.
- ***Transportation.*** Wholesalers can often provide quicker delivery to buyers because they are closer to the buyers.
- ***Financing.*** Wholesalers finance customers by granting credit, and finance suppliers by ordering early and paying bills on time.
- ***Risk bearing.*** Wholesalers absorb some risk by taking title and bearing the cost of theft, damage, spoilage, and obsolescence.
- ***Market information.*** Wholesalers supply information to suppliers and customers regarding competitors' activities, new products, price developments, and so on.
- ***Management services and counseling.*** Wholesalers often help retailers improve their operations by training sales clerks, helping with store layouts and displays, and setting up accounting and inventory-control systems. They may help industrial customers by offering training and technical services.

Trends in Wholesaling

Wholesaler-distributors have faced mounting pressures in recent years from new sources of competition, demanding customers, new technologies, and more direct-buying programs by large industrial, institutional, and retail buyers. Manufacturers' major complaints against wholesalers are: They don't aggressively promote the manufacturer's product line, and they act more like order takers; they don't carry enough inventory and therefore fail to fill customers' orders fast enough; they don't supply the manufacturer with up-to-date market, customer, and competitive information; they don't attract high-caliber managers, bringing down their own costs; and they charge too much for their services.

W.W. Grainger offers its industrial customers an enormous product assortment online, by catalog, and in hundreds of branches and distribution centers linked by satellite for fast service.

Savvy wholesalers have rallied to the challenge and adapted their services to meet their suppliers' and target customers' changing needs. They recognize that they must add value to the channel.

One major drive by wholesalers has been to increase asset productivity by managing inventories and receivables better. They're also reducing operating costs by investing in more advanced materials-handling technology, information systems, and the Internet. Finally, they're improving their strategic decisions about target markets, product assortment and services, price, communications, and distribution.

GRAINGER

W. W. Grainger Inc. is the leading supplier of facilities maintenance products that help 1.8 million North American businesses and institutions stay up and running. Sales for 2006 were $5.9 billion. Grainger serves customers through a network of nearly 600 branches in North America and China, 15 distribution centers, numerous catalogs and direct-mail pieces, and four Web sites to guarantee product availability and quick service. Its 4,000-plus-page catalog features 138,000 products, such as motors, lighting, material handlers, fasteners, tools, and safety supplies, and customers can purchase over 300,000 products at Grainger.com. The distribution centers are linked by satellite network, which has reduced customer-response time and boosted sales. Helped by more than 1,300 suppliers, Grainger offers customers a total of more than 800,000 supplies and repair parts in all.[66]

Narus and Anderson interviewed leading industrial distributors and identified four ways they strengthened their relationships with manufacturers:

1. They sought a clear agreement with their manufacturers about their expected functions in the marketing channel.
2. They gained insight into the manufacturers' requirements by visiting their plants and attending manufacturer association conventions and trade shows.
3. They fulfilled their commitments to the manufacturer by meeting the volume targets, paying bills promptly, and feeding back customer information to their manufacturers.
4. They identified and offered value-added services to help their suppliers.[67]

The wholesaling industry remains vulnerable to one of the most enduring trends—fierce resistance to price increases and the winnowing out of suppliers based on cost and quality. The trend toward vertical integration, in which manufacturers try to control or own their intermediaries, is still strong.

ARROW ELECTRONICS

Arrow Electronics is a global provider of products, services, and solutions to the electronic component and computer product industries. It serves as a supply channel partner for more than 600 suppliers and 140,000 original equipment manufacturers, contract manufacturers, and commercial customers through a global network of 260 locations in 55 countries and territories. With huge contract manufacturers buying more parts directly from suppliers, distributors such as Arrow are being squeezed out. To better compete, Arrow has embraced services, providing financing, on-site inventory management, parts-tracking software, and chip programming. Services helped quadruple Arrow's share price in five years.[68]

::: Market Logistics

Physical distribution starts at the factory. Managers choose a set of warehouses (stocking points) and transportation carriers that will deliver the goods to final destinations in the desired time or at the lowest total cost. Physical distribution has now been expanded into the broader concept of **supply chain management (SCM)**. Supply chain management starts before physical distribution and means strategically procuring the right inputs (raw materials, components, and capital equipment); converting them efficiently into finished products; and dispatching them to the final destinations. An even broader perspective calls for studying how the company's suppliers themselves obtain their inputs. The supply chain perspective can help a company identify superior suppliers and distributors and help them improve productivity, which ultimately brings down the company's costs.

Market logistics includes planning the infrastructure to meet demand, then implementing and controlling the physical flows of materials and final goods from points of origin to points of use, to meet customer requirements at a profit.

Market logistics planning has four steps:[69]

1. Deciding on the company's value proposition to its customers. (What on-time delivery standard should we offer? What levels should we attain in ordering and billing accuracy?)
2. Deciding on the best channel design and network strategy for reaching the customers. (Should the company serve customers directly or through intermediaries? What products should we source from which manufacturing facilities? How many warehouses should we maintain and where should we locate them?)
3. Developing operational excellence in sales forecasting, warehouse management, transportation management, and materials management
4. Implementing the solution with the best information systems, equipment, policies, and procedures

Studying market logistics leads managers to find the most efficient way to deliver value. For example, a software company normally sees its challenge as producing and packaging software disks and manuals, then shipping them to wholesalers—who ship them to retailers, who sell them to customers. Customers bring the software package to the home or office and download the software onto a hard drive. Market logistics would look at two superior delivery systems. The first includes ordering the software to be downloaded directly onto the customer's computer. The second system allows the computer manufacturer to download the software onto its products. Both solutions eliminate the need for printing, packaging, shipping, and stocking millions of disks and manuals. The same solutions are available for distributing music, newspapers, video games, films, and other products that deliver voice, text, data, or images. The newspaper industry, for instance, is rethinking the way it delivers the news to readers who are now becoming accustomed to getting it free over the Internet. Here's what one newspaper company is doing to revamp its market logistics.

THE NEW YORK TIMES

When Ameritech executive Martin Nisenholtz came to the the *New York Times* 10 years ago to take over its digital operations, the *Times*' publisher said to him, "We're not in the ink-on-paper business, we're in the news business. It doesn't matter how we distribute information; what matters is that we can make money out of it." The majority of the *Times*' readers, who cling to their inky two-inch-thick editions of the *Sunday Times*, have been slower to agree. But the *Times* has emerged as one of the most Web-savvy newspapers in the country. The turning point came in 2005, when the company began focusing on building communities rather than pushing information. The *Times* purchased About.com, integrated print and online newsrooms, added blogs, podcasts, and other Web 2.0 technologies, and launched the premium service TimesSelect, which allows only paying users to access the work of certain columnists and selected features. Of 513,000 subscribers in June 2006, almost half were paying the Web-only rate of $49.95 a year, contributing $9.5 million to the *Times*' bottom line. The biggest challenge: making all these changes appealing to the majority of *Times* subscribers who aren't technologically savvy.[70]

Integrated Logistics Systems

The market logistics task calls for **integrated logistics systems (ILS),** which include materials management, material flow systems, and physical distribution, aided by information technology (IT). Third-party suppliers, such as FedEx Logistics Services or Ryder Integrated Logistics, often participate in designing or managing these systems. Volvo, working with FedEx, set up a warehouse in Memphis with a complete stock of truck parts. A dealer, needing a part in an emergency, phones a toll-free number, and the part is flown out the same day and delivered that night at either the airport or the dealer's office, or even at the roadside repair site.

Information systems play a critical role in managing market logistics, especially computers, point-of-sale terminals, uniform product bar codes, satellite tracking, electronic data interchange (EDI), and electronic funds transfer (EFT). These developments have shortened the order-cycle time, reduced clerical labor, reduced the error rate in documents, and provided improved control of operations. They have enabled companies to make a promise such as "the product will be at dock 25 at 10:00 AM tomorrow," and control that promise through information.

Market logistics encompass several activities. The first is sales forecasting, on the basis of which the company schedules distribution, production, and inventory levels. Production plans indicate the materials the purchasing department must order. These materials arrive through inbound transportation, enter the receiving area, and are stored in raw-material inventory. Raw materials are converted into finished goods. Finished-goods inventory is the link between customer orders and manufacturing activity. Customers' orders draw down the finished-goods inventory level, and manufacturing activity builds it up. Finished goods flow off the assembly line and pass through packaging, in-plant warehousing, shipping-room processing, outbound transportation, field warehousing, and customer delivery and servicing.

Management has become concerned about the total cost of market logistics, which can amount to as much as 30% to 40% of the product's cost. The grocery industry alone thinks it can decrease its annual operating costs by 10%, or $30 billion, by revamping its market logistics. A box of breakfast cereal can take 104 days to chug through a labyrinth of wholesalers, distributors, brokers, and consolidators from factory to supermarket.

Many experts call market logistics "the last frontier for cost economies," and firms are determined to wring every unnecessary cost out of the system: In 1982, logistics represented 14.5% of U.S. GDP; by 2006, the share had dropped to just over 8%.[71] Lower market-logistics costs will permit lower prices, yield higher profit margins, or both. Even though the cost of market logistics can be high, a well-planned program can be a potent tool in competitive marketing.

Market-Logistics Objectives

Many companies state their market-logistics objective as "getting the right goods to the right places at the right time for the least cost." Unfortunately, this objective provides little practical guidance. No system can simultaneously maximize customer service and minimize distribution cost. Maximum customer service implies large inventories, premium transportation, and multiple warehouses, all of which raise market-logistics costs.

Nor can a company achieve market-logistics efficiency by asking each market-logistics manager to minimize his or her own logistics costs. Market-logistics costs interact and are often negatively related. For example:

- The traffic manager favors rail shipment over air shipment because rail costs less. However, because the railroads are slower, rail shipment ties up working capital longer, delays customer payment, and might cause customers to buy from competitors who offer faster service.
- The shipping department uses cheap containers to minimize shipping costs. Cheaper containers lead to a higher rate of damaged goods and customer ill will.
- The inventory manager favors low inventories. This increases stockouts, back orders, paperwork, special production runs, and high-cost, fast-freight shipments.

Given that market-logistics activities require strong trade-offs, managers must make decisions on a total-system basis. The starting point is to study what customers require and what competitors are offering. Customers are interested in on-time delivery, supplier willingness to meet emergency needs, careful handling of merchandise, and supplier willingness to take back defective goods and resupply them quickly.

The company must then research the relative importance of these service outputs. For example, service-repair time is very important to buyers of copying equipment. Xerox developed a service delivery standard that "can put a disabled machine anywhere in the continental United States back into operation within three hours after receiving the service request." It then designed a service division of personnel, parts, and locations to deliver on this promise.

The company must also consider competitors' service standards. It will normally want to match or exceed the competitors' service level, but the objective is to maximize profits, not sales. The company must look at the costs of providing higher levels of service. Some companies offer less service and charge a lower price; other companies offer more service and charge a premium price.

The company ultimately must establish some promise it makes to the market. Coca-Cola wants to "put Coke within an arm's length of desire." Lands' End, the giant clothing retailer, aims to respond to every phone call within 20 seconds and to ship every order within 24 hours of receipt. Some companies define standards for each service factor. One appliance manufacturer has established the following service standards: to deliver at least 95% of the dealer's orders within seven days of order receipt, to fill the dealer's orders with 99% accuracy, to answer dealer inquiries on order status within three hours, and to ensure that damage to merchandise in transit does not exceed 1%. Perhaps the king of all logistics is Wal-Mart.

WAL-MART

Wal-Mart Stores Inc. is the largest retailer in the world, with sales of $345 billion in 2006, 1.8 million employees, and 6,500 facilities across 14 countries. Each week, over 100 million customers visit a Wal-Mart store. Sam Walton founded the company in 1962 with a simple goal: Offer low prices to everyone. Wal-Mart keeps prices low through their unrivaled logistics. The company effectively and efficiently coordinates more than 85,000 suppliers, manages billions in inventory in its warehouses, and brings that inventory to its retail shelves. Over 100 million items per day must get to the right store at the right time. To accomplish this goal, Wal-Mart developed several IT systems that work together. Using up-to-the-minute sales information based on point-of-sale (POS) scanner data, Wal-Mart's Inventory Management System calculates the rate of sales, factors in seasonal and promotional elements, and automatically places replenishment orders to distribution centers and vendor partners. Suppliers can use its voluminous POS databases to analyze customers' regional buying habits. Wal-Marts may look the same on the outside, but the company uses its information systems and logistics to customize the offerings inside each store to suit regional demand.[72]

Given the market-logistics objectives, the company must design a system that will minimize the cost of achieving these objectives. Each possible market-logistics system will lead to the following cost:

$$M = T + FW + VW + S$$

where M = total market-logistics cost of proposed system

T = total freight cost of proposed system

FW = total fixed warehouse cost of proposed system

VW = total variable warehouse costs (including inventory) of proposed system

S = total cost of lost sales due to average delivery delay under proposed system

Choosing a market-logistics system calls for examining the total cost (M) associated with different proposed systems and selecting the system that minimizes it. If it is hard to measure S, the company should aim to minimize $T + FW + VW$ for a target level of customer service.

With its network of IT systems customized for each store, Wal-Mart is the king of logistics and the largest retailer in the world.

Market-Logistics Decisions

The firm must make four major decisions about its market logistics: (1) How should we handle orders (order processing)? (2) Where should we locate our stock (warehousing)? (3) How much stock should we hold (inventory)? and (4) How should we ship goods (transportation)?

ORDER PROCESSING Most companies today are trying to shorten the *order-to-payment cycle*—that is, the elapsed time between an order's receipt, delivery, and payment. This cycle has many steps, including order transmission by the salesperson, order entry and customer credit check, inventory and production scheduling, order and invoice shipment, and receipt of payment. The longer this cycle takes, the lower the customer's satisfaction and the lower the company's profits. General Electric operates an information system that checks the customer's credit standing upon receipt of an order and determines whether and where the items are in stock. The computer issues an order to ship, bills the customer, updates the inventory records, sends a production order for new stock, and relays the message back to the sales representative that the customer's order is on its way—all in less than 15 seconds.

WAREHOUSING Every company must store finished goods until they are sold, because production and consumption cycles rarely match. The storage function helps to smooth discrepancies between production and quantities desired by the market. The company must decide on the number of inventory stocking locations. Consumer-packaged-goods companies have been reducing their number of stocking locations from 10–15 to about 5–7; and pharmaceutical and medical distributors have cut their stocking locations from 90 to about 45. On the one hand, more stocking locations means that goods can be delivered to customers more quickly, but it also means higher warehousing and inventory costs. To reduce warehousing and inventory duplication costs, the company might centralize its inventory in one place and use fast transportation to fill orders.

Some inventory is kept at or near the plant, and the rest is located in warehouses in other locations. The company might own private warehouses and also rent space in public warehouses. *Storage warehouses* store goods for moderate to long periods of time. *Distribution warehouses* receive goods from various company plants and suppliers and move them out as soon as possible. *Automated warehouses* employ advanced materials-handling systems under the control of a central computer. When the Helene Curtis Company replaced its six antiquated warehouses with a new $32 million facility, it cut its distribution costs by 40%.[73]

Some warehouses are now taking on activities formerly done in the plant. These include assembly, packaging, and constructing promotional displays. Postponing finalization of the offering can achieve savings in costs and finer matching of offerings to demand.

INVENTORY Inventory levels represent a major cost. Salespeople would like their companies to carry enough stock to fill all customer orders immediately. However, this is not cost-effective. *Inventory cost increases at an accelerating rate as the customer-service level approaches 100%.* Management needs to know how much sales and profits would increase as a result of carrying larger inventories and promising faster order fulfillment times, and then make a decision.

Inventory decision making requires knowing when and how much to order. As inventory draws down, management must know at what stock level to place a new order. This stock level is called the *order* (or *reorder) point.* An order point of 20 means reordering when the stock falls to 20 units. The order point should balance the risks of stockout against the costs of overstock. The other decision is how much to order. The larger the quantity ordered, the less frequently an order needs to be placed. The company needs to balance order-processing costs and inventory-carrying costs. *Order-processing costs* for a manufacturer consist of *setup costs* and *running costs* (operating costs when production is running) for the item. If setup costs are low, the manufacturer can produce the item often, and the average cost per item is stable and equal to the running costs. If setup costs are high, however, the manufacturer can reduce the average cost per unit by producing a long run and carrying more inventory.

Order-processing costs must be compared with *inventory-carrying costs.* The larger the average stock carried, the higher the inventory-carrying costs. These carrying costs include storage charges, cost of capital, taxes and insurance, and depreciation and obsolescence. Carrying costs might run as high as 30% of inventory value. This means that marketing

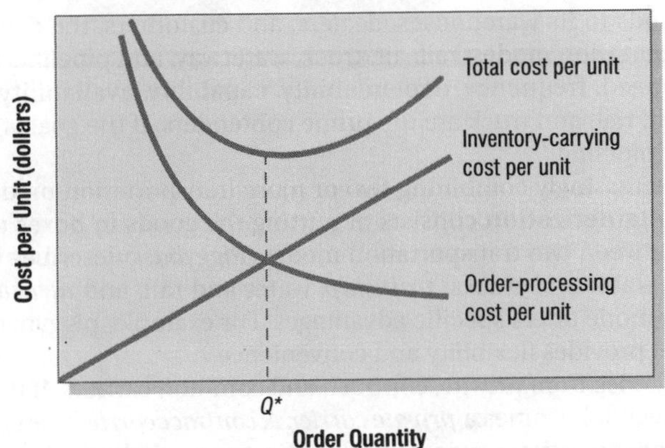

FIG. 16.2

Determining Optimal Order Quantity

managers who want their companies to carry larger inventories need to show that the larger inventories would produce incremental gross profits to exceed incremental carrying costs.

We can determine the optimal order quantity by observing how order-processing costs and inventory-carrying costs sum up at different order levels. Figure 16.2 shows that the order-processing cost per unit decreases with the number of units ordered because the order costs are spread over more units. Inventory-carrying charges per unit increase with the number of units ordered because each unit remains longer in inventory. The two cost curves are summed vertically into a total-cost curve. The lowest point on the total-cost curve is projected down on the horizontal axis to find the optimal order quantity Q^*.[74]

Companies are reducing their inventory costs by treating inventory items differently, positioning them according to risk and opportunity. They distinguish between bottleneck items (high risk, low opportunity), critical items (high risk, high opportunity), commodities (low risk, high opportunity), and nuisance items (low risk, low opportunity).[75] They are also keeping slow-moving items in a central location and carrying fast-moving items in warehouses closer to customers. All these strategies give them more flexibility should anything go wrong, as it often does, be it a dock strike in California, a typhoon in Taiwan, a tsunami in Asia, or a hurricane in New Orleans. [76]

The ultimate answer to carrying *near-zero inventory* is to build for order, not for stock. Sony calls it SOMO, "sell one, make one." Dell, for example, gets the customer to order a computer and pay for it in advance. Then Dell uses the customer's money to pay suppliers to ship the necessary components. As long as customers do not need the item immediately, everyone can save money. Some retailers are using eBay to unload excess inventory. By cutting out the traditional liquidator middleman, retailers can make 60 to 80 cents on the dollar as opposed to 10 cents.[77] And some suppliers are snapping up excess inventory to create opportunity.

CAMERON HUGHES

"If a winery has an eight-barrel lot, it may only use five barrels for its customers," says Cameron Hughes, a wine "negociant" who buys the excess juice from wineries and combines it to make limited edition, premium blends that taste much more expensive than their price tags. Negociants have been around a long time, first as middlemen who sold or shipped wine as wholesalers, but the profession has expanded as opportunists such as Hughes became more involved in effectively making their own wines. Hughes doesn't own any grapes, bottling machines, or trucks. He outsources the bottling, and he sells directly and exclusively to Costco, eliminating middlemen and multiple markups. Hughes never knows which or how many excess lots of wine he will have, but he's turned it to his advantage—he creates a new product with every batch. This rapid turnover is part of Costco's appeal for him. The discount store's customers love the idea of finding a rare bargain, and Hughes promotes his wines through in-store wine tastings and insider e-mails that alert Costoc customers to upcoming numbered lots. Because lots sell out quickly, fans subscribe to Cameron's e-mail alerts at chwine.com that tell them when a new lot will be sold.[78]

TRANSPORTATION Transportation choices will affect product pricing, on-time delivery performance, and the condition of the goods when they arrive, all of which affects customer satisfaction.

In shipping goods to its warehouses, dealers, and customers, the company can choose among five transportation modes: rail, air, truck, waterway, and pipeline. Shippers consider such criteria as speed, frequency, dependability, capability, availability, traceability, and cost. For speed, air, rail, and truck are the prime contenders. If the goal is low cost, then the choice is water or pipeline.

Shippers are increasingly combining two or more transportation modes, thanks to containerization. **Containerization** consists of putting the goods in boxes or trailers that are easy to transfer between two transportation modes. *Piggyback* describes the use of rail and trucks; *fishyback*, water and trucks; *trainship*, water and rail; and *airtruck*, air and trucks. Each coordinated mode offers specific advantages. For example, piggyback is cheaper than trucking alone, yet provides flexibility and convenience.

Shippers can choose from private, contract, and common carriers. If the shipper owns its own truck or air fleet, it becomes a *private carrier.* A *contract carrier* is an independent organization selling transportation services to others on a contract basis. A *common carrier* provides services between predetermined points on a scheduled basis and is available to all shippers at standard rates.

To reduce costly handing at arrival, some firms are putting items into shelf-ready packaging so they don't need to be unpacked from a box and placed on a shelf individually. In Europe, P&G uses a three-tier logistic system to schedule deliveries of fast- and slow-moving goods, bulky items, and small items in the most efficient way.[79]

Organizational Lessons

Market-logistics strategies must be derived from business strategies, rather than solely from cost considerations. The logistics system must be information intensive and establish electronic links among all the significant parties. Finally, the company should set its logistics goals to match or exceed competitors' service standards and should involve members of all relevant teams in the planning process. Getting logistics right can have a big payoff.

PEPSI BOTTLING GROUP

In 2002, Pepsi Bottling Group—Pepsi's largest independent bottler and distributor—was saddled with a creaky supply chain that resulted in many stockouts. It completely overhauled its supply chain, from order taking to truck loading to store deliveries. The new program included technology upgrades, revised work schedules, and a renewed focus on customer service. Warehouse workers, called "pickers," began to wear headsets and barcode scanners on their wrists to create "certified pallets" with close to 100% accuracy. By 2006, stockouts had decreased significantly as a result. As one Pepsi Bottling employee said, "It was almost like when I went to bed I was Fred Flintsone and when I woke up I was George Jetson."[80]

Today's stronger demands for logistical support from large customers will increase suppliers' costs. Customers want more frequent deliveries so they don't have to carry as much inventory. They want shorter order-cycle times, which means that suppliers must carry high in-stock availability. Customers often want direct store delivery rather than shipments to distribution centers. They want mixed pallets rather than separate pallets. They want tighter promised delivery times. They may want custom packaging, price tagging, and display building.

Suppliers can't say no to many of these requests, but at least they can set up different logistical programs with different service levels and customer charges. Smart companies will adjust their offerings to each major customer's requirements. The company's trade group will set up *differentiated distribution* by offering different bundled service programs for different customers.

SUMMARY :::

1. Retailing includes all the activities involved in selling goods or services directly to final consumers for personal, nonbusiness use. Retailers can be understood in terms of store retailing, nonstore retailing, and retail organizations.
2. Like products, retail-store types pass through stages of growth and decline. As existing stores offer more services to remain competitive, costs and prices go up, which opens the door to new retail forms that offer a mix of merchandise and services at lower prices. The major types of retail stores are specialty stores, department stores, supermarkets, convenience stores, discount stores, off-price retailers (factory outlets, independent off-price retailers, and warehouse clubs), superstores (combination stores and supermarkets), and catalog showrooms.
3. Although most goods and services are sold through stores, nonstore retailing has been growing. The major types of nonstore retailing are direct selling (one-to-one selling, one-to-many party selling, and multilevel network marketing), direct marketing (which includes e-commerce and Internet retailing), automatic vending, and buying services.
4. Although many retail stores are independently owned, an increasing number are falling under some form of corporate retailing. Retail organizations achieve many economies of scale, such as greater purchasing power, wider brand recognition, and better-trained employees. The major types of corporate retailing are corporate chain stores, voluntary chains, retailer cooperatives, consumer cooperatives, franchise organizations, and merchandising conglomerates.
5. Like all marketers, retailers must prepare marketing plans that include decisions on target markets, product assortment and procurement, services and store atmosphere, price, promotion, and place. These decisions must take into account major trends, such as the growth of private labels, new retail forms and combinations, growth of intertype retail competition, competition between store-based and non-store-based retailing, growth of giant retailers, decline of middle-market retailers, growing investment in technology, and global presence of major retailers.
6. Wholesaling includes all the activities involved in selling goods or services to those who buy for resale or business use. Wholesalers can perform functions better and more cost-effectively than the manufacturer can. These functions include selling and promoting, buying and assortment building, bulk breaking, warehousing, transportation, financing, risk bearing, dissemination of market information, and provision of management services and consulting.
7. There are four types of wholesalers: merchant wholesalers; brokers and agents; manufacturers' and retailers' sales branches, sales offices, and purchasing offices; and miscellaneous wholesalers such as agricultural assemblers and auction companies.
8. Like retailers, wholesalers must decide on target markets, product assortment and services, price, promotion, and place. The most successful wholesalers are those who adapt their services to meet suppliers' and target customers' needs.
9. Producers of physical products and services must decide on market logistics—the best way to store and move goods and services to market destinations; to coordinate the activities of suppliers, purchasing agents, manufacturers, marketers, channel members, and customers. Major gains in logistical efficiency have come from advances in information technology.

APPLICATIONS :::

Marketing Debate Should National-Brand Manufacturers Also Supply Private-Label Brands?

One controversial move by some marketers of major brands is to supply private-label makers. For example, Ralston-Purina, Borden, ConAgra, and Heinz have all admitted to supplying products—sometimes lower in quality—to be used for private labels. Other marketers, however, criticize this "if you can't beat them, join them" strategy, maintaining that these actions, if revealed, may create confusion or even reinforce a perception by consumers that all brands in a category are essentially the same.

Take a position: Manufacturers should feel free to sell private labels as a source of revenue *versus* National manufacturers should never get involved with private labels.

Marketing Discussion

Think of your favorite stores. What do they do that encourages your loyalty? What do you like about the in-store experience? What further improvements could they make?

PART

7

COMMUNICATING VALUE

IN THIS CHAPTER, WE WILL ADDRESS THE FOLLOWING QUESTIONS:

1. What is the role of marketing communications?
2. How do marketing communications work?
3. What are the major steps in developing effective communications?
4. What is the communications mix and how should it be set?
5. What is an integrated marketing communications program?

CHAPTER 17 ::: DESIGNING AND MANAGING INTEGRATED MARKETING COMMUNICATIONS

seventeen

Modern marketing calls for more than developing a good product, pricing it attractively, and making it accessible. Companies must also communicate with present and potential stakeholders and the general public. For most, therefore, the question is not whether to communicate but rather what to say, how and when to say it, to whom, and how often. But communications get harder and harder as more and more companies clamor to grab an increasingly empowered consumer's divided attention. Consumers themselves are taking a more active role in the communication process and deciding what communications they want to receive and how they want to communicate to others about the products and services they use. To effectively reach and influence target markets, holistic marketers are creatively employing multiple forms of communications.

Dove has been a Unileve stalwart for decades, backed by traditional advertising touting the brand's benefit of one-quarter moisturizing cream and exhorting women to take the seven-day Dove test to discover its effects. A significant shift in strategy occurred for Dove in 2003 with the launch of the Real Beauty campaign, which celebrates "real women" of all shapes, sizes, ages, and colors. The campaign arose from research revealing that only 2% of women worldwide considered themselves beautiful. It featured candid and confident images of curvy, full-bodied women—not traditional models. The ads promoted Dove skin products such as Intensive Firming >>>

The "Evolution" ad video, transforming an ordinary-looking woman's face into the image of a supermodel, was just one of the creative marketing communications that sparked Dove's recent shift in marketing strategy.

Cream, Lotion, and Body Wash. The multimedia campaign was thoroughly integrated. Traditional TV and print ads were combined with all forms of new media, such as real-time voting for models on cell phones and tabulated displays of results on giant billboards. PR was dialed up; paid media was dialed down. The Internet was crucial for creating a dialogue with women. A Web site was launched and supplemented with ad videos. The Dove "Evolution" video showed a rapid-motion view of an ordinary-looking woman transformed by makeup artists, hairdressers, lighting, and digital retouching to look like a model When it was uploaded to YouTube by Dove's ad agency Ogilvy & Mather, it was an instant viral hit, drawing 2.5 million views. A subsequent ad, "No Age Limit," featuring older nude women, also aimed for a primarily online audience. Although the campaign spared much debate, it was credited with boosting Dove sales and share in every country in which it was launched. The Real Beauty campaign received the Grand Effie for the most effective marketing campaign in 2006 from the American Marketing Association.[1]

Done right, marketing communications can have a huge payoff. This chapter describes how communications work and what marketing communications can do for a company. It also addresses how holistic marketers combine and integrate marketing communications. Chapter 18 examines the different forms of mass (nonpersonal) communications (advertising, sales promotion, events and experiences, and public relations and publicity); Chapter 19 examines the different forms of personal communications (direct and interactive marketing, word-of-mouth marketing, and personal selling).

::: The Role of Marketing Communications

Marketing communications are the means by which firms attempt to inform, persuade, and remind consumers—directly or indirectly—about the products and brands they sell. In a sense, marketing communications represent the "voice" of the company and its brands and are a means by which it can establish a dialogue and build relationships with consumers.

Marketing communications also perform many functions for consumers. They can tell or show consumers how and why a product is used, by what kind of person, and where and when. Consumers can learn about who makes the product and what the company and brand stand for; and they can get an incentive or reward for trial or usage. Marketing communications allow companies to link their brands to other people, places, events, brands, experiences, feelings, and things. They can contribute to brand equity—by establishing the brand in memory and creating a brand image—as well as drive sales and even affect shareholder value.[2]

The Changing Marketing Communication Environment

Although marketing communications can play a number of crucial roles, they must do so in an increasingly tough communication environment. Technology and other factors have profoundly changed the way consumers process communications, and even whether they choose to process them at all. The rapid diffusion of powerful broadband Internet connections, ad-skipping digital video recorders, multipurpose cell phones, and portable music and video players have forced marketers to rethink a number of their traditional practices.[3]

These dramatic changes have eroded the effectiveness of the mass media.[4] In 1960, Procter & Gamble could reach 80% of U.S. women with one 30-second Tide commercial aired simultaneously on only three TV networks: NBC, ABC, and CBS. Today, the same ad would have to run on 100 channels to achieve this marketing feat, and even then, it would run an increasing risk of being "zapped" by consumers armed with digital video recorders or DVRs (also called personal video recorders or PVRs). So, although 90% of P&G's global ad spending was on TV in 1994, one of its most successful brand launches in history, for Prilosec OTC in 2003, allocated only about one-quarter of its spending to TV.

Two forces are to blame for the demise of what used to be the most powerful means of hitting the consumer marketing bull's-eye. One is the fragmentation of U.S. audiences and, with the advent of digital technology and the Internet, the media now used to reach them. Prime-time ratings and circulations have been on a downslide since the 1970s. What's new is the proliferation of media and entertainment options—from hundreds of cable TV and radio stations and thousands of magazines and Webzines to uncountable Web sites, blogs, video games, and cell phone screens. Consumers not only have more choices of media to use, they also have a choice about whether and how they want to receive commercial content.

And that's part of the second force leaching oomph out of the 30-second spot. DVRs allow consumers to eliminate commercials with the push of a fast-forward button. Estimates have DVRs in 40% to 50% of U.S. households by 2010, and of those who use them, between 60% and 70% will fast-forward through commercials (the others either like ads, don't mind them, or can't be bothered). The Internet is even more of a threat, with a U.S. penetration of 200 million users who can choose whether to view an ad by clicking on an icon. For all these reasons and others, McKinsey projects that by 2010, traditional TV advertising will be one-third as effective as it was in 1990.[5]

But as some marketers flee traditional media, they still encounter challenges. Commercial clutter is rampant, and it seems the more consumers tune out marketing appeals, the more marketers try to dial them up. The average city dweller is now exposed to 3,000 to 5,000 ad messages a day. Supermarket eggs have been stamped with the name of CBS; subway turnstiles bear the name of Geico; Chinese food cartons promote Continental Airlines; and USAirways is selling ads on its motion sickness bags. Ads in almost every medium and form have been on the rise, and some consumers feel they are becoming increasingly invasive.[6]

Marketing Communications, Brand Equity, and Sales

In this new communication environment, although advertising is often a central element of a marketing communications program, it is usually not the only one—or even the most important one—in terms of building brand equity and driving sales. Consider how Nike chose to introduce the latest version of its successful line of sneakers endorsed by basketball star LeBron James:[7]

NIKE AIR ZOOM LEBRON IV

Nike's launch of the new version of its shoe line was supported by a wide range of traditional and nontraditional communications that included the first episode of "Sports Center" on ESPN to be sponsored by a single advertiser; the distribution of 400,000 copies of DVDs about the making of the shoe and the ad campaign; saturation advertising on espn.com, mtv.com, and some other sites; a "pop-up retail store" in Manhattan; video clips appearing as short programs on the MTV2 cable network; and a retro-chic neon billboard near Madison Square Garden that showed a continuously dunking Mr. James. The campaign also featured television ads and online video featuring James as "the LeBrons," characters who represent four sides of his personality and who first appeared in ads for the Nike Air Zoom LeBron III shoe the previous year, as well as print ads.

A wide range of marketing activities supported the traditional advertising in Nike's latest campaign introducing a new line of sneakers endorsed by basketball star LeBron James

MARKETING COMMUNICATIONS MIX The **marketing communications mix** consists of eight major modes of communication:[8]

1. ***Advertising***—Any paid form of nonpersonal presentation and promotion of ideas, goods, or services by an identified sponsor
2. ***Sales promotion***—A variety of short-term incentives to encourage trial or purchase of a product or service
3. ***Events and experiences***—Company-sponsored activities and programs designed to create daily or special brand-related interactions
4. ***Public relations and publicity***—A variety of programs designed to promote or protect a company's image or its individual products
5. ***Direct marketing***—Use of mail, telephone, fax, e-mail, or Internet to communicate directly with or solicit response or dialogue from specific customers and prospects
6. ***Interactive marketing***—Online activities and programs designed to engage customers or prospects and directly or indirectly raise awareness, improve image, or elicit sales of products and services
7. ***Word-of-mouth marketing***—People-to-people oral, written, or electronic communications that relate to the merits or experiences of purchasing or using products or services
8. ***Personal selling***—Face-to-face interaction with one or more prospective purchasers for the purpose of making presentations, answering questions, and procuring orders

Table 17.1 lists numerous communication platforms. Company communication goes beyond those specific platforms. The product's styling and price, the shape and color of the package, the salesperson's manner and dress, the store décor, the company's stationery—all communicate something to buyers. Every *brand contact* delivers an impression that can strengthen or weaken a customer's view of a company.[9]

As Figure 17.1 shows, marketing communications activities contribute to brand equity and drives sales in many ways: by creating awareness of the brand; linking the right associations to the brand image in consumers' memory; eliciting positive brand judgments or feelings; and/or facilitating a stronger consumer–brand connection.

MARKETING COMMUNICATION EFFECTS The manner in which brand associations are formed does not matter. In other words, if a consumer has an equally strong, favorable, and unique brand association of Subaru with the concepts "outdoors," "active," and "rugged," because of exposure to a TV ad that shows the car driving over rugged terrain at different times of the year, or because of the fact that Subaru sponsors ski, kayak, and mountain bike events, the impact in terms of Subaru's brand equity should be identical.

But these marketing communications activities must be integrated to deliver a consistent message and achieve the strategic positioning. The starting point in planning marketing communications is an audit of all the potential interactions that customers in the target market may have with the company and all its products and services. For example, someone interested in purchasing a new laptop computer might talk to others, see television ads, read articles, look for information on the Internet, and look at laptops in a store.

TABLE 17.1 Common Communication Platforms

Advertising	Sales Promotion	Events & Experiences	Public Relations & Publicity	Direct & Interactive Marketing	Word-of-Mouth Marketing	Personal Selling
Print and broadcast ads	Contests, games, sweepstakes, lotteries	Sports	Press kits	Catalogs	Person-to-person	Sales presentations
Packaging–outer	Premiums and gifts	Entertainment	Speeches	Mailings	Chat rooms	Sales meetings
Packaging inserts	Sampling	Festivals	Seminars	Telemarketing	Blogs	Incentive programs
Motion pictures	Fairs and trade shows	Arts	Annual reports	Electronic shopping		Samples
Brochures and booklets	Exhibits	Causes	Charitable donations	TV shopping		Fairs and trade shows
Posters and leaflets	Demonstrations	Factory tours	Publications	Fax mail		
Directories	Coupons	Company museums	Community relations	E-mail		
Reprints of ads	Rebates	Street activities	Lobbying	Voice mail		
Billboards	Low-interest financing		Identity media	Blogs		
Display signs	Entertainment		Company magazine	Web sites		
Point-of-purchase displays	Trade-in allowances					
Audiovisual material	Continuity programs					
Symbols and logos	Tie-ins					
Videotapes						

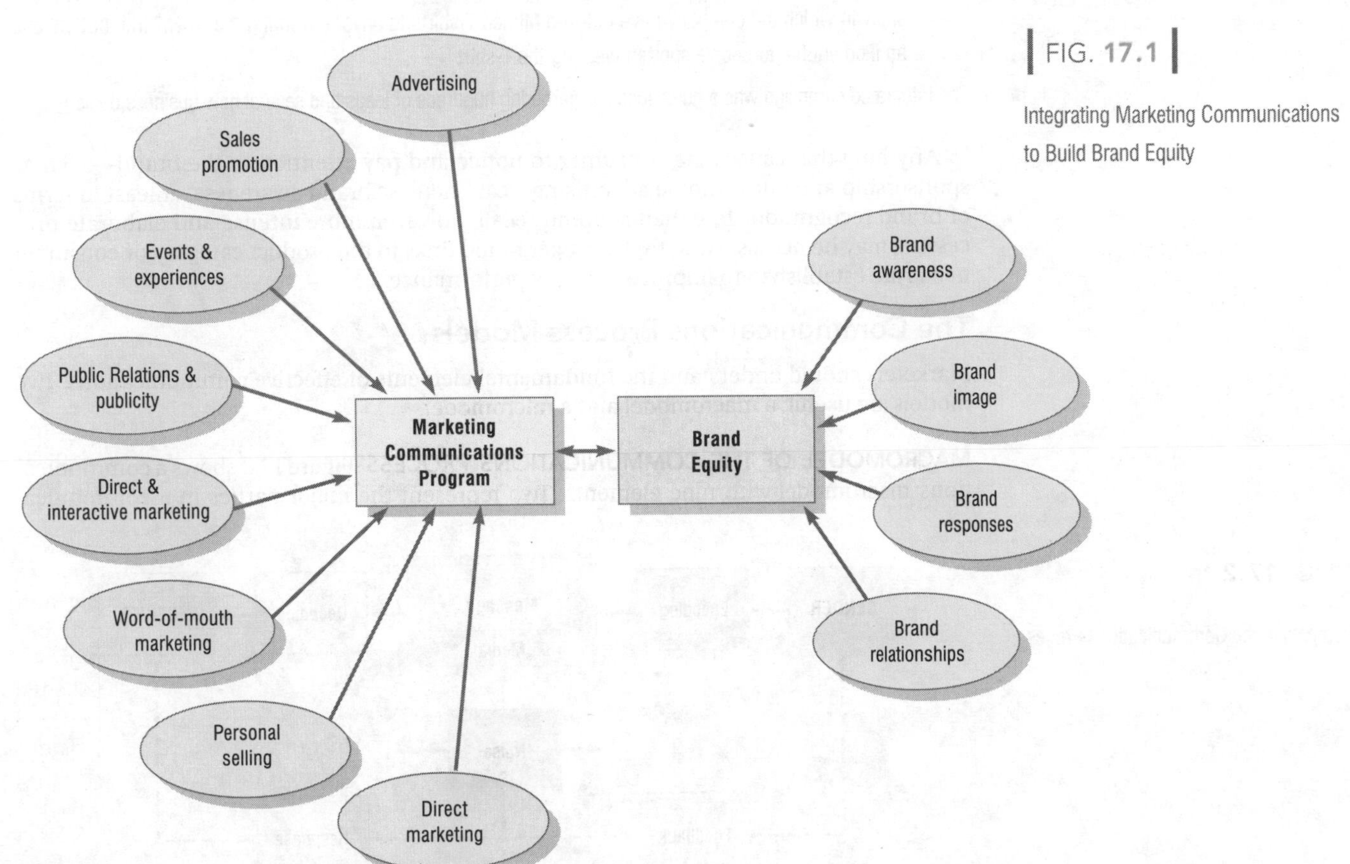

FIG. 17.1

Integrating Marketing Communications to Build Brand Equity

Marketers need to assess which experiences and impressions will have the most influence at each stage of the buying process. This understanding will help them allocate communications dollars more efficiently and design and implement the right communications programs. Armed with these insights, marketers can judge marketing communications according to its ability to affect experiences and impressions, build brand equity, and drive brand sales. For example, how well does a proposed ad campaign contribute to awareness or to creating, maintaining, or strengthening brand associations? Does a sponsorship cause consumers to have more favorable brand judgments and feelings? To what extent does a promotion encourage consumers to buy more of a product? At what price premium?

From the perspective of building brand equity, marketers should be "media neutral" and evaluate *all* the different possible communication options according to effectiveness criteria (how well does it work) as well as efficiency considerations (how much does it cost). This broad view of brand-building activities is especially relevant when marketers are considering strategies to improve brand awareness.[10]

MIMEO.COM

A little-known company called Mimeo.com is hoping to do for commercial printing customers what Moviephone did for film fans—take it online. In 2006, the company had more than 1,500 corporate clients—such as Citigroup, Burger King, and JetBlue—who rely on Mimeo to print training manuals, sales reports, and brochures. Yet with only $26 million in revenues it trails industry leader FedEx Kinko, and the company has almost zero brand awareness. "Mimeo has been around for six years, and no one seemed to know about us," said CEO Adam Slutsky. "Our challenge was to find an agency to partner with that could help us build awareness, figure out positioning, do a totally integrated campaign, and measure everything like a hound." Enter Stein Rogan+Partners and a campaign that featured:

- A new, more dramatic Mimeo.com logo and colors
- A $2 million print-ad campaign in trade publications that target small and mid-size businesses, highlighting case studies of satisfied customers
- A highly original "clown-free" campaign at the American Society of Training and Development (ASTDA) show in which the company gave out free Mimeo T-shirts to anyone wearing the clown-free button, and an iPod shuffle to people spotted wearing the T-shirt

The integrated campaign was a huge success, garnering hundreds of leads and several new business deals.[11]

Anything that causes the consumer to notice and pay attention to the brand—such as sponsorship and out-of-home advertising—can increase brand awareness, at least in terms of brand recognition. To enhance brand recall, however, more intense and elaborate processing may be necessary, so that stronger brand links to the product category or consumer needs are established to improve memory performance.

The Communications Process Models

Marketers should understand the fundamental elements of effective communications. Two models are useful: a macromodel and a micromodel.

MACROMODEL OF THE COMMUNICATIONS PROCESS Figure 17.2 shows a communications macromodel with nine elements. Two represent the major parties in a communica-

Elements in the Communications Process

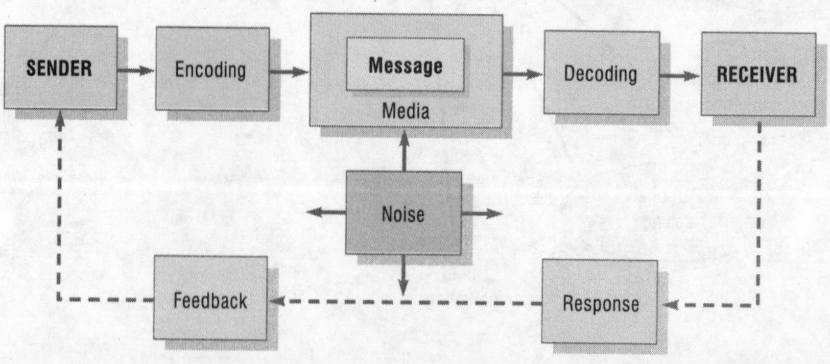

tion—*sender* and *receiver*. Two represent the major communication tools—*message* and *media*. Four represent major communication functions—*encoding, decoding, response,* and *feedback*. The last element in the system is *noise* (random and competing messages that may interfere with the intended communication).[12]

The model emphasizes the key factors in effective communication. Senders must know what audiences they want to reach and what responses they want to get. They must encode their messages so the target audience can decode them. They must transmit the message through media that reach the target audience and develop feedback channels to monitor the responses. The more the sender's field of experience overlaps that of the receiver, the more effective the message is likely to be. Note that selective attention, distortion, and retention processes—concepts first introduced in Chapter 6—may be operating during communication.

MICROMODEL OF CONSUMER RESPONSES Micromodels of marketing communications concentrate on consumers' specific responses to communications. Figure 17.3 summarizes four classic *response hierarchy models.*

All these models assume that the buyer passes through a cognitive, affective, and behavioral stage, in that order. This "learn-feel-do" sequence is appropriate when the audience has high involvement with a product category perceived to have high differentiation, such as an automobile or house. An alternative sequence, "do-feel-learn," is relevant when the audience has high involvement but perceives little or no differentiation within the product category, such as an airline ticket or personal computer. A third sequence, "learn-do-feel," is relevant when the audience has low involvement and perceives little differentiation within the product category, such as salt or batteries. By choosing the right sequence, the marketer can do a better job of planning communications.[13]

Here we will assume the buyer has high involvement with the product category and perceives high differentiation within it. We will illustrate the *hierarchy-of-effects model* (in the second column of Figure 17.3) in the context of a marketing communications campaign for a small Iowa college named Pottsville:

- ***Awareness.*** If most of the target audience is unaware of the object, the communicator's task is to build awareness. Suppose Pottsville seeks applicants from Nebraska but has no name recognition there. There are 30,000 high school juniors and seniors in Nebraska who may potentially be interested in Pottsville College. The college might set the objective of making 70% of these students aware of its name within one year.
- ***Knowledge.*** The target audience might have brand awareness but not know much more. Pottsville may want its target audience to know that it is a private four-year college with excellent programs in English, foreign languages, and history. It needs to learn how

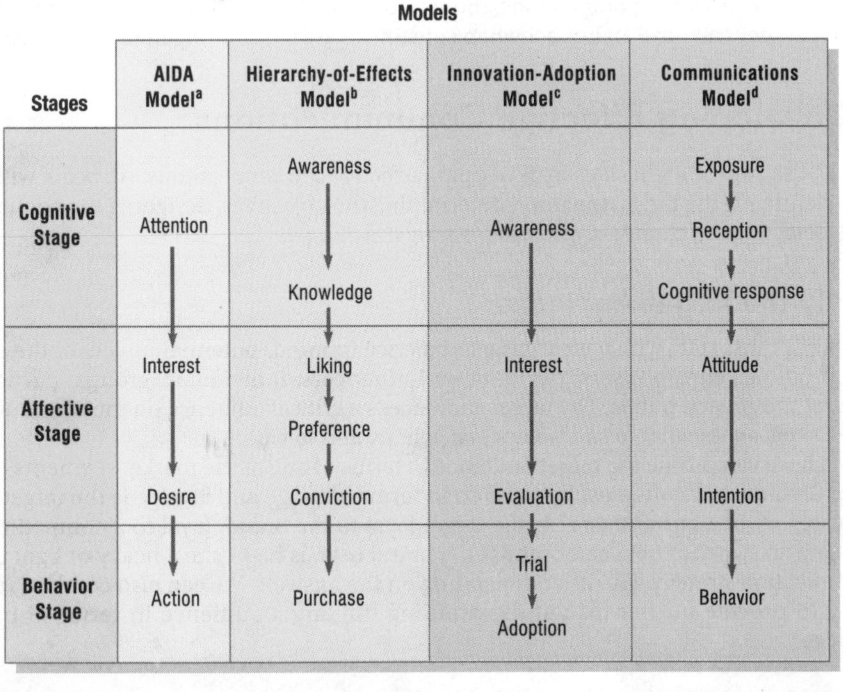

Models

Stages	AIDA Model[a]	Hierarchy-of-Effects Model[b]	Innovation-Adoption Model[c]	Communications Model[d]
Cognitive Stage	Attention	Awareness ↓ Knowledge	Awareness	Exposure ↓ Reception ↓ Cognitive response
Affective Stage	Interest ↓ Desire	Liking ↓ Preference ↓ Conviction	Interest ↓ Evaluation	Attitude ↓ Intention
Behavior Stage	Action	Purchase	Trial ↓ Adoption	Behavior

FIG. 17.3

Response Hierarchy Models

Sources: [a]E. K. Strong, *The Psychology of Selling* (New York: McGraw-Hill, 1925), p. 9; [b]Robert J. Lavidge and Gary A. Steiner, "A Model for Predictive Measurements of Advertising Effectiveness," *Journal of Marketing* (October 1961): 61; [c]Everett M. Rogers, *Diffusion of Innovation* (New York: Free Press, 1962), pp. 79–86; [d]various sources.

many people in the target audience have little, some, or much knowledge about Pottsville. If knowledge is weak, Pottsville may decide to select brand knowledge as its communications objective.

- ***Liking.*** If target members know the brand, how do they feel about it? If the audience looks unfavorably on Pottsville College, the communicator needs to find out why. If the unfavorable view is based on real problems, Pottsville will need to fix its problems and then communicate its renewed quality. Good public relations calls for "good deeds followed by good words."
- ***Preference.*** The target audience might like the product but not prefer it to others. In this case, the communicator must try to build consumer preference by comparing quality, value, performance, and other features to likely competitors.
- ***Conviction.*** A target audience might prefer a particular product but not develop a conviction about buying it. The communicator's job is to build conviction and purchase intent among students interested in Pottsville College.
- ***Purchase.*** Finally, some members of the target audience might have conviction but not quite get around to making the purchase. The communicator must lead these consumers to take the final step, perhaps by offering the product at a low price, offering a premium, or letting consumers try it out. Pottsville might invite selected high school students to visit the campus and attend some classes, or it might offer partial scholarships to deserving students.

To show how fragile the whole communications process is, assume that the probability of *each* of the six steps being successfully accomplished is 50%. The laws of probability suggest that the probability of *all* six steps occurring successfully, assuming they are independent events, is $.5 \times .5 \times .5 \times .5 \times .5 \times .5$, which equals 1.5625%. If the probability of each step occurring was, on average, a more moderate 10%, then the joint probability of all six events occurring would be .0001%—in other words, only 1 in 1,000,000!

To increase the odds for a successful marketing communications campaign, marketers must attempt to increase the likelihood that *each* step occurs. For example, from an advertising standpoint, the ideal ad campaign would ensure that:

1. The right consumer is exposed to the right message at the right place and at the right time.
2. The ad causes the consumer to pay attention to the ad but does not distract from the intended message.
3. The ad properly reflects the consumer's level of understanding of and behaviors with the product and the brand.
4. The ad correctly positions the brand in terms of desirable and deliverable points-of-difference and points-of-parity.
5. The ad motivates consumers to consider purchase of the brand.
6. The ad creates strong brand associations with all these stored communications effects so that they can have an impact when consumers are considering making a purchase.

::: Developing Effective Communications

Figure 17.4 shows the eight steps in developing effective communications. We begin with the basics: identifying the target audience, determining the objectives, designing the communications, selecting the channels, and establishing the budget.

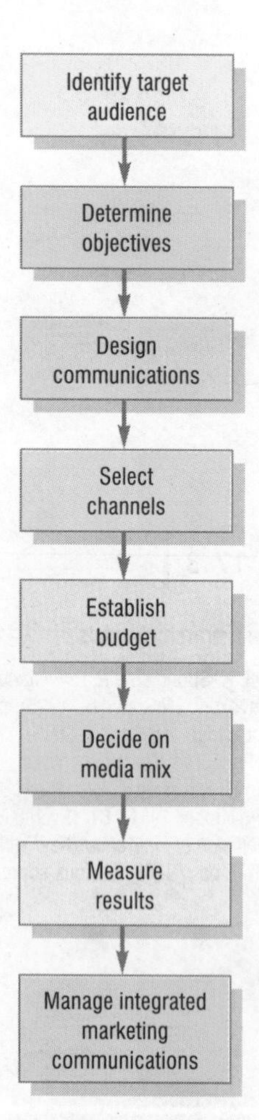

FIG. **17.4**

Steps in Developing Effective Communications

Identify the Target Audience

The process must start with a clear target audience in mind: potential buyers of the company's products, current users, deciders, or influencers; individuals, groups, particular publics, or the general public. The target audience is a critical influence on the communicator's decisions about what to say, how, when, where, and to whom.

Though we can profile the target audience in terms of any of the market segments identified in Chapter 8, it's often useful to do so in terms of usage and loyalty. Is the target new to the category or a current user? Is the target loyal to the brand, loyal to a competitor, or someone who switches between brands? If a brand user, is he or she a heavy or light user? Communication strategy will differ depending on the answers. We can also conduct *image analysis* to provide further insight, by profiling the target audience in terms of brand knowledge.

Determine the Communications Objectives

As we showed with Pottsville College, marketers can set communications objectives at any level of the hierarchy-of-effects model. Rossiter and Percy identify four possible objectives, as follows:[14]

1. ***Category Need***—Establishing a product or service category as necessary to remove or satisfy a perceived discrepancy between a current motivational state and a desired emotional state. A new-to-the-world product such as electric cars would always begin with a communications objective of establishing category need.
2. ***Brand Awareness***—Ability to identify (recognize or recall) the brand within the category, in sufficient detail to make a purchase. Recognition is easier to achieve than recall—consumers asked to think of a brand of frozen entrées are more likely to recognize Stouffer's distinctive orange packages than to recall the brand. Brand recall is important outside the store; brand recognition is important inside the store. Brand awareness provides a foundation for brand equity.
3. ***Brand Attitude***—Evaluating the brand with respect to its perceived ability to meet a currently relevant need. Relevant brand needs may be negatively oriented (problem removal, problem avoidance, incomplete satisfaction, normal depletion) or positively oriented (sensory gratification, intellectual stimulation, or social approval). Household cleaning products often use problem solution; food products, on the other hand, often use sensory-oriented ads emphasizing appetite appeal.
4. ***Brand Purchase Intention***—Self-instructions to purchase the brand or to take purchase-related action. Promotional offers in the form of coupons or two-for-one deals encourage consumers to make a mental commitment to buy a product. But many consumers do not have an expressed category need and may not be in the market when exposed to an ad, so they are unlikely to form buy intentions. For example, in any given week, only about 20% of adults may be planning to buy detergent; only 2% may be planning to buy a carpet cleaner; and only 0.25% may be planning to buy a car.

The most effective communications often can achieve multiple objectives.

Design the Communications

Formulating the communications to achieve the desired response will require solving three problems: what to say (message strategy), how to say it (creative strategy), and who should say it (message source).

To read about the troubled advertising campaigns that Toyota and Nike ran in China, visit www.pearsoned-asia.com/marketingmanagementchina.

MESSAGE STRATEGY In determining message strategy, management searches for appeals, themes, or ideas that will tie into the brand positioning and help to establish points-of-parity or points-of-difference. Some of these may be related directly to product or service performance (the quality, economy, or value of the brand), whereas others may relate to more extrinsic considerations (the brand as being contemporary, popular, or traditional).

John Maloney saw buyers as expecting one of four types of reward from a product: rational, sensory, social, or ego satisfaction.[15] Buyers might visualize these rewards from results-of-use experience, product-in-use experience, or incidental-to-use experience. Crossing the four types of rewards with the three types of experience generates 12 types of messages. For example, the appeal "gets clothes cleaner" is a rational-reward promise following results-of-use experience. The phrase "real beer taste in a great light beer" is a sensory-reward promise connected with product-in-use experience.

CREATIVE STRATEGY Communications effectiveness depends on how a message is being expressed, as well as on the content of the message itself. If a communication is ineffective, it may mean the wrong message was used, or the right one was just poorly expressed. *Creative strategies* are the way marketers translate their messages into a specific communication. We can broadly classify them as either **informational** or **transformational** appeals.[16] These two general categories each encompass several different specific creative approaches.

Informational Appeals An *informational appeal* elaborates on product or service attributes or benefits. Examples in advertising are problem solution ads (Excedrin stops the toughest headache pain), product demonstration ads (Thompson Water Seal can withstand intense rain, snow, and heat), product comparison ads (DirecTV offers better HD options than cable operators), and testimonials from unknown or celebrity endorsers (NBA phenomenon LeBron James pitching Sprite, Powerade, and Nike). Informational appeals assume very rational processing of the communication on the part of the consumer. Logic and reason rule.

Hovland's research at Yale has shed much light on informational appeals and their relationship to such issues as conclusion drawing, one-sided versus two-sided arguments, and order of argument presentation. Some early experiments supported stating conclusions for the audience. Subsequent research, however, indicates that the best ads ask questions and allow readers and viewers to form their own conclusions.[17] If Honda had hammered away that the Element was for young people, this strong definition might have blocked older age groups from buying it. Some stimulus ambiguity can lead to a broader market definition and more spontaneous purchases.

You would think one-sided presentations that praise a product would be more effective than two-sided arguments that also mention shortcomings. Yet two-sided messages may be more appropriate, especially when negative associations must be overcome. Heinz ran the message "Heinz Ketchup is slow good" and Listerine said "Listerine tastes bad twice a day."[18] Two-sided messages are more effective with more educated audiences and those who are initially opposed.[19]

Finally, the order in which arguments are presented is important.[20] In a one-sided message, presenting the strongest argument first has the advantage of arousing attention and interest. This is important in media where the audience often does not attend to the whole message. With a captive audience, a climactic presentation might be more effective. In the case of a two-sided message, if the audience is initially opposed, the communicator might start with the other side's argument and conclude with his or her strongest argument.[21]

Michelin's use of the Michelin Man brand character in its advertising helps to break through the clutter and reinforce the brand's key safety and trust messages.

Transformational Appeals A *transformational appeal* elaborates on a non-product-related benefit or image. It might depict what kind of person uses a brand (VW advertised to active, youthful people with its "Drivers Wanted" campaign) or what kind of experience results from using the brand (Pringles advertised "Once You Pop, the Fun Don't Stop" for years). Transformational appeals often attempt to stir up emotions that will motivate purchase.

Communicators use negative appeals such as fear, guilt, and shame to get people to do things (brush their teeth, have an annual health checkup) or stop doing things (smoking, alcohol abuse, overeating). Fear appeals work best when they are not too strong, when source credibility is high, and when the communication promises to relieve, in a believable and efficient way, the fear it arouses. Messages are most persuasive when they are moderately discrepant with what the audience believes. Stating only what the audience already believes at best only reinforces beliefs, and if the messages are too discrepant, audiences will counterargue and disbelieve them.[22]

Communicators also use positive emotional appeals such as humor, love, pride, and joy. Motivational or "borrowed interest" devices—such as the presence of cute babies, frisky puppies, popular music, or provocative sex appeals—are often employed to attract consumer attention and raise their involvement with an ad. Borrowed-interest techniques are thought to be necessary in the tough new media environment characterized by low-involvement consumer processing and much competing ad and programming clutter.

Although these borrowed-interest approaches can attract attention and create more liking and belief in the sponsor, they may also detract from comprehension, wear out their welcome fast, and overshadow the product.[23] Attention-getting tactics are often *too* effective and distract from brand or product claims. Thus, one challenge in arriving at the best creative strategy is figuring out how to "break through the clutter" to attract the attention of consumers—but still deliver the intended message.

The magic of advertising is to bring concepts on a piece of paper to life in the minds of the consumer target. In a print ad, the communicator must decide on headline, copy, illustration, and color.[24] For a radio message, the communicator must choose words, voice qualities, and vocalizations. The sound of an announcer promoting a used automobile should be different from one promoting a new Cadillac. If the message is to be carried on television or in person, all these elements plus body language (nonverbal clues) must be planned. Presenters need to pay attention to facial expressions, gestures, dress, posture, and hairstyle. If the message is carried by the product or its packaging, the communicator must pay attention to color, texture, scent, size, and shape.

MESSAGE SOURCE Many communications do not use a source beyond the company itself. Others use known or unknown people. Messages delivered by attractive or popular sources can achieve higher attention and recall, which is why advertisers often use celebrities as spokespeople. Celebrities are likely to be effective when they are credible or personify a key product attribute. ABC's *Extreme Makeover* host Ty Pennington for Sears, James Earl Jones for Verizon, and self-proclaimed overweight actress Kirstie Alley for Jenny Craig weight-loss system have all been praised by consumers as good fits.[25] On the other hand, Celine Dion failed to add glamour—or sales—to Chrysler, and even though she was locked into a three-year, $14 million deal, she was let go.

What *is* important is the spokesperson's credibility. What factors underlie source credibility? The three most often identified are expertise, trustworthiness, and likability.[26] *Expertise* is the specialized knowledge the communicator possesses to back the claim. *Trustworthiness* is related to how objective and honest the source is perceived to be. Friends are trusted more than strangers or salespeople, and people who are not paid to endorse a product are viewed as more trustworthy than people who are paid.[27] *Likability* describes the source's attractiveness. Qualities such as candor, humor, and naturalness make a source more likable. Business-to-business marketer Accenture found all these qualities and more in golf pro Tiger Woods.

ACCENTURE

What better symbol for high performance than Tiger Woods, the world's number-one golfer? That's why business consulting firm, Accenture, was persistent in seeking to use the golfer as the linchpin for its rebranding campaign. Enter Tiger Woods and the new tagline "High Performance. Delivered." Accenture's message is that it can help client companies become "high-performing business leaders," like the ones featured on its Web site. The Woods endorsement drives home the importance of high performance, just as Woods drives home yet another tournament championship. The campaign includes ads in 27 countries, capitalizing on Tiger Woods' international appeal; events and sponsorships that are aligned with the idea of high performance, such as the World Golf Championships and the Chicago Marathon; and an interactive Web site that users can personalize to get information and regular updates relevant to their industry. Accenture has also teamed up with the *Wall Street Journal* to produce a series of articles that explore different facets of high-performance business, written by seasoned journalists and featuring Accenture client companies.[28]

The most highly credible source would score high on all three dimensions—expertise, trustworthiness, and likability. Pharmaceutical companies want doctors to testify about product benefits because doctors have high credibility. An expensive ad campaign for cholesterol-lowering drug Lipitor centered on a testimonial from Dr. Robert Jarvik, inventor of the artificial heart. Charles Schwab became the centerpiece of ads for his $4 billion-plus discount brokerage firm via the "Talk to Chuck" corporate advertising campaign. Another credible pitchman turned out to be boxer George Foreman. "Marketing Insight: Celebrity Endorsements as a Strategy" focuses on the use of testimonials.

SALTON AND GEORGE FOREMAN

Salton was a little-known manufacturer of oddball appliances that gained temporary fame in the 1950s with its Salton Hot Tray, a must-have item for every bridal registry at the time. In the early 1990s, the company came up with an indoor grill that seemed destined for obscurity until two-time heavyweight champ George Foreman chose not only to endorse it, but to partner with the company to sell it. Foreman and his Lean, Mean, Fat-Reducing Grilling Machine proved to be a match made in hamburger heaven. Foreman, now presented as a

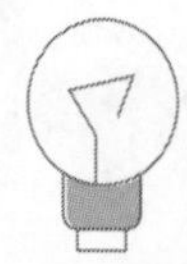

MARKETING INSIGHT | CELEBRITY ENDORSEMENTS AS A STRATEGY

A well-chosen celebrity can draw attention to a product or brand—as when Ameriprise Financial chose '60s movie icon Dennis Hopper to run in its "Dreams Don't Retire" ads going after baby boomers—or the celebrity's mystique can transfer to the brand. To reinforce its prestigious image, American Express used movie legends Robert DeNiro and Martin Scorsese in ads.

The choice of the celebrity is critical. The celebrity should have high recognition, high positive affect, and high appropriateness to the product. Paris Hilton and Donald Trump have high recognition but negative affect among many groups. Robin Williams has high recognition and high positive affect but might not be appropriate for advertising a World Peace Conference. Tom Hanks and Oprah Winfrey could successfully advertise a large number of products because they have extremely high ratings for familiarity and likability (known as the Q factor in the entertainment industry).

Celebrities show up everywhere. In the hotly contested male-impotence drug category, pharmaceutical marketers turned to celebrities to gain product attention and relevance. Initially advertised by retired politician Bob Dole, Pfizer's Viagra was next promoted by 40-year-old baseball slugger Rafael Palmeiro and 45-year-old NASCAR driver Mark Martin to give the market-leading drug a younger appeal. Competitor Levitra led off with famed football coach Iron Mike Ditka to assure its audience of its speed and quality. Only late entrant Cialis eschewed celebrity endorsers, spending $100 million in its launch campaign to run ads showing couples in romantic settings.

Athletes commonly endorse athletic products, beverages, and apparel. One of the premier athletic endorsers has been cyclist Lance Armstrong, who battled and beat testicular cancer on his way to winning six consecutive Tour de France championships. He has endorsed a number of bicycle and sports products and companies, including Trek, PowerBar, and Nike. Armstrong's improbable "against all odds" success story also enabled him to win multimillion-dollar endorsement contracts from companies not affiliated with sports, such as Bristol-Myers Squibb pharmaceuticals, Coca-Cola, Subaru, and 24 Hour Fitness.

Celebrities can play a more strategic role for their brands, not only endorsing a product but also helping to design, position, and sell merchandise and services. Since signing Tiger Woods in 1996, Nike has seen its share of the golf ball market grow steadily. Woods has played a key role in developing a series of golf products and apparel that Nike has periodically altered to reflect his changing personality and design tastes.

Using celebrities poses certain risks. The celebrity might hold out for a larger fee at contract renewal time or withdraw. And just like movies and records, celebrity campaigns can sometimes be expensive flops. Pepsi chose to drop star endorsers Britney Spears and Beyoncé Knowles, whose personalities may have been too overpowering for the brand, to focus on promoting occasions that go well with drinking Pepsi.

The celebrity might lose popularity or, even worse, get caught in a scandal or embarrassing situation. After NBA legend Magic Johnson went public with his HIV diagnosis and his extramarital affairs in 1991, his ads were pulled from the air and his endorsement deals were not renewed. McDonald's chose not to renew a $12 million annual contract with basketball star Kobe Bryant after he faced accusations of rape.

Sources: Keith Naughton, "The Soft Sell," *Newsweek*, February 2, 2004, pp. 46–47; Theresa Howard, "Pepsi Takes Some Fizz off Vanilla Rival," *USA Today*, November 16, 2003; Betsy Cummings, "Star Power," *Sales & Marketing Management* (April 2001): 52–59; Greg Johnson, "Woods' Cautious Approach to the Green," *Los Angeles Times*, July 26, 2000; Bruce Horovitz, "Armstrong Rolls to Market Gold," *USA Today*, May 4, 2000; Irving Rein, Philip Kotler, and Martin Scoller, *The Making and Marketing of Professionals into Celebrities* (Chicago: NTC Business Books, 1997).

lovable lug, was renowned for his love of cheeseburgers. A year after the launch, he went on home shopping channel QVC to sell the grills. The camera caught him in an unscripted moment while presenters were chatting, leaving George with nothing to do except look at the sizzling burgers. He took a roll, grabbed a burger, and started eating, and the phone lines began to buzz. Foreman has helped Salton sell more than 55 million grilling machines since the mid-1990s, and because he gets a share of the proceeds, he has earned more than he did as a boxer—over $150 million.[29]

If a person has a positive attitude toward a source and a message, or a negative attitude toward both, a state of *congruity* is said to exist. What happens if the person holds one attitude toward the source and the opposite one toward the message? Suppose a consumer hears a likable celebrity praise a brand she dislikes. Osgood and Tannenbaum say that *attitude change will take place in the direction of increasing the amount of congruity between the two evaluations.*[30] The consumer will end up respecting the celebrity somewhat less or respecting the brand somewhat more. If a person encounters the same celebrity praising other disliked brands, he or she will eventually develop a negative view of the celebrity and maintain negative attitudes toward the brands. The **principle of congruity** implies that communicators can use their good image to reduce some negative feelings toward a brand but in the process might lose some esteem with the audience.

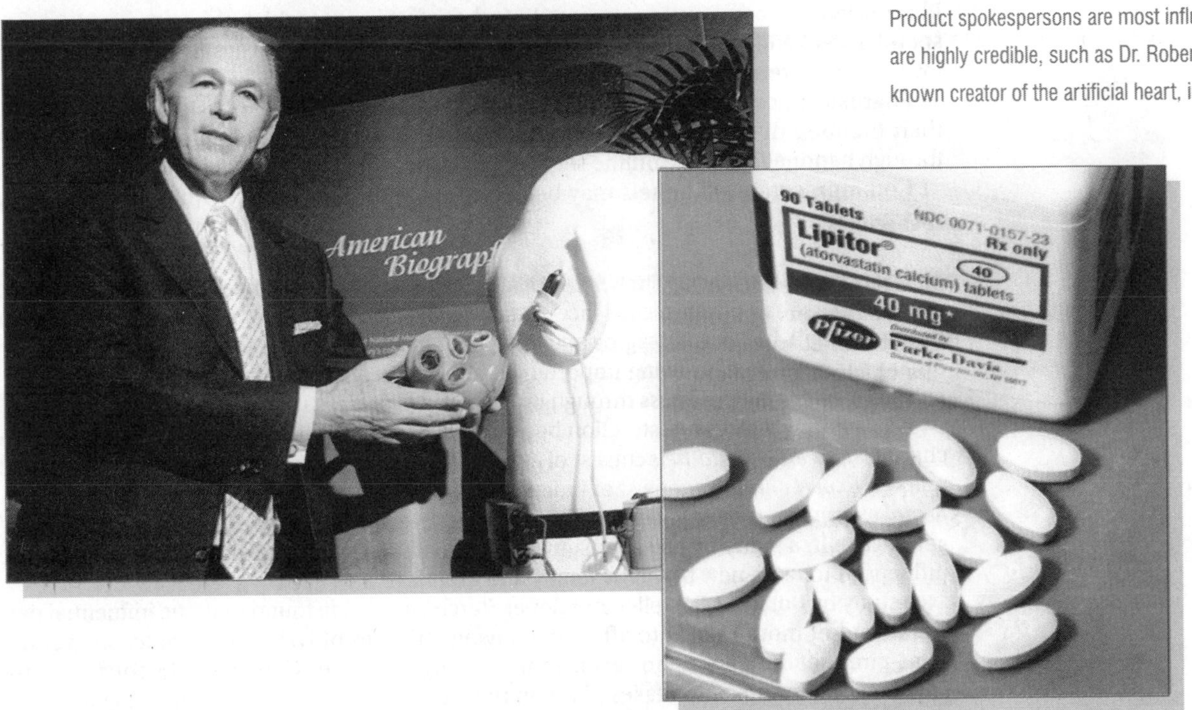

Product spokespersons are most influential when they are highly credible, such as Dr. Robert Jarvik, well-known creator of the artificial heart, in ads for Lipitor.

GLOBAL ADAPTATIONS Multinational companies wrestle with a number of challenges in developing global communications programs: They must decide whether the product is appropriate for a country. They must make sure the market segment they address is both legal and customary. They must decide whether the style of the ad is acceptable, and whether ads should be created at headquarters or locally.[31]

1. ***Product***—Many products are restricted or forbidden in certain parts of the world. Beer, wine, and spirits cannot be advertised or sold in many Muslim countries. Tobacco products are subject to strict regulation in many countries.
2. ***Market Segment***—U.S. toy makers were surprised to learn that in many countries (Norway and Sweden, for example) no TV ads may be directed at children under 12. Sweden lobbied hard to extend that ban to all EU member countries in 2001 but failed. To play it safe, McDonald's advertises itself as a family restaurant in Sweden.
3. ***Style***—Comparative ads, although acceptable and even common in the United States and Canada, are less commonly used in the United Kingdom, unacceptable in Japan, and illegal in India and Brazil. The EU seems to have a very low tolerance for comparative advertising, with a Comparative Advertising Directive that prohibits bashing rivals in ads. PepsiCo had a comparative taste test ad in Japan that was refused by many TV stations and eventually led to a lawsuit.
4. ***Local or Global***—Today, more and more multinational companies are attempting to build a global brand image by using the same advertising in all markets.

Companies that sell their products to different cultures or in different countries must be prepared to vary their messages. In advertising its hair care products in different countries, Helene Curtis adjusts its messages. Middle-class British women wash their hair frequently, whereas the opposite is true among Spanish women. Japanese women avoid overwashing their hair for fear of removing protective oils.

Select the Communications Channels

Selecting efficient means to carry the message becomes more difficult as channels of communication become more fragmented and cluttered. Think of the challenges in the pharmaceutical industry: An army of over 94,000 U.S. sales reps "detail" doctors every day, but only a little over 40% of calls result in seeing the doctor, and then for an average of only 2 minutes or less, which makes sales calling extremely expensive. The industry has had to expand its battery of communications channels to include ads in medical journals, direct mail (including audio and videotapes), free samples, and even telemarketing.

Pharmaceutical companies sponsor clinical conferences at which they pay physicians to spend a weekend listening to leading colleagues extol certain drugs in the morning, followed by an afternoon of golf or tennis.

Pharmaceuticals use all these channels in the hope of building physician preference for their branded therapeutic agent. They are also using new technologies to reach doctors through handheld devices, online services, and videoconferencing equipment.[32]

Communications channels may be personal and nonpersonal. Within each are many subchannels.

PERSONAL COMMUNICATIONS CHANNELS **Personal communications channels** let two or more persons communicate face-to-face, person-to-audience, over the telephone, or through e-mail. Instant messaging and independent sites to collect consumer reviews are another channel, one of growing importance in recent years. Personal communication channels derive their effectiveness through individualized presentation and feedback.

We can draw a further distinction between advocate, expert, and social communications channels. *Advocate channels* consist of company salespeople contacting buyers in the target market. *Expert channels* consist of independent experts making statements to target buyers. *Social channels* consist of neighbors, friends, family members, and associates talking to target buyers. In a study of 7,000 consumers in seven European countries, 60% said they were influenced to use a new brand by family and friends.[33]

A study by Burson-Marsteller and Roper Starch Worldwide found that one influential person's word of mouth tends to affect the buying attitudes of two other people, on average. That circle of influence, however, jumps to eight online. Considerable consumer-to-consumer communication takes place on the Web on a wide range of subjects. Online visitors also increasingly create product information, not just consume it. They join Internet interest groups to share information, so that "word of Web" is joining "word of mouth" as an important buying influence. Word about good companies travels fast; word about bad companies travels even faster. As one marketer noted, "You don't need to reach two million people to let them know about a new product—you just need to reach the right 2,000 people in the right way and they will help you reach two million."[34]

Personal influence carries especially great weight in two situations. One occurs when products are expensive, risky, or purchased infrequently. The other arises when products suggest something about the user's status or taste. People often ask others for a recommendation for a doctor, plumber, hotel, lawyer, accountant, architect, insurance agent, interior decorator, or financial consultant. If we have confidence in the recommendation, we normally act on the referral. In such cases, the recommender has potentially benefited the service provider as well as the service seeker. Service providers clearly have a strong interest in building referral sources.

Here is an example of the power of informal word of mouth:

CHIPOTLE

Denver-based Chipotle Grill eschews TV and other forms of traditional advertising. Founder and CEO M. Steven Ells feels advertising is "not believable," so the company spends less in a year than McDonald's does in 48 hours. Instead, Chipotle relies on word of mouth from loyal customers satisfied with its ample portions, fresh ingredients, and delicious taste. To seed the buzz, Chipotle also samples liberally. When Chipotle entered the Manhattan market, it gave burritos away to 6,000 people, some of whom stood in line for two hours. The event cost $30,000, but also created buzz. And word is getting around. The 573-unit chain is ranked at the top among quick-serve Mexican restaurants in consumer surveys and has experienced double-digit growth in same-store sales for almost a decade.[35]

Sending the right message to the right consumers can be crucial. After experiencing disappointing results from trials of its breakfast cereal Smorz, Kellogg was able to boost samplings by 500,000 through social networking after the company sent samples and DVDs about the making of cereal and the casting of TV ads to 10,000 influential adolescents.[36]

NONPERSONAL COMMUNICATIONS CHANNELS Nonpersonal channels are communications directed to more than one person and include media, sales promotions, events and experiences, and public relations.

- ***Media*** consist of print media (newspapers and magazines); broadcast media (radio and television); network media (telephone, cable, satellite, wireless); electronic media (audiotape, videotape, videodisk, CD-ROM, Web page); and display media (billboards, signs, posters). Most nonpersonal messages come through paid media.
- ***Sales promotions*** consist of consumer promotions (such as samples, coupons, and premiums); trade promotions (such as advertising and display allowances); and business and sales-force promotions (contests for sales reps).
- ***Events and experiences*** include sports, arts, entertainment, and cause events as well as less formal activities that create novel brand interactions with consumers.
- ***Public relations*** include communications directed internally to employees of the company or externally to consumers, other firms, the government, and media.

Much of the recent growth of nonpersonal channels has taken place through events and experiences. A company can build its brand image by creating or sponsoring events. Events marketers who once favored sports events are now using other venues such as art museums, zoos, or ice shows to entertain clients and employees. AT&T and IBM sponsor symphony performances and art exhibits; Visa is an active sponsor of the Olympics; and Harley-Davidson sponsors annual motorcycle rallies.

Companies are searching for better ways to quantify the benefits of sponsorship and demanding greater accountability from event owners and organizers. They are also creating events designed to surprise the public and create a buzz. Many amount to guerrilla marketing tactics. But if not done properly, they can backfire and have unintended consequences.

BOSTON AQUAFORCE PROMOTION

On January 31, 2007, Boston city officials found 38 blinking electronic signs promoting the Cartoon Network's late-night cable TV show "Aqua Teen Hunger Force" on bridges and other high-profile spots across the city. Deeming the devices suspicious, officials closed down major highways and waterways and deployed bomb squads. The 1-foot-tall signs, which were lit up at night, depicted a boxy, cartoon character making an obscene gesture and resembled circuit boards, with batteries and protruding wires. Turner Broadcasting System, which owns the Cartoon Network, later admitted placing the devices in 10 major cities including Boston as part of an elaborate national guerrilla campaign and apologized for the misunderstanding. The company paid one million dollars to the Boston Police Department to cover the cost of its investigation and another million dollars in goodwill funding. Although some people felt city officials overreacted, Turner took these actions to settle any possible criminal and civil claims. The general manager of Cartoon Network also stepped down as a result of the incident.[37]

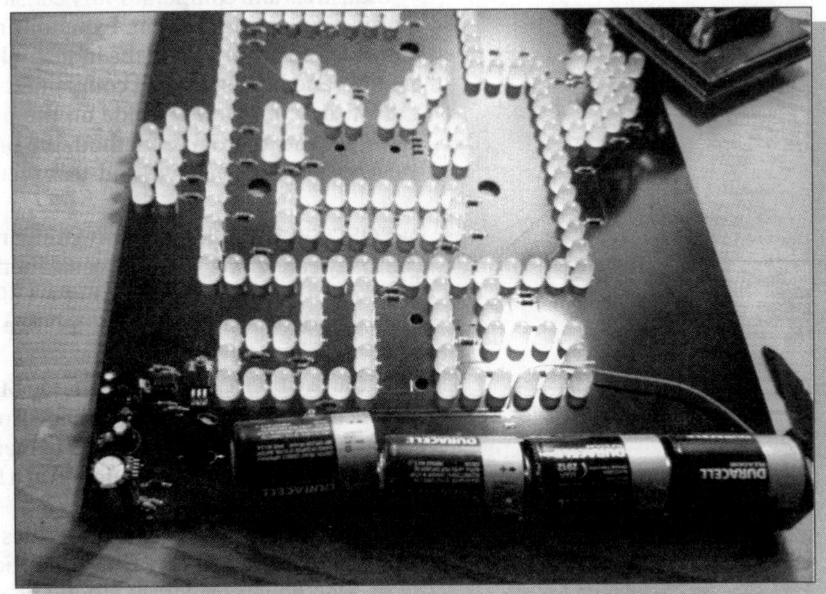

Guerrilla marketing efforts can have unforeseen consequences, as the Cartoon Network found when its cryptic signs for a new late-night show attracted the wrong kind of attention from Boston police.

The increased use of attention-getting events is a response to the fragmentation of media: Consumers can turn to hundreds of cable channels, thousands of magazine titles, and millions of Internet pages. Events can create attention, although whether they have a lasting effect on brand awareness, knowledge, or preference will vary considerably, depending on the quality of the product, the event itself, and its execution.

INTEGRATION OF COMMUNICATIONS CHANNELS Although personal communication is often more effective than mass communication, mass media might be the major means of stimulating personal communication. Mass communications affect personal attitudes and behavior through a two-step process. Ideas often flow from radio, television, and print to opinion leaders, and from these to the less media-involved population groups. This two-step flow has several implications. First, the influence of mass media on public opinion is not as direct, powerful, and automatic as marketers have supposed. It is mediated by opinion leaders, people whose opinions others seek, or who carry their opinions to others. Second, the two-step flow challenges the notion that consumption styles are primarily influenced by a "trickle-down" or "trickle-up" effect from mass media. People interact primarily within their own social groups and acquire ideas from opinion leaders in their groups. Third, two-step communication suggests that mass communicators should direct messages specifically to opinion leaders and let them carry the message to others. Mini developed a clever communication strategy to get people talking and driving.

MINI

The tiny Mini automobile was sold for only seven years in the United States, during the 1960s, before it was withdrawn due to stiff emission regulations. In March 2002, BMW decided to relaunch a new, modernized Mini Cooper in the United States, targeting hip city dwellers who wanted a cool, fun, small car for under $20,000. With only $20 million to spend on the introduction, the Mini marketers decided to launch a guerrilla communications campaign featuring nontraditional uses of billboards, posters, print ads, and grassroots efforts, and no TV ads. The Mini was stacked on top of three Ford Excursion SUVs and driven around national auto shows and 21 major cities. The car showed up in other unusual places, such as inside a sports stadium as seats and inside Playboy as a centerfold. Text-only billboards proclaimed: "THE SUV BACKLASH OFFICIALLY STARTS NOW," "GOLIATH LOST," and "XXL-XL-L-M-S-MINI." Many communications were linked to a cleverly designed Web site that provided necessary product information. The imaginative campaign resulted in a buyer waiting list that was six months long in spring 2002. And Mini hasn't stopped innovating. Using RFID technology, it began to deliver custom messages in January 2007 to Mini owners in four cities on digital signs the company calls "talking billboards." Its 2006 "covert" print campaign, which challenged Mini owners to solve various puzzles in ads, won Grand Prize among the coveted MPA Kelly Awards for excellence and effectiveness in magazine ads, partly because it deepened brand engagement to 21%, its highest level ever, and increased online chat 75%.[38]

Establish the Total Marketing Communications Budget

One of the most difficult marketing decisions is determining how much to spend on marketing communications or promotion. John Wanamaker, the department store magnate, once said, "I know that half of my advertising is wasted, but I don't know which half."

Industries and companies vary considerably in how much they spend on marketing communications or promotion. Expenditures might be 40% to 45% of sales in the cosmetics industry and 5% to 10% in the industrial-equipment industry. Within a given industry, there are low- and high-spending companies.

How do companies decide on the promotion budget? We will describe four common methods: the affordable method, the percentage-of-sales method, the competitive-parity method, and the objective-and-task method.

AFFORDABLE METHOD Many companies set the promotion budget at what they think the company can afford. The affordable method completely ignores the role of promotion as an investment and the immediate impact of promotion on sales volume. It leads to an uncertain annual budget, which makes long-range planning difficult.

PERCENTAGE-OF-SALES METHOD Many companies set promotion expenditures at a specified percentage of sales (either current or anticipated) or of the sales price. Automobile companies typically budget a fixed percentage for promotion based on the planned car price. Oil companies set the appropriation at a fraction of a cent for each gallon of gasoline sold under their own label.

Supporters of the percentage-of-sales method see a number of advantages. First, promotion expenditures will vary with what the company can afford. This satisfies financial managers, who believe expenses should be closely related to the movement of corporate sales over the business cycle. Second, it encourages management to think of the relationship among promotion cost, selling price, and profit per unit. Third, it encourages stability when competing firms spend approximately the same percentage of their sales on promotion.

In spite of these advantages, the percentage-of-sales method has little to justify it. It views sales as the determiner of promotion rather than as the result. It leads to a budget set by the availability of funds rather than by market opportunities. It discourages experimentation with countercyclical promotion or aggressive spending. Dependence on year-to-year sales fluctuations interferes with long-range planning. There is no logical basis for choosing the specific percentage, except what has been done in the past or what competitors are doing. Finally, it does not encourage building the promotion budget by determining what each product and territory deserves.

COMPETITIVE-PARITY METHOD Some companies set their promotion budget to achieve share-of-voice parity with competitors. There are two supporting arguments. One is that competitors' expenditures represent the collective wisdom of the industry. The other is that maintaining competitive parity prevents promotion wars. Neither argument is valid. There are no grounds for believing that competitors know better. Company reputations, resources, opportunities, and objectives differ so much that promotion budgets are hardly a guide. And there is no evidence that budgets based on competitive parity discourage promotion wars.

OBJECTIVE-AND-TAST METHOD The objective-and-task method calls upon marketers to develop promotion budgets by defining specific objectives, determining the tasks that must be performed to achieve these objectives, and estimating the costs of performing these tasks. The sum of these costs is the proposed promotion budget.

For example, suppose Cadbury Schweppes wants to introduce a new natural energy drink, called Sunburst, for the casual athlete.[39]

1. ***Establish the market share goal***—The company estimates 50 million potential users and sets a target of attracting 8% of the market—that is, 4 million users.
2. ***Determine the percentage of the market that should be reached by advertising***—The advertiser hopes to reach 80% (40 million prospects) with the advertising message.
3. ***Determine the percentage of aware prospects that should be persuaded to try the brand***—The advertiser would be pleased if 25% of aware prospects (10 million) tried Sunburst. It estimates that 40% of all triers, or 4 million people, will become loyal users. This is the market goal.
4. ***Determine the number of advertising impressions per 1% trial rate***—The advertiser estimates that 40 advertising impressions (exposures) for every 1% of the population will bring about a 25% trial rate.
5. ***Determine the number of gross rating points that would have to be purchased***—A gross rating point is one exposure to 1% of the target population. Because the company wants to achieve 40 exposures to 80% of the population, it will want to buy 3,200 gross rating points.
6. ***Determine the necessary advertising budget on the basis of the average cost of buying a gross rating point***—To expose 1% of the target population to one impression costs an average of $3,277. Therefore, 3,200 gross rating points will cost $10,486,400 (= $3,277 × 3,200) in the introductory year.

The objective-and-task method has the advantage of requiring management to spell out its assumptions about the relationship among dollars spent, exposure levels, trial rates, and regular usage.

A major question is how much weight marketing communications should receive in relationship to alternatives such as product improvement, lower prices, or better service. The answer depends on where the company's products are in their life cycles, whether they are commodities or highly differentiable products, whether they are routinely needed or must be "sold," and other considerations. Marketing communications budgets tend to be higher when there is low channel support, much change in the marketing program over time, many hard-to-reach customers, more complex customer decision making, differentiated products and nonhomogeneous customer needs, and frequent product purchases in small quantities.[40]

In theory, marketers should establish the total communications budget so that the marginal profit from the last communication dollar just equals the marginal profit from the last dollar in the best noncommunication use. Implementing this principle, however, is not easy.

::: Deciding on the Marketing Communications Mix

Companies must allocate the marketing communications budget over the eight major modes of communication—advertising, sales promotion, public relations and publicity, events and experiences, direct marketing, interactive marketing, word-of-mouth marketing, and the sales force. Within the same industry, companies can differ considerably in their media and channel choices. Avon concentrates its promotional funds on personal selling, whereas Revlon spends heavily on advertising. Electrolux spent heavily on a door-to-door sales force for years, whereas Hoover has relied more on advertising. "Breakthrough Marketing: Ocean Spray" shows how that company has used a variety of communication vehicles to turn their sales fortunes around. Table 17.2 breaks down some major forms of communication.

Companies are always searching for ways to gain efficiency by replacing one communications tool with others. Many companies are replacing some field sales activity with ads, direct mail, and telemarketing. One auto dealer dismissed his five salespeople and cut prices, and sales exploded. The substitutability among communications tools explains why marketing functions need to be coordinated. For example, a new Web site and a coordinated TV ad campaign targeting the greater Los Angeles area sparked record sales for Hawaii's Aloha Airlines, selling over $1 million worth of tickets on one day. The TV ads were designed to create awareness for Aloha and drive traffic to the Web site, where the sale would be closed.[41]

Characteristics of the Marketing Communications Mix

Each communication tool has its own unique characteristics and costs. We briefly review each of these here and discuss them in more detail in Chapters 18 and 19.

ADVERTISING Advertising reaches geographically dispersed buyers. It can build up a long-term image for a product (Coca-Cola ads) or trigger quick sales (a Sears ad for a weekend sale). Certain forms of advertising such as TV can require a large budget, whereas other forms

BREAKTHROUGH MARKETING | **OCEAN SPRAY**

Ocean Spray faced a tough situation in 2004. Domestic sales had been flat for 5 years and there had been a longtime decline in household penetration. Sales in the juice category as a whole suffered from concerns over sugar, increased competition from other types of beverages adding juice, and growing consumer interest in consumption of other beverages such as water and sports drinks. Cranberry juice was known among women as an effective way to keep the urinary tract healthy—not necessarily a product benefit with broad appeal.

Ocean Spray, an agricultural cooperative of growers of cranberries, hired Arnold Worldwide to guide its marketing communications. Working closely with new Ocean Spray COO and experienced marketer Ken Romanzi, Arnold decided to "reintroduce the cranberry to America" as the "surprisingly versatile little fruit that supplies modern-day benefits," through a true "360-degree" campaign that used all facets of marketing communications to reach consumers in a variety of settings. The intent was to support the full range of products—cranberry sauce, fruit juices, and dried cranberries in different forms.

Arnold's strategy was to leverage the unique DNA of the Ocean Spray Cooperative and the realization that the heart of the brand was born in the cranberry bogs and remained there still. The agency decided to focus on the bog to tell an authentic, honest, and perhaps surprising story dubbed "Straight from the Bog." The campaign was designed to also reinforce two key brand benefits—that Ocean Spray products tasted good and were good for you.

PR played a crucial role. Miniature bogs were brought to Manhattan and were featured on an *NBC Today* show morning segment. The event reached over 23 million people through related media pickup. A "Bogs across America Tour" brought the experience to Los Angeles, Chicago, and even London. Television and print advertising featured two natural-looking and natural-sounding growers (depicted by actors) standing waist deep in a bog talking, often humorously, about what they did. The ads were the highest rated ever for Ocean Spray and improved both awareness and persuasion for the two key benefits.

The campaign also included a Web site, in-store displays, and external events for consumers as well as internal ones for members of the growers' cooperative itself. The campaign hit the mark, lifting sales by 10% despite continued decline in the fruit juice category.

Sources: Laurie Peterson, "Breakaway Brands: Ocean Spray Tells It Straight from the Bog," *MediaPost*, October 9, 2006; Francis J. Kelly III and Barry Silverstein, *The Breakaway Brand* (New York: McGraw-Hill, 2005).

Despite a decline in sales of the entire fruit juice category, Ocean Spray's inventive campaign grew sales of all its cranberry products by a remarkable 10%.

such as newspaper do not. Just the presence of advertising might have an effect on sales: Consumers might believe that a heavily advertised brand must offer "good value."[42] Because of the many forms and uses of advertising, it's difficult to make generalizations about it.[43] Yet a few observations are worthwhile:

1. ***Pervasiveness***—Advertising permits the seller to repeat a message many times. It also allows the buyer to receive and compare the messages of various competitors. Large-scale advertising says something positive about the seller's size, power, and success.
2. ***Amplified expressiveness***—Advertising provides opportunities for dramatizing the company and its products through the artful use of print, sound, and color.
3. ***Impersonality***—The audience does not feel obligated to pay attention or respond to advertising. Advertising is a monologue in front of, not a dialogue with, the audience.

SALES PROMOTION Companies use sales promotion tools—coupons, contests, premiums, and the like—to draw a stronger and quicker buyer response, including short-run effects such as highlighting product offers and boosting sagging sales. Sales promotion tools offer three distinctive benefits:

1. ***Communication***—They gain attention and may lead the consumer to the product.
2. ***Incentive***—They incorporate some concession, inducement, or contribution that gives value to the consumer.
3. ***Invitation***—They include a distinct invitation to engage in the transaction now.

PUBLIC RELATIONS AND PUBLICITY Marketers tend to underuse public relations, yet a well-thought-out program coordinated with the other communications-mix elements can be extremely effective, especially if a company needs to challenge consumers' misconceptions.

TABLE 17.2

Advertising and Marketing Communications Forecast for 2007

	2007		
	% Growth	$ (millions)	% Share
Advertising			
Newspapers	–1.8%	47,106	20.4
Broadcast Network Television	–3.0%	18,008	7.8
Cable Network Television	4.0%	17,534	7.6
Broadcast Syndication	1.0%	3,070	1.3
Local & National Spot TV	–5.0%	26,354	11.4
Local / Regional Cable TV	9.0%	6,346	2.8
Branded Entertainment / Product Placement	35.0%	7,335	3.2
Videogame Advertising	90.0%	571	0.2
Cinema Advertising	15.0%	731	0.3
Terrestrial Radio	1.5%	21,416	9.3
Satellite	120.0%	257	0.1
Consumer Magazines	4.2%	14,401	6.2
Business-to-Business Magazines	3.0%	9,268	4.0
Custom Publishing	14.0%	20,876	9.0
Online / Internet	20.0%	16,708	7.2
Out-of-Home	7.0%	6,872	3.0
Mobile Advertising	100.0%	720	0.3
Yellow Pages—Print	0.5%	13,134	5.7
Marketing Communications			100%
Total Advertising	3.7%	230,706	30.6
Direct Mail / Marketing	6.0%	168,477	22.4
Trade Promotion / Slotting Allowances	3.5%	173,612	23.0
Consumer Sales Promotion / Incentives	3.5%	136,828	18.2
Event Marketing	15.0%	17,002	2.3
Public Relations	7.5%	4,284	0.6
Other	–7.5%	22,767	3.0
Total Advertising & Marketing	**4.0%**	**753,674**	**100.0**

Adapted from Jack Myers Media Business Report © copyright 2006/2007 Myers Publishing LLC.

SCIENTIFIC ATLANTA (SA)

Although Forrester Research predicted that high-definition TV (HDTV) sets would be in 16 million homes by the end of 2005, Scientific Atlanta (SA), now a Cisco company, was disappointed in sales of its digital set-top boxes to the country's digital cable TV operators. It turns out consumers weren't demanding set-top boxes because they didn't realize one was required to receive HD programs. As a B2B company, Scientific Atlanta had never needed to communicate directly to consumers before, but it saw the need for a public relations blitz, and fast. The campaign started with SA's commissioning a phone survey of HDTV owners. When the survey revealed all the varied reasons that almost 50% of those surveyed were not taking advantage of HDTV, SA reported the survey results to *USA Today* and the *New York Times.* When the results were published, the company immediately gained credibility by being associated with the survey, but that was only the first step in what became a multimedia campaign. SA's video news release showed friends gathered in living rooms watching HD programs, while a voice-over explained that in order to experience HDTV, you had to "turn on, hook up, and tune in." It ultimately got a respectable 204 broadcast airings, and SA's public relations efforts resulted in a huge jump in the number of HD set-top boxes it shipped.[44]

The appeal of public relations and publicity is based on three distinctive qualities:

1. ***High credibility***—News stories and features are more authentic and credible to readers than ads.

2. ***Ability to catch buyers off guard***—Public relations can reach prospects who prefer to avoid salespeople and advertisements.
3. ***Dramatization***—Public relations has the potential for dramatizing a company or product.

EVENTS AND EXPERIENCES There are many advantages to events and experiences:

1. ***Relevant***—A well-chosen event or experience can be seen as highly relevant because the consumer gets personally involved.
2. ***Involving***—Given their live, real-time quality, events and experiences are more actively engaging for consumers.
3. ***Implicit***—Events are an indirect "soft sell."

DIRECT AND INTERACTIVE MARKETING Direct and interactive marketing takes many forms—over the phone, online, or in person. They share three distinctive characteristics. Direct and interactive marketing messages are:

1. ***Customized***—The message can be prepared to appeal to the addressed individual.
2. ***Up-to-date***—A message can be prepared very quickly.
3. ***Interactive***—The message can be changed depending on the person's response.

WORD-OF-MOUTH MARKETING Word of mouth also takes many forms online or off-line. Three noteworthy characteristics are:

1. ***Credible***—Because people trust others they know and respect, word of mouth can be highly influential.
2. ***Personal***—Word of mouth can be a very intimate dialogue that reflects personal facts, opinions, and experiences.
3. ***Timely***—It occurs when people want it to and when they are most interested, and it often follows noteworthy or meaningful events or experiences.

PERSONAL SELLING Personal selling is the most effective tool at later stages of the buying process, particularly in building up buyer preference, conviction, and action. Personal selling has three distinctive qualities:

1. ***Personal interaction***—Personal selling creates an immediate and interactive episode between two or more persons. Each party is able to observe the other's reactions.
2. ***Cultivation***—Personal selling also permits all kinds of relationships to spring up, ranging from a matter-of-fact selling relationship to a deep personal friendship.
3. ***Response***—The buyer may feel under some obligation for having listened to the sales talk.

Factors in Setting the Marketing Communications Mix

Companies must consider several factors in developing their communications mix: type of product market, consumer readiness to make a purchase, and stage in the product life cycle. Also important is the company's market rank.

TYPE OF PRODUCT MARKET Communications-mix allocations vary between consumer and business markets. Consumer marketers tend to spend comparatively more on sales promotion and advertising; business marketers tend to spend comparatively more on personal selling. In general, personal selling is used more with complex, expensive, and risky goods and in markets with fewer and larger sellers (hence, business markets).

Although marketers use advertising less than sales calls in business markets, advertising still plays a significant role:

- Advertising can provide an introduction to the company and its products.
- If the product has new features, advertising can explain them.
- Reminder advertising is more economical than sales calls.
- Advertisements offering brochures and carrying the company's phone number are an effective way to generate leads for sales representatives.
- Sales representatives can use copies of the company's ads to legitimize their company and products.
- Advertising can remind customers how to use the product and reassure them about their purchase.

A number of studies have underscored advertising's role in business markets. Advertising combined with personal selling can increase sales over what would have resulted if there had been no advertising. Corporate advertising can improve a company's reputation and improve the sales force's chances of getting a favorable first hearing and early adoption of the product.[45] It can also help to position or reposition a business marketer's products or a particular product line, as it did for General Electric.

GENERAL ELECTRIC

Beginning in 2005, GE initiated an integrated marketing campaign that included TV, print, and online advertising as well as events, to let customers know GE products and services help protect the environment. The campaign was dubbed "Ecomagination" and highlighted GE's solar energy products and hybrid locomotives, fuel cells, and lower-emission aircraft. The ads, developed for the company by BBD&O, revolved around this simple, central concept: Although the world's natural resources may be limited, the human imagination is unlimited. In print ads entitled "Shadows," for instance, the shadow of a GE aircraft engine appeared as a giant bird, and the shadow of a GE locomotive as a herd of zebras. Another ad campaign entitled "Audubon" melded GE Ecomagination products with the natural world. The ads, events, and interactive online ads and games all proved extremely successful for GE. Revenue for Ecomagination products in 2005 totaled $10 billion, up 63% from 2004.[46]

Personal selling can also make a strong contribution in consumer-goods marketing. Some consumer marketers use the sales force mainly to collect weekly orders from dealers and to see that sufficient stock is on the shelf. Yet an effectively trained company sales force can make four important contributions:

1. ***Increased stock position***—Sales reps can persuade dealers to take more stock and devote more shelf space to the company's brand.
2. ***Enthusiasm building***—Sales reps can build dealer enthusiasm by dramatizing planned advertising and sales promotion backup.
3. ***Missionary selling***—Sales reps can sign up more dealers.
4. ***Key account management***—Sales reps can take responsibility for growing business with the most important accounts.

BUYER-READINESS STAGE Communication tools vary in cost-effectiveness at different stages of buyer readiness. Figure 17.5 shows the relative cost-effectiveness of three communication tools. Advertising and publicity play the most important roles in the awareness-building stage. Customer comprehension is primarily affected by advertising and personal selling. Customer conviction is influenced mostly by personal selling. Closing the sale is influenced mostly by personal selling and sales promotion. Reordering is also affected mostly by personal selling and sales promotion, and somewhat by reminder advertising.

PRODUCT LIFE-CYCLE STAGE Communication tools also vary in cost-effectiveness at different stages of the product life cycle. In the introduction stage, advertising, events and expe-

FIG. 17.5

Cost-Effectiveness of Three Different Communication Tools at Different Buyer-Readiness Stages

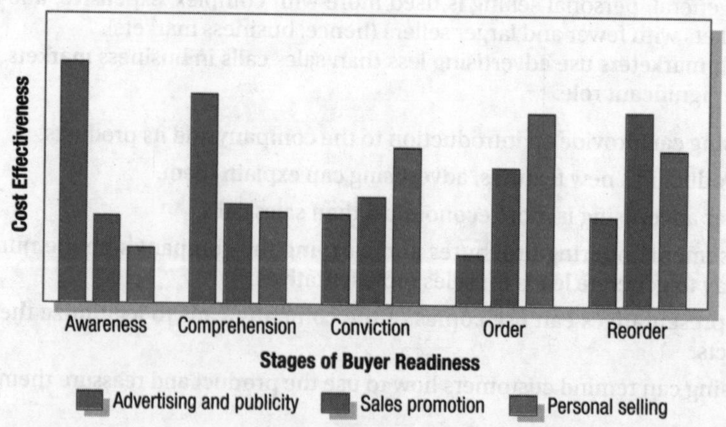

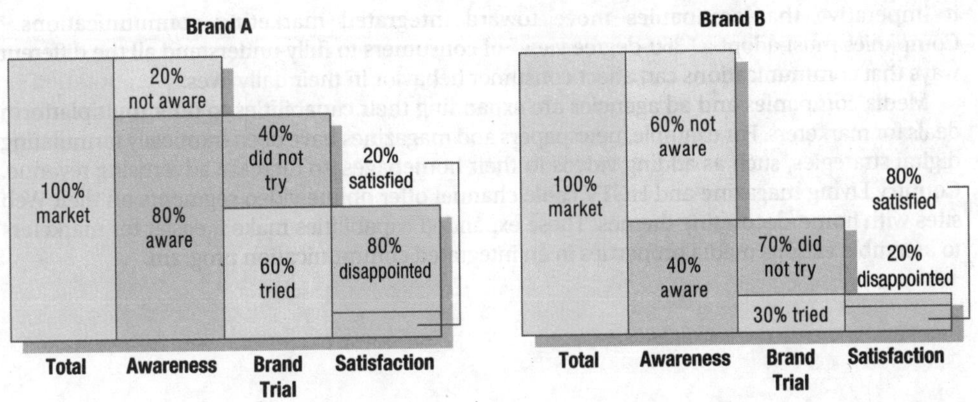

FIG. 17.6

Current Consumer States for Two Brands

riences, and publicity have the highest cost-effectiveness, followed by personal selling to gain distribution coverage and sales promotion and direct marketing to induce trial. In the growth stage, demand has its own momentum through word of mouth. In the maturity stage, advertising, events and experiences, and personal selling all become more important. In the decline stage, sales promotion continues strong, other communication tools are reduced, and salespeople give the product only minimal attention.

Measuring Communication Results

Senior managers want to know the *outcomes* and *revenues* resulting from their communications investments. Too often, however, their communications directors supply only *outputs* and *expenses:* press clipping counts, numbers of ads placed, media costs. In fairness, the communications directors try to translate outputs into intermediate outputs such as reach and frequency, recall and recognition scores, persuasion changes, and cost-per-thousand calculations. Ultimately, behavior-change measures capture the real payoff.

After implementing the communications plan, the communications director must measure its impact on the target audience. Members of the target audience are asked whether they recognize or recall the message, how many times they saw it, what points they recall, how they felt about the message, and their previous and current attitudes toward the product and the company. The communicator should also collect behavioral measures of audience response, such as how many people bought the product, liked it, and talked to others about it.

Figure 17.6 provides an example of good feedback measurement. We find that 80% of the consumers in the total market are aware of brand A, 60% have tried it, and only 20% who have tried it are satisfied. This indicates that the communications program is effective in creating awareness, but the product fails to meet consumer expectations. In contrast, 40% of the consumers in the total market are aware of brand B, and only 30% have tried it, but 80% of those who have tried it are satisfied. In this case, the communications program needs to be strengthened to take advantage of the brand's power.

::: Managing the Integrated Marketing Communications Process

As defined by the American Association of Advertising Agencies, **integrated marketing communications (IMC)** is a concept of marketing communications planning that recognizes the added value of a comprehensive plan. Such a plan evaluates the strategic roles of a variety of communications disciplines—for example, general advertising, direct response, sales promotion, and public relations—and combines these disciplines to provide clarity, consistency, and maximum impact through the seamless integration of messages.

Unfortunately, many companies still rely on one or two communication tools. This practice persists in spite of the fragmenting of mass markets into a multitude of minimarkets, each requiring its own approach; the proliferation of new types of media; and the growing sophistication of consumers. The wide range of communication tools, messages, and audiences makes it imperative that companies move toward integrated marketing communications.[47] Companies must adopt a "360-degree view" of consumers to fully understand all the different ways that communications can affect consumer behavior in their daily lives.

Media companies and ad agencies are expanding their capabilities to offer multiplatform deals for marketers. For example, newspapers and magazines have been frantically formulating digital strategies, such as adding videos to their homepages, to increase advertising revenue. Country Living magazine and HGTV cable channel offer online video segments on their Web sites with home-decorating themes. These expanded capabilities make it easier for marketers to assemble various media properties in an integrated communication program.

GMC & ESPN

General Motors Corp's GMC unit worked with Disney's ABC and ESPN units to develop a promotion that prompted more than 1.5 million people to enter a competition called "GMC Keys to Victory" during *Monday Night Football.* In addition to a large schedule of traditional commercials on ESPN, the promotion included integration of GMC branding and vehicles within the *Monday Night Football* opening sequence. There was a "Keys to the Game" Feature on the *Monday Night Countdown* show and on the episodes of *SportsCenter* that ran just after "MNF" games. GMC ran a season-long promotion for the competition on ESPN.com, and also ran a large gatefold insert in *ESPN the Magazine*, which included a schedule of the *Monday Night Football* games. As part of the deal, GMC gave away a Sierra pickup weekly for 16 weeks on www.keystovictory.com, linked on both www.GMC.com and www.ESPN.com. GMC markers noted that the ESPN deal hit a broad spectrum of media that reached the youthful male target of the GMC truck brand.[48]

Coordinating Media

Media coordination can occur across and within media types, but marketers should combine personal and nonpersonal communications channels to achieve maximum impact. Imagine a marketer using a single tool in a "one-shot" effort to reach and sell a prospect. An example of a *single-vehicle, single-stage campaign* is a one-time mailing offering a cookware item. A *single-vehicle, multiple-stage campaign* would rely on successive mailings to the same prospect. Magazine publishers, for example, send about four renewal notices to a household before giving up. A more powerful approach is the *multiple-vehicle, multiple-stage campaign.* Consider the sequence in Figure 17.7.

Multiple media deployed within a tightly defined time frame can increase message reach and impact. For a Citibank campaign to market home equity loans, instead of using only "mail plus an 800 number," Citibank used "mail plus coupon plus 800 number plus outbound telemarketing plus print advertising." Although the second campaign was more expensive, it resulted in a 15% increase in the number of new accounts compared with direct mail alone.[49]

Research has also shown that promotions can be more effective when combined with advertising.[50] The awareness and attitudes created by advertising campaigns can improve the success of more-direct sales pitches. Many companies are coordinating their online and off-line communications activities. Listing Web addresses in ads (especially print ads) and on packages allows people to more fully explore a company's products, find store locations, and get more product or service information.

For example, Dannon makes it a priority to drive traffic to its Dannon Yogurt homepage, so the company can benefit from the twin paybacks of (1) forging direct relationships with

FIG. 17.7

Example of Multiple-Vehicle, Multiple-Stage Communication Campaign

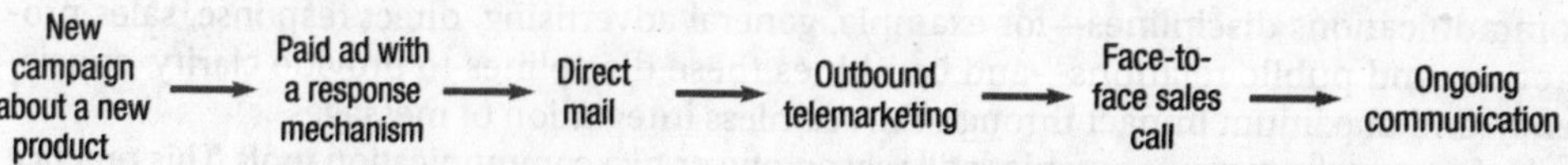

customers and (2) building a database of its best customers, whose loyalty can be strengthened with more targeted coupon and direct-mail promotional efforts.[51] When Dutch financial services firm ING Group launched its brand in the United States, it paired TV and print ads with online ads. In one campaign on financial news sites, all the "ings" in the news text turned orange—matching ING's corporate colors.[52]

Even if consumers don't order online, they can use Web sites in ways that drive them into stores to buy. Best Buy's Web site can function as a research tool for consumers, as surveys revealed that 40% of its customers looked online first before coming into the store.[53]

Implementing IMC

Integrated marketing communications has been slow to take hold for several reasons.[54] Large companies often employ several different communications specialists who may know comparatively little about the other communication tools. Further complicating matters is that many global companies use a large number of ad agencies located in different countries and serving different divisions, resulting in uncoordinated communications and image diffusion. One company that has managed to coordinate the integrated marketing effort of a number of agencies and internal departments is British Gas.

BRITISH GAS

Jane Bednall, head of brand and marketing services at British Gas, holds twice-monthly planning meetings with all the agencies working on various aspects of an integrated marketing campaign—from the ad agency to the PR agency to the company's own internal communications department. One reason Bednall thinks these different factions are truly "integrated" is that British Gas retains them on a project basis and assigns a budget to a specific business initiative rather than to a media channel. Bringing planners from various disciplines together in an open forum to discuss their views shatters preconceptions, Bednall feels. In British Gas's recent campaign around energy efficiency, the company used this collaborative approach and garnered one million responses from people who wanted to learn more about the issue. "We all got behind the single objective and message, starting with advertising, and followed by direct and online marketing. But integration isn't just about marketing communications. It is about everything from PR to the service experience to internal communications," said Bednall. If, in her role as coordinator, Bednall can't coax an agency to be collaborative or if she is forced into a hand-holding role, she makes no bones about finding another agency.[55]

Today, however, a few large agencies have substantially improved their integrated offerings. To facilitate one-stop shopping, major ad agencies have acquired promotion agencies, public relations firms, package-design consultancies, Web site developers, and direct-mail houses. These agencies are redefining themselves as *communications companies* that assist clients to improve their overall communications effectiveness by offering strategic and practical advice on many forms of communication.[56] Many international clients have opted to put a substantial portion of their communications work through one full-service agency. An example is IBM turning all its advertising over to Ogilvy to attain uniform branding. The result is integrated and more-effective marketing communications at a much lower total communications cost.

Integrated marketing communications can produce stronger message consistency and help to build brand equity and create greater sales impact.[57] It forces management to think about every way the customer comes in contact with the company, how the company communicates its positioning, the relative importance of each vehicle, and timing issues. It gives someone the responsibility—where none existed before—to unify the company's brand images and messages as they come through thousands of company activities. IMC should improve the company's ability to reach the right customers with the right messages at the right time and in the right place.[58] "Marketing Memo: How Integrated Is Your IMC Program?" provides some guidelines.

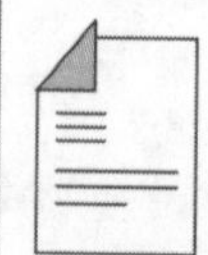

MARKETING MEMO | HOW INTEGRATED IS YOUR IMC PROGRAM?

In assessing the collective impact of an IMC program, the marketer's overriding goal is to create the most effective and efficient communications program possible. The following six criteria can help determine whether communications are truly integrated.

- ***Coverage.*** Coverage is the proportion of the audience reached by each communication option employed, as well as how much overlap exists among communication options. In other words, to what extent do different communication options reach the designated target market and the same or different consumers making up that market?
- ***Contribution.*** Contribution is the inherent ability of a marketing communication to create the desired response and communication effects from consumers in the absence of exposure to any other communication option. How much does a communication affect consumer processing and build awareness, enhance image, elicit responses, and induce sales?
- ***Commonality.*** Commonality is the extent to which *common* associations are reinforced across communication options; that is, the extent to which information conveyed by different communication options share meaning. The consistency and cohesiveness of the brand image is important because it determines how easily existing associations and responses can be recalled and how easily additional associations and responses can become linked to the brand in memory.
- ***Complementarity.*** Communication options are often more effective when used in tandem. Complementarity relates to the extent to which *different* associations and linkages are emphasized across communication options. Different brand associations may be most effectively established by capitalizing on those marketing communication options best suited to eliciting a particular consumer response or establishing a particular type of brand association. As part of their "Now What?" ad campaign showing people dealing with common, but difficult situations, State Farm has used television to introduce a story line that it continued and embellished on its Web site.[59]
- ***Versatility.*** In any integrated communication program, when consumers are exposed to a particular marketing communication, some will have already been exposed to other marketing communications for the brand, and some will not have had any prior exposure. Versatility refers to the extent to which a marketing communication option is robust and "works" for different groups of consumers. The ability of a marketing communication to work at two levels—effectively communicating to consumers who have or have *not* seen other communications—is critically important.
- ***Cost.*** Marketers must weigh evaluations of marketing communications on all these criteria against their cost to arrive at the most effective *and* efficient communications program.

Source: Kevin Lane Keller, *Strategic Brand Management*, 3rd ed. (Upper Saddle River, NJ: Prentice Hall, 2008).

SUMMARY :::

1. Modern marketing calls for more than developing a good product, pricing it attractively, and making it accessible to target customers. Companies must also communicate with present and potential stakeholders and with the general public.
2. The marketing communications mix consists of eight major modes of communication: advertising, sales promotion, public relations and publicity, events and experiences, direct marketing, interactive marketing, word-of-mouth marketing, and personal selling.
3. The communications process consists of nine elements: sender, receiver, message, media, encoding, decoding, response, feedback, and noise. To get their messages through, marketers must encode their messages in a way that takes into account how the target audience usually decodes messages. They must also transmit the message through efficient media that reach the target audience and develop feedback channels to monitor response to the message.
4. Developing effective communications involves eight steps: (1) Identify the target audience, (2) determine the communications objectives, (3) design the communications, (4) select the communications channels, (5) establish the total communications budget, (6) decide on the communications mix, (7) measure the communications results, and (8) manage the integrated marketing communications process.
5. In identifying the target audience, the marketer needs to close any gap that exists between current public perception and the image sought. Communications objectives may involve category need, brand awareness, brand attitude, or brand purchase intention. Formulating the communication requires solving three problems: what to say (message strategy), how to say it (creative strategy), and who should say it (message source). Communications channels may be personal (advocate, expert, and social channels) or nonpersonal (media, atmospheres, and events). The objective-and-task method of setting the promotion budget, which

calls upon marketers to develop their budgets by defining specific objectives, is the most desirable.

6. In deciding on the marketing communications mix, marketers must examine the distinct advantages and costs of each communication tool and the company's market rank. They must also consider the type of product market in which they are selling, how ready consumers are to make a purchase, and the product's stage in the product life cycle. Measuring the effectiveness of the marketing communications mix involves asking members of the target audience whether they recognize or recall the communication, how many times they saw it, what points they recall, how they felt about the communication, and their previous and current attitudes toward the product and the company.

7. Managing and coordinating the entire communications process calls for integrated marketing communications (IMC): marketing communications planning that recognizes the added value of a comprehensive plan that evaluates the strategic roles of a variety of communications disciplines and combines these disciplines to provide clarity, consistency, and maximum impact through the seamless integration of discrete messages.

APPLICATIONS :::

Marketing Debate Has TV Advertising Lost Power?

Long deemed the most successful medium, television advertising has received increased criticism as being too expensive and, even worse, no longer as effective as it once was. Critics maintain that consumers tune out too many ads by zipping and zapping and that it is difficult to make a strong impression. The future, claim some, is with online advertising. Supporters of TV advertising disagree, contending that the multisensory impact of TV is unsurpassed and that no other media option offers the same potential impact.

Take a position: TV advertising has faded in importance *versus* TV advertising is still the most powerful advertising medium.

Marketing Discussion

Pick a brand and go to its Web site. Locate as many forms of communication as you can find. Conduct an informal communications audit. What do you notice? How consistent are the different communications?

IN THIS CHAPTER, WE WILL ADDRESS THE FOLLOWING QUESTIONS:

1. What steps are required in developing an advertising program?
2. How should sales promotion decisions be made?
3. What are the guidelines for effective brand-building events and experiences?
4. How can companies exploit the potential of public relations and publicity?

CHAPTER 18 ::: MANAGING MASS COMMUNICATIONS: ADVERTISING, SALES PROMOTIONS, EVENTS AND EXPERIENCES, AND PUBLIC RELATIONS

eighteen

Although there has been an enormous increase in the use of personal communications by marketers in recent years, due to the rapid penetration of the Internet and other factors, the fact remains that mass media, if used correctly, can still dramatically improve the fortunes of a brand or company. Consider how successful Geico has been at developing a compelling value proposition and brand image for its car insurance via well-conceived mass-media advertising.

Has the $600 million Geico spent on TV advertising been worth it? Geico has nearly quadrupled its size, going from slightly under $3billion in 1998 to more than $11 billion in 2006—making it the fastest-growing car insurance company in the United States. Research also shows that its brand recognition is in the high 90% range. According to Ted Ward, VP of marketing at Geico, this success is due to three things: great employees, breakthrough call-to-action advertising, and a strong brand personality that evolves every day and night on TV and now on video sites such as YouTube. Because Geico needs to appeal to anyone and everyone, it runs three different ad campaigns at once. The popular TV spots advertising Geico's claim that its Web site is "so easy a caveman can use it" feature offended Neanderthals, often dressed improbably in suits, who appeared in additional ads to express frustration and indignation at the prejudice they face. For those who aren't wowed by the caveman spots, there's the gecko series, which establishes Geico's brand personality >>>

Insurance seller Geico has broken out of the pack with its uniquely quirky advertising. Once you've seen the gecko and caveman ads, you never forget them.

as hip and urbane. Finally, a third campaign relies on a tried-and-true format—testimonials—and features people such as Little Richard and Charo paraphrasing the stories of real-life satisfied customers. The multiple campaigns build on each other's success; the company dominates the TV airwaves with so many varied car insurance messages that any competitor's ads are lost.[1]

Although Geico clearly has found great success with its advertising, other marketers are trying to come to grips with how to best use mass media in the new communication environment.[2] In this chapter, we examine the nature and use of four mass-communication tools—advertising, sales promotion, events and experiences, and public relations and publicity.

::: Developing and Managing an Advertising Program

Advertising is any paid form of nonpersonal presentation and promotion of ideas, goods, or services by an identified sponsor. Ads can be a cost-effective way to disseminate messages, whether to build a brand preference or to educate people. Even in today's challenging media environment, good ads can pay off. Ads touting the efficacy of Olay Definity antiaging products and Head & Shoulders Intensive Treatment shampoo helped both P&G brands enjoy double-digit sales gains in recent years.[3]

In developing an advertising program, marketing managers must always start by identifying the target market and buyer motives. Then they can make the five major decisions, known as "the five Ms": *Mission:* What are our advertising objectives? *Money:* How much can we spend? *Message:* What message should we send? *Media:* What media should we use? *Measurement:* How should we evaluate the results? These decisions are summarized in Figure 18.1 and described in the following sections.

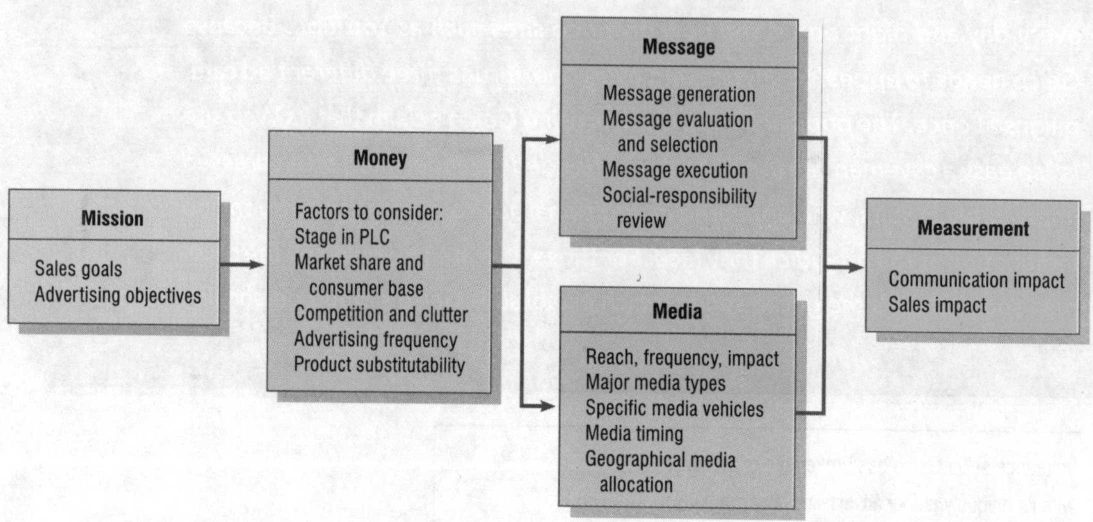

FIG. 18.1 | The Five Ms of Advertising

Setting the Objectives

The advertising objectives must flow from prior decisions on target market, brand positioning, and the marketing program.

An **advertising goal** (or objective) is a specific communications task and achievement level to be accomplished with a specific audience in a specific period of time:[4]

> To increase among 30 million homemakers who own automatic washers the number who identify brand X as a low-sudsing detergent, and who are persuaded that it gets clothes cleaner, from 10% to 40% in one year.

Advertising objectives can be classified according to whether their aim is to inform, persuade, remind, or reinforce. These goals correspond to different stages in the *hierarchy-of-effects* discussed in Chapter 17.

- ***Informative advertising*** aims to create brand awareness and knowledge of new products or new features of existing products. One of the most memorable ads ever starred Australian rugby player Jacko for Energizer batteries. Jacko was dressed as a battery and burst into a subway car, repeatedly shouting out the brand name to helpless early-morning commuters. Unfortunately, although people remembered the brand name—they hated the ad! Brand awareness cannot come at the expense of brand attitudes.
- ***Persuasive advertising*** aims to create liking, preference, conviction, and purchase of a product or service. Some persuasive advertising uses comparative advertising, which makes an explicit comparison of the attributes of two or more brands.[5] Miller Lite took market share from Bud Lite by pointing out that Bud Lite had higher carbs. Comparative advertising works best when it elicits cognitive and affective motivations simultaneously, and when consumers are processing advertising in a detailed, analytical mode.[6]
- ***Reminder advertising*** aims to stimulate repeat purchase of products and services. Expensive, four-color Coca-Cola ads in magazines are intended to remind people to purchase Coca-Cola.
- ***Reinforcement advertising*** aims to convince current purchasers that they made the right choice. Automobile ads often depict satisfied customers enjoying special features of their new car.

The advertising objective should emerge from a thorough analysis of the current marketing situation. If the product class is mature, the company is the market leader, and brand usage is low, the objective is to stimulate more usage. If the product class is new, the company is not the market leader, but the brand is superior to the leader, then the objective is to convince the market of the brand's superiority.

Deciding on the Advertising Budget

How does a company know it's spending the right amount? Some critics charge that large consumer-packaged-goods firms overspend on advertising as a form of insurance against not spending enough, and industrial companies underestimate the power of company and product image building and underspend.[7]

Although advertising is treated as a current expense, part of it is really an investment in building brand equity and customer loyalty. When a company spends $5 million on capital equipment, it may treat the equipment as a five-year depreciable asset and write off only one-fifth of the cost in the first year. When it spends $5 million on advertising to launch a new product, it must write off the entire cost in the first year, reducing its reported profit.

FACTORS AFFECTING BUDGET DECISIONS Here are five specific factors to consider when *setting* the advertising budget:[8]

1. ***Stage in the product life cycle***—New products typically merit large advertising budgets to build awareness and to gain consumer trial. Established brands usually are supported with lower advertising budgets, measured as a ratio to sales.[9]
2. ***Market share and consumer base***—High-market-share brands usually require less advertising expenditure as a percentage of sales to maintain share. To build share by increasing market size requires larger expenditures.

3. ***Competition and clutter***—In a market with a large number of competitors and high advertising spending, a brand must advertise more heavily to be heard. Even simple clutter from advertisements not directly competitive to the brand creates a need for heavier advertising.
4. ***Advertising frequency***—The number of repetitions needed to put across the brand's message to consumers has an obvious impact on the advertising budget.
5. ***Product substitutability***—Brands in less-well-differentiated or commodity-like product classes (beer, soft drinks, banks, and airlines) require heavy advertising to establish a differential image.

In one study of budget allocation, Low and Mohr found that managers allocate less to advertising as brands move to the more mature phase of the product life cycle; when a brand is well differentiated from the competition; when managers are rewarded on short-term results; as retailers gain more power; and when managers have less experience with the company.[10]

ADVERTISING ELASTICITY The predominant response function for advertising is often concave but can be S-shaped.[11] When consumer response is S-shaped, some positive amount of advertising is necessary to generate any sales impact, but sales increases eventually flatten out.[12]

One classic study found that increasing TV advertising budget had a measurable effect on sales only half the time. The success rate was higher on new products or line extensions than on established brands, and when there were changes in copy or in media strategy (such as an expanded target market). When advertising was successful in increasing sales, its impact lasted up to two years after peak spending. Moreover, the long-term incremental sales generated were approximately double the incremental sales observed in the first year of an advertising spending increase.[13]

Other studies reinforce these conclusions. In a 2004 IRI study of 23 brands, advertising often didn't increase sales for mature brands or categories in decline. A review of academic research found that advertising elasticities were estimated to be higher for new (.3) than for established products (.1).[14]

Developing the Advertising Campaign

In designing and evaluating an ad campaign, marketers employ both art and science to develop the *message strategy* or positioning of an ad—*what* the ad attempts to convey about the brand—and its *creative strategy*—*how* the ad expresses the brand claims. Advertisers go through three steps: message generation and evaluation, creative development and execution, and social-responsibility review.

MESSAGE GENERATION AND EVALUATION Many of today's automobile ads have a sameness about them—a car drives at high speed on a curved mountain road or across a desert. The result is that only a weak link forms between the brand and the message. Advertisers are always seeking "the big idea" that connects with consumers rationally and emotionally, sharply distinguishes the brand from competitors, and is broad and flexible enough to translate to different media, markets, and time periods.[15] Fresh insights are important for avoiding using the same appeals and position as others.

A good ad normally focuses on one or two core selling propositions. As part of refining the brand positioning, the advertiser should conduct market research to determine which appeal works best with its target audience and then prepare a *creative brief,* typically covering one or two pages. This is an elaboration of the *positioning statement* and includes: key message, target audience, communications objectives (to do, to know, to believe), key brand benefits, supports for the brand promise, and media.

How many alternative ad themes should the advertiser create before making a choice? The more ads themes explored, the higher the probability of finding an excellent one. Fortunately, the expense of creating rough ads is rapidly falling, thanks to computers. An ad agency's creative department can compose many alternative ads in a short time by drawing from computer files containing still and video images. Marketers can also cut the cost of creative dramatically by using consumers as their creative team, a strategy sometimes called "open source" or "crowdsourcing." However, as the following examples show, this technique can be pure genius or a regrettable failure.

L'OREAL

An in-house-produced ad for cosmetics giant L'Oreal would typically run $164,000 for a 30-second TV spot. Yet in 2006, the company took its inspiration from Current TV, a cable TV channel where user-generated content, in the form of 5-minute segments on any topic, is the programming norm. When Current TV opened up the creative process to commercials, L'Oreal became a Current TV sponsor and paid for an ad produced by someone using the handle "spicytuna." The price tag was a mere $1,000, but you wouldn't know it from the high-concept ad, which featured a Japanese paper fan unfolding across the TV screen. Hidden under the fan was a woman's white-painted face, and when the fan folded up entirely, the face reappeared but with electric-looking green eye shadow. When the ad faded to black, a tagline appeared, "Find color in confidence. L'Oreal Paris."[16]

Other marketers caution that the open-source model doesn't work for every company or every product. Noah Brier, trend tracker at Renegade Marketing of New York, says, "In the future what we'll discover with consumer-generated ads is that if you don't have an insight to back up your big idea, you'll fall flat on your face." Chevrolet did.

GENERAL MOTORS CORP.

In 2006, Chevy directed customers to a special Web site and invited them to create ads for the 2007 Tahoe SUV. The site, www.chevyapprentice.com, was a partnership with the popular TV show, *The Apprentice*, and it allowed apprentice creative directors to choose from a dozen short video clips and almost as many soundtracks and to write their own copy. The ads would then be entered in a contest. But the campaign backfired when Chevy decided to make the spots viral, giving them as much exposure as possible without vetting them first. Instead of singing the Tahoe's praises, many of the spots lambasted Chevy for producing a gas-guzzling contributor to global warming. One said, "This powerful V8 engine only gets 15 miles to the gallon. In a world of limited national resources, you don't need GPS to see where this road is going." One analyst said of the fiasco, "Brands need to be smarter about empowering their brand advocates. In the case of Chevy Tahoe, what you really want to do is take consumers who are most devoted to your product and put them behind the wheel."[17]

CREATIVE DEVELOPMENT AND EXECUTION The ad's impact depends not only on what it says, but often more important, *how* it says it. Execution can be decisive. Every advertising medium has advantages and disadvantages. Here, we review television, print, and radio advertising media.

Television Ads Television is generally acknowledged as the most powerful advertising medium and reaches a broad spectrum of consumers. The wide reach translates to low cost per exposure. TV advertising has two particularly important strengths. First, it can be an effective means of vividly demonstrating product attributes and persuasively explaining their corresponding consumer benefits. Second, it can dramatically portray user and usage imagery, brand personality, and other intangibles.

Because of the fleeting nature of the ad, however, and the distracting creative elements often found in it, product-related messages and the brand itself can be overlooked. Moreover, the high volume of ads and nonprogramming material on television creates clutter that makes it easy for consumers to ignore or forget ads. And although production and placement are expensive, the major networks' share of the prime-time audience has steadily declined, taking the average effectiveness of any one ad with it. For example, research has shown that the number of viewers who said they paid attention to TV ads dropped significantly in the past decade.

Nevertheless, properly designed and executed TV ads can improve brand equity and affect sales and profits. One of the most consistently successful TV advertisers has been Apple. The "1984" ad introducing the Macintosh personal computer—portraying a stark Orwellian future with a feature film look—ran only once on national TV but is one of the best-known ads ever made. In the following years, Apple successfully created awareness and image for a series of products, most recently with its acclaimed iPod ad campaign. A well-done TV commercial can still be a powerful marketing tool.

Aflac's irascible duck is proof that even a commodity product like supplemental insurance can make an impact with the right television campaign.

AFLAC INC.

Insurance companies have a particularly hard time creating brand awareness as well as differentiating themselves from competitors. Aflac Inc. was relatively unknown until a highly creative ad campaign made it one of the most recognized brands in recent history. The lighthearted campaign features an irascible duck incessantly squawking the company's name, "Aflac!" while consumers or celebrities discuss its supplemental health insurance. The duck's frustrated bid for attention appealed to consumers. Sales were up 28% in the first year the duck aired, and name recognition went from 13% to 91%. Aflac has stuck with the duck in its advertising, even incorporating it into its corporate logo in 2005.[18]

Print Ads Print media offer a stark contrast to broadcast media. Because readers consume them at their own pace, magazines and newspapers can provide detailed product information and effectively communicate user and usage imagery. At the same time, the static nature of the visual images in print media makes dynamic presentations or demonstrations difficult, and print media can be fairly passive.

The two main print media—magazines and newspapers—share many advantages and disadvantages. Although newspapers are timely and pervasive, magazines are typically more effective at building user and usage imagery. Newspapers are popular for local—especially retailer—advertising. On an average day, roughly 51 million people buy a newspaper, and 124 million read one, but the numbers have been dropping steadily in recent years.[19] Although advertisers have some flexibility in designing and placing newspaper ads, poor reproduction quality and short shelf life can diminish the ads' impact.

Format elements such as ad size, color, and illustration also affect a print ad's impact. Larger ads gain more attention, though not necessarily by as much as their difference in cost. Four-color illustrations increase ad effectiveness and ad cost. New electronic eye-movement studies show that consumers can be led through an ad by strategic placement of dominant elements.

Researchers studying print advertisements report that the *picture, headline,* and *copy* matter in that order. The picture must be strong enough to draw attention. The headline must reinforce the picture and lead the person to read the copy. The copy must be engaging and the brand's name sufficiently prominent. Even then, less than 50% of the exposed audience will notice even a really outstanding ad. About 30% might recall the headline's main point; about 25% the advertiser's name; and fewer than 10% will read most of the body copy. Ordinary ads don't achieve even these results.

For attracting attention to a print ad, the picture is important, especially if it happens to be a picture of *you.*

UNISYS

Info-tech company Unisys undertook a radical change in ad direction in 2006. The company bought print ads in *Fortune* magazine, but only in select magazines going to about 20 chief information officers at major corporations such as DHL, Subaru of America, Citigroup, and Northwest Airlines. These executives opened the cover wrap of an actual *Fortune* magazine edition to see their own faces smiling up at them. On the reverse side was a customized letter written by a Unisys manager that spoke to the unique challenges in the executive's industry. Also featured were links to mock news videos mentioning the executive's name and a capsule bio focusing on business achievements. Flattery will get you somewhere, according to Unisys's marketing department. To integrate the ads with other forms of marketing communications, Unisys also strategically placed billboard ads (not featuring photos of the executives) so that the executives would see them on their daily commute and even hired field teams to scope out how these high-ranking men and women got to work or where they stopped for coffee.[20]

Given how consumers process print ads, some clear managerial implications emerge, as summarized in "Marketing Memo: Print Ad Evaluation Criteria." One print ad campaign that successfully carved out a brand image is Absolut vodka.

Absolut Vodka created brand awareness for its commodity-like product with a long-running themed campaign, recently replaced with an equally inventive series of new images.

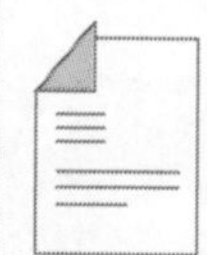

MARKETING MEMO | PRINT AD EVALUATION CRITERIA

In judging the effectiveness of a print ad, in addition to considering the communication strategy (target market, communications objectives, and message and creative strategy), marketers should be able to answer yes to the following questions about the executional elements:

1. Is the message clear at a glance? Can you quickly tell what the advertisement is all about?
2. Is the benefit in the headline?
3. Does the illustration support the headline?
4. Does the first line of the copy support or explain the headline and illustration?
5. Is the ad easy to read and follow?
6. Is the product easily identified?
7. Is the brand or sponsor clearly identified?

Source: Adapted from Philip Ward Burton and Scott C. Purvis, *Which Ad Pulled Best*, 9th ed. (Lincolnwood, IL: NTC Business Books, 2002).

ABSOLUT VODKA

Vodka is generally viewed as a commodity product, yet the amount of brand preference and loyalty in the vodka market is astonishing. Most of this preference and loyalty is attributed to brand image. When the Swedish brand Absolut entered the U.S. market in 1979, the company sold a disappointing 7,000 cases. By 1991, sales had soared to over 2 million cases. Absolut became the largest-selling imported vodka in the United States, with 65% of the market, thanks in large part to its marketing and advertising strategies. In the U.S. market, Absolut aimed for sophisticated, upwardly mobile, affluent drinkers. The vodka comes in a distinctive clear bottle that served as the centerpiece of 15,000 ad executions over a 25-year period. The campaign cleverly juxtaposed a punning caption against a stylized image of the brand's distinctively shaped bottle—for example, "Absolut Texas" under an image of an oversized bottle, or "Absolut 19th" with a bottle made of a golf green. But feeling that consumers were beginning to tune out the message, Absolut vodka replaced the ad campaign with a new global campaign in 2007 that showed what things would be like "In an Absolut World." In this fantasy world, men get pregnant, soap bubbles flow from smokestacks, masterpiece paintings hang in Times Square, protesters and police fight with feather pillows, and perhaps most fantastically of all, the Cubs win the World Series.[21]

Radio Ads Radio is a pervasive medium: Ninety-four percent of all U.S. citizens age 12 and older listen to the radio daily and, on average, for around 20 hours a week, and those numbers have held steady in recent years.[22] Perhaps radio's main advantage is flexibility—stations are very targeted, ads are relatively inexpensive to produce and place, and short closings allow for quick response. Radio is a particularly effective medium in the morning; it can also let companies achieve a balance between broad and localized market coverage.

The obvious disadvantages of radio are the lack of visual images and the relatively passive nature of the consumer processing that results.[23] Nevertheless, radio ads can be extremely creative. Some see the lack of visual images as a plus because they feel the clever use of music, sound, and other creative devices can tap into the listener's imagination to create powerfully relevant and liked images. Here is an example:

MOTEL 6

Motel 6, the nation's largest budget motel chain, was founded in 1962 when the "6" stood for $6 a night. After its business fortunes hit bottom in 1986 with an occupancy rate of only 66.7%, Motel 6 made a number of marketing changes, including the launch of a radio campaign of humorous 60-second ads featuring folksy contractor-turned-writer Tom Bodett delivering the clever tagline "We'll leave the light on for you." The ad campaign is credited with a rise in occupancy and a revitalization of the brand that continues to this day.[24]

LEGAL AND SOCIAL ISSUES Advertisers and their agencies must be sure advertising does not overstep social and legal norms. Public policy makers have developed a substantial body of laws and regulations to govern advertising.

Under U.S. law, advertisers must not make false claims, such as stating that a product cures something when it does not. They must avoid false demonstrations, such as using sand-covered Plexiglas instead of sandpaper to demonstrate that a razor blade can shave sandpaper. It is illegal in the United States to create ads that have the capacity to deceive, even though no one may actually be deceived. For example, a floor wax advertiser can't say the product gives six months' protection unless it does so under typical conditions, and the maker of a diet bread can't say it has fewer calories simply because its slices are thinner. The problem is how to tell the difference between deception and "puffery"—simple exaggerations that are not meant to be believed and that are permitted by law.

SPLENDA VERSUS EQUAL

Splenda's tagline for its artificial sweetener was "Made from sugar, so it tastes like sugar," with "but it's not sugar" in small writing, almost as an afterthought. McNeil Nutritionals, its manufacturer, does begin production of Splenda with pure cane sugar but burns it off in the manufacturing process. However, Merisant, maker of Equal, claimed that Splenda's advertising confuses consumers who are likely to conclude that a product "made from sugar" is healthier than one made from aspartame, Equal's main ingredient. A document used in court and taken from McNeil's own files notes that consumers' perception of Splenda as "not an artificial sweetener" was one of the largest triumphs of the company's marketing campaign, which began in 2003. Splenda became the runaway leader in the sugar-substitute category with 60% of the market, leaving roughly 14% each to Equal (in the blue packets) and Sweet'N Low (pink packets). So, although McNeil agreed to settle the lawsuit and pay Merisant an undisclosed but "substantial" award (and change its advertising), it may be too late for consumers to change their perception of Splenda as something sugary but not sugar free.[25]

Sellers in the United States are legally obligated to avoid bait-and-switch advertising that attracts buyers under false pretenses. Suppose a seller advertises a sewing machine at $149. When consumers try to buy the advertised machine, the seller cannot then refuse to sell it, downplay its features, show a faulty one, or promise unreasonable delivery dates in order to switch the buyer to a more expensive machine.[26]

To be socially responsible, advertisers must be careful not to offend the general public as well as any ethnic groups, racial minorities, or special-interest groups.[27] For example, every year, the nonprofit trade group Advertising Women of New York singles out TV and print ads that it feels portray particularly negative images of women. In 2007, Pizza Hut's ad starring singer Jessica Simpson wearing short shorts and hand-feeding a "Cheesy Bite" to a teenage boy won a Grand Ugly. Converse also got called out for its "Get Chucked" print campaign, as did Carl's Jr. for its Spicy Buffalo Wings Web site and its scantily clad blond hostess, Ashley.[28]

::: Deciding on Media and Measuring Effectiveness

After choosing the message, the advertiser's next task is to choose media to carry it. The steps here are deciding on desired reach, frequency, and impact; choosing among major media types; selecting specific media vehicles; deciding on media timing; and deciding on geographical media allocation. Then the marketer evaluates the results of these decisions.

Deciding on Reach, Frequency, and Impact

Media selection is finding the most cost-effective media to deliver the desired number and type of exposures to the target audience. What do we mean by the desired number of exposures? The advertiser seeks a specified advertising objective and response from the target audience—for example, a target level of product trial. This level depends on, among other things, level of brand awareness. Suppose the rate of product trial increases at a diminishing rate with the level of audience awareness, as shown in Figure 18.2(a). If the advertiser seeks a product trial rate of T^*, it will be necessary to achieve a brand awareness level of A^*.

The next task is to find out how many exposures, E^*, will produce a level of audience awareness of A^*. The effect of exposures on audience awareness depends on the exposures' reach, frequency, and impact:

- ***Reach (R).*** The number of different persons or households exposed to a particular media schedule at least once during a specified time period

FIG. 18.2

Relationship among Trial, Awareness, and the Exposure Function

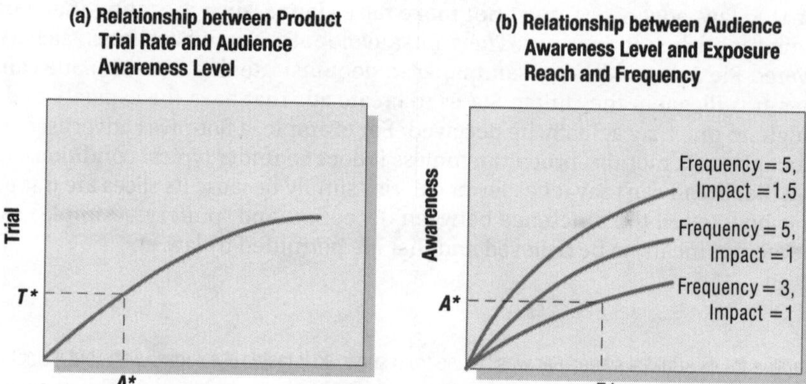

- ***Frequency (F).*** The number of times within the specified time period that an average person or household is exposed to the message
- ***Impact (I).*** The qualitative value of an exposure through a given medium (thus a food ad in *Good Housekeeping* would have a higher impact than in *Fortune* magazine)

Figure 18.2(b) shows the relationship between audience awareness and reach. Audience awareness will be greater, the higher the exposures' reach, frequency, and impact. There are important trade-offs here. Suppose the planner has an advertising budget of $1,000,000 and the cost per thousand exposures of average quality is $5. This means it can buy 200,000,000 exposures ($1,000,000 ÷ [$5/1,000]). If the advertiser seeks an average exposure frequency of 10, it can reach 20,000,000 people (200,000,000 ÷ 10) with the given budget. But if the advertiser wants higher-quality media costing $10 per thousand exposures, it will be able to reach only 10,000,000 people unless it is willing to lower the desired exposure frequency.

The relationship between reach, frequency, and impact is captured in the following concepts:

- ***Total number of exposures (E).*** This is the reach times the average frequency; that is, $E = R \times F$, also called the gross rating points (GRP). If a given media schedule reaches 80% of homes with an average exposure frequency of 3, the media schedule has a GRP of 240 (80 × 3). If another media schedule has a GRP of 300, it has more weight, but we cannot tell how this weight breaks down into reach and frequency.
- ***Weighted number of exposures (WE).*** This is the reach times average frequency times average impact, that is $WE = R \times F \times I$.

Reach is most important when launching new products, flanker brands, extensions of well-known brands, or infrequently purchased brands; or going after an undefined target market. Frequency is most important where there are strong competitors, a complex story to tell, high consumer resistance, or a frequent-purchase cycle.[29] Many advertisers believe a target audience needs a large number of exposures. Others believe that after people see the same ad a few times, they either act on it, get irritated by it, or stop noticing it.[30]

Another reason for repetition is forgetting. The higher the forgetting rate associated with a brand, product category, or message, the higher the warranted level of repetition. However, advertisers should not coast on a tired ad but insist on fresh executions by their ad agency.[31]

Choosing among Major Media Types

The media planner must know the capacity of the major advertising media types to deliver reach, frequency, and impact. The major advertising media along with their costs, advantages, and limitations are profiled in Table 18.1.

Media planners make their choices by considering the following variables:

- ***Target audience media habits.*** Radio and television are the most effective media for reaching teens.
- ***Product characteristics.*** Media types have different potential for demonstration, visualization, explanation, believability, and color. Women's dresses are best shown in color

TABLE 18.1 Profiles of Major Media Types

Medium	Advantages	Limitations
Newspapers	Flexibility; timeliness; good local market coverage; broad acceptance; high believability	Short life; poor reproduction quality; small "pass-along" audience
Television	Combines sight, sound, and motion; appealing to the senses; high attention; high reach	High absolute cost; high clutter; fleeting exposure; less audience selectivity
Direct mail	Audience selectivity; flexibility; no ad competition within the same medium; personalization	Relatively high cost; "junk mail" image
Radio	Mass use; high geographic and demographic selectivity; low cost	Audio presentation only; lower attention than television; nonstandardized rate structures; fleeting exposure
Magazines	High geographic and demographic selectivity; credibility and prestige; high-quality reproduction; long life; good pass-along readership	Long ad purchase lead time; some waste circulation; no guarantee of position
Outdoor	Flexibility; high repeat exposure; low cost; low competition	Limited audience selectivity; creative limitations
Yellow Pages	Excellent local coverage; high believability; wide reach; low cost	High competition; long ad purchase lead time; creative limitations
Newsletters	Very high selectivity; full control; interactive opportunities; relative low costs	Costs could run away
Brochures	Flexibility; full control; can dramatize messages	Overproduction could lead to runaway costs
Telephone	Many users; opportunity to give a personal touch	Relative high cost unless volunteers are used
Internet	High selectivity; interactive possibilities; relatively low cost	Relatively new media with a low number of users in some countries

magazines, but high-tech products requiring dynamic presentation such as digital cameras, printers, or cell phones are best demonstrated on television.

- ***Message characteristics.*** Timeliness and information content will influence media choice. A message announcing a major sale tomorrow will require radio, TV, or newspaper. A message containing a great deal of technical data might require specialized magazines or mailings.
- ***Cost.*** Television is very expensive, whereas newspaper advertising is relatively inexpensive. What counts is the cost per thousand exposures.

Given the abundance of media, the planner must first decide how to allocate the budget to the major media types (see Table 18.2). Consumers are increasingly time starved. Attention is a scarce currency, and advertisers need strong devices to capture people's attention.[32]

TABLE 18.2 Advertising Media Expenditures (United States, 2007, Billions of Dollars)

	$	% of Total
TV	72.1	32%
Radio	20.9	9%
Newspaper	45.8	20%
Magazines	23.7	11%
Yellow Pages	14.4	6%
Internet	16.7	8%
Out-of-Home	7.7	3%
Other	22.5	11%
Total	223.8	

Source: Adapted from www.JackMyers.com Jack Myers Media Business Report.

TABLE 18.3

The Changing Video Environment (percentage of household penetration)

TV/radio/color TV	98%	Home theater sound	36%
VCR	90%	TV/VCR combo	35%
DVD	82%	DTH satellite	31%
Stereo TV	76%	Monochrome TV	29%
Modems	75%	Projection TV	23%
Wireless [mobile] phone	73%	LCD TV	22%
Camcorder	55%		

Source: Consumer Electronics Association (www.ce.org).

Alternative Advertising Options

In recent years, researchers have noticed reduced effectiveness for television due to increased commercial clutter, increased "zipping and zapping" of commercials aided by the arrival of PVRs such as TiVo, and lower viewing owing to the growth in cable and satellite TV and DVD/VCRs.[33] Table 18.3 shows how the home media environment has become significantly wired. Furthermore, television advertising costs have risen faster than other media costs. Many marketers are looking for alternative media.[34] After years of advertising on U.S. television with the "How to Speak Australian" campaign, Foster's decided to completely eliminate TV ads and go online.[35]

PLACE ADVERTISING **Place advertising**, or out-of-home advertising, is a broad category including many creative and unexpected forms to grab consumers' attention. The rationale is that marketers are better off reaching people where they work, play, and, of course, shop. Some of the options include billboards, public spaces, product placement, and point of purchase.

To learn how the Gujarat Cooperative Milk Marketing Federation has enhanced its brand image with a successful billboard compaign over the last 40 years in India, visit www.pearsoned.co.in/marketingmanagementindia.

Billboards Billboards have been transformed and now use colorful, digitally produced graphics, backlighting, sounds, movement, and unusual—even three-dimensional—images.[36] In New York, manhole covers have been reimagined as steaming cups of Folgers coffee; in Belgium, eBay posted "Moved to eBay" stickers on empty storefronts; and in Germany, imaginary workers toiling inside vending machines, ATMs, and photo booths were justification for a German job-hunting Web site to proclaim, "Life is Too Short for the Wrong Job."[37]

Not your grandfather's billboard advertising, but highly effective and entertaining all the same.

BBC WORLD

The Best of Show winner at the OBIE awards sponsored by the Outdoor Advertising Association of America was BBC World television channel and its ad agency BBDO. The BBC World Voting Campaign featured interactive digital billboards designed to introduce BBC World to the U.S. market. The interactive units showed images and headlines that reflected current events. Passersby were then asked to use Bluetooth technology to select one of two available opinions, and a running tally was displayed.[38]

Public Spaces Advertisers are placing ads in unconventional places such as movies, airlines, and lounges, as well as classrooms, sports arenas, office and hotel elevators, and other public places. Billboard-type poster ads are showing up everywhere. Transit ads on buses, subways, and commuter trains—around for years—have become a valuable way to reach working women. "Street furniture"—bus shelters, kiosks, and public areas—is another fast-growing option.

Advertisers can buy space in stadiums and arenas and on garbage cans, bicycle racks, parking meters, airport luggage carousels, elevators, gasoline pumps, the bottom of golf cups, airline snack packages, and supermarket produce in the form of tiny labels on apples and bananas. They can even buy space in toilet stalls and above urinals which, according to research studies, office workers visit an average of three to four times a day for roughly four minutes per visit.[39]

BRITISH AIRPORT AUTHORITY

Ad agency JCDecaux Airport has worked alongside the British Airport Authority (BAA) and architects to build advertising into the very foundation of Heathrow's new Terminal 5. Rather than advertising clutter to besiege the weary traveler, only a small number of advertising sites will carry messages, but they will be massive, including light boxes larger than four double-decker buses. Over three hundred digital ad sites are being installed in the terminal—taking up 50% of the airport's advertising "real estate," and departing from the usual B2B or corporate branding campaigns to introduce a whole range of consumer goods—from chocolates and clothing to perfumes and cosmetics. The intensive use of digital images also means that ad messages can be targeted to different audiences, locations, and times of day. Ads can even appear in different languages to greet arriving and departing flights. BAA director of media, Duncan Tolson, says Terminal 5 is just the beginning. "Terminal 5 will mark the start of a new generation of airport advertising. It will act as a blueprint for the future, and we are looking forward to rolling it out across all BAA airports."[40]

PRODUCT PLACEMENT Product placement has expanded from movies to all types of TV shows.[41] Marketers pay fees of $50,000 to $100,000 and even higher so that their products will make cameo appearances in movies and on television. Sometimes placements are the result of a larger network advertising deal, but other times they are the work of small product-placement shops that maintain ties with prop masters, set designers, and production executives.[42]

The television show *The Apprentice* sold placement rights for millions of dollars to marketers such as Dial, Home Depot, and Lexus to use their products as the basis of competitions on the show. 7-UP, Aston Martin, Finlandia, VISA, and Omega all initiated major promotional pushes based on product-placement tie-ins with the James Bond film "Die Another Day."[43] With over $100 million paid for product-placement rights, some critics called the film "Buy Another Day."

Some firms get product placement at no cost by supplying their product to the movie company (Nike does not pay to be in movies but often supplies shoes, jackets, bags, etc.).[44] Firms sometimes just get lucky and are included in shows for plot reasons. FedEx received a great deal of favorable exposure from the movie *Castaway,* starring Tom Hanks as a marooned FedEx employee.[45]

Marketers are finding inventive ways to advertise during real-time television broadcasts. Sports fans are familiar with virtual logos networks add digitally to the playing field. Invisible to spectators at the event, these ads look just like painted-on logos to home viewers. Ads also appear in best-selling paperback books and movie videotapes. Written material such as annual reports, data sheets, catalogs, and newsletters increasingly carries ads. **Advertorials** are print ads that offer editorial content reflecting favorably on the brand

and are difficult to distinguish from newspaper or magazine content. Many companies include advertising inserts in monthly bills. Some companies mail CDs or DVDs to prospects.

POINT OF PURCHASE There are many ways to communicate with consumers at the ***point of purchase*** (**P-O-P**). In-store advertising includes ads on shopping carts, cart straps, aisles, and shelves, as well as promotion options such as in-store demonstrations, live sampling, and instant coupon machines. Some supermarkets are selling floor space for company logos and experimenting with talking shelves. P-O-P radio provides FM-style programming and commercial messages to thousands of food stores and drugstores nationwide. Programming includes a store-selected music format, consumer tips, and commercials. Ads on Wal-Mart TV run on 125,000 screens in 3,100 stores and appear three times an hour, reaching a potential audience of 127 million shoppers per week. Airtime costs between $50,000 and $300,000 for a four-week flight of ads, depending on frequency.[46]

The appeal of point-of-purchase advertising lies in the fact that in many product categories consumers make the bulk of their final brand decisions in the store, 74% according to one study.[47]

EVALUATING ALTERNATIVE MEDIA Ads now can appear virtually anywhere consumers have a few spare minutes or even seconds to notice them. The main advantage of nontraditional media is that they can often reach a very precise and captive audience in a cost-effective manner. The message must be simple and direct. In fact, outdoor advertising is often called the "15-second sell." It's more effective at enhancing brand awareness or brand image than creating new brand associations.

The challenge with nontraditional media is demonstrating its reach and effectiveness through credible, independent research. Unique ad placements designed to break through clutter may also be perceived as invasive and obtrusive. Consumer backlash often results when people see ads in traditionally ad-free spaces, such as in schools, on police cruisers, and in doctors' waiting rooms.

Not everyone is turned off by the proliferation of advertising. One marketing consultant says, "Kids 18 and under aren't thinking twice about it. Branded merchandise is just the landscape of their lives." Perhaps because of its sheer pervasiveness, some consumers seem to be less bothered by nontraditional media now than in the past.

But consumers must be favorably affected in some way to justify the marketing expenditures for nontraditional media. Some firms offering ad placement in supermarket checkout lines, fast-food restaurants, physicians' waiting rooms, health clubs, and truck stops have suspended business, in part because of a lack of consumer interest. But there will always be room for creative means of placing the brand in front of consumers. The possibilities are endless: "Marketing Insight: Playing Games with Brands" describes the emergence of yet another new media trend.

Selecting Specific Media Vehicles

The media planner must search for the most cost-effective vehicles within each chosen media type. The advertiser who decides to buy 30 seconds of advertising on network television can pay around $100,000 for a new show, almost $500,000 for a popular prime-time show such as *Grey's Anatomy, CSI,* or *Survivor,* or over $2.5 million for an event such as the Super Bowl.[48] These choices are critical: The average cost to produce a national 30-second television commercial in 2005 was about $381,000. It can cost as much to run an ad once on network TV as to make it to start with!

In making choices, the planner must rely on measurement services that provide estimates of audience size, composition, and media cost. Audience size has several possible measures:

- ***Circulation.*** The number of physical units carrying the advertising
- ***Audience.*** The number of people exposed to the vehicle (If the vehicle has pass-on readership, then the audience is larger than circulation.)
- ***Effective audience.*** The number of people with target audience characteristics exposed to the vehicle
- ***Effective ad-exposed audience.*** The number of people with target audience characteristics who actually saw the ad

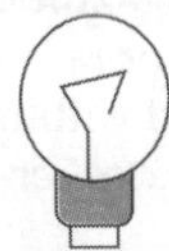

MARKETING INSIGHT | PLAYING GAMES WITH BRANDS

Given the explosive popularity of video games with younger consumers, many advertisers have adopted an "if you can't beat them, join them" attitude. Online games have wide appeal. Today there are 132 million teen and adult gamers in the United States, where nearly half of all households have a game console. As many as 40% of gamers are women. Women seem to prefer puzzles and collaborative games, whereas men seem more attracted to competitive or simulation games.

A top-notch "advergame" can cost between $100,000 and $500,000 to develop. The game can be played on the sponsor's corporate homepage, on gaming portals, or even at restaurants. The Buzztime iTV Network is an out-of-home interactive entertainment network that delivers entertainment and sports games in approximately 3,600 North American hospitality locations such as Applebee's, Bennigan's Irish Grill, T.G.I. Friday's, and others.

7-Up, McDonald's, and Porsche have all been featured in games. Honda developed a game that allowed players to choose a Honda and zoom around city streets plastered with Honda logos. In the first three months, 78,000 people played for an average of eight minutes. The cost per thousand (CPM) of $7 compared favorably to a prime-time TV commercial CPM of $11.65. Marketers collect valuable customer data upon registration and often seek permission to send e-mail. Of game players sponsored by Ford Escape SUV, 54% signed up to receive e-mail.

Marketers are also playing starring roles in popular videogames. In multiplayer videogame Test Drive Unlimited, players can take a break from the races to go shopping, where they can encounter at least 10 real-world brands such as Lexus and Hawaiian Airlines. Tomb Raider's Lara Craft tools around with a Jeep Commander. Mainstream marketers such as Apple, Procter & Gamble, Toyota, and Visa are all jumping on board. Spending on in-game advertising and product placement is expected to grow from $56 million in 2005 to $730 million in 2010, with a typical cost per thousand of $30.

The growing popularity of Second Life and other virtual communities is creating new placement opportunities for marketers. Coca-Cola, H&R Block, IBM, and Toyota are among the first 80 companies that have set up a virtual presence there. The NBA introduced an NBA headquarters in Second Life that included a merchandise store as well as venues and activities sponsored by three existing partners, Cisco Systems, T-Mobile, and Toyota. Getting on board is cheap—it only costs $1,675 plus $295 a month to occupy an island—and advertisers are thrilled at the opportunity to access the hard-to-reach 18- to 34-year-olds and others that make up the 7.1 million registered users. But Second Life is famous too for much racy, edgy content and behaviors. As one online agency executive noted, "If brands go into a space like this, they have to go in with their eyes open about the hazards they might have to deal with."

Sources: "Virtual Worlds Generate Real-Life Benefits for Properties, Sponsors," *IEG Sponsorship Report*, June 11, 2007, pp. 1, 8; Allison Fass, "Sex, Pranks, and Reality," *Forbes*, July 2, 2007, p. 48; Erika Brown, "Game On!" *Forbes*, July 24, 2006, pp. 84–86; David Radd, "Advergaming: You Got It," *BusinessWeek*, October 11, 2006; Stuart Elliott, "Madison's Avenue's Full-Court Pitch to Video Gamers," *New York Times*, October 16, 2005; "Women Get in the Game," www.microsoft.com, January 8, 2004.

Media planners calculate the cost per thousand persons reached by a vehicle. If a full-page, four-color ad in *Newsweek* costs $200,000 and *Newsweek*'s estimated readership is 3.1 million people, the cost of exposing the ad to 1,000 persons is approximately $65. The same ad in *BusinessWeek* may cost $70,000 but reach only 970,000 persons—at a cost-per-thousand of $72. The media planner ranks each magazine by cost-per-thousand and favors magazines with the lowest cost-per-thousand for reaching target consumers. The magazines themselves often put together a "reader profile" for their advertisers, summarizing the characteristics of the magazine's readers with respect to age, income, residence, marital status, and leisure activities.

Virtual communities, such as Second Life pictured here, and videogames are among the new frontiers for advertisers trying to reach young consumers.

Marketers need to apply several adjustments to the cost-per-thousand measure. First, they should adjust the measure for *audience quality.* For a baby lotion ad, a magazine read by one million young mothers has an exposure value of one million; if read by one million teenagers, it would have an exposure value of almost zero. Second, adjust the exposure value for the *audience-attention probability.* Readers of *Vogue* may pay more attention to ads than do readers of *Newsweek*.[49] Third, adjust for the magazine's *editorial quality* (prestige and believability). People are more likely to believe a TV or radio ad and to become more positively disposed toward the brand when the ad is placed within a program they like.[50] Fourth, adjust for the magazine's *ad placement policies and extra services* (such as regional or occupational editions and lead-time requirements).

Media planners are increasingly using more sophisticated measures of effectiveness and employing them in mathematical models to arrive at the best media mix. Many advertising agencies use a computer program to select the initial media and then make further improvements based on subjective factors.[51]

Deciding on Media Timing and Allocation

In choosing media, the advertiser faces both a macroscheduling and a microscheduling problem. The *macroscheduling problem* involves scheduling the advertising in relationship to seasons and the business cycle. Suppose 70% of a product's sales occur between June and September. The firm can vary its advertising expenditures to follow the seasonal pattern, to oppose the seasonal pattern, or to be constant throughout the year.

The *microscheduling problem* calls for allocating advertising expenditures within a short period to obtain maximum impact. Suppose the firm decides to buy 30 radio spots in the month of September. Figure 18.3 shows several possible patterns. The left side shows that advertising messages for the month can be concentrated ("burst" advertising), dispersed continuously throughout the month, or dispersed intermittently. The top side shows that the advertising messages can be beamed with a level, rising, falling, or alternating frequency.

The most effective pattern depends on the communications objectives in relationship to the nature of the product, target customers, distribution channels, and other marketing factors. The timing pattern should consider three factors. *Buyer turnover* expresses the rate at which new buyers enter the market; the higher this rate, the more continuous the advertising should be. *Purchase frequency* is the number of times during the period that the average buyer buys the product; the higher the purchase frequency, the more continuous the advertising should be. The *forgetting rate* is the rate at which the buyer forgets the brand; the higher the forgetting rate, the more continuous the advertising should be.

In launching a new product, the advertiser must choose among continuity, concentration, flighting, and pulsing.

- ***Continuity*** means exposures appear evenly throughout a given period. Generally, advertisers use continuous advertising in expanding market situations, with frequently purchased items, and in tightly defined buyer categories.
- ***Concentration*** calls for spending all the advertising dollars in a single period. This makes sense for products with one selling season or related holiday.
- ***Flighting*** calls for advertising for a period, followed by a period with no advertising, followed by a second period of advertising activity. It is useful when funding is limited, the purchase cycle is relatively infrequent, or items are seasonal.

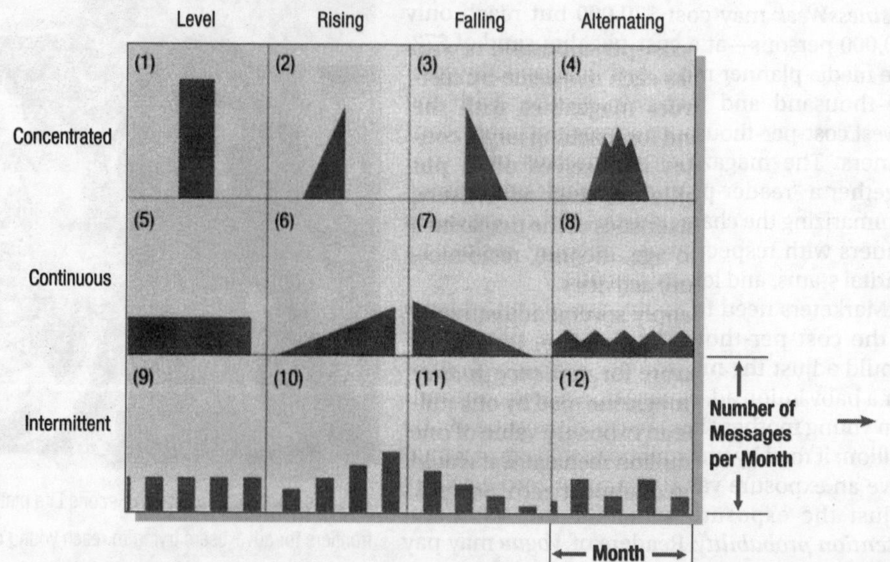

FIG. 18.3 Classification of Advertising Timing Patterns

- ***Pulsing*** is continuous advertising at low-weight levels reinforced periodically by waves of heavier activity. It draws on the strength of continuous advertising and flights to create a compromise scheduling strategy.[52] Those who favor pulsing believe the audience will learn the message more thoroughly, and at a lower cost to the firm.

A company must decide how to allocate its advertising budget over space as well as over time. The company makes "national buys" when it places ads on national TV networks or in nationally circulated magazines. It makes "spot buys" when it buys TV time in just a few markets or in regional editions of magazines. These markets are called *areas of dominant influence* (ADIs) or *designated marketing areas* (DMAs). Ads reach a market 40 to 60 miles from a city center. The company makes "local buys" when it advertises in local newspapers, radio, or outdoor sites.

Evaluating Advertising Effectiveness

Most advertisers try to measure the communication effect of an ad—that is, its potential effect on awareness, knowledge, or preference. They would also like to measure the ad's sales effect.

COMMUNICATION-EFFECT RESEARCH **Communication-effect research**, called *copy testing*, seeks to determine whether an ad is communicating effectively. Marketers should perform this test both before an ad is put into media and after it is printed or broadcast.

There are three major methods of pretesting. The *consumer feedback method* asks consumers questions such as these:

1. What is the main message you get from this ad?
2. What do you think they want you to know, believe, or do?
3. How likely is it that this ad will influence you to undertake the action?
4. What works well in the ad and what works poorly?
5. How does the ad make you feel?
6. Where is the best place to reach you with this message?

Portfolio tests ask consumers to view or listen to a portfolio of advertisements. Consumers are then asked to recall all the ads and their content, aided or unaided by the interviewer. Recall level indicates an ad's ability to stand out and to have its message understood and remembered.

Laboratory tests use equipment to measure physiological reactions—heartbeat, blood pressure, pupil dilation, galvanic skin response, perspiration—to an ad; or consumers may be asked to turn a knob to indicate their moment-to-moment liking or interest while viewing sequenced material.[53] These tests measure attention-getting power but reveal nothing about impact on beliefs, attitudes, or intentions. As we noted in Chapter 4, marketers have begun to explore various neural research methods to study how the brain evaluates different types of ad messages.[54] Table 18.4 describes some specific advertising research techniques.

TABLE 18.4

Advertising Research Techniques

For Print Ads. Starch and Gallup & Robinson Inc. are two widely used print pretesting services. Test ads are placed in magazines, which are then circulated to consumers. These consumers are contacted later and interviewed. Recall and recognition tests are used to determine advertising effectiveness.

For Broadcast Ads. ***In-home tests:*** A video tape is taken or downloaded into the homes of target consumers, who then view the commercials.

Trailer tests: In a trailer in a shopping center, shoppers are shown the products and given an opportunity to select a series of brands. They then view commercials and are given coupons to be used in the shopping center. Redemption rates indicate commercials' influence on purchase behavior.

Theater tests: Consumers are invited to a theater to view a potential new television series along with some commercials. Before the show begins, consumers indicate preferred brands in different categories; after the viewing, consumers again choose preferred brands. Preference changes measure the commercials' persuasive power.

On-air tests: Respondents are recruited to watch a program on a regular TV channel during the test commercial or are selected based on their having viewed the program. They are asked questions about commercial recall.

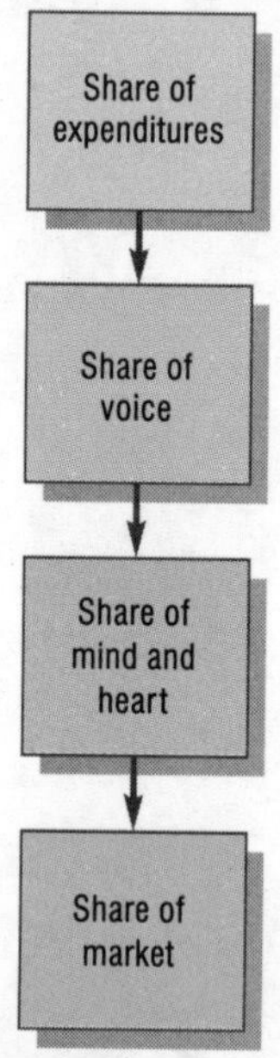

FIG. 18.4

Formula for Measuring Sales Impact of Advertising

Pretest critics maintain that agencies can design ads that test well but may not necessarily perform well in the marketplace. Proponents of ad pretesting maintain that useful diagnostic information can emerge and that pretests should not be used as the sole decision criterion anyway. Widely acknowledged as being one of the best advertisers around, Nike is notorious for doing very little ad pretesting.

Many advertisers use posttests to assess the overall impact of a completed campaign. If a company hoped to increase brand awareness from 20% to 50% and succeeded in increasing it to only 30%, then the company is not spending enough, its ads are poor, or it has overlooked some other factor.

SALES-EFFECT RESEARCH What sales are generated by an ad that increases brand awareness by 20% and brand preference by 10%? The fewer or more controllable other factors such as features and price are, the easier it is to measure advertising's effect on sales. The sales impact is easiest to measure in direct marketing situations and hardest in brand or corporate image-building advertising.

Companies are generally interested in finding out whether they are overspending or underspending on advertising. One approach to answering this question is to work with the formulation shown in Figure 18.4.

A company's *share of advertising expenditures* produces a *share of voice* (proportion of company advertising of that product to all advertising of that product) that earns a *share of consumers' minds and hearts* and, ultimately, a *share of market.*

Researchers try to measure the sales impact through analyzing historical or experimental data. The *historical approach* involves correlating past sales to past advertising expenditures using advanced statistical techniques.[55] Other researchers use an *experimental design* to measure advertising's sales impact. An example follows.

INFORMATION RESOURCES INC.

Information Resources offers a service called BehaviorScan that provides marketers in the United States with data about advertising effectiveness by tracking consumer purchases tied to specific advertising. Consumers in test markets who sign up to be members of IRI's "Shoppers Hotline" panel agree to have microcomputers record when the TV set is on and to which station it is tuned, and electronic scanners record UPC codes of their household purchases at supermarkets. IRI has the capability to send different commercials to different homes. The company also conducts in-store tests in most chains and in most markets in the United States to study the effects of promotions, displays, coupons, store features, and packaging.[56]

A growing number of researchers are striving to measure the sales effect of advertising expenditures instead of settling for communication-effect measures.[57] Millward Brown International has conducted tracking studies for years to help advertisers decide whether their advertising is benefiting their brand.[58] Another research pioneer, Nielsen, has begun tracking commercials electronically.[59]

::: Sales Promotion

Sales promotion, a key ingredient in marketing campaigns, consists of a collection of incentive tools, mostly short term, designed to stimulate quicker or greater purchase of particular products or services by consumers or the trade.[60]

Whereas advertising offers a *reason* to buy, sales promotion offers an *incentive* to buy. Sales promotion includes tools for *consumer promotion* (samples, coupons, cash refund offers, prices off, premiums, prizes, patronage rewards, free trials, warranties, tie-in promotions, cross-promotions, point-of-purchase displays, and demonstrations); *trade promotion* (prices off, advertising and display allowances, and free goods); and *business* and *sales-force promotion* (trade shows and conventions, contests for sales reps, and specialty advertising).

Objectives

Sales promotion tools vary in their specific objectives. A free sample stimulates consumer trial, whereas a free management-advisory service aims at cementing a long-term relationship with a retailer.

Sellers use incentive-type promotions to attract new triers, to reward loyal customers, and to increase the repurchase rates of occasional users. Sales promotions often attract brand switchers, who are primarily looking for low price, good value, or premiums. If some of them would not have otherwise tried the brand, promotion can yield long-term increases in market share.[61]

Sales promotions in markets of high brand similarity can produce a high sales response in the short run but little permanent gain in brand preference over the longer term. In markets of high brand dissimilarity, they may be able to alter market shares permanently. In addition to brand switching, consumers may engage in stockpiling—purchasing earlier than usual (purchase acceleration) or purchasing extra quantities.[62] But sales may then hit a postpromotion dip.[63]

A number of sales promotion benefits flow to manufacturers and consumers.[64] Manufacturers can adjust to short-term variations in supply and demand and test how high a list price they can charge, because they can always discount it. Promotions induce consumers to try new products and lead to more varied retail formats, such as everyday low pricing and promotional pricing. For retailers, promotions may increase sales of complementary categories (cake mix promotions may drive frosting sales) as well as induce store switching. They promote greater consumer awareness of prices. They help manufacturers sell more than normal at the list price and adapt programs to different consumer segments. Service marketers also employ sales promotions to attract new customers and establish loyalty.

Advertising versus Promotion

A decade ago, the advertising-to-sales-promotion ratio was about 60:40. Today, in many consumer-packaged-goods companies, sales promotion accounts for 75% of the combined budget (roughly 50% is trade promotion and 25% is consumer promotion). Sales promotion expenditures increased as a percentage of budget expenditure annually for almost two decades, although its growth has slowed down in recent years.

Several factors contributed to this rapid growth, particularly in consumer markets.[65] Promotion became more accepted by top management as an effective sales tool; the number of brands increased; competitors used promotions frequently; many brands were seen as similar; consumers became more price oriented; the trade demanded more deals from manufacturers; and advertising efficiency declined.

But the rapid growth of sales promotion created clutter. Incessant prices off, coupons, deals, and premiums may devalue the product in buyers' minds. So there is risk in putting a well-known brand on promotion over 30% of the time.[66] Automobile manufacturers turned to 0% financing and hefty cash rebates to ignite sales in the soft economy of 2000–2001 but have found it difficult to wean consumers from discounts ever since.[67] Dominant brands offer deals less frequently, because most deals subsidize only current users.

Loyal brand buyers tend not to change their buying patterns as a result of competitive promotions. Advertising appears to be more effective at deepening brand loyalty, although added-value promotions can be distinguished from price promotions.[68] Certain types of sales promotions may be able to actually enhance brand image.

AMERICAN EXPRESS

In the middle of Christmas shopping season, American Express ran a local sales promotion at the high-traffic Short Hills Mall in New Jersey that swept tired shoppers off their feet, literally. The company created a 3,400-square-foot American Express Members Lounge from November 2006 to January 2007. Furnished with soft leather sofas and lamps emitting a sense of Zen-like serenity, the lounge featured a host of free amenities: stacks of magazines, premium coffee, snacks, Internet access, private restrooms, iPod charging, and even complimentary gift wrapping. Yet, not just any Short Hills shopper could enter the Members Lounge. You needed to either swipe your AmEx card or fill out an application to become an Amex cardholder. The lounge represented American Express's first promotion geared directly to consumers. With so much competing plastic, the company needs to give its brand the concrete feel of exclusivity that it strives to get across in its ads. "This is a test, our way of demonstrating why it's important to keep that card in your wallet," said AmEx's senior VP and general manager of membership rewards for American Express.[69]

Price promotions may not build permanent total-category volume. One study of more than 1,000 promotions concluded that only 16% paid off.[70] Small-share competitors find it advantageous to use sales promotion, because they cannot afford to match the market leaders' large advertising budgets; nor can they obtain shelf space without offering trade allowances or stimulate consumer trial without offering incentives. Price competition is often used by a small brand seeking to enlarge its share, but it is less effective for a category leader whose growth lies in expanding the entire category.

The upshot is that many consumer-packaged-goods companies feel they are forced to use more sales promotion than they wish. They blame the heavy use of sales promotion for decreasing brand loyalty, increasing consumer price sensitivity, brand-quality-image dilution, and a focus on short-run marketing planning. One review of promotion effectiveness concluded, "When the strategic disadvantages of promotions are included, that is, losing control to the trade and training consumers to buy only on deal, the case is compelling for a reevaluation of current practices and the incentive systems responsible for this trend."[71]

Major Decisions

In using sales promotion, a company must establish its objectives, select the tools, develop the program, pretest the program, implement and control it, and evaluate the results.

ESTABLISHING OBJECTIVES Sales promotion objectives derive from broader promotion objectives, which derive from more basic marketing objectives for the product. For consumers, objectives include encouraging purchase of larger-sized units, building trial among nonusers, and attracting switchers away from competitors' brands. Ideally, promotions with consumers would have short-run sales impact as well as long-run brand equity effects. For retailers, objectives include persuading retailers to carry new items and higher levels of inventory, encouraging off-season buying, encouraging stocking of related items, offsetting competitive promotions, building brand loyalty, and gaining entry into new retail outlets. For the sales force, objectives include encouraging support of a new product or model, encouraging more prospecting, and stimulating off-season sales.[72]

SELECTING CONSUMER PROMOTION TOOLS The promotion planner should take into account the type of market, sales promotion objectives, competitive conditions, and each tool's cost-effectiveness. The main consumer promotion tools are summarized in Table 18.5. *Manufacturer promotions* are, for instance in the auto industry, rebates, gifts to motivate test-drives and purchases, and high-value trade-in credit. *Retailer promotions* include price cuts, feature advertising, retailer coupons, and retailer contests or premiums.[73]

We can also distinguish between sales promotion tools that are *consumer franchise building* and those that are not. The former impart a selling message along with the deal, such as free samples, frequency awards, coupons when they include a selling message, and premiums when they are related to the product. Sales promotion tools that typically are *not* brand building include price-off packs, consumer premiums not related to a product, contests and sweepstakes, consumer refund offers, and trade allowances. Consumer franchise-building promotions offer the best of both worlds—they build brand equity while moving product. The following is an example of an award-winning consumer franchise-building promotion.

BODY BY MILK

Although almost every home has milk in the refrigerator, milk consumption by teenagers has been in decline for years. To help teens better understand and appreciate that milk helps them stay lean, toned, and healthy for the "look they want," the "Body by Milk" promotion from the National Fluid Milk Processor Promotion Board was launched in 2006. Milk mustache ads run in magazines read by teenagers featured four celebrities chosen for their physiques and appeal to teenagers: soccer star David Beckham; Yankees third baseman Alex Rodriguez; ice skater Sasha Cohen; and *American Idol* winner Carrie Underwood. The campaign's interactive components included a page on MySpace and banner ads on Web sites such as Alloy.com, Bolt.com, Facebook, and Gamezone.com. The bodybymilk.com Web site featured an "auction" in which visitors could bid each day for merchandise—from companies such as Adidas, the sports apparel maker; Baby Phat, a clothing maker; Fender, the guitar manufacturer; and CCS, which makes skateboards—using bar-code or expiration-date data from milk containers. Visitors to the site could also create their own milk mustache ads. The celebrities also appeared in posters that were distributed, through school food service directors, in more than 100,000 schools, illuminating milk's new message, driving teens to bodybymilk.com for engagement in the Milk Auction. The campaign resulted in much online and off-line activity and a change in teen perceptions.[74]

TABLE 18.5

Major Consumer Promotion Tools

Samples: Offer of a free amount of a product or service delivered door-to-door, sent in the mail, picked up in a store, attached to another product, or featured in an advertising offer.

Coupons: Certificates entitling the bearer to a stated saving on the purchase of a specific product: mailed, enclosed in other products or attached to them, or inserted in magazine and newspaper ads.

Cash Refund Offers (rebates): Provide a price reduction after purchase rather than at the retail shop: Consumer sends a specified "proof of purchase" to the manufacturer who "refunds" part of the purchase price by mail.

Price Packs (cents-off deals): Offers to consumers of savings off the regular price of a product, flagged on the label or package. A *reduced-price pack* is a single package sold at a reduced price (such as two for the price of one). A *banded pack* is two related products banded together (such as a toothbrush and toothpaste).

Premiums (gifts): Merchandise offered at a relatively low cost or free as an incentive to purchase a particular product. A *with-pack premium* accompanies the product inside or on the package. A *free in-the-mail premium* is mailed to consumers who send in a proof of purchase, such as a box top or UPC code. A *self-liquidating premium* is sold below its normal retail price to consumers who request it.

Frequency Programs: Programs providing rewards related to the consumer's frequency and intensity in purchasing the company's products or services.

Prizes (contests, sweepstakes, games): *Prizes* are offers of the chance to win cash, trips, or merchandise as a result of purchasing something. A *contest* calls for consumers to submit an entry to be examined by a panel of judges who will select the best entries. A *sweepstakes* asks consumers to submit their names in a drawing. A *game* presents consumers with something every time they buy—bingo numbers, missing letters—which might help them win a prize.

Patronage Awards: Values in cash or in other forms that are proportional to patronage of a certain vendor or group of vendors.

Free Trials: Inviting prospective purchasers to try the product without cost in the hope that they will buy.

Product Warranties: Explicit or implicit promises by sellers that the product will perform as specified or that the seller will fix it or refund the customer's money during a specified period.

Tie-in Promotions: Two or more brands or companies team up on coupons, refunds, and contests to increase pulling power.

Cross-Promotions: Using one brand to advertise another noncompeting brand.

Point-of-Purchase (P-O-P) Displays and Demonstrations: P-O-P displays and demonstrations take place at the point of purchase or sale.

Sales promotion seems most effective combined with advertising. In one study, a price promotion alone produced only a 15% increase in sales volume. When combined with feature advertising, sales volume increased 19%; when combined with feature advertising and a point-of-purchase display, sales volume increased 24%.[75]

Many large companies have a sales promotion manager whose job is to help brand managers choose the right promotional tools. Some, such as Colgate-Palmolive and Hershey Foods, are also going online with their coupons. One million consumers visit www.CoolSavings.com each month for money-saving coupons and offers from name brands, as well as helpful tips and articles, newsletters, free recipes, sweepstakes, free trials, free samples, and more.

SELECTING TRADE PROMOTION TOOLS Manufacturers use a number of trade promotion tools (see Table 18.6).[76] Manufacturers award money to the trade (1) to persuade the retailer or wholesaler to carry the brand; (2) to persuade the retailer or wholesaler to carry more units than the normal amount; (3) to induce retailers to promote the brand by featuring, display, and price reductions; and (4) to stimulate retailers and their sales clerks to push the product.

The growing power of large retailers has increased their ability to demand trade promotion at the expense of consumer promotion and advertising.[77] The company's sales force and its brand managers are often at odds over trade promotion. The sales force says local retailers will not keep the company's products on the shelf unless they receive more trade promotion money, whereas brand managers want to spend the limited funds on consumer promotion and advertising.

TABLE 18.6

Major Trade Promotion Tools

Price-Off (off-invoice or off-list): A straight discount off the list price on each case purchased during a stated time period.

Allowance: An amount offered in return for the retailer's agreeing to feature the manufacturer's products in some way. An *advertising allowance* compensates retailers for advertising the manufacturer's product. A *display allowance* compensates them for carrying a special product display.

Free Goods: Offers of extra cases of merchandise to intermediaries who buy a certain quantity or who feature a certain flavor or size.

Source: For more information, see Betsy Spethman, "Trade Promotion Redefined," *Brandweek,* March 13, 1995, pp. 25–32.

Manufacturers face several challenges in managing trade promotions. First, they often find it difficult to police retailers to make sure they are doing what they agreed to do. Manufacturers are increasingly insisting on proof of performance before paying any allowances. Second, some retailers are doing *forward buying*—that is, buying a greater quantity during the deal period than they can immediately sell. Retailers might respond to a 10%-off-case allowance by buying a 12-week or longer supply. The manufacturer must schedule more production than planned and bear the costs of extra work shifts and overtime. Third, some retailers are *diverting,* buying more cases than needed in a region in which the manufacturer offered a deal, and shipping the surplus to their stores in nondeal regions. Manufacturers handle forward buying and diverting by limiting the amount they will sell at a discount, or producing and delivering less than the full order in an effort to smooth production.[78]

All said, many manufacturers feel that trade promotion has become a nightmare. It contains layers of deals, is complex to administer, and often leads to lost revenues.

SELECTING BUSINESS AND SALES-FORCE PROMOTION TOOLS Companies spend billions of dollars on business and sales-force promotion tools (see Table 18.7) to gather business leads, impress and reward customers, and motivate the sales force to greater effort. They typically develop budgets for tools that remain fairly constant from year to year. For many new businesses that want to make a splash to a targeted audience, especially in the B2B world, trade shows are an important tool, but the cost per contact is the highest of all communication options. The following example shows how one newcomer in the private jet industry makes trade shows pay.

AVIATION TECHNOLOGY GROUP

To stir interest in the Javelin, its new private jet, ATG paid $200,000 for a 50 by 60-foot booth at an annual industry trade show in Las Vegas to house a full-scale model of the plane and a flight simulator. The company also arranged to send 25 of its executives, technicians, and sales people to the event. Its sales and marketing director, Bob Uhle, learned some valuable lessons there that translate to any business:

Pick the right show. Although the annual Oshkosh Fly-In show in Wisconsin attracts lots of visitors, Uhle read audits showing that the audience didn't include many people willing to drop huge sums of money on a jet.

Meet with your people during the show. Uhle organized staff meetings at the end of each day to talk about everything from visitors' questions to brainstorming answers.

Collect vital data and follow up. ATG collected information via questionnaires and the show's infrared badge-screening system. From the two sets of data, the company created a list of 400 qualified leads and followed up with the most important ones within a few weeks.

Track your ROI. Uhle calculated his ROI for Las Vegas as an impressive $176 in revenue for every $1 spent. His sales team contacts resulted in 17 deposits of $25K each on the Javelin. With a $2.6 million price tag, the projected sales were $44 million.[79]

TABLE 18.7

Major Business and Sales-Force Promotion Tools

Trade Shows and Conventions: Industry associations organize annual trade shows and conventions. Business marketers may spend as much as 35% of their annual promotion budget on trade shows. Over 5,600 trade shows take place every year, drawing approximately 80 million attendees. Trade show attendance can range from a few thousand people to over 70,000 for large shows held by the restaurant or hotel-motel industries. Participating vendors expect several benefits, including generating new sales leads, maintaining customer contacts, introducing new products, meeting new customers, selling more to present customers, and educating customers with publications, videos, and other audiovisual materials.

Sales Contests: A sales contest aims at inducing the sales force or dealers to increase their sales results over a stated period, with prizes (money, trips, gifts, or points) going to those who succeed.

Specialty Advertising: Specialty advertising consists of useful, low-cost items bearing the company's name and address, and sometimes an advertising message that salespeople give to prospects and customers. Common items are ballpoint pens, calendars, key chains, flashlights, tote bags, and memo pads.

DEVELOPING THE PROGRAM In planning sales promotion programs, marketers are increasingly blending several media into a total campaign concept, such as the following promotion that received a gold medal in the 2007 Reggie Award competition from the Promotion Marketing Association.

CANON NENGAJO

With the popularity of e-mail and mobile mail, the Japanese practice of sending Nengajo New Year cards had begun to decline, especially among younger consumers. To reverse this trend, Canon launched the "Enjoy Photo" promotion, which targeted young women and focused on the joy and happiness of printing and sending photos. Three sisters served as "navigators" to guide users through the process. At a product launch party they showed their own digital camera photos, and ads and a Canon catalog portrayed them enjoying Nengajo printing in their daily lives. The ads contained a URL to encourage people to check out a Web site with more detail and featured minidrama movies. Canon printers also appeared in Bals Tokyo, one of the most popular home interior shops among youth in Tokyo, and Odaiba, a popular destination in Tokyo. Canon also created ties with partner hotels at major theme parks in Tokyo. These combined efforts led to an explosion of buzz, press, and Web traffic and a sharp increase in sales.[80]

In deciding to use a particular incentive, marketers must first determine the *size* of the incentive. A certain minimum is necessary if the promotion is to succeed. Second, the marketing manager must establish *conditions* for participation. Incentives might be offered to everyone or to select groups. Third, the marketer must decide on the *duration* of the promotion. According to one researcher, the optimal frequency is about three weeks per quarter, and optimal duration is the length of the average purchase cycle.[81] Fourth, the marketer must choose a *distribution vehicle.* A 15-cents-off coupon can be distributed in the package, in stores, by mail, or in advertising. Fifth, the marketing manager must establish the *timing* of promotion. Finally, the marketer must determine the *total sales promotion budget.* The cost of a particular promotion consists of the administrative cost (printing, mailing, and promoting the deal) and the incentive cost (cost of premium or cents-off, including redemption costs), multiplied by the expected number of units sold. The cost of a coupon deal would recognize that only a fraction of consumers will redeem the coupons.

PRETESTING, IMPLEMENTING, CONTROLLING, AND EVALUATING THE PROGRAM Although most sales promotion programs are designed on the basis of experience, pretests can determine whether the tools are appropriate, the incentive size optimal, and the presentation method efficient. Consumers can be asked to rate or rank different possible deals, or trial tests can be run in limited geographic areas.

Marketing managers must prepare implementation and control plans that cover lead time and sell-in time for each individual promotion. *Lead time* is the time necessary to prepare the program prior to launching it.[82] *Sell-in time* begins with the promotional launch and ends when approximately 95% of the deal merchandise is in the hands of consumers.

Manufacturers can evaluate the program using sales data, consumer surveys, and experiments. Sales (scanner) data helps analyze the types of people who took advantage of the promotion, what they bought before the promotion, and how they behaved later toward the brand and other brands. Sales promotions work best when they attract competitors' customers who then switch. *Consumer surveys* can uncover how many recall the promotion, what they thought of it, how many took advantage of it, and how the promotion affected subsequent brand-choice behavior.[83] *Experiments* vary such attributes as incentive value, duration, and distribution media. For example, coupons can be sent to half the households in a consumer panel. Scanner data can track whether the coupons led more people to buy the product and when.

Additional costs beyond the cost of specific promotions include the risk that promotions might decrease long-run brand loyalty. Second, promotions can be more expensive than they appear. Some are inevitably distributed to the wrong consumers. Third are the costs of special production runs, extra sales-force effort, and handling requirements. Finally, certain promotions irritate retailers, who may demand extra trade allowances or refuse to cooperate.[84]

::: Events and Experiences

According to the IEG Sponsorship Report, $14.9 billion was projected to be spent on sponsorships in North America during 2007, with 66% of this going to sports; another 11% to entertainment tours and attractions; 5% to festivals, fairs, and annual events; 5% to the arts; 3% to associations and membership organizations; and 10% to cause marketing. Becoming part of a personally relevant moment in consumers' lives can broaden and deepen a company's relationship with the target market. See how effectively American Express leveraged its U.S. Open tennis sponsorship.[85]

American Express unrolled a multipronged promotion for the U.S. Open tournament that paid off handsomely.

AMERICAN EXPRESS AND U.S. OPEN TENNIS

American Express had high hopes for its 2006 U.S. Open sponsorship. A key objective was to continue to assert Amex as the brand that brings an event, program, sponsorship, or experience to life at each relevant touch point. Amex cardmembers had exclusive ability to purchase tickets prior to the general public in June. In support of premium card products, unique opportunities were created for cardmembers to meet and greet former top players Monica Seles and Mary Jo Fernandez and enjoy all the action of the U.S. Open from a luxury suite with lavish amenities, including:

- Complimentary pedicab rides from the nearby subway
- Comprehensive tournament information, along with cardmember benefits and concierge services from three on-site locations
- Complimentary radio to listen to live play-by-play commentary, along with continual match updates
- Invitation to attend the following night and experience the U.S. Open like a true VIP

Through *American Express Presents U.S. Open Live* at Rockefeller Center and Madison Square Park (MSP), live matches were shown on a 25'-wide videoboard complete with stadium seating, concessions, U.S. Open merchandise, guest information, and interactive tennis activities and teaching pros. The payoff was considerable:

- Amex received the highest level of sponsor awareness from on-site attendees, despite being a Tier 2-level sponsor.
- The U.S. Open Live platform actively engaged hundreds of thousands of consumers for an average of two hours each, within a fully branded and interactive environment.
- Reported cardmember loyalty improved.
- Millions of PR impressions were generated for Amex around U.S. Open activation, with over 14 unique media outlets citing cardmember-specific benefits.

Daily encounters with brands may also affect consumers' brand attitudes and beliefs. *Atmospheres* are "packaged environments" that create or reinforce leanings toward product purchase. Law offices decorated with Oriental rugs and oak furniture communicate "stability" and "success."[86] A five-star hotel will use elegant chandeliers, marble columns, and other tangible signs of luxury.

Many firms are creating on-site and off-site product and brand experiences. There is Everything Coca-Cola in Las Vegas, M&M World in Times Square in New York, and General Mills Cereal Adventure in Mall of America in Minnesota.[87] Small brands, of necessity, are even more likely to take less obvious and less expensive paths in sponsorship and communications.

Events Objectives

Marketers report a number of reasons to sponsor events:

1. ***To identify with a particular target market or lifestyle***—Customers can be targeted geographically, demographically, psychographically, or behaviorally according to events. Old Spice sponsors college sports and motor sports—including driver Tony Stewart's entries in the Nextel Cup and Busch Series—to highlight product relevancy and sample among its target audience of 16- to 24-year-old males.[88]
2. ***To increase awareness of company or product name***—Sponsorship often offers sustained exposure to a brand, a necessary condition to build brand recognition and enhance brand recall. Frito-Lay used balloon festivals and street parades to sample its Flat Earth baked fruit and vegetable crisps, build awareness, and drive retail traffic.[89]
3. ***To create or reinforce perceptions of key brand image associations***—Events themselves have associations that help to create or reinforce brand associations.[90] To toughen its image and appeal to America's heartland, Toyota Tundra elected to sponsor B.A.S.S. fishing tournaments and a Brooks & Dunn country music tour.
4. ***To enhance corporate image***—Sponsorship can improve perceptions that the company is likable and prestigious. Although Visa views its long-standing Olympic sponsorship as a means of enhancing international brand awareness and increasing usage and volume, it also engenders patriotic goodwill and taps into the emotional Olympic spirit.[91]
5. ***To create experiences and evoke feelings***—The feelings engendered by an exciting or rewarding event may indirectly link to the brand. Online activation accounts for a large portion of LG Electronics MobileComm USA's sponsorship leveraging efforts. The company uses sites such as MySpace and YouTube to extend its personality online and created its own proprietary Web site, LifeWithLG.com, as a central place for information about events and celebrity endorsers and related content for downloading.[92]
6. ***To express commitment to the community or on social issues***—Cause-related marketing sponsors nonprofit organizations and charities. Firms such as Timberland, Stoneyfield Farms, Home Depot, Starbucks, American Express, and Tom's of Maine have made cause-related marketing an important cornerstone of their marketing programs.
7. ***To entertain key clients or reward key employees***—Many events include lavish hospitality tents and other special services or activities only for sponsors and their guests. These perks engender goodwill and establish valuable business contacts. From an employee perspective, events can also build participation and morale or be used as an incentive. BB&T Corp., a major banking and financial services player in the South and Southeast United States, uses its NASCAR Busch Series sponsorship to entertain business customers and its minor league baseball sponsorship to generate excitement among employees.[93]
8. ***To permit merchandising or promotional opportunities***—Many marketers tie in contests or sweepstakes, in-store merchandising, direct response, or other marketing activities with an event. Ford, Coca-Cola, and Cingular Wireless all used their sponsorship of the hit TV show *American Idol* in this way.

Despite these potential advantages, the success of an event can still be unpredictable and beyond the control of the sponsor. Although many consumers will credit sponsors for providing the financial assistance to make an event possible, some may resent the commercialization of events.

Major Sponsorship Decisions

Successful sponsorships require choosing the appropriate events; designing the optimal sponsorship program; and measuring the effects of sponsorship.[94]

PETCO undertook a multilayered sponsorship of the San Diego Padres and their home stadium that went well beyond hanging the company name on the ballpark.

CHOOSING EVENTS Because of the number of opportunities and their huge cost, many marketers are becoming more selective about choosing sponsorship events.

The event must meet the marketing objectives and communication strategy defined for the brand. The audience must match the target market. The event must have sufficient awareness, possess the desired image, and be capable of creating the desired effects. Consumers must make favorable attributions for the sponsor's engagement. An ideal event is also unique but not encumbered with many sponsors, lends itself to ancillary marketing activities, and reflects or enhances the sponsor's brand or corporate image.[95]

More firms are also using their names to sponsor the arenas, stadiums, and other venues that hold the events.[96] Billions of dollars have been spent over the past decade for naming rights to major North American sports facilities. PETCO paid $60 million over 22 years for the rights to have San Diego's new baseball stadium called PETCO Park. But the most important consideration is the additional marketing activities.

PETCO

PETCO is a San Diego-based pet specialty retailer that operates 850+ stores nationwide. The multiyear contract to name San Diego's stadium was designed to elevate the PETCO name nationally—and improve retail sales in the process—as well as show commitment to San Diego at the local level. PETCO also sponsors the San Diego Padres who call the stadium home. The company's marketers attended weekly meetings with the San Diego Padres staff the first year of the sponsorship, with representatives from ballpark operations, promotions, entertainment, ticket sales, and Hispanic marketing, to learn different ways for PETCO to be involved. They met with local government officials, tourism agencies, and baseball associations. They ran local contests for "Top Dog" customers and in-game promotions for "Everybody Wins at PETCO Park." PETCO even sells Padre tickets and employees wear their team jerseys on game days.[97]

DESIGNING SPONSORSHIP PROGRAMS Many marketers believe it's the marketing program accompanying an event sponsorship that ultimately determines its success. At least two to three times the amount of the sponsorship expenditure should be spent on related marketing activities. Jamba Juice augments its running-race sponsorships with bunches of runners in banana costumes. Any runner who finishes the race before a banana gets free smoothies for a year. Jamba Juice banners are displayed all around and smoothies are sampled by race finishers and onlookers.[98]

Event creation is a particularly important skill in publicizing fund-raising drives for nonprofit organizations. Fund-raisers have developed a large repertoire of special events, including anniversary celebrations, art exhibits, auctions, benefit evenings, bingo games, book sales, cake sales, contests, dances, dinners, fairs, fashion shows, parties in unusual places, phonathons, rummage sales, tours, and walkathons. No sooner is one type of event created, such as a walkathon, than competitors spawn new versions, such as readathons, bikeathons, and jogathons.[99]

MEASURING SPONSORSHIP ACTIVITIES As with public relations, measurement of events is difficult. The *supply-side* measurement method focuses on potential exposure to the brand by assessing the extent of media coverage; and the *demand-side* method focuses on reported exposure from consumers.

Supply-side methods approximate the amount of time or space devoted to media coverage of an event, for example, the number of seconds the brand is clearly visible on a television screen or column inches of press clippings covering an event that mention the brand. These potential "impressions" translate into an equivalent value in advertising dollars according to the fees associated in actually advertising in the particular media vehicle. Some industry consultants have estimated that 30 seconds of TV logo exposure during a televised event can be worth 6%, 10%, or as much as 25% of a 30-second TV ad spot.

Although supply-side exposure methods provide quantifiable measures, equating media coverage with advertising exposure ignores the content of the respective communications. The advertiser uses media space and time to communicate a strategically designed message. Media coverage and telecasts only expose the brand and don't necessarily embellish its meaning in any direct way. Although some public relations professionals maintain that positive editorial coverage can be worth 5 to 10 times the equivalent advertising value, sponsorship rarely provides such favorable treatment.[100]

The demand-side method identifies the effect sponsorship has on consumers' brand knowledge. Marketers can survey event spectators to measure sponsor recall of the event as well as resulting attitudes and intentions toward the sponsor. AT&T uses a three-prong approach:[101]

1. ***Direct tracking of sponsorship-related promotions*** (Web data, call center data, online event statistics, other consumer engagements)
2. ***Qualitative research*** (on-site/in-market, pre/post, and participant/nonparticipant, using a proprietary model for brand equity transfer and subsequent impact on purchase intent)
3. ***Quantitative analysis*** (analytics to link sponsorship to brand awareness, sales, and retention and to optimize tactics in sponsorship activation that maximize ROI)

Creating Experiences

A large part of local, grassroots marketing is experiential marketing, which not only communicates features and benefits but also connects a product or service with unique and interesting experiences. "The idea is not to sell something, but to demonstrate how a brand can enrich a customer's life."[102] "Marketing Insight: Experiential Marketing" describes the concept of Customer Experience Management.

Consultants and authors Pine and Gilmore, pioneers on the topic, argue that we are on the threshold of the "Experience Economy," a new economic era in which all businesses must orchestrate memorable events for their customers.[103] They assert:

- If you charge for stuff, then you are in the *commodity business.*
- If you charge for tangible things, then you are in the *goods business.*
- If you charge for the activities you perform, then you are in the *service business.*
- If you charge for the time customers spend with you, then and only then are you in the *experience* business.

Citing a range of companies from Disney to AOL, they maintain that salable experiences come in four varieties: entertainment, education, esthetic, and escapist. Vans, which pioneered slip-on sneakers for skateboarding, has succeeded in that market with an offbeat marketing mix of events, sponsorships, and even a documentary film, all celebrating the skateboard culture.[104] Vans' CEO Gary Schoenfeld proclaims, "Our vision is not to hit our target audience over the head with our ads, but to integrate ourselves into the places they are most likely to be."

Consumers seem to appreciate that. One survey showed four of five respondents found participating in a live event was more engaging than all other forms of communication. The vast majority also felt experiential marketing gave them more information than other forms of communication and would make them more likely to tell others about participating in the event and be receptive to other marketing for the brand.[105]

Companies can even create a strong image by inviting prospects and customers to visit their headquarters and factories. Boeing, Ben & Jerry's, Hershey's, Saturn, and Crayola all sponsor excellent company tours that draw millions of visitors a year.[106] Companies such as Hallmark and Kohler have built corporate museums at their headquarters that display their history and the drama of producing and marketing their products.

::: Public Relations

Not only must the company relate constructively to customers, suppliers, and dealers, it must also relate to a large number of interested publics. A **public** is any group that has an actual or potential interest in or impact on a company's ability to achieve its objectives. **Public relations (PR)** includes a variety of programs to promote or protect a company's image or individual products.

MARKETING INSIGHT | EXPERIENTIAL MARKETING

Through several books and papers, Columbia University's Bernd Schmitt has developed the concept of *Customer Experience Management (CEM)*—the process of strategically managing a customer's entire experience with a product or company. According to Schmitt, brands can help to create five different types of experiences: sense, feel, think, act, relate. In each case, Schmitt distinguishes between hard-wired and acquired experiential response levels. He maintains that marketers can provide experiences for customers through a set of experience providers.

1. ***Communications***—advertising, public relations, annual reports, brochures, newsletters, and magalogs (a combination of a magazine and a catalog)
2. ***Visual/verbal identity***—names, logos, signage, and transportation vehicles
3. ***Product presence***—product design, packaging, and point-of-sale displays
4. ***Co-branding***—event marketing and sponsorships, alliances and partnerships, licensing, and product placement in movies or TV
5. ***Environments***—retail and public spaces, trade booths, corporate buildings, office interiors, and factories
6. ***Web sites and electronic media***—corporate sites, product or service sites, CD-ROMs, automated e-mails, online advertising, and intranets
7. ***People***—salespeople, customer-service representatives, technical support or repair providers, company spokepersons, and CEOs and other executives

The CEM framework is made up of five basic steps:

1. ***Analyzing the experiential world of the customer***—gaining insights into the sociocultural context of consumers or the business context of business customers
2. ***Building the experiential platform***—developing a strategy that includes the positioning for the kind of experience the brand stands for ("what"), the value proposition of what relevant experience to deliver ("why"), and the overall implementation theme that will be communicated ("how")
3. ***Designing the brand experience***—implementing their experiential platform in the look and feel of logos and signage, packaging, and retail spaces, in advertising, collaterals, and online
4. ***Structuring the customer interface***—implementing the experiential platform in the dynamic and interactive interfaces including face-to-face, in stores, during sales visits, at the check-in desk of a hotel, or the e-commerce engine of a Web site
5. ***Engaging in continuous innovation***—implementing the experiential platform in new-product development, creative marketing events for customers, and fine-tuning the experience at every point of contact

Schmitt cites Pret A Manger, the U.K.-based sandwich company, as an example of an attractive brand experience, customer interface, and ongoing innovation: "The Pret A Manger brand is about great tasting, handmade, natural products served by amazing people who are passionate about their work. The sandwiches and stores look appealing and attractive. The company hires only 5% of those who apply and only after they have worked for a day in the shop. This process ensures good fit and good teamwork." He also offers Singapore Airlines, Starbucks, and Amazon.com as outstanding providers of customer experiences.

Sources: www.exgroup.com; Bernd Schmitt, *Customer Experience Management: A Revolutionary Approach to Connecting with Your Customers* (New York: John Wiley and Sons, 2003); Bernd Schmitt, David L. Rogers, and Karen Vrotsos, *There's No Business That's Not Show Business: Marketing in an Experience Culture* (Upper Saddle River, NJ: Prentice Hall, 2003); Bernd Schmitt, *Experiential Marketing: How to Get Companies to Sense, Feel, Think, Act, and Relate to Your Company and Brands* (New York: Free Press, 1999); Bernd Schmitt and Alex Simonson, *Marketing Aesthetics: The Strategic Management of Brands, Identity, and Image* (New York: Free Press, 1997).

The wise company takes concrete steps to manage successful relations with its key publics. Most companies have a public relations department that monitors the attitudes of the organization's publics and distributes information and communications to build goodwill. The best PR departments counsel top management to adopt positive programs and eliminate questionable practices so negative publicity doesn't arise in the first place. They perform the following five functions:

1. ***Press relations***—Presenting news and information about the organization in the most positive light
2. ***Product publicity***—Sponsoring efforts to publicize specific products
3. ***Corporate communications***—Promoting understanding of the organization through internal and external communications
4. ***Lobbying***—Dealing with legislators and government officials to promote or defeat legislation and regulation
5. ***Counseling***—Advising management about public issues, and company positions and image during good times and bad

As "Marketing Insight: Managing a Brand Crisis," explains, sometimes PR must spearhead marketing communication efforts to help when a brand gets into trouble.

MARKETING INSIGHT | MANAGING A BRAND CRISIS

Marketing managers must assume that at some point in time, some kind of brand crisis will arise. Diverse brands such as Firestone tires, Exxon oil, and Martha Stewart have all experienced a potentially crippling brand crises. These may be particularly damaging if there are widespread repercussions: (1) a loss in the product's sales, (2) reduced effectiveness of its marketing activities for the product, (3) an increased sensitivity to rival firms' marketing activities, and (4) reduced effectiveness of its marketing activities on the sales of competing, unaffected brands.

In general, the more strongly brand equity and corporate image have been established—especially corporate credibility and trustworthiness—the more likely that the firm can weather the storm. Careful preparation and a well-managed crisis management program, however, are also critical. As Johnson & Johnson's nearly flawless handling of the Tylenol product-tampering incident suggests, the key to managing a crisis is that consumers see the response by the firm as both *swift* and *sincere*. Customers must feel an immediate sense that the company truly cares. Listening is not enough.

The longer it takes a firm to respond, the more likely that consumers can form negative impressions from unfavorable media coverage or word of mouth. Perhaps worse, consumers may find they don't really like the brand after all and permanently switch brands or products. Getting in front of a problem with PR, and then perhaps ads, can help avoid those problems.

Consider Perrier. In 1994, Perrier was forced to halt production worldwide and recall all existing product when traces of benzene, a known carcinogen, were found in excessive quantities in its bottled water. Over the next few weeks, several explanations of the contamination were offered, creating confusion and skepticism. Perhaps even more damaging, the product itself was off the shelves for over three months. Despite an expensive relaunch featuring ads and promotions, the brand struggled to regain lost market share, and a full year later found sales less than half what they once had been. Part of the problem was that during the time the product was unavailable, consumers and retailers found satisfactory substitutes. With its key "purity" association tarnished—the brand had been advertised as the "Earth's First Soft Drink" and "It's Perfect. It's Perrier."—the brand had no other compelling points-of-difference over competitors. The brand never recovered and eventually was taken over by Nestlé SA.

Second, the more sincere the firm's response— public acknowledgment of the impact on consumers and willingness to take whatever steps are necessary to solve the crisis—the less likely that consumers will form negative attributions. When consumers reported finding shards of glass in some jars of its baby food, Gerber tried to reassure the public that there were no problems in its manufacturing plants but adamantly refused to have products withdrawn from food stores. After market share slumped from 66% to 52% within a couple of months, one company official admitted, "Not pulling our baby food off the shelf gave the appearance that we aren't a caring company."

Sources: Norman Klein and Stephen A. Greyser, "The Perrier Recall: A Source of Trouble," Harvard Business School Case #9-590-104 and "The Perrier Relaunch," Harvard Business School Case #9-590-130; Harald Van Heerde, Kristiaan Helsen, and Marnik G. Dekimpe, "The Impact of a Product-Harm Crisis on Marketing Effectiveness," *Marketing Science* 26 (March–April 2007): 230–45; Michelle L. Roehm and Alice M. Tybout, "When Will a Brand Scandal Spill Over and How Should Competitors Respond?" *Journal of Marketing Research* 43 (August 2006): 366–73; Jill Klein and Niraj Dawar, "Corporate Social Responsibility and Consumers' Attributions and Brand Evaluations in a Product-Harm Crisis," *International Journal of Research in Marketing* 21, no. 3 (September 2004): 203–17; Rohini Ahluwalia, Robert E. Burnkrant, and H. Rao Unnava, "Consumer Response to Negative Publicity: The Moderating Role of Commitment," *Journal of Marketing Research* 37 (May 2000): 203–14; Niraj Dawar and Madan M. Pillutla, "The Impact of Product-Harm Crises on Brand Equity: The Moderating Role of Consumer Expectations," *Journal of Marketing Research* 37 (May 2000): 215–26; Ronald Alsop, "Enduring Brands Hold Their Allure by Sticking Close to Their Roots," *Wall Street Journal Centennial Edition*, June 23, 1989.

Marketing Public Relations

Many companies are turning to **marketing public relations (MPR)** to support corporate or product promotion and image making. MPR, like financial PR and community PR, serves a special constituency, the marketing department.[107]

The old name for MPR was **publicity,** the task of securing editorial space—as opposed to paid space—in print and broadcast media to promote or "hype" a product, service, idea, place, person, or organization. MPR goes beyond simple publicity and plays an important role in the following tasks:

- ***Launching new products.*** The amazing commercial success of toys such as Tickle Me Elmo, Furby, and Leap Frog owes a great deal to strong publicity.
- ***Repositioning a mature product.*** New York City had extremely bad press in the 1970s until the "I Love New York" campaign.
- ***Building interest in a product category.*** Companies and trade associations have used MPR to rebuild interest in declining commodities such as eggs, milk, beef, and potatoes and to expand consumption of such products as tea, pork, and orange juice.
- ***Influencing specific target groups.*** McDonald's sponsors special neighborhood events in Latino and African American communities to build goodwill.

BREAKTHROUGH MARKETING | VIRGIN GROUP

Virgin, the brainchild of England's flamboyant iconoclast Richard Branson, vividly illustrates the power of strong traditional and nontraditional marketing communications. Branson roared onto the British stage in the 1970s with his innovative Virgin Records. He signed unknown artists no one would touch and began a marathon of publicity that continues to this day. He has since sold Virgin Records (to Thorn-EMI for nearly $1 billion in 1992) but created over 200 companies worldwide whose combined revenues exceed $5 billion.

The Virgin name—the third most respected brand in Britain—and the Branson personality help to sell diverse products and services such as planes, trains, finance, soft drinks, music, mobile phones, cars, wines, publishing, even bridal wear. Clearly, Branson can create interest in almost any business he wants by simply attaching the name "Virgin" to it. Virgin Mobile exemplifies this strategy. Branson supplies the brand and a small initial investment and takes a majority control, and big-name partners come up with the cash.

Some marketing and financial critics point out that he is diluting the brand, that it covers too many businesses. Branson has had some fumbles: Virgin Cola, Virgin Cosmetics, and Virgin Vodka have all but disappeared. But despite the diversity, all the lines connote value for money, quality, innovation, fun, and a sense of competitive challenge. The Virgin Group looks for new opportunities in markets with underserved, overcharged customers and complacent competition. Branson called these customer-hostile competitors "big bad wolves." "Wherever we find them, there is a clear opportunity area for Virgin to do a much better job than the competition. We introduce trust, innovation, and customer friendliness where they don't exist," Branson said. And once Virgin finds an opportunity, its vaunted marketing expertise kicks in.

A master of the strategic publicity stunt, Branson took on stodgy, overpriced British Airways by wearing World War I-era flying gear to announce the formation of Virgin Atlantic in 1984. The first Virgin flight took off laden with celebrities and media and equipped with a brass band, waiters from Maxim's in white tie and tails, and free-flowing champagne. The airborne party enjoyed international press coverage and millions of dollars' worth of free publicity. Branson knew that photographers have a job to do and they'd turn up at his events if he gave them a good reason.

Similarly, when Branson launched Virgin Cola in the United States in 1998, he steered an army tank down Fifth Avenue in New York, garnering interviews on each of the network morning TV shows. In 2002, he plunged into Times Square connected to a crane to announce his mobile phone business. In 2004, when introducing a line of hip techie gadgets called Virgin Pulse, Branson again took center stage, this time at a nightclub in New York City. He arrived wearing a pair of flesh-colored tights and a portable CD player to cover the family jewels.

Although Branson eschews traditional market research for a "screw it, let's do it" attitude, he stays in touch through constant customer contact. When he first set up Virgin Atlantic, he called 50 customers every month to chat and get their feedback. He appeared in airports to rub elbows with customers, and if a plane was delayed, he handed out gift certificates to a Virgin Megastore or discounts on future travel. Virgin's marketing campaigns include press and radio ads, direct mail, and point-of-sale material. Virgin Mobile, for example, rolled out a postcard advertising campaign offering consumers discounts on new phones.

To identify where listeners to Virgin's Web-based Virgin Radio reside, the company created a VIP club. Listeners join the club by giving their postal code, which then lets Virgin Radio target promotions and advertising to specific locations, just as a local radio station would. Once known as the "hippie capitalist" and now knighted by the Queen of England, Sir Richard Branson continues to look for new businesses and to generate publicity in his characteristic charismatic style. Remembering a friend's advice about publicity—"If you don't give them a photograph that will get them on the front page, they won't turn up at your next event"—Branson always gives them a reason.

Sources: Peter Elkind, "Branson Gets Grounded," *Fortune*, February 5, 2007, pp. 13–14; Alan Deutschman, "The Enlightenment of Richard Branson," *Fast Company* (September 2006): 49; Andy Serwer, "Do Branson's Profits Equal His *Joie de Vivre*?" *Fortune*, October 17, 2005, p. 57; Kerry Capell with Wendy Zellner, "Richard Branson's Next Big Adventure," *BusinessWeek*, March 8, 2004, pp. 44–45; Melanie Wells, "Red Baron," *Forbes*, July 3, 2000, pp. 151–60; Sam Hill and Glenn Rifkin, *Radical Marketing* (New York: Harper Business, 1999); andwww.virgin.com.

- ***Defending products that have encountered public problems.*** PR professionals must be adept at managing crises, such as the JetBlue Valentine Day's fiasco in 2007 when 2 inches of ice led to 1,000 cancelled flights, massive delays, and passengers stuck on planes for up to nine hours.[108]
- ***Building the corporate image in a way that reflects favorably on its products.*** Bill Gates's speeches and books have helped to create an innovative image for Microsoft Corporation.

As the power of mass advertising weakens, marketing managers are turning to MPR to build awareness and brand knowledge for both new and established products. MPR is also effective in blanketing local communities and reaching specific groups and can be more cost-effective than advertising. Nevertheless, it must be planned jointly with advertising.[109] Marketing managers need to acquire more skill in using MPR resources. As "Breakthrough Marketing Virgin Group" shows, perhaps one of the most accomplished users of MPR is Sir Richard Branson of the Virgin Group.

Clearly, creative public relations can affect public awareness at a fraction of the cost of advertising. The company doesn't pay for media space or time but only for a staff to develop and circulate the stories and manage certain events. An interesting story picked up by the media can be worth millions of dollars in equivalent advertising. Some experts say consumers are five times more likely to be influenced by editorial copy than by advertising. The following is an example of an award-winning PR campaign.

PROJECT ERASE

PR firm Fleishman-Hillard received *PRWeek*'s Campaign of the Year in 2007 for its program "ERASEing the Divide: Giving Underprivileged NYC Kids a Clean Slate in Fighting Asthma," to close the gap in asthma treatment for children. Fleishman discovered a divide in treatment: Specialty care was readily available for those who could afford it, but the underserved faced limited access to even routine medical care. The goal of Project ERASE was to bring specialists to local schools to provide underserved kids access to diagnosis, advice on treatment, and management of asthma and allergies at no cost. Working closely with principals and parent coordinators at two pilot schools, Fleishman created eye-catching posters and placed them throughout the schools. Postcards describing the program and asthma triggers were distributed to parents. ERASE medical and executive directors spoke at school events attended by parents, and group meetings were held with parents and doctors. The specialists were not permitted to prescribe medicine, give injections, or do invasive testing at school, so the firm looked to the kids' primary care physicians to collaborate on treatment—making it a true community outreach effort. Media outreach included a press conference featuring the chancellor, ERASE medical and executive directors, principals from the two schools, and New Jersey Nets' Richard Jefferson, who himself has severe asthma. The ERASE pilot program ran the full school year in both schools. Fifty-one children enrolled, with absences falling from 128 to 57 compared to the previous school year. Hospitalizations also decreased from 26 to 6, and ER visits declined from 40 to 30. That all resulted in savings of approximately $135,000 for New York City.

Major Decisions in Marketing PR

In considering when and how to use MPR, management must establish the marketing objectives, choose the PR messages and vehicles, implement the plan carefully, and evaluate the results. The main tools of MPR are described in Table 18.8.[110]

ESTABLISHING OBJECTIVES MPR can build *awareness* by placing stories in the media to bring attention to a product, service, person, organization, or idea. It can build *credibility* by communicating the message in an editorial context. It can help boost sales force and dealer *enthusiasm* with stories about a new product before it is launched. It can hold down *promotion cost* because MPR costs less than direct-mail and media advertising.

Whereas PR practitioners reach their target publics through the mass media, MPR is increasingly borrowing the techniques and technology of direct-response marketing to reach target audience members one-on-one.

Canny marketing public relations has helped Richard Branson build an empire of successful brands under the Virgin name. Here, with actress Daryl Hannah, he peddles a blender at the 2007 Virgin Festival at Pimlico Racetrack in Baltimore to publicize the festival's efforts to incorporate the highest standards of sustainability and deliver a 'near zero waste' music experience to festival attendees.

CHOOSING MESSAGES AND VEHICLES Suppose a relatively unknown college wants more visibility. The MPR practitioner will search for stories. Do any faculty members have unusual backgrounds, or are any working on unusual projects? Are any new and unusual courses being taught? Are any interesting events taking place on campus? If there are no interesting stories, the MPR practitioner should propose newsworthy events the college could sponsor. Here the challenge is to create news. PR ideas include hosting major academic conventions, inviting expert or celebrity speakers, and developing news conferences. Each event is an opportunity to develop a multitude of stories directed at different audiences. The following is a good example of reaching different audiences.

TABLE 18.8

Major Tools in Marketing PR

Publications: Companies rely extensively on published materials to reach and influence their target markets. These include annual reports, brochures, articles, company newsletters and magazines, and audiovisual materials.
Events: Companies can draw attention to new products or other company activities by arranging special events such as news conferences, seminars, outings, trade shows, exhibits, contests and competitions, and anniversaries that will reach the target publics.
Sponsorships: Companies can promote their brands and corporate name by sponsoring sports and cultural events and highly regarded causes.
News: One of the major tasks of PR professionals is to find or create favorable news about the company, its products, and its people and to get the media to accept press releases and attend press conferences.
Speeches: Increasingly, company executives must field questions from the media or give talks at trade associations or sales meetings, and these appearances can build the company's image.
Public Service Activities: Companies can build goodwill by contributing money and time to good causes.
Identity Media: Companies need a visual identity that the public immediately recognizes. The visual identity is carried by company logos, stationery, brochures, signs, business forms, business cards, buildings, uniforms, and dress codes.

VATTENFALL AB

From its humble roots as a local royal institution and Sweden's electrical company founded in 1909, Vattenfall has become an international brand with 33,000 employees and is now Europe's largest heating firm and fourth-largest electricity firm. This transformation was challenging because it meant mergers and acquisitions with local brands from Germany, Poland, Finland, and Denmark, some as old as from the 1880s. Overcoming suspicion, lack of awareness, and other obstacles required a number of marketing actions, but events and PR played a crucial role. Vattenfall's joint sponsorship and event strategy concentrated in three areas (with themes)—sports (outdoor life and teamwork), human care (life of future generations), and environment (sustainable development and wildlife). These sponsorships and events were set in local markets as well as across all markets. Broader sponsorship includes the National Geographic Society and the World Childhood Foundation. Vattenfall garnered much publicity by also sponsoring a number of local events, such as Brandenburg Gate commemorations in Germany, heated bus stops in Poland, and the 2006 European Athletics (track and field) Championships in Göteborg, Sweden. Through focused and highly integrated activities, Vattenfall was able to enjoy high public awareness, a competitive local image, top financial market performance, and a huge increase in customer satisfaction.[111]

A wide variety of integrated promotions helped Sweden's Vattenfall, a large heating and electricity supplier, reach an equally broad spectrum of audiences and improve its financials.

IMPLEMENTING THE PLAN AND EVALUATING RESULTS MPR's contribution to the bottom line is difficult to measure, because it is used along with other promotional tools.

The easiest measure of MPR effectiveness is the number of *exposures* carried by the media. Publicists supply the client with a clippings book showing all the media that carried news about the product and a summary statement such as the following:

> Media coverage included 3,500 column inches of news and photographs in 350 publications with a combined circulation of 79.4 million; 2,500 minutes of air time on 290 radio stations and an estimated audience of 65 million; and 660 minutes of air time on 160 television stations with an estimated audience of 91 million. If this time and space had been purchased at advertising rates, it would have amounted to $1,047,000.[112]

This measure is not very satisfying because it contains no indication of how many people actually read, heard, or recalled the message and what they thought afterward; nor does it contain information about the net audience reached, because publications overlap in readership. Publicity's goal is reach, not frequency, so it would be more useful to know the number of unduplicated exposures.

A better measure is the *change in product awareness, comprehension, or attitude* resulting from the MPR campaign (after allowing for the effect of other promotional tools). For example, how many people recall hearing the news item? How many told others about it (a measure of word of mouth)? How many changed their minds after hearing it?

SUMMARY :::

1. Advertising is any paid form of nonpersonal presentation and promotion of ideas, goods, or services by an identified sponsor. Advertisers include not only business firms but also charitable, nonprofit, and government agencies.
2. Developing an advertising program is a five-step process: (1) Set advertising objectives; (2) establish a budget; (3) choose the advertising message and creative strategy; (4) decide on the media; and (5) evaluate communication and sales effects.
3. Sales promotion consists of a diverse collection of incentive tools, mostly short term, designed to stimulate quicker or greater purchase of particular products or services by consumers or the trade. Sales promotion includes tools for consumer promotion, trade promotion, and business and sales-force promotion (trade shows and conventions, contests for sales reps, and specialty advertising). In using sales promotion, a company must establish its objectives, select the tools, develop the program, pretest the program, implement and control it, and evaluate the results.
4. Events and experiences are a means to become part of special and more personally relevant moments in consumers' lives. Involvement with events can broaden and deepen the relationship of the sponsor with its target market, but only if managed properly.
5. Public relations (PR) involves a variety of programs designed to promote or protect a company's image or its individual products. Many companies today use marketing public relations (MPR) to support the marketing department in corporate or product promotion and image making. MPR can affect public awareness at a fraction of the cost of advertising and is often much more credible. The main tools of PR are publications, events, news, speeches, public service activities, and identity media.

APPLICATIONS :::

Marketing Debate Should Marketers Test Advertising?

Advertising creatives have long lamented ad pretesting. They believe that it inhibits their creative process and results in much sameness in commercials. Marketers, on the other hand, believe that ad pretesting provides necessary checks and balances as to whether an ad campaign is being developed in a way so that it will connect with consumers and be well received in the marketplace.

Take a position: Ad pretesting in often an unnecessary waste of marketing dollars *versus* Ad pretesting provides an important diagnostic function for marketers as to the likely success of an ad campaign.

Marketing Discussion

What are some of your favorite TV ads? Why? How effective are the message and creative strategies? How are they building brand equity?

IN THIS CHAPTER, WE WILL ADDRESS THE FOLLOWING QUESTIONS:

1. How can companies integrate direct marketing for competitive advantage?
2. How can companies do effective interactive marketing?
3. How can marketers best take advantage of the power of word of mouth?
4. What decisions do companies face in designing and managing a sales force?
5. How can salespeople improve their selling, negotiating, and relationship marketing skills?

CHAPTER 19 ::: MANAGING PERSONAL COMMUNICATIONS: DIRECT AND INTERACTIVE MARKETING, WORD OF MOUTH, AND PERSONAL SELLING

nineteen

Today, marketing communications increasingly occur as a kind of personal dialogue between the company and its customers. Companies must ask not only "How should we reach our customers?" but also "How should our customers reach us?" and even "How can our customers reach each other?" Technological advances allow people and companies to communicate to each other through the Internet, fax machines, cellular phones, pagers, and wireless appliances. By increasing communication effectiveness and efficiency, new technologies have encouraged companies to move from mass communication to more targeted, two-way communications. Consumers now play a much more participatory role in the marketing process.

Newly empowered by the Internet, consumers—especially younger ones—are more actively involved with a firm's marketing. When Coke.com was relaunched by Coca-Cola, it went from a typical corporate Website, with facts, figures, and annual reports, to an interactive community for consumers to share their creativity. Its MyCoke.com site invites visitors to participate in a virtual world, play games. mix music tracks, read or write blog entries, download screen savers, and more. Knowing that not every online feature will gain an audience right away, Coca-Cola—like other advertisers—has been experimenting to discover which site activities will draw audiences most effectively. A Second Life design contest asked consumers to imagine a vending machine that could dispense the essence of Coca-Cola—entertainment, >>>

Consumers are now empowered to become as engaged with a marketer's campaign as technology will allow. Some even create their own ads and commercials. Frito-Lay even ran a consumer-generated ad for its Doritos brand in the most expensive media vehicle around__the Super Bowl.

adventure, or happiness__as well as satisfy curiosities and fulfill virtual wishes. Coke is not alone in getting consumers involved. One of the first major marketers to feature consumer-generated ads was Converse with its award-winning campaign, "Brand Democracy," which used films created by consumers in a series of TV and Web ads. One of the most popular ads during the 2007 Super Bowl broadcast was a homemade contest winner for Doritos that cost all of $12.79 to make. But not all consumer-generated videos will be winners. When H. J. Heinz ran a "Top This TV Challenge" inviting the public to create the next commercial for its Heinz Ketchup brand and win $57,000, entrants clearly ventured into previously uncharted ad territory. One submission had a teenage boy rubbing ketchup over his face like acne cream, another contestant chugged ketchup straight from the bottle, and yet another brushed his teeth, washed his hair, and shaved his face with the condiment.[1]

Personalizing communications and creating dialogues by saying and doing the right thing to the right person at the right time is critical for marketing. In this chapter, we consider how companies personalize their marketing communications to have more impact. We begin by evaluating direct and interactive marketing, then move to word-of-mouth marketing, and finish by considering personal selling and the sales force.

::: Direct Marketing

Direct marketing is the use of consumer-direct (CD) channels to reach and deliver goods and services to customers without using marketing middlemen. Direct marketers can use a number of channels to reach individual prospects and customers: direct mail, catalog marketing, telemarketing, interactive TV, kiosks, Web sites, and mobile devices. They often seek a measurable response, typically a customer order, through **direct-order marketing**.

Today, many direct marketers build long-term relationships with customers.[2] They send birthday cards, information materials, or small premiums. Airlines, hotels, and other businesses build strong customer relationships through frequency reward programs and club programs.[3]

Direct marketing has been a fast-growing avenue for serving customers, partly in response to the high and increasing costs of reaching business markets through a sales force. Sales produced through traditional direct marketing channels (catalogs, direct mail, and telemarketing) have been growing rapidly, along with direct-mail sales, which include sales to the consumer market (53%), B2B (27%), and fund-raising by charitable institutions (20%).[4]

Direct marketing has been outpacing U.S. retail sales. It accounts for almost 48% of total advertising spending, and companies spend more than $161 billion on direct marketing per year, accounting for 10.3% of GDP.[5]

The Benefits of Direct Marketing

Market demassification has resulted in an ever-increasing number of market niches. Consumers short of time and tired of traffic and parking headaches appreciate toll-free phone numbers, Web sites available 24 hours a day and 7 days a week, and direct marketers' commitment to customer service. The growth of next-day delivery via FedEx, Airborne, and UPS has made ordering fast and easy. In addition, many chain stores have dropped slower-moving specialty items, creating an opportunity for direct marketers to promote these items to interested buyers instead.

Sellers benefit as well. Direct marketers can buy a mailing list containing the names of almost any group: left-handed people, overweight people, millionaires. They can customize and personalize messages and build a continuous relationship with each customer. New parents will receive periodic mailings describing new clothes, toys, and other goods as the child grows.

Direct marketing can reach prospects at the right moment and be read by more-interested prospects. It lets marketers test alternative media and messages to find the most cost-effective approach. Direct marketing also makes the direct marketer's offer and strategy less visible to competitors. Finally, direct marketers can measure responses to their campaigns to decide which have been the most profitable. One successful direct marketer is Lands' End.

LANDS' END

A direct merchant of traditionally styled, upscale clothing for the family, as well as soft luggage and products for the home, Lands' End sells its offerings through catalogs, on the Internet, and, after being acquired by Sears in 2002, in stores. Lands' End was an early adopter of the Internet, launching its Web site in 1995. It offers every Lands' End product and is one of the world's largest apparel Web sites in sales volume. A leader in developing new ways to enhance shopping experiences, Lands' End lets customers create a 3-D virtual model of themselves and try clothing on by providing critical measurements such as body shape, build, height, weight, and so on. A "personal wardrobe consultant" is available via text chat or phone to answer questions about clothing preferences. Weekly e-mails with quirky tales and discounts also drive sales. A story of how a customer wore his Lands' End mesh shirt to a preserve for orphaned chimpanzees in the Republic of Ghana led to an increase of 40% in sales of the shirt that week.[6]

Direct marketing must be integrated with other communications and channel activities.[7] Citigroup, AT&T, IBM, Ford, and American Airlines have used integrated direct marketing to build profitable relationships with customers over the years. Retailers such as Nordstrom, Nieman Marcus, Saks Fifth Avenue, and Bloomingdale's regularly send catalogs to supplement

Lands' End has led the way in enhancing the Internet shopping experience, with one of the first 3-D virtual models that lets customers "try" clothing before they order.

in-store sales. Direct marketing companies such as L.L.Bean, Eddie Bauer, Franklin Mint, and The Sharper Image made fortunes building their brands in the direct marketing mail-order and phone-order business and then opened retail stores. They cross-promote their stores, catalogs, and Web sites, for example, by putting their Web addresses on their shopping bags.

Successful direct marketers ensure that customers can contact the company with questions and view a customer interaction as an opportunity to up-sell, cross-sell, or just deepen a relationship. These marketers make sure they know enough about each customer to customize and personalize offers and messages and develop a plan for lifetime marketing to each valuable customer, based on knowledge of life events and transitions. They also carefully integrate each element of their campaigns.

GUINNESS

The Direct Marketing Association's top Diamond ECHO award in 2006 went to Target Marketing for its multimedia/integrated media campaign, "Guinness Relationship Marketing," on behalf of Diageo Ireland. A campaign was designed to maximize the value of the relationship between consumers and pub owners, build brand loyalty, and cross-sell cans of Draught Guinness to consumers who switched brands when drinking at home. Guinness sales reps gave pub owners The Big Black Book, with information about the campaign. Pint vouchers brought consumers back to the pub. Western-themed posters asked "Are you one of the Guinness most wanted?" The campaign also tied in with football (soccer) events, offering home kit boxes for consumers.[8]

We next consider some of the key issues that characterize different direct marketing channels.

Direct Mail

Direct-mail marketing means sending an offer, announcement, reminder, or other item to an individual consumer. Using highly selective mailing lists, direct marketers send out millions of mail pieces each year—letters, flyers, foldouts, and other "salespeople with wings." Some direct marketers mail CDs, DVDs, and computer discs to prospects and customers.

Direct mail is a popular medium because it permits target market selectivity, can be personalized, is flexible, and allows early testing and response measurement. Although the cost per thousand people reached is higher than with mass media, the people reached are much better prospects. The success of direct mail, however, has also become its liability—so many marketers are sending out direct-mail pieces that mailboxes are becoming stuffed, leading some consumers to disregard the blizzard of solicitations they receive. One of the biggest users of direct mail, the financial services industry, has seen its response rates from campaigns drop significantly in recent years.[9]

In constructing an effective direct-mail campaign, direct marketers must decide on their objectives; target markets, and prospects; offer elements; means of testing the campaign; and measures of campaign success.

OBJECTIVES Most direct marketers aim to receive an order from prospects and judge a campaign's success by the response rate. An order-response rate of 2% is normally considered good, although this number varies with product category, price, and the nature of the offering. Direct mail can also produce prospect leads, strengthen customer relationships, inform and educate customers, remind customers of offers, and reinforce recent customer purchase decisions.

TARGET MARKETS AND PROSPECTS Most direct marketers apply the R-F-M formula (*recency, frequency, monetary amount*) to select customers according to how much time has passed since their last purchase, how many times they have purchased, and how much they have spent since becoming a customer. Suppose the company is offering a leather jacket. It might make this offer to the most attractive customers—those who made their last purchase between 30 and 60 days ago, who make three to six purchases a year, and who have spent at least $100 since becoming customers. Points are established for varying R-F-M levels; the more points, the more attractive the customer.[10]

Marketers also identify prospects on the basis of age, sex, income, education, previous mail-order purchases, and occasions. College freshmen will buy laptop computers, backpacks, and compact refrigerators; newlyweds look for housing, furniture, appliances, and bank loans. Another useful variable is consumer lifestyle or "passions" such as computers, cooking, and the outdoors.

Dun & Bradstreet's information service provides a wealth of data for B2B direct marketing. Here the prospect is often not an individual but a group or committee of both decision makers and decision influencers. Each member needs to be treated differently, and the timing, frequency, nature, and format of contact must reflect the member's status and role.

EASTMAN KODAK CO.

Kodak's Creative Network, which offers affordable online design and printing solutions, was designed with the small office/home office (SOHO) market in mind. Direct mail has been a crucial part of an integrated campaign that includes an online component and PR, via both radio and special events. Mailings were personalized for each recipient through digital variable printing. One postcard shows three versions of business cards with the prospect's name and address printed on each and the line, "You're open for business. Now go get your free cards." The reverse side directs the prospect to the Kodak Web page to get free cards printed and find more about Creative Network design tools. Direct mail in this case showed the prospect the print quality as nothing else could. The other plus was the ability to test different concepts. Kodak sent out three test mailings of 10,000 each.[11]

The company's best prospects are customers who have bought its products in the past. The direct marketer can also buy lists of names from list brokers, but these lists often have problems, including name duplication, incomplete data, and obsolete addresses. Better lists include overlays of demographic and psychographic information. Direct marketers typically buy and test a sample before buying more names from the same list. They can build their own lists by advertising a free offer and collecting responses.

OFFER ELEMENTS The offer strategy has five elements—the *product*, the *offer*, the *medium*, the *distribution method*, and the *creative strategy*.[12] Fortunately, all can be tested. The direct-mail marketer also must choose five components of the mailing itself: the outside envelope, sales letter, circular, reply form, and reply envelope. Here are some findings:

1. The outside envelope should contain an illustration, preferably in color, or a catchy reason to open it, such as the announcement of a contest, premium, or benefit. A colorful commemorative stamp, a nonstandard shape or size of envelope, and a handwritten address all attract attention.[13]
2. The sales letter, brief and on good-quality paper, should use a personal salutation and start with a headline in bold type. A computer-typed letter usually outperforms a printed letter, and a pithy P.S. increases response rate, as does the signature of someone whose title is important.
3. A colorful circular accompanying the letter usually increases the response rate by more than its cost.
4. Direct mailers should feature a toll-free number and a Web site where recipients can print coupons.
5. A postage-free reply envelope will dramatically increase the response rate.

Direct mail should be followed up by an e-mail, which is less expensive and less intrusive than a telemarketing call.

TESTING ELEMENTS One of the great advantages of direct marketing is the ability to test, under real marketplace conditions, different elements of an offer strategy, such as products, product features, copy platform, mailer type, envelope, prices, or mailing lists. The following is an example of an informative market test for The Phoenician, a high-end luxury resort in Scottsdale, Arizona.

A test of marketing channels for The Phoenician luxury resort in Arizona showed significantly higher results from boosting the budget for direct mail and inbound telecontact.

THE PHOENICIAN

When research revealed that potetial guests would actually welcome communications directly from The Phoenician, a market test was conducted that increased the emphasis of direct mail and inbound telemarketing (via well-trained reservation agents accessible by phone) with traditional television, newspaper, and magazine image advertising. Specifically, the marketing budget for The Phoenician had been historically allocated as TV (36%), newspaper (32%), magazine (26%), and direct mail (6%). The budget was redeployed for the test as TV (32%), newspaper (31%), magazine (21%), and direct mail plus inbound telecontact (15%). Adding the combination of integrated direct mail and inbound telecontact yielded a significantly higher conversion rate of prospects, 21% versus the historical baseline of 13%. Television generated 5% of the revenue resulting from the campaign, newspapers 21%, magazines 10%, and, despite making up only 15% of the budget, direct mail plus inbound generated 64% of the revenue. The Phoenician concluded that coordinating traditional image advertising and new multichannel direct marketing increased revenue.[14]

Response rates typically understate a campaign's long-term impact. Suppose only 2% of the recipients who receive a direct-mail piece advertising Samsonite luggage place an order. A much larger percentage became aware of the product (direct mail has high readership), and some percentage may have formed an intention to buy at a later date (either by mail or at a retail outlet). Furthermore, some may mention Samsonite luggage to others as a result of the direct-mail piece. To better estimate a promotion's impact, some companies measure the impact of direct marketing on awareness, intention to buy, and word of mouth.

MEASURING CAMPAIGN SUCCESS: LIFETIME VALUE By adding up the planned campaign costs, the direct marketer can determine the needed break-even response rate. This rate must be net of returned merchandise and bad debts.

Even when a specific campaign fails to break even in the short run, it can still be profitable in the long run if customer lifetime value is factored in (see Chapter 5) by calculating the average customer longevity, average customer annual expenditure, and average gross margin, minus the average cost of customer acquisition and maintenance (discounted for the opportunity cost of money).[15]

Catalog Marketing

In catalog marketing, companies may send full-line merchandise catalogs, specialty consumer catalogs, and business catalogs, usually in print form but also sometimes as CDs, videos, or online. Through their catalogs, Avon sells cosmetics, IKEA sells furniture, and Saks

Fifth Avenue sells specialty clothing. Many direct marketers find combining catalogs and Web sites an effective way to sell. Thousands of small businesses also issue specialty catalogs. Large businesses such as Grainger, Merck, and others send catalogs to business prospects and customers.

Catalogs are a huge business—about 71% of U.S. consumers shop from home using catalogs by phone, mail, and Internet.[16] The success of a catalog business depends on managing customer lists carefully to avoid duplication or bad debts, controlling inventory carefully, offering quality merchandise so returns are low, and projecting a distinctive image. Some companies add literary or information features, send swatches of materials, operate a special hotline to answer questions, send gifts to their best customers, and donate a percentage of profits to good causes.

Business marketers are making inroads as well. Putting their entire catalog online provides better access to global consumers than ever before, saving printing and mailing costs. Sales to foreign (mainly European) markets have driven earnings increases at Viking Office Products because, unlike the United States, Europe has few superstores so is very receptive to mail order. Black Box Corporation owes much of its international growth to its customer-service policies, unmatched in Europe, but it doesn't hurt that it also has an award-winning catalog.[17]

BLACK BOX

Black Box is the world's largest technical services company dedicated to designing, building, and maintaining today's complicated data and voice infrastructure systems. It has 175,000 clients in 141 countries with 173 offices throughout the world. Black Box has been recognized as best in its category for 12 years in a row, and in 3 of 4 years it won Catalog of the Year at the Annual Conference for Catalog and Multichannel Merchants. The award recognizes excellence in merchandising, creativity, customer services, and catalog effectiveness. The Black Box catalog, long known as the "Big Book," features 900 pages of data, voice, and networking and communications services and products and is divided into 15 different sections, including comprehensive technical reference information.[18]

Telemarketing

Telemarketing is the use of the telephone and call centers to attract prospects, sell to existing customers, and provide service by taking orders and answering questions. Telemarketing helps companies increase revenue, reduce selling costs, and improve customer satisfaction. Companies use call centers for *inbound telemarketing*—receiving calls from customers—and *outbound telemarketing*—initiating calls to prospects and customers.

Although telemarketing is a major direct marketing tool, its sometimes intrusive nature led to the Federal Trade Commission's establishment of a National Do Not Call Registry in 2003, so consumers could indicate they did not want telemarketing calls at home. Only political organizations, charities, telephone surveyors, or companies with existing relationships with consumers are exempt.[19]

Telemarketing is increasing in business-to-business marketing. Raleigh Bicycles uses telemarketing to reduce personal selling for contacting its dealers. In the first year, sales force travel costs were reduced by 50% and sales in a single quarter went up 34%. As it improves with the use of videophones, telemarketing will increasingly replace, though never eliminate, more expensive field sales calls. Effective telemarketing depends on choosing the right telemarketers, training them well, and providing performance incentives.

USAA

USAA, in San Antonio, Texas, proves that a company can successfully conduct its entire insurance business via phone and Internet without ever meeting customers face-to-face. From its beginnings, USAA focused on selling auto insurance, and later other insurance products, to those with military service. It increased its share of each customer's business by launching a consumer bank, issuing credit cards, opening a discount brokerage, and offering a selection of no-load mutual funds. In spite of now conducting transactions for more than 150 products and services on the phone or online, USAA boasts one of the highest customer satisfaction ratings of any company in the United States. As a result of its outstanding service, it received the prestigious Chairman's Award from J. D. Power & Associates in 2002 and was ranked #1 in *BusinessWeek*'s list of Customer Service Champions in 2007.[20]

Other Media for Direct-Response Marketing

Direct marketers use all the major media. Newspapers and magazines carry abundant print ads offering books, articles of clothing, appliances, vacations, and other goods and services that individuals can order via toll-free numbers. Radio ads present offers 24 hours a day. Some companies prepare 30- and 60-minute *infomercials* to combine the sell of television commercials with the draw of information and entertainment. Infomercials promote products that are complicated or technologically advanced, or require a great deal of explanation (Callaway Golf, Carnival Cruises, Mercedes, Microsoft, Philips Electronics, Universal Studios, and even the online job search site, Monster.com).[21] Some at-home shopping channels are dedicated to selling goods and services on a toll-free number for delivery within 48 hours.

Public and Ethical Issues in Direct Marketing

Direct marketers and their customers usually enjoy mutually rewarding relationships. Occasionally, however, a darker side emerges:

- ***Irritation.*** Many people don't like the large number of hard-sell, direct marketing solicitations. Especially bothersome are dinnertime or late-night phone calls, poorly trained callers, and computerized calls by auto-dial recorded-message players.
- ***Unfairness.*** Some direct marketers take advantage of impulsive or less sophisticated buyers or prey on the vulnerable, especially the elderly.[22]
- ***Deception and fraud.*** Some direct marketers design mailers and write copy intended to mislead. They may exaggerate product size, performance claims, or the "retail price." The Federal Trade Commission receives thousands of complaints each year about fraudulent investment scams or phony charities.
- ***Invasion of privacy.*** It seems that almost every time consumers order products by mail or telephone, enter a sweepstakes, apply for a credit card, or take out a magazine subscription, their names, addresses, and purchasing behavior may be added to several company databases. Critics worry that marketers may know too much about consumers' lives, and that they may use this knowledge to take unfair advantage.

People in the direct marketing industry are addressing the issues. They know that, left unattended, such problems will lead to increasingly negative consumer attitudes, lower response rates, and calls for greater state and federal regulation. In the final analysis, most direct marketers want the same thing consumers want: honest and well-designed marketing offers targeted only to those who appreciate hearing about the offer.

::: Interactive Marketing

The newest channels for communicating and selling directly to customers are electronic.[23] The Internet provides marketers and consumers with opportunities for much greater *interaction* and *individualization.* Few marketing programs are considered complete without some type of prominent online component.

To learn how Stella Artois uses interactive marketing to succeed in Belgium, visit www.pearsoned.co.uk/marketingmanagementeurope.

Advantages and Disadvantages of Interactive Marketing

Interactive marketing offers unique benefits.[24] Companies can send tailored messages that engage consumers by reflecting their special interests and behavior. The Internet is highly accountable and its effects can be easily traced. Eddie Bauer cut its marketing cost per sale 74% by concentrating on higher-performing ads.[25] Online, advertisers can gauge response instantaneously by noting how many unique visitors or "UVs" click on a page or ad, how long they spend with it, where they go afterwards, and so on.[26]

The Web offers the advantage of *contextual placement* and buying ads on sites that are related to the marketer's offerings. Marketers can also place advertising based on keywords from search engines, to reach people when they've actually started the buying process. Light consumers of other media, especially television, can be reached online. The Web is especially effective at reaching people during the day. Young, high-income, high-education customers' total online media consumption exceeds that of TV.[27]

Using the Web also has disadvantages. Consumers can effectively screen out most messages. Marketers may think their ads are more effective than they are if bogus clicks are generated by software-powered Web sites. Advertisers lose some control over what consumers will do with their online messages and activity. Consumers could place a video in undesirable or unseemly places.

But many feel the pros outweight the cons, and the Web is attracting marketers of all kinds. Visa blanketed the Web with rich media ads as a major component of its first new brand campaign in 20 years, "Life Takes Visa." To reinforce its image as a technology innovator, IBM launched an online campaign for two new B2B platforms, "What Makes You Special?" and "Take Back Control." Amgen and Wyeth Pharmaceuticals used a series of online ads to build awareness for the rheumatoid arthritis drug Enbrel.[28]

To capitalize on advertisers' interest, firms are rushing online services and other support to marketers. Microsoft has invested in a broad range of businesses for placing ads on the Web, videogames, mobile phones and alongside Internet search results. "Breakthrough Marketing: Yahoo!" describes that company's online efforts.

For marketers of automobiles, financial services, personal computers, and telecommunications, marketing activities on the Web have become crucial. But others are quickly following. Although beauty pioneer Estée Lauder said she relied on three means of communication to build her multimillion-dollar cosmetics business—"telephone, telegraph, and tell a woman"—she would now have to add the Web, which helps to support brands such as its antiaging treatment, Advanced Night Repair Concentrate.[29] Consumer packaged-goods giants such as Procter & Gamble, General Mills, and Kraft are also significantly increasing their online budgets. Pepsi spent between 5% and 10% of its overall ad budget online in 2006, compared to just 1% in 2001, because of its cost-effectiveness.[30]

BREAKTHROUGH **MARKETING** | YAHOO!

Yahoo! has grown from a tiny upstart surrounded by Silicon Valley heavyweights to a powerful force in Internet media. David Filo and Jerry Yang, two computer science PhD students at Stanford University, created a simple search engine in 1994. Using a homemade filing system, the pair cataloged sites on the newly created World Wide Web and published the directory, called Jerry and David's Guide to the World Wide Web, on the Internet. They named their effort Yahoo! after they left school to devote their full attention to the business.

From its start, Yahoo! conveyed an irreverent attitude that came from the top of the corporate ladder, in the personalities of Filo and Yang. The two had conceived of Yahoo! while housed "in trailers full of pizza boxes," and each of their business cards bore the title "Chief Yahoo!" The name even contains a hidden joke—Yahoo is a self-deprecating acronym meaning "Yet Another Hierarchical Officious Oracle." Yahoo!'s marketing reflected the company's style as well: In one ad, Eskimos ordered a hot tub online. For years, each ad closed with the tagline "Do You Yahoo!?" and the signature "Yahoo!" yodel, an audio cue to reinforce brand recall.

Yahoo! has worked hard to be more than just a search engine. The company proudly proclaims it is, "The only place anyone needs to go to find anything, communicate with anyone, or buy anything." Its wide range of Web services includes e-mail, news, weather, music, photos, games, shopping, auctions, travel, and more.

Yahoo! sees one of its main advantages over rival Google as its vast array of original content. Yahoo! partners with hundreds of premier content providers to offer a personalization option in My Yahoo!, which enables users to specify their favorite Yahoo! features and content to fit a single page. With a database of information about where its millions of registered users live and what their interests are, Yahoo! can present users with both more relevant search results and more relevant advertising. Each month more than 475 million people worldwide visit one of its myriad sites, with billions of page views each day.

Yahoo! continues to expand. Its acquisition of photo-sharing service Flickr in March 2005, social bookmark manager del.icio.us, and online video editing site Jumpcut strengthened the company's capabilities in those areas. In March 2005, it launched its blogging and social network service Yahoo! 360°. Its mobile display advertising platform on the company's Yahoo! Mobile Web service (m.yahoo.com) allows advertisers to reach consumers around the globe on their mobile phones.

A large percentage of revenues comes from advertising, but the company continues to supplement its revenues through subscription sources such as online personal ads, premium e-mail products, and services for small businesses. In February 2007, Yahoo! launched a new search advertising system, Panama, to increase the quality of its search results as well the advertising revenue it generates from search.

Yahoo! attracts a diverse range of advertisers. A long-time fan is Pepsi, an early sign-up for the mobile service. "We've had exceptional results reaching our consumers on Yahoo! online," said John Vail, director of interactive marketing, Pepsi-Cola North America. "Now we can reach consumers when they're on the move and communicate with them in a way we haven't before."

Sources: Catherine Holahan, "Yahoo!'s Bid to Think Small," *BusinessWeek*, February 26, 2007, p. 94; Ben Elgin, "Yahoo!'s Boulevard of Broken Dreams," *BusinessWeek*, March 13, 2006, pp. 76–77; Justin Hibbard, "How Yahoo! Gave Itself a Face-Lift," *BusinessWeek*, October 9, 2006, pp. 74–77; Kevin J. Delaney, "As Yahoo! Falters, Executive's Memo Calls for Overhaul," *Wall Street Journal*, November 18, 2006; "Yahoo!'s Personality Crisis," *Economist*, August 13, 2005, pp. 49–50; Fred Vogelstein, "Yahoo!'s Brilliant Solution," *Fortune*, August 8, 2005, pp. 42–55.

PEPSI

Pepsi North America was able to monitor its "Call upon Yoda" promotion with a Star Wars theme. In one ad, the film's green, pointy-eared Yoda floated across Yahoo!'s homepage to land in a small box near the upper right corner. Users who clicked on the ad box were taken to a Pepsi site, where they were given a chance to win a $100,000 prize. Using marketing research data, Pepsi was able to place its ads on areas of Yahoo!'s site most frequented by heavy buyers of 12-packs and 24-packs of soda, its target for the promotion. Pepsi concluded that sales to that group rose in double-digit percentages as a result of the ads.

Marketers must go where the customers are, and increasingly that's online. U.S. consumers go to the Web about 15% of the time they spend with all media. Customers define the rules of engagement, however, and insulate themselves with the help of agents and intermediaries if they so choose. Customers define what information they need, what offerings they're interested in, and what they're willing to pay.[31]

Online advertising was estimated at a little less than 6% of global ad spending in 2006, but is expected to jump to 10% to become a $25 billion business by 2009. Helping fuel that growth is the emergence of rich media ads that combine animation, video, and sound with interactive features.[32]

AXE

The world's most popular male grooming brand, Axe has won numerous advertising awards. Much of its success can also be attributed to its edgy online efforts. Winner of *Business 2.0*'s 2003 Sweet Spot Award for Most Innovative Campaign, Unilever's Axe Deodorant body spray was launched in the United States in 2002, targeting the 18- to 24-year-old male audience interested in improving their appeal to the opposite sex. The centerpiece of the effort was a set of commercials purporting to be home videos and playing only on Axe's Web site (www.theaxeeffect.com). In each, a pretty young woman is instantly attracted by a whiff of Axe deodorant. Banner ads on targeted Web sites were linked to Axe's Web site to encourage viewership of the video clips. Four months into the campaign, 1.7 million people had visited the site and one-third reported they had been sent there by friends. Engaging young adult males on their own turf, subsequent online efforts used streaming videos, downloads to cell phones, blogs, chat rooms, and video games equally successfully. An ad costing $200,000 featuring men in a small town in Alaska who use Axe to attract women was viewed more than 10 million times. Axe has also used content-integration deals as launch platforms featuring Web sites built around a "Gamekillers" special with MTV and "Order of the Serpentine" on SpikeTV. A global campaign, "Bom Chika Wah Wah," coincided with Axe's ascent to become the leader in what many people had thought was the mature $2.4 billion deodorant category.[33]

Different people have different attitudes and experiences with the Web. "Marketing Memo: Segmenting Tech Users" profiles different groups and their usage of technology. Figure 19.1 provides a recent summary of typical daily Internet activities.

Placing Ads and Promotions Online

A company chooses which forms of interactive marketing will be most cost-effective in achieving communication and sales objectives.

WEB SITES Companies must design Web sites that embody or express their purpose, history, products, and vision.[34] A key challenge is designing a site that's attractive on first viewing and interesting enough to encourage repeat visits.[35] Rayport and Jaworski propose that effective sites feature seven design elements they call the 7Cs (see Figure 19.2):[36] To encourage repeat visits, companies must pay special attention to context and content factors and embrace another "C"—constant change.[37]

Visitors will judge a site's performance on ease of use and physical attractiveness. Ease of use has three attributes: (1) The site downloads quickly, (2) the first page is easy to understand, and (3) it is easy to navigate to other pages that open quickly. Physical attractiveness is determined by these factors: (1) Individual pages are clean and not crammed with content, (2) typefaces and font sizes are very readable, and (3) the site makes good use of color (and sound). Web sites must also be sensitive to security and privacy-protection issues.[38]

Activity	Percent of Internet Users Who Report Doing This "Yesterday"
Use the Internet	65
Send or read e-mail	54
Use a search engine to find information	41
Get news	31
Surf the Web for fun	28
Check the weather	22
Do any type of research for your job	21
Look for information on a hobby or interest	20
Research a product or service before buying it	19
Look online for news or information about politics or the upcoming campaigns	19
Research for school or training	16
Get sports scores and information online	15
Visit a local, state, or federal government Web site	14
Do any banking online	14
Send or receive text messages using a cell phone	11
Send instant messages	10
Log on to the Internet using a wireless device	10
Watch video clip or listen to an audio clip	10
Use an online social networking site, such as MySpace, Facebook, or Friendster	9
Get financial information online, such as stock quotes or mortgage interest rates	9
Play online games	9
Get travel information	8
Read someone else's Web log or "blog"	7
Pay bills online	7
Look up phone number or address	7

FIG. 19.1

Top 25 Daily Internet Activities

Source: www.pewinternet.org. Data collected largely during 2005–2006.

MICROSITES A **microsite** is a limited area on the Web managed and paid for by an external advertiser/company. Microsites are individual Web pages or cluster of pages that function as supplements to a primary site. They're particularly relevant for companies selling low-interest products. People rarely visit an insurance company's Web site, but the

- *Context.* Layout and design
- *Content.* Text, pictures, sound, and video the site contains
- *Community.* How the site enables user-to-user communication
- *Customization.* Site's ability to tailor itself to different users or to allow users to personalize the site
- *Communication.* How the site enables site-to-user, user-to-site, or two-way communication
- *Connection.* Degree that the site is linked to other sites
- *Commerce.* Site's capabilities to enable commercial transactions

FIG. 19.2

Seven Key Design Elements of an Effective Web Site

Source: Jeffrey F. Rayport and Bernard J. Jaworski, *e-commerce* (New York: McGraw-Hill, 2001), p. 116.

MARKETING MEMO — SEGMENTING TECH USERS

It's easy to exaggerate the pervasiveness of technology, yet not everyone is plugged in. The Pew Internet and American Life Project published in 2007 found that U.S. adults fall into three groups:

1. 31% are elite technology users
2. 20% are moderate technology users
3. 49% have little or no usage of the Internet or cell phones

The study also revealed divisions within each group. The high-tech elites, for instance, are almost evenly split into:

1. *Omnivores*, who fully embrace technology and express themselves creatively through blogs and personal Web pages.
2. *Connectors*, who see the Internet and cell phones as communications tools.
3. *Productivity enhancers*, who consider technology as largely ways to better keep up with their jobs and daily lives.
4. *Lackluster veterans*, who use technology frequently but aren't thrilled by it.

The lackluster veterans remain stuck in the decade-old technologies they started with, suggesting much opportunity for companies that can design engaging and practical next-generation technologies that will capture this group's interest. Moderate users were also evenly divided into "mobile centrics," who primarily use cell phones for voice, text messaging, and even games, and the "connected but hassled," who have used technology but find it burdensome.

The Pew study found 15% of all U.S. adults have neither a cell phone nor an Internet connection. Another 15% use some technology and are satisfied with what it currently does for them, whereas 11% use it intermittently and find connectivity annoying. Eight percent—mostly women in their early 50s—occasionally use technology and might use more given more experience. They tend to still be on dial-up access and may represent potential high-speed customers.

Sources: Anick Jedanun, "Survey Defines Split in Technology Use," *Associated Press*, May 5, 2007; John B. Horrigan, "A Typology of Information and Communication Technology Users," *Pew Internet & American Life Project*, May 7, 2007. The telephone study of 4,001 U.S. adults, including 2,822 Internet users, was conducted Feb. 15 to April 6, 2006, and has a margin of sampling error of plus or minus 2 percentage points.

company can create a microsite on used-car sites that offers advice for buyers of used cars and at the same time a good insurance deal. Some microsites have become huge online hits.

BURGER KING'S SUBSERVIENT CHICKEN

To compete with McDonald's wholesome, family-friendly image, Burger King adopted a youthful, irreverent personality and menu-driven positioning via its longtime "Have It Your Way" slogan. To promote its TenderCrisp sandwich, ad agency Crispin, Porter & Bogusky created a Web site featuring a "subservient chicken," an actor dressed in a chicken costume who performed a wide range of wacky actions based on a user's typed commands—dust furniture, play air guitar, or, naturally, lay an egg! The site employed prerecorded footage but looked like an interactive Webcam. Within a week of launch, about 54 million people had checked out the chicken for an average of eight minutes. This program was designed not only to entertain and connect with target market 14- to 25-year-olds, but to help reinforce the brand's customization message and contemporary image. Said one Burger King executive, "We're really trying to do something different and not just give consumers a straight ad over and over."[39]

SEARCH ADS A hot growth area in interactive marketing is **paid-search** or **pay-per-click ads**, which represent 40% of all online ads.[40] Thirty-five percent of all searches are reportedly for products or services. The search terms serve as a proxy for the consumer's consumption interests and trigger relevant links to product or service offerings alongside search results from Google, MSN, and Yahoo!. Advertisers pay only if people click on the links, but marketers believe consumers who have already expressed interest by virtue of the search are prime prospects.

The cost per click depends on how high the link is ranked and the popularity of the keyword. Average click-through is about 2%, much more than for comparable online ads.[41] At an average of 35 cents, paid search is a lot cheaper than the $1-per-lead for Yellow Pages listings. One Samsung executive estimated it was 50 times cheaper to reach 1,000 people online than on TV, and the company shifted 10% of its advertising budget to the Internet.[42]

Some believe the Internet is moving from the era of search to the era of discovery, thanks to recommender sites and systems such as Pandora or Whattorent that suggest music, movies, Web sites, or whatever is meaningful to users whether they've heard of it or even ask.

DISPLAY ADS **Display ads** or **banner ads** are small, rectangular boxes containing text and perhaps a picture that companies pay to place on relevant Web sites. The larger the audience, the more the placement costs. Some banners are accepted on a barter basis. In the early days of the Internet, viewers clicked on 2% to 3% of the banner ads they saw, but that percentage quickly plummeted and advertisers began to explore other forms of communication.[43]

Dispay ads still hold great promise compared to popular search ads. Given that Internet users spend only 5% of their time online actually searching for information, there are many opportunities to reach and influence consumers while they travel the Web. But ads need to be more attention getting and influential, better targeted, and more closely tracked.[44]

The emergence of *behavioral targeting* is allowing companies to track the online behavior of target customers to find the best match between ad and prospect. For example, if a person clicks on three Web sites related to auto insurance, then visits an unrelated site for sports or entertainment, auto insurance ads may show up on that site, in addition to the auto insurance sites. This practice ensures that ads are readily apparent for a potential customer likely to be in the market. Although critics worry about companies knowing too much about customers, Microsoft claims behavioral targeting can increase the likelihood a visitor clicks an ad by as much as 76%.[45]

INTERSTITIALS **Interstitials** are advertisements, often with video or animation, that pop up between changes on a Web site. Ads for Johnson & Johnson's Tylenol headache reliever would pop up on brokers' Web sites whenever the stock market fell by 100 points or more. Because consumers found pop-up ads intrusive and distracting, many computer users such as AOL installed software to block these ads.[46]

INTERNET-SPECIFIC ADS AND VIDEOS With user-generated content sites such as YouTube, MySpace Video, and Google Video, consumers and advertisers can upload ads and videos to be shared virally by millions of people.

BMW FILMS

In North America, BMW is positioned as the "Ultimate Driving Machine" on the basis of its dual benefits of luxury and high performance. Beginning in 2001, it created "The Hire" series, eight short films by famous action movie directors such as John Woo, Guy Ritchie, and Ang Lee and starring actors such as Mickey Rourke and Madonna. Each was less than 10 minutes long and could be downloaded only from a corporate Web site, www.bmwfilms.com and viewed on the Internet. With a budget of $3 million per film, the films were cinematic in look, but also designed to showcase the unique qualities of different BMW models. To build traffic to the site, BMW used television spots that mirrored movie trailers. The response was overwhelming. According to BMW's ad agency, 55.1 million people viewed "The Hire" series, and tremendous PR buzz resulted. Many film critics even gave the films rave reviews. And by having visitors register before downloading the films, BMW was able to collect contact information for a large number of potential buyers, many of whom were younger and not necessarily as well represented in BMW's prior marketing efforts.[47]

Online videos can be cost-effective—costing $50,000 to $200,000—and marketers can take more freedom with them. One of the online hits during the summer of 2006 was "Tea Partay," a music video by Prep-Unit, three preppy-looking New Englanders spitting rhymes Beastie Boy-style about the joys of eating finger sandwiches, playing croquet, and drinking Smirnoff Raw Tea, a flavored malt beverage. The distiller posted the ad on its site, but others posted it on YouTube where it was seen more than 1.3 million times.[48]

SPONSORSHIPS Many companies get their name on the Internet by sponsoring special content on Web sites that carry news, financial information, and so on. **Sponsorships** are best placed in well-targeted sites that offer relevant information or service. The sponsor pays for showing the content and in turn receives acknowledgment as the sponsor of that particular service on the site.

BMW's online videos had cinematic production quality and stars to match. The ads showcased various BMW models and won an enthusiastic response from consumers and film critics alike.

A popular vehicle for sponsorship is *podcasts,* digital media files created for playback on portable MP3 players, laptops, or PCs. Sponsors pay roughly $25 per thousand listeners to run a 15- or 30-second audio ad at the beginning of the podcast. Although these rates are higher than for popular radio shows, because podcasts are able to reach very specific market segments, analysts expect their popularity to grow.[49]

ALLIANCES When one Internet company works with another, they end up advertising each other through **alliances** and **affiliate programs**. AOL has created many successful alliances. Amazon has almost one million affiliates that post its banners on their Web sites. Companies can also undertake guerrilla marketing actions to publicize their site and generate word of mouth. When Yahoo! started its Denmark site, it distributed apples at the country's busiest train station with the message that in the next hours a trip to New York could be won on the Yahoo! site. It also managed to get the offer mentioned in Danish newspapers. Companies can offer to push content and ads to targeted audiences who agree to receive them and are presumably more interested in the product or product category.

ONLINE COMMUNITIES Many companies sponsor online communities whose members communicate through postings, instant messaging, and chat discussions about special interests related to the company's products and brands. These communities can provide companies useful, hard-to-get information. When GlaxoSmithKline prepared to launch its first weight-loss drug, Alli, it sponsored a weight-loss community. The firm felt the feedback it gained was more valuable than what it could have received from traditional focus groups. Kraft learned from its online group that members really wanted the ability to control how much they ate, giving rise to 100-calorie bags and $100 million in sales. A key for success of online communities is to create individual and group activities that help form bonds among community members.[50]

E-MAIL E-mail uses only a fraction of the cost of a "d-mail," or direct mail, campaign. Microsoft spent approximately $70 million a year on paper-driven campaigns. It switched to sending out 20 million pieces of e-mail every month at a significant savings. Consumers are besieged by e-mails though, and many employ spam filters. Following are some important guidelines for productive e-mail campaigns, followed by pioneering e-mail marketers:[51]

- ***Give the customer a reason to respond.*** Offer powerful incentives for reading e-mail pitches and online ads, such as e-mail trivia games, scavenger hunts, and instant-win sweepstakes.
- ***Personalize the content of your e-mails.*** IBM's iSource has been distributed directly to customers' office e-mail each week, delivering only "the news they choose" in Announcements and Weekly Updates. Customers who agree to receive the newsletter select from topics listed on an interest profile.
- ***Offer something the customer can't get via direct mail.*** Because e-mail campaigns can be carried out quickly, they can offer time-sensitive information. Travelocity sends frequent e-mails pitching last-minute cheap airfares. Club Med uses e-mail to pitch unsold, discounted vacation packages to prospects in its database.
- ***Make it easy for customers to "unsubscribe."*** Online customers demand a positive exit experience. According to a Burston-Marsteller and Roper Starch Worldwide study, the top 10% of Web users who communicate much more often online typically share their views by e-mail with 11 friends when satisfied, but contact 17 friends when dissatisfied.[52]

To increase the effectiveness of e-mails, some researchers are employing "heat mapping," by which they can measure what people read on a computer screen by using cameras attached to a computer that track eye movements. One study showed that clickable graphic icons and buttons that linked to more details of a marketing offer increased click-through rates by 60% compared to links that used an Internet address.[53]

MOBILE MARKETING The United States has been relatively late to pick up on the trend of mobile phone marketing. Japanese carrier NTT DoCoMo Inc. began posting ads on mobile Web sites in 2000 and displayed 1.5 billion ads in 2006.

Mobile ad spending was an estimated $871 million worldwide in 2006, most of which went into text messages. But new dual-mode phones will make it increasingly easy to blend cell phones with wireless Internet service. With cell phones' ubiquitous nature and marketers' ability to personalize messages based on demographics, the appeal of mobile marketing is obvious. But some still wonder how consumers will react to ads on the "third screen."[54]

Some marketers are testing the waters. Every two-minute mobile episode of Fox's "Prison Break: Proof of Innocence" starts with a 10-second message that showcases Toyota's new subcompact sedan, Yaris. Unilever ran a campaign on mobile phones for its "I Can't Believe It's Not Butter" brand that placed small banner ads on sites such as the Weather Channel and asked consumers to click on a link to visit the "Kitchen of Love" Web site featuring spokesman Fabio.[55]

::: Word of Mouth

Social networks, such as MySpace and Facebook, have become an important force in both business-to-consumer and business-to-business marketing.[56] A key aspect of social networks is *word of mouth* and the number and nature of conversations and communications between different parties. Consumers talk about dozens of brands each day. Although many are media and entertainment products such as movies, TV shows, and publications, food products, travel services, retail stores, and many other types of products are often mentioned.[57] And although meganetworks such as MySpace and Facebook offer the most exposure, niche social networks offer a more targeted market more likely to spread the brand message.

CAFÉMOM

Started in 2006 by parent company CMI Marketing, CaféMom has several thousand members who participate in dozens of different forums for moms. When the site started a forum for discussing develomentally appropriate play activities, toymaker Playskool sent toy kits to over 2,500 members and encouraged them to share their experiences with each other. "The great thing is you get direct feedback from actual moms," enthuses the director of media at Hasbro, Playskool's parent company. This kind of feedback can be invaluable in the product-development process as well.

TAKKLE

Procter & Gamble has spent only a tiny fraction of its media expenditures touting its Tampax brand on the Internet. Yet, it decided to advertise on Takkle, a brand new social networking site, because the site caters to an important niche for Tampax: female athletes. According to P&G, many girls use tampons for the first time because they want to fully enjoy sports activities. Here's how their Takkle promo works: Tampax sponsored a "battle" in which high school cheerleaders were asked to submit three-minute video clips of their best cheers with users voting on their favorites. Takkle awards the winner $10,000 worth of cheerleading equipment and clothing. P&G promoted the contest on its own online customer community, BeingGirl.com, which attracts 500,000 teen girl visitors a month. The campaign is a win-win for both parties; Takkle gets huge exposure as a new network by being mentioned on the P&G property, and P&G gets a highly targeted venue for a product for which it's difficult to create excitement."The reality is, if an advertiser wants to target on MySpace, it doesn't know who it is reaching," said Takkle CEO David Birnbaum.[58]

Companies are becoming acutely aware of the power of word of mouth. Products and brands as diverse as Hush Puppies shoes, Krispy Kreme doughnuts, and the blockbuster movie *The Passion of the Christ* were built through strong word of mouth,[59] as were companies such as Body Shop, Palm, Red Bull, Starbucks, and Amazon.com. In some cases, positive word of mouth happens organically with little advertising, but in many cases, it is managed and facilitated.[60]

DOUBLETREE HOTELS (HILTON)

Hilton Hotels' Doubletree hotels figured out how to get customers talking about it via an amazingly simple device—a warm cookie. At check-in every guest gets a delicious, freshly baked chocolate chip cookie. Not only does it taste great; it also gives Doubletree a homey, warm reputation. The Doubletree Web site boasts, "More than 125 million served to grateful guests," and "Synonymous with Doubletree hospitality, the cookie has played a starring role in differentiating the Doubletree hotel brand from its competition." After all, what else are guests going to discuss with their friends when they return home from a Doubletree hotel? All hotels in the mid-size range provide the same basic amenities, but Doubletree guests can even purchase gift tins of the cookies for delivery anywhere in the world.[61]

Word of mouth can be particularly effective for smaller businesses for whom customers may feel a more personal relationship.

Social networks in the form of online virtual communities can be a vital resource for companies. Apple has a large number of discussion groups organized by product lines and also by consumer versus professional use. These groups are customers' primary source of product information after warranties expire. Financial advice companies such as Morningstar and The Motley Fool also sponsor discussion groups, normally organized by investment vehicle. Intuit developed a community for its Quickbooks product, which serves the small business market and helps provide useful feedback to upgrade products. Philip Morris developed a 26-million-plus database of Marlboro smokers, partly from necessity as media options dwindled due to legislative actions. It is now the primary means of marketing the brand.[62]

Here we consider how word of mouth is formed and travels.

Buzz and Viral Marketing

Some marketers highlight two particular forms of word of mouth—buzz and viral marketing.[63] *Buzz marketing* generates excitement, creates publicity, and conveys new relevant brand-related information through unexpected or even outrageous means.[64] *Viral marketing* is another form of word of mouth, or "word of mouse," that encourages consumers to pass along company-developed products and services or audio, video, or written information to others online.[65]

Contrary to popular opinion, products don't have to be outrageous or edgy to generate buzz. Companies can help to create buzz; and media or advertising are not always necessary for buzz to occur.[66]

BLENDTEC

Utah-based Blendtec used to be known primarily for its commercial blenders and food mills. The company wasn't really known to the general public until it launched a hilarious series of "Will it blend?" online videos to promote some of its commercial products for home use. The videos feature founder and CEO Tom Dickson wearing a white lab coat and pulverizing objects ranging from golf balls and pens to beer bottles, all in a genial but deadpan manner. The genius of the videos (willitblend.com) is that they tie into current events. As soon as the iPhone was launched with huge media fanfare, Blendtec aired a video in which Dickson smiled and said, "I love my iPhone. It does everything. But will it blend?" After the blender crushed the iPhone to bits, Dickson lifted the lid on the small pile of black dust and said simply, "iSmoke." The clip drew more than 3.5 million downloads on YouTube and gained even more momentum by linking to eBay, where viewers bid on the pulverized iPhone and a $400 Blendtec blender to go with it.[67]

Outrageousness is a two-edged sword. The Blendtec Web site clearly puts its comic videos in the "don't try this at home" category and another set showing how to grind up vegetables for soup, for instance, in the "try this at home," category. Checkers Drive-in Restaurants' "try this at home" effort generated controversy. The popular online promotion encouraged consumers to take pictures of their cats dressed in a paper bag resembling the jersey worn by the chain's scruffy stuffed cat named Rapcat, with cutaway holes for legs and tail. But a city agency in the Florida town where Checkers is headquartered warned that this kind of "animal cruelty" is a felony. Checkers counters that the promo is sound because the bags it distributed for the stunt bear a warning saying, "Caution. Not all cats will be down with wearing this bag. Do not harm or endanger any cat."[68]

Agencies have been created solely to help clients create buzz. P&G has 225,000 teens enlisted in Tremor and 600,000 mothers enrolled in Vocalpoint. Both groups are built on the premise that certain individuals want to learn about products, receive samples and coupons, share their opinions with companies, and, of course, talk up their experiences with others. P&G chooses well-connected people—the Vocalpoint moms have big social networks and generally speak to 25 to 30 other women during the day, compared to an average of 5 for other moms—and their messages carry a strong reason to share product information with a friend.[69] BzzAgent is another buzz-building firm.

BZZAGENT

Boston-based BzzAgent has assembled a nationwide army of 260,000 demographically diverse—but essentially ordinary—people who volunteer to talk up any of the clients' products they deem worth promoting. Once a client signs on, the company searches a database for "agents" matching the demographic and psychographic profile of target customers and offers them the chance to sign up for the buzz campaign. For their efforts they get a sample product and a training manual on methods for creating buzz—from chatting up salespeople at retail outlets to discussing the product with friends and family. Each time an agent completes an activity, he or she is expected to file a report describing the nature of the buzz and its effectiveness. The company claims the buzz is honest because the process requires just enough work that few agents enroll solely for freebies, and agents don't talk up products they don't like. Agents are also supposed to disclose they're connected to BzzAgent. The company has completed over 250 projects, working with clients such as Levi's Dockers, Anheuser-Busch, Cadbury-Schweppes, and the publishers of *Freakonomics* and *Eats, Shoots, and Leaves*, both bestsellers.[70]

Buzz and viral marketing both try to create a splash in the marketplace to showcase a brand and its noteworthy features. Some believe that viral and buzz marketing are driven more by the rules of entertainment than the rules of selling. A successful viral campaign has been characterized as "that addictive, self-propagating advertainment that lives on Web sites, blogs, cell phones, message boards, and even in real-world stunts. . . ."

CAMPFIRE

A viral campaign for Sega's Beta-7 sports video game, featuring a fictitious gamer playing the game nonstop for three months, collected 2.2 million online followers and helped Sega top sales projections by 25% in a category dominated by Electronic Art's *Madden NFL*. The campaign was created by viral experts Campfire, also responsible for *The Blair Witch Project* campaign and Audi's A3 automobile "Art of the Heist" promotion. For Audi, Campfire staged a labyrinthine cross-country heist for a new 2006 A3 "stolen" from its Park Avenue showroom. More than 5,000,000 people tracked the heist online and through live events, resulting in 10,000 leads. Campfire designs its online promotions carefully to have multiple layers of "rabbit holes" for people with varying levels of interest: the "divers" who participate minute-by-minute; the "dippers" who casually check the message boards once a week, and the "skimmers" who accidentally read about it while surfing online.[71]

Opinion Leaders

Communication researchers propose a social-structure view of interpersonal communication.[72] They see society as consisting of *cliques*, small groups whose members interact frequently. Clique members are similar, and their closeness facilitates effective communication but also insulates the clique from new ideas. The challenge is to create more openness so that cliques exchange information with others in the society. This openness is helped by people who function as liaisons and connect two or more cliques without belonging to either, and *bridges*, people who belong to one clique and are linked to a person in another.

Best-selling author Malcolm Gladwell claims three factors work to ignite public interest in an idea.[73] According to the first, "The Law of the Few," three types of people help to spread an idea like an epidemic. First are *Mavens*, people knowledgeable about big and small things. Second are *Connectors*, people who know and communicate with a great number of other people. Third are *Salesmen*, who possess natural persuasive power. Any idea that catches the interest of Mavens, Connectors, and Salesmen is likely to be broadcast far and wide. The second factor is "Stickiness." An idea must be expressed so that it motivates people to act. Otherwise, "The Law of the Few" will not lead to a self-sustaining epidemic. Finally, the third factor, "The Power of Context," controls whether those spreading an idea are able to organize groups and communities around it.

One team of viral marketing experts caution that although influencers or "alphas" start trends, they are often too introspective and socially alienated to spread them. They advise marketers to cultivate "bees," hyperdevoted customers who are not just satisfied knowing about the next trend but live to spread the word.[74] Companies can take several steps to stimulate personal influence channels to work on their behalf. "Marketing Memo: How to Start a Buzz Fire" describes some techniques.

MARKETING MEMO | HOW TO START A BUZZ FIRE

Although many word-of-mouth effects are beyond marketers' control, certain steps improve the likelihood of starting a positive buzz. Figure 19.3 displays more dos and don'ts.

- ***Identify influential individuals and companies and devote extra effort to them.*** In technology, influencers might be large corporate customers, industry analysts and journalists, selected policy makers, and a sampling of early adopters.
- ***Supply key people with product samples.*** When two pediatricians launched MD Moms to market baby skin care products, they liberally sampled the product to physicians and mothers hoping they would mention them on Internet message boards and parenting Web sites. The strategy worked—the company hit year 1 distribution goals by the end of the first month.
- ***Work through community influentials such as local disk jockeys, class presidents, and presidents of women's organizations.*** When Ford introduced the Focus, it handed out cars to DJs and trendy people so they would be seen around town in them. Ford also identified 100 influential young consumers in five key marketing states and gave them cars to drive around.
- ***Develop word-of-mouth referral channels to build business.*** Professionals will often encourage clients to recommend their services. Weight Watchers found that word-of-mouth referrals from someone in the program had a huge impact on business.
- ***Provide compelling information that customers want to pass along.*** Companies shouldn't communicate with customers in terms better suited for a press release. Make it easy and desirable for a customer to borrow elements from an e-mail message or blog. Information should be original and useful. Originality increases the amount of word of mouth, but usefulness determines whether it will be positive or negative.

Sources: Sarit Moldovan, Jacob Goldenberg, and Amitava Chattopadhyay, "What Drives Word of Mouth? The Roles of Product Originality and Usefulness," *MSI Report No. 06-111* (Cambridge, MA: Marketing Science Institute, 2006); Karen J. Bannan, "Online Chat Is a Grapevine That Yields Precious Fruit," *New York Times*, December 25, 2006; John Batelle, "The Net of Influence," *Business 2.0* (March 2004): 70; Ann Meyer, "Word-of-Mouth Marketing Speaks Well for Small Business," *Chicago Tribune*, July 28, 2003; Malcolm Macalister Hall, "Selling by Stealth," *Business Life* (November 2001): 51–55.

"PAY" WITH FEEDBACK

You don't need to pay cash to get someone to say something about your product—they're already doing it. Find a way to let your customers communicate with you, then listen to them and provide them real support and appreciation. They'll volunteer to help a brand that lets them be part of the process.

INSIST ON OPENNESS

Campaign success—and perhaps your company's reputation—hinges on the openness of your word-of-mouth participants. If you're creating an organized word-of-mouth program, require that your volunteers are above board.

DEMAND HONESTY

If you listen closely, you'll realize that honest opinions influence purchasing decisions more so than questionably positive opinions.

HELP CUSTOMERS TELL STORIES

Consumers place products in the context of their daily lives. If a runner's footwear helps her set a personal best in a marathon, she doesn't exclaim, "Just do it!" Rather, she talks about how the sneakers benefited her stride. In a word-of-mouth campaign for Levi's Dockers, participants described the pride of being dressed sharply at social events. Provide your customers with tools to help them share their real stories more effectively.

DON'T SCRIPT

For years marketers have delivered their messages as taglines that make every product sound perfect. Forcing word-of-mouth participants to repeat these messages is awkward and unnatural. Worse still is asking participants to repeat a marketing script of a perfect opinion that's not their own. Communicate the history, benefits, and unique attributes of your product to those who volunteer to experience and discuss it—and then get out of the way.

DON'T PLAN

Word of mouth is a spontaneous event. It can happen at anytime or anywhere—and yes, it can not happen, even when you want it to. If you try to force word of mouth to take place when it's not appropriate or comfortable, the result will no longer resemble real word of mouth. The key is to help people become more conscious of their opinions. They'll share them when others are really listening.

DON'T SELL

Odds are your company employs a trained and qualified sales force. Let them do their job . . . and let word-of-mouth volunteers do theirs. No one likes to be forcibly sold a product. We like to learn about the pros and cons and then arrive at our own decision. Your word-of-mouth volunteers are not salespeople. They are siblings, friends, coworkers, and accidental acquaintances.

DON'T IGNORE

Listening to word of mouth about your product can be like a trip to the dentist: It's uncomfortable for a moment, but the benefits last a lifetime. However difficult the feedback may be to hear, it is even more powerful to incorporate. Honest word of mouth provides you with a unique opportunity to use real opinions as an incredible feedback loop; and the more you listen and perfect your product, the better your word of mouth will become.

FIG. 19.3

BzzAgent's Word-of-Mouth Dos and Dont's

Source: Dave Balter, "Rules of the Game," *Advertising Age Point* (December 2005): 22–23.

Consumers can resent personal communications if unsolicited. Some word-of-mouth tactics walk a fine line between acceptable and unethical. One controversial tactic, sometimes called *shill marketing* or *stealth marketing,* pays people to anonymously promote a product or service in public places without disclosing their financial relationship to the sponsoring firm. They may pretend they're ordinary consumers who happen to like the product, displaying, demonstrating, or talking it up in the process.

Hiring a person to go into a bar and loudly ordering a specific branded drink strikes some as inappropriate.[75] To launch its T681 mobile camera phone, Sony Ericsson hired actors dressed as tourists to approach people at tourist locations and ask to have their photo taken. Handing over the mobile phone was an opportunity to discuss its merits. Although the approach no doubt created positive benefits, some found the deception distasteful.

Blogs

Blogs, regularly updated online journals or diaries, have become an important outlet for word of mouth. They vary widely, some personal for close friends and families, others designed to reach and influence a vast audience. Acccording to blog search leader Technorati, every day over 175,000 new blogs are created and existing blogs are updated with over 1.6 million posts.

One obvious appeal of blogs is bringing together people with common interests. Blog networks such as Gawker Media offer marketers a portfolio of choices. Online celebrity gossip blog PopSugar has spawned a family of breezy blogs on fashion (FabSugar), fitness (FitSugar), and humor (GiggleSugar), attracting college-educated women aged 18 to 44 making more than $60,000.[76] Corporations are creating their own blogs and carefully monitoring those of others.

FORD BOLD MOVES

Ford created a Bold Moves Web site—www.fordboldmoves.com—in the summer of 2006 to better connect with the U.S. car-buying public and convince skeptics that its turnaround plan was gaining traction. The company posted 50 short episodes that bring viewers inside the company. "It's engaging consumers in a conversation," said Mary Lou Quesnell, director of brand DNA for the company's Ford division. "We need to recognize our challenges, and we need to communicate to consumers and our own employees how we're moving forward and to tell our story." In addition to the videos, the Web site featured opinion pieces both critical and complimentary, links to recent news stories about Ford, and space for public feedback. Ford drove viewers to the new site with a marketing initiative focused on digital media and gauged success by monitoring Internet traffic and tracking the online buzz created by the videos.[77]

Blog search engines provide up-to-the-minute analysis of millions of blogs to find out what's on people's minds.[78] Popular blogs on networks Gawker and Weblogs are creating influential opinion leaders. At the Treehugger site, a team of bloggers track green consumer products for 1.6 million visitors, offering video and reference guides and numerous daily posts.[79]

Ford's Bold Moves campaign features a blog-like Web site with short videos, opinion pieces, and a public feedback area.

Roughly a third of Internet users have read blogs.[80] Although many of these consumers examine product information contained in blogs, they may still see information from corporate Web sites or a professional review site such as Edmunds.com as more trustworthy.[81]

Some consumers use blogs and videos as a means of retribution and revenge on companies for bad service and faulty products. Dell's customer-service shortcomings were splashed all over the Internet through a series of "Dell Hell" postings. AOL took some heat when a frustrated customer recorded and broadcasted online a service representative's emphatic resistance to canceling his service. Comcast was embarrassed when a video surfaced of one of its technicians sleeping on a customer's couch.[82]

Measuring the Effects of Word of Mouth[83]

Marketers are exploring a range of measures to capture word-of-mouth effects. Research and consulting firm Keller Fay notes that although 80% of word of mouth occurs off-line, many marketers concentrate on online effects given the ease of tracking them.

In measuring the viral success of its jackrabbit.intuit.com Web site designed to support new small business owners, Intuit identified blogs that either picked up stories originally posted by a few influential bloggers given a special preview, or wrote their own stories. Intuit classified each blog according to *velocity* (whether it took a month or happened in a few days), *share of voice* (how much talk occurred in the blogosphere), *voice quality* (what was said and how positive or negative it was), and *sentiment* (how meaningful the comments were).

DuPont suggests possible measures such as campaign scale (how far it reached); speed (how fast it spread); share of voice in that space; share of voice in that speed; whether it achieved positive lift in sentiment; whether the message was understood; whether it was relevant; whether it had sustainability (and was not a one-shot deal); and how far it moved from its source.

::: Designing the Sales Force

The original and oldest form of direct marketing is the field sales call. Today most industrial companies rely heavily on a professional sales force to locate prospects, develop them into customers, and grow the business, or they hire manufacturers' representatives and agents to carry out the direct-selling task. In addition, many consumer companies such as Allstate, Avon, Amway, Mary Kay, Merrill Lynch, and Tupperware use a direct-selling force.

U.S. firms spend over a trillion dollars annually on sales forces and sales force materials—more than on any other promotional method. Nearly 12% of the total workforce work full-time in sales occupations, both nonprofit and for profit.[84] Hospitals and museums, for example, use fund-raisers to contact donors and solicit donations. For many firms, sales-force performance is critical.

SOBE

John Bello, founder of SoBe nutritionally enhanced teas and juices, has given much credit to his sales force for the brand's success. Bello claims that the superior quality and consistent sales effort from the 150 salespeople the company had at its peak was directed toward one simple goal: "SoBe won in the street because our salespeople were there more often and in greater numbers than the competition, and they were more motivated by far." SoBe's sales force operated at every level of the distribution chain: At the distributor level, steady communication gave SoBe disproportionate focus relative to the other brands; at the trade level, with companies such as 7-Eleven, Costco, and Safeway, most senior salespeople had strong personal relationships; and at the individual store level, the SoBe team was always at work setting and restocking shelves, cutting in product, and putting up point-of-sale displays. According to Bello, bottom-line success in any entrepreneurial endeavor depends on sales execution.[85]

Although no one debates the importance of the sales force in marketing programs, companies are sensitive to the high and rising costs of maintaining one, including salaries, commissions, bonuses, travel expenses, and benefits. Because the average cost of a personal sales call ranges from \$200 to \$300, and closing a sale typically requires four calls, the total cost can range from \$800 to \$1,200.[86] Not surprisingly, companies are trying to increase the

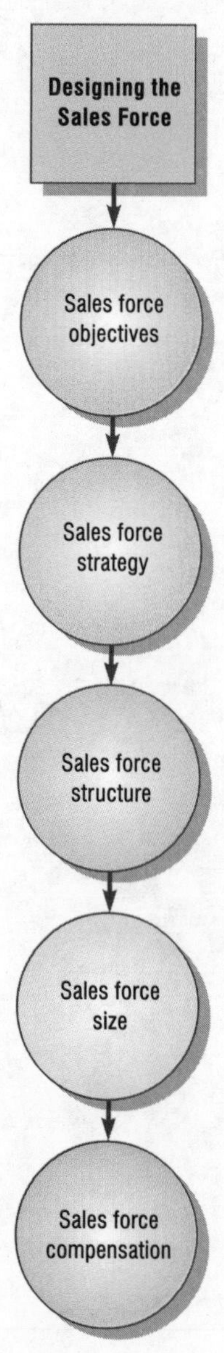

FIG. 19.4

Designing a Sales Force

productivity of the sales force through better selection, training, supervision, motivation, and compensation.

The term *sales representative* covers six positions, ranging from the least to the most creative types of selling:[87]

1. ***Deliverer***—A salesperson whose major task is the delivery of a product (water, fuel, oil).
2. ***Order taker***—An inside order taker (standing behind the counter) or outside order taker (calling on the supermarket manager).
3. ***Missionary***—A salesperson not expected or permitted to take an order but rather to build goodwill or educate the actual or potential user (the medical "detailer" representing an ethical pharmaceutical house).
4. ***Technician***—A salesperson with a high level of technical knowledge (the engineering salesperson who is primarily a consultant to client companies).
5. ***Demand creator***—A salesperson who relies on creative methods for selling tangible products (vacuum cleaners, cleaning brushes, household products) or intangibles (insurance, advertising services, or education).
6. ***Solution vendor***—A salesperson whose expertise is solving a customer's problem, often with a system of the company's products and services (for example, computer and communications systems).

Sales personnel serve as the company's personal link to the customers. Fred Hassan, CEO of global pharmaceutical company Schering-Plough, calls salespeople "active representatives of the company [who] can influence people's perception of it through their ability to interact, to customize, and to build relationships with customers." Hassan also offers first-hand experience of the important feedback role the sales force performs:[88]

> The sales reps are usually the first to spot gaps in the product line. There was a case of this recently in our respiratory business. The sales reps had told me that they would like to be able to offer an antibiotic in addition to our antihistamine line. I remembered this request when the opportunity came up to access an antibiotic called Avelox, which is used to treat pneumonia. Licensing Avelox wasn't a very big deal in terms of its bottom-line effect, but its strategic fit was good. It allowed our salespeople to present a much broader range of respiratory products. . . . If it hadn't been for their input, we would probably have passed on the Avelox opportunity, and Schering-Plough would have struggled longer in respiratory products.

In designing the sales force, the company must consider the development of sales-force objectives, strategy, structure, size, and compensation (see Figure 19.4).

Sales-Force Objectives and Strategy

The days when all the sales force did was "sell, sell, and sell" are long gone. Sales reps need to know how to diagnose a customer's problem and propose a solution. They show a customer-prospect how their company can help improve the customer's profitability.

Companies need to define specific sales-force objectives. For example, a company might want its sales representatives to spend 80% of their time with current customers and 20% with prospects, and 85% of their time on established products and 15% on new products. The specific allocation depends on the kind of products and customers, but regardless of the selling context, salespeople will have one or more of the following specific tasks to perform:

- ***Prospecting.*** Searching for prospects, or leads
- ***Targeting.*** Deciding how to allocate their time among prospects and customers
- ***Communicating.*** Communicating information about the company's products and services
- ***Selling.*** Approaching, presenting, answering questions, overcoming objections, and closing sales
- ***Servicing.*** Providing various services to the customers—consulting on problems, rendering technical assistance, arranging financing, expediting delivery
- ***Information gathering.*** Conducting market research and doing intelligence work
- ***Allocating.*** Deciding which customers will get scarce products during product shortages

Because of the expense, most companies are choosing a *leveraged sales force* that focuses reps on selling the company's more complex and customized products to large accounts and uses inside salespeople and Web ordering for low-end selling. Tasks such as lead generation, proposal writing, order fulfillment, and postsale support are turned over to others. Salespeople handle fewer accounts and are rewarded for key account growth. This is far different from expecting salespeople to sell to every possible account, the common weakness of geographically based sales forces.[89]

Companies must deploy sales forces strategically so they call on the right customers at the right time in the right way. Today's sales representatives act as "account managers" who arrange fruitful contact between people in the buying and selling organizations. Selling increasingly calls for teamwork and the support of others, such as *top management*, especially when national accounts or major sales are at stake; *technical people*, who supply information and service before, during, or after product purchase; *customer-service representatives*, who provide installation, maintenance, and other services; and an *office staff*, consisting of sales analysts, order expediters, and assistants.

To maintain a market focus, salespeople should know how to analyze sales data, measure market potential, gather market intelligence, and develop marketing strategies and plans. Sales representatives, especially at the higher levels of sales management, need analytical marketing skills. Marketers believe sales forces are more effective in the long run if they understand and appreciate marketing as well as selling. Too often marketing and sales are in conflict: marketers complain the sales force isn't converting leads, and the sales force complains marketing isn't generating enough leads (see Figure 19.5). Improved internal collaboration and communication between these two departments can increase revenues and profits.[90]

Once the company chooses an approach, it can use a direct or a contractual sales force. A **direct (company) sales force** consists of full- or part-time paid employees who work exclusively for the company. Inside sales personnel conduct business from the office using the telephone and receive visits from prospective buyers, and field sales personnel travel and visit customers. A **contractual sales force** consists of manufacturers' reps, sales agents, and brokers, who earn a commission based on sales.

Sales-Force Structure

The sales-force strategy has implications for its structure. A company that sells one product line to one end-using industry with customers in many locations would use a territorial structure. A company that sells many products to many types of customers might need a product or market structure. Some companies need a more complex structure. Motorola, for example, manages four types of sales forces: (1) a strategic market sales force composed of technical, applications, and quality engineers and service personnel assigned to major accounts; (2) a geographic sales force calling on thousands of customers in different territories; (3) a distributor sales force calling on and coaching Motorola distributors; and (4) an inside sales force doing telemarketing and taking orders via phone and fax.

Sales: I need leads, but marketing never sends me any good leads. How am I supposed to get new business with no good leads?

Marketing: We deliver tons of leads and they just sit in the system. Why won't sales call on any of them?

Sales: I have nothing new to sell. What is marketing doing? Why can't they figure out what customers want before they give it to us? Why don't they give me anything that's easy to sell?

Marketing: Why won't sales get out and sell my new programs? How do they expect customers to place orders without sales contacts?

Sales: My people spend too much time on administration and paperwork. I need them out selling.

Marketing: We need information to get new ideas. How long does it take to type in a few words? Don't they know their own customers?

Sales: How am I going to hit my number? Marketing is a waste of time. I'd rather have more sales reps.

Marketing: How am I going to hit my number? Sales won't help and I don't have enough people to do it myself.

FIG. 19.5

A Hypothetical (Dysfunctional) Sales-Marketing Exchange

Source: Based on a talk by Scott Sanderude and Jeff Standish, "Work Together, Win Together: Resolving Misconceptions between Sales and Marketing," talk given at Marketing Science Institute's *Marketing, Sales, and Customers* conference, December 7, 2005.

Established companies need to revise their sales-force structures as market and economic conditions change.

HEWLETT-PACKARD

When CEO Mark Hurd took the helm of a troubled Hewlett-Packard, he made it a priority to do a sales-force makeover. He's now credited with transforming HP's sales culture by radically changing its structure. Before, each salesperson was responsible for selling the entire portfolio of HP's products. Although that allowed reps to cross-sell and up-sell and streamlined things for the client, who dealt with only one rep, it was a nearly impossible task for reps and often kept them mired in administrative tasks. Hurd decentralized the sales force and divided sales between HP's three main divisions: IT for large enterprises, printers and printing, and personal computers (including laptops and handhelds). Customers' fairly linear needs mean HP can still keep things streamlined with one contact salesperson per customer. The salesperson, however, is backed up by a "virtual" sales team of specialists who deal with specific areas such as storage, software, and servers. This massive transformation couldn't have taken place without intensive sales training. For instance, a rep who sells to large global enterprise accounts is given a thorough understanding of the client industry in order to converse intelligently about it with both general business executives and IT executives.[91]

Figure 19.6 shows how a company must focus on different aspects of its sales-force structure over the life cycle of the business. SAS, seller of business intelligence software, reorganized its sales force into industry-specific groups such as banks, brokerages, and insurers and saw revenue soar by 14%.[92] "Marketing Insight: Major Account Management" discusses a specialized form of sales-force structure.

Sales-Force Size

Sales representatives are one of the company's most productive and expensive assets. Increasing their number will increase both sales and costs. Once the company establishes the number of customers it wants to reach, it can use a *workload approach* to establish sales-force size. This method has five steps:

1. Group customers into size classes according to annual sales volume.
2. Establish desirable call frequencies (number of calls on an account per year) for each customer class.

| FIG. 19.6 |

The Four Factors for a Successful Sales Force

Source: Andris Zoltners, Prabhakant Sinha, and Sally E. Lorimer, "Match Your Sales-Force Structure to Your Business Life Cycle," *Harvard Business Review* (July–August 2006): 81–89.

	BUSINESS LIFE CYCLE STAGE			
	Start-Up	Growth	Maturity	Decline
EMPHASIS				
ROLE OF SALES FORCE AND SELLING PARTNERS	⇨⇨⇨⇨	⇨⇨	⇨	⇨⇨⇨
SIZE OF SALES FORCE	⇨⇨⇨	⇨⇨⇨⇨	⇨⇨	⇨⇨⇨⇨
DEGREE OF SPECIALIZATION	⇨	⇨⇨⇨⇨	⇨⇨⇨	⇨⇨
SALES FORCE RESOURCE ALLOCATION	⇨⇨	⇨	⇨⇨⇨⇨	⇨
UNDERLYING CUSTOMER STRATEGY	Create awareness and generate quick product uptake	Penetrate deeper into existing segments and develop new ones	Focus on efficiently serving and retaining existing customers	Emphasize efficiency, protect critical customer relationships, exit unprofitable segments

MARKETING INSIGHT | MAJOR ACCOUNT MANAGEMENT

Marketers typically single out for attention major accounts (also called key accounts, national accounts, global accounts, or house accounts). These are important customers with multiple divisions in many locations who are uniform pricing and coordinated service for all divisions. A major account manager (MAM) usually reports to the national sales manager and supervises field reps calling on customer plants within their territories. Large accounts are often handled by a strategic account management team with cross-functional personnel to cover all aspects of the relationship. For example, in 1992, Procter & Gamble stationed a strategic account management team to work with Wal-Mart in its Bentonville, Arkansas, headquarters. By 1998, P&G and Wal-Mart had already jointly saved $30 billion through supply chain improvements. Today, the P&G team in Bentonville consists of approximately 300 staffers, with more stationed at Wal-Mart headquarters in Europe, Asia, and Latin America.

The average company manages about 75 key accounts. If a company has several such accounts, it's likely to organize a major account management division, in which the average MAM handles nine accounts. Some firms such as Rohm and Haas are creating cross-functional strategic account teams that integrate new-product development, technical support, supply chain, marketing activities, and multiple communication channels.

Major account management is growing. As buyer concentration increases through mergers and acquisitions, fewer buyers account for a larger share of a company's sales. Many are centralizing their purchases for certain items, which gives them more bargaining power. Sellers in turn need to devote more attention to these major buyers. And as products become more complex, more groups in the buyer's organization participate in the purchase process. The typical salesperson might not have the skill, authority, or coverage to be effective in selling to the large buyer.

In selecting major accounts, companies look for those that purchase a high volume (especially of more profitable products), purchase centrally, require a high level of service in several geographic locations, may be price sensitive, and may want a long-term partnering relationship. Major account managers act as the single point of contact; develop and grow customer business; understand customer decision processes; identify added-value opportunities; provide competitive intelligence; negotiate sales; and orchestrate customer service.

Favorable pricing based on purchase volume is not enough to retain customer loyalty. Competitors can match or beat a price, or increased costs may necessitate raising prices. Many major accounts look for added value more than a price advantage. They appreciate having a single point of dedicated contact; single billing; special warranties; EDI links; priority shipping; early information releases; customized products; and efficient maintenance, repair, and upgraded service. And there's the value of goodwill. Personal relationships with people who value the major account's business and have a vested interest in the success of that business are compelling reasons for remaining a loyal customer.

Sources: Clare Doyle, Brad McPhee, and Ian Harris, "Marketing, Sales, and Major Account Management: Managing Enterprise Customers as a Portfolio of Opportunities," talk at Marketing Science Institute's *Marketing, Sales, and Customers* conference, December 7, 2005; Sallie Sherman, Joseph Sperry, and Samuel Reese, *The Seven Keys to Managing Strategic Accounts* (New York: McGraw-Hill Trade, 2003); Jack Neff, "Bentonville or Bust," *Advertising Age*, February 24, 2003; Noel Capon, *Key Account Management and Planning: The Comprehensive Handbook for Managing Your Company's Most Important Strategic Asset* (New York: Free Press, 2001). More information can be obtained from NAMA (National Account Management Association); and at www.nasm.com.

3. Multiply the number of accounts in each size class by the corresponding call frequency to arrive at the total workload for the country, in sales calls per year.
4. Determine the average number of calls a sales representative can make per year.
5. Divide the total annual calls required by the average annual calls made by a sales representative, to arrive at the number of sales representatives needed.

Suppose the company estimates that there are 1,000 A accounts and 2,000 B accounts in the nation. A accounts require 36 calls a year, and B accounts require 12 calls a year. The company needs a sales force that can make 60,000 sales calls a year. Suppose the average rep can make 1,000 calls a year. The company would need 60 full-time sales representatives.

Sales-Force Compensation

To attract top-quality sales reps, the company must develop an attractive compensation package. Sales reps want income regularity, extra reward for above-average performance, and fair payment for experience and longevity. Management wants control, economy, and simplicity. Some of these objectives will conflict. No wonder compensation plans exhibit a tremendous variety from industry to industry and even within the same industry.

The company must quantify four components of sales-force compensation—a fixed amount, a variable amount, expense allowances, and benefits. The *fixed amount*, a salary, is intended to satisfy the need for income stability. The *variable amount*, which might be commissions, bonus, or profit sharing, is intended to stimulate and reward effort. *Expense allowances* enable sales reps to meet the expenses involved in travel and entertaining. *Benefits,* such as paid vacations, sickness or accident benefits, pensions, and life insurance, are intended to provide security and job satisfaction.

Fixed compensation is common in jobs with a high ratio of nonselling to selling duties, and jobs where the selling task is technically complex and requires teamwork. Variable compensation works where sales are cyclical or depend on individual initiative. Fixed and variable compensation give rise to three basic types of compensation plans—straight salary, straight commission, and combination salary and commission. One survey revealed that over half of sales reps receive 40% or more of their compensation in variable pay.[93]

Straight-salary plans provide sales reps with a secure income, make them more willing to perform nonselling activities, and give them less incentive to overstock customers. From the company's perspective, these plans represent administrative simplicity and lower turnover. Straight-commission plans attract higher performers, provide more motivation, require less supervision, and control selling costs. On the negative side, they emphasize getting the sale over building the relationship. Combination plans feature the benefits of both plans while reducing their disadvantages.

With compensation plans that combine fixed and variable pay, companies may link the variable portion of a salesperson's pay to a wide variety of strategic goals. One recent trend deemphasizes volume measures in favor of factors such as gross profitability, customer satisfaction, and customer retention. Other companies reward reps partly on a sales team's performance, or even on company-wide performance, increasing the likelihood that reps work closely together for the common good.

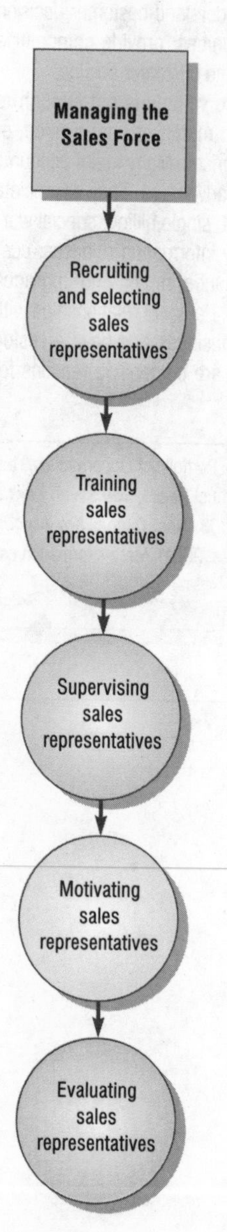

FIG. 19.7

Managing the Sales Force

THRIVENT FINANCIAL

"I don't know how I get paid, I just trust that I'm getting paid right," was typical of the comments Thrivent Financial was hearing from its 2,500-member sales force. This membership-based financial services nonprofit was concerned not only that its reps didn't understand the compensation formula, but also—and mainly—that the formula had not changed with the company. The compensation system, a product of two companies that merged to form Thrivent in 2002, was based on a transactional sales model. But Thrivent now had new sales roles, team-based incentive, and different channels for selling. "We had a one-size-fits-all comp plan, and we don't have a one-size-fits-all world," said Thrivent's VP of field administration. Ultimately the company rolled out a new compensation system with TrueComp, software from vendor Callidus, at the center. The system not only halved the cost of compensating the field sales force and provided more commission transparency, but it also allowed the company to quickly accommodate new product and service introductions and offer new incentive variables, such as degree of customer engagement.[94]

::: Managing the Sales Force

Various policies and procedures guide the firm in recruiting, selecting, training, supervising, motivating, and evaluating sales representatives (see Figure 19.7).

Recruiting and Selecting Representatives

At the heart of any successful sales force is a means of selecting effective representatives. One survey revealed that the top 27% of the sales force brought in over 52% of the sales. Conversely, it's a great waste to hire the wrong people. The average annual turnover rate for all industries is almost 20%. Sales-force turnover leads to lost sales, costs of finding and training replacements, and often a strain on existing salespeople to pick up the slack.

Numerous studies have shown little relationship between sales performance on one hand, and background and experience variables, current status, lifestyle, attitude, personality, and skills on the other. More effective predictors have been composite tests and assessment centers that simulate the working environment so applicants are assessed in an environment similar to the one in which they would work.[95]

After management develops its selection criteria, it must recruit. The human resources department seeks applicants by soliciting names from current sales representatives, using employment agencies, placing job ads, and contacting college students. Selection procedures can vary from a single informal interview to prolonged testing and interviewing.

Although scores from formal tests are only one information element in a set that includes personal characteristics, references, past employment history, and interviewer reactions, tests have been weighted quite heavily by IBM, Prudential, and Procter & Gamble. Gillette claims tests have reduced turnover and scores correlated well with the progress of new reps.

Training and Supervising Sales Representatives

Today's customers expect salespeople to have deep product knowledge, to add ideas to improve the customer's operations, and to be efficient and reliable. These demands have required companies to make a much higher investment in sales training.

New reps may spend a few weeks to several months in training. The median training period is 28 weeks in industrial-products companies, 12 in service companies, and 4 in consumer-products companies. Training time varies with the complexity of the selling task and the type of person recruited. For all sales, new hire "ramp-up" to full effectiveness is taking longer than ever, with 27% taking 3–6 months, 38% taking 6–12 months, and 28% having a 12+ month ramp-up time.

New methods of training are continually emerging, such as the use of audio or video tapes, CDs and CD-ROMs; and programmed learning, distance learning, and films. Some firms are now using role playing and sensitivity or empathy training to help their sales force identify with customers' situations, feelings, and motives.

ALTERA

Altera makes chips that customers can continually reprogram, offering an alternative to custom designs in the computing, car manufacturing, and consumer electronic industries. Over a five-year period beginning in 2002, Altera spent nearly $11 million on empathy training for its sales force using a variety of training methods. The sales force first took the Myers-Briggs type indicator personality test to help form the right sales teams. Next, reps went through a series of exercises to help put themselves in their customers' shoes. One method, "the hot seat," asked salespeople to imagine stepping up behind a person and looking at the world through her eyes. An empathy trainer playing the role of the customer would give the salesperson 10 minutes to ask as many questions as he could to uncover what problems the customer faced. The training and other organizational changes to create greater customer intimacy seemed to pay off: Altera was one of the fastest-growing chip companies in 2005.[96]

Companies vary in how closely they supervise sales reps. Reps paid mostly on commission generally receive less supervision. Those who are salaried and must cover definite accounts are likely to receive substantial supervision. With multilevel selling, used by Avon, Sara Lee, Virgin, AOL Time Warner, and others, independent distributors are also in charge of their own sales force selling company products. These independent contractors or reps are paid a commission not only on their own sales but also on the sales of people they recruit and train.[97]

Some firms are employing empathy training to increase sales reps' understanding of customer problems.

Sales Rep Productivity

How many calls should a company make on a particular account each year? Some research suggests today's sales reps spend too much time selling to smaller, less profitable accounts instead of focusing on larger, more profitable accounts.[98]

NORMS FOR PROSPECT CALLS Companies often specify how much time reps should spend prospecting for new accounts. Spector Freight wants its sales representatives to spend 25% of their time prospecting and to stop calling on a prospect after three unsuccessful calls.

Companies set up prospecting standards for a number of reasons. Left to their own devices, many reps will spend most of their time with current customers, who are known quantities. Reps can depend on them for some business, whereas a prospect might never deliver any. Some companies rely on a missionary sales force instead to open new accounts.

USING SALES TIME EFFICIENTLY The best sales reps manage their time efficiently. *Time-and-duty analysis* helps reps understand how they spend their time and how they might increase their productivity. In the course of a day, sales reps spend time planning, traveling, waiting, selling, and doing administrative tasks (report writing and billing, attending sales meetings, and talking to others in the company about production, delivery, billing, sales performance, and other matters). It's no wonder face-to-face selling time amounts to as little as 29% of total working time![99]

Companies constantly try to improve sales-force productivity. To cut costs, reduce time demands on their outside sales force, and take advantage of computer and telecommunications innovations, many have increased the size and responsibilities of their inside sales force.[100]

Inside salespeople are of three types: *Technical support people* provide technical information and answers to customers' questions. *Sales assistants* provide clerical backup for outside salespersons, call ahead to confirm appointments, run credit checks, follow up on deliveries, and answer customers' questions. *Telemarketers* use the phone to find new leads, qualify them, and sell to them. Telemarketers can call up to 50 customers a day, compared to four for an outside salesperson.

The inside sales force frees the outside reps to spend more time selling to major accounts, identifying and converting new major prospects, placing electronic ordering systems in customers' facilities, and obtaining more blanket orders and systems contracts. Inside salespeople spend more time checking inventory, following up orders, and phoning smaller accounts. Outside sales reps are paid largely on an incentive-compensation basis, and inside reps on a salary or salary-plus-bonus pay.

The salesperson today has truly gone electronic. Not only is sales and inventory information transferred much faster, but specific computer-based decision support systems on CDs have been created for sales managers and sales representatives. Using laptop computers, salespeople can access valuable product and customer information. With a few keystrokes, salespeople can prime themselves on backgrounds of clients; call up prewritten sales letters; transmit orders and resolve customer-service issues on the spot during customer calls; and have samples, pamphlets, brochures, and other materials sent to clients.

One of the most valuable electronic tools for the sales rep is the company Web site, and one of its most useful applications is as a prospecting tool. Company Web sites can help define the firm's relationships with individual accounts and identify those whose business warrants a personal sales call. They provide an introduction to self-identified potential customers and might even receive the initial order. For more complex transactions, the site provides a way for the buyer to contact the seller. Selling over the Internet supports relationship marketing by solving problems that do not require live intervention and thus allows more time to be spent on issues that are best addressed face-to-face.

Motivating Sales Representatives

The majority of sales representatives require encouragement and special incentives, especially those in the field who encounter a number of daily challenges.[101] Most marketers believe that the higher the salesperson's motivation, the greater the effort and the resulting performance, rewards, and satisfaction—all of which further motivation.

Marketers reinforce intrinsic and extrinsic rewards of all types. One research study measuring the importance of different rewards found the reward with the highest value was pay, followed by promotion, personal growth, and sense of accomplishment.[102] The least valued rewards were liking and respect, security, and recognition. In other words, salespeople are highly motivated by pay and the chance to get ahead and satisfy their intrinsic needs, and less motivated by compliments and security.

Many companies set annual sales quotas, developed from the annual marketing plan, on dollar sales, unit volume, margin, selling effort or activity, or product type. Compensation is often tied to degree of quota fulfillment. The company first prepares a sales forecast that becomes the basis for planning production, workforce size, and financial requirements. Management then establishes quotas for regions and territories, which typically add up to more than the sales forecast to encourage managers and salespeople to perform at their best. Even if they fail to make their quotas, the company nevertheless may reach its sales forecast.

Each area sales manager divides the area's quota among its reps. Sometimes a rep's quotas are set high, to spur extra effort, or more modestly, to build confidence. One general view is that a salesperson's quota should be at least equal to the person's last year's sales, plus some fraction of the difference between territory sales potential and last year's sales. The more favorably the salesperson reacts to pressure, the higher the fraction should be.

Conventional wisdom is that profits are maximized by sales reps focusing on the more important products and more profitable products. Reps are unlikely to achieve their quotas for established products when the company is launching several new products at the same time. The company will need to expand its sales force for new-product launches.

Setting sales quotas can create problems. If the company underestimates and the sales reps easily achieve their quotas, it has overpaid them. If the company overestimates sales potential, the salespeople will find it very hard to reach their quotas and be frustrated or quit. Another downside is that quotas can drive reps to get as much business as possible—often ignoring the service side of the business. The company gains short-term results at the cost of long-term customer satisfaction.

Some companies are dropping quotas.[103] Siebel, the leading supplier of sales automation software, judges its sales reps using a number of metrics, such as customer satisfaction, repeat business, and profitable revenues. Almost 40% of incentive compensation is based on customers' reported satisfaction with service and product. The company's close scrutiny of the sales process leads to satisfied customers: Over 50% of Siebel's revenue comes from repeat business.[104] Nortel and AT&T Worldnet also prefer to use a larger set of measures for motivating and rewarding sales reps. Even hard-driving Oracle has changed its approach to sales compensation.

ORACLE

Finding sales flagging and customers griping, Oracle, the second-largest software company in the world, has been overhauling its sales department and practices in recent years. Its rapidly expanding capabilities, with diverse applications such as human resources, supply chain, and CRM, made its account management system difficult. One rep could no longer be responsible for selling all Oracle products to certain customers. Reorganization let reps specialize in a few particular products. To tone down the sales force's reputation as overly aggressive, Oracle changed the commission structure from a range of 2–12% to a flat 4–6% and adopted a set of sales staff guidelines on how to "play nice" with partners, including channels, independent software vendors (ISVs), resellers, integrators, and value-added resellers (VARs). The six principles instructed sales staff to identify and work with partners in accounts and respect their positions and the value they add in those accounts. The principles were intended to address partner feedback that Oracle can and should be more predictable and reliable.[105]

Evaluating Sales Representatives

We have been describing the *feed-forward* aspects of sales supervision—how management communicates what the sales reps should be doing and motivates them to do it. But good feed-forward requires good *feedback,* which means getting regular information from reps to evaluate performance.

SOURCES OF INFORMATION The most important source of information about reps is sales reports. Additional information comes through personal observation, salesperson self-reports, customer letters and complaints, customer surveys, and conversations with other sales representatives.

Sales reports are divided between *activity plans* and *write-ups of activity results.* The best example of the former is the salesperson's work plan, which reps submit a week or month in advance to describe intended calls and routing. This report forces sales reps to plan and schedule their activities and inform management of their whereabouts. It provides a basis for comparing their plans and accomplishments or their ability to "plan their work and work their plan."

Many companies require representatives to develop an annual territory-marketing plan in which they outline their program for developing new accounts and increasing business from existing accounts. Sales managers study these plans, make suggestions, and use them to develop sales quotas. Sales reps write up completed activities on *call reports*. Sales representatives also submit expense reports, new-business reports, lost-business reports, and reports on local business and economic conditions.

These reports provide raw data from which sales managers can extract key indicators of sales performance: (1) average number of sales calls per salesperson per day, (2) average sales call time per contact, (3) average revenue per sales call, (4) average cost per sales call, (5) entertainment cost per sales call, (6) percentage of orders per hundred sales calls, (7) number of new customers per period, (8) number of lost customers per period, and (9) sales-force cost as a percentage of total sales.

FORMAL EVALUATION The sales force's reports along with other observations supply the raw materials for evaluation. There are several approaches to conducting evaluations. One type of evaluation compares current performance to past performance. An example is shown in Table 19.1.

The sales manager can learn many things about a rep from this table. Total sales increased every year (line 3). This does not necessarily mean he is doing a better job. The product breakdown shows he has been able to push the sales of product B further than the sales of product A (lines 1 and 2). According to his quotas for the two products (lines 4 and 5), his success in increasing product B sales could be at the expense of product A sales. According to gross profits (lines 6 and 7), the company earns more selling A than B. The rep might be pushing the higher-volume, lower-margin product at the expense of the more profitable product. Although the rep increased total sales by $1,100 between 2006 and 2007 (line 3), the gross profits on total sales actually decreased by $580 (line 8).

Sales expense (line 9) shows a steady increase, although total expense as a percentage of total sales seems to be under control (line 10). The upward trend in total dollar expense does not seem to be explained by any increase in the number of calls (line 11), although it might be related to success in acquiring new customers (line 14). There is a possibility that in prospecting for new customers, this rep is neglecting present customers, as indicated by an upward trend in the annual number of lost customers (line 15).

The last two lines show the level and trend in sales and gross profits per customer. These figures become more meaningful when compared with overall company averages. If this

TABLE 19.1

Form for Evaluating Sales Representative's Performance

Territory: Midland Sales Representative: John Smith	2004	2005	2006	2007
1. Net sales product A	$251,300	$253,200	$270,000	$263,100
2. Net sales product B	423,200	439,200	553,900	561,900
3. Net sales total	674,500	692,400	823,900	825,000
4. Percent of quota product A	95.6	92.0	88.0	84.7
5. Percent of quota product B	120.4	122.3	134.9	130.8
6. Gross profits product A	$50,260	$50,640	$54,000	$52,620
7. Gross profits product B	42,320	43,920	55,390	56,190
8. Gross profits total	92,580	94,560	109,390	108,810
9. Sales expense	$10,200	$11,100	$11,600	$13,200
10. Sales expense to total sales (%)	1.5	1.6	1.4	1.6
11. Number of calls	1,675	1,700	1,680	1,660
12. Cost per call	$6.09	$6.53	$6.90	$7.95
13. Average number of customers	320	24	328	334
14. Number of new customers	13	14	15	20
15. Number of lost customers	8	10	11	14
16. Average sales per customer	$2,108	$2,137	$2,512	$2,470
17. Average gross profit per customer	$289	$292	$334	$326

rep's average gross profit per customer is lower than the company's average, he could be concentrating on the wrong customers or not spending enough time with each customer. A review of annual number of calls (line 11) shows he might be making fewer annual calls than the average salesperson. If distances in the territory are similar to other territories, the rep might not be putting in a full workday, is poor at sales planning and routing, or is spending too much time with certain accounts.

Even if effective in producing sales, the rep may not rate high with customers. Success may come because competitors' salespeople are inferior, the rep's product is better, or new customers are always found to replace those who dislike the rep. Managers can glean customer opinion of the salesperson, product, and service by mail questionnaires or telephone calls. Sales reps can analyze the success or failure of a sales call and how they would improve the odds on subsequent calls. Their performance could be related to internal factors (effort, ability, and strategy) and external factors (task and luck).[106]

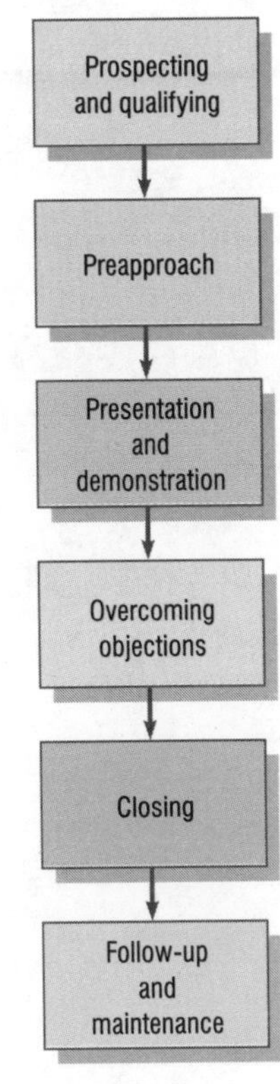

FIG. 19.8

Major Steps in Effective Selling

::: Principles of Personal Selling

Personal selling is an ancient art. Effective salespeople today however have more than instinct; they are trained in methods of analysis and customer management. Companies now spend hundreds of millions of dollars each year to train salespeople and transform them from passive order takers into active order getters. Reps are taught the SPIN method to build long-term relationships with questions such as:[107]

1. ***Situation questions***—These ask about facts or explore the buyer's present situation. For example, "What system are you using to invoice your customers?"
2. ***Problem questions***—These deal with problems, difficulties, and dissatisfactions the buyer is experiencing. For example, "What parts of the system create errors?"
3. ***Implication questions***—These ask about the consequences or effects of a buyer's problems, difficulties, or dissatisfactions. For example, "How does this problem affect your people's productivity?"
4. ***Need-payoff questions***—These ask about the value or usefulness of a proposed solution. For example, "How much would you save if our company could help reduce the errors by 80%?"

Most sales training programs agree on the major steps involved in any effective sales process. We show these steps in Figure 19.8 and discuss their application to industrial selling next.[108]

The Six Steps

PROSPECTING AND QUALIFYING The first step in selling is to identify and qualify prospects. More companies are taking responsibility for finding and qualifying leads so salespeople can use their expensive time doing what they can do best: selling. Companies qualify the leads by contacting them by mail or phone to assess their level of interest and financial capacity. "Hot" prospects are turned over to the field sales force and "warm" prospects to the telemarketing unit for follow-up. Even then, it takes about four calls on a prospect to consummate a business transaction.

PREAPPROACH The salesperson needs to learn as much as possible about the prospect company (what it needs, who is involved in the purchase decision) and its buyers (personal characteristics and buying styles). The rep should set call objectives: to qualify the prospect, gather information, make an immediate sale. Another task is to choose the best contact approach, whether a personal visit, a phone call, or a letter. Finally, the salesperson should plan an overall sales strategy for the account.

PRESENTATION AND DEMONSTRATION The salesperson tells the product "story" to the buyer, using a *features, advantages, benefits,* and *value* approach (FABV). Features describe physical characteristics of a market offering, such as chip processing speeds or memory capacity. Advantages describe why the features provide an advantage to the customer. Benefits describe the economic, technical, service, and social benefits delivered by the offering. Value describes the offering's worth (often in monetary terms). Salespeople often spend too much time on product features (a product orientation) and not enough time stressing benefits and value (a customer orientation).

OVERCOMING OBJECTIONS Customers typically pose objections. *Psychological resistance* includes resistance to interference, preference for established supply sources or brands, apathy, reluctance to giving up something, unpleasant associations created by the sales rep, predetermined ideas, dislike of making decisions, and neurotic attitude toward money. *Logical resistance* might be objections to the price, delivery schedule, or product or company characteristics.

To handle these objections, the salesperson maintains a positive approach, asks the buyer to clarify the objection, questions in such a way that the buyer answers his own objection, denies the validity of the objection, or turns it into a reason for buying. Although price is the most frequently negotiated issue, others include contract completion time; quality of goods and services offered; purchase volume; responsibility for financing, risk taking, promotion, and title; and product safety.

Salespeople sometimes give in too easily when customers demand a discount. One company recognized this problem when sales revenues went up 25% but profit remained flat. The company decided to retrain its salespeople to "sell the price," rather than "sell through price." Salespeople were given richer information about each customer's sales history and behavior. They received training to recognize value-adding opportunities rather than price-cutting opportunities. As a result, the company's sales revenues climbed and so did its margins.[109]

CLOSING Closing signs from the buyer include physical actions, statements or comments, and questions. Reps can ask for the order, recapitulate the points of agreement, offer to help write up the order, ask whether the buyer wants A or B, get the buyer to make minor choices such as color or size, or indicate what the buyer will lose by not placing the order now. The salesperson might offer specific inducements to close, such as a special price, an extra quantity, or a token gift.

FOLLOW-UP AND MAINTENANCE Follow-up and maintenance are necessary to ensure customer satisfaction and repeat business. Immediately after closing, the salesperson should cement any necessary details about delivery time, purchase terms, and other matters important to the customer. The salesperson should schedule a follow-up call after delivery to ensure proper installation, instruction, and servicing and to detect any problems, assure the buyer of the salesperson's interest, and reduce any cognitive dissonance. The salesperson should develop a maintenance and growth plan for the account.

Relationship Marketing

The principles of personal selling and negotiation are largely transaction oriented because their purpose is to close a specific sale. But in many cases the company seeks not an immediate sale, but rather a long-term supplier–customer relationship. Today's customers prefer suppliers who can sell and deliver a coordinated set of products and services to many locations; who can quickly solve problems in different locations; and who can work closely with customer teams to improve products and processes.

Salespeople working with key customers must do more than call only when they think customers might be ready to place orders. They should call or visit at other times, take customers to dinner, and make useful suggestions about the business. They should monitor key accounts, know customers' problems, and be ready to serve them in a number of ways. They must be adaptive and respond to different customer needs or situations.[111]

When a relationship management program is properly implemented, the organization will focus as much on managing its customers as on managing its products. At the same time, companies should realize relationship marketing is not effective in all situations. Ultimately, companies must judge which segments and which customers will respond profitably to relationship management.

SUMMARY :::

1. Direct marketing is an interactive marketing system that uses one or more media to effect a measurable response or transaction at any location. Direct marketing, especially electronic marketing, is showing explosive growth.
2. Direct marketers plan campaigns by deciding on objectives, target markets and prospects, offers, and prices. This is followed by testing and establishing measures to determine the campaign's success.
3. Major channels for direct marketing include face-to-face selling, direct mail, catalog marketing, telemarketing, interactive TV, kiosks, Web sites, and mobile devices.
4. Interactive marketing provides marketers with opportunities for much greater interaction and individualization through well-designed Web sites, as well as online ads and promotions and other approaches.
5. Word-of-mouth marketing finds ways to engage customers so that they choose to talk with others about products, services, and brands.
6. Two notable forms of word-of-mouth marketing are buzz marketing, which seeks to get people talking about a brand by ensuring that a product or service or how it is marketed is out of the ordinary, and viral marketing, which encourages people to exchange information related one way or another to a product or service online.
7. Sales personnel serve as a company's link to its customers. The sales rep *is* the company to many of its customers, and it is the rep who brings back to the company much-needed information about the customer.
8. Designing the sales force requires decisions regarding objectives, strategy, structure, size, and compensation. Objectives may include prospecting, targeting, communicating, selling, servicing, information gathering, and allocating. Determining strategy requires choosing the most effective mix of selling approaches. Choosing the sales-force structure entails dividing territories by geography, product, or market (or some combination of these). Estimating how large the sales force needs to be involves estimating the total workload and how many sales hours (and hence salespeople) will be needed. Compensating the sales force entails determining what types of salaries, commissions, bonuses, expense accounts, and benefits to give, and how much weight customer satisfaction should have in determining total compensation.
9. There are five steps involved in managing the sales force: (1) recruiting and selecting sales representatives; (2) training the representatives in sales techniques and in the company's products, policies, and customer-satisfaction orientation; (3) supervising the sales force and helping reps to use their time efficiently; (4) motivating the sales force and balancing quotas, monetary rewards, and supplementary motivators; (5) evaluating individual and group sales performance.
10. Effective salespeople are trained in the methods of analysis and customer management, as well as the art of sales professionalism. No approach works best in all circumstances, but most trainers agree that selling is a six-step process: prospecting and qualifying customers, preapproach, presentation and demonstration, overcoming objections, closing, and follow-up and maintenance.

APPLICATIONS :::

Marketing Debate Are Great Salespeople Born or Made?

One debate in sales is about the impact of training versus selection in developing an effective sales force. Some observers maintain the best salespeople are born that way and are effective due to their personalities and interpersonal skills developed over a lifetime. Others contend that application of leading-edge sales techniques can make virtually anyone a sales star.

Take a position: The key to developing an effective sales force is selection *versus* The key to developing an effective sales force is training.

Marketing Discussion

Pick a company and go to its Web site. How would you evaluate the Web site? How well does it score on the 7Cs design elements: context, content, community, customization, communication, connection, and commerce?

PART 8

CREATING SUCCESSFUL LONG-TERM GROWTH

IN THIS CHAPTER, WE WILL ADDRESS THE FOLLOWING QUESTIONS:

1. What challenges does a company face in developing new products and services?
2. What organizational structures and processes do managers use to manage new-product development?
3. What are the main stages in developing new products and services?
4. What is the best way to manage the new-product development process?
5. What factors affect the rate of diffusion and consumer adoption of newly launched products and services?

CHAPTER 20 ::: INTRODUCING NEW MARKET OFFERINGS

twenty

Companies need to grow their revenue over time by developing new products and services and expanding into new markets. New-product development shapes the company's future. Improved or replacement products and services can maintain or build sales; new-to-the-world products and services can transform industries and companies and change lives. But the low success rate of new products and services points to the many challenges involved. More and more companies are doing more than just talking about innovation. They are fundamentally changing the way they develop their new products and services. Look what's happening at Johnson & Johnson.[1]

To improve the odds for new-product success in its growing medical device business, Johnson & Johnson is making a number of changes. First, it is trying to replicate the dynamic venture-capital world within the company by creating internal start-ups that seek financing from other J&J units. Teams with a promising idea create a business plan and try to win financing from the company's venture-capital arm, Johnson & Johnson Development Corp., which has invested in outside start-ups for years, as well as from one or more of J&J's existing businesses. J&J is also pushing for greater input from doctors and insurers to provide stronger assurance that any devices it introduces will be highly desirable, feasible, and cost-effective. The Ethicon-Endo unit designed new surgical clips based on >>>

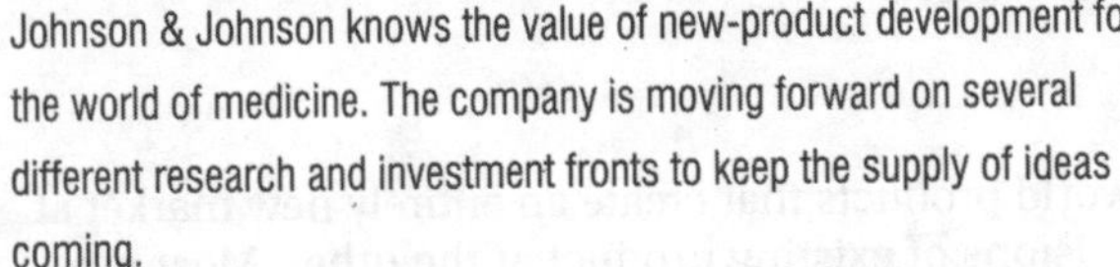

Johnson & Johnson knows the value of new-product development for the world of medicine. The company is moving forward on several different research and investment fronts to keep the supply of ideas coming.

discussions with physicians about the need to find ways to make surgery less invasive. J&J also put one of its most successful scientists in the newly created position of Chief Science and Technology Officer, to encourage collaboration between J&J's different businesses and to overcome the barriers that can prevail in its decentralized structure. One notable success: the $2.6 billion Cypher drug-coated stent. J&J isn't starting from scratch; with 15,000 R&D employees and an R&D budget of $6.3 billion, it has had more than its share of new-product successes through the years, but innovative companies never stand still and are always looking for new and better ways to drive new-product growth.[2]

Firms all over the world are trying to come up with creative ways to develop even better new products and services, faster and more efficiently. Marketers are playing a key role in the development of new products by identifying and evaluating new-product ideas and working with R&D and other areas in every stage of development. This chapter provides a detailed analysis of the new-product development process. Much of the discussion is equally relevant to new products, services, or business models. Chapter 21 considers how marketers can tap into global markets as another source of long-term growth.

::: New-Product Options

There are a variety of types of new products and ways to create them.[3]

Make or Buy

A company can add new products through acquisition or development. The acquisition route can take three forms. The company can buy other companies, it can acquire patents from other companies, or it can buy a license or franchise from another company. Swiss food giant Nestlé increased its presence in North America via its acquisition of such diverse brands as Carnation, Hills Brothers, Stouffer's, Ralston Purina, Dreyer's Ice Cream, and Chef America.[4]

But firms can successfully make only so many acqusitions. At some point, there becomes a pressing need for *organic growth*—the development of new products from within the company. When Praxair, in Danbury, Connecticut, set an ambitious goal of $200 million per year of double-digit new annual sales growth, it achieved that goal only through a healthy dose of organic growth and a large number of smaller but significant $5 million projects.[5]

For product development, the company can create new products in its own laboratories, or it can contract with independent researchers or new-product development firms to develop specific new products or provide new technology.[6] Many firms such as Samsung, GE, Diageo, Hershey, USB, and others have engaged new-product consulting boutiques to provide fresh insights and different points of view.

Types of New Products

New products range from new-to-the-world products that create an entirely new market at one end, to minor improvements or revisions of existing product at the other. Most new-product activity is devoted to improving existing products. At Sony, over 80% of new-product activity is modifying and improving existing products. Some of the most successful new consumer products in recent years have been brand extensions of existing products: Tide with Febreze and Tide Coldwater; Crest ProHealth Rinse and Crest Whitestrips Premium Plus; and Gillette Venus Vibrance.

In many categories, it is becoming increasingly difficult to identify blockbuster products that will transform a market; but continuous innovation to better satisfy consumer needs can force competitors to play catch-up.[7] Continually launching new products as brand extensions into related product categories can also broaden the brand meaning. Nike started as a running-shoe manufacturer but now competes in the sports market with all types of athletic shoes, clothing, and equipment. Armstrong World Industries moved from selling floor coverings to ceilings to total interior surface decoration. Product innovation and effective marketing programs have allowed these firms to expand their "market footprint."

Fewer than 10% to 15% of all new products are truly innovative and new to the world.[8] These products incur the greatest cost and risk because they are new to both the company and the marketplace.[9] Radical innovations can hurt the company's bottom line in the short run, but the good news is that success can create a greater sustainable competitive advantage than more ordinary products. Companies typically must create a strong R&D and marketing partnership to pull off a radical innovation.[10] Few reliable techniques exist for estimating demand for these innovations. Focus groups will provide some perspectives on customer interest and need, but marketers may need to use a probe-and-learn approach based on observation and feedback of early users' experiences and other means.[11]

Many high-tech firms strive for radical innovation.[12] High tech covers a wide range of industries—telecommunications, computers, consumer electronics, biotech, and software. High-tech marketers face a number of challenges in launching their products: high technological uncertainty; high market uncertainty; high competitive volatility; high investment costs; short product life cycles; and difficulty in finding funding sources for risky projects.[13]

PERCEPTIVE PIXEL

At the 2006 TED conference for showcasing the best in new technology, entertainment, and design, Jeff Han earned a reception worthy of a rock star as he moved his hands across a cobalt blue 36-inch wide "multitouch" screen, zooming in on maps with the touch of a finger and manipulating photos as if they were on a tabletop. Han's touch display redefines the way commands go to the computer and uses both movement and pressure from multiple fingertips. To come up with his invention, Han, an engineer, simply explored concepts of interest to him. In forming his company, Perceptive Pixel, he says, "I wanted to create an environment where I can create technology, get it into the hands of someone to market it, and move on to other technologies so I can keep innovating." He already faces stiff competition: Microsoft has its own multitouch version, TouchLight, which GE Healthcare is already using. Mitsubishi's DiamondTouch table targets businesspeople, and Panasonic has developed wall-size interactive touch screens. Yet, Han has two things going for him: well-funded military customers and plans to offer consulting and support services, which will earn even more revenue.[14]

::: Challenges in New-Product Development

New-product introductions have accelerated in recent years. In many industries, such as retailing, consumer goods, electronics, autos, and others, the time it takes to bring a product to market has been cut in half.[15] Luxury leather-goods maker Louis Vuitton implemented a new factory format dubbed Pégase so that it could ship fresh collections to its boutiques every six weeks—more than twice as frequently as in the past—giving customers more new looks to choose from.[16]

To learn how Maple Leafs Sports & Entertainment successfully developed a new product—the Toronto FC—for Major League Soccer, visit www.pearsoned.ca/marketingmanagementcanada.

The Innovation Imperative

In an economy of rapid change, continuous innovation is a necessity. Highly innovative firms are able to identify and quickly seize new market opportunities. Table 20.1 lists the 2007 rankings of the top 25 globally innovative firms on the basis of a *BusinessWeek*-Boston Consulting Group survey. Innovative firms create a positive attitude toward innovation and risk taking, routinize the innovation process, practice teamwork, and allow their people to experiment and even fail.

TABLE 20.1 | The World's Top 25 Most Innovative Companies

2007 Rank	2006 Rank	Company Name	HQ City	HQ Country	HQ Continent	Stock Returns 2001–2006	Revenue Growth 2001–2006	Margin Growth 2001–2006	Patent Citation Index
1	1	APPLE	Cupertino, CA	USA	North America	50.60	29.21	NA	34
2	2	GOOGLE	Mountain View, CA	USA	North America	NA	NA	NA	1
3	4	TOYOTA MOTOR	Toyota	Japan	Asia	20.50	8.30	5.21	361
4	6	GENERAL ELECTRIC	Fairfield, CT	USA	North America	1.11	5.06	1.36	155
5	5	MICROSOFT	Redmond, WA	USA	North America	0.83	11.85	−3.04	174
6	7	PROCTER & GAMBLE	Cincinnati, OH	USA	North America	12.20	11.69	3.70	105
7	3	3M	St. Paul, MN	USA	North America	7.77	7.35	5.49	57
8	43	WALT DISNEY CO	Burbank, CA	USA	North America	11.71	6.29	7.35	8
9	10	IBM	Armonk, NY	USA	North America	−3.48	1.26	4.97	94
10	13	SONY	Tokyo	Japan	Asia	−2.62	0.60	1.14	418
11	20	WAL-MART	Bentonville, AR	USA	North America	−3.35	9.79	3.54	0
12	23	HONDA MOTOR	Tokyo	Japan	Asia	13.61	7.40	0.38	377
13	8	NOKIA	Espoo	Finland	Europe	−9.24	5.68	4.37	287
14	9	STARBUCKS	Seattle, WA	USA	North America	30.04	24.07	1.51	2
15	22	TARGET	Minneapolis, MN	USA	North America	7.55	8.32	4.23	0
16	16	BMW	Munich	Germany	Europe	4.30	4.96	−1.23	84
17	12	SAMSUNG ELECTRONICS	Seoul	South Korea	Asia	36.24	4.60	8.07	1000
18	11	VIRGIN GROUP	London	United Kingdom	Europe	Private	Private	Private	0
19	17	INTEL	Santa Clara, CA	USA	North America	−7.57	5.92	12.55	216
20	21	AMAZON.COM	Seattle, WA	USA	North America	29.53	27.96	NA	0
21	70	BOEING	Chicago, IL	USA	North America	19.91	1.12	−4.23	59
22	14	DELL	Round Rock, TX	USA	North America	1.59	12.87	−5.24	16
23	27	GENENTECH	South San Francisco, CA	USA	North America	24.50	34.85	32.40	4
24	18	EBAY	San Jose, CA	USA	North America	12.45	51.47	4.91	1
25	28	CISCO SYSTEMS	San Jose, CA	USA	North America	8.58	5.02	205.04	20

Source: "The World's Fifty Most Innovative Companies," Special Report, *BusinessWeek,* May 9, 2007.
Note: The *BusinessWeek*-Boston Consulting Group 2007 rankings are based on a senior management survey about innovation distributed electronically to executives worldwide in October 2006. Surveys were sent to their top 10 executives in charge of innovation at the 1,500 largest global corporations, determined by market capitalization in U.S. dollars. Surveys were also distributed to senior management members of the *BusinessWeek* Market Advisory Board, an online panel consisting of *BusinessWeek* readers, and via the Knowledge@Wharton e-mail newsletter. Survey participation was voluntary and anonymous, and the survey closed in March 2007 The survey consisted of 20 general questions on innovation and an optional 12 questions focused on innovation metrics. A total of 2,468 executives answered the survey. Of those indicating their location, 77% were from North America, 12% were from Europe, and 9% were from Asia or the Pacific region.

W. L. GORE

W. L. Gore, best known for its durable Gore-Tex outdoor fabric, has innovated breakthrough new products in a number of diverse areas—guitar strings, dental floss, medical devices, and fuel cells. It has adopted several principles to guide its new-product development. First, it works with potential customers. Its thoracic graft, designed to combat heart disease, was developed in close collaboration with physicians. Second, it lets employees choose projects and appoints few of its actual product leaders and teams. Gore likes to nurture "passionate champions" who convince others a project is worth their time and commitment. The development of the fuel cell rallied over 100 of the company's 6,000 research associates. Third, Gore gives employees "dabble" time. All research associates spend 10% of their work hours developing their own ideas. Promising ideas are pushed forward and judged according to a "Real, Win, Worth" exercise: Is the opportunity real? Can we win? Can we make money? Fourth, it knows when to let go. Sometimes dead ends in one area can spark an innovation in another.

Elixir acoustic guitar strings were a result of a failed venture into bike cables. Even successful ventures may need to move on. Glide shred-resistant dental floss was sold to Procter & Gamble because Gore-Tex knew that retailers would want to deal with a company selling a whole family of health care products.[17]

Companies that fail to develop new products put themselves at risk. Their existing products are vulnerable to changing customer needs and tastes, new technologies, shortened product life cycles, and increased domestic and foreign competition. New technologies are especially threatening. Kodak has worked hard to develop a new business model and product-development processes that work well in a digital photography world. Its new goal is to do for photos what Apple does for music by helping people to organize and manage their personal libraries of images. Table 20.2 displays CEO Antonio M. Perez's philosophy of innovation and transformation.

New-Product Success

Most established companies focus on *incremental innovation.* Incremental innovation can allow companies to enter new markets by tweaking products for new customers, use variations on a core product to stay one step ahead of the market, and create interim solutions for industry-wide problems. Scott Paper and Southwest Airlines have made some notable incremental innovations.

SCOTT PAPER COMPANY

When Scott Paper couldn't compete with Fort Howard Paper Co. on price for the lucrative institutional toilet tissue market, it borrowed a solution from European companies: a dispenser that held bigger rolls of paper. Scott made the larger rolls of paper and provided institutional customers with free dispensers. It later did the same thing with paper towels. Scott not only won over customers in a new market, but it also was less vulnerable to competitors, such as Fort Howard, which could lower prices but weren't offering the larger rolls or tailor-made dispensers.

SOUTHWEST AIRLINES

An airline known for bucking tradition, Southwest used incremental innovation to offset the impact of an important competitor innovation: frequent flier miles. Begun by American Airlines more than 20 years ago to boost customer loyalty, frequent flier rewards programs were soon rolled out by all the major airlines. Southwest, however, decided to tie its rewards to the number of flights taken rather than miles flown. The airline offers mainly short-haul flights for business travelers who often fly the same route over and over. The program was a big hit with this target market.[18]

Newer companies create *disruptive technologies* that are cheaper and more likely to alter the competitive space. Established companies can be slow to react or invest in these disruptive technologies because they threaten their investment. Then they suddenly find themselves

TABLE 20.2

Kodak CEO Antonio Perez's Seven Notions of Innovation

1. See the future through the eyes of your customer.
2. Intellectual property and brand power are key assets.
3. Use digital technology to create tools for customers.
4. Build a championship team, not a group of champions.
5. Innovation is a state of mind.
6. Speed is critical, so push your organization.
7. Partner up if you're not the best in something.

Source: Steve Hamm and William C. Symonds, "Mistakes Made on the Road to Innovation," *BusinessWeek In Inside Innovation* (November 2006): 27–31.

facing formidable new competitors, and many fail.[19] To avoid this trap, incumbent firms must carefully monitor the preferences of both customers and noncustomers over time and uncover evolving, difficult-to-articulate customer needs.[20]

What else can a company do to develop successful new products? In a study of industrial products, new-product specialists Cooper and Kleinschmidt found that the number-one success factor is a unique, superior product. Such products succeed 98% of the time, compared to products with a moderate advantage (58% success) or minimal advantage (18% success). Another key factor is a well-defined product concept. The company carefully defines and assesses the target market, product requirements, and benefits before proceeding. Other success factors are technological and marketing synergy, quality of execution in all stages, and market attractiveness.[21]

CUTS FITNESS FOR MEN

Sometimes creating a new product or service means taking a successful product concept and adapting it for a different audience. This is what John Gennaro tried when he started Cuts Fitness for Men. Cuts gives time-strapped men a quick, full-body workout in a no-frills atmosphere where they're not likely to be intimidated by or embarrassed in front of muscle-bound jocks and fitness freaks. His model is based on Curves, the world's largest women's fitness franchise. Cuts used the same elements Curves did: small space, no-frills, hydraulic exercise equipment, a 30-minute workout, and word-of-mouth marketing. However, with memberships low and franchises closing two years later, Gennaro realized he had to redefine the product concept in some important ways. For one thing, he had to get franchisees with a sound fitness and marketing background. Then he needed to give men what they wanted most, a way to measure their weightlifting progress; he added stacked weights on which you can move the pin down to add more weight. Finally, although men are passionate about fitness, they don't talk about it to other men. Word of mouth wasn't working. Gennaro had to get each franchisee to do grassroots promotions in the community. The jury is still out whether these changes will work. After some initial success, the franchisor ran into some trouble.[22]

Cooper and Kleinschmidt also found that domestic products designed solely for the domestic market tend to show a high failure rate, low market share, and low growth. In contrast, products designed for the world market—or at least to include neighboring countries—achieve significantly more profits, both at home and abroad. Yet only 17% of the products in their study were designed with an international orientation.[23] The implication is that companies should adopt an international focus in designing and developing new products.

New-Product Failure

New-product development can be quite risky. New products continue to fail at a disturbing rate. Recent studies put the rate as high as 50% and potentially as high as 95% in the United States and 90% in Europe.[24]

New products can fail for many reasons: ignored or misinterpreted market research; overestimates of market size; high development costs; poor design; incorrect positioning, ineffective advertising, or wrong price; insufficient distribution support; and competitors who fight back hard. Some additional factors hindering new-product development are:

- ***Shortage of important ideas in certain areas.*** There may be few ways left to improve some basic products (such as steel or detergents).
- ***Fragmented markets.*** Companies must aim their new products at smaller market segments, and this can mean lower sales and profits for each product.
- ***Social and governmental constraints.*** New products must satisfy consumer safety and environmental concerns.
- ***Cost of development.*** A company typically must generate many ideas to find just one worthy of development and often faces high R&D, manufacturing, and marketing costs.
- ***Capital shortages.*** Some companies with good ideas cannot raise the funds needed to research and launch them.
- ***Shorter required development time.*** Companies must learn how to compress development time by using new techniques, strategic partners, early concept tests, and advanced marketing planning.

TABLE 20.3

Causes of New-Product Failure

1. Market/marketing failure
   - Small size of the potential market
   - No clear product differentiation
   - Poor positioning
   - Misunderstanding of customer needs
2. Financial failure
   - Low return on investment
3. Timing failure
   - Late in the market
   - "Too" early—market not yet developed
4. Technical failure
   - Product did not work
   - Bad design
5. Organizational failure
   - Poor fit with the organizational culture
   - Lack of organizational support
6. Environmental failure
   - Government regulations
   - Macroeconomic factors

Source: Dipak Jain, "Managing New-Product Development for Strategic Competitive Advantage," Table 6.1 in chapter 6 in *Kellogg on Marketing*, ed. Dawn Iacobucci (New York: John Wiley, 2001), p. 131.

- ***Shorter product life cycles.*** When a new product is successful, rivals are quick to copy it. Sony used to enjoy a three-year lead on its new products. Now Matsushita will copy the product within six months, barely leaving time for Sony to recoup its investment.

Table 20.3 summarizes causes of new-product failure.

But failure comes with the territory, and truly innovative firms accept it as part of what's needed to be successful. Silicon Valley marketing expert Seth Godin maintains: "It is not just OK to fail; it's imperative to fail."[25] Many Web companies are the result of failed business ventures and experience numerous failed initiatives as they evolve their services. Dogster.com, a social network site for dog lovers, emerged after the spectacular demise of Pets.com. Like.com, a site for people seeking look-alike clothes, fared better than a service for searching for similar-looking photos; and even Google found that a Google Answers service for people seeking specialized information flopped.[26]

Initial product failure is not always the end of the road for an idea. Recognizing that 90% of experimental drugs fail, Eli Lilly has established a corporate culture that looks at failure as an inevitable part of discovery, and its scientists are encouraged to look for new uses for compounds that fail at any stage in a human clinical trial. Evista was a failed contraceptive that became a $1 billion-a-year drug for osteoporosis. Strattera was unsuccessful as an antidepressant but became a top seller for attention deficit/hyperactivity disorder. One promising cardiovascular drug in development started as an asthma project.[27]

::: Organizational Arrangements

Many companies today use *customer-driven engineering* to design new products. This strategy attaches high importance to incorporating customer preferences in the final design.

XEROX

Xerox traditionally developed new products as many firms did in the past: Come up with an idea, develop a prototype, and get some consumer feedback. When Xerox researchers first came up with the idea for a dual-engine commercial printer, they decided to first go straight to the consumer to collect feedback before even developing

Xerox's popular new dual-engine printer was a response to customers' feedback on the value of a commercial printer with a back-up engine.

any prototypes. Lucky they did. Although the Xerox team thought customers would want a second engine for special purposes, the fact that the second engine would be a back-up if the main engine failed turned out to be the biggest draw. As one customer said, "If you're down, you're dead." In introducing the dual-engine Nuvera 288 Digital Perfecting System in April 2007, Xerox chief technology officer Sophie V. Vandebroek cited "customer-led innovation" as a critical driver. Xerox now believes in brainstorming, or "dreaming with the customer," by combining company experts who know technology with customers who know the "pain points" and what the most valuable product features can be. In addition, scientists and engineers are encouraged to meet face to face with customers, in some cases working on-site for a few weeks to see how customers interact with products.[28]

Figure 20.1 shows how three other companies instituted internal changes to try to develop more successful new products and growth initiatives.

New-product development requires senior management to define business domains, product categories, and specific criteria. General Motors has a hefty $400 million benchmark it must apply to new car models—this is what it costs to get a new vehicle into production.[29] One company established the following acceptance criteria:

- The product can be introduced within five years.
- The product has a market potential of at least $50 million and a 15% growth rate.
- The product can provide at least 30% return on sales and 40% on investment.
- The product can achieve technical or market leadership.

Budgeting for New-Product Development

Senior management must decide how much to budget for new-product development. R&D outcomes are so uncertain that it is difficult to use normal investment criteria. Some companies solve this problem by financing as many projects as possible, hoping to achieve a few winners. Other companies apply a conventional percentage-of-sales figure or spend what the competition spends. Still other companies decide how many successful new products they need and work backward to estimate the required investment.

FIG. 20.1

Three Innovation Models

- Whirlpool Corporation launched an effort in 2000 to stimulate greater innovation. The company trained 400 employees from a wide variety of functions in a new process of "ideation." Since the initiative began, Whirlpool has gone from a handful of product introductions per year to dozens, including the highly successful Gladiator line of appliances, workbenches, and storage systems for the garage.
- Shell, in 1996, authorized a team of its employees to allocate $20 million to rule-breaking ideas originating anywhere in the company. Any employee can make a 10-minute pitch followed by a 15-minute Q&A. Greenlight ideas get an average of $100,000 and up to $600,000. Four teams out of 12 received 6-month funding for next-stage development. Of Shell's five largest growth initiatives in 1999, four started this way.
- Samsung Electronics established the Value Innovation Program (VIP) Center in 1998. Core cross-functional team members come together to discuss their strategic projects. In 2003, the center completed 80 projects. Samsung runs an annual Value Innovation conference, and awards are given for the best cases.

TABLE 20.4

Finding One Successful New Product (Starting with 64 new ideas)

Stage	Number of Ideas	Pass Ratio	Cost per Product Idea	Total Cost
1. Idea screening	64	1:4	$ 1,000	$ 64,000
2. Concept testing	16	1:2	20,000	320,000
3. Product development	8	1:2	200,000	1,600,000
4. Test marketing	4	1:2	500,000	2,000,000
5. National launch	2	1:2	5,000,000	10,000,000
			$5,721,000	$13,984,000

Table 20.4 shows how a company might calculate the cost of new-product development. The new-products manager at a large consumer packaged-goods company reviewed the results of 64 ideas. Only one in four, or 16, passed the screening stage. It cost $1,000 to review each idea at this stage. Half these ideas, or eight, survived the concept-testing stage, at a cost of $20,000 each. Half of these, or four, survived the product-development stage, at a cost of $200,000 each. Half of these, or two, did well in the test market, at a cost of $500,000 each. When the two ideas were launched, at a cost of $5 million each, only one was highly successful. Thus, this one successful idea cost the company $5,721,000 to develop.

In the process, 63 other ideas fell by the wayside. The total cost for developing one successful new product from the 64 ideas was $13,984,000. Unless the company can improve the pass ratios and reduce the costs at each stage, it will need to budget nearly $14 million for each successful new idea it hopes to find.

Hit rates vary. Inventor Sir James Dyson claims he made 5,127 prototypes of his bagless, transparent vacuum cleaner before finally getting it right, eventually resulting in the best-selling vacuum cleaner by revenue in the United States. He doesn't lament his failures though: "If you want to discover something that other people haven't, you need to do things the wrong way . . . watching why that fails can take you on a completely different path."[30]

Organizing New-Product Development

Companies handle the organizational aspect of new-product development in several ways.[31] Many companies assign responsibility for new-product ideas to *product managers.* But product managers are often so busy managing existing lines that they give little thought to new products other than line extensions. They also lack the specific skills and knowledge needed to develop and critique new products. Kraft and Johnson & Johnson have employed *new-product managers* who report to category managers. Some companies have a *high-level management committee* charged with reviewing and approving proposals. Large companies often establish a *new-product department* headed by a manager who has substantial authority and access to top management. The department's major responsibilities include generating and screening new ideas, working with the R&D department, and carrying out field testing and commercialization.

ADOBE SYSTEMS INC.

A developer of software solutions for graphic designers and publishers, Adobe established a task force in 2004 to identify all the obstacles company innovators faced in trying to develop new products. The team found the corporate hierarchy resisted ideas needing a new sales channel, new business model, or even new packaging, and the company had grown so large that ideas originating in branch offices were not getting a fair shake. The company then established a New Business Initiatives Group that holds quarterly Adobe Idea Champion Showcases. About 20 product managers and other employees (except top executives who are barred from the proceedings) watch as potential employee-entrepreneurs give brief presentations and Q&A sessions. The ideas are vetted by Adobe entrepreneurs-in-residence, but even one that's nixed can still get a hearing on the company's brainstorming site. Since the new initiative was formed, the event has become extremely popular within Adobe—an American Idol-style way for good ideas to come to the fore.[32]

3M, Dow, and General Mills have assigned new-product development work to **venture teams**, cross-functional groups charged with developing a specific product or business.

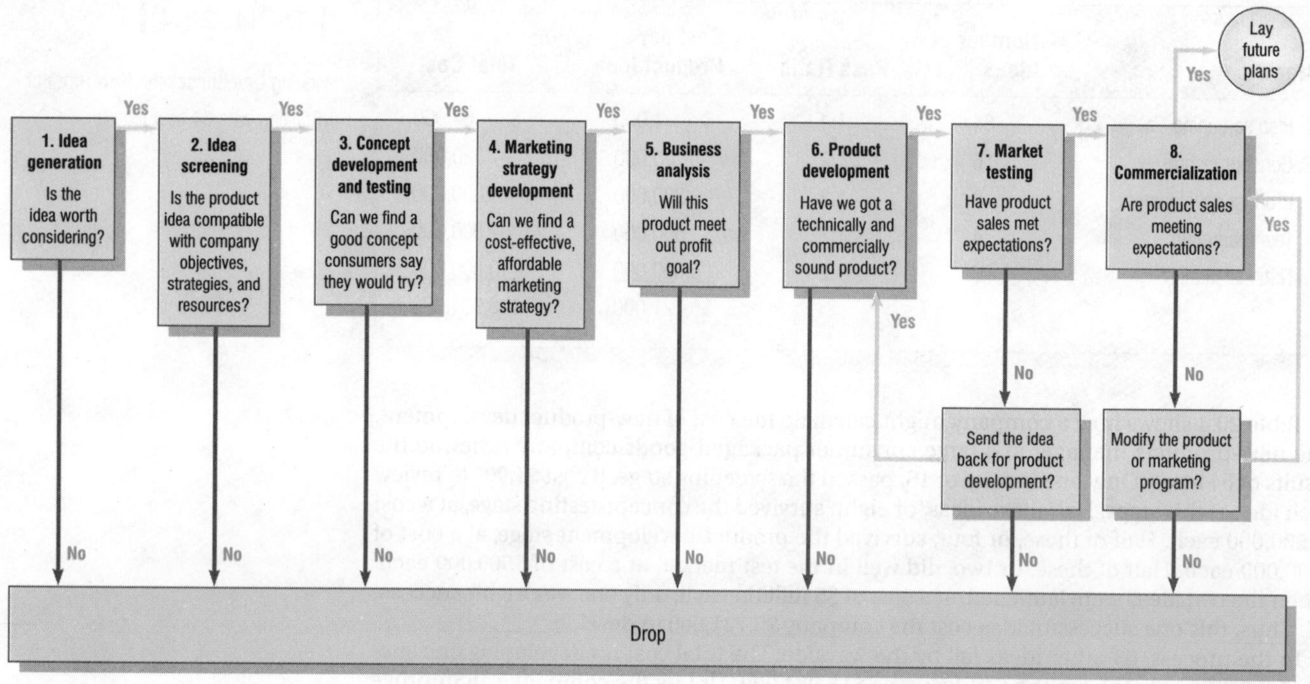

FIG. 20.2 The New-Product Development Decision Process

These "intrapreneurs" are relieved of their other duties and given a budget, time frame, and "skunkworks" setting. *Skunkworks* are informal workplaces, sometimes garages, where intrapreneurial teams attempt to develop new products.

Cross-functional teams can collaborate and use concurrent new-product development to push new products to market.[33] Concurrent product development resembles a rugby match, with team members passing the new product back and forth as they head toward the goal. Using this system, the Allen-Bradley Corporation (a maker of industrial controls) was able to develop a new electrical control device in just two years, as opposed to six under its old system. Cross-functional teams help ensure that engineers are not driven to create a "better mousetrap" when potential customers don't need or want one.

Many top companies use the *stage-gate system* to manage the innovation process.[34] They divide the process into stages, at the end of each being a gate or checkpoint. The project leader, working with a cross-functional team, must bring a set of known deliverables to each gate before the project can pass to the next stage. To move from the business plan stage into product development requires a convincing market research study of consumer needs and interest, a competitive analysis, and a technical appraisal. Senior managers review the criteria at each gate to make one of four decisions: *go, kill, hold,* or *recycle.* Stage-gate systems make the innovation process visible to all involved and clarify the project leader's and team's responsibilities at each stage.[35]

The stages in the new-product development process are shown in Figure 20.2. Many firms have parallel sets of projects working through the process, each at a different stage.[36] Think of the process as a *funnel:* A large number of initial new-product ideas and concepts are winnowed down to a few high-potential products that are ultimately launched. But the process is not always linear. Many firms use a *spiral development process* that recognizes the value of returning to an earlier stage to make improvements before moving forward.[37]

::: Managing the Development Process: Ideas

Idea Generation

The new-product development process starts with the search for ideas. Some marketing experts believe the greatest opportunities and highest leverage with new products are found by uncovering the best possible set of unmet customer needs or technological innovation.[38] New-product ideas can come from interacting with various groups and using creativity-generating techniques.[39] (See "Marketing Memo: Ten Ways to Find Great New-Product Ideas.")

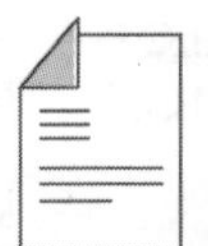

MARKETING MEMO | TEN WAYS TO FIND GREAT NEW-PRODUCT IDEAS

1. Run informal sessions where groups of customers meet with company engineers and designers to discuss problems and needs and brainstorm potential solutions.
2. Allow time off—scouting time—for technical people to putter on their own pet projects. 3M has allowed 15% time off; Rohm & Haas 10%.
3. Make a customer brainstorming session a standard feature of plant tours.
4. Survey your customers: Find out what they like and dislike in your and competitors' products.
5. Undertake "fly-on-the-wall" or "camping out" research with customers, as do Fluke and Hewlett-Packard.
6. Use iterative rounds: a group of customers in one room, focusing on identifying problems, and a group of your technical people in the next room, listening and brainstorming solutions. Immediately test proposed solutions with the group of customers.
7. Set up a keyword search that routinely scans trade publications in multiple countries for new-product announcements.
8. Treat trade shows as intelligence missions, where you view all that is new in your industry under one roof.
9. Have your technical and marketing people visit your suppliers' labs and spend time with their technical people—find out what's new.
10. Set up an idea vault, and make it open and easily accessed. Allow employees to review the ideas and add constructively to them.

Source: Adapted from Robert Cooper, *Product Leadership: Creating and Launching Superior New Products* (New York: Perseus Books, 1998).

INTERACTING WITH OTHERS Encouraged by the *open innovation* movement, many firms are increasingly going outside the company to tap external sources of new ideas,[40] including customers, employees, scientists, engineers, channel members, marketing agencies, top management, and even competitors. "Marketing Insight: P&G's New Connect-and-Develop Approach to Innovation" describes how that company has become more externally focused in its new-product development.

Customer needs and wants are the logical place to start the search.[41] One-on-one interviews and focus-group discussions can explore product needs and reactions. Griffin and Hauser suggest that conducting 10 to 20 in-depth experiential interviews per market segment often uncovers the vast majority of customer needs.[42] But many additional approaches can be profitable (see "Marketing Memo: Seven Ways to Draw New Ideas from Your Customers").

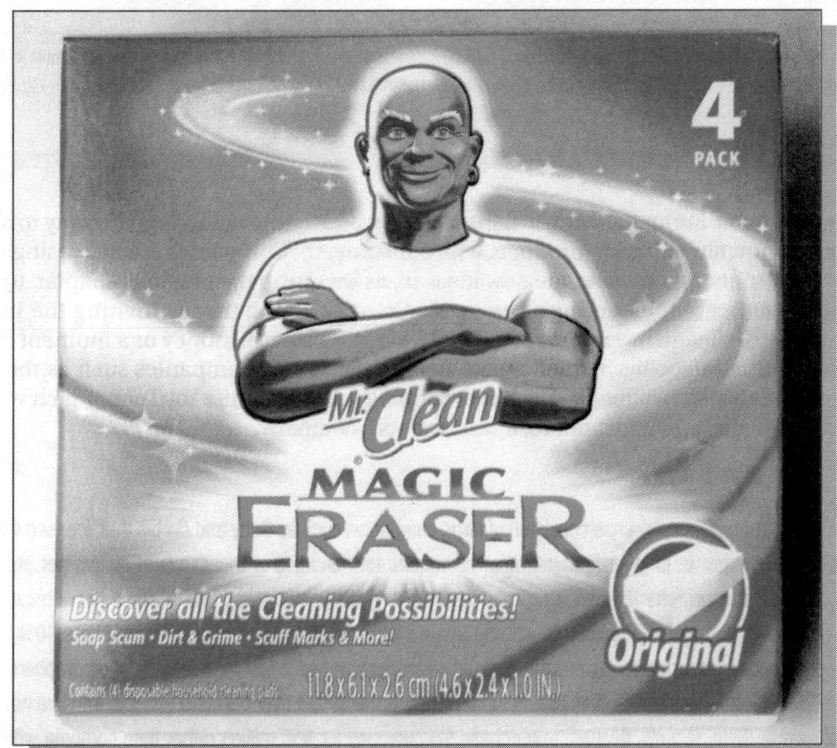

Mr. Clean Magic Eraser is one of Procter & Gamble's most recent innovations. The company has revamped the process by which it researches and develops new products, tapping more external sources than ever before.

MARKETING INSIGHT | P&G'S NEW CONNECT-AND-DEVELOP APPROACH TO INNOVATION

From fiscal years 2000 to 2004, Procter & Gamble's corporate profits jumped by almost 70%, to $9.8 billion, and revenues increased by almost 30%, to $51 billion. Helping fuel that growth were successful new products such as Swiffer (a sweeper for hard floor surfaces), Mr. Clean Magic Eraser (a soft cleaning pad that removes dirt and stains), and Actonel (a prescription medication for osteoporosis). In January 2005, P&G acquired Gillette for $54 billion. But to a large degree P&G's growth in recent years has been driven by what CEO A.G. Lafley calls "the core"—core markets, categories, brands, technologies, and capabilities—and innovation has been at the heart of that.

To more effectively develop its core, P&G adopted a "connect-and-develop" model that emphasizes the pursuit of more externally sourced innovation. Twenty-five percent of new products and technologies come from outside the company; Lafley wants to raise that to 50%, so "half would come out of P&G labs and half would come *through* P&G labs, from the outside."

P&G collaborates with organizations and individuals around the world, systematically searching for proven technologies, packages, and products it can improve, scale up, and market, either on its own or in partnership with other companies. It has forged strong relationships with external designers, distributing product development around the world to increase what P&G calls "consumer sensing," and even bringing John Osher, who invented the successful Crest SpinBrush electric rotating toothbrush, inside the company for a period to help make it more innovative.

To focus its idea search, P&G identifies the top 10 customer needs, closely related products that could leverage or benefit from existing brand equity, and technology "game boards" that map the flow of technology adoption across different product categories. With these sources as boundaries, P&G may consult government and private labs, as well as academic and other research institutions; suppliers, retailers, competitors, development and trade partners; VC firms; and individual entrepreneurs. P&G uses online networks to reach thousands of experts worldwide.

All these connections have helped to produce 100 new products in two years. For example, new ink-jet technology for printing edible images on cakes invented by a professor in Bologona, Italy, was used to create Pringles potato chips with jokes and pictures printed on them. The product was developed two to three years faster than usual at a fraction of the cost and resulted in double-digit growth for the Pringles brand. P&G has identified three core requirements for a successful connect-and-develop strategy:

1. Never assume that "ready-to-go" ideas found outside are truly ready to go. There will always be development work to do, including risky scale-up.
2. Don't underestimate the internal resources required. You'll need a full-time, senior executive to run any connect-and-develop initiative.
3. Never launch without a mandate from the CEO. Connect and develop cannot succeed if it's cordoned off in R&D. It must be a top-down, company-wide strategy.

The connect-and-develop model certainly seems to be working for P&G. Forty-five percent of initiatives in the product-development portfolio have key elements that were discovered externally. Through connect and develop—along with improvements in other aspects of innovation related to product cost, design, and marketing—R&D productivity has increased by nearly 60%. The innovation success rate has more than doubled, and the cost of innovation has fallen. R&D investment as a percentage of sales is down from 4.8% in 2000 to 3.4% today. Since 2000, P&G's share price has doubled, and the company now has a portfolio of twenty-two billion-dollar brands.

Sources: Steve Hamm, "Speed Demons," *BusinessWeek*, March 27, 2006, pp. 69–76; Larry Huston and Nabil Sakkab, "Connect and Develop: Inside Procter & Gamble's New Model for Innovation," *Harvard Business Review* (March 2006): 58–66; Geoff Colvin, "Lafley and Immelt: In Search of Billions," *Fortune*, December 11, 2006, pp. 70–72; Rajat Gupta and Jim Wendler, "Leading Change: An Interview with the CEO of P&G," *McKinsey Quarterly* (July 2005).

The traditional company-centric approach to product innovation is giving way to a world in which companies cocreate products with consumers.[43] Companies are increasingly turning to "crowdsourcing" to generate new ideas or, as we saw in the previous chapter, to create consumer-generated marketing campaigns. Crowdsourcing means inviting the Internet community to help create content or software, often with prize money or a moment of glory involved. This strategy has helped create new products and companies such as the open-source encyclopedia, Wikipedia, the hugely popular video Web site YouTube, which was purchased by Google, and iStockphoto, a "microstock" company.

ISTOCKPHOTO

The stock photography industry once consisted of large companies such as Getty and Corbis that licensed their high-end photos and images to ad agencies and other customers for hundreds or thousands of dollars per photo. Then Calgary, Canada, photographer Bruce Livingstone began giving his photos away online. Once users began trading photos via the site, Livingstone decided to sell the images for a small fee and offer photographers 40% royalties. iStockphoto has been enormously successful, both as a company and as a tool for freelance photographers like Lisa Gagne: In 2006, Gagne became the first iStockphoto photographer to sell over 500,000 images, and she now makes six figures yearly. Getty recently decided to purchase the company for $50 million rather than compete with it.[44]

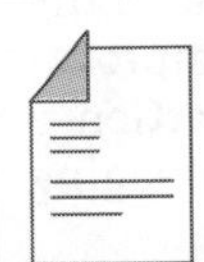

MARKETING MEMO | SEVEN WAYS TO DRAW NEW IDEAS FROM YOUR CUSTOMERS

1. ***Observe how your customers are using your product.*** Medtronic, a medical device company, has salespeople and market researchers regularly observe spine surgeons who use their products and competitive products, to learn how they can be improved. Similarly, GE has gathered ideas for improving CAT scanners by observing their use by skilled medical personnel.
2. ***Ask your customers about their problems with your products.*** Komatsu Heavy Equipment sent a group of engineers and designers to the United States for six months to ride with equipment drivers and learn how to make products better. Procter & Gamble, recognizing consumers were frustrated that potato chips would break and were difficult to save after opening the bag, designed Pringles to be uniform in size and encased in a tennis-ball-type can so consumers could open the can, consume a few unbroken chips, and close it again.
3. ***Ask your customers about their dream products.*** Ask your customers what they want your product to do, even if the ideal sounds impossible. One 70-year-old camera user told Minolta he would like the camera to make his subjects look better and not show their wrinkles and aging. In response, Minolta produced a camera with two lenses, one of which was for rendering softer images of the subjects.
4. ***Use a customer advisory board to comment on your company's ideas.*** Levi Strauss uses youth panels to discuss lifestyles, habits, values, and brand engagements; Cisco runs Customer Forums to improve its offerings; and Harley-Davidson solicits product ideas from its one million H.O.G. (Harley Owners Group) members.
5. ***Use Web sites for new ideas.*** Companies can use specialized search engines such as Technorati and Day Pop to find blogs and postings relevant to their businesses. P&G's site has *We're Listening* and *Share Your Thoughts* sections and Advisory Feedback sessions to gain advice and feedback from customers.
6. ***Form a brand community of enthusiasts who discuss your product.*** Harley-Davidson and Apple have strong brand enthusiasts and advocates; Sony engaged in collaborative dialogues with consumers to codevelop Sony's PlayStation 2. LEGO draws on kids and influential adult enthusiasts for feedback on new-product concepts in early stages of development.
7. ***Encourage or challenge your customers to change or improve your product.*** Salesforce.com wants its users to develop and share new software applications using simple programming tools. International Flavors & Fragrances gives a toolkit to its customers to modify specific flavors, which IFF then manufactures; LSI Logic Corporation also provides customers with do-it-yourself toolkits so that customers can design their own specialized chips; and BMW posted a toolkit on its Web site to let customers develop ideas using telematics and in-car online services.

Source: From an unpublished paper, Philip Kotler, "Drawing New Ideas from Your Customers," 2007.

Besides producing new and better ideas, cocreation can help customers feel closer to and more favorably towards the company, and to tell others of their involvement through favorable word of mouth.[45]

Lead users can be a good source of input when they innovate products without the consent or even the knowledge of the companies that produce them. Mountain bikes developed as a result of youngsters taking their bikes up to the top of a mountain and riding down. When the bikes broke, the youngsters began building more durable bikes and adding things such as motorcycle brakes, improved suspension, and accessories. The youngsters, not the companies, developed these innovations. Some companies, particularly those that want to appeal to hip young consumers, bring the lead users into their product-design process.

KARMALOOP

Karmaloop is one of the most successful retailers of "urban, streetwear, rave, and boutique clothing." Its brands include Triple Five Soul, SpiewaSoul, Kitchen Orange, and Zoo York. One of the keys to its success is that Karmaloop has developed a way for its lead users to spot fashion trends, model Karmaloop clothing, take on Karmaloop's guerrilla marketing, and even create their own clothing designs. Through Karmaloop's Kasbah E-marketplace, launched in 2006, underground and unknown designers can sell their wares. "Some of these guys are making stuff with their own printing presses. You can't get any closer to the ground than that," says Karmaloop founder Greg Selkoe, who works closely with his three-person IT team to keep the infrastructure of Kasbah evolving as quickly as customers' new ideas bubble up. To make sure the company is seen as legitimate, the site sells limited quantities and turns merchandise over quickly to keep offerings exclusive.[46]

Technical companies can learn a great deal by studying customers who make the most advanced use of the company's products and who recognize the need for improvements before other customers do.[47] Microsoft studied 13- to 24-year-olds—the NetGen—and developed its threedegrees software product to satisfy their instant messaging needs.[48]

Not everyone, however, believes a customer focus helps to create better new products. As Henry Ford famously said, "If I'd asked people what they wanted, they would have said a faster horse." Or as Bill Mitchell, the one-time head of GM car design in the 1960s said: "Frank Lloyd Wright did not go around ringing doorbells asking people what kind of houses they wanted! There is not one good-looking car I designed that market research had anything to do with." And some still caution that being overly focused on consumers who may not really know what they want, or what could be possible, can result in short-sighted product development and miss real potential breakthroughs.[49]

Employees throughout the company can be a source of ideas for improving production, products, and services. Toyota claims its employees submit 2 million ideas annually (about 35 suggestions per employee), over 85% of which are implemented. Kodak, Milliken, and other firms give monetary, holiday, or recognition awards to employees who submit the best ideas. Nokia inducts engineers with at least 10 patents into its "Club 10," recognizing them each year in a formal awards ceremony hosted by CEO Jorma Ollila.[50]

A company can motivate its employees to submit new ideas to an *idea manager* whose name and phone number are widely circulated. Internal brainstorming sessions also can be quite effective—if they are conducted correctly. "Marketing Memo: How to Run a Successful Brainstorming Session" provides some brainstorming guidelines.

Companies can find good ideas by researching the products and services of competitors and other companies. They can find out what customers like and dislike about competitors' products. They can buy their competitors' products, take them apart, and build better ones. Company sales representatives and intermediaries are a particularly good source of ideas. These groups have firsthand exposure to customers and are often the first to learn about competitive developments. Electronic retailer Best Buy actually checks with venture capitalists to find out what start-ups are working on.

Top management can be another major source of ideas. Some company leaders, such as former CEO Andy Grove of Intel, take personal responsibility for technological innovation in their companies. New-product ideas can come from inventors, patent attorneys, university and commercial laboratories, industrial consultants, advertising agencies, marketing research firms, and industrial publications. However, although ideas can flow from many sources, their chances of receiving serious attention often depend on someone in the organization taking the role of product champion.

MARKETING MEMO | HOW TO RUN A SUCCESSFUL BRAINSTORMING SESSION

Group brainstorming sessions have much upside, but also downside. If done incorrectly, they are a painful waste of time that can frustrate and antagonize participants; if done correctly, they can create insights, ideas, and solutions that would have been impossible without everyone's participation. To ensure success, experts recommend the following guidelines:

1. There should be a trained facilitator to guide the session.
2. Participants must feel that they can express themselves freely.
3. Participants must see themselves as collaborators working towards a common goal.
4. Rules need to be set up and followed, so conversations don't get off track.
5. Participants must be given proper background preparation and materials so that they can get into the task quickly.
6. Individual sessions before and after the brainstorming workshop can be useful to think and learn about the topic ahead of time as well as reflect afterwards on what happened.
7. Brainstorming sessions must lead to a clear plan of action and implementation, so the ideas that materialize can provide tangible value.
8. Brainstorming sessions can do more than just generate ideas—they can help build teams and leave participants better informed and energized.

Sources: Linda Tischler, "Be Creative: You Have 30 Seconds," *Fast Company* (May 2007): 47–50; Michael Myser, "When Brainstorming Goes Bad," *Business 2.0* (October 2006): 76; Robert I. Sutton, "Eight Rules to Brilliant Brainstorming," *BusinessWeek IN Inside Innovation* (September 2006): 17–21.

CREATIVITY TECHNIQUES The following list is a sampling of techniques for stimulating creativity in individuals and groups.[51]

- ***Attribute listing.*** List the attributes of an object, such as a screwdriver. Then modify each attribute, such as replacing the wooden handle with plastic, providing torque power, adding different screw heads, and so on.
- ***Forced relationships.*** List several ideas and consider each in relation to each other idea. In designing new office furniture, for example, consider a desk, bookcase, and filing cabinet as separate ideas. Then imagine a desk with a built-in bookcase or a desk with built-in files or a bookcase with built-in files.
- ***Morphological analysis.*** Start with a problem, such as "getting something from one place to another via a powered vehicle." Now think of dimensions, such as the type of platform (cart, chair, sling, bed), the medium (air, water, oil, rails), and the power source (compressed air, electric motor, magnetic fields). By listing every possible combination, you can generate many new solutions.
- ***Reverse assumption analysis.*** List all the normal assumptions about an entity and then reverse them. Instead of assuming that a restaurant has menus, charges for food, and serves food, reverse each assumption. The new restaurant may decide to serve only what the chef bought that morning and cooked; may provide some food and charge only for how long the person sits at the table; and may design an exotic atmosphere and rent out the space to people who bring their own food and beverages.
- ***New contexts.*** Take familiar processes, such as people-helping services, and put them into a new context. Imagine helping dogs and cats instead of people with day care service, stress reduction, psychotherapy, animal funerals, and so on. As another example, instead of sending hotel guests to the front desk to check in, greet them at curbside and use a wireless device to register them.
- ***Mind mapping.*** Start with a thought, such as a car, write it on a piece of paper, then think of the next thought that comes up (say Mercedes), link it to car, then think of the next association (Germany), and do this with all associations that come up with each new word. Perhaps a whole new idea will materialize.

Increasingly, new-product ideas arise from *lateral marketing* that combines two product concepts or ideas to create a new offering. Here are some successful examples:

- Gas station stores = gas stations + food
- Cyber cafés = cafeteria + Internet
- Cereal bars = cereal + snacking
- Kinder Surprise = candy + toy
- Sony Walkman = audio + portable

Idea Screening

In screening ideas, the company must avoid two types of errors. A *DROP-error* occurs when the company dismisses a good idea. It is extremely easy to find fault with other people's ideas (Figure 20.3). Some companies shudder when they look back at ideas they dismissed or breathe sighs of relief when they realize how close they came to dropping what eventually became a huge success. This was the case with the hit television show *Friends.*

FRIENDS

The NBC situation comedy *Friends* enjoyed a 10-year run from 1994 to 2004 as a perennial ratings powerhouse. But the show almost didn't see the light of the day. According to an internal NBC research report, the pilot episode was described as "not very entertaining, clever, or original" and was given a failing grade, scoring 41 out of 100. Ironically, the pilot for an earlier hit sitcom, *Seinfeld,* also was rated "weak," although the pilot for the medical drama *ER* scored a healthy 91. Courtney Cox's Monica was the *Friends* character who scored best with test audiences, but characters portrayed by Lisa Kudrow and Matthew Perry were deemed to have marginal appeal, and the Rachel, Ross, and Joey characters scored even lower. Adults 35 and over in the sample found the characters as a whole, "smug, superficial, and self-absorbed."[52]

FIG. 20.3

Forces Fighting New Ideas

Source: With permission of Jerold Panas, Young & Partners Inc.

An idea that almost didn't get off the storyboard was the pilot for *Friends*, one of the longest-running hit comedies on television. The test episode was deemed "not very entertaining, clever, or original." Dismissing an idea that later proves successful is the marketer's nightmare called a DROP-error.

A *GO-error* occurs when the company permits a poor idea to move into development and commercialization. An *absolute product failure* loses money; its sales do not cover variable costs. A *partial product failure* loses money, but its sales cover all its variable costs and some of its fixed costs. A *relative product failure* yields a profit lower than the company's target rate of return.

The purpose of screening is to drop poor ideas as early as possible. The rationale is that product-development costs rise substantially with each successive development stage. Most companies require new-product ideas to be described on a standard form for a new-product committee's review. The description states the product idea, the target market, and the competition and roughly estimates market size, product price, development time and costs, manufacturing costs, and rate of return.

The executive committee then reviews each idea against a set of criteria. Does the product meet a need? Would it offer superior value? Can it be distinctively advertised? Does the company have the necessary know-how and capital? Will the new product deliver the expected sales volume, sales growth, and profit? Consumer input may be necessary to tap into marketplace realities.[53]

Management can rate the surviving ideas using a weighted-index method like that in Table 20.5. The first column lists factors required for successful product launches, and the second column assigns importance weights. The third column scores the product idea on a scale from 0 to 1.0, with 1.0 the highest score. The final step multiplies each factor's importance by the product score to obtain an overall rating. In this example, the product idea scores 0.69, which places it in the "good idea" level. The purpose of this basic rating device is to promote systematic evaluation and discussion. It is not supposed to make the decision for management.

As the idea moves through development, the company will need to constantly revise its estimate of the product's overall probability of success, using the following formula:

$$\text{Overall probability of success} = \text{Probability of technical completion} \times \text{Probability of commercialization given technical completion} \times \text{Probability of economic success given commercialization}$$

For example, if the three probabilities are estimated as 0.50, 0.65, and 0.74, respectively, the overall probability of success is 0.24. The company then must judge whether this probability is high enough to warrant continued development.

TABLE 20.5

Product–Idea Rating Device

Product Success Requirements	Relative Weight (a)	Product Score (b)	Product Rating (c = a × b)
Unique or superior product	.40	.8	.32
High performance-to-cost ratio	.30	.6	.18
High marketing dollar support	.20	.7	.14
Lack of strong competition	.10	.5	.05
Total	1.00		.69[a]

[a]Rating scale: .00–.30 poor; .31–.60 fair; .61–.80 good. Minimum acceptance rate: .61

::: Managing the Development Process: Concept to Strategy

Attractive ideas must be refined into testable product concepts. A *product idea* is a possible product the company might offer to the market. A *product concept* is an elaborated version of the idea expressed in consumer terms.

Concept Development and Testing

CONCEPT DEVELOPMENT Let us illustrate concept development with the following situation: A large food-processing company gets the idea of producing a powder to add to milk to increase its nutritional value and taste. This is a product *idea*, but consumers don't buy product ideas; they buy product *concepts*.

A product idea can be turned into several concepts. The first question is: Who will use this product? The powder can be aimed at infants, children, teenagers, young or middle-aged adults, or older adults. Second, what primary benefit should this product provide? Taste, nutrition, refreshment, energy? Third, when will people consume this drink? Breakfast, midmorning, lunch, midafternoon, dinner, late evening? By answering these questions, a company can form several concepts:

- ***Concept 1.*** An instant breakfast drink for adults who want a quick nutritious breakfast without preparation.
- ***Concept 2.*** A tasty snack for children to drink as a midday refreshment.
- ***Concept 3.*** A health supplement for older adults to drink in the late evening before they go to bed.

Each concept represents a *category concept* that defines the product's competition. An instant breakfast drink would compete against bacon and eggs, breakfast cereals, coffee and pastry, and other breakfast alternatives. A tasty snack drink would compete against soft drinks, fruit juices, sports drinks, and other thirst quenchers.

Suppose the instant-breakfast-drink concept looks best. The next task is to show where this powdered product would stand in relationship to other breakfast products. *Perceptual maps* are a visual way to display consumer perceptions and preferences. They provide quantitative portrayals of market situations and how consumers see different products, services, and brands along various dimensions. By overlaying consumer preferences with brand perceptions, marketers can reveal "holes" or "openings" that suggest unmet consumer needs.

Figure 20.4a uses the two dimensions of cost and preparation time to create a *product-positioning map* for the breakfast drink. An instant breakfast drink offers low cost and quick preparation. Its nearest competitor is cold cereal or breakfast bars; its most distant competitor is bacon and eggs. These contrasts can help communicate and promote the concept to the market.

Next, the product concept becomes a *brand concept*. Figure 20.4b is a *brand-positioning map*, a perceptual map showing the current positions of three existing brands of instant breakfast drinks (A–C), as seen by consumers. It can also be useful to overlay consumer preferences on to the map in terms of their current or desired preferences. Figure 20.4b also shows that there are four segments of consumers (1–4) whose preferences are clustered around the points displayed on the map.

The brand-positioning map helps the company to decide how much to charge and how calorific to make its drink. Three segments (1–3) are well served by existing brands (A–C). The company would not want to position itself next to one of those existing brands, unless that brand is weak or inferior or market demand was high enough to be shared. As it turns out, the new brand would be distinctive in the medium-price, medium-calorie market or in the high-price, high-calorie market. There is also a segment of consumers (4) clustered fairly near the medium-price, medium-calorie market, suggesting that it may offer the greatest opportunity.

CONCEPT TESTING Concept testing means presenting the product concept, symbolically or physically, to target consumers and getting their reactions. The more the tested concepts resemble the final product or experience, the more dependable concept testing is. Concept

(a) Product-positioning Map (Breakfast Market)

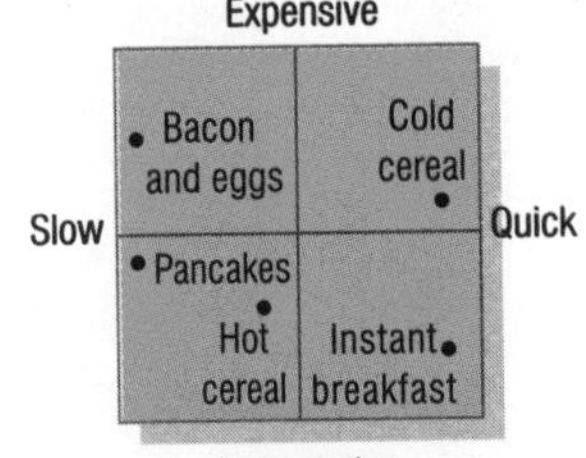

(b) Brand-positioning Map (Instant Breakfast Market)

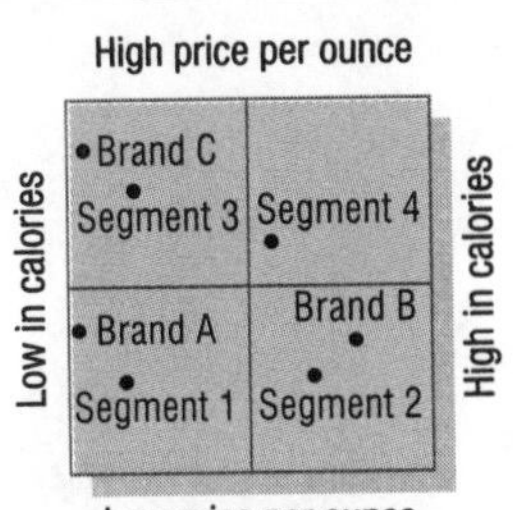

FIG. 20.4

Product and Brand Positioning

Computer-assisted rapid prototyping made it possible for the Kendall-Jackson winery to quickly develop two separate brands that helped it sell an unexpected short-term oversupply of wine.

testing of prototypes can help avoid costly mistakes, but it may be especially challenging with radically different, new-to-the-world products.[54]

In the past, creating physical prototypes was costly and time consuming, but today firms can use *rapid prototyping* to design products on a computer, and then produce rough models of each to show potential consumers for their reactions. In response to a short-term oversupply of wine in the marketplace, the makers of Kendall-Jackson developed two brands by using rapid prototyping to quickly bring its ideas to life, selling 100,000 cases, 10 times more than expected, for each brand in the process.[55] Companies are also using *virtual reality* to test product concepts. Virtual reality programs use computers and sensory devices (such as gloves or goggles) to simulate reality.

Concept testing presents consumers with an elaborated version of the concept. Here is the elaboration of concept 1 in our milk example:

> Our product is a powdered mixture added to milk to make an instant breakfast that gives the person all the day's needed nutrition along with good taste and high convenience. The product comes in three flavors (chocolate, vanilla, and strawberry) and individual packets, six to a box, at $2.49 a box.

After receiving this information, researchers measure product dimensions by having consumers respond to the following types of questions:

1. ***Communicability and believability***—Are the benefits clear to you and believable? If the scores are low, the concept must be refined or revised.
2. ***Need level***—Do you see this product solving a problem or filling a need for you? The stronger the need, the higher the expected consumer interest.
3. ***Gap level***—Do other products currently meet this need and satisfy you? The greater the gap, the higher the expected consumer interest. Marketers can multiply the need level by the gap level to produce a *need-gap score.* A high score means the consumer sees the product as filling a strong need not satisfied by available alternatives.
4. ***Perceived value***—Is the price reasonable in relationship to value? The higher the perceived value, the higher is expected consumer interest.
5. ***Purchase intention***—Would you (definitely, probably, probably not, definitely not) buy the product? Consumers who answered the first three questions positively should answer "Definitely" here.
6. ***User targets, purchase occasions, purchasing frequency***—Who would use this product, when, and how often?

Respondents' answers indicate whether the concept has a broad and strong consumer appeal, what products it competes against, and which consumers are the best targets. The need-gap levels and purchase-intention levels can be checked against norms for the product category to see whether the concept appears to be a winner, a long shot, or a loser. One food manufacturer rejects any concept that draws a definitely-would-buy score lower than 40%.

CONJOINT ANALYSIS We measure consumer preferences for alternative product concepts with **conjoint analysis**, a method for deriving the utility values that consumers attach to varying levels of a product's attributes.[56] Conjoint analysis has become one of the most popular concept-development and testing tools. For example, Marriott used it to design its Courtyard hotel concept.[57]

With conjoint analysis, respondents see different hypothetical offers formed by combining varying levels of the attributes, then rank the various offers. Management can identify the most appealing offer and its estimated market share and profit. Green and Wind have illustrated this approach in connection with developing a new spot-removing, carpet-cleaning agent for home use.[58] Suppose the new-product marketer is considering five design elements:

- Three package designs (A, B, C—see Figure 20.5)
- Three brand names (K2R, Glory, Bissell)
- Three prices ($1.19, $1.39, $1.59)
- A possible *Good Housekeeping* seal (yes, no)
- A possible money-back guarantee (yes, no)

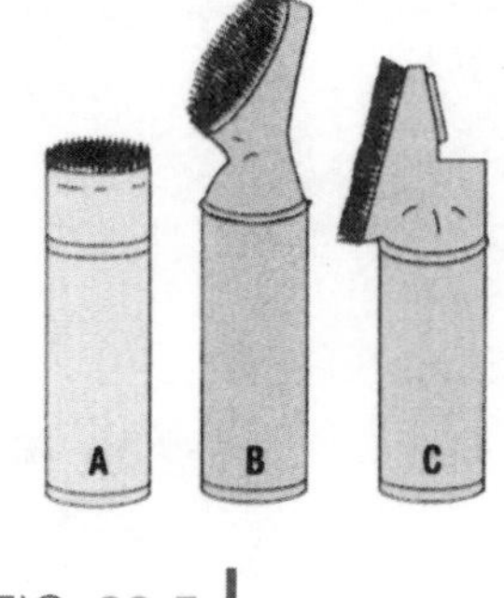

FIG. 20.5

Samples for Conjoint Analysis

Although the researcher can form 108 possible product concepts ($3 \times 3 \times 3 \times 2 \times 2$), it would be too much to ask consumers to rank 108 concepts. A sample of, say, 18 contrasting product concepts is feasible, and consumers would rank them from most to least preferred.

The marketer now uses a statistical program to derive the consumer's utility functions for each of the five attributes (see Figure 20.6). Utility ranges between zero and one; the higher the utility, the stronger the consumer's preference for that level of the attribute. Looking at packaging, we see that package B is the most favored, followed by C and then A (A hardly has any utility). The preferred names are Bissell, K2R, and Glory, in that order. The consumer's utility varies inversely with price. A *Good Housekeeping* seal is preferred, but it does not add that much utility and may not be worth the effort to obtain it. A money-back guarantee is strongly preferred.

The consumer's most desired offer is package design B, brand name Bissell, priced at $1.19, with a *Good Housekeeping* seal and a money-back guarantee. We can also determine the relative importance of each attribute to this consumer—the difference between the highest and lowest utility level for that attribute. The greater the difference, the more important the attribute. Clearly, this consumer sees price and package design as the most important attributes, followed by money-back guarantee, brand name, and a *Good Housekeeping* seal.

Preference data from a sufficient sample of target consumers helps us estimate the market share any specific offer is likely to achieve, given any assumptions about competitive response. Still, the company may not launch the market offer that promises to gain the greatest market share, because of cost considerations. The most customer-appealing offer is not always the most profitable offer to make.

Under some conditions, researchers will collect the data not with a full-profile description of each offer, but by presenting two factors at a time. For example, respondents may see a table with three price levels and three package types and indicate which of the nine

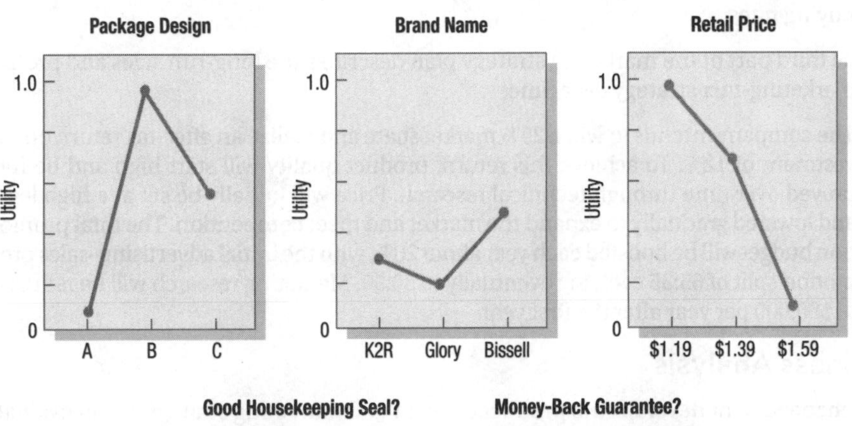

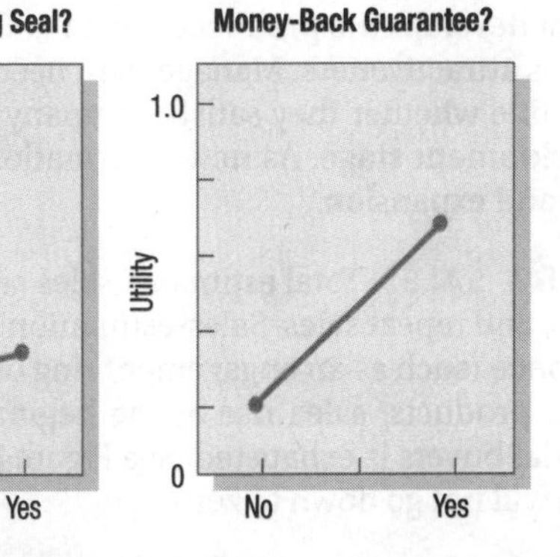

FIG. 20.6

Utility Functions Based on Conjoint Analysis

combinations they would like most, second-best, and so on. A further table consists of trade-offs between two other variables. The trade-off approach may be easier to use when there are many variables and possible offers. However, it is less realistic in that respondents are focusing on only two variables at a time. Adaptive conjoint analysis (ACA) is a "hybrid" data collection technique that combines self-explicated importance ratings with pair-wise trade-off tasks.

Marketing Strategy Development

Following a successful concept test, the new-product manager will develop a preliminary three-part strategy plan for introducing the new product into the market. The first part describes the target market's size, structure, and behavior; the planned product positioning; and the sales, market share, and profit goals sought in the first few years:

> The target market for the instant breakfast drink is families with children who are receptive to a new, convenient, nutritious, and inexpensive form of breakfast. The company's brand will be positioned at the higher-price, higher-quality end of the instant-breakfast-drink category. The company will aim initially to sell 500,000 cases or 10% of the market, with a loss in the first year not exceeding $1.3 million. The second year will aim for 700,000 cases or 14% of the market, with a planned profit of $2.2 million.

The second part outlines the planned price, distribution strategy, and marketing budget for the first year:

> The product will be offered in chocolate, vanilla, and strawberry, in individual packets of six to a box, at a retail price of $2.49 a box. There will be 48 boxes per case, and the case price to distributors will be $24. For the first two months, dealers will be offered one case free for every four cases bought, plus cooperative-advertising allowances. Free samples will be distributed door-to-door. Coupons for 20 cents off will appear in newspapers. The total sales promotional budget will be $2.9 million. An advertising budget of $6 million will be split 50:50 between national and local. Two-thirds will go into television and one-third into newspapers. Advertising copy will emphasize the benefit concepts of nutrition and convenience. The advertising-execution concept will revolve around a small boy who drinks instant breakfast and grows strong. During the first year, $100,000 will be spent on marketing research to buy store audits and consumer-panel information to monitor market reaction and buying rates.

The third part of the marketing strategy plan describes the long-run sales and profit goals and marketing-mix strategy over time:

> The company intends to win a 25% market share and realize an after-tax return on investment of 12%. To achieve this return, product quality will start high and be improved over time through technical research. Price will initially be set at a high level and lowered gradually to expand the market and meet competition. The total promotion budget will be boosted each year about 20%, with the initial advertising–sales promotion split of 65:35 evolving eventually to 50:50. Marketing research will be reduced to $60,000 per year after the first year.

Business Analysis

After management develops the product concept and marketing strategy, it can evaluate the proposal's business attractiveness. Management needs to prepare sales, cost, and profit projections to determine whether they satisfy company objectives. If they do, the concept can move to the development stage. As new information comes in, the business analysis will undergo revision and expansion.

ESTIMATING TOTAL SALES Total estimated sales are the sum of estimated first-time sales, replacement sales, and repeat sales. Sales-estimation methods depend on whether the product is purchased once (such as an engagement ring or retirement home), infrequently, or often. For one-time products, sales rise at the beginning, peak, and approach zero as the number of potential buyers is exhausted (see Figure 20.7a). If new buyers keep entering the market, the curve will not go down to zero.

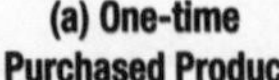

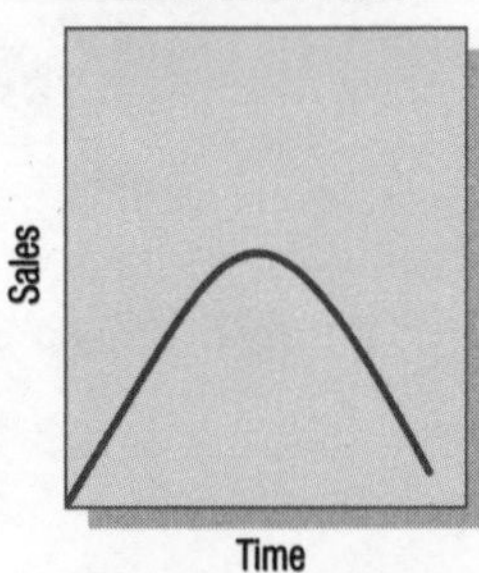

(b) Infrequently
Purchased Product

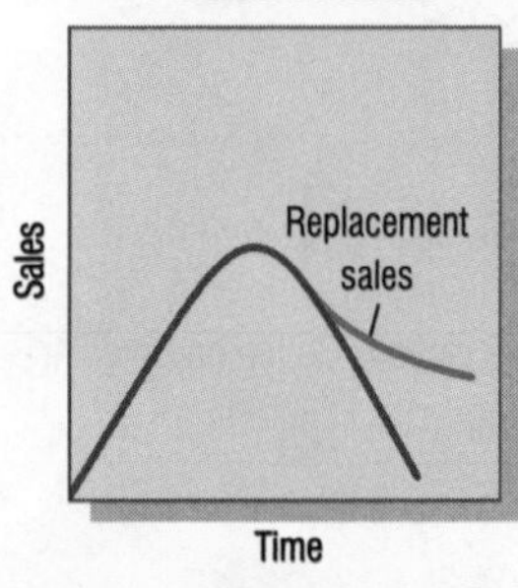

(c) Frequently
Purchased Product

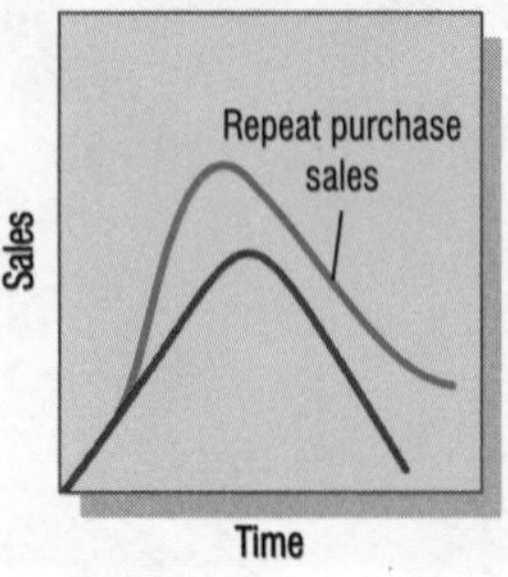

FIG. 20.7

Product Life-Cycle Sales for Three Types of Products

Infrequently purchased products—such as automobiles, toasters, and industrial equipment—exhibit replacement cycles dictated by physical wear or obsolescence associated with changing styles, features, and performance. Sales forecasting for this product category calls for estimating first-time sales and replacement sales separately (see Figure 20.7b).

Frequently purchased products, such as consumer and industrial nondurables, have product life-cycle sales resembling Figure 20.7c. The number of first-time buyers initially increases and then decreases as fewer buyers are left (assuming a fixed population). Repeat purchases occur soon, providing the product satisfies some buyers. The sales curve eventually falls to a plateau representing a level of steady repeat-purchase volume; by this time, the product is no longer a new product.

In estimating sales, the manager's first task is to estimate first-time purchases of the new product in each period. To estimate replacement sales, management researches the product's *survival-age distribution*—that is, the number of units that fail in year one, two, three, and so on. The low end of the distribution indicates when the first replacement sales will take place. Because replacement sales are difficult to estimate before the product is in use, some manufacturers base the decision to launch a new product solely on the estimate of first-time sales.

For a frequently purchased new product, the seller estimates repeat sales as well as first-time sales. A high rate of repeat purchasing means customers are satisfied; sales are likely to stay high even after all first-time purchases take place. The seller should note the percentage of repeat purchases in each repeat-purchase class: those who rebuy once, twice, three times, and so on. Some products and brands are bought a few times and dropped.[59]

ESTIMATING COSTS AND PROFITS Costs are estimated by the R&D, manufacturing, marketing, and finance departments. Table 20.6 illustrates a five-year projection of sales, costs, and profits for the instant breakfast drink.

Row 1 shows projected sales revenue over the five-year period. The company expects to sell $11,889,000 (approximately 500,000 cases at $24 per case) in the first year. Behind this projection is a set of assumptions about the rate of market growth, the company's market share, and the factory-realized price. *Row 2* shows the cost of goods sold, which hovers around 33% of sales revenue. We find this cost by estimating the average cost of labor, ingredients, and packaging per case. *Row 3* shows the expected gross margin, the difference between sales revenue and cost of goods sold.

Row 4 shows anticipated development costs of $3.5 million, including product-development cost, marketing research costs, and manufacturing development costs. *Row 5* shows the estimated marketing costs over the five-year period to cover advertising, sales promotion, and marketing research and an amount allocated for sales-force coverage and

TABLE 20.6 Projected Five-Year Cash Flow Statement (in thousands of dollars)

	Year 0	Year 1	Year 2	Year 3	Year 4	Year 5
1. Sales revenue	$ 0	$11,889	$15,381	$19,654	$28,253	$32,491
2. Cost of goods sold	0	3,981	5,150	6,581	9,461	10,880
3. Gross margin	0	7,908	10,231	13,073	18,792	21,611
4. Development costs	−3,500	0	0	0	0	0
5. Marketing costs	0	8,000	6,460	8,255	11,866	13,646
6. Allocated overhead	0	1,189	1,538	1,965	2,825	3,249
7. Gross contribution	−3,500	−1,281	2,233	2,853	4,101	4,716
8. Supplementary contribution	0	0	0	0	0	0
9. Net contribution	−3,500	−1,281	2,233	2,853	4,101	4,716
10. Discounted contribution (15%)	−3,500	−1,113	1,691	1,877	2,343	2,346
11. Cumulative discounted cash flow	−3,500	−4,613	−2,922	−1,045	1,298	3,644

marketing administration. *Row 6* shows the allocated overhead to this new product to cover its share of the cost of executive salaries, heat, light, and so on.

Row 7, the gross contribution, is gross margin minus the preceding three costs. *Row 8*, supplementary contribution, lists any change in income to other company products caused by the new-product introduction. *Dragalong income* is additional income to them, and *cannibalized income* is reduced income.[60] Table 20.6 assumes no supplementary contributions. *Row 9* shows net contribution, which in this case is the same as gross contribution. *Row 10* shows discounted contribution—that is, the present value of each future contribution discounted at 15% per annum. For example, the company will not receive $4,716,000 until the fifth year. This amount is worth only $2,345,000 today if the company can earn 15% on its money through other investments.[61]

Finally, *row 11* shows the cumulative discounted cash flow, the accumulation of the annual contributions in row 10. Two things are of central interest. First is the maximum investment exposure, the highest loss the project can create. The company will be in a maximum loss position of $4,613,000 in year 1. The second is the payback period, the time when the company recovers all its investment, including the built-in return of 15%. The payback period here is about three and a half years. Management must decide whether to risk a maximum investment loss of $4.6 million and a possible payback period of three and a half years.

Companies use other financial measures to evaluate the merit of a new-product proposal. The simplest is **breakeven analysis**, which estimates how many units the company must sell (or how many years it will take) to break even with the given price and cost structure. If management believes sales could easily reach the break-even number, it is likely to move the project into product development.

A more complex method of estimating profit is **risk analysis**. Here we obtain three estimates (optimistic, pessimistic, and most likely) for each uncertain variable affecting profitability, under an assumed marketing environment and marketing strategy for the planning period. The computer simulates possible outcomes and computes a distribution showing the range of possible rates of returns and their probabilities.[62]

::: Managing the Development Process: Development to Commercialization

Up to now, the product has existed only as a word description, a drawing, or a prototype. The next step represents a jump in investment that dwarfs the costs incurred so far. The company will determine whether the product idea can translate into a technically and commercially feasible product. If not, the accumulated project cost will be lost, except for any useful information gained in the process.

Product Development

The job of translating target customer requirements into a working prototype is helped by a set of methods known as *quality function deployment* (QFD). The methodology takes the list of desired *customer attributes* (CAs) generated by market research and turns them into a list of *engineering attributes* (EAs) that engineers can use. For example, customers of a proposed truck may want a certain acceleration rate (CA). Engineers can turn this into the required horsepower and other engineering equivalents (EAs). The methodology measures the trade-offs and costs of meeting customer requirements. A major contribution of QFD is improved communication between marketers, engineers, and manufacturing people.[63]

PHYSICAL PROTOTYPES The R&D department will develop one or more physical versions of the product concept. Its goal is to find a prototype that embodies the key attributes described in the product-concept statement, that performs safely under normal use and conditions, and that the firm can produce within budgeted manufacturing costs. In the past, developing and manufacturing a successful prototype could take days, weeks, months, or even years. The Web now permits more rapid prototyping and more flexible development processes.[64] Sophisticated virtual-reality technology is also speeding the process. By designing and testing product designs through simulation, for example, companies achieve the flexibility to respond to new information and to resolve uncertainties by quickly exploring alternatives.

BOEING

Boeing designed its 777 aircraft on a totally digital basis. Engineers, designers, and more than 500 suppliers designed the aircraft on a special computer network without ever making a blueprint on paper. Project partners were connected by an extranet enabling them to communicate, share ideas, and work on the design at a distance. A computer-generated "human" could climb inside the three-dimensional design on-screen to show how difficult maintenance access would be for a live mechanic. Such computer modeling allowed engineers to spot design errors that otherwise would have remained undiscovered until a person began to work on a physical prototype. Avoiding the time and cost of building physical prototypes reduced development time and scrappage and rework by 60% to 90%.[65]

Lab scientists must not only design the product's functional characteristics, but also communicate its psychological aspects and brand image through physical cues. How will consumers react to different colors, sizes, and weights? In the case of a mouthwash, historically a yellow color supported an "antiseptic" claim (Listerine), a red color supported a "refreshing" claim (Lavoris), and a green or blue color supported a "cool" claim (Scope). Marketers need to supply lab people with information about what attributes consumers seek and how consumers judge whether these attributes are present.

CUSTOMER TESTS When the prototypes are ready, they must be put through rigorous functional tests and customer tests before they enter the marketplace. *Alpha testing* is testing the product within the firm to see how it performs in different applications. After refining the prototype further, the company moves to *beta testing* with customers.[66]

Consumer testing can take several forms, from bringing consumers into a laboratory to giving them samples to use in their homes. Procter & Gamble has on-site labs such as a diaper-testing center where dozens of mothers bring their babies to be studied. To develop its Cover Girl Outlast all-day lip color, P&G invited 500 women to come to its labs each morning to apply the lipstick, record their activities, and return eight hours later so it could measure remaining lip color, resulting in a product that came with a tube of glossy moisturizer that women can reapply on top of their color without having to look at a mirror. In-home placement tests are common for products ranging from ice cream flavors to new appliances. When DuPont developed its new synthetic carpeting, it installed free carpeting in several homes in exchange for the homeowners' willingness to report their likes and dislikes about the product.

How do we measure customer preferences? The *rank-order* method asks the consumer to rank the options. The *paired-comparison* method presents pairs of options and asks the consumer which one is preferred in each pair. The *monadic-rating* method asks the consumer to rate each product on a scale so marketers can derive the individual's preference order and levels.

Researchers for Hawaii Coffee Company are gathering in the aroma of a dish of coffee during a taste test to help design a new differentiated product for the company.

Market Testing

After management is satisfied with functional and psychological performance, the product is ready to be dressed up with a brand name and packaging and put into a market test. In an authentic setting, marketers can learn how large the market is and how consumers and dealers react to handling, using, and repurchasing the product.

Not all companies undertake market testing. A company officer at Revlon Inc. stated: "In our field—primarily higher-priced cosmetics not geared for mass distribution—it would be unnecessary for us to market test. When we develop a new product, say an improved liquid makeup, we know it's going to sell because we're familiar with the field. And we've got 1,500 demonstrators in department stores to promote it." Many companies, however, believe market testing can yield valuable information about buyers, dealers, marketing program effectiveness, and market potential. The main issues are: How much market testing should be done, and what kind(s)?

The amount of market testing is influenced by the investment cost and risk on the one hand, and the time pressure and research cost on the other. High-investment–high-risk products, where the chance of failure is high, must be market tested; the cost of the market tests will be an insignificant percentage of total project cost. High-risk products—those that create new-product categories (first instant breakfast drink) or have novel features (first gum-strengthening toothpaste)—warrant more market testing than modified products (another toothpaste brand).

The amount of market testing may be severely reduced if the company is under great time pressure because the season is just starting, or because competitors are about to launch their brands. When Kellogg's tracking results showed that General Mills' Toast-Ems toaster pastries were popular in test markets, it launched a nationwide marketing plan with its own Pop-Tarts toaster pastries, taking a large market share.[67] The company may prefer the risk of a product failure to the risk of losing distribution or market penetration on a highly successful product.

CONSUMER-GOODS MARKET TESTING Consumer-products tests seek to estimate four variables: *trial, first repeat, adoption,* and *purchase frequency.* The company hopes to find all these variables at high levels. Many consumers may try the product but few rebuy it; or it might achieve high permanent adoption but low purchase frequency (like gourmet frozen foods).

Here are four major methods of consumer-goods market testing, from least to most costly.

Sales-Wave Research In *sales-wave research,* consumers who initially try the product at no cost are reoffered it, or a competitor's product, at slightly reduced prices. The offer may be made as many as five times (sales waves), while the company notes how many customers selected that product again and their reported level of satisfaction. Sales-wave research can also expose consumers to one or more advertising concepts to measure the impact of that advertising on repeat purchase.

Sales-wave research can be implemented quickly, conducted with a fair amount of security, and carried out without final packaging and advertising. However, it does not indicate trial rates the product would achieve with different sales promotion incentives, because the consumers are preselected to try the product; nor does it indicate the brand's power to gain distribution and favorable shelf position.

Simulated Test Marketing Simulated test marketing calls for finding 30 to 40 qualified shoppers and questioning them about brand familiarity and preferences in a specific product category. These consumers attend a brief screening of both well-known and new TV commercials or print ads. One ad advertises the new product but is not singled out for attention. Consumers receive a small amount of money and are invited into a store where they may buy any items. The company notes how many consumers buy the new brand and competing brands. This provides a measure of the ad's relative effectiveness against competing ads in stimulating trial. Consumers are asked the reasons for their purchases or nonpurchases. Those who did not buy the new brand are given a free sample. Some weeks later, they are interviewed by phone to determine product attitudes, usage, satisfaction, and repurchase intention and are offered an opportunity to repurchase any products.

This method gives fairly accurate results on advertising effectiveness and trial rates (and repeat rates if extended) in a much shorter time and at a fraction of the cost of using real test markets. The results are incorporated into new-product forecasting models to project ultimate sales levels. Marketing research firms have reported surprisingly accurate predictions of sales levels of products that are subsequently launched in the market.[68] In a world where media and channels have become highly fragmented, however, it will become increasingly harder for simulated test marketing to truly simulate market conditions with only traditional approaches.

Controlled Test Marketing In controlled test marketing, a research firm manages a panel of stores that will carry new products for a fee. The company with the new product specifies the number of stores and geographic locations it wants to test. The research firm delivers the product to the participating stores and controls shelf position; number of facings, displays, and point-of-purchase promotions; and pricing. Electronic scanners measure sales at checkout. The company can also evaluate the impact of local advertising and promotions.

Controlled test marketing allows the company to test the impact of in-store factors and limited advertising on buying behavior. A sample of consumers can be interviewed later to give their impressions of the product. The company does not have to use its own sales force, give trade allowances, or "buy" distribution. However, controlled test marketing provides no information on how to sell the trade on carrying the new product. This technique also exposes the product and its features to competitors' scrutiny.

Test Markets The ultimate way to test a new consumer product is to put it into full-blown test markets. The company chooses a few representative cities, and the sales force tries to sell the trade on carrying the product and giving it good shelf exposure. The company puts on a full advertising and promotion campaign similar to the one it would use in national marketing. Test marketing also measures the impact of alternative marketing plans by varying the marketing program in different cities: A full-scale test can cost over $1 million, depending on the number of test cities, the test duration, and the amount of data the company wants to collect.

Management faces several decisions:

1. ***How many test cities?*** Most tests use two to six cities. The greater the possible loss, the greater the number of contending marketing strategies, the greater the regional differences, and the greater the chance of test-market interference by competitors, the more cities management should test.
2. ***Which cities?*** Each company must develop selection criteria such as having good media coverage, cooperative chain stores, and average competitive activity. How representative the city is of other markets must also be considered.
3. ***Length of test?*** Market tests last anywhere from a few months to a year. The longer the average repurchase period, the longer the test period.
4. ***What information to collect?*** Warehouse shipment data will show gross inventory buying but will not indicate weekly sales at the retail level. Store audits will show retail sales and competitors' market shares but will not reveal buyer characteristics. Consumer panels will indicate which people are buying which brands and their loyalty and switching rates. Buyer surveys will yield in-depth information about consumer attitudes, usage, and satisfaction.
5. ***What action to take?*** If the test markets show high trial and repurchase rates, the marketer should launch the product nationally; if a high trial rate and low repurchase rate, redesign or drop the product; if a low trial rate and high repurchase rate, develop marketing communications to convince more people to try it. If trial and repurchase rates are both low, abandon the product. Many managers find it difficult to kill a project that created much effort and attention even if they should, resulting in an unfortunate (and typically unsuccessful) escalation of commitment.[69]

In spite of its benefits, many companies today skip test marketing and rely on faster and more economical testing methods. General Mills prefers to launch new products in perhaps 25% of the country, an area too large for rivals to disrupt. Managers review retail scanner data, which tell them within days how the product is doing and what corrective fine-tuning to do. Colgate-Palmolive often launches a new product in a set of small "lead countries" and keeps rolling it out if it proves successful.

BUSINESS-GOODS MARKET TESTING Business goods can also benefit from market testing. Expensive industrial goods and new technologies will normally undergo alpha testing (within the company) and beta testing (with outside customers). During beta testing, the company's technical people observe how test customers use the product, a practice that often exposes unanticipated problems of safety and servicing and alerts the company to customer training and servicing requirements. The company can also observe how much value the equipment adds to the customer's operation as a clue to subsequent pricing.

The company will ask test customers to express their purchase intention and other reactions after the test. Companies must interpret beta test results carefully, because only a small number of test customers are used, they are not randomly drawn, and tests are somewhat customized to each site. Another risk is that test customers who are unimpressed with the product may leak unfavorable reports about it.

A second common test method for business goods is to introduce the new product at trade shows. The company can observe how much interest buyers show in the new product, how they react to various features and terms, and how many express purchase intentions or place orders.

New industrial products can be tested in distributor and dealer display rooms, where they may stand next to the manufacturer's other products and possibly competitors' products. This method yields preference and pricing information in the product's normal selling atmosphere. The disadvantages are that the customers might want to place early orders that cannot be filled, and those customers who come in might not represent the target market.

Industrial manufacturers come close to using full test marketing when they give a limited supply of the product to the sales force to sell in a limited number of areas that receive promotion support and printed catalog sheets.

Commercialization

If the company goes ahead with commercialization, it will face its largest costs to date.[70] It will need to contract for manufacture or build or rent a full-scale manufacturing facility. Another major cost is marketing. To introduce a major new consumer packaged good into the national market can cost from $25 million to as much as $100 million in advertising, promotion, and other communications in the first year. In the introduction of new food products, marketing expenditures typically represent 57% of sales during the first year. Most new-product campaigns rely on a sequenced mix of market communication tools.

WHEN (TIMING) In commercializing a new product, market-entry timing is critical. Suppose a company has almost completed the development work on its new product and learns that a competitor is nearing the end of its development work. The company faces three choices:

1. ***First entry***—The first firm entering a market usually enjoys the "first mover advantages" of locking up key distributors and customers and gaining leadership. But if the product is rushed to market before it is thoroughly debugged, the first entry can backfire.
2. ***Parallel entry***—The firm might time its entry to coincide with the competitor's entry. The market may pay more attention when two companies are advertising the new product.[71]
3. ***Late entry***—The firm might delay its launch until after the competitor has entered. The competitor will have borne the cost of educating the market, and its product may reveal faults the late entrant can avoid. The late entrant can also learn the size of the market.

The timing decision requires additional considerations.[72] If a new product replaces an older product, the company might delay the introduction until the old product's stock is drawn down. If the product is seasonal, it might be delayed until the right season arrives; often a product waits for a "killer application" to occur. Complicating new-product launches, many companies are encountering competitive "design-arounds"—rivals are imitating inventions but making their own versions just different enough to avoid patent infringement and the need to pay royalties.

WHERE (GEOGRAPHIC STRATEGY) The company must decide whether to launch the new product in a single locality, a region, several regions, the national market, or the international market. Most will develop a planned market rollout over time. Company size is an important factor here. Small companies will select an attractive city and put on a blitz campaign, entering other cities one at a time. Large companies will introduce their product into a whole region and then move to the next region. Companies with national distribution networks, such as auto companies, will launch their new models in the national market.

Most companies design new products to sell primarily in the domestic market. If the product does well, the company considers exporting to neighboring countries or the world market, redesigning if necessary. In choosing rollout markets, the major criteria are market potential, the company's local reputation, the cost of filling the pipeline, the cost of communication media, the influence of the area on other areas, and competitive penetration.

The presence of strong competitors will influence rollout strategy. Suppose McDonald's wants to launch a new chain of fast-food "McPizza" pizza parlors. Historically, Pizza Hut has been strongly entrenched on the East Coast, Domino's and Little Caesar's in the Midwest, Papa John's in the South, with all looking to compete in the West. McDonald's must carefully select a geographic rollout strategy that balances consumer, competitive, and company considerations.

With the Web connecting far-flung parts of the globe, competition is more likely to cross national borders. Companies are increasingly rolling out new products simultaneously across the globe, rather than nationally or even regionally. However, masterminding a global launch poses challenges, and a sequential rollout across countries may still be the best option.[73]

TO WHOM (TARGET-MARKET PROSPECTS) Within the rollout markets, the company must target its initial distribution and promotion to the best prospect groups. The company will have profiled these, and ideally they should be early adopters, heavy users, and opinion leaders who can be reached at low cost.[74] Few groups have all these characteristics. The company should rate the various prospect groups on these characteristics and target the best group. The aim is to generate strong sales as soon as possible to attract further prospects.

HOW (INTRODUCTORY MARKET STRATEGY) The company must develop an action plan for introducing the new product into the rollout markets. Because new-product launches often take longer and cost more money than expected, many potentially successful offerings suffer from underfunding. It's important to allocate sufficient time and resources—but also not to overspend—as the new product gains traction in the marketplace.[75]

A master of new-product introductions, Apple Computer staged a massive marketing blitz in 1998 to launch the iMac, its reentry into the computer PC business after a hiatus of 14 years. Five years later, Apple struck gold again with the launch of the iPod, as described in "Breakthrough Marketing: Apple iPod."

To coordinate the many activities involved in launching a new product, management can use network-planning techniques such as **critical path scheduling (CPS)**. This calls for developing a master chart showing the simultaneous and sequential activities that must take place to launch the product. By estimating how much time each activity takes, the planners estimate completion time for the entire project. Any delay in any activity on the critical path—the shortest route to completion—will cause the project to be delayed. If the launch must be completed earlier, the planner searches for ways to reduce time along the critical path.[77]

BREAKTHROUGH MARKETING | APPLE IPOD

In a few short years, the iPod MP3 music player has truly become a cultural phenomenon. Few people are without one. The iPod exemplified Apple's innovative design skills and looked, felt, and operated like no other. With the launch of iTunes Music Store, a dynamic duo of legally downloadable music and a cutting-edge portable music player caused iPod sales to skyrocket. To the delight of Apple (and the chagrin of competitor Sony), the iPod has become "the Walkman of the 21st century."

Beyond spurring sales, the iPod has been central in changing the way people listen to and use music. The shuffle feature of iPods helped people make connections between different genres of music. According to musician John Mayer, "People feel they're walking through musicology" when they use their iPods, leading them to listen to more music, and with more passion.[76] Podcasting enables users to replace radio broadcasts and listen to DJ sets without commercial interruption. The new video, photo, and phone features have the potential to change how people interact with those media as well.

Apple reached this impressive state of market domination through a combination of shrewd product innovation and clever marketing. It defined a broad access point for its target market—music lovers who wanted *their* music, whenever and wherever. The marketing effort was designed to appeal to Mac fans as well as people who had not used Apple products in the past. This broader access required a shift in Apple's channel strategies. Adding "mass electronic" retailers such as Best Buy and Circuit City to Apple's existing channels and company stores resulted in an increase of outlets from 4,000 to 21,000.

Besides this enhanced "push" effort, Apple also developed memorable, creative "pull" advertising that helped drive the popularity of the iPod. The Silhouettes campaign ran all over the world with a message simple enough to work across cultures, portraying the iPod as cool, but not so cool as to be beyond the reach of anyone who enjoyed music. Television commercials featured people in silhouette listening to iPods and dancing in front of neon backgrounds. Similar images populated print ads, billboards, and posters. Ad text such as "*iPod. Welcome to the digital music revolution. 10,000 songs in your pocket. Mac or PC*" told the story of iPod's capabilities in a simple, appealing way.

Apple's campaign also flooded a handful of big cities such as San Francisco and Shanghai with iPod billboards, bus posters, print ads, and TV commercials that were intended to spread the message "iPod is everywhere." The brand enjoyed exceedingly strong PR, buzz, and word of mouth. Apple has continually updated the iPod and released new versions, spawning an "iPod economy" of third-party accessories and add-ons. Even though some analysts thought sales might slow, consumers have continued to snap up the music players. By October 2007, more than 119 million iPod's had been sold worldwide and the iPod contributed one-third of Apple's corporate revenue. A halo effect from iPod was thought to help explain Apple's increase in market share in retail computers of more than 3 percentage points in recent years. With a wave of positive buzz and a promising sales start in the summer of 2007, Apple hoped to repeat the success of the iPod with its launch of the iPhone.

Sources: Terril Yue Jones, "How Long Can the iPod Stay on Top?" *Los Angeles Times*, March 5, 2006; Beth Snyder Bulik, "Grab an Apple and a Bag of Chips," *Advertising Age*, May 23, 2005; Jay Parsons, "A Is for Apple on iPod," *Dallas Morning News*, October 6, 2005; Peter Burrows, "Rock On, iPod," *BusinessWeek*, June 7, 2004, pp. 130–31; Jay Lyman, "Mini iPod Moving Quickly, Apple Says," *TechNewsWorld*, February 26, 2004; Steven Levy, "iPod Nation," *Newsweek*, July 25, 2004; www.apple.com; www.effie.org; "Apple Computer: iPod Silhouettes," New York Marketing Association.

The campaign for the Apple iPod was a masterful new-product introduction that helped the product quickly achieve a dominant market share.

::: The Consumer-Adoption Process

Adoption is an individual's decision to become a regular user of a product. The *consumer-adoption process* is followed by the *consumer-loyalty process,* which is the concern of the established producer. Years ago, new-product marketers used a *mass-market approach* to launch products, which had two main drawbacks: It called for heavy marketing expenditures, and it wasted many exposures. These drawbacks led to a second approach, *heavy-user target marketing.* This approach makes sense, provided that heavy users are identifiable and are early adopters. However, even within the heavy-user group, many heavy users are loyal to existing brands. New-product marketers now aim at early adopters and use the theory of innovation diffusion and consumer adoption to identify them.

Stages in the Adoption Process

An **innovation** is any good, service, or idea that someone *perceives* as new, no matter how long its history. Innovations take time to spread. Everett Rogers defines the **innovation diffusion process** as "the spread of a new idea from its source of invention or creation to its ultimate users or adopters."[78] The consumer-adoption process is the mental steps through which an individual passes from first hearing about an innovation to final adoption.[79]

Adopters of new products move through five stages:

1. ***Awarenes***—The consumer becomes aware of the innovation but lacks information about it.
2. ***Interest***—The consumer is stimulated to seek information about the innovation.
3. ***Evaluation***—The consumer considers whether to try the innovation.
4. ***Trial***—The consumer tries the innovation to improve his or her estimate of its value.
5. ***Adoption***—The consumer decides to make full and regular use of the innovation.

The new-product marketer should facilitate movement through these stages. A portable electric-dishwasher manufacturer might discover that many consumers are stuck in the interest stage; they do not buy because of their uncertainty and the large investment cost.[80] But these same consumers would be willing to use an electric dishwasher on a trial basis for a small monthly fee. The manufacturer should consider offering a trial-use plan with option to buy.

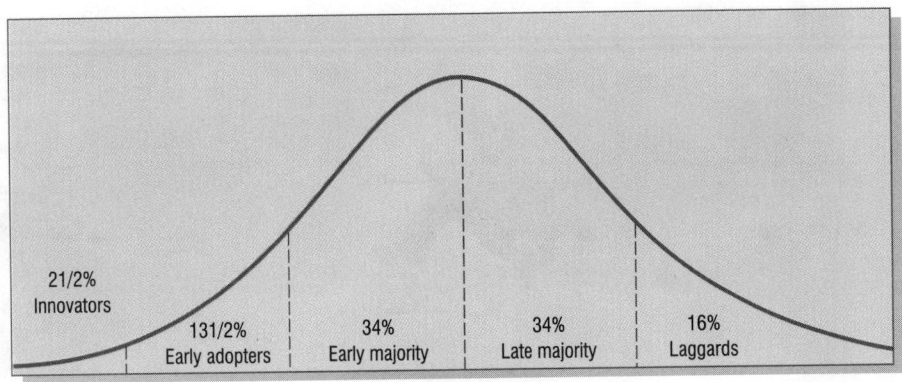

FIG. 20.8

Adopter Categorization on the Basis of Relative Time of Adoption of Innovations

Source: Redrawn from Everett M. Rogers, *Diffusion of Innovations* (New York: Free Press, 1983). Reprinted with permission of The Free Press, a Division of Simon & Schuster Adult Publishing Group, from *Diffusion of Innovations* by Everett M. Rogers.

Factors Influencing the Adoption Process

Marketers recognize the following characteristics of the adoption process: differences in individual readiness to try new products; the effect of personal influence; differing rates of adoption; and differences in organizations' readiness to try new products. Some researchers are focusing on use-diffusion processes as a complement to adoption process models, to see how consumers actually use new products.[81]

READINESS TO TRY NEW PRODUCTS AND PERSONAL INFLUENCE Everett Rogers defines a person's level of innovativeness as "the degree to which an individual is relatively earlier in adopting new ideas than the other members of his social system." In each product area, there are pioneers and early adopters. Some people are the first to adopt new clothing fashions or new appliances; some doctors are the first to prescribe new medicines; some farmers are the first to adopt new farming methods.[82] People fall into the adopter categories in Figure 20.8. After a slow start, an increasing number of people adopt the innovation, the number reaches a peak, and then it diminishes as fewer nonadopters remain. The five adopter groups differ in their value orientations and their motives for adopting or resisting the new product.[83]

- ***Innovators*** are technology enthusiasts; they are venturesome and enjoy tinkering with new products and mastering their intricacies. In return for low prices, they are happy to conduct alpha and beta testing and report on early weaknesses.
- ***Early adopters*** are opinion leaders who carefully search for new technologies that might give them a dramatic competitive advantage. They are less price sensitive and willing to adopt the product if given personalized solutions and good service support.
- ***Early majority*** are deliberate pragmatists who adopt the new technology when its benefits are proven and a lot of adoption has already taken place. They make up the mainstream market.
- ***Late majority*** are skeptical conservatives who are risk averse, technology shy, and price sensitive.
- ***Laggards*** are tradition-bound and resist the innovation until they find that the status quo is no longer defensible.

Each group must be approached with a different type of marketing if the firm wants to move its innovation through the full product life cycle.[84]

Personal influence is the effect one person has on another's attitude or purchase probability. Its significance is greater in some situations and for some individuals than others, and it is more important in the evaluation stage than the other stages. It has more influence on late adopters than early adopters and is more important in risky situations.

Companies often target innovators and early adopters with product rollouts. For Vespa scooters, Piaggio hired models to go around cafés and clubs in trendy Los Angeles areas to talk up the brand.[85] When Nike entered the skateboarding market, it recognized an anti-establishment, big-company bias from the target market could present a sizable challenge. To gain "street cred" with teen skaters, it sold exclusively to independent shops, advertised nowhere but skate magazines, and gained sponsorships from well-admired pro riders by engaging them in product design.[86]

Nike used carefully selected retail outlets and advertising media to avoid looking like a big corporation when it started marketing skateboards to the skeptical teen skater market. Pro riders who helped with product design also tailored the company's appeal.

CHARACTERISTICS OF THE INNOVATION Some products catch on immediately (rollerblades), whereas others take a long time to gain acceptance (diesel engine autos). Five characteristics influence the rate of adoption of an innovation. We will consider them in relation to the adoption of personal video recorders (PVRs) for home use, as exemplified by TiVo.[87]

The first characteristic is *relative advantage*—the degree to which the innovation appears superior to existing products. The greater the perceived relative advantage of using a PVR, say, for easily recording favorite shows, pausing live TV, or skipping commercials, the more quickly it will be adopted. The second is *compatibility*—the degree to which the innovation matches the values and experiences of the individuals. PVRs, for example, are highly compatible with the preferences of avid television watchers. Third is *complexity*—the degree to which the innovation is difficult to understand or use. PVRs are somewhat complex and will therefore take a slightly longer time to penetrate into home use. Fourth is *divisibility*—the degree to which the innovation can be tried on a limited basis. This provides a sizable challenge for PVRs—sampling can only occur in a retail store or perhaps a friend's house. Fifth is *communicability*—the degree to which the benefits of use are observable or describable to others. The fact that PVRs have some clear advantages can help create interest and curiosity.

Other characteristics that influence the rate of adoption are cost, risk and uncertainty, scientific credibility, and social approval. The new-product marketer must research all these factors and give the key ones maximum attention in designing the new product and marketing program.[88]

ORGANIZATIONS' READINESS TO ADOPT INNOVATIONS The creator of a new teaching method would want to identify innovative schools. The producer of a new piece of medical equipment would want to identify innovative hospitals. Adoption is associated with variables in the organization's environment (community progressiveness, community income), the organization itself (size, profits, pressure to change), and the administrators (education level, age, sophistication). Other forces come into play in trying to get a product adopted into organizations that receive the bulk of their funding from the government, such as public schools. A controversial or innovative product can be squelched by negative public opinion.

SUMMARY :::

1. Once a company has segmented the market, chosen its target customer groups and identified their needs, and determined its desired market positioning, it is ready to develop and launch appropriate new products and services. Marketing should participate with other departments in every stage of new-product development.
2. Successful new-product development requires the company to establish an effective organization for managing the development process. Companies can choose to use product managers, new-product managers, new-product committees, new-product departments, or new-product venture teams. Increasingly, companies are adopting cross-functional teams, connecting to individuals and organizations outside the company, and developing multiple product concepts.
3. Eight stages take place in the new-product development process: idea generation, screening, concept development and testing, marketing strategy development, business analysis, product development, market testing, and commercialization. At each stage, the company must determine whether the idea should be dropped or moved to the next stage.
4. The consumer-adoption process is the process by which customers learn about new products, try them, and adopt or reject them. Today many marketers are targeting heavy users and early adopters of new products, because both groups can be reached by specific media and tend to be opinion leaders. The consumer-adoption process is influenced by many factors beyond the marketer's control, including consumers' and organizations' willingness to try new products, personal influences, and the characteristics of the new product or innovation.

APPLICATIONS :::

Marketing Debate **Whom Should You Target with New Products?**

Some new-products experts maintain that getting close to customers through intensive research is the only way to develop successful new products. Other experts disagree and maintain that customers can't possibly provide useful feedback on what they don't know and can't provide insights that will lead to breakthrough products.

Take a position: Consumer research is critical to new-product development *versus* Consumer research may not be all that helpful in new-product development.

Marketing Discussion

Think about the last new product you bought. How do you think its success will be affected by the five characteristics of an innovation: relative advantage, compatibility, complexity, divisibility, and communicability?

IN THIS CHAPTER, WE WILL ADDRESS THE FOLLOWING QUESTIONS:

1. What factors should a company review before deciding to go abroad?
2. How can companies evaluate and select specific foreign markets to enter?
3. What are the major ways of entering a foreign market?
4. To what extent must the company adapt its products and marketing program to each foreign country?
5. How should the company manage and organize its international activities?

CHAPTER 21 ::: TAPPING INTO GLOBAL MARKETS

twenty-one

With faster communication, transportation, and financial flows, the world is rapidly shrinking. Products and services developed in one country are finding enthusiastic acceptance in others. A German businessman may wear an Italian suit to meet an English friend at a Japanese restaurant, who later returns home to drink Russian vodka and watch an American movie on a Korean TV. More and more countries are becoming increasingly multicultural. Companies need to be able to cross boundaries within and outside their country. Consider the international success of Nokia.

Nokia has made a remarkable transformation from an obscure Finnish conglomerate into the world's largest maker of mobile phones. Part of Nokia's success is due to the broad view it takes of its business, selling a wide range of products to consumers of all kinds all over the world. Nokia also takes a broad perspective on competition, viewing Apple, Sony, and Canon as threats as much as traditional rivals Motorola and Samsung. To sustain its market leadership, Nokia has launched a range of handsets, the Nseries, with advanced features such as music playing, video recording, and computing (e-mail). But Nokia wants to be a leader in all global markets, so it can't afford to sell just high-end products. With the bulk of industry growth coming from developing markets, Nokia has made sure its cheapest handsets are appealing—and profitable—in markets such >>>

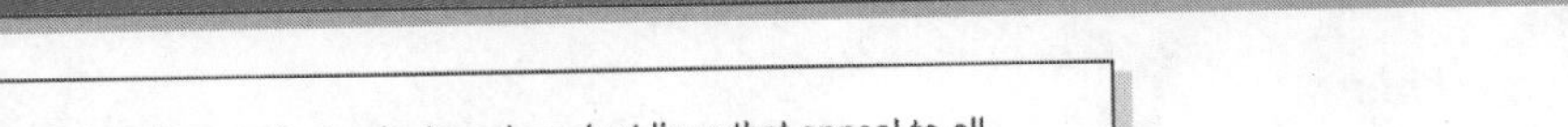

Nokia's global view motivates its broad product lines that appeal to all kinds of customers and price ranges all over the world.

as China, India, and Latin America. Along with a $750 handset with built-in global-positioning receivers, it also sells basic models that cost just $45. Although Nokia has struggled some in North America—in part because many networks there use a different wireless standard (CDMA) than in Europe (GSM)—its global footprint is still impressive. Of the 900 million mobile phones sold worldwide in 2006, 320 million were made by Nokia.[1]

Although opportunities to enter and compete in international markets are significant, the risks can also be high. Companies selling in global industries, however, have no choice but to internationalize their operations. In this chapter, we review the major decisions in expanding into global markets.

::: Competing on a Global Basis

Two hundred giant corporations, most larger than many national economies, together have sales that exceed a quarter of the world's economic activity. Altria, including its main subsidiary Philip Morris, is about the same size as the economy of New Zealand and operates in over 160 countries. Exports accounted for over one-quarter of U.S. GDP growth in 2006.[2]

Many companies have conducted international marketing for decades—firms such as Nestlé, Shell, Bayer, and Toshiba have been familiar around the world for years. But global competition is intensifying as new firms make their mark on the international stage. "Breakthrough Marketing: Samsung" describes the swift global ascent of that company.

Domestic companies that never thought about foreign competitors suddenly find them in their backyards. Newspapers report on the success of Japanese, German, Swedish, and Korean car imports in the U.S. market, and the loss of textile and shoe markets to imports from developing countries in Latin America, Eastern Europe, and Asia. Many companies thought of as U.S. firms are really foreign. Dannon, Red Roof Inn, Motel 6, Wild Turkey, Interscope, Houghton Mifflin, and L'Oréal, for example, are all French owned.[3]

Although some U.S. businesses may want to eliminate foreign competition through protective legislation, the better way to compete is to continuously improve products at home and expand into foreign markets. In a **global industry**, competitors' strategic positions in major geographic or national markets are affected by their overall global positions.[4] A **global firm** operates in more than one country and captures R&D, production, logistical, marketing, and financial advantages not available to purely domestic competitors.

Global firms plan, operate, and coordinate their activities on a worldwide basis. Otis Elevator uses door systems from France, small geared parts from Spain, electronics from Germany, and motor drives from Japan; systems integration happens in the United States. One successful global company is ABB, formed by a merger between Swedish company ASEA and Swiss company Brown Boveri.[5]

ABB

ABB's products include power transformers, electrical installations, instrumentation, auto components, air-conditioning equipment, and railroad equipment. The company has annual revenues of $24 billion and 108,000 employees in 87 countries. Its motto: "ABB is a global company local everywhere." English is its official language (all ABB managers must be conversant in English), and all financial results must be reported in dollars. ABB aims

BREAKTHROUGH MARKETING | SAMSUNG

Korean consumer electronics giant Samsung has made a remarkable transformation, from a provider of value-priced commodity products that original equipment manufacturers (OEMs) sold under their own brands, to a global marketer of premium-priced Samsung-branded consumer electronics such as flat-screen TV's, digital cameras, and cell phones. Its high-end cell phones have been a growth engine, and Samsung has released a steady stream of innovations, popularizing the PDA phone and the first cell phone with an MP3 player.

Samsung used to stress volume and market domination rather than profitability. Yet during the Asian financial crisis of the late 1990s, when other Korean *chaobols* collapsed beneath a mountain of debt, Samsung took a different tack. It cut costs and reemphasized product quality and manufacturing flexibility, which allowed its consumer electronics to go from project phase to store shelves within six months. It also refocused on innovation, using technological leapfrogging to produce best-selling mobile handsets for Asia, Europe, and the United States.

Samsung's success has been driven by well-designed, path-breaking products, but also by an upgrade in its brand image. From 1998–2006, it spent $6 billion in marketing, sponsoring the past five Olympics, running a global ad campaign themed "Imagine," and even erecting a large video screen in Times Square. Samsung views its brand message as "technology," "design," and "sensation" (human). With increasing digital convergence, it's been able to introduce a wide range of electronic products under its strong brand umbrella. The company has poured money into R&D, with a $40 billion budget for 2005–2010, and more than doubled its number of researchers between 2000 and 2006.

Its greatest sign of success, though, may be that longtime market leader Sony has been courting Samsung for joint ventures, partnering on a $2 billion state-of-the-art LCD factory in South Korea and agreeing to share 24,000 basic patents covering a range of components and production processes. Perhaps this is not surprising given that in 2005, for the first time, brand valuation experts Interband valued the Samsung brand as worth more than the Sony brand. To maintain its market leadership, however, Samsung cannot rest on its laurels and must continue to successfully expand via new products and new markets.

Sources: Moon Ihlwan, "Samsung Is Having a Sony Moment," *BusinessWeek*, July 30, 2007, p. 38; Martin Fackler, "Raising the Bar at Samsung," *New York Times*, April 25, 2006; "Brand New," *Economist*, January 15, 2005, pp. 10–11; Patricia O'Connell, "Samsung's Goal: Be Like BMW," *BusinessWeek*, August 1, 2005; Heidi Brown and Justin Doeble, "Samsung's Next Act," *Forbes*, July 26, 2004; John Quelch and Anna Harrington, "Samsung Electronics Company: Global Marketing Operations," Harvard Business School Case 9-504-051.

to reconcile three contradictions: to be global and local; to be big and small; and to be radically decentralized with centralized reporting and control. It has fewer than 200 staff at company headquarters in Switzerland, compared to the 3,000 people who populate competitor Siemens' headquarters. The company's product lines are organized into 8 business segments, 65 business areas, 1,300 companies, and 5,000 profit centers; the average employee belongs to a profit center of around 50 employees. Managers are regularly rotated among countries, and mixed-nationality teams are encouraged. Depending on the type of business, some units are treated as superlocal businesses with lots of autonomy, whereas others are global businesses governed through central control.[6]

Small and medium-sized firms can practice global nichemanship. The Poilane Bakery sells 15,000 loaves of old-style bread each day in Paris—2.5% of all bread sold in that city—via company-owned delivery trucks. But each day, Poilane-branded bread is also shipped via FedEx to loyal customers in roughly 20 countries around the world.[7]

Service businesses increasingly fuel the world economy, and, in turn, a globalizing economy fuels the service industry. The world market for services is growing at double the rate of world merchandise trade. Although some countries have erected entry barriers or regulations, the World Trade Organization, consisting of 150 countries, continues to press for more free trade in international services and other areas.[8]

Large firms in accounting, advertising, banking, communications, construction, insurance, law, management consulting, and retailing are pursuing global expansion. Pricewaterhouse, American Express, Citigroup, Club Med, Hilton, and Thomas Cook are all known worldwide. Merrill Lynch has 740 offices in 37 countries, with non-U.S. revenue making up 54% of total revenue of its global markets and investment banking group. For global service firms, diversity has become a business imperative, but it has become true for all firms too. As one former Colgate executive says, "The speed of global business is accelerating diversity. All business processes cut across country borders now, with virtual teams in North America, Latin America, and Asia."[9]

For a company of any size or any type to go global, it must make a series of decisions (see Figure 21.1). We'll examine each of these decisions here.

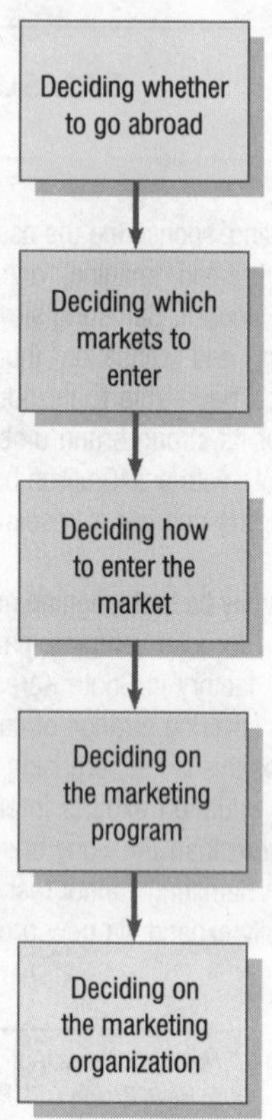

FIG. 21.1

Major Decisions in International Marketing

::: Deciding Whether to Go Abroad

Most companies would prefer to remain domestic if their domestic market were large enough. Managers would not need to learn other languages and laws, deal with volatile currencies, face political and legal uncertainties, or redesign their products to suit different customer needs and expectations. Business would be easier and safer. Yet several factors draw companies into the international arena:

- Some international markets present higher profit opportunities than the domestic market.
- The company needs a larger customer base to achieve economies of scale.
- The company wants to reduce its dependence on any one market.
- The company decides to counterattack global competitors in their home markets.
- Customers are going abroad and require international service.

Before making a decision to go abroad, the company must be aware of and weigh several risks:

- The company might not understand foreign preferences and could fail to offer a competitively attractive product.
- The company might not understand the foreign country's business culture.
- The company might underestimate foreign regulations and incur unexpected costs.
- The company might lack managers with international experience.
- The foreign country might change its commercial laws, devalue its currency, or undergo a political revolution and expropriate foreign property.

Some companies don't act until events thrust them into the international arena.

The *internationalization process* typically has four stages:[10]

1. No regular export activities
2. Export via independent representatives (agents)
3. Establishment of one or more sales subsidiaries
4. Establishment of production facilities abroad

The first task is to move from stage 1 to stage 2. Most firms work with an independent agent and enter a nearby or similar country. Later, the firm establishes an export department to manage its agent relationships. Still later, it replaces agents with its own sales subsidiaries in its larger export markets. This increases investment and risk, but also earning potential.

To manage subsidiaries, the company replaces the export department with an international department. If markets are large and stable, or the host country requires local production, the company will locate production facilities in those markets. By this time, it's operating as a multinational and is optimizing its global sourcing, financing, manufacturing, and marketing. According to some researchers, top management begins to pay more attention to global opportunities when over 15% of revenues comes from international markets.[11]

::: Deciding Which Markets to Enter

In deciding to go abroad, the company needs to define its marketing objectives and policies. What proportion of international to total sales will it seek? Most companies start small when they venture abroad. Some plan to stay small; others have bigger plans.

How Many Markets to Enter

To learn about Billabong and how it has grown from its start selling boardshorts in Australia into an international brand offering many more products, visit www.pearsoned.com.au/marketingmanagementaustralia.

The company must decide how many countries to enter and how fast to expand. Typical entry strategies are the *waterfall* approach, gradually entering countries in sequence, and the *sprinkler* approach, entering many countries simultaneously. Increasingly, firms—especially technology-intensive firms—are born *global* and market to the entire world from the outset.[12]

Matsushita, BMW, General Electric, Benetton, and The Body Shop followed the waterfall approach. It allows firms to carefully plan expansion and is less likely to strain human and financial resources. When first-mover advantage is crucial and a high degree of competitive intensity prevails, such as when Microsoft introduces a new version of Windows software, the sprinkler approach is better. The main risk is the substantial resources needed and the difficulty of planning entry strategies into many diverse markets.

The company must also decide on the countries to consider. Their attractiveness is influenced by the product and by geography, income and population, and political climate.

Developed versus Developing Markets

One of the sharpest distinctions in global marketing is between developed and developing or less mature markets such as Brazil, Russia, India, China, and South Africa.[13] The unmet needs of the emerging or developing world represent huge potential markets for food, clothing, shelter, consumer electronics, appliances, and many other goods. Market leaders rely on developing markets to fuel their growth. Unilever and Colgate have generated 40% of their business in developing markets.[14]

Developed nations and the prosperous parts of developing nations account for about 20% of the world's population. Can marketers serve the other 80%, which has much less purchasing power and living conditions ranging from mild deprivation to severe deficiency?[15] This imbalance is likely to get worse, as more than 90% of future population growth is projected to occur in the less developed countries.

Successfully entering developing markets requires a special set of skills and plans. Consider how the following companies pioneered ways to serve these "invisible" consumers:[16]

- Grameen-Phone marketed cell phones to 35,000 villages in Bangladesh by hiring village women as agents who leased phone time to other villagers, one call at a time.
- Colgate-Palmolive rolled into Indian villages with video vans that showed the benefits of toothbrushing.
- Fiat developed a "third-world car," the Palio, to sell in developing nations. The car is produced in Brazil, India, Turkey, South Africa, China, and other countries.
- Corporacion GEO builds low-income housing in Mexico. The two-bedroom homes are modular and can be expanded. The company has moved into Chile.

Many market-leading firms are relying on developing markets to fuel their future growth. Fiat, for example, sells its Palio car only in developing areas such as India and Latin America.

These marketers capitalize on the potential of developing markets by changing their conventional marketing practices.[17] Selling in developing areas can't be "business as usual." Economic and cultural differences abound; a marketing infrastructure may barely exist; and local competition can be surprisingly stiff.[18] In China, PC maker Lenovo, mobile-phone provider TCL, and appliance manufacturer Haier have thrived despite strong foreign competition. Besides their sharp grasp of Chinese tastes, these companies have vast distribution networks, especially in rural areas. Competition is also growing from other developing markets. China has been exporting cars to Africa, Southeast Asia, and the Middle East. Tata of India, Cemex of Mexico, and Petronas of Malaysia have emerged from developing markets to become strong multinationals selling in many countries.[19] Table 21.1 identifies 25 firms that have made similar journeys.

Eighty percent of consumers in emerging markets buy their products from tiny bodegas, stalls, kiosks, and mom-and-pop stores not much bigger than a closet, which Procter & Gamble calls "high-frequency stores." Smaller packaging and lower sales prices are often critical when incomes and housing spaces are limited. Unilever's 4-cent sachets of detergent and shampoo have been a big hit in rural India, where 70% of the country's population still lives. When Coca-Cola moved to a smaller, 200 ml bottle in India, selling it for 10 to 12 cents in small shops, bus-stop stalls, and roadside eateries, sales jumped.[20] A Western image can also be helpful, as Coca-Cola discovered in China. Part of its success against local cola brand Jianlibao was due to its symbolic values of modernity and affluence.[21]

TABLE 21.1

Twenty-Five Leading Global Firms Based in Developing Markets

Company	Country	Industry	Revenues in Billions
América Móvil	Mexico	Telecom services	$17.0
Cemex	Mexico	Building materials	15.3
China Mobile	China	Telecom services	30.1
CNOOC	China	Oil and gas	8.7
CVRD	Brazil	Mining	15.1
Embraer	Brazil	Aerospace	3.8
Gazprom	Russia	Oil and gas	48.9
Haier	China	Home appliances	12.8
Hisense	China	Electronics, appliances	4.2
Huawei Technologies	China	Telecom equipment	5.9
Infosys Technologies	India	IT services	2.0
Koc Holding	Turkey	Diversified industries	18.0
Lenovo Group	China	Computers, IT components	13.4
MMC Norilsk Nickel	Russia	Nonferrous metals	7.2
Mahindra & Mahindra	India	Tractors, autos	2.9
Orascom Telecom	Egypt	Telecom services	3.3
Petrobras	Brazil	Oil and gas	56.3
Ranbaxy Laboratories	India	Pharmaceuticals	1.2
Sadia	Brazil	Food and beverages	3.6
Severstal	Russia	Steel	4.9
Shanghai Baosteel	China	Steel	15.8
Tata Consultancy Service	India	IT services	2.8
Tata Motors	India	Autos	5.8
Techtronic Industries	Hong Kong/China	Power tools	3.0
Wipro	India	IT services	2.3

Source: Peter Engardio, "Emerging Giants," *BusinessWeek*, July 31, 2006, p. 43. Rankings based on data from Boston Consulting Group, company reports, Bloomberg, and *BusinessWeek*.

Recognizing that its cost structure made it difficult to compete effectively in developing markets, Procter & Gamble devised cheaper, clever ways to make the right kinds of products to suit consumer demand. It now uses contract manufacturers in certain markets and gained eight market-share points in Russia for Always feminine protection pads by responding to consumer wishes for a thicker pad.[22] In Mexico, Cemex received kudos for helping to actually improve housing in poor areas by introducing a pay-as-you-go system for buying building supplies.[23]

DANONE

In Bangladesh, French food giant Danone recently partnered with Muhammed Yunus' Nobel-prize-winning microcredit organization, Grameen Bank, to make and sell low-cost, nutrionally fortified yogurts under the brand name Shoktidoi. The joint venture will provide income to thousands of local farmers who supply the milk (and who raise cows by borrowing small amounts of money from Grameen) and to villagers who distribute the yogurt. At 8 cents per 80-gram pot, Shoktidoi will not likely net profits for Danone right now. Yet, the firm is confident tangible returns will match the intangible returns of feeding the poor. Danone has transformed Bangladesh into a laboratory in which it develops new food products for malnourished children in very poor countries, but it could also churn out new products there for mature and richer markets, all at low cost.[24]

The challenge is to think creatively about how marketing can fulfill the dreams of most of the world's population for a better standard of living. Many companies are betting they can do that. "Marketing Insight: Spotlight on Key Developing Markets" highlights some important developments in the five key emerging market areas often called "BRICS" for short: Brazil, Russia, India, China, and South Africa.

Regional economic integration—the creation of trading agreements between blocs of countries—has intensified in recent years. This means companies are more likely to enter entire regions at the same time. Certain countries have formed free trade zones or economic communities—groups of nations organized to work toward common goals in the regulation of international trade.

THE EUROPEAN UNION Formed in 1957, the European Union set out to create a single European market by reducing barriers to the free flow of products, services, finances, and labor among member countries, and by developing trade policies with nonmember nations. Today, it's one of the world's largest single markets, with 25 member countries, a common currency—the euro—and more than 454 million consumers, accounting for 23% of the world's exports. Companies that plan to create "pan-European" marketing campaigns should proceed with caution, however. Even as the EU standardizes its general trade regulations and currency, creating an economic community will not create a homogeneous market. Companies marketing in Europe face 14 different languages, 2,000 years of historical and cultural differences, and a daunting mass of local rules.

NAFTA In January 1994, the North American Free Trade Agreement (NAFTA) unified the United States, Mexico, and Canada in a single market of 360 million people who produce and consume $6.7 trillion worth of goods and services annually. As it is implemented over a 15-year period, NAFTA will eliminate all trade barriers and investment restrictions among the three countries. Before NAFTA, tariffs on U.S. products entering Mexico averaged 13%, whereas U.S. tariffs on Mexican goods averaged 6%.

MERCOSUR Other free trade areas are forming in Latin America. MERCOSUR (or MERCOSUL) links Brazil, Argentina, Paraguay, Uruguay, and Venezuela to promote free trade and the fluid movement of goods, peoples, and currency. Bolivia, Chile, Columbia, Ecuador, and Peru are associate members. NAFTA will likely eventually merge with this and other arrangements to form an all-Americas free trade zone. Chile and Mexico have already formed a successful free trade zone.

APEC Twenty-one countries, as well as the NAFTA members, Japan, and China, are working to create a pan-Pacific free trade area under the auspices of the Asian Pacific Economic Cooperation forum (APEC). Heads of government of APEC members meet at an annual summit to discuss regional economy, cooperation, trade, and investment.

MARKETING INSIGHT | SPOTLIGHT ON KEY DEVELOPING MARKETS

Brazil

The vast majority of people in Latin America have little to spend. According to the World Bank, 25% live on less than $2 a day, and many millions more earn only a few hundred dollars a month. In Brazil, the region's biggest market and 12th-largest economy in the world, low-income groups make up 87% of the population, but earn only 53% of the income. Marketers in the region are finding innovative ways to sell products and services to these poor and low-income residents.

Nestlé Brazil saw sales of Bono cookies jump 40% after it shrank the package from 200 grams to 140 grams and lowered the price. Recognizing that illiteracy is a problem, Unilever launched a brand of soap in northeast Brazil with the simple name, "Ala." Brazilian firms that have succeeded internationally include brewer and beverage producer AmBev, which merged with Interbrew to form Imbev, aircraft manufacturer Embraer, national airline Varig, and sandal maker Havaianas. The world famous Rio Carnival and world-champion soccer (football) team have helped create an image of fun and physical fitness for Brazil.

Brazil has already experienced some "go-go" growth years in the 1960s and 1970s, when it was the world's second-fastest-growing large economy. It also differs from other emerging markets in being a full-blown democracy, unlike Russia and China, and it has no serious disputes with neighbors, unlike India. But Brazil's growth in recent years has been slower, and a number of obstacles exist that are popularly called *custo Brasil* ("the cost of Brazil"). For example, the cost of transporting products eats up nearly 13% of Brazil's GDP, five percentage points more than in the United States. Most observers see Brazil's economic, social, and political transformation as still a work in process.

Russia

Russia has seen a recent rise in foreign investment and, importantly, not just in its traditionally strong markets in natural resources such as oil and gas. Dutch brewer Heineken, Swedish retailer IKEA, U.S. banker Citibank, and more than a dozen carmakers have ramped up operations in Russia. Their target is Russia's growing middle class, which expanded from 8 million in 2000 to 55 million in 2006 and now accounts for over one-third of the population. The mood in the country has become more upbeat too—the share of Russians who think life is "not bad' has risen to 23% in 2006 from just 7% in 1999. Salaries are rising fast, savings are comparatively low, and consumer credit is increasingly available even for small purchases.

But not everyone has participated in this increased prosperity. The average Russian earns $330 a month, just 10% of the U.S. average, and only a third own cars. Many elderly feel they have been left behind, as do those who live far from Moscow, the capital. Concerns about the business climate remain. Although the economy has produced 7% annual growth in GDP, the Organization for Economic Cooperation & Development (OECD) cautions that economic reforms have been stagnant and ranks Russia as one of the most corrupt countries in the world. Many feel the government under Vladimir Putin has been unpredictable and sometimes difficult to work with.

Motorola's recent experience in Russia is instructive. In 2006, 167,500 Motorola handsets were seized on arrival at Moscow airport, alleged to be smuggled and counterfeit; to violate a Russian patent; and to be a danger to public health. Around 50,000 were supposedly destroyed by the interior ministry, though some were later said to have turned up on the black market. Eventually most of the handsets were returned, but perhaps more telling was Motorola's reaction. With Russia being the company's third-biggest handset market in the world (behind the United States and China), Motorola takes a fairly sanguine attitude towards the ups and downs inherent in doing business there and plans to stay the course.

India

India's recent growth rate has been as explosive as its neighbor China's. Reforms in the early 1990s that significantly lowered barriers to trade and liberalized capital markets have brought booming investment and consumption. But it's not all about demand. With its large numbers of low-cost, high-IQ, English-speaking employees, India is snapping up programming and call center jobs once held by U.S. workers in a wave of outsourcing that shows no signs of stopping. By 2008, IT services and back-office work in India will swell fivefold, to a $57 billion annual export industry employing four million people and accounting for 7% of India's GDP.

Although India's ascent inevitably means lost jobs for U.S. white-collar workers, it also means a larger market for U.S. and Western goods—and pain for traditional Indian families. Along with training in U.S. accents and geography, India's legions of call center employees are absorbing new ideas about family, material possessions, and romance and questioning conservative traditions. They want to watch Hollywood movies, listen to Western music, chat on cell phones, buy on credit rather than save, and eat in restaurants or cafés. They're being targeted relentlessly by companies that have waited to see India develop a Western-style consumer class.

India still struggles with poor infrastructure and highly restrictive labor laws. Its retail channel structure, although improving, still lags. The quality of public services—education, health, provision of water—is also often lacking. But all these obstacles have not prevented global firms such as Mittal, Reliance, Tata, WiPro, and Infosys from achieving varying degrees of international success.

China

China's 1.3 billion people have marketers scrambling to gain a foothold there, and competition has been heating up between domestic and international firms. Initial gains in the Chinese market didn't necessarily spell long-term success for many international firms. After investing to establish the markets, foreign pioneers in television sets and motorcycles saw domestic Chinese firms emerge as rivals. In 1995, virtually all mobile phones in China were made by global giants Nokia, Motorola, and Ericsson. Within 10 years, their market share had dropped to 60%. China's 2001 entry into the World Trade Organization has eased manufacturing and investment rules and modernized retail and logistics industries. Greater competition in pricing, products, and channels have resulted.

Selling in China means going beyond the big cities to the 700 million potential consumers who live in small villages, towns, and cities in the rural interior. About half of potential PC buyers live outside major cities; only one-third of overall retail revenues come from China's 24 largest cities. Rural consumers can be challenging though, as they have lower incomes, are less sophisticated buyers, and often cling to local cultural and buying habits.

Luxury cars, however, are the fastest-growing segment of the auto market thanks to China's growing ranks of millionaires and booming stock market and economy. China's emerging middle class consists of more active and more discerning consumers who demand higher-quality products. Although the mainland's population is four times that of the United States, Chinese consumers spent just 12% of what U.S. consumers did in 2006.

South Africa

One of the toughest places in the world to do business is Africa. According to the World Bank, of the 35 least business-friendly countries, 27 are in sub-Saharan Africa. Sierra Leone imposes harsh taxes; in the Democratic Republic of Congo, registering a business takes 155 days and costs almost five times the average Congolese's annual income of $120; and in Angola, enforcing a contract takes over 1,000 days. To avoid all the government red tape and restrictions, 42% of the region's economy is informal, the highest proportion in the world. Bad roads—if there are roads at all—a lack of reliable electricity, and volatile currency fluctuations add to the logistical and financial challenges. War, famine, AIDS, and disaster are even more significant human difficulties.

But some successful businesses are emerging, especially in banking, retailing, and mobile telephones, and many are using South Africa as a launch pad. Although many Africans are poor, they will still pay for what they need. Mobile phone operator Celtel invested in rural services by introducing the Me2U service, by which callers could send airtime credit to other mobile phones. Because most Africans don't have bank accounts, it's become a convenient and cheap way to transfer money, even substituting for cash in some villages. South Africa's MTN, the largest mobile phone company in the region, built its own microwave transmission backbone and power supplies in Nigeria, and the first solar pay phone in Lake Victoria, Uganda. South Africa's Net 1 has built a customer base of 3.6 million accounts by issuing free smart cards to indigent people who have no bank accounts or credit cards, taking tiny percentages of their transactions for revenue.

The payoff for companies willing to deal with the complications and risk associated with doing business in Africa is often large margins and a lack of competition. SABMiller, the world's second-largest brewer, enjoys its best operating margins (over 42%) in Africa. Local knowledge is key, and South African companies are well placed to take advantage of opportunities. Finding a local partner can help in terms of expertise and contacts. SABMiller's African operations are joint ventures with locals, some of them government.

Sources: Brazil: Antonio Regalado, "Marketers Pursue the Shallow Pocketed," *Wall Street Journal,* January 26, 2007; "Land of Promise," *Economist,* April 12, 2007; Melissa Campanelli, "Marketing to Latin America? Think Brazil," *DMNEWS,* June 20, 2006. *Russia:* "Dancing with the Bear," *Economist,* February 3, 2007, pp. 63–64; Jason Bush, "Russia: How Long Can the Fun Last?" *BusinessWeek,* December 18, 2006, pp. 50–51. *India:* "India on Fire," *Economist,* February 3, 2007, pp. 69–71; Joanna Slater, "Call of the West," *Wall Street Journal,* January 2, 2004; Manjeet Kripalani and Pete Engardio, "The Rise of India," *BusinessWeek,* December 8, 2003, pp. 66–76. *China:* Dexter Roberts, "Cadillac Floors It in China," *BusinessWeek,* June 4, 2007, p. 52; Bruce Einhorn, "Grudge Match in China," *BusinessWeek,* April 2, 2007, pp. 42–43; Russell Flannery, "Watch Your Back," *Forbes,* April 23, 2007, pp. 104–5; Dexter Roberts, "Cautious Consumers," *BusinessWeek,* April 30, 2007, pp. 32–34; Seung Ho Park and Wilfried R. Vanhonacker, "The Challenge for Multinational Corporations in China: Think Local, Act Global," *MIT Sloan Management Review,* May 31, 2007; Dexter Roberts, "Scrambling to Bring Crest to the Masses," *BusinessWeek,* June 25, 2007, pp. 72–73. *South Africa:* Helen Coster, "Great Expectations," *Forbes,* February 12, 2007, pp. 56–58; "The Flicker of a Brighter Future," *Economist,* September 9, 2006, pp. 60–62; "Going Global," *Economist,* July 15, 2006, pp. 59–60.

ASEAN Ten countries make up the Association of Southeast Asian Nations: Brunei Darussalam, Cambodia, Indonesia, Laos, Malaysia, Myanmar, Philippines, Singapore, Thailand, and Vietnam. The region is an attractive market of over 550 million people and the member countries are aiming to work together to enhance its area as a major production and export center.

Active attempts at regional economic integration are underway in the Caribbean and parts of Africa.

Evaluating Potential Markets

Although the world is becoming flatter, there is still some "roundedness." However much nations and regions integrate their trading policies and standards, each nation still has unique features. Its readiness for different products and services, and its attractiveness as a market, depend on its economic, political-legal, and cultural environments.

Suppose a company has assembled a list of potential markets to enter. How does it choose among them? Many companies prefer to sell to neighboring countries because they understand these countries better and can control their costs more effectively. It's not surprising that the two largest U.S. export markets are Canada and Mexico, or that Swedish companies first sold to their Scandinavian neighbors.

At other times, *psychic proximity* determines choices. Many U.S. firms prefer to sell in Canada, England, and Australia—rather than in larger markets such as Germany and France—because they feel more comfortable with the language, laws, and culture. Companies should be careful, however, in choosing markets according to cultural distance. Besides overlooking

Singapore meets most but not all of Bechtel's criteria for overseas investment; its population is relatively small.

potentially better markets, firms may perform superficial analysis of some very real differences among countries and adopt predictable marketing actions that put them at a disadvantage.[25]

It often makes sense to operate in fewer countries, with a deeper commitment and penetration in each. In general, a company prefers to enter countries (1) that rank high on market attractiveness, (2) that are low in market risk, and (3) in which it possesses a competitive advantage. Here is how Bechtel Corporation, the construction giant, goes about evaluating overseas markets.

BECHTEL CORPORATION

Bechtel provides premier technical, management, and related services to develop, manage, engineer, build, and operate installations for customers in nearly 60 countries worldwide. Before it ventures into new markets, Bechtel starts with a detailed strategic market analysis. It looks at its markets and tries to determine where it should be in four or five years' time. A management team does a cost-benefit analysis that factors in the position of competitors, infrastructure, regulatory and trade barriers, and the tax situation (both corporate and individual). Ideally, the new market should be a country with an untapped need for its products or services, a skilled labor pool capable of manufacturing the product, and a welcoming environment (governmental and physical).

Are there countries that meet Bechtel's requirements? Although Singapore has an educated, English-speaking labor force, enjoys political stability, and encourages foreign investment, it has a small population of 5 million. Many countries in Central Europe possess an eager labor pool hungry to learn, but their infrastructures create difficulties. The team evaluating a new market must determine whether the company could earn enough on its investment to cover the risks and negatives.

::: Deciding How to Enter the Market

Once a company decides to target a particular country, it must determine the best mode of entry. Its broad choices are *indirect exporting, direct exporting, licensing, joint ventures,* and *direct investment.* These five market-entry strategies are shown in Figure 21.2. Each succeeding strategy entails more commitment, risk, control, and profit potential.

Indirect and Direct Export

The normal way to get involved in an international market is through export. Companies typically start with *indirect exporting*—that is, they work through independent intermediaries. *Domestic-based export merchants* buy the manufacturer's products and then sell them abroad. *Domestic-based export agents* seek and negotiate foreign purchases for a commission. Included in this group are trading companies. *Cooperative organizations* carry on exporting activities on behalf of several producers—often of primary products such as fruits or nuts—and are partly under their administrative control. *Export-management companies* agree to manage a company's export activities for a fee.

Indirect export has two advantages. First, there is less investment: The firm doesn't have to develop an export department, an overseas sales force, or a set of international contacts. Second, there's less risk: Because international marketing intermediaries bring know-how and services to the relationship, the seller will make fewer mistakes.

Companies eventually may decide to handle their own exports.[26] The investment and risk are somewhat greater, but so is the potential return. A company can carry on direct exporting in several ways:

- ***Domestic-based export department or division.*** This might evolve from a purely service function into a self-contained export department operating as its own profit center.

- ***Overseas sales branch or subsidiary.*** The sales branch handles sales and distribution and perhaps warehousing and promotion as well. It often serves as a display and customer-service center.
- ***Traveling export sales representatives.*** Home-based sales representatives travel abroad to find business.
- ***Foreign-based distributors or agents.*** These distributors and agents can hold limited or exclusive rights to represent the company in that country.

Many companies use direct or indirect exporting as a way to "test the waters" before building a plant and manufacturing a product overseas. Here's one small business marketer that got into direct exporting indirectly.

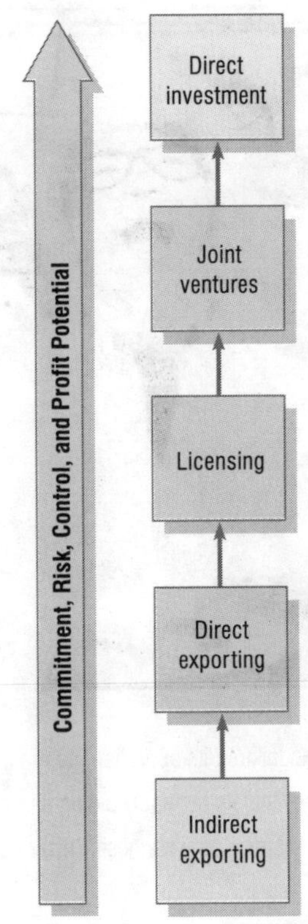

FIG. 21.2

Five Modes of Entry into Foreign Markets

M.A.G. MANUFACTURING

M.A.G. Manufacturing, based in California, is a leading supplier of home security hardware that outsources some of its manufacturing in China. Mark Allengaugh, after inheriting the business from his father, needed to make sure one of the firm's factories could ramp up supply for a Home Depot order. On his arrival in China, however, he had what he calls a "life-changing experience." "What I saw when I got there was the U.S. on steroids. I realized: This is not just a country to outsource from, this is a country to sell to." By the end of that year, M.A.G. had established a Shanghai office with six local employees, which Allenbaugh upped to 15 the following year. Now M.A.G. sells products manufactured in Chinese factories to do-it-yourself retailers in China—a burgeoning market in China's economic and housing boom. It's also able to sell its U.S.-made door hardware directly to Chinese construction firms. Expanding into China has been life-changing in more than a business sense: Allenbaugh is studying Mandarin and Cantonese and has hired a Mandarin-speaking nanny to care for his two toddlers who, like their dad, may wind up at the helm of an increasingly international business one day.[27]

Using a Global Web Strategy

With the Web, it's now not even necessary to attend international trade shows to show your wares abroad: Electronic communication via the Internet is extending the reach of companies large and small, allowing them to attract new customers outside their home countries, support existing customers who live abroad, source from international suppliers, and build global brand awareness.

These companies adapt their Web sites to provide country-specific content and services to their best potential international markets, ideally in the local language. The number of Internet users is rising quickly as access costs decline, local-language content increases, and infrastructure improves. After going online, upscale retailer and cataloger The Sharper Image found that more than 25% of its online business came from overseas customers.[28]

The Internet has become an effective means of conducting market research and offering customers a secure process for ordering and paying for products across time zones. Finding free information about trade and exporting has never been easier. Here are some places to start a search:

www.ita.doc.gov	U.S. Department of Commerce's International Trade Administration
www.exim.gov	Export-Import Bank of the United States
www.sba.gov	U.S. Small Business Administration
www.bis.doc.gov	Bureau of Industry and Security, a branch of the Commerce Department

Many states' export-promotion offices also have online resources and allow businesses to link to their sites.

Licensing

Licensing is a simple way to engage in international marketing. The licensor issues a license to a foreign company to use a manufacturing process, trademark, patent, trade secret, or other item of value for a fee or royalty. The licensor gains entry at little risk; the licensee gains production expertise or a well-known product or brand name.

Licensing has potential disadvantages. The licensor has less control over the licensee than it does over its own production and sales facilities. If the licensee is very successful, the

KFC has tailored its approach, its menu, and even its mascot to appeal to Chinese tastes and has become China's fastest-growing and most popular fast-food chain. But it still retains some of its iconic imagery, as with these Chinese children dressed as Colonel Sanders as part of a promotion.

firm has given up profits, and if and when the contract ends, the company might find it has created a competitor. To prevent this, the licensor usually supplies some proprietary product ingredients or components (as Coca-Cola does). But the best strategy is to lead in innovation so the licensee will continue to depend on the licensor.

There are variations on a licensing arrangement. Companies such as Hyatt and Marriott sell *management contracts* to owners of foreign hotels to manage these businesses for a fee. The management firm may have the option to purchase some share in the managed company within a stated period.

In *contract manufacturing,* the firm hires local manufacturers to produce the product. When Sears opened department stores in Mexico and Spain, it found qualified local manufacturers to produce many of its products. Contract manufacturing gives the company less control over the manufacturing process and risks loss of potential profits on manufacturing. However, it offers a chance to start faster, with the opportunity to form a partnership or buy out the local manufacturer later.

Finally, a company can enter a foreign market through *franchising,* a more complete form of licensing. The franchisor offers a complete brand concept and operating system. In return, the franchisee invests in and pays certain fees to the franchisor. McDonald's, KFC, and Avis have entered scores of countries by franchising their retail concepts and making sure their marketing is culturally relevant.

KFC CORPORATION

KFC is the world's largest fast-food chicken chain, owning or franchising 11,000 outlets in 80 countries and territories—60% of them outside the United States—and serving 8 million customers daily. KFC had a number of obstacles to overcome when it entered the Japanese market. The Japanese saw fast food as artificial, made by mechanical means, and unhealthy. To build trust in the KFC brand, advertising showed scenes depicting Colonel Sanders' beginnings in Kentucky that conveyed Southern hospitality, old American tradition, and authentic home cooking. The campaign was hugely successful, and in less than eight years KFC expanded its presence from 400 locations to more than 1,000. KFC is China's largest, oldest, most popular, and fastest-growing quick-service restaurant chain, with over 1,800 locations. It has set up its own supply and distribution system in China, allowing it to expand quickly into ever-smaller cities. The company has also tailored its menu to local tastes with items such as the Dragon Twister, a sandwich stuffed with chicken strips, Peking duck sauce, cucumbers, and scallions. KFC even has a Chinese mascot—a kid-friendly character named Chicky, which the company boasts has become "the Ronald McDonald of China."[29]

Joint Ventures

Historically, foreign investors have often joined with local investors to create a **joint venture** company in which they share ownership and control. For instance:[30]

- Coca-Cola and Nestlé joined forces to develop the international market for "ready-to-drink" tea and coffee, which currently they sell in significant amounts in Japan.
- Procter & Gamble formed a joint venture with its Italian archrival Fater to cover babies' bottoms in the United Kingdom and Italy.
- Whirlpool took a 53% stake in the Dutch electronics group Philips's white-goods business to leapfrog into the European market.

A joint venture may be necessary or desirable for economic or political reasons. The foreign firm might lack the financial, physical, or managerial resources to undertake the venture alone; or the foreign government might require joint ownership as a condition for entry. Joint ownership has certain drawbacks. The partners might disagree over investment, marketing, or other policies. One might want to reinvest earnings for growth, and the other to declare more dividends. Joint ownership can also prevent a multinational company from carrying out specific manufacturing and marketing policies on a worldwide basis.

Direct Investment

The ultimate form of foreign involvement is direct ownership of foreign-based assembly or manufacturing facilities. The foreign company can buy part or full interest in a local company or build its own facilities. General Motors has invested billions of dollars in auto manufacturers around the world, such as Shangai GM, Fiat Auto Holdings, Isuzu, Daewoo, Suzuki, Saab, Fuji Heavy Industries, Jinbei GM Automotive Co., and AvtoVAZ.[31]

If the market appears large enough, foreign production facilities offer distinct advantages. First, the firm secures cost economies in the form of cheaper labor or raw materials, foreign-government investment incentives, and freight savings. Second, the firm strengthens its image in the host country because it creates jobs. Third, the firm develops a deeper relationship with government, customers, local suppliers, and distributors, enabling it to better adapt its products to the local environment. Fourth, the firm retains full control over its investment and therefore can develop manufacturing and marketing policies that serve its long-term international objectives. Fifth, the firm assures itself access to the market in case the host country insists locally purchased goods have domestic content.

The main disadvantage of direct investment is that the firm exposes a large investment to risks such as blocked or devalued currencies, worsening markets, or expropriation. It can be expensive to reduce or close down operations, because the host country might require substantial severance pay to employees.

::: Deciding on the Marketing Program

International companies must decide how much to adapt their marketing strategy to local conditions.[32] At one extreme are companies that use a globally *standardized marketing mix* worldwide. Standardization of the product, communication, and distribution channels promises the lowest costs. Table 21.2 summarizes some pros and cons of standardizing the marketing program. At the other extreme is an *adapted marketing mix,* where the producer, consistent with the marketing concept, holds that consumer needs vary and tailors marketing programs to each target group.

TABLE 21.2

Global Marketing Pros and Cons

Advantages

- Economies of scale in production and distribution
- Lower marketing costs
- Power and scope
- Consistency in brand image
- Ability to leverage good ideas quickly and efficiently
- Uniformity of marketing practices

Disadvantages

- Ignores differences in consumer needs, wants, and usage patterns for products
- Ignores differences in consumer response to marketing-mix elements
- Ignores differences in brand and product development and the competitive environment
- Ignores differences in the legal environment
- Ignores differences in marketing institutions
- Ignores differences in administrative procedures

The development of the Web, the rapid spread of cable and satellite TV around the world, and the global linking of telecommunications networks have led to a convergence of lifestyles. Increasingly common needs and wants have created global markets for standardized products, particularly among the young middle class. Consider Red Bull.

RED BULL

A billion-dollar brand in less than 15 years, Red Bull has gained 70% of the worldwide energy drink market by skillfully connecting with global youth. Founded in Austria by Dietrich Mateschitz, Red Bull was introduced into its first foreign market, Hungary, in 1992, and is now sold in over 100 countries. Red Bull consists of amino acid taurine, B-complex vitamins, caffeine, and carbohydrates. The drink was sold originally in only one size—the silver 250 ml (8.3 oz.) can—and received little traditional advertising support beyond animated television commercials with the tagline "Red Bull Gives You Wiiings." Red Bull built buzz about the product through its "seeding program": the company microtargets "in" shops, clubs, bars, and stores, gradually moves to convenience stores and restaurants, and finally enters supermarkets. It targets opinion leaders by making Red Bull available at sports competitions, in limos before award shows, and at exclusive after-parties. Red Bull also built its cool image through sponsorship of extreme sports such as its X-Fighters events, and unique grassroots efforts. In cities throughout the world, for example, the company sponsors an annual Flugtag where contestants build flying machines that they launch off ramps into water, true to the brand's slogan![33]

Although many companies have tried to launch their version of a world product, most products require at least some adaptation. Toyota's Corolla will exhibit some differences in styling. Even Coca-Cola is sweeter or less carbonated in certain countries. Rather than assuming it can introduce its domestic product "as is" in another country, the company should review the following elements and determine which add more revenue than cost:

- Product features
- Labeling
- Colors
- Materials
- Sales promotion
- Advertising media
- Brand name
- Packaging
- Advertising execution
- Prices
- Advertising themes

Red Bull relies on many nontraditional marketing activities to expand worldwide from its European base. The annual Flugtag contest is just one. Here a competitor is seen flying his camel machine in the Dubai Creek as part of the Flying Day Red Bull Flugtag competition there. Flying machines were launched from a six-meter-high runway using only human power.

Consumer behavior can dramatically differ across markets. One of the highest per-capita consumers of carbonated soft drinks is the United States, at 204 liters; Italy is among the lowest. But Italy is one of the highest per-capita drinkers of bottled water, with 203 liters, whereas the United Kingdom uses only 23 liters. When it comes to beer, Ireland and the Czech Republic lead the pack, with 157 and 131 liters per capita, respectively, and France is among the lowest at 36 liters.[34]

Cultural differences can be pronounced across countries. Hofstede identifies four cultural dimensions that differentiate countries:[35]

1. ***Individualism vs. collectivism***—In collectivist societies, such as Japan, the self-worth of an individual is rooted more in the social system than in individual achievement.
2. ***High vs. low power distance***—High power distance cultures tend to be less egalitarian.
3. ***Masculine vs. feminine***—This dimension measures how much the culture is dominated by assertive males versus nurturing females.
4. ***Weak vs. strong uncertainty avoidance***—Uncertainty avoidance indicates how risk-tolerant or risk-aversive people are.

Besides demand-side differences, supply-side differences can prevail. Flexible manufacturing techniques make it easier to produce many different product versions, tailored to particular countries.

Most brands are adapted to some extent to reflect significant differences in consumer behavior, brand development, competitive forces, and the legal or political environment.[36] Even global brands undergo some changes in product features, packaging, channels, pricing, or communications in different global markets.[37] (See "Marketing Memo: The Ten Commandments of Global Branding.") Firms must make sure their message is relevant to consumers in every market.

WESTERN UNION

With economic migration booming, so is the remittance—money transfer—market. Western Union introduced the first electronic money transfer service more than 150 years ago in 1871, but it set up shop outside the United States only in 1990. It's now located in more than 200 countries, with a customer base of economic migrants who send funds home to their families. A key to Western Union's success in the burgeoning global market is its realization that along with money transfers, it's providing a perhaps more important intangible benefit. To Western Union's customers, a money transfer can mean providing for a child's education or medical treatment for an ailing relative. This emotional aspect of its service is emphasized in Western Union's very successful international ad campaign. The company also uses its customer knowledge to build loyalty by supporting popular events such as community festivals and religious celebrations. For instance, it supports its Jamaican customers by sponsoring the Notting Hill Carnival in London and similar events in other Jamaican enclaves of the United Kingdom. Western Union also sponsored the Albanian Football Federation and Africa's football (soccer) competition, the Africa Cup of Nations. With an estimated 185 million global migrants accounting for 6% to 10% of the population in European countries, Western Union will likely be doing even more to connect with potential customers.[38]

Western Union offers its money-transfer customers, mostly migrant workers, the intangible benefit of safely sending money to family back home. Its many sponsorship events build customer loyalty among this group. The Western Union sign can be seen here in the background of an African Nations Cup soccer match between Nigeria and Sengal in 2006.

Product

Some types of products travel better across borders than others—food and beverage marketers must contend with widely varying tastes.[39] Warren Keegan has distinguished five adaptation strategies of product and communications to a foreign market (see Figure 21.3).[40]

Straight extension introduces the product in the foreign market without any change. It's been successful with cameras, consumer electronics, and many machine tools. In other cases, it has been a disaster. General Foods introduced its standard powdered Jell-O in the British market only to find that British consumers prefer the solid wafer or cake form. Campbell Soup Company lost an estimated $30 million in introducing condensed soups in England; consumers saw expensive small-sized cans and didn't realize water needed to be added. Straight extension is tempting because it requires no additional R&D expense, manufacturing retooling, or promotional modification; but it can be costly in the long run.

Communications	Product: Do Not Change Product	Product: Adapt Product	Product: Develop New Product
Do Not Change Communications	Straight extension	Product adaptation	Product invention
Adapt Communications	Communication adaptation	Dual adaptation	

FIG. 21.3

Five International Product and Communication Strategies

MARKETING MEMO | THE TEN COMMANDMENTS OF GLOBAL BRANDING

For many companies, global branding has been both a blessing and a curse. A global branding program can lower marketing costs, realize greater economies of scale in production, and provide a long-term source of growth. If not designed and implemented properly, however, it may ignore important differences in consumer behavior and/or the competitive environment in the individual countries. These suggestions can help a company retain the advantages of global branding while minimizing potential disadvantages:

1. ***Understand similarities and differences in the global branding landscape***—International markets can vary in terms of brand development, consumer behavior, competitive activity, legal restrictions, and so on.
2. ***Do not take shortcuts in brand building***—Build a brand in new markets from the "bottom up," both strategically (building awareness before brand image) and tactically (creating sources of brand equity in new markets).
3. ***Establish a marketing infrastructure***—A company must either build marketing infrastructure "from scratch" or adapt to existing infrastructure in other countries.
4. ***Embrace integrated marketing communications***—A company must often use many forms of communication in overseas markets, not just advertising.
5. ***Establish brand partnerships***—Most global brands have marketing partners in their international markets that help companies achieve advantages in distribution, profitability, and added value.
6. ***Balance standardization and customization***—Some elements of a marketing program can be standardized (packaging, brand name); others typically require greater customization (distribution channels).
7. ***Balance global and local control***—Companies must balance global and local control within the organization and distribute decision making between global and local managers.
8. ***Establish operable guidelines***—Brand definition and guidelines must be established, communicated, and properly enforced so marketers everywhere know what they are expected to do and not do. The goal is to set rules for how the brand should be positioned and marketed.
9. ***Implement a global brand-equity measurement system***—A global brand-equity system is a set of research procedures designed to provide timely, accurate, and actionable information for marketers so they can make the best possible short-run tactical decisions and long-run strategic decisions.
10. ***Leverage brand elements***—Proper design and implementation of brand elements (brand name and trademarked brand identifiers) can be an invaluable source of brand equity worldwide.

Source: Adapted from Kevin Lane Keller and Sanjay Sood, "The Ten Commandments of Global Branding," *Asian Journal of Marketing* 8, no. 2 (2001): 97–108.

Product adaptation alters the product to meet local conditions or preferences. There are several levels of adaptation.

- A company can produce a *regional version* of its product, such as a Western European version. Finnish cellular phone superstar Nokia customized its 6100 series phone for every major market. Developers built in rudimentary voice recognition for Asia, where keyboards are a problem, and raised the ring volume so the phone could be heard on crowded Asian streets.
- A company can produce a *country version* of its product. In Japan, Mister Donut's coffee cup is smaller and lighter to fit the hand of the average Japanese consumer; even the doughnuts are a little smaller. Kraft blends different coffees for the British (who drink their coffee with milk), the French (who drink their coffee black), and Latin Americans (who want a chicory taste).
- A company can produce a *city version* of its product—for instance, a beer to meet Munich tastes or Tokyo tastes.
- A company can produce different *retailer versions* of its product, such as one coffee brew for the Migros chain store and another for the Cooperative chain store, both in Switzerland.

Some companies have learned the importance of adapting the hard way. When Walt Disney launched the Euro Disney theme park outside Paris in 1992, it was harshly criticized as an example of U.S. cultural imperialism. A number of local French customs and values, such as serving wine with meals, were ignored. As one Euro Disney executive noted, "When we first launched, there was the belief that it was enough to be Disney. Now we realize our guests need to be welcomed on the basis of their own culture and travel habits." Renamed Disneyland Paris, the theme park eventually has become Europe's biggest tourist attraction—even more popular than the Eiffel Tower—by making a number of changes and adding more local touches.[41]

Product invention consists of creating something new. It can take two forms:

- **Backward invention** is reintroducing earlier product forms that are well adapted to a foreign country's needs. The National Cash Register Company reintroduced its crank-operated cash register at half the price of a modern cash register and sold substantial numbers in Latin America and Africa.

BERTELSMANN

In Ukraine, where the average person makes $8,000 a year and bookstores are few and far between, the old-fashioned book club is enjoying huge popularity. German book-publishing giant Bertelsmann has seen a decline in its Book-of-the-Month and Literary Guild units in both the United States and Europe. In Ukraine, however, these clubs are seeing profit margins triple the 4% global average. Bertelsmann has been astute at marketing its "old" media to 20- to 30-year-old consumers there, and the clubs draw a younger following than in the United States. They recruit hot young Ukrainian authors and serve as their exclusive distributor, a masterstroke in a country with only 300 bookstores. The publisher also keeps prices low because its main competition in Ukraine is the open-air book market, where books sell very cheaply. Its Family Leisure book club titles go for under $5, for instance. To keep costs down, Bertelsmann delivers books to post offices where customers pick them up.[42]

- **Forward invention** is creating a new product to meet a need in another country. Less developed countries need low-cost, high-protein foods. Companies such as Quaker Oats, Swift, and Monsanto have researched these countries' nutrition needs, formulated new foods, and developed advertising campaigns to gain product trial and acceptance.

Product invention is a costly strategy, but the payoffs can be great, particularly if a company can parlay a product innovation into other countries. Sometimes the innovation even works at home.

HÄAGEN-DAZS

Häagen-Dazs developed an ice cream flavor for sale solely in Argentina, called "dulce de leche." Translated literally as "sweet of milk," it was named for the caramelized milk that is one of the most popular flavors in Argentina. Just one year later, the company rolled out dulce de leche in supermarkets from Boston to Los Angeles to Paris. The co-opted flavor soon did $1 million a month in the United States, becoming one of the company's top 10 flavors. It was particularly popular in Miami, where it sold twice as fast as any other flavor.[43]

When they launch products and services globally, marketers may need to change certain brand elements. When Clairol introduced the "Mist Stick," a curling iron, in Germany, it found that *mist* is slang for manure. Brand slogans or ad taglines sometimes need to be changed too:[44]

- When Coors put its brand slogan "Turn it loose" into Spanish, some read it as "suffer from diarrhea."
- A laundry soap ad claiming to wash "really dirty parts" was translated in French-speaking Quebec to read "a soap for washing private parts."
- Perdue's slogan—"It takes a tough man to make a tender chicken"—was rendered into Spanish as "It takes a sexually excited man to make a chick affectionate."
- Electrolux's British ad line for its vacuum cleaners—"Nothing sucks like an Electrolux"—would certainly not lure customers in the United States!

Table 21.3 lists some other famous blunders in this area.

Communications

Companies can run the same marketing communications programs they use in the home market or change them for each local market, a process called **communication adaptation**. If it adapts both the product and the communications, the company engages in **dual adaptation**.

TABLE 21.3

Blunders in International Marketing

- Hallmark cards failed when they were introduced in France. The French dislike syrupy sentiment and prefer writing their own cards.
- Philips began to earn a profit in Japan only after it reduced the size of its coffeemakers to fit into smaller Japanese kitchens and its shavers to fit smaller Japanese hands.
- Coca-Cola withdrew its two-liter bottle in Spain after discovering that few Spaniards owned refrigerators with large enough compartments to accommodate it.
- General Foods' Tang initially failed in France because it was positioned as a substitute for orange juice at breakfast. The French drink little orange juice and almost none at breakfast.
- Kellogg's Pop-Tarts failed in Britain because the percentage of British homes with toasters was significantly lower than in the United States, and the product was too sweet for British tastes.
- Procter & Gamble's Crest toothpaste initially failed in Mexico when it used the U.S. campaign. Mexicans did not care as much for the decay-prevention benefit, nor did scientifically oriented advertising appeal to them.
- General Foods squandered millions trying to introduce packaged cake mixes to Japanese consumers. The company failed to note that only 3% of Japanese homes were equipped with ovens.
- S.C. Johnson's wax floor polish initially failed in Japan. The wax made the floors too slippery, and Johnson had overlooked the fact that Japanese do not wear shoes in their homes.

Consider the message. The company can use one message everywhere, varying only the language, name, and perhaps colors to avoid taboos in some countries.[45] Purple is associated with death in Burma and some Latin American nations; white is a mourning color in India; and green is associated with disease in Malaysia.[46]

The second possibility is to use the same creative theme globally but adapt the specific execution to appropriate local markets. Apple Computer's "Mac vs. PC," which was voted the best U.S. ad campaign of 2006 by *Adweek* magazine, features two actors bantering. One is hip looking (Apple), the other nerdy looking (PC). Apple dubbed the ads for Spain, France, Germany, and Italy but chose to reshoot and rescript for the United Kingdom and Japan—two important markets with unique advertising and comedy cultures. The U.K. ads followed a similar formula but tweaked the jokes to reflect British humor; the Japanese ads avoided direct comparisons and were more subtle in tone.[47] Here is another example of communication adaptation from a business-to-business marketer.

ACOPIA NETWORKS

Data management company Acopia Networks is breaking into European and Asian markets with a targeted e-mail marketing campaign. Tim Pitcher, VP of international sales, realized early that he wouldn't be able to use the same messages or strategies that Acopia uses to market in the United States. For instance, European buyers are more receptive to marketing that comes from Acopia's local representatives or partners, so Pitcher created a one-size-fits-all e-mail marketing template that his local people change based on what they know about prospects. The firm also uses local translators in each market, including the United Kingdom, where English spellings and meanings are sometimes different. Acopia makes sure its e-mails are timed to arrive first thing in the morning to account for the different work habits of Europeans—from the British habit of long pub lunches to Southern European siestas—and never before, during, or right after a local or national holiday. So far Acopia's strategy is working well. In less than six months the e-mail campaign drew a 10% conversion rate, which means it results in an in-person sales call 10% of the time.[48]

The third approach consists of developing a global pool of ads, from which each country selects the most appropriate. Coca-Cola and Goodyear have used this approach. Finally, some companies allow their country managers to create country-specific ads—within guidelines, of course. The challenge is to make sure the message is as compelling and effective as in the home market.

NIKE

China's state-owned media actively enforce rules on what communications can and cannot say. In 2004, Nike ran afoul of those rules with its "Chamber of Fear" commercial, which was banned for "insulting national pride." It showed the NBA star LeBron James fighting a Kung-Fu character, two women in Chinese dress, and a pair of dragons (considered sacred symbols). The Chinese interpretation of the ad was that LeBron was trying to defeat Chinese culture. The State Administration for Radio, Film, and Television said the ad "violates regulations that mandate all advertisement in China should uphold national dignity and interest and respect the motherland's culture." Censorship aside, Nike has recently decided its Chinese ad campaigns need to focus less on U.S. or even Chinese athletes with "you should . . ." or "try this . . ." messages intended for China's younger generation, which is rapidly creating its own style. Instead, Nike is trying to get its "Just Do It" tagline across by saluting unknown Chinese youngsters who have surmounted obstacles to play basketball, to skateboard, or to cycle. In addition to being able to watch the gritty ads featuring genuinely moving stories of kids, Internet-connected Chinese tweens and teens can send their personal stories to the Nike Web site. So instead of insulting national pride, Nike is tapping into the vast store of "personal pride" of China's newest generation of consumers.[49]

In Hong Kong, a women talks on her mobile phone in front of a Nike advertisement featuring NBA player LeBron James. China officials objected to Nike television commercials featuring James battling animated characters, prompting the company to focus on adapting its powerful "Just Do It" message instead.

The use of media also requires international adaptation because media availability varies from country to country. Norway, Belgium, and France don't allow cigarettes and alcohol to be advertised on TV. Austria and Italy regulate TV advertising to children. Saudi Arabia does not want advertisers to use women in ads. India has taxed advertising. Magazines vary in availability and effectiveness; they play a major role in Italy and a minor one in Austria.

In developing markets, high cell phone penetration makes mobile marketing attractive. A pioneer in China, Coca-Cola China created a national campaign asking Beijing residents to send text messages guessing the high temperature in the city every day for just over a month, for a chance to win a one-year supply of Coke products. The campaign attracted more than four million messages over the course of 35 days.[50]

Personal selling tactics may need to change too. The direct, no-nonsense approach favored in the United States (characterized by a "let's get down to business" and "what's in it for me" stance) may not work as well in Europe, Asia, and other places where an indirect, subtle approach can be more effective.[51] With younger, more worldly employees, however, such cultural differences may be less pronounced.

Price

Multinationals face several pricing problems when selling abroad. They must deal with price escalation, transfer prices, dumping charges, and gray markets.

MICROSOFT

When Microsoft entered China 15 years ago, the company made its first big blunder by trying to sell its Windows operating system at the same high price it commands in the developed world. Yet, pirated copies were available at rock bottom prices. Microsoft spent the next 10 years trying to crack down on piracy in China, suing companies for using its software illegally and always losing in court. The Chinese government grew ever more mistrustful of Microsoft—even suspecting the United States was spying via the software—and put open-source Linux operating systems on all workers' PCs. So how did Microsoft become so respected in China that CEO Bill Gates is now a celebrity? For one thing, by doing a complete turnaround and tolerating piracy. "It's easier for our software to compete with Linux when there's piracy than when there's not," says Gates. Yet, the best move Microsoft made was to collaborate with the Chinese government and open a research center in Beijing, which today lures the country's top computer scientists. Rather than being known as a company that comes to China to sue people, it's regarded as a company with long-term vision.[52]

When companies sell their goods abroad, they face a **price escalation** problem. A Gucci handbag may sell for $120 in Italy and $240 in the United States. Why? Gucci must add the cost of transportation, tariffs, importer margin, wholesaler margin, and retailer margin to its factory price. Depending on these added costs, as well as the currency-fluctuation risk, the product might sell for two to five times as much in another country to make the same profit for the manufacturer. Companies have three choices for setting prices in different countries:

1. ***Set a uniform price everywhere***—Coca-Cola might want to charge 75 cents for Coke everywhere in the world, but then it would earn quite different profit rates in different countries. Also, this strategy would make the price too high in poor countries and not high enough in rich countries.
2. ***Set a market-based price in each country***—Here Coca-Cola would charge what each country could afford, but this strategy ignores differences in the actual cost from country to country. Also, it could lead to a situation in which intermediaries in low-price countries reship their Coca-Cola to high-price countries.
3. ***Set a cost-based price in each country***—Here Coca-Cola would use a standard markup of its costs everywhere, but this strategy might price Coca-Cola out of the market in countries where its costs are high.

A different problem arises when one unit charges another unit in the same company a **transfer price** for goods it ships to its foreign subsidiaries. If the company charges a subsidiary too *high* a price, it may end up paying higher tariff duties, although it may pay lower income taxes in the foreign country. If the company charges too *low* a price to its subsidiary, it can be accused of **dumping**, charging either less than its costs or less than it charges at home in order to enter or win a market. Stelco, a Canadian steelmaker, successfully fought dumping of steel products by steelmakers in Brazil, Finland, India, Indonesia, Thailand, and Ukraine. A Canadian tribunal found that cut-price steel imports from these countries caused "material injury to Canadian producers, including Stelco."[53]

When the U.S. Customs Bureau finds evidence of dumping, it can levy a dumping tariff on the guilty company. Various governments are watching for abuses and often force companies to charge the **arm's-length price**—the price charged by other competitors for the same or a similar product.

Disney has worked hard to fight piracy in China. Here are some Disney books, with Chinese translation, sold at a department store in Beijing, China.

Many multinationals are plagued by the gray market problem. The **gray market** consists of branded products diverted from normal or authorized distributions channels in the country of product origin or across international borders. Dealers in the low-price country find ways to sell some of their products in higher-price countries, thus earning more. Often a company finds some enterprising distributors buying more than they can sell in their own country and reshipping the goods to another country to take advantage of price differences. "Marketing Insight: Unauthorized Sales—Dealing with the Gray Market and Counterfeit Products" describes some issues with gray markets, as well as product fakes.

When companies sell their wares over the Internet, price becomes transparent, and price differentiation between countries declines: Consider an online training course. Whereas the price of a classroom-delivered day of training can vary significantly from the United States to France to Thailand, the price of an online-delivered day of training would be similar.

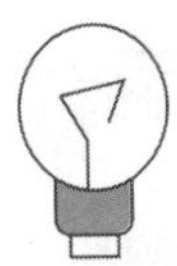

MARKETING INSIGHT | UNAUTHORIZED SALES – DEALING WITH THE GRAY MARKET AND COUNTERFEIT PRODUCTS

One of the downsides of globalization is that someone, somewhere, could be making money from your products and services, without your authorization or even knowledge. Two particularly thorny problems exist with gray markets and counterfeits.

The Gray Market

Research suggests that gray market activity—sales of genuine trademarked products through distribution channels unauthorized by the manufacturer or brand owner—accounts for over $40 billion in revenue each year. Gray markets create a "free-riding problem" and make legitimate distributors' investments in supporting a manufacturer's product less productive. Gray markets also make a selective distribution system more intensive. Gray markets harm distributor relations, tarnish the manufacturer's brand equity, and undermine the integrity of the distribution channel.

Multinationals try to prevent gray markets by policing the distributors, by raising their prices to lower-cost distributors, or by altering the product characteristics or service warranties for different countries. 3Com successfully sued several companies in Canada (for a total of $10 million) that provided written and oral misrepresentations to get deep discounts on 3Com networking equipment. The equipment, worth millions of dollars, was to be sold to a U.S. education software company and sent to China and Australia, but instead ended up back in the United States.

One research study found that gray market activity was most effectively deterred when the penalties were severe, when manufacturers were able to detect violations or mete out punishments in a timely fashion, or both.

Counterfeit Products

With the latest technology available everywhere, it's no surprise that fakes and imitations have become a major problem. Counterfeiting, estimated to cost businesses $600 billion a year, is expected to increase to $1.2 trillion by 2009. The Chinese have been prime offenders. According to U.S. Customs and Border Protection, 88% of all goods seized by Customs in a recent year originated in China (81%), Hong Kong (6%), or Taiwan (1%).

Fakes take a big bite of the profits of luxury brands such as Hermès, LVMH Moët Hennesy Louis Vuitton, and Tiffany, but faulty counterfeits can literally kill people. Cell phones with counterfeit batteries, fake brake pads made of compressed grass trimmings, and counterfeit airline parts pose safety risks to consumers. Virtually every product is vulnerable. As one anti-counterfeit consultant observed, "If you can make it, they can fake it." Defending against counterfeiters is difficult; some observers estimate that a new security system can be just months old before counterfeiters start nibbling at sales again.

The Web has been especially problematic. One estimate put Web sales of knockoff goods from watches to pharmacueticals at $119 billion in 2007—up from $84 billion the year before. EBay has come under heavy criticism from some manufacturers. Based on a survey of thousands of items, LVMH estimated 90% of Louis Vuitton and Christian Dior items listed on eBay were fakes, prompting the firm to sue.

Manufacturers are fighting back online with Web-crawling software that detects fraud and automatically sends warnings to apparent violaters without the need for any human intervention. Acushnet, maker of Titleist golf clubs and balls, shut down 75 auctions of knock-off gear in one day with just one mouse click. Web-crawling technology searches for counterfeit storefronts and sales by detecting domain names similar to legitimate brands and unauthorized Web sites that plaster brand trademarks and logos all over their homepages. It also checks for keywords such as "cheap," "discount," "authentic," and "factory variants," as well as colors that products were never made in and prices that are far too low.

Dealing with counterfeits is a never-ending struggle, and firms are trying all kinds of tacks online and off-line to fight back. To combat piracy in China, Disney developed a "Disney Magical Journey" rewards program. Consumers had to peel red hologram-covered stickers off legitimate Disney products, attach them to a form with some personal details, and mail them in to enter a contest for free Disney DVDs, television sets, and a trip to Hong Kong Disneyland. In addition to raising awareness of legitimate products and developing a database of Disney-friendly Chinese consumers, the promotion helped clean up some of Disney's channels as consumers would call to alert the company to retailers that, perhaps even unknowingly, were selling product fakes.

Sources: Gray Markets: www.agmaglobal.org; David Blanchard, "Just in Time—How to Fix a Leaky Supply Chain," *IndustryWeek*, May 1, 2007; Kersi D. Antia, Mark E. Bergen, Shantanu Dutta, and Robert J. Fisher, "How Does Enforcement Deter Gray Market Incidence?" *Journal of Marketing* 70 (January 2006): 92–106; Matthew B. Myers and David A. Griffith, "Strategies for Combating Gray Market Activity," *Business Horizons* 42 (November–December 1999): 2–8. *Counterfeiting:* Deborah Kong, "Smart Tech Fights Fakes," *Business 2.0* (March 2007): 30; Eric Shine, "Faking Out the Fakers," *BusinessWeek*, June 4, 2007, pp. 76–80; Geoffrey A. Fowler, "Disney Tries New Antipiracy Tack," *Wall Street Journal*, May 31, 2006; Carol Matlack, "Fed Up with Fakes," *BusinessWeek*, October 9, 2006, pp. 56–57.

Another new global pricing challenge is that countries with overcapacity, cheap currencies, and the need to export aggressively have pushed prices down and devalued their currencies. For multinational firms this poses challenges: Sluggish demand and reluctance to pay higher prices make selling in these emerging markets difficult. Instead of lowering prices and taking a loss, some multinationals have found more lucrative and creative means of coping.[54]

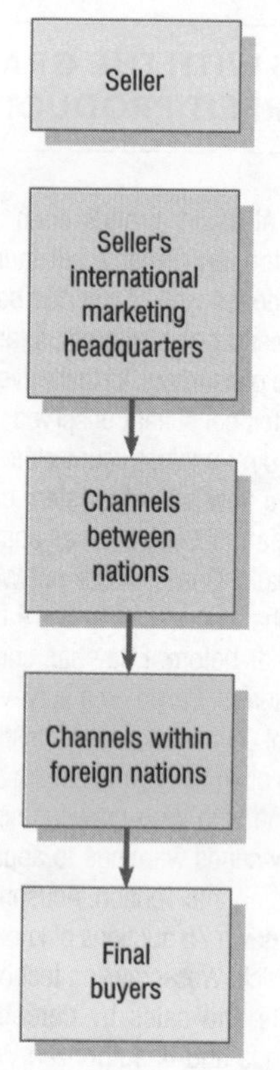

FIG. 21.4

Whole-Channel Concept for International Marketing

GENERAL ELECTRIC COMPANY

Rather than striving for larger market share, GE's power systems unit focused on winning a larger percentage of each customer's expenditures. The unit asked its top 100 customers what services were most critical and how GE could provide or improve them. The answers prompted the company to cut response time for replacing old or damaged parts from 12 weeks to 6. It began advising customers on the nuances of doing business in Europe and Asia and providing maintenance staff for occasional equipment upgrades. By adding value and helping customers reduce costs and become more efficient, GE avoided a move to commodity pricing and generated bigger margins and record revenues.[55]

Distribution Channels

Too many U.S. manufacturers think their job is done once the product leaves the factory. They should instead note how the product moves within the foreign country and take a whole-channel view of distributing products to final users. Figure 21.4 shows three links between seller and ultimate buyer. In the first, *seller's international marketing headquarters,* the export department or international division makes decisions about channels and other marketing activities. The second link, *channels between nations,* gets the products to the borders of the foreign nation. Decisions made in this link include the types of intermediaries (agents, trading companies), type of transportation (air, sea), and financing and risk management. The third link, *channels within foreign nations,* gets products from their entry point to final buyers and users.

Distribution channels within countries vary considerably. To sell consumer products in Japan, companies must work through one of the most complicated distribution systems in the world. They sell to a general wholesaler, who sells to a product wholesaler, who sells to a product-specialty wholesaler, who sells to a regional wholesaler, who sells to a local wholesaler, who finally sells to retailers. All these distribution levels can make the consumer's price double or triple the importer's price. Taking these same consumer products to tropical Africa, the company might sell to an import wholesaler, who sells to several jobbers, who sell to petty traders (mostly women) working in local markets.

Another difference is the size and character of retail units abroad. Large-scale retail chains dominate the U.S. scene, but much foreign retailing is in the hands of small, independent retailers. In India, millions of retailers operate tiny shops or sell in open markets. Their markups are high, but the real price comes down through haggling. Incomes are low, and people shop daily for small amounts, limited to whatever they can carry home on foot or bicycle. Most homes lack storage space and refrigeration. Packaging costs are kept low in order to keep prices low. In India, people often buy one cigarette at a time. Breaking bulk remains an important function of intermediaries and helps perpetuate the long channels of distribution, which are a major obstacle to the expansion of large-scale retailing in developing countries.

Retail outlets vary widely in size and character, forcing marketers to adapt their package sizes, price, and distribution channels to environments such as rural India.

When multinationals first enter a country, they prefer to work with local distributors who have good local knowledge, but friction often arises later.[56] The multinational complains that the local distributor doesn't invest in business growth, doesn't follow company policy, and doesn't share enough information. The local distributor complains of insufficient corporate support, impossible goals, and confusing policies. The multinational must choose the right distributors, invest in them, and set up performance goals to which they can agree.[57]

Some companies choose to invest in infrastructure to ensure they benefit from the right channels. Peruvian cola company Kola Real has been able to compete with Coca-Cola and Pepsi-Cola in Mexico by setting up its own distribution network of 600 leased lorries, 24 distribution centers, and 800 salespeople. Many retailers are trying to make inroads into global markets. France's Carrefour, Germany's Metro, and United Kingdom's Tesco have all established global positions. But some of the world's most successful retailers have had mixed success meeting the challenges of going abroad.

ALDI

Germany's Aldi follows a simple formula globally. It stocks only about 1,000 of the most popular everyday grocery and household items, compared with more than 20,000 at a traditional grocer such as Royal Ahold's Albert Heijin. Almost all the products carry Aldi's own exclusive label. Because it sells so few items, Aldi can exert strong control over quality and price and can simplify shipping and handling, leading to large margins. Retail experts expect Aldi to have 1,000 stores in the United States by 2010, with as much as 2% of the U.S. grocery market. With more than 7,500 stores worldwide currently, Aldi brings in about $35 billion in annual sales.[58]

WAL-MART

The world's largest retailer, Wal-Mart generates 20% of its total sales from international operations. Although this is the fastest-growing segment of its business, it has had mixed success globally. When it first went overseas in the early 1990s, Wal-Mart tried to bring a little Americana wherever it went: In soccer-crazed Brazil, it pushed golf clubs; in blazing hot Mexico, it promoted ice skates; in staid Germany, it instructed its cashiers to smile, prompting suspicions they were flirting. Wal-Mart's tried-and-true formula of low prices, tight inventory control, and big selection doesn't always pay off in markets where consumers have different shopping habits, discount competitors are already entrenched, and employees and suppliers are less subservient. After struggling for years, Wal-Mart withdrew from Germany and South Korea. In some countries, such as Mexico or England with its Asda subsidiary, the traditional formula of "cheap, steep, and deep" has worked well. But Wal-Mart has learned to adapt in those markets where more challenges exist. After realizing its suburban supercenter concept would not be the answer in Brazil, it purchased chains with an assortment of formats to better satisfy the diverse domestic market, and it has also made inroads in the enormous Chinese market.[59]

::: Country-of-Origin Effects

In an increasingly connected, highly competitive global marketplace, government officials and marketers are concerned with how attitudes and beliefs about their country affect consumer and business decision making. *Country-of-origin perceptions* are the mental associations and beliefs triggered by a country. Government officials want to strengthen their country's image to help domestic marketers who export, and to attract foreign firms and investors. Marketers want to use positive country-of-origin perceptions to sell their products and services.

Building Country Images

Governments now recognize that the images of their cities and countries affect more than tourism and have important value in commerce. Attracting foreign business can improve the local economy, provide jobs, and improve infrastructure. City officials in Kobe, Japan, were able to entice multinationals Procter & Gamble, Nestlé, and Eli Lilly to locate their Japanese headquarters in the city through traditional marketing techniques, with careful targeting and positioning.[60] Across the globe, after seeing its name being used to help sell everything from pizza to perfume to window blinds, the city of Venice made it a priority to capitalize on its image. City officials developed a trademark that could be licensed to product marketers.[61] Hong Kong officials also developed a symbol—a stylized dragon—to represent their city's core brand values.[62]

Countries all over the world are being marketed like any other brand.[63] New Zealand has developed concerted marketing programs to both sell its products outside the country, via its New Zealand Way program, and to attract tourists by showing the dramatic landscapes featured in "The Lord of the Rings" film trilogy. Both efforts reinforce the image of New Zealand as fresh and pure. But not all films can help the image of a country. Although Kazakhstan has a story to tell given its huge size, rich natural resources, and

The spectacular landscapes of New Zealand were brought to millions of viewers through the hugely successful "Lord of the Rings" film trilogy, shot there in its entirety. Marketing for a new surge of tourism to New Zealand has carefully played on the films' popularity.

rapid modernization, British comedian Sacha Baron Cohen's mock documentary "Borat" portrayed the country in an entirely different, sometimes crude and vulgar, light.[64]

Attitudes toward country of origin can change over time. Before World War II, Japan had a poor quality image. The success of Sony and its Trinitron TV sets and Japanese automakers Honda and Toyota helped change people's opinions. A strong company that emerges as a global player can do wonders for the image of a country. Relying partly on the global success of Nokia, Finland launched a campaign to enhance its image as a center of high-tech innovation.[65] "Marketing Insight: The Ups and Downs of Brand America" describes some of the issues that arose due to the anti-U.S. sentiment after the commencement of the Iraq war in 2003.

Consumer Perceptions of Country of Origin

Global marketers know that buyers hold distinct attitudes and beliefs about brands or products from different countries.[66] These country-of-origin perceptions can affect consumer decision making directly and indirectly. The perceptions may be included as an attribute in decision making or influence other attributes in the process ("if it's French, it must be stylish"). The mere fact that a brand is perceived as successful on a global stage may lend credibility and respect.[67] Several studies have found the following:[68]

- People are often ethnocentric and favorably predisposed to their own country's products, unless they come from a less developed country.
- The more favorable a country's image, the more prominently the "Made in . . ." label should be displayed.
- The impact of country of origin varies with the type of product. Consumers want to know where a car was made, but not the lubricating oil.
- Certain countries enjoy a reputation for certain goods: Japan for automobiles and consumer electronics; the United States for high-tech innovations, soft drinks, toys, cigarettes, and jeans; France for wine, perfume, and luxury goods.
- Sometimes country-of-origin perception can encompass an entire country's products. In one study, Chinese consumers in Hong Kong perceived U.S. products as prestigious, Japanese products as innovative, and Chinese products as cheap.

Marketers must look at country-of-origin perceptions from both a domestic and a foreign perspective. In the domestic market, these perceptions may stir consumers' patriotic notions or remind them of their past. As international trade grows, consumers may view certain brands as symbolically important in their own cultural heritage and identity. Patriotic appeals have been the basis of marketing strategies all over the world, but they can lack uniqueness and even be overused. During the Reagan administration in the 1980s, a number of U.S. brands in a diverse range of product categories (cars, beer, clothing) used pro-American themes in their advertising, perhaps diluting the efforts of all as a result.

In some cases, consumers don't know where brands come from, because the brand has become intertwined with multiple countries or the country of origin is not widely known. In surveys, consumers routinely guess that Heineken is German and Nokia is Japanese (they are Dutch and Finnish, respectively). Few consumers know Häagen-Dazs and Estée Lauder originated in the United States.

With so much outsourcing and foreign manufacturing, it's hard to know what the actual country of origin really is anyway. Only 65% of the content of a Ford Mustang comes from the United States or Canada, whereas the Toyota Sienna is assembled in Indiana with 90% local

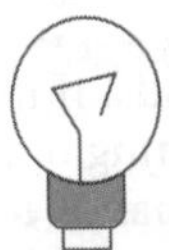

MARKETING INSIGHT | THE UPS AND DOWNS OF BRAND AMERICA

One concern for global marketers is how political issues about their domestic country can spill over to influence consumers' perceptions of their products and services in overseas markets. As the United States found itself at odds with other countries in recent years over various issues, including the war in Iraq, marketers wondered how that might influence the effectiveness of their marketing programs.

Initially, the answer appeared to be little. As one protester against the U.S. policy on North Korea observed, "Calling for political independence is one thing, and liking American brands is another. I like IBM, Dell, Microsoft, Starbucks, and Coke." Many consumers seemed willing to separate politics and products. U.S. technology was widely admired and young people all over the world continued to embrace U.S. youth culture. Perhaps the most compelling example of the power of U.S. brands overseas is the fact that McDonald's most successful market in Europe has been France, a country often dismissive of U.S. politics and culture.

Part of the explanation for this mental compartmentalization may be the way global U.S. brands have been built and marketed over the years. Many successfully tapped into universal consumer values and needs—such as Nike with athletic performance, MTV with youth culture, and Coca-Cola with youthful optimism. These firms hire thousands of employees abroad and make sure their products and marketing activities are consistent with local sensibilities.

Many brands have gone to great lengths to weave themselves into the cultural fabric of their foreign markets. One Coca-Cola executive tells of a young child visiting the United States from Japan who commented to her parents on seeing a Coca-Cola vending machine—"Look, they have Coca-Cola too!" As far as she was concerned, Coca-Cola was a Japanese brand.

Although some U.S. brands such as McDonald's, Coca-Cola, Microsoft, and Yahoo! did sustain some tarnishing of their images as time and the war ground on, the resilience of U.S. brands surprised many observers. One mid-2006 study of brand preferences in emerging markets found that even if the United States was not necessarily always that popular, its brands were. In Saudi Arabia, Kraft packaged cheese, Lay's potato chips, and McDonald's restaurants were all viewed as top brands in their categories. Overall, the study found that 70% of consumers in developing countries, ranging from Argentina to the United Arab Emirates, felt local products weren't as good as international brands. As one marketer said of the study, "Regardless of all the problems we have as a country, we are still looked to as the consumer capital of the world."

Sources: Kenneth Hein, "Emerging Markets Still Like U.S. Brands," *Brandweek*, April 16, 2007, p. 4; Parija Bhatnagar, "U.S. Brands Losing Luster," *CNN/Money*, May 21, 2004; "Burgers and Fries a la Francaise," *Economist*, April 17, 2004, pp. 60–61; Janet Guyon, "Brand America," *Fortune*, October 27, 2003, pp. 179–82; Richard Tompkins, "As Hostility towards America Grows, Will the World Lose Its Appetite for Coca-Cola, McDonald's, and Nike?" *Financial Times*, March 27, 2003, p. 13; Gerry Kermouch and Diane Brady, "Brands in an Age of Anti-Americanism," *BusinessWeek*, August 4, 2003, pp. 69–78.

components. Foreign auto makers are pouring money into North America, investing in plants, suppliers, and dealerships as well as design, testing, and research centers. But what makes a product more "American"—having a higher percentage of North American components or creating more jobs in North America? The two measures may not lead to the same conclusion.[69]

Companies can target niches to establish a footing in new markets. China's leading maker of refrigerators, washing machines, and air conditioners, Haier, is building a beachhead in the United States with U.S. college students who loyally buy its minifridges at Wal-Mart and elsewhere.[70] Haier's long-term plans are to introduce innovative products in other areas, such as flat-screen TV sets and wine-cooling cabinets.

As they make progress, companies can start to build local roots to increase relevance, as Toyota has done.

TOYOTA

Toyota has made sales in North America a top priority. As one executive bluntly stated, "We must Americanize." As proof of its conviction, consider the following. Toyota produces one of every six cars sold in the United States, and 60% of its cars sold in North America are made in North America. It has the top-selling car (the Camry) and hybrid (the Prius). To publicize its efforts and its convictions, Toyota has run ads touting its $16.6 billion investment in 13 North American factories and its 37,000-plus U.S. employee base. As much as 60% of its corporate operating profit comes from the United States, and it sells more cars there than in Japan.[71]

::: Deciding on the Marketing Organization

Companies manage their international marketing activities in three ways: through export departments, international divisions, or a global organization.

Export Department

A firm normally gets into international marketing by simply shipping out its goods. If its international sales expand, the company organizes an export department, consisting of a sales manager and a few assistants. As sales increase, the export department expands to include various marketing services so the company can go after business more aggressively. If the firm moves into joint ventures or direct investment, the export department will no longer be adequate to manage international operations.

International Division

Many companies engage in several international markets and ventures. Sooner or later they create international divisions to handle all their international activity. The international division is headed by a division president who sets goals and budgets and is responsible for the company's international growth.

The international division's corporate staff consists of functional specialists who provide services to various operating units. Operating units can be organized in several ways. First, they can be *geographical organizations*. Reporting to the international-division president might be regional vice presidents for North America, Latin America, Europe, Africa, the Middle East, and the Far East. Reporting to the regional vice presidents are country managers responsible for a sales force, sales branches, distributors, and licensees in the respective countries. The operating units may be *world product groups*, each with an international vice president responsible for worldwide sales of each product group. The vice presidents may draw on corporate-staff area specialists for expertise on different geographical areas. Finally, operating units may be *international subsidiaries*, each headed by a president. The various subsidiary presidents report to the president of the international division.

Global Organization

Several firms have become truly global organizations. Their top corporate management and staff plan worldwide manufacturing facilities, marketing policies, financial flows, and logistical systems. The global operating units report directly to the chief executive or executive committee, not to the head of an international division. The firm trains its executives in worldwide operations, recruits management from many countries, purchases components and supplies where it can obtain them at least cost, and makes investments where anticipated returns are greatest.

These companies face several organizational complexities. For example, when the firm is pricing a company's mainframe computers to a large banking system in Germany, how much influence should the headquarters product manager have? And the company's market manager for the banking sector? And the company's German country manager?

Different circumstances will dictate different approaches.[72] When forces for "global integration" (capital-intensive production, homogeneous demand) are strong and forces for "national responsiveness" (local standards and barriers, strong local preferences) are weak, a global strategy that treats the world as a single market can make sense (for example, with consumer electronics). When the reverse is true, then a multinational strategy that treats the world as a portfolio of national opportunities can be more appropriate (such as for food or cleaning products).

When both forces prevail to some extent, a "glocal" strategy that standardizes certain elements and localizes other elements can be the way to go (for instance, with telecommunications). As this is often the case, many firms seek a blend of centralized global control from corporate headquarters with input from local and regional marketers. Finding that balance can be tricky, though. Coca-Cola's "think local, act local" philosophy, which decentralized much of the power and responsibility for designing marketing programs and activities, fell apart because many local managers lacked the necessary skills or discipline to do the job. Decidedly un-Coke-like ads appeared—such as skinny-dippers streaking down a beach in Italy—and sales stalled. The pendulum swung back, and Coke executives in Atlanta began to play a stronger strategic role again.[73]

SUMMARY :::

1. Despite the many challenges in the international arena (shifting borders, unstable governments, foreign-exchange problems, corruption, and technological pirating), companies selling in global industries need to internationalize their operations. Companies cannot simply stay domestic and expect to maintain their markets.
2. In deciding to go abroad, a company needs to define its international marketing objectives and policies. The company must determine whether to market in a few countries or many countries. It must decide which countries to consider. In general, the candidate countries should be rated on three criteria: market attractiveness, risk, and competitive advantage. Developing countries offer a unique set of opportunities and risks.
3. Once a company decides on a particular country, it must determine the best mode of entry. Its broad choices are indirect exporting, direct exporting, licensing, joint ventures, and direct investment. Each succeeding strategy involves more commitment, risk, control, and profit potential.
4. In deciding on the marketing program, a company must decide how much to adapt its marketing program. At the product level, firms can pursue a strategy of straight extension, product adaptation, or product invention. At the communication level, firms may choose communication adaptation or dual adaptation. At the price level, firms may encounter price escalation, dumping, gray markets, and discounted counterfeit products. At the distribution level, firms need to take a whole-channel view of the challenge of distributing products to the final users. In creating all elements of the marketing program, firms must be aware of the cultural, social, political, technological, environmental, and legal limitations they face in other countries.
5. Country-of-origin perceptions can affect consumers and businesses alike. Managing those perceptions in the most advantageous way possible is an important marketing priority.
6. Depending on the level of international involvement, companies manage their international marketing activity in three ways: through export departments, international divisions, or a global organization.

APPLICATIONS :::

Marketing Debate Is the World Coming Closer Together?

Many social commentators maintain that youth and teens are becoming more and more alike across countries as time goes on. Others, although not disputing that fact, point out that differences between cultures at even younger ages by far exceed the similarities.

Take a position: People are becoming more and more similar *versus* The differences between people of different cultures far outweigh their similarities.

Marketing Discussion

Think of some of your favorite brands. Do you know where they come from? Where and how they are made or provided? Do you think knowing these answers would affect your perceptions of quality or satisfaction?

IN THIS CHAPTER, WE WILL ADDRESS THE FOLLOWING QUESTIONS:

1. What are important trends in marketing practices?
2. What are the keys to effective internal marketing?
3. How can companies be responsible social marketers?
4. How can a company improve its marketing skills?
5. What tools are available to help companies monitor and improve their marketing activities?

CHAPTER 22 ::: MANAGING A HOLISTIC MARKETING ORGANIZATION FOR THE LONG RUN

twenty-two

Healthy long-term growth for a brand requires that the marketing organization be managed properly. Holistic marketers must engage in a host of carefully planned, interconnected marketing activities and satisfy an increasingly broader set of constituents.[1] They must also consider a wider range of effects of their actions. Corporate social responsibility and sustainability have become a priority as organizations grapple with the short-term and long-term effects of their marketing. Some firms have embraced this new vision of corporate enlightenment and made it the very core of what they do. Consider Stonyfield Farm.[2]

Stonyfield Farm's roots go back to a time in the mid-1980s when local farms were disappearing in New England. Gary Hirshberg sat on the board of directors of an organic dairy farming school and convinced its founder there was a business opportunity in selling organic dairy products while "restoring the environment." Social responsibility has been at the core of the company from the start. As Hirshberg acknowledges, "Profits . . . are a means to an end. My highest goal is to save the planet for my children." Towards that end, Stonyfield is willing to live with the low margins that result from using higher-priced ingredients purchased from organic farmers. Stonyfield's suppliers eschew the productivity practices of agribusiness, including antibiotics, growth hormones, pesticides, and fertilizers. After calculating the amount of energy used to run its plant, Stonyfield decided to >>>

From its beginnings, Stonyfield Farm's commitment to holistic marketing has paid off in terms of concrete results that help the environment, like its reduced use of plastic and its loyalty to its organic suppliers, and in solid profitability. Its Yo Bany organic yogurt is made with whole milk and is packaged in 4-ounce containers for smaller appetites.

make an equivalent investment in environmental projects such as reforestation and wind farms. The company has dropped the plastic lids on its yogurt, saving about a million pounds of plastic a year, and added on-package messages about global warming, the perils of hormones, and genetically modified foods. Even after being purchased by France's Groupe Danone in 2001, the company has retained its core values. It hasn't lost sight of the products it sells either. It's added cultures or dietary supplements to help the immune system fight off illness and makes low-fat versions of its products. It has also introduced new flavors such as Vanilla Chi and Raspberry White Chocolate Chunk frozen yogurt, as well as new product lines such as Organic Greek yogurt and Shift dairy energy drink. The attitudes and beliefs that Stonyfield adopted have not hurt its financial performance. In fact, sales increased 22.3% in 2004, 28.5% in 2005, and 18.9% in 2006, making it the number-three yogurt brand in the United States.

Other brands such as Whole Foods, Ben & Jerry's, Patagonia, Timberland, and Odwalla have embraced similar philosophies and practices. Successful holistic marketing requires effective relationship marketing, integrated marketing, internal marketing, and performance marketing. Preceding chapters addressed the first two topics and the strategy and tactics of marketing.[3] In this chapter, we consider the latter two topics and how to conduct marketing responsibly. In our discussion, we look at how firms organize, implement, evaluate, and control marketing activities. We also discuss the increased importance of social responsibility. We begin by examining changes in how companies conduct marketing today.

::: Trends in Marketing Practices

Chapters 1 and 3 describe some important changes in the marketing macroenvironment, such as globalization, deregulation, technological advances, customer empowerment, and market fragmentation. In response to this rapidly changing environment, companies have restructured their business and marketing practices in many ways:

- ***Reengineering.*** Appointing teams to manage customer-value-building processes and break down walls between departments
- ***Outsourcing.*** Buying more goods and services from outside domestic or foreign vendors
- ***Benchmarking.*** Studying "best practice companies" to improve performance
- ***Supplier partnering.*** Partnering with fewer but better value-adding suppliers
- ***Customer partnering.*** Working more closely with customers to add value to their operations
- ***Merging.*** Acquiring or merging with firms in the same or complementary industries to gain economies of scale and scope

- ***Globalizing.*** Increasing efforts to "think global" and "act local"
- ***Flattening.*** Reducing the number of organizational levels to get closer to the customer
- ***Focusing.*** Determining the most profitable businesses and customers and focusing on them
- ***Accelerating.*** Designing the organization and setting up processes to respond more quickly to changes in the environment
- ***Empowering.*** Encouraging and empowering personnel to produce more ideas and take more initiative

The role of marketing in the organization is also changing.[4] Traditionally, marketers have played the roles of middlemen, charged with understanding customer needs and transmitting the voice of the customer to various functional areas in the organization. But in a networked enterprise, *every* functional area can interact directly with customers. Marketing no longer has sole ownership of customer interactions; rather, marketing needs to integrate all the customer-facing processes so customers see a single face and hear a single voice when they interact with the firm.

::: Internal Marketing

Internal marketing requires that everyone in the organization buy into the concepts and goals of marketing and engage in choosing, providing, and communicating customer value. Over the years, marketing has evolved from work done by the sales department into a complex group of activities spread through the organization.[5]

To learn about how the Haier Group implemented the "market-chain based Business Process Re-engineering"—a comprehensive internal marketing strategy—to transform itself into a top ranking company in China, visit www.pearsoned-asia.com/marketingmanagementchina.

HAMPTON INN

A unit of Hilton Hotels headquartered in Beverly Hills, California, Hampton Inn embarked on a major marketing campaign in 2004 that included strategic communication, experiential marketing, and a new tagline, "Make It Happen." The campaign was solely an internal one, however, created by Hampton Inn to sell its own general managers on 122 changes it was making to products and services. "We wanted it to be an internal rallying cry that by doing these things, we were making [the customer's stay] unique to Hampton," said the VP of brand management. The 122 changes ranged from serving better breakfasts to installing new shower rods. General managers and franchisees were able to see the improvements for themselves at a 2004 Hampton Inn show, via a gigantic model of the hotel. The company walked employees through every change, with the idea that only by experiencing it could they really understand and promote it to guests. With the managers and franchisees on board and enthused, the roll-out to customers lifted Hampton Inn's market share by five percentage points, and the percent of customers who rated Hampton a 9 or 10 for overall satisfaction went up by the same amount.[6]

A company can have an excellent marketing department, however, and fail at marketing. Much depends on how *other* company departments view customers. If they point to the marketing department and say, "They do the marketing," the company has not implemented effective marketing. Only when *all* employees realize their job is to create, serve, and satisfy customers does the company become an effective marketer.[7] "Marketing Memo: Characteristics of Company Departments That Are Truly Customer Driven" presents a tool that evaluates which company departments are truly customer driven.[8]

Let's look at how marketing departments are being organized, how they can work effectively with other departments, and how firms can foster a creative marketing culture within the entire organization.

Organizing the Marketing Department

Modern marketing departments can be organized in a number of different, sometimes overlapping ways:[9] functionally, geographically, by product or brand, by market, or in a matrix.

FUNCTIONAL ORGANIZATION The most common form of marketing organization consists of functional specialists reporting to a marketing vice president, who coordinates their

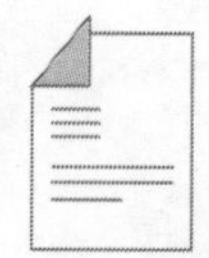

MARKETING MEMO | CHARACTERISTICS OF COMPANY DEPARTMENTS THAT ARE TRULY CUSTOMER DRIVEN

R&D	___	They spend time meeting customers and listening to their problems.
	___	They welcome the involvement of marketing, manufacturing, and other departments on each new project.
	___	They benchmark competitors' products and seek "best of class" solutions.
	___	They solicit customer reactions and suggestions as the project progresses.
	___	They continuously improve and refine the product on the basis of market feedback.
Purchasing	___	They proactively search for the best suppliers rather than choose only from those who solicit their business.
	___	They build long-term relations with fewer but more reliable high-quality suppliers.
	___	They do not compromise quality for price savings.
Manufacturing	___	They invite customers to visit and tour their plants.
	___	They visit customer factories to see how customers use the company's products.
	___	They willingly work overtime when it is important to meet promised delivery schedules.
	___	They continuously search for ways to produce goods faster and/or at lower costs.
	___	They continuously improve product quality, aiming for zero defects.
	___	They meet customer requirements for "customization" where this can be done profitably.
Marketing	___	They study customer needs and wants in well-defined market segments.
	___	They allocate marketing effort in relation to the long-run profit potential of the targeted segments.
	___	They develop winning offerings for each target segment.
	___	They measure company image and customer satisfaction on a continuous basis.
	___	They continuously gather and evaluate ideas for new products, product improvements, and services to meet customers' needs.
	___	They influence all company departments and employees to be customer centered in their thinking and practice.
Sales	___	They have specialized knowledge of the customer's industry.
	___	They strive to give the customer "the best solution."
	___	They make only promises they can keep.
	___	They feed back customers' needs and ideas to those in charge of product development.
	___	They serve the same customers for a long period of time.
Logistics	___	They set a high standard for service delivery time and they meet this standard consistently.
	___	They operate a knowledgeable and friendly customer-service department that can answer questions, handle complaints, and resolve problems in a satisfactory and timely manner.
Accounting	___	They prepare periodic "profitability" reports by product, market segment, geographic areas (regions, sales territories), order sizes, and individual customers.
	___	They prepare invoices tailored to customer needs and answer customer queries courteously and quickly.
Finance	___	They understand and support marketing expenditures (e.g., image advertising) that represent marketing investments that produce long-term customer preference and loyalty.
	___	They tailor the financial package to the customers' financial requirements.
	___	They make quick decisions on customer creditworthiness.
Public Relations	___	They disseminate favorable news about the company and they "damage control" unfavorable news.
	___	They act as an internal customer and public advocate for better company policies and practices.
Other Customer-Contact Personnel	___	They are competent, courteous, cheerful, credible, reliable, and responsive.

activities. Figure 22.1 shows five specialists. Additional specialists might include a customer service manager, a marketing planning manager, a market logistics manager, a direct marketing manager, and a digital marketing manager.

The main advantage of a functional marketing organization is its administrative simplicity. It can be quite a challenge to develop smooth working relationships, however, within the marketing department.[10] This form also can lose its effectiveness as the number of products and markets increases. A functional organization often leads to inadequate planning for specific products and markets. Then, each functional group competes with others for budget and status. The marketing vice president constantly weighs the claims of competing functional specialists and faces a difficult coordination problem.

GEOGRAPHIC ORGANIZATION A company selling in a national market often organizes its sales force (and sometimes other functions, including marketing) along geographic lines. The

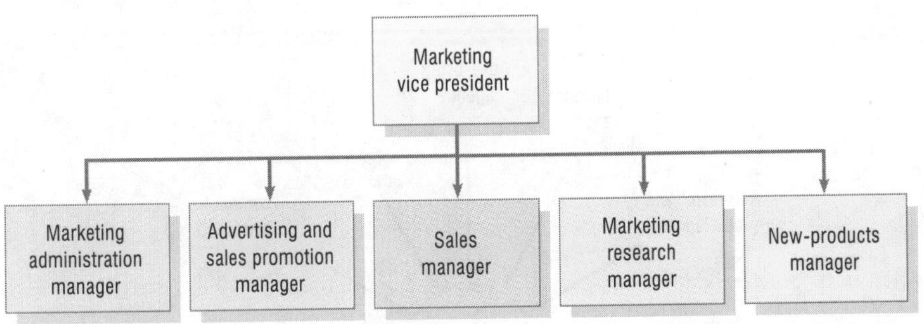

FIG. 22.1

Functional Organization

national sales manager may supervise 4 regional sales managers, who each supervise 6 zone managers, who in turn supervise 8 district sales managers, who each supervise 10 salespeople.

Several companies are now adding *area market specialists* (regional or local marketing managers) to support the sales efforts in high-volume markets. One such market might be Miami, Florida, where roughly 44% of the households are Hispanic. The Miami specialist would know Miami's customer and trade makeup, help marketing managers at headquarters adjust their marketing mix for Miami, and prepare local annual and long-range plans for selling all the company's products in Miami.

Companies that have shifted to a greater regional marketing emphasis are McDonald's, which now spends about 50% of its total advertising budget regionally; American Airlines, which realized that the travel needs of Chicagoans and Southwesterners are very different in the winter months; and Anheuser-Busch, which has subdivided its regional markets into ethnic and demographic segments, with different ad campaigns for each. Some companies must develop different marketing programs in different parts of the country because their brand development varies so much.

PACE

In 1947, a young Texan named David Pace had a passion for producing the freshest-tasting picante sauce. After experimenting with ingredients, bottling techniques, and a unique production process, he produced a special blend of tomatoes, onions, and jalapeños he called Pace Picante Sauce. Campbell Soup Company acquired the firm in 1994. Pace's historical strength, however, lies west of the Mississippi. The brand registers only single digits in market share in the Northeast. The vast disparity in regional strengths has led to tailored marketing programs in different parts of the country. Pace's trailgating tour, blending cowboy-style chuckwagon cooking and tailgate barbecuing, coincides with its rodeo event sponsorship and appeals to the core customer base out West. New England promotions are designed for trial and market penetration.[11]

Widely divergent degrees of market penetration east and west of the Rockies dictates two different marketing approaches for Pace Picante Sauce, such as with this promotional event, Pace Picante Pro Rodeo Chute Out, in Las Vegas.

PRODUCT- OR BRAND-MANAGEMENT ORGANIZATION Companies producing a variety of products and brands often establish a product- (or brand-) management organization. The product-management organization does not replace the functional organization, but serves as another layer of management. A product manager supervises product category managers, who in turn supervise specific product and brand managers.

A product-management organization makes sense if the company's products are quite different, or if the sheer number of products is beyond the ability of a functional organization to handle. Kraft has used a product-management organization in its Post division, with separate product category managers in charge of cereals, pet food,

FIG. 22.2

The Product Manager's Interactions

and beverages. Within the cereal-product group, Kraft has had separate subcategory managers for nutritional cereals, children's presweetened cereals, family cereals, and miscellaneous cereals.

Product and brand management is sometimes characterized as a **hub-and-spoke system**. The brand or product manager is figuratively at the center, with spokes emanating out to various departments (see Figure 22.2). Some tasks that product or brand managers may perform include:

- Developing a long-range and competitive strategy for the product
- Preparing an annual marketing plan and sales forecast
- Working with advertising and merchandising agencies to develop copy, programs, and campaigns
- Increasing support of the product among the sales force and distributors
- Gathering continuous intelligence on the product's performance, customer and dealer attitudes, and new problems and opportunities
- Initiating product improvements to meet changing market needs

The product-management organization lets the product manager concentrate on developing a cost-effective marketing mix and react more quickly to new products in the marketplace; it also gives the company's smaller brands a product advocate. However, this organization has disadvantages too:

- Product and brand managers may lack enough authority to carry out their responsibilities.
- Product and brand managers become experts in their product area but rarely achieve functional expertise.
- The product-management system often turns out to be costly. One person is appointed to manage each major product or brand, and soon more are appointed to manage even minor products and brands.
- Brand managers normally manage a brand for only a short time. Short-term involvement leads to short-term planning and fails to build long-term strengths.
- The fragmentation of markets makes it harder to develop a national strategy. Brand managers must please regional and local sales groups, transferring power from marketing to sales.
- Product and brand managers focus the company on building market share rather than the customer relationship.

A second alternative in a product-management organization is *product teams*. There are three types of structures: vertical product team, triangular product team, and the horizontal product team (see Figure 22.3).

The triangular and horizontal product-team approaches let each major brand be run by a **brand-asset management team (BAMT)** consisting of key representatives from functions that affect the brand's performance. The company is made of several BAMTs that periodically report to a BAMT directors committee, which itself reports to a chief branding officer. This is quite different from the way brands have traditionally been handled.

A third alternative for product-management organization is to eliminate product manager positions for minor products and assign two or more products to each remaining manager. This is feasible where two or more products appeal to a similar set of needs. A cosmetics company doesn't need product managers for each product because cosmetics serve one major need—beauty. A toiletries company needs different managers for headache remedies, toothpaste, soap, and shampoo, because these products differ in use and appeal.

A fourth alternative is to introduce *category management*, in which a company focuses on product categories to manage its brands. Procter & Gamble, pioneers of the brand-management system, and several other top firms made a significant shift to category management.[12]

P&G cites a number of advantages. By fostering internal competition among brand managers, the traditional brand-management system created strong incentives to excel, but also much internal competition for resources and a lack of coordination. The new scheme was designed to ensure that all categories would be able to receive adequate resources.

Another rationale for category management is the increasing power of the trade. Because the retail trade has tended to think of profitability in terms of product categories, P&G felt it only made sense to deal along similar lines. Retailers and regional grocery chains such as Wal-Mart and Dominick's respectively have embraced category management as a means to define a particular product category's strategic role within the store and address logistics, the role of private-label products, and the trade-offs between product variety and inefficient duplication.

Category management is not a panacea. It is still a product-driven system. Colgate has moved from brand management (Colgate toothpaste) to category management (toothpaste category) to a new stage called "customer-need management" (mouth care). This last step finally focuses the organization on a basic customer need.[13]

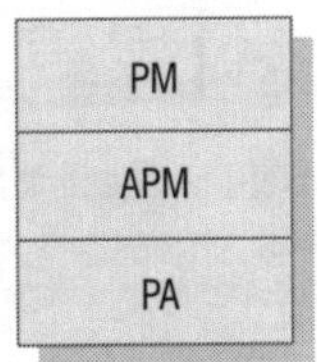

(a) Vertical Product Team

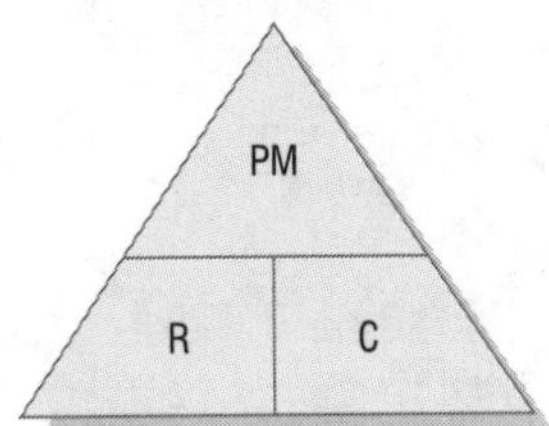

(b) Triangular Product Team

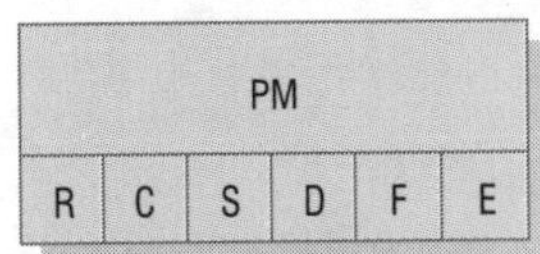

(c) Horizontal Product Team

PM = product manager
AP = associate product manager
PA = product assistant
R = market researcher
C = communication specialist
S = sales manager
D = distribution specialist
F = finance/accounting specialist
E = engineer

FIG. 22.3

Three Types of Product Teams

MARKET-MANAGEMENT ORGANIZATION Many companies sell to different markets. Canon sells fax machines to consumer, business, and government markets. U.S. Steel sells to the railroad, construction, and public utility industries. When customers fall into different user groups with distinct buying preferences and practices, a **market-management organization** is desirable. Market managers supervise several market-development managers, market specialists, or industry specialists and draw on functional services as needed. Market managers of important markets might even have functional specialists reporting to them.

Market managers are staff (not line) people, with duties similar to those of product managers. They develop long-range and annual plans for their markets. Their performance is judged by their market's growth and profitability. This system shares many advantages and disadvantages of product-management systems. Its strongest advantage is organizing marketing activity to meet the needs of distinct customer groups rather than focusing on marketing functions, regions, or products. Many companies are reorganizing along market lines and becoming **market-centered organizations**. Xerox has converted from geographic selling to selling by industry, as have IBM and Hewlett-Packard.

In a **customer-management organization**, companies can organize themselves to understand and deal with individual customers rather than with the mass market or even market segments.[14] When a close relationship is advantageous, such as when customers have diverse and complex requirements and buy an integrated bundle of products and services, customer-management organizations should prevail. IBM's Global Services and General Electric's Power Systems are organized in this fashion because of their need to interact closely with customers. One study showed that companies organized by customer groups reported much higher accountability for the overall quality of relationships and employees' freedom to take actions to satisfy individual customers.[15]

MATRIX-MANAGEMENT ORGANIZATION Companies that produce many products for many markets may adopt a matrix organization. Some provide the context in which a matrix can thrive—flat, lean team organizations focused around business processes that cut horizontally across functions.[16] DuPont was a pioneer in developing the matrix structure (see Figure 22.4).

FIG. 22.4

Product/Market-Management Matrix System

		Market Managers			
		Menswear	Women's wear	Home furnishings	Industrial markets
Product Managers	Rayon				
	Acetate				
	Nylon				
	Orlon				
	Dacron				

DUPONT

Before it was spun off, DuPont's textile fibers department consisted of separate product managers for rayon, acetate, nylon, orlon, and dacron; and separate market managers for menswear, women's wear, home furnishings, and industrial markets. The product managers planned sales and profits for their respective fibers. They asked market managers to estimate how much of their fiber they could sell in each market at a proposed price. Market managers, however, were generally more interested in meeting their market's needs than pushing a particular fiber. In preparing their market plans, they asked each product manager about the fiber's planned prices and availabilities. The final sales forecast of the market managers and the product managers should have added up to the same grand total.

Companies like DuPont can go one step further and view the market managers as the main marketers, and their product managers as suppliers. The menswear market manager, for example, would be empowered to buy textile fibers from DuPont's product managers or, if DuPont's price is too high, from outside suppliers, forcing DuPont product managers to become more efficient. If a DuPont product manager couldn't match the "arm's-length pricing" levels of competitive suppliers, then perhaps DuPont should not produce that fiber.

A matrix organization seems desirable in a multiproduct, multimarket company. The rub is that it's costly and often creates conflicts. There's the cost of supporting all the managers, and questions about where authority and responsibility for marketing activities should reside—at headquarters or in the division?[17] Some corporate marketing groups assist top management with overall opportunity evaluation, provide divisions with consulting assistance on request, help divisions that have little or no marketing, and promote the marketing concept throughout the company.

Relations with Other Departments

Under the marketing concept, all departments need to "think customer" and work together to satisfy customer needs and expectations. The marketing department must drive this point home. The marketing vice president, or CMO, has two tasks: (1) to coordinate the company's internal marketing activities and (2) to coordinate marketing with finance, operations, and other company functions to serve the customer.

Yet, there is little agreement on how much influence and authority marketing should have over other departments. Departments define company problems and goals from their viewpoint, so conflicts of interest and communications problems are unavoidable. Typically, the marketing vice president must work through persuasion rather than authority.

To develop a balanced orientation in which marketing and other functions jointly determine what is in the company's best interests, companies can provide joint seminars to understand each others' viewpoints, joint committees and liaison personnel, personnel exchange programs, and analytical methods to determine the most profitable course of action.[18]

Many companies now focus on key processes rather than departments, because departmental organization can be a barrier to the smooth performance of fundamental business processes. They appoint process leaders, who manage cross-disciplinary teams that include marketing and sales people. As a result, marketing personnel may have a solid-line responsibility to their teams and a dotted-line responsibility to the marketing department.

JONES LANG LASALLE (JLL)

A global property and investment management company, Jones Lang Lasalle (JLL) moved in stages to transform its organizational structure to a customer-centric, rather than a product-management, organization. JLL added an overarching "Corporate Solutions" group of all three of its service units and an account management function, run by high-ranking officers influential with big clients such as Bank of America. JLL's revenue from the Corporate Solutions group grew more than 50% between 2000 and 2005, but the service unit managers didn't like ceding authority to account managers lacking experience in their service. And single-transaction customers thought the small number of JLL account managers in their local markets was problematic. JLL then made a more dramatic move; it dispensed with service-focused units altogether and organized its business into two groups: Clients and Markets. This restructuring put more employees in the field, where they were closer to and more responsive to clients, and got all internal groups and processes focused on customer needs above all.[19]

Building a Creative Marketing Organization

Many companies realize they're not yet really market and customer driven—they are product and sales driven. Baxter, General Motors, Shell, and J.P. Morgan are attempting to transform into true market-driven companies. This requires:

1. Developing a company-wide passion for customers
2. Organizing around customer segments instead of products
3. Understanding customers through qualitative and quantitative research

The task is not easy, but the payoffs can be considerable.[20] It won't happen as a result of the CEO making speeches and urging every employee to "think customer." See "Marketing Insight: The Marketing CEO" for actions a CEO can take to improve marketing capabilities.

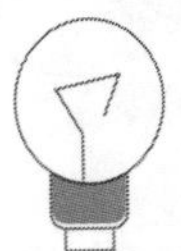

MARKETING INSIGHT | THE MARKETING CEO

What steps can a CEO take to create a market- and customer-focused company?

1. ***Convince senior management of the need to become customer focused.*** The CEO personally exemplifies strong customer commitment and rewards those in the organization who do likewise. For example, former CEOs Jack Welch of GE and Lou Gerstner of IBM are said to have spent 100 days a year visiting customers, in spite of their many strategic, financial, and administrative burdens; current Starbucks CEO Jim Donald visits 10–20 stores a week to go to the back of the counter and talk to store partners (employees) and customers.
2. ***Appoint a senior marketing officer and marketing task force.*** The marketing task force should include the CEO; the vice presidents of sales, R&D, purchasing, manufacturing, finance, and human resources; and other key individuals.
3. ***Get outside help and guidance.*** Consulting firms have considerable experience in helping companies move toward a marketing orientation.
4. ***Change the company's reward measurement and system.*** As long as purchasing and manufacturing are rewarded for keeping costs low, they will resist accepting some costs required to serve customers better. As long as finance focuses on short-term profit, it will oppose major investments designed to build satisfied, loyal customers.
5. ***Hire strong marketing talent.*** The company needs a strong marketing vice president who not only manages the marketing department but also gains respect from and influence with the other vice presidents. A multidivisional company will benefit from establishing a strong corporate marketing department.
6. ***Develop strong in-house marketing training programs.*** The company should design well-crafted marketing training programs for corporate management, divisional general managers, marketing and sales personnel, manufacturing personnel, R&D personnel, and others. GE, Motorola, and Accenture run these programs.
7. ***Install a modern marketing planning system.*** The planning format will require managers to think about the marketing environment, opportunities, competitive trends, and other forces. These managers then prepare strategies and sales-and-profit forecasts for specific products and segments and are accountable for performance.
8. ***Establish an annual marketing excellence recognition program.*** Business units that believe they've developed exemplary marketing plans should submit a description of their plans and results. Winning teams should be rewarded at a special ceremony and the plans disseminated to the other business units as "models of marketing thinking." Accenture, Becton-Dickenson, and DuPont follow this strategy.
9. ***Shift from a department focus to a process-outcome focus.*** After defining the fundamental business processes that determine its success, the company should appoint process leaders and cross-disciplinary teams to reengineer and implement these processes.
10. ***Empower the employees.*** Progressive companies encourage and reward their employees for coming up with new ideas and empower them to settle customer complaints to save the customer's business. IBM, for example, lets its frontline employees spend up to $5,000 to solve a customer problem on the spot.

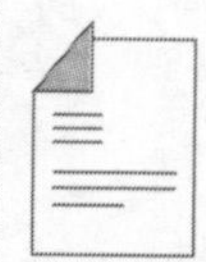

MARKETING MEMO | FUELING STRATEGIC INNOVATION

Professor Stephen Brown of Ulster University has challenged a number of fundamental assumptions underlying the marketing concept. He thinks marketers make too much of researching and satisfying consumers, and they risk losing marketing imagination and significant consumer impact. How can companies build a capability for strategic innovation? Here are some approaches he advocates:

- Hire marketers who are unusually creative to counterbalance the majority who do marketing by the textbook. These people may be unconventional, rule breaking, risk taking, and even more argumentative, but their ideas will at least present a challenge.
- Train your employees in the use of creativity techniques, for groups (brainstorming, synectics) and individuals (visualization, attribute listing, forced relationships, morphological analysis, mind mapping).
- Note trends such as longer working hours, single parenting, and new life styles, and tease out their implications for your firm.
- List unmet customer needs and imagine new offerings or solutions: how to help people lose weight, stop smoking, relieve stress, meet others.
- Run a "best idea" competition once a month. Give a cash reward, extra vacation time, or travel awards to those who come up with the best ideas.
- Have senior managers take small sets of employees out to lunch or dinner once a week to discuss ideas for improving the business. Go to new settings, such as a wrestling match, a drug rehabilitation center, a poor neighborhood.
- Set up groups of employees to critique the company's and competitors' products and services. Let them critique the company's cherished beliefs and consider turning them upside down.
- Occasionally hire creative resources from outside the firm. Many large advertising agencies, such as Leo Burnett, run a creativity service for clients.

Sources: For more on Brown's views, see Stephen Brown, *Marketing—The Retro Revolution* (Thousand Oaks, CA: Sage, 2001). For more on creativity, see Pat Fallon and Fred Senn, *Juicing the Orange: How to Turn Creativity into a Powerful Business Advantage* (Boston: Harvard Business School Press, 2006); Bob Schmetterer, *Leap: A Revolution in Creative Business Strategy* (Hoboken, NJ: John Wiley & Sons, 2003); Jean-Marie Dru, *Beyond Disruption: Changing the Rules in the Marketplace* (Hoboken, NJ: John Wiley & Sons, 2002); Michael Michalko, *Cracking Creativity: The Secrets of Creative Genius* (Berkeley, CA: Ten Speed Press, 1998); James M. Higgins, *101 Creative Problem-Solving Techniques* (New York: New Management Publishing, 1994); and all the books by Edward DeBono.

Although it's *necessary* to be customer oriented, it's not *enough*. The organization must also be creative. Companies today copy each others' advantages and strategies with increasing speed. Differentiation gets harder to achieve, let alone maintain, and margins fall when firms become more alike. The only answer is to build a capability in strategic innovation and imagination (see "Marketing Memo: Fueling Strategic Innovation"). This capability comes from assembling tools, processes, skills, and measures that let the firm generate more and better new ideas than its competitors.[21]

Companies must watch trends and be ready to capitalize on them. Motorola was 18 months late in moving from analog to digital cellular phones, giving Nokia and Ericsson a big lead. Barnes & Noble was late to recognize online ordering of books and music, letting Amazon.com gain a head start. Nestlé was late seeing the trend toward coffeehouses such as Starbucks. Coca-Cola was slow to pick up beverage trends toward fruit-flavored drinks such as Snapple, energy drinks such as Gatorade, and designer water brands. Market leaders tend to miss trends when they are risk averse, obsessed about protecting their existing markets and physical resources, and more interested in efficiency than innovation.[22]

::: Socially Responsible Marketing

Effective internal marketing must be matched by a strong sense of ethics, values, and social responsibility.[23] A number of forces are driving companies to practice a higher level of corporate social responsibility: rising customer expectations, evolving employee goals and ambitions, tighter government legislation and pressure, developing investor interest in social criteria, relentless media scrutiny, and changing business procurement practices.[24] The commercial success of Al Gore's 2006 documentary, *An Inconvenient Truth*, shows how the general public has become more concerned about environmental issues.

Virtually all firms have decided to take a more active, strategic role with corporate responsibility. As Wal-Mart CEO Lee Scott said, "We thought we could sit in Bentonville [Arkansas], take care of customers, take care of associates—and the world would leave us alone. It doesn't work that way anymore." Former Home Depot CEO Robert Nardelli similarly observed: "Things have become a lot more interdependent. There are a broader range of constituents."[25] Even banana producer Chiquita, which once had a poor reputation for exploiting farmworkers, contaminating water, and destroying rain forest, has improved workers conditions; significantly reduced pesticide use, reduced erosion and chemical runoff; and even implemented a major recycling program on its farms.[26]

There were not always these beliefs in the value of social responsibility. In 1776, Adam Smith proclaimed, "I have never known much good done by those who profess to trade for the public good." Legendary economist Milton Friedman famously declared social initiatives "fundamentally subversive" because he felt they undermined the profit-seeking purpose of public companies and wasted shareholders' money. Some critics worry that important business investment in areas such as R&D could suffer as a result of a focus on social responsibility.[27]

But these critics are in the vast minority. Many now believe that satisfying customers, employees, and other stakeholders and achieving business success are closely tied to the adoption and implementation of high standards of business and marketing conduct. Firms are finding that one benefit of being seen as a socially responsible company is the ability to attract employees, especially younger people who want to work for companies they feel good about. The most admired—and increasingly most successful—companies in the world abide by a code of serving people's interests, not only their own.

FIRMS OF ENDEARMENT

Researchers Sisodia, Wolfe, and Sheth believe humanistic companies make great companies. They define "Firms of Endearment" as those that have a culture of caring and serve the interests of their stakeholders. Stakeholders are defined in terms of the acronym, SPICE: Society, Partners, Investors, Customers, and Employees. Firms of Endearment create a love affair with stakeholders. Their senior managers run an open-door policy, are passionate about customers, and their compensation is modest. They pay more to their employees, relate more closely to a smaller group of excellent suppliers, and give back to the communities in which they work. The researchers assert that Firms of Endearment actually spend less on marketing as a percentage but yet earn greater profits. It appears that the customers who love the company do most of the marketing. The authors see the 21st-century marketing paradigm as creating value for all stakeholders and becoming a beloved firm.

Table 22.1 displays firms receiving top marks as firms of endearment from a sample of thousands of customers, employees, and suppliers.[28] "Breakthrough Marketing: Starbucks" describes the practices of one high scorer on that list. But many smaller firms excel too. Boston's Dancing Deer Baking is an $8 million company whose customers rave about its popular all-natural sweets. It also receives much praise for its philanthropic efforts to assist homeless people; its use of recycled fiber in packaging; and its commitment to its 65 employees in low-income Roxbury (inner-city Boston).[29] The experience of another Boston-based business, Life is Good, shows how effective philanthropy can be when it is aligned with the company's mission.

TABLE 22.1 Top Firms of Endearment

Best Buy	BMW	CarMax	Caterpillar
Commerce Bank	Container Store	Costco	eBay
Google	Harley-Davidson	Honda	IDEO
IKEA	JetBlue	Johnson & Johnson	Jordan's Furniture
L.L.Bean	New Balance	Patagonia	Progressive Insurance
REI	Southwest	Starbucks	Timberland
Toyota	Trader Joe's	UPS	Wegmans
Whole Foods			

Source: Raj Sisodia, David B. Wolfe, and Jag Sheth, *Firms of Endearment: How World-Class Companies Profit from Passion and Purpose* (Upper Saddle River, NJ: Wharton Schcol Publishing, 2007).

Dancing Deer Baking in inner-city Boston has made its reputation as a producer of popular all-natural sweets and as an eco-friendly and generous neighbor.

LIFE IS GOOD®

Life Is Good morphed from two brothers selling hand-screen-printed "Life Is Good" T-shirts at a Cambridge street fair in 1994 to an $80 million business with 5,000 distributors and 200 employees. Although Bert and John Jacobs market everything from T-shirts to dog dishes emblazoned with their stick figure mascot Jake and "Life Is Good" slogan, they see themselves as essentially selling optimism. Yet, in the aftermath of 9/11, employees wondered how they could sell such a cheery message. The Jacobs brothers responded by taking $30,000 they had set aside for their first advertising campaign and giving it to a fund for the families of 9/11 victims. The next year, the company continued its family-centric philanthropy efforts by donating to Project Joy, which offers play therapy for traumatized children, and Camp Sunshine, a retreat for children with life-threatening diseases. Now, to raise funds for these and similar causes, Life Is Good hosts seasonal feel-good festivals around the country. Not only do festivalgoers live the Life Is Good motto by enjoying life's simple pleasures at a pumpkin or watermelon festival, but they also get a worthy cause to promote and, in turn, Life Is Good raises its public profile.[30]

Companies are increasingly working with public interest groups to avoid perceptions of "greenwashing"—insincere, phony efforts to appear more environmentally sensitive than they really are. Alliances with environmentalists can achieve more satisfying solutions that both address public concerns and increase the firm's image and profits. DuPont once viewed Greenpeace as an enemy; the firm now uses Greenpeace's former head as a consultant. Greenpeace has also worked with McDonald's, Cargill, and others to stop farmers cutting down the Amazon rainforest to grow soybeans. When Greenpeace called out Coca-Cola on the eve of the 2000 Sydney Olympics for using a potent greenhouse gas in its nearly

BREAKTHROUGH MARKETING | STARBUCKS

Starbucks opened in Seattle in 1971 at a time when coffee consumption in the United States had been declining for a decade and rival coffee brands used cheaper coffee beans to compete on price. Starbucks' founders decided to experiment with a new concept: a store that would sell only the finest imported coffee beans and coffee-brewing equipment. The original store didn't sell coffee by the cup, only beans.

Howard Schultz came to Starbucks in 1982. While in Milan on business, he walked into an Italian coffee bar and had an epiphany with his espresso. "There was nothing like this in America. It was an extension of people's front porch. It was an emotional experience," he said. He knew right away that he wanted to bring this concept to the United States. Schultz set about creating an environment for Starbucks coffeehouses that would reflect Italian elegance melded with U.S. informality. He envisioned Starbucks as a "personal treat" for its customers, a "Third Place"—a comfortable, sociable gathering spot bridging the workplace and the home.

From its launch in Seattle, Starbucks' expansion throughout the United States was carefully planned. The management team agreed that all stores would be owned and operated by the company, ensuring complete control to cultivate an unparalleled image of quality. Starbucks employed a "hub" expansion strategy, in which coffeehouses entered a new market in a clustered group. Although this deliberate saturation often cannibalized 30% of one store's sales by introducing a store nearby, any drop in revenue was offset by efficiencies in marketing and distribution costs, and the enhanced image of convenience. A typical customer would stop by Starbucks 18 times a month. No U.S. retailer has had a higher frequency of customer visits.

Part of the success of Starbucks undoubtedly lies in its products and services, and its relentless commitment to providing customers with the richest possible sensory experiences. But another key is the enlightened sense of responsibility that manifests itself in a number of different ways.

Schultz believes, to exceed the expectations of customers that it is first necessary to exceed the expectations of employees. As far back as 1990, Starbucks provided comprehensive health care to all employees, including part-timers. Health insurance now costs Starbucks more each year than coffee. The firm also introduced a stock option plan called "Bean Stock," which allows Starbucks' employees to participate in the company's financial success.

The company donates millions of dollars to charities via The Starbucks Foundation, created in 1997 with proceeds from the sale of Schultz's book. The mission of the foundation is to "create hope, discovery, and opportunity in communities where Starbucks partners [employees] live and work." The primary focus of the foundation has been on improving young peoples' lives by supporting literacy programs for children and families. By 2007, the foundation had provided over $12 million to more than 700 youth-focused organizations in the United States and Canada. Starbucks also has donated 5 cents of every sale of its Ethos bolted water to improving the quality of water in poor countries as part of a five-year, $10 million pledge.

Starbucks believes that by focusing and aligning the giving priorities of Starbucks Coffee Company with The Starbucks Foundation, a separate 501(c)(3) charitable organization, its contributions will have greater impact and provide more benefit to communities around the world. The Starbucks Foundation celebrated its 10-year anniversary in 2007 with the announcement of Starbucks About Youth, a global Philanthropic endeavor focused on supporting educational initiatives and youth leadership in Starbucks retail markets around the world.

Starbucks also promotes "fair-trade" export practices with third-world coffee bean producers—no other retailer in North America sells more fair-trade coffee—and pays its producers in those countries an average of 23% above market price. It took the company 10 years of development to create the world's first recycled beverage cup made from 10% postconsumer fiber, conserving five million pounds of paper or approximately 78,000 trees a year. The company has 87 urban locations co-owned by Earvin "Magic" Johnson.

Howard Schultz stepped down as CEO in 2000, but he remains chairman and "Chief Global Strategist." Starbucks currently has over 12,400 stores worldwide, with 115,000 employees and almost $8 billion in revenue. The company hopes to expand to 40,000 outlets, cafés, and kiosks worldwide, half of them outside the United States. No matter what the growth trajectory, Schultz believes Starbucks must retain a passion for coffee and a sense of humanity, to remain small even as it gets big, and to always treat workers as individuals.

Sources: Howard Schultz, "Dare to Be a Social Entrepreneur," *Business 2.0* (December 2006): 87; Edward Iwata, "Owner of Small Coffee Shop Takes On Java Titan Starbucks," *USA Today*, December 20, 2006; "Staying Pure: Howard Schultz's Formula for Starbucks," *Economist*, February 25, 2006, p. 72; Diane Anderson, "Evolution of the Eco Cup," *Business 2.0* (June 2006): 50; Bruce Horovitz, "Starbucks Nation," *USA Today*, May 19, 2006; Theresa Howard, "Starbucks Takes Up Cause for Safe Drinking Water," *USA Today*, August 2, 2005; Howard Schultz and Dori Jones Yang, *Pour Your Heart into It: How Starbucks Built a Company One Cup at a Time* (New York: Hyperion, 1997); www.starbucks.com.

Adobe Systems' award-winning headquarters in San Jose is the greenest corporate site on record. Adobe has dramatically reduced electricity and gas consumption in the building over a five-year period.

10 million coolers and vending machines, Coke, along with PepsiCo, Unilever, and McDonald's, invested $30 million in a less damaging system that now displays a "technology approved by Greenpeace" banner.[31]

Firms are fundamentally changing the way they conduct their business, sometimes even where they work. In 2006, $2 billion software maker Adobe Systems became the first company to receive a platinum award from the U.S. Green Building Council, making the firm's San Jose headquarters the greenest corporate site on record. By retrofitting its building with automatic faucets, waterless urinals, timed outages, energy-saver compact fluorescent lights, weather-controlled irrigation systems, and motion sensors, Adobe reduced electricity use by 35% and gas consumption by 41% over a five-year period while still increasing its head count by 80%.[32]

Corporate Social Responsibility

Raising the level of socially responsible marketing calls for making a three-pronged attack that relies on proper legal, ethical, and social responsibility behavior.

LEGAL BEHAVIOR Organizations must ensure every employee knows and observes relevant laws. For example, it's illegal for salespeople to lie to consumers or mislead them about the advantages of buying a product. Salespeople's statements legally must match advertising claims. Salespeople may not offer bribes to purchasing agents or others influencing a B2B sale. They may not obtain or use competitors' technical or trade secrets through bribery or industrial espionage. Finally, they must not disparage competitors or their products by suggesting things that are not true. Managers must make sure every sales representative knows the law and acts accordingly.[33]

ETHICAL BEHAVIOR Business practices come under attack because business situations routinely pose tough ethical dilemmas: It's not easy to draw a clear line between normal marketing practice and unethical behavior. Some issues sharply divide critics. Though Kraft chose to stop advertising some of its less healthy products such as Oreos and Chips Ahoy! on television programs targeted to children ages 6 to 11, some watch groups felt that was not enough.[34]

At the same time, certain business practices are clearly unethical or illegal. These include bribery, theft of trade secrets, false and deceptive advertising, exclusive dealing and tying agreements, quality or safety defects, false warranties, inaccurate labeling, price-fixing or undue discrimination, and barriers to entry and predatory competition.

Companies must adopt and disseminate a written code of ethics, build a company tradition of ethical behavior, and hold people fully responsible for observing ethical and legal guidelines.[35] Companies that don't perform ethically or well are at greater risk of being exposed, thanks to the Internet. In the past, a disgruntled customer might bad-mouth a firm to 12 other people; today he or she can reach thousands. Microsoft, for example, has attracted scores of anti-Microsoft sites, including Hate Microsoft and Boycott Microsoft. The general distrust of companies among U.S. consumers is evident in research showing that between 2001 and 2005, the number who viewed corporations unfavorably increased 20%.

SOCIAL RESPONSIBILITY BEHAVIOR Individual marketers must practice a "social conscience" in specific dealings with customers and stakeholders. Increasingly, people want information about a company's record on social and environmental responsibility to help decide which companies to buy from, invest in, and work for.[36] Table 22.2 lists companies receiving high marks for social responsibility.

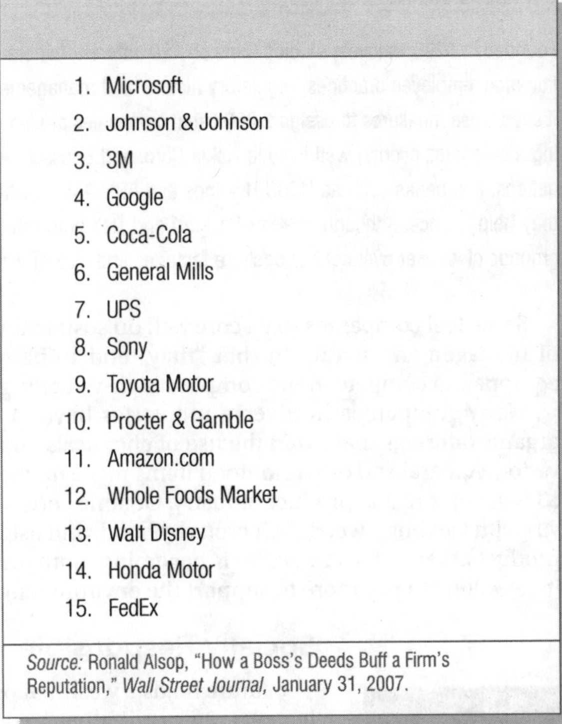

TABLE 22.2
Top-Rated Companies for Social Responsibility

1. Microsoft
2. Johnson & Johnson
3. 3M
4. Google
5. Coca-Cola
6. General Mills
7. UPS
8. Sony
9. Toyota Motor
10. Procter & Gamble
11. Amazon.com
12. Whole Foods Market
13. Walt Disney
14. Honda Motor
15. FedEx

Source: Ronald Alsop, "How a Boss's Deeds Buff a Firm's Reputation," *Wall Street Journal*, January 31, 2007.

Deciding how to communicate corporate social responsibility can be difficult. Once a firm touts an environmental initiative, it can become a target for criticism. When Levi's launched its Eco organic jeans line, it added organic cotton to its products quietly for several years until it reached 100%, because it feared drawing attention to the fact that according to USDA and EPA data, a third of a pound of chemicals is used to grow a pound of the regular, nonorganic cotton in the United States used in some of its other jeans lines. Many well-intentioned product or marketing initiatives attract unforeseen negative consequences. Palm oil was hailed as a renewable fuel for food companies looking to find a solution to a trans fat ban, until its use was linked to the potential extinction of the orangutan and the sun bear.[37]

Corporate philanthropy also can pose problems.[38] Merck, DuPont, Wal-Mart, and Bank of America have donated $100 million or more to charities in a year. Yet good deeds can be overlooked—even resented—if the company is seen as exploitive or fails to live up to a "good guys" image.[39] Philip Morris Company's $250 million ad campaign touting its charitable activities was met with skepticism because of its negative corporate image.

SUSTAINABILITY *Sustainability*—the importance of meeting humanity's needs without harming future generations—has risen to the top of many corporate agendas. Major corporations now outline in great detail how they are trying to improve the long-term impact of their actions on communities and the environment. As one sustainability consultant put it, "There is a triple bottom line—people, planet, and profit—and the people part of the equation must come first. Sustainability means more than being eco-friendly, it also means you are in it for the long haul."[40]

Many CEOs believe embracing sustainability can avoid the negative consequences of environmental disasters, political protests, and human rights or workplace abuses. Often a target of environmental criticism in the past, DuPont has moved through two phases of sustainability in the past 15 years: first, drastically reducing the emission of greenhouse gases, release of carcinogens, and discharge of hazardous wastes; and second, embracing sustainability as a strategic goal via the introduction of alternative biofuels and energy-saving materials such as its new bio-PDO fiber.[41]

Investors are even demanding more concrete information about what firms are doing to achieve sustainability. Sustainability ratings exist, although there is little agreement about what the appropriate metrics might be.[42]

INNOVEST

Founded in 1995, Innovest studies firms on 120 different factors, such as energy use, health and safety records, litigation, employee practices, regulatory history, and management systems for dealing with supplier problems. It uses these measures to assign 2,200 listed companies grades ranging from AAA to CCC, much like a bond rating. Companies scoring well include Nokia Corp. and Ericsson, which excel at tailoring products for developing nations, and banks such as HSBC Holdings and ABN-AMRO, which study the environmental impact of projects they help finance. Although Hewlett-Packard and Dell both rate AAA, Apple gets a middling BBB rating on the grounds of weaker oversight of offshore factories and lack of a "clear environmental business strategy."

Some feel companies that score well on sustainability factors typically exhibit high levels of management quality in that "they tend to be more strategically nimble and better equipped to compete in the complex, high-velocity, global environment."[43]

Many companies in diverse industries beyond edible food products are embracing organic offerings that avoid the use of chemicals and pesticides to stress ecological preservation. Apparel and other nonfood items make up the second-fastest growth category of the $3.5 billion organic product industry. Organic cotton grown by farmers who fight boll weevils with ladybugs, weed their crops by hand, and use manure for fertilizer has become a hot product at retail. Sustainability is becoming more mainstream, and consumers are increasingly willing to pay more to support the environment.[44]

Socially Responsible Business Models

The future holds a wealth of opportunities.[45] Technological advances in solar energy, online networks, cable and satellite television, biotechnology, and telecommunications promise to change the world as we know it. At the same time, forces in the socioeconomic, cultural, and natural environments will impose new limits on marketing and business practices. Companies that innovate solutions and values in a socially responsible way are the most likely to succeed.[46]

Many companies such as The Body Shop, Working Assets, and Smith and Hawken are giving social responsibility a more prominent role. Actor Paul Newman's homemade salad dressing has grown to a huge business. The Newman's Own brand is on additional products such as pasta sauce, salsa, popcorn, and lemonade and is sold in 15 countries. The company has given away all its profits and royalties after tax—$200 million so far—to educational and charitable programs such as the Hole in the Wall Gang camps Newman created for children with serious illnesses.[47]

Corporate philanthropy as a whole is on the rise, increasing 22% to total $13.7 billion in cash and in-kind support in 2005. In the United States health and human services get more than half of corporate support, followed by education, with giving by the pharmaceutical industry surpassing all other industries.[48] More firms are coming to the belief that corporate social responsibility in the form of cash donations, in-kind contributions, cause marketing, and employee volunteerism programs is not just the "right thing" but also the "smart thing to do."[49] "Marketing Insight: New Views on Corporate Social Responsibility" offers two high-profile perspectives on how to make progress in that area.

As part of a global launch of products made of 100% organic cotton, Levi's introduced its new Eco jeans for customers who want to "minimize their personal impact on the environment." Even the garment tags and packaging are made of organic fabric or recycled paper and printed with soy-based ink.

Cause-Related Marketing

Many firms blend corporate social responsibility initiatives with marketing activities.[50] **Cause-related marketing** links the firm's contributions to a designated cause to customers' engaging directly or indirectly in revenue-producing transactions with the firm.[51] Cause marketing is part of *corporate societal marketing (CSM)*, which Drumwright and Murphy define as marketing efforts "that have at least one noneconomic objective related to social welfare and use the resources of the company and/or of its partners."[52] They also

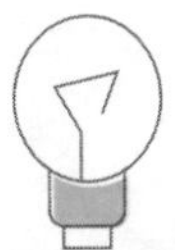

MARKETING INSIGHT | NEW VIEWS ON CORPORATE SOCIAL RESPONSIBILITY

Two of management's most renowned thinkers have turned their attention to corporate social responsibility, offering some unique perspectives that builds on their past management research and thinking.

Michael Porter

Harvard's Michael Porter and Mark Kramer, managing director of FSG Social Impact Advisors, believe good corporate citizenship can be a source of opportunity, innovation, and competitive advantage, as long as firms evaluate it using the same frameworks and concepts that guide their core business strategies. They feel corporate social responsibility must mesh with a firm's strengths, capabilities, and positioning. They assert that *strategic corporate social responsibility* results when firms (1) transform value chain activities to benefit society while reinforcing strategy and (2) engage in strategic philanthropy that leverages capabilities to improve salient areas of competitive context.

According to the authors, firms should select causes that intersect their particular businesses to create shared value for the firm and society. For example, Toyota addressed public concerns about auto emissions by creating a competitively strong and environmentally friendly hybrid vehicle, Prius; Mexican construction company Urbi prospered by using novel financing approaches to build housing for disadvantaged buyers; and French banking giant Crédit Agricole differentiated itself through specialized environmentally friendly financial products.

Porter and Kramer note that, "By providing jobs, investing capital, purchasing goods, and doing business every day, corporations have a profound and positive influence on society. The most important thing a corporation can do for society, and for any community, is contribute to a prosperous economy." Although companies can address hundreds of social issues, only a handful offer the opportunity to build focused, proactive, and integrated social initiatives that link with core business strategies to make a real difference to society and create a competitive advantage in the marketplace.

Clayton Christensen

Harvard's Clayton Christensen, along with his research colleagues, advocates *catalytic innovations* to address social sector problems. Like Christensen's disruptive innovations—which challenge industry incumbents by offering simpler, good enough alternatives to an underserved group of customers—catalytic innovations offer good enough solutions to inadequately addressed social problems. Catalytic innovators share five qualities:

1. They create systemic social change through scaling and replication.
2. They meet a need that is either overserved (because the existing solution is more complex than many people require) or not served at all.
3. They offer simpler, less costly products and services that may have a lower level of performance, but that users consider to be good enough.
4. They generate resources, such as donations, grants, volunteer manpower, or intellectual capital, in ways that are initially unattractive to competitors.
5. They are often ignored, disparaged, or even encouraged by existing players for whom the business model is unprofitable or otherwise unattractive and who therefore avoid or retreat from the market segment.

As support for their approach, the authors note how community colleges have dramatically changed the shape of higher education in the United States by providing a low-cost alternative of choice for 44% of the nation's undergraduates. The Minneapolis-based MinuteClinic provides affordable walk-in diagnosis and treatment for common health problems, as well as vaccinations, via 87 clinics located in CVS stores in 10 states.

To find organizations that are creating a catalytic innovation for investment or other purposes, Christensen and his colleagues offer some guidelines:

1. ***Look for signs of disruption in the process***—Although not necessarily easily observed, preexisting catalytic innovators may already be present in a market.
2. ***Identify specific catalytic innovations***—Apply the five criteria listed.
3. ***Assess the business model***—Determine whether the organization can effectively introduce the innovation and scale it up and sustain it.

Sources: Michael F. Porter and Mark R. Kramer, "Strategy & Society," *Harvard Business Review* (December 2006): 78-82; Clayton M. Christensen, Heiner Baumann, Rudy Ruggles, and Thomas M. Stadtler, "Disruption Innovation for Social Change," *Harvard Business Review* (December 2006): 94-101. See also, Richard Steckel, Elizabeth Ford, Casey Hilliard, and Traci Sanders, *Cold Cash for Warm Hearts: 101 Best Social Marketing Initiatives* (Homewood, IL: High Tide Press, 2004).

include other activities such as traditional and strategic philanthropy and volunteerism as part of CSM.

Tesco, a leading U.K. retailer, has created a "Computers for Schools" program: Customers receive vouchers for every 10 pounds spent, which they can donate to the school of their choice; the school exchanges the vouchers for new computer equipment. Dawn, the top dishwashing liquid in the United States, introduced a campaign highlighting the fact that the product's grease-cleaning power had an unusual side benefit—it could clean birds caught in oil spills. A Web site launched in 2006, www.DawnSavesWildlife.com, drew 130,000 people who formed virtual groups to encourage friends and others to stop gas and oil leaks from their cars into the environment.[53] British Airways has a particularly successful and highly visible program.

The MinuteClinic walk-in medical treatment centres at 87 CVS stores around the country exemplify the idea of "catalytic innovation" described by Harvard's Clayton Christensen, by offering a low-cost available alternative that customers consider "good enough" for their needs.

BRITISH AIRWAYS

British Airways partnered with UNICEF and developed a cause-marketing campaign called Change for Good. Passengers on British Airways flights are encouraged to donate leftover foreign currency from their travels. The scheme is simple: Passengers deposit their surplus currency in envelopes provided by British Airways, which collects the deposits and donates them directly to UNICEF. British Airways advertises its program during an in-flight video, on the backs of seat cards, and with in-flight announcements. The company also developed a television ad that featured a child thanking British Airways for its contribution to UNICEF. Because Change for Good can be directly targeted to passengers and can produce immediate results, it does not require extensive advertising or promotion and is highly cost-efficient. Since 1994, it has distributed almost $45 million around the world.[54]

CAUSE-MARKETING BENEFITS AND COSTS A successful cause-marketing program can improve social welfare; create differentiated brand positioning; build strong consumer bonds; enhance the company's public image with government officials and other decision makers; create a reservoir of goodwill; boost internal morale and galvanizing employees; drive sales; and increase the market value of the firm.[55]

Consumers may develop a strong, unique bond with the firm that transcends normal marketplace transactions.[56] Specifically, cause marketing can (1) build brand awareness, (2) enhance brand image, (3) establish brand credibility, (4) evoke brand feelings, (5) create a sense of brand community, and (6) elicit brand engagement.[57] Cause marketing has a particular interested audience in civic-minded 13- to 25-year-old Millennial consumers (see Table 22.3).

The danger, however, is that a cause-related marketing program could backfire if cynical consumers question the link between the product and the cause and see the firm as self-serving and exploitive.[58]

TABLE 22.3

Millennial Generation Cause Attitudes

Percentage of 13–25-year-olds who say they:	
Feel personally responsible for making a difference in the world	61%
Feel companies should join in the effort to make a difference in the world	75%
Are likely to switch brands (given equal price and quality) to support a cause	89%
Are more likely to pay attention to messages of companies deeply committed to a cause	74%
Consider a company's social commitment when deciding where to shop	69%
Consider a company's social commitment when recommending products	64%

Source: Cone Inc./AMP Insights survey of 1,800 13–25-year-olds as reported in *BusinessWeek*, November 6, 2006, p. 13.

CADBURY SCHWEPPES PLC

Cadbury's "Sports for Schools" promotion offered sports and fitness equipment for schools in exchange for tokens. The problem was, the public and media saw a perverse incentive for children to eat more chocolate, a product associated with obesity. As Britain's Food Commission, a nongovernmental organization, said, "Cadbury wants children to eat two million kilograms of fat—to get fit." The commission estimated that to generate the 90 tokens to purchase a £5 netball would require spending £38 on Cadbury candies and consuming more than 20,000 calories and over 1,000 grams of fat. The product and the cause seemed to be at war. Cadbury Schweppes quickly discontinued the token program, but it continued its "Get Active" campaign offering teachers tips for sporty games in conjunction with the Youth Sport Trust and sponsored events such as Get Active Day with British sports stars. Putting a positive spin on the bad press, a Cadbury spokesperson insisted, "The ensuing debate was very welcome. We have been trying to promote Get Active for two months. I don't think there can be anyone in the country who hasn't heard of it this week."[59]

Nike's alliance with the Lance Armstrong Foundation for cancer research has sold over 70 million yellow LIVE**STRONG** bracelets for $1, but deliberately, the famed Nike swoosh logo is nowhere to be seen.[60] One of the more interesting cause programs in recent years is the Project Red campaign.[61]

(RED)

2006 saw the highly publicized launch of (RED), championed by U2 singer and activist Bono and Bobby Shriver, Chairman of DATA. (RED) was created to raise awareness and money for The Global Fund by teaming with some of the world's most iconic branded products—American Express cards, Motorola phones, Converse sneakers, Gap T-shirts, Apple iPods, and Emperio Armani sunglasses—to produce (PRODUCT)RED branded products. Up to 50% of the profits from the sale of (PRODUCT)RED products are given to The Global Fund to help women and children affected by HIV/AIDS in Africa. The parentheses or brackets in the logo were designed to signify "the embrace"—each company that becomes (RED) places its logo in this embrace and is then "elevated to the power of red." Although some critics felt the project was overmarketed, in the first 18 months of its existence, (RED) contributed more than $36 million to The Global Fund, more than seven times the amount businesses had contributed since it was founded in 2002.

The brainchild of U2's Bono and Bobby Shriver, chairman of DATA, (RED) was a highly publicized effort to raise money for AIDS relief in Africa through partnerships with iconic brands such as Apple, Motorola, American Express, and Gap. Bono and talk show host Oprah Winfrey are shown here shopping at the Red launch in Chicago.

The knowledge, skills, resources, and experiences of a top firm may even be more important to a nonprofit or community group than funding. Nonprofits must be clear about what their goals are, communicate clearly what they hope to accomplish, and have an organizational structure in place to work with different firms. Developing a long-term relationship with a firm can take a long time. As one consultant noted, "What's often a problem between corporations and nonprofits is different expectations and different understanding about the amount of time everything will take."[62]

Firms must make a number of decisions in designing and implementing a cause-marketing program, such as how many and which cause(s) to choose and how to brand the cause program.

CHOOSING A CAUSE Some experts believe the positive impact of cause-related marketing is reduced by sporadic involvement with numerous causes. For example, Cathy Chizauskas, Gillette's director of civic affairs, states: "When you're spreading out your giving in fifty-dollar to one-thousand-dollar increments, no one knows what you are doing. . . . It doesn't make much of a splash."[63]

Many companies choose to focus on one or a few main causes to simplify execution and maximize impact. One such focused marketer is McDonald's. Ronald McDonald Houses in more than 27 countries offer more than 6,000 rooms each night to families needing support while their child is in the hospital. The Ronald McDonald House program has provided a "home away from home" for nearly 10 million family members since its beginning in 1974.

Limiting support to a single cause, however, may limit the pool of consumers or other stakeholders who can transfer positive feelings from the cause to the firm. In addition, many popular causes already have numerous corporate sponsors. Over 300 companies, including Avon, Ford, Estée Lauder, Revlon, Lee Jeans, Polo Ralph Lauren, Yoplait, Saks, BMW, and American Express, have associated themselves with breast cancer as a cause.[64] As a consequence, the brand may find itself "lost in the shuffle," overlooked in a sea of symbolic pink ribbons.

Opportunities may be greater with "orphan causes"—diseases that afflict fewer than 200,000 people.[65] Another option is overlooked diseases, such as pancreatic cancer, which is the fourth-deadliest form of cancer behind skin, lung, and breast, yet has received little or no corporate support. Even major killers such as prostate cancer for men and heart disease for women have been relatively neglected compared to breast cancer, but a number of firms have begun to fill the void. Recent years have seen a dozen new sponsors such as Gillette and Grolsch beer join longtime supporters Safeway and Major League Baseball in the fight against prostate cancer. The American Heart Association launched a marketing program "Go Red for Women" with a Red Dress symbol to heighten awareness and attract interest from corporations and others to a disease that kills roughly 12 times more women than breast cancer each year.[66]

Most firms choose causes that fit their corporate or brand image and matter to their employees and shareholders. LensCrafters' Give the Gift of Sight program is a family of charitable vision care programs that provides free vision screenings, eye exams, and glasses to more than 3 million needy people in North America and developing countries around the world. All stores are empowered to deliver free glasses in their communities. In addition, Give the Gift of Sight sponsors two traveling Vision Vans targeting children in North America as well as monthly two-week optical missions overseas. "Marketing Memo: Making A Difference" provides some tips from a top cause-marketing firm.

Social Marketing

Cause-related marketing supports a cause. **Social marketing** by nonprofit or government organizations *furthers* a cause, such as "say no to drugs" or "exercise more and eat better."[67]

Social marketing goes back many years. In the 1950s, India started family planning campaigns. In the 1970s, Sweden ran social marketing campaigns to turn the country into a nation of nonsmokers and nondrinkers, the Australian government ran "Wear Your Seat Belt" campaigns, and the Canadian government launched campaigns to "Say No to Drugs," "Stop Smoking," and "Exercise for Health." In the 1980s, the World Bank, World Health Organization, and Centers for Disease Control and Prevention started to use the term and promote interest in social marketing. Some notable global social marketing successes include these:

- Oral rehydration therapy in Honduras significantly decreased deaths from diarrhea in small children under the age of five.

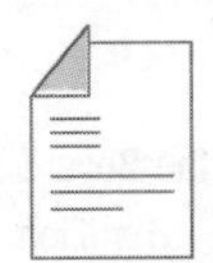

MARKETING MEMO | MAKING A DIFFERENCE

One of the most accomplished cause-marketing consulting firms, Boston's Cone Inc., offers perspectives on the current state of cause marketing and how it should best be practiced:

> With new vigor, consumers, customers, employees, investors, and communities are closely watching how companies behave in relation to them and to society. Influential groups such as Business for Social Responsibility, Dow Jones Sustainability Index, *Fortune* magazine, and others are judging companies based on a complex series of global standards. Business practices such as governance, philanthropy, sourcing, the environment, employee relations, and community relations have moved from behind the scenes to center stage. For executives today, appropriately defining, executing, and communicating corporate social responsibility (CSR) has never been more important.

To help execute and communicate CSR more effectively, Cone offers the following considerations:

- ***Define CSR for your company.*** Make sure that your senior executives are all talking about the same thing. CSR includes a broad range of complex internal and external business practices. Although they are vital components of the CSR mix, corporate philanthropy and community relations alone don't define CSR.
- ***Build a diverse team.*** The development and execution of CSR strategies require a collaborative, concerted team effort. Create a decision-making task force that integrates and brings together a range of expertise and resources, including marketing, public affairs, community relations, legal, human resources, manufacturing, and others. Put a formal process in place to approach CSR strategy development, ongoing implementation, and continuous improvement.
- ***Analyze your current CSR-related activities and revamp them if necessary.*** Do your due diligence at the outset to understand CSR gaps and risks specific to your company. Research industry examples and cull best practices from leading case studies. Make sure to consider global trends, as Europe is far advanced of the United States.
- ***Forge and strengthen NGO relationships.*** The more than 300,000 nongovernmental organizations (NGOs) around the world are a powerful force on corporate policies and behavior, serving as both advocates and loud critics. Forge sincere partnerships with organizations that can offer you independent, unbiased insight into and evaluation of your CSR activities, provide expertise on social issues and developing global markets, and offer access to key influentials.
- ***Develop a cause-branding initiative.*** Create a public face for your citizenship activities through a signature cause-branding initiative that integrates philanthropy, community relations, marketing, and human resources assets. ConAgra Foods' Feeding Children Better program, for example, is a multiyear initiative created to feed millions of hungry children through innovative partnerships, grant making, employee volunteerism, and education and awareness. This program recently earned ConAgra Foods the U.S. Chamber of Commerce's Corporate Citizenship Award.
- ***Walk your talk.*** Critics often assert that companies exploit CSR as a PR smokescreen to conceal or divert attention from corporate misdeeds and blemishes. Before introducing any new CSR initiative or drawing attention to good corporate behavior, make sure that your company is addressing stakeholder expectations of CSR at the most basic level.
- ***Don't be silent.*** Not only do Americans expect businesses to behave socially, the majority want companies to tell them how they are doing so. An overwhelming majority also say they prefer to find out about CSR activities from a third-party source, particularly the media.
- ***Beware.*** Greater public awareness for your corporate citizenship record can be double-edged. Claims of socially responsible behavior, even sincere ones, often invite public scrutiny. Be prepared. Even if your company is not ready to proactively communicate about your CSR activities, be ready to respond to public inquiries immediately. Don't let the threat of public scrutiny keep you mute, though. More often than not, silence regarding CSR issues is translated as indifference, or worse, inaction.

Sources: Cone Buzz (April 2004). See also, Carol L. Cone, Mark A. Feldman, and Alison T. DaSilva, "Cause and Effects," *Harvard Business Review* (July 2003): 95–101.

- Social marketers created booths in marketplaces where Ugandan midwives sold contraceptives at affordable prices.
- Population Communication Services created and promoted two extremely popular songs in Latin America, "Stop" and "When We Are Together," to help young women "say no."
- The National Heart, Lung, and Blood Institute successfully raised awareness about cholesterol and high blood pressure, which helped to significantly reduce deaths.

A number of different types of organizations conduct social marketing in the United States. Government agencies include the Centers for Disease Control and Prevention, Departments of Health, Social, and Human Services, Department of Transportation, and the U.S. Environmental Protection Agency. Literally hundreds of nonprofit organizations conduct social marketing, including the American Red Cross, the World Wildlife Fund, and the American Cancer Society.

The Boys & Girls Club of America partners with many different individuals and organizations to help raise awareness of their programs to bring recreation, fitness, educational, and leadership activities to millions of U.S. children. Denzel Washington, a prominent spokesperson, is shown here with New York City Mayor Michael Bloomberg at a gala dinner.

BOYS & GIRLS CLUB OF AMERICA

Known as "The Positive Place for Kids," the Boys & Girls Club of America serves more than 4.6 million young people annually in over 4,000 club locations in all 50 states and on military bases worldwide. The children's time in the program is spent on such activities as sports, recreation, and fitness, as well as on schoolwork, and even on programs centered on character development, leadership, and life skills. Distinguished alumni of the Boys & Girls Club include Bill Cosby, Brad Pitt, and Denzel Washington, who serves as a spokesperson. In a little over a decade, the organization built a roster of roughly 40 corporate partners to help provide programs and services for its members. The Crest Cavity-Free Zone improves dental health of underserved children; Club Tech uses a $100 million cash and in-kind grant from Microsoft to place computers and software in clubs; and Blockbuster's support of the Boys & Girls Clubs' National Kids Day promotion has generated millions in funding.[68]

Choosing the right goal or objective for a social marketing program is critical. Should a family-planning campaign focus on abstinence or birth control? Should a campaign to fight air pollution focus on ride sharing or mass transit? Social marketing campaigns may have objectives related to changing people's cognitions, values, actions, or behaviors. The following examples illustrate the range of possible objectives.

Cognitive campaigns

- Explain the nutritional value of different foods.
- Explain the importance of conservation.

Action campaigns

- Attract people for mass immunization.
- Motivate people to vote "yes" on a certain issue.
- Motivate people to donate blood.
- Motivate women to take a pap test.

Behavioral campaigns

- Demotivate cigarette smoking.
- Demotivate usage of hard drugs.
- Demotivate excessive consumption of alcohol.

Value campaigns

- Alter ideas about abortion.
- Change attitudes of bigoted people.

Social marketing uses a number of different tactics to achieve its goals.[69] The planning process follows many of the same steps as for traditional products and services (see Table 22.4). Some key success factors in developing and implementing a social marketing program include:

- Study the literature and previous campaigns.
- Choose target markets that are most ready to respond.

TABLE 22.4

Social Marketing Planning Process

Where Are We?
- Determine program focus.
- Identify campaign purpose.
- Conduct an analysis of strengths, weaknesses, opportunities, and threats (SWOT).
- Review past and similar efforts.

Where Do We Want to Go?
- Select target audiences.
- Set objectives and goals.
- Analyze target audiences and the competition.

How Will We Get There?
- Product: Design the market offering.
- Price: Manage costs of behavior change.
- Distribution: Make the product available.
- Communications: Create messages and choose media.

How Will We Stay on Course?
- Develop a plan for evaluation and monitoring.
- Establish budgets and find funding sources.
- Complete an implementation plan.

- Promote a single, doable behavior in clear, simple terms.
- Explain the benefits in compelling terms.
- Make it easy to adopt the behavior.
- Develop attention-grabbing messages and media.
- Consider an education-entertainment approach.

One organization that has accomplished most of these goals via an unusual targeted campaign is the Global Water Foundation.

GLOBAL WATER FOUNDATION

The average denizen of Second Life, the Web-based virtual world in which residents interact via computer-animated "avatars," is 33, lives in the United States or Europe, is tech savvy, and has a relatively high disposable income—a perfect market for the Global Water Foundation (GWF) to launch a campaign. Its Virtual Education Center features streaming video and audio supporting its cause—ensuring clean, drinkable water for the developing world—and photos highlighting its work. Interested visitors click on GWF's Web site and pick up free virtual GWF T-shirts, enabling their avatars to spread the word. In just six months since the campaign began on Second Life, GWF logged more than 77,000 Web hits. In the next phase, the organization plans to use the growing Second Life economy, based on virtual currency and purchased with real-world money, to collect visitor donations that it will reward with virtual premiums such as wristbands and pet dolphins.[70]

Social marketing programs are complex; they take time and may require phased programs or actions. For example, recall the steps in discouraging smoking: cancer reports, labeling of cigarettes, banning cigarette advertising, education about secondary smoke effects, no smoking in homes, no smoking in restaurants, no smoking on planes, raising taxes on cigarettes to pay for antismoking campaigns, and states suing cigarette companies.

Social marketing organizations should evaluate program success in terms of objectives. Criteria might include incidence of adoption, speed of adoption, continuance of adoption, low cost per unit of adoption, and absence of counterproductive consequences.

::: Marketing Implementation

Table 22.5 summarizes the characteristics of a great marketing company, great not for "what it is," but for "what it does." **Marketing implementation** is the process that turns marketing plans into action assignments and ensures they accomplish the plan's stated objectives.[71]

A brilliant strategic marketing plan counts for little if not implemented properly. Strategy addresses the *what* and *why* of marketing activities; implementation addresses the *who, where, when,* and *how*. They are closely related: One layer of strategy implies certain tactical implementation assignments at a lower level. For example, top management's strategic decision to "harvest" a product must be translated into specific actions and assignments.

Companies today are striving to make their marketing operations more efficient and their return on marketing investment more measurable (see Chapter 4). Marketing costs can amount to 20% to 40% of a company's total operating budget. Marketers need better templates for marketing processes, better management of marketing assets, and better allocation of marketing resources. Certain repetitive processes can be automated under such names as *marketing resource management (MRM), marketing investment management (MIM), enterprise marketing management (EMM),* and *marketing automation systems (MAS)*.[72]

Marketing resource management (MRM) software provides a set of Web-based applications that automate and integrate such activities as project management, campaign management, budget management, asset management, brand management, customer relationship management, and knowledge management. The knowledge management component consists of process templates, how-to wizards, and best practices.

Software packages are Web hosted and available to users with passwords. They add up to what some have called *desktop marketing* and give marketers whatever information and decision structures they need on computer dashboards. MRM software lets marketers improve spending and investment decisions, bring new products to market more quickly, and reduce decision time and costs.

RYDEX INVESTMENTS

In one year, the marketing department of Rydex Investments, a Maryland fund-management company, had over 800 projects in the works, ranging from simple updates of marketing pieces to full-scale campaign launches. It was getting harder to complete projects on time because 30 to 35 people needed to sign off on them. Paper folders went through the marketing group, design department, communications, and then the legal department. As Rydex doubled its staff over two years, it was clear it had outgrown this cumbersome manual process, so it adopted a Web-based marketing resource management system (MRS) from MarketingCentral of Georgia. The system lets Rydex create a centralized space for marketing projects, organized by folders, that managers in all departments can collaborate on. It lets them create schedules and track approvals to make sure all regulatory steps are taken, and it even gives participants a chance to comment on the projects as they're being finished. Since adopting the MRS, Rydex has seen the time it takes to get a message to market shrink by 20%.[73]

TABLE 22.5

Characteristics of a Great Marketing Company

- The company selects target markets in which it enjoys superior advantages and exits or avoids markets where it is intrinsically weak.
- Virtually all the company's employees and departments are customer and market minded.
- There is a good working relationship between marketing, R&D, and manufacturing.
- There is a good working relationship between marketing, sales, and customer service.
- The company has installed incentives designed to lead to the right behaviors.
- The company continuously builds and tracks customer satisfaction and loyalty.
- The company manages a value delivery system in partnership with strong suppliers and distributors.
- The company is skilled in building its brand name(s) and image.
- The company is flexible in meeting customers' varying requirements.

::: Evaluation and Control

In spite of the need to monitor and control marketing activities, many companies have inadequate control procedures. Table 22.6 lists four types of needed marketing control: annual-plan control, profitability control, efficiency control, and strategic control. We consider each.

Annual-Plan Control

Annual-plan control ensures the company achieves the sales, profits, and other goals established in its annual plan. At its heart is management by objectives. There are four steps (see Figure 22.5). First, management sets monthly or quarterly goals. Second, management monitors its performance in the marketplace. Third, management determines the causes of serious performance deviations. Fourth, management takes corrective action to close gaps between goals and performance.

This control model applies to all levels of the organization. Top management sets annual sales and profit goals; each product manager, regional district manager, sales manager, and sales rep is committed to attaining specified levels of sales and costs. Each period, top management reviews and interprets the results.

Marketers today have better marketing metrics for measuring the performance of marketing plans (see Table 22.7 for some sample ones).[74] They can use four tools to check on plan performance: sales analysis, market share analysis, marketing expense-to-sales analysis, and financial analysis.

SALES ANALYSIS **Sales analysis** measures and evaluates actual sales in relationship to goals. Two specific tools make it work.

Sales-variance analysis measures the relative contribution of different factors to a gap in sales performance. Suppose the annual plan called for selling 4,000 widgets in the first quarter

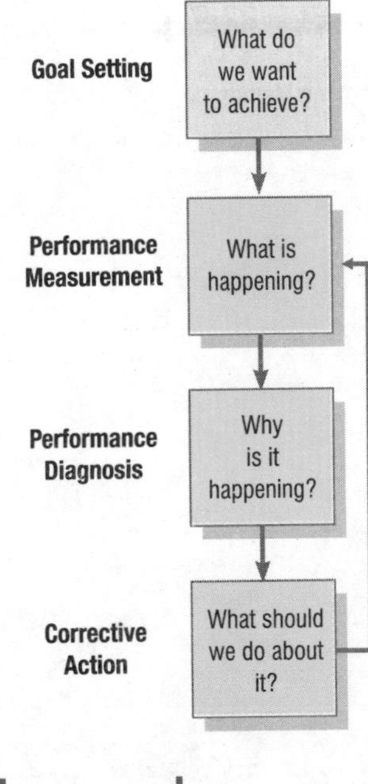

FIG. 22.5

The Control Process

TABLE 22.6 Types of Marketing Control

Type of Control	Prime Responsibility	Purpose of Control	Approaches
I. Annual-plan control	Top management Middle management	To examine whether the planned results are being achieved	■ Sales analysis ■ Market share analysis ■ Sales-to-expense ratios ■ Financial analysis ■ Market-based scorecard analysis
II. Profitability control	Marketing controller	To examine where the company is making and losing money	Profitability by: ■ product ■ territory ■ customer ■ segment ■ trade channel ■ order size
III. Efficiency control	Line and staff management Marketing controller	To evaluate and improve the spending efficiency and impact of marketing expenditures	Efficiency of: ■ sales force ■ advertising ■ sales promotion ■ distribution
IV. Strategic control	Top management Marketing auditor	To examine whether the company is pursuing its best opportunities with respect to markets, products, and channels	■ Marketing effectiveness rating instrument ■ Marketing audit ■ Marketing excellence review ■ Company ethical and social responsibility review

TABLE 22.7

Marketing Metrics

Sales Metrics	Distribution Metrics
■ Sales growth	■ Number of outlets
■ Market share	■ Share in shops handling
■ Sales from new products	■ Weighted distribution
Customer Readiness to Buy Metrics	■ Distribution gains
■ Awareness	■ Average stocks volume (value)
■ Preference	■ Stocks cover in days
■ Purchase intention	■ Out of stock frequency
■ Trial rate	■ Share of shelf
■ Repurchase rate	■ Average sales per point of sale
Customer Metrics	***Communication Metrics***
■ Customer complaints	■ Spontaneous (unaided) brand awareness
■ Customer satisfaction	■ Top of mind brand awareness
■ Number of promoters to detractors	■ Prompted (aided) brand awareness
■ Customer acquisition costs	■ Spontaneous (unaided) advertising awareness
■ New-customer gains	■ Prompted (aided) advertising awareness
■ Customer losses	■ Effective reach
■ Customer churn	■ Effective frequency
■ Retention rate	■ Gross rating points (GRP)
■ Customer lifetime value	■ Response rate
■ Customer equity	
■ Customer profitability	
■ Return on customer	

at $1 per widget, for total revenue of $4,000. At quarter's end, only 3,000 widgets were sold at $.80 per widget, for total revenue of $2,400. How much of the sales performance gap is due to the price decline, and how much to the volume decline? This calculation answers the question:

Variance due to price decline = ($1.00–$.80) (3,000) =	$600	37.5%
Variance due to volume decline = ($1.00) (4,000–3,000) =	$1,000	62.5%
	$1,600	100.0%

Almost two-thirds of the variance is due to failure to achieve the volume target. The company should look closely at why it failed to achieve expected sales volume.

Microsales analysis looks at specific products, territories, and so forth that failed to produce expected sales. Suppose the company sells in three territories, and expected sales were 1,500 units, 500 units, and 2,000 units, respectively. Actual volumes were 1,400 units, 525 units, and 1,075 units, respectively. Thus territory 1 showed a 7% shortfall in terms of expected sales; territory 2, a 5% improvement over expectations; and territory 3, a 46% shortfall! Territory 3 is causing most of the trouble. Maybe territory 3's sales rep is underperforming; a major competitor has entered this territory; or business is in a recession there.

MARKET SHARE ANALYSIS Company sales don't reveal how well the company is performing relative to competitors. For this purpose, management needs to track its market share in one of three ways.

Overall market share expresses the company's sales as a percentage of total market sales. **Served market share** is sales as a percentage of the total sales to the market. The **served market** is all the buyers able and willing to buy the product, and served market share is always larger than overall market share. A company could capture 100% of its served market and yet have a relatively small share of the total market. **Relative market share** is market share in relationship to the largest competitor. A relative market share over 100% indicates a market leader. A relative market share of exactly 100% means the company is tied for the lead. A rise in relative market share means a company is gaining on its leading competitor.

Conclusions from market share analysis, however, are subject to certain qualifications:

- ***The assumption that outside forces affect all companies in the same way is often not true.*** The U.S. Surgeon General's Report on the harmful consequences of cigarette smoking caused total cigarette sales to falter, but not equally for all companies.
- ***The assumption that a company's performance should be judged against the average performance of all companies is not always valid.*** A company's performance is best judged against that of its closest competitors.
- ***If a new firm enters the industry, every existing firm's market share might fall.*** A decline in market share might not mean the company is performing any worse than other companies. Share loss depends on the degree to which the new firm hits the company's specific markets.
- ***Sometimes a market share decline is deliberately engineered to improve profits.*** For example, management might drop unprofitable customers or products.
- ***Market share can fluctuate for many minor reasons.*** For example, it can be affected by whether a large sale occurs on the last day of the month or at the beginning of the next month. Not all shifts in market share have marketing significance.[75]

A useful way to analyze market share movements is in terms of four components:

$$\textit{Overall market share} = \textit{Customer penetration} \times \textit{Customer loyalty} \times \textit{Customer selectivity} \times \textit{Price selectivity}$$

where:

Customer penetration	Percentage of all customers who buy from the company
Customer loyalty	Purchases from the company by its customers as a percentage of their total purchases from all suppliers of the same products
Customer selectivity	Size of the average customer purchase from the company as a percentage of the size of the average customer purchase from an average company
Price selectivity	Average price charged by the company as a percentage of the average price charged by all companies

Now suppose the company's dollar market share falls during the period. The overall market share equation provides four possible explanations: The company lost some customers (lower customer penetration); existing customers are buying less from the company (lower customer loyalty); the company's remaining customers are smaller in size (lower customer selectivity); or the company's price has slipped relative to competition (lower price selectivity).

MARKETING EXPENSE-TO-SALES ANALYSIS Annual-plan control requires making sure the company isn't overspending to achieve sales goals. The key ratio to watch is *marketing expense-to-sales.* In one company, this ratio was 30% and consisted of five component expense-to-sales ratios: sales force-to-sales (15%); advertising-to-sales (5%); sales promotion-to-sales (6%); marketing research-to-sales (1%); and sales administration-to-sales (3%).

Fluctuations outside normal range are cause for concern. Management needs to monitor period-to-period fluctuations in each ratio on a *control chart* (see Figure 22.6). This chart shows the advertising expense-to-sales ratio normally fluctuates between 8% and 12%, say 99 out of 100 times. In the 15th period, however, the ratio exceeded the upper control limit. One of two hypotheses can explain: (1) The company still has good expense control, and this situation represents a rare chance event. (2) The company has lost control over this expense and should find the cause. If there is no investigation, the risk is that some real change might have occurred, and the company will fall behind. An investigation may also uncover nothing and be a waste of time and effort.

Managers should watch the behavior of successive observations even within the upper and lower control limits. Note in Figure 22.6 that the level of the expense-to-sales ratio rose steadily from the 9th period onward. The probability of encountering six successive increases in what should be independent events is only 1 in 64.[76] This unusual pattern should have led to an investigation sometime before the 15th observation.

FIG. 22.6

The Control-Chart Model

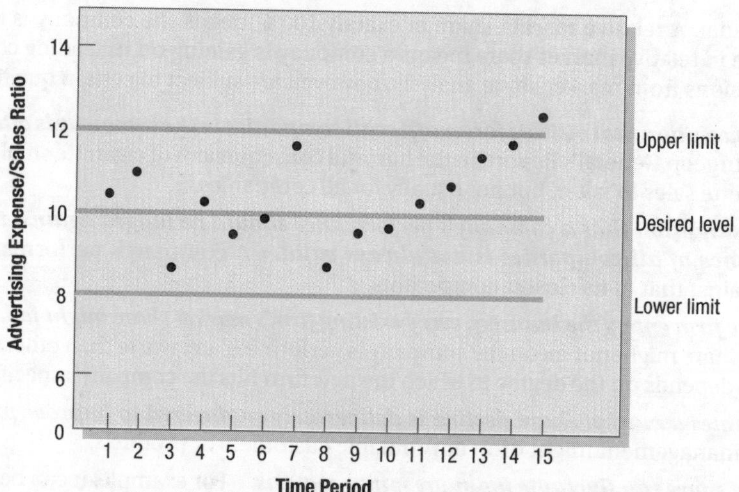

FINANCIAL ANALYSIS Marketers should analyze the expense-to-sales ratios in an overall financial framework to determine how and where the company is making its money. They can, and are increasingly, using financial analysis to find profitable strategies beyond building sales.

Management uses financial analysis to identify factors that affect the company's *rate of return on net worth.*[77] The main factors are shown in Figure 22.7, along with illustrative numbers for a large chain-store retailer. The retailer is earning a 12.5% return on net worth. The return on net worth is the product of two ratios, the company's *return on assets* and its *financial leverage.* To improve its return on net worth, the company must increase its ratio of net profits to assets, or increase the ratio of assets to net worth. The company should analyze the composition of its assets (cash, accounts receivable, inventory, and plant and equipment) and see whether it can improve its asset management.

The return on assets is the product of two ratios, the *profit margin* and the *asset turnover.* The profit margin in Figure 22.7 seems low, whereas the asset turnover is more normal for retailing. The marketing executive can seek to improve performance in two ways: (1) Increase the profit margin by increasing sales or cutting costs; and (2) increase the asset turnover by increasing sales or reducing assets (inventory, receivables) held against a given level of sales.[78]

Profitability Control

Companies can benefit from deeper financial analysis and should measure the profitability of their products, territories, customer groups, segments, trade channels, and order sizes. This information can help management determine whether to expand, reduce, or eliminate any products or marketing activities.

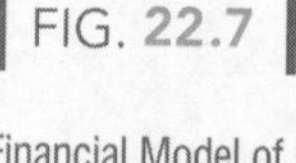
FIG. 22.7

Financial Model of Return on Net Worth

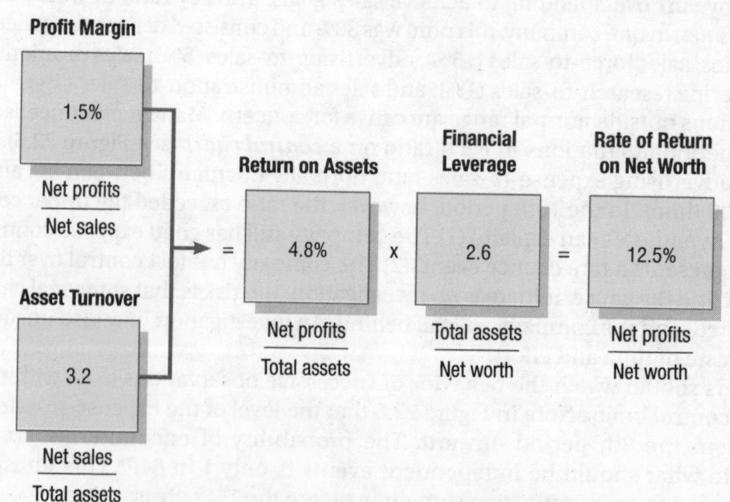

TABLE 22.8

A Simplified Profit-and-Loss Statement

Sales		$60,000
Cost of goods sold		39,000
Gross margin		$21,000
Expenses		
Salaries	$9,300	
Rent	3,000	
Supplies	3,500	
		15,800
Net profit		$5,200

MARKETING PROFITABILITY ANALYSIS We will illustrate the steps in marketing profitability analysis with the following example: The marketing vice president of a lawn mower company wants to determine the profitability of selling through three types of retail channels: hardware stores, garden supply shops, and department stores. The company's profit-and-loss statement is shown in Table 22.8.

Step 1: Identifying Functional Expenses Assume the expenses listed in Table 22.8 are incurred to sell the product, advertise it, pack and deliver it, and bill and collect for it. The first task is to measure how much of each expense was incurred in each activity.

Suppose most of the salary expense went to sales representatives and the rest to an advertising manager, packing and delivery help, and an office accountant. Let the breakdown of the $9,300 be $5,100, $1,200, $1,400, and $1,600, respectively. Table 22.9 shows the allocation of the salary expense to these four activities.

Table 22.9 also shows the rent account of $3,000 allocated to the four activities. Because the sales reps work away from the office, none of the building's rent expense is assigned to selling. Most of the expenses for floor space and rented equipment are for packing and delivery. The supplies account covers promotional materials, packing materials, fuel purchases for delivery, and home office stationery. The $3,500 in this account is reassigned to functional uses of the supplies.

Step 2: Assigning Functional Expenses to Marketing Entities The next task is to measure how much functional expense was associated with selling through each type of channel. Consider the selling effort, indicated by the number of sales in each channel. This number is in the selling column of Table 22.10. Altogether, 275 sales calls were made during the period. Because the total selling expense amounted to $5,500 (see Table 22.10), the selling expense averaged $20 per call.

We can allocate advertising expense according to the number of ads addressed to different channels. Because there were 100 ads altogether, the average ad cost $31.

The packing and delivery expense is allocated according to the number of orders placed by each type of channel. This same basis was used for allocating billing and collection expense.

Step 3: Preparing a Profit-and-Loss Statement for Each Marketing Entity We can now prepare a profit-and-loss statement for each type of channel (see Table 22.11). Because hardware stores accounted for half of total

TABLE 22.9

Mapping Natural Expenses into Functional Expenses

Natural Accounts	Total	Selling	Advertising	Packing and Delivery	Billing and Collecting
Salaries	$9,300	$5,100	$1,200	$1,400	$1,600
Rent	3,000	—	400	2,000	600
Supplies	3,500	400	1,500	1,400	200
	$15,800	$5,500	$3,100	$4,800	$2,400

TABLE 22.10

Bases for Allocating Functional Expenses to Channels

Channel Type	Selling	Advertising	Packing and Delivery	Billing and Collecting
Hardware	200	50	50	50
Garden supply	65	20	21	21
Department stores	10	30	9	9
	275	**100**	**80**	**80**
Functional expense	$5,500	$3,100	$4,800	$2,400
÷ No. of Units				
	275	100	80	80
Equals	**$ 20**	**$ 31**	**$ 60**	**$ 30**

sales ($30,000 out of $60,000), charge this channel with half the cost of goods sold ($19,500 out of $39,000). This leaves a gross margin from hardware stores of $10,500. From this we deduct the proportions of functional expenses hardware stores consumed. According to Table 22.10, hardware stores received 200 of 275 total sales calls. At an imputed value of $20 a call, hardware stores must bear a $4,000 selling expense. Table 22.10 also shows hardware stores were the target of 50 ads. At $31 an ad, the hardware stores are charged with $1,550 of advertising. The same reasoning applies in computing the share of the other functional expenses. The result is that hardware stores gave rise to $10,050 of the total expenses. Subtracting this from gross margin, we find the profit of selling through hardware stores is only $450.

Repeat this analysis for the other channels. The company is losing money in selling through garden supply shops and makes virtually all its profits through department stores. Notice that gross sales is not a reliable indicator of the net profits for each channel.

DETERMINING CORRECTIVE ACTION It would be naive to conclude the company should drop garden supply shops and possibly hardware stores so that it can concentrate on department stores. We need to answer the following questions first:

- To what extent do buyers buy on the basis of type of retail outlet versus brand?
- What are the trends with respect to the importance of these three channels?
- How good are the company marketing strategies directed at the three channels?

On the basis of the answers, marketing management can evaluate five alternatives:

1. Establish a special charge for handling smaller orders.
2. Give more promotional aid to garden supply shops and hardware stores.
3. Reduce the number of sales calls and the amount of advertising going to garden supply shops and hardware stores.

TABLE 22.11

Profit-and-Loss Statements for Channels

	Hardware	Garden Supply	Dept. Stores	Whole Company
Sales	$30,000	$10,000	$20,000	$60,000
Cost of goods sold	19,500	6,500	13,000	39,000
Gross margin	$10,500	$ 3,500	$ 7,000	$21,000
Expenses				
Selling ($20 per call)	$ 4,000	$ 1,300	$ 200	$ 5,500
Advertising ($31 per advertisement)	1,550	620	930	3,100
Packing and delivery ($60 per order)	3,000	1,260	540	4,800
Billing ($30 per order)	1,500	630	270	2,400
Total expenses	$10,050	$ 3,810	$ 1,940	$ 15,800
Net profit or loss	$ 450	$ (310)	$ 5,060	$ 5,200

4. Do not abandon any channel entirely, but only the weakest retail units in each channel.
5. Do nothing.

In general, marketing profitability analysis indicates the relative profitability of different channels, products, territories, or other marketing entities. It does not prove that the best course of action is to drop the unprofitable marketing entities, nor does it capture the likely profit improvement if these marginal marketing entities are dropped.

DIRECT VERSUS FULL COSTING Like all information tools, marketing profitability analysis can lead or mislead marketing executives, depending on how well they understand its methods and limitations. The lawn mower company showed some arbitrariness in its choice of bases for allocating the functional expenses to its marketing entities. It used "number of sales calls" to allocate selling expenses, generating less recordkeeping and computation, when in principle "number of sales working hours" is a more accurate indicator of cost.

Far more serious is another judgmental element affecting profitability analysis—whether to allocate full costs or only direct and traceable costs in evaluating a marketing entity's performance. The lawn mower company sidestepped this problem by assuming only simple costs that fit in with marketing activities, but we cannot avoid the question in real-world analyses of profitability. We distinguish three types of costs:

1. ***Direct costs***—We can assign direct costs directly to the proper marketing entities. Sales commissions are a direct cost in a profitability analysis of sales territories, sales representatives, or customers. Advertising expenditures are a direct cost in a profitability analysis of products to the extent that each advertisement promotes only one product. Other direct costs for specific purposes are sales-force salaries and traveling expenses.
2. ***Traceable common costs***—We can assign traceable common costs only indirectly, but on a plausible basis, to the marketing entities. In the example, we analyzed rent this way.
3. ***Nontraceable common costs***—Common costs whose allocation to the marketing entities is highly arbitrary are nontraceable common costs. To allocate "corporate image" expenditures equally to all products would be arbitrary, because all products don't benefit equally. To allocate them proportionately to the sales of the various products would be arbitrary, because relative product sales reflect many factors besides corporate image making. Other examples are top management salaries, taxes, interest, and other overhead.

No one disputes the inclusion of direct costs in marketing cost analysis. There is some controversy about including traceable common costs, which lump together costs that would and would not change with the scale of marketing activity. If the lawn mower company drops garden supply shops, it would probably continue to pay the same rent. In this event, its profits would not rise immediately by the amount of the present loss in selling to garden supply shops ($310).

The major controversy is about whether to allocate the nontraceable common costs to the marketing entities. Such allocation is called the *full-cost approach*, and its advocates argue that all costs must ultimately be imputed in order to determine true profitability. However, this argument confuses the use of accounting for financial reporting with its use for managerial decision making. Full costing has three major weaknesses:

1. The relative profitability of different marketing entities can shift radically when we replace one arbitrary way to allocate nontraceable common costs by another.
2. The arbitrariness demoralizes managers, who feel their performance is judged adversely.
3. The inclusion of nontraceable common costs could weaken efforts at real cost control.

Operating management is most effective in controlling direct costs and traceable common costs. Arbitrary assignments of nontraceable common costs can lead managers to spend their time fighting cost allocations instead of managing controllable costs well.

Companies show growing interest in using marketing profitability analysis, or its broader version, activity-based cost accounting (ABC), to quantify the true profitability of different activities.[79] Managers can then reduce the resources required to perform various activities, make the resources more productive, acquire them at lower cost, or raise prices on products that consume heavy amounts of support resources. The contribution of ABC is to refocus management's attention away from using only labor or material standard costs to allocate full cost, and toward capturing the actual costs of supporting individual products, customers, and other entities.

Efficiency Control

Suppose a profitability analysis reveals the company is earning poor profits in certain products, territories, or markets. Are there more efficient ways to manage the sales force, advertising, sales promotion, and distribution in connection with these marketing entities?

Some companies have established a *marketing controller* position to work out of the controller's office but specialize in improving marketing efficiency. At companies such as General Foods, DuPont, and Johnson & Johnson, they perform a sophisticated financial analysis of marketing expenditures and results. They examine adherence to profit plans, help prepare brand managers' budgets, measure the efficiency of promotions, analyze media production costs, evaluate customer and geographic profitability, and educate marketing personnel on the financial implications of marketing decisions.[80] They can examine the efficiency of the channel, sales force, advertising, or any other form of marketing communication.

For example, in assessing channel efficiency, management needs to search for distribution economies in inventory control, warehouse locations, and transportation modes. It should track such measures as:

- Logistics costs as a percentage of sales
- Percentage of orders filled correctly
- Percentage of on-time deliveries
- Number of billing errors

Management should strive to reduce inventory while at the same time speeding up the order-to-delivery cycle. Dell Computer shows how to do both simultaneously.

DELL

A customer-customized computer ordered from Dell's Web site at 9:00 AM on Wednesday can be on the delivery truck by 9:00 PM Thursday. In that short period, Dell electronically orders the computer components from its suppliers' warehouses. Equally impressive, Dell gets paid electronically within 24 hours, whereas Compaq, supplying its computers to retailers, receives payment days later.

Strategic Control

Each company should periodically reassess its strategic approach to the marketplace with a good marketing audit. Companies can also perform marketing excellence reviews and ethical/social responsibility reviews.

THE MARKETING AUDIT The average U.S. corporation loses half its customers in five years, half its employees in four years, and half its investors in less than one year. Clearly, this points to some weaknesses. Companies that discover weaknesses should undertake a thorough study known as a marketing audit.[81] A **marketing audit** is a comprehensive, systematic, independent, and periodic examination of a company's or business unit's marketing environment, objectives, strategies, and activities, with a view to determining problem areas and opportunities and recommending a plan of action to improve the company's marketing performance.

Let's examine the marketing audit's four characteristics:

1. ***Comprehensive***—The marketing audit covers all the major marketing activities of a business, not just a few trouble spots. It would be called a functional audit if it covered only the sales force, pricing, or some other marketing activity. Although functional audits are useful, they sometimes mislead management. Excessive sales-force turnover, for example, could be a symptom not of poor sales-force training or compensation but of weak company products and promotion. A comprehensive marketing audit usually is more effective in locating the real source of problems.
2. ***Systematic***—The marketing audit is an orderly examination of the organization's macro- and micromarketing environments, marketing objectives and strategies, marketing systems, and specific activities. The audit indicates the most-needed improvements, incorporating them into a corrective-action plan with short- and long-run steps to improve overall effectiveness.

3. ***Independent***—Marketers can conduct a marketing audit in six ways: self-audit, audit from across, audit from above, company auditing office, company task-force audit, and outsider audit. Self-audits, in which managers use a checklist to rate their own operations, lack objectivity and independence.[82] The 3M Company has made good use of a corporate auditing office, which provides marketing audit services to divisions on request.[83] Generally speaking, however, the best audits come from outside consultants who have the necessary objectivity, broad experience in a number of industries, some familiarity with the industry being audited, and undivided time and attention.
4. ***Periodic***—Typically, firms initiate marketing audits only after sales have turned down, sales-force morale has fallen, and other problems have occurred. Companies are thrown into a crisis partly because they failed to review their marketing operations during good times. A periodic marketing audit can benefit companies in good health as well as those in trouble.

A marketing audit starts with a meeting between the company officer(s) and the marketing auditor(s) to work out an agreement on the audit's objectives, coverage, depth, data sources, report format, and time frame. It includes a detailed plan of who is to be interviewed, the questions to be asked, and where and when to minimize time and cost. The cardinal rule in marketing auditing is: Don't rely solely on company managers for data and opinions. Ask customers, dealers, and other outside groups. Many companies don't really know how their customers and dealers see them, nor do they fully understand customer needs.

The marketing audit examines six major components of the company's marketing situation. Table 22.12 lists the major questions.

THE MARKETING EXCELLENCE REVIEW The three columns in Table 22.13 distinguish among poor, good, and excellent business and marketing practices. Management can place a checkmark to indicate its perception of where the business stands. The profile that results from this marketing excellence review exposes weaknesses and strengths, highlighting where the company might make changes to become a truly outstanding player in the marketplace.

::: The Future of Marketing

Top management recognizes that past marketing has been highly wasteful and demands more accountability. "Marketing Memo: Major Marketing Weaknesses" summarizes companies' major deficiencies in marketing, and how to find and correct them.

Going forward, marketing must be "holistic" and less departmental. Marketers must achieve larger influence in the company if they are to be the main architects of business strategy. They must continuously create new ideas if the company is to prosper in a hyper-competitive economy. They must strive for customer insight and treat customers differently but appropriately. Marketers must build their brands through performance, more than through promotion. Marketers must go electronic and win through building superior information and communication systems.

In these ways, modern marketing will continue to evolve and confront new challenges and opportunities. As a result, the coming years will see:

- The demise of the marketing department and the rise of holistic marketing
- The demise of free-spending marketing and the rise of ROI marketing
- The demise of marketing intuition and the rise of marketing science
- The demise of manual marketing and the rise of automated marketing
- The demise of mass marketing and the rise of precision marketing

To accomplish these changes and become truly holistic, marketers need a new set of skills and competencies in areas such as:

- Customer relationship management (CRM)
- Partner relationship management (PRM)
- Database marketing and datamining
- Contact center management and telemarketing
- Public relations marketing (including event and sponsorship marketing)
- Brand-building and brand-asset management

TABLE 22.12 | Components of a Marketing Audit

Part I. Marketing Environment Audit	
Macroenvironment	
A. Demographic	What major demographic developments and trends pose opportunities or threats to this company? What actions has the company taken in response to these developments and trends?
B. Economic	What major developments in income, prices, savings, and credit will affect the company? What actions has the company been taking in response to these developments and trends?
C. Environmental	What is the outlook for the cost and availability of natural resources and energy needed by the company? What concerns have been expressed about the company's role in pollution and conservation, and what steps has the company taken?
D. Technological	What major changes are occurring in product and process technology? What is the company's position in these technologies? What major generic substitutes might replace this product?
E. Political	What changes in laws and regulations might affect marketing strategy and tactics? What is happening in the areas of pollution control, equal employment opportunity, product safety, advertising, price control, and so forth, that affects marketing strategy?
F. Cultural	What is the public's attitude toward business and toward the company's products? What changes in customer lifestyles and values might affect the company?
Task Environment	
A. Markets	What is happening to market size, growth, geographical distribution, and profits? What are the major market segments?
B. Customers	What are the customers' needs and buying processes? How do customers and prospects rate the company and its competitors on reputation, product quality, service, sales force, and price? How do different customer segments make their buying decisions?
C. Competitors	Who are the major competitors? What are their objectives, strategies, strengths, weaknesses, sizes, and market shares? What trends will affect future competition and substitutes for the company's products?
D. Distribution and Dealers	What are the main trade channels for bringing products to customers? What are the efficiency levels and growth potentials of the different trade channels?
E. Suppliers	What is the outlook for the availability of key resources used in production? What trends are occurring among suppliers?
F. Facilitators and Marketing Firms	What is the cost and availability outlook for transportation services, warehousing facilities, and financial resources? How effective are the company's advertising agencies and marketing research firms?
G. Publics	Which publics represent particular opportunities or problems for the company? What steps has the company taken to deal effectively with each public?
Part II. Marketing Strategy Audit	
A. Business Mission	Is the business mission clearly stated in market-oriented terms? Is it feasible?
B. Marketing Objectives and Goals	Are the company and marketing objectives and goals stated clearly enough to guide marketing planning and performance measurement? Are the marketing objectives appropriate, given the company's competitive position, resources, and opportunities?
C. Strategy	Has the management articulated a clear marketing strategy for achieving its marketing objectives? Is the strategy convincing? Is the strategy appropriate to the stage of the product life cycle, competitors' strategies, and the state of the economy? Is the company using the best basis for market segmentation? Does it have clear criteria for rating the segments and choosing the best ones? Has it developed accurate profiles of each target segment? Has the company developed an effective positioning and marketing mix for each target segment? Are marketing resources allocated optimally to the major elements of the marketing mix? Are enough resources or too many resources budgeted to accomplish the marketing objectives?
Part III. Marketing Organization Audit	
A. Formal Structure	Does the marketing vice president have adequate authority and responsibility for company activities that affect customers' satisfaction? Are the marketing activities optimally structured along functional, product, segment, end user, and geographical lines?

TABLE 22.12 Continued

B. Functional Efficiency	Are there good communication and working relations between marketing and sales? Is the product-management system working effectively? Are product managers able to plan profits or only sales volume? Are there any groups in marketing that need more training, motivation, supervision, or evaluation?
C. Interface Efficiency	Are there any problems between marketing and manufacturing, R&D, purchasing, finance, accounting, and/or legal that need attention?
Part IV. Marketing Systems Audit	
A. Marketing Information System	Is the marketing intelligence system producing accurate, sufficient, and timely information about marketplace developments with respect to customers, prospects, distributors and dealers, competitors, suppliers, and various publics? Are company decision makers asking for enough marketing research, and are they using the results? Is the company employing the best methods for market measurement and sales forecasting?
B. Marketing Planning System	Is the marketing planning system well conceived and effectively used? Do marketers have decision support systems available? Does the planning system result in acceptable sales targets and quotas?
C. Marketing Control System	Are the control procedures adequate to ensure that the annual-plan objectives are being achieved? Does management periodically analyze the profitability of products, markets, territories, and channels of distribution? Are marketing costs and productivity periodically examined?
D. New-Product Development System	Is the company well organized to gather, generate, and screen new-product ideas? Does the company do adequate concept research and business analysis before investing in new ideas? Does the company carry out adequate product and market testing before launching new products?
Part V. Marketing Productivity Audit	
A. Profitability Analysis	What is the profitability of the company's different products, markets, territories, and channels of distribution? Should the company enter, expand, contract, or withdraw from any business segments?
B. Cost-Effectiveness Analysis	Do any marketing activities seem to have excessive costs? Can cost-reducing steps be taken?
Part VI. Marketing Function Audits	
A. Products	What are the company's product-line objectives? Are they sound? Is the current product line meeting the objectives? Should the product line be stretched or contracted upward, downward, or both ways? Which products should be phased out? Which products should be added? What are the buyers' knowledge and attitudes toward the company's and competitors' product quality, features, styling, brand names, and so on? What areas of product and brand strategy need improvement?
B. Price	What are the company's pricing objectives, policies, strategies, and procedures? To what extent are prices set on cost, demand, and competitive criteria? Do the customers see the company's prices as being in line with the value of its offer? What does management know about the price elasticity of demand, experience-curve effects, and competitors' prices and pricing policies? To what extent are price policies compatible with the needs of distributors and dealers, suppliers, and government regulation?
C. Distribution	What are the company's distribution objectives and strategies? Is there adequate market coverage and service? How effective are distributors, dealers, manufacturers' representatives, brokers, agents, and others? Should the company consider changing its distribution channels?
D. Marketing Communications	What are the organization's advertising objectives? Are they sound? Is the right amount being spent on advertising? Are the ad themes and copy effective? What do customers and the public think about the advertising? Are the advertising media well chosen? Is the internal advertising staff adequate? Is the sales promotion budget adequate? Is there effective and sufficient use of sales promotion tools such as samples, coupons, displays, and sales contests? Is the public relations staff competent and creative? Is the company making enough use of direct, online, and database marketing?
E. Sales Force	What are the sales force's objectives? Is the sales force large enough to accomplish the company's objectives? Is the sales force organized along the proper principles of specialization (territory, market, product)? Are there enough (or too many) sales managers to guide the field sales representatives? Do the sales compensation level and structure provide adequate incentive and reward? Does the sales force show high morale, ability, and effort? Are the procedures adequate for setting quotas and evaluating performance? How does the company's sales force compare to competitors' sales forces?

TABLE 22.13

The Marketing Excellence Review: Best Practices

Poor	Good	Excellent
Product driven	Market driven	Market driving
Mass-market oriented	Segment oriented	Niche oriented and customer oriented
Product offer	Augmented product offer	Customer solutions offer
Average product quality	Better than average	Legendary
Average service quality	Better than average	Legendary
End-product oriented	Core-product oriented	Core-competency oriented
Function oriented	Process oriented	Outcome oriented
Reacting to competitors	Benchmarking competitors	Leapfrogging competitors
Supplier exploitation	Supplier preference	Supplier partnership
Dealer exploitation	Dealer support	Dealer partnership
Price driven	Quality driven	Value driven
Average speed	Better than average	Legendary
Hierarchy	Network	Teamwork
Vertically integrated	Flattened organization	Strategic alliances
Stockholder driven	Stakeholder driven	Societally driven

- Experiential marketing
- Integrated marketing communications
- Profitability analysis by segment, customer, and channel

It is an exciting time for marketing. In the relentless pursuit of marketing superiority and dominance, new rules and practices are emerging. The benefits of successful 21st-century marketing are many, but will only come with hard work, insight, and inspiration. The words of 19th-century U.S. author Ralph Waldo Emerson may never have been more true: "This time like all times is a good one, if we but know what to do with it."

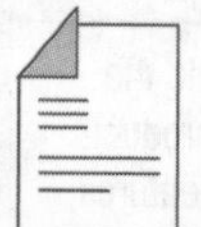

MARKETING MEMO | MAJOR MARKETING WEAKNESSES

A number of "deadly sins" signal that the marketing program is in trouble. Here are 10 deadly sins, the signs, and some solutions.

Deadly Sin: The company is not sufficiently market focused and customer driven.

Signs: There is evidence of poor identification of market segments, poor prioritization of market segments, no market segment managers, employees who think it is the job of marketing and sales to serve customers, no training program to create a customer culture, and no incentives to treat the customer especially well.

Solutions: Use more advanced segmentation techniques, prioritize segments, specialize the sales force, develop a clear hierarchy of company values, foster more "customer consciousness" in employees and company agents, and make it easy for customers to reach the company and respond quickly to any communication.

Deadly Sin: The company does not fully understand its target customers.

Signs: The latest study of customers is three years old; customers are not buying your product like they once did; competitors' products are selling better; and there is a high level of customer returns and complaints.

Solutions: Do more sophisticated consumer research, use more analytical techniques, establish customer and dealer panels, use customer relationship software, and do datamining.

Deadly Sin: The company needs to better define and monitor its competitors.

Signs: The company focuses on near competitors, misses distant competitors and disruptive technologies, and has no system for gathering and distributing competitive intelligence.

Solutions: Establish an office for competitive intelligence, hire competitors' people, watch for technology that might affect the company, and prepare offerings like those of competitors.

Deadly Sin: The company does not properly manage relationships with stakeholders.

Signs: Employees, dealers, and investors are not happy; and good suppliers do not come.

Solutions: Move from zero-sum thinking to positive-sum thinking; and do a better job of managing employees, supplier relations, distributors, dealers, and investors.

Deadly Sin: The company is not good at finding new opportunities.

Signs: The company has not identified any exciting new opportunities for years, and the new ideas the company has launched have largely failed.

Solutions: Set up a system for stimulating the flow of new ideas.

Deadly Sin: The company's marketing planning process is deficient.

Signs: The marketing plan format does not have the right components, there is no way to estimate the financial implications of different strategies, and there is no contingency planning.

Solutions: Establish a standard format including situational analysis, SWOT, major issues, objectives, strategy, tactics, budgets, and controls; ask marketers what changes they would make if they were given 20% more or less budget; and run an annual marketing awards program with prizes for best plans and performance.

Deadly Sin: Product and service policies need tightening.

Signs: There are too many products and many are losing money; the company is giving away too many services; and the company is poor at cross-selling products and services.

Solutions: Establish a system to track weak products and fix or drop them; offer and price services at different levels; and improve processes for cross-selling and up-selling.

Deadly Sin: The company's brand-building and communications skills are weak.

Signs: The target market does not know much about the company; the brand is not seen as distinctive; the company allocates its budget to the same marketing tools in about the same proportion each year; and there is little evaluation of the ROI impact of promotions.

Solutions: Improve brand-building strategies and measurement of results; shift money into effective marketing instruments; and require marketers to estimate the ROI impact in advance of funding requests.

Deadly Sin: The company is not organized for effective and efficient marketing.

Signs: Staff lacks 21st-century marketing skills, and there are bad vibes between marketing/sales and other departments.

Solutions: Appoint a strong leader and build new skills in the marketing department, and improve relationships between marketing and other departments.

Deadly Sin: The company has not made maximum use of technology.

Signs: There is evidence of minimal use of the Internet, an outdated sales automation system, no market automation, no decision-support models, and no marketing dashboards.

Solutions: Use the Internet more, improve the sales automation system, apply market automation to routine decisions, and develop formal marketing decision models and marketing dashboards.

Source: Philip Kotler, *Ten Deadly Marketing Sins: Signs and Solutions* (Hoboken, NJ: John Wiley & Sons, 2004).

SUMMARY :::

1. The modern marketing department has evolved through the years from a simple sales department to an organizational structure where marketing personnel work mainly on cross-disciplinary teams.
2. Modern marketing departments can be organized in a number of ways. Some companies are organized by functional specialization, whereas others focus on geography and regionalization. Still others emphasize product and brand management or market-segment management. Some companies establish a matrix organization consisting of both product and market managers. Finally, some companies have strong corporate marketing, others have limited corporate marketing, and still others place marketing only in the divisions.
3. Effective modern marketing organizations are marked by a strong cooperation and customer focus among the company's departments: marketing, R&D, engineering, purchasing, manufacturing, operations, finance, accounting, and credit.
4. Companies must practice social responsibility through their legal, ethical, and social words and actions. Cause marketing can be a means for companies to productively link social responsibility to consumer marketing programs. Social marketing is done by a nonprofit or government organization to directly address a social problem or cause.
5. A brilliant strategic marketing plan counts for little if it is not implemented properly. Implementing marketing plans calls for skills in recognizing and diagnosing a problem, assessing the company level where the problem exists, and evaluating results.
6. The marketing department must monitor and control marketing activities continuously. Marketing plan control involves analysis to ensure that the company achieves the sales, profits, and other goals established in its annual plan. The main tools are sales analysis, market share analysis, marketing expense-to-sales analysis, and financial analysis of the marketing plan. Profitability control seeks

to measure and control the profitability of various products, territories, customer groups, trade channels, and order sizes. An important part of controlling for profitability is assigning costs and generating profit-and-loss statements. Efficiency control focuses on finding ways to increase the efficiency of the sales force, advertising, sales promotion, and distribution. Strategic control entails a periodic reassessment of the company and its strategic approach to the marketplace using the tools of the marketing effectiveness and marketing excellence reviews, as well as the marketing audit.

7. Achieving marketing excellence in the future will require new challenges and oppportunities. The resulting marketing imperatives will require a new set of skills and competencies.

APPLICATIONS :::

Marketing Debate Is Marketing Management an Art or a Science?

Some marketing observers maintain that good marketing is something that is more than anything an art and does not lend itself to rigorous analysis and deliberation. Others strongly disagree and contend that marketing management is a highly disciplined enterprise that shares much in common with other business disciplines.

Take a position: Marketing management is largely an artistic exercise and therefore highly subjective *versus* Marketing management is largely a scientific exercise with well-established guidelines and criteria.

Marketing Discussion

How does cause or corporate societal marketing affect your personal consumer behavior? Do you ever buy or not buy any products or services from a company because of its environmental policies or programs? Why or why not?

APPENDIX

::: SONIC MARKETING PLAN AND EXERCISES

The Marketing Plan: An Introduction

As a marketer, you'll need a good marketing plan to provide direction and focus for your brand, product, or company. With a detailed plan, any business will be better prepared to launch an innovative new product or increase sales to current customers. Nonprofit organizations also use marketing plans to guide their fundraising and outreach efforts. Even government agencies put together marketing plans for initiatives such as building public awareness of proper nutrition and stimulating area tourism.

The Purpose and Content of a Marketing Plan

A marketing plan has a more limited scope than a business plan, which offers a broad overview of the entire organization's mission, objectives, strategy, and resource allocation. The marketing plan documents how the organization's strategic objectives will be achieved through specific marketing strategies and tactics, with the customer as the starting point. It is also linked to the plans of other organizational departments. Suppose a marketing plan calls for selling 200,000 units annually. The production department must gear up to make that many units, finance must arrange funding to cover the expenses, human resources must be ready to hire and train staff, and so on. Without the appropriate level of organizational support and resources, no marketing plan can succeed.

Although the exact length and layout varies from company to company, a marketing plan usually contains the sections described in Chapter 2. Smaller businesses may create shorter or less formal marketing plans, whereas corporations generally require highly structured marketing plans. To guide implementation effectively, every part of the plan must be described in considerable detail. Sometimes a company will post its marketing plan on an internal Web site so managers and employees in different locations can consult specific sections and collaborate on additions or changes.

The Role of Research

To develop innovative products, successful strategies, and action programs, marketers need up-to-date information about the environment, the competition, and the selected market segments. Often, analysis of internal data is the starting point for assessing the current marketing situation, supplemented by marketing intelligence and research investigating the overall market, the competition, key issues, threats, and opportunities. As the plan is put into effect, marketers use research to measure progress toward objectives and to identify areas for improvement if results fall short of projections.

Finally, marketing research helps marketers learn more about their customers' requirements, expectations, perceptions, satisfaction, and loyalty. This deeper understanding provides a foundation for building competitive advantage through well-informed segmenting, targeting, and positioning decisions. Thus, the marketing plan should outline what marketing research will be conducted and when, as well as how the findings will be applied.

The Role of Relationships

Although the marketing plan shows how the company will establish and maintain profitable customer relationships, it also affects both internal and external relationships. First, it influences how marketing personnel work with each other and with other departments to deliver value and satisfy customers. Second, it affects how the company works with suppliers, distributors, and partners to achieve the plan's objectives. Third, it influences the company's dealings with other stakeholders, including government regulators, the media, and the community at large. All these relationships are important to the organization's success and must be considered when developing a marketing plan.

From Marketing Plan to Marketing Action

Most companies create yearly marketing plans, although some plans cover a longer period. Marketers start planning well in advance of the implementation date to allow time for marketing research, analysis, management review, and coordination between departments. Then, after each action program begins, marketers monitor ongoing results, investigate any deviation from the projected outcome, and take corrective steps as needed. Some marketers also prepare contingency plans for implementation if certain conditions emerge. Because of inevitable and sometimes unpredictable environmental changes, marketers must be ready to update and adapt marketing plans at any time.

For effective implementation and control, the marketing plan should define how progress toward objectives will be measured. Managers typically use budgets, schedules, and marketing metrics for monitoring and evaluating results. With budgets, they can compare planned expenditures with actual expenditures for a given period. Schedules allow management to see when tasks were supposed to be completed and when they were actually completed. Marketing metrics track the actual outcomes of marketing programs to see whether the company is moving forward toward its objectives.

Sample Marketing Plan for Sonic

This section takes you inside the sample marketing plan for Sonic, a hypothetical start-up company. The company's first product is the Sonic 1000, a multimedia, cellular/Wi-Fi-enabled personal digital assistant (PDA), also known as a handheld computer. Sonic will be competing with Palm, Hewlett-Packard, Motorola, Apple, and other well-established rivals in a crowded, fast-changing marketplace where smart phones and many other electronics devices have PDA functionality as well as entertainment capabilities. The annotations explain more about what each section of the plan should contain.

This section summarizes market opportunities, marketing strategy, and marketing and financial objectives for senior managers who will read and approve the marketing plan.

1.0 Executive Summary

Sonic is preparing to launch a new multimedia, dual-mode PDA product, the Sonic 1000, in a mature market. We can compete with both PDAs and smart phones because our product offers a unique combination of advanced features and functionality at a value-added price. We are targeting specific segments in the consumer and business markets, taking advantage of the growing interest in a single device with communication, organization, and entertainment benefits.

The primary marketing objective is to achieve first-year U.S. market share of 3 percent with unit sales of 240,000. The primary financial objectives are to achieve first-year sales revenues of $60 million, keep first-year losses to less than $10 million, and break even early in the second year.

The situation analysis describes the market, the company's capability to serve targeted segments, and the competition.

2.0 Situation Analysis

Sonic, founded 18 months ago by two entrepreneurs with telecommunications experience, is about to enter the now mature PDA market. Multifunction cell phones, e-mail devices, and wireless communication devices are increasingly popular for both personal and professional use, with more than 5 million PDAs and 22 million smart phones sold worldwide each year. Competition is increasingly intense even as technology evolves, industry consolidation continues, and pricing pressures squeeze profitability. Palm, a PDA pioneer, is one of several key players having difficulty adapting to the smart-phone challenge. To gain market share in this dynamic environment, Sonic must carefully target specific segments with valued features and plan for a next-generation product to keep brand momentum going.

Market summary includes size, needs, growth and trends. Describing the targeted segments in detail provides context for marketing strategies and programs discussed later in the plan.

2.1 MARKET SUMMARY Sonic's market consists of consumers and business users who prefer to use a single device for communication, information storage and exchange, organization, and entertainment on the go. Specific segments being targeted during the first year include professionals, corporations, students, entrepreneurs, and medical users. Exhibit A-1 shows how the Sonic 1000 addresses the needs of targeted consumer and business segments.

PDA purchasers can choose between models based on several different operating systems, including systems from Palm, Microsoft, and Symbian, plus Linux variations. Sonic licenses a Linux-based system because it is somewhat less vulnerable to attack by hackers and viruses. Storage capacity (hard drive or flash drive) is an expected feature for PDAs, so Sonic is equipping its first product with an ultra-fast 20-gigabyte drive that can be supplemented by extra storage. Technology costs are decreasing even as capabilities are increasing, which makes value-priced models more appealing to consumers and to business users with older PDAs who want to trade up to new, high-end multifunction units.

2.2 STRENGTHS, WEAKNESSES, OPPORTUNITIES, AND THREAT ANALYSIS Sonic has several powerful strengths on which to build, but our major weakness is lack of brand awareness and image. The major opportunity is demand for multifunction communication, organization, and entertainment devices that deliver a number of valued benefits. We also face the threat of ever-higher competition and downward pricing pressure.

Strengths Sonic can build on three important strengths:

Strengths are internal capabilities that can help the company reach its objectives.

1. ***Innovative product***—The Sonic 1000 offers a combination of features that would otherwise require customers to carry multiple devices, such as speedy, hands-free dual-mode cell/Wi-Fi telecommunications capabilities, and digital video/music/TV program storage/playback.
2. ***Security***—Our PDA uses a Linux-based operating system that is less vulnerable to hackers and other security threats that can result in stolen or corrupted data.
3. ***Pricing***—Our product is priced lower than competing multifunction PDAs—none of which offer the same bundle of features—which gives us an edge with price-conscious customers.

Weaknesses By waiting to enter the PDA market until considerable consolidation of competitors has occurred, Sonic has learned from the successes and mistakes of others. Nonetheless, we have two main weaknesses:

Weaknesses are internal elements that may interfere with the company's ability to achieve its objectives.

1. ***Lack of brand awareness***—Sonic has no established brand or image, whereas Palm, Apple, and others have strong brand recognition. We will address this issue with aggressive promotion.
2. ***Heavier and thicker unit***—The Sonic 1000 is slightly heavier and thicker than most competing models because it incorporates many multimedia features and offers far more storage capacity than the average PDA. To counteract this weakness, we will emphasize our product's benefits and value-added pricing, two compelling competitive strengths.

EXHIBIT A-1 | Needs and Corresponding Features/Benefits of Sonic PDA

Targeted Segment	Customer Need	Corresponding Feature/Benefit
Professionals (consumer market)	■ Stay in touch while on the go	■ Wireless e-mail to conveniently send and receive messages from anywhere; cell phone capability for voice communication from anywhere
	■ Record information while on the go	■ Voice recognition for no-hands recording
Students (consumer market)	■ Perform many functions without carrying multiple gadgets	■ Compatible with numerous applications and peripherals for convenient, cost-effective functionality
	■ Express style and individuality	■ Case wardrobe of different colors and patterns allows users to make a fashion statement
Corporate users (business market)	■ Input and access critical data on the go	■ Compatible with widely available software
	■ Use for proprietary tasks	■ Customizable to fit diverse corporate tasks and networks
Entrepreneurs (business market)	■ Organize and access contacts, schedule details	■ No-hands, wireless access to calendar and address book to easily check appointments and connect with contacts
Medical users (business market)	■ Update, access, and exchange medical records	■ No-hands, wireless recording and exchange of information to reduce paperwork and increase productivity

Opportunities are areas of buyer need or potential interest in which the company might perform profitably.

Opportunities Sonic can take advantage of two major market opportunities:

1. ***Increasing demand for multimedia devices with communication functions***—The market for multimedia, multifunction devices is growing much faster than the market for single-use devices. Growth is accelerating as dual-mode capabilities become mainstream, giving customers the flexibility to make phone calls over cell or Internet connections. PDAs and smart phones are already commonplace in public, work, and educational settings; in fact, users who bought entry-level models are now trading up.
2. ***Lower technology costs***—Better technology is now available at a lower cost than ever before. Thus, Sonic can incorporate advanced features at a value-added price that allows for reasonable profits.

Threats are challenges posed by an unfavorable trend or development that could lead to lower sales and profits.

Threats We face three main threats at the introduction of the Sonic 1000:

1. ***Increased competition***—More companies are offering devices with some but not all of the features and benefits provided by the Sonic PDA. Therefore, Sonic's marketing communications must stress our clear differentiation and value-added pricing.
2. ***Downward pressure on pricing***—Increased competition and market share strategies are pushing PDA prices down. Still, our objective of seeking a 10% profit on second-year sales of the original model is realistic, given the lower margins in the PDA market.
3. ***Compressed product life cycle***—PDAs have reached the maturity stage of their life cycle more quickly than earlier technology products. Because of this compressed life cycle, we plan to introduce a media-oriented second product during the year following the Sonic 1000's launch.

This section identifies key competitors, describes their market positions, and provides an overview of their strategies.

2.3 COMPETITION The emergence of new multifunction smart phones, including the Apple iPhone, has increased competitive pressure. Dell has already left the PDA market; the remaining competitors are continually adding features and sharpening price points. Competition from specialized devices for text and e-mail messaging, such as Blackberry devices, is another major factor. Key competitors:

- ***Palm.*** As the PDA market leader, with a 34 percent share, Palm has excellent distribution in multiple channels and alliances with a number of U.S. and European telecommunications carriers. However, Palm's smart phone share is well below that of Nokia and other handset marketers. Palm products use either the proprietary Palm operating system or Windows.
- ***Hewlett-Packard.*** HP holds 22 percent of the PDA market and targets business segments with its numerous iPAQ Pocket PC devices. Some of its PDAs can send documents to Bluetooth-equipped printers and prevent data loss if batteries run down. For extra security, one model allows access by fingerprint match as well as by password. HP enjoys widespread distribution and offers a full line of PDAs at various price points.
- ***Motorola.*** Motorola sold 100 million of its RAZR clamshell phones worldwide in three years and now offers the RAZR2, smaller and lighter than earlier models and with two operating system options. The Motorola Q targets professionals and business users with PDA and e-mail functions, a tiny keyboard, Bluetooth connections, multimedia capabilities, and more.
- ***Apple.*** The iPhone, a smart phone with a 3.5-inch color screen, has been designed with entertainment enthusiasts in mind. It's well equipped for music, video, and Web access, plus calendar and contact management functions. Apple initially partnered only with the AT&T network and cut the product's price to $399 two months after introduction to speed market penetration. Its iPod Touch media player has iPhone styling without phone functionality.
- ***RIM.*** Research in Motion makes the lightweight BlackBerry wireless phone/PDA products that are popular among corporate users. RIM's continuous innovation and solid customer service support strengthen its competitive standing as it introduces more smart phones and PDAs.

EXHIBIT A-2 | Selected PDA Products and Pricing

Competitor	Model	Features	Price
PalmOne	Tungsten C	PDA functions, wireless capabilities, color screen, tiny keyboard, wireless capabilities	$499
PalmOne	M130	PDA functions, color screen, expandable functionality	$199
Handspring	Treo 270	PDA and cell phone functions, color screen, tiny keyboard, speakerphone capabilities; no expansion slot	$499
Samsung	i500	PDA functions, cell phone functions, MP3 player, color screen, video capabilities	$599
Garmin	iQue 3600	PDA functions, global positioning system technology, voice recorder, expansion slot, MP3 player	$589
Dell	Axim X5	PDA functions, color screen, e-mail capable, voice recorder, speaker, expandable	$199
Sony	Clie PEG-NX73V	PDA functions, digital camera, tiny keyboard, games, presentation software, MP3 player, voice recorder	$499

- ***Samsung.*** Value, style, function: Samsung is a powerful competitor, offering a variety of smart phones and Ultra mobile PCs for consumer and business segments. Some of its smart phones are available for specific telecommunications carriers and some are "unlocked," ready for any compatible telecommunications network.

Despite strong competition, Sonic can carve out a definite image and gain recognition among targeted segments. Our voice-recognition system for hands-off operation is a critical point of differentiation for competitive advantage. Our second product will have PDA functions but will be more media-oriented to appeal to segments where we will have strong brand recognition. Exhibit A-2 shows a sample of competitive products and prices.

2.4 PRODUCT OFFERINGS The Sonic PDA 1000 offers the following standard features:

This section summarizes the main features of the company's various products.

- Voice recognition for hands-free operation
- Organization functions, including calendar, address book, synchronization
- Built-in dual cell phone/Internet phone and push-to-talk instant calling
- Digital music/video/television recording, wireless downloading, and instant playback
- Wireless Web and e-mail, text messaging, instant messaging
- Three-inch color screen for easy viewing
- Ultra-fast 20-gigabyte drive and expansion slots
- Four megapixel camera with flash and photo editing/sharing tools

First-year sales revenues are projected to be $60 million, based on sales of 240,000 of the Sonic 1000 model at a wholesale price of $250 each. Our second-year product will be the Sonic All Media 2000, stressing multimedia communication, networking, and entertainment functions with PDA capabilities as secondary features. The Sonic All Media 2000 will include Sonic 1000 features plus:

- Built-in media beaming to share music, video, television files with other devices
- Web cam for instant video capture and uploading to popular video Web sites
- Voice-command access to popular social networking Web sites
- Integrated eight megapixel camera, flash, and photo editing/sharing tools

2.5 DISTRIBUTION Sonic-branded products will be distributed through a network of retailers in the top 50 U.S. markets. Among the most important channel partners being contacted are:

Distribution explains each channel for the company's products and mentions new developments and trends.

- ***Office supply superstores.*** Office Max and Staples will both carry Sonic products in stores, in catalogs, and online.
- ***Computer stores.*** CompUSA and independent computer retailers will carry Sonic products.

■ ***Electronics specialty stores.*** Best Buy will feature Sonic PDAs in its stores, online, and in its media advertising.

■ ***Online retailers.*** Amazon.com will carry Sonic PDAs and, for a promotional fee, will give Sonic prominent placement on its home page during the introduction.

Distribution will initially be restricted to the United States, with appropriate sales promotion support. Later, we plan to expand into Canada and beyond.

3.0 Marketing Strategy

Objectives should be defined in specific terms so management can measure progress and take corrective action to stay on track.

3.1 OBJECTIVES We have set aggressive but achievable objectives for the first and second years of market entry.

■ ***First-year Objectives.*** We are aiming for a 3 percent share of the U.S. PDA market through unit sales volume of 240,000.

■ ***Second-year Objectives.*** Our second-year objective is to achieve break-even on the Sonic 1000 and launch our second model.

All marketing strategies start with segmentation, targeting, and positioning.

3.2 TARGET MARKETS Sonic's strategy is based on a positioning of product differentiation. Our primary consumer target for the Sonic 1000 is middle- to upper-income professionals who need one device to coordinate their busy schedules, stay in touch with family and colleagues, and be entertained on the go. Our secondary consumer target is high school, college, and graduate students who want a multimedia, dual-mode device. This segment can be described demographically by age (16–30) and education status. Our Sonic All Media 2000 will be aimed at teens and twenty-somethings who want a device with features to support social networking and heavier entertainment media consumption.

The primary business target for the Sonic 1000 is mid- to large-sized corporations that want to help their managers and employees stay in touch and input or access critical data when out of the office. This segment consists of companies with more than $25 million in annual sales and more than 100 employees. A secondary target is entrepreneurs and small-business owners. Also we will target medical users who want to update or access patients' medical records.

Each of the marketing-mix strategies conveys Sonic's differentiation to these target market segments.

Positioning identifies the brand, benefits, points of difference, and parity for the product or line.

3.3 POSITIONING Using product differentiation, we are positioning the Sonic PDA as the most versatile, convenient, value-added model for personal and professional use. Our marketing will focus on the hands-free operation of multiple communication, entertainment, and information capabilities differentiating the Sonic 1000.

3.4 STRATEGIES

Product strategy includes decisions about product mix and lines, brands, packaging and labeling, and warranties.

Product The Sonic 1000, including all the features described in the earlier Product Review section, will be sold with a one-year warranty. We will introduce the Sonic All Media 2000 during the following year, after we have established our Sonic brand. The brand and logo (Sonic's distinctive yellow thunderbolt) will be displayed on our products and packaging as well as in all marketing campaigns.

Pricing strategy covers decisions about setting initial prices and adapting prices in response to opportunities and competitive challenges.

Pricing The Sonic 1000 will be introduced at $250 wholesale/$350 estimated retail price per unit. We expect to lower the price of this model when we expand the product line by launching the Sonic All Media 2000, to be priced at $350 wholesale per unit. These prices reflect a strategy of (1) attracting desirable channel partners and (2) taking share from established competitors.

Distribution strategy includes selection and management of channel relationships to deliver value to customers.

Distribution Our channel strategy is to use selective distribution, marketing Sonic PDAs through well-known stores and online retailers. During the first year, we will add channel partners until we have coverage in all major U.S. markets and the product is included in the major electronics catalogs and Web sites. We will also investigate distribution through cell-phone outlets maintained by major carriers such as Verizon Wireless. In support of channel partners, we will provide demonstration products, detailed specification handouts, and full-color photos and displays featuring the product. Finally, we plan to arrange special payment terms for retailers that place volume orders.

Marketing Communications By integrating all messages in all media, we will reinforce the brand name and the main points of product differentiation. Research about media consumption patterns will help our advertising agency choose appropriate media and timing to reach prospects before and during product introduction. Thereafter, advertising will appear on a pulsing basis to maintain brand awareness and communicate various differentiation messages. The agency will also coordinate public relations efforts to build the Sonic brand and support the differentiation message. To generate buzz, we will host a user-generated video contest on our Web site. To attract, retain, and motivate channel partners for a push strategy, we will use trade sales promotions and personal selling. Until the Sonic brand has been established, our communications will encourage purchases through channel partners rather than from our Web site.

Marketing communications strategy covers all efforts to communicate to target audiences and channel members.

3.5 MARKETING MIX The Sonic 1000 will be introduced in February. Here are summaries of action programs we will use during the first six months to achieve our stated objectives.

The marketing mix includes tactics and programs that support product, pricing, distribution, and marketing communications strategy.

- ***January*** We will launch a $200,000 trade sales promotion campaign and participate in major industry trade shows to educate dealers and generate channel support for the product launch in February. Also, we will create buzz by providing samples to selected product reviewers, opinion leaders, influential bloggers, and celebrities. Our training staff will work with retail sales personnel at major chains to explain the Sonic 1000's features, benefits, and advantages.
- ***February*** We will start an integrated print/radio/Internet campaign targeting professionals and consumers. The campaign will show how many functions the Sonic PDA can perform and emphasize the convenience of a single, powerful handheld device. This multimedia campaign will be supported by point-of-sale signage as well as online-only ads and video tours.
- ***March*** As the multimedia advertising campaign continues, we will add consumer sales promotions such as a contest in which consumers post videos to our Web site, showing how they use the Sonic in creative and unusual ways. We will also distribute new point-of-purchase displays to support our retailers.
- ***April*** We will hold a trade sales contest offering prizes for the salesperson and retail organization that sells the most Sonic PDAs during the 4-week period.
- ***May*** We plan to roll out a new national advertising campaign this month. The radio ads will feature celebrity voices telling their Sonic PDAs to perform functions such as initiating a phone call, sending an e-mail, playing a song or video, and so on. The stylized print and online ads will feature avatars of these celebrities holding their Sonic PDAs. We plan to reprise this theme for next year's product launch.
- ***June*** Our radio campaign will add a new voice-over tag line promoting the Sonic 1000 as a graduation gift. We will exhibit at the semiannual electronics trade show and provide retailers with new competitive comparison handouts as a sales aid. In addition, we will analyze the results of customer satisfaction research for use in future campaigns and product development efforts.

Programs should coordinate with the resources and activities of other departments that contribute to customer value for each product.

3.6 MARKETING RESEARCH Using research, we will identify specific features and benefits our target market segments value. Feedback from market tests, surveys, and focus groups will help us develop and fine-tune the Sonic All Media 2000. We are also measuring and analyzing customers' attitudes toward competing brands and products. Brand awareness research will help us determine the effectiveness and efficiency of our messages and media. Finally, we will use customer satisfaction studies to gauge market reaction.

This section shows how marketing research will support the development, implementation, and evaluation of marketing strategies and programs.

4.0 Financials

Total first-year sales revenue for the Sonic 1000 is projected at $60 million, with an average wholesale price of $250 per unit and variable cost per unit of $150 for unit sales volume of 240,000. We anticipate a first-year loss of up to $10 million. Break-even calculations indicate

Financials include budgets and forecasts to plan for marketing expenditures, scheduling, and operations.

that the Sonic 1000 will become profitable after the sales volume exceeds 267,500 during the product's second year. Our break-even analysis assumes per-unit wholesale revenue of $250 per unit, variable cost of $150 per unit, and estimated first-year fixed costs of $26,750,000. With these assumptions, the break-even calculation is:

$$\frac{26{,}750{,}000}{\$250 - \$150} = 267{,}500 \text{ units}$$

Controls help management measure results and identify any problems or performance variations that need corrective action.

5.0 Controls

Controls are being established to cover implementation and the organization of our marketing activities.

5.1 IMPLEMENTATION We are planning tight control measures to closely monitor quality and customer service satisfaction. This will enable us to react very quickly in correcting any problems that may occur. Other early warning signals that will be monitored for signs of deviation from the plan include monthly sales (by segment and channel) and monthly expenses.

The marketing department may be organized by function, as in this sample, or by geography, product, customer, or some combination of these.

5.2 MARKETING ORGANIZATION Sonic's chief marketing officer, Jane Melody, holds overall responsibility for all of the company's marketing activities. Exhibit A-3 shows the structure of the eight-person marketing organization. Sonic has hired Worldwide Marketing to handle national sales campaigns, trade and consumer sales promotions, and public relations efforts.

Sonic Marketing Plan Chapter Assignments [1]

Chapter 2

As an assistant to Jane Melody, Sonic's chief marketing officer, you've been assigned to draft a mission statement for top management's review. This should cover the competitive spheres within which the firm will operate and your recommendation of an appropriate generic competitive strategy. Using your knowledge of marketing, the information you have about Sonic, and library or Internet resources, answer the following questions.

- What should Sonic's mission be?
- In what competitive spheres (industry, products and applications, competence, market-segment, vertical, and geographic) should Sonic operate?

EXHIBIT A-3
Sonic's Marketing Organization

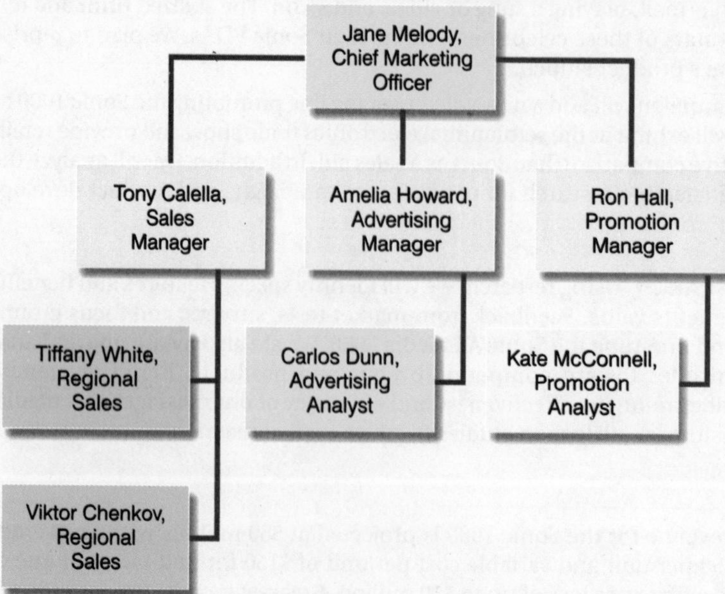

- Which of Porter's generic competitive strategies would you recommend Sonic follow in formulating overall strategy?

As your instructor directs, enter your answers and supporting information in a written marketing plan or use *Marketing Plan Pro* software to document your ideas.

Chapter 3

Jane Melody asks you to scan Sonic's external environment for early warning signals of new opportunities and emerging threats that could affect the success of the Sonic 1000 PDA. Using Internet or library sources (or both), locate information to answer three questions about key areas of the macroenvironment.

- What demographic changes are likely to affect Sonic's targeted segments?
- What economic trends might influence buyer behavior in Sonic's targeted segments?
- How might the rapid pace of technological change/alter Sonic's competitive situation?

Enter your answers about Sonic's environment in the appropriate sections of a written marketing plan or use the *Marketing Plan Pro* software to record your comments.

Chapter 4

Your next task is to consider how marketing research can help Sonic support its marketing strategy. Jane Melody also asks you how Sonic can measure results after the marketing plan is implemented. She wants you to answer the following three questions.

- What surveys, focus groups, observation, behavioral data, or experiments will Sonic need to support its marketing strategy? Be specific about the questions or issues that Sonic needs to resolve using marketing research.
- Where can you find suitable secondary data about total demand for PDAs over the next two years? Identify at least two sources (online or off-line), describe what you plan to draw from each source, and indicate how the data would be useful for Sonic's marketing planning.
- Recommend three specific marketing metrics for Sonic to apply in determining marketing effectiveness and efficiency.

Enter this information in the marketing plan you've been writing or use the *Marketing Plan Pro* software to document your responses.

Chapter 5

Sonic has decided to focus on total customer satisfaction as a way of encouraging brand loyalty in a highly competitive marketplace. With this in mind, you've been assigned to analyze three specific issues as you continue working on Sonic's marketing plan.

- How (and how often) should Sonic monitor customer satisfaction?
- Would you recommend that Sonic use the Net Promoter method? Explain your reasoning.
- Which customer touch points should Sonic pay particularly close attention to, and why?

Consider your answers in the context of Sonic's current situation and the objectives it has set. Then enter your latest decisions in the written marketing plan or using *Marketing Plan Pro* software.

Chapter 6

You're responsible for researching and analyzing the consumer market for Sonic's PDA product. Look again at the data you've already entered about the company's current situation and macroenvironment, especially the market being targeted. Now answer these questions about the market and buyer behavior.

- What cultural, social, and personal factors are likely to most influence consumer purchasing of PDAs? What research tools would help you better understand the effect on buyer attitudes and behavior?
- Which aspects of consumer behavior should Sonic's marketing plan emphasize and why?

■ What marketing activities should Sonic plan to coincide with each stage of the consumer buying process?

After you've analyzed these aspects of consumer behavior, consider the implications for Sonic's marketing efforts to support the launch of its PDA. Finally, document your findings and conclusions in a written marketing plan or with *Marketing Plan Pro.*

Chapter 7

You've been learning more about the business market for Sonic's PDA. Jane Melody has defined this market as mid- to large-sized corporations that want their employees to stay in touch and be able to input or access data from any location. Respond to the following three questions based on your knowledge of Sonic's current situation and business-to-business marketing.

■ What types of businesses appear to fit Melody's market definition? How can you research the number of employees and find other data about these types of businesses?

■ What type of purchase would a Sonic PDA represent for these businesses? Who would participate in and influence this type of purchase?

■ Would demand for PDAs among corporate buyers tend to be inelastic? What are the implications for Sonic's marketing plan?

Your answers to these questions will affect how Sonic plans marketing activities for the business segments to be targeted. Take a few minutes to note your ideas in a written marketing plan or using *Marketing Plan Pro.*

Chapter 8

Identifying suitable market segments and selecting targets are critical to the success of any marketing plan. As Jane Melody's assistant, you're responsible for market segmentation and targeting. Look back at the market information, buyer behavior data, and competitive details you previously gathered as you answer the following questions.

■ Which variables should Sonic use to segment its consumer and business markets?

■ How can Sonic evaluate the attractiveness of each identified segment? Should Sonic market to one consumer segment and one business segment or target more than one in each market? Why?

■ Should Sonic pursue full market coverage, market specialization, product specialization, selective specialization, or single-segment concentration? Why?

Next, consider how your decisions about segmentation and targeting will affect Sonic's marketing efforts. Depending on your instructor's directions, summarize your conclusions in a written marketing plan or use *Marketing Plan Pro.*

Chapter 9

Sonic is a new brand with no prior brand associations, which presents a number of marketing opportunities and challenges. Jane Melody has given you responsibility for making recommendations about three brand equity issues that are important to Sonic's marketing plan.

■ What brand elements would be most useful for differentiating the Sonic brand from competing brands?

■ How can Sonic sum up its brand promise for the new PDA?

■ Should Sonic add a brand for its second product or retain the Sonic name?

Be sure your brand ideas are appropriate in light of what you've learned about your targeted segments and the competition. Then add this information to your written marketing plan or the plan you've been developing with *Marketing Plan Pro* software.

Chapter 10

As before, you're working with Jane Melody on Sonic's marketing plan for launching a new PDA. Now you're focusing on Sonic's positioning and product life-cycle strategies by answering three specific questions.

- In a sentence or two, what is an appropriate positioning statement for the Sonic 1000 PDA?
- Knowing the stage of Sonic's PDA in the product life cycle, what are the implications for pricing, promotion, and distribution?
- In which stage of its evolution does the PDA market appear to be? What does this mean for Sonic's marketing plans?

Document your ideas in a written marketing plan or in *Marketing Plan Pro*. Note any additional research you may need to determine how to proceed after the Sonic 1000 has been launched.

Chapter 11

Sonic is a new entrant in an established industry characterized by competitors with relatively high brand identity and strong market positions. Use research and your knowledge of how to deal with competitors to consider three issues that will affect the company's ability to successfully introduce its first product:

- What factors will you use to determine Sonic's strategic group?
- Should Sonic select a class of competitor to attack on the basis of strength versus weakness, closeness versus distance, or good versus bad? Why is this appropriate in the PDA market?
- As a start-up company, what competitive strategy would be most effective as Sonic introduces its first product?

Take time to analyze how Sonic's competitive strategy will affect its marketing strategy and tactics. Now summarize your ideas in a written marketing plan or using *Marketing Plan Pro* software.

Chapter 12

Introducing a new product entails a variety of decisions about product strategy, including differentiation, ingredient branding, packaging, labeling, warranty, and guarantee. Your next task is to answer the following questions about Sonic's product strategy.

- Which aspect of product differentiation would be most valuable in setting Sonic apart from its competitors, and why?
- Should Sonic use ingredient branding to tout the Linux-based operating system that it says makes its PDA more secure than PDAs based on some other operating systems?
- How can Sonic use packaging and labeling to support its brand image and help its channel partners sell the PDA product more effectively?

Once you've answered these questions, incorporate your ideas into the marketing plan you've been writing or document them using the *Marketing Plan Pro* software.

Chapter 13

You're planning customer support services for Sonic's new PDA product. Review what you know about your target market and its needs; also think about what Sonic's competitors are offering. Then respond to these three questions about designing and managing services.

- What support services are buyers of PDA products likely to want and need?
- How can Sonic manage gaps between perceived service and expected service to satisfy customers?
- What post-sale service arrangements must Sonic make and how would you expect these to affect customer satisfaction?

Consider how your service strategy will support Sonic's overall marketing efforts. Summarize your recommendations in a written marketing plan or use *Marketing Plan Pro* to document your ideas.

Chapter 14

You're in charge of pricing Sonic's product for its launch early next year. Review the SWOT analysis you previously prepared as well as Sonic's competitive environment, targeting strategy, and product positioning. Now continue working on your marketing plan by responding to the following questions.

- What should Sonic's primary pricing objective be? Explain your reasoning.
- Are PDA customers likely to be price sensitive? What are the implications for your pricing decisions?
- What price adaptations (such as discounts, allowances, and promotional pricing) should Sonic include in its marketing plan?

Make notes about your answers to these questions and then document the information in a written marketing plan or use *Marketing Plan Pro* software, depending on your instructor's directions.

Chapter 15

At Sonic, you have been asked to develop a marketing channel system for the new Sonic 1000 PDA. Based on what you know about designing and managing integrated marketing channels, answer the three questions that follow.

- Do you agree with Jane Melody's decision to use a push strategy for the new product? Explain your reasoning.
- How many channel levels are appropriate for Sonic's targeted consumer and business segments?
- In determining the number of channel members, should you use exclusive, selective, or intensive distribution? Why?

Be sure your marketing channel ideas support the product positioning and are consistent with the goals that have been set. Record your recommendations in a written marketing plan or use *Marketing Plan Pro.*

Chapter 16

At this point, you need to make more specific decisions about managing the marketing intermediaries for Sonic's first product. Formulate your ideas by answering the following questions.

- What types of retailers would be most appropriate for distributing Sonic's PDA? What are the advantages and disadvantages of selling through these types of retailers?
- What role should wholesalers play in Sonic's distribution strategy? Why?
- What market-logistics issues must Sonic consider for the launch of its first PDA?

Summarize your decisions about retailing, wholesaling, and logistics in the marketing plan you've been writing or in the *Marketing Plan Pro* software.

Chapter 17

Jane Melody has assigned you to plan integrated marketing communications for Sonic's new product introduction. Review the data, decisions, and strategies you previously documented in your marketing plan before you answer the next three questions.

- What communications objectives are appropriate for Sonic's initial campaign?
- How can Sonic use personal communications channels to influence its target audience?
- Which communication tools would you recommend using after Sonic's initial product has been in the market for six months? Why?

Confirm that your marketing communications plans make sense in light of Sonic's overall marketing efforts. Now, as your instructor directs, summarize your thoughts in a written marketing plan or in the *Marketing Plan Pro* software.

Chapter 18

Mass communications will play a key role in Sonic's product introduction. After reviewing your earlier decisions and thinking about the current situation (especially your competitive circumstances), respond to the following questions to continue planning Sonic's marketing communications strategy.

- Once Sonic begins to use consumer advertising, what goals would be appropriate?
- Should Sonic continue consumer and trade sales promotion after the new product has been in the market for six months? Explain your reasoning.
- Jane Melody wants you to recommend an event sponsorship possibility that would be appropriate for the new product campaign. What type of event would you suggest and what objectives would you set for the sponsorship?

Record your ideas about mass communications in the marketing plan you've been writing or use *Marketing Plan Pro.*

Chapter 19

Sonic needs a strategy for managing personal communications during its new product launch. This is the time to look at interactive marketing, word-of-mouth, and personal selling. Answer these three questions as you consider Sonic's personal communications strategy.

- Which forms of interactive marketing are appropriate for Sonic, given its objectives, mass communications arrangements, and channel decisions?
- How should Sonic use word-of-mouth to generate brand awareness and encourage potential buyers to visit retailers to see the new PDA in person?
- Does Sonic need a direct sales force or can it sell through agents and other outside representatives?

Look back at earlier decisions and ideas before you document your comments about personal communications in your written marketing plan or using *Marketing Plan Pro* software.

Chapter 20

Knowing that the PDA market isn't growing as quickly as the market for multimedia, multifunction communication devices, Jane Melody wants you to look ahead at Sonic how can develop new products outside the PDA market. Review the competitive situation and the market situation before you continue working on the Sonic marketing plan.

- List three new-product ideas that build on Sonic's strengths and the needs of its various target segments. What criteria should Sonic use to screen these ideas?
- Develop the most promising idea into a product concept and explain how Sonic can test this concept. What particular dimensions must be tested?
- Assume that the most promising idea tests well. Now develop a marketing strategy for introducing it, including: a description of the target market; the product positioning; the estimated sales, profit, and market share goals for the first year; your channel strategy; and the marketing budget you will recommend for this new product introduction. If possible, estimate Sonic's costs and conduct a break-even analysis.

Document all the details of your new-product development ideas in the written marketing plan or use *Marketing Plan Pro* software.

Chapter 21

As Jane Melody's assistant, you're researching how to market the Sonic 1000 PDA product outside the United States within a year. You've been asked to answer the following questions about Sonic's use of global marketing.

- As a start-up company, should Sonic use indirect or direct exporting, licensing, joint ventures, or direct investment to enter the Canadian market next year? To enter other markets? Explain your answers.

- If Sonic starts marketing its PDA in other countries, which of the international product strategies is most appropriate? Why?
- Although some components are made in Asia, Sonic's PDAs will be assembled in Mexico through a contractual arrangement with a local factory. How are country-of-origin perceptions likely to affect your marketing recommendations?

Think about how these global marketing issues fit into Sonic's overall marketing strategy. Now document your ideas in the marketing plan you've been writing or using *Marketing Plan Pro*.

Chapter 22

With the rest of the marketing plan in place, you're ready to make recommendations about how to manage Sonic's marketing activities. Here are some specific questions Jane Melody wants you to consider.

- How can Sonic drive customer-focused marketing and strategic innovation throughout the organization?
- What role should social responsibility play in Sonic's marketing?
- How can Sonic evaluate its marketing? Suggest several specific steps the company should take.

To complete your marketing plan, enter your answers to these questions in the written marketing plan or in *Marketing Plan Pro* software. Finally, draft the executive summary of the plan's highlights.

ENDNOTES

Chapter 1

1. The Conference Board, "The CEO Challenge 2006 – Top Ten Challenges," Research Report R-1380-05-RR, 2006.
2. Sandra Ward, "Warming Up the Copier," *Barron's* 18, May 1, 2006, Vol. 86, pp. 19, 21.
3. American Marketing Association, 2004.
4. Peter Drucker, *Management: Tasks, Responsibilities, Practices* (New York: Harper and Row, 1973), pp. 64–65.
5. Richard Verrier, "Actor Plays His Cards Right," *Los Angeles Times*, July 5, 2006.
6. B. Joseph Pine II and James Gilmore, *The Experience Economy* (Boston: Harvard Business School Press, 1999); Bernd Schmitt, *Experience Marketing* (New York: Free Press, 1999); Philip Kotler, "Dream Vacations: The Booming Market for Designed Experiences," *The Futurist* (October 1984): 7–13.
7. Irving J. Rein, Philip Kotler, Michael Hamlin, and Martin Stoller, *High Visibility*, 3rd ed. (New York: McGraw-Hill, 2006).
8. Philip Kotler, Christer Asplund, Irving Rein, and Donald H. Haider, *Marketing Places in Europe: Attracting Investments, Industries, Residents, and Visitors to European Cities, Communities, Regions, and Nations* (London: Financial Times Prentice-Hall, 1999); Philip Kotler, Irving J. Rein, and Donald Haider, *Marketing Places: Attracting Investment, Industry, and Tourism to Cities, States, and Nations* (New York: Free Press, 1993).
9. Michael McCarthy, "Vegas Goes Back to Naughty Roots," *USA Today*, April 11, 2005; Julie Dunn, "Vegas Hopes for Payoff with Denverites," *Denver Post*, June 16, 2005; John M. Broder, "The Pied Piper of Las Vegas Seems to Have Perfect Pitch," *New York Times*, June 4, 2004.
10. Kerry Capell, "Thinking Simple at Philips," *BusinessWeek*, December 11, 2006, p. 50; www.philips.com.
11. Carl Shapiro and Hal R. Varian, "Versioning: The Smart Way to Sell Information," *Harvard Business Review* (November–December 1998): 106–14.
12. John R. Brandt, "Dare to Be Different," *Chief Executive*, May 2003, pp. 34–38.
13. Margaret Bauman, "Alaska Salmon Debuts in Chinese Wal-Marts," *Knight Ridder Tribune Business News*, September 3, 2006.
14. Jeffrey Rayport and John Sviokla, "Exploring the Virtual Value Chain," *Harvard Business Review* (November–December 1995): 75–85. Also see their "Managing in the Marketspace," *Harvard Business Review* (November–December 1994): 141–150.
15. Mohan Sawhney, *Seven Steps to Nirvana* (New York: McGraw-Hill, 2001).
16. Constantine von Hoffman, "Armed With Intelligence," *Brandweek*, May 29 2006, pp. 17–20.
17. Ibid., 19.
18. Richard Rawlinson, "Beyond Brand Management," *Strategy+Business*, Summer 2006.
19. Gail McGovern and John A. Quelch, "The Fall and Rise of the CMO," *Strategy+Business*, Winter 2004.
20. Adam Lashinsky, "Shoutout in Gadget Land," *Fortune*, November 10, 2003, pp. 77–86.
21. "2005 Marketing Receptivity Survey," Yankelovich Partners Inc., April 18, 2005.
22. Danielle Sacks, MAC Cosmetics Inc., *Fast Company*, September 2006, p. 62.
23. David Kiley, "Advertisers, Start Your Engines," *BusinessWeek*, March 6, 2006, p. 26.
24. Anya Kamenetz, "The Network Unbound," *Fast Company*, June 2006, pp. 69–73.
25. "The Blogs in the Corporate Machine," *Economist*, February 11, 2006, pp. 55–56.
26. Bruce Einhorn, "Mad as Hell in China's Blogosphere," *BusinessWeek*, August 14, 2006, p. 39.
27. Todd Wasserman, "Word Games," *Brandweek*, April 24, 2006, pp. 24–28.
28. Linda Tischler, "What's The Buzz?" *Fast Company*, May 2004, p. 76.
29. Brian Morrissey, "Banking on the Internet for Better Brand Building," *Adweek*, February 3, 2006.
30. Laura Mazur, "Personal Touch Is Now Crucial to Growing Profits," *Marketing*, November 27, 2003, p. 18.
31. Kenneth Hein, "Marketers Map Out Their GPS Ad Plans," *Brandweek*, April 24, 2006, p. 4.
32. Suzanne Vranica, "Marketers Aim New Ads at Video iPod Users," *Wall Street Journal*, January 31, 2006.
33. Li Yuan and Brian Steinberg, "Sales Call: More Ads Hit Cell Phone Screens," *Wall Street Journal*, February 2, 2006.
34. Bruce Horovitz, "In Trend Toward Vanity Food, It's Getting Personal," *USA Today*, August 9, 2006.
35. Stanley Holmes, "Into the Wild Blog Yonder," *BusinessWeek*, May 22, 2006, pp. 84–85.
36. Gerry Khermouch, "Breaking into the Name Game," *BusinessWeek*, April 7, 2003, p. 54; Anonymous, "China's Challenge," *Marketing Week*, October 2, 2003, pp. 22–24.
37. Bruce I. Newman, ed., *Handbook of Political Marketing* (Thousand Oaks, CA: Sage Publications, 1999); and Bruce I. Newman, *The Mass Marketing*

of Politics (Thousand Oaks, CA: Sage Publications, 1999).

38. Robert J. Keith, "The Marketing Revolution," *Journal of Marketing* (January 1960): 35–38; John B. McKitterick, "What Is the Marketing Management Concept?" In Frank M. Bass, ed. *The Frontiers of Marketing Thought and Action* (Chicago: American Marketing Association, 1957), pp. 71–82; Fred J. Borch, "The Marketing Philosophy as a Way of Business Life," *The Marketing Concept: Its Meaning to Management* (Marketing series, no. 99; New York: American Management Association, 1957), pp. 3–5.

39. Theodore Levitt, "Marketing Myopia," *Harvard Business Review* (July–August 1960): 50.

40. Rohit Deshpande and John U. Farley, "Measuring Market Orientation: Generalization and Synthesis," *Journal of Market-Focused Management* 2 (1998): 213–32; Ajay K. Kohli and Bernard J. Jaworski, "Market Orientation: The Construct, Research Propositions, and Managerial Implications," *Journal of Marketing* (April 1990): 1–18; John C. Narver and Stanley F. Slater, "The Effect of a Market Orientation on Business Profitability," *Journal of Marketing* (October 1990): 20–35.

41. John C. Narver, Stanley F. Slater, and Douglas L. MacLachlan, "Responsive and Proactive Market Orientation and New-Product Success," *Journal of Product Innovation Management* 21, no. 5 (September 2004): 334–47. See also, Ken Matsuno and John T. Mentzer, "The Effects of Strategy Type on the Market Orientation–Performance Relationship," *Journal on Marketing* (October 2000): 1–16.

42. Evert Gummesson, *Total Relationship Marketing* (Boston: Butterworth-Heinemann, 1999); Regis McKenna, *Relationship Marketing* (Reading, MA: Addison-Wesley, 1991); Martin Christopher, Adrian Payne, and David Ballantyne, *Relationship Marketing: Bringing Quality, Customer Service, and Marketing Together* (Oxford, UK: Butterworth-Heinemann, 1991).

43. James C. Anderson, Hakan Hakansson, and Jan Johanson, "Dyadic Business Relationships within a Business Network Context," *Journal of Marketing* (October 15, 1994): 1–15.

44. Larry Selden and Yoko S. Selden, "Profitable Customer: The Key to Great Brands," *Advertising Age* (July 10, 2006): S7.

45. Kim Cross, "Fill It to the Brim," *Business 2.0*, March 6, 2001.

46. For another framework, see George S. Day, "The Capabilities of Market-Driven Organizations," *Journal of Marketing* 58, no. 4 (October 1994): 37–52; Neil H. Borden, "The Concept of the Marketing Mix," *Journal of Advertising Research* 4 (June 1964): 2–7.

47. E. Jerome McCarthy and William D. Perreault, *Basic Marketing: A Global-Managerial Approach*, 14th ed. (Homewood, IL: McGraw-Hill Irwin, 2002).

48. Chekitan S. Dev and Don E. Schultz, "A Customer-Focused Approach Can Bring the Current Marketing Mix into the 21st Century," *Marketing Management* 14 (January/February 2005).

49. Allison Fass, "Theirspace.com," *Forbes*, May 8, 2006, pp. 122–24.

50. Christian Homburg, John P. Workman Jr., and Harley Krohmen, "Marketing's Influence within the Firm," *Journal of Marketing* (January 1999): 1–15.

51. Samar Farah, "Future Tense," Editorial, *CMO Magazine*, May 2005.

52. Robert Shaw and David Merrick, *Marketing Payback: Is Your Marketing Profitable?* (London, UK: Pearson Education, 2005).

53. Rajendra Sisodia, David Wolfe, and Jagdish Sheth, *Firms of Endearment: How World-Class Companies Profit from Passion* (Upper Saddle River, NJ: Wharton School Publishing, 2007).

54. June 2005, *Point*, p. 4.

55. John Ehernfield, "Feeding the Beast," *Fast Company* (December 2006/January 2007): 41–43.

56. If choosing to develop a strategic corporate social responsibility program, see Michael E. Porter and Mark R. Kramer, "Strategy and Society: The Link between Competitive Advantage and Corporate Social Responsibility," *Harvard Business Review* (December 2006): 78–92.

57. Jeffrey Hollender and Stephen Fenichell, *What Matters Most* (New York: Basic Books, 2004), p. 168.

58. Jonathan Glancey, "The Private World of the Walkman," The *Guardian*, October 11, 1999.

59. Joann Muller, "Ford: Why It's Worse Than You Think," *BusinessWeek*, June 25, 2001; Ford *1999 Annual Report;* Greg Keenan, "Six Degrees of Perfection," *The Globe and Mail*, December 20, 2000.

Chapter 2

1. Jack Ewing, "Nokia, Siemens Plan to Join and Conquer," *Business Week*, June 20, 2006; Abraham Lustgarten, "Remaking a German Giant with American-Style Tactics," *Fortune*, August 7, 2006; Jack Ewing, "Siemen's Tough Guy Gets Going," *Business Week*, June 27, 2005.

2. Nirmalya Kumar, *Marketing As Strategy: The CEO's Agenda for Driving Growth and Innovation* (Boston: Harvard Business School Press, 2004).

3. Frederick E. Webster Jr., "The Future Role of Marketing in the Organization," in *Reflections on the Futures of Marketing*, edited by Donald R. Lehmann and Katherine Jocz (Cambridge, MA: Marketing Science Institute, 1997), pp. 39–66.

4. Michael E. Porter, *Competitive Advantage: Creating and Sustaining Superior Performance* (New York: Free Press, 1985).

5. Robert Hiebeler, Thomas B. Kelly, and Charles Ketteman, *Best Practices: Building Your Business with Customer-Focused Solutions* (New York: Simon and Schuster, 1998).

6. James Carbone, "At Today's Cisco Systems, the Fewer Suppliers the Better" *Purchasing*, April 20, 2006, pp. 18-21.

7. Michael Hammer and James Champy, *Reengineering the Corporation: A Manifesto for Business Revolution* (New York: Harper Business, 1993).

8. Ibid.; Jon R. Katzenbach and Douglas K. Smith, *The Wisdom of Teams: Creating the High-Performance Organization* (Boston: Harvard Business School Press, 1993).

9. Michelle L. Kirsche, "Retailers Look to Reshape Patient Care," *Drug Store News*, March 1, 2004; Michael Johnsen, "
Profiting from a First-Place Focus," *Drug Store News*, January 20, 2003, p. 26.

10. C. K. Prahalad and Gary Hamel, "The Core Competence of the Corporation," *Harvard Business Review* (May–June 1990): 79–91.

11. J. Gloria Goodale, "Netflix: From Movies in the Mall to Movies on Demand?" *The Christian Science Monitor*, September 1, 2006, p. 11; Timothy J. Mullaney, "The Mail Order House That Clobbered Blockbuster," *BusinessWeek*, June 5, 2006, pp. 56-57; "Movies To Go," *The Economist*, July 9, 2005, p. 57.

12. George S. Day, "The Capabilities of Market-Driven Organizations," *Journal of Marketing* (October 1994): 38.

13. George S. Day and Paul J. H. Schoemaker, *Peripheral Vision: Detecting the Weak Signals That Will Make or Break Your Company* (Cambridge, MA: Harvard Business School Press, 2006).

14. "Kodak Plans to Cut Up to 5,000 More Jobs," *Bloomberg News*, February 8, 2007; Leon Lazaroff, "Kodak's Big Picture Focusing on Image Change," *Chicago Tribune*, January 29, 2006.

15. *Pew Internet and American Life Project Survey*, November–December 2000.

16. Kasuaki Ushikubo, "A Method of Structure Analysis for Developing Product Concepts and Its Applications," *European Research* 14, no. 4 (1986): 174–175.

17. Yoram J. Wind and Vijay Mahajan with Robert E. Gunther, *Convergence Marketing: Strategies for Reaching the New Hybrid Consumer* (Upper Saddle River, NJ: Prentice Hall PTR, 2002).

18. Peter Drucker, *Management: Tasks, Responsibilities and Practices* (New York: Harper and Row, 1973), chapter 7.

19. Ralph A. Oliva, "Nowhere to Hide," *Marketing Management* (July/August 2001): 44–46.

20. *Pew Internet and American Life Project Survey*, November–December 2000.

21. He also humorously suggests checking out comic strip character Dilbert's mission statement generator first if one has to be developed by the organization: www.dilbert.com/comics/dilbert/games/career/bin/ms.cgi.

22. Source: *The Economist: Business Miscellany* (London: Profile Books Ltd, 2005), pp. 32-33.

23. Jeffrey F. Rayport and Bernard J. Jaworski, *e-commerce* (New York: McGraw-Hill, 2001), p. 116.

24. Tilman Kemmler, Monika Kubicová, Robert Musslewhite, and Rodney Prezeau, "E-Performance II—The Good, the Bad, and the Merely Average," an exclusive to *mckinseyquarterly.com*, 2001.

25. This section is based on Chapter 16 of Robert M. Grant's, *Contemporary Strategy Analysis*, 5th ed. (Malden, MA: Blackwell Publishing, 2005).

26. The same matrix can be expanded into nine cells by adding modified products and modified markets. See S. J. Johnson and Conrad Jones, "How to Organize for New Products," *Harvard Business Review* (May–June 1957): 49–62.

27. www.starbucks.com; Andy Serwer, "Hot Starbucks to Go," *Fortune*, January 26, 2004, pp. 60–74; Howard Schultz, *Pour Your Heart into It* (New York: Hyperion, 1997).

28. Tim Goodman, "NBC Everywhere?" *San Francisco Chronicle*, September 4, 2003.

29. Bobby White, "Expanding into Consumer Electronics, Cisco Aims to Jazz Up Its Stodgy Image," *Wall Street Journal*, September 6, 2006.

30. Andi Atwater, "HealthSouth to Rid Itself of Some Wichita Centers," *Knight Ridder Tribune Business News*, August 15, 2006.

31. "The Consumer-Centric Marketer as Guru of Exponential Growth: Kelly Styring," *KNOW*, Spring/Summer 2006; www.knowledgenetworks.com.

32. Jena McGregor, "The World's Most Innovative Companies," *BusinessWeek*, April 24, 2006, pp. 63-74.

33. E. Jerome McCarthy, *Basic Marketing: A Managerial Approach*, 12th ed. (Homewood, IL: Irwin, 1996).

34. Dev Patnaik, "Insight," *In* (June 2006): 32.

35. Paul J. H. Shoemaker, "Scenario Plannning: A Tool for Strategic Thinking," *Sloan Management Review* (Winter 1995): 25–40.

36. Philip Kotler, *Kotler on Marketing* (New York: Free Press, 1999).
37. Ibid.
38. Phaedra Hise, "Was It Time to Go Downmarket?" *Inc.* (September 2006): 47.
39. Dominic Dodd and Ken Favaro, "Managing the Right Tension," *Harvard Business Review* (December 2006): 62-74.
40. Ram Charan and Noel M. Tichy, *Every Business Is a Growth Business: How Your Company Can Prosper Year after Year* (New York: Times Business, Random House, 1998).
41. Michael E. Porter, *Competitive Strategy: Techniques for Analyzing Industries and Competitors* (New York: Free Press, 1980), chapter 2.
42. Stephen C. Miller, "It Protects Electronic Devices from Power Surges and Gives Dust Bunnies No Place to Hide," *The New York Times*, September 14, 2006; www.belkin.com/pressroom/releases/uploads/08_15_06Concealed_CompactSurge.html.
43. Michael E. Porter, "What Is Strategy?" *Harvard Business Review* (November–December 1996): 61–78.
44. For some readings on strategic alliances, see John R. Harbison and Peter Pekar , *Smart Alliances: A Practical Guide to Repeatable Success*, (San Francisco, CA: Jossey-Bass, 1998); Peter Lorange and Johan Roos, *Strategic Alliances: Formation, Implementation and Evolution* (Cambridge, MA: Blackwell, 1992); Jordan D. Lewis, *Partnerships for Profit: Structuring and Managing Strategic Alliances* (New York: The Free Press, 1990).
45. Anonymous, "Trends Report: Looking for the Pharmaceutical-Biotechnology Alliance Creates a Win–Win," *Health and Medicine Week*, December 29, 2003, p. 726.
46. Robin Cooper and Robert S. Kalpan, "Profit Priorities from Activity-Based Costing," *Harvard Business Review* (May–June 1991): 130–135.
47. See Robert S. Kaplan and David P. Norton, *The Balanced Scorecard: Translating Strategy into Action* (Boston: Harvard Business School Press, 1996) as a tool for monitoring stakeholder satisfaction.
48. Thomas J. Peters and Robert H. Waterman Jr., *In Search of Excellence: Lessons from America's Best-Run Companies* (New York: Harper and Row, 1982), pp. 9–12.
49. John P. Kotter and James L. Heskett, *Corporate Culture and Performance* (New York: Free Press, 1992); Stanley M. Davis, *Managing Corporate Culture* (Cambridge, MA: Ballinger, 1984); Terrence E. Deal and Allan A. Kennedy, *Corporate Cultures: The Rites and Rituals of Corporate Life* (Reading, MA: Addison-Wesley, 1982); "Corporate Culture," *BusinessWeek*, October 27, 1980, pp. 148–160.
50. Nitin Nohria, William Joyce, and Bruce Roberson, "What Really Works," *Harvard Business Review* 81, no. 7 (2003): 42–53.
51. Marian Burk Wood, *The Marketing Plan: A Handbook* (Upper Saddle River, NJ: Prentice Hall, 2003).
52. Donald R. Lehmann and Russell S. Winer, *Product Management*, 3rd ed. (Boston: McGraw-Hill/Irwin, 2001).

Chapter 3

1. Marc Gunther, "Wal-Mart Sees Green," *Fortune*, August 7, 2006, pp. 42–57; "Wal-Mart Goes Crunchy," *Economist*, June 10, 2006, p. 60; Jerry Adler, "Going Green," *Newsweek*, July 17, 2006, pp. 43–52.
2. Susan Warren, "Pillow Talk: Stackers Outnumber Plumpers; Don't Mention Drool," *Wall Street Journal*, January 8, 1998.
3. A. Mukund, "Cisco Systems – The Supply Chain Story," ICFAI Center for Management Research, 2003; www.icmrindia.org.
4. Charles Babcock, "Data, Data Everywhere," *InformationWeek*, January 9, 2006.
5. Charles Fishman, "The Wal-Mart You Don't Know," *Fast Company* (December 2003): 68–80.
6. Kelly Shermach, "Growing Acceptance of Cookies," *Sales and Marketing Management* 158, no. 7 (September 2006): 20.
7. Heather Green, "TaylorMade," *BusinessWeek*, November 24, 2003, p. 94.
8. Mara Der Hovanesian, "Wells Fargo," *BusinessWeek*, November 24, 2004, p. 96.
9. Jennifer Esty, "Those Wacky Customers!" *Fast Company* (January 2004): 40.
10. Sara Steindorf, "Shoppers Spy on Those Who Serve," *Christian Science Monitor*, May 28, 2002; Edward F. McQuarrie, *Customer Visits: Building a Better Market Focus*, 2nd ed. (Newbury Park, CA: Sage Press, 1998).
11. Julie Forster, "You Deserve a Better Break Today," *BusinessWeek*, September 30, 2002, p. 42.
12. Shirely S. Wang, "Heath Care Taps 'Mystery Shoppers'," *Wall Street Journal*, August 10, 2006.
13. Kim Girard, "Strategies to Turn Stealth into Wealth," *Business 2.0* (May 2003): 66.
14. Leonard M. Fuld, "Staying a Step Ahead of the Rest," *Chief Executive* 218 (June 2006): 32.
15. Sacha Pfeiffer, "A Little Market Strategy Can Go a Long Way," *Boston Globe*, July 9, 2006.

16. Andy Serwer, "P&G's Covert Operation," *Fortune*, September 17, 2001, pp. 42–44.
17. Amy Merrick, "Counting on the Census," *Wall Street Journal*, February 14, 2001.
18. Kim Girard, "Strategies to Turn Stealth into Wealth," *Business 2.0*, May 2003, p. 66.
19. Robin T. Peterson and Zhilin Yang, "Web Product Reviews Help Strategy," *Marketing News*, April 7, 2004, p. 18.
20. Heather Green, "It Takes a Web Village," *Business Week*, September 4, 2006, p. 66.
21. American Productivity & Quality Center, "User-Driven Competitive Intelligence: Crafting the Value Proposition," December 3–4, 2002.
22. See www.badfads.com for examples of fads and collectibles through the years.
23. John Naisbitt and Patricia Aburdene, *Megatrends 2000* (New York: Avon Books, 1990).
24. Indata, *IN* (June 2006): 27.
25. World POPClock, U.S. Census Bureau, www.census.gov, September 1999.
26. Although over 10 years old, this breakdown provides useful perspective. See Donella H. Meadows, Dennis L. Meadows, and Jorgen Randers, *Beyond Limits:* (White River Junction, VT: Chelsea Green, 1993) for some commentary.
27. "Survey: Forever Young," *The Economist*, March 27, 2004, pp. 53–54.
28. Brian Grow, "Hispanic Nation," *BusinessWeek*, March 15, 2004, pp. 58–70.
29. Queena Sook Kim, "Fisher Price Reaches for Hispanics," *Wall Street Journal*, November 1, 2004.
30. Mireya Navarro, "Focusing on an Attitude Rather Than a Language," *New York Times*, September 25, 2006.
31. For descriptions on the buying habits and marketing approaches to African Americans and Hispanics, see M. Isabel Valdes, *Marketing to American Latinos: A Guide to the In-Culture Approach, Part II* (Ithaca, NY: Paramount Market Publishing, 2002); Alfred L. Schreiber, *Multicultural Marketing* (Lincolnwood, IL: NTC Business Books, 2001).
32. Jacquelyn Lynn, "Tapping the Riches of Bilingual Markets," *Management Review* (March 1995): 56–61; Mark R. Forehand and Rohit Deshpandé, "What We See Makes Us Who We Are: Priming Ethnic Self-Awareness and Advertising Response," *Journal of Marketing Research* (August 2001): 336–348.
33. Tennille M. Robinson, "Tapping into Black Buying Power," *Black Enterprise* 36, no. 6 (January 2006): 64.
34. The Central Intelligence Agency's World Factbook
35. "Population of the Number of Households and Families in the United States: 1995-2010," P25–1129, U.S. Department of Commerce.
36. Michelle Conlin, "Unmarried America," *BusinessWeek*, October 20, 2003, pp. 106–116; James Morrow, "A Place for One," *American Demographics* (November 2003): 25–30.
37. Rebecca Gardyn, "A Market Kept in the Closet," *American Demographics* (November 2001): 37–43.
38. Laura Koss-Feder, "Out and About," *Marketing News*, May 25, 1998, pp. 1, 20.
39. Nanette Byrnes, "Secrets of the Male Shopper," *Business Week*, September 4, 2006, p. 44.
40. "Rural Population and Migration: Overview," Economic Research Service, U.S. Department of Agriculture.
41. Christopher Reynolds, "Magnetic South," *Forecast* (September 2003): 6.
42. Robert H. Franc, "Yes the Rich Get Richer, but There's More to the Story," *Columbia Journalism Review*, November 1, 2000; David Leonhardt, "Two-Tier Marketing," *BusinessWeek*, March 17, 1997, pp. 82–90.
43. Julie Schlosser, "Infosys U.," *Fortune*, March 20, 2006, pp. 41–42.
44. Pamela Paul, "Corporate Responsibility," *American Demographics* (May 2002): 24–25.
45. Stephen Baker, "Wiser about the Web," *Business Week*, March 27, 2006, pp. 53–57.
46. "Clearing House Suit Chronology," *Associated Press*, January 26, 2001; Paul Wenske, "You Too Could Lose $19,000!" *Kansas City Star*, October 31, 1999.
47. Laura Zinn, "Teens: Here Comes the Biggest Wave Yet," *BusinessWeek*, April 11, 2004, pp. 76–86.
48. Clay Chandler, "Full Speed Ahead," *Fortune*, February 7, 2005, pp. 78–84; "What You Can Learn from Toyota," *Business 2.0* (January–February 2005 67–72; Keith Naughton, "Red, White, and Bold," *Newsweek*, April 25, 2005, pp. 34–36.
49. Rebecca Gardyn, "Eco-Friend or Foe," *American Demographics* (October 2003): 12–13. See also, Rebecca Gardyn, "Being Green," *American Demographics* (September 2002): 10–11.
50. Subhabrata Bobby Banerjee, Easwar S. Iyer, and Rajiv K Kashyap, "Corporate Enviromentalism: Antecedents and Influence of Industry Type," *Journal of Marketing* 67 (April 2003), 106–22.
51. See Dorothy Cohen, *Legal Issues on Marketing Decision Making* (Cincinnati: South-Western, 1995).
52. Rebecca Gardyn, "Swap Meet," *American Demographics* (July 2001): 51–55.
53. Pamela Paul, "Mixed Signals," *American Demographics* (July 2001): 45–49.

Chapter 4

1. A.G. Lafley, interview, "It Was a No-Brainer," *Fortune*, February 21, 2005, p. 96; Naomi Aoki, "Gillette Hopes to Create a Buzz with Vibrating Women's Razor," *Boston Globe*, December 17, 2004; Chris Reidy, "The Unveiling of a New Venus," *Boston Globe*, November 3, 2000.
2. See Robert Schieffer, *Ten Key Customer Insights: Unlocking the Mind of the Market* (Mason, OH: Thomson, 2005) for a comprehensive, in-depth discussion of how to generate customer insights to drive business results.
3. Esomar, "2005 Global Market Research Report."
4. Melanie Haiken, "Tuned In to CrowdCasting," *Business 2.0* (November 2006): 66–68.
5. Kevin J. Clancy and Robert S. Shulman, *Marketing Myths That Are Killing Business* (New York: McGraw-Hill, 1994), p. 58; Phaedra Hise, "Comprehensive CompuServe," *Inc.* (June 1994): 109; "Business Bulletin: Studying the Competition," *Wall Street Journal*, March 19, 1995.
6. "Would You Fly in Chattering Class?" *The Economist*, September 9, 2006, p. 63.
7. For some background information on in-flight Internet service, see "Boeing In-Flight Internet Plan Goes Airborne," *The Associated Press*, April 18, 2004; John Blau, "In-Flight Internet Service Ready for Takeoff," *IDG News Service*, June 14, 2002; "In-Flight Dogfight," *Business2.Com*, January 9, 2001, pp. 84–91.
8. For a discussion of the decision-theory approach to the value of research, see Donald R. Lehmann, Sunil Gupta, and Joel Steckel, *Market Research* (Reading, MA: Addison-Wesley, 1997).
9. Gregory Solman, "Finding Car Buyers at Their Home (sites)," *Adweek*, Aug 21–Aug 28, 2006, p. 8.
10. Linda Tischler, "Every Move You Make," *Fast Company* (April 2004): 73–75; Allison Stein Wellner, "Look Who's Watching," *Continental* (April 2003): 39–41.
11. For a detailed review of relevant academic work, see Eric J. Arnould and Amber Epp, "Deep Engagement with Consumer Experience," in the *Handbook of Marketing Research*, ed. Rajiv Grover and Marco Vriens (Thousand Oaks, CA: Sage Publications, 2006). For a range of academic discussion, see the following special issue, "Can Ethnography Uncover Richer Consumer Insights?" *Journal of Advertising Research* 46 (September 2006). For some practical tips, see Richard Durante and Michael Feehan, "Leverage Ethnography to Improve Strategic Decision Making," *Marketing Research* (Winter 2005).
12. Eric J. Arnould and Linda L. Price, "Market-Oriented Ethnography Revisited," *Journal of Advertising Research* 46 (September 2006): 251-62; Eric J. Arnould and Melanie Wallendorf, "Market-Oriented Ethnography: Interpretation Building and Marketing Strategy Formulation," *Journal of Marketing Research* 31 (November 1994): 484–504.
13. "Case Study: Bank of America," Inside Innovation, *BusinessWeek*, June 19, 2006; Spencer E. Ante, "Inprogress," *IN* (June 2006): 28–29.
14. Spencer E. Ante, "The Science of Desire," *BusinessWeek*, June 5, 2006, pp. 98–106.
15. Michael Fielding, "Shift the Focus," *Marketing News*, September 1, 2006, pp. 18–20.
16. Eric Pfanner, "Agencies Look beyond Focus Groups to Spot Trends," *New York Times*, January 2, 2006.
17. Eric Schellhorn, "A Tsunami of Surveys Washes over Consumers," *The Christian Science Monitor*, October 2, 2006, p. 13.
18. Georgia Mullen, "Teens Talk Back to Mobile Industry," *Telecommunications America* 40, no. 9 (September 2006): 14.
19. Louise Witt, "Inside Intent," *American Demographics* (March 2004): 34–39; Andy Raskin, "A Face Any Business Can Trust," *Business 2.0* (December 2003): 58–60; Gerald Zaltman, "Rethinking Market Research: Putting People Back In," *Journal of Marketing Research* 34 (November 1997): 424–37; Wally Wood, "The Race to Replace Memory," *Marketing and Media Decisions* (July 1986): 166–67; Roger D. Blackwell, James S. Hensel, Michael B. Phillips, and Brian Sternthal, *Laboratory Equipment for Marketing Research* (Dubuque, IA: Kendall/Hunt, 1970).
20. Stephen Baker, "Wiser about the Web," *BusinessWeek*, March 27, 2006, pp. 54–62.
21. www.asientertainment.com.
22. Michael Fielding, "Shift the Focus," *Marketing News*, September 1, 2006, pp. 18–20.
23. Kate Maddox, "The ROI of Research," *B to B*, pp. 25, 28.
24. Bradley Johnson, "Forget Phone and Mail: Online's the Best Place to Administer Surveys," *Advertising Age*, July 17, 2006, p. 23.
25. Deborah L. Vence, "In an Instant: More Researchers Use IM for Fast, Reliable Results," *Marketing News*, March 1, 2006, p. 53–55.
26. Allison Enright, "Make the Connection," *Marketing News*, April 1, 2006, p. 21.
27. Catherine Arnold, "Global Perspective: Synovate Exec Discusses Future of International Research," *Marketing News*, May 15, 2004, p. 43; Michael Erard, "For Technology, No Small World after All," *New York Times*, May 6, 2004; Deborah L. Vence, "Global Consistency: Leave It to the Experts," *Marketing News*, April 28, 2003, p. 37.

28. Michael Fielding, "Global Insights: Synovate's Chedore Discusses MR Trends," *Marketing News*, May 15, 2006, pp. 41–42.

29. Dale Buss, "Reflections of Reality," *Point* (June 2006): 10-11; Todd Wasserman, "Unilever, Whirlpool Get Personal with Personas," *Brandweek*, September 18, 2006, p. 13.

30. Kevin J. Clancy and Peter C. Krieg, *Counterintuitive Marketing: How Great Results Come from Uncommon Sense* (New York: The Free Press, 2000).

31. See "Special Issue on Managerial Decision Making," *Marketing Science* 18, no. 3 (1999) for some contemporary perspectives. See also John D. C. Little, "Decision Support Systems for Marketing Managers," *Journal of Marketing* (Summer 1979): 11.

32. Leonard M. Lodish, "CALLPLAN: An Interactive Salesman's Call Planning System," *Management Science* (December 1971): 25–40.

33. Rajiv Grover and Marco Vriens, "Trusted Advisor: How It Helps Lay the Foundation for Insight," in *Handbook of Marketing Research* (Thousand Oaks, CA: Sage Publications, 2006), 3–17; Christine Moorman, Gerald Zaltman, and Rohit Deshpandé, "Relationships between Providers and Users of Market Research: The Dynamics of Trust within and between Organizations," *Journal of Marketing Research* 29 (August 1992): 314–28.

34. Adapted from Arthur Shapiro, "Let's Redefine Market Research," *Brandweek*, June 21, 2004, p. 20.

35. Robert Shaw and David Merrick, *Marketing Payback: Is Your Marketing Profitable* (London: FT Prentice Hall, 2005).

36. John McManus, "Stumbling into Intelligence," *American Demographics* (April 2004): 22–25.

37. Lisa Sanders, "Measuring ROI Eludes Half of Top Marketers," *Marketing News*, July 7, 2006, p. 4.

38. Tim Ambler, *Marketing and the Bottom Line: The New Metrics of Corporate Wealth* (London: FT Prentice Hall, 2000).

39. Paul Farris, Neil T. Bendle, Phillip E. Pfeifer, and David J. Reibstein, *Marketing Metrics: 50+ Metrics Every Executive Should Master* (Upper Saddle River, NJ: Pearson Education, 2006); John Davis, *Magic Numbers for Consumer Marketing: Key Measures to Evaluate Marketing Success* (Singapore: John Wiley & Sons, 2005).

40. Bob Donath, "Employ Marketing Metrics with a Track Record," *Marketing News*, September 15, 2003, p. 12.

41. Tim Ambler, *Marketing and the Bottom Line: The New Methods of Corporate Wealth*, 2nd ed. (London: Pearson Education, 2003).

42. Kusum L. Ailawadi, Donald R. Lehmann, and Scott A. Neslin, "Revenue Premium as an Outcome Measure of Brand Equity," *Journal of Marketing* 67 (October 2003): 1–17.

43. Stephen Baker, "Wiser about the Web," *Business Week*, March 27, 2006, pp. 53–57.

44. Tim Ambler, *Marketing and the Bottom Line: The New Methods of Corporate Wealth*, 2nd ed. (London: Pearson Education, 2003).

45. Gerard J. Tellis, "Modeling Marketing Mix," in *Handbook of Marketing Research*, ed. Rajiv Grover and Marco Vriens (Thousand Oaks, CA: Sage Publications, 2006).

46. Jack Neff, "P&G, Clorox Rediscover Modeling," *Advertising Age*, March 29, 2004, p. 10.

47. Laura Q. Hughes, "Econometrics Take Root," *Advertising Age*, August 5, 2002, p. S-4.

48. David J. Reibstein, "Connect the Dots," *CMO Magazine* (May 2005).

49. Jeff Zabin, "Marketing Dashboards: The Visual Display of Marketing Data," *Chief Marketer* .

50. Robert S. Kaplan and David P. Norton, *The Balanced Scorecard* (Boston: Harvard Business School Press, 1996).

51. Spencer Ante, "Giving the Boss the Big Picture," *BusinessWeek*, February 13, 2006, pp. 48–50.

52. Conference Summary, "Excelling in Today's Multimedia World," Economist Conferences' Fourth Annual Marketing Roundtable, Landor, March 2006.

53. For a good discussion and illustration, see Roger J. Best, *Market-Based Management*, 4th ed. (Upper Saddle River, NJ: Prentice Hall, 2005).

54. For further discussion, see Gary L. Lilien, Philip Kotler, and K. Sridhar Moorthy, *Marketing Models* (Upper Saddle River, NJ: Prentice Hall, 1992).

55. www.naics.com, http://www.census.gov/epcd/naics02>.

56. Stanley F. Slater and Eric M. Olson, "Mix and Match," *Marketing Management* (July–August 2006): 32–37; Brian Sternthal and Alice M. Tybout, "Segmentation and Targeting," in *Kellogg on Marketing*, ed. Dawn Iacobucci (New York: John Wiley & Sons, 2001), 3–30.

57. For an excellent overview of market forecasting, see Scott Armstrong, ed., *Principles of Forecasting: A Handbook for Researchers and Practitioners* (Norwell, MA: Kluwer Academic Publishers, 2001) and his Web site: http://fourps.wharton.upenn.edu/forecast/handbook.html; Also see Roger J. Best, "An Experiment in Delphi Estimation in Marketing Decision Making," *Journal of Marketing Research* (November 1974): 447–52; Norman Dalkey and Olaf Helmer, "An Experimental Application of the Delphi Method to the Use of Experts," *Management Science* (April 1963): 458–67.

Chapter 5

1. www.ritzcarlton.com; www.brandkeys.com.
2. Robert Schieffer, *Ten Key Consumer Insights* (Mason, OH: Thomson, 2005).
3. Don Peppers and Martha Rogers, "Customers Don't Grow on Trees," *Fast Company* (July 2005): 25–26.
4. For discussion of some of the issues involved, see Glen Urban, *Don't Just Relate—Advocate* (Upper Saddle River, NJ: Pearson Education Wharton School Publishing, 2005).
5. See Glen L. Urban and John R. Hauser, "'Listening In' to Find and Explore New Combinations of Customer Needs," *Journal of Marketing* 68 (April 2004): 72–87.
6. Oliver Ryan, "Putting Your Customer to Work," *Fortune*, March 20, 2006, p. 30.
7. Deborah L. Vence, "Shopping Portal Moves Customer Surveys Online; Metrics Soar," *AMA Marketing News*, June 15, 2006, p. 9.
8. Glen L. Urban, "The Emerging Era of Customer Advocacy," Sloan Management Review, 45 (2), 2004, pp. 77–82.
9. Steven Burke, "Dell's vs. HP's Value," *CRN*, May 15, 2006, p. 46; David Kirkpatrick, "Dell in the Penalty Box," *Fortune* 154, no. 6, September 18, 2006, p. 70+.
10. Irwin P. Levin and Richard D. Johnson, "Estimating Price–Quality Tradeoffs Using Comparative Judgments," *Journal of Consumer Research*, June 11, 1984, pp. 593–600. Customer-perceived value can be measured as a difference or as a ratio. If total customer value is $20,000 and total customer cost is $16,000, then the customer-perceived value is $4,000 (measured as a difference) or 1.25 (measured as a ratio). Ratios that are used to compare offers are often called *value–price ratios*.
11. For more on customer-perceived value, see David C. Swaddling and Charles Miller, *Customer Power* (Dublin, OH: The Wellington Press, 2001).
12. Gary Hamel, "Strategy as Revolution," *Harvard Business Review* (July–August 1996): 69–82.
13. www.brandkeys.com/awards/index.cfm; Jim Edwards, "Customer Loyalty Index: Broken Promises," *Brandweek*, May 22, 2006.
14. Michael J. Lanning, *Delivering Profitable Value* (Oxford, UK: Capstone, 1998).
15. Vikas Mittal, Eugene W. Anderson, Akin Sayrak, and Pandu Tadilamalla, "Dual Emphasis and the Long-Term Financial Impact of Customer Satisfaction," *Marketing Science* 24 (Fall 2005): 544–55.
16. Fred Crawford and Ryan Mathews, *The Myth of Excellence: Why Great Companies Never Try to Be the Best of Everything* (New York: Crown Business, 2001), pp. 85–100.
17. Michael Tsiros, Vikas Mittal, and William T. Ross Jr., "The Role of Attributions in Customer Satisfaction: A Reexamination," *Journal of Consumer Research* 31 (September 2004): 476–83.
18. For a succinct review, see Richard L. Oliver, "Customer Satisfaction Research," in *Handbook of Marketing Research*, ed. Rajiv Grover and Marco Vriens (Thousand Oaks, CA: Sage Publications, 2006), pp. 569–87.
19. For some provocative analysis and discussion, see Praveen K. Kopalle and Donald R. Lehmann, "Setting Quality Expectations When Entering a Market: What Should the Promise Be?" *Marketing Science* 25 (January–February 2006): 8–24; and Susan Fournier and David Glenmick, "Rediscovering Satisfaction," *Journal of Marketing* (October 1999): 5–23.
20. Jennifer Aaker, Susan Fournier, and S. Adam Brasel, "When Good Brands Do Bad," *Journal of Consumer Research* 31 (June 2004): 1–16; Pankaj Aggrawal, "The Effects of Brand Relationship Norms on Consumer Attitudes and Behavior," *Journal of Consumer Research* 31 (June 2004): 87–101.
21. For in-depth discussion, see Michael D. Johnson and Anders Gustafsson, *Improving Customer Satisfaction, Loyalty, and Profit* (San Francisco: Josey-Bass, 2000).
22. For an interesting analysis of the effects of different types of expectations, see William Boulding, Ajay Kalra, and Richard Staelin, "The Quality Double Whammy," *Marketing Science* 18, no. 4 (April 1999): 463–84.
23. Alice Z. Cuneo, "Magazines as Muses: Hotelier Finds Inspiration in Titles such as Wired," *Advertising Age*, November 6, 2006, p. 10.
24. As quoted in Neal Templin, "Boutique-Hotel Group Thrives on Quirks," *Wall Street Journal*, March 18, 1999.
25. As quoted in Clifford Carlsen, "Joie de Vivre Resorts to New Hospitality Strategy," *San Francisco Business Times*, June 18, 1999.
26. Neil A. Morgan, Eugene W. Anderson, and Vikas Mittal, "Understanding Firms' Customer Satisfaction Information Usage," *Journal of Marketing* 69 (July 2005): 131–51.
27. Jim Edwards, "Broken Promises," *Brandweek*, May 22, 2006, pp. 23–28.
28. Although for moderating factors, see Kathleen Seiders, Glenn B. Voss, Dhruv Grewal, and Andrea L. Godfrey, "Do Satisfied Customers Buy More? Examining Moderating Influences in a Retailing Context," *Journal of Marketing* 69 (October 2005): 26–43.
29. See, for example, Christian Homburg, Nicole Koschate, and Wayne D. Hoyer, "Do Satisfied Customers Really Pay More? A Study of the

Relationship between Customer Satisfaction and Willingness to Pay," *Journal of Marketing* 69 (April 2005): 84–96.

30. Claes Fornell, Sunil Mithas, Forrest V. Morgeson III, and M.S. Krishnan, "Customer Satisfaction and Stock Prices: High Returns, Low Risk," *Journal of Marketing* 70 (January 2006): 3–14. See also, Thomas S. Gruca and Lopo L. Rego, "Customer Satisfaction, Cash Flow, and Shareholder Value," *Journal of Marketing* 69 (July 2005): 115–30; Eugene W. Anderson, Claes Fornell, and Sanal K. Mazvancheryl, "Customer Satisfaction and Shareholder Value," *Journal of Marketing* 68 (October 2004): 172–85.

31. Thomas O. Jones and W. Earl Sasser Jr., "Why Satisfied Customers Defect," *Harvard Business Review* (November–December 1995): 88–99.

32. Companies should also note that managers and salespeople can manipulate customer satisfaction ratings. They can be especially nice to customers just before the survey. They can also try to exclude unhappy customers. Another danger is that if customers know the company will go out of its way to please them, some may express high dissatisfaction in order to receive more concessions.

33. Anne Chen, "Customer Feedback Key for Theme Park: Inquisite Lets Visitors Sound Off," *eWeek*, December 15, 2003, p. 58.

34. For an empirical comparison of different methods to measure customer satisfaction, see Neil A. Morgan and Lopo Leotto Rego, "The Value of Different Customer Satisfaction and Loyalty Metrics in Predicting Business Performance," *Marketing Science* 25 (September–October 2006) 426–39.

35. Frederick K. Reichheld, "The One Number You Need to Grow," *Harvard Business Review* (December 2003): 46–54.

36. James C. Ward and Amy L. Ostrom, "Complaining to the Masses: The Role of Protest Framing in Customer-Created Complaint Sites," *Journal of Consumer Research* 33 (September 2006): 220–30; Kim Hart, "Angry Customers Use Web to Shame Firms," *Washington Post*, July 5, 2006.

37. Eugene W. Anderson and Claes Fornell, "Foundations of the American Customer Satisfaction Index," *Total Quality Management* 11, no. 7 (September 2000): S869–S882; Claes Fornell, Michael D. Johnson, Eugene W. Anderson, Jaaesung Cha, and Barbara Everitt Bryant, "The American Customer Satisfaction Index: Nature, Purpose, and Findings," *Journal of Marketing* (October 1996): 7–18.

38. Jennifer Rooney, "Winning Hearts and Minds," *Advertising Age* 77, no. 28, July 10, 2006, p. S10+.

39. Technical Assistance Research Programs (Tarp), *U.S. Office of Consumer Affairs Study on Complaint Handling in America*, 1986.

40. Stephen S. Tax and Stephen W. Brown, "Recovering and Learning from Service Failure," *Sloan Management Review* 40, no. 1 (Fall 1998): 75–88; Ruth Bolton and Tina M. Bronkhorst, "The Relationship between Customer Complaints to the Firm and Subsequent Exit Behavior," in *Advances in Consumer Research*, vol. 22 (Provo, UT: Association for Consumer Research, 1995), pp. unknown; Roland T. Rust, Bala Subramanian, and Mark Wells, "Making Complaints a Management Tool," *Marketing Management* 1, no. 3 (March 1992): 40–45; Karl Albrecht and Ron Zemke, *Service America!* (Homewood, IL: Dow Jones-Irwin, 1985), pp. 6–7.

41. Christian Homburg and Andreas Fürst, "How Organizational Complaint Handling Drives Customer Loyalty: An Analysis of the Mechanistic and the Organic Approach," *Journal of Marketing* 69 (July 2005): 95–114.

42. Philip Kotler, *Kotler on Marketing* (New York: The Free Press, 1999), pp. 21–22.

43. Cyndee Miller, "U.S. Firms Lag in Meeting Global Quality Standards," *Marketing News*, February 15, 1993.

44. Roland R. Rust, Anthony J. Zahorik, and Timothy L. Keiningham, "Return on Quality (ROQ): Making Service Quality Financially Accountable," *Journal of Marketing* 59, no. 2 (April 1995): 58–70; "Quality: The U.S. Drives to Catch Up," *BusinessWeek*, November 1, 1982, pp. 66–80.

45. Robert D. Buzzell and Bradley T. Gale, *The PIMS Principles: Linking Strategy to Performance* (New York: The Free Press, 1987), chapter 6. (PIMS stands for Profit Impact of Market Strategy.)

46. Brian Hindo, "Satisfaction Not Guaranteed," *BusinessWeek*, June 19, 2006, pp. 32–36.

47. Lerzan Aksoy, Timothy L. Keiningham, and Terry G. Vavra, "Nearly Everything You Know about Loyalty Is Wrong," *Marketing News*, October 1, 2005, p. 20–21; Timothy L. Keiningham, Terry G. Vavra, Lerzan Aksoy, and Henri Wallard, *Loyalty Myths* (Hoboken, NJ: John Wiley & Sons, 2005).

48. Werner J. Reinartz and V. Kumar, "The Impact of Customer Relationship Characteristics on Profitable Lifetime Duration," *Journal of Marketing* 67 (January 2003): 77–99; Werner J. Reinartz and V. Kumar, "On the Profitability of Long-Life Customers in a Noncontractual Setting: An Empirical Investigation and Implications for Marketing," *Journal of Marketing* 64 (October 2000): 17–35.

49. Rakesh Niraj, Mahendra Gupta, and Chakravarthi Narasimhan, "Customer Profitability in a Supply Chain," *Journal of Marketing* (July 2001): 1–16.

50. Thomas M. Petro, "Profitability: The Fifth 'P' of Marketing," *Bank Marketing* (September 1990): 48–52; "Who Are Your Best Customers?" *Bank Marketing* (October 1990): 48–52.

51. Michael D. Johnson, and Fred Selnes, "Diversifying Your Customer Portfolio," *MIT Sloan Management Review* 46, no. 3 (Spring 2005): 11–14.

52. Michael D. Johnson, and Fred Selnes, "Customer Portfolio Management," *Journal of Marketing* 68, no. 2 (April 2004): 1–17.

53. Ravi Dhar and Rashi Glazer, "Hedging Customers," *Harvard Business Review* (May 2003): 86–92.

54. V. Kumar, "Customer Lifetime Value," in *Handbook of Marketing Research*, ed. Rajiv Grover and Marco Vriens (Thousand Oaks, CA: Sage Publications, 2006), pp. 602–27; Sunil Gupta, Donald R. Lehmann, and Jennifer Ames Stuart, "Valuing Customers," *Journal of Marketing Research* 61 (February 2004): 7–18; Rajkumar Venkatesan and V. Kumar, "A Customer Lifetime Value Framework for Customer Selection and Resource Allocation Strategy," *Journal of Marketing* 68 (October 2004): 106–25.

55. V. Kumar, "Profitable Relationships," *Marketing Research* 18 (Fall 2006): 41–46.

56. For some recent analysis and discussion, see Michael Haenlein, Andreas M. Kaplan, and Detlef Schoder, "Valuing the Real Option of Abandoning Unprofitable Customers When Calculating Customer Lifetime Value," *Journal of Marketing* 70 (July 2006): 5–20; Teck-Hua Ho, Young-Hoon Park, and Yong-Pin Zhou, "Incorporating Satisfaction into Customer Value Analysis: Optimal Investment in Lifetime Value," *Marketing Science* 25 (May–June 2006): 260–77; and Peter S. Fader, Bruce G. S. Hardie, and Ka Lok Lee, "RFM and CLV: Using Iso-Value Curves for Customer Base Analysis," *Journal of Marketing Research* 62 (November 2005): 415–30.

57. Nicole E. Coviello, Roderick J. Brodie, Peter J. Danaher, and Wesley J. Johnston, "How Firms Relate to Their Markets: An Empirical Examination of Contemporary Marketing Practices," *Journal of Marketing* 66 (July 2002):

58. For an up-to-date view of academic perspectives, see the articles contained in the Special Section on Customer Relationship Management, *Journal of Marketing* 69 (October 2005). For a study of the processes involved, see Werner Reinartz, Manfred Kraft, and Wayne D. Hoyer, "The Customer Relationship Management Process: Its Measurement and Impact on Performance," *Journal of Marketing Research* 61 (August 2004): 293–305.

59. Nora A. Aufreiter, David Elzinga, and Jonathan W. Gordon, "Better Branding," *The McKinsey Quarterly* 4 (2003): 29–39.

60. Eric Krell, "The 6 Most Overlooked Customer Touch Points," *Customer Relationship Management*, January 2005. Vol. 9, Iss. 1; p. 40+.

61. Lanning, *Delivering Profitable Value.*

62. Louis Columbus, "Lessons Learned in Las Vegas: Loyalty Programs Pay," *CRM Buyer*, July 29, 2005; Mark Leon, "Catering to True-Blue Customers," *Computerworld*, August 11, 2003, p. 37; John R. Brandt, "Dare to Be Different," *Chief Executive* (May 2003): 34–38; Joe Ashbrook Nickell, "Welcome to Harrah's," *Business 2.0* (April 2002): 49–54; Del Jones, "Client Data Means Little without Good Analysis," *USA Today*, December 24, 2001.

63. Don Peppers and Martha Rogers, *One-to-One B2B: Customer Development Strategies for the Business-To-Business World* (New York: Doubleday, 2001); Peppers and Rogers, *The One-to-One Future: Building Relationships One Customer at a Time;* Don Peppers and Martha Rogers, *The One-to-One Manager: Real-World Lessons in Customer Relationship Management* (New York: Doubleday, 1999); Don Peppers, Martha Rogers, and Bob Dorf, *The One-to-One Fieldbook: The Complete Toolkit for Implementing a One-to-One Marketing Program* (New York: Bantam, 1999); Don Peppers and Martha Rogers, *Enterprise One to One: Tools for Competing in the Interactive Age* (New York: Currency, 1997).

64. Katherine O'Brien, "Differentiation Begins with Customer Knowledge," *American Printer* (July 2003): 8.

65. Tom Ostenon, *Customer Share Marketing* (Upper Saddle River, NJ: Prentice-Hall, 2002); Alan W. H. Grant and Leonard A. Schlesinger, "Realize Your Customer's Full Profit Potential," *Harvard Business Review* (September–October 1995): 59–72.

66. Donna M. Airoldi, "Bank Taps Consumers' Hearts (and Wallets) through Their Dogs' Stomachs," *Incentive* 180, no. 10 (October 2006): 120.

67. Michael Lewis, "Customer Acquisition Promotions and Customer Asset Value," *Journal of Marketing Research* 63 (May 2006): 195–203.

68. Werner Reinartz, Jacquelyn S. Thomas, and V. Kumar, "Balancing Acquisition and Retention Resources to Maximize Customer Profitability," *Journal of Marketing* 69 (January 2005): 63–79.

69. Frederick F. Reichheld, "Learning from Customer Defections," *Harvard Business Review* (March–April 1996): 56–69.

70. Frederick F. Reichheld, *Loyalty Rules* (Boston: Harvard Business School Press, 2001); Frederick F. Reichheld, *The Loyalty Effect* (Boston: Harvard Business School Press, 1996).

71. Leonard L. Berry and A. Parasuraman, *Marketing Services: Computing through Quality* (New York:

The Free Press, 1991), pp. 136–142. For an academic examination in a business-to-business context, see Robert W. Palmatier, Srinath Gopalakrishna, and Mark B. Houston, "Returns on Business-to-Business Relationship Marketing Investments: Strategies for Leveraging Profits," *Marketing Science* 25 (September–October 2006): 477–93.

72. Reichheld, "Learning from Customer Defections," pp. 56–69.

73. Jim Edwards, "Broken Promises," *Brandweek*, May 22, 2006, pp. 23–28.

74. Utpal M. Dholakia, "How Consumer Self-Determination Influences Relational Marketing Outcomes: Evidence from Longitudinal Field Studies," *Journal of Marketing Research* 43 (February 2006): 109–20.

75. Allison Enright, "Serve Them Right," *Marketing News*, May 1, 2006, pp. 21–22.

76. For a review, see Grahame R. Dowling and Mark Uncles, "Do Customer Loyalty Programs Really Work?" *Sloan Management Review* 38, no. 4 (Summer 1997): 71–82.

77. Thomas Lee, "Retailers Look for a Hook," *St. Louis Post-Dispatch*, December 4, 2004.

78. Theresa Howard, "Hershey's, eBay Team to Reward Customers," *USA Today*, April 21, 2006; Angelo Fernando, "Why Punish, When You Can Reward?" *Communication World* 23, no. 5 (September–October 2006): 14+.

79. www.apple.com.

80. www.hog.com.

81. James H. Donnelly Jr., Leonard L. Berry, and Thomas W. Thompson, *Marketing Financial Services—A Strategic Vision* (Homewood, IL: Dow Jones–Irwin, 1985), p. 113.

82. www.ameritrade.com; Rebecca Buckman, "Ameritrade Unveils Index That Tracks Customer Trends," *Wall Street Journal*, December 2, 1999; Sean Michael Kerner, "Ameritrade Tops List of Best Online Brokerages," *Finance*, July 26, 2005. For a contrast, see Susan Stellin, "For Many Online Companies, Customer Service Is Hardly a Priority," *New York Times*, February 19, 2001.

83. Susan Stellin, "For Many Online Companies, Customer Service Is Hardly a Priority," *New York Times*, February 19, 2001; Michelle Johnson, "Getting Ready for the Onslaught," *Boston Globe*, November 4, 1999.

84. Kerry Capell, "BBC: Step Right into the Telly," *BusinessWeek*, July 24, 2006, p. 52; http://backstage.bbc.co.uk.

85. Michael Totty, "E-Commerce (A Special Report): Business Solutions," *Wall Street Journal*, October 20, 2003.

86. Jeffrey Pfeffer, "The Face of Your Business," *Business 2.0* (December 2002–January 2003): 58.

87. Jacquelyn S. Thomas, Robert C. Blattberg, and Edward J. Fox, "Recapturing Lost Customers," *Journal of Marketing Research* 61 (February 2004): 31–45.

88. Werner Reinartz and V. Kumar, "The Impact of Customer Relationship Characteristics on Profitable Lifetime Duration," *Journal of Marketing* 67, no. 1 (January 2003): 77–99; Werner Reinartz and V. Kumar, "The Mismanagement of Customer Loyalty," *Harvard Business Review* (July 2002): 86–97.

89. V. Kumar, Rajkumar Venkatesan, and Werner Reinartz, "Knowing What to Sell, When, and to Whom," *Harvard Business Review* (March 2006): 131–37.

90. Christopher R. Stephens and R. Sukumar, "An Introduction to Data Mining," in *Handbook of Marketing Research*, ed. Rajiv Grover and Marco Vriens (Thousand Oaks, CA: Sage Publications, 2006), pp. 455–86; Pang-Ning Tan, Michael Steinbach, and Vipin Kumar, *Introduction to Data Mining* (Upper Saddle River, NJ: Addison Wesley, 2005); Michael J. A. Berry and Gordon S. Linoff, *Data Mining Techniques: For Marketing, Sales, and Customer Relationship Management*, 2nd ed. (Hoboken, NJ: Wiley Computer, 2004); James Lattin, Doug Carroll, and Paul Green, *Analyzing Multivariate Data* (Florence, KY: Thomson Brooks/Cole, 2003).

91. Werner Reinartz and V. Kumar, "The Mismanagement of Customer Loyalty," *Harvard Business Review* (July 2002): 86–94; Susan M. Fournier, Susan Dobscha, and David Glen Mick, "Preventing the Premature Death of Relationship Marketing," *Harvard Business Review* (January–February 1998): 42–51.

92. Jon Swartz, "Ebay Faithful Expect Loyalty in Return," *USA Today*, July 1, 2002.

93. George S. Day, "Creating a Superior Customer-Relating Capability," *Sloan Management Review* 44, no. 3 (Spring 2003): 77–82.

94. Darrell K. Rigby, Frederick F. Reichheld, and Phil Schefter, "Avoid the Four Perils of CRM," *Harvard Business Review* (February 2002): 101–9.

95. George S. Day, "Creating a Superior Customer-Relating Capability," *Sloan Management Review* 44, no. 3 (Spring 2003): 77–82; George S. Day, "Creating a Superior Customer-Relating Capability," *MSI Report No. 03–101* (Cambridge, MA: Marketing Science Institute, 2003); "Why Some Companies Succeed at CRM (and Many Fail)," *Knowledge at Wharton*, http://knowledge.wharton.upenn.edu, accessed January 15, 2003.

Chapter 6

1. Alice Cuneo, "P&G Tries Out Mobile Marketing," *Advertising Age*, June 19, 2006, p. 2; Alice Cuneo, "Dot-com vs. Dot-mobi Debate Divides Industry," *Advertising Age*, June 19, 2006, p. 10; Marguerite Reardon, "Advertising Seeps into the Cell Phone," *CNET News.com*, September 14, 2006; Camille Ricketts, "Dialing into the Youth Market," *Wall Street Journal*, August 3, 2006.
2. Input on this chapter from Duke University's Jim Bettman and John Lynch and Stanford University's Itamar Simonson is gratefully acknowledged. For an academic overview of the field of consumer research, see Itamar Simonson, Ziv Carmon, Ravi Dhar, Aimee Drolet, and Stephen M Nowlis, "Consumer Research: In Search of Identity," *Annual Review of Psychology* 52 (2001): 249–75.
3. Leon G. Schiffman and Leslie Lazar Kanuk, *Consumer Behavior*, 9th ed. (Upper Saddle River, NJ: Prentice Hall, 2006).
4. Rob Walker, "The Princess Buy," *The New York Times Magazine*, Oct 15, 2006, http://select.nytimes.com/.
5. Sonya A. Grier, Anne Brumbaugh, and Corliss G. Thornton, "Crossover Dreams: Consumer Responses to Ethnic-Oriented Products," *Journal of Marketing* 70 (April 2006): 35–51.
6. Richard P. Coleman, "The Continuing Significance of Social Class to Marketing," *Journal of Consumer Research* (December 1983): 265–80; Richard P. Coleman and Lee P. Rainwater, *Social Standing in America: New Dimension of Class* (New York: Basic Books, 1978).
7. Schiffman and Kanuk, *Consumer Behavior.*
8. Steven Power, "Chrysler to Take Its Cars to Church; Deal with Patti LaBelle Offers Tickets, Test Drives to Sunday Worshipers," *The Wall Street Journal*, October 19, 2006.
9. Kimberly L. Allers, "Retail's Rebel Yell," *Fortune*, November 10, 2003, p. 137.
10. Elizabeth S. Moore, William L. Wilkie, and Richard J. Lutz, "Passing the Torch: Intergenerational Influences as a Source of Brand Equity," *Journal of Marketing* (April 2002): 17–37; Robert Boutilier, "Pulling the Family's Strings," *American Demographics* (August 1993): 44–48; David J. Burns, "Husband-Wife Innovative Consumer Decision Making: Exploring the Effect of Family Power," *Psychology & Marketing* (May–June 1992): 175–89; Rosann L. Spiro, "Persuasion in Family Decision Making," *Journal of Consumer Research* (March 1983): 393–402. For cross-cultural comparisons of husband–wife buying roles, see John B. Ford, Michael S. LaTour, and Tony L. Henthorne, "Perception of Marital Roles in Purchase-Decision Processes: A Cross-Cultural Study," *Journal of the Academy of Marketing Science* (Spring 1995): 120–31.
11. Kay M. Palan and Robert E. Wilkes, "Adolescent-Parent Interaction in Family Decision Making," *Journal of Consumer Research* 24, no. 2 (March1997): 159–69; Sharon E. Beatty and Salil Talpade, "Adolescent Influence in Family Decision Making: A Replication with Extension," *Journal of Consumer Research* 21 (September 1994): 332–41.
12. Chenting Su, Edward F. Fern, and Keying Ye, "A Temporal Dynamic Model of Spousal Family Purchase-Decision Behavior," *Journal of Marketing Research* 40 (August 2003): 268–81.
13. Anonymous, "Retailers Learn that Electronics Shopping Isn't Just a Guy Thing," *Wall Street Journal*, January 15, 2004.
14. Hillary Chura, "Failing to Connect: Marketing Messages for Women Fall Short," *Advertising Age*, September 23, 2002, pp. 13–14.
15. "Trillion-Dollar Kids," *The Economist*, December 2, 2006, p. 66.
16. Jennifer Bayot, "The Teenage Market; Young, Hip, and Looking for a Bargain," *New York Times*, December 1, 2003.
17. Jennifer Saranow, "'This Is the Car We Want, Mommy'; Car Makers Direct More Ads at Kids (and Their Parents); A 5-Year-Old's Toy Hummer," *The Wall Street Journal*, November 9, 2006.
18. Susan Linn, *Consuming Kids: The Hostile Takeover of Childhood* (New York: The New Press, 2004).
19. Deborah Roedder John, "Consumer Socialization of Children: A Retrospective Look at Twenty-Five Years of Research," *Journal of Consumer Research* (December 1999); Lan Nguyen Chaplin and Deborah Roedder John, "The Development of Self-Brand Connections in Children and Adolescents," *Journal of Consumer Research* (June 2005).
20. Courtney Kane, "TV and Movie Characters Sell Children's Snacks," *New York Times*, December 8, 2003.
21. Rex Y. Du and Wagner A. Kamakura, "Household Life Cycles and Lifestyles in the United States," *Journal of Marketing Research* 48 (February 2006): 121–32; Lawrence Lepisto, "A Life Span Perspective of Consumer Behavior," in *Advances in Consumer Research*, vol. 12, ed. Elizabeth Hirshman and Morris Holbrook (Provo, UT: Association for Consumer Research, 1985), p. 47. Also see Gail Sheehy, *New Passages: Mapping Your Life across Time* (New York: Random House, 1995).
22. See Frederick Herzberg, *Work and the Nature of Man* (Cleveland: William Collins, 1966); Henk Thierry and Agnes M. Koopman-Iwerna, "Motivation and Satisfaction," in *Handbook of Work and Organizational Psychology*, ed. P. J. Drenth (New York: John Wiley, 1984), pp. 141–42.

23. Harold H. Kassarjian and Mary Jane Sheffet, "Personality and Consumer Behavior: An Update," in *Perspectives in Consumer Behavior,* ed. Harold H. Kassarjian and Thomas S. Robertson (Glenview, IL: Scott, Foresman, 1981), pp. 160–80.
24. Jennifer Aaker, "Dimensions of Measuring Brand Personality," *Journal of Marketing Research* 34 (August 1997): 347–56.
25. Jennifer L. Aaker, Veronica Benet-Martinez, and Jordi Garolera, "Consumption Symbols as Carriers of Culture: A Study of Japanese and Spanish Brand Personality Constructs," *Journal of Personality and Social Psychology* 81, no. 3 (March 2001): 492–508.
26. Yongjun Sung and Spencer F. Tinkham, "Brand Personality Structures in the United States and Korea: Common and Culture-Specific Factors," *Journal of Consumer Psychology* 15, no. 4 (December 2005): 334–50.
27. M. Joseph Sirgy, "Self Concept in Consumer Behavior: A Critical Review," *Journal of Consumer Research* 9 (December 1982): 287–300.
28. Timothy R. Graeff, "Consumption Situations and the Effects of Brand Image on Consumers' Brand Evaluations," *Psychology & Marketing* 14, no. 1 (January 1997): 49–70; Timothy R. Graeff, "Image Congruence Effects on Product Evaluations: The Role of Self-Monitoring and Public/Private Consumption," *Psychology & Marketing* 13, no. 5 (August 1996): 481–99.
29. Jennifer L. Aaker, "The Malleable Self: The Role of Self-Expression in Persuasion," *Journal of Marketing Research* 36, no. 1 (February 1999): 45–57.
30. Anonymous, "16m. Young High-Earning Consumers Are Targets of High-End Lifestyle Products," *News India—Times* 37, no. 31, August 4, 2006, p. 16.
31. Amy Cortese, "They Care about the World (and They Shop Too)," *New York Times,* July 20, 2003.
32. Anthony Banco and Wendy Zellner, "Is Wal-Mart Too Powerful?" *BusinessWeek,* October 6, 2003, p. 100.
33. Toby Weber, "All Three? Gee," *Wireless Review* (May 2003): 12–14.
34. Noel C. Paul, "Meal Kits in Home," *Christian Science Monitor,* June 9, 2003, p. 13.
35. For a review of current academic research on consumer behavior, see "Consumer Psychology: Categorization, Inferences, Affect, and Persuasion," *Annual Review of Psychology* 57 (2006): 453–95. To learn more about how consumer behavior theory can be applied to policy decisions, see "Special Issue on Helping Consumers Help Themselves: Improving the Quality of Judgments and Choices," *Journal of Public Policy & Marketing* 25, no. 1 (Spring 2006).
36. Thomas J. Reynolds and Jonathan Gutman, "Laddering Theory, Method, Analysis, and Interpretation," *Journal of Advertising Research* (February–March 1988): 11–34.
37. Ernest Dichter, *Handbook of Consumer Motivations* (New York: McGraw-Hill, 1964).
38. Jan Callebaut et al., *The Naked Consumer: The Secret of Motivational Research in Global Marketing* (Antwerp, Belgium: Censydiam Institute, 1994).
39. Melanie Wells, "Mind Games," *Forbes,* September 1, 2003, p. 70.
40. Clotaire Rapaille, "Marketing to the Reptilian Brain," *Forbes,* July 3, 2006.
41. Abraham Maslow, *Motivation and Personality* (New York: Harper and Row, 1954), pp. 80–106.
42. See Frederick Herzberg, *Work and the Nature of Man* (Cleveland: William Collins, 1966); Thierry and Koopman-Iwerna, "Motivation and Satisfaction," pp. 141–42.
43. Bernard Berelson and Gary A. Steiner, *Human Behavior: An Inventory of Scientific Findings* (New York: Harcourt Brace Jovanovich, 1964), p. 88.
44. J. Edward Russo, Margaret G. Meloy, and Victoria Husted Medvec, "The Distortion of Product Information during Brand Choice," *Journal of Marketing Research* 35 (November 1998): 438–52.
45. Leslie de Chernatony and Simon Knox, "How an Appreciation of Consumer Behavior Can Help in Product Testing," *Journal of Market Research Society* (July 1990): 333. See also, Chris Janiszewski and Stiju M. J. Osselar, "A Connectionist Model of Brand–Quality Association,". *Journal of Marketing Research* (August 2000): 331–51.
46. Florida's Chris Janiszewski has developed a fascinating research program looking at preconscious processing effects. See Chris Janiszewski, "Preattentive Mere Exposure Effects," *Journal of Consumer Research* 20 (December 1993): 376–92, as well as some of his earlier and subsequent research. For more perspectives, see also John A. Bargh and Tanya L. Chartrand, "The Unbearable Automaticity Of Being," *American Psychologist* 54 (1999): 462–79 and the research programs of both authors. For lively academic debate, see Research Dialogue section of the July 2005 issue of the *Journal of Consumer Psychology.*
47. See Timothy E. Moore, "Subliminal Advertising: What You See Is What You Get," *Journal of Marketing* 46 (Spring 1982): 38–47 for an early classic; and Andrew B. Aylesworth, Ronald C. Goodstein, and Ajay Kalra, "Effect of Archetypal Embeds on Feelings: An Indirect Route to Affecting Attitudes?" *Journal of Advertising* 28, no. 3 (Fall 1999): 73–81 for a more current treatment.

48. Robert S. Wyer Jr. and Thomas K. Srull, "Person Memory and Judgment," *Psychological Review* 96, no. 1 (January 1989): 58–83; John R. Anderson, *The Architecture of Cognition* (Cambridge, MA: Harvard University Press, 1983).

49. Kyle James, "Getting That Crunching Sound Juuust Right," American Public Media's *Marketplace*, December 15, 2006.

50. For additional discussion, see John G. Lynch Jr. and Thomas K. Srull, "Memory and Attentional Factors in Consumer Choice: Concepts and Research Methods," *Journal of Consumer Research* 9 (June 1982): 18–36; and Joseph W. Alba, J. Wesley Hutchinson, and John G. Lynch Jr., "Memory and Decision Making," in *Handbook of Consumer Theory and Research*, ed. Harold H. Kassarjian and Thomas S. Robertson (Englewood Cliffs, NJ: Prentice Hall, 1992), pp. 1–49.

51. Robert S. Lockhart, Fergus I. M. Craik, and Larry Jacoby, "Depth of Processing, Recognition, and Recall," in *Recall and Recognition*, ed. John Brown (New York: John Wiley & Sons, 1976); Fergus I. M. Craik and Endel Tulving, "Depth of Processing and the Retention of Words in Episodic Memory," *Journal of Experimental Psychology* 104, no. 3 (September 1975): 268–94; Fergus I. M. Craik and Robert S. Lockhart, "Levels of Processing: A Framework for Memory Research," *Journal of Verbal Learning and Verbal Behavior* 11 (1972): 671–84.

52. Leonard M. Lodish, Magid Abraham, Stuart Kalmenson, Jeanne Livelsberger, Beth Lubetkin, Bruce Richardson, and Mary Ellen Stevens, "How T.V. Advertising Works: A Meta-Analysis of 389 Real World Split Cable T.V. Advertising Experiments," *Journal of Marketing Research* 32 (May 1995): 125–39.

53. Elizabeth F. Loftus and Gregory R. Loftus, "On the Permanence of Stored Information in the Human Brain," *American Psychologist* 35 (May 1980): 409–20.

54. Kathryn A. Braun, "Postexperience Advertising Effects on Consumer Memory," *Journal of Consumer Research* 25 (March 1999): 319–32.

55. For a comprehensive review of the academic literature on decision making, see J. Edward Russo and Kurt A. Carlson, "Individual Decision Making," in *Handbook of Marketing*, ed. Bart Weitz and Robin Wensley (London: Sage Publications, 2002), pp. 372–408.

56. Benson Shapiro, V. Kasturi Rangan, and John Sviokla, "Staple Yourself to an Order," *Harvard Business Review* (July–August 1992): 113–22. See also, Carrie M. Heilman, Douglas Bowman, and Gordon P. Wright, "The Evolution of Brand Preferences and Choice Behaviors of Consumers New to a Market," *Journal of Marketing Research* (May 2000): 139–55.

57. Alison Stein Wellner, "Research on a Shoestring," *American Demographics* (April 2001): 38–39.

58. Marketing scholars have developed several models of the consumer buying process. See; Mary Frances Luce, James R. Bettman, and John W. Payne, *Emotional Decisions: Tradeoff Difficulty and Coping in Consumer Choice* (Chicago: University of Chicago Press, 2001); James F. Engel, Roger D. Blackwell, and Paul W. Miniard, *Consumer Behavior*, 8th ed. (Fort Worth, TX: Dryden, 1994); John A. Howard and Jagdish N. Sheth, *The Theory of Buyer Behavior* (New York: Wiley, 1969).

59. William P. Putsis Jr. and Narasimhan Srinivasan, "Buying or Just Browsing? The Duration of Purchase Deliberation," *Journal of Marketing Research* (August 1994): 393–402.

60. Chem L. Narayana and Rom J. Markin, "Consumer Behavior and Product Performance: An Alternative Conceptualization," *Journal of Marketing* (October 1975): 1–6. See also, Lee G. Cooper and Akihiro Inoue, "Building Market Structures from Consumer Preferences," *Journal of Marketing Research* 33, no. 3 (August 1996): 293–306; Wayne S. DeSarbo and Kamel Jedidi, "The Spatial Representation of Heterogeneous Consideration Sets," *Marketing Science* 14, no. 3, pt. 2 (Summer 1995): 326–42.

61. For a market-structure study of the hierarchy of attributes in the coffee market, see Dipak Jain, Frank M. Bass, and Yu-Min Chen, "Estimation of Latent Class Models with Heterogeneous Choice Probabilities: An Application to Market Structuring," *Journal of Marketing Research* (February 1990): 94–101. For an application of means-end chain analysis to global markets, see Frenkel Ter Hofstede, Jan-Benedict E. M. Steenkamp, and Michel Wedel, "International Market Segmentation Based on Consumer–Product Relations," *Journal of Marketing Research* (February 1999): 1–17.

62. Virginia Postrel, "The Lessons of the Grocery Shelf Also Have Something to Say about Affirmative Action," *New York Times*, January 30, 2003.

63. David Krech, Richard S. Crutchfield, and Egerton L. Ballachey, *Individual in Society* (New York: McGraw-Hill, 1962), chapter 2.

64. Jeff Manning, "Got Milk?" *Associations Now*, July 1, 2006, pp. 56–61; Jeff Manning and Kevin Lane Keller, "Making Advertising Work: How GOT MILK? Marketing Stopped a 20-Year Sales Decline," *Marketing Management* (January–February 2003); Jeff Manning, *Got Milk? The Book* (New York: Prima Lifestyles, 1999).

65. See Leigh McAlister, "Choosing Multiple Items from a Product Class," *Journal of Consumer Research* (December 1979): 213–24; Paul E. Green and Yoram

Wind, *Multiattribute Decisions in Marketing: A Measurement Approach* (Hinsdale, IL: Dryden, 1973), chapter 2; Richard J. Lutz, "The Role of Attitude Theory in Marketing," in *Perspectives in Consumer Behavior*, ed. Kassarjian and Robertson, pp. 317–39.

66. This expectancy-value model was originally developed by Martin Fishbein, "Attitudes and Prediction of Behavior," in *Readings in Attitude Theory and Measurement*, ed. Martin Fishbein (New York: John Wiley, 1967), pp. 477–92. For a critical review, see Paul W. Miniard and Joel B. Cohen, "An Examination of the Fishbein-Ajzen Behavioral-Intentions Model's Concepts and Measures," *Journal of Experimental Social Psychology* (May 1981): 309–39.
67. Michael R. Solomon, *Consumer Behavior: Buying, Having, and Being*, 7th ed. (Upper Saddle River, NJ: Prentice Hall, 2007).
68. James R. Bettman, Eric J. Johnson, and John W. Payne, "Consumer Decision Making," in *Handbook of Consumer Theory and Research*, ed. Kassarjian and Robertson, pp. 50–84.
69. Jagdish N. Sheth, "An Investigation of Relationships among Evaluative Beliefs, Affect, Behavioral Intention, and Behavior," in *Consumer Behavior: Theory and Application*, ed. John U. Farley, John A. Howard, and L. Winston Ring (Boston: Allyn & Bacon, 1974), pp. 89–114.
70. Fishbein, "Attitudes and Prediction of Behavior."
71. Margaret C. Campbell and Ronald C. Goodstein, "The Moderating Effect of Perceived Risk on Consumers' Evaluations of Product Incongruity: Preference for the Norm," *Journal of Consumer Research* 28 (December 2001): 439–49; Grahame R. Dowling, "Perceived Risk," in *The Elgar Companion to Consumer Research and Economic Psychology*, ed. Peter E. Earl and Simon Kemp (Cheltenham, UK: Edward Elgar, 1999), pp. 41924; Grahame R. Dowling, "Perceived Risk: The Concept and Its Measurement," *Psychology and Marketing* 3 (Fall 1986): 193210; James R. Bettman, "Perceived Risk and Its Components: A Model and Empirical Test," *Journal of Marketing Research* 10 (May 1973): 18490; Raymond A. Bauer, "Consumer Behavior as Risk Taking," in *Risk Taking and Information Handling in Consumer Behavior*, ed. Donald F. Cox (Boston: Division of Research, Harvard Business School, 1967).
72. Richard L. Oliver, "Customer Satisfaction Research," in *Handbook of Marketing Research*, ed. Rajiv Grover and Marco Vriens (Thousand Oaks, CA: Sage Publications, 2006), pp. 569–87.
73. Ralph L. Day, "Modeling Choices among Alternative Responses to Dissatisfaction," *Advances in Consumer Research* 11 (1984): 496–99. Also see Philip Kotler and Murali K. Mantrala, "Flawed Products: Consumer Responses and Marketer Strategies," *Journal of Consumer Marketing* (Summer 1985): 27–36.
74. Albert O. Hirschman, *Exit, Voice, and Loyalty* (Cambridge, MA: Harvard University Press, 1970).
75. John D. Cripps, "Heuristics and Biases in Timing the Replacement of Durable Products," *Journal of Consumer Research* 21 (September 1994): 304–18.
76. Richard E. Petty, *Communication and Persuasion: Central and Peripheral Routes to Attitude Change* (New York: Springer-Verlag, 1986); Richard E. Petty and John T. Cacioppo, *Attitudes and Persuasion: Classic and Contemporary Approaches* (New York: McGraw-Hill, 1981).
77. Herbert E. Krugman, "The Impact of Television Advertising: Learning without Involvement," *Public Opinion Quarterly* (Fall 1965): 349–56.
78. For a detailed review of the practical significance of consumer decision making, see Itamar Simonson, "Get Close to Your Customers by Understanding How They Make Their Choices," *California Management Review* 35 (Summer 1993): 78–79.
79. Frank R. Kardes, *Consumer Behavior and Managerial Decision Making*, 2nd ed. (Upper Saddle River, NJ: Prentice Hall, 2003).
80. See Richard Thaler, "Mental Accounting and Consumer Choice," *Marketing Science* 4, no. 3 (Summer 1985): 199–214 for a seminal piece; and Richard Thaler, "Mental Accounting Matters," *Journal of Behavioral Decision Making* 12, no. 3 (September 1999): 183–206 for more contemporary perspectives.
81. Gary L. Gastineau and Mark P. Kritzman, *Dictionary of Financial Risk Management*, 3rd ed. (New York: John Wiley & Sons, 1999).
82. Example adapted from Daniel Kahneman and Amos Tversky, "Prospect Theory: An Analysis of Decision under Risk," *Econometrica* 47 (March 1979): 263–91.
83. Harper W. Boyd Jr. and Sidney Levy, "New Dimensions in Consumer Analysis," *Harvard Business Review*, (November–December 1963): 129–40.
84. Sandra Vandermerwe, *Customer Capitalism: Increasing Returns in New Market Spaces* (London: Nicholas Brealey Publishing), chapter 11.
85. Patricia B. Seybold, "Get Inside the Lives of Your Customers," *Harvard Business Review* (May 2001): 81–89.

Chapter 7

1. Kate Maddox, "BMA Conference Showcases Innovation," *B to B*, June 12, 2006, p. 3.
2. For a comprehensive review of the topic, see James C. Anderson and James A. Narus, *Business Market Management: Understanding, Creating, and Delivering Value*, 2nd ed. (Upper Saddle River, NJ:

Prentice Hall, 2004). Comments on a draft of this chapter from Northwestern University's Jim Anderson and University of Wisconsin's Jan Heide are gratefully acknowledged.

3. Frederick E. Webster Jr. and Yoram Wind, *Organizational Buying Behavior* (Upper Saddle River, NJ: Prentice Hall, 1972), p. 2. For a review of recent academic literature on the topic, see Håkan Håkansson and Ivan Snehota, "Marketing in Business Markets," in *Handbook of Marketing*, ed. Bart Weitz and Robin Wensley (London: Sage Publications, 2002), pp. 513–26.
4. Bob Donath, "Customer Knowledge Takes Priority in Study," *Marketing News*, December 15, 2005, p. 7.
5. Jennifer Gilbert, "Small but Mighty," *Sales & Marketing Management* (January 2004): 30–35.
6. Peter Lewis, "Texas Instruments' Lunatic Fringe," *Fortune*, 154, no. 5, September 4, 2006, p. 120.
7. Susan Avery, *Purchasing* 135, no. 16, November 2, 2006, p. 36.
8. Michael Collins, "Breaking into the Big Leagues," *American Demographics* (January 1996): 24.
9. Patrick J. Robinson, Charles W. Faris, and Yoram Wind, *Industrial Buying and Creative Marketing* (Boston: Allyn & Bacon, 1967).
10. Michele D. Bunn, "Taxonomy of Buying Decision Approaches," *Journal of Marketing* 57 (January 1993):38–56; Daniel H. McQuiston, "Novelty, Complexity, and Importance as Causal Determinants of Industrial Buyer Behavior," *Journal of Marketing* (April 1989): 66–79; Peter Doyle, Arch G. Woodside, and Paul Mitchell, "Organizational Buying in New Task and Rebuy Situations," *Industrial Marketing Management* (February 1979): 7–11.
11. Urban B. Ozanne and Gilbert A. Churchill Jr., "Five Dimensions of the Industrial Adoption Process," *Journal of Marketing Research* (August 1971): 322–28.
12. To learn more about how business-to-business firms can improve their branding, see Philip Kotler and Waldemar Pfoertsch, *B2B Brand Management* (Berlin: Springer, 2006).
13. Steve Hamm, "The Fine Art of Tech Mergers," *BusinessWeek*, July 10, 2006, pp. 70–71.
14. Niraj Dawar and Mark Vandenbosch, "The Seller's Hidden Advantage," *MIT Sloan Management Review* (Winter 2004): 83–88.
15. Jeffrey E. Lewin and Naveen Donthu, "The Influence of Purchase Situation on Buying Center Structure and Involvement: A Select Meta-Analysis of Organizational Buying Behavior Research," *Journal of Business Research* 58 (October 2005): 1381–90; R. Venkatesh and Ajay K. Kohli, "Influence Strategies in Buying Centers," *Journal of Marketing* 59 (October 1995): 71–82.
16. Donald W. Jackson Jr., Janet E. Keith, and Richard K. Burdick, "Purchasing Agents' Perceptions of Industrial Buying Center Influence: A Situational Approach," *Journal of Marketing* (Fall 1984): 75–83.
17. Webster and Wind, *Organizational Buying Behavior*, p. 6.
18. James C. Anderson and James A. Narus, *Business Market Management: Understanding, Creating, and Delivering Value*, 2nd ed. (Upper Saddle River, NJ: Prentice Hall, 2004); Frederick E. Webster Jr. and Yoram Wind, "A General Model for Understanding Organizational Buying Behavior," *Journal of Marketing* 36 (April 1972): 12–19; Webster and Wind, *Organizational Buying Behavior.*
19. Allison Enright, "It Takes a Committee to Buy into B-to-B," *Marketing News*, February 15, 2006, pp. 12–13.
20. David Welch, "Renault-Nissan: Say Hello to Bo," *BusinessWeek*, July 31, 2006, p. 56.
21. Frederick E. Webster Jr. and Kevin Lane Keller, "A Roadmap for Branding in Industrial Markets," *Journal of Brand Management* 11 (May 2004): 388–402.
22. Scott Ward and Frederick E. Webster Jr., "Organizational Buying Behavior" in *Handbook of Consumer Behavior*, ed. Tom Robertson and Hal Kassarjian (Upper Saddle River, NJ: Prentice Hall, 1991), chapter 12, pp. 419–58.
23. Bob Donath, "Emotions Play Key Role in Biz Brand Appeal," *Marketing News*, June 1, 2006, p. 7.
24. Michael Krauss, "Warriors of the Heart," *Marketing News*, February 1, 2006, p. 7.
25. Bob Lamons, "Branding, B-to-B Style," *Sales and Marketing Management* 157, no. 9 (September 2005): 46–50.
26. Webster and Wind, *Organizational Buying Behavior*, p. 6.
27. Erin Strout, "Safe and Sound," *Sales & Marketing Management* (September 2003): 38.
28. James C. Anderson, James A. Narus, and Wouter van Rossum, "Customer Value Proposition in Business Markets," *Harvard Business Review* (March 2006): 2–10; James C. Anderson, "From Understanding to Managing Customer Value in Business Markets," in *Rethinking Marketing: New Marketing Tools*, ed. H. Håkansson, D. Harrison, and A. Waluszewski (London: John Wiley & Sons, 2004), pp. 137–59.
29. Susan Caminiti, "Drivers of the Economy," *Fortune* 153, no. 7, April 17, 2006, p. C1+.
30. David Hannon, "Lockheed Martin: Negotiators Inc.," *Purchasing*, February 5, 2004, pp. 27–30.

31. Wayne Forrest, "McDonald's Applies SRM Strategy to Global Technology Buy," *Purchasing* 135, no. 12, September 7, 2006, p. 16.

32. Tim Minahan, "OEM Buying Survey—Part 2: Buyers Get New Roles but Keep Old Tasks," *Purchasing,* July 16, 1998, pp. 208–9.

33. Robinson, Faris, and Wind, *Industrial Buying and Creative Marketing.*

34. Rajdeep Grewal, James M. Comer, and Raj Mehta, "An Investigation into the Antecedents of Organizational Participation in Business-to-Business Electronic Markets," *Journal of Marketing* 65 (July 2001): 17–33.

35. Knowledge@Wharton, "Open Sesame? Or Could the Doors Slam Shut for Alibaba.com?" July 27, 2005; Julia Angwin, "Top Online Chemical Exchange Is Unlikely Success Story," *Wall Street Journal,* January 8, 2004; Olga Kharif, "B2B, Take 2," *BusinessWeek,* November 25, 2003; George S. Day, Adam J. Fein, and Gregg Ruppersberger, "Shakeouts in Digital Markets: Lessons from B2B Exchanges," *California Management Review* 45, no. 2 (Winter 2003): 131–51.

36. Brian J. Carroll, *Lead Generation for the Complex Sale* (New York: McGraw-Hill, 2006).

37. Allison Enright, "It Takes a Committee to Buy into B-to-B," *Marketing News,* February 15, 2006, pp. 12–13.

38. Robert Hiebeler, Thomas B. Kelly, and Charles Ketteman, *Best Practices: Building Your Business with Customer-Focused Solutions* (New York: Arthur Andersen/Simon & Schuster, 1998), pp. 122–24.

39. Daniel J. Flint, Robert B. Woodruff, and Sarah Fisher Gardial, "Exploring the Phenomenon of Customers' Desired Value Change in a Business-to-Business Context," *Journal of Marketing* 66 (October 2002): 102–17.

40. Ruth N. Bolton and Matthew B. Myers, "Price-Based Global Market Segmentation for Services," *Journal of Marketing* 67 (July 2003): 108–28.

41. Wolfgang Ulaga and Andreas Eggert, "Value-Based Differentiation in Business Relationships: Gaining and Sustaining Key Supplier Status," *Journal of Marketing* 70 (January 2006): 119–36.

42. Christopher Palmeri, "Serving Two (Station) Masters," *BusinessWeek,* July 24, 2006, p. 46.

43. David Kiley, "Small Print Jobs for Peanuts," *BusinessWeek,* July 17, 2006, p. 58.

44. Nirmalya Kumar, *Marketing as Strategy: Understanding the CEO's Agenda for Driving Growth and Innovation* (Boston: Harvard Business School Press, 2004).

45. Kumar, *Marketing as Strategy.*

46. See William Atkinson, "Now That's Value Added," *Purchasing,* December 11, 2003, p. 26; James A. Narus and James C. Anderson, "Turn Your Industrial Distributors into Partners," *Harvard Business Review* (March–April 1986): 66–71.

47. For foundational material, see Lloyd M. Rinehart, James A. Eckert, Robert B. Handfield, Thomas J. Page Jr., and Thomas Atkin, "An Assessment of Buyer–Seller Relationships," *Journal of Business Logistics* 25, no. 1 (2004): 25–62; F. Robert Dwyer, Paul Schurr, and Sejo Oh, "Developing Buyer–Supplier Relationships," *Journal of Marketing* 51 (April 1987): 11–28; and Barbara Bund Jackson, *Winning & Keeping Industrial Customers: The Dynamics of Customer Relations* (Lexington, MA: D. C. Heath, 1985).

48. Arnt Buvik and George John, "When Does Vertical Coordination Improve Industrial Purchasing Relationships?" *Journal of Marketing* 64 (October 2000): 52–64.

49. Das Narayandas and V. Kasturi Rangan, "Building and Sustaining Buyer–Seller Relationships in Mature Industrial Markets," *Journal of Marketing* 68 (July 2004): 63–77.

50. Robert W. Palmatier, Rajiv P. Dant, Dhruv Grewal, and Kenneth R. Evans, "Factors Influencing the Effectiveness of Relationship Marketing: A Meta-Analysis," *Journal of Marketing* 70 (October 2006): 136–53; Jean L. Johnson, Ravipreet S. Sohli, and Rajdeep Grewal, "The Role of Relational Knowledge Stores in Interfirm Partnering," *Journal of Marketing* 68 (July 2004): 21–36; Fred Selnes and James Sallis, "Promoting Relationship Learning," *Journal of Marketing* 67 (July 2003): 80–95; Patricia M. Doney and Joseph P. Cannon, "An Examination of the Nature of Trust in Buyer–Seller Relationships," *Journal of Marketing* 61 (April 1997): 35–51; Shankar Ganesan, "Determinants of Long-Term Orientation in Buyer–Seller Relationships," *Journal of Marketing* 58 (April 1994): 1–19.

51. John H. Sheridan, "An Alliance Built on Trust," *Industry Week,* March 17, 1997, pp. 66–70.

52. William W. Keep, Stanley C. Hollander, and Roger Dickinson, "Forces Impinging on Long-Term Business-to-Business Relationships in the United States: An Historical Perspective," *Journal of Marketing* 62 (April 1998): 31–45.

53. Joseph P. Cannon and William D. Perreault Jr., "Buyer–Seller Relationships in Business Markets," *Journal of Marketing Research* 36 (November 1999): 439–60.

54. Jan B. Heide and Kenneth H. Wahne, "Friends, Businesspeople, and Relationship Roles: A Conceptual Framework and Research Agenda," *Journal of Marketing* 70 (July 2006): 90–103.

55. Cannon and Perreault Jr., "Buyer–Seller Relationships in Business Markets," pp. 439–60.

56. Thomas G. Noordewier, George John, and John R. Nevin, "Performance Outcomes of Purchasing

Arrangements in Industrial Buyer–Vendor Arrangements," *Journal of Marketing* 54 (October 1990): 80–93; Buvik and John, "When Does Vertical Coordination Improve Industrial Purchasing Relationships?" pp. 52–64.

57. Akesel I. Rokkan, Jan B. Heide, and Kenneth H. Wathne, "Specific Investment in Marketing Relationships: Expropriation and Bonding Effects," *Journal of Marketing Research* 40 (May 2003): 210–24.

58. Kenneth H. Wathne and Jan B. Heide, "Relationship Governance in a Supply Chain Network," *Journal of Marketing* 68 (January 2004): 73–89; Douglas Bowman and Das Narayandas, "Linking Customer Management Effort to Customer Profitability in Business Markets," *Journal of Marketing Research* 61 (November 2004): 433–47; Mrinal Ghosh and George John, "Governance Value Analysis and Marketing Strategy," *Journal of Marketing* 63 (Special Issue, 1999): 131–45.

59. Sandy Jap, "Pie Expansion Effects: Collaboration Processes in Buyer–Seller Relationships," *Journal of Marketing Research* 36 (November 1999): 461–75.

60. Buvik and John, "When Does Vertical Coordination Improve Industrial Purchasing Relationships?" pp. 52–64.

61. Kenneth H. Wathne and Jan B. Heide, "Opportunism in Interfirm Relationships: Forms, Outcomes, and Solutions," *Journal of Marketing* 64 (October 2000): 36–51.

62. Mary Walton, "When Your Partner Fails You," *Fortune*, May 26, 1997, pp. 151–54.

63. Mark B. Houston and Shane A. Johnson, "Buyer–Supplier Contracts versus Joint Ventures: Determinants and Consequences of Transaction Structure," *Journal of Marketing Research* 37 (February 2000): 1–15.

64. Rokkan, Heide, and Wathne, "Specific Investment in Marketing Relationships: Expropriation and Bonding Effects," pp. 210–24.

65. Paul King, "Purchasing: Keener Competition Requires Thinking outside the Box," *Nation's Restaurant News*, August 18, 2003, p. 87.

66. Matthew Swibel and Janet Novack, "The Scariest Customer," *Forbes*, November 10, 2003, pp. 96–97.

67. Laura M. Litvan, "Selling to Uncle Sam: New, Easier Rules," *Nation's Business* (March 1995): 46–48.

68. Ellen Messmer, "Feds Do E-Commerce the Hard Way," *Network World*, April 13, 1998, pp. 31–32.

1. Louise Lee, "Love Those Boomers," *BusinessWeek*, October 24, 2005, p. 94; Bob Moos, "Last of Boomers Turn 40," *Dallas Morning News*, January 1, 2005; Linda Tischler, "Where the Bucks Are," *Fast Company* (March 2004): 71–77; Michael J. Weiss, "Chasing Youth," *American Demographics* (October 2002): 35–40; Becky Ebenkamp, "When They're 64," *Brandweek*, October 7, 2002, pp. 22–25.

2. James C. Anderson and James A. Narus, "Capturing the Value of Supplementary Services," *Harvard Business Review* (January–February 1995): 75–83.

3. Tevfik Dalgic and Maarten Leeuw, "Niche Marketing Revisited: Concept, Applications, and Some European Cases," *European Journal of Marketing* 28, no. 4 (April 1994): 39–55.

4. Robert D. Hof, "There's Not Enough 'Me' in MySpace," *Business Week*, December 4, 2006, p. 40; Abbey Klaassen, "Niche-Targeted Social Networks Find Audiences," *Advertising Age* 77, no. 45, November 6, 2006, p. 15.

5. Jerry Harkavy, "Colgate Buying Control of Tom's of Maine for $100 Million," *Associated Press*, Boston.com, March 21, 2006.

6. Robert Blattberg and John Deighton, "Interactive Marketing: Exploiting the Age of Addressibility," *Sloan Management Review* 33, no. 1 (Fall 1991): 5–14.

7. Brian Morrissey, "Dan Myrick on the Spot," *Adweek*, May 8, 2006, p. 28.

8. Dale Buss, "Brands in the Hood," *Point* (December 2005): 1924.

9. Don Peppers and Martha Rogers, *One-to-One B2B: Customer Development Strategies for the Business-To-Business World* (New York: Doubleday, 2001); Mark Rechtin, "Aston Martin Woos Customers One by Jerry Wind and A. Rangaswamy, "Customerization: The Second Revolution in Mass Customization," Wharton School working paper, June 1999.

10. Anderson and Narus, "Capturing the Value of Supplementary Services," pp. 75–83.

11. Itamar Simonson, "Determinants of Customers' Responses to Customized Offers: Conceptual Framework and Research Propositions," *Journal of Marketing* 69 (January 2005): 32–45.

12. Joann Muller, "Kmart con Salsa: Will It Be Enough?" *BusinessWeek*, September 9, 2002.

13. Steve Friedman, "You Paid How Much for That Bike?" *New York Times*, November 9, 2006.

14. Nanette Byrnes, "What's Beyond for Bed Bath & Beyond?" *BusinessWeek*, January 19, 2004, pp. 45–50; Andrea Lillo, "Bed Bath Sees More Room for Growth," *Home Textiles Today*, July 7, 2003, p. 2.

15. Kate Kane, "It's a Small World," *Working Woman* (October 1997): 22.

16. By visiting the company's sponsored site, MyBestSegments.com, you can enter in a zip code and discover the top five clusters for that area. Note that another leading supplier of geodemographic data is ClusterPlus (Strategic Mapping).

17. Becky Ebenkamp, "Urban America Redefined," *Brandweek*, October 6, 2003, pp. 12–13.
18. www.claritas.com.
19. Art Weinstein, *Handbook of Market Segmentation: Strategic Targeting for Business and Technology Firms*, 3rd ed. (Binghamton, NY: Haworth Press, 2004); Michael J. Weiss, *The Clustered World* (Boston: Little, Brown & Co., 2000).
20. Michael J. Weiss, "To Be about to Be," *American Demographics* (September 2003): 29–36.
21. Gina Chon, "Car Makers Talk 'Bout G-G-Generations," *Wall Street Journal*, May 9, 2006.
22. Brooks Barnes and Monica M. Clark, "Tapping into the Wedding Industry to Sell Broadway Seats," *Wall Street Journal*, July 3, 2006.
23. Sarah Allison and Carlos Tejada, "Mr., Mrs., Meet Mr. Clean," *Wall Street Journal*, January 30, 2003.
24. For some consumer behavior perspectives on gender, see Jane Cunningham and Philippa Roberts, "What Woman Want," *Brand Strategy* (December 2006–January 2007): 40–41; Robert J. Fisher and Laurette Dube, "Gender Differences in Responses to Emotional Advertising: A Social Desirability Perspective," *Journal of Consumer Research* 31 (March 2005): 850–58; Joan Meyers-Levy and Durairaj Maheswaran, "Exploring Males' and Females' Processing Strategies: When and Why Do Differences Occur in Consumers' Processing of Ad Claims," *Journal of Consumer Research* 18 (June 1991): 63–70; Joan Meyers-Levy and Brian Sternthal, "Gender Differences in the Use of Message Cues and Judgments," *Journal of Marketing Research* 28 (February 1991): 84–96.
25. Jim Rendon, "Rear Window," *Business 2.0* (August 2003): 72.
26. Tom Lowry, "Young Man, Your Couch Is Calling," *BusinessWeek*, July 28, 2003, pp. 68–69.
27. Constantine von Hoffman, "So Long Unisex, Make It His or Hers," *Brandweek* 47, no. 25, June 19, 2006, p. S50.
28. Jessica Hopper, "The Dove Campaign: Conforming or Transforming?" *National NOW Times* 38, no. 3 (Fall 2006): 16+.
29. Dawn Klingensmith, "Marketing Gurus Try to Read Women's Minds," *Chicago Tribune*, April 19, 2006.
30. Marti Barletta, "Who's Really Buying That Car? Ask Her," *Brandweek*, September 4, 2006, p. 20; Robert Craven, Kiki Maurey, and John Davis, "What Women Really Want," *Critical Eye* 15 (July 2006): 50–53.
31. Aixa Pascual, "Lowe's Is Sprucing Up Its House," *BusinessWeek*, June 3, 2002, pp. 56–57; Pamela Sebastian Ridge, "Tool Sellers Tap Their Feminine Side," *Wall Street Journal*, June 16, 2002.
32. Louise Lee, "She's Not an Also Ran," *BusinessWeek*, June 12, 2006, p. 79.
33. Constantine Van Hoffman, "For Some Marketers, Low Income Is Hot," *Brandweek*, September 11, 2006, p. 6.
34. Ian Zack, "Out of the Tube," *Forbes*, November 26, 2001, p. 200.
35. Gregory L. White and Shirley Leung, "Middle Market Shrinks as Americans Migrate toward the Higher End," *Wall Street Journal*, March 29, 2002.
36. Linda Tischler, "The Price Is Right," *Fast Company* (November 2003): 83–91.
37. Christopher Noxon, "Toyification Nation," *Brandweek*, October 9, 2006; Rod O'Connor, "Adulthood: Are We There Yet? If You're Still Watching Cartoons or Playing Kickball, Then You, Kiddo, Just Might Be a 'Rejuvenile'," *Chicago Tribune*, August 6, 2006.
38. Andrew E. Serwer, "42,496 Secrets Bared," *Fortune*, January 24, 1994, pp. 13–14; Kenneth Labich, "Class in America," *Fortune*, February 7, 1994, pp. 114–26.
39. www.sric-bi.com.
40. Harold Thorkilsen, "Manager's Journal: Lessons of the Great Cranberry Crisis," *Wall Street Journal*, December 21, 1987.
41. Pam Danziger, "Getting More for V-Day," *Brandweek*, February 9, 2004, p. 19.
42. Andrew Kaplan, "A Fruitful Mix," *BeverageWorld* (May 2006): 28–36.
43. This classification was adapted from George H. Brown, "Brand Loyalty: Fact or Fiction?" *Advertising Age* (June 1952–January 1953), a series. See also, Peter E. Rossi, Robert E. McCulloch, and Greg M. Allenby, "The Value of Purchase History Data in Target Marketing," *Marketing Science* 15, no. 4 (Fall 1996): 321–40.
44. Chip Walker, "How Strong Is Your Brand," *Marketing Tools* (January–February 1995): 46–53.
45. www.conversionmodel.com.
46. Daniel Yankelovich and David Meer, "Rediscovering Market Segmentation," *Harvard Business Review* (February 2006), pp. 122-131.
47. For a review of many of the methodological issues in developing segmentation schemes, see William R. Dillon and Soumen Mukherjee, "A Guide to the Design and Execution of Segmentation Studies," in *Handbook of Marketing Research*, ed. Rajiv Grover and Marco Vriens (Thousand Oaks, CA: Sage, 2006); and Michael Wedel and Wagner A. Kamakura, *Market Segmentation: Conceptual and Methodological Foundations* (Boston: Kluwer, 1997).
48. Wendell R. Smith, "Product Differentiation and Market Segmentation as Alternative Marketing Strategies," *Journal of Marketing* (July 1956): 4.

49. www.esteelauder.com.
50. Christopher Hosford, "A Transformative Experience," *Sales and Marketing Management* 158, no. 5 (June 2006): 32–36.
51. Bart Macchiette and Roy Abhijit, "Sensitive Groups and Social Issues," *Journal of Consumer Marketing* 11, no. 4 (Fall 1994): 55–64.
52. Roger O. Crockett, "They're Lining Up for Flicks in the 'Hood'," *BusinessWeek*, June 8, 1998, pp. 75–76.
53. Caroline E. Mayer, "Nurturing Brand Loyalty; with Preschool Supplies, Firms Woo Future Customers—and Current Parents," *Washington Post*, October 12, 2003.

Chapter 9

1. Tom Lowry, "ESPN's Cell Phone Fumble," *BusinessWeek*, October 30, 2006, p. 26.
2. For foundational work on branding, see Jean-Noel Kapferer, *Strategic Brand Management*, 2nd ed. (New York: Free Press, 2005); David A. Aaker and Erich Joachimsthaler, *Brand Leadership* (New York: Free Press, 2000); David A. Aaker, *Building Strong Brands* (New York: Free Press, 1996); David A. Aaker, *Managing Brand Equity* (New York: Free Press, 1991).
3. Interbrand Group, *World's Greatest Brands: An International Review* (New York: John Wiley, 1992). See also Karl Moore and Susan E. Reid, "The Birth of a Brand," Working paper, Desautels Faculty of Management, McGill University, 2006.
4. Rajneesh Suri and Kent B. Monroe, "The Effects of Time Pressure on Consumers' Judgments of Prices and Products," *Journal of Consumer Research* 30 (June 2003): 92–104.
5. Rita Clifton and John Simmons, eds., *The Economist on Branding* (New York: Bloomberg Press, 2004); Rik Riezebos, *Brand Management: A Theoretical and Practical Approach* (Essex, England: Pearson Education, 2003); and Paul Temporal, *Advanced Brand Management: From Vision to Valuation* (Singapore: John Wiley & Sons, 2002).
6. Constance E. Bagley, *Managers and the Legal Environment: Strategies for the 21st Century*, 3rd ed. (Cincinnati, OH: Southwestern College/West Publishing, 2005). For a marketing academic point of view of some important legal issues, see Judith Zaichkowsky, *The Psychology behind Trademark Infringement and Counterfeiting* (Mahwah, NJ: LEA Publishing, 2006) and Maureen Morrin and Jacob Jacoby, "Trademark Dilution: Empirical Measures for an Elusive Concept," *Journal of Public Policy & Marketing* 19, no. 2 (May 2000): 265–76.
7. Tulin Erdem, "Brand Equity as a Signaling Phenomenon," *Journal of Consumer Psychology* 7, no. 2 (1998): 131–57.
8. Scott Davis, *Brand Asset Management: Driving Profitable Growth through Your Brands*, (San Francisco: Jossey-Bass, 2000); Mary W. Sullivan, "How Brand Names Affect the Demand for Twin Automobiles," *Journal of Marketing Research* 35 (May 1998): 154–65; D. C. Bello and M. B. Holbrook, "Does an Absence of Brand Equity Generalize across Product Classes?" *Journal of Business Research* 34 (October 1996): 125–31; Adrian J. Slywotzky and Benson P. Shapiro, "Leveraging to Beat the Odds: The New Marketing Mindset," *Harvard Business Review* (September–October 1993): 97–107.
9. The power of branding is not without its critics, however, some of whom reject the commercialism associated with branding activities. See Naomi Klein, *No Logo: Taking Aim at the Brand Bullies* (New York: Picador, 2000).
10. Libby Sander, "Chicago Journal: Loss of Marhsall Field's Has Store Loyalists Seeing Red," *New York Times*, at www.nytimes.com, January 17, 2007; Judy Artunian, "Change of Name Can Come with Risk: Customer Loyalty Often Diminished," *Chicago Tribune*, May 29, 2006.
11. Natalie Mizik and Robert Jacobson, "Talk about Brand Strategy," *Harvard Business Review* (October 2005): 1; Baruch Lev, *Intangibles: Management, Measurement, and Reporting* (Washington, DC: Brookings Institute, 2001).
12. For an academic discussion of how consumers become so strongly attached to people as brands, see Matthew Thomson, "Human Brands: Investigating Antecedents to Consumers' Stronger Attachments to Celebrities," *Journal of Marketing* 70 (July 2006): 104–19. For some practical branding tips from the world of rock and roll, see Roger Blackwell and Tina Stephan, *Brands That Rock*, (Hoboken, NJ: John Wiley & Sons, 2004), and from the world of sports, see Irving Rein, Philip Kotler, and Ben Shields, *The Elusive Fan: Reinventing Sports in a Crowded Marketplace*, (New York: McGraw-Hill, 2006).
13. Other approaches are based on economic principles of signaling (e.g., Tulin Erdem, "Brand Equity as a Signaling Phenomenon," *Journal of Consumer Psychology* 7, no. 2 [1998]: 131–57); or more of a sociological, anthropological, or biological perspective (e.g., Grant McCracken, *Culture and Consumption II: Markets, Meaning, and Brand Management* [Bloomington: Indiana University Press, 2005]; or Susan Fournier, "Consumers and Their Brands: Developing Relationship Theory in Consumer Research,"

Journal of Consumer Research 24 [September 1998]: 343–73).

14. Kevin Lane Keller, *Strategic Brand Management,* 3rd ed. (Upper Saddle River, NJ: Prentice Hall, 2008); David A. Aaker and Erich Joachimsthaler, *Brand Leadership* (New York: Free Press 2000); David A. Aaker, *Building Strong Brands* (New York: Free Press, 1996); David A. Aaker, *Managing Brand Equity* (New York: Free Press, 1991).

15. Jennifer L. Aaker, "Dimensions of Brand Personality," *Journal of Marketing Research* (August 1997): 347–56; Jean-Noel Kapferer, *Strategic Brand Management: New Approaches to Creating and Evaluating Brand Equity* (London: Kogan Page, 1992), p. 38; Davis, *Brand Asset Management.* For an overview of academic research on branding, see Kevin Lane Keller, "Branding and Brand Equity," in *Handbook of Marketing,* ed. Bart Weitz and Robin Wensley (London: Sage Publications, 2002), pp. 151–78.

16. Keller, *Strategic Brand Management.*

17. Theodore Levitt, "Marketing Success through Differentiation—of Anything," *Harvard Business Review* (January–February 1980): 83–91.

18. Kusum Ailawadi, Donald R. Lehmann, and Scott Neslin, "Revenue Premium as an Outcome Measure of Brand Equity," *Journal of Marketing* 67 (October 2003): 1-17.

19. Alice Z. Cuneo, "Apple Transcends as Lifestyle Brand," *Advertising Age,* June 15, 2003, pp. S2, S6.

20. Jon Miller and David Muir, *The Business of Brands* (West Sussex, England: John Wiley & Sons, 2004).

21. Douglas Holt, *How Brands Become Icons: The Principle of Cultural Branding* (Cambridge, MA: Harvard Business School Press, 2004); Douglas Holt, "Branding as Cultural Activism," zibs.com; Douglas Holt, "What Becomes an Icon Most," *Harvard Business Review* 81 (March 2003): 43–49.

22. Stuart Elliott, "Letting Consumers Control Marketing: Priceless," *New York Times,* October 9, 2006; Elizabeth Holmes, "On MySpace, Millions of Users Make 'Friends' with Ads," *Wall Street Journal,* August 7, year?.

23. David A. Aaker and Erich Joachimsthaler, *Brand Leadership* (New York: Free Press, 2000).

24. David A. Aaker, *Building Strong Brands* (New York: Free Press, 1996).

25. Kevin Lane Keller, "Building Customer-Based Brand Equity: A Blueprint for Creating Strong Brands," *Marketing Management* 10 (July–August 2001): 15–19.

26. For some academic insights, see Matthew Thomson, Deborah J. MacInnis, and C. W. Park, "The Ties That Bind: Measuring the Strength of Consumers' Emotional Attachments to Brands," *Journal of Consumer Psychology* 15, no. 1 (2005): 77–91; and Jennifer Edson Escalas, "Narrative Processing: Building Consumer Connections to Brands," *Journal of Consumer Psychology* 14, no. 1 & 2 (1996): 168–79. For some managerial guidelines, see Kevin Roberts, *Lovemarks: The Future beyond Brands* (New York: Powerhouse Books, 2004); and Douglas Atkins, *The Culting of Brands* (New York: Penguin Books, 2004).

27. Paul Rittenberg and Maura Clancey, "Testing the Value of Media Engagement for Advertising Effectiveness," at www.knowledgenetworks.com (Spring–Summer 2006): 35–42.

28. Marketers of the Next Generation," *Brandweek,* April 17, 2006, p. 30.

29. Rachel Dodes, "From Tracksuits to Fast Track," *Wall Street Journal,* September 13, 2006.

30. "42 Below," accessed at www.betterbydesign.org.nz, September 14, 2007.

31. Alina Wheeler, *Designing Brand Identity* (Hoboken, NJ: John Wiley & Sons, 2003).

32. Pat Fallon and Fred Senn, *Juicing the Orange: How to Turn Creativity into a Powerful Business Advantage* (Cambridge, MA: Harvard Business School Press, 2006).

33. Robert Salerno, "We Try Harder: An Ad Creates a Brand," *Brandweek,* September 8, 2003, p. 32–33.

34. John R. Doyle and Paul A. Bottomly, "Dressed for the Occasion: Font-Product Congruity in the Perception of Logotype," *Journal of Consumer Psychology* 16, no. 2 (2006): 112–23; Kevin Lane Keller, Susan Heckler, and Michael J. Houston, "The Effects of Brand Name Suggestiveness on Advertising Recall," *Journal of Marketing* 62 (January 1998): 48–57. For an in-depth examination of how brand names get developed, see Alex Frankel, *Wordcraft: The Art of Turning Little Words into Big Business* (New York: Crown Publishers, 2004).

35. Don Schultz and Heidi Schultz, *IMC: The Next Generation* (New York: McGraw-Hill, 2003); Don E. Schultz, Stanley I. Tannenbaum, and Robert F. Lauterborn, *Integrated Marketing Communications* (Lincolnwood, IL: NTC Business Books, 1993).

36. Mohanbir Sawhney, "Don't Harmonize, Synchronize," *Harvard Business Review* (July–August 2001): 101–8.

37. David C. Court, John E. Forsyth, Greg C. Kelly, and Mark A. Loch, "The New Rules of Branding: Building Strong Brands Faster," *McKinsey White Paper Fall 1999*; Scott Bedbury, *A New Brand World* (New York: Viking Press, 2002).

38. Sonia Reyes, "Cheerios: The Ride," *Brandweek,* September 23, 2002, pp. 14–16.

39. Christopher Locke, Rick Levine, Doc Searls, and David Weinberger, *The Cluetrain Manifesto: The End of Business as Usual* (Cambridge, MA: Perseus Press, 2000).

40. Kenneth Hein, "Satisfying a Publicity Jones with Hemp, Love Potions," *Brandweek*, March 13, 2006, p. 14; Corporate Design Foundation, "Keep Up with the Jones, Dude!" *BusinessWeek*, October 26, 2005; Ryan Underwood, "Jones Soda Secret," *Fast Company* (March 2005): 74.

41. Seth Godin, *Permission Marketing: Turning Strangers into Friends, and Friends into Customers* (New York: Simon & Schuster, 1999). See also Susan Fournier, Susan Dobscha, and David Mick, "Preventing the Premature Death of Relationship Marketing," *Harvard Business Review* (January–February 1998): 42–51.

42. Dawn Iacobucci and Bobby Calder, eds., *Kellogg on Integrated Marketing* (New York: John Wiley & Sons, 2003).

43. Drew Madsen, "Olive Garden: Creating Value through an Integrated Brand Experience," presentation at Marketing Science Institute Conference, *Brand Orchestration*, Orlando, Florida, December 4, 2003.

44. Pete Engardio, "Taking a Brand Name Higher," *BusinessWeek*, July 31, 2006, p. 48; Rob Walker, "Haier Goals," *New York Times Magazine*, November 20, 2005.

45. Michael Dunn and Scott Davis, "Building Brands from the Inside," *Marketing Management* (May–June 2003): 32–37; Scott Davis and Michael Dunn, *Building the Brand-Driven Business* (New York: John Wiley & Sons, 2002).

46. Stan Maklan and Simon Knox, *Competing on Value* (Upper Saddle River, NJ: Financial Times, Prentice Hall, 2000).

47. Coeli Carr, "Seeking to Attract Top Prospects, Employers Brush Up on Brands," *New York Times*, September 10, 2006.

48. Sherrie Bossung and Mark Pocharski, "Building a Communication Strategy: Marketing the Brand to Employees," presentation at Marketing Science Institute Conference, *Brand Orchestration*, Orlando, Florida, December 4, 2003.

49. The principles and examples from this passage are based on Colin Mitchell, "Selling the Brand Inside," *Harvard Business Review* (January 2002): 99–105. For an in-depth discussion of how two organizations, QuikTrip and Wawa, have developed stellar internal branding programs, see Neeli Bendapudi and Venkat Bendapudi, "Creating the Living Brand," *Harvard Business Review* (May 2005): 124–32.

50. Deborah Roeddder John, Barbara Loken, Kyeong-Heui Kim, and Alokparna Basu Monga, "Brand Concept Maps: A Methodology for Identifying Brand Association Networks," *Journal of Marketing Research* 43 (November 2006): 549–63.

51. In terms of related empirical insights, see Manoj K. Agrawal and Vithala Rao "An Empirical Comparison of Consumer-Based Measures of Brand Equity," *Marketing Letters* 7, no. 3 (July 1996): 237–47; and Walfried Lassar, Banwari Mittal, and Arun Sharma, "Measuring Customer-Based Brand Equity," *Journal of Consumer Marketing* 12, no. 4 (1995): 11–19.

52. "The Best Global Brands," *BusinessWeek*, August 7, 2006. The article ranks and critiques the 100 best global brands using the valuation method developed by Interbrand. For more discussion on some brand winners and losers, see Matt Haig, *Brand Royalty: How the Top 100 Brands Thrive and Survive* (London: Kogan Page, 2004); and Matt Haig, *Brand Failures: The Truth about the 100 Biggest Branding Mistakes of All Time* (London: Kogan Page, 2003). For an academic discussion of valuing brand equity, see V. Srinivasan, Chan Su Park, and Dae Ryun Chang, "An Approach to the Measurement, Analysis, and Prediction of Brand Equity and Its Sources," *Management Science* 51 (September 2005): 1433–48.

53. Mark Sherrington, *Added Value: The Alchemy of Brand-Led Growth* (Hampshire, UK: Palgrave Macmillan, 2003).

54. For an up-to-date discussion of what factors determine long-term branding success, see Allen P. Adamson, *Brand Simple* (New York: Palgrave Macmillan, 2006).

55. David Kiley, "To Boost Sales, Volvo Returns to Its Roots: Safety," *USA Today*, August 26, 2002.

56. Natalie Mizik and Robert Jacobson, "Trading Off between Value Creation and Value Appropriation: The Financial Implications of Shifts in Strategic Emphasis," *Journal of Marketing* 67 (January 2003): 63–76.

57. Mark Speece, "Marketer's Malady: Fear of Change," *Brandweek*, August 19, 2002, p. 34.

58. Joseph Weber, "Harley Just Keeps on Cruisin'," *BusinessWeek*, November 6, 2006, pp. 71–72.

59. Keith Naughton, "Fixing Cadillac," *Newsweek*, May 28, 2001, pp. 36–37.

60. Peter Farquhar, "Managing Brand Equity," *Marketing Research* 1 (September 1989): 24–33.

61. Steven M. Shugan, "Branded Variants," 1989 AMA Educators' Proceedings (Chicago: American Marketing Association, 1989), pp. 33–38; also M. Bergen, S. Dutta, and S. M. Shugan, "Branded Variants: A Retail Perspective," *Journal of Marketing Research* 33 (February 1996): 9–21.

62. Adam Bass, "Licensed Extension – Stretching to Communicate," *Journal of Brand Management* 12 (September 2004): 31–38. Also see Aaker, *Building Strong Brands*.

63. Jean Halliday, "Troubled Automakers' Golden Goose," *AutoWeek*, August 14, 2006; Becky Ebenkamp, "The Creative License," *Brandweek*, June 9, 2003, pp. 36–40.
64. Dan Reed, "Low-Fare Rivals Keep a Close Eye on Song," *USA Today*, November 25, 2003.
65. William J. Holstein, "The Incalculable Value of Building Brands," *Chief Executive* (April–May 2006): 52+.
66. For comprehensive corporate branding guidelines, see James R. Gregory, *The Best of Branding: Best Practices in Corporate Branding* (New York: McGraw-Hill, 2004). For some international perspectives, see *The Expressive Organization: Linking Identity, Reputation, and Corporate Brand*, ed. Majken Schultz, Mary Jo Hatch, and Mogens Holten Larsen (Oxford, UK: Oxford University Press, 2000); and *Corporate Branding: Purpose, People, and Process*, ed. Majken Schultz, Yun Mi Antorini, and Fabian F. Csaba (Denmark: Copenhagen Business School Press, 2005).
67. Guido Berens, Cees B. M. van Riel, and Gerrit H. van Bruggen, "Corporate Associations and Consumer Product Responses: The Moderating Role of Corporate Brand Dominance," *Journal of Marketing* 69 (July 2005): 35–48; Zeynep Gürhan-Canli and Rajeev Batra, "When Corporate Image Affects Product Evaluations: The Moderating Role of Perceived Risk," *Journal of Marketing Research* 41 (May 2004): 197–205; Kevin Lane Keller and David A. Aaker, "Corporate-Level Marketing: The Impact of Credibility on a Company's Brand Extensions," *Corporate Reputation Review* 1 (August 1998): 356–78; Thomas J. Brown and Peter Dacin, "The Company and the Product: Corporate Associations and Consumer Product Responses," *Journal of Marketing* 61 (January 1997): 68–84.
68. Vithala R. Rao, Manoj K. Agarwal, and Denise Dalhoff, "How Is Manifest Branding Strategy Related to the Intangible Value of a Corporation?" *Journal of Marketing* 68 (October 2004): 126–41. For an examination of the financial impact of brand portfolio decisions, see Neil A. Morgan and Lopo L. Rego, "The Marketing and Financial Performance Consequences of Firms' Brand Portfolio Strategy," Working paper, Kelley School of Business, Indiana University, 2006.
69. Byung-Do Kim and Mary W. Sullivan, "The Effect of Parent Brand Experience on Line Extension Trial and Repeat Purchase," *Marketing Letters* 9 (April 1998): 181–93.
70. John Milewicz and Paul Herbig, "Evaluating the Brand Extension Decision Using a Model of Reputation Building," *Journal of Product & Brand Management* 3, no. 1 (January 1994): 39–47; Kevin Lane Keller and David A. Aaker, "The Effects of Sequential Introduction of Brand Extensions," *Journal of Marketing Research* 29 (February 1992): 35–50.
71. Valarie A. Taylor and William O. Bearden, "Ad Spending on Brand Extensions: Does Similarity Matter?" *Journal of Brand Management* 11 (September 2003): 63–74; Sheri Bridges, Kevin Lane Keller, and Sanjay Sood, "Communication Strategies for Brand Extensions: Enhancing Perceived Fit by Establishing Explanatory Links," *Journal of Advertising* 29 (Winter 2000): 1–11; Daniel C. Smith, "Brand Extension and Advertising Efficiency: What Can and Cannot Be Expected," *Journal of Advertising Research* (November–December 1992): 11–20; Daniel C. Smith and C. Whan Park, "The Effects of Brand Extensions on Market Share and Advertising Efficiency," *Journal of Marketing Research* 29 (August 1992): 296–313.
72. Bruce Meyer, "Rubber Firms Extend Brands to Gain Customers, Revenue," *B to B* 90, no. 12, October 10, 2005, p. 6.
73. Subramanian Balachander and Sanjoy Ghose, "Reciprocal Spillover Effects: A Strategic Benefit of Brand Extensions," *Journal of Marketing* 67, no. 1 (January 2003): 4–13.
74. Bharat N. Anand and Ron Shachar, "Brands as Beacons: A New Source of Loyalty to Multiproduct Firms," *Journal of Marketing Research* 41 (May 2004): 135–50.
75. Kevin Lane Keller and David A. Aaker, "The Effects of Sequential Introduction of Brand Extensions," *Journal of Marketing Research* 29 (February 1992): 35–50. For consumer processing implications, see Huifung Mao and H. Shanker Krishnan, "Effects of Prototype and Exemplar Fit on Brand Extension Evaluations: A Two-Process Contingency Model," *Journal of Consumer Research* 33 (June 2006): 41–49.
76. Maureen Morrin, "The Impact of Brand Extensions on Parent Brand Memory Structures and Retrieval Processes," *Journal of Marketing Research* 36, no. 4 (November 1999): 517–25; John A. Quelch and David Kenny, "Extend Profits, Not Product Lines," *Harvard Business Review* (September–October 1994): 153–60; Perspectives from the Editors, "The Logic of Product-Line Extensions," *Harvard Business Review* (November–December 1994): 53–62;
77. Al Ries and Jack Trout, *Positioning: The Battle for Your Mind, 20th Anniversary Edition* (New York: McGraw-Hill, 2000).
78. David A. Aaker, *Brand Portfolio Strategy: Creating Relevance, Differentiation, Energy, Leverage, and Clarity* (New York: Free Press, 2004).
79. "Lego's Turnaround: Picking Up the Pieces," *The Economist*, October 28, 2006, p. 76.

80. Mary W. Sullivan, "Measuring Image Spillovers in Umbrella-Branded Products," *Journal of Business* 63, no. 3 (July 1990): 309–29.

81. Deborah Roedder John, Barbara Loken, and Christopher Joiner, "The Negative Impact of Extensions: Can Flagship Products Be Diluted," *Journal of Marketing* (January 1998): 19–32; Susan M. Broniarcyzk and Joseph W. Alba, "The Importance of the Brand in Brand Extension," *Journal of Marketing Research* (May 1994): 214–28 (this entire issue of *JMR* is devoted to brands and brand equity); Barbara Loken and Deborah Roedder John, "Diluting Brand Beliefs: When Do Brand Extensions Have a Negative Impact?" *Journal of Marketing* (July 1993): 71–84. See also, Chris Pullig, Carolyn Simmons, and Richard G. Netemeyer, "Brand Dilution: When Do New Brands Hurt Existing Brands?" *Journal of Marketing* 70 (April 2006): 52–66; R. Ahluwalia and Z. Gürhan-Canli, "The Effects of Extensions on the Family Brand Name: An Accessibility-Diagnosticity Perspective," *Journal of Consumer Research* 27 (December 2000): 371–81; Z. Gürhan-Canli and M. Durairaj, "The Effects of Extensions on Brand Name Dilution and Enhancement," *Journal of Marketing Research* 35 (November 1998): 464–73; S. J. Milberg, C. W. Park, and M. S. McCarthy, "Managing Negative Feedback Effects Associated with Brand Extensions: The Impact of Alternative Branding Strategies," *Journal of Consumer Psychology* 6 (1997): 119–40.

82. See also, Franziska Völckner and Henrik Sattler, "Drivers of Brand Extension Success," *Journal of Marketing* 70 (April 2006): 1–17.

83. Andrea Rothman, "France's Bic Bets U.S. Consumers Will Go for Perfume on the Cheap," *Wall Street Journal*, January 12, 1989.

84. David A. Aaker, *Brand Portfolio Strategy: Creating Relevance, Differentiation, Energy, Leverage, and Clarity* (New York: Free Press, 2004).

85. Jack Trout, *Differentiate or Die: Survival in Our Era of Killer Competition* (New York: John Wiley, 2000).

86. Nirmalya Kumar, "Kill a Brand, Keep a Customer," *Harvard Business Review* (December 2003): 87–95.

87. For a methodological approach for assessing the extent and nature of cannibalization, see Charlotte H. Mason and George R. Milne, "An Approach for Identifying Cannibalization within Product Line Extensions and MultiBrand Strategies," *Journal of Business Research* 31 (October–November 1994): 163–70.

88. Paul W. Farris, "The Chevrolet Corvette," Case UVA-M-320, The Darden Graduate Business School Foundation, University of Virginia, Charlottesville.

89. Roland T. Rust, Valerie A. Zeithaml, and Katherine A. Lemon, "Measuring Customer Equity and Calculating Marketing ROI," in *Handbook of Marketing Research*, ed. Rajiv Grover and Marco Vriens (Thousand Oaks, CA: Sage Publications, 2006), pp. 588–601; Roland T. Rust, Valerie A. Zeithaml, and Katherine A. Lemon, *Driving Customer Equity* (New York: Free Press, 2000).

90. Robert C. Blattberg and John Deighton, "Manage Marketing by the Customer Equity Test," *Harvard Business Review* (July–August 1996): 136–44.

91. Robert C. Blattberg and Jacquelyn S. Thomas, "Valuing, Analyzing, and Managing the Marketing Function using Customer Equity Principles," in *Kellogg on Marketing*, ed. Dawn Iacobucci (New York: John Wiley & Sons, 2002); Robert C. Blattberg, Gary Getz, and Jacquelyn S. Thomas, *Customer Equity: Building and Managing Relationships as Valuable Assets* (Boston: Harvard Business School Press, 2001).

92. Much of this section is based on: Robert Leone, Vithala Rao, Kevin Lane Keller, Man Luo, Leigh McAlister, and Rajendra Srivatstava, "Linking Brand Equity to Customer Equity," *Journal of Service Research* 9 (November 2006): 125–38. This special issue is devoted to customer equity and has a number of thought-provoking articles.

93. Niraj Dawar, "What Are Brands Good For?" *MIT Sloan Management Review* (Fall 2004): 31–37.

Chapter 10

1. Michael J. Silverstein and Neil Fiske, *Trading Up: The New American Luxury* (New York: Portfolio, 2003); Dylan Machan, "Sharing Victoria's Secret," *Forbes*, June 5, 1995, p. 132.

2. Darrell Dunn, "Aligned at Last," *InformationWeek*, March 15, 2004; Kortney Stringer, "Hard Lesson Learned: Premium and No-Frills Don't Mix," *Wall Street Journal*, November 3, 2003.

3. Al Ries and Jack Trout, *Positioning: The Battle for Your Mind, 20th Anniversary Edition* (New York: McGraw-Hill, 2000).

4. Theresa Howard, "DiGiorno's Campaign Delivers Major Sales," *USA Today*, April 1, 2002; Alice M. Tybout and Brian Sternthal, "Brand Positioning," in *Kellogg on Marketing*, ed. Dawn Iacobucci (New York: John Wiley & Sons, 2001), p. 35.

5. Kevin Lane Keller, Brian Stenthal, and Alice Tybout, "Three Questions You Need to Ask about Your Brand," *Harvard Business Review* 80 (September 2002): 80–89.

6. Thomas A. Brunner and Michaela Wänke, "The Reduced and Enhanced Impact of Shared Features on Individual Brand Evaluations," *Journal of Consumer Psychology* 16 (April 2006): 101–11.

7. Professor Brian Sternthal, "Miller Lite Case," Kellogg Graduate School of Management, Northwestern University.

8. Patrick Tickle, Kevin Lane Keller, and Keith Richey, "Branding in High-Technology Markets," *Market Leader* 22 (Autumn 2003): 21–26.

9. Janet Bigham Bernstel, "A New Blend of Bank," *ABA Bank Marketing* 38, no. 2 (March 2006): 14+; Pat Allen, "How Umpqua Sustains and Builds on Its 'Pretty Cool' Status," *BAI Online Banking Strategies* (November–December 2006), at http://www.bai.org/bankingstrategies/2006-nov-dec/UmpquaSustains/print.asp.

10. Jim Hopkins, "When the Devil Is in the Design," *USA Today,* December 31, 2001.

11. Keith Naughton, "Ford's 'Perfect Storm'," *Newsweek,* September 17, 2001, pp. 48–50.

12. Dale Buss, "Sweet Success," *Brandweek,* May 12, 2003, pp. 22–23.

13. Susan M. Broniarczyk and Andrew D. Gershoff, "The Reciprocal Effects of Brand Equity and Trivial Attributes," *Journal of Marketing Research* 40 (May 2003): 161–75; Gregory S. Carpenter, Rashi Glazer, and Kent Nakamoto, "Meaningful Brands from Meaningless Differentiation: The Dependence on Irrelevant Attributes," *Journal of Marketing Research* 31 (August 1994): 339–50.

14. Michael Applebaum, "Comfy to Cool: A Brand Swivel," *Brandweek,* May 2, 2005, pp. 18–19.

15. Cecilie Rohwedder, "Playing Down the Plaid," *Wall Street Journal,* July 7, 2006, at http://online.wsj.com/article_print/SB115222828906800109.html.

16. Michael E. Porter, *Competitive Strategy: Techniques for Analyzing Industries and Competitors* (New York: Free Press, 1980).

17. Willow Duttge, "Counting Sleep," *Advertising Age,* June 5, 2006, pp. 4, 50.

18. Patrick Barwise, *Simply Better: Winning and Keeping Customers by Delivering What Matters Most* (Cambridge, MA: Harvard Business School Press, 2004).

19. *Fortune,* April 17, 2006; Katrina Brooker, "The Chairman of the Board Looks Back," *Fortune,* May 28, 2001.

20. "The 25 Best Sales Forces," *Sales & Marketing Management* (July 1998): 32–50.

21. Some authors distinguished additional stages. Wasson suggested a stage of competitive turbulence between growth and maturity. See Chester R. Wasson, *Dynamic Competitive Strategy and Product Life Cycles* (Austin, TX: Austin Press, 1978). Maturity describes a stage of sales growth slowdown and saturation, a stage of flat sales after sales have peaked.

22. John E. Swan and David R. Rink, "Fitting Market Strategy to Varying Product Life Cycles," *Business Horizons* (January–February 1982): 72–76; Gerald J. Tellis and C. Merle Crawford, "An Evolutionary Approach to Product Growth Theory," *Journal of Marketing* (Fall 1981): 125–34.

23. William E. Cox Jr., "Product Life Cycles as Marketing Models," *Journal of Business* (October 1967): 375–84.

24. Jordan P. Yale, "The Strategy of Nylon's Growth," *Modern Textiles Magazine* (February 1964): 32. Also see Theodore Levitt, "Exploit the Product Life Cycle," *Harvard Business Review* (November–December 1965): 81–94.

25. Chester R. Wasson, "How Predictable Are Fashion and Other Product Life Cycles?" *Journal of Marketing* (July 1968): 36–43.

26. Wasson, "How Predictable Are Fashion and Other Product Life Cycles?"

27. William H. Reynolds, "Cars and Clothing: Understanding Fashion Trends," *Journal of Marketing* (July 1968): 44–49.

28. Bryan Curtis, "Trivial Pursuit," *Slate.com,* April 13, 2005; Patrick Butters, "What Biggest-Selling Adult Game Still Cranks Out Vexing Questions?" *Insight on the News,* January 26, 1998, p. 39.

29. Robert D. Buzzell, "Competitive Behavior and Product Life Cycles," in *New Ideas for Successful Marketing,* ed. John S. Wright and Jack Goldstucker (Chicago: American Marketing Association, 1956), p. 51.

30. Rajesh J. Chandy, Gerard J. Tellis, Deborah J. MacInnis, and Pattana Thaivanich, "What to Say When: Advertising Appeals in Evolving Markets," *Journal of Marketing Research* 38 (November 2001): 399–414.

31. As reported in Joseph T. Vesey, "The New Competitors: They Think in Terms of Speed to Market." *Academy of Management Executive* 5, no. 2 (May 1991): 23–33; and Brian Dumaine, "How Managers Can Succeed through Speed," *Fortune,* February 13, 1989, pp. 54–59.

32. Glen L. Urban et al., "Market Share Rewards to Pioneering Brands: An Empirical Analysis and Strategic Implications," *Management Science* (June 1986): 645–59; William T. Robinson and Claes Fornell, "Sources of Market Pioneer Advantages in Consumer Goods Industries," *Journal of Marketing Research* (August 1985): 305–17.

33. Gregory S. Carpenter and Kent Nakamoto, "Consumer Preference Formation and Pioneering Advantage," *Journal of Marketing Research* (August 1989): 285–98.

34. William T. Robinson and Sungwook Min, "Is the First to Market the First to Fail? Empirical Evidence for Industrial Goods Businesses," *Journal of Marketing Research* 39 (February 2002): 120–28.

35. Frank R. Kardes, Gurumurthy Kalyanaram, Murali Chankdrashekaran, and Ronald J. Dornoff, "Brand Retrieval, Consideration Set Composition,

Consumer Choice, and the Pioneering Advantage," *Journal of Consumer Research* (June 1993): 62–75. See also, Frank H. Alpert and Michael A. Kamins, "Pioneer Brand Advantage and Consumer Behavior: A Conceptual Framework and Propositional Inventory," *Journal of the Academy of Marketing Science* (Summer 1994): 244–53.

36. Thomas S. Robertson and Hubert Gatignon, "How Innovators Thwart New Entrants into Their Market," *Planning Review* (September–October 1991): 4–11, 48; Douglas Bowman and Hubert Gatignon, "Order of Entry as a Moderator of the Effect of Marketing Mix on Market Share," *Marketing Science* 15, no. 3 (Summer 1996): 222–42.

37. Venkatesh Shankar, Gregory S. Carpenter, and Lakshman Krishnamurthi, "Late Mover Advantage: How Innovative Late Entrants Outsell Pioneers," *Journal of Marketing Research* 35 (February 1998): 54–70.

38. Mark Ritson, "It Sometimes Pays to Come Second," *Marketing*, October 25, 2006, p. 23; Richard Waters, "Wikipedia Founder Plans Rival 'Citizendium' Aims to Introduce Order to Chaos of Web Encyclopedias; Editors Will Control the Posting of Articles," *Financial Times*, October 17, 2006, p. 19.

39. Steven P. Schnaars, *Managing Imitation Strategies* (New York: Free Press, 1994). See also, Jin K. Han, Namwoon Kim, and Hony-Bom Kin, "Entry Barriers: A Dull-, One-, or Two-Edged Sword for Incumbents? Unraveling the Paradox from a Contingency Perspective," *Journal of Marketing* (January 2001): 1–14.

40. Victor Kegan, "Second Sight: Second Movers Take All," *The Guardian*, October 10, 2002.

41. Peter N. Golder, "Historical Method in Marketing Research with New Evidence on Long-Term Market Share Stability," *Journal of Marketing Research* 37 (May 2000): 156–72; Peter N. Golder and Gerald J. Tellis, "Pioneer Advantage: Marketing Logic or Marketing Legend?" *Journal of Marketing Research* (May 1992): 34–46. See also, Shi Zhang and Arthur B. Markman, "Overcoming the Early Advantage: The Role of Alignable and Nonalignable Differences," *Journal of Marketing Research* (November 1998): 1–15.

42. Gerald Tellis and Peter Golder, *Will and Vision: How Latecomers Can Grow to Dominate Markets* (New York: McGraw-Hill, 2001); Rajesh K. Chandy and Gerald J. Tellis, "The Incumbent's Curse? Incumbency, Size, and Radical Product Innovation," *Journal of Marketing Research* (July 2000): 1–17.

43. Sungwook Min, Manohar U. Kalwani, and William T. Robinson, "Market Pioneer and Early Follower Survival Risks: A Contingency Analysis of Really New Versus Incrementally New Product-Markets," *Journal of Marketing* 70 (January 2006): 15–35. See also Raji Srinivasan, Gary L. Lilien, and Arvind Rangaswamy, "First In, First Out? The Effects of Network Externalities on Pioneer Survival," *Journal of Marketing* 68 (January 2004): 41–58.

44. Oliver Ryan, "The Bush Who Pays the Bills," *Fortune* 155, no. 1, January 22, 2007, p. 124.

45. Ben Elgin, "Yahoo!'s Boulevard of Broken Dreams," *BusinessWeek*, March 13, 2006, pp. 76–77; Fred Vogelstein, Yahoo!'s Brilliant Solution," *Fortune*, August 8, 2005, pp. 42–56; "Yahoo!'s Personality Crisis," *The Economist*, August 13, 2005, pp. 49–50; Ben Elgin, "The Search War Is About to Get Bloody," *BusinessWeek*, July 28, 2003, pp. 72–73.

46. Trond Riiber Knudsen, "Escaping the Middle-Market Trap: An Interview with CEO of Electrolux," *McKinsey Quarterly* (December 2006): 72–79.

47. Stephanie Thompson, "Coffee Brands Think outside of the Can," *Advertising Age*, July 28, 2003, p. 26.

48. Allen J. McGrath, "Growth Strategies with a '90s Twist," *Across the Board* (March 1995): 43–46.

49. Brian Wansink and Michael L. Ray, "Advertising Strategies to Increase Usage Frequency," *Journal of Marketing* (January 1996): 31–46. Also see Brian Wansink, "Expansion Advertising," in *How Advertising Works*, ed. John Philip Jones (Thousand Oaks, CA: Sage Publications), pp. 95–103.

50. Stephen M. Nowlis and Itamar Simonson, "The Effect of New Product Features on Brand Choice," *Journal of Marketing Research* (February 1996): 36–46.

51. Rajan Varadarajan, Mark P. DeFanti, and Paul S. Busch, "Brand Portfolio, Corporate Image, and Reputation: Managing Brand Deletions," *Journal of the Academy of Marketing Science* 34 (Spring 2006): 195–205; Stephen J. Carlotti Jr., Mary Ellen Coe, and Jesko Perrey, "Making Brand Portfolios Work," *McKinsey Quarterly* 4 (2004): 24–36; Nirmalya Kumar, "Kill a Brand, Keep a Customer," *Harvard Business Review* 81 (December 2003): 86–95; George J. Avlonitis, "Product Elimination Decision Making: Does Formality Matter," *Journal of Marketing* (Winter 1985): 41–52; Philip Kotler, "Phasing Out Weak Products," *Harvard Business Review* (March–April 1965): 107–18.

52. Kathryn Rudie Harrigan, "The Effect of Exit Barriers upon Strategic Flexibility," *Strategic Management Journal* 1 (February 1980): 165–76.

53. Laurence P. Feldman and Albert L. Page, "Harvesting: The Misunderstood Market Exit Strategy," *Journal of Business Strategy* (Spring 1985): 79–85; Philip Kotler, "Harvesting Strategies for Weak Products," *Business Horizons* (August 1978): 15–22.

54. Peter N. Golder and Gerard J. Tellis, "Growing, Growing, Gone: Cascades, Diffusion, and Turning Points in the Product Life Cycle," *Marketing Science* 23 (Spring 2004): 207–18.
55. Youngme Moon, "Break Free from the Product Life Cycle," *Harvard Business Review* (May 2005): 87–94.
56. Hubert Gatignon and David Soberman, "Competitive Response and Market Evolution," in *Handbook of Marketing*, ed. Barton A. Weitz and Robin Wensley (London, UK: Sage Publications, 2002), pp. 126–47; Robert D. Buzzell, "Market Functions and Market Evolution," *Journal of Marketing* 63 (Special Issue 1999): 61–63.
57. For a discussion of the evolution of the minivan market between 1982 and 1998, see Jose Antonio Rosa, Joseph F. Porac, Jelena Runser-Spanjol, and Michael S. Saxon, "Sociocognitive Dynamics in a Product Market," *Journal of Marketing* 63 (Special Issue 1999): 64–77.
58. Daniel Fisher, "Six Feet Under," *Forbes*, July 7, 2003, pp. 66–68.

Chapter 11

1. Louise Lee, "Can Progressive Stay in Gear?" *BusinessWeek*, August 8, 2004, p. 44; Robert J. Dolan and Hermann Simon, "Power Pricers," *Across the Board* (May 1997): 18–19; Carol J. Loomis, "Sex. Reefer? And Auto Insurance," *Fortune*, August 7, 1995, p. 76; www.progressive.com.
2. For a detailed academic treatment of a number of issues on competition, see the Special Issue on Competitive Responsiveness, *Marketing Science* 24 (Winter 2005).
3. Michael E. Porter, *Competitive Strategy* (New York: Free Press, 1980), pp. 22–23.
4. Tarun Khanna and Krishna G. Palepu, "Emerging Giants," *Harvard Business Review* 84, no. 10 (October 2006): 60–69.
5. Ibid.
6. Allan D. Shocker, "Determining the Structure of Product-Markets: Practices, Issues, and Suggestions," in *Handbook of Marketing*, ed. Barton A. Weitz and Robin Wensley (London: Sage, 2002), pp. 106–25. See also, Bruce H. Clark and David B. Montgomery, "Managerial Identification of Competitors," *Journal of Marketing* 63 (July 1999): 67–83.
7. "What Business Are You In? Classic Advice from Theodore Levitt," *Harvard Business Review* (October 2006): 127–37. See also Theodore Levitt's seminal article, "Marketing Myopia," *Harvard Business Review* (July–August 1960): 45–56.
8. Jeffrey F. Rayport and Bernard J. Jaworski, *e-Commerce* (New York: McGraw-Hill, 2001), p. 53.
9. Richard A. D'Aveni, "Competitive Pressure Systems: Mapping and Managing Multimarket Contact," *MIT Sloan Management Review* (Fall 2002): 39–49.
10. Porter, *Competitive Strategy*, chapter 7.
11. For discussion of some of the long-term implications of marketing activities, see Koen Pauwels, "How Dynamic Consumer Response, Competitor Response, Company Support, and Company Inertia Shape Long-Term Marketing Effectiveness," *Marketing Science* 23 (Fall 2004): 596–610; Koen Pauwels, Dominique M. Hanssens, and S. Siddarth, "The Long-Term Effects of Price Promotions on Category Incidence, Brand Choice, and Purchase Quantity," *Journal of Marketing Research* 34 (November 2002): 421–39; and Marnik Dekimpe and Dominique Hanssens, "Sustained Spending and Persistent Response: A New Look at Long-term Marketing Profitability," *Journal of Marketing Research* 36 (November 1999): 397–412.
12. Rajendra S. Sisodia, David B. Wolfe, and Jagdish N. Sheth, *Firms of Endearment: How World-Class Companies Benefit Profit from Passion & Purpose* (Upper Saddle River, NJ: Wharton School Publishing, 2007).
13. For an academic treatment of benchmarking, see Douglas W. Vorhies and Neil A. Morgan, "Benchmarking Marketing Capabilities for Sustained Competitive Advantage," *Journal of Marketing* 69, no. 1 (January 2005): 80–94.
14. Michael E. Porter, *Competitive Strategy* (New York: Free Press, 1980), chapter 7.
15. These taxonomy and the Telstra example come from the writings of Australian marketing academic John H. Roberts: John H. Roberts, "Defensive Marketing: How a Strong Incumbent Can Protect Its Position," *Harvard Business Review* (November 2005): 150–57; John Roberts, Charlie Nelson, and Pamela Morrison, "Defending the Beachhead: Telstra vs. Optus," *Business Strategy Review* 12 (Spring 2001): 19–24.
16. Michael Barbaro and Hillary Chura, "The Gap Is in Need of a Niche." *New York Times*, January 27, 2007 p. C1 Copyright ©2007 *The New York Times*. Reprinted by permission.
17. www.starbucks.com/aboutus/overview.asp, accessed March 7, 2007.
18. Brian Wansink, "Can Package Size Accelerate Usage Volume?" *Journal of Marketing* 60 (July 1996): 1–14. See also, Priya Raghubir and Eric A. Greenleaf, "Ratios in Proportion: What Should the Shape of the Package Be?" *Journal of Marketing* 70 (April 2006): 95–107; and Valerie Folkes and Shashi Matta, "The Effect of Package Shape on Consumers' Judgments of Product Volume: Attention as a Mental Contaminant," *Journal of Consumer Research* 31 (September 2004): 390–401.
19. John D. Cripps, "Heuristics and Biases in Timing the Replacement of Durable Products," *Journal of Consumer Research* 21 (September 1994): 304–18.

20. "Business Bubbles," *The Economist*, October 12, 2002.

21. George Stalk Jr. and Rob Lachanauer, "Hardball: Five Killer Strategies for Trouncing the Competition," *Harvard Business Review* 82 (April 2004): 62–71; Richard D'Aveni, "The Empire Strikes Back: Counterrevolutionary Strategies for Industry Leaders," *Harvard Business Review* (November 2002): 66–74.

22. Robert D. Hof, "There's Not Enough 'Me' in MySpace," *BusinessWeek*, December 4, 2006, p. 40; Patricia Sellers, "MySpace Cowboys," *Fortune*, September 4, 2006, pp. 66–74; Aaron Pressman, "MySpace for Baby Boomers," *BusinessWeek*, October 16, 2006, pp. 120–22.

23. John Tagliabue, "Yeah, They Torture Jeans. But It's All for the Sake of Fashion," *New York Times*, July 12, 2006 p. C1. Copyright ©2006 *The New York Times*. Reprinted by permission.

24. Brian Morrissey, "R/GA," *Adweek*, January 22, 2007, p. 20+.

25. Jonathan Glancey, "The Private World of the Walkman," *Guardian*, October 11, 1999.

26. These six defense strategies, as well as the five attack strategies, are taken from Philip Kotler and Ravi Singh, "Marketing Warfare in the 1980s," *Journal of Business Strategy* (Winter 1981): 30–41.

27. Porter, *Competitive Strategy*, chapter 4; Jaideep Prabhu and David W. Stewart, "Signaling Strategies in Competitive Interaction: Building Reputations and Hiding the Truth," *Journal of Marketing Research* 38 (February 2001): 62–72.

28. Roger J. Calantone and Kim E. Schatzel, "Strategic Foretelling: Communication-Based Antecedents of a Firm's Propensity to Preannounce," *Journal of Marketing* 64 (January 2000): 17–30; Jehoshua Eliashberg and Thomas S. Robertson, "New Product Preannouncing Behavior: A Market Signaling Study," *Journal of Marketing Research* 25 (August 1988): 282–92.

29. Thomas S. Robertson, Jehoshua Eliashberg, and Talia Rymon, "New-Product Announcement Signals and Incumbent Reactions," *Journal of Marketing* 59 (July 1995): 1–15.

30. Yuhong Wu, Sridhar Balasubramanian, and Vijay Mahajan, "When Is a Preannounced New Product Likely to Be Delayed?" *Journal of Marketing* 68 (April 2004): 101–13; Barry L. Bayus, Sanjay Jain, and Ambar G. Rao, "Truth or Consequences: An Analysis of Vaporware and New-Product Announcements," *Journal of Marketing Research* 38 (February 2001): 3–13.

31. Kevin Kelleher, "Why FedEx Is Gaining Ground," *Business 2.0* (October 2003): 56–57; Charles Haddad, "FedEx: Gaining on Ground," *BusinessWeek*, December 16, 2002, pp. 126–28.

32. "Sara Lee Cleans Out Its Cupboards," *Fortune*, March 7, 2005, p. 38; Jane Sassen, "How Sara Lee Left Hanes in Its Skivvies," *BusinessWeek*, September 18, 2006, p. 40.

33. J. Scott Armstrong and Kesten C. Green, "Competitor-Oriented Objectives: The Myth of Market Share," *International Journal of Business* 12, no. 1 (Winter 2007): 115–34; Stuart E. Jackson, *Where Value Hides: A New Way to Uncover Profitable Growth for Your Business* (New York: John Wiley & Sons, 2006).

34. Nirmalya Kumar, *Marketing as Strategy* (Cambridge, MA: Harvard Business School Press, 2004); Philip Kotler and Paul N. Bloom, "Strategies for High-Market-Share Companies," *Harvard Business Review* (November–December 1975): 63–72.

35. Robert D. Buzzell and Frederick D. Wiersema, "Successful Share-Building Strategies," *Harvard Business Review* (January–February 1981): 135–44.

36. Robert J. Dolan, "Models of Competition: A Review of Theory and Empirical Evidence," in *Review of Marketing*, ed. Ben M. Enis and Kenneth J. Roering (Chicago: American Marketing Association, 1981), pp. 224–34.

37. Linda Hellofs and Robert Jacobson, "Market Share and Customer's Perceptions of Quality: When Can Firms Grow Their Way to Higher versus Lower Quality?" *Journal of Marketing* 63 (January 1999): 16–25.

38. Jon Birger, "Second-Mover Advantage," *Fortune*, March 20, 2006, pp. 20–21.

39. Venkatesh Shankar, Gregory Carpenter, and Lakshman Krishnamurthi, "Late-Mover Advantage: How Innovative Late Entrants Outsell Pioneers," *Journal of Marketing Research* 35 (February 1998): 54–70; Gregory S. Carpenter and Kent Nakamoto, "The Impact of Consumer Preference Formation on Marketing Objectives and Competitive Second-Mover Strategies," *Journal of Consumer Psychology* 5, no. 4 (1996): 325–58; Gregory S. Carpenter and Kent Nakamoto, "Competitive Strategies for Late Entry into a Market with a Dominant Brand," *Management Science* (October 1990): 1268–78.

40. Megan Johnston, "The Ketchup Strategy," *Forbes*, November 13, 2006, p. 185.

41. Michael V. Copeland, "These Boots Really Were Made for Walking," *Business 2.0* (October 2004): 72–74.

42. Abby Klassen, "Search Davids Take Aim at Goliath Google," *Advertising Age*, January 8, 2007, p. 1+; Anonymous, "Cha-Cha—Ceo Interview," *CEO Wire*, January 9, 2007.

43. Katrina Booker, "The Pepsi Machine," *Fortune*, February 6, 2006, pp. 68–72.

44. Jonathan Last, "Setting the Stage for Another Flop?" *philly.com*, June 4, 2006; Eryn Brown,

"Sony's Big Bazooka," *Fortune*, December 30, 2002, pp. 111–14.

45. Suzanne Smalley and Raja Mishra, "Froth, Fear, and Fury," *Boston Globe*, February 1, 2007.
46. Theodore Levitt, "Innovative Imitation," *Harvard Business Review* (September–October 1966): 63. Also see, Steven P. Schnaars, *Managing Imitation Strategies: How Later Entrants Seize Markets from Pioneers* (New York: Free Press, 1994).
47. Stuart F. Brown, "The Company That Out-Harleys Harley," *Fortune*, September 28, 1998, pp. 56–57; www.sscycle.com.
48. Melita Marie Garza, "Illinois Tool Works Stock Continues to Suffer Since Acquisition of Firm," *Chicago Tribune*, November 16, 2000; www.itw.com/about_home.html.
49. Jayne O'Donnell, "Family Rolling to Success on Tire Rack," *USA Today*, December 8, 2003.
50. Mark Morrison, "This Wildcatter Feels Right at Home in Gabon," *BusinessWeek*, June 5, 2006, p. 63.
51. Reported in E. R. Linneman and L. J. Stanton, *Making Niche Marketing Work* (New York: McGraw-Hill, 1991).
52. Thomas A. Fogarty, "Keeping Zippo's Flame Eternal," *USA Today*, June 24, 2003; www.zippo.com.
53. Kathleen Kingsbury, "The Cell Islands," *Time* 168, no. 21, November 20, 2006, p. G20.
54. Robert Spector, *Amazon.com: Get Big Fast* (New York: HarperBusiness, 2000), p. 151.

Chapter 12

1. Bruce Upbin, "Sharpening the Claws," *Forbes*, July 26, 1999, pp. 102–5.
2. This discussion is adapted from Theodore Levitt, "Marketing Success through Differentiation: Of Anything," *Harvard Business Review* (January–February 1980): 83–91. The first level, core benefit, has been added to Levitt's discussion.
3. Harper W. Boyd Jr. and Sidney Levy, "New Dimensions in Consumer Analysis," *Harvard Business Review* (November–December 1963): 129–40.
4. Joe Iannarelli, "Jamestown Container Thinks outside the Box," *Business First*, October 3, 2003, p. 4.
5. For some definitions, see Peter D. Bennett, ed., *Dictionary of Marketing Terms* (Chicago: American Marketing Association, 1995). Also see, Patrick E. Murphy and Ben M. Enis, "Classifying Products Strategically," *Journal of Marketing* (July 1986): 24–42.
6. Some of these bases are discussed in David A. Garvin, "Competing on the Eight Dimensions of Quality," *Harvard Business Review* (November–December 1987): 101–9.
7. Paul Kedrosky, "Simple Minds," *Business 2.0* (April 2006): 38; Debora Viana Thompson, Rebecca W. Hamilton, and Roland Rust, "Feature Fatigue: When Product Capabilities Become Too Much of a Good Thing," *Journal of Marketing Research* 42 (November 2005): 431–42.
8. James H. Gilmore and B. Joseph Pine, *Markets of One: Creating Customer-Unique Value through Mass Customization*, (Boston: Harvard Business School Press, 2000).
9. Daniel Schodel, Martin Bechtold, James Kimo Griggs, Kenneth Kao, and Marco Steinberg, *Digital Design and Manufacturing: CAD/CAM Applications in Architecture and Design* (New York: John Wiley, 2005).
10. Stuart Elliott, "Letting Consumers Control Marketing: Priceless," *New York Times*, October 9, 2006.
11. Paul Grimaldi, "Consumers Design Products Their Way." *Knight Ridder Tribune Business News*, November 25, 2006; Michael A. Prospero, *Fast Company* (September 2005): 35.
12. Gail Edmondson, "Mercedes Gets Back up to Speed," *BusinessWeek*, November 13, 2006, pp. 46–47.
13. Bernd Schmitt and Alex Simonson, *Marketing Aesthetics: The Strategic Management of Brand, Identity, and Image* (New York: Free Press, 1997).
14. Bruce Nussbaum, "The Power of Design," *BusinessWeek*, May 17, 2004, pp. 88–94; "Masters of Design," *Fast Company* (June 2004): 61–75. Also see, Philip Kotler, "Design: A Powerful but Neglected Strategic Tool," *Journal of Business Strategy* (Fall 1984): 16–21.
15. Ilana DeBare, "Cleaning Up without Dot-Coms/Belittled Entrepreneurs Choose Household Products over the High-Tech Industry and Become Highly Successful," [Final Edition 1] *San Francisco Chronicle*, October 8, 2006. Reprinted by permission.
16. A. G. Lafley, "Delivering Delight," *Fast Company* (June 2004): 51; Frank Nuovo, "A Call for Fashion," *Fast Company* (June 2004): 52; Bobbie Gossage, "Strategies: Designing Success," *Inc.* (May 2004): 27–29; Jerome Kathman, "Building Leadership Brands by Design," *Brandweek*, December 1, 2003, p. 20; Bob Parks, "Deconstructing Cute," *Business 2.0* (December 2002–January 2003): 47–50; J. Lynn Lunsford and Daniel Michaels, "Masters of Illusion," *Wall Street Journal*, November 25, 2002; Jim Hopkins, "When the Devil Is in the Design," *USA Today*, December 31, 2001.
17. Stanley Reed, "Rolls Royce at Your Service," *BusinessWeek*, November 15, 2005, pp. 92–93.

18. For a comprehensive discussion of Cemex, see Adrian J. Slywotzky and David J. Morrison, *How Digital Is Your Business* (New York: Crown Business, 2000), chapter 5.
19. Mark Sanchez, "Herman Miller Offers Training to Its Furniture Users," *Grand Rapids Business Journal*, December 2, 2002, p. 23.
20. Linda Knapp, "A Sick Computer?" *Seattle Times*, January 28, 2001.
21. Matthew Boyle, "Best Buy's Giant Gamble," *Fortune*, April 3, 2006, pp. 69–75. Geoffrey Colvin, "Talking Shop," *Fortune*, August 21, 2006, pp. 73–80; "Best Buy Turns on the Geek Appeal," *DSN Retailing Today*, February 24, 2003, p. 22.
22. Leslie Earnest and Adrian G. Uribarri, "Costco Halts Liberal Electronics Return Policy; Refunds Were Costing the Warehouse Store Chain 'Tens of Millions of Dollars' a Year," *Los Angeles Times*, February 28, 2007, p. C1. Reprinted by permission.
23. This section is based on a comprehensive treatment of product returns, James Stock and Thomas Speh, "Managing Product Returns for Competitive Advantage," *MIT Sloan Management Review* (Fall 2006): 57–62.
24. Robert Bordley, "Determining the Appropriate Depth and Breadth of a Firm's Product Portfolio," *Journal of Marketing Research* 40 (February 2003): 39–53; Peter Boatwright and Joseph C. Nunes, "Reducing Assortment: An Attribute-Based Approach," *Journal of Marketing* 65 (July 2001): 50–63.
25. Adapted from a Hamilton Consultants White Paper, December 1, 2000.
26. This illustration is found in Benson P. Shapiro, *Industrial Product Policy: Managing the Existing Product Line* (Cambridge, MA: Marketing Science Institute, 1977), pp. 3–5, 98–101.
27. "Brand Challenge," *The Economist*, April 6, 2002, p. 68.
28. Amna Kirmani, Sanjay Sood, and Sheri Bridges, "The Ownership Effect in Consumer Responses to Brand-Line Stretches," *Journal of Marketing* 63 (January 1999): 88–101; T. Randall, K. Ulrich, and D. Reibstein, "Brand Equity and Vertical Product-Line Extent," *Marketing Science* 17 (Fall 1998): 356–79; David A. Aaker, "Should You Take Your Brand to Where the Action Is?" *Harvard Business Review* (September–October 1997): 135–43.
29. France Leclerc, Christopher K. Hsee, and Joseph C. Nunes, "Narrow Focusing: Why the Relative Position of a Good in Its Category Matters More Than It Should," *Marketing Science* 24 (Spring 2005): 194–205.
30. Neal E. Boudette, "BMW's Push to Broaden Line Hits Some Bumps in the Road," *Wall Street Journal*, January 25, 2005; Alex Taylor III, "The Ultimate Fairly Inexpensive Driving Machine," *Fortune*, November 1, 2004, pp. 130–40.
31. Steuart Henderson Britt, "How Weber's Law Can Be Applied to Marketing," *Business Horizons* (February 1975): 21–29.
32. Stanley Holmes, "All the Rage Since Reagan," *BusinessWeek*, July 25, 2005, p. 68.
33. Nirmalya Kumar, "Kill a Brand, Keep a Customer," *Harvard Business Review* (December 2003): 86–95; Brad Stone, "Back to Basics," *Newsweek*, August 4, 2003, pp. 42–44.
34. Laurens M. Sloot, Dennis Fok, and Peter Verhoef, "The Short- and Long-Term Impact of an Assortment Reduction on Category Sales," *Journal of Marketing Research* 43 (November 2006): 536–48.
35. Patricia O'Connell, "A Chat with Unilever's Niall FitzGerald," *BusinessWeek Online*, August 2, 2001; John Willman, "Leaner, Cleaner, and Healthier Is the Stated Aim," *Financial Times*, February 23, 2000; "Unilever's Goal: 'Power Brands'," *Advertising Age*, January 3, 2000.
36. George Rädler, Jan Kubes, and Bohdan Wojnar, "Skoda Auto: From 'No-Class' to World-Class in One Decade," *Critical EYE* 15 (July 2006); Scott D. Upham, "Beneath the Brand," *Automotive Manufacturing & Production* (June 2001).
37. Ben Elgin, "Can HP's Printer Biz Keep Printing Money?" *BusinessWeek*, July 14, 2003, pp. 68–70; Simon Avery, "H-P Sees Room for Growth in Printer Market," *Wall Street Journal*, June 28, 2001; Lee Gomes, "Computer-Printer Price Drop Isn't Starving Makers," *Wall Street Journal*, August 16, 1996.
38. See Gerald J. Tellis, "Beyond the Many Faces of Price: An Integration of Pricing Strategies," *Journal of Marketing* (October 1986): 155. Also see, Dilip Soman and John T. Gourville, "Transaction Decoupling: How Price Bundling Affects the Decision to Consume," *Journal of Marketing Research* 38 (February 2001): 30–44.
39. Adapted from George Wuebker, "Bundles Effectiveness Often Undermined," *Marketing News*, March 18, 2002, pp. 9–12. See, Stefan Stremersch and Gerard J. Tellis, "Strategic Bundling of Products and Prices," *Journal of Marketing* 66 (January 2002): 55–72.
40. Akshay R. Rao, Lu Qu, and Robert W. Ruekert, "Signaling Unobservable Quality through a Brand Ally," *Journal of Marketing Research* 36, no. 2 (May 1999): 258–68; Akshay R. Rao and Robert W. Ruekert, "Brand Alliances as Signals of Product Quality," *Sloan Management Review* (Fall 1994): 87–97.
41. Bernard L. Simonin and Julie A. Ruth, "Is a Company Known by the Company It Keeps? Assessing the Spillover Effects of Brand Alliances on Consumer Brand Attitudes," *Journal of*

Marketing Research (February 1998): 30–42; see also, C. W. Park, S. Y. Jun, and A. D. Shocker, "Composite Branding Alliances: An Investigation of Extension and Feedback Effects," *Journal of Marketing Research* 33 (November 1996): 453–66.

42. Park, Jun, and Shocker, "Composite Branding Alliances: An Investigation of Extension and Feedback Effects," pp. 453–66; Lance Leuthesser, Chiranjier Kohli, and Rajneesh Suri, "2 + 2 = 5? A Framework for Using Co-Branding to Leverage a Brand," *Journal of Brand Management* 2, no. 1 (September 2003): 35–47.

43. Based in part on a talk by Nancy Bailey, "Using Licensing to Build the Brand," Brand Masters conference, December 7, 2000.

44. Barry Schlacter, "Giving Break a Boost; New Additives Are Touted as Way to Help Lower Bad Cholesterol, Aid Health," *Knight Ridder Tribune Business News,* April 4, 2007.

45. Kalpesh Kaushik Desai and Kevin Lane Keller, "The Effects of Brand Expansions and Ingredient Branding Strategies on Host Brand Extendibility," *Journal of Marketing* 66 (January 2002): 73–93; D. C. Denison, "Ingredient Branding Puts Big Names in the Mix," *Boston Globe,* May 26, 2002.

46. www.dupont.com.

47. Seth Goldin, "In Praise of Purple Cows," *Fast Company* (February 2003): 74–85.

48. Susan B. Bassin, "Value-Added Packaging Cuts Through Store Clutter," *Marketing News,* September 26, 1988, p. 21.

49. Karen Springen, "Nancy's Still Nice," *Newsweek,* February 16, 2004, p. 9; Judith Rosen, "Classics Strategies; Classics Sale," *Publishers Weekly,* October 6, 2003, pp. 16–18.

50. Susanna Hamner, "Packaging That Pays," *Business 2.0* (July 2006): 68–69.

51. Mya Frazier, "How Can Your Package Stand Out? Eye Tracking Looks Hard for Answers," *Advertising Age,* October 16, 2006, p. 14.

52. Kate Fitzgerald, "Packaging Is the Capper," *Advertising Age,* May 5, 2003, p. 22.

53. Kate Novack, "Tomato Soup with a Side of Pop Art," *Time,* May 10, 2004; "Campbell Soup Co. Changes the Look of Its Famous Cans," *Wall Street Journal,* August 26, 1999.

54. John C. Kozup, Elizabeth H. Creyer, and Scot Burton, "Making Healthful Food Choices: The Influence of Health Claims and Nutrition Information on Consumers' Evaluations of Packaged Food Products and Restaurant Menu Items," *Journal of Marketing* 67 (April 2003): 19–34; Siva K. Balasubramanian and Catherine Cole, "Consumers' Search and Use of Nutrition Information: The Challenge and Promise of the Nutrition Labeling and Education Act," *Journal of Marketing* 66 (July 2002): 112–27.

55. Jason Stein, "10-year Mitsubishi Warranty Is Small Part of a Larger Plan," *Automotive News,* January 12, 2004, p. 16.

56. Dee Gill, ". . . Or Your Money Back," *Inc.* 27, no. 9 (September 2005): 46. Reprinted by permission of *Inc.* via Copyright Clearance Center.

57. Robert Berner, "Watch Out, Best Buy and Circuit City," *BusinessWeek,* November 21, 2005, pp. 46–48.

58. Barbara Ettore, "Phenomenal Promises Mean Business," *Management Review* (March 1994): 18–23; "More Firms Pledge Guaranteed Service," *Wall Street Journal,* July 17, 1991; Also see, Sridhar Moorthy and Kannan Srinivasan, "Signaling Quality with a Money-Back Guarantee: The Role of Transaction Costs," *Marketing Science* 14, no. 4 (Fall 1995): 442–46; Christopher W. L. Hart, *Extraordinary Guarantees* (New York: Amacom, 1993).

Chapter 13

1. Leonard L. Berry, *On Great Service: A Framework for Action* (New York: Free Press, 2006); Leonard L. Berry, *Discovering the Soul of Service: The Nine Drivers of Sustainable Business Success* (New York: Free Press, 1999); Fred Wiersema, ed., *Customer Service: Extraordinary Results at Southwest Airlines, Charles Schwab, Lands' End, American Express, Staples, and USAA* (New York: HarperBusiness, 1998).

2. Leonard L. Berry and Kent D. Seltman, "Building a Strong Services Brand: Lessons from Mayo Clinic," *Business Horizons* 50 (May 2007): 199–209; Leonard L. Berry, "Leadership Lessons from Mayo Clinic," *Organizational Dynamics* 33 (August 2004): 228–42; Leonard L. Berry and Neeli Bendapudi, "Clueing in Customers," *Harvard Business Review* (February 2003): 100–106; John La Forgia, Kent Seltman, and Scott Swanson, "Mayo Clinic: Sustaining a Legacy Brand and Leveraging Its Equity in the 21st-Century Market," Presentation at the Marketing Science Institute's Conference on Brand Orchestration, Orlando, FL, December 4–5, 2003.

3. www.bls.gov/emp/home.htm.

4. Benjamin Scheider and David E. Bowen, *Winning the Service Game* (Boston: Harvard Business School Press, 1995); Leonard L. Berry, "Services Marketing Is Different," *Business* (May–June 1980): 24–30. For a thorough review of academic research into services, see Roland T. Rust and Tuck Siong Chung, "Marketing Models of Service and Relationships," *Marketing Science* 25 (November–December 2006): 560–80.

5. Jena McGregor, "Customer Service Champs," *BusinessWeek,* March 5, 2007, pp. 52–64; Mohanbir Sawhney, Sridhar Balasubramanian, and Vish V.

Krishnan, "Creating Growth with Services," *MIT Sloan Management Review* (Winter 2004): 34–43.

6. *Marketing News* Special Section, Webby Awards, June 1, 2006, pp. 15–22.
7. Further classifications of services are described in Christopher H. Lovelock, *Services Marketing*, 3rd ed. (Upper Saddle River, NJ: Prentice Hall, 1996). Also see John E. Bateson, *Managing Services Marketing: Text and Readings*, 3rd ed. (Hinsdale, IL: Dryden, 1995).
8. Valarie A. Zeithaml, "How Consumer Evaluation Processes Differ between Goods and Services," in *Marketing of Services*, ed. J. Donnelly and W. R. George (Chicago: American Marketing Association, 1981), pp. 186–90.
9. Amy Ostrom and Dawn Iacobucci, "Consumer Trade-Offs and the Evaluation of Services," *Journal of Marketing* (January 1995): 17–28.
10. For discussion of how the blurring of the line distinguishing products and services changes the meaning of this taxonomy, see Christopher Lovelock and Evert Gummesson, "Whither Services Marketing? In Search of a New Paradigm and Fresh Perspectives," *Journal of Service Research* 7 (August 2004): 20–41; and Stephen L. Vargo and Robert F. Lusch, "Evolving to a New Dominant Logic for Marketing," *Journal of Marketing* 68 (January 2004): 1–17.
11. Theodore Levitt, "Marketing Intangible Products and Product Intangibles," *Harvard Business Review* (May–June 1981): 94–102; Berry, "Services Marketing Is Different."
12. B. H. Booms and M. J. Bitner, "Marketing Strategies and Organizational Structures for Service Firms," in *Marketing of Services*, ed. J. Donnelly and W. R. George (Chicago: American Marketing Association, 1981), pp. 47–51.
13. Lewis P. Carbone and Stephan H. Haeckel, "Engineering Customer Experiences," *Marketing Management* 3 (Winter 1994): 17.
14. Bernd H. Schmitt, *Customer Experience Management* (New York: John Wiley & Sons, 2003).
15. Kimberly L. Allers, "A New Banking Model," *Fortune*, March 31, 2003, pp. 102–4; Linda Tischler, "Bank of (Middle) America," *Fast Company* (March 2003): 104–9; Anders Gronstedt, "Washington Mutual Energizes 54,000 Brand Ambassadors," at www.gronstedtgroup.com, accessed .
16. Irene Lacher, "Blue Man Group: With Flying Colors," *Hollywood Reporter*, May 16, 2006; Rob Walker, "Brand Blue," *Fortune*, April 28, 2003.
17. Gila E. Fruchter and Eitan Gerstner, "Selling with 'Satisfaction Guaranteed,'" *Journal of Service Research* 1, no. 4 (May 1999): 313–23. See also, Rebecca J. Slotegraaf and J. Jeffrey Inman, "Longitudinal Shifts in the Drivers of Satisfaction with Product Quality: The Role of Attribute Resolvability," *Journal of Marketing Research* 41 (August 2004): 269–80.
18. For a similar list, see Leonard L. Berry and A. Parasuraman, *Marketing Services: Competing through Quality* (New York: Free Press, 1991), p. 16.
19. G. Pascal Zachary and Dick Kovacevich, "Bank Different," *Business 2.0* (June 2006): 101–3; Greg Farrell, "Banking on Success as a One-Stop Shop," *USA Today*, March 26, 2007.
20. The material in this paragraph is based in part on Valarie Zeithaml, Mary Jo Bitner, and Dwayne D. Gremler, *Services Marketing: Integrating Customer Focus across the Firm*, 4th ed. (New York: McGraw-Hill, 2006), chapter 9.
21. G. Lynn Shostack, "Service Positioning through Structural Change," *Journal of Marketing* (January 1987): 34–43.
22. Vikas Mittal, Wagner A. Kamakura, and Rahul Govind, "Geographical Patterns in Customer Service and Satisfaction: An Empirical Investigation," *Journal of Marketing* 68 (July 2004): 48–62.
23. Jeffrey F. Rayport, Bernard J. Jaworski, and Ellie J. Kyung, "Best Face Forward: Improving Companies' Service Interface with Customers," *Journal of Interactive Marketing* 19 (Autumn 2005): 67–80; Asim Ansari and Carl F. Mela, "E-Customization," *Journal of Marketing Research* 40 (May 2003): 131–45.
24. W. Earl Sasser, "Match Supply and Demand in Service Industries," *Harvard Business Review* (November–December 1976): 133–40.
25. Steven M. Shugan and Jinhong Xie, "Advance Selling for Services," *California Management Review* 46, no. 3 (Spring 2004): 37–54; Eyal Biyalogorsky and Eitan Gerstner, "Contingent Pricing to Reduce Price Risks," *Marketing Science* 23, no. 1 (Winter 2003): 146–55; Steven M. Shugan and Jinhong Xie, "Advance Pricing of Services and Other Implications of Separating Purchase and Consumption," *Journal of Service Research* 2, no. 3 (February 2000): 227–39.
26. Carol Krol, "Case Study: Club Med Uses E-Mail to Pitch Unsold, Discounted Packages," *Advertising Age*, December 14, 1998, p. 40; www.clubmed.com.
27. Seth Godin, "If It's Broke, Fix It," *Fast Company* (October 2003): 131.
28. Diane Brady, "Why Service Stinks," *BusinessWeek*, October 23, 2000, pp. 119–28.
29. Kenneth Hein, "Communications Breakdown: Why Brands Can't Connect," *Brandweek*, February 19, 2007, p. 10.
30. Mary Clingman, "Turkey Talker," *Fortune*, November 27, 2006, p. 70.

31. Hannah Clark, "Customer Service Hell," *Forbes*, March 30, 2006.

32. Hannah Clark, "Customer Service Hell," *Forbes*, March 30, 2006.

33. Horovitz, "Whatever Happened to Customer Service? Automated Answering, Long Waits Irk Consumers."

34. Michelle Slatella, "Toll-Free Apology Soothes Savage Beast," *New York Times*, February 12, 2004; Jane Spencer, "Cases of Customer Rage Mount as Bad Service Prompts Venting," *Wall Street Journal*, September 17, 2003; Judi Ketteler, "Grumbling Groundswell," *Cincinnati Business Courier*, September 8, 2003; Richard Halicks, "You Can Count on Customer Disservice," *Atlanta Journal Constitution*, June 29, 2003; Bruce Horovitz, "Whatever Happened to Customer Service?" *USA Today*, September 26, 2003.

35. David Lazarus, "JetBlue Response Praised," *San Francisco Chronicle*, February 25, 2007, B1. Reprinted by permission.

36. Stephen S. Tax, Mark Colgate, and David Bowen, "How to Prevent Your Customers from Failing," *MIT Sloan Management Review* (Spring 2006): 30–38; Mei Xue and Patrick T. Harker, "Customer Efficiency: Concept and Its Impact on E-Business Management," *Journal of Service Research* 4, no. 4 (May 2002): 253–67; Matthew L. Meuter, Amy L. Ostrom, Robert I. Roundtree, and Mary Jo Bitner, "Self-Service Technologies: Understanding Customer Satisfaction with Technology-Based Service Encounters," *Journal of Marketing* 64, no. 3 (July 2000): 50–64.

37. Valarie Zeithaml, Mary Jo Bitner, and Dwayne D. Gremler, *Services Marketing: Integrating Customer Focus across the Firm*, 4th ed. (New York: McGraw-Hill, 2006).

38. Stephen S. Tax, Mark Colgate, and David Bowen, "How to Prevent Your Customers from Failing," *MIT Sloan Management Review* (Spring 2006): 30–38.

39. Susan M. Keaveney, "Customer Switching Behavior in Service Industries: An Exploratory Study," *Journal of Marketing* (April 1995): 71–82. See also, Jaishankar Ganesh, Mark J. Arnold, and Kristy E. Reynolds, "Understanding the Customer Base of Service Providers: An Examination of the Differences between Switchers and Stayers," *Journal of Marketing* 64 (July 2000): 65–87; Michael D. Hartline and O. C. Ferrell, "The Management of Customer-Contact Service Employees: An Empirical Investigation," *Journal of Marketing* (October 1996): 52–70; Linda L. Price, Eric J. Arnould, and Patrick Tierney, "Going to Extremes: Managing Service Encounters and Assessing Provider Performance," *Journal of Marketing* (April 1995): 83–97; Lois A. Mohr, Mary Jo Bitner, and Bernard H. Booms, "Critical Service Encounters: The Employee's Viewpoint," *Journal of Marketing* (October 1994): 95–106.

40. Christian Gronroos, "A Service-Quality Model and Its Marketing Implications," *European Journal of Marketing* 18, no. 4 (1984): 36–44.

41. Leonard Berry, "Big Ideas in Services Marketing," *Journal of Consumer Marketing* (Spring 1986): 47–51. See also, Jagdip Singh, "Performance Productivity and Quality of Frontline Employees in Service Organizations," *Journal of Marketing* 64 (April 2000): 15–34; John R. Hauser, Duncan I. Simester, and Birger Wernerfelt, "Internal Customers and Internal Suppliers," *Journal of Marketing Research* (August 1996): 268–80; Walter E. Greene, Gary D. Walls, and Larry J. Schrest, "Internal Marketing: The Key to External Marketing Success," *Journal of Services Marketing* 8, no. 4 (1994): 5–13.

42. Justin Doebele, "The Engineer," *Forbes*, January 9, 2006, pp. 122–24; Stanley Holmes, "Creature Comforts at 30,000 Feet," *BusinessWeek*, December 18, 2006, p. 138; Anonymous, "What Makes Singapore a Service Champion?" *Strategic Direction* (April 2003): 26–28.

43. Christian Gronroos, "A Service-Quality Model," pp. 38–39; Michael D. Hartline, James G. Maxham III, and Daryl O. McKee, "Corridors of Influence in the Dissemination of Customer-Oriented Strategy to Customer-Contact Service Employees," *Journal of Marketing* (April 2000): 35–50.

44. Ad de Jong, Ko de Ruyter, and Jos Lemmink, "Antecedents and Consequences of the Service Climate in Boundary-Spanning Self-Managing Service Teams," *Journal of Marketing* 68 (April 2004): 18-35; Michael D. Hartline and O. C. Ferrell, "The Management of Customer-Contact Service Employees: An Empirical Investigation," *Journal of Marketing* 60 (October 1996): 52-70.

45. Andrea Tortora, "High Tech, High Touch," *Cincinnati Business Courier*, July 4, 2003.

46. John Batelle, "Charles Schwab, Back from the Brink," *Business 2.0* (March 2006); "Q&A with Becky Saeger, CMO, Charles Schwab," *ANA Marketing Musings*, September 11, 2006; Betsy Morris, "Charles Schwab's Big Challenge," *Fortune*, May 30, 2005.

47. Roland T. Rust and Katherine N. Lemon, "E-Service and the Consumer," *International Journal of Electronic Commerce* 5, no. 3 (Spring 2001): 83–99. See also, Balaji Padmanabhan and Alexander Tuzhilin, "On the Use of Optimization for Data Mining: Theoretical Interactions and ECRM opportunities," *Management Science* 49, no. 10 (October 2003): 1327–43; B. P. S. Murthi and Sumit Sarkar, "The Role of the Management Sciences in Research on Personalization," *Management Science* 49, no. 10 (October 2003): 1344–62.

48. Roland T. Rust, P. K. Kannan, and Na Peng, "The Customer Economics of Internet Privacy," *Journal of the Academy of Marketing Science* 30, no. 4 (2002): 455–64.

49. Glenn B. Voss, A. Parasuraman, and Dhruv Grewal, "The Role of Price, Performance, and Expectations in Determining Satisfaction in Service Exchanges," *Journal of Marketing* 62 (October 1998): 46–61.

50. Roland T. Rust and Richard L. Oliver, "Should We Delight the Customer?" *Journal of the Academy of Marketing Science* 28, no. 1 (Fall 2002): 86–94.

51. www.ritzcarlton.com; Carmine Gallo, "How Ritz-Carlton Maintains Its Mystique," *BusinessWeek*, February 13, 2007; Special Issue on Service Excellence, *Expert Magazine* 3, no. 6 (2006); Roger Crockett, "Keeping Ritz-Carlton at the Top of Its Game," *BusinessWeek*, May 29, 2006.

52. A. Parasuraman, Valarie A. Zeithaml, and Leonard L. Berry, "A Conceptual Model of Service Quality and Its Implications for Future Research," *Journal of Marketing* (Fall 1985): 41–50. See also, Michael K. Brady and J. Joseph Cronin Jr., "Some New Thoughts on Conceptualizing Perceived Service Quality," *Journal of Marketing* 65 (July 2001): 34–49; Susan J. Devlin and H. K. Dong, "Service Quality from the Customers' Perspective," *Marketing Research* (Winter 1994): 4–13.

53. Leonard L. Berry and A. Parasuraman, *Marketing Services: Competing through Quality* (New York: Free Press, 1991), p. 16.

54. Parasuraman, Zeithaml, and Berry, "A Conceptual Model of Service Quality and Its Implications for Future Research," pp. 41–50.

55. Alison Overholt, "Cuckoo for Customers," *Fast Company* (June 2004): 86–87; www.rackspace.com/support/.

56. Jena McGregor, "Customer Service Champs," *BusinessWeek*, March 5, 2007, pp. 52–64.

57. James L. Heskett, W. Earl Sasser Jr., and Christopher W. L. Hart, *Service Breakthroughs* (New York: Free Press, 1990).

58. William C. Copacino, *Supply Chain Management* (Boca Raton, FL: St. Lucie Press, 1997).

59. Leonard L. Berry, Kathleen Seiders, and Dhruv Grewal, "Understanding Service Convenience," *Journal of Marketing* 66 (July 2002): 1–17.

60. Mary Jo Bitner, "Self-Service Technologies: What Do Customers Expect?" *Marketing Management* (Spring 2001): 10–11; Matthew L. Meuter, Amy L. Ostrom, Robert J. Roundtree, and Mary Jo Bitner, "Self-Service Technologies: Understanding Customer Satisfaction with Technology-Based Service Encounters," *Journal of Marketing* 64 (July 2000): 50–64.

61. Peter Burrows, "The Era of Efficiency," *BusinessWeek*, June 18, 2001, pp. 94–98.

62. Matthew L. Meuter, Mary Jo Bitner, Amy L. Ostrom, and Stephen W. Brown, "Choosing among Alternative Service Delivery Modes: An Investigation of Customer Trial of Self-Service Technologies," *Journal of Marketing* 69 (April 2005): 61–83.

63. John McCormick, "Roadblock: The Customer; Airlines, Railroads, Grocery Stores, and Hotels Racing to Deploy Self-Service Check-In Devices Have Discovered Two Things," *Baseline*, April 1, 2003.

64. Michelle Higgins, "Go Directly to Your Room Key! Pass the Desk!" *New York Times*, August 20, 2006, pp. 5-6. Copyright © 2006 The New York Times. Reprinted by permission.

65. John A. Martilla and John C. James, "Importance-Performance Analysis," *Journal of Marketing* (January 1977): 77–79.

66. Jeffrey G. Blodgett and Ronald D. Anderson, "A Bayesian Network Model of the Customer Complaint Process," *Journal of Service Research* 2, no. 4 (May 2000): 321–38; Stephen S. Tax and Stephen W. Brown, "Recovering and Learning from Service Failures," *Sloan Management Review* (Fall 1998): 75–88; Claes Fornell and Birger Wernerfelt, "A Model for Customer Complaint Management," *Marketing Science* 7 (Summer 1988): 271–86.

67. James G. Maxham III and Richard G. Netemeyer, "Firms Reap What They Sow: The Effects of Shared Values and Perceived Organizational Justice on Customers' Evaluations of Complaint Handling," *Journal of Marketing* 67 (January 2003): 46–62; Singh, "Performance Productivity and Quality of Frontline Employees in Service Organizations," pp. 15–34; Barry J. Rabin and James S. Boles, "Employee Behavior in a Service Environment: A Model and Test of Potential Differences between Men and Women," *Journal of Marketing* 62 (April 1998): 77–91.

68. Tax, Brown, and Chandrashekaran, "Customer Evaluations of Service Complaint Experiences: Implications for Relationship Marketing," pp. 60–76; Tax and Brown, "Recovering and Learning from Service Failures," pp. 75–88.

69. Tania Padgett, "Some Automated Voice Systems Are More Human Than Others," *Chicago Tribune*, January 28, 2007; www.gethuman.com.

70. D. Todd Donovan, Tom J. Brown, and John C. Mowen, "Internal Benefits of Service Worker Customer Orientation: Job Satisfaction, Commitment, and Organizational Citizenship Behaviors," *Journal of Marketing* 68 (January 2004): 128–46.

71. Philip Walzer, "'Best to Work for' Companies Have Happy, and Loyal, Employees," *Knight Ridder Tribune Business News*, January 28, 2007, p. 1; http://media.paychex.com/article_print.cfm?article_id=3369; http://media.paychex.com/article_print.cfm?article_id=2383.

72. Amy Barrett, "Vanguard Gets Personal," *BusinessWeek*, October 3, 2005, pp. 115–18; Carolyn Marconi and Donna MacFarland, "Growth by Marketing under the Radar," Presentation made at Marketing Science Institute Board of Trustees Meeting: Pathways to Growth, Tucson, AZ, November 7, 2002.

73. Christopher Rowland, "The Pharmacists in Chains Promote Personal Touch to Keep Edge Over Mail-Order Firms," *Boston Globe*, December 10, 2003.

74. www.schneider.com/; www.informs.org; Todd Raphael, "Facing 'Fierce Competition,' Schneider National Struggles to Fill Trucking Jobs," *Inside Recruiting*, May 31, 2006.

75. Susanna Hamner, "Checking In at the Hotel of Tomorrow," *Business 2.0* (November 2006): 38–40.

76. Mike Beirne and Javier Benito, "Starwood Uses Personnel to Personalize Marketing," *Brandweek*, April 24, 2006, p. 9.

77. Linda Tischler, "Join the Circus," *Fast Company* (July 2005): 53–58; "Cirque du Soliel," *America's Greatest Brands* 3 (2004); Geoff Keighley, "The Phantasmagoria Factory," *Business 2.0* (February 2004): 102; Robin D. Rusch, "Cirque du Soleil—Contorts," *brandchannel.com*, December 1, 2003.

78. Mark Vandenbosch and Niraj Dawar, "Beyond Better Products: Capturing Value in Customer Interactions," *MIT Sloan Management Review* 43 (Summer 2002): 35–42; Milind M. Lele and Uday S. Karmarkar, "Good Product Support Is Smart Marketing," *Harvard Business Review* 61 (November–December 1983): 124–32.

79. For recent research on the effects of delays in service on service evaluations, see Michael K. Hui and David K. Tse, "What to Tell Consumers in Waits of Different Lengths: An Integrative Model of Service Evaluation," *Journal of Marketing* (April 1996): 81–90; Shirley Taylor, "Waiting for Service: The Relationship between Delays and Evaluations of Service," *Journal of Marketing* (April 1994): 56–69.

80. Byron G. Auguste, Eric P. Harmon, and Vivek Pandit, "The Right Service Strategies for Product Companies," *McKinsey Quarterly* 1 (2006): 41–51.

Chapter 14

1. Dan Beucke, "A Blade Too Far," *BusinessWeek*, August 14, 2006; Jenn Abelson, "And Then There Were Five," *Boston Globe*, September 15, 2005; Jack Neff, "Six-Blade Blitz," *Advertising Age*, September 19, 2005, pp. 3, 53; Editorial, "Gillette Spends Smart on Fusion," *Advertising Age*, September 26, 2005, p. 24.

2. "The Price Is Wrong," *Economist*, May 25, 2002.

3. Xavier Dreze and Joseph C. Nunes, "Using Combined-Currency Prices to Lower Consumers' Perceived Cost," *Journal of Marketing Research* 41 (February 2004): 59–72.

4. Jack Neff, "Moving to Margins in a New Marketing Age," *Advertising Age*, July 24, 2006, pp. 1, 21.

5. Michael Menduno, "Priced to Perfection," *Business 2.0*, March 6, 2001, pp. 40–42.

6. Paul Markillie, "A Perfect Market: A Survey of E-Commerce," *Economist*, May 15, 2004, pp. 3–20; David Kirpatrick, "How the Open-Source World Plans to Smack Down Microsoft, and Oracle, and . . . ," *Fortune*, February 23, 2004, pp. 92–100; Faith Keenan, "The Price Is Really Right," *BusinessWeek*, March 31, 2003, pp. 61–67; Michael Menduno, "Priced to Perfection," *Business 2.0*, March 6, 2001, pp. 40–42; Amy E. Cortese, "Good-Bye to Fixed Pricing?" *BusinessWeek*, May 4, 1998, pp. 71–84. For a discussion of some of the academic issues involved, see Florian Zettelmeyer, "Expanding to the Internet: Pricing and Communication Strategies When Firms Compete on Multiple Channels," *Journal of Marketing Research* 37 (August 2000): 292–308; John G. Lynch Jr. and Dan Ariely, "Wine Online: Search Costs Affect Competition on Price, Quality, and Distribution," *Marketing Science* (Winter 2000): 83–103; Rajiv Lal and Miklos Sarvary, "When and How Is the Internet Likely to Decrease Price Competition?" *Marketing Science* 18, no. 4 (Fall 1999): 485–503.

7. "Growth as a Process," Interview with Jeffrey Immelt, *Harvard Business Review* (June 2006).

8. "Pricing Benchmarks for the Future: How General Electric Does It," White paper, Simon-Kucher Partners, March 6, 2007.

9. For a thorough, up-to-date review of pricing research, see Chezy Ofir and Russell S. Winer, "Pricing: Economic and Behavioral Models," in *Handbook of Marketing*, ed. Bart Weitz and Robin Wensley (London: Sage Publications, 2002).

10. Pia Sarkar, "Which Shirt Costs $275?—Brand Loyalty, Bargain Hunting, and Unbridled Luxury All Play a Part in the Price You'll Pay for a T-Shirt," *Final Edition*, March 15, 2007, p. C1. Reprinted by permission.

11. Peter R. Dickson and Alan G. Sawyer, "The Price Knowledge and Search of Supermarket Shoppers," *Journal of Marketing* (July 1990): 42–53. For a methodological qualification, however, see Hooman Estalami, Alfred Holden, and Donald R. Lehmann, "Macro-Economic Determinants of Consumer Price Knowledge: A Meta-Analysis of Four Decades of Research," *International Journal of Research in Marketing* 18 (December 2001): 341–55.

12. For a comprehensive review, see Tridib Mazumdar, S. P. Raj, and Indrajit Sinha, "Reference Price Research: Review and Propositions," *Journal of*

Marketing 69 (October 2005), 84–102. For a different point of view, see Chris Janiszewski and Donald R. Lichtenstein, "A Range Theory Account of Price Perception," *Journal of Consumer Research* (March 1999): 353–68.

13. For a discussion of how "incidental" prices outside the category can serve as contextual reference prices, see Joseph C. Nunes and Peter Boatwright, "Incidental Prices and Their Effect on Willingness to Pay," Journal *of Marketing Research* 41 (November 2004): 457–66.

14. K. N. Rajendran and Gerard J. Tellis, "Contextual and Temporal Components of Reference Price," *Journal of Marketing* (January 1994): 22–34; Gurumurthy Kalyanaram and Russell S. Winer, "Empirical Generalizations from Reference-Price Research," *Marketing Science* 14, no. 3 (Summer 1995): G161–69.

15. Robert Strauss, "Prices You Just Can't Believe," *New York Times*, January 17, 2002.

16. Gurumurthy Kalyanaram and Russell S. Winer, "Empirical Generalizations from Reference-Price Research," *Marketing Science* 14, no. 3 (Summer 1995): 161–69.

17. Glenn E. Mayhew and Russell S. Winer, "An Empirical Analysis of Internal and External Reference-Price Effects Using Scanner Data," *Journal of Consumer Research* (June 1992): 62–70.

18. Robert Ziethammer, "Forward-Looking Buying in Online Auctions," *Journal of Marketing Research* 43 (August 2006): 462–76.

19. John T. Gourville, "Pennies-a-Day: The Effect of Temporal Reframing on Transaction Evaluation," *Journal of Consumer Research* (March 1998): 395–408.

20. Gary M. Erickson and Johny K. Johansson, "The Role of Price in Multi-Attribute Product-Evaluations," *Journal of Consumer Research* (September 1985): 195–99.

21. Wilfred Amaldoss and Sanjay Jain, "Pricing of Conspicuous Goods: A Competitive Analysis of Social Effects," *Journal of Marketing Research* 42 (February 2005); Angela Chao and Juliet B. Schor, "Empirical Tests of Status Consumption: Evidence from Women's Cosmetics," *Journal of Economic Psychology* 19, no. 1 (January 1998): 107–31.

22. Ellen Byron, "Fashion Victim: To Refurbish Its Image, Tiffany Risks Profits; After Silver Took Off, Jeweler Raises Prices to Discourage Teens," *Wall Street Journal*, January 10, 2007, p. A1. Reprinted by permission of Dow Jones via Copyright Clearance Center.

23. Mark Stiving and Russell S. Winer, "An Empirical Analysis of Price Endings with Scanner Data," *Journal of Consumer Research* (June 1997): 57–68.

24. Eric T. Anderson and Duncan Simester, "Effects of $19 Price Endings on Retail Sales: Evidence from Field Experiments," *Quantitative Marketing and Economics* 1, no. 1 (March 2003): 93–110.

25. Eric Anderson and Duncan Simester, "Mind Your Pricing Cues," *Harvard Business Review* (September 2003): 96–103.

26. Robert M. Schindler and Patrick N. Kirby, "Patterns of Rightmost Digits Used in Advertised Prices: Implications for Nine-Ending Effects," *Journal of Consumer Research* (September 1997): 192–201.

27. Anderson and Simester, "Mind Your Pricing Cues," pp. 96–103.

28. Anderson and Simester, "Mind Your Pricing Cues," pp. 96–103.

29. Daniel J. Howard and Roger A. Kerin, "Broadening the Scope of Reference-Price Advertising Research: A Field Study of Consumer Shopping Involvement," *Journal of Marketing* 70 (October 2006): 185–204.

30. Robert C. Blattberg and Kenneth Wisniewski, "Price-Induced Patterns of Competition," *Marketing Science* 8 (Fall 1989): 291–309.

31. Shantanu Dutta, Mark J. Zbaracki, and Mark Bergen, "Pricing Process as a Capability: A Resource-Based Perspective," *Strategic Management Journal* 24, no. 7 (July 2003): 615–30.

32. Mei Fong, "IKEA Hits Home in China: The Swedish Design Giant, Unlike Other Retailers, Slashes Prices for the Chinese," *Wall Street Journal*, March 3, 2006, p. B1. Reprinted by permission of Dow Jones via Copyright Clearance Center.

33. Michael Silverstein and Neil Fiske, *Trading Up: The New American Luxury* (New York: Portfolio, 2003).

34. Christopher Lawton, "A Liquor Maverick Shakes Up Industry with Pricey Brands," *Wall Street Journal*, May 21, 2003.

35. David Leonhardt, "Seeing Art: What's It Worth to You?" *New York Times*, July 21, 2006; Stephanie Cash, "Point of View: The High Price of Looking," *Art in America* 94, no. 8 (September 2006): 37; Roberta Smith, "Should Museums Always Be Free?" *New York Times*, July 22, 2006.

36. Timothy Aeppel, "Seeking Perfect Prices, CEO Tears Up the Rules," *Wall Street Journal*, March 27, 2007.

37. Florian Zettelmeyer, Fiona Scott Morton, and Jorge Silva-Risso, "How the Internet Lowers Prices: Evidence from Matched Survey and Automobile Transaction Data," *Journal of Marketing Research* 43 (May 2006): 168–81; Jeffrey R. Brown and Austan Goolsbee, "Does the Internet Make Markets More Competitive? Evidence from the Life Insurance Industry," *Journal of Political Economy* 110, no. 5 (October 2002): 481–507.

38. Walter Baker, Mike Marn, and Craig Zawada, "Price Smarter on the Net," *Harvard Business Review* (February 2001): 122–27.
39. Victoria Murphy Barret, "What the Traffic Will Bear," *Forbes*, July 3, 2006, pp. 69–70.
40. Thomas T. Nagle and Reed K. Holden, *The Strategy and Tactics of Pricing*, 3rd ed. (Upper Saddle River, NJ: Prentice Hall, 2002).
41. For a summary of elasticity studies, see Dominique M. Hanssens, Leonard J. Parsons, and Randall L. Schultz, *Market Response Models: Econometric and Time Series Analysis* (Boston: Kluwer, 1990), pp. 187–91.
42. Tammo H. A. Bijmolt, Harald J. Van Heerde, and Rik G. M. Pieters, "New Empirical Generalizations on the Determinants of Price Elasticity," *Journal of Marketing Research* 42 (May 2005): 141–56.
43. "Easier Than ABC," *Economist*, October 25, 2003, p. 56.
44. William W. Alberts, "The Experience Curve Doctrine Reconsidered," *Journal of Marketing* (July 1989): 36–49.
45. Michael Sivy, "Japan's Smart Secret Weapon," *Fortune*, August 12, 1991, p. 75.
46. Adapted from Robert J. Dolan and Hermann Simon, "Power Pricers," *Across the Board* (May 1997): 18–19.
47. Kusum L. Ailawadi, Donald R. Lehmann, and Scott A. Neslin, "Market Response to a Major Policy Change in the Marketing Mix: Learning from Procter & Gamble's Value Pricing Strategy," *Journal of Marketing* 65 (January 2001): 44–61.
48. Timothy Aeppel, "Seeking Perfect Prices, CEO Tears Up the Rules," *Wall Street Journal*, March 27, 2007.
49. Tung-Zong Chang and Albert R. Wildt, "Price, Product Information, and Purchase Intention: An Empirical Study," *Journal of the Academy of Marketing Science* (Winter 1994): 16–27. See also, G. Dean Kortge and Patrick A. Okonkwo, "Perceived Value Approach to Pricing," *Industrial Marketing Management* (May 1993): 133–40.
50. James C. Anderson, Dipak C. Jain, and Pradeep K. Chintagunta, "Customer Value Assessment in Business Markets: A State-of-Practice Study," *Journal of Business-to-Business Marketing* 1, no. 1 (Spring 1993): 3–29.
51. Bill Saporito, "Behind the Tumult at P&G," *Fortune*, March 7, 1994, pp. 74–82. For empirical analysis of its effects, see Kusim L. Ailawadi, Donald R. Lehmann, and Scott A. Neslin, "Market Response to a Major Policy Change in the Marketing Mix: Learning from Procter & Gamble's Value Pricing Strategy," *Journal of Marketing* 65 (January 2001): 44–61.
52. Stephen J. Hoch, Xavier Dreze, and Mary J. Purk, "EDLP, Hi-Lo, and Margin Arithmetic," *Journal of Marketing* (October 1994): 16–27; Rajiv Lal and R. Rao, "Supermarket Competition: The Case of Everyday Low Pricing," *Marketing Science* 16, no. 1 (Winter 1997): 60–80.
53. Joseph W. Alba, Carl F. Mela, Terence A. Shimp, and Joel E. Urbany, "The Effect of Discount Frequency and Depth on Consumer Price Judgments," *Journal of Consumer Research* (September 1999): 99–114.
54. John Dobosz, "Putting Family Dollar on the Shopping List," *Forbes*, August 23, 2006; Jeff Meyer, "The Mad Dash to the Dollar Shop," *Christian Science Monitor*, August 4, 2003, p. 13; "Low Prices, Treasure Hunts Build Dollar Empire," *DSN Retailing Today*, November 24, 2003, pp. 23–24.
55. Ethan Smith and Sara Silver, "To Protect Its Box-Office Turf, Ticketmaster Plays Rivals' Tune," *Wall Street Journal*, September 12, 2006.
56. "Royal Mail Drives Major Cost Savings through Free Markets," Free Markets press release, December 15, 2003.
57. Sandy D. Jap, "The Impact of Online Reverse Auction Design on Buyer-Supplier Relationships," *Journal of Marketing* 71 (January 2007): 146–59; Sandy D. Jap, "An Exploratory Study of the Introduction of Online Reverse Auctions," *Journal of Marketing* 67 (July 2003): 96–107.
58. Paul W. Farris and David J. Reibstein, "How Prices, Expenditures, and Profits Are Linked," *Harvard Business Review* (November–December 1979): 173–84. See also, Makoto Abe, "Price and Advertising Strategy of a National Brand against Its Private-Label Clone: A Signaling Game Approach," *Journal of Business Research* (July 1995): 241–50.
59. J. P. Morgan Report, "E-Tailing and the Five Cs," (March 2000).
60. Eugene H. Fram and Michael S. McCarthy, "The True Price of Penalties," *Marketing Management* (October 1999): 49–56.
61. Joel E. Urbany, "Justifying Profitable Pricing," *Journal of Product and Brand Management* 10, no. 3 (2001): 141–57; Charles Fishman, "The Wal-Mart You Don't Know," *Fast Company* (December 2003): 68–80.
62. Normandy Madden, "P&G Adapts Attitude toward Local Markets," *Advertising Age*, February 23, 2004, pp. 28–29; "China: Let a Thousand Brands Bloom," *BusinessWeek*, October 17, 2005.
63. P. N. Agarwala, *Countertrade: A Global Perspective* (New Delhi: Vikas, 1991); Michael Rowe, *Countertrade* (London: Euromoney Books, 1989); Christopher M. Korth, ed., *International Countertrade* (New York: Quorum Books, 1987).

64. For an interesting discussion of a quantity surcharge, see David E. Sprott, Kenneth C. Manning, and Anthony Miyazaki, "Grocery Price Settings and Quantity Surcharges," *Journal of Marketing* 67 (July 2003): 34–46.

65. Michael V. Marn and Robert L. Rosiello, "Managing Price, Gaining Profit," *Harvard Business Review* (September–October 1992): 84–94. See also, Kusum L. Ailawadi, Scott A. Neslin, and Karen Gedenk, "Pursuing the Value-Conscious Consumer: Store Brands versus National-Brand Promotions," *Journal of Marketing* 65 (January 2001): 71–89; Gerard J. Tellis, "Tackling the Retailer Decision Maze: Which Brands to Discount, How Much, When, and Why?" *Marketing Science* 14, no. 3, pt. 2 (Summer 1995): 271–99.

66. Kevin J. Clancy, "At What Profit Price?" *Brandweek,* June 23, 1997.

67. Carol J. Loomis, "The Bloomberg," *Fortune,* April 16, 2007, pp. 60–70.

68. Jay E. Klompmaker, William H. Rogers, and Anthony E. Nygren, "Value, Not Volume," *Marketing Management* (May–June 2003): 45–48; www.landsend.com.

69. Bill Ordine, "The Price Is . . . : Single-Game Cost Rises for Yankee Games, Red Sox Weekend Dates, and Opening Day," *Knight Ridder Tribune Business News,* January 19, 2007, p. 1.

70. Ramarao Deesiraju and Steven M. Shugan, "Strategic Service Pricing and Yield Management," *Journal of Marketing* 63 (January 1999): 44–56; Robert E. Weigand, "Yield Management: Filling Buckets, Papering the House," *Business Horizons* (September–October 1999): 55–64.

71. Charles Fishman, "Which Price Is Right?" *Fast Company* (March 2003): 92–102; Bob Tedeschi, "E-Commerce Report," *New York Times,* September 2, 2002; Faith Keenan, "The Price Is Really Right," *BusinessWeek,* March 31, 2003, pp. 62–67; Peter Coy, "The Power of Smart Pricing," *BusinessWeek,* April 10, 2000, pp. 160–64. For a review of recent and seminal work linking pricing decisions with operational insights, see Moritz Fleischmann, Joseph M. Hall, and David F. Pyke, "Research Brief: Smart Pricing," *MIT Sloan Management Review* (Winter 2004): 9–13.

72. Mike France, "Does Predatory Pricing Make Microsoft a Predator?" *BusinessWeek,* November 23, 1998, pp. 130–32. Also see Joseph P. Guiltinan and Gregory T. Gundlack, "Aggressive and Predatory Pricing: A Framework for Analysis," *Journal of Advertising* (July 1996): 87–102.

73. For more information on specific types of price discrimination that are illegal, see Henry Cheesman, *Business Law,* 6th ed. (Upper Saddle River, NJ: Prentice Hall, 2007).

74. Bob Donath, "Dispel Major Myths about Pricing," *Marketing News,* February 3, 2003, p. 10.

75. For a classic review, see Kent B. Monroe, "Buyers' Subjective Perceptions of Price," *Journal of Marketing Research* (February 1973): 70–80. See also, Z. John Zhang, Fred Feinberg, and Aradhna Krishna, "Do We Care What Others Get? A Behaviorist Approach to Targeted Promotions," *Journal of Marketing Research* 39 (August 2002): 277–91.

76. Margaret C. Campbell, "Perceptions of Pricing Unfairness: Antecedents and Consequences," *Journal of Marketing Research* 36 (May 1999): 187–99.

77. Lan Xia, Kent B. Monroe, and Jennifer L. Cox, "The Price Is Unfair! A Conceptual Framework of Price Fairness Perceptions," *Journal of Marketing* 68 (October 2004): 1–15.

78. Eric Mitchell, "How Not to Raise Prices," *Small Business Reports* (November 1990): 64–67.

79. Stephanie Thompson, "Big G Yields on Cereal-Price Cuts," *Advertising Age* 78, no. 12, March 19, 2007, p. 6.

Chapter 15

1. Kerry Capell, "Thinking Simple at Philips," *BusinessWeek,* December 11, 2006, p. 50; Royal Philips Electronics Annual Report, 2006; "Philips—Unfulfilled," *brandchannel.com,* June 20, 2005; Jennifer L. Schenker, "Fine-Tuning a Fuzzy Image," *TIMEeurope.com* (Spring 2002).

2. Anne T. Coughlan, Erin Anderson, Louis W. Stern, and Adel I. El-Ansary, *Marketing Channels,* 6th ed. (Upper Saddle River, NJ: Prentice Hall, 2001).

3. Louis W. Stern and Barton A. Weitz, "The Revolution in Distribution: Challenges and Opportunities," *Long Range Planning* 30, no. 6 (December 1997): 823–29.

4. For an insightful summary of academic research, see Erin Anderson and Anne T. Coughlan, "Channel Management: Structure, Governance, and Relationship Management," in *Handbook of Marketing,* ed. Bart Weitz and Robin Wensley (London: Sage, 2001), pp. 223–47. See also, Gary L. Frazier, "Organizing and Managing Channels of Distribution," *Journal of the Academy of Marketing Sciences* 27, no. 2 (Spring 1999): 226–40.

5. Laura Petrecca, "We Should Be Feeling Very Sleepy, Considering Flood of Sleep Aids," *USA Today,* March 12, 2007; Daniel Yi, "Wake Up: You May Not Need a Pill to Sleep," *Los Angeles Times,* August 8, 2006; Diedtra Henderson, "With Advertising under Siege, Drug Marketers Rethink Their Marketing Message," *Boston Globe,* July 31, 2005.

6. Peter Child, Suzanne Heywood, and Michael Kilger, "Do Retail Brands Travel?" *McKinsey Quarterly* (January 2002): 11–13.

7. David Whitford, "Uh . . . Maybe Should I Drive," *Fortune*, April 30, 2007, pp. 125–28; Louise Lee, "It's Dell vs. the Dell Way," *BusinessWeek*, March 6, 2006, pp. 61–62; David Kirkpatrick, "Dell in the Penalty Box," *Fortune*, September 18, 2006, pp. 70–78; Nanette Byrnes, Peter Burrows, and Louise Lee, "Dark Days at Dell," *BusinessWeek*, September 4, 2006, pp. 27–30; Elizabeth Corcoran, "A Bad Spell for Dell," *Forbes*, June 19, 2006, pp. 44–46.

8. "Click to Download," *The Economist*, August 19, 2006, pp. 57–58.

9. Martin Wildberger, "Multichannel Business Basics for Successful E-Commerce," *Electronic Commerce News*, September 16, 2002, p. 1; Matthew Haeberle, "REI Overhauls Its E-Commerce," *Chain Store Age* (January 2003): 64.

10. Asim Ansari, Carl F. Mela, and Scott A. Neslin, "Customer Channel Migration," *Journal of Marketing Research*, 45, (February 2008), forthcoming; Jacquelyn S. Thomas and Ursula Y. Sullivan, "Managing Marketing Communications," *Journal of Marketing* 69 (October 2005): 239–51; Sridhar Balasubramanian, Rajagopal Raghunathan, and Vijay Mahajan, "Consumers in a Multichannel Environment: Product Utility, Process Utility, and Channel Choice," *Journal of Interactive Marketing* 19, no. 2 (Spring 2005): 12–30; Edward J. Fox, Alan L. Montgomery, and Leonard M. Lodish, "Consumer Shopping and Spending across Retail Formats," *The Journal of Business* 77, no. 2 (April 2004): S25–S60.

11. Paul F. Nunes and Frank V. Cespedes, "The Customer Has Escaped," *Harvard Business Review* (November 2003): 96–105.

12. Peter Child, Suzanne Heywood, and Michael Kilger, "Do Retail Brands Travel?" *McKinsey Quarterly* (January 2002): 11–13.

13. John Helyar, "The Only Company Wal-Mart Fears," *Fortune*, November 24, 2003, pp. 158–66. See also, Michael Silverstein and Neil Fiske, *Trading Up: The New American Luxury* (New York: Portfolio, 2003).

14. Chekitan S. Dev and Don E. Schultz, "In the Mix: A Customer-Focused Approach Can Bring the Current Marketing Mix into the 21st Century," *Marketing Management* 14 (January–February 2005).

15. Coughlan, Anderson, Stern, and El-Ansary, *Marketing Channels*, pp. 5–6.

16. For additional information on backward channels, see Marianne Jahre, "Household Waste Collection as a Reverse Channel: A Theoretical Perspective," *International Journal of Physical Distribution and Logistics* 25, no. 2 (1995): 39–55; Terrance L. Pohlen and M. Theodore Farris II, "Reverse Logistics in Plastics Recycling," *International Journal of Physical Distribution and Logistics* 22, no. 7 (1992): 35–37.

17. John Colapinto, "When I'm Sixty-Four," *New Yorker*, June 4, 2007.

18. Irving Rein, Philip Kotler, and Martin Stoller, *High Visibility* (New York: Dodd, Mead, 1987).

19. William M. Bulkeley, "Kodak Revamps Wal-Mart Kiosks," *Wall Street Journal*, September 6, 2006; Faith Keenan, "Big Yellow's Digital Dilemma," *BusinessWeek*, March 24, 2003, pp. 80–81.

20. Coughlan, Anderson, Stern, and El-Ansary, *Marketing Channels*.

21. Louis P. Bucklin, *A Theory of Distribution Channel Structure* (Berkeley: Institute of Business and Economic Research, University of California, 1966).

22. Katrijn Gielens and Marnik G. Dekimpe, "The Entry Strategies Retail Firms into Transition Economies," *Journal of Marketing* 71 (April 2007): 196–212.

23. Bridget Finn, "A Quart of Milk, a Dozen Eggs, and a 2.6-GHz Laptop," *Business 2.0* (October 2003): 58.

24. Allison Enright, "Shed New Light," *Marketing News*, May 1, 2006, pp. 9–10.

25. "Exclusives Becoming a Common Practice," *DSN Retailing Today*, February 9, 2004, pp. 38, 44.

26. "Trouser Suit," *Economist*, November 24, 2001, p. 56.

27. "2001 Industry Forecasts," *Outdoor Power Equipment*, January 1, 2001.

28. "Nike Says No to Blue-Light Specials," *Fortune*, May 4, 2005.

29. For more on relationship marketing and the governance of marketing channels, see Jan B. Heide, "Interorganizational Governance in Marketing Channels," *Journal of Marketing* (January 1994): 71–85.

30. Robert K. Heady, "Online Bank Offers Best Rates," *South Florida Sun-Sentinel*, November 22, 2004.

31. Duff McDonald, "Customer, Support Thyself," *Business 2.0* (April 2004): 56.

32. Anderson and Coughlan, "Channel Management: Structure, Governance, and Relationship Management," pp. 223–47.

33. These bases of power were identified in John R. P. French and Bertram Raven, "The Bases of Social Power," in *Studies in Social Power*, ed. Dorwin Cartwright (Ann Arbor: University of Michigan Press, 1959), pp. 150–67.

34. Bert Rosenbloom, *Marketing Channels: A Management View*, 5th ed. (Hinsdale, IL: Dryden, 1995).

35. Daniel Corsten and Nirmalya Kumar, "Do Suppliers Benefit from Collaborative Relationships with Large Retailers? An Empirical Investigation of Efficient Consumer Response Adoption," *Journal of Marketing* 69 (July 2005): 80–94.

36. Jerry Useem, "Simply Irresistible," *Fortune*, March 19, 2007, pp. 107–12; Nick Wingfield, "How

Apple's Store Strategy Beat the Odds," *Wall Street Journal*, May 17, 2006; Tobi Elkin, "Apple Gambles with Retail Plan," *Advertising Age*, June 24, 2001.

37. Thomas H. Davenport and Jeanne G. Harris, *Competing on Analytics: The New Science of Winning* (Boston: Harvard Business School Press, 2007).

38. Junhong Chu, Pradeep K. Chintagunta, and Naufel J. Vilcassim, "Assessing the Economic Value of Distribution Channels: An Application to the Personal Computer Industry," *Journal of Marketing Research* 44 (February 2007): 29–41.

39. Stefan Wuyts, Stefan Stremersch, Christophe Van Den Bulte, and Philip Hans Franses, "Vertical Marketing Systems for Complex Products: A Triadic Perspective," *Journal of Marketing Research* 41 (November 2004): 479–87.

40. Russell Johnston and Paul R. Lawrence, "Beyond Vertical Integration: The Rise of the Value-Adding Partnership," *Harvard Business Review* (July–August 1988): 94–101. See also, Arnt Bovik and George John, "When Does Vertical Coordination Improve Industrial Purchasing Relationships," *Journal of Marketing* 64 (October 2000): 52–64; Judy A. Siguaw, Penny M. Simpson, and Thomas L. Baker, "Effects of Supplier Market Orientation on Distributor Market Orientation and the Channel Relationship: The Distribution Perspective," *Journal of Marketing* (July 1998): 99–111; Narakesari Narayandas and Manohar U. Kalwani, "Long-Term Manufacturer–Supplier Relationships: Do They Pay Off for Supplier Firms?" *Journal of Marketing* (January 1995): 1–16.

41. Raji Srinivasan, "Dual Distribution and Intangible Firm Value: Franchising in Restaurant Chains," *Journal of Marketing* 70 (July 2006): 120–35.

42. http://www.citizensbank.com/.

43. http://www.disney.com/; Edward Helmore, "Media: Why House of Mouse Is Haunted by Failures," *Observer*, February 11, 2001, p. 10.

44. Rajkumar Venkatesan, V. Kumar, and Nalini Ravishanker, "Multichannel Shopping: Causes and Consequences," *Journal of Marketing* 71 (April 2007): 114–32.

45. Based on Rowland T. Moriarty and Ursula Moran, "Marketing Hybrid Marketing Systems," *Harvard Business Review* (November–December 1990): 146–55.

46. Louise Lee, "Catalogs, Catalogs, Everywhere," *BusinessWeek*, December 4, 2006, pp. 32–34.

47. Susan Casey, "Eminence Green," *Fortune*, April 2, 2007, pp. 64–70.

48. Barbara Darow, "Oracle's New Partner Path," *CRN*, August 21, 2006, p. 4.

49. Coughlan and Stern, "Marketing Channel Design and Management," pp. 247–69.

50. Matthew Boyle, "Brand Killers," *Fortune*, August 11, 2003, pp. 51–56; for an opposing view, see Anthony J. Dukes, Esther Gal-Or, and Kannan Srinivasan, "Channel Bargaining with Retailer Asymmetry," *Journal of Marketing Research* 43 (February 2006): 84–97.

51. Jerry Useem, Julie Schlosser, and Helen Kim, "One Nation under Wal-Mart," *Fortune* (Europe), March 3, 2003.

52. Alberto Sa Vinhas and Erin Anderson, "How Potential Conflict Drives Channel Structure: Concurrent (Direct and Indirect) Channels," *Journal of Marketing Research* 42 (November 2005): 507–15.

53. For an example of when conflict can be viewed as helpful, see Anil Arya and Brian Mittendorf, "Benefits of Channel Discord in the Sale of Durable Goods," *Marketing Science* 25 (January–February 2006): 91–96; and Nirmalya Kumar, "Living with Channel Conflict," *CMO Magazine* (October 2004).

54. Fareena Sultan and Andrew J. Rohm, "The Evolving Role of the Internet in Marketing Strategy: An Exploratory Study," *Journal of Interactive Marketing* (Spring 2004): 6–19.

55. This section draws on Stern and El-Ansary, *Marketing Channels*, chapter 6. See also, Jonathan D. Hibbard, Nirmalya Kumar, and Louis W. Stern, "Examining the Impact of Destructive Acts in Marketing Channel Relationships," *Journal of Marketing Research* 38 (February 2001): 45–61; Kersi D. Antia and Gary L. Frazier, "The Severity of Contract Enforcement in Interfirm Channel Relationships," *Journal of Marketing* 65 (October 2001): 67–81; James R. Brown, Chekitan S. Dev, and Dong-Jin Lee, "Managing Marketing Channel Opportunism: The Efficiency of Alternative Governance Mechanisms," *Journal of Marketing* 64 (April 2001): 51–65.

56. Andrew Kaplan, "All Together Now?" *Beverage World* (March 2007): 14–16.

57. Allison Fass, "Trading Up," *Forbes*, January 29, 2007, pp. 48–49; Diane Brady, "Coach's Split Personality," *BusinessWeek*, November 7, 2005, pp. 60–62.

58. Christina Passriello, "Fashionably Late? Designer Brands Are Starting to Embrace E-Commerce," *Wall Street Journal*, May 19, 2006.

59. Greg Johnson, "Gray Wail: Southern California Companies Are among the Many Upscale Manufacturers Voicing Their Displeasure about Middlemen Delivering Their Goods into the Hands of Unauthorized Discount Retailers," *Los Angeles Times*, March 30, 1997. Also see Paul R. Messinger and Chakravarthi Narasimhan, "Has Power Shifted in the Grocery Channel?" *Marketing Science* 14, no. 2 (Spring 1995): 189–223.

60. William G. Zikmund and William J. Stanton, "Recycling Solid Wastes: A Channels-of-Distribution Problem," *Journal of Marketing* (July 1971): 34.

61. Joel C. Collier and Carol C. Bienstock, "How Do Customers Judge Quality in an E-Tailer," *MIT Sloan Management Review* (Fall 2006): 35–40.

62. Nielsen/NetRatings, "Online Retail Report Card," press release, April 7, 2005.

63. Alexis K. J. Barlow, Noreen Q. Siddiqui, and Mike Mannion, "Development in Information and Communication Technologies for Retail Marketing Channels," *International Journal of Retail and Distribution Management* 32 (March 2004): 157–63; G&J Electronic Media Services, *7th Wave of the GfK-Online-Monitor* (Hamburg: GfK Press, 2001).

64. Heather Green, "Lessons of the Cyber Survivors," *BusinessWeek*, April 22, 2002, p. 42.

65. Sidra Durst, "Shoe In," *Business 2.0* (December 2006): 54.

66. Kate Maddox, "Online Marketing Summit Probes New Technologies," *BtoB* 92, no. 3, March 12, 2007, pp. 3, 39. Reprinted by permission.

67. Martin Holzwarth, Chris Janiszewski, and Marcus M. Newmann, "The Influence of Avatars on Online Consumer Shopping Behavior," *Journal of Marketing* 70 (October 2006): 19–36.

68. http://marketplace.publicradio.org/shows/2007/05/23/AM200705232.

69. Ann E. Schlosser, Tiffany Barnett White, and Susan M. Lloyd, "Converting Web Site Visitors into Buyers: How Web Site Investment Increases Consumer Trusting Beliefs and Online Purchase Intentions," *Journal of Marketing* 70 (April 2006): 133–48.

70. Steve Bodow, "The Care and Feeding of a Killer App," *Business 2.0* (August 2002): 76–78.

71. Ronald Abler, John S. Adams, and Peter Gould, *Spatial Organizations: The Geographer's View of the World* (Upper Saddle River, NJ: Prentice Hall, 1971), pp. 531–32.

72. "China's Pied Piper," *The Economist*, September 23, 2006, p. 80; www.alibaba.com.

73. For an in-depth academic examination, see John G. Lynch Jr. and Dan Ariely, "Wine Online: Search Costs and Competition on Price, Quality, and Distribution," *Marketing Science* 19 (Winter 2000): 83–103.

74. Described in *Inside 1-to-1*, Peppers and Rogers Group newsletter, May 14, 2001.

75. Bob Tedeshi, "How Harley Revved Online Sales," *Business 2.0* (December 2002–January 2003): 44.

76. Marc Weingarten, "The Medium Is the Instant Message," *Business 2.0* (February 2002): 98–99; Douglas Lamont, *Conquering the Wireless World: The Age of M-Commerce* (New York: Wiley, 2001).

77. Louise Story, "New Form of Impulse: Shopping via Text Message," *New York Times*, April 16, 2007; Todd Wasserman, "Publishers Test Out Text-to-Buy Feature," *Brandweek*, November 20, 2006, p. 4.

Chapter 16

1. Kerry Capell, "Fashion Conquistador," *BusinessWeek*, September 4, 2006, pp. 38–39; Rachel Tipaldy, "Zara: Taking the Lead in Fast-Fashion," *BusinessWeek*, April 4, 2006; Kasra Ferdows, Michael A. Lewis, and Jose A. D. Machuca, "Zara's Secret for Fast Fashion," *Harvard Business School Working Knowledge*, February 21, 2005; Vivian Manning-Schaffel, "Zara-Zesty," *brandchannel.com*, August 23, 2004.

2. William R. Davidson, Albert D. Bates, and Stephen J. Bass, "Retail Life Cycle," *Harvard Business Review* (November–December 1976): 89–96.

3. Stanley C. Hollander, "The Wheel of Retailing," *Journal of Marketing* (July 1960): 37–42.

4. "Click to Download," *Economist*, August 19, 2006, pp. 57–58.

5. Richard Gibson, "Even 'Copycat' Businesses Require Creativity and Flexibility," *Wall Street Journal Online*, March 2004; www.entrepreneur.com.

6. Robert Curran, "Comfort Keepers Fills Vital Niche for 'Boomers,'" *Northeast Pennsylvania Business Journal*, January 1, 2007, p. 20; www.comfortkeepers.com.

7. Anne D'Innocenzio, "Upscale Bloomingdale's Heads Down to Soho," *New York Times*, April 23, 2004.

8. Amy Merrick, Jeffrey Trachtenberg, and Ann Zimmerman, "Department Stores Fight to Preserve Role That May Be Outdated," *Wall Street Journal*, March 12, 2002; Ann Zimmerman, "Dillard's Counts on House Brands to Recapture Reputation," *Wall Street Journal*, March 2001.

9. Charles Fishman, "The Anarchist's Cookbook," *Fast Company* (July 2004): 70–78.

10. Theresa Howard, "Retail Stores Pop Up for Limited Time Only," *USA Today*, May 28, 2004.

11. "Reinventing the Store—the Future of Retailing," *Economist*, November 22, 2003, pp. 65–68.

12. "Storm Clouds over the Mall," *Economist*, October 8, 2005, pp. 71–72.

13. Wendy Liebmann, "Consumers Push Back," *Brandweek*, February 23, 2004, pp. 19–20.

14. Liebmann, "Consumers Push Back," pp. 19–20.

15. Teri Agins, "Todd Does Target," *Wall Street Journal*, April 11, 2002.

16. Cheryl Lu-Lien Tan, "Hot Kohl's," *Wall Street Journal*, April 16, 2007.

17. "Reinventing the Store—the Future of Retailing," *Economist*, November 22, 2003, pp. 65–68.

18. Jenn Abelson, "Miles Away, 'I'll Have a Burger,' " *Knight Ridder Tribune Business News*, November 5, 2006, p. 1.

19. Catherine Yang, "Maybe They Should Call Them Scammers," *BusinessWeek*, January 16, 1995, pp. 32–33; Ronald C. Goodstein, "UPC Scanner Pricing Systems: Are They Accurate?" *Journal of Marketing* (April 1994): 20–30.

20. For a listing of the key factors involved in success with an EDI system, see R. P. Vlosky, D. T. Wilson, and P. M. Smith, "Electronic Data Interchange Implementation Strategies: A Case Study," *Journal of Business & Industrial Marketing* 9, no. 4 (1994): 5–18.

21. "Business Bulletin: Shopper Scanner," *Wall Street Journal*, February 18, 1995.

22. Michael Freedman, "The Eyes Have It," *Forbes*, September 4, 2006, p. 70.

23. Matthew Boyle, "IBM Goes Shopping," *Fortune*, November 27, 2006, pp. 77–78.

24. For further discussion of retail trends, see Anne T. Coughlan, Erin Anderson, Louis W. Stern, and Adel I. El-Ansary, *Marketing Channels*, 6th ed. (Upper Saddle River, NJ: Prentice Hall, 2001).

25. Carla Rapoport with Justin Martin, "Retailers Go Global," *Fortune*, February 20, 1995, pp. 102–8; Shelley Donald Coolidge, "Facing Saturated Home Markets, Retailers Look to Rest of World," *Christian Science Monitor*, February 14, 1994, p. 7.

26. Amy Merrick, "Asking 'What Would Ann Do?' " *Wall Street Journal*, September 15, 2006.

27. Ann Zimmerman and Kris Hudson, "Chasing Upscale Customers Tarnishes Mass-Market Jeweler," *Wall Street Journal*, June 26, 2006; Kris Hudson, "Signet Sparkles with Jewelry Strategy," *Wall Street Journal*, June 26, 2006.

28. Jessi Hempel, "Urban Outfitters, Fashion Victim," *BusinessWeek*, July 17, 2006, p. 60.

29. Robert Berner, "To Lure Teenager Mall Rats, You Need the Right Cheese," *BusinessWeek*, June 7, 2004, pp. 96–101.

30. Kimberly L. Allers, "Retail's Rebel Yell," *Fortune*, November 10, 2003, pp. 137–42.

31. Laurence H. Wortzel, "Retailing Strategies for Today's Marketplace," *Journal of Business Strategy* (Spring 1987): 45–56.

32. Mark Tatge, "Fun & Games," *Forbes*, January 12, 2004, pp. 138–44.

33. Nanette Byrnes, "What's Beyond for Bed Bath & Beyond," *BusinessWeek*, January 19, 2004, pp. 48–50.

34. Robert Berner, "JCPenney Gets the Net," *BusinessWeek*, May 7, 2007, p. 70; Anne D'Innocenzio, "Penney's Uses Net to Boost Traffic and Image," *Marketing News*, April 1, 2006, pp. 29–30; Robert Berner, "Penney: Back in Fashion," *BusinessWeek*, January 9, 2006, pp. 82–84.

35. Uta Werner, John McDermott, and Greg Rotz, "Retailers at the Crossroads: How to Develop Profitable New Growth Strategies," *Journal of Business Strategy* 25, no. 2 (2004): 10–17.

36. Robert Berner, "Chanel's American in Paris," *BusinessWeek*, January 29, 2007, pp. 70–71.

37. Cecilie Rohwedder, "Viva la Differenza," *Wall Street Journal*, January 29, 2003.

38. Deborah Orr, "The Cheap Gourmet," *Forbes*, April 10, 2006, pp. 76–77; Amy Wu, "A Specialty Food Store with a Discount Attitude," *New York Times*, July 27, 2003.

39. Venkatesh Shankar and Ruth N. Bolton, "An Empirical Analysis of Determinants of Retailer Pricing Strategy," *Marketing Science* 23 (Winter 2004): 28–49.

40. Duncan Simester, "Signaling Price Image Using Advertised Prices," *Marketing Science* 14 (Summer 1995): 166–88; see also, Jiwoong Shin, "The Role of Selling Costs in Signaling Price Image," *Journal of Marketing Research* 42 (August 2005): 305–12.

41. Frank Feather, *The Future Consumer* (Toronto: Warwick Publishing, 1994), p. 171. Also see David R. Bell and James M. Lattin, "Shopping Behavior and Consumer Preference for Retail Price Format: Why 'Large Basket' Shoppers Prefer EDLP," *Marketing Science* 17 (Spring 1998): 66–68; Stephen J. Hoch, Xavier Dreeze, and Mary E. Purk, "EDLP, Hi-Lo, and Margin Arithmetic," *Journal of Marketing* (October 1994): 1–15.

42. Sarah Fister Gale, "The Bookstore Battle," *Workforce Management* (January 2004): 51–53.

43. Constance L. Hays, "Retailers Seeking to Lure Customers with Service," *New York Times*, December 1, 2003.

44. Amy Gillentine, "Marketing Groups Ignore Women at Their Own Peril," *Colorado Springs Business Journal*, January 20, 2006; Mary Lou Quinlan, "Women Aren't Buying It," *Brandweek*, June 2, 2003, pp. 20–22.

45. Cametta Coleman, "Kohl's Retail Racetrack," *Wall Street Journal*, March 1, 2000.

46. Justin Hibbard, "Put Your Money Where Your Mouth Is," *BusinessWeek*, September 18, 2006, pp. 61–63.

47. Mindy Fetterman and Jayne O'Donnell, "Just Browsing at the Mall? That's What *You* Think," *USA Today*, September 1, 2006.

48. "Reinventing the Store," *Economist*, November 22, 2003, pp. 65–68; Moira Cotlier, "Census Releases First E-Commerce Report," *Catalog Age*, May 1, 2001; Associated Press, "Online Sales Boomed at End of 2000," *Star-Tribune of Twin Cities*, February 17, 2001; Kenneth T. Rosen and Amanda L. Howard, "E-Tail: Gold Rush or Fool's Gold?" *California Management Review*, April 1, 2000, pp. 72–100.

49. Velitchka D. Kaltcheva and Barton Weitz, "When Should a Retailer Create an Exciting Store Environment?" *Journal of Marketing* 70 (January 2006): 107–18.

50. For more discussion, see Philip Kotler, "Atmospherics as a Marketing Tool," *Journal of Retailing* (Winter 1973–1974): 48–64. Also see B. Joseph Pine II and James H. Gilmore, *The Experience Economy* (Boston: Harvard Business School Press, 1999).

51. Jeff Cioletti, "Super Marketing," *Beverage World* (November 2006): 60–61.

52. Carol Tice, "Anchors Away: Department Stores Lose Role at Malls," *Puget Sound Business Journal*, February 13, 2004, p. 1.

53. R. L. Davies and D. S. Rogers, eds., *Store Location and Store Assessment Research* (New York: John Wiley, 1984).

54. Sara L. McLafferty, *Location Strategies for Retail and Service Firms* (Lexington, MA: Lexington Books, 1987).

55. www.plma.com (accessed May 2007).

56. Sonia Reyes, "Saving Private Labels," *Brandweek*, May 8, 2006, pp. 30–34.

57. Matthew Boyle, "Brand Killers," *Fortune*, August 11, 2003, pp. 88–100.

58. Kusum Ailawadi and Bari Harlam, "An Empirical Analysis of the Determinants of Retail Margins: The Role of Store-Brand Share," *Journal of Marketing* 68 (January 2004): 147–65.

59. Boyle, "Brand Killers," pp. 88–100; William C. Copacino, *Supply Chain Management* (Boca Raton, FL: St. Lucie Press, 1997).

60. Kenji Hall, "Zen and the Art of Selling Minimalism," *BusinessWeek*, April 9, 2007, p. 45; Rob Walker, "Musuem Quality," *New York Times Magazine*, January 9, 2005, p. 25.

61. Jeanne Whalen, "Betting $10 Billion on Generics, Novartis Seeks to Inject Growth," *Wall Street Journal*, May 4, 2006.

62. Michael Felding, "No Longer Plain, Simple," *Marketing News*, May 15, 2006, pp. 11–13; Rob Walker, "Shelf Improvement," *New York Times*, May 7, 2006.

63. Sonia Reyes, "Saving Private Labels," *Brandweek*, May 8, 2006, pp. 30–34.

64. James A. Narus and James C. Anderson, "Contributing as a Distributor to Partnerships with Manufacturers," *Business Horizons* (September–October 1987). Also see James D. Hlavecek and Tommy J. McCuistion, "Industrial Distributors—When, Who, and How," *Harvard Business Review* (March–April 1983): 96–101.

65. Nirmalya Kumar and Jan-Benedict E. M. Steenkamp, *Private Label Strategy: How to Meet the Store-Brand Challenge* (Boston: Harvard Business School Press, 2007).

66. www.grainger.com.

67. Narus and Anderson, "Contributing as a Distributor to Partnerships with Manufacturers." Also see Hlavecek and McCuistion, "Industrial Distributors—When, Who, and How," pp. 96–101.

68. Brett Nelson, "Stuck in the Middle," *Forbes*, August 15, 2005, p. 88.

69. Copacino, *Supply Chain Management*.

70. John Heilemann, "All the News That's Fit for Bits," *Business 2.0* 7, no. 8 (September 2006): 40.

71. "Cargo Cults," *Economist: A Survey of Logistics*, June 17, 2006, pp. 9–14.

72. Anthony Bianco, "Wal-Mart's Midlife Crisis," *BusinessWeek*, April 30, 2007, pp. 46–56; Matthew Maier, "How to Beat Wal-Mart," *Business 2.0* (May 2005); Jerry Useem, "Should We Admire Wal-Mart?" *Fortune*, March 8, 2004, pp. 118–21; www.walmart.com.

73. Rita Koselka, "Distribution Revolution," *Forbes*, May 25, 1992, pp. 54–62.

74. The optimal order quantity is given by the formula $Q^* = 2DS/IC$, where D=annual demand, S=cost to place one order, and I=annual carrying cost per unit. Known as the economic-order quantity formula, it assumes a constant ordering cost, a constant cost of carrying an additional unit in inventory, a known demand, and no quantity discounts. For further reading on this subject, see Richard J. Tersine, *Principles of Inventory and Materials Management*, 4th ed. (Upper Saddle River, NJ: Prentice Hall, 1994).

75. Copacino, *Supply Chain Management*, pp. 122–23.

76. "Shining Examples," *Economist: A Survey of Logistics*, June 17, 2006, pp. 4–6.

77. Renee DeGross, "Retailers Try eBay Overstocks, Returns for Sale Online," *Atlanta Journal-Constitution*, April 10, 2004.

78. Chuck Salter, "Savvy, with Hints of Guile and Resourcefulness," *Fast Company* 112 (February 2007): 50; Heather Mcpherson, "Lots to Like about This Concept: As a Wine Negociant, Cameron Hughes Can Offer Premium Wines at Affordable Prices," *Knight Ridder Tribune Business News*, February 21, 2007, p. 1.

79. "Manufacturing Complexity," *Economist: A Survey of Logistics*, June 17, 2006, pp. 6–9.

80. Chad Terhune, "Pepsi's Supply Chain Fix," *Wall Street Journal*, June 6, 2006.

Chapter 17

1. Randall Rothenberg, "Dove Effort Gives Packaged-Goods Marketers Lessons for the Future," *Advertising Age*, March 5, 2007; Theresa Howard, "Ad Campaign Tells Women to Celebrate Who They Are," *USA Today*, July 8, 2005; Jack Neff, "In Dove Ads, Normal Is the New Beautiful," *Advertising Age*, September 27, 2004; www.campaignforrealbeauty.com.
2. Xueming Luo and Naveen Donthu, "Marketing's Credibility: A Longitudinal Investigation of Marketing Communication Productivity and Shareholder Value," *Journal of Marketing* 70 (October 2006): 70–91.
3. David Kiley, "Hey Advertisers, TiVo Is Your Friend," *BusinessWeek*, October 17, 2005, pp. 97–98; Linda Kaplan Thaler and Robin Koval with Delia Marshall, *Bang! Getting Your Message Heard in a Noisy World* (New York: Currency, 2003).
4. Anthony Bianco, "The Vanishing Mass Market," *BusinessWeek*, July 12, 2004, pp. 60–68; Susan Thea Posnock, "It Can Control Madison Avenue," *American Demographics* (February 2004): 28–33; Jennifer Pendleton, "Multi TASKERS," *Advertising Age*, March 29, 2004, pp. S1, S8; Christopher Reynolds, "Game Over," *American Demographics* (February 2004): 34–38; Noreen O'Leary, "The 30-Second Spot Is Dead, Long Live the 30-Second Spot," *Adweek*, November 17, 2003, pp. 12–21; Hank Kim, "Madison Ave. Melds Pitches and Content," *Advertising Age*, October 7, 2002, pp. 1, 14.
5. Louise Story, "Viewers Fast-Forwarding Past Ads? Not Always," *New York Times*, February 16, 2007; Abbey Klaassen, "Major Turnoff: McKinsey Slams TV Selling Power," *Advertising Age*, August 7, 2006, pp. 1, 33. See also, Ron Briggs and Greg Stuart, *What Sticks: Why Most Advertising Fails and How to Guarantee Yours Succeeds* (New York: Kaplan Business, 2006).
6. Louise Story, "Anywhere the Eye Can See, It's Likely to See an Ad," *New York Times*, January 15, 2007; Laura Petrecca, "Product Placement–You Can't Escape It," *USA Today*, October 11, 2006.
7. Stuart Elliott, "Nike Reaches Deeper into New Media to Find Young Buyers," *Wall Street Journal*, October 31, 2006.
8. Some of these definitions are adapted from Peter D. Bennett, ed., *Dictionary of Marketing Terms* (Chicago: American Marketing Association, 1995).
9. Tom Duncan and Sandra Moriarty, "How Integrated Marketing Communication's 'Touch Points' Can Operationalize the Service-Dominant Logic," in *The Service-Dominant Logic of Marketing: Dialog, Debate, and Directions*, ed. Robert F. Lusch and Stephen L. Vargo (Armonk, NY: M.E. Sharpe, 2006); Tom Duncan, *Principles of Advertising and IMC*, 2nd ed. (New York, NY: McGraw-Hill/Irwin, 2005).
10. Joseph W. Alba and J. Wesley Hutchinson, "Dimensions of Consumer Expertise," *Journal of Consumer Research* 13 (March 1987): 411–53.
11. Amanda Fung, "Duplication Effort," *Crain's New York Business* 22, no. 37, September 11, 2006, p. 2; Kate Maddox, "Integrated Marketing Success Stories," *BtoB* 91, no. 28, August 14, 2006, p. 28.
12. For an alternate communications model developed specifically for advertising communications, see Barbara B. Stern, "A Revised Communication Model for Advertising: Multiple Dimensions of the Source, the Message, and the Recipient," *Journal of Advertising* (June 1994): 5–15. For some additional perspectives, see Tom Duncan and Sandra E. Morarity, "A Communication-Based Marketing Model for Managing Relationships," *Journal of Marketing* (April 1998): 1–13.
13. Demetrios Vakratsas and Tim Ambler, "How Advertising Works: What Do We Really Know?" *Journal of Marketing* 63, no. 1 (January 1999): 26–43.
14. This section is based on the excellent text, John R. Rossiter and Larry Percy, *Advertising and Promotion Management*, 2nd ed. (New York: McGraw-Hill, 1997).
15. James F. Engel, Roger D. Blackwell, and Paul W. Minard, *Consumer Behavior*, 9th ed. (Fort Worth, TX: Dryden, 2001).
16. Rossiter and Percy, *Advertising and Promotion Management*.
17. Engel, Blackwell, and Minard, *Consumer Behavior*.
18. Ayn E. Crowley and Wayne D. Hoyer, "An Integrative Framework for Understanding Two-Sided Persuasion," *Journal of Consumer Research* (March 1994): 561–74.
19. C. I. Hovland, A. A. Lumsdaine, and F. D. Sheffield, *Experiments on Mass Communication*, vol. 3 (Princeton, NJ: Princeton University Press, 1948), chapter 8; Crowley and Hoyer, "An Integrative Framework for Understanding Two-Sided Persuasion." For an alternative viewpoint, see George E. Belch, "The Effects of Message Modality on One- and Two-Sided Advertising Messages," in *Advances in Consumer Research*, ed. Richard P. Bagozzi and Alice M. Tybout (Ann Arbor, MI: Association for Consumer Research, 1983), pp. 21–26.
20. Curtis P. Haugtvedt and Duane T. Wegener, "Message Order Effects in Persuasion: An Attitude Strength Perspective," *Journal of Consumer Research* (June 1994): 205–18; H. Rao Unnava, Robert E. Burnkrant, and Sunil Erevelles, "Effects of Presentation Order and Communication Modality on Recall and Attitude," *Journal of Consumer Research* (December 1994): 481–90.

21. Sternthal and Craig, *Consumer Behavior,* pp. 282–84.

22. Michael R. Solomon, *Consumer Behavior,* 7th ed. (Upper Saddle River, NJ: Prentice Hall, 2007).

23. Some recent research on humor in advertising, for example, includes: Haseeb Shabbir and Des Thwaites, "The Use of Humor to Mask Deceptive Advertising: It's No Laughing Matter," *Journal of Advertising* 36 (Summer 2007): 75–85; Thomas W. Cline and James J. Kellaris, "The Influence of Humor Strength and Humor Message Relatedness on Ad Memorability: A Dual Process Model;" *Journal of Advertising* 36 (Spring 2007): 55–67; H. Shanker Krishnan and Dipankar Chakravarti, "A Process Analysis of the Effects of Humorous Advertising Executions on Brand Claims Memory," *Journal of Consumer Psychology* 13, no. 3 (2003): 230–45.

24. Rik Pieters and Michel Wedel, "Attention Capture and Transfer in Advertising: Brand, Pictorial, and Text-Size Effects," *Journal of Marketing* 68 (April 2004): 36–50.

25. NPD Celebrity Influence Study 2005, NPD Group.

26. Herbert C. Kelman and Carl I. Hovland, "Reinstatement of the Communication in Delayed Measurement of Opinion Change," *Journal of Abnormal and Social Psychology* 48 (July 1953): 327–35.

27. David J. Moore, John C. Mowen, and Richard Reardon, "Multiple Sources in Advertising Appeals: When Product Endorsers Are Paid by the Advertising Sponsor," *Journal of the Academy of Marketing Science* (Summer 1994): 234–43.

28. www.accenture.com; Mary Ellen Podmolik, "Accenture Turns to Tiger for Global Marketing Effort," *BtoB* 89, no. 12, October 25, 2004; Sean Callahan, "Tiger Tees Off in New Accenture Campaign," *BtoB* 88, no. 11, October 13, 2003.

29. Julie Sloane, "Gorgeous George," *Fsb: Fortune Small Business* (June 2003): 36.

30. C. E. Osgood and P. H. Tannenbaum, "The Principles of Congruity in the Prediction of Attitude Change," *Psychological Review* 62 (January 1955): 42–55.

31. "EU to Try Again on Tobacco Advertising Ban," *Associated Press,* May 9, 2001; Richard C. Morais, "Mobile Mayhem," *Forbes,* July, 6 1998, p. 138; "Working in Harmony," *Soap Perfumery & Cosmetics,* July 1, 1998, p. 27; Rodger Harrabin, "A Commercial Break for Parents," *Independent,* September 8, 1998, p. 19; Naveen Donthu, "A Cross-Country Investigation of Recall of and Attitude toward Comparative Advertising," *Journal of Advertising* 27 (June 1998): 111.

32. "Rebirth of a Salesman," *Economist,* April 14, 2001.

33. Michael Kiely, "Word-of-Mouth Marketing," *Marketing* (September 1993): 6. See also, Aric Rindfleisch and Christine Moorman, "The Acquisition and Utilization of Information in New Product Alliances: A Strength-of-Ties Perspective," *Journal of Marketing* (April 2001): 1–18.

34. Ian Mount, "Marketing," *Business 2.0* (August–September 2001): 84.

35. Michael Arndt, "Burrito Buzz–And So Few Ads," *BusinessWeek,* March 12, 2007, pp. 84–85.

36. David Kiley, "Hey Advertisers, TiVo Is Your Friend," *BusinessWeek,* October 17, 2005, pp. 97–98.

37. www.msnbc.msn.com/id/16921137/.

38. Steve Miller, "Mini Making Big Claims about Mileage in New Push," *Brandweek,* June 4, 2007, p. 7; Barnaby Feder, "Billboards That Know You by Name," *New York Times,* January 29, 2007; www.kellyawardsgallery.org/; Burt Helm, "For Your Eyes Only," *BusinessWeek,* July 31, 2006, pp. 66–67; Warren Berger, "Dare-Devils," *Business 2.0* (April 2004): 111–16; Karen Lundegaard, "BMW 'Mini' Campaign: Odd to the Max," *Wall Street Journal,* February 28, 2002; John Gaffney, "Most Innovative Campaign," *Business 2.0* (May 2002): 98–99.

39. Adapted from G. Maxwell Ule, "A Media Plan for 'Sputnik' Cigarettes," *How to Plan Media Strategy* (American Association of Advertising Agencies, 1957 Regional Convention), pp. 41–52.

40. Thomas C. Kinnear, Kenneth L. Bernhardt, and Kathleen A. Krentler, *Principles of Marketing,* 6th ed. (New York: HarperCollins College Div., 1995).

41. Terrence Sing, "Integrated Marketing More Than Just an Internet Brochure," *Pacific Business News,* February 18, 2004, p. 23.

42. K. Sridhar Moorthy and Scott A. Hawkins, "Advertising Repetition and Quality Perceptions," *Journal of Business Research* 58 (March 2005): 354–60; Amna Kirmani and Akshay R. Rao, "No Pain, No Gain: A Critical Review of the Literature on Signaling Unobservable Product Quality," *Journal of Marketing* 64 (April 2000): 66–79; Amna Kirmani, "The Effect of Perceived Advertising Costs on Brand Perceptions," *Journal of Consumer Research* 17, September 17, 1990, pp. 160–71; Amna Kirmani and Peter Wright, "Money Talks: Perceived Advertising Expense and Expected Product Quality," *Journal of Consumer Research* 16 (December 1989): 344–53.

43. Demetrios Vakratsas and Tim Ambler, "How Advertising Works: What Do We Really Know?" *Journal of Marketing* 63, no. 1 (January 1999): 26–43.

44. Chris Daniels, "B-to-B Creaks Comms Barrier," *PRweek* 10, no. 22, June 4, 2007.

45. Levitt, *Industrial Purchasing Behavior: A Study in Communication Effects.*

46. Kate Maddox, "Integrated Marketing Success Stories," *BtoB* 91, no. 10, August 14, 2006.

47. Prasad A. Naik and Kalyan Raman, "Understanding the Impact of Synergy in Multimedia Communications," *Journal of Marketing Research* 40 (November 2003): 375–88. See also, Prasad A. Naik, Kalyan Raman, and Russell S. Winer, "Planning Marketing-Mix Strategies in the Presence of Interaction Effects," *Marketing Science* 24 (January 2005): 25–34.

48. Janet Stilson, "Wide-Ranging Deals Help ESPN Score with Marketers," *Advertising Age*, March 12, 2007, p. S-2.

49. Ernan Roman, *Integrated Direct Marketing: The Cutting Edge Strategy for Synchronizing Advertising, Direct Mail, Telemarketing, and Field Sales* (Lincolnwood, IL: NTC Business Books, 1995).

50. Scott Neslin, *Sales Promotion*, MSI Relevant Knowledge Series (Cambridge, MA: Marketing Science Institute, 2002).

51. Gerry Khermouch, "The Top 5 Rules of the Ad Game," *BusinessWeek*, January 20, 2003, pp. 72–73.

52. Heather Green, "Online Ads Take Off Again," *BusinessWeek*, May 5, 2003, p. 75.

53. Maria Puente, "Online Experience Is Now a Much Better Fit," *USA Today*, December 4, 2002.

54. "A White Paper on the Status, Scope, and Future of IMC," eds. Tom Duncan and Frank Mulhern.

55. Suzy Bashford, "Collaboration Is Imperative," *Marketing*, December 13, 2006, p. 4.

56. Ellen Neuborne, "Ads That Actually Sell Stuff," *Business 2.0* (June 2004): 78.

57. Sreedhar Madhavaram, Vishag Badrinarayanan, and Robert E. McDonald, "Integrated Marketing Communication (IMC) and Brand Identity as Critical Components of Brand Equity Strategy," *Journal of Advertising* 34 (Winter 2005): 69–80; Mike Reid, Sandra Luxton, and Felix Mavondo, "The Relationship between Integrated Marketing Communication, Market Orientation, and Brand Orientation," *Journal of Advertising* 34 (Winter 2005): 11–23.

58. Don E. Schultz and Heidi Schultz, *IMC, The Next Generation: Five Steps for Delivering Value and Measuring Financial Returns* (New York: McGraw-Hill, 2003); Don E. Shultz, Stanley I. Tannenbaum, and Robert F. Lauterborn, *Integrated Marketing Communications: Putting It Together and Making It Work* (Lincolnwood, IL: NTC Business Books, 1992).

59. Deborah L. Vance, "Better Coverage," *Marketing News*, January 15, 2007, pp. 13–14; Barry Janoff, "State Farm Asks, 'Now What?' " *Brandweek*, August 8, 2006.

Chapter 18

1. Adam Armbruster, "Geico Takes Varied Roads to Consumers," *Television Week*, March 12, 2007, p. 10; Rob Walker, "Pop-Culture Evolution," *New York Times Magazine*, April 15, 2007.

2. Paul F. Nunes and Jeffrey Merrihue, "The Continuing Power of Mass Advertising," *Sloan Management Review* (Winter 2007): 63–69.

3. Jack Neff, " 'Broken' Ad Model Holds Big Advantages for P&G," *Advertising Age*, March 5, 2007.

4. Russell H. Colley, *Defining Advertising Goals for Measured Advertising Results* (New York: Association of National Advertisers, 1961).

5. William L. Wilkie and Paul W. Farris, "Comparison Advertising: Problem and Potential," *Journal of Marketing* (October 1975): 7–15.

6. "Responses to Comparative Advertising," *Journal of Consumer Research* 32 (March 2006): 530–40; Dhruv Grewal, Sukumar Kavanoor, and James Barnes, "Comparative versus Noncomparative Advertising: A Meta-Analysis," *Journal of Marketing* (October 1997): 1–15; Randall L. Rose, Paul W. Miniard, Michael J. Barone, Kenneth C. Manning, and Brian D. Till, "When Persuasion Goes Undetected: The Case of Comparative Advertising," *Journal of Marketing Research* (August 1993): 315–30.

7. For a good discussion, see David A. Aaker and James M. Carman, "Are You Overadvertising?" *Journal of Advertising Research* (August–September 1982): 57–70.

8. Donald E. Schultz, Dennis Martin, and William P. Brown, *Strategic Advertising Campaigns* (Chicago: Crain Books, 1984), pp. 192–97.

9. Rajesh Chandy, Gerard J. Tellis, Debbie MacInnis, and Pattana Thaivanich, "What to Say When: Advertising Appeals in Evolving Markets," *Journal of Marketing Research* 38, no. 4 (November 2001); Gerard J. Tellis, Rajesh Chandy, and Pattana Thaivanich, "Decomposing the Effects of Direct Advertising: Which Brand Works, When, Where, and How Long?" *Journal of Marketing Research* 37 (February 2000): 32–46.

10. See, George S. Low and Jakki J. Mohr, "Brand Managers' Perceptions of the Marketing Communications Budget Allocation Process" (Cambridge, MA: Marketing Science Institute, Report No. 98-105, March 1998); and their "The Advertising Sales Promotion Trade-Off: Theory and Practice" (Cambridge, MA: Marketing Science Institute, Report No. 92-127, October 1992). Also see Gabriel J. Beihal and Daniel A. Sheinen, "Managing the Brand in a Corporate Advertising Environment: A Decision-Making Framework for

Brand Managers," *Journal of Advertising* 17, June 22, 1998, p. 99.

11. For an excellent review, see Greg Allenby and Dominique Hanssens, "Advertising Response," Marketing Science Institute, *Special Report*, No. 05-200, 2005.

12. Demetrios Vakratsas, Fred M. Feinberg, Frank M. Bass, and Gurumurthy Kalyanaram, "The Shape of Advertising Response Functions Revisited: A Model of Dynamic Probabilistic Thresholds," *Marketing Science* 23, no. 1 (Winter 2004): 109–19.

13. Leonard M. Lodish, Magid Abraham, Stuart Kalmenson, Jeanne Livelsberger, Beth Lubetkin, Bruce Richardson, and Mary Ellen Stevens, "How T.V. Advertising Works: A Meta-Analysis of 389 Real-World Split Cable T.V. Advertising Experiments," *Journal of Marketing Research* 32 (May 1995): 125–39.

14. Greg Allenby and Dominique Hanssens, "Advertising Response," Marketing Science Institute, *Special Report*, No. 05-200, 2005; Jack Neff, "TV Doesn't Sell Package Goods," *Advertising Age*, May 24, 2004, pp. 1, 30.

15. Cleve Langton, "Searching for the Holy Global Ad Grail," *Brandweek*, June 5, 2006, p. 16.

16. Jessi Hempel, "Crowdsourcing: Milk the Masses for Inspiration," *BusinessWeek*, September 25, 2006, p. 38.

17. Todd Wasserman, "Intelligence Gathering," *Brandweek* 47, no. 25, June 19, 2006, pp. S8–S15, S18; Catherine P. Taylor, "Chevy's Crash, Burn," *Adweek* 47, no. 16, April 17, 2006, p. 14.

18. Kathleen Sampey, "Q&A: Aflac CMO Herbert," *Adweek*, October 16, 2006; Ron Insana, "Insurance Business Just Ducky for AFLAC," *USA Today*, July 5, 2005; Chad Bray, "If It Quacks, It May Be an Insurance Ad," *Wall Street Journal*, April 2, 2003; Stuart Elliott, "Why a Duck? Because It Sells Insurance," *New York Times*, June 24, 2002.

19. www.stateofthenewsmedia.org/2007/narrative_newspapers_intro.asp?media=3.

20. Brian Steinberg, "Unisys Pitch Finds the I in Niche: Key Executives Are Targeted with *Fortune* 'Cover Shots,' Billboards on Commutes." *Wall Street Journal*, Oct. 24, 2006, p. B4. Reprinted by permission of Dow Jones via Copyright Clearance Center.

21. Andrew McMains, " 'Absolut World' Debuts," *Adweek*, April 27, 2007; Stuart Elliott, "In an 'Absolut World,' " a Vodka Could Use the Same Ads for More than 25 Years," *New York Times*, April 27, 2007; Theresa Howard, "Absolut Gets into Spirit of Name Play with New Ads," *USA Today*, January 16, 2006.

22. www.stateofthenewsmedia.org/2007/narrative_radio_audience.asp?cat=2&media=9.

23. David Ogilvy, *Ogilvy on Advertising* (New York: Vintage Books, 1983).

24. "Motel 6 Receives Hermes and Silver GALAXY Awards for 2002 Advertising Campaigns," Business Editors/Travel Writers, *Business Wire*, November 22, 2002.

25. James P. Miller, "Bitter Sweets Fight Ended," *Chicago Tribune*, May 12, 2007; Avery Johnson, "How Sweet It Isn't: Maker of Equal Says Ads for J&J's Splenda Misled; Chemistry Lesson for Jurors," *Wall Street Journal*, April 6, 2007.

26. For further reading, see Dorothy Cohen, *Legal Issues in Marketing Decision Making* (Cincinnati, OH: South-Western, 1995).

27. Kim Bartel Sheehan, *Controversies in Contemporary Advertising* (Thousand Oaks, CA: Sage, 2003).

28. Eleftheria Parpis, "Dove's 'Evolution' Is All to the Good," *Adweek*, April 25, 2007; www.awny.org/.

29. Schultz et al., *Strategic Advertising Campaigns*, p. 340.

30. Herbert E. Krugman, "What Makes Advertising Effective?" *Harvard Business Review* (March–April 1975): 98.

31. Prashant Malaviya, "The Moderating Influence of Advertising Context on Ad Repetition Effects: The Role of Amount and Type of Elaboration," *Journal of Consumer Research* 34 (June 2007): 32–40.

32. Thomas H. Davenport and John C. Beck, *The Attention Economy: Understanding the New Currency of Business* (Boston: Harvard Business School Press, 2000).

33. Susan Thea Posnock, "It Can Control Madison Avenue," *American Demographics* (February 2004): 29–33.

34. James Betzold, "Jaded Riders Are Ever-Tougher Sell," *Advertising Age*, July 9, 2001; Michael McCarthy, "Ads Are Here, There, Everywhere," *USA Today*, June 19, 2001; Michael McCarthy, "Critics Target 'Omnipresent' Ads," *USA Today*, April 16, 2001; Kipp Cheng, "Captivating Audiences," *Brandweek*, November 29, 1999.

35. Jeremy Mullman, "Foster's Wants to Be Your Drinking Buddy," *Advertising Age*, August 7, 2006, p. 8; Aaron O. Patrick, "Foster's to Launch Web-Only U.S. Ad Strategy," *Wall Street Journal*, August 3, 2006.

36. Sam Jaffe, "Easy Riders," *American Demographics* (March 2004): 20–23.

37. Max Chafkin, "Ads and Atmospherics," *Inc.* (February 2007).

38. www.oaaa.org/.

39. Jeff Pelline, "New Commercial Twist in Corporate Restrooms," *San Francisco Chronicle*, October 6, 1986.

40. Belinda Archer, "Outdoor Media: Digital Formats: Weblinks: Airport Advertising Flies into the Future," *Guardian*, June 25, 2007, p. 2.

41. www.prwebdirect.com/releases/2007/3/prweb511540.htm.

42. Brian Steinberg and Suzanne Vranica, "Prime-Time TV's New Guest Stars: Products," *Wall Street Journal*, January 13, 2004.

43. Jane Weaver, "A License to Shill," *MSNBC News*, November 17, 2002.

44. John Lippman and Rick Brooks, "Hot Holiday Flick Pairs FedEx, Hanks," *Wall Street Journal*, December 11, 2000; Joanne Lipman, "Product Placement Can Be Free Lunch," *Wall Street Journal*, November 25, 1991.

45. Warren Berger, "That's Advertainment," *Business 2.0* (March 2003): 91–95.

46. Laura Petrecca, "Wal-Mart TV Sells Marketers Flexibility," *USA Today*, March 29, 2007; Matthew Boyle, "Hey Shoppers: Ads on Aisle 7!" *Fortune*, November 24, 2003.

47. www.popai.com/AM/Template.cfm?Section=Industry.

48. Richard Linnett, " 'Friends' Tops TV Price Chart," *Advertising Age*, September 15, 2003, pp. 1, 46.

49. For more on other media context effects, see Michael A. Kamins, Lawrence J. Marks, and Deborah Skinner, "Television Commercial Evaluation in the Context of Program-Induced Mood: Congruency versus Consistency Effects," *Journal of Advertising* (June 1991): 1–14; see also, Jing Wang and Bobby J. Calder, "Media Transportation and Advertising," *Journal of Consumer Research* 33 (September 2006): 151–62.

50. Kenneth R. Lord, Myung-Soo Lee, and Paul L. Sauer, "Program Context Antecedents of Attitude toward Radio Commercials," *Journal of the Academy of Marketing Science* (Winter 1994): 3–15; Kenneth R. Lord and Robert E. Burnkrant, "Attention versus Distraction: The Interactive Effect of Program Involvement and Attentional Devices on Commercial Processing," *Journal of Advertising* (March 1993): 47–60.

51. Roland T. Rust, *Advertising Media Models: A Practical Guide* (Lexington, MA: Lexington Books, 1986).

52. Hani I. Mesak, "An Aggregate Advertising Pulsing Model with Wearout Effects," *Marketing Science* (Summer 1992): 310–26; Fred M. Feinberg, "Pulsing Policies for Aggregate Advertising Models," *Marketing Science* (Summer 1992): 221–34.

53. Josephine L. C. M. Woltman Elpers, Michel Wedel, and Rik G. M. Pieters, "Why Do Consumers Stop Viewing Television Commercials? Two Experiments on the Influence of Moment-to-Moment Entertainment and Information Value," *Journal of Marketing Research* 40 (November 2003): 437–53.

54. See, for example, Antonio G. Chessa and Jaap M. J. Murre, "A Neurocognitive Model of Advertisement Content and Brand-Name Recall," *Marketing Science* 26 (January–February 2007): 130–41.

55. David B. Montgomery and Alvin J. Silk, "Estimating Dynamic Effects of Market Communications Expenditures," *Management Science* (June 1972): 485–501; Kristian S. Palda, *The Measurement of Cumulative Advertising Effect* (Upper Saddle River, NJ: Prentice Hall, 1964), p. 87.

56. www.infores.com; Lodish et al., "How T.V. Advertising Works."

57. Gerard J. Tellis, Rajesh K. Chandy, and Pattana Thaivanich, "Which Ad Works, When, Where, and How Often? Modeling the Effects of Direct Television Advertising," *Journal of Marketing Research* 37 (February 2000): 32–46; Ajay Kalra and Ronald C. Goodstein, "The Impact of Advertising Positioning Strategies on Consumer Price Sensitivity," *Journal of Marketing Research* (May 1998): 210–24; Anil Kaul and Dick R. Wittink, "Empirical Generalizations about the Impact of Advertising on Price Sensitivity and Price," *Marketing Science* 14, no. 3, pt. 1 (Summer 1995): G151–60; David Walker and Tony M. Dubitsky, "Why Liking Matters," *Journal of Advertising Research* (May–June 1994): 9–18; Abhilasha Mehta, "How Advertising Response Modeling (ARM) Can Increase Ad Effectiveness," *Journal of Advertising Research* (May–June 1994): 62–74; John Deighton, Caroline Henderson, and Scott Neslin, "The Effects of Advertising on Brand Switching and Repeat Purchasing," *Journal of Marketing Research* (February 1994): 28–43; Karin Holstius, "Sales Response to Advertising," *International Journal of Advertising* 9, no. 1 (September 1990): 38–56.

58. Nigel Hollis, "The Future of Tracking Studies," *Admap* (October 2004): 151–53.

59. Laura Petrecca and Theresa Howard, "Nielsen Wants to Track Who Watches Commercials," *USA Today*, July 11, 2006.

60. From, Robert C. Blattberg and Scott A. Neslin, *Sales Promotion: Concepts, Methods, and Strategies* (Upper Saddle River, NJ: Prentice Hall, 1990). This text provides the most comprehensive and analytical treatment of sales promotion to

date. An extremely up-to-date and comprehensive review of academic work on sales promotions can be found in Scott Neslin, "Sales Promotion," in *Handbook of Marketing*, ed. Bart Weitz and Robin Wensley (London: Sage, 2002), pp. 310–38.

61. Kusum Ailawadi, Karen Gedenk, and Scott A. Neslin, "Heterogeneity and Purchase Event Feedback in Choice Models: An Empirical Analysis with Implications for Model Building," *International Journal of Research in Marketing* 16 (September 1999): 177–98. See also, Kusum L. Ailawadi, Karen Gedenk, Christian Lutzky, and Scott A. Neslin, "Decomposition of the Sales Impact of Promotion-Induced Stockpiling," *Journal of Marketing Research* 44 (August 2007); Eric T. Anderson and Duncan Simester, "The Long-Run Effects of Promotion Depth on New versus Established Customers: Three Field Studies," *Marketing Science* 23, no. 1 (Winter 2004): 4–20; Luc Wathieu, A. V. Muthukrishnan, and Bart J. Bronnenberg. "The Asymmetric Effect of Discount Retraction on Subsequent Choice," *Journal of Consumer Research* 31 (December 2004): 652–65; Praveen Kopalle, Carl F. Mela, and Lawrence Marsh, "The Dynamic Effect of Discounting on Sales: Empirical Analysis and Normative Pricing Implications," *Marketing Science* 18 (Summer 1999): 317–32.

62. Carl Mela, Kamel Jedidi, and Douglas Bowman, "The Long-Term Impact of Promotions on Consumer Stockpiling," *Journal of Marketing Research* 35, no. 2 (May 1998): 250–62.

63. Harald J. Van Heerde, Sachin Gupta, and Dick Wittink, "Is 75% of the Sales Promotion Bump Due to Brand Switching? No, Only 33% Is," *Journal of Marketing Research* 40 (November 2003): 481–91; Harald J. Van Heerde, Peter S. H. Leeflang, and Dick R. Wittink, "The Estimation of Pre- and Postpromotion Dips with Store-Level Scanner Data," *Journal of Marketing Research* 37, no. 3 (August 2000): 383–95.

64. Paul W. Farris and John A. Quelch, "In Defense of Price Promotion," *Sloan Management Review* (Fall 1987): 63–69.

65. Roger A. Strang, "Sales Promotion: Fast Growth, Faulty Management," *Harvard Business Review* (July–August 1976): 116–19.

66. For a good summary of the research on whether promotion erodes the consumer franchise of leading brands, see Blattberg and Neslin, *Sales Promotion*.

67. AutoVIBES, *AutoBeat Daily*, March 3, 2004; Karen Lundegaard and Sholnn Freeman, "Detroit's Challenge: Weaning Buyers from Years of Deals," *Wall Street Journal*, January 6, 2004.

68. Robert George Brown, "Sales Response to Promotions and Advertising," *Journal of Advertising Research* (August 1974): 36–37. Also see Kamel Jedidi, Carl F. Mela, and Sunil Gupta, "Managing Advertising and Promotion for Long-Run Profitability," *Marketing Science* 18, no. 1 (Winter 1999): 1–22; Carl F. Mela, Sunil Gupta, and Donald R. Lehmann, "The Long-Term Impact of Promotion and Advertising on Consumer Brand Choice," *Journal of Marketing Research* (May 1997): 248–61; Purushottam Papatla and Lakshman Krishnamurti, "Measuring the Dynamic Effects of Promotions on Brand Choice," *Journal of Marketing Research* (February 1996): 20–35.

69. "Bronze Reggie: Winners," *Brandweek* 48, no. 73, March 26, 2007, pp. R21+; Tammy la Gorce, "For Card-Carrying Members, Lounging at the Mall," *New York Times*, December 24, 2006.

70. Magid M. Abraham and Leonard M. Lodish, "Getting the Most out of Advertising and Promotion," *Harvard Business Review* (May–June 1990): 50–60. See also, Shuba Srinivasan, Koen Pauwels, Dominique Hanssens, and Marnik Dekimpe, "Do Promotions Benefit Manufacturers, Retailers, or Both?" *Management Science* 50, no. 5 (May 2004): 617-629.

71. Lodish et al., "How T.V. Advertising Works."

72. For a model for setting sales promotions objectives, see David B. Jones, "Setting Promotional Goals: A Communications Relationship Model," *Journal of Consumer Marketing* 11, no. 1 (1994): 38–49.

73. Kusum L. Ailawadi, Bari A. Harlam, Jacques Cesar, and David Trounce, "Promotion Profitability for a Retailer: The Role of Promotion, Brand, Category, and Store Characteristics," *Journal of Marketing Research* 43 (November 2006): 518–36.

74. www.pmalink.org/awards/; Jane L. Levere, "Body by Milk: More Than Just a White Mustache," *New York Times*, August 30, 2006.

75. See, John C. Totten and Martin P. Block, *Analyzing Sales Promotion: Text and Cases*, 2nd ed. (Chicago: Dartnell, 1994), pp. 69–70.

76. Miguel Gomez, Vithala Rao, and Edward McLaughlin, "Empirical Analysis of Budget and Allocation of Trade Promotions in the U.S. Supermarket Industry," *Journal of Marketing Research* 44 (August 2007); Norris Bruce, Preyas S. Desai, and Richard Staelin, "The Better They Are, the More They Give: Trade Promotions of Consumer Durables," *Journal of Marketing Research* 42 (February 2005): 54–66.

77. Kusum L. Ailawadi and Bari Harlam, "An Empirical Analysis of the Determinants of Retail Margins: The Role of Store Brand Share," *Journal of Marketing* 68 (January 2004): 147–66; Kusum L. Ailawadi, "The Retail Power-Performance Conundrum: What Have We Learned?" *Journal of Retailing* 77, no. 3 (Fall 2001): 299–318; Paul W. Farris and Kusum L. Ailawadi, "Retail Power: Monster or Mouse?" *Journal of Retailing* (Winter 1992): 351–69; Koen Pauwels, "How Retailer and Competitor Decisions Drive the Long-Term Effectiveness of Manufacturer Promotions," *Journal of Retailing*, in press.

78. Rajiv Lal, J. Little, and J. M. Vilas-Boas, "A Theory of Forward Buying, Merchandising, and Trade Deals," *Marketing Science* 15, no. 1 (Winter 1996): 21–37; "Retailers Buy Far in Advance to Exploit Trade Promotions," *Wall Street Journal*, October 9, 1986.

79. Christopher Hosford, "Avoiding Trade Show Faux Pas: Six Tips Exhibitors Should Know," *Inc.* (June 2007): 33–34. Reprinted by permission of Inc. via Copyright Clearance Center.

80. www.pmalink.org/awards/.

81. Arthur Stern, "Measuring the Effectiveness of Package-Goods Promotion Strategies," paper presented to the Association of National Advertisers, Glen Cove, New York, February 1978.

82. Kurt H. Schaffir and H. George Trenten, *Marketing Information Systems* (New York: Amacom, 1973), p. 81.

83. Joe A. Dodson, Alice M. Tybout, and Brian Sternthal, "Impact of Deals and Deal Retraction on Brand Switching," *Journal of Marketing Research* (February 1978): 72–81.

84. Books on sales promotion include Totten and Block, *Analyzing Sales Promotion: Text and Cases;* Don E. Schultz, William A. Robinson, and Lisa A. Petrison, *Sales Promotion Essentials*, 2nd ed. (Lincolnwood, IL: NTC Business Books, 1994); John Wilmshurst, *Below-the-Line Promotion* (Oxford, England: Butterworth/Heinemann, 1993); Blattberg and Neslin, *Sales Promotion: Concepts, Methods, and Strategies.* For an expert systems approach to sales promotion, see John W. Keon and Judy Bayer, "An Expert Approach to Sales Promotion Management," *Journal of Advertising Research* (June–July 1986): 19–26.

85. From internal company sources.

86. Philip Kotler, "Atmospherics as a Marketing Tool," *Journal of Retailing* (Winter 1973–1974): 48–64.

87. Kathleen Kerwin, "When the Factory Is a Theme Park," *BusinessWeek*, May 3, 2004, p. 94; Vanessa O'Connell, " 'You-Are-There' Advertising," *Wall Street Journal*, August 5, 2002.

88. "Personal Care Marketers: Who Does What," *IEG Sponsorship Report*, April 16, 2007, p. 4.

89. "New Frito-Lay Brand Seeks to Rise above Pack with Event Ties," *IEG Sponsorship Report*, April 16, 2007, p. 7.

90. Bettina Cornwell, Michael S. Humphreys, Angela M. Maguire, Clinton S. Weeks, and Cassandra Tellegen, "Sponsorship-Linked Marketing: The Role of Articulation in Memory," *Journal of Consumer Research* 33 (December 2006): 312–21.

91. Hilary Cassidy, "So You Want to Be an Olympic Sponsor?" *Brandweek*, November 7, 2005, pp. 24–28.

92. "The Biggest Thing: Activation Holds Key to Sponsorship Success," *IEG Sponsorship Report*, April 2, 2007, pp. 1–3.

93. "Bank's New Department, Deals Reflect Elevated Sponsorship Status," *IEG Sponsorship Report*, April 16, 2007, pp. 1, 8.

94. The Association of National Advertisers has a useful source: *Event Marketing: A Management Guide*, which is available at www.ana.net/bookstore.

95. Cornwell et al., "Sponsorship-Linked Marketing."

96. Constantine von Hoffman, "Buying Up the Bleachers," *Brandweek*, February 19, 2007, pp. 18–21.

97. Clint White, "Making Your Sponsorship Work Harder," talk given at IEG 24th Annual Sponsorship Conference, March 13, 2007.

98. Kelley Gates, "Wild in the Streets," *Brand Marketing* (February 2001): 54.

99. Dwight W. Catherwood and Richard L. Van Kirk, *The Complete Guide to Special Event Management* (New York: John Wiley, 1992).

100. William L. Shankin and John Kuzma, "Buying That Sporting Image," *Marketing Management* (Spring 1992): 65.

101. "The Sponsorship Factor," *IEG Sponsorship Report*, April 2, 2007, p. 7.

102. Peter Post, "Beyond Brand—The Power of Experience Branding," *ANA/ Advertiser* (October–November 2000).

103. B. Joseph Pine and James H. Gilmore, *The Experience Economy: Work Is Theatre and Every Business a Stage* (Cambridge, MA: Harvard University Press, 1999).

104. Arlene Weintrub, "Chairman of the Board," *BusinessWeek*, May 28, 2001, p. 96.

105. "2006 Experiential Marketing Study," www.jackmorton.com.

106. Karen Axelrod and Bruce Brumberg, *Watch It Made in the U.S.A.* (Santa Fe, NM: John Muir Publications, 1997).

107. For an excellent account, see Thomas L. Harris, *The Marketer's Guide to Public Relations* (New York: John Wiley, 1991). Also see Harris, *Value-Added Public Relations* (Chicago: NTC Business Books, 1998).
108. Chuck Salter, "Lessons from the Tarmac," *Fast Company* (May 2007): 31–32.
109. "Do We Have a Story for You!" *Economist*, January 21, 2006, pp. 57–58; Al Ries and Laura Ries, *The Fall of Advertising and the Rise of PR* (New York: HarperCollins, 2002).
110. For further reading on cause-related marketing, see P. Rajan Varadarajan and Anil Menon, "Cause-Related Marketing: A Co-Alignment of Marketing Strategy and Corporate Philanthropy," *Journal of Marketing* (July 1988): 58–74.
111. Stefan Nurpin, "From Brand out of Mind to Brand in Hand: Brand Unification by Icons, Totems, and Titans," talk given at IEG's 24th Annual Sponsorship Conference, March 13, 2007.
112. Arthur M. Merims, "Marketing's Stepchild: Product Publicity," *Harvard Business Review* (November–December 1972): 111–12. Also see Katherine D. Paine, "There Is a Method for Measuring PR," *Marketing News*, November 6, 1987, p. 5.

Chapter 19

1. Louise Story, "The High Price of Creating Free Ads," *New York Times*, May 26, 2007; Laura Petrecca, "Madison Avenue Wants You! (or at Least Your Videos)," *USA Today*, June 21, 2007; Eric Pfanner, "Leave It to the Professionals? Hey, Let Consumers Make Their Own Ads," *New York Times*, August 4, 2006; Kenneth Hein, "Coke's Web Formula Is a Work in Progress," *Brandweek*, September 4, 2006, p. 9.
2. The terms *direct-order marketing* and *direct-relationship marketing* were suggested as subsets of direct marketing by Stan Rapp and Tom Collins in *The Great Marketing Turnaround* (Upper Saddle River, NJ: Prentice Hall, 1990).
3. Ran Kivetz and Itamar Simonson, "The Idiosyncratic Fit Heuristic: Effort Advantage as a Determinant of Consumer Response to Loyalty Programs," *Journal of Marketing Research* 40 (November 2003): 454–67; Ran Kivetz and Itamar Simonson, "Earning the Right to Indulge: Effort as a Determinant of Customer Preferences toward Frequency Program Rewards," *Journal of Marketing Research* 39 (May 2002): 155–70.
4. Michael McCarthy, "Direct Marketing Gets Cannes Do Spirit," *USA Today*, June 17, 2002.
5. "DMA's 2006 'Power of Direct Marketing' Reports," *Direct Marketing Association*, June 5, 2007; "Direct Marketing's Growth Rate to Cushion Cooling U.S. Economy," *Direct Marketing Association*, October 17, 2006; Carol Krol, "Direct Hits It Big." *BtoB*, October 10, 2005, pp. 29–31.
6. "Lands' End Shines a Beacon on Its Brand," *BusinessWeek*, November 9, 2005; Amy Merrick, "Sears Orders Fashion Makeover from the Lands' End Catalog," *Wall Street Journal*, January 28, 2004; Chana R. Schoenberger, "Web? What Web?" *Forbes*, June 10, 2002, p. 132; Amy Merrick, "Keep It Fresh," *Wall Street Journal*, December 10, 2001.
7. Stan Rapp and Thomas L. Collins, *Maximarketing* (New York: McGraw-Hill, 1987).
8. www.the-dma.org.
9. "On the Mat," *Economist*," November 26, 2005, p. 78.
10. Bob Stone, *Successful Direct Marketing Methods*, 6th ed. (Lincolnwood, IL: NTC Business Books, 1996). Also see David Shepard Associates, *The New Direct Marketing*, 2nd ed. (Chicago: Irwin, 1995); Amiya K. Basu, Atasi Basu, and Rajeev Batra, "Modeling the Response Pattern to Direct Marketing Campaigns," *Journal of Marketing Research* (May 1995): 204–12.
11. Carol Krol, "Kodak Develops Direct for SOHO," *BtoB* 92, no. 4, April 2, 2007, p. 14.
12. Edward L. Nash, *Direct Marketing: Strategy, Planning, Execution*, 4th ed. (New York: McGraw-Hill, 2000).
13. Rachel McLaughlin, "Get the Envelope Opened!" *Target Marketing* (September 1998): 37–39.
14. "Case Study: The Phoenician Utilizes IDM," *Relationship Marketing Insights Newsletter*, Issue #5, 2006.
15. The *average customer longevity* (*N*) is related to the *customer retention rate* (*CR*). Suppose the company retains 80% of its customers each year. Then the average customer longevity is given by: $N = 1/(1 - CR) = 1/.2 = 5$.
16. Lorie Grant, "Niche Catalogs' Unique Gifts Make Money Less of an Object," *USA Today*, November 20, 2003; Olivia Barker, "Catalogs Are Complementary with Online Sales, Purchases," *USA Today*, December 4, 2002.
17. Cacilie Rohwedder, "U.S. Mail-Order Firms Shake Up Europe—Better Service, Specialized Catalogs Find Eager Shoppers," *Wall Street Journal*, January 6, 1998; Kathleen Kiley, "B-to-B Marketers High on Overseas Sales," *Catalog Age*, January 1, 1997, p. 8.
18. www.blackbox.com; www.multichannelmerchant.com.
19. www.ftc.gov/donotcall/.

20. "Customer Service Champs," *BusinessWeek*, March 5, 2007; "USAA Receives Chairman's Award," *San Antonio Business Journal*, June 20, 2002.

21. Jim Edwards, "The Art of the Infomercial," *Brandweek*, September 3, 2001, pp. 14–19.

22. Charles Duhigg, "Telemarketing Thieves Sharpen Their Focus on the Elderly," *New York Times*, May 20, 2007.

23. Tony Case, "Growing Up," *Interactive Quarterly*, April 19, 2004, pp. 32–34.

24. David L. Smith and Karen McFee, "Media Mix 101: Online Media for Traditional Marketers," accessed September 2003, at http://advantage.msn.com/articles/MediaMix101_2.asp.

25. Kenneth Hein, "Industry Turns Page on Page View Stats," *Brandweek*, June 4, 2007, p. 6; Paul C. Judge, "Will Online Ads Ever Click?" *Fast Company* (March 2001): 181–92.

26. Emily Steel, "Advertising's Brave New World," *Wall Street Journal*, May 25, 2007; Johnnie L. Roberts, "How to Count Eyeballs," *Newsweek*, November 27, 2006, p. 42.

27. Online Publisher's Association, "OPA Media Consumption Study," January 2002.

28. Michael Applebaum, "A Matter of Timing," *Brandweek IQ*, July 10, 2006, pp. 22–24.

29. Ellen Byron, "Estée Lauder Tests Web-Ad Waters," *Wall Street Journal*, September 19, 2006.

30. Kevin J. Delaney, "Once-Wary Industry Giants Embrace Internet Advertising," *Wall Street Journal*, April 17, 2006.

31. Asim Ansari and Carl F. Mela, "E-Customization," *Journal of Marketing Research* 40, no. 2 (May 2003): 131–45.

32. Daniel Michaels and J. Lynn Lunsford, "Ad-Sales Woes Likely to Continue," *Wall Street Journal*, December 4, 2006; Jack Neff, "Axe Cuts Past Competitors, Claims Market Lead," *Advertising Age*, May 14, 2006; Byron Acohido, "Rich Media Enriching PC Ads," *USA Today*, February 25, 2004.

33. Catherine Holahan, "Raising the Bar on Viral Web Ads," *BusinessWeek*, July 23, 2006; Robert Berner, "How Unilever Scored with Young Guys," *BusinessWeek*, May 23, 2005; Thomas Mucha, "Spray Here. Get Girl," *Business 2.0* (June 2003).

34. Philip Kotler, *According to Kotler* (New York: American Management Association, 2005).

35. Peter J. Danaher, Guy W. Mullarkey, and Skander Essegaier, "Factors Affecting Web Site Visit Duration: A Cross-Domain Analysis," *Journal of Marketing Research* 43 (May 2006): 182–94.

36. Jeffrey F. Rayport and Bernard J. Jaworski, *e-commerce* (New York: McGraw-Hill, 2001), p. 116.

37. Bob Tedeschi, "E-Commerce Report," *New York Times*, June 24, 2002.

38. Jan-Benedict E. M. Steenkamp and Inge Geyskens, "How Country Characteristics Affect the Perceived Value of Web Sites," *Journal of Marketing* 70 (July 2006): 136–50.

39. Allison Fass, "A Kingdom Seeks Magic," *Forbes*, October 16, 2006, pp. 68–70; David Kiley, "The Craziest Ad Guys in America," *BusinessWeek*, May 22, 2006, pp. 72–80; www.subservientchicken.com.

40. "Prime Clicking Time," *Economist*, May 31, 2003, p. 65; Ben Elgin, "Search Engines Are Picking Up Steam," *BusinessWeek*, March 24, 2003, pp. 86–87.

41. Ned Desmond, "Google's Next Runaway Success," *Business 2.0* (November 2002): 73.

42. Heather Green, "Online Ads Take Off Again," *BusinessWeek*, May 5, 2003, p. 75.

43. Puneet Manchanda, Jean-Pierre Dubé, Khim Yong Goh, and Pradeep K. Chintagunta, "The Effects of Banner Advertising on Internet Purchasing," *Journal of Marketing Research* 43 (February 2006): 98–108; "Pay per Sale," *Economist*, October 1, 2005, p. 62.

44. Paul Sloan, "The Quest for the Perfect Online Ad," *Business 2.0* (March 2007): 88–93; Catherine Holahan, "The Promise of Online Display Ads," *BusinessWeek*, May 1, 2007.

45. Jessica Mintz, "Microsoft Adds Behavioral Targeting," *Associated Press*, December 28, 2006.

46. Stephen Baker, "Pop-Up Ads Had Better Start Pleasing," *BusinessWeek*, December 8, 2003, p. 40.

47. Youngme Moon, "BMW Films," Harvard Business School Case #9-5-2-046.

48. Brian Morrissey, "Clients Try to Manipulate 'Unpredictable' Viral Buzz," *Adweek*, March 22, 2007; Devin Leonard, "Viral Ads: It's an Epidemic," *Fortune*, October 2, 2006, pp. 61–62.

49. Heather Green, "Searching for the Pod of Gold," *BusinessWeek*, November 14, 2005, pp. 88–90.

50. Heather Green, "It Takes a Web Village," *BusinessWeek*, September 4, 2006, p. 66; Paul Dwyer, "Measuring the Value of Word of Mouth and Its Impact in Consumer Communities," MSI Report No. 06-118, *Marketing Science Institute*, Cambridge, MA.

51. Seth Godin, *Permission Marketing: Turning Strangers into Friends and Friends into Customers* (New York: Simon & Schuster, 1999).

52. Chana R. Schoenberger, "Web? What Web?" *Forbes*, June 10, 2002, p. 132.

53. Suzanne Vranica, "Marketers Give E-Mail Another Look," *Wall Street Journal*, July 17, 2006.

54. Amol Sharma, "Companies Vie for Ad Dollars on Mobile Web," *Wall Street Journal*, January 17, 2007; Amol Sharma, "T-Mobile Readies New Web Phones and Hangs Up on a Star Pitchwoman," *Wall Street Journal*, September 26, 2006.

55. Brooks Barnes, "Toyota Aims Young, Sponsors Fox Spinoff for Cell Phone Screens," *Wall Street Journal*, April 24, 2006; Matt Richtel, "Verizon to Allow Ads on Its Mobile Phones," *New York Times*, December 26, 2006.

56. For a thorough review of relevant academic literature, see Christophe Van Den Bulte and Stefan Wuyts, *Social Networks and Marketing*, Marketing Science Institute Relevant Knowledge Series, Cambridge, MA, 2007.

57. Louise Story, "What We Talk About When We Talk About Brands," *New York Times*, November 24, 2006.

58. Brian Morrisey, "Niche Social Networks Offer Target Practice," *Adweek* 48, no. 15, April 9, 2007, p. 11; www.adweek.com/aw/iq_interactive/article_display.jsp?vnu_content_id=1003556820.

59. Elizabeth Wellington, "Freebies and Chitchat Are Hot Marketing Tools," *Philadelphia Inquirer*, December 31, 2003; Bob Sperber, "Krispy Kreme Word-of-Mouth Tactics Continue to Go against the Grain," *Brandweek*, October 21, 2002, p. 9.

60. Renée Dye, "The Buzz on Buzz," *Harvard Business Review* (November–December 2000): 139–46.

61. Chip Heath, "Give 'Em Something to Talk About," *Fast Company* 116 (June 2007): 58+.

62. http://discussions.apple.com/index.jspa; http://socialize.morningstar.com/newsocialize/asp/coverpage.asp?pgid=hetabdi; www.fool.com/; Nanette Byrnes, "Leader of the Packs," *BusinessWeek*, October 31, 2005; www.quickbooksgroup.com.

63. Dave Balter and John Butman, "Clutter Cutter," *Marketing Management* (July–August 2006): 49–50.

64. Emanuel Rosen, *The Anatomy of Buzz* (New York: Currency, 2000).

65. George Silverman, *The Secrets of Word-of-Mouth Marketing* (New York: Amacom, 2001); Emanuel Rosen, *The Anatomy of Buzz* (New York: Currency, 2000), chapter 12; "Viral Marketing," *Sales & Marketing Automation* (November 1999): 12–14.

66. Renée Dye, "The Buzz on Buzz," *Harvard Business Review* (November–December 2000): 139.

67. www.willitblend.com; www.blendtec.com; Jon Fine, "Ready to Get Weird, Advertisers?" *BusinessWeek*, January 8, 2007, p. 24; Paul Gillin, "Podcasting, Blogs Cause Major Boost," *BtoB* 92, no. 5 (May 2007): 32.

68. Gregg Cebryznisky, "Checkers' Rapcat Raises Issue of 'Edginess' in Online Promos," *Nation's Restaurant News* 41, no. 10, March 5, 2007, pp. 4+.

69. Robert Berner, "I Sold It through the Grapevine," *BusinessWeek*, May 29, 2006, pp. 32–34.

70. Barbara Kiviat, "Word on the Street," *Time*, April 12, 2007; Dave Balter, "Rules of the Game," *Advertising Age Point* (December 2005): 22–23; Scott Kirsner, "How Much Can You Trust Buzz?" *Boston Globe*, November 14, 2005; Linda Tischler, "What's the Buzz?" *Fast Company* (May 2004): 76–77.

71. Danielle Sacks, "Down the Rabbit Hole," *Fast Company* (November 2006): 86–93; "Fast Talk," *Fast Company* (September 2006): 21–24.

72. Jacqueline Johnson Brown, Peter M. Reingen, and Everett M. Rogers, *Diffusion of Innovations*, 4th ed. (New York: Free Press, 1995); J. Johnson Brown and Peter Reingen, "Social Ties and Word-of-Mouth Referral Behavior," *Journal of Consumer Research* 14, 3 (December 1987): 350–62; Peter H. Riengen and Jerome B. Kernan, "Analysis of Referral Networks in Marketing: Methods and Illustration," *Journal of Marketing Research* (November 1986): 37–78.

73. Malcolm Gladwell, *The Tipping Point: How Little Things Can Make a Big Difference* (Boston: Little, Brown & Company, 2000).

74. Douglas Atkin, *The Culting of Brands: When Customers Become True Believers* (New York: Penguin, 2004); Marian Salzman, Ira Matathia, and Ann O'Reilly, *Buzz: Harness the Power of Influence and Create Demand* (New York: John Wiley, 2003).

75. Dave Balter and John Butman, "Clutter Cutter," *Marketing Management* (July–August 2006): 49–50; "Is There a Reliable Way to Measure Word-of-Mouth Marketing?" *Marketing NPV* 3, no. 3 (2006): 3–9.

76. Claire Cain Miller, "The Sweet Spot," *Forbes*, April 23, 2007, p. 41.

77. David Kiley, "Ford on the Web, Warts and All," *BusinessWeek*, October 30, 2006, pp. 68–71; Jonathan Fahey, "Candid Camera," *Forbes*, November 13, 2006, pp. 124–26.

78. Stephen Baker, "Looking for a Blog in a Haystack," *BusinessWeek*, July 25, 2006, p. 38.

79. Heather Green, "The Big Shots of Blogdom," *BusinessWeek*, May 7, 2007.

80. Pew Internet & American Life Project, July 2006; www.pewinternet.org/.

81. Todd Wasserman, "Report: Consumers Don't Trust Blogs," *Brandweek*, September 4, 2006, p. 10; For an academic discussion of chat rooms, recommendation sites, and customer review sections online, see Dina Mayzlin, "Promotional

Chat on the Internet," *Marketing Science* 25 (March–April 2006): 155–63; and Judith Chevalier and Dina Mayzlin, "The Effect of Word of Mouth on Sales: Online Book Reviews," *Journal of Marketing Research* 43 (August 2006): 345–54.

82. Kim Hart, "Angry Customers Use Web to Shame Firms," *Washington Post*, July 5, 2006.

83. This section is based on an excellent summary, "Is There a Reliable Way to Measure Word-of-Mouth Marketing?" *Marketing NPV* 3, no. 3 (2006): 3–9, available at www.marketingnpv.com.

84. www.bls.gov/oco/reprints/ocor012.pdf.

85. Jon Bello, "Sell Like Your Outfit Is at Stake. It Is," *BusinessWeek Online*, February 5, 2004.

86. Bill Keenan, "Cost-per-Call Data Deserve Scrutiny," *Industry Week*, January 10, 2000.

87. Adapted from Robert N. McMurry, "The Mystique of Super-Salesmanship," *Harvard Business Review* (March–April 1961): 114. Also see William C. Moncrief III, "Selling Activity and Sales Position Taxonomies for Industrial Sales Forces," *Journal of Marketing Research* (August 1986): 261–70.

88. Thomas A. Stewart and David Champion, "Leading Change from the Top Line," *Harvard Business Review* (July–August 2006): 90–97.

89. Lawrence G. Friedman and Timothy R. Furey, *The Channel Advantage: Going to Marketing with Multiple Sales Channels* (Oxford, UK: Butterworth-Heinemann, 1999).

90. Philip Kotler, Neil Rackham, and Suj Krishnaswamy, "Ending the War between Sales & Marketing," *Harvard Business Review* (July–August 2006): 68–78; Timothy M. Smith, Srinath Gopalakrishna, and Rubikar Chaterjee, "A Three-Stage Model of Integrated Marketing Communications at the Marketing-Sales Interface," *Journal of Marketing Research* 43 (November 2006): 546–79.

91. Christopher Hosford, "Rebooting Hewlett-Packard," *Sales and Marketing Management* 158, no. 6 (July–August 2006): 32+.

92. Michael Copeland, "Hits and Misses," *Business 2.0* (April 2004): 142.

93. "Sales Performance Benchmarks," *Go-to-Market Strategies*, June 5, 2007.

94. Julia Chang, "Sales 2.0," *Sales and Marketing Management* (April 2007): 31–34.

95. Sonke Albers, "Sales-Force Management—Compensation, Motivation, Selection, and Training," in *Handbook of Marketing*, ed. Bart Weitz and Robin Wensley (London: Sage, 2002), pp. 248–66.

96. Cliff Edwards, "Death of a Pushy Salesman," *BusinessWeek*, July 3, 2006, pp. 108–9.

97. Nanette Byrnes, "Avon Calling—Lots of New Reps," *BusinessWeek*, June 2, 2003, pp. 53–54.

98. Michael R. W. Bommer, Brian F. O'Neil, and Beheruz N. Sethna, "A Methodology for Optimizing Selling Time of Salespersons," *Journal of Marketing Theory and Practice* (Spring 1994): 61–75. See also, Lissan Joseph, "On the Optimality of Delegating Pricing Authority to the Sales Force," *Journal of Marketing* 65 (January 2001): 62–70.

99. Dartnell Corporation, 30th Sales-Force Compensation Survey. Other breakdowns show that 12.7% is spent in service calls, 16% in administrative tasks, 25.1% in telephone selling, and 17.4% in waiting/traveling.

100. James A. Narus and James C. Anderson, "Industrial Distributor Selling: The Roles of the Outside and Inside Sales Forces," *Industrial Marketing Management* 15, 1 (February 1986): 55–62.

101. Willem Verbeke and Richard P. Bagozzi, "Sales-Call Anxiety: Exploring What It Means When Fear Rules a Sales Encounter," *Journal of Marketing* 64 (July 2000): 88–101.

102. Gilbert A. Churchill Jr., Neil M. Ford, Orville C. Walker Jr., Mark W. Johnston, and John F. Tanner, *Sales-Force Management*, 6th ed. (Homewood, IL: Irwin, 1998). Also see Eric G. Harris, John C. Mowen, and Tom J. Brown, "Reexamining Salesperson Goal Orientations: Personality Influencers, Customer Orientation, and Work Satisfaction," *Journal of the Academy of Marketing Science* 33, no. 1 (Winter 2005): 19–35; Manfred Krafft, "An Empirical Investigation of the Antecedents of Sales-Force Control Systems," *Journal of Marketing* 63 (July 1999): 120–34; Wujin Chu, Eitan Gerstner, and James D. Hess, "Costs and Benefits of Hard Sell," *Journal of Marketing Research* (February 1995): 97–102; Murali K. Mantrala, Prabhakant Sinha, and Andris A. Zoltners, "Structuring a Multiproduct Sales Quota-Bonus Plan for a Heterogeneous Sales Force: A Practical Model-Based Approach," *Marketing Science* 13, no. 2 (Spring 1994): 121–44; Jhinuk Chowdhury, "The Motivational Impact of Sales Quotas on Effort," *Journal of Marketing Research* (February 1993): 28–41.

103. Eilene Zimmerman, "Quota Busters," *Sales & Marketing Management* (January 2001): 59–63.

104. Peter Burrows, "The Era of Efficiency," *BusinessWeek*, June 18, 2001, p. 92; Melanie Warner, "Confessions of a Control Freak," *Fortune*, September 4, 2000, p. 30.

105. Lisa Vaas, "Oracle Teaches Its Sales Force to Play Nice," *eWeek*, July 28, 2004; Lisa Vaas, "Oracle's Sales Force Reorg Finally Bears Fruit," *eWeek*, December 17, 2003; Ian Mount, "Out of Control," *Business 2.0* (August 2002): 38–44.

106. Philip M. Posdakoff and Scott B. MacKenzie, "Organizational Citizenship Behaviors and Sales-Unit Effectiveness," *Journal of Marketing Research* (August 1994): 351–63. See also, Andrea L. Dixon, Rosann L. Spiro, and Magbul Jamil, "Successful and Unsuccessful Sales Calls: Measuring Salesperson Attributions and Behavioral Intentions," *Journal of Marketing* 65 (July 2001): 64–78; Willem Verbeke and Richard P. Bagozzi, "Sales-Call Anxiety: Exploring What It Means When Fear Rules a Sales Encounter," *Journal of Marketing* 64 (July 2000): 88–101.

107. Neil Rackham, *SPIN Selling* (New York: McGraw-Hill, 1988). Also see his *The SPIN Selling Fieldbook* (New York: McGraw-Hill, 1996); James Lardner, "Selling Salesmanship," *Business 2.0* (December 2002–January 2003): 66; Sharon Drew Morgen, *Selling with Integrity: Reinventing Sales through Collaboration, Respect, and Serving* (New York: Berkeley Books, 1999); Neil Rackham and John De Vincentis, *Rethinking the Sales Force* (New York: McGraw-Hill, 1996).

108. Some of the following discussion is based on W. J. E. Crissy, William H. Cunningham, and Isabella C. M. Cunningham, *Selling: The Personal Force in Marketing* (New York: John Wiley, 1977), pp. 119–29.

109. Joel E. Urbany, "Justifying Profitable Pricing," Working Paper Series, Marketing Science Institute, Report No. 00-117, 2000, pp. 17–18.

110. George R. Franke and Jeong-Eun Park, "Salesperson Adaptive Selling Behavior and Customer Orientation: A Meta-Analysis," *Journal of Marketing Research* 43 (November 2006): 693–702; Richard G. McFarland, Goutam N. Challagalla, and Tasadduq A. Shervani, "Influence Tactics for Effective Adaptive Selling," *Journal of Marketing* 70 (October 2006): 103–17.

Chapter 20

1. Michael Arndt, "3M's Rising Star," *BusinessWeek*, April 12, 2004, pp. 62–74; Mark Tatge, "Prescription for Growth," *Forbes*, February 17, 2003, pp. 65–66; Michael Arndt, "3M: A Lab for Growth?" *BusinessWeek*, January 21, 2002, pp. 50–51.

2. Amy Barrett, "J&J: Reinventing How It Invents," *BusinessWeek*, April 17, 2006, pp. 60–61.

3. For some scholarly reviews, see Ely Dahan and John R. Hauser, "Product Development: Managing a Dispersed Process," in *Handbook of Marketing*, ed. Bart Weitz and Robin Wensley (London: Sage, 2002), pp. 179–222; Dipak Jain, "Managing New-Product Development for Strategic Competitive Advantage," chapter 6 in *Kellogg on Marketing*, ed. Dawn Iacobucci (New York: John Wiley, 2001), pp. 130–48; Jerry Wind and Vijay Mahajan, "Issues and Opportunities in New-Product Development: An Introduction to the Special Issue," *Journal of Marketing Research* 34 (February 1997): 1–12.

4. Deborah Ball and Sarah Ellison, "Nestlé's Appetite for Acquisitions Quickens," *Wall Street Journal*, August 7, 2002.

5. Scott Sanderude, "Growth from Harvesting the Sky: The $200 Million Challenge," talk at Marketing Science Institute Conference: New Frontiers for Growth, Boston, MA, April 2005.

6. Stephen J. Carson, "When to Give Up Control of Outsourced New-Product Development," *Journal of Marketing* 71 (January 2007): 49–66.

7. "Don't Laugh at Gilded Butterflies," *Economist*, April 24, 2004, pp. 71–73. For some academic discussion of the effects of new-product introductions on markets, see Harald J. Van Heerde, Carl F. Mela, and Puneet Manchanda, "The Dynamic Effect of Innovation on Market Structure," *Journal of Marketing Research* 41 (May 2004): 166–83.

8. www-935.ibm.com/services/us/gbs/bus/pdf/g510-6310-executive-brief-enabling-multifaceted.pdf.

9. Sungwook Min, Manohar U. Kalwani, and William T. Robinson, "Market Pioneer and Early Follower Survival Risks: A Contingency Analysis of Really New versus Incrementally New Product-Markets," *Journal of Marketing* 70 (January 2006): 15–33; C. Page Moreau, Arthur B. Markman, and Donald R. Lehmann, " 'What Is It?' Category Flexibility and Consumers' Response to Really New Products," *Journal of Consumer Research* 27 (March 2001): 489–98.

10. Stefan Wuyts, Shantanu Dutta, and Stefan Stremersch, "Portfolios of Interfirm Agreements in Technology-Intensive Markets: Consequences for Innovation and Profitability," *Journal of Marketing* 68 (April 2004): 88–100; Aric Rindfleisch and Christine Moorman, "The Acquisition and Utilization of Information in New-Product Alliance: A Strength-of-Ties Perspective," *Journal of Marketing* 65 (April 2001): 1–18.

11. Steve Hoeffler, "Measuring Preferences for Really New Products," *Journal of Marketing Research* 40 (November 2003): 406–20; Glen Urban, Bruce Weinberg, and John R. Hauser, "Premarket Forecasting of Really New Products," *Journal of Marketing* 60 (January 1996): 47–60.

12. Ashish Sood and Gerard J. Tellis, "Technological Evolution and Radical Innovation," *Journal of Marketing* 69 (July 2005): 152–68.

13. For more discussion, see Jakki Mohr, *Marketing of High-Technology Products and Innovations*, 2nd ed. (Upper Saddle River, NJ: Prentice Hall, 2005).

14. Adam L. Penenberg, "Can't Touch This," *Fast Company* (February 2007): 86.
15. Steve Hamm, "Speed Demons," *BusinessWeek*, March 27, 2006, pp. 69–76.
16. Christina Passariello, "Brand New Bag: Louis Vuitton Tries Modern Methods on Factory Lines," *Wall Street Journal*, October 9, 2006.
17. Brad Weiners, "Gore-Tex Tackles the Great Indoors," *Business 2.0* (April 2004): 32; Ann Harrington, "Who's Afraid of a New Product," *Fortune*, November 10, 2003, pp. 189–92.
18. Rajan Varadarajan, "Business Insight (A Special Report); Think Small: Every Company Wants to Hit It Big with Market-Shattering Innovations; But the Little Changes, Too, Can Make a Huge Difference," *Wall Street Journal*, March 3, 2007.
19. Clayton M. Christensen, *The Innovator's Dilemma: When New Technologies Cause Great Firms to Fail* (Boston: Harvard University Press, 1997).
20. Ely Dahan and John R. Hauser, "Product Development: Managing a Dispersed Process," in *Handbook of Marketing*, ed. Bart Weitz and Robin Wensley (London: Sage, 2002), pp. 179–222.
21. Robert G. Cooper and Elko J. Kleinschmidt, *New Products: The Key Factors in Success* (Chicago: American Marketing Association, 1990).
22. Jill Agostino, "A Fitness Formula That Makes the Cut," *New York Times*, September 12, 2006.
23. Cooper and Kleinschmidt, *New Products*, pp. 35–38.
24. Susumu Ogama and Frank T. Piller, "Reducing the Risks of New-Product Development," *MIT Sloan Management Review* (Winter 2006): 65–71; A. C. Nielsen, "New-Product Introduction—Successful Innovation/Failure: Fragile Boundary," A. C. Nielsen BASES and Ernst & Young Global Client Consulting, June 24, 1999; Deloitte and Touche, "Vision in Manufacturing Study," Deloitte Consulting and Kenan-Flagler Business School, March 6, 1998.
25. Hamm, "Speed Demons."
26. Tom McNichol, "A Start-Up's Best Friend? Failure," *Business 2.0* (March 2007): 39–41.
27. Thomas N. Burton, "By Learning from Failures Lilly Keeps Drug Pipelines Full," *Wall Street Journal*, April 21, 2004.
28. Nanette Byrnes, "Xerox's New Design Team Customers," *BusinessWeek*, May 7, 2007, p. 72.
29. David Welch, "Can Stodgy GM Turn Stylish?" *BusinessWeek*, November 11, 2002, pp. 111–12.
30. Chuck Salter, "Failure Doesn't Suck," *Fast Company* (May 2007): 44.
31. Doug Ayers, Robert Dahlstrom, and Steven J. Skinner, "An Exploratory Investigation of Organizational Antecedents to New-Product Success," *Journal of Marketing Research* (February 1997): 107–16; David S. Hopkins, *Options in New-Product Organization* (New York: Conference Board, 1974).
32. Danielle Sacks, Chuck Salter, Alan Deutschman, and Scott Kirsner, "Innovation Scouts," *Fast Company* (May 2007): 90+.
33. Rajesh Sethi, Daniel C. Smith, and C. Whan Park, "Cross-Functional Product Development Teams, Creativity, and the Innovativeness of New Consumer Products," *Journal of Marketing Research* 38 (February 2001): 73–85.
34. Robert G. Cooper, "Stage-Gate Systems: A New Tool for Managing New Products," *Business Horizons* (May–June 1990): 44–54. See also, Robert G. Cooper, "The NewProd System: The Industry Experience," *Journal of Product Innovation Management* 9 (June 1992): 113–27.
35. Robert G. Cooper, *Product Leadership: Creating and Launching Superior New Products* (New York: Perseus Books, 1998).
36. Dahan and Hauser, "Product Development: Managing a Dispersed Process."
37. Another alternative approach to the funnel process advocates "rocketing." See, David Nichols, *Return on Ideas* (West Sussex, England: Wiley, 2007).
38. John Hauser, Gerard J. Tellis, and Abbie Griffin, "Research on Innovation: A Review and Agenda for Marketing Science," *Marketing Science* 25 (November–December 2006): 687–717.
39. Byron Acohido, "Microsoft Cultures Creativity in Unique Lab," *USA Today*, July 11, 2007; Erich Joachimsthaler, *Hidden in Plain Sight: How to Find and Execute Your Company's Next Big Growth Strategy* (Boston: Harvard Business School Press, 2007); Subin Im and John P. Workman Jr., "Market Orientation, Creativity, and New-Product Performance in High-Technology Firms," *Journal of Marketing* 68 (April 2004): 114–32.
40. Henry Chesbrough, *Open Business Models: How to Thrive in the New-Innovation Landscape* (Boston: Harvard University Press, 2006); Eric Von Hippel, *Democratizing Innovation* (Cambridge, MA: MIT Press, 2005); Burt Helm, "Inside a White-Hot Idea Factory," *BusinessWeek*, January 15, 2005, pp. 72–73; C. K. Prahalad and Venkat Ramaswamy, *The Future of Competition: Cocreating Unique Value with Customers* (Boston: Harvard University Press, 2004); Henry Chesbrough, *Open Innovation: The New Imperative for Creating and Profiting from Technology* (Boston: Harvard University Press, 2003).
41. Bruce Horovitz, "Marketers Zooming in on Your Daily Routines," *USA Today*, April 30, 2007; Ashwin W. Joshi and Sanjay Sharma, "Customer Knowledge Development: Antecedents and Impact on New-

Product Performance," *Journal of Marketing* 68 (October 2004): 47–59.

42. Abbie J. Griffin and John Hauser, "The Voice of the Customer," *Marketing Science* (Winter 1993): 1–27.

43. Peter C. Honebein and Roy F. Cammarano, "Customers at Work," *Marketing Management* (January–February 2006): 26–31; Peter C. Honebein and Roy F. Cammarano, *Creating Do-It-Yourself Customers: How Great Customer Experiences Build Great Companies* (Mason, OH: Texere Southwestern Educational Publishing, 2005).

44. Robert Levine, "You Ought to Be in Pictures," *Business 2.0* 8, no. 3 (April 2007): 90; Kim Peterson, "Microstock Photography Represents a New Business Model," *Knight Ridder Tribune Business News*, May 28, 2007, p. 1; "World's Most Successful 'Crowdsourcing' Stock Photographer Reaches Half a Million Images Sold on iStockphoto," *Business Wire*, June 5, 2007.

45. Patricia Seybold, *Outside Innovation: How Your Customers Will Codesign Your Company's Future* (New York: Collins, 2006).

46. Patricia Seybold, "Customer-Controlled Innovation—Collaboration with Customers Is Transforming Product-Development Strategies and Unlocking New Ways for Companies to Innovate," *Optimize* 6, no. 2 (February 2007): 26; Jessica Pallay, Nola Sarkisian-Miller, Brenda Lloyd, and Gillian Koenig, "From Surf to Street: The Best of Young Men's Retail," *DNR* 37, no. 11, March 12, 2007, p. 16.

47. Eric von Hippel, "Lead Users: A Source of Novel Product Concepts," *Management Science* (July 1986): 791–805. Also see *The Sources of Innovation* (New York: Oxford University Press, 1988); and "Learning from Lead Users," in *Marketing in an Electronic Age*, ed. Robert D. Buzzell (Cambridge, MA: Harvard Business School Press, 1985), pp. 308–17.

48. Steven Levy, "Microsoft Gets a Clue from Its Kiddie Corps," *Newsweek*, February 24, 2003, pp. 56–57.

49. Kevin Zheng Zhou, Chi Kin (Bennett) Yim, and David K. Tse, "The Effects of Strategic Orientations on Technology- and Market-Based Breakthrough Innovations," *Journal of Marketing* 69 (April 2005): 42–60; Michael Treacy, "Ignore the Consumer," *Advertising Age Point* (September 2005): 15–19.

50. "The World's Fifty Most Innovative Companies," Special Report, *BusinessWeek*, May 9, 2007.

51. Darren W. Dahl and Page Moreau, "The Influence and Value of Analogical Thinking during New-Product Ideation," *Journal of Marketing Research* 39 (February 2002): 47–60; Michael Michalko, *Cracking Creativity: The Secrets of Creative Genius* (Berkeley, CA: Ten Speed Press, 1998); James M. Higgins, *101 Creative Problem-Solving Techniques* (New York: New Management, 1994).

52. www.smokinggun.com.

53. Olivier Toubia and Laurent Florès, "Adaptive Idea Screening Using Consumers," *Marketing Science* 26 (May–June 2007): 342–60; Melanie Wells, "Have It Your Way," *Forbes*, February 14, 2005.

54. Steve Hoeffler, "Measuring Preferences for Really New Products," *Journal of Marketing Research* 40 (November 2003): 406–20; Dahl and Moreau, "The Influence and Value of Analogical Thinking during New-Product Ideation"; Michelle L. Roehm and Brian Sternthal, "The Moderating Effect of Knowledge and Resources on the Persuasive Impact of Analogies," *Journal of Consumer Research* 28 (September 2001): 257–72; Darren W. Dahl, Amitava Chattopadhyay, and Gerald J. Gorn, "The Use of Visual Mental Imagery in New-Product Design," *Journal of Marketing Research* 36 (February 1999): 18–28; Jennifer Gregan-Paxton and Deborah Roedder John, "Consumer Learning by Analogy: A Model of Internal Knowledge Transfer," *Journal of Consumer Research* 24 (December 1997): 266–84.

55. Hamm, "Speed Demons."

56. For additional information, also see David Bakken and Curtis L. Frazier, "Conjoint Analysis: Understanding Consumer Decision Making," in *The Handbook of Marketing Research*, ed. Rajiv Grover and Marco Vriens (Thousand Oaks, CA: Sage, 2006); Vithala R. Rao and John R. Hauser, "Conjoint Analysis, Related Modeling, and Application," in *Market Research and Modeling: Progress and Prospects: A Tribute to Paul Green*, ed. Yoram Wind and Paul E. Green (New York: Springer, 2004), pp. 141–68; Jordan J. Louviere, David A. Hensher, and Joffre D. Swait, *Stated Choice Models: Analysis and Applications* (New York: Cambridge University Press, 2000); Paul E. Green and V. Srinivasan, "Conjoint Analysis in Marketing: New Developments with Implications for Research and Practice," *Journal of Marketing* (October 1990): 3–19; www.sawtoothsoftware.com.

57. Jerry Wind, Paul Green, Douglas Shifflet, and Marsha Scarbrough, "Courtyard by Marriott: Designing a Hotel Facility with Consumer-Based Marketing Models," *Interfaces* 19 (January–February 1989): 25–47. For another interesting application, see Paul E. Green, Abba M. Krieger, and Terry Vavra, "Evaluating EZ-Pass: Using Conjoint Analysis to Assess Consumer Response to a New Tollway Technology," *Marketing Research* (Summer 1999): 5–16.

58. The full-profile example was taken from Paul E. Green and Yoram Wind, "New Ways to Measure Consumers' Judgments," *Harvard Business Review* (July–August 1975): 107–17.

59. Peter N. Golder and Gerald J. Tellis, "Will It Ever Fly? Modeling the Takeoff of Really New Consumer

Durables," *Marketing Science* 16, no. 3 (Summer 1997): 256–70; Glen L. Urban, Bruce D. Weinberg, and John R. Hauser, "Premarket Forecasting of Really New Products," *Journal of Marketing* (January 1996): 47–60; Robert Blattberg and John Golany, "Tracker: An Early Test-Market Forecasting and Diagnostic Model for New-Product Planning," *Journal of Marketing Research* (May 1978): 192–202.

60. Roger A. Kerin, Michael G. Harvey, and James T. Rothe, "Cannibalism and New-Product Development," *Business Horizons* (October 1978): 25–31.

61. The present value (V) of a future sum (I) to be received t years from today and discounted at the interest rate (r) is given by $V = I_t/(1 + r)^t$. Thus $\$4,716,000/(1.15)^5 = \$2,345,000$.

62. David B. Hertz, "Risk Analysis in Capital Investment," *Harvard Business Review* (January–February 1964): 96–106.

63. John Hauser, "House of Quality," *Harvard Business Review* (May–June 1988): 63–73. Customer-driven engineering is also called "quality function deployment." See, Lawrence R. Guinta and Nancy C. Praizler, *The QFD Book: The Team Approach to Solving Problems and Satisfying Customers through Quality Function Deployment* (New York: AMACOM, 1993); and V. Srinivasan, William S. Lovejoy, and David Beach, "Integrated Product Design for Marketability and Manufacturing," *Journal of Marketing Research* (February 1997): 154–63.

64. Tom Peters, *The Circle of Innovation* (New York: Alfred A. Knopf, 1997), p. 96. For more general discussion, see also, Rajesh Sethi, "New-Product Quality and Product-Development Teams," *Journal of Marketing* (April 2000): 1–14; Christine Moorman and Anne S. Miner, "The Convergence of Planning and Execution Improvisation in New-Product Development," *Journal of Marketing* (July 1998): 1–20; and Ravinchoanath MacChavan and Rajiv Graver, "From Embedded Knowledge to Embodied Knowledge: New-Product Development as Knowledge Management," *Journal of Marketing* (October 1998): 1–12.

65. Marco Iansiti and Alan MacCormack, "Developing Products on Internet Time," *Harvard Business Review* (September–October 1997): 108–17; Srikant Datar, C. Clark Jordan, and Kannan Srinivasan, "Advantages of Time-Based New-Product Development in a Fast-Cycle Industry," *Journal of Marketing Research* (February 1997): 36–49; Christopher D. Ittner and David F. Larcker, "Product-Development Cycle Time and Organizational Performance," *Journal of Marketing Research* (February 1997): 13–23.

66. Peters, *The Circle of Innovation*, p. 96. For more general discussion, see also, Sethi, "New Product Quality and Product Development Teams," pp. 1–14; Moorman and Miner, "The Convergence of Planning and Execution Improvisation in New-Product Development," pp. 1–20; and MacChavan and Graver, "From Embedded Knowledge to Embodied Knowledge," pp. 1–12.

67. Merle Crawford and Anthony Di Benedetto, *New-Products Management*, 8th ed. (Burr Ridge, IL: McGraw-Hill/Irwin, 2006).

68. Kevin J. Clancy, Peter C. Krieg, and Marianne McGarry Wolf, *Marketing New Products Successfully: Using Simulated Test Marketing Methodology* (New York: Lexington Books, 2005); Glen L. Urban, John R. Hauser, and Roberta A. Chicos, "Information Acceleration: Validation and Lessons from the Field," *Journal of Marketing Research* (February 1997): 143–53; V. Mahajan and Jerry Wind, "New Product Models: Practice, Shortcomings, and Desired Improvements," *Journal of Product Innovation Management* 9 (June 1992): 129–39.

69. Eyal Biyalogorsky, William Boulding, and Richard Staelin, "Stuck in the Past: Why Managers Persist with New-Product Failures," *Journal of Marketing* 70 (April 2006): 108–21.

70. Rajesh Chandy, Brigette Hopstaken, Om Narasimhan, and Jaideep Prabhu, "From Invention to Innovation: Conversion Ability in Product Development," *Journal of Marketing Research* 43 (August 2006): 494–508.

71. Remco Prins and Peter C. Verhoef, "Marketing Communication Drivers of Adoption Timing of a New E-Service among Existing Customers," *Journal of Marketing* 71 (April 2007): 169–83.

72. For further discussion, see Yuhong Wu, Sridhar Balasubramanian, and Vijay Mahajan, "When Is a Preannounced New Product Likely to Be Delayed?" *Journal of Marketing* 68 (April 2004): 101–13; Raji Srinivasan, Gary L. Lilien, and Arvind Rangaswamy, "First in First out? The Effects of Network Externalities on Pioneer Survival," *Journal of Marketing* 68 (January 2004): 41–58; Barry L. Bayus, Sanjay Jain, and Ambar Rao, "Consequences: An Analysis of Truth or Vaporware and New-Product Announcements," *Journal of Marketing Research* (February 2001): 3–13; Thomas S. Robertson, Jehoshua Eliashberg, and Talia Rymon, "New-Product Announcement Signals and Incumbent Reactions," *Journal of Marketing* (July 1995): 1–15; Frank H. Alpert and Michael A. Kamins, "Pioneer Brand Advantages and Consumer Behavior: A Conceptual Framework and Propositional Inventory," *Journal of the Academy of Marketing Science* (Summer 1994): 244–336; Robert J. Thomas, "Timing: The Key to Market Entry," *Journal of Consumer Marketing* (Summer 1985): 77–87.

73. Katrijn Gielens and Jan-Benedict E. M. Steenkamp, "What Drives New-Product Success? An Investigation across Products and Countries," Marketing Science Institute Working Paper 04-108, Cambridge, MA; Katrijn Gielens and Jan-Benedict E. M. Steenkamp, "Drivers of Consumer Acceptance of New Packaged Goods: An Investigation across Products and Countries," *International Journal of Research in Marketing* 24 (June 2007): 97–111; Marc Fischer, Venkatesh Shankar, and Michael Clement, "Can a Late Mover Use International Market Entry Strategy to Challenge the Pioneer?" Marketing Science Institute Working Paper 05-118, Cambridge, MA; Venkatesh Shankar, Gregory S. Carpenter, and Lakshman Krishnamukthi, "Late Mover Advantages: How Innovative Late Entrants Outsell Pioneers," *Journal of Marketing Research* 35 (February 1998): 54–70.

74. Philip Kotler and Gerald Zaltman, "Targeting Prospects for a New Product," *Journal of Advertising Research* (February 1976): 7–20.

75. Mark Leslie and Charles A. Holloway, "The Sales Learning Curve," *Harvard Business Review* (July–August 2006): 114–23.

76. Steven Levy, "iPod Nation," *Newsweek*, July 25, 2004.

77. For details, see Keith G. Lockyer, *Critical Path Analysis and Other Project Network Techniques* (London: Pitman, 1984). Also see Arvind Rangaswamy and Gary L. Lilien, "Software Tools for New-Product Development," *Journal of Marketing Research* (February 1997): 177–84.

78. The following discussion leans heavily on Everett M. Rogers, *Diffusion of Innovations* (New York: Free Press, 1962). Also see his third edition, published in 1983.

79. C. Page Moreau, Donald R. Lehmann, and Arthur B. Markman, "Entrenched Knowledge Structures and Consumer Response to New Products," *Journal of Marketing Research* 38 (February 2001): 14–29.

80. John T. Gourville, "Eager Sellers & Stony Buyers," *Harvard Business Review* (June 2006): 99–106.

81. Chuan-Fong Shih and Alladi Venkatesh, "Beyond Adoption: Development and Application of a Use-Diffusion Model," *Journal of Marketing* 68 (January 2004): 59–72.

82. Michal Herzenstein, Steven S. Posavac, and J. Joškon Brakuz, "Adoption of New and Really New Products: The Effects of Self-Regulation Systems and Risk Salience," *Journal of Marketing Research* 44 (May 2007): 251–60; Christophe Van den Bulte and Yogesh V. Joshi, "New-Product Diffusion with Influentials and Imitators," *Marketing Science* 26 (May–June 2007): 400–21; Steve Hoeffler, "Measuring Preferences for Really New Products," *Journal of Marketing Research* 40 (November 2003): 406–20.

83. Rogers, *Diffusion of Innovations*, p. 192; Geoffrey A. Moore, *Crossing the Chasm: Marketing and Selling High-Tech Products to Mainstream Customers* (New York: HarperBusiness, 1999).

84. A. Parasuraman and Charles L. Colby, *Techno-Ready Marketing* (New York: Free Press, 2001); Jakki Mohr, *Marketing of High-Technology Products and Innovations* (Upper Saddle River, NJ: Prentice Hall, 2001).

85. Malcolm Macalister Hall, "Selling by Stealth," *Business Life* (November 2001): 51–55.

86. Jordan Robertson, "How Nike Got Street Cred," *Business 2.0* (May 2004): 43–46.

87. Cliff Edwards, "Will Souping Up TiVo Save It?" *BusinessWeek*, May 17, 2004, pp. 63–64; Cliff Edwards, "Is TiVo's Signal Still Fading?" *BusinessWeek*, September 10, 2001, pp. 72–74.

88. Fareena Sultan, John U. Farley, and Donald R. Lehman, "Reflection on 'A Meta-Analysis of Applications of Diffusion Models,' " *Journal of Marketing Research* (May 1996): 247–49; Vijay Mahajan, Eitan Muller, and Frank M. Bass, "Diffusion of New Products: Empirical Generalizations and Managerial Uses," *Marketing Science* 14, no. 3, part 2 (Summer 1995): G79–G89; Minhi Hahn, Sehoon Park, and Andris A. Zoltners, "Analysis of New-Product Diffusion Using a Four-Segment Trial-Repeat Model," *Marketing Science* 13, no. 3 (Summer 1994): 224–47; Hubert Gatignon and Thomas S. Robertson, "A Propositional Inventory for New Diffusion Research," *Journal of Consumer Research* (March 1985): 849–67.

Chapter 21

1. Jack Ewing, "Nokia: Lesson Learned, Reward Reaped," *BusinessWeek*, July 30, 2007, p. 32; "Face Value," *Economist*, May 27, 2006, p. 64.

2. www.ita.doc.gov/.

3. "The List," *BusinessWeek*, April 21, 2003, p. 14.

4. Michael E. Porter, *Competitive Strategy* (New York: Free Press, 1980), p. 275.

5. Richard Tomlinson, "Dethroning Percy Barnevik," *Fortune*, April 1, 2002; Charles Fleming and Leslie Lopez, "The Corporate Challenge—No Boundaries: ABB's Dramatic Plan to Recast Its Business Structure along Global Lines: It May Not Be Easy—or Wise," *Wall Street Journal*, September 28, 1998.

6. www.abb.com.

7. Ron Lieber, "Give Us This Day Our Global Bread," *Fast Company* (March 2001): 158.

8. Charles P. Wallace, "Charge!" *Fortune*, September 28, 1998, pp. 189–96; www.wto.org.

9. Edward Iwata, "Companies Find Gold inside Melting Pot," *USA Today*, July 9, 2007.

10. Jan Johanson and Finn Wiedersheim-Paul, "The Internationalization of the Firm," *Journal of Management Studies* (October 1975): 305–22.

11. Michael R. Czinkota and Ilkka A. Ronkainen, *International Marketing*, 5th ed. (New York: Harcourt Brace Jovanovich, 1999).

12. For a timely and thorough review of academic research on global marketing, see Johny K. Johansson, "Global Marketing: Research on Foreign Entry, Local Marketing, Global Management," in *Handbook of Marketing*, ed. Bart Weitz and Robin Wensley (London: Sage, 2002), pp. 457–83. Also see Johny K. Johansson, *Global Marketing*, 2nd ed. (New York: McGraw-Hill, 2003). For some global marketing research issues, see Susan Douglas and Samuel R. Craig, *International Marketing Research*, 2nd ed. (Upper Saddle River, NJ: Prentice Hall, 2000).

13. According to the CIA World Factbook (www.cia.gov/library/publications/the-world-factbook/index.html), there are 34 developed countries: Andorra, Australia, Austria, Belgium, Bermuda, Canada, Denmark, Faroe Islands, Finland, France, Germany, Greece, Holy See, Iceland, Ireland, Israel, Italy, Japan, Liechtenstein, Luxembourg, Malta, Monaco, Netherlands, New Zealand, Norway, Portugal, San Marino, South Africa, Spain, Sweden, Switzerland, Turkey, United Kingdom, and United States. They note that DCs are similar to the new International Monetary Fund (IMF) term "advanced economies" that adds Hong Kong, South Korea, Singapore, and Taiwan but drops Malta, Mexico, South Africa, and Turkey.

14. Jack Neff, "Submerged," *Advertising Age*, March 4, 2002, p. 14.

15. www.populationmedia.org/issues/issues.htm.

16. Adapted from Vijay Mahajan, Marcos V. Pratini De Moraes, and Jerry Wind, "The Invisible Global Market," *Marketing Management* (Winter 2000): 31–35. See also, Tarun Khanna and Krishna G. Palepu, "Emerging Giants: Building World-Class Companies in Developing Countries," *Harvard Business Review* (October 2006): 60–69.

17. C. K. Prahalad, *The Fortune at the Bottom of the Pyramid: Eradicating Poverty through Profits* (Upper Saddle River, NJ: Wharton School Publishing, 2005); Niraj Dawar and Amitava Chattopadhyay, "Rethinking Marketing Programs for Emerging Markets," *Long Range Planning* 35, (October 2002).

18. Bart J. Bronnenberg, Jean-Pierre Dubé, and Sanjay Dhar, "Consumer Packaged Goods in the United States: National Brands, Local Branding," *Journal of Marketing Research* 44 (February 2007): 4–13; Bart J. Bronnenberg, Jean-Pierre Dubé, and Sanjay Dhar, "National Brands, Local Branding: Conclusions and Future Research Opportunities," *Journal of Marketing Research* 44 (February 2007): 26–28; Bart J. Bronnenberg, Jean-Pierre Dubé, and Sanjay Dhar, "Market Structure and the Geographic Distribution of Brand Shares in Consumer Package Goods Industries," working paper, UCLA Graduate School of Management.

19. Bruce Einhorn, "Grudge Match in China," *BusinessWeek*, April 2, 2007, pp. 42–43; Russell Flannery, "Watch Your Back," *Forbes*, April 23, 2007, pp. 104–5; Steve Hamm and Dexter Roberts, "China's First Global Capitalist," *BusinessWeek*, December 11, 2006, pp. 52–57; "The Fast and the Furious," *Economist*, November 25, 2006, pp. 63–64.

20. Manjeet Kripalani, "Finally, Coke Gets It Right," *BusinessWeek*, February 10, 2003, p. 47; Manjeet Kripalani, "Battling for Pennies in India's Villages," *BusinessWeek*, June 10, 2002, p. 22.

21. Ellen Byron, "P&G's Global Target: Shelves of Tiny Stores," *Wall Street Journal*, July 16, 2007; "Not So Fizzy," *Economist*, February 23, 2002, pp. 66–67; Rajeev Batra, Venkatram Ramaswamy, Dana L. Alden, Jan-Benedict E. M. Steenkamp, and S. Ramachander, "Effects of Brand Local and Nonlocal Origin on Consumer Attitudes in Developing Countries," *Journal of Consumer Psychology* 9, no. 2 (2000): 83–95.

22. Patricia Sellers, "P&G: Teaching an Old Dog New Tricks," *Fortune*, May 31, 2004, pp. 167–80.

23. Antonio Regalado, "Marketers Pursue the Shallow-Pocketed," *Wall Street Journal*, January 26, 2007.

24. Paul Betts, "Danone's Taste for Microfinance Pays Dividends," *Financial Times*, March 30, 2007, p. 24; "The Bottom of the Pyramid Is Where the Real Gold Is Hidden," *Marketing Week*, February 8, 2007, p. 18; Adam Jones, "Danone and Yunus Extend Partnership," *Financial Times*, December 19, 2006, p. 19.

25. Johny K. Johansson, "Global Marketing: Research on Foreign Entry, Local Marketing, Global Management," in *Handbook of Marketing*, ed. Bart Weitz and Robin Wensley (London: Sage, 2002), pp. 457–83.

26. For an academic review, see Leonidas C. Leonidou, Constantine S. Katsikeas, and Nigel F. Piercy, "Identifying Managerial Influences on Exporting: Past Research and Future Directions," *Journal of International Marketing* 6, no. 2 (Summer 1998): 74–102.

27. Ellen Neuborne, "The Best New World Markets for Selling," *Sales and Marketing Management* 158, no. 2 (March 2006): 38+.

28. Brandon Mitchener, "E-Commerce: Border Crossings," *Wall Street Journal*, November 22, 1999.

29. Michael Arndt and Dexter Roberts, "A Finger-Lickin' Good Time in China," *BusinessWeek*,

October 30, 2006, p. 50; "Cola down Mexico Way," *Economist*, October 11, 2003, pp. 69–70.

30. Laura Mazur and Annik Hogg, *The Marketing Challenge* (Wokingham, England: Addison-Wesley, 1993), pp. 42–44; Jan Willem Karel, "Brand Strategy Positions Products Worldwide," *Journal of Business Strategy* 12, no. 3 (May–June 1991): 16–19.

31. Joann Muller, "Global Motors," *Forbes*, January 12, 2004, pp. 62–68.

32. "Burgers and Fries a la Francaise," *Economist*, April 17, 2004, pp. 60–61; Johny K. Johansson, "Global Marketing: Research on Foreign Entry, Local Marketing, Global Management," in *Handbook of Marketing*, ed. Bart Weitz and Robin Wensley (London: Sage, 2002), pp. 457–83; Shaoming Zou and S. Tamer Cavusgil, "The GMS: A Broad Conceptualization of Global Marketing Strategy and Its Effect on Firm Performance," *Journal of Marketing* 66 (October 2002): 40–56; "What Makes a Company Great?" *Fortune*, October 26, 1998, pp. 218–26; Bernard Wysocki Jr., "The Global Mall: In Developing Nations, Many Youths Splurge, Mainly on U.S. Goods," *Wall Street Journal*, June 26,1997; David M. Szymanski, Sundar G. Bharadwaj, and P. Rajan Varadarajan, "Standardization versus Adaptation of International Marketing Strategy: An Empirical Investigation," *Journal of Marketing* (October 1993):1–17; Theodore Levitt, "The Globalization of Markets," *Harvard Business Review* (May–June 1983): 92–102.

33. Kevin Lane Keller, "Red Bull: Managing a High-Growth Brand," in *Best Practice Cases in Branding*, 3rd ed. (Upper Saddle River, NJ: Prentice Hall, 2008).

34. www.beverageworld.com; www.beveragemarketing.com.

35. Geert Hofstede, *Culture's Consequences* (Beverley Hills, CA: Sage, 1980).

36. For some recent treatments of branding in Asia in particular, see S. Ramesh Kumar, *Marketing & Branding: The Indian Scenario* (Delhi: Pearson Education, 2007); Martin Roll, *Asian Brand Strategy: How Asia Builds Strong Brands* (New York: Palgrave MacMillan, 2006); Paul Temporal, *Branding in Asia: The Creation, Development, and Management of Asian Brands for the Global Market* (Singapore: John Wiley & Sons, 2001).

37. Pankaj Ghemawat, "Globalization: The Strategy of Differences," *Harvard Business School Working Knowledge*, November 10, 2003; Pankaj Ghemawat, "The Forgotten Strategy," *Harvard Business Review* 81 (November 2003): 76–84.

38. "Brand Strategy Briefing: Remittance Goes Global," *Brand Strategy*, November 2, 2005, p. 50.

39. Arundhati Parmar, "Dependent Variables: Sound Global Strategies Rely on Certain Factors," *Marketing News*, September 16, 2002, p. 4.

40. Walter J. Keegan and Mark C. Green, *Global Marketing*, 4th ed. (Upper Saddle River, NJ: Prentice Hall, 2005); Warren J. Keegan, *Global Marketing Management*, 7th ed. (Upper Saddle River, NJ: Prentice Hall, 2002).

41. Paulo Prada and Bruce Orwall, "A Certain 'Je Ne Sais Quoi' at Disney's New Park," *Wall Street Journal*, March 12, 2003.

42. Jack Ewing, "Where the Business Is Humming: Bertlesmann Is Making a Bundle off Old Media in Former Soviet Bloc Countries," *BusinessWeek*, May 14, 2007, p. 50.

43. Marlene Parrish, "Taste Buds Tango at New Squirrel Hill Café," *Pittsburgh Post-Gazette*, February 6, 2003; David Leonhardt, "It Was a Hit in Buenos Aires—So Why Not Boise?" *BusinessWeek*, September 7, 1998, pp. 56–58.

44. Mark Lasswell, "Lost in Translation," *Business 2.0* (August 2004): 68–70; Richard P. Carpenter and the *Globe* Staff, "What They Meant to Say Was . . . ," *Boston Globe*, August 2, 1998.

45. For an interesting distinction based on the concept of global consumer culture positioning, see Dana L. Alden, Jan-Benedict E. M. Steenkamp, and Rajeev Batra, "Brand Positioning through Advertising in Asia, North America, and Europe: The Role of Global Consumer Culture," *Journal of Marketing* 63 (January 1999): 75–87.

46. Thomas J. Madden, Kelly Hewett, and Martin S. Roth, "Managing Images in Different Cultures: A Cross-National Study of Color Meanings and Preferences," *Journal of International Marketing* 8, no. 4 (Winter 2000): 90–107; Zeynep Gürhan-Canli and Durairaj Maheswaran, "Cultural Variations in Country-of-Origin Effects," *Journal of Marketing Research* 37 (August 2000): 309–17.

47. Geoffrey Fowler, Brian Steinberg, and Aaron O. Patrick, "Globalizing Apple's Ads," *Wall Street Journal*, March 1, 2007.

48. Karen J. Bannan, "Acopia Tailors E-Mail for Int'l Audience," *BtoB* 91, no. 15, November 13, 2006, p. 20.

49. Noreen O'Leary, "Bright Lights, Big Challenge," *Adweek*, January 15, 2007, p. 22; Normandy Madden, "Nike Drops Its American Idols," *Advertising Age*, March 20, 2006, p. 12.

50. Loretta Chao, "Cell Phone Ads Are Easier Pitch in China Interactive Campaigns," *Wall Street Journal*, January 4, 2007.

51. John L. Graham, Alma T. Mintu, and Waymond Rogers, "Explorations of Negotiations Behaviors in Ten Foreign Cultures Using a Model Developed in the United States," *Management Science* 40 (January 1994): 72–95.

52. David Kirkpatrick, "How Microsoft Conquered China," *Fortune* 156, no. 2, July 23, 2007, pp. 78–84.

53. Tony Van Alphen, "Some U.S. Makers Dumping Steel in Canada," *Toronto Star,* May 2, 2001.

54. Ram Charan, "The Rules Have Changed," *Fortune,* March 16, 1998, pp. 159–62.

55. www.ge.com.

56. David Arnold, "Seven Rules of International Distribution," *Harvard Business Review* (November–December 2000): 131–37.

57. Arnold, "Seven Rules of International Distribution."

58. Jack Ewing, "The Next Wal-Mart?" *BusinessWeek,* April 26, 2004, pp. 60–62.

59. Geraldo Samor, Cecilie Rohwedder, and Ann Zimmerman, "Innocents Abroad," *Wall Street Journal,* May 10, 2006; Mark Landler and Michael Barbaro, "Wal-Mart's Overseas Push Can Be Lost in Translation," *International Herald Tribune,* August 2, 2006; "Heading for the Exit," *Economist,* August 5, 2006, p. 52; Keith Naughton, "The Great Wal-Mart of China," *Newsweek,* October 30, 2006, pp. 50–52; "Trouble at Till," *Economist,* November 4, 2006, p. 18.

60. "From Head & Shoulders to Kobe," *Economist,* March 27, 2004, p. 64.

61. Alessandra Galloni, "Venice: Gondoliers, Lagoons, Moonlight—and Meatballs?" *Wall Street Journal,* August 9, 2002.

62. "A Dragon with Core Values," *Economist,* March 30, 2002.

63. "The Shock of Old," *Economist,* July 13, 2002, p. 49.

64. "From Fantasy Worlds to Food," *Economist,* November 11, 2006, p. 73; "A New Sort of Beauty Contest," *Economist,* November 11, 2006, p. 68.

65. Jim Rendon, "When Nations Need a Little Marketing," *New York Times,* November 23, 2003.

66. Zeynep Gurhan-Canli and Durairaj Maheswaran, "Cultural Variations in Country-of-Origin Effects," *Journal of Marketing Research* 37 (August 2000): 309–17.

67. Douglas B. Holt, John A. Quelch, and Earl L. Taylor, "How Global Brands Compete," *Harvard Business Review* 82 (September 2004): 68–75; Jan-Benedict E. M. Steenkamp, Rajeev Batra, and Dana L. Alden, "How Perceived Brand Globalness Creates Brand Value," *Journal of International Business Studies* 34 no. 1 (January 2003): 53–65.

68. Gürhan-Canli and Maheswaran "Cultural Variations in Country-of-Origin Effects"; Johny K. Johansson, "Global Marketing: Research on Foreign Entry, Local Marketing, Global Management," in *Handbook of Marketing,* ed. Barton A. Weitz and Robin Wensley (London: Sage, 2002), pp. 457–83; "Old Wine in New Bottles," *Economist,* February 21, 1998, p. 45; Johny K. Johansson, "Determinants and Effects of the Use of 'Made in' Labels," *International Marketing Review (UK)* 6, no. 1 (January 1989): 47–58; Warren J. Bilkey and Erik Nes, "Country-of-Origin Effects on Product Evaluations," *Journal of International Business Studies* (Spring–Summer 1982): 89–99.

69. Jathon Sapsford and Norihiko Shirouzo, "Mom, Apple Pie and . . . Toyota?" *Wall Street Journal,* May 11, 2006.

70. "Haier's Purpose," *Economist,* March 20, 2004, p. 72; Gerry Kermouch, "Breaking into the Name Game," *BusinessWeek,* April 7, 2003, p. 54.

71. Charles Fishman, "No Satisfaction at Toyota," *Fast Company* (December 2006–January 2007); Roben Farzad, "The Toyota Enigma," *BusinessWeek,* July 10, 2006, p. 30; Keith Naughton, "Red, White, & Bold," *Newsweek,* April 25, 2005, pp. 34–36; Alex Taylor III, "The Americanization of Toyota," *Fortune,* December 8, 2003, pp. 165–70.

72. Christopher A. Bartlett and Sumantra Ghoshal, *Managing across Borders* (Cambridge, MA: Harvard Business School Press, 1989).

73. Betsy McKay, "Coke Hunts for Talent to Re-Establish Its Marketing Might," *Wall Street Journal,* March 6, 2002.

Chapter 22

1. Keith Fox, Katherine Jocz, and Bernard Jaworski, "A Common Language," *Marketing Management* (May–June 2003): 14–17.

2. Tara Weiss, "Special Report: Going Green," *Forbes.com,* July 3, 2007; Matthew Grimm, "Progressive Business," *Brandweek,* November 28, 2005, pp. 16–26.

3. For additional updates on the latest academic thinking on marketing strategy and tactics, see *Kellogg on Integrated Marketing,* ed. Dawn Iacobucci and Bobby Calder (New York: Wiley, 2003); and *Kellogg on Marketing,* ed. Dawn Iacobucci (New York: Wiley, 2001).

4. Frederick E. Webster Jr., Alan J. Malter, and Shankar Ganesan, "Can Marketing Regain Its Seat at the Table?" *Marketing Science Institute Report No. 03-113* (Cambridge, MA: Marketing Science Institute, 2003).

5. For a broad historical treatment of marketing thought, see D. G. Brian Jones and Eric H. Shaw, "A History of Marketing Thought," in *Handbook of Marketing,* ed. Barton A. Weitz and Robin Wensley (London: Sage, 2002), pp. 39–65.

6. Julia Chang, "From the Inside Out," *Sales and Marketing Management* 157, no. 8 (August 2005): 14.

7. Hamish Pringle and William Gordon, *Beyond Manners: How to Create the Self-Confident Organisation to Live the Brand* (West Sussex, England: John Wiley & Sons, 2001); Frederick E. Webster Jr., "The Changing Role of Marketing in the Corporation," *Journal of Marketing* (October 1992): 1–17. Also see John P. Workman Jr., Christian Homburg, and Kjell Gruner, "Marketing Organization: An Integrative Framework of Dimensions and Determinants," *Journal of Marketing* (July 1998): 21–41; Ravi S. Achrol, "Evolution of the Marketing Organization: New Forms for Turbulent Environment," *Journal of Marketing* (October 1991): 77–93. For some contemporary perspectives, see Special Issue 1999 of *Journal of Marketing Fundamental Issues and Directions for Marketing.*

8. For an excellent account of how to convert a company into a market-driven organization, see George Day, *The Market-Driven Organization: Aligning Culture, Capabilities, and Configuration to the Market* (New York: Free Press, 1989).

9. Frederick E. Webster Jr., "The Role of Marketing and the Firm," in *Handbook of Marketing*, ed. Barton A. Weitz and Robin Wensley (London: Sage, 2002), pp. 39–65.

10. Frank V. Cespedes, *Managing Marketing Linkages: Text, Cases, and Readings* (Upper Saddle River, NJ: Prentice Hall, 1996); Frank V. Cespedes, *Concurrent Marketing: Integrating Product, Sales, and Service* (Boston: Harvard Business School Press, 1995).

11. Theresa Howard, "Pace Pokes More Fun at NYC," *USA Today*, November 7, 2004.

12. Laurie Freeman, "P&G Widens Power Base: Adds Category Managers," *Advertising Age*; Michael J. Zenor, "The Profit Benefits of Category Management," *Journal of Marketing Research* 31 (May 1994): 202–13; Gerry Khermouch, "Brands Overboard," *Brandweek*, August 22, 1994, pp. 25–39; Zachary Schiller, "The Marketing Revolution at Procter & Gamble," *BusinessWeek*, July 25, 1988, pp. 72–76.

13. For further reading, see Robert Dewar and Don Shultz, "The Product Manager, an Idea Whose Time Has Gone," *Marketing Communications* (May 1998): 28–35; George S. Low and Ronald A. Fullerton, "Brands, Brand Management, and the Brand Manager System: A Critical Historical Evaluation," *Journal of Marketing Research* (May 1994): 173–90; Michael J. Zanor, "The Profit Benefits of Category Management," *Journal of Marketing Research* (May 1994): 202–13.

14. Larry Selden and Geoffrey Colvin, *Angel Customers & Demon Customers* (New York: Portfolio [Penguin], 2003).

15. For an in-depth discussion of issues around implementing a customer-based organization on which much of this paragraph is based, see George S. Day, "Aligning the Organization with the Market," *MIT Sloan Management Review* (Fall 2006): 41–49.

16. Richard E. Anderson, "Matrix Redux," *Business Horizons* (November–December 1994): 6–10.

17. Frederick E. Webster Jr., "The Role of Marketing and the Firm," in *Handbook of Marketing*, ed. Barton A. Weitz and Robin Wensley (London: Sage, 2002), pp. 39–65.

18. Benson P. Shapiro, "Can Marketing and Manufacturing Coexist?" *Harvard Business Review* (September–October 1977): 104–14. Also see Robert W. Ruekert and Orville C. Walker Jr., "Marketing's Interaction with Other Functional Units: A Conceptual Framework with Other Empirical Evidence," *Journal of Marketing* (January 1987): 1–19.

19. Ranjay Gulati, "Silo Busting: How to Execute on the Promise of Customer Focus," *Harvard Business Review* 85, no. 5, May 1, 2007, pp. 98+.

20. Erik Brynjolfsson and Lorin Hitt, "The Customer Counts," *InformationWeek*, September 9, 1996.

21. Gary Hamel, *Leading the Revolution* (Boston: Harvard Business School Press, 2000).

22. Jagdish N. Sheth, *The Self-Destructive Habits of Good Companies . . . And How to Break Them* (Upper Saddle River, NJ: Wharton School Publishing, 2007).

23. William L. Wilkie and Elizabeth S. Moore, "Marketing's Relationship to Society," in *Handbook of Marketing*, ed. Barton A. Weitz and Robin Wensley (London: Sage, 2002), pp. 1–38.

24. "Special Report: Corporate Social Responsibility," *Economist*, December 14, 2002, pp. 62–63.

25. Brian Grow, "The Debate over Doing Good," *BusinessWeek*, August 15, 2005, pp. 76–78.

26. Jennifer Alsever, "Chiquita Cleans Up Its Act, *Business 2.0* (August 2006): 56–58.

27. Grow, "The Debate over Doing Good."

28. Raj Sisodia, David B. Wolfe, and Jag Sheth, *Firms of Endearment: How World-Class Companies Profit from Passion and Purpose* (Upper Saddle River, NJ: Wharton School Publishing, 2007).

29. Stacy Pearman, "Scones and Social Responsibility," *BusinessWeek*, August 21–28, 2006, p. 38.

30. Leigh Buchanan, "Life Lessons," *Inc.* 28, no. 10 (October 2006): 86+.

31. John Carey, "Hugging the Tree Huggers," *BusinessWeek*, March 12, 2007, pp. 66–68.

32. Jeff Nachtigal, "It's Easy and Cheap Being Green," *Fortune*, October 16, 2006, p. 53.

33. For further reading, see Dorothy Cohen, *Legal Issues in Marketing Decision Making* (Cincinnati, OH: South-Western College Publishing, 1995).

34. Sarah Ellison, "Kraft Limits on Kids' Ads May Cheese Off Rivals," *Wall Street Journal*, January 13, 2005.

35. Shelby D. Hunt and Scott Vitell, "The General Theory of Marketing Ethics: A Retrospective and Revision," in *Ethics in Marketing*, ed. John Quelch and Craig Smith (Chicago: Irwin, 1992).

36. Majken Schultz, Yun Mi Antorini, and Fabian F. Csaba, *Corporate Branding: Purpose, People, and Process* (Køge, Denmark: Copenhagen Business School Press, 2005); Ronald J. Alsop, *The 18 Immutable Laws of Corporate Reputation: Creating, Protecting, and Repairing Your Most Valuable Asset* (New York: Free Press, 2004); Marc Gunther, "Tree Huggers, Soy Lovers, and Profits," *Fortune*, June 23, 2003, pp. 98–104; Ronald J. Alsop, "Perils of Corporate Philanthropy," *Wall Street Journal*, January 16, 2002.

37. Mya Frazier, "Going Green? Plant Deep Roots," *Advertising Age*, April 30, 2007, pp. 1, 54–55.

38. Michael E. Porter and Mark R. Kramer, "The Competitive Advantage of Corporate Philanthropy," *Harvard Business Review* (December 2002): 5–16.

39. Dwane Hal Deane, "Associating the Corporation with a Charitable Event through Sponsorship: Measuring the Effects on Corporate Community Relations," *Journal of Advertising* (Winter 2002): 77–87.

40. Sandra O'Loughlin, "The Wearin' o' the Green," *Brandweek*, April 23, 2007, pp. 26–27. For a critical response, see also, John R. Ehrenfield, "Feeding the Beast," *Fast Company* (December 2006–January 2007): 42–43.

41. Nicholas Varchaver, "Chemical Reaction," *Fortune*, April 2, 2007, pp. 53–58.

42. Pete Engardio, "Beyond the Green Corporation," *BusinessWeek*, January 29, 2007, pp. 50-64.

43. Engardio, "Beyond the Green Corporation."

44. Kenneth Hein, "The World on a Platter," *Brandweek*, April 23, 2007, pp. 27–28; Megan Johnston, "Hard Sell for a Soft Fabric," *Forbes*, October 30, 2006, pp. 73–80.

45. See, Philip Kotler and Nancy Lee, *Corporate Social Responsibility: Doing the Most Good for Your Company and Your Cause* (New York: John Wiley, 2005).

46. Lynn Upshaw, *Truth: The New Rules for Marketing in a Skeptical World* (New York: Amacon, 2007); Cheryl Dahle, "A More Powerful Path," *Fast Company* (December 2006–January 2007): 68–81.

47. Jennifer Barrett, "A Secret Recipe for Success," *Newsweek*, November 3, 2003, pp. 48–49; Paul Newman and A. E. Hotchner, *Shameless Exploitation in Pursuit of the Common Good: The Madcap Business Adventure by the Truly Oddest Couple* (Waterville, ME: Thorndike Press, 2003); http://newmansown.com/.

48. Todd Cohen, "Corporations Aim for Strategic Engagement," *Philanthropy Journal*, September 20, 2006.

49. Robert Berner, "Smarter Corporate Giving," *BusinessWeek*, November 28, 2005, pp. 68–76; Craig N. Smith, "Corporate Social Responsibility: Whether or How?" *California Management Review* 45, no. 4 (Summer 2003): 52–76.

50. Larry Chiagouris and Ipshita Ray, "Saving the World with Cause-Related Marketing," *Marketing Management* (July–August 2007): 48–51; Hamish Pringle and Marjorie Thompson, *Brand Spirit: How Cause-Related Marketing Builds Brands* (New York: John Wiley & Sons, 1999); Sue Adkins, *Cause-Related Marketing: Who Cares Wins* (Oxford, England: Butterworth-Heineman, 1999); "Marketing, Corporate Social Initiatives, and the Bottom Line," Marketing Science Institute Conference Summary, *MSI Report No. 01-106*, 2001.

51. Rajan Varadarajan and Anil Menon, "Cause-Related Marketing: A Co-Alignment of Marketing Strategy and Corporate Philanthropy," *Journal of Marketing* 52 (July 1988): 58–74.

52. Minette Drumwright and Patrick E. Murphy, "Corporate Societal Marketing," in *Handbook of Marketing and Society*, ed. Paul N. Bloom and Gregory T. Gundlach (Thousand Oaks, CA: Sage, 2001), pp. 162–83. See also, Minette Drumwright, "Company Advertising with a Social Dimension: The Role of Noneconomic Criteria," *Journal of Marketing* 60 (October 1996): 71–87.

53. Jack Neff and Stephanie Thompson, "Eco-Marketing Has Staying Power This Time Around," *Advertising Age*, April 30, 2007, p. 55.

54. www.britishairways.com.

55. Xueming Luo and C. B. Bhattacharya, "Corporate Social Responsibility, Customer Satisfaction, and Market Value," *Journal of Marketing* 70 (October 2006): 1–18; Pat Auger, Paul Burke, Timothy Devinney, and Jordan J. Louviere, "What Will Consumers Pay for Social Product Features?" *Journal of Business Ethics* 42 (February 2003): 281–304.

56. Dennis B. Arnett, Steve D. German, and Shelby D. Hunt, "The Identity Salience Model of Relationship Marketing Success: The Case of Nonprofit Marketing," *Journal of Marketing* 67 (April 2003): 89–105; C. B. Bhattacharya and Sankar Sen, "Consumer-Company Identification: A Framework for Understanding Consumers' Relationships with Companies," *Journal of Marketing* 67 (April 2003): 76–88; Sankar Sen and C. B. Bhattacharya, "Does Doing Good Always Lead to Doing Better? Consumer Reactions to Corporate Social

Responsibility," *Journal of Marketing Research* 38, no. 2 (May 2001): 225–44.

57. Paul N. Bloom, Steve Hoeffler, Kevin Lane Keller, and Carlos E. Basurto, "How Social-Cause Marketing Affects Consumer Perceptions," *MIT Sloan Management Review* (Winter 2006): 49–55; Carolyn J. Simmons and Karen L. Becker-Olsen, "Achieving Marketing Objectives through Social Sponsorships," *Journal of Marketing* 70 (October 2006): 154–69; Guido Berens, Cees B. M. van Riel, and Gerrit H. van Bruggen, "Corporate Associations and Consumer Product Responses: The Moderating Role of Corporate Brand Dominance," *Journal of Marketing* 69 (July 2005): 35–48; Donald R. Lichtenstein, Minette E. Drumwright, and Bridgette M. Braig, "The Effect of Social Responsibility on Customer Donations to Corporate-Supported Nonprofits," *Journal of Marketing* 68 (October 2004): 16–32; Stephen Hoeffler and Kevin Lane Keller, "Building Brand Equity through Corporate Societal Marketing," *Journal of Public Policy and Marketing* 21, no. 1 (Spring 2002): 78–89. See also, Special Issue: Corporate Responsibility, *Journal of Brand Management* 10, nos. 4–5 (May 2003).

58. Mark R. Forehand and Sonya Grier, "When Is Honesty the Best Policy? The Effect of Stated Company Intent on Consumer Skepticism," *Journal of Consumer Psychology* 13, no. 3 (2003): 349–56; Dwane Hal Dean, "Associating the Corporation with a Charitable Event through Sponsorship: Measuring the Effects on Corporate Community Relations," *Journal of Advertising* 31, no. 4 (Winter 2002): 77–87.

59. N. Craig Smith, "Out of Left Field," *Business Strategy Review* 18, no. 2 (Summer 2007): 55–59; Adam Jones, "Choc Horror over Cadbury Tokens," *Financial Times*, May 3, 2003, p. 14.

60. Lauren Gard, "We're Good Guys, Buy from Us," *BusinessWeek*, November 22, 2004, pp. 72–74.

61. Mya Frazier, "Costly Red Campaign Reaps Meager $18 Million," *Advertising Age*, March 5, 2007; Viewpoint: Bobby Shriver, "CEO: Red's Raised Lots of Green," *Advertising Age*, March 12, 2007; Michelle Conlin, "Shop (in the Name of Love)," *BusinessWeek*, October 2, 2006, p. 9.

62. Todd Cohen, "Corporations Aim for Strategic Engagement," *Philanthropy Journal*, September 20, 2006; John A. Quelch and Nathalie Laidler-Kylander, *The New Global Brands: Managing Non-Governmental Organizations in the 21st Century* (Cincinnati, OH: South-Western College Publishing, 2005).

63. Alsop, *The 18 Immutable Laws of Corporate Reputation: Creating, Protecting, and Repairing Your Most Valuable Asset*, p. 125.

64. Susan Orenstein, "The Selling of Breast Cancer," *Business 2.0* (February 2003): 88–94; H. Meyer, "When the Cause Is Just," *Journal of Business Strategy* (November–December 1999): 27–31.

65. Christine Bittar, "Seeking Cause and Effect," *Brandweek*, November 11, 2002, pp. 18–24.

66. Paula Andruss, " 'Think Pink' Awareness Much Higher Than Threat," *Marketing News*, February 15, 2006, pp. 14–16; Jessi Hempel, "Selling a Cause, Better Make It Pop," *BusinessWeek*, February 13, 2006, p. 75; Elizabeth Woyke, "Prostate Cancer's Higher Profile," *BusinessWeek*, October 9, 2006, p. 14.

67. Philip Kotler, Ned Roberto, and Nancy Lee, *Social Marketing: Improving the Quality of Life* (Thousand Oaks, CA: Sage, 2002); Michael L. Rothschild, "Carrots, Sticks, and Promises: A Conceptual Framework for the Management of Public Health and Social Issue Behaviors," *Journal of Marketing* 63 (October 1999): 24–37.

68. www.causemarketingforum.com.

69. See, Rothschild, "Carrots, Sticks, and Promises: A Conceptual Framework for the Management of Public Health and Social Issue Behaviors," pp. 24–37.

70. Amy Syracuse, "Social Marketing for a Cause," *Target Marketing* 30, no. 7 (July 2007): 13.

71. For more on developing and implementing marketing plans, see H. W. Goetsch, *Developing, Implementing, and Managing an Effective Marketing Plan* (Chicago: NTC Business Books, 1993). See also, Thomas V. Bonoma, *The Marketing Edge: Making Strategies Work* (New York: Free Press, 1985). Much of this section is based on Bonoma's work.

72. C. Marcus, "Marketing Resource Management: Key Components," *Gartner Research Note*, August 22, 2001.

73. Julia Chang, "Cover Your Tracks," *Sales and Marketing Management* (June 2007): 12.

74. For other examples, see Paul W. Farris, Neil T. Bendle, Phillip E. Pfeifer, and David J. Reibstein, *Marketing Metrics: 50+ Metrics Every Executive Should Master* (Upper Saddle River, NJ: Wharton School Publishing, 2006); Marion Debruyne and Katrina Hubbard, "Marketing Metrics," working paper series, Conference Summary, Marketing Science Institute, Report No. 00-119, 2000.

75. Alfred R. Oxenfeldt, "How to Use Market-Share Measurement," *Harvard Business Review* (January–February 1969): 59–68.

76. There is a one-half chance that a successive observation will be higher or lower. Therefore, the probability of finding six successively higher values is given by (1/2) to the sixth, or 1/64.

77. Alternatively, companies need to focus on factors affecting shareholder value. The goal of marketing planning is to increase shareholder value, which is the present value of the future income stream created by the company's present actions. Rate-of-return analysis usually focuses on only one year's results. See, Alfred Rapport, *Creating Shareholder Value*, rev. ed. (New York: Free Press, 1997).
78. For additional reading on financial analysis, see Peter L. Mullins, *Measuring Customer and Product-Line Profitability* (Washington, DC: Distribution Research and Education Foundation, 1984).
79. Robin Cooper and Robert S. Kaplan, "Profit Priorities from Activity-Based Costing," *Harvard Business Review* (May–June 1991): 130–35.
80. Sam R. Goodman, *Increasing Corporate Profitability* (New York: Ronald Press, 1982), chapter 1. Also see Bernard J. Jaworski, Vlasis Stathakopoulos, and H. Shanker Krishnan, "Control Combinations in Marketing: Conceptual Framework and Empirical Evidence," *Journal of Marketing* (January 1993): 57–69.
81. Philip Kotler, William Gregor, and William Rodgers, "The Marketing Audit Comes of Age," *Sloan Management Review* (Winter 1989): 49–62. Frederick Reichheld, *The Loyalty Effect* (Boston: Harvard Business School Press, 1996) discusses attrition of the figures.
82. Useful checklists for a marketing self-audit can be found in Aubrey Wilson, *Aubrey Wilson's Marketing Audit Checklists* (London: McGraw-Hill, 1982); Mike Wilson, *The Management of Marketing* (Westmead, England: Gower Publishing, 1980). A marketing audit software program is described in Ben M. Enis and Stephen J. Garfein, "The Computer-Driven Marketing Audit," *Journal of Management Inquiry* (December 1992): 306–18.
83. Kotler, Gregor, and Rodgers, "The Marketing Audit Comes of Age," pp. 49–62.

Appendix

1. Background information and market data adapted from Sascha Segan, "Motorola RAZR2: The RAZR2 Cuts Four Ways," *PC Magazine*, October 2, 2007, pp. 32–33; Walter S. Mossberg, "Apple's iPod Touch Is a Beauty of a Player Short on Battery Life," *Wall Street Journal*, September 20, 2007, p. B1; "Roam If You Want To," *PC World*, September 2007, p. 134; Sascha Segam, "Exclusive: One RAZR2, Four Ways to Cut It," *PC Magazine Online*, August 13, 2007, www.pcmag.com; "Apple Unlikely to Budge Anytime Soon on iPhone Pricing," *InformationWeek*, July 26, 2007; "Smartphones Get Smarter, Thanks in Part to the iPhone," *InformationWeek*, July 21, 2007; "Nine Alternatives to Apple's iPhone," *InformationWeek*, June 28, 2007; "Hospital Uses PDA App for Patient Transport," *Health Data Management*, June 2007, p. 14; Jessica E. Vascellaro and Pui-Wing Tam, "RIM's New Gear Fuels Profit Surge; Palm Sputters," *Wall Street Journal*, June 29, 2007, p. B4; "Smart Phones Force Dell from Handhelds," *MicroScope*, April 23, 2007; "2005 PDA Shipments Set Record," *Business Communications Review*, April 2006, p. 6; "Smartphone Market Grows Fast Despite Challenges," *Appliance*, March 2006, p. 16.

GLOSSARY

A

activity-based cost (ABC) accounting procedures that can quantify the true profitability of different activities by identifying their actual costs.

advertising any paid form of nonpersonal presentation and promotion of ideas, goods, or services by an identified sponsor.

advertorials print ads that offer editorial content that reflects favorably on the brand and resemble newspaper or magazine content.

anchoring and adjustment heuristic when consumers arrive at an initial judgment and then make adjustments of their first impressions based on additional information.

arm's-length price the price charged by other competitors for the same or a similar product.

aspirational groups groups a person hopes or would like to join.

associative network memory model a conceptual representation that views memory as consisting of a set of nodes and interconnecting links where nodes represent stored information or concepts and links represent the strength of association between this information or concepts.

attitude a person's enduring favorable or unfavorable evaluation, emotional feeling, and action tendencies toward some object or idea.

augmented product a product that includes features that go beyond consumer expectations and differentiate the product from competitors.

available market the set of consumers who have interest, income, and access to a particular offer.

availability heuristic when consumers base their predictions on the quickness and ease with which a particular example of an outcome comes to mind.

average cost the cost per unit at a given level of production; it is equal to total costs divided by production.

B

backward invention reintroducing earlier product forms that can be well adapted to a foreign country's needs.

banner ads (Internet) small, rectangular boxes containing text and perhaps a picture to support a brand.

basic product what specifically the actual product is.

belief a descriptive thought that a person holds about something.

brand a name, term, sign, symbol, or design, or a combination of them, intended to identify the goods or services of one seller or group of sellers and to differentiate them from those of competitors.

brand associations all brand-related thoughts, feelings, perceptions, images, experiences, beliefs, attitudes, and so on that become linked to the brand node.

brand audit a consumer-focused exercise that involves a series of procedures to assess the health of the brand, uncover its sources of brand equity, and suggest ways to improve and leverage its equity.

brand awareness consumers' ability to identify the brand under different conditions, as reflected by their brand recognition or recall performance.

brand contact any information-bearing experience a customer or prospect has with the brand, the product category, or the market that relates to the marketer's product or service.

brand development index (BDI) the index of brand sales to category sales.

brand dilution when consumers no longer associate a brand with a specific product or highly similar products or start thinking less favorably about the brand.

brand elements those trademarkable devices that serve to identify and differentiate the brand such as a brand name, logo, or character.

brand equity the added value endowed to products and services.

brand extension a company's use of an established brand to introduce a new product.

brand image the perceptions and beliefs held by consumers, as reflected in the associations held in consumer memory.

brand knowledge all the thoughts, feelings, images, experiences, beliefs, and so on that become associated with the brand.

brand line all products, original as well as line and category extensions, sold under a particular brand name.

brand mix the set of all brand lines that a particular seller makes available to buyers.

brand personality the specific mix of human traits that may be attributed to a particular brand.

brand portfolio the set of all brands and brand lines a particular firm offers for sale to buyers in a particular category.

brand promise the marketer's vision of what the brand must be and do for consumers.

brand valuation an estimate of the total financial value of the brand.

brand value chain a structured approach to assessing the sources and outcomes of brand equity and the manner in which marketing activities create brand value.

branded entertainment using sports, music, arts, or other entertainment activities to build brand equity.

branded variants specific brand lines uniquely supplied to different retailers or distribution channels.

branding endowing products and services with the power of a brand.

branding strategy the number and nature of common and distinctive brand elements applied to the different products sold by the firm.

breakeven analysis a means by which management estimates how many units of the product the company would have to sell to break even with the given price and cost structure.

brick-and-click existing companies that have added an online site for information and/or e-commerce.

business database complete information about business customers' past purchases; past volumes, prices, and profits.

business market all the organizations that acquire goods and services used in the production of other products or services that are sold, rented, or supplied to others.

C

capital items long-lasting goods that facilitate developing or managing the finished product.

captive products products that are necessary to the use of other products, such as razor blades or film.

category extension Using the parent brand to brand a new product outside the product category currently served by the parent brand.

category membership the products or sets of products with which a brand competes and which function as close substitutes.

cause-related marketing marketing that links a firm's contributions to a designated cause to customers' engaging directly or indirectly in revenue-producing transactions with the firm.

channel advantage when a company successfully switches its customers to lower-cost channels, while assuming no loss of sales or deterioration in service quality.

channel conflict when one channel member's actions prevent the channel from achieving its goal.

channel coordination when channel members are brought together to advance the goals of the channel, as opposed to their own potentially incompatible goals.

channel power the ability to alter channel members' behavior so that they take actions they would not have taken otherwise.

communication adaptation changing marketing communications programs for each local market.

communication-effect research determining whether an ad is communicating effectively.

company demand the company's estimated share of market demand at alternative levels of company marketing effort in a given time period.

company sales forecast the expected level of company sales based on a chosen marketing plan and an assumed marketing environment.

competitive advantage a company's ability to perform in one or more ways that competitors cannot or will not match.

conformance quality the degree to which all the produced units are identical and meet the promised specifications.

conjoint analysis a method for deriving the utility values that consumers attach to varying levels of a product's attributes.

conjunctive heuristic the consumer sets a minimum acceptable cutoff level for each attribute and chooses the first alternative that meets the minimum standard for all attributes.

consumer involvement the level of engagement and active processing undertaken by the consumer in responding to a marketing stimulus.

consumerist movement an organized movement of citizens and government to strengthen the rights and powers of buyers in relation to sellers.

consumption system the way the user performs the tasks of getting and using products and related services.

containerization putting the goods in boxes or trailers that are easy to transfer between two transportation modes.

content-target advertising links ads not to keywords but to the contents of Web pages.

contractual sales force manufacturers' reps, sales agents, and brokers, who are paid a commission based on sales.

convenience goods goods the consumer purchases frequently, immediately, and with a minimum of effort.

conventional marketing channel an independent producer, wholesaler(s), and retailer(s).

core benefit the service or benefit the customer is really buying.

core competency attribute that (1) is a source of competitive advantage in that it makes a significant contribution to perceived customer benefits, (2) has applications in a wide variety of markets, (3) is difficult for competitors to imitate.

core values the belief systems that underlie consumer attitudes and behavior, and that determine people's choices and desires over the long term.

corporate culture the shared experiences, stories, beliefs, and norms that characterize an organization.

corporate retailing corporately owned retailing outlets that achieve economies of scale, greater purchasing power, wider brand recognition, and better-trained employees.

cues stimuli that determine when, where, and how a person responds.

culture the fundamental determinant of a person's wants and behavior.

customer-based brand equity the differential effect that brand knowledge has on a consumer response to the marketing of that brand.

customer churn high customer defection.

customer consulting data, information systems, and advice services that the seller offers to buyers.

customer database an organized collection of comprehensive information about individual customers or prospects that is current, accessible, and actionable for marketing purposes.

customer lifetime value (CLV) the net present value of the stream of future profits expected over the customer's lifetime purchases.

customer mailing list a set of names, addresses, and telephone numbers.

customer perceived value (CPV) the difference between the prospective customer's evaluation of all the benefits and all the costs of an offering and the perceived alternatives.

customer-performance scorecard how well the company is doing year after year on particular customer-based measures.

customer profitability analysis (CPA) a means of assessing and ranking customer profitability through accounting techniques such as Activity-Based Costing (ABC).

customer training training the customer's employees to use the vendor's equipment properly and efficiently.

customer value analysis report of the company's strengths and weaknesses relative to various competitors.

customer value hierarchy five product levels that must be addressed by marketers in planning a market offering.

customerization combination of operationally driven mass customization with customized marketing in a way that empowers consumers to design the product and service offering of their choice.

D

data warehouse a collection of current data captured, organized, and stored in a company's contact center.

database marketing the process of building, maintaining, and using customer databases and other databases for the purpose of contacting, transacting, and building customer relationships.

datamining the extracting of useful information about individuals, trends, and segments from the mass of data.

delivery how well the product or service is delivered to the customer.

demand chain planning the process of designing the supply chain based on adopting a target market perspective and working backward.

direct marketing the use of consumer-direct (CD) channels to reach and deliver goods and services to customers without using marketing middlemen.

direct-order marketing marketing in which direct marketers seek a measurable response, typically a customer order.

direct product profitability (DDP) a way of measuring a product's handling costs from the time it reaches the warehouse until a customer buys it in the retail store.

direct (company) sales force full- or part-time paid employees who work exclusively for the company.

discrimination the process of recognizing differences in sets of similar stimuli and adjusting responses accordingly.

dissociative groups those groups whose values or behavior an individual rejects.

distribution programming building a planned, professionally managed, vertical marketing system that meets the needs of both manufacturer and distributors.

drive a strong internal stimulus impelling action.

dual adaptation adapting both the product and the communications to the local market.

dumping situation in which a company charges either less than its costs or less than it charges in its home market, in order to enter or win a market.

durability a measure of a product's expected operating life under natural or stressful conditions.

E

e-business the use of electronic means and platforms to conduct a company's business.

e-commerce a company or site offers to transact or facilitate the selling of products and services online.

e-marketing company efforts to inform buyers, communicate, promote, and sell its products and services over the Internet.

e-purchasing purchase of goods, services, and information from various online suppliers.

elimination-by-aspects heuristic situation in which the consumer compares brands on an attribute selected probabilistically, and brands are eliminated if they do not meet minimum acceptable cutoff levels.

environmental threat a challenge posed by an unfavorable trend or development that would lead to lower sales or profit.

everyday low pricing (EDLP) in retailing, a constant low price with few or no price promotions and special sales.

exchange the process of obtaining a desired product from someone by offering something in return.

exclusive distribution severely limiting the number of intermediaries, in order to maintain control over the service level and outputs offered by resellers.

expectancy-value model consumers evaluate products and services by combining their brand beliefs—positive and negative—according to their weighted importance.

expected product a set of attributes and conditions buyers normally expect when they purchase this product.

experience curve (learning curve) a decline in the average cost with accumulated production experience.

F

fad a craze that is unpredictable, short-lived, and without social, economic and political significance.

family brand situation in which the parent brand is already associated with multiple products through brand extensions.

family of orientation parents and siblings.

family of procreation spouse and children.

features things that enhance the basic function of a product.

fixed costs (overhead) costs that do not vary with production or sales revenue.

flexible market offering (1) a naked solution containing the product and service elements that all segment members value, and (2) discretionary options that some segment members value.

focus group a gathering of six to ten people who are carefully selected based on certain demographic, psychographic, or other considerations and brought together to discuss various topics of interest.

forecasting the art of anticipating what buyers are likely to do under a given set of conditions.

form the size, shape, or physical structure of a product.

forward invention creating a new product to meet a need in another country.

frequency programs (FPs) designed to provide rewards to customers who buy frequently and in substantial amounts.

G

global firm a firm that operates in more than one country and captures R&D, production, logistical, marketing, and financial advantages in its costs and reputation that are not available to purely domestic competitors.

global industry an industry in which the strategic positions of competitors in major geographic or national markets are fundamentally affected by their overall global positions.

goal formulation the process of developing specific goals for the planning period.

going-rate pricing price based largely on competitors' prices.

gray market branded products diverted from normal or authorized distributions channels in the country of product origin or across international borders.

H

heuristics rules of thumb or mental shortcuts in the decision process.

high-low pricing charging higher prices on an everyday basis but then running frequent promotions and special sales.

holistic marketing a concept based on the development, design, and implementation of marketing programs, processes, and activities that recognizes their breadth and interdependencies.

horizontal marketing system two or more unrelated companies put together resources or programs to exploit an emerging market opportunity.

hybrid channels use of multiple channels of distribution to reach customers in a defined market.

I

image the set of beliefs, ideas, and impressions a person holds regarding an object.

industry a group of firms that offer a product or class of products that are close substitutes for one another.

ingredient branding a special case of co-branding that involves creating brand equity for materials, components, or parts that are necessarily contained within other branded products.

innovation any good, service, or idea that is perceived by someone as new.

innovation diffusion process the spread of a new idea from its source of invention or creation to its ultimate users or adopters.

installation the work done to make a product operational in its planned location.

institutional market schools, hospitals, nursing homes, prisons, and other institutions that must provide goods and services to people in their care.

integrated logistics systems (ILS) materials management, material flow systems, and physical distribution, abetted by information technology (IT).

integrated marketing mixing and matching marketing activities to maximize their individual and collective efforts.

integrated marketing communications (IMC) a concept of marketing communications planning that recognizes the added value of a comprehensive plan.

intensive distribution the manufacturer placing the goods or services in as many outlets as possible.

internal branding activities and processes that help to inform and inspire employees.

interstitials advertisements, often with video or animation, that pop up between changes on a Web site.

J

joint venture a company in which multiple investors share ownership and control.

L

learning changes in an individual's behavior arising from experience.

lexicographic heuristic a consumer choosing the best brand on the basis of its perceived most important attribute.

licensed product one whose brand name has been licensed to other manufacturers who actually make the product.

life-cycle cost the product's purchase cost plus the discounted cost of maintenance and repair less the discounted salvage value.

lifestyle a person's pattern of living in the world as expressed in activities, interests, and opinions.

line extension the parent brand is used to brand a new product that targets a new market segment within a product category currently served by the parent brand.

line stretching a company lengthens its product line beyond its current range.

long-term memory (LTM) a permanent repository of information.

loyalty a commitment to rebuy or re-patronize a preferred product or service.

M

maintenance and repair the service program for helping customers keep purchased products in good working order.

market-buildup method identifying all the potential buyers in each market and estimating their potential purchases.

market demand the total volume of a product that would be bought by a defined customer group in a defined geographical area in a defined time period in a defined marketing environment under a defined marketing program.

market forecast the market demand corresponding to the level of industry marketing expenditure.

market logistics planning the infrastructure to meet demand, then implementing and controlling the physical flows or materials and final goods from points of origin to points of use, to meet customer requirements at a profit.

market opportunity analysis (MOA) system used to determine the attractiveness and probability of success.

market partitioning the process of investigating the hierarchy of attributes consumers examine in choosing a brand if they use phased decision strategies.

market penetration index a comparison of the current level of market demand to the potential demand level.

market-penetration pricing pricing strategy where prices start low to drive higher sales volume from price-sensitive customers and produce productivity gains.

market potential the upper limit to market demand whereby increased marketing expenditures would not be expected to stimulate further demand.

market-skimming pricing pricing strategy where prices start high and are slowly lowered over time to maximize profits from less price-sensitive customers.

marketer someone who seeks a response (attention, a purchase, a vote, a donation) from another party, called the prospect.

marketing process of planning and executing the conception, pricing, promotion, and distribution of ideas, goods, and services to create exchanges that satisfy individual and organizational goals.

marketing audit a comprehensive, systematic, independent, and periodic examination of a company's or business unit's marketing environment, objectives, strategies, and activities.

marketing channel system the particular set of marketing channels employed by a firm.

marketing channels sets of interdependent organizations involved in the process of making a product or service available for use or consumption.

marketing communications the means by which firms attempt to inform, persuade, and remind consumers—directly or indirectly—about products and brands that they sell.

marketing communications mix advertising, sales promotion, events and experiences, public relations and publicity, direct marketing, and personal selling.

marketing decision support system (MDSS) a coordinated collection of data, systems, tools, and techniques with supporting software and hardware by which an organization gathers and interprets relevant information from business and the environment and turns it into a basis for marketing action.

marketing implementation the process that turns marketing plans into action assignments and ensures that such assignments are executed in a manner that accomplishes the plan's stated objectives.

marketing information system (MIS) people, equipment, and procedures to gather, sort, analyze, evaluate, and distribute information to marketing decision makers.

marketing intelligence system a set of procedures and sources managers use to obtain everyday information about developments in the marketing environment.

marketing management the art and science of choosing target markets and getting, keeping, and growing customers through creating, delivering, and communicating superior customer value.

marketing metrics the set of measures that helps firms to quantify, compare, and interpret their marketing performance.

marketing network the company and its supporting stakeholders, with whom it has built mutually profitable business relationships.

marketing opportunity an area of buyer need and interest in which there is a high probability that a company can profitably satisfy that need.

marketing plan written document that summarizes what the marketer has learned about the marketplace, indicates how the firm plans to reach its marketing objectives, and helps direct and coordinate the marketing effort.

marketing public relations (MPR) publicity and other activities that build corporate or product image to facilitate marketing goals.

marketing research the systematic design, collection, analysis, and reporting of data and findings relevant to a specific marketing situation facing the company.

markup pricing an item by adding a standard increase to the product's cost.

materials and parts goods that enter the manufacturer's product completely.

media selection finding the most cost-effective media to deliver the desired number and type of exposures to the target audience.

megamarketing the strategic coordination of economic, psychological, political, and public relations skills, to gain the cooperation of a number of parties in order to enter or operate in a given market.

megatrends large social, economic, political, and technological changes that are slow to form, and once in place, have an influence for seven to ten years or longer.

membership groups groups having a direct influence on a person.

memory encoding how and where information gets into memory.

memory retrieval how and from where information gets out of memory.

mental accounting the manner by which consumers code, categorize, and evaluate financial outcomes of choices.

microsales analysis examination of specific products and territories that fail to produce expected sales.

microsite a limited area on the Web managed and paid for by an external advertiser/company.

mission statements statements that organizations develop to share with managers, employees, and (in many cases) customers.

mixed bundling the seller offers goods both individually and in bundles.

multichannel marketing a single firm uses two or more marketing channels to reach one or more customer segments.

multitasking doing two or more things at the same time.

N

net price analysis analysis that encompasses company list price, average discount, promotional spending, and co-op advertising to arrive at net price.

noncompensatory models in consumer choice, when consumers do not simultaneously consider all positive and negative attribute considerations in making a decision.

Online alliances and affiliate programs when one Internet company works with another one and they advertise each other.

opinion leader the person in informal, product-related communications who offers advice or information about a specific product or product category.

ordering ease how easy it is for the customer to place an order with the company.

organization a company's structures, policies, and corporate culture.

organizational buying the decision-making process by which formal organizations establish the need for purchased products and services and identify, evaluate, and choose among alternative brands and suppliers.

overall market share the company's sales expressed as a percentage of total market sales.

P

parent brand an existing brand that gives birth to a brand extension.

partner relationship management (PRM) activities the firm undertakes to build mutually satisfying long-term relations with key partners such as suppliers, distributors, ad agencies, and marketing research suppliers.

penetrated market the set of consumers who are buying a company's product.

perceived value the value promised by the company's value proposition and perceived by the customer.

perception the process by which an individual selects, organizes, and interprets information inputs to create a meaningful picture of the world.

performance quality the level at which the product's primary characteristics operate.

personal communications channels two or more persons communicating directly face-to-face, person-to-audience, over the telephone, or through e-mail.

personal influence the effect one person has on another's attitude or purchase probability.

personality a set of distinguishing human psychological traits that lead to relatively consistent responses to environmental stimuli.

place advertising (also out-of-home advertising) ads that appear outside of home and where consumers work and play.

point-of-purchase (P-O-P) the location where a purchase is made, typically thought of in terms of a retail setting.

potential market the set of consumers who profess a sufficient level of interest in a market offer.

potential product all the possible augmentations and transformations the product or offering might undergo in the future.

price discrimination a company sells a product or service at two or more prices that do not reflect a proportional difference in costs.

price escalation an increase in the price of a product due to added costs of selling it in different countries.

primary groups groups with which a person interacts continuously and informally, such as family, friends, neighbors, and co-workers.

principle of congruity psychological mechanism that states that consumers like to see seemingly related objects as being as similar as possible in their favorability.

private label brand brands that retailers and wholesalers develop and market.

product adaptation altering the product to meet local conditions or preferences.

product assortment the set of all products and items a particular seller offers for sale.

product invention creating something new via product development or other means.

product mix see product assortment.

product penetration percentage the percentage of ownership or use of a product or service in a population.

product system a group of diverse but related items that function in a compatible manner.

profitable customer a person, household, or company that over time yields a revenue stream that exceeds by an acceptable amount the company's cost stream of attracting, selling, and servicing that customer.

prospect theory when consumers frame decision alternatives in terms of gains and losses according to a value function.

public any group that has an actual or potential interest in or impact on a company's ability to achieve its objectives.

public relations (PR) a variety of programs designed to promote or protect a company's image or its individual products.

publicity the task of securing editorial space—as opposed to paid space—in print and broadcast media to promote something.

pull strategy when the manufacturer uses advertising and promotion to persuade consumers to ask intermediaries for the product, thus inducing the intermediaries to order it.

purchase probability scale a scale to measure the probability of a buyer making a particular purchase.

pure bundling a firm only offers its products as a bundle.

pure-click companies that have launched a Web site without any previous existence as a firm.

push strategy when the manufacturer uses its sales force and trade promotion money to induce intermediaries to carry, promote, and sell the product to end users.

R

reference groups all the groups that have a direct or indirect influence on a person's attitudes or behavior.

reference prices pricing information a consumer retains in memory which is used to interpret and evaluate a new price.

relational equity the cumulative value of the firm's network of relationships with its customers, partners, suppliers, employees, and investors.

relationship marketing building mutually satisfying long-term relationships with key parties, in order to earn and retain their business.

relative market share market share in relation to a company's largest competitor.

reliability a measure of the probability that a product will not malfunction or fail within a specified time period.

repairability a measure of the ease of fixing a product when it malfunctions or fails.

representativeness heuristic when consumers base their predictions on how representative or similar an outcome is to other examples.

risk analysis a method by which possible rates of returns and their probabilities are calculated by obtaining estimates for uncertain variables affecting profitability.

role the activities a person is expected to perform.

S

sales analysis measuring and evaluating actual sales in relation to goals.

sales budget a conservative estimate of the expected volume of sales, used for making current purchasing, production, and cash flow decisions.

sales promotion a collection of incentive tools, mostly short term, designed to stimulate quicker or greater purchase of particular products or services by consumers or the trade.

sales quota the sales goal set for a product line, company division, or sales representative.

sales-variance analysis a measure of the relative contribution of different factors to a gap in sales performance.

satisfaction a person's feelings of pleasure or disappointment resulting from comparing a product's perceived performance or outcome in relation to his or her expectations.

scenario analysis developing plausible representations of a firm's possible future that make different assumptions about forces driving the market and include different uncertainties.

search-related ads ads in which search terms are used as a proxy for the consumer's consumption interests and relevant links to product or service offerings are listed alongside the search results.

secondary groups groups which tend to be more formal and require less interaction than primary groups, such as religious, professional, and trade-union groups.

selective attention the mental process of screening out certain stimuli while noticing others.

selective distortion the tendency to interpret product information in a way that fits consumer perceptions.

selective distribution the use of more than a few but less than all of the intermediaries who are willing to carry a particular product.

selective retention good points about a product that consumers like are remembered and good points about competing products are forgotten.

served market all the buyers who are able and willing to buy a company's product.

served market share a company's sales expressed as a percentage of the total sales to its served market.

service any act or performance that one party can offer to another that is essentially intangible and does not result in the ownership of anything.

share penetration index a comparison of a company's current market share to its potential market share.

shopping goods goods that the consumer, in the process of selection and purchase, characteristically compares on such bases as suitability, quality, price, and style.

short-term memory (STM) a temporary repository of information.

social classes homogeneous and enduring divisions in a society, which are hierarchically ordered and whose members share similar values, interests, and behavior.

social marketing marketing done by a nonprofit or government organization to further a cause, such as "say no to drugs."

specialty goods goods that have unique characteristics or brand identification for which a sufficient number of buyers are willing to make a special purchasing effort.

sponsorship financial support of an event or activity in return for recognition and acknowledgment as the sponsor.

stakeholder-performance scorecard a measure to track the satisfaction of various constituencies who have a critical interest in and impact on the company's performance.

status one's position within his or her own hierarchy or culture.

straight extension introducing a product in a foreign market without any change in the product.

strategic brand management the design and implementation of marketing activities and programs to build, measure, and manage brands to maximize their value.

strategic business units (SBUs) a single business or collection of related businesses that can be planned separately from the rest of the company, with its own set of competitors and a manager who is responsible for strategic planning and profit performance.

strategic group firms pursuing the same strategy directed to the same target market.

strategic marketing plan laying out the target markets and the value proposition that will be offered, based on analysis of the best market opportunities.

strategy a company's game plan for achieving its goals.

style a product's look and feel to the buyer.

sub-brand a new brand combined with an existing brand.

subculture subdivisions of a culture that provide more specific identification and socialization, such as nationalities, religions, racial groups, and geographical regions.

subliminal perception receiving and processing subconscious messages that affect behavior.

supersegment a set of segments sharing some exploitable similarity.

supplies and business services short-term goods and services that facilitate developing or managing the finished product.

supply chain management (SCM) procuring the right inputs (raw materials, components, and capital equipment); converting them efficiently into finished products; and dispatching them to the final destinations.

T

tactical marketing plan marketing tactics, including product features, promotion, merchandising, pricing, sales channels, and service.

target costing deducting the desired profit margin from the price at which a product will sell, given its appeal and competitors' prices.

target market the part of the qualified available market the company decides to pursue.

target-return pricing determining the price that would yield the firm's target rate of return on investment (ROI).

telemarketing the use of telephone and call centers to attract prospects, sell to existing customers, and provide service by taking orders and answering questions.

total costs the sum of the fixed and variable costs for any given level of production.

total customer cost the bundle of costs customers expect to incur in evaluating, obtaining, using, and disposing of the given market offering, including monetary, time, energy, and psychic costs.

total customer value the perceived monetary value of the bundle of economic, functional, and psychological benefits customers expect from a given market offering.

total quality management (TQM) an organizationwide approach to continuously improving the quality of all the organization's processes, products, and services.

tracking studies collecting information from consumers on a routine basis over time.

transaction a trade of values between two or more parties: A gives X to B and receives Y in return.

transfer in the case of gifts, subsidies, and charitable contributions: A gives X to B but does not receive anything tangible in return.

transfer price the price a company charges another unit in the company for goods it ships to foreign subsidiaries.

trend a direction or sequence of events that has some momentum and durability.

two-part pricing a fixed fee plus a variable usage fee.

tying agreements agreement in which producers of strong brands sell their products to dealers only if dealers purchase related products or services, such as other products in the brand line.

U

unsought goods those the consumer does not know about or does not normally think of buying, like smoke detectors.

V

value-delivery network a company's supply chain and how it partners with specific suppliers and distributors to make products and bring them to markets.

value-delivery system all the expectancies the customer will have on the way to obtaining and using the offering.

value network a system of partnerships and alliances that a firm creates to source, augment, and deliver its offerings.

value pricing winning loyal customers by charging a fairly low price for a high-quality offering.

value proposition the whole cluster of benefits the company promises to deliver.

variable costs costs that vary directly with the level of production.

venture team a cross-functional group charged with developing a specific product or business.

vertical integration situation in which manufacturers try to control or own their suppliers, distributors, or other intermediaries.

vertical marketing system (VMS) producer, wholesaler(s), and retailer(s) acting as a unified system.

viral marketing using the Internet to create word of mouth effects to support marketing efforts and goals.

Y

yield pricing situation in which companies offer (1) discounted but limited early purchases, (2) higher-priced late purchases, and (3) the lowest rates on unsold inventory just before it expires.

Z

zero-level channel (direct-marketing channel) a manufacturer selling directly to the final customer.

IMAGE CREDITS

Chapter 1
2: Dallas and John Heaton/The Stock Connection; 6: © Ruaridh Stwart/ZUMA/Corbis; 8: Ad used with the permission of the United Negro College Fund; 11: © Edmunds Inc. Reprinted with permission; 13: Ric Francis/AP Wide World Photos; 18: © 2005 Jones Soda Company. All Rights Reserved. Used with permission; 19: Bill Aron/PhotoEdit, Inc.; 24: Reprinted by permission of Carnival Cruise Lines.

Chapter 2
32: Siemens press picture, courtesy of Siemens; 36: A. Ramey/PhotoEdit Inc.; 37: Paul Sakuma/AP Wide World Photos; 37: Reproduced by permission of Netflix, Inc., Copyright © 2007 Netflix, Inc. All rights reserved; 41: © 2007 Intel Corporation. All rights reserved. Photographer: Trevor Pearson. Used with permission; 48: © Rick Chard/ CORBIS. All Rights Reserved; 50: Getty Images, Inc.

Chapter 3
64: Photo by J.D Pooley/Getty Images, Inc.; 69: Ford Motor Company; 71: Ben Margot/AP Wide World Photos; 74: HO/AFP/Getty Images; 79: Bill Aron/PhotoEdit Inc.; 81: © Sergio Pitamitz/ CORBIS. All Rights Reserved; 86: James Kirkikis.

Chapter 4
88: Courtesy of Gillette; 92: Noridicphotos/Alamy Images; 93: Jae C. Hong/AP Wide World Photos; 94: Spencer Grant/PhotoEdit Inc.; 98: Norman H. Olson, Purdue University; 105: Steven Moeder/IDEO; 110: Dennis MacDonald/PhotoEdit Inc.

Chapter 5
118: Spencer Grant/PhotoEdit Inc.; 123: Reprinted by permission of Volvo Car Corporation; 125: © Kenneth Johansson/CORBIS. All Rights Reserved; 127: Reprinted by permission of Enterprise Rent-a-Car, Inc.; 128: Used by permission of Benjamin Moore & Co.; 134: Text and artwork copyright ©1998 by Yahoo! Inc. All rights reserved. YAHOO! and the YAHOO! logo are trademarks of YAHOO! Inc.; 140: © John. G Mabanglo/ CORBIS. All Rights Reserved; 144: Guang Niu/Getty Images, Inc.

Chapter 6
148: CORBIS. All Rights Reserved; 155: Reed Saxon/ AP Wide World Photos; 158: © Andy Warhole Foundation/ CORBIS. All Rights Reserved; 162: Alamy Images; 159: Reprinted with permission of Betty Crocker/General Mills; 170: With permission from Lowe Worldwide, Inc. As Agent for National Fluid Milk Processor Promotion Board.

Chapter 7
180: Reprinted by permission of Cisco Systems; 183: The Goodyear Tire & Rubber Company; 186: Alamy Images; 189: Courtesy of Emerson Electric; 196: Courtesy of Rockwell Automation; 197: Jenny Ogborn/Lincoln Electric Co.; 203: Matt Rourke/AP Wide World Photos.

Chapter 8
206: Onne van der Wal/Corbis/Bettmann; 210: Orlin Wagner/AP Wide World Photos; 211: © Tony Kurdzuk/Star Ledger/ Corbis; 213: Tony Freeman/PhotoEzit Inc.; 215: Kevork Djansezian/AP Wide World Photos; 216: American Honda Motor Co., Inc. Photography by Uwe Breitkpof. Illustration by Matt Wood; 218: ©Sara Krulwhich/The New York Times; 219: Used by permission of Kendall-Jackson Winery; 223: Rudi Von Briel/PhotoEdit Inc.; 230: Reprinted by permission of Proter & Gamble, Inc.

Chapter 9
234: AP Wide World Photos; 237: SuperStock, Inc.; 238: © (Nik Wheeler)/CORBIS. All Rights Reserved; 239: Amy Etra/PhotoEdit Inc; 240: Alamy Images; 244: © 2006 MasterCard. All rights reserved; 248: Courtesy of the Jones Soda Company; 255: Harley-Davidson Motor Company; 262: © Daniele La Monaca/ Rueters/ Corbis.

Chapter 10
266: AP Wide World Photos; 270: AP Wide World Photos; 273: Used by permission of BMW NA; 271: Used by permission of American Express; 272: AP Wide World Photos; 276: PhotoEdit Inc.; 281: Used by permission of Wikipedia; 285: Park Street/PhotoEdit Inc.

Chapter 11
292: Progressive www. progressive.com. Used by permission; 297: Howard Koby Photography; 301: PhotoEdit Inc.; 304: Stephan F. Faust/ www.photographersdirect.com; 305: © Stefano Rellandini/ CORBIS. All Rights Reserved; 311: S & S Cycle.

Chapter 12
316: Douglas C. Pizac/AP Wide World Photos; 320: Alamy Images; 323: DaimlerChrysler Corporation; 324: © John van Hasselt/ CORBIS. All Rights Reserved; 327: Courtesy of Herman Miller, Inc.; 332: Michael Newman/PhotoEdit Inc.; 335: Martin Meissner/AP Wide World Photos; 338: AP Wide World Photos; 340: Bill Aron/PhotoEdit Inc.

Chapter 13
344: © America/Alamy; 349: AP Wide World Photos; 350: Stringer/Agence France Presse/Getty Images; 354: Time Boyle/Getty Images, Inc.; 356: ROSLAN RAHMAN/AFP/Getty Images, Inc.; 358: Used by permission of Charles Schwab; 368: Daniel Shanken/AP Wide World Photos; 369: Robert E. Klein/AP Wide World Photos.

Chapter 14
374: Don Ryan/AP Wide World Photos; 377: Getty Images, Inc.; 378: Alamy Images; 381: Alamy Images; 382: KAZUHIRO NOGIA/Agence France Presse/Getty Images; 384: ABSOLUT®VODKA. Absolut Country of Sweden Vodka & Logo, Absolut, Absolut Bottle Design and Absolut Calligraphy are trademarks owned by V&S VIN & SPRIT AB (publ.) © 2006 V&S VIN & SPRIT AB (publ); 395: Courtesy of eBay; 397: Adam J. Shane/Howard Koby Photography; 400: © Joseph Sohm//Visions of America/ CORBIS. All Rights Reserved.

Chapter 15
408: Getty Images, Inc.; 411: Alamy Images; 419: Harry & David; 420: Charlie Riedel/AP Wide World Photos; 425: Alamy Images; 426: Jay LaPrete/AP Wide World Photos; 428: Max SIVYI Photography/Howard Koby Photography; 432: David Zalubowski/AP Wide World Photos.

Chapter 16
440: INDITEK; 442: Alamay Images; 444: Paul Chesley/Getty Images Inc.–Stone Allstock; 446: Getty Images, Inc.; 449: Mark Lennihan/AP Wide World Photos; 452: Michael Nagle/ Getty Images, Inc.; 455: Corbis/Bettmann; 456: Loblaw Brands Limited; 460: W. W. Grainger, Inc.; 463: Getty Images, Inc.

Chapter 17
468: Used by permission of Unilever; 472: Used by permission of Nike; 478: Used with permission of Michelin North America, Inc.; 481: Karen Bleier/Agence France Presse/Getty Images; 481: © Tannen Maury/ CORBIS. All Rights Reserved; 483: Todd Vanderlin/AP Wide World Photos; 487: Used by permission of Ocean Spray.

Chapter 18
496: Used by permission of GEICO; 502: Reprinted by permission of Aflac; 503: ABSOLUT®VODKA. Absolut Country of Sweden Vodka & Logo, Absolut, Absolut Bottle Design and Absolut Calligraphy are trademarks owned by V&S VIN & SPRIT AB (publ.) © 2006 V&S VIN & SPRIT AB (publ); 508: Gareth Cattermole/Getty Images, Inc.; 511: Copyright 2007, Linden Research, Inc. All Rights Reserved; 520: © (Photographer)/CORBIS. All Rights Reserved; 522: Rob

Leiter/MLB Photos via Getty Images, Inc.; 527: © Shawn Thew/epa/CORBIS. All Rights Reserved; 528: Lowe Brindfors AB.

Chapter 19

530: Jim Whitmer Photography; 533: Joe Raymond; 536: © Karen Huntt/ CORBIS. All Rights Reserved; 544: BMW/ Ritta & Associates; 550: Courtesy of Ford Motor Company; 557: Jupiterimages/NewsCom.

Chapter 20

564: Miker Derer/AP Wide World Photos; 572: Courtesy Xerox Corporation; 575: Zuma Press/NewsCom; 580: Warner Brothers TV/Bright/Kauffman/ Crane Pro/The Kobal Collection/Chris Haston; 582: Robert Glusic/NewsCom; 587: Honolulu Star-Bulletin, Craig T. Kojima/AP Wide World Photos; 592: Getty Images; 594: Used by permission of Nike.

Chapter 21

596: Panos Pictures; 601: Courtesy of Fiat Auto India; 606: David Noton Photography/ Alamy Images; 608: Zhu Gang-FeatureChina/NewsCom/ NewsCom; 610: Tamara Abdul Hadi/Reuters Limited; 611: Radu Sigheti/Reuters Limited; 615: Mike Clarke/Agence France Presse/Getty Images; 616: Claro Cortes IV CC/Reuters Limited; 618: Robert Harding Library/Alamy Images; 620: New Line/Saul Zaentz/Wing Nut/The Kobal Collection.

Chapter 22

624: James F. Quinn/Chicago Tribune/NewsCom; 629: U. S. Army Photograph; 636: Michael Tercha/Chicago Tribune/MCT/ NewsCom; 637: Used by permission of Starbucks Corporation; 638: Paul Sakuma/ AP Wide World Photos; 640: Ross Hailey/Fort Warth Star Telegram/MCT/NewsCom; 642: Andy King/AP Wide World Photos; 643: M. Spencer Green/AP Wide World Photos; 646: Tina Fineberg/AP Wide World Photos.

INDEX

Name

Company, Brand, and Organization Index

Subject Index